EDITORIAL BOARD

SAUL LEVMORE
DIRECTING EDITOR
William B. Graham Distinguished Service Professor of Law and
Former Dean of the Law School
University of Chicago

DANIEL A. FARBER
Sho Sato Professor of Law
University of California at Berkeley

HEATHER K. GERKEN
Dean and the Sol & Lillian Goldman Professor of Law
Yale University

SAMUEL ISSACHAROFF
Bonnie and Richard Reiss Professor of Constitutional Law
New York University

HAROLD HONGJU KOH
Sterling Professor of International Law and
Former Dean of the Law School
Yale University

THOMAS W. MERRILL
Charles Evans Hughes Professor of Law
Columbia University

ROBERT L. RABIN
A. Calder Mackay Professor of Law
Stanford University

HILLARY A. SALE
Professor of Law and Affiliated Faculty
McDonough School of Business, Georgetown University

UNIVERSITY CASEBOOK SERIES®

CIVIL PROCEDURE

FIFTH EDITION

THOMAS D. ROWE, JR.
Elvin R. Latty Professor of Law Emeritus
Duke University School of Law

SUZANNA SHERRY
Herman O. Loewenstein Professor of Law
Vanderbilt University Law School

JAY TIDMARSH
Judge James J. Clynes, Jr., Professor of Law
Notre Dame Law School

The publisher is not engaged in rendering legal or other professional advice, and this publication is not a substitute for the advice of an attorney. If you require legal or other expert advice, you should seek the services of a competent attorney or other professional.

University Casebook Series is a trademark registered in the U.S. Patent and Trademark Office.

© 2004 FOUNDATION PRESS
© 2008, 2012 THOMSON REUTERS/FOUNDATION PRESS
© 2016 LEG, Inc. d/b/a West Academic
© 2020 LEG, Inc. d/b/a West Academic
    444 Cedar Street, Suite 700
    St. Paul, MN 55101
    1-877-888-1330

Printed in the United States of America

ISBN: 978-1-68467-038-3

To Susan, Sarah, Ellie, and Dylan
— T.R.

To Hannah and Joshua
— S.S.

To Chris, David, Kevin, and Clare
— J.T.

PREFACE TO THE FIFTH EDITION

Across the five editions of this book, we have introduced students to the enduring traditions of American civil litigation, while also chronicling the ongoing changes intended to improve our civil-justice system. In this fifth edition, we include one new Supreme Court opinion as a principal case, and we discuss more than a dozen recent Court decisions in the notes. As part of our commitment to give students a sense of the current state of American litigation, we also include seven new principal cases from the lower federal courts, and we discuss or cite more than one hundred new lower-court opinions and law-review articles. The most recent amendments to the Federal Rules of Civil Procedure are accounted for.

Civil procedure is not a simple subject. We have always aimed for a book that provides a sophisticated treatment of the subject but is short enough to allow students to focus on core principles. We have worked hard to make this edition as clear, informative, and readable as possible. We have relentlessly edited this edition from the first page to the last, and in the process we have eliminated twenty pages of material.

In our endeavors we have had considerable help. Our own students served as guinea pigs as we tried out material, and in that process they have taught us more than we have taught them. Our adopters shared comments about things that worked and things that didn't in their classrooms. Graham Pilotte, a student at Notre Dame Law School, proofread the text. Finally, Staci Herr at Foundation Press provided continuing support.

The intelligence, intellectual curiosity, and enthusiasm of the students who use this book inspire us and drive us to become ever better teachers and authors. To all of you, we owe our greatest debt of gratitude.

Marina del Rey, California
Nashville, Tennessee
Notre Dame, Indiana
February, 2020

PREFACE TO THE FIRST EDITION

As is often the case, this book had its source in the authors' desire to provide a new perspective on Civil Procedure. We wanted to write a book that was short and intellectually sophisticated, exploring both doctrinal and theoretical themes in a book of manageable length. We have therefore tried to combine — both in the choice and editing of cases and in our own text — depth, brevity, and clarity. We also aimed for adaptability, adding modularity to our structure to allow teachers to pick and choose what to teach and what to omit. The reader can judge whether we have accomplished our goals.

A word on the cases and other non-original material: We follow the ordinary convention of signaling substantive changes or omissions with brackets and ellipses. But we have omitted citations and footnotes without notice, and we have also added or altered citations and non-emphatic italicization within cases to conform to modern academic usage. Readers should therefore not assume that the materials as printed are identical in form to the originals.

Finally, this book could not have been written without the help of many other people. We would especially like to thank our deans — Katharine Bartlett at Duke, Kent Syverud at Vanderbilt, and Patricia O'Hara at Notre Dame — for providing both tangible and intangible encouragement and support. Steve Errick and the members of the editorial board at Foundation brought the authors together and helped make the project a reality. Six Vanderbilt law students tirelessly and conscientiously citechecked, proofread, and generally kept us honest and consistent: Christine Anthony, Amy Bohannon, Charles Canter, Meredith Capps, Brendan McLaughlin, and Liza Wirtz. Jesse Schomer at Notre Dame provided additional research assistance. We are also grateful to the department of Information Technology Services and Solutions at the Vanderbilt University Law School, especially Michael Curatolo, who set up a Web-based document library for the three of us to share, taught us (and retaught us) to use it, and responded to all our emergency calls for help. Our assistants — Maya Jackson at Duke, Janelle Steele at Vanderbilt, Debbie Sumption and Debbie Blasko at Notre Dame, and Peggie Flynn at Harvard — took charge of the voluminous correspondence inevitably generated by three authors at different schools, made multiple copies of multiple drafts, and generally provided on-the-spot assistance. Professor Rowe would also like to thank his mother-in-law, Senior Ninth Circuit Judge Betty Fletcher, for editorial suggestions on Chapter 6, Appeals. Finally, we thank our students at Duke, Harvard, Michigan, Minnesota, Notre Dame, and Vanderbilt for providing the inspiration for this book and for keeping us on our toes.

Durham, North Carolina
Nashville, Tennessee
Notre Dame, Indiana
May, 2004

ACKNOWLEDGMENTS

We acknowledge with thanks the copyright owners who have graciously granted us permission to reprint excerpts from the following works:

AMERICAN LAW INSTITUTE/UNIDROIT, PRINCIPLES OF TRANSNATIONAL PROCEDURE, copyright © 2006, by the American Law Institute.

AMERICAN LAW INSTITUTE, RESTATEMENT (SECOND) OF JUDGMENTS, copyright © 1982, by the American Law Institute.

Robert G. Bone, *The Process of Making Process: Court Rulemaking, Democratic Legitimacy, and Procedural Efficacy*, 87 GEO. L.J. 887. Reprinted with permission of the publisher, Georgetown Law Journal copyright © 1999.

Abram Chayes, *The Role of the Judge in Public Law Litigation*, 89 HARV. L. REV. 1281, copyright © 1976, by permission of Antonia Chayes and by the Harvard Law Review Association.

CHARLES E. CLARK, HANDBOOK OF THE LAW OF CODE PLEADING (2d ed.) copyright © 1947. Reprinted with permission of West Publishing Co.

John Hart Ely, *The Irrepressible Myth of* Erie, 87 HARV. L. REV. 693, copyright © 1974, by the Harvard Law Review Association.

Richard A. Epstein, *Of Pleading and Discovery: Reflections on* Twombly *and* Iqbal *with Special Reference to Antitrust*, 2011 U. ILL. L. REV. 187, copyright © 2011. Reprinted by permission of the University of Illinois Law Review.

Christopher M. Fairman, *Heightened Pleading*, 81 TEX. L. REV. 551, copyright © 2002. Reprinted by permission of the Texas Law Review Association and the author.

Owen M. Fiss, *Against Settlement*, 93 YALE L.J. 1073. Reprinted by permission of The Yale Journal Company and Fred B. Rothman & Company, from *The Yale Law Journal*, copyright © 1984, Vol. 93, pages 1073-90.

Lawrence Friedman, *Some Notes on the Civil Jury in Historical Perspective*, 48 DEPAUL L. REV. 201, copyright © 1998, by the De Paul Law Review.

Lon L. Fuller, *The Forms and Limits of Adjudication*, 92 HARV. L. REV. 353, copyright © 1978, by the Harvard Law Review Association.

Geoffrey C. Hazard, Jr., *Discovery and the Role of the Judge in Civil Law Jurisdictions*, Volume 73, Number 4, NOTRE DAME L. REV. (May 1998) 1017. Reprinted with permission © by *Notre Dame Law Review*, University of Notre Dame.*

STEPHAN LANDSMAN, READINGS ON ADVERSARIAL JUSTICE: THE AMERICAN APPROACH TO LITIGATION copyright © 1988. Reprinted with permission of West Publishing Co.

John H. Langbein, *The German Advantage in Civil Procedure*, 52 U. CHI. L. REV. 823, copyright © 1985, by the University of Chicago Law Review.

JULIUS BYRON LEVINE, DISCOVERY copyright © 1982. By permission of Oxford University Press.

Carrie Menkel-Meadow, *Whose Dispute Is It Anyway? A Philosophical and Democratic Defense of Settlement (In Some Cases)*, 83 GEO. L.J. 2663. Reprinted with permission of the publisher, Georgetown Law Journal copyright © 1995.

Burt Neuborne, *The Myth of Parity*, 90 HARV. L. REV. 1105, copyright © 1977, by the Harvard Law Review Association.

Wendy Collins Perdue, *Personal Jurisdiction and the Beetle in the Box*, 32 B.C. L. REV. 529, copyright © 1991, reprinted by permission of the author.

EDWARD A. PURCELL, JR., BRANDEIS AND THE PROGRESSIVE CONSTITUTION, copyright © 2000, by Yale University Press. Reprinted by permission.

Judith Resnik, *Managerial Judges*, 92 HARV. L. REV. 353, copyright © 1982, by the Harvard Law Review Association.

LEONARD L. RISKIN & JAMES E. WESTBROOK, DISPUTE RESOLUTION AND LAWYERS (5th ed.) copyright © 2014. Reprinted with permission of West Academic.

William W Schwarzer, *The Federal Rules, the Adversary Process, and Discovery Reform*, 50 U. PITT. L. REV. 703 copyright © 1989. Reprinted with permission by the University of Pittsburgh Law Review.

Gil Seinfeld, *The Federal Courts as a Franchise: Rethinking The Justifications for Federal Question Jurisdiction*, 97 CAL. L. REV. 95 copyright © 2009 by the California Law Review, Inc. Reprinted by permission of the California Law Review.

David L. Shapiro, *Class Actions: The Class as Party and Client*, Volume 73, Number 4, NOTRE DAME L. REV. (May 1998) 913. Reprinted with permission © by *Notre Dame Law Review*, University of Notre Dame.*

Stephen N. Subrin, *Discovery in Global Perspective: Are We Nuts?*, 52 DEPAUL L. REV. 299, copyright © 2002, by the DePaul Law Review.

* Foundation Press and the authors bear responsibility for any errors which have occurred in reprinting or editing.

Summary of Contents

Preface to the Fifth Edition... v
Preface to the First Edition.. vii
Acknowledgments.. ix
Table of Contents... xvii
Table of Cases... xxix
Table of Authorities... xliii

CHAPTER ONE: An Introduction to Civil Procedure......... 1

Sec.

A. The Goals of a Procedural System 2
B. A Brief History of the American Procedural System 11
    1. English Antecedents...................................... 11
    2. American Antecedents 14
    3. The Modern American System............................... 15
C. An Overview of the American Judicial System................. 16
    1. Dual System of Courts 16
    2. Source of Law 18
    3. Processing the Lawsuit................................... 19
    4. Finality 20
    5. Challenging the Standard Litigation Paradigm............. 20
D. American Civil Procedure in Comparative Perspective 21
E. The Social Significance of Civil Dispute Resolution 22

CHAPTER TWO: Pleading................................... 24

Sec.

A. Perspectives on Pleading 24
B. The Complaint.. 26
    1. A Sample Complaint....................................... 27
    2. The Sufficiency of the Complaint......................... 28
    3. Filing and Serving the Complaint......................... 58
C. Responding to the Complaint.................................. 67
    1. Rule 12 Motions 67
    2. The Answer... 70
D. Amending the Pleadings....................................... 80
E. Policing Pleadings and Motions 90

CHAPTER THREE: DISCLOSURE AND DISCOVERY 107

Sec.

- A. Perspectives on Discovery. 108
- B. The Mechanics of Disclosure and Discovery 113
  1. Party-Initiated Discovery Devices. 113
  2. Required Initial Disclosure 117
  3. Supplementing Disclosures and Responses 118
- C. The Scope of and Limits on Discovery. 118
  1. Relevance and Proportionality. 120
  2. Privilege and Work Product. 140
- D. Handling Disclosure and Discovery Disputes: Herein of Sanctions. 160
  1. Motions to Compel 161
  2. Motions for Protective Orders 166
  3. Certifications in the Discovery Process. 171
  4. Other Sanctions 172

CHAPTER FOUR: CASE MANAGEMENT, SETTLEMENT, AND ALTERNATIVE DISPUTE RESOLUTION 174

Sec.

- A. Perspectives on Case Management, Settlement, and Alternative Dispute Resolution 176
- B. Case Management. 184
  1. The Scheduling Order 184
  2. Some Basic Case-Management Techniques 189
  3. Final Disclosures and the Final Pretrial Order 195
- C. Settlement and Alternative Dispute Resolution 200
  1. An Overview 201
  2. Settlement. 205
  3. Using ADR Techniques in Litigation. 213
  4. Arbitration, Unconscionability, and Preemption 219

CHAPTER FIVE: JUDGE AND JURY. 231

Sec.

- A. Perspectives on Jury Trial 232
- B. Summary Judgment 236
- C. Jury Trial. 249
  1. The Right to Trial by Jury in Federal Civil Cases 250
  2. Selecting a Jury 266
  3. Motion for Judgment as a Matter of Law 272
  4. Jury Instructions, Special Verdicts, and General Verdicts with Answers to Written Questions 281
  5. Renewed Motion for Judgment as a Matter of Law and Motion for a New Trial. 283

		a.	Renewed Motion for Judgment as a Matter of Law......	283
			i. Timing	283
			ii. Grounds	283
			iii. Limits on Renewed Motion	283
		b.	New Trial	284
			i. Timing	284
			ii. Grounds	284
			iii. Limits on Motion for New Trial	285
		c.	Constitutional Considerations........................	285
		d.	Relationship Between Judgment as a Matter of Law and New Trial	285
D.	Factfinding in Trials Without a Jury......................			291
	1.	Selecting the Factfinder: The Advisory Jury and Special Masters		292
	2.	Findings of Fact and Conclusions of Law		292
	3.	Motions to Terminate Trial and Post-Trial Motions		293
E.	Relief from a Judgment or Order...........................			294

CHAPTER SIX: APPEALS 301

Sec.

A.	The Structure and Functions of Appellate Courts		301
	1.	Structure of Appellate-Court Systems	301
	2.	Correcting Error, Settling Conflicts, and Articulating the Law	303
B.	Basic Concepts...		305
	1.	Appealability..	305
	2.	Reviewability..	309
	3.	Standard of Review......................................	310

CHAPTER SEVEN: JUDGMENTS 313

Sec.

A.	Perspectives on Judgments	314
B.	Claim Preclusion..	320
C.	Issue Preclusion...	329
D.	Interjurisdictional Preclusion................................	342
E.	Law of the Case and Stare Decisis...........................	345
	1. Law of the Case..	345
	2. Stare Decisis	347

CHAPTER EIGHT: JOINDER OF CLAIMS AND PARTIES........... 349

Sec.

A.	Perspectives on Joinder	350

B. A Primer on Jurisdiction	353
C. Claim Joinder	355
1. Asserting Multiple Claims Against the Defendant	355
2. Asserting Multiple Defenses Against the Plaintiff	357
3. Asserting Claims Against the Plaintiff	357
D. Party Joinder	363
1. Permissive Party Joinder	364
a. Joining Additional Plaintiffs and Defendants	364
b. Impleading Third-Party Defendants	369
c. Asserting Additional Claims	375
2. Required Joinder Under Rule 19	380
3. Intervention	388
4. Other Joinder Rules	395
a. Interpleader	396
b. Class Actions	397

CHAPTER NINE: PERSONAL JURISDICTION AND VENUE 399

Sec.

A. Perspectives on Personal Jurisdiction	400
B. From Presence to Contacts	405
C. Applying Minimum Contacts	419
1. The First Step: Statutes or Court Rules as the Authority for Exercising Personal Jurisdiction	419
2. The Second Step: Constitutional Authority and Minimum-Contacts Analysis	420
D. Beyond Minimum Contacts: Other Bases for Personal Jurisdiction	461
1. General Jurisdiction	461
2. "Presence": Service in the Forum State	472
3. Consent and Waiver	479
E. The Requirement of Notice	485
F. Personal Jurisdiction in Federal Court	494
G. Venue	495
1. Original Venue	495
2. Change of Venue	498

CHAPTER TEN: SUBJECT-MATTER JURISDICTION 508

Sec.

A. Perspectives on Subject-Matter Jurisdiction	508
B. Federal-Question Jurisdiction	516
1. The "Well-Pleaded Complaint" Rule	516
2. Sufficiency of the Federal Question	521
C. Diversity Jurisdiction	534
1. Diversity of Citizenship	534

		a.	The Complete-Diversity Rule	534
		b.	Determining Citizenship	535
	2.	Amount in Controversy		547

D. Supplemental Jurisdiction 551
E. Removal Jurisdiction and Procedure 567

CHAPTER ELEVEN: STATE LAW IN FEDERAL COURTS (THE *ERIE* DOCTRINE) 574

Sec.

A. Perspectives on *Erie* 574
B. Developing and Applying *Erie* in the Procedural Context 586
C. Ascertaining the Content of State Law 623

CHAPTER TWELVE: CLASS ACTIONS 631

Sec.

A. Perspectives on Class Actions............................... 632
B. Class Actions: The Basics 636
    1. Rule 23(a) 636
    2. Rule 23(g) 639
    3. Rule 23(b) 639
    4. Applying Rule 23...................................... 642
C. Procedural Doctrines Reconsidered 657
    1. Personal Jurisdiction 658
    2. Subject-Matter Jurisdiction 665
    3. Preclusion 676
    4. *Erie* 682
    5. Trial.. 686
D. Settlement Class Actions: Resolving Widespread Disputes Without Adversary Litigation 688

INDEX 701

TABLE OF CONTENTS

PREFACE TO THE FIFTH EDITION... v
PREFACE TO THE FIRST EDITION... vii
ACKNOWLEDGMENTS.. ix
SUMMARY OF CONTENTS.. xi
TABLE OF CASES... xxix
TABLE OF AUTHORITIES... xliii

CHAPTER ONE: AN INTRODUCTION TO CIVIL PROCEDURE......... 1
Sec.

A. The Goals of a Procedural System............................... 2
Robert G. Bone, *The Process of Making Process: Court Rulemaking, Democratic Legitimacy, and Procedural Efficacy*............. 2
Notes and Questions 4
Stephan Landsman, *Readings on Adversarial Justice: The American Approach to Adjudication* 6
John H. Langbein, *The German Advantage in Civil Procedure* 7
Notes and Questions 9

B. A Brief History of the American Procedural System 11
1. English Antecedents....................................... 11
2. American Antecedents 14
3. The Modern American System.............................. 15

C. An Overview of the American Judicial System 16
1. Dual System of Courts 16
2. Source of Law 18
3. Processing the Lawsuit.................................... 19
4. Finality 20
5. Challenging the Standard Litigation Paradigm............. 20

D. American Civil Procedure in Comparative Perspective 21

E. The Social Significance of Civil Dispute Resolution 22

CHAPTER TWO: PLEADING 24
Sec.

A. Perspectives on Pleading 24
Charles E. Clark, *Handbook of the Law of Code Pleading* 25
Notes and Questions 25

B. The Complaint 26
1. A Sample Complaint 27
2. The Sufficiency of the Complaint 28
   Conley v. Gibson 28
   Notes and Questions 30
   Swierkiewicz v. Sorema N.A. 31
   Notes and Questions 34
   Bell Atlantic Corp. v. Twombly 36
   Notes and Questions 43
   Ashcroft v. Iqbal 45
   Notes and Questions 53
3. Filing and Serving the Complaint 58
   Rio Properties, Inc. v. Rio International Interlink 59
   Notes and Questions 64

C. Responding to the Complaint 67
1. Rule 12 Motions 67
2. The Answer 70
   Milton v. General Dynamics Ordnance and Tactical Systems, Inc. 70
   Notes and Questions 72
   GEOMC Co. v. Calmare Therapeutics Inc. 74
   Notes and Questions 78

D. Amending the Pleadings 80
Williams v. Citigroup Inc. 80
Notes and Questions 84
Neita v. City of Chicago 86
Notes and Questions 88

E. Policing Pleadings and Motions 90
Patsy's Brand, Inc. v. I.O.B. Realty, Inc. 90
In re Pennie & Edmonds LLP 95
Notes and Questions 98
Frantz v. United States Powerlifting Federation 102
Notes and Questions 105

CHAPTER THREE: DISCLOSURE AND DISCOVERY	107

Sec.

A. **Perspectives on Discovery** 108

    Julius Byron Levine, *Discovery* 108
    Geoffrey C. Hazard, Jr., *Discovery and the Role of the Judge in Civil Law Jurisdictions* 108
    Stephen N. Subrin, *Discovery in Global Perspective: Are We Nuts?* 109
    Notes and Questions 110

B. **The Mechanics of Disclosure and Discovery** 113

    1. Party-Initiated Discovery Devices 113
        Notes and Questions 114
    2. Required Initial Disclosure 117
    3. Supplementing Disclosures and Responses 118

C. **The Scope of and Limits on Discovery** 118

    1. Relevance and Proportionality 120
        Oxbow Carbon & Minerals LLC v. Union Pacific R.R. 121
        Notes and Questions 128
        United States ex rel. Guardiola v. Renown Health 130
        Notes and Questions 137
    2. Privilege and Work Product 140
        Hickman v. Taylor 141
        Notes and Questions 149
        Republic of Ecuador v. Hinchee 152
        Notes and Questions 157

D. **Handling Disclosure and Discovery Disputes: Herein of Sanctions** 160

    1. Motions to Compel 161
        National Hockey League v. Metropolitan Hockey Club, Inc. ... 161
        Notes and Questions 163
    2. Motions for Protective Orders 166
        In re National Prescription Opiate Litigation 167
        Notes and Questions 170
    3. Certifications in the Discovery Process 171
    4. Other Sanctions 172

CHAPTER FOUR: CASE MANAGEMENT, SETTLEMENT, AND ALTERNATIVE DISPUTE RESOLUTION	174

Sec.

A. **Perspectives on Case Management, Settlement, and Alternative Dispute Resolution** 176

Sec.

A. Perspectives on Case Management, Settlement, and Alternative Dispute Resolution — Continued

William W Schwarzer, *The Federal Rules, the Adversary Process, and Discovery Reform* 176
Judith Resnik, *Managerial Judges* 177
Owen M. Fiss, *Against Settlement* 178
Notes and Questions 180

B. Case Management 184

1. The Scheduling Order 184
   McKeague v. One World Technologies, Inc. 185
   Notes and Questions 188
2. Some Basic Case-Management Techniques 189
   Manual for Complex Litigation, Fourth 189
   Acuna v. Brown & Root Inc. 190
   Ocean Atlantic Woodland Corp. v. DRH Cambridge Homes, Inc. 192
   Notes and Questions 193
3. Final Disclosures and the Final Pretrial Order 195
   R.M.R. v. Muscogee County School District 196
   Notes and Questions 199

C. Settlement and Alternative Dispute Resolution 200

1. An Overview 201
   Leonard L. Riskin et al., *Dispute Resolution and Lawyers* 201
   Notes 203
2. Settlement 205
   Marek v. Chesny 206
   Notes and Questions 211
3. Using ADR Techniques in Litigation 213
   United States v. Tenacious Holdings, Inc. 214
   Notes and Questions 217
4. Arbitration, Unconscionability, and Preemption 219
   AT&T Mobility LLC v. Concepcion 220
   Notes and Questions 227

CHAPTER FIVE: JUDGE AND JURY 231

Sec.

A. Perspectives on Jury Trial 232

Lawrence M. Friedman, *Some Notes on the Civil Jury in Historical Perspective* 232
Notes and Questions 234

Sec.

B. **Summary Judgment** 236
    Celotex Corp. v. Catrett 236
    Notes and Questions 239
    Scott v. Harris 243
    Notes and Questions 247

C. **Jury Trial** 249
  1. The Right to Trial by Jury in Federal Civil Cases 250
      Chauffeurs, Teamsters and Helpers, Local No. 391 v. Terry .. 250
      Notes and Questions 256
      Markman v. Westview Instruments, Inc. 259
      Notes and Questions 263
  2. Selecting a Jury 266
      Edmonson v. Leesville Concrete Co. 267
      Notes and Questions 272
  3. Motion for Judgment as a Matter of Law 272
      Reeves v. Sanderson Plumbing Products, Inc. 273
      Notes and Questions 280
  4. Jury Instructions, Special Verdicts, and General Verdicts with Answers to Written Questions 281
  5. Renewed Motion for Judgment as a Matter of Law and Motion for a New Trial 283
    a. Renewed Motion for Judgment as a Matter of Law 283
        i. Timing 283
        ii. Grounds 283
        iii. Limits on Renewed Motion 283
    b. New Trial 284
        i. Timing 284
        ii. Grounds 284
        iii. Limits on Motion for New Trial 285
    c. Constitutional Considerations 285
    d. Relationship Between Judgment as a Matter of Law and New Trial 285
      Unitherm Food Systems, Inc. v. Swift-Eckrich, Inc. 286
      Notes and Questions 289

D. **Factfinding in Trials Without a Jury** 291
  1. Selecting the Factfinder: The Advisory Jury and Special Masters 292
  2. Findings of Fact and Conclusions of Law 292
  3. Motions to Terminate Trial and Post-Trial Motions 293

Sec.

E. Relief from a Judgment or Order 294
    Ackermann v. United States 295
    Notes and Questions 298

CHAPTER SIX: APPEALS 301
Sec.

A. The Structure and Functions of Appellate Courts 301
    1. Structure of Appellate-Court Systems 301
    2. Correcting Error, Settling Conflicts, and Articulating the Law 303

B. Basic Concepts 305
    1. Appealability 305
    2. Reviewability 309
    3. Standard of Review 310

CHAPTER SEVEN: JUDGMENTS 313
Sec.

A. Perspectives on Judgments 314
    Restatement (Second) of Judgments 314
    Notes 319

B. Claim Preclusion 320
    Restatement (Second) of Judgments 320
    Notes 321
    Rush v. City of Maple Heights 323
    Notes and Questions 328

C. Issue Preclusion 329
    Restatement (Second) of Judgments 329
    Notes and Questions 330
    Parklane Hosiery Co. v. Shore 333
    Notes and Questions 338

D. Interjurisdictional Preclusion 342
    Questions 345

E. Law of the Case and Stare Decisis 345
    1. Law of the Case 345
    2. Stare Decisis 347

CHAPTER EIGHT: JOINDER OF CLAIMS AND PARTIES 349
Sec.

A. Perspectives on Joinder 350
Abram Chayes, *The Role of the Judge in Public Law Litigation* 350
Lon L. Fuller, *The Forms and Limits of Adjudication* 351
Notes and Questions 352

B. A Primer on Jurisdiction 353

C. Claim Joinder 355
1. Asserting Multiple Claims Against the Defendant 355
2. Asserting Multiple Defenses Against the Plaintiff 357
3. Asserting Claims Against the Plaintiff 357
   Painter v. Harvey 357
   Notes and Questions 360

D. Party Joinder 363
1. Permissive Party Joinder 364
   a. Joining Additional Plaintiffs and Defendants 364
      Griggs v. Holt 364
      Notes and Questions 367
   b. Impleading Third-Party Defendants 369
      Lehman v. Revolution Portfolio LLC 370
      Notes and Questions 373
   c. Asserting Additional Claims 375
      Luyster v. Textron, Inc. 375
      Notes and Questions 379
2. Required Joinder Under Rule 19 380
   Makah Indian Tribe v. Verity 381
   Notes and Questions 385
3. Intervention 388
   Grutter v. Bollinger 388
   Notes and Questions 393
4. Other Joinder Rules 395
   a. Interpleader 396
   b. Class Actions 397

CHAPTER NINE: PERSONAL JURISDICTION AND VENUE 399
Sec.

A. Perspectives on Personal Jurisdiction 400

Sec.

A. Perspectives on Personal Jurisdiction — Continued

Wendy Collins Perdue, *Personal Jurisdiction and the Beetle in the Box*... 400
Notes and Questions 405

B. From Presence to Contacts 405

Pennoyer v. Neff 406
Notes and Questions 410
International Shoe Co. v. Washington 412
Notes and Questions 415

C. Applying Minimum Contacts 419

1. The First Step: Statutes or Court Rules as the Authority for Exercising Personal Jurisdiction 419
2. The Second Step: Constitutional Authority and Minimum-Contacts Analysis 420

   Notes and Questions 423
   World–Wide Volkswagen Corp. v. Woodson 424
   Notes and Questions 432
   J. McIntyre Machinery, Ltd. v. Nicastro 437
   Notes and Questions 444
   Bristol–Myers Squibb Co. v. Superior Court of California 446
   Notes and Questions 451
   Shippitsa Ltd. v. Slack 453
   Notes and Questions 458

D. Beyond Minimum Contacts: Other Bases for Personal Jurisdiction 461

1. General Jurisdiction 461

   Daimler AG v. Bauman 461
   Notes and Questions 470

2. "Presence": Service in the Forum State 472

   Burnham v. Superior Court of California 472
   Notes and Questions 476

3. Consent and Waiver 479

   Carnival Cruise Lines, Inc. v. Shute 479
   Notes and Questions 484

E. The Requirement of Notice 485

Mullane v. Central Hanover Bank & Trust Co. 486
Notes and Questions 492

F. Personal Jurisdiction in Federal Court 494

G. Venue 495

1. Original Venue 495

Sec.

G. **Venue** — Continued

    2. Change of Venue 498

        Piper Aircraft Co. v. Reyno 500
        Notes and Questions 506

CHAPTER TEN: SUBJECT-MATTER JURISDICTION 508

Sec.

A. **Perspectives on Subject-Matter Jurisdiction** 508

    Burt Neuborne, *The Myth of Parity* 509
    Gil Seinfeld, *The Federal Courts as a Franchise: Rethinking the Justifications for Federal Question Jurisdiction* 511
    Larry Kramer, *Diversity Jurisdiction* 512
    Notes and Questions 515

B. **Federal-Question Jurisdiction** 516

    1. The "Well-Pleaded Complaint" Rule 516

        Louisville & Nashville Railroad Co. v. Mottley 516
        Notes and Questions 518

    2. Sufficiency of the Federal Question 521

        Grable & Sons Metal Products, Inc. v. Darue Engineering & Manufacturing 522
        Notes and Questions 527
        Gunn v. Minton 527
        Notes and Questions 532

C. **Diversity Jurisdiction** 534

    1. Diversity of Citizenship 534

        a. The Complete-Diversity Rule 534
        b. Determining Citizenship 535

            Sheehan v. Gustafson 535
            Notes and Questions 537
            Hertz Corp. v. Friend 540
            Notes and Questions 546

    2. Amount in Controversy 547

        JTH Tax, Inc. v. Frashier 547
        Notes and Questions 550

D. **Supplemental Jurisdiction** 551

    United Mine Workers of America v. Gibbs 552
    Notes and Questions 554
    Exxon Mobil Corp. v. Allapattah Services, Inc. 557
    Notes and Questions 565

Sec.

E. Removal Jurisdiction and Procedure 567
   Spencer v. U.S. District Court for the Northern District of California... 567
   Notes and Questions 569

CHAPTER ELEVEN: STATE LAW IN FEDERAL COURTS (THE *ERIE* DOCTRINE) 574

Sec.

A. Perspectives on *Erie*.................................... 574
   Rules of Decision Act..................................... 575
   Swift v. Tyson 575
   Erie Railroad Co. v. Tompkins............................ 577
   Edward A. Purcell, Jr., *Brandeis and the Progressive Constitution*... 582
   Notes and Questions 584

B. Developing and Applying *Erie* in the Procedural Context . 586
   Guaranty Trust Co. of New York v. York................... 586
   Ragan v. Merchants Transfer & Warehouse Co............... 588
   Notes and Questions 590
   Hanna v. Plumer... 594
   Notes and Questions 600
   Walker v. Armco Steel Corp............................... 603
   Notes and Questions 607
   Gasperini v. Center for Humanities, Inc.................. 609
   Notes and Questions 612
   Shady Grove Orthopedic Associates, P.A. v. Allstate Insurance Co. 614
   Notes and Questions 622

C. Ascertaining the Content of State Law 623
   Webber v. Sobba.. 623
   Notes and Questions 627

CHAPTER TWELVE: CLASS ACTIONS 631

Sec.

A. Perspectives on Class Actions 632
   David L. Shapiro, *Class Actions: The Class as Party and Client*.. 632
   Notes and Questions 635

B. Class Actions: The Basics................................ 636
   1. Rule 23(a) 636
   2. Rule 23(g) 639

Sec.

B. Class Actions: The Basics— Continued

   3. Rule 23(b) 639
   4. Applying Rule 23... 642
      Haley v. Medtronic, Inc. 642
      Notes and Questions.. 647
      Wal–Mart Stores, Inc. v. Dukes 648
      Notes 656

C. Procedural Doctrines Reconsidered..................... 657

   1. Personal Jurisdiction 658
      Phillips Petroleum Co. v. Shutts 658
      Notes and Questions.. 663
   2. Subject-Matter Jurisdiction.............................. 665
      Standard Fire Insurance Co. v. Knowles............ 667
      Preston v. Tenet Healthsystem Memorial Medical Center, Inc. 669
      Notes 673
   3. Preclusion 676
      Stephenson v. Dow Chemical Co....................... 676
      Notes and Questions.. 680
   4. *Erie* 682
      In re Rhone–Poulenc Rorer, Inc. 683
      Shady Grove Orthopedic Associates, P.A. v. Allstate Insurance Co. 684
      Notes and Questions.. 684
   5. Trial.. 686

D. Settlement Class Actions: Resolving Widespread Disputes Without Adversary Litigation 688
   Amchem Products, Inc. v. Windsor........................ 689
   Notes and Questions 696

INDEX 701

TABLE OF CASES

Principal cases appear in bold typeface.
References are to page number.

721 Bourbon, Inc. v. House of Auth, LLC, 140 F. Supp. 3d 586 (E.D. La. 2015), 423

A Corp. v. All Am. Plumbing, Inc., 812 F.3d 54 (1st Cir. 2016), 461
Abbas v. Foreign Policy Group, LLC, 783 F.3d 1328 (D.C. Cir. 2015), 609, 622
Abood v. Detroit Bd. of Educ., 431 U.S. 209 (1977), 347
Abrazinski v. DuBois, 876 F. Supp. 313 (D. Mass. 1995), 74
Absolute Activist Value Master Fund Ltd. v. Devine, 262 F. Supp. 3d 1312 (M.D. Fla. 2017), 159
Acevedo v. Allsup's Convenience Stores, Inc., 600 F.3d 516 (5th Cir. 2010), 367
Ackermann, United States v., 53 F. Supp. 611 (W.D. Tex. 1943), 298
Ackermann v. United States, 340 U.S. 193 (1950), **295**
Acorda Therapeutics Inc. v. Mylan Pharm. Inc., 817 F.3d 755 (Fed. Cir. 2016), 461
Acuna v. Brown & Root Inc., 200 F.3d 335 (5th Cir. 2000), **190**
Adam v. Saenger, 303 U.S. 59 (1938), 479
Adams v. Robertson, 520 U.S. 83 (1997), 663
Adickes v. S.H. Kress & Co., 398 U.S. 144 (1970), 240
Advance Magazine Publishers, Inc. v. Tinsley, 2019 WL 1285089 (E.D. Mich. Mar. 20, 2019), 65
AE *ex rel.* Hernandez v. Cty. of Tulare, 666 F.3d 631 (9th Cir. 2012), 85
AFTG–TG, LLC v. Nuvoton Tech. Corp., 689 F.3d 1358 (Fed. Cir. 2012), 445
"Agent Orange" Prod. Liab. Litig., *In re*, 821 F.2d 139 (2d Cir. 1987), 171

Aguilar v. Immigration & Customs Enforcement Div., 255 F.R.D. 350 (S.D.N.Y. 2008), 137
Ainsworth v. Moffett Eng'g, Ltd., 716 F.3d 174 (5th Cir. 2013), 445
AK Ssteele Corp. v. PAC Operation L.P., 2017 WL 3314294 (D. Kan. Aug. 3, 2017), 484
Aldinger v. Howard, 427 U.S. 1 (1976), 555
Alicea-Hernandez v. Catholic Bishop of Chi., 320 F.3d 698 (7th Cir. 2003), 69
ALS Scan, Inc. v. Digital Serv. Consultants, Inc., 293 F.3d 707 (4th Cir. 2002), 458
Alumax Mill Prods., Inc. v. Cong. Fin. Corp., 912 F.2d 996 (8th Cir. 1990), 379
Amchem Prods., Inc. v. Windsor, 521 U.S. 591 (1997), 685, **689**
American Elec. Power Co. v. Connecticut, 564 U.S. 410 (2011), 347
American Express Co. v. Italian Colors Rest., 570 U.S. 228 (2013), 228
American Life Ins. Co. v. Stewart, 300 U.S. 203 (1937), 264
American Med. Sys., Inc., *In re*, 75 F.3d 1069 (6th Cir. 1996), 648
American Nat'l Red Cross v. S.G., 505 U.S. 247 (1992), 519
American Nurses' Ass'n v. Illinois, 783 F.2d 716 (7th Cir. 1986), 57
American Trucking Ass'n v. N.Y. State Thruway Auth., 795 F.3d 351 (2d Cir. 2015), 387
Americold Realty Trust v. ConAgra Foods, Inc., 577 U.S. —, 136 S. Ct. 1012 (2016), 547
Amgen Inc. v. Conn. Ret. Plans & Trust Funds, 568 U.S. 455 (2013), 656

Ammons v. Ally Fin., Inc. 305 F. Supp. 3d 818 (M.D. Tenn. 2018), 362, 566

Anderson v. City of Bessemer City, 470 U.S. 564 (1985), 293, 294

Anderson v. Liberty Lobby, Inc., 477 U.S. 242 (1986), 240

Anderson Group v. City of Saratoga Springs, 803 F.3d 34 (2d Cir. 2015), 285

Ariel Invs. v. Ariel Capital Advisors, 881 F.3d 520 (7th Cir. 2018), 461

Arizona v. California, 530 U.S. 392 (2000), 320

Armstrong v. Pomerance, 423 A.2d 174 (Del. 1980), 418

Artis v. Dist. of Columbia, 583 U.S. —, 138 S. Ct. 594 (2018), 567

Asahi Metal Indus. Co. v. Superior Court of Cal., 480 U.S. 102 (1987), 436

ASARCO, LLC v. Union Pac. R.R., 765 F.3d 999 (9th Cir. 2014), 88

Asbestos Prods. Liab. Litig., *In re*, 384 F. Supp. 3d 532 (E.D. Pa. 2019), 485

Ashcroft v. Iqbal, 556 U.S. 662 (2009), **45**

Atlantic Marine Constr. Corp. v. U.S. District Court, 571 U.S. 49 (2013), 499, 628

Atlantic Pipe Corp., *In re*, 304 F.3d 135 (1st Cir. 2002), 217

Atlantis Dev. Corp. v. United States, 379 F.2d 818 (5th Cir. 1967), 394

ATSI Commc'ns, Inc. v. Shaar Fund, Ltd., 579 F.3d 143 (2d Cir. 2009), 98

AT&T Mobility LLC v. Concepcion, 563 U.S. 333 (2011), **220**

A.T. *ex rel.* Travis v. Hahn,, 341 F. Supp. 3d 1031 (E.D. Mo. 2018), 452

Avandia Mktg., Sales Practices & Prods. Liab. Litig., *In re*, 924 F.3d 662 (3d Cir. 2019), 171

Avista Mgmt., Inc. v. Wausau Underwriters Ins. Co., 2006 WL 1562246 (M.D. Fla. June 6, 2006), 165

Axiom Foods, Inc. v. Acerchem Int'l, Inc. 874 F.3d 1064 (9th Cir. 2017), 461

Baker v. Gold Seal Liquors, Inc., 417 U.S. 467 (1974), 361

Banco Nacional de Cuba v. Sabbatino, 376 U.S. 398 (1964), 585

Bandemer v. Ford Motor Co., 931 N.W. 2d 744 (Minn. 2019), 452

Bank of the United States v. Planters' Bank of Ga., 22 U.S. (9 Wheat.) 904 (1824), 519

Bartels *ex rel.* Bartels v. Saber Healthcare Grp., LLC, 880 F.3d 668 (4th Cir. 2018), 675

B & B Hardware, Inc. v. Hargis Indus., Inc., 575 U.S. 138 (2015), 332

Beacon Theatres, Inc. v. Westover, 359 U.S. 500 (1959), 264, 308

Bell Atlantic Corp. v. Twombly, 550 U.S. 544 (2007), **36**

Bell v. Johnson, 404 F.3d 997 (6th Cir. 2005), 285

Beneficial Nat'l Bank v. Anderson, 539 U.S. 1 (2003), 572

Benitez v. JMC Recycling Sys., Ltd., 97 F. Supp. 3d 576 (D.N.J. 2015), 446

Bergeron v. Nw. Publ'ns Inc., 165 F.R.D. 518 (D. Minn. 1996), 101

Best Van Lines, Inc. v. Walker, 490 F.3d 239 (2d Cir. 2007), 458

Betzel v. State Farm Lloyds, 480 F.3d 704 (5th Cir. 2007), 188

Blair v. Equifax Check Servs., Inc., 181 F.3d 832 (7th Cir. 1999), 657

BNSF Ry. Co. v. Tyrrell, 581 U.S. —, 137 S. Ct. 1549 (2017), 470

Boulger v. Woods, 917 F.3d 471 (6th Cir. 2019), 69

Bowers v. Nat'l Collegiate Athletic Ass'n, 475 F.3d 524 (3d Cir. 2007), 118

Boyle v. United Techs. Corp., 487 U.S. 500 (1988), 585

Braddock v. Orlando Reg'l Health Care Sys., Inc., 881 F. Supp. 580 (M.D. Fla. 1995), 608

Branch Consultants, L.L.C., United States *ex rel.* v. Allstate Ins. Co. v., 265 F.R.D. 266 (E.D. La. 2010), 360

Breslin v. Brainard, 2002 WL 31513429 (E.D. Pa. Nov. 1, 2002), 194

Bridgeport Music, Inc. v. Still N The Water Publ'g, 327 F.3d 472 (6th Cir. 2003), 436

Bristol–Myers Squibb Co. v. Super. Ct. of Cal., 582 U.S. —, 137 S. Ct. 1773 (2017), 445, **446**

Brown v. Lockheed Martin Corp., 814 F.3d 619 (2d Cir. 2016), 484

Bryant v. Egan, 890 F.3d 382 (2d Cir. 2018), 290

Burger King Corp. v. Rudzewicz, 471 U.S. 462 (1985), 434

Burks v. Wis. Dep't of Transp., 464 F.3d 744 (7th Cir. 2006), 243

Burlington N. R.R. v. Woods, 480 U.S. 1 (1987), 608

Burnham v. Superior Court of Cal., 495 U.S. 604 (1990), **472**

Business Guides, Inc. v. Chromatic Commc'ns Enters., Inc., 498 U.S. 533 (1991), 101
Byrd v. Blue Ridge Rural Elec. Coop., Inc., 356 U.S. 525 (1958), 591

C.B. v. City of Sonora, 769 F.3d 1005 (9th Cir. 2014), 282
Cable News Network L.P. v. cnnews.com, 162 F. Supp. 2d 484 (E.D. Va. 2001), 418
Calder v. Jones, 465 U.S. 783 (1984), 459
Camacho v. Major League Baseball, 297 F.R.D. 457 (S.D. Cal. 2013), 386
Campbell–Ewald Co. v. Gomez, 577 U.S. —, 136 S. Ct. 663 (2016), 213, 656
Canada Life Assurance Co. v. Converium Ruckversicherung (Deutschland) AG, 335 F.3d 52 (2d Cir. 2003), 533
Capitol Hill Group v. Pillsbury, Winthrop, Shaw, Pittman, LLC, 569 F.3d 485 (D.C. Cir. 2009), 361
Carbone v. Cable News Network, Inc., 910 F.3d 1345 (11th Cir. 2018), 609
Carden v. Arkoma Assocs., 494 U.S. 185 (1990), 547
Carlsbad Tech., Inc. v. HIF Bio, Inc., 556 U.S. 635 (2009), 566, 570
Carlson v. Green, 446 U.S. 14 (1980), 256
Carnival Cruise Lines, Inc. v. Shute, 499 U.S. 585 (1991), **479**
Carolina Power & Light Co. v. Uranex, 451 F. Supp. 1044 (N.D. Cal. 1977), 419
Carrera v. Bayer Corp., 727 F.3d 300 (3d Cir. 2013), 638
Castano v. Am. Tobacco Co., 84 F.3d 734 (5th Cir. 1996), 648, 684
Caterpillar Inc. v. Lewis, 519 U.S. 61 (1996), 539
Catrett v. Johns–Manville Sales Corp., 826 F.2d 33 (D.C. Cir. 1987), 239
Cat3, LLC v. Black Lineage, Inc., 164 F. Supp. 3d 488 (S.D.N.Y. 2016), 165
Celli v. Cole, 699 F. App'x 88 (2d Cir. 2017), 57
Celotex Corp. v. Catrett, 477 U.S. 317 (1986), **236**
Certain Real Prop. Located at Route 1, United States v., 126 F.3d 1314 (11th Cir. 1997), 164
Chalick v. Cooper Hosp./Univ. Med. Ctr., 192 F.R.D. 145 (D.N.J. 2000), 117
Chambers v. NASCO, Inc., 501 U.S. 32 (1991), 101, 165
Channell v. Citicorp. Nat'l. Servs., Inc. 89 F.3d 379 (7th Cir. 1996), 566

Chase Nat'l Bank v. City of Norwalk 291 U.S. 431 (1934), 349
Chauffeurs, Teamsters & Helpers, Local No. 391 v. Terry, 494 U.S. 558 (1990), **250**
Checking Account Overdraft Litig., In re, 685 F.3d 1269 (11th Cir. 2012), 229
Checking Account Overdraft Litig., In re, 485 F. App'x 403 (11th Cir. 2012), 229
Checuti v. Conrail, 291 F. Supp. 2d 664 (N.D. Ohio 2003), 85
Chen v. Allstate Ins. Co., 819 F.3d 1136 (9th Cir. 2016), 213
Chevron Corp., In re, 633 F.3d 153 (3d Cir. 2011), 152, 159
Chevron U.S.A., Inc., In re, 109 F.3d 1016 (5th Cir. 1997), 688
Christiansburg Garment Co. v. EEOC, 434 U.S. 412 (1978), 212
Christianson v. Colt Indus. Operating Corp., 486 U.S. 800 (1988), 346
Cimino v. Raymark Indus., Inc., 151 F.3d 297 (5th Cir. 1998), 687
Circuit City Stores, Inc. v. Adams, 532 U.S. 105 (2001), 219
Citicorp Leasing, Inc. v. United Am. Funding, Inc., 2004 WL 102761 (S.D.N.Y. Jan. 21, 2004), 498
City of (see name of city)
Clark v. Paul Gray, Inc., 306 U.S. 583 (1939), 557
Clarke, United States v., 573 U.S. 248 (2014), 312
Clearfield Trust Co. v. United States, 318 U.S. 363 (1943), 585
Cleveland Hous. Renewal Project v. Deutsche Bank Trust Co., 621 F.3d 554 (6th Cir. 2010), 550
Cohen v. Office Depot, Inc., 184 F.3d 1292 (11th Cir. 1999), 608
Colby v. Umbrella, Inc., 955 A.2d 1082 (Vt. 2008), 57
Coleman v. Md. Court of Appeals, 626 F.3d 187 (4th Cir. 2010), 54
CollegeSource, Inc. v. AcademyOne, Inc., 653 F.3d 1066 (9th Cir. 2011), 458
Comcast Corp. v. Behrend, 569 U.S. 27 (2013), 656
Commil USA, LLC v. Cisco Sys., Inc., 575 U.S. 632 (2015), 79
Commissioner v. Sunnen, 333 U.S. 591 (1948), 333
Community Dental Servs. v. Tani, 282 F.3d 1164 (9th Cir. 2002), 300
Compass Bank v. Katz, 287 F.R.D. 392 (S.D. Tex. 2012), 66

Concrete Pipe & Prods. of Cal., Inc. v. Constr. Laborers Pension Trust for S. Cal., 508 U.S. 602 (1993), 294

Conley v. Gibson, 355 U.S. 41 (1957), **28**

Connecticut v. Doehr, 501 U.S. 1 (1991), 493

Construction Prods. Research, Inc., United States v., 73 F.3d 464 (2d Cir. 1996), 159

Coon v. The Medical Ctr., Inc., 797 S.E.2d 828 (Ga. 2017), 585

Cooper v. Fed. Reserve Bank of Richmond, 467 U.S. 867 (1984), 682

Cooper v. Glasser, 419 S.W.3d 924 (Tenn. 2013), 344

Cooper Tire & Rubber Co., In re, 568 F.3d 1180 (10th Cir. 2009), 128

Cooter & Gell v. Hartmarx Corp., 496 U.S. 384 (1990), 101

Correspondent Servs. Corp. v. First Equities Corp. of Fla., 442 F.3d 767 (2d Cir. 2006), 550

County of (see name of county)

Crossman v. Marcoccio, 806 F.2d 329 (1st Cir. 1986), 212

Cunningham Charter Corp. v. Learjet, Inc., 592 F.3d 805 (7th Cir. 2010), 676

Curran v. Price, 150 F.R.D. 85 (D. Md. 1993), 100

Daggett v. Comm'n on Governmental Ethics & Election Practices, 172 F.3d 104 (1st Cir. 1999), 394

D'Agostino, United States ex rel. v. EV3, Inc., 802 F.3d 188 (1st Cir. 2015), 189

Daimler AG v. Bauman, 571 U.S.117 (2014), **461**

Dairy Queen, Inc. v. Wood, 369 U.S. 469 (1962), 264

Damsky v. Zavatt, 289 F.2d 46 (2d Cir. 1961), 257

Dart Cherokee Basin Operating Co. v. Owens, 574 U.S. 81 (2014), 572, 675

Da Silva Moore v. Publicis Groupe, 287 F.R.D. 182 (S.D.N.Y. 2012), 137

Data Key Partners v. Permira Advisers LLC, 849 N.W.2d 693 (Wis. 2014), 57

Daubert v. Merrell Dow Pharm., Inc., 509 U.S. 579 (1993), 158

Davis v. Morris–Walker, Ltd, 922 F.3d 868 (8th Cir. 2019), 85

Deloitte LLP, United States v., 610 F.3d 129 (D.C. Cir. 2010), 151

Delta Air Lines, Inc. v. August, 450 U.S. 346 (1981), 213

Desert Empire Bank v. Ins. Co. of N. Am., 623 F.2d 1371 (9th Cir. 1980), 368

Dice v. Akron, Canton & Youngstown R.R., 342 U.S. 359 (1952), 623

Diet Drugs (Phentermine/Fenfluramine/Dexfenfluramine) Prods. Liab. Litig., In re, 431 F.3d 141 (3d Cir. 2005), 682

Digitek® Prod. Liab. Litig., In re, 264 F.R.D. 249 (S.D. W. Va. 2010), 194

Dimick v. Schiedt, 293 U.S. 474 (1935), 285

DirecTV, Inc. v. Imburgia, 577 U.S. —, 136 S. Ct. 463 (2015), 228

DLC Mgmt. Corp. v. Town of Hyde Park, 163 F.3d 124 (2d Cir. 1998), 286

Dukes v. Wal–Mart Stores, Inc., 964 F. Supp. 2d 1115 (N.D. Cal. 2013), 657

Edmonson v. Leesville Concrete Co., 500 U.S. 614 (1991), **267**

Ehrenhaus v. Reynolds, 965 F.2d 916 (10th Cir. 1992), 166

Eisen v. Carlisle & Jacquelin, 417 U.S. 156 (1974), 641

Eldee-K Rental Props., LLC v. DirecTV, Inc., 748 F.3d 943 (9th Cir. 2014), 497

Elmaghraby v. United States, No. 04 CV 1809 (JG) (SMG) (E.D.N.Y. Nov. 10, 2009), 54

Elyse v. Bridgeside, Inc., 367 F. App'x 266 (2d Cir. 2010), 290

EMC Corp. In re, 677 F.3d 1351 (Fed. Cir. 2012), 367

Empire HealthChoice Assurance, Inc. v. McVeigh, 547 U.S. 677 (2006), 527

Encompass Ins. Co. v. Stone Mansion Rest. Inc., 902 F.3d 147 (3d Cir. 2018), 570

Engel Cases, In re, 283 F. Supp. 3d 1174 (M.D. Fla. 2017), 98, 100

Epic Sys. Corp. v. Lewis, 584 U.S. —, 138 S. Ct. 1612 (2018), 228

Epstein v. MCA, Inc., 179 F.3d 461 (9th Cir. 1999), 680

Erica P. John Fund, Inc. v. Halliburton Co., 563 U.S. 804 (2011), 656

Erie R.R. v. Tompkins, 304 U.S. 64 (1938), **577**

Esfeld v. Costa Crociere, S.P.A., 289 F.3d 1300 (11th Cir. 2002), 592

Estate of Klieman v. Palestinian Auth., 932 F.3d 1115 (D.C. Cir. 2019), 485

Evergreen Square of Cudahy v. Wisc. Housing & Econ. Dev. Auth., 776 F.3d 463 (7th Cir. 2015), 533

Ex parte (see name of party)
Exxon Mobil Corp. v. Allapattah Servs., Inc., 545 U.S. 546 (2005), **557**, 666, 676
Exxon Shipping Co. v. Baker, 554 U.S. 471 (2008), 284

Faludi v. U.S. Shale Sols, L.L.C., 936 F.3d 215 (5th Cir. 2019), 249
Fed. Treasury Enter. Sojuzplodoimport v. SPI Spirits Ltd., 726 F.3d 62 (2d Cir. 2013), 622
Feltner v. Columbia Pictures Television, Inc., 523 U.S. 340 (1998), 257
Ferens v. John Deere Co., 494 U.S. 516 (1990), 628
Fesler v. Whelen Eng'g Co., 794 F. Supp. 2d 994 (S.D. Iowa 2011), 241
Fid. & Deposit Co. of Md. v. United States, 187 U.S. 315 (1902), 243
Finley v. United States, 490 U.S. 545 (1989), 556
First Nat'l Bank of Pulaski v. Curry, 301 F.3d 456 (6th Cir. 2002), 571
FleetBoston Fin. Corp. v. fleetbostonfinancial.com, 138 F. Supp. 2d 121 (D. Mass. 2001), 418
Foman v. Davis, 371 U.S. 178 (1962), 84
Ford Motor Co. v. Mont. Eighth Judicial Dist. Ct., 443 P.3d 407 (Mont. 2019), 452
Foreign Candy Co. v. Tropical Paradise, Inc., 950 F. Supp. 2d 1017 (N.D. Iowa 2013), 423
Fox v. Vice, 563 U.S. 826 (2011), 212
Frantz v. U.S. Powerlifting Fed'n, 836 F.2d 1063 (7th Cir. 1987), **102**
Freeland v. Liberty Mut. Fire Ins. Co., 632 F.3d 250 (6th Cir. 2011), 550
Fuentes v. Shevin, 407 U.S. 67 (1972), 493

Galloway v. United States, 319 U.S. 372 (1943), 242, 280
Garibaldi, United States *ex rel.* v. Orleans Parish Sch. Bd., 397 F.3d 334 (5th Cir. 2005), 320
Garman v. Campbell Cty. Sch. Dist. No. 1, 630 F.3d 977 (10th Cir. 2010), 622, 685
Garst, United States *ex rel.* v. Lockheed–Martin Corp., 328 F.3d 374 (7th Cir. 2003), 58
Gasperini v. Ctr. for Humanities, Inc., 518 U.S. 415 (1996), 285, **609**
Geiserman v. MacDonald, 893 F.2d 787 (5th Cir. 1990), 188

Gelboim v. Bank of Am. Corp., 574 U.S. 405 (2015), 307
General Tel. Co. of Sw. v. Falcon, 457 U.S. 147 (1982), 638
Genuine Parts Co. v. Cepec, 137 A.3d 123 (Del. 2016), 485
GEOMC Co. v. Calmare Therapeutics Inc., 918 F.3d 92 (2d Cir. 2019), **74**
Gibbons v. Bristol–Myers Squibb Co., 919 F.3d 699 (2d Cir. 2019), 570
Gilead Sciences, Inc. v. Merck & Co., 2016 WL 146574 (N.D. Cal. Jan. 13, 2016), 129
Global Naps, Inc. v. Verizon New Eng., Inc., 603 F.3d 71 (1st Cir. 2010), 362, 566
Global Tech. & Trading, Inc. v. Tech Mahindra Ltd., 789 F.3d 730 (7th Cir. 2015), 79
GN Network, Inc. v. Plantronics, Inc., 930 F.3d 76 (3d Cir. 2019), 166
Goldlawr, Inc. v. Heiman, 369 U.S. 463 (1962), 499
Gonzalez-Servin v. Ford Motor Co., 662 F.3d 931 (7th Cir. 2011), 106
Goodlett v. Kalishek, 223 F.3d 32 (2d Cir. 2000), 629
Goodyear Tire & Rubber Co. v. Haeger, 581 U.S. —, 137 S. Ct. 1178 (2017), 165
Gough v. Transamerica Life Ins. Co., 781 F. Supp. 2d 498 (W.D. Ky. 2011), 682
Grable & Sons Metal Prods., Inc. v. Darue Eng'g & Mfg., 545 U.S. 308 (2005), **522**
Grace v. MacArthur, 170 F. Supp. 442 (E.D. Ark. 1959), 478
Granfinanciera, S.A. v. Nordberg, 492 U.S. 33 (1989), 256, 263
Gratz v. Bollinger, 539 U.S. 244 (2003), 393
Great Lakes Gas Transmission Ltd. P'ship v. Essar Steel Minn., LLC,103 F. Supp. 3d 1000 (D. Minn. 2015), 533
Greene v. Lindsey, 456 U.S. 444 (1982), 492
Griggs v. Holt, 2018 WL 5283448 (S.D. Ga. Oct. 24, 2018), **364**
Grutter v. Bollinger, 188 F.3d 394 (6th Cir. 1999), **388**
Grutter v. Bollinger, 539 U.S. 306 (2003), 393
Guaranty Trust Co. of N.Y. v. York, 326 U.S. 99 (1945), **586**
Guardiola, United States *ex rel.*, v. Renown Health, 2015 WL 5056726 (D. Nev. Aug. 25, 2015), **130**

Guidry v. Kem Mfg. Co., 598 F.2d 402 (5th Cir. 1979), 282
Gully v. First Nat'l Bank, 299 U.S. 109 (1936), 522
Gunn v. Minton, 568 U.S. 251 (2013), **527**
Gwinn, United States v., 2006 WL 3377636 (S.D. W. Va. Nov. 20, 2006), 72

Hagans v. Lavine, 415 U.S. 528 (1974), 534
Haley v. Medtronic, Inc., 169 F.R.D. 643 (C.D. Cal. 1996), **642**
Hall v. Hall, 584 U.S. —, 138 S. Ct. 1118 (2018), 308
Hamilton v. Atlas Turner, Inc., 197 F.3d 58 (2d Cir. 1999), 69
Hana Fin., Inc. v. Hana Bank, 574 U.S. 418 (2015), 263
Hanlon v. Chrysler Corp., 150 F.3d 1011 (9th Cir. 1998), 697
Hanna v. Plumer, 380 U.S. 460 (1965), **594**
Hannaford Bros. Co. Customer Data Sec. Breach Litig., *In re*, 564 F.3d 75 (1st Cir. 2009), 675
Hansberry v. Lee, 311 U.S. 32 (1940), 637
Hanson v. Denckla, 357 U.S. 235 (1958), 421
Harborside Refrigerated Servs., Inc. v. Vogel, 959 F.2d 368 (2d Cir. 1992), 322
Harris v. Balk, 198 U.S. 215 (1905), 417
Harris v. Sec'y, U.S. Dep't of Veterans Affairs, 126 F.3d 339 (D.C. Cir. 1997), 79
Harvey v. Grey Wolf Drilling Co., 542 F.3d 1077 (5th Cir. 2008), 547
Havel v. Honda Motor Eur. Ltd., 2014 WL 4967229 (S.D. Tex. Sept. 30, 2014), 461
Herbert v. Nat'l Acad. of Scis., 974 F.2d 192 (D.C. Cir. 1992), 69
Hertz Corp. v. Friend, 559 U.S. 77 (2010), **540**
Hess v. Pawloski, 274 U.S. 352 (1927), 411
Hickman v. Taylor, 329 U.S. 495 (1947), **141**
Hilao v. Estate of Marcos, 103 F.3d 767 (9th Cir. 1996), 687
Holmes v. United States, 898 F.3d 785 (8th Cir. 2018), 299
Home Depot U.S.A., Inc., v. Jackson, 587 U.S. —, 139 S. Ct. 1743 (2019), 571, 674

Horne v. Flores, 557 U.S. 433 (2009), 299
Hospitality Mgmt. Assocs., Inc. v. Shell Oil Co., 591 S.E.2d 611 (S.C. 2004), 682
Hu v. City of New York, 927 F.3d 81 (2d Cir. 2019), 69
Hunt v. Cromartie, 526 U.S. 541 (1999), 248
Husky Ventures, Inc. v. B55 Invs., Ltd., 911 F.3d 1000 (10th Cir. 2018), 86

Iannacchino v. Ford Motor Co., 888 N.E.2d 879 (Mass. 2008), 57
Illinois v. Hemi Group LLC, 622 F.3d 754, 759 (7th Cir. 2010), 458
Improvement Co. v. Munson, 81 U.S. (14 Wall.) 442 (1871), 242
In re **(see name of party)**
Insurance Corp. of Ir. v. Compagnie des Bauxites de Guinee, 456 U.S. 694 (1982), 433
Intellectual Ventures I LLC v. Capital One Fin. Corp., 937 F.3d 1359 (Fed. Cir. 2019), 332
International Shoe Co. v. Washington, 326 U.S. 310 (1945), **412**
Iqbal v. Ashcroft, 574 F.3d 820 (2d Cir. 2009), 54

James River Ins. Co. v. Rapid Funding, LLC, 658 F.3d 1207 (10th Cir. 2011), 622
Janus v. Am. Fed'n of State, Cty., & Mun. Emps., 585 U.S. —, 138 S. Ct. 2448 (2018), 347
Javeler Marine Servs. LLC v. Cross, 175 F. Supp. 2d 756 (S.D. Tex. 2016), 138
Jean Alexander Cosmetics, Inc. v. L'Oreal USA, Inc., 458 F.3d 244 (3d Cir. 2006), 332
J.E.B. v. Alabama *ex rel*. T.B., 511 U.S. 127 (1994), 272
Jenkins v. Methodist Hosps. of Dallas, Inc., 478 F.3d 255 (5th Cir. 2007), 98
Jennings v. Jones, 587 F.3d 430 (1st Cir. 2009), 286
J. Lyons & Co. v. Republic of Tea, Inc., 892 F. Supp. 486 (S.D.N.Y. 1995), 498
J. McIntyre Mach., Ltd. v. Nicastro, 564 U.S. 873 (2011), **437**
Johnson v. City of Shelby, 574 U.S. 10 (2014), 56
Johnson Creative Arts, Inc. v. Wool Masters, Inc., 743 F.2d 947 (1st Cir. 1984), 495

Johnson v. SmithKline Beecham Corp., 724 F.3d 337 (3d Cir. 2013), 546
Jones v. Bock, 549 U.S. 199 (2007), 79
Jones v. Flowers, 547 U.S. 220 (2006), 493
Jones v. Ford Motor Credit Co., 358 F.3d 205 (2d Cir. 2004), 370, 566
Jones v. Krautheim, 208 F. Supp. 2d 1173 (D. Colo. 2002), 608
JTH Tax, Inc. v. Frashier, 624 F.3d 635 (4th Cir. 2010), **547**
Jumpsport, Inc. v. Jumpking, Inc., 213 F.R.D. 329 (N.D. Cal. 2003), 150
Juris v. Inamed Corp., 685 F.3d 1294 (11th Cir. 2012), 665

Katchen v. Landy, 382 U.S. 323 (1966), 265
Kaufman v. Allstate N.J. Ins. Co., 561 F.3d 144 (3d Cir. 2009), 675
Keeton v. Hustler Magazine, Inc., 465 U.S. 770 (1984), 433
Keranos, LLC. v. Analog Devices, Inc., 2011 WL 4027427 (E.D. Tex. Sept. 12, 2011), 445
King Vision Pay Per View, Ltd. v. J.C. Dimitri's Rest., Inc., 180 F.R.D. 332 (N.D. Ill. 1998), 72
Kircher v. Putnam Funds Trust, 547 U.S. 633 (2006), 333
Klaxon Co. v. Stentor Elec. Mfg. Co., 313 U.S. 487 (1941), 628
Klipsch Grp., Inc. v. ePRO E–Commerce Ltd., 880 F.3d 620 (2d Cir. 2018), 160
Klocke v. Watson, 936 F.3d 240 (5th Cir. 2019), 609
Knowlton v. Allied Van Lines, Inc., 900 F.2d 1196 (8th Cir. 1990), 484
Kohler v. Flava Enters., 779 F.3d 1016 (9th Cir. 2015), 78
Koon v. United States, 518 U.S. 81 (1996), 312
Kossick v. United Fruit Co., 365 U.S. 731 (1961), 585
KPS & Assocs., Inc. v. Designs by FMC, Inc., 318 F.3d 1 (1st Cir. 2003), 300
Krupski v. Costa Crociere S. p. A., 560 U.S. 538 (2010), 89

La Buy v. Howes Leather Co., 352 U.S. 249 (1957), 292
Lakes v. Bath & Body Works LLC, 2018 WL 533915 (E.D. Cal. Jan. 23, 2018), 129
Lamarque v. Fairbanks Capital Corp., 927 A.2d 753 (R.I. 2007), 682

Lamps Plus, Inc. v. Varela, 587 U.S. —, 139 S. Ct. 1407 (2019), 227
Lear Corp. v. Johnson Elec. Holdings Ltd., 353 F.3d 580 (7th Cir. 2003), 547
Lehman v. Nakshian, 453 U.S. 156 (1981), 256
Lehman v. Revolution Portfolio LLC, 166 F.3d 389 (1st Cir. 1999), **370**
Lewis v. Windsor Door Co., 926 F.2d 729 (8th Cir. 1991), 571
Leybovich v. SecureAlert, Inc., 237 So. 3d 1104 (Fla. Dist. Ct. App. 2017), 242
Life of the S. Ins. Co. v. Carzell, 851 F.3d 1341 (11th Cir. 2017), 675
Liggon-Redding v. Estate of Sugarman, 659 F.3d 258 (3d Cir. 2011), 608
Lindsley v. Am. Honda Motor Co., 2017 WL 3217140 (E.D. Pa. July 28, 2017), 452
Link v. Wabash R.R., 370 U.S. 626 (1962), 165
Lipscher v. LRP Publ'ns, Inc., 266 F.3d 1305 (11th Cir. 2001), 171
Lockheed Martin Corp. v. United States, 973 F. Supp. 2d 591 (D. Md. 2013), 78
Louisville & Nashville R.R. v. Mottley, 211 U.S. 149 (1908), **516**
Louisville & Nashville R.R. v. Mottley, 219 U.S. 467 (1911), 519
Lundquist v. Precision Valley Aviation, Inc., 946 F.2d 8 (1st Cir. 1991), 537
Lutz v. Glendale Union High Sch., 403 F.3d 1061 (9th Cir. 2005), 256
Luv n' care, Ltd. v. Insta–Mix, Inc., 438 F.3d 465 (5th Cir. 2006), 436
Luyster v. Textron, Inc., 266 F.R.D. 54 (S.D.N.Y. 2010), **375**

Makaeff v. Trump Univ. LLC, 736 F.3d 1180 (9th Cir. 2013)
Makah Indian Tribe v. Verity, 910 F.2d 555 (9th Cir. 1990), **381**
Manganella v. Evanston Ins. Co., 700 F.3d 585 (1st Cir. 2012), 339
Manley v. AmBase Corp., 337 F.3d 237 (2d Cir. 2003), 290
Marbury v. Madison, 5 U.S. (1 Cranch) 137 (1803), 55
Marcello v. Maine, 238 F.R.D. 113 (D. Me. 2006), 65
Marek v. Chesny, 473 U.S. 1 (1985), **206**
Markman v. Westview Instruments, Inc., 517 U.S. 370 (1996), **259**
Marks v. United States, 430 U.S. 188 (1977), 445, 622

Martin v. Behr Dayton Thermal Prods. LLC, 896 F.3d 405 (6th Cir. 2018), 657

Martin v. Wilks, 490 U.S. 755 (1989), 341, 350

Martinez v. Aero Caribbean, 764 F.3d 1062 (9th Cir. 2014), 477

Mason v. Am. Emery Wheel Works, 241 F.2d 906 (1st Cir. 1957), 627

Massachusetts, United States v., 781 F. Supp. 2d 1 (D. Mass. 2011), 180

Massachusetts Sch. of Law at Andover, Inc. v. Am. Bar Ass'n, 914 F. Supp. 1172 (E.D. Pa. 1996), 159

Mathews v. Eldridge, 424 U.S. 319 (1976), 494

Matsushita Elec. Indus. Co. v. Zenith Radio Corp., 475 U.S. 574 (1986), 240

Mayle v. Felix, 545 U.S. 644 (2005), 88

McCulloch v. Maryland, 17 U.S. (4 Wheat.) 316 (1819), 519

McCurry ex rel. Turner v. Adventist Health Sys./Sunbelt, Inc., 298 F.3d 586 (6th Cir. 2002), 300

McDonald v. City of Chi., 561 U.S. 742 (2010), 256

McGee v. Int'l Life Ins. Co., 355 U.S. 220 (1957), 421

McKeague v. One World Techs., Inc., 858 F.3d 703 (1st Cir. 2017), **185**

McMahan v. Toto, 311 F.3d 1077 (11th Cir. 2002), 630

McNabb v. United States, 318 U.S. 332 (1943), 26

Meacham v. Knolls Atomic Power Lab., 554 U.S. 84 (2008), 79

Menard v. CSX Transp., Inc., 698 F.3d 40 (1st Cir. 2012), 45

Mendoza, United States v., 464 U.S. 154 (1984), 340

Merrell Dow Pharm. Inc. v. Thompson, 478 U.S. 804 (1986), 522

Mesa v. California, 489 U.S. 121 (1989), 520

Microsoft Corp. Antitrust Litig., *In re*, 355 F.3d 322 (4th Cir. 2004), 338

Microsoft Corp. v. Baker, 582 U.S. —, 137 S. Ct. 1702 (2017), 657

Microvote Corp. v. Montgomery Cty., 942 F. Supp. 1046 (E.D. Pa. 1996), 627

Milliken v. Meyer, 311 U.S. 457 (1940), 411

Milton v. Gen. Dynamics Ordnance & Tactical Sys., Inc., 2011 WL 4708637 (S.D. Ill. Oct. 4, 2011), **70**

Mims v. Arrow Fin. Servs., LLC, 565 U.S. 368 (2012), 520

Mississippi, United States v., 380 U.S. 128 (1965), 369

Missouri *ex rel.* Pemiscot Cty. v. W. Sur. Co., 51 F.3d 170 (8th Cir. 1995), 550

Mitchell v. Eli Lilly & Co., 159 F. Supp. 3d 967 (E.D. Mo. 2016), 484

Mitchell v. Forsyth, 472 U.S. 511 (1985), 308

Mitchell v. W. T. Grant Co., 416 U.S. 600 (1974), 493

Mobil Corp., United States v., 149 F.R.D. 533 (N.D. Tex. 1993), 152

Mohammad, United States v., 249 F. Supp. 3d 450 (D.D.C. 2017), 67

Mohawk Indus., Inc. v. Carpenter, 558 U.S. 100 (2009), 308

Monfore v. Phillips, 778 F.3d 849 (10th Cir. 2015), 199

Monterey, City of v. Del Monte Dunes at Monterey, Ltd., 526 U.S. 687 (1999), 256

Montgomery Ward & Co. v. Duncan, 311 U.S. 243 (1940), 284

Moore v. Chesapeake & Ohio Ry., 291 U.S. 205 (1934), 521

Moore v. N.Y. Cotton Exch., 270 U.S. 593 (1926), 362, 554

MSC Recovery Claims v. Plymouth Rock Assurance Corp., 404 F. Supp. 3d 470 (D. Mass. 2019), 638

Mullane v. Cent. Hanover Bank & Trust Co., 339 U.S. 306 (1950), 67, **486,** 664

Mullin v. Balicki, 875 F.3d 140 (3d Cir. 2018), 84

Mullins v. Direct Digital, LLC, 795 F.3d 654 (7th Cir. 2015), 638

Murphy Bros. v. Michetti Pipe Stringing, Inc., 526 U.S. 344 (1999), 572

Mwani v. bin Laden, 417 F.3d 1 (D.C. Cir. 2005), 495

N.A. Burkitt, Inc. v. J.I. Case Co., 597 F. Supp. 1086 (D. Me. 1984), 627

National Ass'n of Life Underwriters, Inc. v. Comm'r, 30 F.3d 1526 (D.C. Cir. 1994), 74

National Football League Players Concussion Injury Litig., *In re*, 821 F.3d 410 (3d Cir. 2016), 697

National Hockey League v. Metro. Hockey Club, Inc., 427 U.S. 639 (1976), **161**

National Prescription Opiate Litigation, *In re*, 927 F.3d 919 (6th Cir. 2019), **167**
National Prescription Opiate Litig., 332 F.R.D. 532 (N.D. Ohio 2019), 698
Nationwide Mut. Ins. Co. v. Buffetta, 230 F.3d 634 (3d Cir. 2000), 627
Neita v. City of Chicago, 830 F.3d 494 (7th Cir. 2016), **86**
Newburyport Water Co. v. City of Newburyport, 193 U.S. 561 (1904), 533
Newman–Green, Inc. v. Alfonzo-Larrain, 490 U.S. 826 (1989), 547, 565
Newsham v. Lockheed Missiles & Space Co., United States *ex rel.*, 190 F.3d 963 (9th Cir. 1999), 609
Nolan v. Transocean Air Lines, 276 F.2d 280 (2d Cir. 1960), 628
Norris v. Alabama, 294 U.S. 587 (1935), 266
Northern Ins. Co. of N.Y. v. Constr. Navale Bordeaux, 2011 WL 2682950 (S.D. Fla. July 11, 2011), 445
Northern Light Tech., Inc. v. N. Lights Club, 236 F.3d 57 (1st Cir. 2001), 477
North Ga. Finishing, Inc. v. Di–Chem, Inc., 419 U.S. 601 (1975), 493
Nuesse v. Camp, 385 F.2d 694 (D.C. Cir. 1967), 394

Ocean Atl. Woodland Corp. v. DRH Cambridge Homes, Inc., 2004 WL 609326 (N.D. Ill. Mar. 23, 2004), **192**
O'Connor v. Sandy Lane Hotel Co., 496 F.3d 312 (3d Cir. 2007), 451
Oliveras v. Am. Exp. Isbrandtsen Lines, Inc., 431 F.2d 814 (2d Cir. 1970), 285
Omni Capital Int'l, Ltd. v. Rudolf Wolff & Co., 484 U.S. 97 (1987), 495
Oppenheimer Fund, Inc. v. Sanders, 437 U.S. 340 (1978), 119
Original Creations, Inc. v. Ready Am., Inc., 836 F. Supp. 2d 711 (N.D. Ill. 2011), 445
Ortiz v. Fibreboard Corp., 527 U.S. 815 (1999), 664, 685, 697
Ortiz v. Jordan, 562 U.S. 180 (2011), 291
Osborn v. Bank of the United States, 22 U.S. (9 Wheat.) 738 (1824), 519
Osborn v. Haley, 549 U.S. 225 (2007), 570
Oticon, Inc. v. Sebotek Hearing Sys., LLC, 865 F. Supp. 2d 501 (D.N.J. 2011), 445
Owen Equip. & Erection Co. v. Kroger, 437 U.S. 365 (1978), 555

Oxbow Carbon & Minerals LLC v. Union Pac. R.R., 322 F.R.D. 1 (D.D.C. 2017), **121**
Oxford Global Res., LLC v. Hernandez, 106 N.E.2d 556 (Mass. 2018), 507

Pace v. Timmermann's Ranch & Saddle Shop, Inc., 795 F.3d 748 (7th Cir. 2015), 363
Painter v. Harvey, 863 F.2d 329 (4th Cir. 1988), **357**
PA Prison Soc'y v. Cortes, 622 F.3d 215 (3d Cir. 2010), 395
Parchman v. SLM Corp., 896 F.3d 728 (6th Cir. 2018), 85
Parklane Hosiery Co. v. Shore, 439 U.S. 322 (1979), **333**
Patsy's Brand, Inc. v. I.O.B. Realty, Inc., 317 F.3d 209 (2d Cir. 2003), 101
Patsy's Brand, Inc. v. I.O.B. Realty, Inc., 2002 WL 59434 (S.D.N.Y. Jan. 16, 2002), **90**
Patsy's Brand, Inc. v. I.O.B. Realty, Inc., 2001 WL 1154669 (S.D.N.Y. Oct. 1, 2001), 102
Payment Card Interchange Fee & Merch. Discount Antitrust Litig., *In re*, 827 F.3d 223 (2d Cir. 2016), 682
Peabody v. Hamilton, 106 Mass. 217 (1870), 478
Pennie & Edmonds LLP, *In re*, 323 F.3d 86 (2d Cir. 2003), **95**
Pennoyer v. Neff, 95 U.S. 714 (1878), **406**
Peterson, *Ex parte*, 253 U.S. 300 (1920), 258
Peterson v. Temple, 918 P.2d 413 (Or. 1996), 328
Pharmaceutical Indus. Average Wholesale Price Litig., *In re*, 582 F.3d 156 (1st Cir. 2009), 688
PHC, Inc. S'holder Litig., *In re*, 894 F.3d 419 (1st Cir. 2018), 285
Philip Morris USA, Inc., United States v., 327 F. Supp. 2d 21 (D.D.C. 2004), 165
Phillips Petroleum Co. v. Shutts, 472 U.S. 797 (1985), **658**
Pioneer Inv. Servs. Co. v. Brunswick Assocs. Ltd., 507 U.S. 380 (1993), 299
Piper Aircraft Co. v. Reyno, 454 U.S. 235 (1981), **500**
Plouffe v. Ligon, 606 F.3d 890 (8th Cir. 2010), 312
Plumhoff v. Pickard, 572 U.S. 765 (2014), 247

Poller v. Columbia Broad. Sys., Inc., 368 U.S. 464 (1962), 240
Potomac Elec. Power Co. v. Elec. Motor Supply, Inc., 190 F.R.D. 372 (D. Md. 1999), 188
Powerex Corp. v. Reliant Energy Servs., Inc., 551 U.S. 224 (2007), 570
Preston v. Ferrer, 552 U.S. 346 (2008), 219
Preston v. Tenet Healthsystem Mem'l Med. Ctr., Inc., 485 F.3d 804 (5th Cir. 2007), **669**
Price v. Hartford Life & Accident Ins. Co., 746 F. Supp. 2d 860 (E.D. Mich. 2010), 119
Priester v. JP Morgan Chase Bank, N.A., 927 F.3d 912 (5th Cir. 2019), 300
Provident Tradesmens Bank & Trust Co. v. Patterson, 390 U.S. 102 (1968), 387
P & S Bus. Machs., Inc. v. Canon USA, Inc., 331 F.3d 804 (11th Cir. 2003), 499
Purkett v. Elem, 514 U.S. 765 (1995), 272

Ragan v. Merchs. Transfer & Warehouse Co., 337 U.S. 530 (1949), **588**, 602
Ramirez v. County of San Bernardino, 806 F.3d 1002 (9th Cir. 2015), 84
Ray v. City of Rock Hill, 834 S.E.2d 464 (S.C. 2019), 242
Ray Haluch Gravel Co. v. Cent. Pension Fund of Int'l Union of Operating Eng'rs & Participating Emp'rs, 571 U.S. 177 (2014), 305
Reed v. Columbia St. Mary's Hosp., 915 F.3d 473 (7th Cir. 2019), 79
Reeves v. Sanderson Plumbing Prods., Inc., 530 U.S. 133 (2000), **273**
Rent-A-Center, W., Inc. v. Jackson, 561 U.S. 63 (2010), 219, 227
Republic of Ecuador v. Hinchee, 741 F.3d 1185 (11th Cir. 2013), **152**
Republic of the Philippines v. Pimentel, 553 U.S. 851 (2008), 387
Reynolds v. City of Chicago, 296 F.3d 524 (7th Cir. 2002), 294
Rhoads Indus., Inc. v. Bldg. Materials Corp. of Am., 254 F.R.D. 216 (E.D. Pa. 2008), 159
Rhodes v. MacDonald, 670 F. Supp. 2d 1363 (M.D. Ga. 2009), 105
Rhone–Poulenc Rorer, Inc., *In re*, 51 F.3d 1293 (7th Cir. 1995), 635, 648, **683**

Rimbert v. Eli Lilly & Co., 647 F.3d 1247 (10th Cir. 2011), 188
Rio Props., Inc. v. Rio Int'l Interlink, 284 F.3d 1007 (9th Cir. 2002), **59**, 492
Rivet v. Regions Bank of La., 522 U.S. 470 (1998), 572
R.M.R. v. Muscogee Cty. Sch. Dist., 165 F.3d 812 (11th Cir. 1999), **196**
Roadway Express, Inc. v. Piper, 447 U.S. 752 (1980), 165
Rose v. Giamatti, 721 F. Supp. 906 (S.D. Ohio 1989), 538
Ross v. Bernhard, 396 U.S. 531 (1970), 258, 265
Royce v. Michael R. Needle, P.C., 158 F. Supp. 3d 708 (N.D. Ill. 2016), 99
Rufo v. Inmates of Suffolk Cty. Jail, 502 U.S. 367 (1992), 299
Rush v. City of Maple Heights, 147 N.E.2d 599 (Ohio 1958), **323**

S Indus., Inc. v. Centra 2000, Inc., 249 F.3d 625 (7th Cir. 2001), 128
St. Francis Assis v. Kuwait Fin. House, 2016 WL 5725002 (N.D. Cal. Sept. 30, 2016), 67
St. Jude Med., Inc., Silzone Heart Valve Prods. Liab. Litig., *In re*, 425 F.3d 1116 (8th Cir. 2005), 648
Salazar *ex rel.* Salazar v. Dist. of Columbia, 633 F.3d 1110 (D.C. Cir. 2011), 300
Salus v. Sivan, 534 F. Supp. 2d 430 (S.D.N.Y. 2008), 248
Salve Regina Coll. v. Russell, 499 U.S. 225 (1991), 627
Samovsky v. Nordstrom, Inc., 619 F. App'x 547 (7th Cir. 2015), 54
Sartor v. Ark. Natural Gas Corp., 321 U.S. 620 (1944), 242, 258
Scott v. Harris, 550 U.S. 372 (2007), **243**
Seattle Times Co. v. Rhinehart, 467 U.S. 20 (1984), 170
SEB S.A. v. Montgomery Ward & Co., 594 F.3d 1360 (Fed. Cir. 2010), 284
Semtek Int'l Inc. v. Lockheed Martin Corp., 531 U.S. 497 (2001), 344
September 11th Liab. Ins. Coverage Cases, *In re*, 243 F.R.D. 114 (S.D.N.Y. 2007), 165
Shady Grove Orthopedic Assocs., P.A. v. Allstate Ins. Co., 559 U.S. 393 (2010), 228, 602, **614, 684**
Shaffer v. Heitner, 433 U.S. 186 (1977), 417

Shamrock Oil & Gas Corp. v. Sheets, 313 U.S. 100 (1941), 570
Sheehan v. Gustafson, 967 F.2d 1214 (8th Cir. 1992), **535**
Shippitsa Ltd. v. Slack, 2019 WL 2372687 (N.D. Tex. June 5, 2019), **453**
Shoshone Mining Co. v. Rutter, 177 U.S. 505 (1900), 533
Shuker v. Smith & Nephew, 885 F.3d 760 (3d Cir. 2017), 452
Sibbach v. Wilson & Co., 312 U.S. 1 (1941), 593
Sibley v. Choice Hotels Int'l, 2015 WL 9413101 (E.D.N.Y. Dec. 22, 2015), 120
Sinclair Refining Co. v. Howell, 222 F.2d 637 (5th Cir. 1955), 74
Smilow v. Sw. Bell Mobile Sys., Inc., 323 F.3d 32 (1st Cir. 2003), 687
Smith v. Bayer Corp., 564 U.S. 299 (2011), 664
Smith v. Kansas City Title & Trust Co., 255 U.S. 180 (1921), 521
Smith v. Vaughn, 171 F.R.D. 323 (M.D. Fla.1997), 212
Smith & Fuller P.A. v. Cooper Tire & Rubber Co., 685 F.3d 486 (5th Cir. 2012), 171
SmithKline Beecham Corp. v. Abbott Labs., 740 F.3d 471 (9th Cir. 2014), 272
Sniadach v. Family Fin. Corp. of Bay View, 395 U.S. 337 (1969), 493
Snyder v. Harris, 394 U.S. 332 (1969), 665
Soberay Mach. & Equip. Co. v. MRF Ltd., 181 F.3d 759 (6th Cir. 1999), 386
Sound of Music Co. v. Minn. Mining & Mfg. Co., 477 F.3d 910 (7th Cir. 2007), 85
Southern Pac. Co. v. Jensen, 244 U.S. 205 (1917), 584
Spencer v. U.S. Dist. Court, 393 F.3d 867 (9th Cir. 2004), **567**
Sprague Farms, Inc. v. Providian Corp., 929 F. Supp. 1125 (C.D. Ill. 1996), 106
Standard Fire Ins. Co. v. Knowles, 568 U.S. 588 (2013), **667**
State of (see name of state)
State Farm Fire & Cas. Co. v. Tashire, 386 U.S. 523 (1967), 534
State Farm Mut. Auto. Ins. Co. v. Fayda, 2015 WL 7871037 (S.D.N.Y. Dec. 3, 2015), 129
State Farm Mut. Auto. Ins. Co. v. Riley, 199 F.R.D. 276 (N.D. Ill. 2001), 73
Stein, United States v., 881 F.3d 853 (11th Cir. 2018), 249

Stephenson v. Dow Chem. Co., 273 F.3d 249 (2d Cir. 2001), **676**
Stevens v. City of Brockton, 676 F. Supp. 26 (D. Mass. 1987), 100
Stewart Org., Inc. v. Ricoh Corp., 487 U.S. 22 (1988), 485, 608
Stojcevski v. Cty. of Macomb, 143 F. Supp. 3d (E..D. Mich. 2015), 368
Stolt–Nielsen S.A. v. AnimalFeeds Int'l Corp., 559 U.S. 662 (2010), 227
Stone & Downer Co., United States v., 274 U.S. 225 (1927), 333
Strawbridge v. Curtiss, 7 U.S. (3 Cranch) 267 (1806), 354, 534
Students for Fair Admissions, Inc. v. President & Fellows of Harvard College, 807 F.3d 472 (1st Cir. 2015), 395
Suffolk, County of v. Long Island Lighting Co., 907 F.2d 1295 (2d Cir. 1990), 664
Sullivan v. DB Invs., Inc., 667 F.3d 273 (3d Cir. 2011), 685
Sulzer Mixpac AG v. Medenstar Indus. Co., 312 F.R.D. 329 (S.D.N.Y. 2015), 66
Supreme Tribe of Ben–Hur v. Cauble, 255 U.S. 356 (1921), 665
Swierkiewicz v. Sorema N. A., 534 U.S. 506 (2002), **31**
Swift v. Tyson, 41 U.S. (16 Pet.) 1 (1842), **575**
Swift & Co., United States v., 286 U.S. 106 (1932), 299
Swiger v. Allegheny Energy, Inc., 540 F.3d 179 (3d Cir. 2008), 547
Syngenta Crop Prot., Inc. v. Henson, 537 U.S. 28 (2002), 572

Taylor v. Sturgell, 553 U.S. 880 (2008), 79, 341
Teleglobe Commc'ns Corp., In re, 493 F.3d 345 (3d Cir. 2007), 159
Tellabs, Inc. v. Makor Issues & Rights, Ltd., 551 U.S. 308 (2007), 258
Temple v. Synthes Corp., 498 U.S. 5 (1990), 369, 387
Tenacious Holdings, Inc., United States v., 6 F. Supp. 3d 1374 (Ct. Int'l Trade 2014), **214**
Texas ex rel. Bd. of Regents v. Walker, 142 F.3d 813 (5th Cir. 1998), 571
Textile Workers Union v. Lincoln Mills of Ala., 353 U.S. 448 (1957), 520
Thermtron Prods., Inc. v. Hermansdorfer, 423 U.S. 336 (1976), 570
Thomas v. Albright, 139 F.3d 227 (D.C. Cir. 1998), 664
Thomas v. Shelton, 740 F.2d 478 (7th Cir. 1984), 571

Thompson v. Dept. of Hous. & Urban Dev., 199 F.R.D. 168 (D. Md. 2001), 129
Ticor Title Ins. Co. v. Brown, 511 U.S. 117 (1994), 664
Tiggle–Lockhart v. Specialized Loan Servicing, LLC, 2015 WL 12734791 (C.D. Cal. Mar. 3, 2015), 66
Tiso v. Blumenthal, 371 F. Supp. 2d 135 (D. Conn. 2005), 248
Tolan v. Cotton, 572 U.S. 650 (2014), 247
Torres v. Mercer Canyons, Inc., 835 F.3d 1125 (9th Cir. 2016), 657
Touchcom, Inc. v. Bereskin & Parr, 574 F.3d 1403 (Fed. Cir. 2009), 495
Town of Chester v. Laroe Estates, Inc., 581 U.S. —, 137 S. Ct. 1645 (2017), 395
Toys "R" Us, Inc. v. Step Two, S.A., 318 F.3d 446 (3d Cir. 2003), 458
Tull v. United States, 481 U.S. 412 (1987), 263
Tyson Foods, Inc. v. Bouaphakeo, 577 U.S. —, 136 S. Ct. 1036 (2016), 656, 687

U.S. Bank Nat'l Assn. *ex rel.* CWCapital Asset Mgmt. LLC v. Vill. at Lakeridge, LLC, 583 U.S. —, 138 S. Ct. 960 (2018), 310
Ungar v. Arafat, 634 F.3d 46 (1st Cir. 2011), 394
United Mine Workers of Am. v. Gibbs, 383 U.S. 715 (1966), **552,** 675
United States v. — (see opposing party)
United States *ex rel.* v. — (see relator and opposing party)
United States Gypsum Co., United States v., 333 U.S. 364 (1948), 293, 311
Unitherm Food Sys., Inc. v. Swift–Eckrich, Inc., 546 U.S. 394 (2006), **286**
Upjohn Co. v. United States, 449 U.S. 383 (1981), 150

Vallejo v. Amgen, Inc., 903 F.3d 733 (8th Cir. 2018), 128
Van Dusen v. Barrack, 376 U.S. 612 (1964), 498, 628
Vang v. PNC Mortg., Inc., 517 F. App'x 523 (8th Cir. 2013), 622
Vega v. T–Mobile USA, Inc., 564 F.3d 1256 (11th Cir. 2009), 676
Vega-Castillo, United States v., 540 F.3d 1235 (11th Cir. 2008), 302
Vehicle 2007 Mack 600 Dump Truck, United States v., 680 F. Supp. 2d 816 (E.D. Mich. 2010), 72
Verlinden B.V. v. Cent. Bank of Nigeria, 461 U.S. 480 (1983), 519
Victor Stanley, Inc. v. Creative Pipe, Inc., 250 F.R.D. 251 (D. Md. 2008), 160
Volkswagen "Clean Diesel" Mktg. Sales Practices & Prods. Liab. Litig, *In re*, 229 F. Supp. 3d 1052 (N.D. Cal. 2017), 697

Waite v. All Acquisition Corp., 901 F.3d 1307 (11th Cir. 2018), 484
Wakim, *Re* [1999] 198 CLR 511 (Austl.), 405
Walden v. Fiore, 571 U.S. 277 (2014), 460
Waldman v. Palestinian Liberation Org., 835 F.3d 317 (2d Cir. 2016), 485
Walker v. Armco Steel Corp., 446 U.S. 740 (1980), **603**
Wal–Mart Stores, Inc. v. Dukes, 564 U.S. 338 (2011), **648,** 664, 685, 687
Wal–Mart Stores, Inc. v. Visa U.S.A., Inc., 396 F.3d 96 (2d Cir. 2005), 682
Walsh v. U.S. Bank, N.A., 851 N.W.2d 598 (Minn. 2014), 57
Washington v. Ryan, 833 F.3d 1087 (9th Cir. 2016), 300
Water Splash, Inc. v. Menon, 581 U.S. —, 137 S. Ct. 1504 (2017), 66
W.E. Aubuchon Co. v. BeneFirst, LLC, 245 F.R.D. 38 (D. Mass. 2007), 139
Webber v. Sobba, 322 F.3d 1032 (8th Cir. 2003), **623**
Weisgram v. Marley Co., 528 U.S. 440 (2000), 291
Weissman v. Dawn Joy Fashions, Inc., 214 F.3d 224 (2d Cir. 2000), 283
West v. Conrail, 481 U.S. 35 (1987), 607
Whitlock v. Jackson, 754 F. Supp. 1394 (S.D. Ind. 1991), 283
Williams v. Citigroup Inc., 659 F.3d 208 (2d Cir. 2011), **80**
Williams v. KFC Nat'l Mgmt. Co., 391 F.3d 411 (2d Cir. 2004), 248
Williams v. S. Towing Co., 2004 WL 60314 (E.D. La. Jan 4, 2004), 499
Williamson v. Osenton, 232 U.S. 619 (1914), 539
Winforge, Inc. v. Coachmen Indus., Inc., 691 F.3d 856 (7th Cir. 2012), 79
World Trade Ctr. Props., L.L.C. v. Hartford Fire Ins. Co., 345 F.3d 154 (2d Cir. 2003), 533
World–Wide Volkswagen Corp. v. Woodson, 444 U.S. 286 (1980), **424**
Wylam v. Trader Joe's Co., 2018 WL 473022 (M.D. Pa. 2018), 445

Wynder v. McMahon, 360 F.3d 73 (2d Cir. 2004), 194

Yates-Williams v. El Nihum, 268 F.R.D. 566 (S.D. Tex. 2010), 622
Yohannon v. Keene Corp., 924 F.2d 1255 (3d Cir. 1991), 285
Young v. City of Providence *ex rel.* Napolitano, 404 F.3d 33 (1st Cir. 2005), 98

Zahn v. Int'l Paper Co., 414 U.S. 291 (1973), 557, 665
Zippo Mfg. Co. v. Zippo Dot Com, Inc., 952 F. Supp. 1119 (W.D. Pa. 1997), 458
Zofran (Ondansetron) Prods. Liab. Litig., *In re*, 392 F. Supp. 3d 179 (D. Mass 2019), 158
Zubulake v. UBS Warburg LLC, 217 F.R.D. 309 (S.D.N.Y. 2003), 139

TABLE OF AUTHORITIES

Principal authorities appear in bold typeface.
References are to page number.

ADMINISTRATIVE OFFICE OF U.S. COURTS, STATISTICAL TABLES FOR THE FEDERAL JUDICIARY (2019), 235, 304

ALI/UNIDROIT, PRINCIPLES OF TRANSNATIONAL CIVIL PROCEDURE (2006), 21, 356

American Bar Ass'n, Metadata Ethics Opinions Around the U.S., 137

Megan Barbero, Note, *Interpreting Rule 68 to Conform with the Rules Enabling Act*, 57 STAN. L. REV. 2017 (2005), 212

Robert G. Bone, *Plausibility Pleading Revisited and Revised: A Comment on Ashcroft v. Iqbal*, 85 NOTRE DAME L. REV. 849 (2010), 54

Robert G. Bone, *Rule 68, Offers of Judgment, and the History of the Federal Rules of Civil Procedure*, 102 NW. U. L. REV. 1561 (2008), 212

Robert G. Bone, *The Process of Making Process: Court Rulemaking, Democratic Legitimacy, and Procedural Efficacy*, 87 GEO. L.J. 887 (1999), 2

Patrick J. Borchers, *The Origins of Diversity Jurisdiction, The Rise of Legal Positivism, and a Brave New World for Erie and Klaxon*, 72 TEX. L. REV. 79 (1993), 584

Wayne D. Brazil, *ADR and the Courts, Now and in the Future*, 17 ALTERNATIVES TO THE HIGH COST OF LITIGATION 85 (1999), 219

KENNETH S. BROUN ET AL., MCCORMICK ON EVIDENCE (7th ed. 2014), 140

Stephen B. Burbank, *Of Rules and Discretion: The Supreme Court, Federal Rules and The Common Law*, 63 NOTRE DAME L. REV. 693 (1988), 585

Stephen B. Burbank, *The Costs of Complexity*, 85 MICH. L. REV. 1463 (1987), 4

Stephen B. Burbank, *The Rules Enabling Act of 1934*, 130 U. PA. L. REV. 1015 (1982), 15

Stephen B. Burbank & Stephen N. Subrin, *Litigation and Democracy: Restoring a Realistic Prospect of Trial*, 46 HARV. C.R.–C.L. L. REV. 399 (2011), 235

Robert A. Bush, *Dispute Resolution Alternatives and Achieving the Goals of Civil Justice: Jurisdictional Principles for Process Choice*, 1984 WIS. L. REV. 893, 4

Paul D. Carrington, *Self-Deregulation, the "National Policy" of the Supreme Court*, 3 NEV. L.J. 259 (2002–03), 230

Joe S. Cecil et al., *A Quarter Century of Summary Judgment Practice in Six Federal District Courts*, 4 J. EMPIRICAL LEGAL STUD. 861 (2007), 240

JOE S. CECIL ET AL., MOTIONS TO DISMISS FOR FAILURE TO STATE A CLAIM AFTER *IQBAL*: REPORT TO THE JUDICIAL CONFERENCE ADVISORY COMMITTEE (2011), 55

JOE S. CECIL, UPDATE ON RESOLUTION OF RULE 12(b)(6) MOTIONS GRANTED WITH LEAVE TO AMEND (2011), 55, 85

Oscar G. Chase, *Consent to Judicial Jurisdiction: The Foundation of "Registration" Statutes*, 73 N.Y.U. ANN. SURV. AM. L. 159 (2018), 485

Abram Chayes, *The Role of the Judge in Public Law Litigation*, 89 HARV. L. REV. 1281 (1976), 10, 350

Edward K. Cheng, *When 10 Trials Are Better Than 10,000: An Evidentiary Perspective on Trial Sampling*, 160 U. PA. L. REV. 955 (2012), 687

Steven Alan Childress, *Standards of Review Primer: Federal Civil Appeals*, 229 F.R.D. 267 (2005), 310

CHARLES E. CLARK, HANDBOOK OF THE LAW OF CODE PLEADING (2d ed. 1947), **25**

Charles E. Clark, *Special Pleading in the "Big Case,"* 21 F.R.D. 45 (1957), 58

Kevin M. Clermont, *Res Judicata as Requisite for Justice*, 68 RUTGERS L. REV. 1067 (2016), 314

Zachary D. Clopton, *Procedural Retrenchment and the States*, 106 CALIF. L. REV. 411 (2018), 57

JOHN C. COFFEE, JR., ENTREPRENEURIAL LITIGATION (2015), 636

COMPLEX LITIGATION ch. 6 (AM. L. INST. 1994), 685

Alyssa L. Eisenberg, Comment, *Keep Your Facebook Friends Close and Your Process Server Closer: The Expansion of Social Media Service of Process to Cases Involving Domestic Defendants*, 51 SAN DIEGO L. REV. 779 (2014), 67

Theodore Eisenberg et al., *Arbitration's Summer Soldiers: An Empirical Study of Arbitration Clauses in Consumer and Nonconsumer Contracts*, 41 U. MICH. J. L. REFORM 871 (2008), 230

Theodore Eisenberg & Michael Heise, *Plaintiphobia in State Courts: An Empirical Study of State Court Trials on Appeal*, 38 J. LEGAL STUD. 121 (2009), 235

Theodore Eisenberg & Charlotte Lanvers, *Summary Judgment Rates Over Time, Across Case Categories, and Across Districts: An Empirical Study of Three Large Federal Districts*, in EMPIRICAL STUDIES OF JUDICIAL SYSTEMS 2008 (K.C. Huang ed. 2009), 240

John Hart Ely, *The Irrepressible Myth of Erie*, 87 HARV. L. REV. 693 (1974), 602

Nora Freeman Engstrom, *The Lessons of Lone Pine*, 129 Yale L.J. 2 (2019), 194

Howard M. Erichson, *Interjurisdictional Preclusion*, 96 MICH. L. REV. 945 (1998), 343

Owen M. Fiss, *Against Settlement*, 93 YALE L.J. 1073 (1984), 178

Owen M. Fiss, *The History of an Idea*, 78 FORDHAM L. REV. 1273 (2009), 183

Brian T. Fitzpatrick, *Originalism and Summary Judgment*, 71 OHIO ST. L.J. 919 (2010), 258

BRIAN T. FITZPATRICK, THE CONSERVATIVE CASE FOR CLASS ACTIONS (2020), 636

Fourth Annual Litigation Trends Survey Findings (2007), 139

JEROME FRANK, COURTS ON TRIAL: MYTH AND REALITY IN AMERICAN JUSTICE (1949), 10

Marvin E. Frankel, *The Search for Truth: An Umpireal View*, 123 U. PA. L. REV. 1031 (1975), 10

Lawrence M. Friedman, *Some Notes on the Civil Jury in Historical Perspective*, 48 DE PAUL L. REV. 201 (1998), 232

Brian L. Frye, *The Ballad of Harry James Tompkins*, 52 AKRON L. REV. 531 (2019), 585

Lon L. Fuller, *The Forms and Limits of Adjudication*, 92 HARV. L. REV. 353 (1978), 10, 351, 699

Marc Galanter, *Why the "Haves" Come Out Ahead: Speculations on the Limits of Legal Change*, 9 L. & SOC'Y REV. 95 (1974), 230

Jonah B. Gelbach, Note, *Locking the Doors to Discovery? Assessing the Effects of* Twombly *and* Iqbal *on Access to Discovery*, 121 YALE L.J. 2270 (2012), 56

Steven S. Gensler, *Bifurcation Unbound*, 75 WASH. L. REV. 705 (2000), 194

Eric J. Hamilton, Note, *Federalism and the State Civil Jury Trial Rights*, 65 STAN. L. REV. 851 (2013), 266

Milton Handler, *The Shift from Substantive to Procedural Innovations in Antitrust Suits — The Twenty-Third Annual Antitrust Review*, 71 COLUM. L. REV. 1, 9 (1971), 635

Valerie P. Hans & Stephanie Albertson, *Empirical Research and Civil Jury Reform*, 78 NOTRE DAME L. REV. 1497 (2003), 281

Geoffrey C. Hazard, Jr., *Discovery and the Role of the Judge in Civil Law Jurisdictions*, 73 NOTRE DAME L. REV. 1017 (1998), 108

GEOFFREY C. HAZARD, JR., ETHICS IN THE PRACTICE OF LAW (1978), 10

GEOFFREY C. HAZARD, JR. ET AL., CIVIL PROCEDURE (6th ed. 2011), 320

Larry Heuer & Steven Penrod, *Trial Complexity: A Field Investigation of Its Meaning and Its Effects*, 18 L. & HUM. BEHAV. 29 (1994), 281

PETER T. HOFFMAN & STUART M. ISRAEL, EFFECTIVE DISCOVERY (2017), 115

Oliver Wendell Holmes, *The Path of the Law*, 10 HARV. L. REV. 457 (1897), 479

William H.J. Hubbard, *Testing for Change in Procedural Standards, with Application to* Bell Atlantic v. Twombly, 42 J. LEGAL STUD. 35 (2013), 56

William H.J. Hubbard, *The Effects of* Twombly *and* Iqbal, 14 J. EMPIRICAL LEGAL STUD. 474 (2017), 56

INTERIM REPORT ON THE JOINT PROJECT OF THE AMERICAN COLLEGE OF TRIAL LAWYERS TASK FORCE ON DISCOVERY AND THE INSTITUTE FOR THE ADVANCEMENT OF THE AMERICAN LEGAL SYSTEM (2008), 113

Samuel Issacharoff & George Loewenstein, *Second Thoughts About Summary Judgment*, 100 YALE L.J. 73 (1990), 240

GREGORY P. JOSEPH, SANCTIONS: THE FEDERAL LAW OF LITIGATION ABUSE (5th ed. 2013), 106

Dan M. Kahan et al., *Whose Eyes Are You Going to Believe?* Scott v. Harris *and the Perils of Cognitive Illiberalism*, 122 HARV. L. REV. 837 (2009), 247

James S. Kakalik et al., *Discovery Management: Further Analysis of the Civil Justice Reform Act Evaluation Data*, 39 B.C. L. REV. 613 (1998), 112, 117, 182

JAMES S. KAKALIK ET AL., AN EVALUATION OF JUDICIAL CASE MANAGEMENT UNDER THE CIVIL JUSTICE REFORM ACT (1996), 182

JAMES S. KAKALIK ET AL., AN EVALUATION OF MEDIATION AND EARLY NEUTRAL EVALUATION UNDER THE CIVIL JUSTICE REFORM ACT (1996), 184

HARRY KALVEN JR. & HANS ZEISEL, THE AMERICAN JURY (1966), 281

Louis Kaplow, *Multistage Adjudication*, 126 HARV. L. REV. 1179 (2013), 241

Robert H. Klonoff, *Class Actions for Monetary Relief Under Rule 23(b)(1)(A) and (b)(1)(B): Does Due Process Require Notice and Opt-Out Rights?*, 82 GEO. WASH. L. REV. 798 (2014), 663

Robert H. Klonoff, *The Decline of Class Actions*, 90 WASH. U. L. REV. 729 (2013), 656

Larry Kramer, *Diversity Jurisdiction*, 1990 B.Y.U. L. REV. 97, 512

Anthony T. Kronman, *Mistake, Disclosure, Information and the Law of Contracts*, 7 J. LEG. STUD. 1 (1978), 118

Alexandra D. Lahav, *Bellwether Trials*, 76 GEO. WASH. L. REV. 576 (2008), 688

STEPHAN LANDSMAN, READINGS ON ADVERSARIAL JUSTICE: THE AMERICAN APPROACH TO ADJUDICATION (1988), 6

John H. Langbein, *The Disappearance of Civil Trial in the United States*, 122 YALE L.J. 522 (2012), 181, 235

John H. Langbein, *The German Advantage in Civil Procedure*, 52 U. CHI. L. REV. 823 (1985), 7

EMERY G. LEE III & THOMAS E. WILLGING, FED. JUD. CTR., NATIONAL, CASE-BASED CIVIL RULES SURVEY (2009), 112

EMERY G. LEE III & THOMAS E. WILLGING, FED. JUD. CTR., LITIGATION COSTS IN CIVIL CASES: MULTIVARIATE ANALYSIS (2010), 112

JULIUS BYRON LEVINE, DISCOVERY (1982), 108

KARL LLEWELLYN, THE BRAMBLE BUSH (3d ed. 1960), 1

DAVID LUBAN, LEGAL ETHICS AND HUMAN DIGNITY (2007), 9

Jonathan R. Macey & Geoffrey P. Miller, *The Plaintiffs' Attorney's Role in Class Action and Derivative Litigation: Economic Analysis and Recommendations for Reform*, 58 U. CHI. L. REV. 1 (1991), 636

MANUAL FOR COMPLEX LITIGATION, FOURTH, 189

David Marcus, *Flawed but Noble: Desegregation Litigation and Its Implications for the Modern Class Action*, 63 FLA. L. REV. 657 (2011), 640

Richard Marcus, *Procedural Postcard from America*, 1 RUSS. L.J. 9 (2013), 5

John Markoff, *Armies of Expensive Lawyers, Replaced by Cheaper Software*, N.Y. TIMES, Mar. 5, 2011, 140

Luke McCloud & David Rosenberg, *A Solution to the Choice of Law Problem of Differing State Laws in Class Actions: Average Law*, 79 GEO. WASH. L. REV. 374 (2011), 685

Andrew McThenia & Thomas Shaffer, *For Reconciliation*, 94 YALE L.J. 1660 (1985), 182

Carrie Menkel-Meadow, *Do the Haves Come Out Ahead in Alternative Judicial Systems? Repeat Players in ADR*, 15 OHIO ST. J. DISP. RESOL. 19 (1999), 230

Carrie Menkel-Meadow, *Whose Dispute Is It Anyway? A Philosophical and Democratic Defense of Settlement (In Some Cases)*, 83 GEO. L.J. 2663 (1995), 183, 218

Roger Michalski, *The Clash of Procedural Values*, 22 LEWIS & CLARK L. REV. 61 (2018), 5

Roger Michalski & Abby K. Wood, *Twombly and Iqbal at the State Level*, 14 J. EMPIRICAL LEGAL STUD. 474 (2017), 56

Frank I. Michelman, *The Supreme Court and Litigation Access Fees: The Right to Protect One's Rights — Part I*, 1973 DUKE L.J. 1153, 4

Darrell A.H. Miller, *Text, History, and Tradition: What the Seventh Amendment Can Teach Us About the Second*, 122 YALE L.J. 852 (2013), 257

Paul J. Mishkin, *The Federal "Question" in the District Courts*, 53 COLUM. L. REV. 157 (1953), 520

MODEL CODE OF PROF'L RESPONSIBILITY, 105

Michael Moffitt, *Three Things To Be Against ("Settlement" Not Included)*, 78 FORDHAM L. REV. 1203 (2009), 183

Tanya J. Monestier, *Registration Statutes, General Jurisdiction, and the Fallacy of Consent*, 36 CARDOZO L. REV. 1343 (2015), 485

3 JAMES WM. MOORE ET AL., MOORE'S FEDERAL PRACTICE (3d ed. 2016), 200

16 JAMES WM. MOORE ET AL., MOORE'S FEDERAL PRACTICE (3d ed. 2016), 419, 472

18 JAMES WM. MOORE ET AL., MOORE'S FEDERAL PRACTICE (3d ed. 2016), 340, 346

Richard A. Nagareda, *The Litigation-Arbitration Dichotomy Meets the Class Action*, 86 NOTRE DAME L. REV. 1069 (2011), 230

Burt Neuborne, *The Myth of Parity*, 90 HARV. L. REV. 1105 (1977), 509

JAMES OLDHAM, TRIAL BY JURY (2006), 263

David B. Owens, *Civil Rights Foe or Frivolous Litigation Enabler? An Empirical Study of Rule 11 Practice Under the 1983 and 1993 Version* (2010), 106

NICHOLAS PACE & LAURA ZAKARAS, RAND CORP., WHERE THE MONEY GOES (2012), 140

Wendy Collins Perdue, *Personal Jurisdiction and the Beetle in the Box*, 32 B.C. L. REV. 529 (1991), 400

Wendy Collins Perdue, *Sin, Scandal, and Substantive Due Process: Personal Jurisdiction and Pennoyer Reconsidered*, 62 WASH. L. REV. 479 (1987), 410

PRINCIPLES OF THE LAW OF AGGREGATE LITIGATION (AM. L. INST. 2010), 636, 682

EDWARD A. PURCELL, JR., BRANDEIS AND THE PROGRESSIVE CONSTITUTION (2000), 582

Martin H. Redish, *Judicial Parity, Litigant Choice, and Democratic Theory: A Comment on Federal Jurisdiction and Constitutional Rights*, 36 UCLA L. REV. 329 (1988), 515

MARTIN H. REDISH, WHOLESALE JUSTICE (2009), 636

Alexander A. Reinert, *Measuring the Impact of Plausibility Pleading*, 101 VA. L. REV. 2117 (2015), 56

Judith Resnik, *Fairness in Numbers: A Comment on AT&T v. Concepcion, Wal-Mart v. Dukes, and Turner v. Rogers*, 125 HARV. L. REV. 78 (2011), 183

Judith Resnik, *Managerial Judges*, 96 HARV. L. REV. 374 (1982), 177

RESTATEMENT (SECOND) OF JUDGMENTS (AM. LAW INST. 1982), 314, 320, 322, 329, 338, 339

LEONARD L. RISKIN ET AL., DISPUTE RESOLUTION AND LAWYERS (5th ed. 2014), 201

WILFRED J. RITZ, REWRITING THE HISTORY OF THE JUDICIARY ACT OF 1789: EXPOSING MYTHS, CHALLENGING PREMISES, AND USING NEW EVIDENCE (1990), 584

Thomas D. Rowe, Jr., *Authorized Managerialism Under the Federal Rules — and the Extent of Convergence with Civil-Law Judging*, 36 SW. U. L. REV. 191 (2007), 181

Thomas D. Rowe, Jr., *Not Bad For Government Work: Does Anyone Else Think the Supreme Court is Doing a Halfway Decent Job in its* Erie-Hanna *Jurisprudence?*, 73 NOTRE DAME L. REV. 963 (1998), 602, 607, 613

William B. Rubenstein, *The Concept of Equality in Civil Procedure*, 23 CARDOZO L. REV. 1865 (2002), 4

Stephen E. Sachs, Pennoyer *Was Right*, 95 TEX. L. REV. 1249 (2017), 416

William W Schwarzer, *The Federal Rules, the Adversary Process, and Discovery Reform*, 50 U. PITT. L. REV. 703 (1989), 176

Gil Seinfeld, *The Federal Courts as a Franchise: Rethinking the Justifications for Federal Question Jurisdiction*, 97 CAL. L. REV. 95 (2009), 511

DAVID L. SHAPIRO, CIVIL PROCEDURE: PRECLUSION IN CIVIL ACTIONS (2001), 314, 320, 332, 339

David L. Shapiro, *Class Actions: The Class as Party and Client*, 73 NOTRE DAME L. REV. 913 (1998), 632, 684

David L. Shapiro, *The Story of* Celotex: *The Role of Summary Judgment in the Administration of Justice*, *in* CIVIL PROCEDURE STORIES 359 (Kevin M. Clermont ed., 2d ed. 2008), 239

Suzanna Sherry, *A Pox on Both Your Houses: Why the Court Can't Fix the* Erie *Doctrine*, 10 J. L. ECON & POL'Y 173 (2013), 623

Suzanna Sherry, *Hogs Get Slaughtered at the Supreme Court*, 2011 SUP. CT. REV. 1, 230, 657

Suzanna Sherry, *Overruling* Erie: *Nationwide Class Actions and National Common Law*, 156 U. PA. L. REV. 2135 (2008), 685

Suzanna Sherry, *Wrong, Out of Step, and Pernicious:* Erie *as the Worst Decision of All Time*, 39 PEPP. L. REV. 129 (2011), 584

Linda J. Silberman, *Judicial Jurisdiction in the Conflict of Laws Course: Adding a Comparative Dimension*, 28 VAND. J. TRANSNAT'L L. 389 (1995), 405

Linda Silberman, Shaffer v. Heitner: *The End of an Era*, 53 N.Y.U. L. REV. 33 (1978), 405

Charles Silver, *We're Scared to Death: Class Certification and Blackmail*, 78 N.Y.U. L. REV. 1357 (2003), 635

Jason M. Solomon, *The Political Puzzle of the Civil Jury*, 61 EMORY L.J. 1331 (2012), 235

Lawrence B. Solum, *Procedural Justice*, 78 S. CAL. L. REV. 181 (2004), 4

Brian Soucek & Remington B. Lamons, *Heightened Pleading Standards for Defendants: A Case Study of Court-Counting Precedent*, 70 ALA. L. REV. 875 (2018), 78

Norman W. Spaulding, *The Rule of Law in Action: A Defense of Adversary System Values*, 93 CORNELL L. REV. 1377 (2008), 9

Adam N. Steinman, *The Irrepressible Myth of* Celotex; *Reconsidering Summary Judgment Burdens Twenty Years after the Trilogy*, 63 WASH. & LEE L. REV. 81 (2006), 241

Subcommittee on Long-Range Planning, *A Self-Study of Federal Judicial Rulemaking*, 168 F.R.D. 679 (1995), 4

Stephen N. Subrin, *A Traditionalist Looks at Mediation: It's Here to Stay and Much Better than I Thought*, 3 NEV. L.J. 196 (2002–03), 218

Stephen N. Subrin, *Discovery in Global Perspective: Are We Nuts?* 52 DE PAUL L. REV. 299 (2002), 109

Stephen N. Subrin, *How Equity Conquered Common Law: The Federal Rules of Civil Procedure in Historical Perspective*, 135 U. PA. L. REV. 909 (1987), 235

Stephen N. Subrin & Thomas O. Main, *The Fourth Era of American Civil Procedure*, 162 U. PA. L. REV. 1839 (2014), 180

Symposium, Against Settlement: *Twenty-Five Years Later*, 78 FORDHAM L. REV. 1117 (2009), 183

Symposium, *The Future of Discovery*, 71 VAND. L. REV. 1775 (2018), 130

The Sedona Conference Best Practices Commentary on the Use of Search & Information Retrieval Methods in E-Discovery, 8 SEDONA CONF. J. 200 (2007), 160

The Supreme Court 1995 Term, 110 HARV. L. REV. 1 (1996), 263

Suja A. Thomas, *Why Summary Judgment Is Unconstitutional*, 93 VA. L. REV. 140 (2007), 258

Suja A. Thomas, *Why the Motion to Dismiss Is Now Unconstitutional*, 92 MINN. L. REV. 1851 (2008), 258

Jay Tidmarsh, *Procedure, Substance, and Erie*, 64 VAND. L. REV. 877 (2011), 602

JAY TIDMARSH & ROGER H. TRANGSRUD, MODERN COMPLEX LITIGATION (2d ed. 2010), 685, 687

NEIL VIDMAR & VALERIE P. HANS, AMERICAN JURIES: THE VERDICT (2007), 235

Herbert Wechsler, *Federal Jurisdiction and the Revision of the Judicial Code*, 13 LAW & CONTEMP. PROBS. 216 (1948), 520

Thomas E. Willging et al., *An Empirical Study of Discovery and Disclosure Practices Under the 1993 Federal Rule Amendments*, 39 B.C. L. REV. 525 (1998), 112

Thomas E. Willging & Shannon R Wheatman, *Attorney Choice of Forum in Class Action Litigation: What Difference Does It Make?*, 81 NOTRE DAME L. REV. 591 (2006), 636

THOMAS E. WILLGING ET AL., EMPIRICAL STUDY OF CLASS ACTIONS IN FOUR FEDERAL DISTRICT COURTS (1996), 636

6 CHARLES A. WRIGHT ET AL., FEDERAL PRACTICE AND PROCEDURE (3d ed. 2010), 85, 361, 379

7 CHARLES ALAN WRIGHT & ARTHUR R. MILLER, FED. PRACTICE AND PROCEDURE (3d ed. 2001), 387

8 CHARLES ALAN WRIGHT ET AL., FEDERAL PRACTICE AND PROCEDURE (3d ed. 2010), 128

9 CHARLES A. WRIGHT & ARTHUR R. MILLER, FEDERAL PRACTICE AND PROCEDURE (3d ed. 2008), 392

9B CHARLES A. WRIGHT & ARTHUR R. MILLER, FEDERAL PRACTICE AND PROCEDURE (3d ed. 2008), 290

11 CHARLES A. WRIGHT ET AL., FEDERAL PRACTICE AND PROCEDURE (3d ed. 2012), 284, 290, 293

14AA CHARLES ALAN WRIGHT ET AL., FEDERAL PRACTICE AND PROCEDURE (4th ed. 2011), 551

18 CHARLES ALAN WRIGHT ET AL., FEDERAL PRACTICE AND PROCEDURE (2d ed. 2002), 338

Ernest A. Young, *A General Defense of Erie Railroad Co. v. Tompkins*, 10 J.L. ECON. & POL'Y 17 (2013), 623

Hans Zeisel & Thomas Callahan, *Split Trials and Time Saving: A Statistical Analysis*, 76 HARV. L. REV. 1606 (1963), 194

UNIVERSITY CASEBOOK SERIES®
CIVIL PROCEDURE

FIFTH EDITION

Chapter One

An Introduction To Civil Procedure

This book describes how the American system of civil justice works. Your other courses focus on the substance of the law: rights and duties, crimes, how our governmental structure operates. Without a system of procedure, however, a society cannot implement its substantive law. "You must read each substantive course, so to speak, through the spectacles of . . . procedure. For what substantive law says should be means nothing except in terms of what procedure says that you can make real."* If I crash my car into yours, the substantive law may say that you can recover from me — but different procedural regimes can make it easier or harder for you to obtain justice.

Studying procedure at the beginning of your legal career is therefore crucial, but it is also challenging. You have some sense of what a crime is, and what property is. Contracts seem like formal promises. Even torts is just an unfamiliar name for the accidents and harms that people cause. But procedure has no analogue outside the law. Most students have never been involved in litigation and have never seen a trial in person. Moreover, most newsworthy cases are criminal. This is a course in *civil* procedure, which concerns the somewhat different rules and vocabulary governing lawsuits that are not criminal and that often involve only private parties.

Learning civil procedure at this stage is a little like trying to learn the rules of baseball from a book without ever having seen the game played. To make matters worse, each rule of civil procedure is part of a larger whole; only after you have studied the entire system do the component parts begin to make sense. Sometimes this course will feel as though you are trying to understand the infield-fly rule with no knowledge of the rules of the rest of the game. To top things off, you will learn that many of the "rules" of civil procedure are not so much rules as guidelines. It can seem like a game in

---

* Karl Llewellyn, The Bramble Bush 9 (3d ed. 1960).

which the umpires are told to call each pitch a ball or a strike, but can define for themselves, pitch by pitch, where the strike zone is.

Whether you are studying baseball or civil procedure, however, it helps to keep in mind three things: the goals of the rules, the rules' historical development, and the social context in which they operate.

Section A: The Goals of a Procedural System

Every society creates institutions, such as courts and administrative tribunals, to resolve disputes. Procedural rules establish the structure and methods by which these institutions resolve disputes. This book focuses primarily on one branch of procedure: the structure and methods by which American courts resolve (or *adjudicate*) civil disputes.

Civil adjudication requires a court to perform four functions: first, determine the relevant legal principles; second, find the facts that bear on these legal principles; third, apply the law to the facts to determine the winner; and fourth, when appropriate, provide a remedy (usually, either money (*damages*) or a court order (*injunction*)). A procedural system seeks to accomplish these functions in a way that is consistent with a society's norms and values. You might think that designing such a system is a simple task on which reasonable minds would rarely disagree. In fact, the "right" way to design a procedural system is controversial.

Robert G. Bone, The Process of Making Process: Court Rulemaking, Democratic Legitimacy, and Procedural Efficacy

87 Geo. L.J. 887, 919-20, 933-34, 939-40 (1999)

[W]e need a metric for judging the quality of procedural rules. There are three such metrics, which differ according to what they assume is valuable about procedure: an efficiency metric that values procedure in terms of its effect on aggregate social costs; a rights-based metric that values procedure in terms of its contribution to enforcement of individual rights[;] and a process-based metric that values procedure in terms of its intrinsic regard for the dignity and autonomy of litigating parties. . . .

Efficiency requires a tradeoff between the costs of error and the costs of process to safeguard against error. Adding procedure reduces error costs by reducing the risk of mistakes, but it also increases process costs. An optimal procedural system minimizes the sum of error costs and process costs.

From an efficiency point of view, there is no fundamental difference between substance and procedure. Both types of rules share a common goal — minimization of social costs — and both operate in tandem to further that goal. Substantive law creates incentives for efficient behavior by adjusting the payoffs from different courses of action, and procedural law facilitates the substantive goal by increasing the likelihood of accurate enforcement. The rational actor decides what to do by comparing the expected costs of alternative actions, and those costs are a product of the sanction imposed by the substantive law and the probability of enforcement created by the procedural law.

Thus, a lawmaker can induce efficient behavior by tinkering with substance, or by holding substance constant and tinkering with procedure. As a result, what we call "substance" and "procedure" are from an efficiency perspective simply different tools for achieving the same goal. . . .

The goal of adjudication in a rights-based theory is to enforce the substantive rights of the parties rather than to minimize social costs. A substantive right gives the individual rightholder a claim that society must honor, even if doing so increases social costs and reduces aggregate welfare. Thus, rights trump or act as side-constraints on the pursuit of utilitarian goals; a right cannot be limited merely because doing so would create greater net benefits for all.

The existence of substantive rights implies procedural rights. Because effective enforcement is critical to respecting a substantive right, limiting procedure for reasons of utility would be tantamount to limiting the substantive right on utilitarian grounds. Put differently, without the constraint of procedural rights, courts could undermine substantive rights in order to serve utilitarian goals by denying the costly procedures necessary to their enforcement.

It is no easy matter, however, to specify the content of a party's procedural rights. At first glance, it might seem that a party should have a procedural right to a *perfectly accurate* outcome, since anything less would violate her substantive rights. The problem with this approach is that . . . error is an inevitable feature of any procedural system no matter how well designed. Moreover, any effort to achieve perfect accuracy would commit most of the public treasury to financing procedure at the expense of other public goods. . . .

[Finally,] many proceduralists believe that litigants enjoy process-based procedural rights unrelated to outcome quality . . . .

To illustrate, consider the participation right. In its process-based form, this right derives from the state's obligation to respect the dignity and autonomy of persons affected by adjudication. For one committed to this view, the challenge is to define the specific participation opportunities the right guarantees. One might reason from a general theory of democratic participation, but it is hard to imagine a general theory specific enough to prescribe the working details of [procedural rules]. These institutional details are developed through institutional practice. . . .

. . . [R]easonable people disagree about the metric, and this creates an analytic and practical problem: how should we choose a proper metric if the right choice is not obvious?

Notes and Questions

1. Somewhat echoing Professor's Bone's three metrics, Professor Solum posits three models of adjudication: a balancing model, an accuracy model, and a participation model. Professor Solum argues for the primacy of the participation model. Lawrence B. Solum, *Procedural Justice*, 78 S. CAL. L. REV. 181 (2004). Professor Michelman lists four procedural values: dignity values, participation values, deterrence values, and effectuation values; all but deterrence seem to be "process-based values" according to Professor Bone's nomenclature. Frank I. Michelman, *The Supreme Court and Litigation Access Fees: The Right to Protect One's Rights — Part I*, 1973 DUKE L.J. 1153. Professor Bush lists seven goals for a civil-justice system: resource allocation (or efficiency), promoting social or distributive justice, protecting fundamental rights, maintaining public order, developing positive human relations, legitimacy, and ease of administration. Robert A. Bush, *Dispute Resolution Alternatives and Achieving the Goals of Civil Justice: Jurisdictional Principles for Process Choice*, 1984 WIS. L. REV. 893. A subcommittee of the Judicial Conference of the United States, which is composed of leading federal judges, suggested "five related norms" for procedural rules adopted in federal courts: efficiency, fairness, simplicity, consensus, and uniformity. Subcommittee on Long Range Planning, *A Self-Study of Federal Judicial Rulemaking*, 168 F.R.D. 679, 693 (1995).

2. Professor Burbank has suggested that equality of treatment and consistency with democratic theory are additional goals of a procedural system. Stephen B. Burbank, *The Costs of Complexity*, 85 MICH. L. REV. 1463 (1987). These values may not have universal appeal, but they resonate strongly within the American tradition — a fact suggesting that the design of a procedural system may be, to some extent, culture-specific.

3. As a procedural goal, "equality" may sound desirable, but different understandings of "equality" can lead to different rules of procedure. In one sense, procedural rules are "equal" when they are facially neutral and apply to all types of civil disputes (torts, contracts, and so on). Such a system of rules is called "trans-substantive," meaning that the same rules apply across substantive fields of law. In a different sense, rules are "equal" when both parties in a lawsuit enjoy equal access to proof or equal opportunities to present their cases to the decision maker, even if the rules used for different types of disputes are different. "Equality" can also refer to equality of outcome, so that the procedural rules should seek to ensure that cases with similar facts arrive at similar outcomes. Procedural rules implementing the first type of equality might look very different from rules implementing the second or third types. *Cf.* William B. Rubenstein, *The Concept of Equality in Civil Procedure*, 23 CARDOZO L. REV. 1865 (2002) (discussing different meanings of procedural equality).

4. All of these goals seem worthy, but, as Professor Bone points out, they can be in tension with each other. Therefore, an evident initial problem in designing a procedural system is selecting the relevant goal(s). Professor Michalski surveyed 1,200 judges and litigants to determine the procedural

goals that they valued and those that they did not. He reported a consensus on speed, cost, and privacy: no groups valued them highly. At this point, differences emerged. Federal judges valued fairness and participation, corporations valued accuracy and finality, and *pro se* litigants (i.e., those not represented by lawyers) rated accessibility and simplicity highly. The author concludes that favoring certain values may amount to favoring certain litigants. *See* Roger Michalski, *The Clash of Procedural Values*, 22 LEWIS & CLARK L. REV. 61 (2018).

Even when goals are selected, translating a goal (say, fairness) into a specific rule presents problems. For instance, in the American federal-court system a lawsuit begins when a *plaintiff* (the person claiming a violation of legal right) files a document called a *complaint*. What should a fair procedural system require this document to contain?

5. Another example of the slippage between general principles and the specifics of a procedural system involves the degree to which the parties and their lawyers should control the development of a lawsuit. One approach, known as the adversarial model, posits that the parties should remain in charge of presenting the evidence and arguments, while the neutral decision-maker (judge or jury) listens passively. An adversarial approach is employed, to some degree, in most common-law countries, including the United States.* Its competitor, the inquisitorial model, places more control over the gathering of evidence and framing of arguments in the hands of the judge; this model is employed in the civil-law systems of continental Europe and elsewhere around the world. The differences between the two systems are largely ones of degree along a continuum. Civil-law systems are less inquisitorial than many Americans tend to assume. Conversely, recent innovations in American procedure deviate somewhat from the adversarial model. *See* Richard Marcus, *Procedural Postcard from America*, 1 RUSS. L.J. 9 (2013) (describing increasing harmonization among systems). Indeed, the story of American procedure in the last century is largely one of reforms to curb the perceived excesses of the adversarial system and to replace its purported win-by-any-means, get-off-on-any-technicality mentality with norms such as efficiency and resolution of cases on their substantive merits.

---

* You will frequently encounter the phrase "common law." Unfortunately, it is not a phrase of single or simple meaning. In one sense, "common law" refers to the method of creating legal rules through judicial decisions that guide future similar cases. This method contrasts with lawmaking by constitution, code, statute, regulation, or executive order; here, a legal authority other than a judicial decision is the source of the law.

In another meaning, the "common law" contrasts the legal systems of English heritage with the "civil law" systems, whose roots lie in ancient Rome and continental Europe. The civil-law approach is employed in most of the world, and relies more on inquisitorial as opposed to adversarial modes of proceeding, places greater emphasis on codes, and eschews common law made by courts.

In a third sense, the phrase "common law" refers to the English courts, known as the "common-law courts," that heard disputes (including tort and eventually contract cases) usually seeking money. Other courts (such as equity, which typically awarded injunctions; ecclesiastical and admiralty courts; and a hodgepodge of others) resolved other disputes.

Despite these reforms, the American procedural system is the most adversarial in the world today. The following readings discuss some of the advantages and disadvantages of an adversarial approach.

STEPHAN LANDSMAN, READINGS ON ADVERSARIAL JUSTICE: THE AMERICAN APPROACH TO ADJUDICATION

33-36, 39 (1988)

A number of reasons, apart from the historical, warrant reliance on adversarial methods. The adversary process provides litigants with the means to control their lawsuits. The parties are preeminent in choosing the forum, designating the proofs, and running the process. The courts, as a general rule, pursue the questions the parties propound. Ultimately, the whole procedure yields results tailored to the litigants' needs and in this way reinforces individual rights. . . . [T]his sort of procedure also enhances the economic efficiency of adjudication . . . .

Party control yields other benefits as well. Perhaps most important, it promotes litigant and societal acceptance of decisions rendered by the courts. Adversary theory holds that if a party is intimately involved in the adjudicatory process and feels that he has been given a fair opportunity to present his case, he is likely to accept the results whether favorable or not. Assuming this theory is correct, the adversary process will serve to reduce post-litigation friction and to increase compliance with judicial mandates.

Adversary theory identifies litigant control as important to satisfy not only the parties but society as well. When litigants direct the proceedings, there is little opportunity for the judge to pursue her own agenda or to act on her biases. . . . Her detachment preserves the appearance of fairness as well as fairness itself. . . .

. . . [Empirical evidence has shown that] litigant control produces other sorts of benefits. First, it tends to encourage desirable conduct on the part of litigants and their counsel. Psychological experimentation has shown that an advocate working in an adversarial context who finds his client at a factual disadvantage will expend significant effort to improve his client's position. This is to be contrasted with the behavior of the advocate working in an inquisitorial setting who will seldom undertake an extensive search for better evidence to bolster a weak case. . . .

[Empirical evidence has] also found that adversarial emphasis on party presentation tends to counteract the bias of the decision maker more effectively than does an approach requiring the active participation of the [decision maker] in marshaling the proof. . . .

Party control has another beneficial effect as well. It affirms human individuality. It mandates respect for the opinions of each party rather than those of his attorney, of the court, or of society at large. It provides the litigant a neutral forum in which to air his views and promises that those views will be heard and considered. . . .

Generally, inquisitorial process will not serve as a check on government power. Inquisitorial judges (at least throughout Europe) are bureaucrats who identify with the government and whose advancement in the judicial hierarchy depends on accommodation rather than confrontation. Such officials are not likely to identify novel rights against the government or expand rights previously established.

JOHN H. LANGBEIN, THE GERMAN ADVANTAGE IN CIVIL PROCEDURE

52 U. CHI. L. REV. 823, 826, 830-34, 843-46, 848 (1985)

There are two fundamental differences between German and Anglo-American civil procedure, and these differences lead in turn to many others. First, the court rather than the parties' lawyers takes the main responsibility for gathering and sifting evidence, although the lawyers exercise a watchful eye over the court's work. Second, there is no distinction between pretrial and trial, between discovering evidence and presenting it. Trial is not a single continuous event. Rather, the court gathers and evaluates evidence over a series of hearings, as many as the circumstances require. . . .*

From the standpoint of comparative civil procedure, the most important consequence of having judges direct fact-gathering in this episodic fashion is that . . . in German procedure the court ranges over the entire case, constantly looking for the jugular — for the issue of law or fact that might dispose of the case. Free of constraints that arise from party presentation of evidence, the court investigates the dispute in the fashion most likely to narrow the inquiry. A major job of counsel is to guide the search by directing the court's attention to particularly cogent lines of inquiry. . . .

The episodic character of German civil procedure — [Professor] Benjamin Kaplan called it the "conference method" of adjudication — has other virtues: It lessens tension and theatrics, and it encourages settlement. Countless novels, movies, plays, and broadcast serials attest to the dramatic potential of the Anglo-American trial. . . . German civil proceedings have the tone not of the theatre, but of a routine business meeting — serious rather than tense. When the court inquires and directs, it sets no stage for advocates to perform. The forensic skills of counsel can wrest no material advantage . . . .

---

* The serial-trial system that Professor Langbein describes existed in West Germany at the time that he wrote. Subsequent reforms have moved German procedure somewhat in the direction of the common-law single-event trial, although other civil-law countries still retain the serial-trial model. Professor Langbein's main theme about German procedure — the dominant role of the judge in fact-gathering — remains a feature of German and some other civil-law systems. — ED.

In this business-like system of civil procedure the tradition is strong that the court promotes compromise. The judge who gathers the facts soon knows the case as well as the litigants do, and he concentrates each subsequent increment of fact-gathering on the most important issues still unresolved. As the case progresses the judge discusses it with the litigants, sometimes indicating provisional views of the likely outcome. He is, therefore, strongly positioned to encourage a litigant to abandon a case that is turning out to be weak or hopeless, or to recommend settlement....

Adversary control of fact-gathering in our procedure entails a high level of conflict between partisan advantage and orderly disclosure of the relevant information. [Former federal judge] Marvin Frankel put this point crisply when he said that "it is the rare case in which either side yearns to have the witnesses, or anyone, give *the whole truth.*"

If we had deliberately set out to find a means of impairing the reliability of witness testimony, we could not have done much better than the existing system of having partisans prepare witnesses in advance of trial and examine and cross-examine them at trial.... "[T]he partisan nature of trials tends to make partisans of the witnesses."

Cross-examination at trial — our only substantial safeguard against this systematic bias in the testimony that reaches our courts — is a frail and fitful palliative. Cross-examination is too often ineffective to undo the consequences of skillful coaching. Further, because cross-examination allows so much latitude for bullying and other truth-defeating stratagems, it is frequently the source of fresh distortion when brought to bear against truthful testimony....

Equality of representation. The German system gives us a good perspective on another great defect of adversary theory, the problem that the Germans call "Waffenungleichheit" — literally, inequality of weapons, or in this instance, inequality of counsel.... The simple truth is that very little in our adversary system is designed to match combatants of comparable prowess, even though adversarial prowess is a main factor affecting the outcome of litigation. Adversary theory thus presupposes a condition that adversary practice achieves only indifferently.... Disparity in the quality of legal representation can make a difference in Germany, too, but the active role of the judge places major limits on the extent of the injury that bad lawyering can work on a litigant. In German procedure both parties get the same fact-gatherer — the judge....

Prejudgment. Perhaps the most influential justification for adversary domination of fact-gathering [is that] [n]onadversarial procedure risks prejudgment — that is, prematurity in judgment....

In German procedure counsel oversees and has means to prompt a flagging judicial inquiry; but quite apart from that protection, is it really true that a "familiar pattern" would otherwise beguile the judge into investigating too sparingly? If so, it seems odd that this asserted "natural human tendency" towards premature judgment does not show up in ordinary business and personal decision-making, whose patterns of inquiry resemble the fact-gathering process in German civil procedure. . . .

Depth. [C]oncern about prematurity shades into a different issue: how to achieve appropriate levels of depth in fact-gathering. Extra investment in search can almost always turn up further proofs that would be at least tenuously related to the case. Adversary domination of fact-gathering privatizes the decision about what level of resources to invest in the case. . . .

[German fact-gathering] does indeed contrast markedly with the inclination of American litigators "to leave no stone unturned, provided, of course, they can charge by the stone." The primary reason that German courts do less fact-gathering than American lawyers is that the Germans eliminate the waste. . . .

Because German procedure places upon the judge the responsibility for fact-gathering, the danger arises that the job will not be done well. The American system of partisan fact-gathering has the virtue of its vices: It aligns responsibility with incentive. Each side gathers and presents proofs according to its own calculation of self-interest. This privatization is an undoubted safeguard against official sloth. After all, who among us has not been treated shabbily by some lazy bureaucrat in a government department? And who would want to have that ugly character in charge of one's lawsuit?

The answer to that concern in the German tradition is straightforward: The judicial career must be designed in a fashion that creates incentives for diligence and excellence. The idea is to attract very able people to the bench, and to make their path of career advancement congruent with the legitimate interests of the litigants.

Notes and Questions

1. In an adversarial system lawyers owe a duty of loyalty to their clients. The system could not work if lawyers were pure partisans, able to do anything (such as lying, bribing witnesses, or destroying evidence) to further their clients' interests. At the same time, lawyers are expected to advance the interests of the client by means that lawyers might not employ in their own lives, such as attacking the credibility of a witness whom the lawyer believes to be truthful. Defining and policing the limits of lawyers' conduct in the representation of their clients are the job of a system of legal ethics. One criticism of the adversarial system is its distinction between lawyers' "ordinary morality" (how they act in private life) and their "professional morality" (how they act in representing clients). Denying that such a distinction is coherent, Professor Luban argues that lawyers' conduct should be judged by the moral worth of the ends that they seek to achieve for their clients. *See* DAVID LUBAN, LEGAL ETHICS AND HUMAN DIGNITY (2007). For a thoughtful response, see Norman W. Spaulding, *The Rule of Law in Action: A Defense of Adversary System Values*, 93 CORNELL L. REV. 1377 (2008). Professor Spaulding points out that Luban's criticism is strongest when the moral reprehensibility of a lawyer's conduct is clear, but

lawyers typically work in a pluralistic society in which the truth of disputed events is often unknown and the values at stake are contested and complex.

2. Another way to describe the ethical difficulty is to consider lawyers' dual obligations: They are bound relationally and financially to their clients, yet they must ensure the fair and impartial administration of justice. Indeed, two of the foundational ethical tenets in American law are that lawyers must "competently" represent their clients and that lawyers are "officers of the court." Can lawyers fulfill both roles? According to a leading scholar of legal ethics and procedure:

> So long as the advocate in the American system is supposed to be at once a champion in forensic roughhouse and a guardian of the temple of justice, he can fulfill his responsibilities only if he combines extraordinary technical skill with an unusually disciplined sense of probity. That seems to be asking too much of any profession.

GEOFFREY C. HAZARD, JR., ETHICS IN THE PRACTICE OF LAW 135 (1978).

3. Most of the arguments raised by Professors Landsman and Langbein are instrumental in form, arguing that the adversarial system is (or is not) better at achieving desired procedural goals. It is also possible to make noninstrumental arguments for an adversarial process. Professor Fuller contended that the adversarial approach is intrinsic to the nature of adjudication. *See* Lon L. Fuller, *The Forms and Limits of Adjudication*, 92 HARV. L. REV. 353 (1978). The classic rejoinder to Professor Fuller is Abram Chayes, *The Role of the Judge in Public Law Litigation*, 89 HARV. L. REV. 1281 (1976). Professor Chayes argues that, in important ways, modern American litigation does not conform to the adversarial model.

4. When you came to law school, you might have thought that accuracy was the *only* goal of adjudication. As you now realize, this goal has its limits. Suppose that perfectly correct outcomes could be guaranteed, but at a cost of $1,000,000 per dispute. Or suppose that correct outcomes could be guaranteed by administering a truth serum that killed the witnesses. At some point, truth-seeking comes into conflict with other important values.

Indeed, Professor Landsman does not stake his defense of adversarial process entirely, or even primarily, on its truth-seeking capacity. Nor does Professor Langbein base his criticism of the adversarial system entirely on its supposed indifference to truth. Perhaps the most sustained criticisms of the adversarial system's truth-finding capacity came from two American judges, Jerome Frank and Marvin Frankel. *See* JEROME FRANK, COURTS ON TRIAL: MYTH AND REALITY IN AMERICAN JUSTICE (1949); Marvin E. Frankel, *The Search for Truth: An Umpireal View*, 123 U. PA. L. REV. 1031 (1975). Judge Frankel's article gives a flavor of their criticism:

> The advocate in the trial courtroom is not engaged much more than half the time — and then only coincidentally — in the search for truth. The advocate's prime loyalty is to his client, not to truth as such. . . .
>
> . . . [W]e know that others searching after facts — in history, geography, medicine, whatever — do not emulate our adversary system. We know that most countries of the world seek justice by different

routes. What is much more to the point, we know that many of the rules and devices of adversary litigation as we conduct it are not geared for, but are often aptly suited to defeat, the development of the truth. [*Id.* at 1035-36.]

5. We do not expect you to have answers to the difficult questions of selecting and implementing procedural norms that this section has raised. Nevertheless, because many of the issues we study in this book implicate these questions, now is the time to begin to think about their answers.

SECTION B: A BRIEF HISTORY OF THE AMERICAN PROCEDURAL SYSTEM

Another way to understand a procedural system is to study how it developed. This section describes the history of American civil procedure.

1. English Antecedents. After their conquest of England in 1066, the Normans sought to consolidate their power. One method was to bring the most important types of disputes (often involving title to land) before the king's agents. Eventually this administrative process evolved into a judicial one, giving rise to the English common-law courts.

In order for one of the king's courts to hear a case, the plaintiff needed to obtain a *writ* from the Chancery. The Chancery was administered by the Chancellor, who was one of the king's closest advisors. Until the middle of the thirteenth century, complainants with a good reason for seeking the king's assistance could obtain a writ, thus multiplying the number and types of writs issued. Eventually the royal courts, which had developed some independence from the crown, began to refuse to hear disputes that did not fit within the terms of an existing writ. The issue was settled in 1285, when Parliament decided that the Chancellor could issue writs only if the dispute either invoked one of the writs that had been issued previously or involved facts that were similar to the established writs. With that decision, the shape of the English common law began to harden into definite form.

Out of these writs grew the great common-law subjects that still define our legal system: property, torts, and contracts. But the systematization of the writs into these legal categories lay centuries in the future. In the meantime, each writ developed its own procedures and remedies. Some writs entitled the winner to possession of property, others to money or a declaration of title. Some permitted the plaintiff to seize an asset, others did not. Some writs entitled the plaintiff to trial before a new institution based on Anglo-Saxon and possibly Norman precursors — a jury. Other writs relied on quainter dispute-resolution methods, such as trial by ordeal (in which a defendant was thrown into the water; the innocent defendant sank), wager by battle (in which the adversaries or their agents fought each other, with God granting victory to the rightful side), or wager of law (in which a defendant could take an oath to deny responsibility, as long as eleven people would swear that they believed him).

Cases began with the *pleadings*. Initially, pleading involved oral discussions between the lawyers and the judge; by the sixteenth century, lawyers reduced their pleadings to writing. The point of *common-law pleading* was to narrow the case to a single issue of fact or law. Each writ had its own pleading requirements. In general, the case began with the plaintiff's *declaration*, which stated facts intended to demonstrate the plaintiff's entitlement to relief. The defendant's responsive plea usually took one of four forms: (1) a *traverse* (denying that some or all the alleged conduct had occurred); (2) a *demurrer* (admitting the acts alleged, but denying that the conduct was a legal wrong); (3) a *confession and avoidance* (admitting the acts alleged, but providing a reason why the defendant bore no responsibility); or (4) a *dilatory plea* (claiming a defect in the court's ability to decide the case). The defendant had to choose one, and only one, of these options, even if two or more might apply. Depending on the writ and the nature of the defendant's plea, the parties sometimes pleaded further.

As the centuries went on, pleading became a complicated, precise ritual with no tolerance for miscues. A plaintiff who chose the wrong writ lost, even if using a different writ would have been successful. A defendant who lost after choosing the wrong plea couldn't go back and try another plea, even if the latter plea would have led to victory. In part driven by concerns for the fallibility of juries, the point of this draconian operation was to leave a single issue to decide. If the parties chose one pleading route, all that remained was what we would today call a *question of law*, which the court decided. If the parties chose a different set of pleas, all that remained was what we would today call a *question of fact*, which trial by jury, ordeal, battle, or wager resolved. For that reason, common-law pleading is often called *single-issue pleading*.

Rigid enforcement of procedural technicalities was not the only problem with common-law pleading. As a general matter, the parties had no mechanisms by which they could force other parties or witnesses to disclose information that might assist in resolving the case; as a result, the parties might have little notice about the true nature of the dispute. Moreover, with its ossified writ system, the common law had limited capacity to respond to demands for new forms of law. For instance, the common law did not enforce most contracts until the seventeenth century.

In short, common-law pleading often resulted in cases not being resolved on their merits. Pleading rules were so complex and intricate that procedure ended up dominating the substance of disputes. Although seemingly illogical, the writ system stood for more than eight centuries. One reason was tradition. Another was the system's ability to resolve common disputes tolerably well. A third was the popularity of jury trial, which eventually replaced ordeal, battle, and wager as the decision-making procedure.

A final factor that prolonged the writ system was that it was not the only procedural game in town. The principal alternative system was known as *equity*. People whose claims fit within no existing writ or who distrusted common-law procedures sometimes petitioned to have the Chancellor hear their cases. Thus was the system of equity born. Because early Chancellors were trained in canon law, equity had a Roman flavor. There were no juries. In the early years, pleadings were minimal, and pleading technicalities never kept the Chancellor from reaching the merits of the dispute. To do complete justice, equity was also willing to bring all interested parties into the suit and to entertain more complicated party structures than the standard one-plaintiff, one-defendant structure of the common law. The Chancellor also had the power to send out functionaries to obtain documents, and eventually to take written statements from witnesses. The Chancellor then reviewed these materials and rendered a decision without a formal trial. Without the common law's culminating trial, the Chancellor could examine the evidence on one matter, make a decision, and then move to the next issue in a piecemeal fashion.

Over time, the jurisdiction of the Chancellor expanded. The common-law courts did not always take kindly to the intrusion. Complicated by power struggles between the crown and Parliament, the skirmishes between common law and equity — between two very different procedural systems — lasted for more than four hundred years. Although equity finally gained a more dominant position in the eighteenth century, it was still the tail on the dog; the most common disputes, such as damage claims in property, tort, and contract, fell to the law courts.

Equity was not without its own problems. First, equity's commitment to individualized justice meant, as some wags have put it, that justice was measured by the "Chancellor's foot"; because each Chancellor had a different sense of justice, results in similar cases could vary markedly. Relatedly, because the Chancellor was committed to deciding cases on their merits, he could always revisit decisions; equity lacked the virtue of finality. For this reason and because the Chancellor was a busy government official, the pace of equity practice was excruciatingly slow; the decades-old case lampooned in Dickens' *Bleak House* was a suit in equity, and Dickens did not overstate the problem. Equity was also expensive for the parties. Like many bureaucracies, the Chancery was riven from time to time with scandal, and bribery was not uncommon. Another problem was equity's lack of effective issue-narrowing devices or a culminating event with the drama and ritual of trial by jury. Equity was also limited in its remedies. Equity could issue an injunction to prevent a party from engaging in certain conduct, but typically could not award common-law remedies, such as damages or declarations about ownership of real property. (Conversely, common-law courts could not typically award injunctions.) A final problem was that, in its mature nineteenth-century form, equity had lost much of its flexibility and had taken on the common law's rigor.

In many ways equity was the opposite of the common law. Common-law pleading was certain and efficient (even ruthless) in winnowing a case to a decidable issue, and it vaulted procedural compliance over legal merit. In spirit if not always in practice, equity used flexible procedures, always with an eye toward resolving cases on the substantive merits. The common law had no means to uncover information before trial; equity did. The common law had simple party structures; equity allowed more complex ones. The common law used juries; equity did not. The common law awarded damages; equity awarded injunctions and specific performance. The strengths of each system were the weaknesses of the other. The two systems were symbiotic; neither could have lasted without the other.

2. *American Antecedents*. With adjustments, colonists imported law and equity to America. For the most part, the dual systems survived the American Revolution. When Congress created the federal courts in 1789, it required that, with regard to common-law claims, a federal court should follow the rules of procedure of the state in which it was located. Suits in equity presented a muddier picture. In the early nineteenth century Congress gave the United States Supreme Court the power to promulgate rules of procedure for federal-court suits in equity. For the most part, the Supreme Court declined the invitation, choosing to create only a few interstitial rules. Federal equity suits tended to follow state-court practice.

Over the first half of the nineteenth century, substance emerged from the shadow of procedure. Jeremy Bentham spearheaded a movement to reform the English court system. New York, then the most influential American jurisdiction, adopted a comprehensive procedural code in 1848. The Field Code (named after David Dudley Field, its principal proponent) merged law and equity into one system. The writ system's issue pleading gave way to an approach under which the parties were to plead enough facts to demonstrate that they could prove each element of each claim or defense they raised. This system was called *code pleading* (or, because of its emphasis on pleading facts, *fact pleading*). By the turn of the twentieth century, twenty-seven states had adopted some version of code pleading.

Although some states (notably California and New York) still use code pleading today, all that needs to be said about early code pleading is that it became bogged down in technicalities as mind-numbing as the common-law system that it was supposed to simplify. Therefore, a new wave of American reform commenced early in the twentieth century. One significant manifestation was the 1912 revision to the Federal Equity Rules.

The 1912 Equity Rules established a comprehensive procedural system. They swept aside arcane and complex pleading rules, and typically permitted only two pleadings: the plaintiff's bill of complaint and the defendant's answer. Requiring only a "short and simple" statement of the controversy, the pleadings were intended to give an opponent notice of the nature of the claims or defenses. Known as *notice pleading*, this system relied on other methods to narrow issues and develop facts. In particular, the 1912 Rules permitted parties to inspect documents, to promulgate written questions to other parties, and to take the testimony of witnesses before trial. The Rules authorized the joinder of additional claims and parties on liberal terms. Rejecting equity practice of long standing, the 1912 Rules also permitted a judge to hear live testimony at the trial, thus making the trial in equity resemble a common-law trial (but for the jury).

The Equity Rules were revolutionary. They returned to the ancient spirit of equity practice; at the same time, they blended in elements of the common-law trial. The immediate impact of the Equity Rules, however, was modest. Equity practice was a small part of the federal docket; for its much larger common-law docket, a federal court still employed the procedures of the state in which it sat. And state procedure was all over the lot, with various procedural systems employed across the country.

3. The Modern American System. Over the next two decades, reformers tried to convince Congress to enact legislation giving the United States Supreme Court the power to craft procedural rules for all federal cases. Congress finally enacted the Rules Enabling Act of 1934, which provided this power. The principal restriction on this power was that "[s]aid rules shall neither abridge, enlarge, nor modify the substantive rights of any litigant."*

The Supreme Court appointed a committee to draft a procedural code. Led by two professors, Charles Clark and Edson Sunderland, the committee drafted, and the Supreme Court promulgated, a new code known as the Federal Rules of Civil Procedure. The Federal Rules took effect in 1938.

The Federal Rules abolished the distinction between law and equity in federal court (though, as we shall see, the distinction is still salient for some purposes). *See* Fed. R. Civ. P. 2. In many ways, the Federal Rules patterned themselves after the 1912 Equity Rules. Pleadings were short and plain, parties had full discovery of facts before trial, procedural rules were not supposed to frustrate decisions on a case's merits, and judges had broad discretion. But the new Rules also tried to preserve common-law traditions, including the use of a single culminating trial and the reliance on adversaries to collect evidence and shape the arguments.

The Federal Rules of Civil Procedure remain in force to this day. The Court has amended the substance and clarified the language of many of the Rules over the years. Despite these changes, the Rules' vision of American civil litigation remains intact more than eighty years after their adoption.

The Federal Rules have also influenced state procedure. Because the Federal Rules apply only in federal courts, state courts are not required to follow them. Nevertheless, many states adopted most of the provisions of the Federal Rules as their own. There are important exceptions — we have already mentioned California and New York — and in recent years the finer details of federal and state procedure have tended to diverge more significantly. Despite these differences, the basic vision of the Federal Rules — simplified pleading, broad discovery, culminating trial, and avoidance of procedural technicality — prevails in the states as well.

For this reason, this casebook focuses largely on procedure at the federal level. In establishing this focus, we are not denigrating the importance or the procedural contributions of state courts, which handle approximately 98% of civil litigation. But as a single, coherent procedural code, the Federal Rules of Civil Procedure are an excellent vehicle for exploring the common issues and challenges that American litigation poses.

---

* The heart of the present version of the Rules Enabling Act is 28 U.S.C. § 2072, which you might profitably read now. For a history of the Enabling Act, see Stephen B. Burbank, *The Rules Enabling Act of 1934*, 130 U. Pa. L. Rev. 1015 (1982).

Section C: An Overview of the American Judicial System

Like a machine, a procedural system consists of separate parts. To comprehend the significance of each part, you must understand how it fits into the overall structure. This reality presents a dilemma for those who learn, and those who teach, civil procedure. To understand the point of a rule, you often need information about other rules that you haven't yet studied. Although we cannot completely resolve this pedagogical dilemma, this section provides a brief roadmap of the book — and in the process, of the American procedural system — so that you might begin to understand at the outset how each procedural piece fits into the machine. The description here is simplistic; subsequent chapters flesh out vital details.

1. Dual System of Courts. The two main systems of courts in the United States are the federal courts and the state courts. For the most part, the structures of the court systems are similar. On the federal side, cases usually begin in the *district courts*. Congress has divided the United States into ninety-four federal judicial districts, each of which covers a certain geographical territory (every state and territory has at least one district; populous states have as many as four). Assuming that a case does not settle and otherwise terminate through the action of the parties, the district court — either after trial or through other processes — will enter a *judgment* reflecting its decision about the lawsuit's outcome. In some but not all cases, the court uses a jury to determine the facts relevant to the outcome.

In most civil cases, a party who loses the judgment has a right of appeal to an appellate court. In the federal system, these courts are the *courts of appeals* — often (but technically incorrectly) called the *circuit courts*. There are presently thirteen federal courts of appeals. Twelve of them are regional; they handle the appeals from the district courts in their territory. The thirteenth court — the United States Court of Appeals for the Federal Circuit — handles appeals from all ninety-four federal districts in cases involving patents, government contracts, and a few other types of claims.

Courts of appeals are constrained in their functions. They can review the alleged legal errors made by district courts, but they cannot conduct a trial. If the district court made no prejudicial errors, the court of appeals *affirms* the judgment of the district court; the losing party in the district court loses as well on appeal. If prejudicial errors occurred, the court of appeals usually *reverses* the judgment of the district court. In some cases, this means that the party that lost in the district court now wins; in other cases, a court of appeals *vacates* the judgment and *remands* the case to the district court in order for that court to determine the dispute under the proper principles.

Above the federal courts of appeals sits the United States Supreme Court. In unusual cases, a party can commence a case in the Supreme Court. Typically, however, the Supreme Court acts, like the courts of appeals, as an appellate court reviewing the claimed legal errors in the judgment of the court immediately below. Infrequently, a party can seek direct Supreme

Court review of a district-court decision. For virtually all federal-court cases, however, the Supreme Court reviews the judgment of a court of appeals. In these cases, a party gains Supreme Court review by obtaining a *writ of certiorari*. Writs of certiorari are discretionary; a losing party below must *petition* the Supreme Court to grant the writ, and the Supreme Court is not required to grant anyone's petition. Under present practice, at least four of the nine Supreme Court justices must vote to "grant cert" before the Court can hear a case. Recently the Court has been hearing about 70 cases a year, out of more than 8,000 cases in which petitions are filed. Typically the Supreme Court chooses to hear cases because of their broad legal significance, not because the lower courts made errors — even serious errors. Like other courts of appeals, the Supreme Court typically affirms, reverses, or vacates the decision of the court immediately below it.

To illustrate, assume that you want to file a case in federal court in your home town — Nashville, Tennessee. The federal court in which you would file the case is the United States District Court for the Middle District of Tennessee. Suppose that you lose the case, and the district court enters judgment against you. Unless the case involves a patent or government contract, you usually have a right of appeal to the United States Court of Appeals for the Sixth Circuit, which covers the district courts in Michigan, Ohio, Kentucky, and Tennessee. Let's say that the court of appeals agrees with your opponent's position, and affirms the judgment. You can now petition the United States Supreme Court to grant a writ of certiorari. Unless the Supreme Court does so and reverses the court of appeals, you have lost your case.

The same three-tier structure of courts, including the last level of discretionary review, is also typical of state-court systems (although sometimes there may be as few as two or as many as four tiers, and other local differences also exist). The United States Supreme Court can review, by means of a writ of certiorari, the judgment of the highest state court — but only when the state court decides an issue of federal law.

An obvious question is how these two systems of courts relate to each other. This question implicates the doctrine of *subject-matter jurisdiction*. As the name imperfectly implies, different courts have *jurisdiction* over (or authority to hear) certain types of cases. In the federal system, Article III of the United States Constitution describes nine different types of cases that federal courts can hear. For the district courts, this constitutional authority is not self-executing; Congress must also pass legislation that gives the district courts jurisdiction to hear a particular type of case. The two main types of civil cases that district courts have jurisdiction to hear are cases arising under federal law and cases arising under state law in which the parties in the case are citizens of different states and the amount at stake exceeds $75,000. The first kind of jurisdiction is called *federal-question jurisdiction*; the latter is called *diversity jurisdiction*. We study these rules of federal subject-matter jurisdiction in Chapter Ten. (A third important category of subject-matter jurisdiction for federal courts involves cases in which the United States government, or one of its agencies or officers, is a party, but that subject lies beyond this basic course.)

In contrast to federal courts, whose subject-matter jurisdiction is *limited*, state courts are courts of *general jurisdiction*: they have authority to hear all kinds of disputes, regardless of whether they involve questions of federal law and regardless of the citizenship of the parties. The phrase "general jurisdiction" is really a misnomer, for state legislatures may designate certain state courts to hear only certain kinds of cases (consider, for instance, probate and juvenile courts). State-court jurisdiction is *general* only in the sense that, when looked at as a whole, some court somewhere in the state system can nearly always hear a particular dispute.

The relationship between the state and federal courts is complex. The jurisdiction of the federal and state courts often overlaps, so that a plaintiff whose case fits within federal jurisdiction may have a choice of bringing the case in state court or in federal court. This system of *concurrent jurisdiction* gives rise to a series of doctrines, only some of which we examine in this course, under which a defendant who does not like the court system chosen by the plaintiff can seek to move the case into the other court system. As if this were not trouble enough, some types of cases can be filed only in federal court; federal courts have *exclusive jurisdiction* in these areas.

The geographical boundaries of state and federal courts give rise to other issues. For instance, suppose that, while driving in your home state, you hit Smith, a citizen of a neighboring state. Smith has learned that the isolated country of Lower Slobbovia has a justice system with a friendly attitude toward car-accident victims. So she sues you there. The next thing that you know, you have an official piece of paper commanding you to come to Lower Slobbovia to defend yourself. Your immediate reaction probably is "Smith can't get away with this!" The problem that you have intuited is not one of subject-matter jurisdiction, for Lower Slobbovia's courts have the power to hear claims involving car accidents. Rather, the problem is that Lower Slobbovian courts have no power over *you* — in other words, they have no *jurisdiction over the person* (or *personal jurisdiction*).

The same reaction that you had to being sued in Lower Slobbovia carries over to domestic situations. If the car accident with Smith occurred in your home state of Maine and if Smith lived in New Hampshire, the State of Hawai'i cannot force you to appear in its courts to defend the case. On the other hand, courts in Maine, and arguably in New Hampshire, have an interest in deciding the case. The doctrine of personal jurisdiction, which we examine in Chapter Nine, defines the limits of a court's authority to require defendants to appear before it.

Even if a court has power over you, it might be inconvenient for you to appear before it. Rules of *venue*, which Chapter Nine also explores, help to ensure that a court has enough connection with the parties or the lawsuit to make it a convenient forum.

2. Source of Law. A separate problem created by the existence of a federal structure is the capacity of multiple governments and government institutions to create substantive and procedural law that might govern a case. One set of questions — when courts must apply rules created by the legislature or the executive and when they may create "common-law" rules — lies beyond this course. So does another tricky issue: Whose law should a court choose when each of two or more states has a legitimate interest in the application of its law? A third difficult question, which this book explores in Chapter Eleven, is to determine whether and when federal courts must apply state substantive and procedural law, and state courts must apply federal substantive and procedural law.

3. Processing the Lawsuit. Until now, we have focused on describing issues of judicial structure. Once a plaintiff has chosen the claims and the proper court, the court can turn to resolving the case. In general, American litigation contains five stages: the *pleading* stage, the *pretrial* stage, *trial*, the *post-trial* stage in the trial court, and *appeal*. The vast majority of cases never proceed through all five stages. Due to settlements, abandonment of cases by plaintiffs, defaults by defendants, and resolutions on pretrial motions, less than 1% of all federal civil cases reach trial today. Despite that statistic, however, the critical phase in designing a civil-procedure system is the trial, which remains the default mechanism for determining disputed facts, applying the law to the facts, and deciding the appropriate remedy for the winner. As a result, the structure of the trial influences the design of the procedural system that surrounds it.

Our Anglo-American heritage gave us two very different methods of trial: the common-law trial, in which all disputes were resolved in one sitting, and equity's "continuous trial," in which issues were determined seriatim through a series of hearings. Juries were employed in the common-law trial, but not in equity. Two of the critical decisions made in the Federal Rules of Civil Procedure were to merge law and equity, *see* Fed. R. Civ. P. 2, and to adopt the common-law all-issues trial as the default method for trying a case.

But the drafters of the 1938 Rules also adopted pretrial processes for investigating and narrowing issues before trial that had their origin in equity's continuous-trial method. In the pleading stage, which Chapter Two examines, the parties obtain notice of the claims or defenses raised against them; and claims and defenses that are implausible can be terminated at that point. With regard to factual investigation, the Federal Rules created perhaps the most extensive fact-gathering system in history. Known as *disclosure and discovery*, this system provides the parties with tools — such as powers to inspect documents and take pretrial testimony from witnesses — to uncover information. Chapter Three examines the methods and limitations of this system. The original Federal Rules included few issue-narrowing devices. The principal device was *summary judgment*; later amendments to the Rules have strengthened judges' issue-narrowing capacity. Chapters Four and Five discuss these developments.

In the pretrial stage, the parties must also establish the structure of the lawsuit — in other words, the claims and the persons who will be involved in the case. The writ system usually allowed a plaintiff to assert only one claim against one defendant at a time. Equity, with its attitude of doing complete justice among parties, liberally permitted the joinder of multiple claims and multiple parties in one case. Hewing to the equitable principle that procedure should not get in the way of substance, the Federal Rules have adopted and even expanded on equity's approach. We examine the rules of *claim joinder* and *party joinder* in Chapter Eight.

Once the pretrial phase is over, the trial is ready to begin. Most issues concerning trial are the subject of other law-school courses, such as Evidence and Trial Advocacy. Chapter Five focuses on a few matters — most particularly, on the scope of a party's right to have a jury determine the facts and on doctrines, both during and after trial, that try to ensure that juries come to rationally justified decisions.

In Chapter Six, we briefly examine the final stage of the litigation process: the appeal, in which the work of the trial court can be reviewed.

4. *Finality.* An important principle for a procedural system is finality. It is neither efficient from society's viewpoint nor fair to a party if another party, displeased with the judgment on a claim or issue, can contest the claim or issue over and over in new lawsuits. Chapter Seven examines the common-law principles and statutes that define the law of *preclusion* used in American courts.

5. *Challenging the Standard Litigation Paradigm.* Most of this book focuses on describing and understanding the rules governing American civil litigation. At the same time, it is important to take a critical stance toward these rules, and to ask whether the present procedural system is the best one for the future. This book provides introductory materials on two of the challenges to the American litigation system.

First, this course focuses mostly on routine litigation — litigation involving small numbers of parties on each side. Some disputes, however, involve great numbers of parties whose individual cases might clog the court system. Examples include litigation against a corporation by shareholders and litigation against a manufacturer of a chemical that has contaminated a neighborhood's air or water. These types of cases are often brought as *class actions,* in which one plaintiff (or a small group of plaintiffs) represents the interests of a class of similarly situated people. This type of litigation can be efficient, but it also robs the members of the class of their autonomy and their adversarial right to control their cases. Chapter Twelve introduces the basics of class actions and discusses the controversy surrounding their use.

Second, critics believe that American litigation is too expensive and takes too long. Interest in new models of adjudication and alternatives to adjudication is rising. Under the concept of *case management,* many judges have become more active participants in shaping lawsuits than traditional adversarial theory permits. Courts are also sponsoring methods other than adjudication, such as arbitration and mediation, to resolve disputes. Chapter Four introduces various forms of *alternative dispute resolution* (or "ADR").

SECTION D: AMERICAN CIVIL PROCEDURE IN COMPARATIVE PERSPECTIVE

American civil procedure is the focus of this book. But American civil procedure does not exist in a vacuum, and in a globalizing world other systems interact with our own. The American system has both much in common with foreign procedural systems and a good deal that sets it apart. It is probably fair to say that among developed nations, if you could somehow come up with an "average" procedural system, America's is farther away from that average than any other country's. The American differences can be viewed more or less positively as an instance of what is often referred to as American exceptionalism. Some, especially lawyers in civil-law systems in Europe and elsewhere, may be inclined to view them as another product of those crazy Americans. For better or worse — and some in the United States are among the critics — we do seem to be the outlier.

So as not to exaggerate the differences, let us start with some major common features among procedural systems. According to one law-harmonization effort:

> The fundamental similarities among procedural systems can be summarized as follows:
> - Standards governing assertion of personal jurisdiction and subject-matter jurisdiction
> - Specifications for a neutral adjudicator
> - Procedure for notice to defendant
> - Rules for formulation of claims
> - Explication of applicable substantive law
> - Establishment of facts through proof
> - Provision for expert testimony
> - Rules for deliberation, decision, and appellate review
> - Rules of finality of judgments[.]

ALI/UNIDROIT, PRINCIPLES OF TRANSNATIONAL CIVIL PROCEDURE 5 (2006).

This source goes on to list major ways in which American civil procedure differs from that in the rest of the world, including other systems of English common-law heritage:

> The American system is unique in the following respects:
> - Jury trial is a broadly available right in the American federal and state courts. No other country routinely uses juries in civil cases.
> - American rules of discovery give wide latitude for exploration of potentially relevant information and evidence, including through oral deposition.

- The American adversary system generally affords the advocates far greater latitude in presentation of a case than is customary in other common-law systems.

- The American adversary system operates through a cost rule under which each party ordinarily pays that party's own lawyer and cannot recover that expense from a losing opponent. In almost all other countries, except Japan and China, the winning party, whether plaintiff or defendant, [is entitled to recover] at least a substantial portion of litigation costs.

- American judges are selected through a variety of ways in which political affiliation plays an important part. In most other common-law countries judges are selected on the basis of professional standards. [*Id.* at 6-7.]

We can add to this list three additional differences. First, among countries with federal rather than unitary governments, the American system probably suffers from the most complexity in the relations between its state and federal courts. Second, although interest in their use elsewhere is increasing, class actions remain more prevalent in America despite decisions somewhat cutting back on them. Third, in America opposing parties usually call expert witnesses; the rest of the world tends to view this approach as excessively partisan and favors neutral experts that courts designate.

Although this book does not dwell on the fact that major differences among systems exist, it is worthwhile to keep in mind that ours is far from the only way of doing things. It is especially useful to be aware of the differences if you deal with transnational civil litigation. Just because an American court orders broad discovery against a foreign party, for example, doesn't mean that foreign courts will be eager to enforce that order if you need to go after documents located abroad. On a policy level, practices in other advanced nations may provide a basis for critique of what seems wrong with American civil litigation, and a source for reform ideas; conversely, the rest of the world may be able to learn from what we do well.

SECTION E: THE SOCIAL SIGNIFICANCE OF CIVIL DISPUTE RESOLUTION

Much of what you have read to this point may leave you with the impression that civil procedure involves an awful lot of technical stuff. Well, it does (and thus calls for rigorous thinking on your part). Whatever the amount of nitty-gritty, though, it is important not to lose sight of the role that a system of procedure plays on the larger societal stage. Mechanisms for resolving disputes are among the most ancient and basic institutions in civilized societies; our ancestors understood that such institutions lessened resort to violence and provided a means for exercising control over important social issues. Today civil courts serve multiple goals and perform numerous functions. To give a nonexhaustive (and perhaps not entirely uncontroversial) list: enforcing substantive law; advancing public policy; promoting productive economic activity; maintaining civic order and legitimating government through the righting of wrongs; protecting property rights; effectuating change to bring law and institutions into greater harmony with social norms; and, most broadly, promoting justice.

[margin note: goals of civil courts]

Systems of civil procedure make great differences in whether the courts can serve such purposes well or badly. On the one hand, it is important that persons with potentially valid claims that aren't being honored voluntarily can have reasonable access to justice, so that people don't too often have to "lump it." Further, the United States relies to an unusual degree on private plaintiffs, sometimes referred to as "private attorneys general," to bring cases as a way of complementing government litigation to enforce public policy. Access to justice requires not only formal availability of judicial redress but also reasonable efficiency and dispatch, lest justice be denied by cost and delay. It also requires ways of trying to keep resource disparities between parties from giving the side with more wealth or a better lawyer a victory every time. Access to civil justice is important not just for claims by one private party against another, but also for cases involving the government as defendant or plaintiff; despite the old adage, sometimes you *can* fight City Hall, and much government enforcement of public policy takes place in civil rather than criminal litigation.

On the other hand, civil litigation can be subject to excess and abuse, which can call for controls lest access to justice come to seem too much of a good thing. Problems of excess may be raised most prominently by the claim, strongly pressed by some and strongly contested by others, that America suffers from a civil "litigation explosion." One need not buy the litigation-explosion view in strong form to acknowledge that ease of access to civil justice can come with problems, such as weak claims that are so expensive to litigate that defendants settle instead of fighting them; high discovery costs in some big-stakes cases; subjecting people to the often considerable psychological aggravations of litigation; taking decisions on public-policy issues away from the people's democratically elected representative bodies; and heavy use of scarce resources invested in courts rather than in other government services (or not taken as taxes in the first place).

[margin note: concerns w/ access to the system]

Trying to achieve an appropriate balance of the concerns just listed brings forth regular efforts at reform of the civil-justice system, in which many of you will participate through bar-association groups, law-reform organizations, legislative and judicial rulemaking bodies, and even scholarship. Such work can be professionally fulfilling as well as socially valuable, albeit at times frustrating and patience-trying. The interests affected by the ways that civil cases are processed — such as those of corporations, unions, governments, and consumer, environmental, or civil-rights groups — can make civil-justice reform, even if it is not the very most hot-button of areas, surprisingly politicized. That this is so reflects how civil procedure is not some autonomous mass of technicalities, but rather plays an important role in how people and institutions involved in disputes subject to legal regulation, as well as the citizenry and government, relate to each other.

Chapter Two

Pleading

A civil lawsuit begins when a *plaintiff* files a document called a *complaint*. What exactly should this complaint say? Should it provide all of the factual information that the plaintiff knows about a case, or just a sketch? Should it contain the legal authorities on which the plaintiff intends to rely? Must some magic formula or legal incantation be invoked? To whom should the complaint be given, and how? What, if anything, can or must the *defendant* (the person sued by the plaintiff) say to respond to the complaint? Can the parties change these initial statements? Can they be punished for saying things that turn out not to be true?

A system of *pleading* addresses these questions. Understanding this system begins with an appreciation of the purposes that the pleadings serve in the structure and resolution of a lawsuit.

Section A: Perspectives on Pleading

Because the American legal system separates the pretrial stage of civil litigation from the trial stage, a major function of the pretrial stage is to ready the case for trial. Basic notions of fairness, as well as the need for a well-run trial, demand at a minimum that each party notify the court and the other parties about the nature of the legal and factual assertions that the party will make. Beyond the minimum, a pretrial process should also uncover information relevant to the legal and factual contentions and narrow down these contentions to those that are serious enough to invoke the machinery of trial. Unfortunately, given the finiteness of time, money, and knowledge, no pretrial system can perfectly perform the tasks of notice, developing facts, and narrowing issues.

The *pleadings*, which are the formal written exchanges that set out the parties' claims and defenses, are the first step in the pretrial process. If the pleadings are also the only step in the pretrial process (so that the trial begins when the pleadings close), then the pleading system bears the entire burden of accomplishing the pretrial functions. If other pretrial processes follow the pleadings, then the pleadings need to accomplish less. How much less depends on what the remainder of the pretrial process does.

The following reading describes the approach taken in the Federal Rules of Civil Procedure and parallel state-court rules, as well as the approaches of the common-law and code-pleading regimes that the modern pleading system replaced.

CHARLES E. CLARK, HANDBOOK OF THE LAW OF CODE PLEADING

3-4, 56-58 (2d ed. 1947)

The *pleadings* . . . serve the primary purpose of acquainting the court and the parties with the facts in dispute. In so doing they should point out the actual issues to be settled. Several other purposes may also be served by the pleadings . . . : (1) To serve as a formal basis for the judgment to be entered; (2) to separate issues of fact from questions of law; (3) to give the litigants the advantage of the plea of res judicata if again molested; (4) to notify the parties of the claims, defenses, and cross-demands of their adversaries. . . . [T]he purpose especially emphasized has varied from time to time. Thus in common-law pleading especial emphasis was placed upon the *issue-formulating* function of pleadings; under the earlier code pleading like emphasis was placed upon *stating the material, ultimate facts* in the pleadings; while at the present time the emphasis seems to have shifted to the *notice* function of pleading. . . .

. . . [Notice pleading] differs in the main in the extent of generality of statement permitted. Thus, instead of describing the particulars of an accident, only the time and date of the accident are referred to. There is not so much a change in the kind of pleading as a change in emphasis. The common-law pleading both set forth facts and gave notice, but stressed mainly the framing of the issue; the code produced one or more issues and gave notice, but did this while setting forth the facts. So notice pleading, giving some facts, presents a very broad issue. . . .

. . . The code purpose of stating the facts did not work. . . . It may therefore properly give place to the purpose of fair notice.

Notes and Questions

1. Professor (later Judge) Clark was the principal drafter of the Federal Rules of Civil Procedure, as well as a noted authority on pleading. Behind his support for notice pleading was a fundamental jurisprudential commitment. Professor Clark believed that procedural rules "should perform the office only of *aiding* in the enforcement of substantive legal relations. . . . It is a means to an end, not an end in itself — the 'handmaid rather than the

mistress' of justice." Clark, *supra*, at 54. Contrast with this view Justice Frankfurter's statement that "[t]he history of liberty has largely been the history of observance of procedural safeguards." McNabb v. United States, 318 U.S. 332, 347 (1943). Consider as well the less lofty view of a former Congressman: "I'll let you write the substance . . . and you let me write the procedure, and I'll screw you every time." Rep. John Dingell, Hearings on H.R. 2327 Before the Subcomm. on Admin. Law and Governmental Relations of the House Comm. on the Judiciary, 98th Cong. 312 (1983).

2. One of the standard criticisms of the systems of common-law and code pleading was their penchant to decide cases on the basis of pleading technicalities rather than substantive merits. Without doubt, imposing a lot of pleading technicalities will cause some parties to lose cases that, in an ideal world, they "should have" won. But these hurdles will also cause parties to lose cases that they "should have" lost — and with much less expense than the cost of full-blown pretrial and trial. Does Clark fail to balance the benefits of a stricter pleading regime against its costs? Or is a hallmark of modern procedural justice the accurate enforcement of substantive rights, regardless of cost?

3. Notice pleading facilitates access to courts. Open access to courts is a two-edged sword. Critics of the American system of civil justice sometimes claim that the United States is the most litigious society in history, and that the United States witnessed a "litigation explosion" in the latter half of the twentieth century. The truth of these claims is hotly debated, but notice pleading probably does foster more litigation. That fact hardly makes notice pleading the root cause of American litigiousness. Other reasons include changes in substantive law that gave people more rights and changes in social attitudes about suing corporations and governments.

4. Evaluating the merits of notice pleading requires knowledge of the other steps in the pretrial process. The Federal Rules of Civil Procedure contain post-pleading devices to uncover the facts, identify the law, and narrow the issues for trial. The system of *disclosure and discovery* allows each side to investigate the factual basis of the case. The systems of *case management* and *summary judgment* frame and winnow the issues. How accurate and inexpensive these devices are — questions that Chapters Three, Four, and Five explore — is relevant in deciding whether a notice-pleading approach is best.

Section B: The Complaint

The pleading provisions are found in Federal Rules of Civil Procedure 7-15. According to Rule 7(a), the only pleadings are *complaints*, *answers*, and (in rare cases when courts order them) *replies* to the answer. Rule 7(b) distinguishes pleadings from *motions*, which are requests for a court order.

According to Rule 3, a case "is commenced by filing a complaint with the court." Rule 4 prescribes the way(s) in which the plaintiff must *serve* (in other words, provide a copy of) the complaint to the defendant. Rule 12 then requires the served defendant either to file an answer to the complaint or to file a motion. (A defendant can also do nothing, and the court will enter a default. *See* Fed. R. Civ. P. 55. Default is a very risky strategy except in limited circumstances that we discuss *infra* pp. 477-78, Note 4.)

This section examines the issues surrounding a complaint and its service. Section C explores motions and answers.

1. A Sample Complaint

Virginia Rose walks into your law firm. She says that, while she was crossing the street, a car hit her and she suffered significant injuries. She wants to sue the driver, David Young. After investigation, your firm agrees to represent her. You draft the following complaint for your partner:

IN THE UNITED STATES DISTRICT COURT
FOR THE DISTRICT OF MASSACHUSETTS

VIRGINIA ROSE, Plaintiff,)
)
v.   )   Civil No. 20-CIV-220-B
)
DAVID YOUNG, Defendant   )

COMPLAINT

1. Plaintiff Virginia Rose is a citizen of the state of Massachusetts.

2. Defendant David Young is a citizen of the state of Rhode Island.

3. The amount in controversy in this case exceeds $75,000.

4. On August 14, 2019, on Boylston Street in Boston, Massachusetts, defendant drove a motor vehicle against the plaintiff while she was crossing the street.

5. As a result, the plaintiff was physically injured, lost wages, incurred medical expenses, and suffered physical and mental pain.

6. Plaintiff demands judgment against defendant for at least $200,000, plus costs and such other relief as the Court deems proper.

Plaintiff demands a jury trial.

Dated: June 1, 2020

Respectfully Submitted,

_____
Fenton Fletcher
1 Lawyers Square
Boston, Massachusetts
trssjt@gmail.com
888-555-1212

Because you are filing the case in federal court, your complaint must pass muster under the pleading requirements of the Federal Rules of Civil Procedure. Does it? The principal Rules that describe the contents of a complaint are Fed. R. Civ. P. 8(a), 8(d), 8(e), 9, and 10.

These Rules provide general guidance, but they are not a cookbook that lists every legal and factual ingredient that every adequate complaint must contain. Nor do they specify magic language whose presence immunizes a complaint from attack or whose absence automatically constitutes a fatal defect. Therefore, you must use your judgment to determine whether your complaint complies with the Federal Rules. Among the aids that can guide you are prior cases that have interpreted the same Rules.

2. The Sufficiency of the Complaint

CONLEY V. GIBSON

355 U.S. 41 (1957)

■ MR. JUSTICE BLACK delivered the opinion for a unanimous Court.

Once again Negro employees are here under the Railway Labor Act asking that their collective bargaining agent be compelled to represent them fairly. In a series of cases beginning with *Steele v. Louisville & Nashville R.R.*, 323 U.S. 192 (1944), this Court has emphatically and repeatedly ruled that an exclusive bargaining agent under the Railway Labor Act is obligated to represent all employees in the bargaining unit fairly and without discrimination because of race and has held that the courts have power to protect employees against such invidious discrimination.

. . . [T]he complaint made the following allegations relevant to our decision: Petitioners were employees of the Texas and New Orleans Railroad at its Houston Freight House. Local 28 of the Brotherhood was the designated bargaining agent under the Railway Labor Act for the bargaining unit to which petitioners belonged. A contract existed between the Union and the Railroad which gave the employees in the bargaining unit certain protection from discharge and loss of seniority. In May 1954, the Railroad purported to abolish 45 jobs held by petitioners or other Negroes all of whom were either discharged or demoted. In truth the 45 jobs were not abolished at all but instead filled by whites as the Negroes were ousted, except for a few instances where Negroes were rehired to fill their old jobs but with loss of seniority. Despite repeated pleas by petitioners, the Union . . . did nothing to protect them against these discriminatory discharges and refused to give them protection comparable to that given white employees. The complaint then went on to allege that the Union had failed in general to represent Negro employees equally and in good faith. It charged that such discrimination constituted a violation of petitioners' right under the Railway Labor Act to fair representation from their bargaining agent. And it concluded by asking for relief in the nature of declaratory judgment, injunction and damages.

[The petitioners sued the union, its local, and some of its officers in the United States District Court for the Southern District of Texas. The defendants moved to dismiss the complaint for numerous reasons, including the complaint's failure to state a claim upon which relief could be granted. The district court granted the motion on one of the other grounds. The United States Court of Appeals for the Fifth Circuit affirmed. After reversing this determination, the Supreme Court turned to the union's argument that the complaint failed to state a claim.]

. . . [W]e hold that under the general principles laid down in the *Steele* [and subsequent] cases the complaint adequately set forth a claim upon which relief could be granted. In appraising the sufficiency of the complaint we follow, of course, the accepted rule that a complaint should not be dismissed for failure to state a claim unless it appears beyond doubt that the plaintiff can prove no set of facts in support of his claim which would entitle him to relief. Here, the complaint alleged, in part, that petitioners were discharged wrongfully by the Railroad and that the Union, acting according to plan, refused to protect their jobs as it did those of white employees or to help them with their grievances all because they were Negroes. If these allegations are proven there has been a manifest breach of the Union's statutory duty to represent fairly and without hostile discrimination all of the employees in the bargaining unit. This Court squarely held in *Steele* and subsequent cases that discrimination in representation because of race is prohibited by the Railway Labor Act.

The respondents also argue that the complaint failed to set forth specific facts to support its general allegations of discrimination and that its dismissal is therefore proper. The decisive answer to this is that the Federal Rules of Civil Procedure do not require a claimant to set out in detail the facts upon which he bases his claim. To the contrary, all the Rules require is "a short and plain statement of the claim" that will give the defendant fair notice of what the plaintiff's claim is and the grounds upon which it rests. Such simplified "notice pleading" is made possible by the liberal opportunity for discovery and the other pretrial procedures established by the Rules to disclose more precisely the basis of both claim and defense and to define more narrowly the disputed facts and issues. Following the simple guide of Rule 8(f) that "all pleadings shall be so construed as to do substantial justice,"* we have no doubt that petitioners' complaint adequately set forth a claim and gave the respondents fair notice of its basis. The Federal Rules reject the approach that pleading is a game of skill in which one misstep by counsel may be decisive to the outcome and accept the principle that the purpose of pleading is to facilitate a proper decision on the merits. . . .

The judgment is reversed and the cause is remanded to the District Court for further proceedings not inconsistent with this opinion.

---

* In 2007, as part of the general restyling of the Federal Rules, Rule 8(f) was re-numbered as Rule 8(e), and its language was slightly altered to read: "Pleadings must be construed so as to do justice." — ED.

Notes and Questions

1. We are studying the sufficiency of the complaint, not the responses that a defendant can make to the complaint. Almost invariably, however, cases evaluating the sufficiency of a complaint arise when a defendant files a *motion to dismiss* under Rule 12(b)(6). We will have more to say about Rule 12(b) motions soon (*see infra* pp. 67-69).

2. Rule 8(a) provides that a sufficient complaint must contain three elements: "a short and plain statement of the grounds for the court's jurisdiction," Fed. R. Civ. P. 8(a)(1); "a short and plain statement of the claim showing that the pleader is entitled to relief," Fed. R. Civ. P. 8(a)(2); and "a demand for the relief sought," Fed. R. Civ. P. 8(a)(3). The union made two arguments why the complaint failed to meet the Rule 8(a)(2) requirement. The first concerned the legal merit of the plaintiffs' case: whether the complaint alleged behavior by the defendant for which the substantive law affords the plaintiffs a remedy. The second concerned notice: whether the complaint met the goal of notice pleading by providing the defendant enough details about the nature of the plaintiffs' claim.

Conley responded to both arguments. It stated two different tests, one to determine the sufficiency of the plaintiffs' complaint on its legal merits and the other to determine the sufficiency of the notice it provided. Make sure that you understand each test, and how it differs from the other.

3. Given the *Steele* case, the complaint in *Conley* had legal merit. The complaint also provided more than enough specifics to meet the goal of notice pleading. So why did the union move to dismiss the case? One reason might have been that, before *Conley*, the Supreme Court had never decided a case describing a plaintiff's pleading burden under Rule 8(a)(2). Another reason might have been tactical. In responding to a motion to dismiss, a plaintiff will often describe the complaint's legal and factual basis in more detail than the complaint did. Thus, even if the union expected to lose, the motion to dismiss got the plaintiffs to say more about their case than the complaint had — and more than Rule 8(a)(2) required.

Is such a tactic a proper use of a motion to dismiss? You will want to ask this question again after you study Section E of this chapter (*infra* pp. 90-106), which examines sanctions for baseless or improperly motivated pleadings and motions. But the possibility of such tactics is an important object lesson: in an adversarial system, a party can almost always find a way to take a rule intended to serve one purpose (here, to eliminate insufficient pleadings) and turn it toward a different purpose (here, to extract more information from a plaintiff than the rules of pleading require).

4. Does the sample complaint pass muster under the *Conley* tests?

5. The following three cases continue to explore the requirements for a sufficient complaint. As you read the cases, ask yourself which of type of sufficiency (sufficiency of the complaint's legal merits or of the notice given) is at issue and what test the Supreme Court adopts to govern the issue.

SWIERKIEWICZ V. SOREMA N. A.
534 U.S. 506 (2002)

■ JUSTICE THOMAS delivered the opinion for a unanimous Court.

This case presents the question whether a complaint in an employment discrimination lawsuit must contain specific facts establishing a . . . case of discrimination under the framework set forth by this Court in *McDonnell Douglas Corp. v. Green*, 411 U.S. 792 (1973). We hold that an employment discrimination complaint need not include such facts and instead must contain only "a short and plain statement of the claim showing that the pleader is entitled to relief." Fed. R. Civ. P. 8(a)(2).

I

Petitioner Akos Swierkiewicz is a native of Hungary, who at the time of his complaint was 53 years old.[1] [The complaint alleged that SOREMA was a reinsurance company principally owned and controlled by a French parent corporation. SOREMA's Chief Executive Officer was François M. Chavel, a French national. The following numbered paragraphs are reproduced verbatim from the complaint:

16. On April 17, 1989 Mr. Swierkiewicz began his employment with SOREMA in the position of Senior Vice President and Chief Underwriting Officer ("CUO").

17. In all respects, Mr. Swierkiewicz performed his job in a satisfactory and exemplary manner.

18. Despite plaintiff's stellar performance, in February 1995 Mr. Chavel demoted him from his CUO position to a marketing and services position and transferred the bulk of his underwriting responsibilities to another French national, Nicholas Papadopoulo, who was 32 years old at the time (and 16 years younger than plaintiff).

19. Mr. Chavel demoted Mr. Swierkiewicz on account of his national origin (Hungarian) and his age (he was 49 at the time). . . .

21. Mr. Papadopoulo was far less experienced and less qualified to be SOREMA's CUO than was Mr. Swierkiewicz. Indeed, Mr. Papadopoulo had just one year of underwriting experience prior to being appointed CUO by Mr. Chavel. By contrast, plaintiff had more than 26 years of broad based experience in the insurance and reinsurance industry.

22. At the time Mr. Papadopoulo assumed plaintiff's duties as CUO, Mr. Chavel stated that he wanted to "energize" the underwriting department — clearly implying that plaintiff was too old for the job. . . .

---

1. Because we review here a decision granting respondent's motion to dismiss, we must accept as true all of the factual allegations contained in the complaint. *See, e.g.*, Leatherman v. Tarrant County Narcotics Intelligence and Coordination Unit, 507 U.S. 163, 164 (1993).

28. Mr. Swierkiewicz was isolated by Mr. Chavel following his demotion . . . .

32. In the morning, on Tuesday April 29, 1997, Mr. Chavel and [SOREMA's counsel] met with Mr. Swierkiewicz and gave him two options: either resign his job (with no severance package) or be fired.

33. Mr. Swierkiewicz refused to resign his employment with SOREMA.

34. As a result, he was fired by Mr. Chavel, effective that very day.

35. SOREMA had no valid basis to fire Mr. Swierkiewicz. . . .

42. SOREMA terminated Mr. Swierkiewicz's employment on account of his national origin and thereby violated his right to equal employment opportunity as protected by Title VII . . . .

44. SOREMA terminated Mr. Swierkiewicz's employment on account of his age and thereby violated his right to equal employment opportunity as protected by the [Age Discrimination in Employment Act of 1967 ("ADEA")].

. . . The United States District Court for the Southern District of New York dismissed petitioner's complaint because it found that he "ha[d] not adequately alleged . . . circumstances that support an inference of discrimination." The United States Court of Appeals for the Second Circuit affirmed the dismissal. The Court of Appeals held that petitioner had failed to meet his burden because his allegations were "insufficient as a matter of law to raise an inference of discrimination." We granted certiorari to resolve a split among the Courts of Appeals concerning the proper pleading standard for employment discrimination cases, and now reverse.

II

Applying Circuit precedent, the Court of Appeals required petitioner to plead a . . . case of discrimination in order to survive respondent's motion to dismiss. In the Court of Appeals' view, petitioner was thus required to allege in his complaint: (1) membership in a protected group; (2) qualification for the job in question; (3) an adverse employment action; and (4) circumstances that support an inference of discrimination. *McDonnell Douglas*, 411 U.S. at 802.

. . . *McDonnell Douglas*, however, [states] an evidentiary standard, not a pleading requirement. . . . In subsequent cases, this Court has reiterated that the [*McDonnell Douglas* standard] relates to the employee's burden of presenting evidence that raises an inference of discrimination. . . .

This Court has never indicated that the requirements for establishing a prima facie case under *McDonnell Douglas* also apply to the pleading standard that plaintiffs must satisfy in order to survive a motion to dismiss. For instance, we have rejected the argument that a Title VII complaint requires greater "particularity," because this would "too narrowly constric[t] the role of the pleadings." Consequently, the ordinary rules for assessing the sufficiency of a complaint apply. *See, e.g.*, Scheuer v. Rhodes, 416 U.S. 232,

236 (1974) ("When a federal court reviews the sufficiency of a complaint, before the reception of any evidence either by affidavit or admissions, its task is necessarily a limited one. The issue is not whether a plaintiff will ultimately prevail but whether the claimant is entitled to offer evidence to support the claims[.]")....

Furthermore, imposing the Court of Appeals' heightened pleading standard in employment discrimination cases conflicts with Federal Rule of Civil Procedure 8(a)(2), which provides that a complaint must include only "a short and plain statement of the claim showing that the pleader is entitled to relief." Such a statement must simply "give the defendant fair notice of what the plaintiff's claim is and the grounds upon which it rests." Conley v. Gibson, 355 U.S. 41, 47 (1957) [*supra* p. 28]. This simplified notice pleading standard relies on liberal discovery rules and summary judgment motions to define disputed facts and issues and to dispose of unmeritorious claims. "The provisions for discovery are so flexible and the provisions for pretrial procedure and summary judgment so effective, that attempted surprise in federal practice is aborted very easily, synthetic issues detected, and the gravamen of the dispute brought frankly into the open for the inspection of the court." 5 C. WRIGHT & A. MILLER, FEDERAL PRACTICE AND PROCEDURE § 1202, p. 76 (2d ed. 1990).

Rule 8(a)'s simplified pleading standard applies to all civil actions, with limited exceptions. Rule 9(b), for example, provides for greater particularity in all averments of fraud or mistake. This Court, however, has declined to extend such exceptions to other contexts.... Thus, complaints in these cases, as in most others, must satisfy only the simple requirements of Rule 8(a).

Other provisions of the Federal Rules of Civil Procedure are inextricably linked to Rule 8(a)'s simplified notice pleading standard. Rule 8(e)(1) states that "[n]o technical forms of pleading or motions are required," and Rule 8(f) provides that "[a]ll pleadings shall be so construed as to do substantial justice."* Given the Federal Rules' simplified standard for pleading, "[a] court may dismiss a complaint only if it is clear that no relief could be granted under any set of facts that could be proved consistent with the allegations." Hishon v. King & Spalding, 467 U.S. 69, 73 (1984). If a pleading fails to specify the allegations in a manner that provides sufficient notice, a defendant can move for a more definite statement under Rule 12(e) before responding. Moreover, claims lacking merit may be dealt with through summary judgment under Rule 56. The liberal notice pleading of Rule 8(a) is the starting point of a simplified pleading system, which was adopted to focus litigation on the merits of a claim.

Applying the relevant standard, petitioner's complaint easily satisfies the requirements of Rule 8(a) because it gives respondent fair notice of the basis for petitioner's claims. Petitioner alleged that he had been terminated

---

* The 2007 stylistic amendments to the Federal Rules of Civil Procedure slightly changed these provisions. Former Rule 8(e)(1) is now found in Rule 8(d)(1). It states: "No technical form is required." Former Rule 8(f) is now found in Rule 8(e). It states: "Pleadings must be construed so as to do justice." — ED.

on account of his national origin in violation of Title VII and on account of his age in violation of the ADEA. His complaint detailed the events leading to his termination, provided relevant dates, and included the ages and nationalities of at least some of the relevant persons involved with his termination. These allegations give respondent fair notice of what petitioner's claims are and the grounds upon which they rest. In addition, they state claims upon which relief could be granted under Title VII and the ADEA.

Respondent argues that allowing lawsuits based on conclusory allegations of discrimination to go forward will burden the courts and encourage disgruntled employees to bring unsubstantiated suits. Whatever the practical merits of this argument, the Federal Rules do not contain a heightened pleading standard for employment discrimination suits. A requirement of greater specificity for particular claims is a result that "must be obtained by the process of amending the Federal Rules, and not by judicial interpretation." *Leatherman*, 507 U.S. at 168. Rule 8(a) establishes a pleading standard without regard to whether a claim will succeed on the merits. "Indeed it may appear on the face of the pleadings that a recovery is very remote and unlikely but that is not the test." *Scheuer*, 416 U.S. at 236.

For the foregoing reasons, we hold that an employment discrimination plaintiff need not plead a prima facie case of discrimination and that petitioner's complaint is sufficient to survive respondent's motion to dismiss. Accordingly, the judgment of the Court of Appeals is reversed, and the case is remanded for further proceedings consistent with this opinion.

Notes and Questions

1. In *Swierkiewicz*, Sorema did not argue that the discrimination claims were factually false. Nor did it argue that the law of employment discrimination failed to cover the acts it was alleged to have committed. In other words, Sorema did not argue that it should win the case on its factual or legal merits. Instead, it argued that the plaintiff had made a procedural gaffe; the complaint failed to say enough. According to Sorema, what should the complaint have said? What test did the Supreme Court use to evaluate Sorema's argument? Under this test, could the complaint have said even less and still been sufficient? Or was it scraping by at the bare minimum?

2. To answer these questions, you must interpret the "short and plain statement of the claim showing that the pleader is entitled to relief" language in Rule 8(a), the pleading rule that governs most complaints. (As the Court notes, Rule 9(b) governs some allegations in some complaints; but Rule 9(b) did not apply to any of the allegations in the *Swierkiewicz* complaint.) Look at the tools that *Swierkiewicz* used to interpret the phrase "short and plain statement": the language of the Rule, the purpose of the Rule, the context supplied by surrounding rules, a well-known treatise on civil procedure (*Wright & Miller*), and prior cases. Should the Court also

have used other interpretive tools (such as philosophers' theories of justice or economists' analyses of the most efficient rule)? Did it need to use all of these interpretive methods? What if one method (say, context) suggests a different interpretation from another method (say, purpose)?

In this book, courts are constantly interpreting procedural rules, statutes, or constitutional provisions. You should always focus on the tools of interpretation that each opinion uses, and ask whether the methods of interpretation vary in predictable and principled ways among the cases.

3. *Swierkiewicz* refers to the "burdens" that a plaintiff must shoulder both in making allegations in the complaint and in presenting evidence at trial. The term "burden" is used in multiple senses. With respect to pleading, it has two meanings. First, one of the parties must raise an issue for it to be included in the case; that party has the "burden" of pleading that issue. For instance, if the substantive law treats the plaintiff's contributory negligence as a bar to recovery even if the defendant was negligent, pleading rules may either require the defendant to plead the plaintiff's contributory negligence as a defense (thus putting the pleading burden on the defendant) or require the plaintiff to plead a lack of contributory negligence (putting the pleading burden on the plaintiff). Second, the term "burden" refers to how much a party must include in a pleading. In federal court and in state systems that adopt notice pleading, the plaintiff's burden is modest; as we have seen, a plaintiff does not need to allege every fact or include every legal authority on which the plaintiff will rely.

Distinct from these two *pleading burdens* are *evidentiary burdens* that are often referred to under the label *burden of proof*. That term can be imprecise, as it may refer either to a *burden of production* or to a *burden of persuasion*. The law allocates to one party the obligation to introduce enough evidence to create a factual dispute. The party who must introduce evidence has the burden of production. Usually plaintiffs have that burden as to each element of each of their claims. On affirmative defenses, however, defendants usually have the burden of production. Sometimes a party with the initial burden presents such strong evidence that, absent countervailing evidence, a rational factfinder could decide only its way, thus shifting the burden of production to show a factual dispute to the other side. The decision whether a party has satisfied the burden of producing evidence is made by the judge, who leaves a matter to the factfinder if the burden is met but who takes it away from the factfinder if the burden is not.

Sometimes you will see the term *prima facie case*. A prima facie case refers to the bundle of elements that a plaintiff must prove in order to prevail on a particular claim. For instance, in most states, the prima facie case for a nonintentional tort contains four elements: duty, negligence, causation, and damage. When the plaintiff produces evidence on each of these elements, then the plaintiff has made a prima facie case. A plaintiff who cannot make a prima facie case loses. But the converse is not necessarily true: making a prima facie case does not mean that the plaintiff wins. Rather, the defendant can still win either by proving a defense or by introducing evidence that discredits or disputes the plaintiff's evidence.

When an opposing party introduces evidence that discredits or disputes the other side's evidence, the burden of persuasion becomes relevant. A burden of persuasion involves the factfinder's weighing of the evidence that the parties produce. The persuasion burden with which you may be most familiar is the criminal one: the prosecution must prove each element of a crime "beyond a reasonable doubt." The usual burden of persuasion in a civil case is "fair preponderance of the evidence," a less exacting standard that requires a party with the burden to persuade the factfinder that the evidence "more likely than not" supports its view. Typically, the plaintiff bears the burden of persuasion for the elements of a claim; the defendant bears the burden of persuasion for the elements of a defense. Thus, for a plaintiff to win on a claim, the factfinder must be persuaded to a slightly more than 50% degree of confidence that the plaintiff's evidence supporting the claim is credible. On the other hand, if the factfinder thinks the evidence is a tie (a 50% chance that either side is right) or that the defendant's evidence is more persuasive (a less than 50% chance that the plaintiff's evidence is right), the plaintiff should lose. The converse propositions hold for matters on which the defendant has the persuasion burden. In jury cases, the court determines the persuasion burden and instructs the jury about the standard it should apply in weighing the evidence.

Your courses in substantive law (Torts, Contracts, Property, and so on) will explore the prima facie elements of various claims and defenses. A course in Evidence will explore burdens of proof in more detail.

4. As long as a threat of dismissal under Rule 12(b)(6) exists, lawyers must know how to plead "well enough." The next two principal cases provide more details about this pleading burden.

BELL ATLANTIC CORP. V. TWOMBLY

550 U.S. 544 (2007)

■ JUSTICE SOUTER delivered the opinion of the Court.

Liability under § 1 of the Sherman Act, 15 U.S.C. § 1, requires a "contract, combination . . . , or conspiracy, in restraint of trade or commerce." The question in this putative class action is whether a § 1 complaint can survive a motion to dismiss when it alleges that major telecommunications providers engaged in certain parallel conduct unfavorable to competition, absent some factual context suggesting agreement, as distinct from identical, independent action. We hold that such a complaint should be dismissed.

I

The upshot of the 1984 divestiture of the American Telephone & Telegraph Company's (AT&T) local telephone business was a system of regional service monopolies (variously called "Regional Bell Operating Companies," "Baby Bells," or "Incumbent Local Exchange Carriers"

(ILECs)), and a separate, competitive market for long-distance service from which the ILECs were excluded. [In 1996, Congress enacted the Telecommunications Act of 1996 (1996 Act), which withdrew the local monopolies enjoyed by the ILECs. A critical provision in the 1996 Act required each ILEC to share its network with certain competitors, known as "competitive local exchange carriers" (CLECs). The ILECs vigorously litigated the scope of this obligation during the ensuing decade.]

Respondents William Twombly and Lawrence Marcus (hereinafter plaintiffs) represent a putative class consisting of all "subscribers of local telephone and/or high speed internet services ... from February 8, 1996 to present." In this action against petitioners, a group of ILECs, plaintiffs seek treble damages and declaratory and injunctive relief for claimed violations of § 1 of the Sherman Act....

The complaint alleges that the ILECs conspired to restrain trade in two ways.... Plaintiffs say, first, that the ILECs "engaged in parallel conduct" in their respective service areas to inhibit the growth of upstart CLECs....

Second, the complaint charges agreements by the ILECs to refrain from competing against one another....

[The complaint recited the ways in which the ILECs had sought to block entry of the CLECs into their markets. It also alleged that the ILECs did not compete with each other, even though, in some cases, one defendant completely surrounded another defendant's territory. On this latter point, the complaint quoted a newspaper interview with Richard Notebaert, a CEO of one of the ILECs; according to the complaint, Notebaert said that "it would be fundamentally wrong to compete in [another ILEC's] territory, adding 'it might be a good way to turn a quick dollar but that doesn't make it right.'" The complaint concluded in Paragraph 51:

> In the absence of any meaningful competition between the [defendants] in one another's markets, and in light of the parallel course of conduct that each engaged in to prevent competition from CLECs within their respective local telephone and/or high speed internet services markets and the other facts and market circumstances alleged above, Plaintiffs allege upon information and belief that Defendants have entered into a contract, combination or conspiracy to prevent competitive entry in their respective local telephone and/or high speed internet services markets and have agreed not to compete with one another and otherwise allocated customers and markets to one another.]

The United States District Court for the Southern District of New York dismissed the complaint for failure to state a claim upon which relief can be granted....

The Court of Appeals for the Second Circuit reversed.... Although the Court of Appeals took the view that plaintiffs must plead facts that "include conspiracy among the realm of 'plausible' possibilities in order to survive a motion to dismiss," it then said that "to rule that allegations of parallel anticompetitive conduct fail to support a plausible conspiracy claim, a court would have to conclude that there is no set of facts that would permit a plaintiff to demonstrate that the particular parallelism asserted was the product of collusion rather than coincidence."

We granted certiorari to address the proper standard for pleading an antitrust conspiracy through allegations of parallel conduct, and now reverse.

II

A

Because § 1 of the Sherman Act "does not prohibit [all] unreasonable restraints of trade . . . but only restraints effected by a contract, combination, or conspiracy," "[t]he crucial question" is whether the challenged anticompetitive conduct "stem[s] from independent decision or from an agreement, tacit or express." While a showing of parallel "business behavior is admissible circumstantial evidence from which the fact finder may infer agreement," it falls short of "conclusively establish[ing] agreement or . . . itself constitut[ing] a Sherman Act offense." Even "conscious parallelism," a common reaction of "firms in a concentrated market [that] recogniz[e] their shared economic interests and their interdependence with respect to price and output decisions" is "not in itself unlawful." . . .

Accordingly, we have previously hedged against false inferences from identical behavior at a number of points in the trial sequence. An antitrust conspiracy plaintiff with evidence showing nothing beyond parallel conduct is not entitled to a directed verdict; proof of a § 1 conspiracy must include evidence tending to exclude the possibility of independent action; and at the summary judgment stage a § 1 plaintiff's offer of conspiracy evidence must tend to rule out the possibility that the defendants were acting independently.

B

This case presents the antecedent question of what a plaintiff must plead in order to state a claim under § 1 of the Sherman Act. Federal Rule of Civil Procedure 8(a)(2) requires only "a short and plain statement of the claim showing that the pleader is entitled to relief," in order to "give the defendant fair notice of what the . . . claim is and the grounds upon which it rests," Conley v. Gibson, 355 U.S. 41, 47 (1957) [*supra* p. 28]. While a complaint attacked by a Rule 12(b)(6) motion to dismiss does not need detailed factual allegations, a plaintiff's obligation to provide the "grounds" of his "entitle[ment] to relief" requires more than labels and conclusions, and a formulaic recitation of the elements of a cause of action will not do. Factual allegations must be enough to raise a right to relief above the speculative level,[3] on the assumption that all the allegations in the complaint are true

3. The dissent greatly oversimplifies matters by suggesting that the Federal Rules somehow dispensed with the pleading of facts altogether. While, for most types of cases, the Federal Rules eliminated the cumbersome requirement

(even if doubtful in fact), *see, e.g.,* Swierkiewicz v. Sorema N. A., 534 U.S. 506, 508 n.1 (2002) [*supra* p. 31].

In applying these general standards to a § 1 claim, we hold that stating such a claim requires a complaint with enough factual matter (taken as true) to suggest that an agreement was made. Asking for plausible grounds to infer an agreement does not impose a probability requirement at the pleading stage; it simply calls for enough fact[s] to raise a reasonable expectation that discovery will reveal evidence of illegal agreement.[4] And, of course, a well-pleaded complaint may proceed even if it strikes a savvy judge that actual proof of those facts is improbable, and "that a recovery is very remote and unlikely." In identifying facts that are suggestive enough to render a § 1 conspiracy plausible, we have the benefit of the prior rulings and considered views of leading commentators . . . that lawful parallel conduct fails to bespeak unlawful agreement. It makes sense to say, therefore, that an allegation of parallel conduct and a bare assertion of conspiracy will not suffice. Without more, parallel conduct does not suggest conspiracy, and a conclusory allegation of agreement at some unidentified point does not supply facts adequate to show illegality. Hence, when allegations of parallel conduct are set out in order to make a § 1 claim, they must be placed in a context that raises a suggestion of a preceding agreement, not merely parallel conduct that could just as well be independent action.

The need at the pleading stage for allegations plausibly suggesting (not merely consistent with) agreement reflects the threshold requirement of Rule 8(a)(2) that the "plain statement" possess enough heft to "sho[w] that the pleader is entitled to relief." . . . An allegation of parallel conduct is thus much like a naked assertion of conspiracy in a § 1 complaint: it gets the complaint close to stating a claim, but without some further factual enhancement it stops short of the line between possibility and plausibility of "entitle[ment] to relief."

. . . [W]hen the allegations in a complaint, however true, could not raise a claim of entitlement to relief, "this basic deficiency should . . . be exposed at the point of minimum expenditure of time and money by the parties and the court."

Thus, it is one thing to be cautious before dismissing an antitrust complaint in advance of discovery, but quite another to forget that proceeding to antitrust discovery can be expensive. "[A] district court must

---

that a claimant "set out *in detail* the facts upon which he bases his claim," Conley v. Gibson, 355 U.S. 41, 47 (1957) (emphasis added), Rule 8(a)(2) still requires a "showing," rather than a blanket assertion, of entitlement to relief. Without some factual allegation in the complaint, it is hard to see how a claimant could satisfy the requirement of providing not only "fair notice" of the nature of the claim, but also "grounds" on which the claim rests.

4. Commentators have offered several examples of parallel conduct allegations that would state a § 1 claim under this standard. . . . The parties in this case agree that "complex and historically unprecedented changes in pricing structure made at the very same time by multiple competitors, and made for no other discernible reason" would support a plausible inference of conspiracy.

retain the power to insist upon some specificity in pleading before allowing a potentially massive factual controversy to proceed." That potential expense is obvious enough in the present case: plaintiffs represent a putative class of at least 90 percent of all subscribers to local telephone or high-speed Internet service in the continental United States, in an action against America's largest telecommunications firms (with many thousands of employees generating reams and gigabytes of business records) for unspecified (if any) instances of antitrust violations that allegedly occurred over a period of seven years.

It is no answer to say that a claim just shy of a plausible entitlement to relief can, if groundless, be weeded out early in the discovery process through "careful case management," given the common lament that the success of judicial supervision in checking discovery abuse has been on the modest side. And it is self-evident that the problem of discovery abuse cannot be solved by "careful scrutiny of evidence at the summary judgment stage," much less "lucid instructions to juries"; the threat of discovery expense will push cost-conscious defendants to settle even anemic cases before reaching those proceedings. Probably, then, it is only by taking care to require allegations that reach the level suggesting conspiracy that we can hope to avoid the potentially enormous expense of discovery in cases with no "reasonably founded hope that the [discovery] process will reveal relevant evidence" to support a § 1 claim.

... [Plaintiffs'] main argument against the plausibility standard at the pleading stage is its ostensible conflict with an early statement of ours construing Rule 8. Justice Black's opinion for the Court in *Conley v. Gibson* spoke not only of the need for fair notice of the grounds for entitlement to relief but of "the accepted rule that a complaint should not be dismissed for failure to state a claim unless it appears beyond doubt that the plaintiff can prove no set of facts in support of his claim which would entitle him to relief." This "no set of facts" language can be read in isolation as saying that any statement revealing the theory of the claim will suffice unless its factual impossibility may be shown from the face of the pleadings; and the Court of Appeals appears to have read *Conley* in some such way when formulating its understanding of the proper pleading standard.

... *Conley*'s "no set of facts" language has been questioned, criticized, and explained away long enough. To be fair to the *Conley* Court, the passage should be understood in light of the opinion's preceding summary of the complaint's concrete allegations, which the Court quite reasonably understood as amply stating a claim for relief. But the passage so often quoted fails to mention this understanding on the part of the Court, and after puzzling the profession for 50 years, this famous observation has earned its retirement. The phrase is best forgotten as an incomplete, negative gloss on an accepted pleading standard: once a claim has been stated adequately, it may be supported by showing any set of facts consistent with the allegations in the complaint. *Conley*, then, described the breadth of opportunity to prove what an adequate complaint claims, not the minimum standard of adequate pleading to govern a complaint's survival.

III

When we look for plausibility in this complaint, we agree with the District Court that plaintiffs' claim of conspiracy in restraint of trade comes up short. To begin with, the complaint leaves no doubt that plaintiffs rest their § 1 claim on descriptions of parallel conduct and not on any independent allegation of actual agreement among the ILECs. Although in form a few stray statements speak directly of agreement, on fair reading these are merely legal conclusions resting on the prior allegations. . . .[10] The nub of the complaint, then, is the ILECs' parallel behavior, consisting of steps to keep the CLECs out and manifest disinterest in becoming CLECs themselves, and its sufficiency turns on the suggestions raised by this conduct when viewed in light of common economic experience.

We think that nothing contained in the complaint invests either the action or inaction alleged with a plausible suggestion of conspiracy. As to the ILECs' supposed agreement to disobey the 1996 Act and thwart the CLECs' attempts to compete, we agree with the District Court that nothing in the complaint intimates that the resistance to the upstarts was anything more than the natural, unilateral reaction of each ILEC intent on keeping its regional dominance. . . . The economic incentive to resist was powerful, but resisting competition is routine market conduct . . .

[On the second theory, the ILECs' failure to compete with each other] was not suggestive of conspiracy, not if history teaches anything. . . . In the decade preceding the 1996 Act and well before that, monopoly was the norm in telecommunications, not the exception. The ILECs were born in that world, doubtless liked the world the way it was, and surely knew the adage about him who lives by the sword. Hence, a natural explanation for the noncompetition alleged is that the former Government-sanctioned monopolists were sitting tight, expecting their neighbors to do the same thing. . . .

. . . We agree with the District Court's assessment that antitrust conspiracy was not suggested by the facts adduced under either theory of the complaint, which thus fails to state a valid § 1 claim.[14]

---

10. If the complaint had not explained that the claim of agreement rested on the parallel conduct described, we doubt that the complaint's references to an agreement among the ILECs would have given the notice required by Rule 8. Apart from identifying a seven-year span in which the § 1 violations were supposed to have occurred (i.e., "[b]eginning at least as early as February 6, 1996, and continuing to the present"), the pleadings mentioned no specific time, place, or person involved in the alleged conspiracies. . . . [T]he complaint here furnishes no clue as to which of the four ILECs (much less which of their employees) supposedly agreed, or when and where the illicit agreement took place. A defendant . . . seeking to respond to plaintiffs' conclusory allegations . . . would have little idea where to begin.

14. In reaching this conclusion, we do not apply any "heightened" pleading standard, nor do we seek to broaden the scope of Federal Rule of Civil Procedure 9, which can only be accomplished "by the process of amending the Federal Rules, and not by judicial interpretation." Swierkiewicz v. Sorema N. A., 534 U.S. 506, 515 (2002). On certain subjects understood to raise a high risk of abusive litigation, a plaintiff must state factual allegations with greater particularity than Rule 8 requires. Fed. R.

Plaintiffs say that our analysis runs counter to *Swierkiewicz v. Sorema N. A.*, 534 U.S. 506, 508 (2002) . . . . [*Swierkiewicz*] reversed on the ground that the Court of Appeals had impermissibly applied what amounted to a heightened pleading requirement by insisting that Swierkiewicz allege "specific facts" beyond those necessary to state his claim and the grounds showing entitlement to relief.

Here, in contrast, we do not require heightened fact pleading of specifics, but only enough facts to state a claim to relief that is plausible on its face. Because the plaintiffs here have not nudged their claims across the line from conceivable to plausible, their complaint must be dismissed.

* * *

The judgment of the Court of Appeals for the Second Circuit is reversed, and the cause is remanded for further proceedings consistent with this opinion.

■ JUSTICE STEVENS, with whom JUSTICE GINSBURG joins . . . , dissenting. . . .

The Court and petitioners' legal team are no doubt correct that the parallel conduct alleged is consistent with the absence of any contract, combination, or conspiracy. But that conduct is also entirely consistent with the *presence* of the illegal agreement alleged in the complaint. . . . [T]he Federal Rules of Civil Procedure, our longstanding precedent, and sound practice mandate that the District Court at least require some sort of response from petitioners before dismissing the case.

Two practical concerns presumably explain the Court's dramatic departure from settled procedural law. Private antitrust litigation can be enormously expensive, and there is a risk that jurors may mistakenly conclude that evidence of parallel conduct has proved that the parties acted pursuant to an agreement when they in fact merely made similar independent decisions. Those concerns merit careful case management, including strict control of discovery, careful scrutiny of evidence at the summary judgment stage, and lucid instructions to juries; they do not, however, justify the dismissal of an adequately pleaded complaint without even requiring the defendants to file answers denying a charge that they in fact engaged in collective decisionmaking. More importantly, they do not justify an interpretation of Federal Rule of Civil Procedure 12(b)(6) that seems to be driven by the majority's appraisal of the plausibility of the ultimate factual allegation rather than its legal sufficiency. . . .

Consistent with the design of the Federal Rules, *Conley*'s "no set of facts" formulation permits outright dismissal only when proceeding to discovery or beyond would be futile. . . . Today, however, in its explanation of a decision to dismiss a complaint that it regards as a fishing expedition, the Court scraps *Conley*'s "no set of facts" language. . . .

Civ. P. 9(b)-(c). Here, our concern is not that the allegations in the complaint were insufficiently "particular[ized]"; rather, the complaint warranted dismissal because it failed in toto to render plaintiffs' entitlement to relief plausible.

If *Conley*'s "no set of facts" language is to be interred, let it not be without a eulogy. That exact language, which the majority says has "puzzl[ed] the profession for 50 years," has been cited as authority in a dozen opinions of this Court.... In not one of those ... opinions was the language "questioned," "criticized," or "explained away." Indeed, today's opinion is the first by any Member of this Court to express any doubt as to the adequacy of the *Conley* formulation. Taking their cues from the federal courts, 26 States and the District of Columbia utilize as their standard for dismissal of a complaint the very language the majority repudiates....

Petitioners have not requested that the *Conley* formulation be retired .... I would not ... call into doubt the pleading rules of most of [the] States without far more informed deliberation as to the costs of doing so. Congress has established a process — a rulemaking process — for revisions of that order. *See* 28 U.S.C. §§ 2072-2074.

Notes and Questions

1. *Conley* provided two tests by which to judge the sufficiency of a complaint: "fair notice" and "no set of facts." Be clear about what each test measures. *Twombly* "retires" the "no set of facts" test, replacing it with a "plausibility" test: a complaint must state facts showing a plausible (i.e., more than a "conceivable") claim. But *Twombly* says that the "fair notice" test survives. Would *Swierkiewicz* come out the same after *Twombly*?

2. In thinking through this question, consider three complaints that make only the following allegations of wrongdoing:

- In a suit against your boss: "My boss discriminated against me."
- In a suit against your best friend: "My friend inflicted emotional distress on me when she did not say hi at school this morning."
- In a suit against the CIA: "Martians controlled by the CIA tortiously abducted me from my home on January 1 of this year."

The three sets of allegations present different issues. The first may well have factual and legal merit, but you have not provided enough factual detail for a court to know. The second allegation lacks legal merit; tort law provides no remedy for friends who snub each other. The third allegation lacks factual merit; Martians don't exist, at least not yet.

The "fair notice" test leads to dismissal of the first complaint because the complaint does not provide enough detail about what happened and what law, if any, was broken. The "fair notice" test does not strike down the latter two complaints, which plead enough facts to give notice of the events and the legal theories on which the claims rest. Conversely, the "no set of facts" test allows a court to dismiss the second and third complaints because neither claim has substantive merit. But the "no set of facts" test does not strike down a complaint making the first allegation because some set of facts might show that your boss illegally discriminated against you. The "no set of facts" test had been criticized for its ineffectiveness in responding to complaints of the first type — complaints that formally were inadequate but substantively *might* have merit — but the criticism may have been a straw man: the "no set of facts" test was probably not designed to deal with failures in providing sufficient notice of the facts and grounds of a claim. The "fair notice" test handled formally insufficient complaints.

Applying a "plausibility" test results in dismissal of all three complaints.

3. The *Twombly* complaint was not as deficient as the three complaints in the last Note. Although the majority noted that the *Twombly* complaint's vagueness on names, dates, and places presented a "fair notice" problem, it did not hold that the complaint failed to give fair notice. (Why not?) Rather, the majority held that the complaint lacked substantive merit: the allegations did not plausibly allege that a violation of the law had occurred. Recall that *Swierkiewicz* had held that, when ruling on a motion to dismiss, a court must accept the plaintiff's factual allegations as true. In *Twombly*, Paragraph 51 specifically alleged that the defendants entered into a conspiracy. Why wasn't that allegation enough to assert a plausible right to relief?

4. Once the Court determined that it would not automatically take the allegation of a conspiracy as true, it needed to decide whether the remaining allegations plausibly alleged a right to relief. How much more did the complaint need to say to meet the plausibility test? Did it need just one fact showing the existence of a conspiracy rather than conscious parallelism? Was the interview by Richard Notebaert such a fact? Suppose that the complaint had alleged: "On February 1, 1996, the chief executive officers of each of the defendants participated in a telephone call and agreed to the conspiracy alleged in this complaint." Would this allegation have pushed the complaint across the plausibility line? Would it have made the allegation of conspiracy no longer "conclusory," and therefore required the court to take it as true? Isn't that essentially what the allegations in Paragraph 51 state, albeit without the specificity of the exact date and people involved? Would *Twombly* allow a court to reject the telephone-call allegation because it seems unlikely?

5. Unless the plaintiffs' lawyers had evidence that this alleged phone call occurred, they would have faced ethical problems and possible legal sanctions for making the allegation. *See infra* pp. 90-102. On the other hand, without such an allegation, they stood to lose the case, unable ever to get the evidence that might actually prove a conspiracy. They tried to avoid the horns of this dilemma by making the conclusory conspiracy allegation in Paragraph 51 "upon information and belief." For the purpose of avoiding legal sanctions, Rule 11(b)(3) allows a lawyer to make factual contentions in a complaint that either "have evidentiary support, or, if specifically so identified, will likely have evidentiary support after a reasonable opportunity for further investigation or discovery." The "information and belief" allegation of Paragraph 51 arguably might have been enough to prevent a court from sanctioning the plaintiffs' lawyers, but it was not sufficient to meet the terms of the plausibility test. Should the Court have discussed whether its plausibility test was consistent with Rule 11(b)(3)? *Cf.*

Menard v. CSX Transp., Inc., 698 F.3d 40, 45 (1st Cir. 2012) (" '[S]ome latitude' may be appropriate where a plausible claim may be indicated 'based on what is known,' at least where, as here, 'some of the information needed may be in the control of [the] defendants.' ")

6. In *Twombly*, the Court said that trying to block the entry of new competitors is ordinary competitive behavior, and that the defendants, having operated in a regulated monopolist environment before the 1996 Act, preferred not to compete with each other. The Court's "natural explanation" of the defendants' behavior relied on "common economic experience." Even if independent, rational economic actors would behave this way, should the Court have assumed that the defendants acted for this reason?

7. Sometimes the best way to deal with abstract questions like those in the last few notes is to see how they bear on a real-world problem. Look again at the sample complaint on p. 27. Would the complaint pass muster in federal court after *Twombly*? As you think about this question, pay attention to the tools that the Court (and Justice Stevens in dissent) used. Both opinions relied on language and purpose, as well as the relationship between pleading rules and other pretrial rules — although *Twombly*'s majority seemed less sanguine about the ability of pretrial rules to eliminate meritless claims than *Swierkiewicz* had been five years earlier. Both opinions relied on precedent. Both opinions relied on procedural values (efficiency for the majority, resolving cases on the merits for Justice Stevens).

8. If you are still unsure about *Twombly*'s effect, you are not alone. It seemed as though the case had shaken the foundation of notice pleading in federal court, but no one could be sure. For many judicial opinions that appear to be seismic in nature, it can take time for the import of a case to become clear. Two years later, the Supreme Court re-entered the fray.

ASHCROFT V. IQBAL

556 U.S. 662 (2009)

■ JUSTICE KENNEDY delivered the opinion of the Court.

[Following the September 11, 2001, terrorist attacks, respondent Javaid Iqbal, a Pakistani Muslim, was arrested on criminal charges and detained by federal officials under restrictive conditions. He was designated a person "of high interest" and held in a maximum-security unit known as the Administrative Maximum Special Housing Unit (ADMAX SHU), where he was allegedly mistreated. Iqbal filed a suit in federal court pursuant to *Bivens v. Six Unknown Named Agents of Federal Bureau of Narcotics*, 403 U.S. 388 (1971), which allows people to sue officials of the federal government for violation of constitutional rights. His suit named numerous federal officials as defendants, including John Ashcroft, the former Attorney General, and Robert Mueller, the Director of the Federal Bureau of Investigation (FBI).]

Respondent [Iqbal's] account of his prison ordeal could, if proved, demonstrate unconstitutional misconduct by some governmental actors. But the allegations and pleadings with respect to these actors are not before us here. This case instead turns on a narrower question: Did respondent, as the plaintiff in the District Court, plead factual matter that, if taken as true, states a claim that petitioners [Ashcroft and Mueller] deprived him of his . . . constitutional rights. We hold respondent's pleadings are insufficient.

I

The allegations against petitioners are the only ones relevant here. The complaint contends that petitioners designated respondent a person of high interest on account of his race, religion, or national origin, in contravention of the First and Fifth Amendments to the Constitution. The complaint alleges that "the [FBI], under the direction of Defendant MUELLER, arrested and detained thousands of Arab Muslim men . . . as part of its investigation of the events of September 11." It further alleges that "[t]he policy of holding post-September-11th detainees in highly restrictive conditions of confinement until they were 'cleared' by the FBI was approved by Defendants ASHCROFT and MUELLER in discussions in the weeks after September 11, 2001." Lastly, the complaint posits that petitioners "each knew of, condoned, and willfully and maliciously agreed to subject" respondent to harsh conditions of confinement "as a matter of policy, solely on account of [his] religion, race, and/or national origin and for no legitimate penological interest." The pleading names Ashcroft as the "principal architect" of the policy, and identifies Mueller as "instrumental in [its] adoption, promulgation, and implementation."

Petitioners moved to dismiss the complaint for failure to state sufficient allegations to show their own involvement in . . . unconstitutional conduct. The District Court denied their motion. Accepting all of the allegations in respondent's complaint as true, the court held that "it cannot be said that there [is] no set of facts on which [respondent] would be entitled to relief as against" petitioners (relying on *Conley v. Gibson*, 355 U.S. 41 (1957)) [*supra* p. 28]. . . . [P]etitioners filed an interlocutory appeal in the United States Court of Appeals for the Second Circuit. While that appeal was pending, this Court decided *Bell Atlantic Corp. v. Twombly*, 550 U.S. 544 (2007) [*supra* p. 36], which discussed the standard for evaluating whether a complaint is sufficient to survive a motion to dismiss.

The Court of Appeals considered *Twombly*'s applicability to this case. Acknowledging that *Twombly* retired the *Conley* no-set-of-facts test relied upon by the District Court, the Court of Appeals' opinion discussed at length how to apply this Court's "standard for assessing the adequacy of pleadings." It concluded that *Twombly* called for a "flexible 'plausibility standard,' which obliges a pleader to amplify a claim with some factual allegations in those contexts where such amplification is needed to render the claim *plausible*." The court found that petitioners' appeal did not present one of "those contexts" requiring amplification. As a consequence, it held respondent's pleading adequate to allege petitioners' personal involvement in discriminatory decisions which, if true, violated clearly established constitutional law....

III

... [W]e begin by taking note of the elements a plaintiff must plead to state a claim of unconstitutional discrimination against [government] officials....

The factors necessary to establish a *Bivens* violation will vary with the constitutional provision at issue. Where the claim is invidious discrimination in contravention of the First and Fifth Amendments, our decisions make clear that the plaintiff must plead and prove that the defendant acted with discriminatory purpose. Under extant precedent purposeful discrimination requires more than "intent as volition or intent as awareness of consequences." Personnel Administrator of Mass. v. Feeney, 442 U.S. 256, 279 (1979). It instead involves a decisionmaker's undertaking a course of action "'because of,' not merely 'in spite of,' [the action's] adverse effects upon an identifiable group." *Id.* It follows that, to state a claim based on a violation of a clearly established right, respondent must plead sufficient factual matter to show that petitioners adopted and implemented the detention policies at issue not for a neutral, investigative reason but for the purpose of discriminating on account of race, religion, or national origin....

IV

A

We turn to respondent's complaint. Under Federal Rule of Civil Procedure 8(a)(2), a pleading must contain a "short and plain statement of the claim showing that the pleader is entitled to relief." As the Court held in *Twombly,* the pleading standard Rule 8 announces does not require "detailed factual allegations," but it demands more than an unadorned, the-defendant-unlawfully-harmed-me accusation. A pleading that offers "labels and conclusions" or "a formulaic recitation of the elements of a cause of action will not do." Nor does a complaint suffice if it tenders "naked assertion[s]" devoid of "further factual enhancement."

To survive a motion to dismiss, a complaint must contain sufficient factual matter, accepted as true, to "state a claim to relief that is plausible on its face." A claim has facial plausibility when the plaintiff pleads factual content that allows the court to draw the reasonable inference that the defendant is liable for the misconduct alleged. The plausibility standard is not akin to a "probability requirement," but it asks for more than a sheer possibility that a defendant has acted unlawfully. Where a complaint pleads facts that are "merely consistent with" a defendant's liability, it "stops short of the line between possibility and plausibility of 'entitlement to relief.'"

CHAPTER TWO   PLEADING

Two working principles underlie our decision in *Twombly*. First, the tenet that a court must accept as true all of the allegations contained in a complaint is inapplicable to legal conclusions. Threadbare recitals of the elements of a cause of action, supported by mere conclusory statements, do not suffice. 550 U.S. at 555 ([a]lthough for the purposes of a motion to dismiss we must take all of the factual allegations in the complaint as true, we "are not bound to accept as true a legal conclusion couched as a factual allegation"). Rule 8 marks a notable and generous departure from the hyper-technical, code-pleading regime of a prior era, but it does not unlock the doors of discovery for a plaintiff armed with nothing more than conclusions. Second, only a complaint that states a plausible claim for relief survives a motion to dismiss. Determining whether a complaint states a plausible claim for relief will . . . be a context-specific task that requires the reviewing court to draw on its judicial experience and common sense. But where the well-pleaded facts do not permit the court to infer more than the mere possibility of misconduct, the complaint has alleged — but it has not "show[n]" — "that the pleader is entitled to relief." Fed. R. Civ. P. 8(a)(2).

In keeping with these principles a court considering a motion to dismiss can choose to begin by identifying pleadings that, because they are no more than conclusions, are not entitled to the assumption of truth. While legal conclusions can provide the framework of a complaint, they must be supported by factual allegations. When there are well-pleaded factual allegations, a court should assume their veracity and then determine whether they plausibly give rise to an entitlement to relief.

Our decision in *Twombly* illustrates the two-pronged approach. There, we considered the sufficiency of a complaint alleging that incumbent telecommunications providers had entered an agreement not to compete and to forestall competitive entry, in violation of the Sherman Act, 15 U.S.C. § 1. . . . The complaint also alleged that the defendants' "parallel course of conduct . . . to prevent competition" and inflate prices was indicative of the unlawful agreement alleged.

The Court held the plaintiffs' complaint deficient under Rule 8. In doing so it first noted that the plaintiffs' assertion of an unlawful agreement was a "legal conclusion" and, as such, was not entitled to the assumption of truth. Had the Court simply credited the allegation of a conspiracy, the plaintiffs would have stated a claim for relief and been entitled to proceed perforce. The Court next addressed the "nub" of the plaintiffs' complaint — the well-pleaded, nonconclusory factual allegation of parallel behavior — to determine whether it gave rise to a "plausible suggestion of conspiracy." Acknowledging that parallel conduct was consistent with an unlawful agreement, the Court nevertheless concluded that it did not plausibly suggest an illicit accord because it was not only compatible with, but indeed was more likely explained by, lawful, unchoreographed free-market behavior. Because the well-pleaded fact of parallel conduct, accepted as true, did not plausibly suggest an unlawful agreement, the Court held the plaintiffs' complaint must be dismissed.

B

Under *Twombly*'s construction of Rule 8, we conclude that respondent's complaint has not "nudged [his] claims" of invidious discrimination "across the line from conceivable to plausible."

We begin our analysis by identifying the allegations in the complaint that are not entitled to the assumption of truth. Respondent pleads that petitioners "knew of, condoned, and willfully and maliciously agreed to subject [him]" to harsh conditions of confinement "as a matter of policy, solely on account of [his] religion, race, and/or national origin and for no legitimate penological interest." Complaint ¶ 96. The complaint alleges that Ashcroft was the "principal architect" of this invidious policy, *id.* ¶ 10, and that Mueller was "instrumental" in adopting and executing it, *id.* ¶ 11. These bare assertions, much like the pleading of conspiracy in *Twombly*, amount to nothing more than a "formulaic recitation of the elements" of a constitutional discrimination claim, 550 U.S. at 555, namely, that petitioners adopted a policy "'because of,' not merely 'in spite of,' its adverse effects upon an identifiable group." *Feeney*, 442 U.S. at 279. As such, the allegations are conclusory and not entitled to be assumed true. To be clear, we do not reject these bald allegations on the ground that they are unrealistic or nonsensical. We do not so characterize them any more than the Court in *Twombly* rejected the plaintiffs' express allegation of a "contract, combination or conspiracy to prevent competitive entry" because it thought that claim too chimerical to be maintained. It is the conclusory nature of respondent's allegations, rather than their extravagantly fanciful nature, that disentitles them to the presumption of truth.

We next consider the factual allegations in respondent's complaint to determine if they plausibly suggest an entitlement to relief. The complaint alleges that "the [FBI], under the direction of Defendant MUELLER, arrested and detained thousands of Arab Muslim men . . . as part of its investigation of the events of September 11." Complaint ¶ 47. It further claims that "[t]he policy of holding post-September-11th detainees in highly restrictive conditions of confinement until they were 'cleared' by the FBI was approved by Defendants ASHCROFT and MUELLER in discussions in the weeks after September 11, 2001." *Id.* ¶ 69. Taken as true, these allegations are consistent with petitioners' purposefully designating detainees "of high interest" because of their race, religion, or national origin. But given more likely explanations, they do not plausibly establish this purpose.

The September 11 attacks were perpetrated by 19 Arab Muslim hijackers who counted themselves members in good standing of al Qaeda, an Islamic fundamentalist group. Al Qaeda was headed by another Arab Muslim — Osama bin Laden — and composed in large part of his Arab Muslim disciples. It should come as no surprise that a legitimate policy directing law enforcement to arrest and detain individuals because of their suspected link to the attacks would produce a disparate, incidental impact on Arab Muslims, even though the purpose of the policy was to target neither Arabs nor Muslims. On the facts respondent alleges the arrests

Mueller oversaw were likely lawful and justified by his nondiscriminatory intent to detain aliens who were illegally present in the United States and who had potential connections to those who committed terrorist acts. As between that "obvious alternative explanation" for the arrests, *Twombly*, 550 U.S. at 567, and the purposeful, invidious discrimination respondent asks us to infer, discrimination is not a plausible conclusion.

But even if the complaint's well-pleaded facts give rise to a plausible inference that respondent's arrest was the result of unconstitutional discrimination, that inference alone would not entitle respondent to relief. It is important to recall that respondent's complaint challenges neither the constitutionality of his arrest nor his initial detention . . . . Respondent's constitutional claims against petitioners rest solely on their ostensible "policy of holding post-September-11th detainees" in the ADMAX SHU once they were categorized as "of high interest." Complaint ¶ 69. To prevail on that theory, the complaint must contain facts plausibly showing that petitioners purposefully adopted a policy of classifying post-September-11 detainees as "of high interest" because of their race, religion, or national origin.

This the complaint fails to do. Though respondent alleges that various other defendants, who are not before us, may have labeled him a person of "of high interest" for impermissible reasons, his only factual allegation against petitioners accuses them of adopting a policy approving "restrictive conditions of confinement" for post-September-11 detainees until they were "'cleared' by the FBI." Accepting the truth of that allegation, the complaint does not show, or even intimate, that petitioners purposefully housed detainees in the ADMAX SHU due to their race, religion, or national origin. All it plausibly suggests is that the Nation's top law enforcement officers, in the aftermath of a devastating terrorist attack, sought to keep suspected terrorists in the most secure conditions available until the suspects could be cleared of terrorist activity. Respondent does not argue, nor can he, that such a motive would violate petitioners' constitutional obligations. He would need to allege more by way of factual content to "nudg[e]" his claim of purposeful discrimination "across the line from conceivable to plausible." . . .

. . . [R]espondent's complaint does not contain any factual allegation sufficient to plausibly suggest petitioners' discriminatory state of mind. His pleadings thus do not meet the standard necessary to comply with Rule 8. . . .

C

Respondent offers three arguments that bear on our disposition of his case, but none is persuasive.

1

Respondent first says that our decision in *Twombly* should be limited to pleadings made in the context of an antitrust dispute. This argument is not supported by *Twombly* and is incompatible with the Federal Rules of Civil Procedure. Though *Twombly* determined the sufficiency of a complaint sounding in antitrust, the decision was based on our interpretation and application of Rule 8. That Rule in turn governs the pleading standard "in all civil actions and proceedings in the United States district courts." Fed. R. Civ. P. 1. Our decision in *Twombly* expounded the pleading standard for "all civil actions," and it applies to antitrust and discrimination suits alike.

2

Respondent next implies that our construction of Rule 8 should be tempered where, as here, the Court of Appeals has "instructed the district court to cabin discovery [to avoid interfering with governmental functions]." We have held, however, that the question presented by a motion to dismiss a complaint for insufficient pleadings does not turn on the controls placed upon the discovery process. *Twombly*, 550 U.S. at 559 . . . .

3

Respondent finally maintains that the Federal Rules expressly allow him to allege petitioners' discriminatory intent "generally," which he equates with a conclusory allegation. It follows, respondent says, that his complaint is sufficiently well pleaded because it claims that petitioners discriminated against him "on account of [his] religion, race, and/or national origin and for no legitimate penological interest." Were we required to accept this allegation as true, respondent's complaint would survive petitioners' motion to dismiss. But the Federal Rules do not require courts to credit a complaint's conclusory statements without reference to its factual context.

It is true that Rule 9(b) requires particularity when pleading "fraud or mistake," while allowing "[m]alice, intent, knowledge, and other conditions of a person's mind [to] be alleged generally." But "generally" is a relative term. In the context of Rule 9, it is to be compared to the particularity requirement applicable to fraud or mistake. Rule 9 merely excuses a party from pleading discriminatory intent under an elevated pleading standard. It does not give him license to evade the less rigid — though still operative — strictures of Rule 8. And Rule 8 does not empower respondent to plead the bare elements of his cause of action, affix the label "general allegation," and expect his complaint to survive a motion to dismiss.

V

We hold that respondent's complaint fails to plead sufficient facts to state a claim for purposeful and unlawful discrimination against petitioners. The Court of Appeals should decide in the first instance whether to remand to the District Court so that respondent can seek leave to amend his deficient complaint.

The judgment of the Court of Appeals is reversed, and the case is remanded for further proceedings consistent with this opinion.

CHAPTER TWO   PLEADING

■   JUSTICE SOUTER, with whom JUSTICE STEVENS, JUSTICE GINSBURG, and JUSTICE BREYER join, dissenting. . . .

. . . The complaint . . . alleges, at a bare minimum, that Ashcroft and Mueller knew of and condoned the discriminatory policy their subordinates carried out. Actually, the complaint goes further in alleging that Ashcroft and Mueller affirmatively acted to create the discriminatory detention policy. If these factual allegations are true, Ashcroft and Mueller were, at the very least, aware of the discriminatory policy being implemented and deliberately indifferent to it.

Ashcroft and Mueller argue that these allegations fail to satisfy the "plausibility standard" of *Twombly*. They contend that Iqbal's claims are implausible because such high-ranking officials "tend not to be personally involved in the specific actions of lower-level officers down the bureaucratic chain of command." But this response bespeaks a fundamental misunderstanding of the enquiry that *Twombly* demands. *Twombly* does not require a court at the motion-to-dismiss stage to consider whether the factual allegations are probably true. We made it clear, on the contrary, that a court must take the allegations as true, no matter how skeptical the court may be. *See Twombly*, 550 U.S. at 555; *see also* Neitzke v. Williams, 490 U.S. 319, 327 (1989) ("Rule 12(b)(6) does not countenance . . . dismissals based on a judge's disbelief of a complaint's factual allegations"). The sole exception to this rule lies with allegations that are sufficiently fantastic to defy reality as we know it: claims about little green men, or the plaintiff's recent trip to Pluto, or experiences in time travel. That is not what we have here.

Under *Twombly*, the relevant question is whether, assuming the factual allegations are true, the plaintiff has stated a ground for relief that is plausible. That is, in *Twombly*'s words, a plaintiff must "allege facts" that, taken as true, are "suggestive of illegal conduct." . . . Here, by contrast [to *Twombly*], the allegations in the complaint are neither confined to naked legal conclusions nor consistent with legal conduct. The complaint alleges that FBI officials discriminated against Iqbal solely on account of his race, religion, and national origin, and it alleges the knowledge and deliberate indifference that, by Ashcroft and Mueller's own admission, are sufficient to make them liable for the illegal action. Iqbal's complaint therefore contains "enough facts to state a claim to relief that is plausible on its face."

I do not understand the majority to disagree with this understanding of "plausibility" under *Twombly*. Rather, the majority discards the allegations discussed above with regard to Ashcroft and Mueller as conclusory, and is left considering only two statements in the complaint: that "the [FBI], under the direction of Defendant MUELLER, arrested and detained thousands of Arab Muslim men . . . as part of its investigation of the events of September 11," and that "[t]he policy of holding post-September-11th detainees in highly restrictive conditions of confinement until they were 'cleared' by the FBI was approved by Defendants ASHCROFT and MUELLER in discussions in the weeks after September 11, 2001." I think the majority is right in saying that these allegations suggest only that Ashcroft and Mueller "sought to keep suspected terrorists in the most secure conditions available until the suspects could be cleared of terrorist activity," and that this produced "a disparate, incidental impact on Arab Muslims." And I agree that the two allegations selected by the majority, standing alone, do not state a plausible entitlement to relief for unconstitutional discrimination.

But these allegations do not stand alone as the only significant, nonconclusory statements in the complaint, for the complaint contains many allegations linking Ashcroft and Mueller to the discriminatory practices of their subordinates. *See* Complaint ¶ 10 (Ashcroft was the "principal architect" of the discriminatory policy); *id.* ¶ 11 (Mueller was "instrumental" in adopting and executing the discriminatory policy); *id.* ¶ 96 (Ashcroft and Mueller "knew of, condoned, and willfully and maliciously agreed to subject" Iqbal to harsh conditions "as a matter of policy, solely on account of [his] religion, race, and/or national origin and for no legitimate penological interest").

The majority says that these are "bare assertions" that, "much like the pleading of conspiracy in *Twombly*, amount to nothing more than a 'formulaic recitation of the elements' of a constitutional discrimination claim" and therefore are "not entitled to be assumed true." The fallacy of the majority's position, however, lies in looking at the relevant assertions in isolation. The complaint contains specific allegations that, in the aftermath of the September 11 attacks, the Chief of the FBI's International Terrorism Operations Section and the Assistant Special Agent in Charge for the FBI's New York Field Office implemented a policy that discriminated against Arab Muslim men, including Iqbal, solely on account of their race, religion, or national origin. Viewed in light of these subsidiary allegations, the allegations singled out by the majority as "conclusory" are no such thing. Iqbal's claim is not that Ashcroft and Mueller "knew of, condoned, and willfully and maliciously agreed to subject" him to a discriminatory practice that is left undefined; his allegation is that "they knew of, condoned, and willfully and maliciously agreed to subject" him to a particular, discrete, discriminatory policy detailed in the complaint. Iqbal does not say merely that Ashcroft was the architect of some amorphous discrimination, or that Mueller was instrumental in an ill-defined constitutional violation; he alleges that they helped to create the discriminatory policy he has described. Taking the complaint as a whole, it gives Ashcroft and Mueller "'fair notice of what the . . . claim is and the grounds upon which it rests.'" *Twombly*, 550 U.S. at 555 (quoting *Conley v. Gibson*, 355 U.S. 41, 47 (1957)).

Notes and Questions

1. Because of their close relationship, some lawyers have taken to referring to the *Twombly* and *Iqbal* cases as "*Twiqbal*."

2. Justice Souter, who wrote the opinion for a seven-Justice majority in *Twombly*, wrote the dissent in *Iqbal*. Justice Breyer, who was in the majority in *Twombly*, also moved into dissent in *Iqbal*. None of the dissenters — not even Justices Stevens and Ginsburg, who had dissented in

Twombly — argued for a return to the "no set of facts" test that *Twombly* jettisoned. Rather, all nine Justices now acceded to *Twombly*'s "plausibility" test. So what divided the majority from the dissent? The dissent believed that the complaint's nonconclusory factual allegations established a plausible claim for relief. Justice Souter focused on allegations that the majority failed to address before it decided that an innocent, as opposed to a discriminatory, reason motivated the defendants' design of the detention program. The majority, on the other hand, thought that these allegations were not relevant to the specific claim of discrimination in the case: that the plaintiff was unlawfully detained, as opposed to unlawfully arrested.

Note the majority's statement that conducting a plausibility inquiry is "a context-specific task that requires the reviewing court to draw on its judicial experience and common sense." Can such an inquiry yield clear answers when nine Justices, with an array of judicial experience and no small measure of common sense, split five to four on the plausibility of a complaint's claim for relief? Should a plaintiff's chances of surviving a motion to dismiss depend on the judge who hears the motion?

3. The majority in *Iqbal* states that the plausibility test contains two steps: first, strike all legal conclusions (which include both pure statements of law and "threadbare" or "conclusory" factual allegations) from the complaint; and second, apply the plausibility analysis to the allegations that remain. Both steps can be teased out of *Twombly*, but breaking the analysis into two steps — with the screening out of conclusory allegations at the first step — arguably increases the plaintiff's pleading burden. *See* Robert G. Bone, *Plausibility Pleading Revisited and Revised: A Comment on* Ashcroft v. Iqbal, 85 NOTRE DAME L. REV. 849 (2010).

Lower courts have had a difficult time determining whether allegations are so "conclusory" that they should be disregarded. Consider, for instance, the allegations in *Swierkiewicz* that the plaintiff had been discriminated against on the basis of his age and national origin. Which of his allegations must be accepted as true for purposes of testing the sufficiency of his complaint, and do they plausibly state a claim for relief? *Compare* Samovsky v. Nordstrom, Inc., 619 F. App'x 547, 548 (7th Cir. 2015) ("'I was turned down for a job because of my race' is all a complaint has to say.") (internal quotation marks omitted), *with* Coleman v. Md. Ct. of Appeals, 626 F.3d 187, 190-91 (4th Cir. 2010) (disregarding allegations in a complaint that "conclusorily allege[d] that Coleman was terminated based on his race"), *aff'd on other grounds*, 566 U.S. 30 (2012).

4. Although it found the complaint insufficient, the Court remanded *Iqbal* to the Court of Appeals so that it could consider whether to allow Iqbal to amend the complaint and fix its deficiencies. The court of appeals in turn remanded the case to the district court so that it could decide the issue in the first instance. Iqbal v. Ashcroft, 574 F.3d 820 (2d Cir. 2009) (per curiam). Before the trial court ruled on the motion to amend, the parties settled and the court dismissed the case pursuant to the settlement. Elmaghraby v. United States, No. 04 CV 1809 (JG) (SMG) (E.D.N.Y. Nov. 10, 2009) (order of dismissal). The amount of the settlement was not disclosed, but some

sources have put the figure at $265,000, paid by the United States. The settlement ended the litigation against all government officials involved in Iqbal's detention, not just Ashcroft and Mueller.

5. *Twombly* and *Iqbal* have generated enormous debate. Some Supreme Court commentators have described *Iqbal* as one of the most important (or most dangerous, depending on the perspective) decisions in the past decade. We could fill pages with the titles of excellent articles and blog posts about *Twombly* and *Iqbal*, and more pages with citations to thoughtful opinions that have addressed the cases — and still not come close to covering them all. Here is one lens through which to understand the impact of the cases. According to the WestlawNext database, in the ten years after the Court issued *Iqbal* (thus, May 17, 2009 through May 17, 2019), federal courts issued more than 169,000 reported opinions citing *both* *Twombly* and *Iqbal*. (Many more cases cite one or the other but not both.) To compare, from February 1803 through May 17, 2019, only 2,877 reported federal cases had cited *Marbury v. Madison*, 5 U.S. (1 Cranch) 137 (1803), often said to be the most famous Supreme Court decision. *Twombly* and *Iqbal* easily rank at the top of the Court's most-cited decisions. Raw citation numbers do not determine the importance of a case, but the extent to which federal judges and litigators have engaged with *Twombly* and *Iqbal* is clear.

6. The debate about *Twombly* and *Iqbal* hinges, to some extent, on their effect: whether they have resulted in the dismissal of more cases than during the *Conley* regime or have discouraged more litigants from filing claims in federal court (sometimes referred to as the "selection effect"). Some commentators who looked at reported decisions noted an increase in successful motions to dismiss in some areas. But examining only reported cases can be deceiving. Hence, the Federal Judicial Center studied reported and unreported cases in twenty-three federal districts from 2006 until 2010. The rate of filing motions to dismiss for failure to state a claim increased over this period. But the rate at which motions were granted without leave to amend showed a statistically significant increase in only one area: cases challenging mortgage loans. Likely because of the collapse in housing markets, the number of these cases tripled from 2006 to 2010. *See* JOE S. CECIL ET AL., MOTIONS TO DISMISS FOR FAILURE TO STATE A CLAIM AFTER *IQBAL*: REPORT TO THE JUDICIAL CONFERENCE ADVISORY COMMITTEE (2011). A follow-up study confirmed these findings, but also noted that the "findings do not rule out the possibility that the pleading standards established in *Twombly* and *Iqbal* may have a greater effect in narrower categories of cases in which respondents must obtain the facts from movants in order to state a claim." JOE S. CECIL ET AL., UPDATE ON RESOLUTION OF RULE 12(b)(6) MOTIONS GRANTED WITH LEAVE TO AMEND 1 (2011).

In a similar vein, the Administrative Office of United States Courts studied trends in motions to dismiss through the end of 2010. Based on our own extrapolation of its quarterly data, we estimate that, in the four months before *Twombly*, motions to dismiss were filed in 33.8% of cases. In the nineteen months after *Iqbal*, motions to dismiss were filed in 36.5% of cases. Overall, the number of successful motions to dismiss rose from slightly over

12% of cases filed before *Twombly* to 13.8% of cases filed after *Iqbal*. The success rate on motions to dismiss remained fairly steady, at about 37%; the increase in the number of successful motions to dismiss relates principally to the fact that more motions were filed. By the last study period (October-December 2010), successful motions to dismiss fell off to pre-*Twombly* levels. One limitation to note: the data include all motions to dismiss, not just motions to dismiss for failure to state a claim of the *Twombly-Iqbal* variety.

Using two different models and two data sets (one with 250,000 pre-*Twombly* cases and another with 12,000 post-*Twombly* cases), Professor Hubbard found "no (significant) change in the willingness of courts to dismiss cases, even after accounting for selection effects" as a result of *Twombly*. *See* William H.J. Hubbard, *Testing for Change in Procedural Standards, with Application to* Bell Atlantic v. Twombly, 42 J. LEGAL STUD. 35, 57 (2013). With certain caveats given the limits of the data, his analysis "strongly rejects the view that *Twombly* constitutes a major change in how district courts have applied the law of pleading." *Id.* at 59. His later work confirmed that *Twombly* and *Iqbal* had no major effect on dismissal rates, the number of motions to dismiss, or settlement and filing patterns in cases in which lawyers represent plaintiffs, but it did find some evidence of potentially major effects on *unrepresented* plaintiffs. William H.J. Hubbard, *The Effects of* Twombly *and* Iqbal, 14 J. EMPIRICAL LEGAL STUD. 474 (2017). *See also* Roger Michalski & Abby K. Wood, Twombly *and* Iqbal *at the State Level,* 14 J. EMP. LEG. STUD. 424 (2017) (comparing Nebraska, which raised pleading standards, to several other states that did not; finding no effects on plaintiffs' behavior, defense strategies, or judicial responses).

On the other hand, Professor Reinert examined 4,200 cases filed in fifteen federal district courts between 2006 and 2010, and found that dismissals of employment-discrimination and civil-rights cases rose significantly after *Iqbal*. *See* Alexander A. Reinert, *Measuring the Impact of Plausibility Pleading*, 101 VA. L. REV. 2117 (2015). Finally, using economic modeling, now-Professor Gelbach argued that focusing on the rates at which motions to dismiss are granted fails to capture the full effect of *Twombly* and *Iqbal* on the willingness of plaintiffs to file suit. His model estimates that *Twombly* and *Iqbal* have had, at a minimum, a "negative effect" — defined as the failure to obtain discovery after a motion to dismiss in the post-*Twombly-Iqbal* period when the case would have obtained discovery before *Twombly* — in fifteen to twenty-one percent of cases, depending on the type of claims the plaintiffs would have filed. *See* Jonah B. Gelbach, Note, *Locking the Doors to Discovery? Assessing the Effects of* Twombly *and* Iqbal *on Access to Discovery*, 121 YALE L.J. 2270 (2012).

7. In *Johnson v. City of Shelby*, 574 U.S. 10 (2014) (per curiam*), the Court rejected an aggressive reading of *Twombly* and *Iqbal*. In *Johnson* police officers alleged that they were fired, in violation of their Fourteenth Amendment due-process rights, because they uncovered evidence of criminal behavior by an alderman. The officers' complaint did not specifically

---

* In a per curiam opinion, none of the members of a court is listed as the author; instead, the opinion emerges "from the court." — ED.

mention that they were seeking relief under 42 U.S.C. § 1983 (a federal statute authorizing civil-rights actions against state and local officials and local governments), even though that statute was the obvious legal basis for their claim. Due to this failing, the district court dismissed their complaint and the court of appeals affirmed. The Supreme Court summarily and unanimously reversed, holding that "no heightened pleading rule requires plaintiffs seeking damages for violations of constitutional rights to invoke § 1983 expressly in order to state a claim." 574 U.S. at 11. The Court observed that "[o]ur decisions in *Twombly* and *Iqbal* are not in point, for they concern the factual allegations a complaint must contain to survive a motion to dismiss. . . . Petitioners' complaint was not deficient in that regard. Petitioners stated simply, concisely, and directly events that, they alleged, entitled them to damages from the city." *Id.* at 12.

8. Although this casebook does not focus on state-court procedure, the debate about the standards under which to judge a complaint's sufficiency is also playing out in state courts. For instance, in *Iannacchino v. Ford Motor Co.*, 888 N.E.2d 879, 889-90 (Mass. 2008), the Supreme Judicial Court of Massachusetts adopted *Twombly*'s "plausibility" test and overturned a prior decision that had adopted *Conley*'s "no set of facts" formulation. Neighboring Vermont rejected *Twombly*, and affirmed its reliance on *Conley*'s "no set of facts" standard. Colby v. Umbrella, Inc., 955 A.2d 1082, 1086 n.1 (Vt. 2008) (noting that "we . . . are in no way bound by federal jurisprudence in interpreting our state pleading rules"). For another neighborly disagreement, compare Walsh v. U.S. Bank, N.A., 851 N.W.2d 598, 601-06 (Minn. 2014) (rejecting the *Twombly-Iqbal* pleading standard), *with* Data Key Partners v. Permira Advisers LLC, 849 N.W.2d 693 (Wis. 2014) (adopting the *Twombly-Iqbal* pleading standard). *See* Zachary D. Clopton, *Procedural Retrenchment and the States*, 106 CALIF L. REV. 411, 425-26 (2018) (noting that six states had adopted the *Twombly-Iqbal* plausibility standard and nineteen states had rejected or criticized it).

9. Until now, our focus has been on pleadings that arguably say too little. Lawyers in an adversarial system do not like to tip their hands unless doing so serves their interests. That fact suggests that pleadings will often come close to the Rule 8(a)(2) minimum. Most complaints, however, plead far more than the minimum. The reasons are usually tactical: "Plaintiffs' lawyers, knowing that some judges read a complaint as soon as it is filed in order to get a sense of the suit, hope by pleading facts to 'educate' (that is to say, influence) the judge with regard to the nature and probable merits of the case, and also hope to set the stage for an advantageous settlement by showing the defendant what a powerful case they intend to prove." Am. Nurses' Ass'n v. Illinois, 783 F.2d 716, 723-24 (7th Cir. 1986).

But can a plaintiff get in trouble for saying too much? In *Celli v. Cole*, 699 F. App'x 88, 89 (2d Cir. 2017), the plaintiff filed a 95-page third amended complaint "that was ill structured and largely indecipherable." After the district court told the plaintiff that the complaint failed to comply with Rule 8 and suggested how to cure the problem, the plaintiff filed a 197-page complaint "that was more prolix and confusing that the last one." The court of appeals affirmed the district judge's dismissal of the complaint. It probably didn't help that the plaintiff "attacked the judge with profane insults." *Id.*; *see also* United States *ex rel.* Garst v. Lockheed–Martin Corp., 328 F.3d 374, 378 (7th Cir. 2003) (dismissing a rambling 155-page, 400-paragraph complaint that did not "alert either the district judge or the defendants to the principal contested matters"; noting that "judges and adverse parties need not try to fish a gold coin from a bucket of mud").

10. Charles Clark, the scholar and judge who was the principal force behind the notice-pleading provisions in the Federal Rules, observed near the end of his career:

> . . . I fear that every age must learn its lesson that special pleading cannot be made to do the service of trial and that live issues between active litigants are not to be disposed of or evaded on the paper pleadings . . . . [E]xperience is wholly clear that such quickie justice always breaks down . . . .
>
> [The motion to dismiss a complaint] is normal trial practice to be expected as long as our adversary system lasts. But the objects of defense tactics and of judicial expedition of business are not the same . . . . And so to my colleagues as they reach for an order of dismissal rather than for a pre-trial conference, I feel I must say "Don't!" You will get there more expeditiously if instead of pausing to beautify the pleadings you turn to pre-trial . . . .

Charles E. Clark, *Special Pleading in the "Big Case,"* 21 F.R.D. 45, 46-47, 53 (1957).

3. Filing and Serving the Complaint

The plaintiff *files* the complaint by giving it to the clerk of the court, along with a filing fee (presently $350 for federal court — *see* 28 U.S.C. § 1914). Next, the plaintiff must *serve* (or provide) the defendant with certain papers about the lawsuit. Why do we require service? Return to first principles. We employ an adversarial system, which affords parties an opportunity to make arguments and introduce evidence — in other words, the *opportunity to be heard*. But a defendant's opportunity to be heard is meaningless unless the defendant receives *notice* of the case.

Service also accomplishes another function. If someone hands you an invitation to a party, you are not thereby compelled to attend. So what compels a defendant who receives a complaint to do anything? The answer is that, when the plaintiff files the complaint, the court issues a *summons* — an order telling the defendant to respond to the complaint (or face a default judgment). The plaintiff must serve on the defendant both a copy of the complaint and the summons. *See* Fed. R. Civ. P. 4(c)(1). Thus, service both provides notice to the defendant and acts as the means by which the court asserts its power, or jurisdiction, over a defendant.

Rules of the court or statutes describe in detail exactly how a defendant must be served and under what circumstances a court may exercise jurisdiction over a defendant. A second source of law also affects both of these issues: the United States Constitution, whose guarantee of due process has been interpreted to require that a defendant *both* receive adequate notice *and* be subject to the court's jurisdiction. Therefore, for service to be effective, it must meet four distinct criteria: (1) Notice must be provided in the manner prescribed in a court rule or statute; (2) Notice must be provided in a way that comports with due process; (3) jurisdiction over the defendant must be asserted in a manner authorized by statute or court rule; and (4) jurisdiction over the defendant must satisfy the requirement of due process. Because the jurisdictional issues of (3) and (4) raise distinct concerns, we defer their consideration until Chapter Nine. For now, we focus on issues (1) and (2): the steps that a plaintiff must take to give adequate notice.

Federal Rule of Civil Procedure 4 addresses how a plaintiff accomplishes *service of process* in federal court. Read Rules 4(a)-(j), –(l), and –(m). (For now, you can ignore Rule 4(k), to which we return later (*see infra* pp. 494-95), and Rule 4(n); both address issue (3).) Also read the Rule 4 Notice of a Lawsuit and Request to Waive Service of Summons and the Rule 4 Waiver of the Service of Summons, both of which follow Rule 4. Rules 4(a) and (b) describe the content of the summons and how the court issues it. Rules 4(c)(2)-(3) describe the persons who can serve the summons and complaint. Rules 4(e)-(j) describe how to serve different types of defendants (adults; minors and incompetent persons; corporations; and foreign, federal, and state governments). Rule 4(d) provides an alternative to service. Finally, note Rule 4(m): if the plaintiff does not accomplish service within ninety days after filing the complaint, the district court must dismiss the case unless "the plaintiff shows good cause for the failure."

90 days or dismissed

RIO PROPERTIES, INC. V. RIO INTERNATIONAL INTERLINK

284 F.3d 1007 (9th Cir. 2002)

Before GOODWIN, SNEED, and TROTT, Circuit Judges.

TROTT, Circuit Judge.

Las Vegas hotel and casino operator Rio Properties, Inc. ("RIO") sued Rio International Interlink ("RII"), a foreign Internet business entity, asserting various statutory and common law trademark infringement claims. The district court entered default judgment against RII.... RII now appeals the sufficiency of the service of process, effected via email and regular mail pursuant to Federal Rule of Civil Procedure 4(f)(3) ....

PH

BACKGROUND

RIO owns the RIO All Suite Casino Resort.... In addition to its elegant hotel, RIO's gambling empire consists of the Rio Race & Sports Book, which allows customers to wager on professional sports. To protect its exclusive rights in the "RIO" name, RIO registered numerous trademarks with the United States Patent and Trademark Office. When RIO sought to expand its presence onto the Internet, it registered the domain name, *www.playrio.com*. At that address, RIO operates a website that informs prospective customers about its hotel and allows those enticed by Lady Luck to make reservations.

RII is a Costa Rican entity that participates in an Internet sports gambling operation . . . . RII enables its customers to wager on sporting events online or via a 1-800 telephone number. Far from a penny ante operation, RII grosses an estimated $3 million annually.

RIO became aware of RII's existence by virtue of RII's advertisement in the *Football Betting Guide '98 Preview*. RIO later discovered, in the Nevada edition of the *Daily Racing Form*, another RII advertisement which invited customers to visit RII's website, *www.riosports.com*. RII also ran radio spots in Las Vegas as part of its comprehensive marketing strategy.

Upon learning of RII, RIO fired off an epistle demanding that RII cease and desist from operating the *www.riosports.com* website. Although RII did not formally respond, it promptly disabled the objectionable website. Apparently not ready to cash in its chips, RII soon activated the URL *http://www.betrio.com* to host an identical sports gambling operation. Perturbed, RIO filed the present action alleging various trademark infringement claims and seeking to enjoin RII from the continued use of the name "RIO."

To initiate suit, RIO attempted to locate RII in the United States for service of process. RIO discovered that RII claimed an address in Miami, Florida when it registered the allegedly infringing domain names. As it turned out, however, that address housed only RII's international courier, IEC, which was not authorized to accept service on RII's behalf. Nevertheless, IEC agreed to forward the summons and complaint to RII's Costa Rican courier.

After sending a copy of the summons and complaint through IEC, RIO received a telephone call from Los Angeles attorney John Carpenter ("Carpenter") inquiring about the lawsuit. Apparently, RII received the summons and complaint from IEC and subsequently consulted Carpenter about how to respond. Carpenter indicated that RII provided him with a partially illegible copy of the complaint and asked RIO to send him a complete copy. RIO agreed to resend the complaint and, in addition, asked Carpenter to accept service for RII; Carpenter politely declined. Carpenter did, however, request that RIO notify him upon successful completion of service of process on RII.

Thus thwarted in its attempt to serve RII in the United States, RIO investigated the possibility of serving RII in Costa Rica. Toward this end, RIO searched international directory databases looking for RII's address in Costa Rica. These efforts proved fruitless however; the investigator learned only that RII preferred communication through its email address, *email@betrio.com*, and received snail mail, including payment for its services, at the IEC address in Florida.

Unable to serve RII by conventional means, RIO filed an emergency motion for alternate service of process. RII opted not to respond to RIO's motion. The district court granted RIO's motion, and pursuant to Federal Rules of Civil Procedure 4(h)(2) and 4(f)(3), ordered service of process on RII through the mail to Carpenter and IEC and via RII's email address, *email@betrio.com*.

Court order in hand, RIO served RII by these court-sanctioned methods. RII filed a motion to dismiss for insufficient service of process.... The parties fully briefed the issues, and the district court denied RII's motion without a hearing. RII then filed its answer, denying RIO's allegations and asserting twenty-two affirmative defenses....

[As a sanction for abuses during the discovery process, the district court entered default judgment against RII.] RII now appeals the sufficiency of the court-ordered service of process....

DISCUSSION

I. ALTERNATIVE SERVICE OF PROCESS

A. *Applicability of Rule 4(f)(3)*

We review for an abuse of discretion the district court's decision regarding the sufficiency of service of process. Federal Rule of Civil Procedure 4(h)(2) authorizes service of process on a foreign business entity in the manner prescribed by Rule 4(f) for individuals. The subsection of Rule 4(f) relevant to our decision, Rule 4(f)(3), permits service in a place not within any judicial district of the United States "by ... means not prohibited by international agreement as may be directed by the court."*

As [is] obvious from its plain language, service under Rule 4(f)(3) must be (1) directed by the court; and (2) not prohibited by international agreement. No other limitations are evident from the text....

RII argues that Rule 4(f) should be read to create a hierarchy of preferred methods of service of process. RII's interpretation would require that a party attempt service of process by those methods enumerated in Rule 4(f)(2), including by diplomatic channels and letters rogatory, before petitioning the court for alternative relief under Rule 4(f)(3). We find no support for RII's position. No such requirement is found in the Rule's text, implied by its structure, or even hinted at in the advisory committee notes.

By all indications, court-directed service under Rule 4(f)(3) is as favored as service available under Rule 4(f)(1) or Rule 4(f)(2).[4] Indeed, Rule 4(f)(3)

---

* After amendment in 2007, Rule 4(f)(3) now reads: "by other means not prohibited by international agreement, as the court orders." — ED.

4. A federal court would be prohibited from issuing a Rule 4(f)(3) order in contravention of an international agreement, including the Hague Convention referenced in Rule 4(f)(1). The parties agree, however, that the Hague Convention does not apply in this case because Costa Rica is not a signatory.

is one of three separately numbered subsections in Rule 4(f), and [Rule 4(f)(3) is separated from the prior subsections] by the simple conjunction "or." Rule 4(f)(3) is not subsumed within or in any way dominated by Rule 4(f)'s other subsections; it stands independently, on equal footing. Moreover, no language in Rules 4(f)(1) or 4(f)(2) indicates their primacy, and certainly Rule 4(f)(3) includes no qualifiers or limitations which indicate its availability only after attempting service of process by other means.

The advisory committee notes ("advisory notes") bolster our analysis. Beyond stating that service ordered under Rule 4(f)(3) must comport with constitutional notions of due process and must not be prohibited by international agreement, the advisory notes indicate the availability of alternate service of process under Rule 4(f)(3) without first attempting service by other means. Specifically, the advisory notes suggest that in cases of "urgency," Rule 4(f)(3) may allow the district court to order a "special method of service," even if other methods of service remain incomplete or unattempted.

Thus, examining the language and structure of Rule 4(f) and the accompanying advisory committee notes, we are left with the inevitable conclusion that service of process under Rule 4(f)(3) is neither a "last resort" nor "extraordinary relief." It is merely one means among several which enables service of process on an international defendant.

. . . [W]e hold that Rule 4(f)(3) is an equal means of effecting service of process under the Federal Rules of Civil Procedure, and we commit to the sound discretion of the district court the task of determining when the particularities and necessities of a given case require alternate service of process under Rule 4(f)(3).

Applying this proper construction of Rule 4(f)(3) . . . , trial courts have authorized a wide variety of alternative methods of service including publication, ordinary mail, mail to the defendant's last known address, delivery to the defendant's attorney, telex, and most recently, email. . . .

Contrary to RII's assertions, RIO need not have attempted every permissible means of service of process before petitioning the court for alternative relief. Instead, RIO needed only to demonstrate that the facts and circumstances of the present case necessitated the district court's intervention. Thus, when RIO presented the district court with its inability to serve an elusive international defendant, striving to evade service of process, the district court properly exercised its discretionary powers to craft alternate means of service. We expressly agree with the district court's handling of this case and its use of Rule 4(f)(3) to ensure the smooth functioning of our courts of law.

B. Reasonableness of the Court Ordered Methods of Service

Even if facially permitted by Rule 4(f)(3), a method of service of process must also comport with constitutional notions of due process. To meet this requirement, the method of service crafted by the district court must be "reasonably calculated, under all the circumstances, to apprise interested

parties of the pendency of the action and afford them an opportunity to present their objections." Mullane v. Cent. Hanover Bank & Trust Co., 339 U.S. 306, 314 (1950) (Jackson, J.) [*infra* p. 486].

Without hesitation, we conclude that each alternative method of service of process ordered by the district court was constitutionally acceptable. In our view, each method of service was reasonably calculated, under these circumstances, to apprise RII of the pendency of the action and afford it an opportunity to respond.

In particular, service through IEC was appropriate because RII listed IEC's address as its own when registering the allegedly infringing domain name. The record also reflects that RII directed its customers to remit payment to IEC's address. Moreover, when RIO sent a copy of the summons and complaint to RII through IEC, RII received it. All told, this evidence indicates that RII relied heavily upon IEC to operate its business in the United States and that IEC could effectively pass information to RII in Costa Rica.

Service upon Carpenter was also appropriate because he had been specifically consulted by RII regarding this lawsuit. He knew of RII's legal positions, and it seems clear that he was in contact with RII in Costa Rica. Accordingly, service to Carpenter was also reasonably calculated in these circumstances to apprise RII of the pendency of the present action.

Finally, we turn to the district court's order authorizing service of process on RII by email at *email@betrio.com*. We acknowledge that we tread upon untrodden ground. The parties cite no authority condoning service of process over the Internet or via email, and our own investigation has unearthed no decisions by the United States Courts of Appeals dealing with service of process by email and only one case anywhere in the federal courts. Despite this dearth of authority, however, we do not labor long in reaching our decision. Considering the facts presented by this case, we conclude not only that service of process by email was proper — that is, reasonably calculated to apprise RII of the pendency of the action and afford it an opportunity to respond — but in this case, it was the method of service most likely to reach RII.

To be sure, the Constitution does not require any particular means of service of process, only that the method selected be reasonably calculated to provide notice and an opportunity to respond. *See Mullane,* 339 U.S. at 314. In proper circumstances, this broad constitutional principle unshackles the federal courts from anachronistic methods of service . . . .

Although communication via email and over the Internet is comparatively new, such communication has been zealously embraced within the business community. RII particularly has embraced the modern e-business model and profited immensely from it. In fact, RII structured its business such that it could be contacted *only* via its email address. RII listed no easily discoverable street address in the United States or in Costa Rica. Rather, on its website and print media, RII designated its email address as its preferred contact information.

... If any method of communication is reasonably calculated to provide RII with notice, surely it is email.... In addition, email was the only court-ordered method of service aimed directly and instantly at RII, as opposed to methods of service effected through intermediaries like IEC and Carpenter. Indeed, when faced with an international e-business scofflaw, playing hide-and-seek with the federal court, email may be the only means of effecting service of process. Certainly in this case, it was a means reasonably calculated to apprise RII of the pendency of the lawsuit, and the Constitution requires nothing more.

... RII contends that email is never an approved method of service under Rule 4. We disagree. . Although RII is correct that a plaintiff may not generally resort to email service on his own initiative, in this case ... email service was properly ordered by the district court using its discretion under Rule 4(f)(3).

Despite our endorsement of service of process by email in this case, we are cognizant of its limitations. In most instances, there is no way to confirm receipt of an email message.... [W]e leave it to the discretion of the district court to balance the limitations of email service against its benefits in any particular case. In our case, the district court performed the balancing test admirably, crafting methods of service reasonably calculated under the circumstances to apprise RII of the pendency of the action.[8] ...

[In Part II of the opinion, the court of appeals held that the district court had personal jurisdiction over RII. In Part III, it held that the district court did not abuse its discretion in entering a default judgment as a sanction for RII's failure to obey its discovery orders.]

For the reasons delineated above, we affirm the district court's decision in all respects.

Notes and Questions

1. In *Rio*, the defendant lost the case by default because it failed to abide by its obligations in discovery. We will examine that issue in Chapter Three. Having lost the case on this ground, RII then appealed because it believed that it had not been properly served. Its theory was that, without proper service, it was not a proper defendant in the case; therefore, the district court had no power to enter judgment against it.

2. As a result of Rio's first efforts to serve RII, RII had actual notice of the lawsuit. *Rio* shows that actual notice is insufficient; service also must comply with Rule 4. If actual notice is the point of Rule 4, what difference does it make whether the technical requirements of Rule 4 have been met? We could replace the complex provisions in Rules 4(d)-(j) with this simple service rule: "Unless circumstances make actual notice too difficult, a person

---

[8]. Notably, RII does not argue that it did not receive notice of the present lawsuit or that such notice was incomplete, delayed or in any way prejudicial to its ability to respond effectively and in a timely manner.

serving a complaint must provide a defendant with actual notice of the summons and complaint. When actual notice is too difficult, the court may authorize the use of one or more alternative methods of service reasonably calculated to result in actual notice." Would this rule be adequate? Could you draft an even better one?

3. For individuals, handing the summons and complaint directly to the defendant is the Cadillac of service; it guarantees actual notice. But such *personal service* is neither costless nor always successful. The tricks process servers use to effect personal service on dodgy defendants, and the countermeasures dodgy defendants take to avoid service, make wonderful reading. *See, e.g.,* Advance Magazine Publishers, Inc. v. Tinsley, 2019 WL 1285089, at *1 (E.D. Mich. Mar. 20, 2019) (defendant successfully evaded service of process ten times, at one point calling plaintiff's counsel and "pretend[ing] to be someone else named 'Katrina' to avoid service of process and obstruct further service attempts"; the court deemed service effective after counsel noticed that the phone number "Katrina" used was the same number the defendant used in a YouTube video).

Alternatives to personal service, such as *substituted service* on "someone of suitable age and discretion who resides" at the defendant's "dwelling or usual place of abode," *see* Fed. R. Civ. P. 4(e)(2)(B), are also possible. Personal service need not be attempted first. With alternative methods of service, however, the risk exists that the defendant will not receive notice. Should the Rules require an attempt at personal service before authorizing an alternative method?

Serving corporations, governments, and other creatures of the law raises other issues that have led to particular methods by which they are properly served, as Rules 4(f), –(h), –(i), and –(j) reflect. For individuals whose age or mental disability may make them incapable of understanding a legal notice, Rule 4(g) provides still other means of service.

4. Rule 4(f) applies to individuals and (by cross-reference in Rule 4(h)(2)) corporations served outside the United States. *See also* Fed. R. Civ. P. 4(g) (limiting service options for minors and incompetent persons served outside the United States), –(h)(2) (limiting service options for corporations served outside the United States). Other service rules, such as Rule 4(e) (governing service on individuals within the United States) and Rule 4(h)(1) (governing service on corporations generally), do not have a catch-all clause comparable to Rule 4(f)(3), so that e-mail service would be possible. Should a court have a power akin to Rule 4(f)(3) to order that a dodgy domestic defendant be served by alternate means?

5. Although it is unlikely to be helpful against the dodgy defendant, Rule 4(d) avoids some of the difficulties of service by allowing the defendant to waive formal service of process and accept service through ordinary first-class mail. As inducements to agree to this waiver, a defendant gets a carrot (*compare* Rule 4(d)(3) *and* Rule 12(a)(1)(A)(ii) *with* Rule 12(a)(1)(A)(i)), and is threatened with a stick (*see* Rule 4(d)(2)). *See* Marcello v. Maine, 238 F.R.D. 113 (D. Me. 2006) (imposing costs for failing to waive service even though the lawsuit was frivolous).

6. What other provisions of Rule 4 ameliorate the difficulties inherent in serving domestic defendants? (Hint: some states permit methods of service other than those mentioned in the Federal Rules. *See* Rule 4(e)(1); Tiggle–Lockhart v. Specialized Loan Servicing, LLC, 2015 WL 12734791, at *2 (C.D. Cal. Mar. 3, 2015) ("California state law provides for service by [first-class] mail, and the Federal Rules permit Plaintiff to avail herself of that state law procedure.")

7. On the case's particular facts, *Rio* upholds service effected in part by e-mail. This possibly handy mode of service may not always be valid. In *Compass Bank v. Katz*, 287 F.R.D. 392 (S.D. Tex. 2012), the district court refused to authorize service by e-mail on the defendants, who had borrowed money from the plaintiff to purchase a vacation home in Mexico. The plaintiff claimed that, although it was aware that the defendants resided in Tijuana, Mexico, the defendants' addresses were unknown. The court noted that the defendant had failed to attempt physical service at two locations where the defendants might have been located and that Mexico had objected to service by postal channels when it signed the Hague Convention.

This latter holding raises an issue that, because Costa Rica had not signed the Hague Convention, *Rio* was able to sidestep. Article 10(a) of the Convention permits service "of judicial documents[ ] by postal channels" as long as "the State of destination does not object." There was some dispute about whether this language applied to service of process — in other words, whether the Hague Convention allowed service of process by mail, or whether service of process could be accomplished only through the judicial or governmental machinery of the country of destination. In *Water Splash, Inc. v. Menon*, 581 U.S. —, 137 S. Ct. 1504, 1513 (2017), the Supreme Court held that the Hague Convention authorized service of process by mail "if two conditions are met: first, the receiving state has not objected to service by mail; and second, service by mail is authorized under otherwise-applicable law." Thus, even if Rule 4(f)(3) permits it, service by e-mail is ineffective in a country that is a signatory to the Hague Convention unless e-mail is a "postal channel" and the country has not objected to e-mail service.

More broadly, even if a court can validly order service by e-mail, neither courts nor plaintiffs should always regard such service as preferable despite its simplicity. Traditional methods will often be easy, reliable, and likely to withstand challenge in American courts. Counsel must also consider the problem of collecting the judgment abroad. When a lawyer uses a foreign court to collect an American judgment from a foreign defendant, the law of the foreign country determines whether the judgment is enforceable. Something as innovative as e-mail service — although yielding a judgment that American courts will say is valid — might make the foreign court reluctant to enforce the judgment against one of its citizens. A good lawyer avoids appealing shortcuts that create problems down the line. *Cf.* Sulzer Mixpac AG v. Medenstar Indus. Co., 312 F.R.D. 329 (S.D.N.Y. 2015) (refusing under Rule 4(f)(3) to authorize postal-mail service on a Chinese defendant due to China's view that the Hague Convention prohibits such service, but authorizing service by e-mail).

8. *Rio* was the first federal appellate decision to countenance service by e-mail, and its interpretation of Rule 4 and the Due Process clause remains influential. But who reads e-mail any more? A more certain means to reach many people is social media. Should service through Facebook, Instagram, or Twitter be allowed when customary means of service are ineffective? *See* United States v. Mohammad, 249 F. Supp. 3d 450 (D.D.C. 2017) (entering summary judgment against defendant who failed to appear after the court authorized service via e-mail and Facebook message); St. Francis Assisi v. Kuwait Fin. House, 2016 WL 5725002 (N.D. Cal. Sept. 30, 2016) (permitting service through Twitter, on which nonprofit organization that allegedly financed ISIS terrorists maintained an active presence); Alyssa L. Eisenberg, Comment, *Keep Your Facebook Friends Close and Your Process Server Closer: The Expansion of Social Media Service of Process to Cases Involving Domestic Defendants*, 51 SAN DIEGO L. REV. 779 (2014) (arguing for expanded use of service through social media).

9. *Mullane v. Central Hanover Bank & Trust Co.*, 339 U.S. 306 (1950) (*infra* p. 486), is the classic case describing the constitutional requirement for adequate notice. In general, the service methods described in Rule 4 meet this requirement. *Mullane* held that publication in a newspaper was insufficient notice to trust beneficiaries whose names and addresses were known to the trustee, but sufficient for unknown beneficiaries. In *Rio*, would publication in a Costa Rican newspaper have satisfied due process?

10. Rule 5(b)(2)(E) permits electronic service of pleadings and motions other than the summons and complaint on parties who consent in writing to such service.

SECTION C: RESPONDING TO THE COMPLAINT

Until now, you have worn the hat of the plaintiff's lawyer. Now switch hats, and assume the role of the defendant's lawyer. After your client has either been served or waived service, what do you do? Read Rule 12. Begin with the question of timing: how long do you have to respond? *See* Fed. R. Civ. P. 12(a)(1)(A). Now consider your possible responses. Taken together, Rules 12(a)-(b), –(e), and –(f) indicate two permissible options: (1) file an *answer*, or (2) file a *motion* in lieu of an answer. An answer is a pleading, *see* Fed. R. Civ. P. 7(a); a motion is not, *see* Fed. R. Civ. P. 7(b). We begin with motions, and then study answers.

1. Rule 12 Motions

Rule 12 Motions and Rule 12(b) Defenses. Rule 12 describes three motions that a defendant can file in lieu of an answer: a motion to dismiss under Rule 12(b), a motion seeking a more definite statement of the complaint under Rule 12(e), and a motion to strike "redundant, immaterial, impertinent, or scandalous matter" under Rule 12(f). Motions under Rules

12(e) and –(f) are rare — and even more rarely successful. Motions under Rule 12(b) are a different matter. As we described above (*see supra* pp. 55-56, Note 6), defendants often move to dismiss a case — or at least one or more claims in the case — due to a perceived defect in the complaint.

In total, Rule 12(b) lists seven defects that can be the basis for a motion to dismiss. Litigators know these seven defenses by heart. Look at the list, and begin to commit the defenses to memory.

We have already examined three of the Rule 12(b) defenses. In studying the sufficiency of the complaint (*supra* pp. 28-58), we explored the Rule 12(b)(6)'s motion to dismiss "for failure to state a claim upon which relief can be granted." In studying the summons and service of process (*supra* pp. 58-67), we saw the grounds for Rule 12(b)(4) and 12(b)(5) motions. We will examine the other four defenses in later chapters, when we encounter doctrines of subject-matter jurisdiction (the Rule 12(b)(1) motion), personal jurisdiction (the Rule 12(b)(2) motion), venue (the Rule 12(b)(3) motion), and the joinder of a required party under Rule 19 (the Rule 12(b)(7) motion).

With the exception of Rule 12(b)(6), none of the Rule 12(b) defenses goes to the merits of the case. They seek dismissal for preliminary matters (such as subject-matter jurisdiction, personal jurisdiction, or venue) or procedural flaws (such as defects in the summons, in the service of process, or in the joinder of parties). These defenses nonetheless raise important concerns — concerns that our system regards as so significant that dismissal of the case without reaching the merits is proper.

In many cases, a judge has discretion to grant a Rule 12(b) motion *with prejudice* or *without prejudice*. Dismissal with prejudice means that the plaintiff usually cannot bring the claim again. A dismissal without prejudice allows a plaintiff to file an amended complaint correcting the deficiency. If the plaintiff does not or cannot correct the problem, a judge may then dismiss the defective claim with prejudice.

Raising Rule 12(b) Defenses. A defendant can raise these defenses in either of two ways: by making a motion or by pleading the defenses in the answer. *See* Fed. R. Civ. P. 12(b). A defendant can assert as many of the defenses as is appropriate.

Waiving Rule 12(b) Defenses. When pleading these defenses or raising them by motion, the defendant must negotiate the minefields of Rules 12(g) and –(h). The defenses listed in Rules 12(b)(2)-(5) are lost if they are not properly preserved in either a motion or an answer. The same defenses are also lost if the defendant makes a motion under Rule 12 but fails to raise any of the other defenses then available. In contrast, a failure to preserve or raise the defenses under Rules 12(b)(6) and –(b)(7) may limit a defendant's opportunity to raise them later, but does not bar them. And in further contrast, a defendant can never lose a Rule 12(b)(1) defense.

Try parsing Rules 12(g) and –(h) with this hypothetical: After being served with a complaint, Dee files a Rule 12(b)(3) motion alleging improper venue. The court denies the motion. Dee would now like to raise additional defenses by motion. Which of the following defenses may Dee still assert?

- Lack of subject-matter jurisdiction;
- Lack of personal jurisdiction; and
- Failure to state a claim.

Even if a defendant preserves them in the answer, some 12(b) defenses can be forfeited through the passage of time. *See,, e.g.*, Boulger v. Woods, 917 F.3d 471, 477-78 (6th Cir. 2019) (forfeiture of Rule 12(b)(2) and 12(b)(5) defenses by filing a Rule 12(c) motion for judgment on the pleadings); Hamilton v. Atlas Turner, Inc., 197 F.3d 58, 60-63 (2d Cir. 1999) (forfeiture of a Rule 12(b)(2) defense by participating in litigation for four years).

Resolving Factual Disputes. Can a defendant who asserts a Rule 12 defense contest the truthfulness of the factual allegations in the complaint? To an extent, the answer depends on the defense. We have already seen that, for Rule 12(b)(6) motions for failure to state a claim, courts must accept as true all well-pleaded factual assertions, although they need not accept unbelievable assertions or legal conclusions. In addition, courts draw all reasonable inferences from properly alleged facts in favor of the plaintiff. *See, e.g.*, Hu v. City of New York, 927 F.3d 81, 88 (2d Cir. 2019). If the court considers matters not referenced in the complaint (documents, affidavits, and the like), Rule 12(d) requires the motion to be "treated as one for summary judgment under Rule 56." The standard for granting summary judgment is different from the Rule 12(b)(6) standard; one difference is that a Rule 56 motion cannot usually be granted until the opposing party has had adequate time to conduct discovery. *See infra* p. 237; p. 242, Note 8.

Rule 12 motions besides those under Rule 12(b)(6) concern matters other than the merits of the dispute, so a court will typically rule on these defenses before trial. To do so accurately, a court sometimes must consider evidence beyond the four corners of the complaint. The parties often present such evidence in the form of affidavits. In *Herbert v. National Academy of Sciences*, 974 F.2d 192, 197-98 (D.C. Cir. 1992), the court observed:

> ... [T]he District Court may in appropriate cases dispose of a motion to dismiss for lack of subject matter jurisdiction under Fed. R. Civ. P. 12(b)(1) on the complaint standing alone. But where necessary, the court may consider the complaint supplemented by undisputed facts evidenced in the record, or the complaint supplemented by undisputed facts plus the court's resolution of disputed facts.

Until a defendant raises a factual dispute that requires a court to "look beyond the jurisdictional allegations of the complaint," however, the court "must accept as true all well-pleaded factual allegations and draw all reasonable inferences in favor of the plaintiff." Alicea-Hernandez v. Catholic Bishop of Chi., 320 F.3d 698, 701 (7th Cir. 2003).

Motion for Judgment on the Pleadings. Rule 12(c) permits either party to move for judgment on the pleadings. This motion can be filed "[a]fter the pleadings close — but early enough not to delay trial." For a plaintiff, a Rule 12(c) motion is the equivalent of a Rule 12(b)(6) motion. A plaintiff may believe that the defendant's answer, coupled with the complaint, proves the plaintiff's entitlement to judgment (for example, if the answer admits the facts and pleads only a legally insufficient defense). The Rule 12(c) motion allows the court to enter judgment in favor of the plaintiff when appropriate.

For defendants, a Rule 12(c) motion often acts as a delayed Rule 12(b) motion. Recall that a defendant can file an answer asserting its Rule 12(b) defenses rather than filing a 12(b) motion. After the defendant files an answer, the time for filing a Rule 12(b) motion has passed. *See* Fed. R. Civ. P. 12(b) (stating that a motion asserting a Rule 12(b) defense "must be made before pleading"). The Rule 12(c) motion serves as the vehicle for raising certain Rule 12(b) defenses that were not raised in an earlier Rule 12(b) motion. *See* Fed. R. Civ. P. 12(h)(2)(B) (mentioning the use of the Rule 12(c) motion to raise the defenses available under Rules 12(b)(6) and –(7)).

Whether the motion is filed by a plaintiff or a defendant, "the standard for dismissal under Rule 12(c) is the same as under Rule 12(b)(6)." Magee v. Reed, 912 F.3d 820, 822 (5th Cir. 2019).

2. The Answer

In many cases the defendant has no Rule 12 motions to raise; in other cases, the defendant, for tactical reasons or due to the press of time, chooses not to file a Rule 12 motion; in still other cases, the court denies a Rule 12 motion. In each of these situations, the defendant must now answer the complaint. What must the answer contain? Read Rules 8(b)-(e), especially –(b) and –(c). Rule 8(b)(1) imposes two requirements: first, an answer must "admit or deny the allegations" in the complaint (Rule 8(b)(1)(B)), and second, it must state "in short and plain terms its defenses" (Rule 8(b)(1)(A)). Rules 8(b)(2)-(5) describe in detail the first requirement, while Rule 8(c) (as supplemented by Rule12(b)) lays out in detail the second requirement. The following two cases examine the content of these two requirements.

MILTON V. GENERAL DYNAMICS ORDNANCE AND TACTICAL SYSTEMS, INC.

2011 WL 4708637 (S.D. Ill. Oct. 4, 2011)

■ WILKERSON, United States Magistrate Judge.

Now pending before the Court is Plaintiff Bobby E. Milton's Motion to Admit Paragraphs 6–52 of Count III of the Amended Complaint. . . .

Plaintiff Bobby E. Milton filed an amended complaint in this action on September 2, 2011. The complaint alleged three counts: I) for retaliation in violation of Title VII against Defendant Ira E. Clark; II) for racial discrimination and retaliation in violation of 42 U.S.C. § 1981 against Defendant Ira E. Clark; and III) for racial discrimination and retaliation in violation of Title VII against Defendant General Dynamics Ordnance and Tactical Systems, Inc. ("General Dynamics"). The third line of the heading for Count I of the complaint reads (in bold text): (DEFENDANT IRA E. CLARK). The allegations, listed in numbered paragraphs 7-52, pertain to the Plaintiff's employment relationship with Defendant Ira E. Clark. Some of the allegations, however, refer to and name General Dynamics. Count III of the complaint incorporates by reference paragraphs 1-52 of Count I as paragraphs 1-52 of Count III.

Defendant General Dynamics answered the allegations of paragraphs 6-52 of Count I by stating as its answer for each: "General Dynamics states that it is not required to answer the allegations contained in paragraph[s] [6-52] because they are directed to Defendant Ira E. Clark." For its answer to paragraphs 1-52 of Count III, General Dynamics stated: "General Dynamics realleges and incorporates its answers to Paragraphs 1-52 of Count I as though fully set forth herein." At the conclusion of its answer, General Dynamics stated: "Each and every allegation of the Complaint not specifically admitted or denied is hereby denied."

Plaintiff now asks the Court to deem admitted paragraphs 6-52 of Count III, because General Dynamics did not admit or deny the allegations as required under Fed. R. Civ. P. 8(b)(6). Defendant General Dynamics argues in response that Plaintiff's motion is meritless because General Dynamics was not required to answer allegations directed to its co-defendant, and even if it were so required, it did sufficiently answer those allegations with the statement "[e]ach and every allegation of the Complaint not specifically admitted or denied is hereby denied." . . .

The only permissible responses to a complaint under Fed. R. Civ. P. 8(b) are admission, denial, or a statement of the absence of both knowledge and information sufficient to form a belief. The rules do not approve or permit other types of responses. Under Rule 8(b)(6), an allegation is admitted "if a responsive pleading is required and the allegation is not denied." Under Rule 8(b)(1)(B), however, a party is required to respond only to allegations asserted against it by an opposing party.

Count I of the Plaintiff's amended complaint, by its own heading, is directed against Defendant Ira E. Clark. At the same time, allegations described under that count refer to or involve Defendant General Dynamics. In the Court's view Plaintiff should have been clearer in specifying allegations against Defendant General Dynamics, but Defendant General Dynamics should have admitted, denied, or stated insufficient knowledge for each allegation in paragraphs 6-52 that Plaintiff incorporated from Count I into Count III.

The Court is not interested in placing blame on or punishing the parties for unintentional, non-prejudicial errors. But it is in the interest of both the Court and the parties that the litigation commences with a complaint that clearly sets out the factual and legal bases for relief. The Court is mindful that its ultimate goal is to allow the case to proceed on its merits. . . .

Accordingly, Plaintiff's Motion to Admit Paragraphs 6-52 of Count III of the Amended Complaint is denied. Defendant General Dynamics is ordered to amend its answer by October 18, 2011. The amended answer shall admit, deny, or state insufficient knowledge of each allegation described in paragraphs 6-52 of Count III of the amended complaint.

Notes and Questions

1. United States magistrate judges perform important work within the federal judiciary. Unlike Supreme Court Justices, judges on the courts of appeals, or district judges — who are often called "Article III judges" because Article III of the United States Constitution grants them life tenure and salary protection — magistrate judges are neither nominated by the President nor confirmed by the Senate. Instead, they are appointed by the judges of the district in which they serve. 28 U.S.C. § 631(a). They do not enjoy the life tenure of Article III judges; generally their term is eight years. *Id.* § 631(e). In part because they lack the constitutional stature of Article III judges, Congress has imposed certain limits on what rulings magistrate judges can render. *Id.* § 636(b)(1). In civil and criminal cases, they handle pretrial motions that do not dispose of a case, and can also make recommendations to district judges about case-dispositive rulings. If the parties consent, a magistrate judge can also rule on case-dispositive motions and preside at civil trials, both jury and nonjury. *Id.* § 636(b)(1), –(c).

2. In *King Vision Pay Per View, Ltd. v. J.C. Dimitri's Restaurant, Inc.*, 180 F.R.D. 332 (N.D. Ill. 1998), a defendant responded to thirty of a complaint's thirty-five paragraphs with the statement: "Neither admit nor deny the allegations of said Paragraph —, but demand strict proof thereof." After noting that this response was not one of the three responses permitted by Rule 8(b), the district judge ordered that all thirty paragraphs be deemed admitted. The judge was frustrated by the frequency with which he encountered this pleading response in cases in his courtroom, and after years of cajoling lawyers to bring their answers into compliance with Rule 8(b), he announced: "This is it. . . . Future Rule 8(b) violators are hereby placed on constructive notice that their similarly defective pleadings will encounter like treatment." *Id.* at 333.

In contrast, other judges have treated demands for "strict proof" or comparable phrases as denials, on the theory that these phrases adequately placed the plaintiff on notice about the defendant's disagreement with the complaint's allegations. *See, e.g.*, United States v. Gwinn, 2006 WL 3377636 (S.D. W. Va. Nov. 20, 2006).

Milton agrees with *King Vision* about the unacceptability of a response other than an admission, a denial, or a lack of knowledge; but in allowing the defendant to amend the answer, *Milton* tempers *King Vision*'s harsh result. In *United States v. Vehicle 2007 Mack 600 Dump Truck*, 680 F. Supp. 2d 816 (E.D. Mich. 2010), a defendant responded to numerous allegations by stating "Neither admit nor deny the allegations in these paragraphs and leave the Plaintiff to its proofs." The court ordered the allegations admitted, but only after concluding that the defendant's bad faith in using evasive and dilatory tactics deprived him of the opportunity to amend the answer.

King Vision and *Dump Truck* follow the letter of the law, *Gwinn* and *Milton* the spirit of notice pleading. An answer deemed deficient in one courtroom might be deemed sufficient in another; a defendant might lose a case on the pleadings in the first court and prevail on the merits in the second. Is this result desirable?

3. One way to think about this problem is to ask whether clients should bear the consequences of the errors of their counsel. In a later case, the judge who decided *King Vision* changed tack and prepared a list of common pleading errors (with the one in *King Vision* among those topping the list). He then gave the list to defense counsel who filed answers making any of these errors, along with an instruction to correct the mistakes. He also ordered the lawyers not to charge their clients for making the corrections and to tell the clients in writing what they were doing. *See* State Farm Mut. Auto. Ins. Co. v. Riley, 199 F.R.D. 276 (N.D. Ill. 2001).

4. Rule 8(b)(1)(B)'s requirement imposes a minimal obligation that can often be satisfied with one word ("Admit" or "Deny"). Even Rule 8(b)(5)'s alternative — an allegation of insufficient knowledge — takes no more than a sentence. So the answer should be fairly short, right? Usually it is, but sometimes defense attorneys use the answer to put their own "spin" on the case, much as plaintiffs' attorneys sometimes use complaints (*see supra* pp. 57-58, Note 9). For example, in its antitrust case against Microsoft, the United States alleged the following in Paragraph 11 of its complaint:

> 11. Because of its resources and programming technology, Microsoft was well positioned to develop and market a browser in competition with Netscape. Indeed, continued competition on the merits between Netscape's Navigator and Microsoft's Internet Explorer would have resulted in greater innovation and the development of better products at lower prices. Moreover, in the absence of Microsoft's anticompetitive product [the Windows operating system bundled with the Internet Explorer browser], the offsetting advantages of Microsoft's size and dominant position in desktop software and Netscape's position as the browser innovator and the leading browser supplier, and the benefit to consumers of product differentiation, could have been expected to sustain competition on the merits between these companies, and perhaps others that have entered and might enter the browser market.

Here is Microsoft's answer to this paragraph:

> 11. Denies the allegations of Paragraph 11 of the Complaint, except (a) admits on information and belief that Netscape has been and still is "the leading browser supplier," as defined by share of usage; (b) admits that Microsoft was well positioned to develop and market software providing web browsing functionality in competition with Netscape; and (c) avers that (i) there are sound reasons for Microsoft's decision to integrate Internet-related technologies into its Windows operating systems rather than to develop a free-standing product (akin to Netscape Navigator) that provides web browsing functionality to end users; (ii) the competition between Microsoft and Netscape continues to be vigorous and has resulted in the development of innovative products at lower prices, the ultimate objective of the federal antitrust laws; and (iii) other companies have entered and will continue to enter the business of supplying software providing web browsing functionality.

What are both parties trying to accomplish with these pleadings?

5. Rule 8(b) has some traps for the unwary pleader. First, suppose that a defendant erroneously admits the truth of an allegation in the plaintiff's complaint. Can the defendant litigate the case on the basis of the true state of affairs? The usual answer is "no"; an admission binds the defendant from then on — unless the defendant can amend the answer (a subject we cover in the following section). *See, e.g.*, Nat'l Ass'n of Life Underwriters, Inc. v. Comm'r, 30 F.3d 1526 (D.C. Cir. 1994).

Second, suppose that the answer denies an allegation with such generality that the plaintiff lacks notice of the nature of the defendant's disagreement with the allegation. In *Sinclair Refining Co. v. Howell*, 222 F.2d 637 (5th Cir. 1955), a plaintiff alleged that the defendant was not subject to the state's workers' compensation act. This was an important issue: if the defendant was covered by the act, the plaintiff's case was doomed. The answer did not deny the allegation, but rather stated: "Defendant denies that the plaintiff is entitled to recover any damages in this cause." The court held that this statement was not an effective denial; hence, the allegation was admitted. Some courts have suggested a familiar principle for judging the sufficiency of denials: an adequate answer must provide notice of those matters that are not in dispute and those that remain to be determined. *See* Abrazinski v. DuBois, 876 F. Supp. 313 (D. Mass. 1995). This principle, of course, is the flip side of the notice-pleading principle that applies to complaints.

6. A third trap for the unwary exists in Rule 8(b)(1)(A), which requires the defendant to "state" the "defenses" to each claim "in short and plain terms." Some defenses are not a denial of the plaintiff's allegations, but an independent reason why the defendant contends it is not liable. Many such reasons can exist. Perhaps the statute of limitations has run, or the defendant has already paid the plaintiff. Such grounds, known as *affirmative defenses*, have a common theme: they are a reason to deny recovery to the plaintiff even if everything in the complaint is true. Some common affirmative defenses are listed in Rule 8(c). If the affirmative defense is sound, the no-liability conclusion follows. Suppose a defendant pleads an affirmative defense without specifying its legal or factual basis. Does the "plausibility" hurdle that *Twombly* and *Iqbal* impose on the claims in a complaint apply to defenses in the answer? Is sauce for the goose sauce for the gander? Consider the following case.

GEOMC CO. V. CALMARE THERAPEUTICS INC.

918 F.3d 92 (2d Cir. 2019)

Before NEWMAN, JACOBS, and POOLER, Circuit Judges.

NEWMAN, Circuit Judge. . . .

Defendant-Appellant Calmare Therapeutics, Inc. ("Calmare"), a Delaware corporation, appeals from the Sept. 29, 2017, judgment of the

District Court for the District of Connecticut (Victor A. Bolden, District Judge) in favor of Plaintiff-Appellee GEOMC Co., Ltd. ("GEOMC"), a South Korean corporation, entered after a bench trial. The litigation concerns a dispute arising from sales of medical devices for managing pain.

BACKGROUND

. . . GEOMC filed an amended complaint in October 2014, asserting five causes of action. Calmare filed an answer in December 2014, asserting nine affirmative defenses, but no counterclaims. In September 2015, almost a year later, Calmare sought leave to amend its answer to the amended complaint to add several additional affirmative defenses and several counterclaims. . . .

On June 15, 2016, GEOMC filed a second amended complaint, adding, as a sixth cause of action, a claim for breach of contract. On June 30, 2016, Calmare filed an answer to the second amended complaint, adding six affirmative defenses and six counterclaims. On July 25, 2016, GEOMC moved to strike all of Calmare's six new affirmative defenses and five of its six new counterclaims. On Oct. 19, 2016, the District Court granted in part and denied in part GEOMC's motion to strike. The Court denied the motion with respect to four affirmative defenses, and, pertinent to the pending appeal, struck Calmare's sixth and seventh affirmative defenses and five counterclaims. Calmare seeks review of that ruling.

DISCUSSION

. . .

The starting point for analysis is Rule 12(f), which provides that a court may strike "from a pleading" any "insufficient defense or any redundant, immaterial, impertinent, or scandalous matter." After the adoption of the Federal Rules of Civil Procedure in 1938, the first time we considered the propriety of striking an affirmative defense appears to be *United States v. Oswego Falls Corp.*, 113 F.2d 322 (2d Cir. 1940). We there ruled that a defense, apparently timely filed, was properly stricken because no facts were pleaded to support the defense. Shortly thereafter, we ruled, apparently for the first time, that an affirmative defense was properly stricken because it was legally insufficient.

Not until many years later did we endeavor to expand, even briefly, on the pleading standard necessary for an affirmative defense to survive a motion to strike. In *William Z. Salcer, Panfeld, Edelman v. Envicon Equities Corp.*, 744 F.2d 935 (2d Cir. 1984), *vacated on other grounds*, 478 U.S. 1015 (1986), we stated that a motion to strike an affirmative defense, apparently timely filed, will not be granted unless "it appears to a certainty that plaintiffs would succeed despite any state of the facts which could be proved in support of the defense." *Id.* at 939 (internal quotation marks omitted). This formulation expansively phrased the pleading standard with the wording then used by the Supreme Court in *Conley v. Gibson*, 355 U.S. 41

(1957) [*supra* p. 28], for testing the sufficiency of a complaint: "[A] complaint should not be dismissed for failure to state a claim unless it appears beyond doubt that the plaintiff can prove no set of facts in support of his claim which would entitle him to relief." That wording, the Court ruled in *Bell Atlantic Corp. v. Twombly*, 550 U.S. 544 (2007) [*supra* p. 36], "is best forgotten," and was replaced with a "plausibility standard"; *see* Ashcroft v. Iqbal, 556 U.S. 662, 678 (2009) [*supra* p. 45] (same).

Fifteen years after *Salcer*, a District Court in this Circuit purported to extract from that opinion a three-part test for striking a timely filed affirmative defense:

> In order to prevail on a motion to strike [an affirmative defense], a plaintiff must show that: (1) there is no question of fact which might allow the defense to succeed; (2) there is no question of law which might allow the defense to succeed; and (3) the plaintiff would be prejudiced by inclusion of the defense.

SEC v. McCaskey, 56 F. Supp. 2d 323, 326 (S.D.N.Y. 1999). This formulation divided *Salcer*'s reference to facts into two factors, one concerned with facts, and the other concerned with law. The *McCaskey* formulation also added a third factor, prejudice to the plaintiff, a factor not mentioned in *Salcer*. . . .

Before adjudicating the propriety of the District Court's striking two of Calmare's affirmative defenses, we take this occasion to clarify the factors relevant to striking an affirmative defense. To avoid having district courts continue to repeat the three-factor formulation as worded in *McCaskey*, we consider each of those factors in turn.

Whether the first of the *McCaskey* factors should be reworded in light of *Twombly*, *i.e.*, whether *Twombly* applies to the pleading of affirmative defenses, is an issue that has divided the many district courts[8] and commentators that have considered it. . . .

We conclude that the plausibility standard of *Twombly* applies to determining the sufficiency of all pleadings, including the pleading of an affirmative defense, but with recognition that, as the Supreme Court explained in *Iqbal*, applying the plausibility standard to any pleading is a "context-specific" task. 556 U.S. at 679. The Court described the context of *Iqbal* as one "where we are impelled to give real content to the concept of qualified immunity for high-level officials who must be neither deterred nor detracted from the vigorous performance of their duties." 556 U.S. at 686.

The key aspect of the context relevant to the standard for pleading an affirmative defense is that an affirmative defense, rather than a complaint, is at issue. This is relevant to the degree of rigor appropriate for testing the pleading of an affirmative defense. The pleader of a complaint has the entire

---

8. *Compare, e.g.*, Perez v. Gordon & Wong Law Grp., 2012 WL 1029425, at *6-8 (N.D. Cal. Mar. 26, 2012) (*Twombly* applicable to affirmative defenses), [and] HCRI TRS Acquirer, LLC v. Iwer, 708 F. Supp. 2d 687, 691 (N.D. Ohio 2010) (same), *with e.g.*, Leviton Mfg. Co. v. Pass & Seymour, Inc., 264 F. Supp. 3d 421, 427 (E.D.N.Y. 2017) (*Twombly* not applicable to pleading affirmative defenses), [and] Lane v. Page, 272 F.R.D. 581, 588-97 (D.N.M. 2011) (same).

time of the relevant statute of limitations to gather facts necessary to satisfy the plausibility standard. By contrast, the pleader of an affirmative defense has only the 21-day interval to respond to an original complaint, *see* Fed. R. Civ. P. 12(a)(1)(A)(i), the 21-day interval to amend, without court permission, an answer that requires a responsive pleading, *see* Fed. R. Civ. P. 15(a)(1)(B), or the 14-day interval to file a required response to an amended pleading that makes a new claim, *see* Fed. R. Civ. P. 15(a)(3). That aspect of the context matters. In addition, the relevant context will be shaped by the nature of the affirmative defense. For example, the facts needed to plead a statute-of-limitations defense will usually be readily available; the facts needed to plead an ultra vires defense, for example, may not be readily known to the defendant, a circumstance warranting a relaxed application of the plausibility standard.

The second factor identified in *McCaskey* needs no revision. There is no dispute that an affirmative defense is improper and should be stricken if it is a legally insufficient basis for precluding a plaintiff from prevailing on its claims.

Whether the third of the *McCaskey* factors, prejudice, should be a basis for dismissing or opposing the addition of an otherwise valid affirmative defense will normally depend on when the defense is presented. A factually sufficient and legally valid defense should always be allowed if timely filed even if it will prejudice the plaintiff by expanding the scope of the litigation. A defendant with such a defense is entitled to a full opportunity to assert it and have it adjudicated before a plaintiff may impose liability. On the other hand, prejudice may be considered and, in some cases, may be determinative, where a defense is presented beyond the normal time limits of the Rules, especially at a late stage in the litigation, and challenged by a motion to dismiss or opposed by opposition to a Rule 15(a) motion.

With these considerations in mind, we consider the District Court's ruling in this case. Granting in part a motion by GEOMC, the District Court struck Calmare's sixth and seventh affirmative defenses asserted in its answer to GEOMC's second amended complaint. The sixth defense alleged that GEOMC's damages were caused by its own negligence; the seventh defense alleged that GEOMC failed to join a necessary party. . . .

Striking these two affirmative defenses was within the District Court's discretion. The sixth defense lacked any indication of what conduct by GEOMC or others might have been a defense to the breach of contract claim added by the second amended complaint. The seventh defense lacked any indication of which party needed to be joined or why. Calmare needed to support these defenses with some factual allegations to make them plausible. Moreover, both affirmative defenses were presented at a late stage of the litigation. Although the defenses were presented soon after GEOMC filed its second amended complaint, they were not aimed at the one new cause of action in that complaint but sought to challenge claims made nearly a year earlier in the first amended complaint. Expanding the litigation at that stage would have been prejudicial to GEOMC.

[The court of appeals then held that the district court was within its discretion to strike Calmare's counterclaims.]

CONCLUSION

The ruling striking Calmare's two affirmative defenses and rejecting its five counterclaims is affirmed. The case is remanded for further proceedings consistent with a summary order filed this day.

Notes and Questions

1. As *GEOMC* states, the level of detail that an affirmative defense must contain has divided courts in the wake of *Twombly* and *Iqbal*. The number of district-court opinions to address the issue is vast. Courts on both sides of the issue have claimed that their view represents the majority position. According to one article, a majority (62%) of 925 district-court cases reaching the question in the decade after *Twombly* held that *Twombly* and *Iqbal* do *not* apply to affirmative defenses. Brian Soucek & Remington B. Lamons, *Heightened Pleading Standards for Defendants: A Case Study of Court-Counting Precedent*, 70 ALA. L. REV 875 (2018).

GEOMC is the first decision from a court of appeals squarely on point. *But see* Kohler v. Flava Enters., 779 F.3d 1016, 1019 (9th Cir. 2015) (noting, without citing *Twombly* or *Iqbal*, that "the 'fair notice' required by the pleading standards only requires describing the [affirmative] defense 'in general terms.'"). Whether *GEOMC* will swing the tide toward applying *Twombly* and *Iqbal* to affirmative defenses remains to be seen.

2. Courts that have argued against applying *Twombly* and *Iqbal* to affirmative defenses have used a combination of textual and policy arguments. As a matter of text, Rule 8(a)(2) requires a plaintiff to make a "showing" of entitlement to relief, while Rule 8(b)(1)(A) requires a defendant only to "state" its defenses. In addition, Rule 8(b)(3) allows a defendant to respond with a general denial; and, "[a]lthough Rule 8(b)(3) does not speak to affirmative defenses directly, it . . . would be anomalous if Rule 8(b) allowed parties to generally deny the allegations in the complaint yet required them to plead facially plausible affirmative defenses." Lockheed Martin Corp. v. United States, 973 F. Supp. 2d 591, 594 (D. Md. 2013). As a matter of policy, these courts have emphasized the point that *GEOMC* also made: the difficulty that the defendant has in investigating the facts in the limited period allowed before filing an answer.

Courts arguing that *Twombly* and *Iqbal* apply to affirmative defenses have tended to emphasize a couple of policy justifications. One is the "sauce for the goose is sauce for the gander" argument: if plaintiffs must be more specific in their pleadings, so must defendants. The other argument is litigation efficiency; boilerplate affirmative defenses clutter the docket and force defendants to undertake wasteful discovery.

In a sense, *GEOMC* splits the difference. Formally, it sides with the courts applying *Twombly and Iqbal* and ignores the arguably pertinent textual differences within Rule 8. But *GEOMC*'s emphasis on context suggests that, as a practical matter, it has sympathy with the concerns of those courts that decline to apply *Twombly* and *Iqbal*: not a lot of specificity will be expected for affirmative defenses that may require the defendant to engage in significant investigation and discovery. Note that plaintiffs do not get a similar break with respect to claims that they cannot plausibly state without the benefit of discovery.

3. We have been talking about the pleading requirements for defenses, but exactly what are these defenses? Rule 8(b)(1) says that a defending party "must" state "its defenses." Rule 8(c)(1) says that a defending party "must affirmatively state any avoidance or affirmative defense." Is there a difference between a "defense" and an "affirmative defense"? Between an "avoidance" and a "defense"? The Federal Rules never define these terms. Rule 8(c) lists eighteen avoidances or defenses, but the list is not exhaustive. *See* Commil USA, LLC v. Cisco Sys., Inc., 575 U.S. 632 (2015) (recognizing patent invalidity, which is not listed in Rule 8(c), as an "affirmative defense"); Jones v. Bock, 549 U.S. 199, 212 (2007) (noting that the list in Rule 8(c) is "nonexhaustive"; holding that failure to exhaust administrative remedies is an affirmative defense). The seven grounds listed in Rule 12(b) are also defenses.

In two cases, the Supreme Court intimated a rough-and-ready test for an affirmative defense: a legal doctrine that allows a defendant to avoid liability, for which the defendant bears the burden of proof at trial. *See* Meacham v. Knolls Atomic Power Lab., 554 U.S. 84 (2008); Taylor v. Sturgell, 553 U.S. 880 (2008). In *Winforge, Inc. v. Coachmen Industries, Inc.*, 691 F.3d 856, 872 (7th Cir. 2012), the court "identified two approaches for determining whether a defense not specifically enumerated in Rule 8(c) is an affirmative defense: . . . (a) if the defendant bears the burden of proof under state law or (b) if [the defense does] not controvert the plaintiff's proof" (internal quotation marks omitted).

4. Rule 8(c) is silent on the consequences of failing to plead an affirmative defense. The standard view is that the defendant loses any defense that is not properly pleaded. *See* Reed v. Columbia St. Mary's Hosp., 915 F.3d 473, 478 (7th Cir. 2019) ("A defendant's failure to plead an affirmative defense may result in a waiver of the defense if the defendant has relinquished it knowingly and intelligently, or forfeiture if the defendant merely failed to preserve the defense by pleading it."). There is also a generally accepted corollary to the forfeiture rule: forfeiture is not proper if the plaintiff suffers no prejudice from the court's allowing the defense. *See*, *e.g.*, Global Tech. & Trading, Inc. v. Tech Mahindra Ltd., 789 F.3d 730, 731 (7th Cir. 2015) ("[A] district court may (though it need not) permit an untimely affirmative defense, provided the plaintiff does not suffer prejudice from the delay."). Some courts do not accept the prejudice corollary, and disallow any defense that is not properly pleaded. *See* Harris v. Sec'y, U.S. Dep't of Veterans Affairs, 126 F.3d 339, 345 (D.C. Cir. 1997). *Harris*

suggested that the defendant's only way around forfeiture was to seek leave to amend the answer. As you will learn in the following section, leave to amend is usually allowed in the absence of prejudice, so functionally the two approaches come to the same place. *See Global Technology*, 789 F.3d at 732.

5. In many cases, the only pleadings filed are the complaint and the answer. At that point, the pleading stage closes, and the parties move on to the remainder of the pretrial process. In some cases, however, other pleadings are filed. First, the plaintiff may amend the complaint, or the defendant the answer — a process we examine in the next section. Second, a defendant may assert a claim against a third party, a co-defendant, or even the plaintiff. We consider the assertion of these claims in Chapter Eight. After the defendant asserts this claim (sometimes in the answer, sometimes in a separate pleading), the party against whom the claim is asserted must answer it. *See* Fed. R. Civ. P. 7(a)(1)-(6).

Third, a court may also order a complaining party to file a *reply* to an answer. Fed. R. Civ. P. 7(a)(7). Federal courts rarely order replies, although the device has received some favorable attention as a means to address the problem of a complaint that passes muster under Rule 8 but is still vague. *See* Crawford-El v. Britton, 523 U.S. 574, 597-98 (1998) (recommending the use of a reply in certain civil-rights cases). Can you reconcile this use of the reply with the notice-pleading requirement of Rule 8?

SECTION D: AMENDING THE PLEADINGS

A process to amend the pleadings addresses two concerns. First, as we have seen, pleading still has potential pitfalls for the unwary. These pitfalls are less serious if we allow a pleader to amend a deficient pleading. Second, the pretrial process sometimes uncovers facts that suggest additional claims or defenses. Again, an amendment process permits the court to resolve the case on its merits, not on the basis of an initial incomplete pleading.

You would expect the Federal Rules, with their focus on merits-based resolutions, to permit parties to amend their pleadings without imposing substantial obstacles. Read Rule 15(a), which is the basic rule governing amendments, and then consider its application in the following case.

WILLIAMS V. CITIGROUP INC.

659 F.3d 208 (2d Cir. 2011)

Before LEVAL, KATZMANN, [and] HALL, Circuit Judges.

■ PER CURIAM.

Plaintiff-Appellant Linda Grant Williams appeals from a November 3, 2009 judgment of the United States District Court for the Southern District of New York dismissing her complaint and from the district court's February 8, 2010 order denying her postjudgment motion for reargument and reconsideration of this dismissal and for leave to replead.... We hold that the district court, in denying the postjudgment motion, applied a standard that overemphasized considerations of finality at the expense of the liberal amendment policy embodied in the Federal Rules of Civil Procedure. Accordingly, we vacate the order denying the postjudgment motion....[1] We remand for further proceedings consistent with this opinion.

BACKGROUND

[The plaintiff was an attorney who specialized in structured finance.] She has developed a patent-pending structure for Airline Special Facility bonds ("ASF bonds"), which are issued by municipalities to finance the construction and renovation of airport terminals. According to Williams, her structure is superior to that of existing ASF bonds and would provide benefits to airlines, municipalities, bondholders, and underwriting banks if it were adopted.

Defendant-Appellee Citigroup Inc. . . . is a major underwriter of ASF bonds. Williams [performed work for Citigroup at two law firms. While at the second firm, Pillsbury Winthrop Shaw Pittman, LLP ("Pillsbury"),] Williams marketed her structure to Citigroup. Although a Citigroup executive responsible for ASF bond underwriting initially responded to her proposal with enthusiasm, Citigroup ultimately declined to adopt Williams's structure. Eventually, Pillsbury "forced" Williams to leave the firm....

The complaint alleges that Citigroup, along with various rating agencies, airlines, and municipalities, conspired to block the use of Williams's structure to issue ASF bonds.... Williams avers that Citigroup and its coconspirators took these actions to protect the profits that they derived from the existing secondary trading market for ASF bonds, which she claims would disappear if her structure were adopted.

[Williams's complaint asserted eight claims. The first five (the "federal claims") alleged that the conspiracy to monopolize the ASF bond market violated the Sherman Act, 15 U.S.C. §§ 1-2. The other three claims (the "state law claims") alleged violations of New York statutory and common law. Citigroup moved to dismiss all the claims under Rule 12(b)(6).]

By memorandum and order dated November 2, 2009, the district court granted the motion to dismiss. It dismissed the federal claims on the ground that Williams failed to satisfy the pleading standard set forth in *Ashcroft v. Iqbal*, 556 U.S. 662 (2009) [*supra* p. 45], and *Bell Atlantic Corp. v. Twombly*, 550 U.S. 544 (2007) [*supra* p. 36], due to the absence of factual allegations plausibly suggesting that Citigroup violated the Sherman Act. Notwithstanding Citigroup's request that the state law claims be dismissed without prejudice so as to allow reassertion in state court, the district court

---

1. In an accompanying summary order filed today, we affirm the district court's dismissal of Williams's federal claims.

[dismissed them with prejudice as well]. On the day following the district court's ruling, the clerk entered final judgment.

On November 17, 2009, Williams timely moved for reargument and reconsideration pursuant to Federal Rules of Civil Procedure 59(e) and 60(b) . . . . Through this motion (the "postjudgment motion"), Williams sought to reopen the judgment and obtain leave to amend her original complaint so as to attempt to remedy the pleading defects identified in the dismissal order. Williams's counsel previewed the proposed amendments in a fifteen-page declaration accompanying the motion.

The district court denied the postjudgment motion in a brief order dated February 8, 2010 . . . . This appeal followed.

DISCUSSION

. . .

. . . We review the district court's denial of a postjudgment motion for leave to replead for abuse of discretion. A district court abuses its discretion when its ruling "rests on an error of law" or "cannot be located within the range of permissible decisions."

In reviewing the district court's denial of this motion, we are mindful of the nature of the relief that Williams sought: namely, leave to amend her complaint. In the ordinary course, the Federal Rules of Civil Procedure provide that courts "should freely give leave" to amend a complaint "when justice so requires." Fed. R. Civ. P. 15(a)(2). This permissive standard is consistent with our "strong preference for resolving disputes on the merits." Where, however, a party does not seek leave to file an amended complaint until after judgment is entered, Rule 15's liberality must be tempered by considerations of finality. As a procedural matter, "[a] party seeking to file an amended complaint postjudgment must first have the judgment vacated or set aside pursuant to [Rules] 59(e) or 60(b)." . . .

The standards . . . for evaluating postjudgment motions generally place significant emphasis on the "value of finality and repose." . . . [H]owever, . . . considerations of finality do not always foreclose the possibility of amendment, even when leave to replead is not sought until after the entry of judgment. . . .

Particularly instructive in this respect is the Supreme Court's decision in *Foman v. Davis*, 371 U.S. 178 (1962). *Foman* involved an action to enforce an alleged oral agreement regarding the amount that the plaintiff stood to inherit from her father's estate. The district court dismissed the complaint for failure to state a claim on the ground that the alleged oral agreement was unenforceable under the statute of frauds. The day after judgment was entered, the plaintiff moved to vacate the judgment and to amend her complaint to seek recovery in quantum meruit. The district court denied that motion. The Supreme Court reversed, construing the motion to vacate as filed pursuant to Rule 59(e) and holding that the district court abused its discretion in denying leave:

Rule 15(a) declares that leave to amend "shall be freely given when justice so requires";* this mandate is to be heeded. If the underlying facts or circumstances relied upon by a plaintiff may be a proper subject of relief, he ought to be afforded an opportunity to test his claim on the merits. In the absence of any apparent or declared reason — such as undue delay, bad faith or dilatory motive on the part of the movant, repeated failure to cure deficiencies by amendments previously allowed, undue prejudice to the opposing party by virtue of allowance of the amendment, futility of amendment, etc. — the leave sought should, as the rules require, be "freely given." Of course, the grant or denial of an opportunity to amend is within the discretion of the District Court, but outright refusal to grant the leave without any justifying reason appearing for the denial is not an exercise of discretion; it is merely abuse of that discretion and inconsistent with the spirit of the Federal Rules. . . .

We conclude that the denial of [Williams's postjudgment motion] was not a proper exercise of the district court's discretion, as the district court applied a standard that cannot be reconciled with the Supreme Court's holding in *Foman*. The district court apparently believed that a motion for leave to replead is not timely unless made "in the first instance." The court did not explain precisely what it meant by "in the first instance." In the circumstances of this case, however, it can only have meant one of two things: that the plaintiff was under obligation to seek leave to replead either immediately upon answering the motion to dismiss the complaint (without yet knowing whether the court will grant the motion, or, if so, on what ground), or immediately upon receipt of the court's ruling granting the motion and prior to the entry of judgment thereupon. Regardless which of the two the court had in mind, *Foman* makes unmistakably clear there is no such rule. The plaintiff in *Foman* did not seek leave to replead either together with her response to the motion to dismiss, or indeed prior to the district court's entry of judgment. The motion was made postjudgment. Nonetheless, the Supreme Court, identifying "undue delay" as an appropriate reason that might be given for denial of such a motion, ruled that the district court abused its discretion and violated the liberal spirit of Rule 15 by denying the motion. The *Foman* holding cannot be reconciled with the proposition that the liberal spirit of Rule 15 necessarily dissolves as soon as final judgment is entered.

Citigroup also argues that the denial of the postjudgment motion was justified on the ground that the proposed amendments would not remedy the deficiencies in Williams's claims. It is well established that "[l]eave to amend need not be granted . . . where the proposed amendment would be 'futil[e].'" Therefore, on remand, the district court should address whether the proposed amendments would be futile.

[The court of appeals then held that, even if the district court refused to permit the amendment, it should consider whether to dismiss the state-law

---

* At the time of *Foman*, Rule 15(a) contained this phrase. The 2007 amendments restyled the phrase in Rule 15(a)(2), which the court quoted earlier. — ED.

claims without prejudice. The court of appeals noted that dismissal without prejudice gave the plaintiff the opportunity to pursue the state-law claims in the New York state courts, where the *Twombly-Iqbal* pleading standard had not been adopted.]

Notes and Questions

1. The issue of seeking leave to amend is never reached if a party can amend the pleading "as a matter of course." Fed. R. Civ. P. 15(a)(1). In general, a party has twenty-one days to amend a pleading after serving it. Fed. R. Civ. P. 15(a)(1)(A). If the pleading is one to which a responsive pleading is required (for instance, an answer), that time is extended to twenty-one days after an opponent serves a responsive pleading or a motion under Rule 12(b), –(e), or –(f), whichever occurs earlier. Fed. R. Civ. P. 15(a)(1)(B). A party can exercise the opportunity to amend a pleading as a matter of course only once. Otherwise, the party must obtain either the opposing party's written consent or the court's leave. Fed. R. Civ. P. 15(a)(2). It is usually thought that the opportunity to amend as a matter of course exists only with respect to the original pleading. In *Ramirez v. County of San Bernardino*, 806 F.3d 1002 (9th Cir. 2015), however, a plaintiff who had previously filed his original complaint obtained the consent of the defendant to file a First Amended Complaint. Twenty-one days after the defendant moved to dismiss the First Amended Complaint, the plaintiff filed a Second Amended Complaint as a matter of course. The court appeals stated that Rule 15(a)(1), read literally, permitted this amendment, thus suggesting that the time-limited right to amend as a matter of course persists until the party has exercised it once.

2. As *Williams* says, the classic case interpreting Rule 15(a)(2)'s direction — that a court "should freely give leave when justice so requires" — is *Foman v. Davis*, 371 U.S. 178 (1962). *Foman* defines justice in a negative sense; it lists five circumstances that can lead a court not to grant leave. If none of these factors is present, *Foman* stated that a judge should ordinarily permit the amendment: "It is too late in the day and entirely contrary to the spirit of the Federal Rules of Civil Procedure for decisions on the merits to be avoided on the basis of such mere technicalities." *Id.* at 181.

3. Are *Foman*'s factors of equal weight? Many courts says that delay alone is insufficient, unless the presence of another factor makes the delay "undue." *See* Mullin v. Balicki, 875 F.3d 140, 151 (3d Cir. 2018) ("While simple delay cannot justify denying leave to amend by itself, delay that is 'undue' — a delay that is protracted and unjustified — can place a burden on the court or counterparty, or can indicate a lack of diligence sufficient to justify a discretionary denial of leave.").

4. The principal reasons that courts cite when denying leave to amend are undue prejudice and futility. Prejudice usually occurs when the amendment would cause a significant and unforeseen shift in the nature of the case after the parties have finished most of the discovery, or when the

amendment introduces matters that might prolong the case or confuse the jury. *See* 6 CHARLES A. WRIGHT ET AL., FEDERAL PRACTICE AND PROCEDURE § 1487 (3d ed. 2010). Futility occurs when the pleading as amended would not survive a motion to dismiss or for summary judgment. *See* Parchman v. SLM Corp., 896 F.3d 728, 738 (6th Cir. 2018); Sound of Music Co. v. Minn. Mining & Mfg. Co., 477 F.3d 910, 923 (7th Cir. 2007).

5. Are *Foman*'s factors the only measures of injustice? *Foman* uses the ambiguous word "etc." Most opinions recite only the factors that *Foman* lists. One court, however, has mentioned as additional factors "the need for discovery, strain on the court's docket, or the lack of prejudice as the issue is already known." Checuti v. Conrail, 291 F. Supp. 2d 664, 667 (N.D. Ohio 2003). The first and third factors fit into existing *Foman* categories. Is the second factor relevant?

6. As *Williams* notes, the decision to grant or deny a motion for leave to amend lies within the discretion of the district court. Thus, a court of appeals can reverse a district court's decision to grant or deny leave to amend only when the district court has abused its discretion. Other common *standards of review* are "clear error" with respect to facts that a judge finds and "de novo" with respect to questions of law. *See, e.g.*, Davis v. Morris–Walker. Ltd., 922 F.3d 868, 870 (8th Cir. 2019) ("We review the district court's legal conclusions de novo, its factual findings for clear error, and its denial of the motion for leave to amend for abuse of discretion."). The standards of "clear error" and "abuse of discretion" insulate a district court's judgment from reversal unless the district court makes a fairly egregious mistake, while de novo review provides no deference to the district court. When reading an appellate decision, always pay attention to the standard of review. For further discussion of standards of review, see *infra* Chapter 6, Part B.3.

Was the district court's decision in *Williams* so out of line that it amounted to an abuse? If *Williams* is correct, must a district court always grant a plaintiff's timely request to amend a complaint that fails to meet the requirements of *Twombly* and *Iqbal*? *Cf.* AE ex rel. Hernandez v. Cty. of Tulare, 666 F.3d 631, 636 (9th Cir. 2012) ("A district court abuses its discretion by denying leave to amend unless amendment would be futile or the plaintiff has failed to cure the complaint's deficiencies despite repeated opportunities."); JOE S. CECIL ET AL., UPDATE ON RESOLUTION OF RULE 12(b)(6) MOTIONS GRANTED WITH LEAVE TO AMEND 1 (2011) (noting that, after *Iqbal*, district courts granted motions to amend more frequently than before *Twombly*, thus mitigating to some extent defendants' greater success on motions to dismiss after *Iqbal*).

7. Rule 15 is not the only rule that controls the amendment process. Beginning in 1983, the Federal Rules codified a practice known as *case management*. The theory of case management is that, in order to reduce cost, delay, and abuse, judges need to manage the pretrial process actively. One of the management techniques that was thought to be particularly effective was establishing firm deadlines for accomplishing pretrial tasks. Hence, Rule 16(b)(1) now requires that, in most cases, the judge issue a

scheduling order early in the case. This order "must limit the time" for performing various pretrial activities, including the time to "amend the pleadings." Fed. R. Civ. P. 16(b)(3)(A); *see infra* pp. 184-89 (discussing scheduling orders). Once established, the deadline can be changed "only for good cause and with the judge's consent." Fed. R. Civ. P. 16(b)(4).

A tension exists between the "easy amendment" philosophy of Rule 15(a) and the "strict deadline" philosophy of Rule 16(b). Courts wrestling with this tension have tended to say that the standard of Rule 15(a) applies to an amendment requested within the Rule 16(b) deadline; if it is sought after the deadline, the amendment must satisfy both the Rule 15(a) and the Rule 16(b) standards. *See* Husky Ventures, Inc. v. B55 Invs., Ltd., 911 F.3d 1000, 1019 (10th Cir. 2018).

8. One question that frequently arises is whether an amendment can add a claim if, between the filing of the original claim and the amendment, the statute of limitations has expired on the new claim. Read Rule 15(c) and consider the following case.

Neita v. City of Chicago

830 F.3d 494 (7th Cir. 2016)

Before Easterbrook, Manion, and Sykes, Circuit Judges.

Sykes, Circuit Judge.

. . .

I. BACKGROUND

[Vaughn] Neita formerly owned and operated a dog-grooming business and rescue shelter called A Doggie Business. On February 14, 2012, he brought two dogs to Chicago's Department of Animal Care and Control. One of the dogs, Osa, had become overly aggressive and attacked and killed another dog in Neita's care. The other dog, Olive Oil, had become ill after whelping a litter of puppies.

When Neita arrived with the dogs, Cherie Travis, an Animal Control employee, called the police. Chicago Police Officers Jane Raddatz and Melissa Uldrych responded to the call and, after speaking with Travis, arrested Neita. The officers then searched Neita, his vehicle, and later his business premises. The State's Attorney charged Neita with two counts of animal cruelty and thirteen counts of violating an animal owner's duties under Illinois law. An Illinois judge found him not guilty on all counts.

After his acquittal Neita filed this action against Travis, Officers Raddatz and Uldrych, and the City of Chicago, among others. The complaint alleged that the individual defendants were liable under § 1983 for false arrest and illegal searches in violation of the Fourth Amendment and under Illinois law for malicious prosecution and intentional infliction of emotional

SECTION D   AMENDING THE PLEADINGS

distress. The complaint also sought statutory indemnification from the City of Chicago for the acts of its employees. Neita twice amended his complaint, and the defendants moved to dismiss each iteration for failure to state a claim. See Fed. R. Civ. P. 12(b)(6).

The judge granted the motions. He dismissed the first amended complaint without prejudice, giving Neita an opportunity to replead. But the second amended complaint fared no better. The judge dismissed the federal claims with prejudice, holding that Neita had failed to adequately plead any constitutional violation and that further amendment would be futile. The judge then relinquished supplemental jurisdiction over the remaining state-law claims, dismissing them without prejudice to refiling in state court. This appeal followed.

II. DISCUSSION

Our review of a Rule 12(b)(6) dismissal is de novo. To survive a motion to dismiss, a complaint must contain sufficient factual allegations to state a claim for relief that is legally sound and plausible on its face. Ashcroft v. Iqbal, 556 U.S. 662, 678 (2009) [*supra* p. 45]. The federal claims in Neita's second amended complaint consist of a false-arrest claim against the individual defendants and several illegal-search claims against Officers Raddatz and Uldrych. . . .

To prevail on a false-arrest claim under § 1983, a plaintiff must show that there was no probable cause for his arrest. [The court of appeals held that the plaintiff's complaint adequately pleaded a lack of probable cause.]

Neita next alleges that Officers Raddatz and Uldrych illegally searched his person [and] vehicle . . . . Warrantless searches are per se unreasonable, subject to a few carefully defined exceptions. One exception is for searches conducted incident to a lawful arrest. . . . Because Neita has stated a plausible claim for false arrest, his claim for illegal search incident to his arrest also may go forward.

The claims for illegal search of Neita's vehicle . . . require somewhat more attention. Neita alleges that after arresting and searching him, Officers Uldrych and Raddatz retrieved his keys from his pocket and searched his vehicle. The judge held that this claim was time-barred because it first appeared in the second amended complaint, which Neita filed well after the statute of limitations had run.

Neita did file his second amended complaint after the statute of limitations had run. Claims brought under § 1983 are governed by the statute of limitations for personal-injury claims in the state where the plaintiff's injury occurred. In Illinois the statute of limitations for personal-injury actions is two years from when the cause of action accrued, and a Fourth Amendment claim accrues at the time of the search or seizure. Neita was arrested and his vehicle searched on February 14, 2012. He filed his initial complaint on February 14, 2014, exactly two years later. While his initial complaint was thus timely, it did not allege that the officers illegally searched his vehicle; that claim first appears in the second amended complaint, which Neita filed on November 25, 2014, more than nine months after the limitations period had run.

Conceding this point, Neita argues that his claim relates back to the date of the original pleading under Rule 15(c)(1)(B) of the Federal Rules of Civil Procedure. We agree. Rule 15(c)(1)(B) provides that an amendment relates back to the date of the original pleading when "the amendment asserts a claim or defense that arose out of the conduct, transaction, or occurrence set out — or attempted to be set out — in the original pleading." "The criterion of relation back is whether the original complaint gave the defendant enough notice of the nature and scope of the plaintiff's claim that he shouldn't have been surprised by the amplification of the allegations of the original complaint in the amended one." Santamarina v. Sears, Roebuck & Co., 466 F.3d 570, 573 (7th Cir. 2006).

Here the relevant transaction is properly understood as Neita's arrest at Animal Control on February 14, 2012. The searches all flowed directly from that arrest. The original complaint, which described Neita's arrest and the subsequent searches of his person and business, was sufficient to put the defendant officers on notice that they would have to defend against all claims arising out of this encounter, including the related search of Neita's vehicle. . . .

* * *

For the foregoing reasons, we reverse the dismissal of Neita's false-arrest and illegal-search claims and remand for further proceedings. With the federal claims now reinstated, the state-law claims are revived.

Notes and Questions

1. *Neita* examines how broadly or narrowly Rule 15(c)(1)(B)'s phrase "conduct, transaction, or occurrence" should be construed. In this course, you will come across other situations in which a Federal Rule or other doctrine requires a court to determine whether two events are part of the same "transaction or occurrence." This phrase can shift meanings in different contexts, depending on the purpose underlying the Federal Rule or doctrine at issue. For Rule 15(c), the meaning of the phrase is largely determined by two sets of considerations: on one hand, a policy, reflected in liberal rules of pleading and amendment, of resolving cases on their merits; on the other, the policies that underlie statutes of limitations, such as giving defendants repose and avoiding the risks of inaccurate decisions based on stale evidence and faulty memories. *See* ASARCO, LLC v. Union Pac. R.R., 765 F.3d 999, 1005 (9th Cir. 2014).

2. In *Mayle v. Felix*, 545 U.S. 644, 660 (2005), the Supreme Court held that a new claim did not relate back to an existing claim when the two claims involved "separate episodes." The majority opinion observed:

> The majority of Circuits . . . allow relation back only when the claims added by amendment arise from the same core facts as the timely filed

claims, and not when the new claims depend upon events separate in "both time and type" from the originally raised episodes. . . .

. . . [Rule 15(c)(1)(B)] relaxes, but does not obliterate, the statute of limitations; hence relation back depends on the existence of a common "core of operative facts" uniting the original and newly asserted claims. [*Id.* at 657, 659.]

Mayle was focused on defining "conduct, transaction, or occurrence" in the context of a petition for habeas corpus, but courts have said essentially the same thing about the Rule 15(b)(1)(B) language in other contexts. *See, e.g., ASARCO*, 765 F.3d at 1004 ("To relate back, the original and amended pleadings [must] share a common core of operative facts so that the adverse party has fair notice of the transaction, occurrence, or conduct called into question.") (internal quotation marks omitted). Does *Mayle* help you to understand the meaning of "conduct, transaction, or occurrence," or does it substitute one set of conclusory phrases for another?

3. Why might the district court in *Neita* have thought that the search of the plaintiff's car did not arise out of the same transaction, occurrence, or conduct as the search of the plaintiff's person? Having made that ruling, was the district judge entitled to any deference from the court of appeals? *Neita* states that, with respect to a Rule 12(b)(6) dismissal, the standard of review is de novo — in other words, the court of appeals does not give any deference to the decision of the district court. *Neita* fails to state the standard of review for a district court's Rule 15(c)(1)(B) relation-back decision. Suppose that the standard were abuse of discretion. As an appellate judge, would you have reversed the judgment in *Neita* under that standard? The Supreme Court has never decided the issue, but the usual approach of the courts of appeals — and apparently *Neita* — is to review a district court's decision on relation back de novo. *See ASARCO*, 765 F.3d at 1004.

4. Aside from Rule 15(c)(1)(B), Rule 15(c) allows relation back in two circumstances: when "the law that provides the relevant statute of limitations allows relation back," Fed. R. Civ. P. 15(c)(1)(A); and when the amendment seeks to change the party because the complaint named the wrong defendant, Fed. R. Civ. P. 15(c)(1)(C). In the latter case, a complaint can name a new party if three requirements are met: first, that the "conduct, transaction, or occurrence" requirement of Rule 15(c)(1)(B) is satisfied; second, that within the period allowed under Rule 4(m) for serving a complaint (usually ninety days), the new party receives "such notice of the action that it will not be prejudiced in defending on the merits," *see* Fed. R. Civ. P. 15(c)(1)(C)(i); and third, that within this same period, the new party knew or should have known that "the action would have been brought against it, but for a mistake concerning the proper party's identity," *see* Fed. R. Civ. P. 15(c)(1)(C)(ii).

With respect to the last requirement, *Krupski v. Costa Crociere S. p. A.*, 560 U.S. 538 (2010), held that a Rule 15(c)(1)(C) inquiry must focus solely on the what the newly added defendant knew or should have known, and not on what the plaintiff knew or should have known. The Court then suggested that if a plaintiff makes a deliberate, fully informed choice to sue one party rather than another, rather than a "mistake," "the requirements of Rule 15(c)(1)(C)(ii) are not met." *Id.* at 552.

5. *Krupski* also rejected the argument that Krupski's delay in filing the amended complaint deprived her of the ability to relate the claim back. Rule 15(c)(1) "sets forth an exclusive list of requirements for relation back, and the amending party's diligence is not among them." 560 U.S. at 553. In contrast to Rule 15(a), the "mandatory nature of the inquiry for relation back" leaves no room for "the district court's equitable discretion." *Id.*

6. You may have noticed Rule 15(b), which pertains to amendments to the pleadings during or after trial. At common law, if the evidence introduced at trial deviated from the claim that was pleaded in a material and prejudicial way, this *variance* was regarded as fatal to the case. Consistent with the policy of resolving cases on their merits, Rule 15(b) allows a court to "freely permit" an amendment at trial that "aid[s] in presenting the merits," as long as the opposing party cannot show prejudice. *See* Fed. R. Civ. P. 15(b)(1). Likewise, the pleadings may be amended even after the trial if an unpleaded issue "is tried by the parties' express or implied consent." *See* Fed. R. Civ. P. 15(b)(2); *In re* Fustolo, 896 F.3d 76 (1st Cir. 2018) (holding that bankruptcy court abused its discretion in amending the complaint after trial when the defendant "did not have fair notice of the unpleaded claim and was prejudiced by its addition").

SECTION E: POLICING PLEADINGS AND MOTIONS

A well-functioning adversarial system demands of the parties and lawyers who shape the case for trial that their pleadings and motions have factual and legal merit. Traditionally, the scope and enforcement of these obligations fell to the field of legal ethics and to the disciplinary rules of the jurisdiction in which the lawyer practiced. Today Rule 11 also speaks to the matter. Read Rule 11.

PATSY'S BRAND, INC. V. I.O.B. REALTY, INC.

2002 WL 59434 (S.D.N.Y. Jan. 16, 2002), *vacated* sub nom.
In re Pennie & Edmonds LLP, 323 F.3d 86 (2d Cir. 2003) [*infra* p. 95]

■ MARTIN, District Judge.

This relatively mundane trademark litigation concerning the right to the trademark "Patsy's" for use on sauce has been turned into a minor legal epic, primarily as a result of the perjury and obstruction of justice engaged in by the principals of the corporate defendants. This final chapter of that epic arises from this Court's sua sponte issuance of an order requiring Pennie & Edmonds, the attorneys for the principal defendants, to show cause why it should not be sanctioned for permitting its client to submit a false affidavit.

At the outset, the Court recognizes that the respondent firm, Pennie & Edmonds, enjoys a good reputation in the New York legal community, and the Court does not dispute counsel's assertion that they acted with subjective good faith. In the end, however, the Court concludes that, rather than risk offending and possibly losing a client, counsel simply closed their eyes to the overwhelming evidence that statements in the client's affidavit were not true.

FACTS

Plaintiff Patsy's Brand, Inc., ("Patsy's") commenced this action for trademark infringement against the owner of Patsy's Pizzeria, I.O.B. Realty, Inc. ("I.O.B."), its principals, Frank Brija and John Brecevich, and one of its licensees. The case first came before the Court on Plaintiff's application for a preliminary injunction, in which it asserted it had been selling sauce under the name Patsy's since 1994, and that subsequently the defendants began selling sauce under the same name. In opposing the application for a preliminary injunction, I.O.B. submitted an affidavit from one of its principals, Mr. Brija, in which he swore:

15. In the spring of 1992, I decided to jar my sauces and sell them at retail in my restaurant. These labels were to be used on packaged goods, such as my home made cheeses and sauces. The design for both labels were taken directly from PATSY'S® old menu covers and other features of our restaurant that we have been using for over six decades. The labels display an exact copy of PATSY'S® restaurant's logo, colors and artwork that we have been using since we opened in 1933. Both labels have the name Patsy's written in script, exactly as it was written on our menus in 1933 and other menus since that time. The sauce label also contains a picture of a woman drinking from a wine glass, exactly as it appeared on our menu in 1933 and other later menus.

16. In February of 1993, I contacted Keller Label & Ticket Company (hereinafter, "Keller") to help us design and print PATSY[S]® labels. On or about March 3, 1993, we received a price quote on the artwork, plates and printing for the labels. I immediately accepted Keller's quote. Attached as Exhibit O is a true copy of this quote from Keller.

17. After accepting the quote from Keller, I provided Rich Mazzella with a copy of our logos as they appeared on our menu, and asked them to make the label in a dark green color since this was the color PATSY'S is famous for using, an institutional dark green color. In short, the logo on the face of our menu was transferred to our labels. Likewise, I instructed Keller to put the exact image of the woman holding a glass as it appears on early menu and other menus.

18. On March 18, 1993, Keller invoiced PATSY'S® for 5,000 cheese labels, which were immediately delivered. A true copy of this invoice is attached hereto as Exhibit P. . . .

Relying on these factual assertions, I.O.B.'s brief asserted that: "Defendants have been selling sauce in a mason jar with the label at issue since at least the spring of 1993."

When Plaintiff's reply papers pointed out that 1) Defendants' sauce label contained a bar code that did not exist until 1998; 2) the statement on the label, "For over 65 years PATSY'S Restaurant has served its faithful clientele", would not have been true until 1998 because the restaurant opened in 1933; and 3) the "1993" invoices from the printer listed a telephone number with an area code that did not come into existence until several years later, [I.O.B.'s] then counsel disclaimed any reliance on the documents and later withdrew from representing I.O.B. . . .

[In early 2000, the court granted a preliminary injunction prohibiting I.O.B. from using its labels.] After the preliminary injunction was granted, Pennie & Edmonds appeared for the I.O.B. defendants. Recognizing the significance of the false statements contained in I.O.B.'s prior submissions to the Court, the attorneys at Pennie & Edmonds questioned Messrs. Brija and Brecevich, who continued to insist that the sauce label had been created in 1993 or 1994. Mr. Brija said that he had simply been confused and attached a label created in 1999 to his papers rather than the original label he created in 1993. When asked about the phony documents produced from the printer, Mr. Brija blamed Richard Mazzella, the person at Keller Labels who handled his account. According to Mr. Brija, Richard Mazzella took it upon himself to fabricate the records because he no longer had his records from 1993, and he did not tell this to Mr. Brija. To support his story, Mr. Brija produced a signed statement from Mr. Mazzella to that effect.

When Pennie & Edmonds contacted Mr. Mazzella's lawyer, they were told that Mr. Mazzella did not want to get involved, that the statement he signed was done without the involvement of counsel, and that if Mazzella were subpoenaed, he would testify that he had not even done business with the defendants in [1993].

Thereafter, Plaintiff moved for summary judgment. . . .

The . . . papers submitted by Pennie & Edmonds [to oppose summary judgment] . . . included an affidavit from Mr. Brija in which he swore:

17. I designed the label that we used on the sauces we sold in our restaurants. There were two versions. The first version was created in 1993 or 1994. I simply took the PATSY'S logo exactly as it appears on our menus, and transposed it onto a green background — the same color green as the outside of our restaurant. The labels were printed by [Keller]. Attached as Exhibit I is a copy of this label. In 1999, I designed a newer label. This label has the same script PATSY'S logo on the same colored green background. I also used the design of the woman holding a glass of wine that appeared on the original PATSY'S menu. I added additional text that states "For over 65 years PATSY'S Restaurant has served its faithful clientele the best of its legendary cuisine. Now, PATSY'S offers its famous sauces directly to you at home . . . Enjoy!" Also, I placed on the label

our toll free number for gift orders; the "Nutritional Facts" section, required by the FDA; and, at the suggestion of my attorney, a U.P.C. bar code. These labels were also printed by Keller Label. A copy of the 1999 label is attached as Exhibit J.

18. Last year, in connection with the plaintiff's preliminary injunction motion, my counsel requested that I obtain documentation showing the first order for sauce labels placed with the label manufacturer. I called Richard Mazzella at Keller Label and asked for a copy of the earliest purchase order or invoice. Mr. Mazzella did not have a copy of the invoice, so he recreated it to reflect, the best of his recollection, our first order for sauce labels. I never requested that the invoice or any other document be falsified. I did not learn from Mr. Mazzella that he recreated the document until after the documents was [sic] submitted to the Court. . . .

In the Opinion granting Plaintiff summary judgment and ordering counsel to show cause why sanctions under Rule 11 should not be imposed, the Court noted [that this affidavit] of Mr. Brija was also false, stating:

> I.O.B.'s counsel overlooks the irrefutable evidence that Brija's current story concerning an earlier label which he now claims he used in 1993 is as false as his claim that the current label had been in use since 1993. . . . [T]he label . . . also contains on its face clear evidence that what Brija says is not true. . . .

DISCUSSION

The court has set forth the background facts at great length and in the specific language contained in the various documents because they are so important in assessing whether counsel had a reasonable basis for accepting the false statements of their client. . . .

Pennie & Edmonds argues . . . that because Rule 11 was amended in 1993 to require only that "the allegations or other factual contentions have evidentiary support," they can not be sanctioned because Mr. Brija was willing to swear to the truth of his assertions, and his partner, Mr. Brecevich, was willing to corroborate him.

There are few precepts governing a lawyer's conduct that are as firmly established as the rule that a lawyer shall not "offer evidence that the lawyer knows to be false." Model Rules of Prof'l Conduct R. 3.3(a)(4). Surely, it could not have been the intention of the Rules Committee that wrote the 1993 Amendments to protect an attorney from sanctions for making false statements of fact simply because a witness was willing to sign an affidavit that any reasonable lawyer would recognize as perjury. As noted above, subsequent to the 1993 Amendments to Rule 11, the Second Circuit reaffirmed that "[a]n attorney is entitled to rely on his or her client's statements as to factual claims *when those statements are objectively reasonable.*"

The question thus becomes whether, in light of all the information available to them, Pennie & Edmonds could reasonably rely on the factual representations of Mr. Brija and his partner to the effect that they had sold sauce under the Patsy's label in 1993 and that they had no responsibility for the false documents submitted in connection with the preliminary injunction motion.

In assessing Pennie & Edmonds' conduct, it is important to note that this is not a case where the client was telling a story for the first time and counsel had only vague suspicions that the client's assertions were not true. By the time Pennie & Edmonds took on the representation of I.O.B., a highly detailed affidavit of Mr. Brija had been conclusively proven to be false in very material respects, and had been disavowed by predecessor counsel who then withdrew from representing I.O.B.

While, as noted above, the court accepts the firm's assertion that it acted in subjective good faith, the entire record leaves the Court convinced that the firm could not have had a reasonable belief that the statements in Mr. Brija's affidavit were true. . . .

In sum, all of the facts available to Pennie & Edmonds should have convinced a lawyer of even modest intelligence that there was no reasonable basis on which they could rely on Mr. Brija's statements, even if his partner, Mr. Brecevich, was prepared to support him. . . .

. . . Since the court has concluded that objective reasonableness is the proper standard on which to judge counsel's conduct and that counsel did not have an objectively reasonable basis to believe in the truth of the facts they put into Mr. Brija's affidavit, Rule 11 sanctions are appropriate. The questions that remain are who is the appropriate party to be sanctioned — the individual lawyer who handled the litigation or the law firm — and what the appropriate sanction should be.

The Court is familiar enough with large law firm practice in New York to know that this is a typical large law firm situation in which a client is introduced to the firm by one partner but the litigation is handled by another. The Court is also aware of the substantial economic benefits that flow to "finders," the partners who find the clients, and the pressure to please the client that is felt by the "minders," the lawyers that actually do the client's work. Thus, the litigating partner in this case no doubt felt an obligation to his partners not to jeopardize the firm's relationship with the client by telling the client that the client's factual statements were not credible in light of all of the contrary evidence. While the record does not clearly reflect the extent to which the originating partner was involved in the decision to allow the client to submit the false affidavit, it seems clear that the ultimate responsibility should rest with the firm and not its litigating partner. Given the economic pressures of big firm practice, it is the responsibility of the firm to insure [sic] that each of its partners is aware that it is firm policy that its partners and associates adhere to the highest ethical standards and that if a lawyer's adherence to those standards results in the loss of a client, large or small, the lawyer will not suffer any adverse consequence. If the lawyers involved in the preparation of Mr. Brija's affidavit truly believed their firm had such a policy then they might not have closed their eyes to the significance of all of the facts which established that they could not reasonably accept Mr. Brija['s] false statements.

Pennie & Edmonds' fine reputation in the New York legal community and the fact that the firm has been candid with the Court in admitting the damaging information it learned from the lawyer for the printer are highly relevant in determining what sanction the Court should impose. . . .

. . . [T]he Court is persuaded that little sanction beyond the publication of this Opinion is required to prevent repetition of similar conduct. Thus all that the Court will require is that a partner of the firm submit to the Court an affidavit stating that a copy of this Opinion has been delivered to each of the lawyers in the firm with a memorandum that states that it is firm policy that its partners and associates adhere to the highest ethical standards and that if a lawyer's adherence to those standards results in the loss of a client, large or small, the lawyer will not suffer any adverse consequence.

. . . In this age, where law firms have become bottom line oriented, it is important for lawyers to be reminded that there are certain lines lawyers can not cross in their endeavor to increase the bottom line, and that their duty of candor toward the Court can not be sacrificed to please a client.

IN RE PENNIE & EDMONDS LLP

323 F.3d 86 (2d Cir. 2003)

Before NEWMAN and F.I. PARKER, Circuit Judges, and UNDERHILL, District Judge.*

■ NEWMAN, Circuit Judge.

This appeal presents . . . [the] issue whether[, when a trial judge, sua sponte, initiates a post-trial Rule 11 sanction proceeding,] the lawyer's liability for the sanction requires a mental state of bad faith or only objective unreasonableness [when] the lawyer has no opportunity to withdraw or correct the challenged submission. . . . We conclude that [when] a sua sponte Rule 11 sanction denies a lawyer the opportunity to withdraw the challenged document pursuant to the "safe harbor" provision of Rule 11(c)(1)(A) [now Rule 11(c)(2) — ED.], the appropriate standard is subjective bad faith. In this case, the District Court accepted the firm's assertion that it acted in subjective good faith. We therefore vacate the sanction ruling. . . .

Rule 11 was amended in 1993 in two respects relevant to the pending appeal. First, the standard for imposing sanctions because of written factual submissions submitted to a district court was changed. . . . Under the current standard, presenting a document to the court certifies "that to the best of the person's knowledge, information, and belief, formed after an inquiry reasonable under the circumstances, . . . (3) the allegations and

---

* Honorable Stefan R. Underhill of the United States District Court for the District of Connecticut, sitting by designation.

other factual contentions have evidentiary support...." Fed. R. Civ. P. 11(b) (as amended 1993).*

Second, a "safe harbor" provision was added, providing an opportunity to withdraw or correct a challenged submission. Where a sanction is initiated by a party's motion, this provision requires initial service of the motion but delays filing or presentation of the motion to the court for 21 days; filing of the motion is permitted 21 days after service only if the challenged submission is not "withdrawn or appropriately corrected."...

A sanction proceeding may also be initiated by a court on its own motion by issuance of a show cause order, but no "safe harbor" opportunity exists to withdraw or correct a submission challenged in a court-initiated proceeding.

In recommending the "safe harbor" provision, the rule-makers explicitly noted its unavailability for sanction proceedings initiated by a court and expressed their view that, as a result, court-initiated sanction proceedings would be used only in more egregious circumstances:

> Since show cause orders will ordinarily be issued only in situations that are akin to a contempt of court, the rule does not provide a "safe harbor" to a litigant for withdrawing a claim, defense, etc., after a show cause order has been issued on the court's own initiative.

Fed. R. Civ. P. 11 advisory committee's note to 1993 Amendments. We have noted that the Advisory Committee's "akin to a contempt" standard is applicable to sanction proceedings initiated by a court.... Courts have taken the Advisory Committee's note to mean that sua sponte Rule 11 sanctions must be reviewed with "particular stringency."...

The mental state applicable to liability for Rule 11 sanctions initiated by motion is objective unreasonableness, i.e., liability may be imposed if the lawyer's claim to have evidentiary support is not objectively reasonable. That standard is appropriate [when] the lawyer whose submission is challenged by motion has the opportunity, afforded by the "safe harbor" provision, to correct or withdraw the challenged submission. P & E contends that, because the "safe harbor" protection does not exist when a lawyer's submission is challenged in a show cause proceeding initiated by a trial judge, the more rigorous standard of bad faith should apply....

... [W]hen a lawyer's submission, unchallenged by an adversary, is subject to sanction by a court, the absence of a "safe harbor" opportunity to reconsider risks shifting the balance [between severity and leniency in a sanction regime] to the detriment of the adversary process. The risk is that lawyers will sometimes withhold submissions that they honestly believe have plausible evidentiary support for fear that a trial judge, perhaps at the conclusion of a contentious trial, will erroneously consider their claimed belief to be objectively unreasonable. This risk is appropriately minimized, as the Advisory Committee contemplated, by applying a "bad faith" standard

---

* The 2007 stylistic amendments slightly altered Rule 11(b)(3), which now reads: "(3) the factual contentions have evidentiary support...." — ED.

to submissions sanctioned without a "safe harbor" opportunity to reconsider. . . . It is better to apply a heightened *mens rea* standard to unchallenged submissions and take the slight risk with respect to such submissions that, on occasion, a jury will give unwarranted weight to a few submissions that a judge would consider objectively unreasonable than to withhold from the jury many submissions that are objectively reasonable but that cautious lawyers dare not present. . . .

Judge Martin gave several reasons for applying an "objective unreasonableness" standard . . . . [H]e emphasized the [Advisory] Committee's use of the word "ordinarily" in its identification of contempt-like circumstances as those that warrant court-initiated sanctions. . . . [H]e reasoned that "[s]ince the Court as an institution has a far greater interest in weeding out abuses than does any individual litigant, there is no reason not to apply the well-established 'objective unreasonableness' standard to Rule 11 proceedings initiated by the Court." . . .

We do not regard the Advisory Committee's use of "ordinarily" as indicating that the Committee had some particular category of cases in mind where court-initiated Rule 11 sanctions could be imposed in the absence of conduct "akin to contempt." The word "ordinarily" is frequently used . . . simply to reflect a natural reluctance of rule-makers to say "always," in candid recognition of their inability to anticipate every imaginable set of circumstances that might one day arise. . . .

As for Judge Martin's appropriate concern for a court's responsibility to "weed out abuses," we believe . . . that his application of an "objectively unreasonable" standard, in the absence of either an explicit "safe harbor" protection or an equivalent opportunity where a court initiates a Rule 11 proceeding at an early stage of litigation, risks more damage to the robust functioning of the adversary process than the benefit it would achieve. . . .

Because Judge Martin accepted P & E's representation that its lawyers acted with subjective good faith, the Rule 11 sanction must be vacated. . . .

■ UNDERHILL, District Judge, dissenting. . . .

Interpretation of Rule 11 begins with its text, because this Court must "interpret Rule 11 according to its plain meaning." Cooter & Gell v. Hartmarx Corp., 496 U.S. 384, 391 (1990). A plain reading of Rule 11 demonstrates that a single *mens rea* requirement applies to sanctionable conduct, regardless of whether a court or a party initiates sanctions proceedings and regardless of whether counsel had an opportunity to withdraw the offending submission.

The fundamental flaw in the majority's interpretation of Rule 11 is that it seeks to use procedural distinctions drawn in section (c), regarding *how* sanctions can be imposed with and without a motion, to modify the substantive requirements of section (b), which controls *whether* a violation of Rule 11 has occurred. Under a plain reading of Rule 11, the procedural distinctions set forth in section (c) have no bearing whatever on the state-of-mind requirements of section (b).

Notes and Questions

1. Does it seem likely to you that the Pennie & Edmonds lawyers were acting in subjective good faith? Assuming that they were, should "pure heart, empty head" be a good defense in this type of situation? Did the majority or the dissent in the court of appeals have the better of the argument on how to interpret Rule 11?

2. Be careful about the holding in *Pennie & Edmonds*. The court of appeals does not say that a lawyer can always employ a defense of "subjective good faith." Rather, a lawyer can use the defense only when the lawyer does not have the 21-day "safe harbor," provided in Rule 11(c)(2), to correct or retract a sanctionable statement. When the lawyer has the safe harbor, but fails to act during the 21-day period, the standard of objective reasonableness applies. "Subjective good faith" is the Second Circuit's standard only for conduct sanctioned under the sua sponte authority of Rule 11(c)(3).

Courts elsewhere have expressed skepticism about the "subjective good faith" defense, finding instead that Rule 11 always requires lawyers to abide by a standard of objective reasonableness. *See* Young v. City of Providence *ex rel.* Napolitano, 404 F.3d 33, 39 (1st Cir. 2005) (holding a lawyer to a standard of "falsity and serious carelessness" in a sua sponte Rule 11 proceeding); *In re* Engle Cases, 283 F. Supp. 3d 1174, 1214 (M.D. Fla. 2017) ("[A] subjective standard finds no support in the language of Rule 11."); *see also* Jenkins v. Methodist Hosps. of Dallas, Inc., 478 F.3d 255 (5th Cir. 2007) (applying an objective standard to counsel sanctioned sua sponte). The Second Circuit has itself limited the scope of *Pennie & Edmonds*. The Private Securities Litigation Reform Act of 1995 (PSLRA) *requires* judges to consider Rule 11 sanctions in cases governed by the PSLRA, even if no party has moved for sanctions. Because parties know in advance that the district court will be considering sanctions, the Second Circuit has concluded that an objective-reasonableness standard is applicable to sua sponte sanctions issued under the PSLRA. *See* ATSI Commc'ns, Inc. v. Shaar Fund, Ltd., 579 F.3d 143 (2d Cir. 2009).

3. Why does Rule 11(c)(2) contain a "safe harbor" provision? Answering that question requires some background on Rule 11. The present Rule 11 is the product of two main rounds of amendments, in 1983 and 1993. Before 1983, Rule 11 was a short and sleepy rule that required all pleadings, motions, and papers to be signed. The signature constituted a certification "that to the best of [the signer's] knowledge, information, and belief, there is good ground to support it; and that it is not interposed for delay." The rule also contemplated an "appropriate disciplinary sanction" against an attorney "[f]or a wilful violation of this rule."

In the 1970s and early 1980s, concerns about abusive tactics, cost, and delay in litigation increased. As a result, the 1983 amendment to Rule 11 did three main things. First, it bulked up the certification standards by making the signature attest that the pleading, motion, or paper was factually and legally justified, and that it was not being filed for an improper purpose.

Second, it switched from a subjective to an objective standard of liability. Third, the 1983 amendment provided for mandatory sanctions for violations of the certification standards, and stated that an award of attorneys' fees and costs was often an appropriate sanction. This award of fees was a substantial change: although much of the world requires the losing party to pay the winning party's attorneys' fees, the "American Rule" generally requires each side to bear its own fees and costs, win or lose.

To some degree, the 1983 amendment backfired. Driven largely by the promise of recouping attorneys' fees that were previously unrecoverable, parties that won lawsuits or successfully resisted motions filed large numbers of Rule 11 motions against losing parties. Rule 11 became a focus of litigation. Various concerns — including the volume of Rule 11 "satellite litigation," the tactical use and misuse of the motion, the possibility that Rule 11 was chilling innovative claims (especially in the civil-rights area), and the fear that the Rule was becoming a back-door way of collecting attorneys' fees — led to revisions that took effect in 1993.

Two key features softened the impact of Rule 11. First, the 1993 amendment introduced the "safe harbor" idea now found in Rule 11(c)(2): a party that believes another party's motion or paper has violated one of the Rule 11(b) certifications must serve its Rule 11 motion on the other party, but not file the motion with the court. The other party then has a 21-day safe harbor to fix the problem without sanction; only if he or she does not do so can the party file the Rule 11 motion with the court. Second, the 1993 amendment limited sanctions. Sanctions are no longer mandatory. *See* Fed. R. Civ. P. 11(c)(1) ("[T]he court may impose an appropriate sanction . . . ."). Moreover, the award of attorneys' fees is now listed as only one among several possible sanctions, which "must be limited to what suffices to deter repetition of the conduct or comparable conduct by others similarly situated." Fed. R. Civ. P. 11(c)(4). Nonetheless, courts often recognize that the best deterrent is payment of the opponent's fees and costs. *See* Royce v. Michael R. Needle, P.C., 158 F. Supp. 3d 708, 713 (N.D. Ill. 2016) (noting that "[c]ompensation and deterrence are not only not mutually exclusive, they are sometimes compatible") (internal quotation marks omitted).

4. If you are a lawyer who observes a Rule 11 violation, don't the "safe harbor" and limited-sanction provisions substantially reduce your incentive to spend your time — and your client's money — writing a Rule 11 motion? If you don't write the motion, it will be up to an already busy judge, acting sua sponte, to catch many Rule 11 violations. But if the standard in sua sponte cases is "subjective good faith" (as *Pennie & Edmonds* holds), only clear, wilful violations are subject to sanction.

Has Rule 11 lost too much of its bite? Some members of Congress believe so, and regularly introduce bills to roll back the 1993 amendments to Rule 11. These bills would make Rule 11 sanctions mandatory, eliminate the safe-harbor provision of Rule 11(c)(2), and (in addition to permitting other appropriate sanctions) require the payment of attorney's fees, expenses, and other costs. One such bill recently passed in the House, but died in the Senate. *See* Lawsuit Abuse Reduction Act, H.R. 720, 115th Cong. (2017).

5. When they apply, Rule 11's monetary sanctions can be substantial. For instance, *Engle Cases* was a part of a long-running litigation brought by thousands of smokers against tobacco companies in Florida. Two law firms together filed more than 3,700 personal-injury complaints. There were problems with many of the complaints — including the small difficulty that 588 of the plaintiffs were dead (most for at least a year). The complaints made it sound as if the plaintiffs were still alive, and the lawyers did not have authorization to file the suits either from the plaintiffs (when they were alive) or the representatives of their estates (after they died). The court (or in some instances counsel) eventually dismissed the complaints. The district court then issued a show-cause order to impose sanctions sua sponte.

Relying principally on Rule 11 but also on other sanction powers, the district court found that the law firms' conduct was willful and reckless. It considered disgorging all of the fees that the law firms had earned in representing clients in the litigation (an amount that, depending on some matters yet to be determined, might have been as much as $15.6 million). But it ultimately imposed a monetary sanction of $9,164,404.12, paid into the court's registry, and further referred the matter to the Florida Bar for investigation.

6. Although monetary sanctions remain common, courts can be creative in reprimanding lawyers. Here are a few examples:

- "That defendant's counsel, Timothy F. Umbreit, Esq., will copy out, legibly, in his own handwriting, and within 30 days of the date hereof, the text (i.e., *without footnotes*) of section 3722 in 14A C. Wright, A. Miller, and E. Cooper, Federal Practice and Procedure: Civil (1985), together with the text of that section's update at page 43 of the 1993 pocket part of volume 14A..." Curran v. Price, 150 F.R.D. 85, 87 (D. Md. 1993).

- "Happily, the solution is at hand. On September 26, 1987, MCLE will hold a day-long program on federal trial practice at Boston College Law School at which many of the district judges will be presenting various facets of our practice. As a sanction in this case, I order both attorneys, Frank A. Smith, III, Esquire and Jerry B. Plumb, Esquire to attend this session for the full day. This is an order of the court, violation of which will lead to more serious sanctions. Not later than September 30, 1987, both attorneys shall submit verification of their attendance, by affidavit or otherwise. Perhaps some appreciation of precise pleading will rub off on them, if they have not already gotten the point." Stevens v. City of Brockton, 676 F. Supp. 26, 27 (D. Mass. 1987).

- "Pursuant to Rule 11 of the Federal Rules of Civil Procedure, the Court imposes a sanction on Michael A. Pinotti. He is required, at his own expense, to successfully complete a course in the Federal Rules of Civil Procedure, and the Local Rules of this Court.... The course shall be taught by a professor at an accredited law school, including any of the three Minnesota law schools. It shall consist of at least 40 hours of individualized instruction, and may require more if the professor finds additional instruction is necessary for successful completion of the course.... On or before August 5, 1996, Mr. Pinotti and his professor shall file with the Court an Affidavit certifying that he successfully completed the course and is proficient in the practice of law under these Rules." Bergeron v. Nw. Publ'ns Inc., 165 F.R.D. 518, 523 (D. Minn. 1996).

A court's imposition of Rule 11 sanctions is generally reviewable on appeal only for abuse of discretion. *See* Cooter & Gell Co. v. Hartmarx Corp., 496 U.S. 384, 405 (1990).

7. Imagine that, as an associate at a law firm representing I.O.B., you are asked to prepare the response to the plaintiff's summary-judgment motion. When you approach the partner in charge with your suspicion that the client's affidavit is not truthful, he tells you that he does not want to hear that. What should you do?

8. A set of facts comparable to *Patsy's* arose in *Business Guides, Inc. v. Chromatic Communications Enterprises, Inc.*, 498 U.S. 533 (1991). In *Business Guides*, the lawyer submitted a motion and affidavit, only to discover subsequently that three (of the ten) significant statements in the client's affidavit were false. The lawyer nevertheless did not investigate the remaining statements, later submitting a supplemental affidavit from the client repeating the remaining seven statements. It turned out that six of those seven were also false. *Business Guides* upheld the award of sanctions.

In both *Business Guides* and *Patsy's*, the lawyer's principal sin was failing to investigate adequately. How much must a lawyer investigate in order to satisfy Rule 11(b)'s obligation to conduct "an inquiry reasonable under the circumstances"? Would you have caught the disparities in bar-coding practices, years of operation, and telephone area codes in *Patsy's*? Must a lawyer hire Sherlock Holmes to look for holes in a client's evidence and statements? Is the suspicion that Rule 11 requires of a lawyer consistent with the lawyer's adversarial responsibilities to be a zealous advocate of the client's interests?

9. Would Rule 11 have allowed the district court to sanction I.O.B. for the role of its principal, Brija, in preparing the false affidavit? *Compare* Fed. R. Civ. P. 11(b) *with* Fed. R. Civ. P. 11(c)(1) *and* 11(c)(5)(A). Could the court have sanctioned Brija himself under Rule 11? *See* Fed. R. Civ. P. 11(c)(1). In fact, the court sanctioned Brija under a different authority: the court's contempt power. The amount of the sanction was one-half of the attorneys' fees incurred by Patsy's after Brija presented false information. *See* Patsy's Brand, Inc. v. I.O.B. Realty, Inc., 317 F.3d 209 (2d Cir. 2003); *see generally* Chambers v. NASCO, Inc., 501 U.S. 32 (1991) (holding that a court's inherent power to sanction bad-faith conduct by a nonparty survived specific sanctioning powers such as Rule 11).

In the same decision, the Second Circuit also upheld a $5,000 sanction imposed against the Pennie & Edmonds lawyer representing I.O.B. The lawyer had filed a frivolous motion seeking sanctions against counsel for Patsy's. According to the district court, the lawyer said that he brought the motion "in order to prove to his client how tough he could be," Patsy's Brand, Inc. v. I.O.B. Realty, Inc., 2001 WL 1154669 (S.D.N.Y. Oct. 1, 2001); in the court of appeals, he said it was brought "'to apply pressure on Plaintiff and its counsel' to produce some billing records that [the lawyer] was endeavoring to obtain after the discovery deadline had passed," *Patsy's*, 317 F.3d at 222. The district court did not impose sanctions under Rule 11, because the plaintiff had not complied with the "safe harbor" provision. The court instead issued sanctions under another of the federal courts' sanctioning authorities, 28 U.S.C. § 1927, finding that the conduct of the lawyer "multiplied 'the proceedings unreasonably and vexatiously.'"

10. Does the presence of other sanctions (which also include the state-law tort of malicious prosecution, as well as attorney disciplinary proceedings) suggest that Rule 11 violates the Rules Enabling Act? In particular, 28 U.S.C. § 2072(b) commands that the Federal Rules "shall not abridge, enlarge or modify any substantive right." Since other sanction provisions use standards different from Rule 11, doesn't Rule 11 modify litigants' substantive rights? *See Business Guides*, 498 U.S. at 552 (rejecting Enabling Act challenge because "Rule 11 is reasonably necessary to maintain the integrity of the system of federal practice and procedure, and ... any effect on substantive rights is incidental").

11. *Patsy's* involved factually unsupportable contentions. The next case considers the application of Rule 11 to unsupportable legal arguments.

FRANTZ V. UNITED STATES POWERLIFTING FEDERATION

836 F.2d 1063 (7th Cir. 1987)

Before EASTERBROOK, RIPPLE, and KANNE, Circuit Judges.

■ EASTERBROOK, Circuit Judge.

The complaint charged the International Powerlifting Federation (IPF), its American affiliate the United States Powerlifting Federation (USPF), and Conrad Cotter, the president of the USPF, with conspiring to monopolize the sport of weight lifting. The plaintiffs include two weight lifters who were disqualified from participating in events sponsored by the IPF because they participated in events sponsored by the American Powerlifting Federation (APF), a rival to the USPF. . . .

The IPF did not file an appearance, and a default judgment was entered against it. The district court dismissed the complaint against the USPF and Cotter under Fed. R. Civ. P. 12(b)(6) for failure to state a claim on which relief may be granted, after plaintiffs' counsel conceded that the complaint was insufficient. The plaintiffs then filed an amended complaint against USPF, dropping Cotter as a defendant. The district court dismissed this complaint under Rule 12(b)(6), finding it dependent on a theory of conspiracy between the USPF and the IPF that could not be sustained. The court also held that Cotter is entitled to attorneys' fees as a sanction under Fed. R. Civ. P. 11 for the initial complaint against him, because the plaintiffs did not have a plausible argument about how the USPF could conspire with its officers. The court denied the USPF's request for sanctions, however, because it concluded that the plaintiffs' amended complaint had a colorable, though unsuccessful, theory.

[The district court later vacated its award of fees after Cotter requested $4,289.48 in fees. The district judge stated:]

[T]he court granted Cotter's request for sanctions [because] . . . the law is clear that a corporate officer is not capable of conspiring with his corporation about antitrust violations. Sanctions were awarded because it was extremely clear to the court that there was no legal or factual basis for naming Cotter as a defendant. Cotter's attorneys, however, contend that they have spent at least 39.535 hours drafting that portion of the motion to dismiss, memorandum in support of the motion and summary of the motion which pertained to Cotter. They have requested $4,289.48 in fees as to this activity. . . . Apparently, the issues regarding Cotter's legal and factual involvement in the case were vastly more complicated than this court had determined. The issues must also have been more complicated than appeared from the briefs of the parties. Therefore, the court is sua sponte reconsidering the award of attorneys' fees under Rule 11, Fed. R. Civ. P., and is hereby denying the award of attorneys' fees in toto.

Cotter appeals from the vacation of the award in his favor, and the USPF appeals the denial of its request for sanctions.

I

The suit against Cotter was frivolous, given *Copperweld Corp. v. Independence Tube Corp.,* 467 U.S. 752 (1984), decided a year before this suit began. [*Copperweld* held that a corporation or association cannot conspire with its own officers under the antitrust laws.] Rule 11 requires counsel to do legal research before filing, and to be aware of legal rules established by the Supreme Court. A party may not strike out blindly and rely on its opponent to do the research to make the case or expose its fallacies. . . . The complaint was sanctionable on two bases: it was frivolous, and it was filed without a prior, reasonable inquiry into the law. . . .

The court vacated the sanction because the request for fees showed that counsel spent about 40 hours preparing and filing the motion to dismiss. This showed, according to the court, that the case was "vastly more complicated" than the court had believed. Perhaps this is a droll way to say that Cotter's total bill was out of line. We consider this possibility later. If the court meant the remark seriously, it is insufficient. Whether the complaint violated Rule 11 depends on what the plaintiffs and their lawyer did — whether they performed the legal and factual work necessary to avoid filing an unwarranted paper — not on what the defendants did with the complaint. That the defendants may have taken too long to find *Copperweld* does not absolve plaintiffs; the violation of Rule 11 exists at the moment the paper is filed. . . . The complaint was based on a conspiracy between officer and corporation; this was doomed after *Copperweld*, and sanctions were in order.

For what it is worth, we doubt that 40 hours is preposterous for preparing a response to this complaint. Cotter's lawyers had to find *Copperweld* and then consider the possibility that plaintiffs were trying to create an exception to that case. This might entail researching the treatment of *Copperweld* in later cases and interviewing Cotter, a resident of Florida, to discover whether there were facts (and therefore a theory) lurking behind the outline provided by the complaint. Antitrust suits are easy to file yet notoriously costly to defend, and achieving the dismissal of an antitrust case in under 40 hours is unusual. . . .

The complaint in this case was frivolous, which calls at a minimum for censure of Victor D. Quilici, the plaintiffs' lawyer. Whether it calls for amercement [an old-fashioned legal term for "a fine" — ED.] — and, if so, whether Cotter or the Treasury is the appropriate beneficiary — is something the district court should consider as an initial matter. . . .

II

. . .

[In rejecting USPF's request for sanctions, the district court] appears to be making two points. One is that if a complaint contains any formally correct statement of a legal theory, then the pleader's obligation under Rule 11 has been satisfied. This is incorrect. A claim may be sufficient in form but sanctionable because, for example, counsel failed to conduct a reasonable investigation before filing. And the inclusion of one sufficient (and adequately investigated) claim does not permit counsel to file a stream of unsubstantiated claims as riders.

Each claim takes up the time of the legal system and the opposing side. A single claim in an antitrust case may occasion the expenditure of hundreds or thousands of hours, as opposing counsel try to verify or refute the allegations and theories. Rule 18(a) permits the liberal joinder of claims, but each joined claim, potentially the basis of separate litigation, must have a foundation — the same foundation it would have needed if the claims had been pursued separately. Just as evidence that Perkins is a thief does not justify an accusation that he is a murderer, so a colorable legal theory about boycotts of weight lifters does not excuse a baseless allegation about price fixing in the television business. Rule 11 applies to all statements in papers it covers. Each claim must have sufficient support; each must be investigated and researched before filing.

The court's other point is that the complaint contains sufficient facts from which the judge may discern the legal claims. The USPF takes issue with this, arguing that the complaint was shy the necessary facts. The USPF's reply brief asserts: "This court has made clear that even if Mr. Quilici possessed sufficient information in his files to support plaintiffs' claims, his failure to include it in the complaint violated Rule 11." The USPF does not cite the cases where we "made clear" this proposition. There aren't any such cases. The USPF has confused Rule 8 with Rule 11. Rule 8 determines how much information has to be in the complaint — not much, as . . . the language of Rule 8 . . . show[s]. The complaint should contain a "short and plain statement of the claim showing that the pleader is entitled to relief", Rule 8(a)(2). It is not only unnecessary but also undesirable to plead facts beyond limning the nature of the claim (with exceptions, see Rule 9, that do not concern us). Bloated, argumentative pleadings are a bane of modern practice. Rule 11 requires not that counsel *plead* facts but that counsel *know* facts after conducting a reasonable investigation — and then only enough to make it reasonable to press litigation to the point of seeking discovery. Rule 11 neither modifies the "notice pleading" approach of the federal rules nor requires counsel to prove the case in advance of discovery.

This is a fine line. Rule 11 must not bar the courthouse door to people who have some support for a complaint but need discovery to prove their case, yet the need for discovery does not excuse the filing of a vacuous complaint. No matter how such inquiries come out, however, courts must ask the right question: whether the side filing the pleading knew enough at the time, not whether it spread all on the record. Rule 11 states that the signature verifies that the paper is "well grounded in fact", not that all the facts are contained in the paper.

The case is remanded for a further inquiry . . . into the support for each of the theories contained in the complaint.

Notes and Questions

1. How is the lawyer's conduct in *Frantz* different from the lawyer's conduct in *Patsy's*? For another case about sanctions because of a lawyer's frivolous legal claims, see Rhodes v. MacDonald, 670 F. Supp. 2d 1363 (M.D. Ga. 2009) (imposing $20,000 monetary penalty on counsel for bringing "birther" suit alleging that her client's deployment orders were void because Barack Obama was not validly elected and thus could not be Commander in Chief), *aff'd*, 368 F. App'x 949 (11th Cir. 2010) (per curiam).

2. What specific provision of Rule 11 did the lawyer in *Frantz* violate in suing Cotter? Look at Rule 11(b)(2). Can you ever make a legal argument contrary to existing precedent? Imagine that the plaintiff's lawyer in *Frantz* had a plausible theory about how *Copperweld* was distinguishable. At what point in the litigation process would the lawyer have to present this theory to the court? Should the theory be raised in the complaint? If not, how might the defendant respond to the complaint in light of *Copperweld*, and what should the plaintiff's lawyer do then?

If the defendant moved to dismiss under Rule 12(b)(6), but did not mention *Copperweld* or the rule that corporations cannot conspire with their officers, does the plaintiff's lawyer have any obligation to bring *Copperweld* or the lawyer's basis for distinguishing it to the court's attention? *See, e.g.*, MODEL RULES OF PROF'L CONDUCT r. 3.3(a)(2) (AM. BAR ASS'N 1983) ("A lawyer shall not knowingly . . . fail to disclose to the tribunal legal authority in the controlling jurisdiction known to the lawyer to be directly adverse to the position of the client and not disclosed by opposing counsel . . . ."). *Cf.* Gonzalez-Servin v. Ford Motor Co., 662 F.3d 931, 934 (7th Cir. 2011) (criticizing plaintiffs' counsel for the "ostrich-like tactic of pretending that potentially dispositive authority against a litigant's contention does not exist").

3. Rule 8(d)(2) allows parties to plead two or more claims or defenses "alternatively or hypothetically," even if they are inconsistent with each other. Can a party plead in the alternative and not run afoul of Rule 11(b)(2)? As long as a party has a sufficient basis for each alternative, the answer is "yes"; otherwise, Rule 11 sanctions might attach. *See* Sprague Farms, Inc. v. Providian Corp., 929 F. Supp. 1125 (C.D. Ill. 1996).

4. All of the principal cases in this section involved sanctions on the *court's* initiative under Rule 11(c)(3). Unlike party-initiated motions under Rule 11(c)(2), Rule 11(c)(3) provides no 21-day safe harbor. Federal trial judges acting on their own may sanction conduct they find to have violated Rule 11 without first giving parties a chance to correct it, although the Rule does require that they give parties notice and an opportunity to show why they should not be found in violation. What do you think about Rule 11 giving judges a roving commission to review the work of the lawyers? Is such a role consistent with the judge's passive role in an adversarial system, as well as the lawyers' role in shaping legal arguments? *Cf.* 15 U.S.C. § 78u-4(c)(1) (obligating federal courts to review for Rule 11 violations all complaints and answers, as well as certain motions, filed in certain private cases alleging securities fraud).

5. Does Rule 11's present structure strike a good balance in the effort to control litigation misconduct without having the control device itself become a source of abuse? For an empirical examination of the question, see David B. Owens, *Civil Rights Foe or Frivolous Litigation Enabler? An Empirical Study of Rule 11 Practice Under the 1983 and 1993 Version*, available at http://papers.ssrn.com/sol3/papers.cfm?abstract_id=1622061 (2010) (finding that "the 1993 amendments have well served their intended purpose of deterring both frivolous litigation and needless collateral litigation over sanctions, without opening the courthouse doors to a flood of baseless suits"). In an adversarial system, rules will be used when they lead to private, not public, benefit. Framing rules that harness self-interested behavior to the general good is a great challenge.

6. For a treatise examining the many issues surrounding the federal courts' power to sanction lawyers and parties for abusive litigation behavior, see GREGORY P. JOSEPH, SANCTIONS: THE FEDERAL LAW OF LITIGATION ABUSE (5th ed. 2013).

CHAPTER THREE

DISCLOSURE AND DISCOVERY

The pleading stage has now closed. As we have seen, pleadings can sometimes be bare-bones documents. Unless the plaintiff and defendant gain better knowledge of the facts and the legal issues, a trial would be a helter-skelter affair. Therefore, our procedural system uses a *pretrial process* to give the parties an opportunity to obtain the facts about what really happened, and to narrow the case down to the critical legal and factual disputes still dividing the parties.

Unfortunately, the twin goals of pretrial — the discovery of relevant facts and the narrowing of the issues in dispute — are not always consistent with each other. In an ideal world broad discovery promotes decisions on the merits, vindicating the interest in an accurate and fully participatory process. But if we allow the parties an unfettered ability to discover facts, the number of issues in the case might proliferate rather than narrow; moreover, unfettered discovery is likely to be quite expensive, and an adversary could easily misuse it as a way to force a poorly financed party to capitulate. Narrow, sharply focused proceedings may also foster efficient dispute resolution. If we narrow the issues with great rigor before we permit the parties to discover the facts, however, we may preclude a party from obtaining the information to create the theory that will win the case. How should we balance the interests in broad discovery of information on the one hand and focused dispute resolution on the other?

This chapter focuses on the process of disclosure and discovery: the information that the parties can obtain and the techniques by which the parties can obtain it. Federal Rules of Civil Procedure 26-37 and 45 govern this process. Controversy surrounds these rules; many people, both here and abroad, believe that the American legal system permits discovery on too broad a scale. To some extent, whether it does depends on the courts' ability to narrow issues efficiently and accurately during pretrial. Portions of the next two chapters describe techniques for narrowing issues. After you have studied all three chapters, you should have a better idea about the merits and demerits of American-style discovery.

SECTION A: PERSPECTIVES ON DISCOVERY

JULIUS BYRON LEVINE, DISCOVERY

1-2 (1982)

English authorities have recognized several ways in which discovery may be beneficial by providing parties with information bearing on litigation. For instance, it enables them to make a more accurate evaluation of their own case and that of their opponent. As a result of such enlightened evaluations English authorities believe that the parties may reach compromise settlements or agree to narrow the issues, or that one side may concede defeat. American federal authorities too have pointed out these benefits of discovery.

Another benefit from discovery . . . is that it may permit a party to expose false or misleading evidence which would otherwise surprise him at trial, when he would have neither the time nor opportunity to demonstrate its unreliable nature. . . .

The third and most obvious benefit from discovery is that it may provide, or lead to, evidence a party presents at trial . . . . The party might not come upon this evidence at all were it not for discovery. Even if he could acquire it by other means, such means might be more expensive and time-consuming than discovery. . . . The upshot is not insignificant, for it may well be injustice.

Since an intended benefit of discovery . . . is to eliminate surprise and to promote adjudication in the light of all relevant facts rather than in various degrees of darkness, discovery is intended to blunt some of the rough edges of the adversary system. That is, discovery . . . is an antidote to the "sporting theory" of justice.

GEOFFREY C. HAZARD, JR., DISCOVERY AND THE ROLE OF THE JUDGE IN CIVIL LAW JURISDICTIONS

73 NOTRE DAME L. REV. 1017, 1021-22 (1998)

[T]he function of preview (discovery) in a jury trial system is to permit the parties and their advocates to make estimates of the kind, degree, and extent of evidence that will suffice to convince a jury without incurring undue risk of boring or confusing the jury. These estimates by the opposing advocates are derived with regard for counter-maneuvers and counter-estimates in the opposing camp. Pretrial discovery, therefore, is a system whose primary function is to inform the advocates, rather than informing either the judge (who ordinarily knows little or nothing of the proofs until trial commences and who will be essentially a neutral umpire come trial) or the jury (which will receive only a small refined residue of the material processed by counsel in discovery).

In contrast, in the civil law system, the critically important function of exploring and sifting evidence is performed by the judge. The judge needs to know the facts necessary to decide the case, but needs to know only that much. The civil law judge's inquiry is not "What evidence should be heard to understand the whole case?" but "What evidence do I require to reach a justifiable decision?" The information needed to decide a case could concern only one or two issues . . . . Considerations of efficiency would lead the civil law judge to approach complicated litigation in precisely this fashion — that is, issue by issue. The mind of the judge in a civil law jurisdiction, thus, is the medium of forensic exploration as well as the medium of forensic determination.

In this light, we can better understand the negative reaction of civil law systems to the outreach of American discovery. The immediate impact of American discovery in a civil law jurisdiction is experienced by the judges as an invasion of their role and responsibility.

STEPHEN N. SUBRIN, DISCOVERY IN GLOBAL PERSPECTIVE: ARE WE NUTS?

52 DEPAUL L. REV. 299, 307-10 (2002)

I suppose that much of the world does think we are nuts when it comes to civil discovery. A consistent theme of those comparing American discovery to that in other countries is that the latter avoid and condemn discovery "fishing expeditions." . . .

The foreign critics of American discovery say very little about why "fishing expeditions" are bad. Fishermen, after all, see such excursions in a positive light. I suppose the negative connotations include wasted time and expense for both private individuals and the court system, invasions of privacy, and the unfairness of forcing defendants to expend resources when plaintiffs do not have advance information of liability.

. . . What neither foreign commentators on American discovery nor homegrown conservative critics tend to mention is the extensive empirical research in our country demonstrating that in many American civil cases, often approaching fifty percent, there is no discovery, and in most of the remainder of the cases there is remarkably little. A study by the Federal Judicial Center summarizes the findings of empiricists: "[T]he typical case has relatively little discovery, conducted at costs that are proportionate to the stakes of litigation, and . . . discovery generally — but with notable exceptions — yields information that aids in the just disposition of cases."

This does not mean that our use of discovery resembles most other countries — it does not. Nor does it mean that we do not have discovery abuse — we do. . . . [I]n a substantial subset of cases, in the neighborhood of five to ten percent, or possibly even fifteen percent, lawyers abuse the discovery rules both by over-discovery and by hiding and obfuscating information. There is frequent distortion of evidence, as a result of lawyer interventions including the type of witness coaching that is forbidden in other countries. But even here, it is important to put American discovery in a larger perspective that includes the nature of our government, the composition of the bench and bar, the constitutional right to a jury, methods of lawyer compensation, ideology and beliefs about power, the degree of safety provided by the welfare state, attitudes about government regulation, and the place of discovery in the overall procedural scheme. In short, to label our system as one that wrongly permits "fishing expeditions" is to miss much of the point. . . .

. . . Consider our historic distrust of concentrated power. Our doctrines of federalism and separation of powers, the right to a jury trial, and the adversary system, including party control, reflect our historic distrust of residing power in one person or limited groups. We do not think that judges would ferret out negative aspects of our opponent's case and positive information to prove our own claims or defenses with the same motivation and intensity that self-interest propels. Perhaps if we had more experience with career judges, elevated as the result of performance based on objective criteria, as opposed to politically-appointed or elected judges, we would have more confidence in turning over discovery to the judiciary. But one must be cautious here. Professor Marcus quotes Professor Damaska on the European experience:

> As Professor Damaska has recognized, Continental civil procedure exhibits "a considerable degree of tolerance — almost insouciance, to common law eyes — for the incompleteness of evidentiary material." Assigning fact gathering to the judge does not solve this problem; "the protagonist who tends to monopolize fact gathering — the judge — is not really very energetic or resolute in his probing. His exercise of his near-monopoly power to develop evidence seems lazy."

Notes and Questions

1. Pretrial discovery is *the* central feature of modern American civil litigation. Most federal cases end at some point during the pretrial process; not even one in fifty goes to trial. Once upon a time, lawyers who practiced in the civil arena called themselves "trial lawyers"; now they call themselves "litigators." Pretrial matters consume the working day, and most of those matters concern discovery.

'Twas not always so. Broad discovery was perhaps the most important invention of the Federal Rules. Discovery had been available in equity, and at common law in some states, but nowhere was discovery available with the breadth or bounty of devices that the Federal Rules made available. Discovery was the grand experiment of the Rules, suited to an age that believed in the power, and the objectivity, of facts.

The rest of the world was, and remains, less impressed with this grand experiment. As Professors Hazard and Subrin note, no other country uses pretrial discovery with anything approaching the enthusiasm of the United States. For instance, in the Hague Convention on the Taking of Evidence Abroad in Civil and Commercial Matters, which has been signed by the United States and sixty-one other countries, forty-four countries either refuse to "execute" letters requesting information from a national of a foreign country "for the purpose of obtaining pretrial discovery of documents as known in the common law countries" or impose limits on discovery.

2. Discovery, which permits an opponent to rummage through file cabinets, medical records, corporate board rooms, and the like, can be a significant invasion of someone's privacy and pocketbook. Should a party have access to discovery simply by filing a complaint that satisfies notice pleading? Could the criticism of American discovery be reduced by heightening pleading requirements? Which seems worse — countenancing such invasions or cutting off some meritorious cases at the pleading stage?

3. Another common criticism of discovery is that it is too expensive. Assuming that lawyers make $250 per hour and that only one lawyer works for each party, every hour in which the parties are mutually engaged in discovery costs $500 — and this does not include other expenses such as transcripts of testimony (which will often cost around $200 per hour), the time of employees or parties assembling documents and appearing for testimony, or the time of additional lawyers. Of course, some of this expense is easier to tolerate if it shortens or obviates altogether the need for trial, but it is often hard to know whether discovery has had that effect.

4. There have been attempts to determine, as an empirical matter, how expensive and how effective discovery is. One study, conducted by the Federal Judicial Center and mentioned by Professor Subrin, examined 1,000 federal cases closed in the last quarter of 1996. The other, conducted by the RAND Corporation, studied 5,222 federal cases filed in 1992 and 1993. The studies used different methods and came to somewhat different conclusions, but they contained significant areas of agreement:

- In many cases, no discovery was conducted at all. Both studies tended to exclude certain kinds of cases in which discovery rarely occurs. Nonetheless, in 38% of the cases in the RAND study and 15% in the FJC study, there was no discovery. The RAND study, which examined a broader array of cases, also found that discovery activity was either absent or very minimal in a majority of cases.

- The usual amount of time and money spent on discovery was not large. The RAND study found that the mean amount of attorney time spent on discovery, per litigant, was 83 hours for cases that lasted at least 270 days. (This figure was 36% of the mean total hours attorneys spent working on a case, and was the largest percentage of time spent working on any single aspect of the case.) The FJC study found that the median total costs for litigation expenses (including fees, transcript, and so forth) were $13,000 per client, about half of which went to discovery expenses. In the FJC study, the median estimate by attorneys was that discovery costs amounted to only 3% of the total at stake in the litigation, though 5% of the attorneys thought that discovery expenses amounted to 32% or more of the stakes.

- By and large, attorneys did not report dissatisfaction with the present discovery system. In the FJC study, 54% of attorneys thought that the expense of discovery was about right in relation to the stakes of the case, 15% thought the expenses too high, 20% thought them too low, and the rest had no opinion. About 80% of attorneys thought that discovery generated the right amount of information to resolve the case fairly, with 10% thinking that it generated too much and 10% thinking that it generated too little. The RAND study focused more on attorney satisfaction with respect to specific aspects of discovery, but did state that "subjective information from our interviews with lawyers also suggests that the median or typical case is not 'the problem.'"

- Both studies suggested that a small minority of cases did present significant discovery problems. The FJC study also reported that attorneys thought that 19% of discovery expenses, constituting 4% of litigation expenses, were unnecessary.

See Thomas E. Willging et al., *An Empirical Study of Discovery and Disclosure Practices Under the 1993 Federal Rule Amendments*, 39 B.C. L. REV. 525 (1998); James S. Kakalik et al., *Discovery Management: Further Analysis of the Civil Justice Reform Act Evaluation Data*, 39 B.C. L. REV. 613 (1998).

Other empirical research has studied the costs associated with discovering electronically stored information (information on computers or other digital media). One FJC study found that "e-discovery" occurred in 30% to 40% of federal civil cases in which any discovery occurred; that cases in which e-discovery occurred had higher reported discovery costs; and that the median costs of e-discovery were about 5% of plaintiffs' total costs and 10% of defendants' total costs of discovery. *See* EMERY G. LEE III & THOMAS E. WILLGING, FED. JUD. CTR., NATIONAL, CASE-BASED CIVIL RULES SURVEY 1, 36, 40 (2009). A later report by the same authors, analyzing the same data in more detail, concluded that "for plaintiffs, electronic discovery was associated with higher costs for all parties requesting ESI, even after controlling for other factors." EMERY G. LEE III & THOMAS E. WILLGING, FED. JUD. CTR., LITIGATION COSTS IN CIVIL CASES: MULTIVARIATE ANALYSIS 5 (2010). For defendants, however, "one cannot conclude that these parties had higher costs than parties in non-ESI cases, once factors such as case complexity, firm size, and stakes, among others, are controlled for." *Id.* at 7. The latter study also found that the costs of litigation (including but not limited to the costs of discovery) increased when the stakes of the litigation were higher, when the case took longer to be resolved, when the case went to trial, and when large law firms were involved. *Id.* at 1. Other studies have painted a less rosy picture. *See, e.g.*, INTERIM REPORT ON THE JOINT PROJECT OF THE AMERICAN COLLEGE OF TRIAL LAWYERS TASK FORCE ON DISCOVERY AND THE INSTITUTE FOR THE ADVANCEMENT OF THE AMERICAN LEGAL SYSTEM 3-5 (2008) (describing survey results that "confirm[ ] that there are serious problems in many parts of the civil justice system, especially the rules governing discovery").

The empirical data tell a cautionary tale: be careful of knee-jerk claims that discovery either does or does not cost too much.

5. The discovery process is not the only way to obtain information. Formal discovery can be supplemented with other methods for finding information — private investigation, interviews, surveys, voluntary disclosure of information, Web searches, requests for information from government agencies, and the like. Good lawyers always supplement formal discovery with informal investigation. Because discovery is the default mechanism, however, the following materials concentrate on it.

SECTION B: THE MECHANICS OF DISCLOSURE AND DISCOVERY

In designing a system to obtain information, three issues are crucial:

- *Method:* What specific devices are available to obtain information?
- *Scope:* What type of information can, and cannot, be obtained?
- *Enforcement:* What happens if persons refuse to provide requested information, or ask for information to which they are not entitled?

This section addresses the methods used to obtain information; the following two sections discuss, respectively, the scope of discovery and the enforcement of the parties' disclosure and discovery obligations.

Rules 26(a) and 30-36 describe the principal ways in which parties can obtain information. These methods divide into two types: *discovery* that a party must initiate (Rule 30-36), and *required disclosures* that occur even without a party's request for the information (Rule 26(a)).

1. Party-Initiated Discovery Devices

Depending on how they are counted, the Federal Rules contain between four and six discovery devices. The four "card-carrying" methods are depositions (Rules 30-32), interrogatories (Rule 33), requests for production of documents and tangible things or inspection of premises (Rule 34), and requests for physical or mental examinations (Rule 35). The two other

CHAPTER THREE   DISCLOSURE AND DISCOVERY

devices are the Rule 36 request for admission and the Rule 45 subpoena to obtain information from nonparties.

Rather than trying to teach the details of each of the party-initiated rules one-by-one — a task that might exhaust you long before you have finished — we have created the following chart. The chart is designed to assist you in learning basic information on each of party-initiated discovery devices, to contrast the various devices, and to suggest some common patterns. The information to fill in each box can be gleaned, either directly or by implication, from the relevant Federal Rules.

leave = 10

	Oral deposition	Written deposition	Interrogatories 214	Request for production 217	Physical/mental exam 222	Request for admission 36 224
Which Federal Rule(s)?	27, 28, 30, 32 (45 for nonparties)		33	34	35	36
From whom is information sought?	Witness (includes party)		any party	any party nonparty	med prof	any party
What type of information is obtained?	Oral testimony		same scope as 26B	scope of 26(b)	mental + phys	truth of any matters
Limits on number or frequency of requests?	10 per side (Rule 30a2 7 hrs per depo 30d1)		25 written	NO	NO? - phys mostly 1	No?
Is prior court approval required?	NO		No?	NO	yes - court ordered?	NO
What response if party believes that request is improper?	?		within 30 days	object	?	object

Notes and Questions

1. Different discovery methods produce different types of information (documents, testimony, written answers). Some methods are more effective than others for getting certain kinds of information. For instance, which of

the following two interrogatories would be more effective at obtaining the requested information?

- State the name and address of every person who has knowledge or information regarding the claims and defenses involved in this litigation.
- Were you negligent in operating your car?

Likewise, what type of issues would you expect a request for admission to be best at eliminating from the case? Consider the following two requests:

- Admit that the attached letter of June 1, 2000 is authentic; and
- Admit that the defendant was negligent in the operation of his car at the time of the accident.

The effective use of discovery — in terms of both cost and obtaining information — is an art form that takes years of practice to perfect. It is possible to state some general principles, *see, e.g.*, PETER T. HOFFMAN & STUART M. ISRAEL, EFFECTIVE DISCOVERY (2017), but for every rule myriad exceptions exist.

2. From the viewpoint of the litigator in an adversarial system, the goals of discovery are to obtain the information necessary to tell a coherent story at trial (and to create a strong bargaining position for settlement), to make sure that the other parties are not hiding information that might destroy the coherence of that story or bargaining position, and to reveal only the information about your own case that you want the other parties to know. Because discovery is costly, a temptation always exists for an adversary to use discovery not to seek information but for a more nefarious purpose: to impose costs on an opponent. It is far from clear how much of this *impositional discovery* in fact occurs, but the notion of impositional discovery has attained something of a mythic quality and is a common criticism of the discovery system.

This view of discovery as an aggressive and uncooperative enterprise is a caricature. Even if lawyers are tempted to be obstreperous, they know that judges will require the production of information despite the lawyers' resistance. A recalcitrant lawyer often increases costs for the client without obtaining any corresponding benefit, and damages his or her ability to obtain reciprocal information without an equal struggle. Most lawyers also cherish, and would never sacrifice, their reputation for playing fair.

Nevertheless, many people see the adversarial system as fundamentally at odds with the cooperative orientation needed for discovery.

3. Here is a test case to ponder as you think about the interplay of adversarialism and discovery. Suppose that your opponent has limited resources; your client is well off. You are deciding whether to *notice* (i.e., schedule) four depositions in four parts of the country. The witnesses have useful information, but you could prove the same points with other, readily available evidence. You believe that the opposing party could not easily afford to pay her lawyer to attend these depositions, and might be willing to settle the case immediately on terms favorable to your client rather than

incur these expenses. Do you notice the depositions? Think first about your answer; then read Fed. R. Civ. P. 26(g)(1)(B)(ii)-(iii), and think again. *See also* Fed. R. Civ. P. 30(b)(4) (on taking depositions by remote means).

4. Depositions are often the best way to obtain information. They are similar to trial testimony in the sense that lawyers ask the *deponents* (or *witnesses*) questions, which deponents answer under oath or affirmation. The deposition is recorded (either by a court reporter or by means such as videotape). Unlike trial testimony, the deposition is usually conducted in an office; the judge is present only in rare instances. Moreover, at trial the lawyer presenting a witness will lead with direct examination, turning the witness over to the adversary's lawyer for cross examination. In depositions lawyers usually ask few questions of their own clients or friendly witnesses; the lawyer for the other side leads the questioning.

Because deposition testimony can sometimes be used at trial, *see* Fed. R. Civ. P. 32(a), lawyers must object to other lawyers' questions, just as they would at trial, if they believe that these questions are improper either in their form or in their substance. If the deposition testimony is offered into evidence, the judge will rule on the objections at that time. Therefore, even if a lawyer objects to a question, the person being deposed must answer it except in the three narrow circumstances listed in Rule 30(c)(2).

In the American system, it is probably malpractice for a lawyer not to meet a client before a deposition in order to "prep" the client for the questions that might be asked. "Preps" of sympathetic nonparty witnesses are also fairly common. (This practice contrasts with the approach of many legal systems, which regard any pre-testimony contact between a lawyer and a witness to be unethical or at least highly suspicious behavior.) Although a lawyer cannot ethically tell a witness what to say, there is nothing that prevents a lawyer from explaining the consequences of answering a question in one fashion or another or from critiquing the deponent's proposed answer. One of the basic rules that many lawyers give to putative deponents is, "Answer truthfully, but don't volunteer information." Given this reality, how likely is the deposition — the pinnacle of American discovery — to lead to the unvarnished truth?

Depositions are also costly. Some of the costs are replicated if the witness testifies at the trial. Does it make sense for witnesses to testify once at deposition and again (assuming that Rule 32(a) does not pertain) at trial?

5. Near the beginning of most federal cases, the parties must confer and plan the course of discovery. Under Rule 16(b), a judge must issue a *scheduling order* that sets deadlines for accomplishing various pretrial tasks. Typically the judge issues the order after conducting a *scheduling conference* with the parties. Fed. R. Civ. P. 16(b)(1). The order must issue within "the earlier of 90 days after any defendant has been served with the complaint or 60 days after any defendant has appeared." Fed. R. Civ. P. 16(b)(2). Rule 26(f)(1) requires the parties to conduct a *discovery-planning conference* at least twenty-one days before the scheduling conference or order. Fed. R. Civ. P. 26(f)(1). They must then submit a joint *discovery report* outlining the parties' *discovery plan* within fourteen days of the

discovery-planning conference. Fed. R. Civ. P. 26(f)(2). Thus, the judge has at least seven days to examine the discovery report before conducting the scheduling conference or issuing the scheduling order; and if the parties disagree about how discovery should be conducted, they may raise the matter with the judge before the issuance of the scheduling order. Although there is little empirical evidence about this process, surveys of federal-court litigators tend to show that the planning and conference requirements are helpful.

6. The discovery-planning conference is one manifestation of a more general movement, known as *case management*, that began to be reflected in the Federal Rules in the early 1980s. The point of case management is to reduce the expense and delay thought to be associated with the pretrial system — and especially with the adversary-controlled discovery system. Case-management techniques, such as discovery-planning conferences under Rule 26(f) and pretrial conferences under Rule 16, are intended to bring the judge more actively into the pretrial process and to head off time-consuming and expensive conflicts over discovery. We study case management in more depth in Chapter Four (*infra* pp. 184-200).

2. Required Initial Disclosure

Read Rule 26(a). You can skim Rules 26(a)(2) and –(a)(3) for now; we will examine them in more detail later. *See infra* p. 158, Notes 2-3; p. 195. Concentrate on Rule 26(a)(1).

Rule 26(a)(1)'s required *initial disclosure* was an invention of the 1993 amendments to the Federal Rules. Except for cases exempt from the process, *see* Fed. R. Civ. P. 26(a)(1)(B), Rule 26(a)(1) requires each party to disclose the identity of witnesses and documents that "the disclosing party may use to support its claims or defenses, unless the use would be solely for impeachment," as well as a computation of damages and any insurance policies. Initial disclosures usually occur either at or within fourteen days after the parties' discovery-planning conference under Rule 26(f). *See* Fed. R. Civ. P. 26(a)(1)(C). If a party fails to make the required disclosures, Rules 37(a)(3)(A) and –(c)(1) govern sanctions for failures to disclose.

Initial disclosure constituted a shift in the thinking that had dominated the discovery rules since their inception: that discovery was party-initiated. *See* Chalick v. Cooper Hosp./Univ. Med. Ctr, 192 F.R.D. 145, 150 (D.N.J. 2000) ("The purpose [of Rule 26(a)] . . . is to streamline discovery and thereby avoid the practice of serving multiple, boilerplate interrogatories and document requests, which themselves bring into play a concomitant set of delays and costs."). How effective would you predict that the initial-disclosure system will be in achieving better, more efficient exchanges of information? *See* James S. Kakalik et al., *Discovery Management: Further Analysis of the Civil Justice Reform Act Evaluation Data*, 39 B.C. L. REV. 613 (1998) (finding no significant difference in either lawyer work hours or the time it takes to resolve a case under a required initial-disclosure policy).

3. Supplementing Disclosures and Responses

Often parties uncover additional documents, witnesses, or information as they continue to investigate their case and prepare for trial. Assume that when the required initial disclosures were made, a party was aware of only two witnesses and five documents that support the party's claims, and the party disclosed that information. Later the party locates three more witnesses and ten more documents. Must the party reveal this additional information? What if a party answers an interrogatory, according to the best of its abilities, but later information now comes to light and makes the original answer, viewed in hindsight, inaccurate?

Originally, the Federal Rules contained no requirement to supplement. Rule 26(e), which required supplementation for the first time, was added in 1970. But that duty was a limited one. In 1993, Rule 26(e) was amended, essentially into its present form, to expand the duty to supplement.

Even now, Rule 26(e) is vague in its particulars. The obligation to supplement kicks in when "the disclosure or discovery response is incomplete or inaccurate," *see* Fed. R. Civ. P. 26(e)(1)(A), but Rule 26(e) provides no definition of these terms. How often must a party supplement discovery? What if a party becomes aware of information that is in the possession of a third person? Does the duty to supplement extend to information of which a party reasonably should have known? Most of the cases discussing Rule 26(e) do not examine these questions; the cases usually involve an abject failure to disclose information that unquestionably should have been disclosed. *See* Bowers v. Nat'l Collegiate Athletic Ass'n, 475 F.3d 524 (3d Cir. 2007) (noting that "the duty of supplementation under Rule 26(e)(2) does not require that a party volunteer information that was not encompassed within the scope of an earlier discovery request," but holding that the withheld information fell within the earlier request).

Isn't there a risk that supplementation imposes a penalty on a diligent party and rewards a lazy party who makes a few basic discovery requests and then lives off the work and wits of the diligent party? Should the issue of supplementation ultimately depend on whether a no-supplementation, a limited-supplementation, or a broad-supplementation rule overall generates more information? *Cf.* Anthony T. Kronman, *Mistake, Disclosure, Information and the Law of Contracts*, 7 J. LEG. STUD. 1 (1978) (arguing that a duty to disclose "deliberately acquired information" — as opposed to "casually acquired information" — during contract negotiations does not promote economic efficiency or a socially optimal level of information).

SECTION C: THE SCOPE OF AND LIMITS ON DISCOVERY

The next issue is the type of information that can legitimately be obtained through discovery. Read Rule 26(b). The second sentence of Rule 26(b)(1) describes the basic scope of discovery:

Parties may obtain discovery regarding any nonprivileged matter that is relevant to any party's claim or defense and proportional to the needs of the case, considering the importance of the issues at stake in the action, the amount in controversy, the parties' relative access to relevant information, the parties' resources, the importance of the discovery in resolving the issues, and whether the burden or expense of the proposed discovery outweighs its likely benefit.

Parsing out this language, Rule 26(b)(1) establishes three limits on the information that the parties can gather in discovery: *relevance*, *privilege*, and *proportionality*. Rule 26(b)(2) provides additional limits on discovery, including limits regarding electronically stored information. Rules 26(b)(3) and –(b)(4) introduce another limit: *work product*.

At trial, the information that the factfinder properly receives is referred to as *admissible evidence*. During pretrial, however, the information that can be obtained is broader than the information that could be presented to the factfinder at trial. The last sentence of Rule 26(b)(1) makes this point clear: "Information within this scope of discovery need not be admissible in evidence to be discoverable." But this sentence is not a *carte blanche* to gather any information. Even if evidentiary admissibility is not required, the information sought in discovery must fit within the limits of Rule 26(b) (relevance, proportionality, no privilege, and no work product).

Relevance and privilege are not defined in Rule 26(b). The concepts of both relevance and privilege, however, have a long and rich history in common-law trials. You might naturally think that relevance and privilege have the same meaning during discovery. For privilege, you are correct: Federal Rule of Evidence 1101(c) states that "[t]he rules on privilege apply to all stages of a case or proceeding," thus equating privilege in the pretrial and trial contexts. The same equivalence is not true for relevance. Federal Rule of Evidence 401 provides a capacious definition of "relevance":

> Evidence is relevant if:
>
> (a) it has any tendency to make a fact more or less probable than it would be without the evidence; and
>
> (b) the fact is of consequence in determining the action.

(Evidence Rules 403-15 provide refinements on this definition that need not concern us.) Courts have generally held that "relevance" has at least as broad a meaning under Civil Rule 26(b)(1) as under Evidence Rule 401. *See Oppenheimer Fund, Inc. v. Sanders*, 437 U.S. 340, 351 (1978) (noting that Rule 26(b)(1)'s relevance requirement "has been construed broadly to encompass any matter that bears on, or that reasonably could lead to other matter that could bear on, any issue that is or may be in the case"); *Price v. Hartford Life & Accident Ins. Co.*, 746 F. Supp. 2d 860, 866 (E.D. Mich. 2010) ("Relevance is . . . a broader concept in the context of discovery compared to evidentiary relevancy.").

Of course, these general considerations do not tell us very much about what "relevance," "privilege," "proportionality," and "work product" mean, or about how much discovery you can obtain from the other side. Invariably, the answers to these questions are case-specific. The following materials provide further guidance.

1. Relevance and Proportionality

For relevance, the critical question is often "relevant to what"? From the inception of the Federal Rule in 1938 until 2000, the answer was "relevant to the subject matter involved in the pending action." In 2000 that standard was changed, so that discovery was limited to information "relevant to the claim or defense of any party"; but discovery "relevant to the subject matter" could still be obtained if the requesting lawyer showed "good cause" (a phrase not defined in Federal Rules). In 2015 the ability to obtain discovery "relevant to the subject matter" was eliminated; discovery requests must now be "relevant to any party's claim or defense."

Once information is deemed "relevant," it must then pass through the screen of proportionality. Proportionality is a concept of more recent vintage, first making its appearance in Rule 26(b)(1) in 1983. It has had a peripatetic existence ever since, moving to the newly created Rule 26(b)(2) in 1993, splitting itself between Rule 26(b)(1) and Rule 26(b)(2) in an amendment in 2000, expanding into the newly drafted e-discovery amendment of Rule 26(b)(2)(B) in 2006, and ultimately returning back to Rule 26(b)(1)'s core definition of the scope of discovery (while still retaining a foothold in Rule 26(b)(2)(C)(iii)) in 2015.

Why has the scope of discovery undergone the tinkering and marginal cutbacks? In *Sibley v. Choice Hotels International,* 2015 WL 9413101, at *2 (E.D.N.Y. Dec. 22, 2015), the court noted that amendments to Rule 26 "reflect evolving judgments as to the proper scope of discovery. Over time, these amendments have been aimed at striking the proper balance between the need for evidence, and the avoidance of undue burden or expense."

As always, the critical issue is how lawyers and judges apply the concepts of relevance and proportionality to their cases. Before you read the following cases on the present scope of discovery, you should know that most of the cases defining the parties' discovery obligations arise when a person fails to provide requested discovery. When the party from whom discovery is sought believes that the request exceeds the permissible scope of discovery, the party generally has two ways to seek to limit the discovery. The first, and typical, way is to file an *objection*. An objection puts the ball back in the court of the party seeking discovery. The seeking party who decides to pursue the discovery must then file a *motion to compel* under Rule 37. Second, and less commonly, the person from whom discovery is sought can file a *motion for a protective order* under Rule 26(c). This motion asks the court to relieve it of — or to limit or condition — the obligation to provide discovery. If the court believes that the discovery should be provided, it grants the motion to compel (or denies the motion for a protective order); the converse is true if the court determines that discovery should not be permitted.

OXBOW CARBON & MINERALS LLC v. UNION PACIFIC R.R.

322 F.R.D. 1 (D.D.C. 2017)

■ HARVEY, United States Magistrate Judge.

This matter was referred to the undersigned for the resolution of all discovery disputes. Presently ripe for resolution is Defendants' motion to compel, requesting that the Court order Plaintiffs to produce all documents belonging to their CEO, the production of which Plaintiffs, in turn, argue would be unduly burdensome and disproportionate to any value the documents might possess to Defendants in this litigation. . . . [T]he Court finds that Defendants' motion to compel should be granted.

BACKGROUND

Plaintiffs are five related companies (collectively, "Oxbow") that mine and sell coal and petroleum coke ("petcoke"). They allege in the Amended Complaint that Union Pacific ("UP") and BNSF Railway Company ("BNSF") — both railroad companies with which Oxbow contracts to ship coal and petcoke — conspired to engage in anticompetitive conduct from 2004 to 2012 in violation of the Sherman Antitrust Act, codified at 15 U.S.C. §§ 1 and 2, that forced Oxbow to pay higher prices to ship coal and petcoke. Specifically, Oxbow believes that UP and BNSF conspired to (1) fix fuel rates applied to commercial rail freight service above competitive levels through a uniform fuel surcharge and (2) allocate certain markets for coal shipment to each other, granting UP a monopoly in at least one region of the country. Oxbow claims it paid Defendants more than $50,000,000 in illegal fuel surcharges as a result of the conspiracy. Oxbow seeks to recover treble damages under 15 U.S.C. § 15, as well as its "lost business and profits" that proximately resulted from the conspiracy.

In their motion, Defendants request that the Court compel Oxbow to add William I. Koch ("Koch"), Oxbow's founder, CEO, and [principal] owner as a document custodian whose records will be searched for material responsive to Plaintiffs' discovery requests. Defendants maintain that Koch indisputably possesses relevant, unique information responsive to their requests, and argue that Oxbow has improperly refused to produce this information based on the unsupported theory that production of his documents would be disproportionately burdensome and duplicative of the documents produced from the search of the nineteen other Oxbow document custodians' files. Based upon its review of the documents already produced from the other Oxbow custodians, Defendants believe that Koch's records contain information that would, among other things, reveal that market forces — as opposed to Defendants' alleged collusion — contributed to the increasing rail freight costs and any of Oxbow's lost profits. Relatedly, Defendants assert that their discovery request is proportionate and reasonable in light of the facts of this case, including the tens of millions of dollars that Oxbow seeks in damages.

In their opposition, Oxbow argues that Defendants have failed to satisfy their burden of demonstrating that the discovery they seek is responsive and not unduly burdensome. Based on their calculations, Oxbow estimated that adding Koch as a document custodian would result in roughly 130 gigabytes of additional documents to be filtered through the parties' previously-agreed-upon search terms, a process that Oxbow initially estimated would cost $250,000. Oxbow further contends that many of Koch's documents would likely be duplicative of the other custodians' documents or only marginally responsive given Koch's senior position over a conglomerate of Oxbow companies, only some of which are involved in the coal and petcoke businesses. Despite these arguments, Oxbow represented at the first hearing on Defendants' motion that it was open to analyzing a random sample of Koch's records using the agreed-upon search terms to provide the parties with concrete numbers regarding the responsiveness of Koch's documents to the terms and with a basis to negotiate new search terms if necessary. Accordingly, the undersigned held Defendants' motion in abeyance pending the analysis of a sample of Koch's documents and the parties' attempt to negotiate a resolution of the dispute themselves.

Following the hearing, Oxbow collected a total of 467,614 documents from Koch's electronic and physical files and provided them to a vendor for processing. After removing any duplicative records, the vendor searched Koch's documents using the previously-agreed-upon search terms, which yielded 45,639 document hits — 82,600 documents in total when including "families" of documents. The vendor collected a random sample of ten percent of these hits and any associated families — 12,074 documents in total — and provided them to Oxbow for review for privilege and responsiveness. Of these 12,074 documents, Oxbow determined that approximately 1,300 documents — 11.67 percent of them — were actually responsive to the search terms and produced them to Defendants. In total, the initial processing of Koch's records and review of the sample documents cost Oxbow $57,197.95. Based on its experience reviewing the sample documents, Oxbow now estimates that it will cost approximately $85,000 to process, review, and produce the remainder of Koch's documents to the Defendants, bringing the total cost of the effort, including the review of the sample documents, to approximately $142,000 — significantly less than Oxbow's original estimate of $250,000. . . .

Unfortunately, the sampling effort did not result in the parties resolving the dispute without further intervention of the Court. . . . Accordingly, Plaintiffs asked again for the Court to deny the motion to compel or, in the alternative, order Defendants to bear the cost of the production of the documents it seeks. . . .

LEGAL STANDARD

Rule 37 of the Federal Rules of Civil Procedure provides that, "[o]n notice to other parties and all affected persons, a party may move for an order compelling disclosure of discovery" from a party who fails to comply with its discovery obligations. Fed. R. Civ. P. 37(a). The party that brings the motion to compel bears the initial burden of "proving that the opposing party's answers were incomplete," Equal Rights Ctr. v. Post Prop., Inc., 246 F.R.D. 29, 32 (D.D.C. 2007) (internal citations omitted), and "explaining how the requested information is relevant." Jewish War Veterans of the United States of Am., Inc. v. Gates, 506 F. Supp. 2d 30, 42 (D.D.C. 2007). If the movant satisfies this burden, the burden then shifts to the non-movant "to explain why discovery should not be permitted." *Id*.

[The court briefly discussed the "broad sweep of Rule 26(b)(1)."] The broad presumption in favor of discovery of relevant information embodied in Rule 26 is not without limits, however. Instead, under the amended Rule 26, discovery must be relevant and "proportional to the needs of the case." Fed. R. Civ. P. 26(b)(1). To determine whether a discovery request is proportional, courts weigh the following six factors: "(1) the importance of the issues at stake in this action; (2) the amount in controversy; (3) the parties' relative access to relevant information; (4) the parties' resources; (5) the importance of the discovery in resolving the issues; and (6) whether the burden or expense of the proposed discovery outweighs its likely benefit." Williams v. BASF Catalysts, LLC, 2017 WL 3317295, at *4 (D.N.J. Aug. 3, 2017).

"[N]o single factor is designed to outweigh the other factors in determining whether the discovery sought is proportional," and all proportionality determinations must be made on a case-by-case basis. *Williams*, 2017 WL 3317295, at *4 (internal citations omitted). To be sure, however, "the amendments to Rule 26(b) do not alter the basic allocation of the burden on the party resisting discovery to — in order to successfully resist a motion to compel — specifically object and show that . . . a discovery request would impose an undue burden or expense or is otherwise objectionable." Mir v. L–3 Commc'ns Integrated Sys., L.P., 319 F.R.D. 220, 226 (N.D. Tex. 2016).

DISCUSSION

. . .

. . . In its briefing, Oxbow declines to address any of the other proportionality factors highlighted in Rule 26 — namely, the importance of the issues at stake in this action, the amount in controversy, the parties' relative access to relevant information, the parties' resources, or the importance of the discovery in resolving the issues in this case, see Fed. R. Civ. P. 26(b)(1) — stressing only that the burden and cost of complying with Defendants' request would outweigh its likely benefit. Weighing the six Rule 26 proportionality factors, however, demonstrates that adding Koch as a custodian of documents to be searched for material responsive to Defendants' discovery requests in this matter will be neither unduly burdensome nor unreasonably expensive in light of the facts of this case. Likewise, the Court finds that the instant circumstances do not warrant shifting the costs of doing so to Defendants. . . .

A. The Proportionality of Defendants' Discovery Request

1. *The Importance of the Issues at Stake*

This first Rule 26 factor calls for the Court to "examine[ ] 'the significance of the substantive issues [at stake in the litigation], as measured in philosophic, social, or institutional terms.'" [Arrow Enter. Computing Solutions, Inc. v.] BlueAlly, 2017 WL 876266, at *4 [(E.D.N.C. Mar. 3, 2017)] (quoting Fed. R. Civ. P. 26 advisory committee's note). For example, courts should carefully scrutinize discovery requests in "cases in public policy spheres, such as employment practices, free speech, and other matters," which often "seek[ ] to vindicate vitally important personal and public values" and "may have importance far beyond the monetary amount involved." By Oxbow's own suggestion, the instant case involves important issues and has the potential to broadly impact a wide range of third parties not involved in the litigation. Oxbow has stated that a favorable ruling from this Court "could benefit all of America's shippers and consumers, saving billions of dollars a year in reduced rail freight charges in the United States." What is more, Koch himself has publicly accused Defendants of long relying on "overreaching and abusive behavior" to "shortchange[ ] the American consumer," and of "using aggressive tactics to prevent competition and intimidate customers," including "American farmers, miners[,] and shippers[.]"

Defendants, for their part, do not disagree with Oxbow's estimation of the significance of this case, noting that Oxbow has made serious allegations against Defendants that have the potential to impact many people. Accordingly, the undersigned finds that the importance of the issues at stake here weighs in favor of granting Defendants' discovery request, which Oxbow concedes will produce documents that are relevant to the resolution of this case's claims.

2. *The Amount in Controversy*

Under the second proportionality factor, courts should "compare[ ] the cost of discovery to the amount in controversy to determine [the proposed discovery's] proportionality." Here, Oxbow seeks to recover the more than $50,000,000 in illegal fuel surcharges it alleges were the result of the Defendants' collusion. It also seeks recovery of its "lost business and profits," and a trebling of its damages under 15 U.S.C. § 15. While Oxbow does not specifically quantify these damages in its Amended Complaint, Defendants have suggested that Oxbow seeks to recover over $150 million . . . . Meanwhile, Oxbow's estimated cost of complying with Defendants' proposed discovery is approximately $140,000, including the $57,197.95 that Oxbow has already spent on sampling Koch's documents. Given the very substantial amount of damages that Oxbow seeks to recover in this case, its cost of complying with the discovery request to produce information relevant to Defendants' defense of Oxbow's claims does not strike the undersigned as excessive. Accordingly, the Court finds that this factor, too, favors granting Defendants' discovery request.

3. The Parties' Relative Access to the Relevant Information

In considering this factor, courts look for "information asymmetry" — a circumstance in which one party has very little discoverable information while the other party has vast amounts of discoverable information. In such a case, "the burden of responding to discovery lies heavier on the party who has more information, and properly so." To the extent this factor is applicable here, any informational asymmetry favors Oxbow. Indeed, neither party disputes that Koch is in possession of relevant, unique information, and there appears to be no other way for Defendants to obtain this information than moving to compel Oxbow to produce it. Accordingly, the Court finds that this factor militates in favor of granting Defendants' request.

4. The Parties' Resources

Taking into account the parties' resources, the Court again concludes that this factor weighs in favor of granting Defendants' request. While discovery should not be used to "wage a war of attrition or as a device to coerce a party," regardless of whether the party is "financially weak or affluent," Oxbow represented at the hearing in this matter that it does not object to Defendants' request based on an inability to pay for it. Accordingly, the undersigned sees no reason to deny Defendants' request on this basis.

5. The Importance of the Discovery in Resolving the Issues

This fifth factor requires courts to determine whether "[t]he issues at stake are at the very heart of [the] litigation." Labrier v. State Farm Fire and Cas. Co., 314 F.R.D. 637, 643 (W.D. Mo. 2016). Though Oxbow initially objected to the relevance of any documents in Koch's possession, it has since acknowledged that Koch's records contain relevant and unique documents, although not in the same ratio as other Oxbow custodians' records, and has produced a portion of these documents to Defendants. The Court appreciates that Koch's files do not appear to contain as a high a proportion of responsive documents as the files of custodians who dealt exclusively with Oxbow's coal and petcoke business, but it strains reason to suggest that the principal owner and CEO of a company, who has publicly commented on the importance and magnitude of litigation to which his company is a party and in which the financial health of his company is at issue, would have no unique information relevant to that litigation in his possession. While it may be too early in the production process to determine exactly how significant Koch's records are, the categories of relevant documents identified by Defendants after reviewing the approximately 1,300 documents produced from Koch's files indicates to the Court that

Defendants' discovery request has merit and is not intended to be the first strike in a war of attrition or a coercion tactic. Accordingly, the Court concludes that this factor favors granting Defendants' proposed discovery.

6. Whether the Burden or Expense of the Proposed Discovery Outweighs its Likely Benefit

Oxbow rests its argument entirely on this final factor, asserting that it is the most important of the Rule 26 proportionality factors and counsels against granting Defendants' proposed discovery. In support of its argument, Oxbow contends that its random sampling analysis suggests that approximately half of the agreed-upon search terms' hits on Koch's documents are false positives with no or only marginal relevance to the litigation. . . . [I]t asserts that the $85,000 that it estimates it will take to review and produce the remaining responsive documents from Koch's files is prohibitively burdensome.

The Court disagrees. The cost of reviewing and producing Koch's documents does not strike the undersigned as unduly burdensome or disproportionate, especially given the discovery conducted to date and the damages that Oxbow seeks in this action. Plaintiffs' counsel explained at the second hearing in this matter that Oxbow has spent $1.391 million to date on reviewing and producing approximately 584,000 documents from its nineteen other custodians and Oxbow's email archive. And again, Oxbow seeks tens of millions of dollars from Defendants. Through that lens, the estimated cost of reviewing and producing Koch's responsive documents — even considering the total approximate cost of $142,000 for that effort, which includes the expense of the sampling effort — while certainly high, is not so unreasonably high as to warrant rejecting Defendants' request out of hand. *See* Zubulake v. UBS Warburg, LLC, 217 F.R.D. 309, 321 (S.D.N.Y. 2003) (explaining, in the context of a cost-shifting request, that "[a] response to a discovery request costing $100,000 sounds (and is) costly, but in a case potentially worth millions of dollars, the cost of responding may not be unduly burdensome"). Moreover, based on the parties' representations at the second hearing in this matter, the projected number of responsive and unique documents in Koch's files — approximately 10,000 — is largely consistent with the number of responsive and unique documents produced by the other Oxbow custodians, and the responsiveness rate of Koch's documents — 11.67 percent — while low, is not the lowest among Oxbow's custodians.

In light of the above analysis — including the undersigned's assessment of each of the Rule 26 proportionality factors, all of which weigh in favor of granting Defendants' motion — the Court is unwilling to find that the burden of reviewing the remaining 65,000 responsive documents for a fraction of the cost of discovery to date should preclude Defendants' proposed request. For all of the reasons stated above, and absent any evidence establishing that Defendants are using the discovery of Koch's records to wage a war of attrition or as a device to coerce Oxbow, the Court finds that Defendants' motion must be granted.

B. *Oxbow's Request to Shift Discovery Costs to Defendants*

... "The presumption under the Federal Rules of Civil Procedure is that the producing party bears the costs of complying with a discovery request," but "the Court may shift a portion of the costs to the requesting party in the event that the discovery request would unduly burden the producing party." D'Onofrio v. SFX Sports Group, Inc., 254 F.R.D. 129, 134 (D.D.C. 2008). While the seminal case on cost-shifting in electronic discovery disputes focused its analysis on the shifting of expenses arising from the compelled production of "inaccessible" electronic information, *see Zubulake*, 217 F.R.D. at 318, courts have, over the years, looked beyond accessibility to determine whether to shift discovery costs.

Reflecting this development, Rule 26 was amended in 2015 to expressly recognize the courts' capacity to order cost-shifting in the hopes of forestalling "the temptation [that] some parties may feel to contest" the courts' authority to do so. *See* Fed. R. Civ. P. 26 advisory committee's notes. Specifically, the amendment added subsection 26(c)(1)(B), which permits a court to issue an order, for good cause, to protect a party from "annoyance, embarrassment, oppression, or undue burden or expense," by specifying the terms of discovery, "including time and place or the allocation of expenses[.]" In considering this amendment, courts have found that determining whether a discovery request warrants cost-shifting based on its burdensomeness turns on: the needs of the case; the amount in controversy; the parties' resources; the importance of the issues at stake; and the importance of the proposed discovery in resolving those issues. To be sure, however, this amendment does not "imply that cost-shifting should become a common practice," and "[c]ourts and parties should continue to assume that a responding party ordinarily bears the costs of responding." Fed. R. Civ. P. 26 advisory committee's notes.

Oxbow has failed to rebut the presumption imposed by the Federal Rules of Civil Procedure that it should bear the cost of complying with Defendants' proposed discovery. The above analysis of the Rule 26(b) proportionality factors, which are essentially identical to the factors courts have considered in determining whether to shift discovery costs under Rule 26(c), confirms that Defendants' proposed discovery does not impose an undue burden or expense that warrants a reallocation of expenses. Suffice it to say that, in this case, Oxbow must bear the cost of producing the unique and relevant discovery in its possession, custody and control needed by Defendants to defend against the allegations it raises in the Amended Complaint. Accordingly, Oxbow's request to shift discovery fees to Defendants in whole or in part is denied.

CONCLUSION

For the foregoing reasons, Defendants' motion to compel the production of documents from Koch's records is granted. Oxbow shall produce all unique and relevant documents from Koch's records within 30 days of the entry of this Memorandum Opinion.

Notes and Questions

1. Federal district judges often refer disputes regarding disclosure or discovery to magistrate judges. A party dissatisfied with a magistrate judge's order can ask the district judge to review it. Because the magistrate judge's order is not dispositive (i.e., the order does not result in judgment for a party on a claim or defense), 28 U.S.C. § 636(b)(1) and Rule 72(a) provide a deferential standard of review: the district judge may reject the ruling only when it is "clearly erroneous" or "contrary to law." Under that standard, a district judge reviews de novo any legal determinations that a magistrate judge makes, but cannot overturn a magistrate judge's factual findings or discretionary application of law to fact "unless it strikes us as wrong with the force of a 5 week old, unrefrigerated, dead fish." S Indus., Inc. v. Centra 2000, Inc., 249 F.3d 625, 627 (7th Cir. 2001).

Because disclosure-and-discovery rulings of the magistrate judge or district judge are not dispositive, the losing party has no immediate right to appeal an adverse ruling to the court of appeals. This fact can put the losing party in a bind; especially when that party is ordered to provide disclosure or discovery, the horse will have left the barn long before the court of appeals ever decides whether the order was correct. As Chapter Six will discuss in more detail, the losing party can employ some mechanisms to seek to obtain immediate review of non-final decisions. In the discovery area, the most common is the writ of mandamus, but courts of appeals "will grant a writ only when the district court has acted wholly without jurisdiction or so clearly abused its discretion as to constitute usurpation of power." *See In re* Cooper Tire & Rubber Co., 568 F.3d 1180, 1186 (10th Cir. 2009) (internal quotation marks omitted). When the losing party appeals from a discovery ruling on relevance or proportionality grounds, courts of appeals review the decision using an abuse-of-discretion standard. *See, e.g.,* Vallejo v. Amgen, Inc., 903 F.3d 733, 742 (8th Cir. 2018) ("We review a district court's discovery rulings for abuse of discretion. Our review is both narrow and deferential, and relief will be granted on the basis of erroneous discovery rulings only where the errors amount to a gross abuse of discretion resulting in fundamental unfairness.") (internal quotation marks and brackets omitted). In short, the district court has great sway over the shape of discovery in most cases.

2. Do the proportionality factors require judicial omniscience? For instance, to calculate "whether the burden or expense of proposed discovery outweighs its likely benefit" — the basic concept of proportionality that seems reasonable enough in theory — the court must know what the expected value of the case would be without the information, how much the information will change the expected value, and what the cost of collecting the information will be. As *Oxbow* shows, the court might have some sense of the last variable, but it is in a poor position to assess the first variable, and it cannot begin to assess the second variable without knowing what the information is. Does *Oxbow* even try to strike the balance? *See* 8 CHARLES ALAN WRIGHT ET AL., FEDERAL PRACTICE AND PROCEDURE § 2008.1, at 155 (3d ed. 2010) (noting that "the proportionality concept . . . seemed to require

great familiarity with the case," thus stymying its implementation); *cf.* Thompson v. Dept. of Hous. & Urban Dev., 199 F.R.D. 168, 171 (D. Md. 2001) (noting that, "[d]espite the obvious utility of [the proportionality factors] in tailoring discovery," they "have tended largely to be ignored by the litigants, and, less frequently than desirable, used by the courts").

3. Given the challenges in arguing whether discovery is (or is not) proportional, the burden of proof on the issue may be crucial. After the 2015 amendment to Rule 26(b), some courts have held that "a party seeking discovery of relevant, non-privileged information must show, before anything else, that the discovery sought is proportional to the needs of the case." Gilead Scis., Inc. v. Merck & Co., 2016 WL 146574, at *1 (N.D. Cal. Jan. 13, 2016). Most cases, however, "require proportionality input from *both* sides with the court ultimately responsible for the correct balancing." Lakes v. Bath & Body Works LLC, 2018 WL 533915 (E.D. Cal. Jan. 23, 2018). Courts adopting the latter view often allocate the burden on a particular proportionality factor to the party with better access to information on that issue.

4. Test your grasp of proportionality with these hypotheticals:

- The plaintiff was permanently scarred when a triple-wick candle with a eucalyptus-spearmint scent exploded. She sought discovery on defects for all candles sold by the defendant (including single-wick, double-wick, triple-wick, taper, and votive candles and also including all fragrances). The defendant estimated that it had sold millions of candles and also raised privacy concerns about disclosing the identities of consumers who had contacted it with complaints. Is this discovery proportional? *See Lakes*, 2018 WL 533915.

- The plaintiff sued the defendant on a patent claim involving a chemical compound. A critical issue was the date on which each party had first synthesized the compound. A 2003 photograph showed the plaintiff in possession of a tube of a chemical with the molecular weight of 259.2, which was the weight of the compound at issue, along with a number of other tubes. The plaintiff provided evidence from witnesses that the tube in the photograph was not the disputed chemical. Unwilling to take the plaintiff's word for it, the defendant sought discovery regarding all of the tubes in the photograph and their contents. Proportional? *See Gilead*, 2016 WL 146574.

- The plaintiff claimed that it had reimbursed the defendants for medically unnecessary services that the defendants fraudulently submitted. The scheme involved a landlord who allegedly supplied patients to the defendants in return for kickbacks, which were disguised as rent payments. The plaintiff sought bank records and tax returns from the defendants in an attempt to prove that these referrals constituted a large portion of the defendants' income, making them financially dependent on the landlord's scheme. Proportional? *See* State Farm Mut. Auto. Ins. Co. v. Fayda, 2015 WL 7871037 (S.D.N.Y. Dec. 3, 2015).

5. As *Oxbow* shows, even if a party is entitled to discovery, a separate issue is who must pay for it. Traditionally the party *responding* to disclosure or discovery bears the cost of doing so. The 2015 amendments bulked up Rule 26(c)(1)(B) by allowing a court to enter a protective order that specifies "the allocation of expenses" regarding disclosure or discovery. Before 2015 courts possessed this power, but the new language made more explicit the court's power to order the party requesting discovery or benefitting from disclosure to bear some or all of the cost. As with the amendment to Rule 26(b)(1), it remains to be seen how courts will exercise this power; *Oxbow*, for example, declined to invoke it. As a principled matter, should we make someone who wants something (discoverable information) pay for it? Would a "requester pays" approach cut down on excessive discovery requests? Would it give the responding party an incentive to jack up the costs of responding? Would it make it too hard for parties without substantial resources (the little guys) to prevail against parties that hold significant amounts of information (the fat cats)?

6. For a series of creative proposals to cut down on the cost of discovery, see Symposium, *The Future of Discovery*, 71 Vand. L. Rev. 1775 (2018).

7. A modern context that has become fertile ground for testing the limits of relevance and proportionality is electronically stored information. Read Rule 26(b)(2)(B) and the following case.

UNITED STATES EX REL. GUARDIOLA V. RENOWN HEALTH

2015 WL 5056726 (D. Nev. Aug. 25, 2015)

■ COOKE, United States Magistrate Judge.

Before the court is the motion of relator Cecilia Guardiola ("relator") to compel production of "gap period" emails, which are email communications for the period from April 2011 through February 28, 2013. . . .

I. PROCEDURAL HISTORY

This is a *qui tam* action under the False Claims Act, 31 U.S.C. §§ 3729-33. Relator alleges that, while working at Renown from June 2006 through June 2014, she discovered the existence of a scheme whereby Renown knowingly submitted false inpatient reimbursement claims to Medicare that should have been billed on a less expensive, outpatient basis.

Initially, relator sent two document production requests to Renown. The court set the relevant timespan for production as June 1, 2006 through June 30, 2014, an eight-year period. Over the ensuing months, the parties reached compromises on a variety of issues, such as narrowing of search terms and limiting the production of relevant emails to certain individuals. Renown has produced or will produce emails for (1) June 2006 through March 2011 and (2) February 2013 through June 2014. However, as explained below, Renown has not produced emails for a so-called "gap period" between April 2011 and February 2013.

Renown explains technology, email retention policy, and cost as the reasons for the existence of the gap period. Between April 2011 and February 2013, Renown used Arcserve, a then-leading backup solution system, to back up email and other data. Prior to April 2011, the beginning of the gap period, Renown lacked an email retention policy and retained all emails. Thus, as of March 2011, Renown possessed email for every employee from the beginning of their employment until that date, and all of these emails were backed up and are now located on the March 2011 backup tapes. With the advent of Arcserve in April 2011, Renown also adopted an email retention period of six months: as emails became six-months old, they became inactive data and were then stored on a backup tape. Because Renown began routinely backing up its network servers and stored emails, the gap-period emails are presently located on a variety of backup tapes that post-date March 2011.

On the belief that the March 2011 tapes held the greatest number and scope of historical emails relevant to this litigation, Renown restored the March 2011 backup tapes, via a third-party vendor, and produced emails contained therein. Renown indicates that the restoration cost alone, i.e., excluding attorney review and production, exceeded $35,000. Including review and production, the cost surpassed $100,000.

Due to time and expense, Renown has not attempted, and remains unwilling, to restore the gap-period tapes. It avers that its IT department cannot restore the gap-period emails in-house; therefore, it would have to outsource the work for a total cost of at least $248,000, which includes data processing and contract attorney review. Relator's position is that Renown should be ordered to produce them because they are highly relevant to her claims.

II. LEGAL STANDARD

. . .

... [W]hen considering a motion to compel production of [electronically stored information, or "ESI"], the court conducts a three-part inquiry. First, the court determines whether the party opposing production has demonstrated that the ESI is not reasonably accessible due to undue burden or undue cost. See Fed. R. Civ. P. 26(b)(2)(B). Second, upon a requisite showing, the court asks whether the party seeking production has demonstrated, notwithstanding the inaccessibility, good cause for production in light of the factors discussed in Rule 26(b)(2)(C) and the Advisory Committee notes. See 2006 Advisory Committee Notes to FRCP 26(b) (listing seven factors).

Finally, if the ESI is not reasonably accessible, the court may consider whether cost sharing is appropriate. When considering cost shifting, courts in this circuit rely on the seminal *Zubulake* factors. See Zubulake v. UBS

Warburg LLC, 217 F.R.D. 309, 324 (S.D.N.Y. 2003) ("*Zubulake I*") (identifying seven factors); Zubulake v. UBS Warburg LLC, 216 F.R.D. 280, 284 (S.D.N.Y. 2003) ("*Zubulake II*") (applying those factors).

III. DISCUSSION AND ANALYSIS

The court considers in turn each step of the tripartite inquiry.

A. *Are the gap-period emails not reasonably accessible because of burden or cost?*

1. *Undue Burden*

Under Rule 26(b)(2)(B), it is Renown's burden to show that the gap-period emails are not reasonably accessible due to undue burden. . . . Renown contends that the fact of "backup tapes" alone establishes that the emails are not reasonably accessible, and it relies on a string of cases that have held backup tapes are inaccessible. *See Zubulake I,* 217 F.R.D. at 319–20; OpenTV v. Liberate Techs., 219 F.R.D. 474, 477 (N.D. Cal. 2003) ("backup tapes are considered inaccessible, because they are not organized for retrieval of individual documents or files."). On the weight of this authority, Renown urges that backup tapes are inaccessible *per se.* . . .

As a preliminary matter, the plain language of Rule 26(b)(2)(B) instructs that "undue burden," rather than the format of the ESI, is to guide the court's analysis. Technological features of the storage media do enter the analysis, but only as they relate to the undue burden inquiry. Stated differently, undue burden is fact specific and no format is inaccessible *per se.* Even if a particular format typically yields an inaccessibility finding, the party opposing production, who bears the burden at this step, must establish that restoration and production of its particular tapes or other storage media, due to their particular aspects and features, would impose undue burden or cost. . . .

The court concludes that Renown has failed to show that the gap-period emails are not reasonably accessible because of undue burden. As described above, Renown has produced emails from the restored March 2011 backup tapes. In so doing, Renown has demonstrated that it is technologically feasible to restore and produce the gap-period emails. Renown argues that the burden of restoration is so great that it . . . must and will again use a third-party vendor. By implication, Renown will ameliorate the burdens of in-house production, though at some cost. As Renown acknowledges, the tapes containing the gap-period emails have already been identified. Accordingly, the court cannot fathom what burden accompanies third-party restoration. Renown has not stated that use of a vendor will nevertheless impose burdens — in terms of staff resources, delay of other critical IT projects, or inadequate attention to existing technology infrastructure.

At bottom, there will be a burden *or* a cost, but not both. . . . [T]he remaining question is only whether undue cost of the third-party vendor makes the gap-period emails not reasonably accessible.

2. *Undue Cost*

Undue cost is the second factor that the court considers in the reasonable inaccessibility analysis. As above observed, Renown indicated at oral argument that it will use a third-party vendor to restore the gap-period emails, a decision that it deems "the most cost-effective method." On the basis of a quote for the restoration, Renown states that the likely cost is $136,000, with a range of $96,000 to $147,400. Because this sum includes only data services, without storage or attorney review time, Renown estimates that the actual cost is between $248,000 and $310,000. At oral argument, relator argued that the relevant cost is only that of data production, excluding any review or storage costs, and that the smaller sum is a minuscule expense to an entity with $2.6 billion in annual patient revenues.

The court rejects Renown's argument that "cost" under Rule 26(b)(2)(B) includes document review and storage. Renown cites no authority for the proposition that review costs — ordinarily borne by the producing party — fall into cost under Rule 26(b)(2)(B). . . .

The $136,000 figure for restoration is not an undue cost that renders the gap-period emails reasonably inaccessible. Undue cost is examined not as a number alone, but instead within context of myriad facts. . . .

. . . [T]he context of this case demands a finding that restoration is not unduly costly. During the gap period, Renown elected to store typical disaster recovery tapes with archival data. This is an important distinction because archival data may contain the only remaining copies of relevant documents. . . . ESI is now a common part and cost of business. Businesses are best situated to weigh for themselves the costs and benefits of various technology solutions in light of their needs. These needs should include some thought to the risk of litigation and corresponding discovery obligations. To the extent that restoration costs in this case owe to Renown's failure to earlier implement a sensible email retention policy and its choice to use an archival/backup solution that did not maintain ESI in an indexed or otherwise searchable manner — a conclusion that Renown itself advances — Renown must bear some responsibility within the consideration of whether the restoration cost is undue. . . .

Renown had a records retention policy before and after the gap period that allowed for searching, reviewing, and printing documents relevant to discovery requests and Renown's own business needs. The policy and corresponding technology features simultaneously served as a backup system for disaster recovery and also an archival system of documents kept for future business purposes. . . . [D]uring the gap period, Renown in effect stored randomly hundreds of thousands of documents, no differently than if had tossed files into banker's boxes without labels or organization. . . .

. . . [T]he court concludes that the ESI in this case is not reasonably inaccessible due to undue cost. In light of the court's discussion of Renown's practices, $136,000 is not an unreasonable sum. *Compare* Gen. Elec. Co. v. Wilkins, 2012 WL 570048, at *5 (E.D. Cal. Feb. 21, 2012) (finding reasonable inaccessibility due to undue cost where backup restoration estimates exceeded $2,000,000). The restoration cost, as relator correctly notes, is an infinitesimally small portion of Renown's annual revenues. Absent a demonstration through authority or other cogent arguments that a $136,000 bill makes the cost undue in light of Renown's decisions and gap-period practices, the court is compelled by Rule 26 to find that the emails are reasonably accessible and discoverable. Relator's motion to compel shall be granted.

B. Does good cause support production of the gap-period emails?

Although the court's step-one finding regarding reasonable accessibility ends the inquiry, the court nevertheless considers in the alternative whether good cause supports discoverability of the gap-period emails. . . .

To decide whether good cause exists, the court must apply a "balancing test of the costs and potential benefits of the requested discovery under Rule 26(b)(2)(B)," taking into account seven factors: (1) the specificity of the discovery request; (2) the quantity of information available from other and more easily accessed sources; (3) the failure to produce relevant information that seems likely to have existed but is no longer available on more easily accessed sources; (4) the likelihood of finding relevant, responsive information that cannot be obtained from other, more easily accessed sources; (5) predictions as to the importance and usefulness of further information; (6) the importance of the issues at stake in the litigation; and (7) the parties' resources. 2006 Advisory Committee Notes to Fed. R. Civ. P. 26(b). The court considers each factor in turn.

1. The Specificity of the Discovery Request

Relator argues that she has dramatically narrowed the scope of this case by limiting her claims to a subset of specialties and procedures. Correspondingly, she has repeatedly and consistently narrowed her discovery requests and worked with Renown to reduce their production burden. . . .

This factor favors relator. The parties have worked diligently for the past several months to narrow, clarify, and/or remove from consideration many areas of dispute, including deciding on keyword searches and limiting custodians. Because of the agreement regarding the search terms, the court finds that the discovery relator seeks in her motion is sufficiently specific. . . .

2. Quantity of Information Available from Other and More Easily Accessed Sources

. . . [R]elator argues that there is no alternative or readily accessible source of the communications contained in the gap-period emails. Renown's position is that it has searched and produced over 68,000 documents from other, more easily accessible sources, including its internal server system and individual employees' personal hard drives. In restoring, cataloguing, searching, reviewing, and producing these documents, Renown avers that it has spent over $850,000. Renown suggests that this information is comparable to the gap-period emails, and it argues that relator has not identified any particular documents that she believes are missing from their existing production, either specifically or by category.

This factor favors relator. That thousands of other documents have been produced does not supplant the need for the gap-period emails. The court agrees with relator that email has become the principal form of workplace communication. As the court in *Zubulake II* noted, "an email contains the precise words used by the author. Because of that, it is a particularly powerful form of proof at trial [when] offered as an admission of a party opponent." 216 F.R.D. at 287. . . . The gap-period emails are highly and, very likely, uniquely relevant to relator's claims.

3. *Failure to Produce Relevant Information that Seems Likely to Have Existed but Is No Longer Available on More Easily Accessed Sources*

The parties agree that this factor is neutral. The court concurs.

4. *The Likelihood of Finding Relevant, Responsive Information that Cannot Be Obtained from Other, More Easily Accessed Sources*

Relator asserts that the gap period represents a critical span of time because significant events occurred during that gap period that are highly relevant to her claims. . . .

This factor also favors relator. She has demonstrated in great detail the events that occurred during that gap period and how email communications during this time span might well relate to her claims. Because of the role of email communications at Renown, it is highly likely that the gap-period emails contain relevant statements regarding these events. The court is persuaded that the gap-period emails likely contain communications unavailable from other sources.

5. *Predictions of the Importance and Usefulness of Further Information*

For similar reasons as those already discussed, relator predicts the gap-period emails will provide important information, and she provides several examples of discussions that the emails likely contain. Renown responds that these examples are merely speculative, and the likely usefulness is diminished due to the volume of prior production.

Based upon the discussion of factor four, this factor favors relator.

[6]. *Importance of Issues at Stake in the Litigation*

The parties strongly differ in their analyses of the importance of issues at stake in this case. Not surprisingly, relator points out that the False

Claims Act is a potent tool for rooting out waste and fraud in government and that preventing, reporting, and prosecuting fraud against the government is an issue of great importance. In contrast, Renown characterizes this case as one of mere wealth transfer. It notes that the United States declined to intervene and that proper classification of inpatients is already being addressed through regulatory proceedings: the government has adopted audits to detect and recover payments for mistaken classification of inpatients.

This factor favors relator. The court disagrees with Renown that this case is simply about a transfer of wealth from one party to another. Instead, *qui tam* actions are an important means of addressing fraud claims on behalf of taxpayers and the United States. That fact imbues this case with heightened importance.

7. *The Parties' Resources*

Renown argues that the final factor is neutral because both parties have resources. It contrasts its position as Reno's only non-profit hospital with relator's recovery of $1.1 million in a prior *qui tam* lawsuit. . . . [R]elator again observes that Renown "generates in excess of $2.6 billion in total patient revenue annually."

This factor is neutral. Although Renown's resources are substantially greater than those of relator, the record suggests that she is not penniless.

8. *Conclusion*

As the court has described, five of the relevant factors favor relator, while two are neutral. Consequently, the court finds that relator has carried her step-two burden of demonstrating good cause. The court holds in the alternative that, even were the gap-period emails reasonably inaccessible due to undue burden or undue cost, good cause supports their discoverability.

C. *Is cost shifting appropriate?*

The third and final step is an examination of cost shifting. . . .

Zubulake I held that courts should consider seven factors in the cost-shifting analysis, weighted in the following order: (1) the extent to which the request is specifically tailored to discover relevant information; (2) the availability of such information from other sources; (3) the total cost of production, compared to the amount in controversy; (4) the total cost of production, compared to the resources available to each party; (5) the relative ability of each party to control costs and its incentive to do so; (6) the importance of the issues at stake in the litigation; and (7) the relative benefits to the parties of obtaining the information. Many of these factors mirror those of the good-cause inquiry . . . .

[After examining these factors, the court determined that cost shifting was unwarranted.]

Notes and Questions

1. Electronically stored information ("ESI") is proving to be one of the most vexing problem areas in civil litigation. Think of how much information passes across your computer, tablet, and cell phone on any given day. Multiply that amount of information by dozens or hundreds of employees, and then multiply that amount by the hundreds or thousands of days that are at issue in a lawsuit — and then you have some sense of the quantity of ESI that a single Rule 34 request for production can involve.

Quantity is just the tip of the iceberg. Sometimes, as hardware or software no longer supports a method of storage, a company decides not to convert the information from a "legacy" format. Moreover, companies must balance cost issues when deciding how to store electronic information; storing information in a readily retrievable format is more expensive than storage in archival formats or on backup tapes, although using these less accessible formats can become very expensive if data need to be retrieved in later litigation.

Another unique problem of ESI is metadata — data about the data. Metadata can be information as basic as when a document was created or modified, or what formula was used to generate the number in a cell on a spreadsheet. Parties who produce ESI often scrub the metadata for reasons such as relevance, expense, privacy, client confidentiality, and trade secrecy, so that a party who has reason to want the metadata usually must request it specifically. *See generally* Aguilar v. Immigration & Customs Enforcement Div., 255 F.R.D. 350 (S.D.N.Y. 2008) (discussing forms of metadata; ordering the production of some, but not all, metadata). Sometimes documents inadvertently include metadata, so the receiving party must decide whether to go to the expense of mining the document for its metadata. Some jurisdictions have issued ethics opinions stating that such mining is unethical; other jurisdictions, and the American Bar Association, have taken the opposite position. *See* FORMAL OPINION 06-442 (AM. BAR ASS'N 2006).

Production of ESI can also create issues. ESI often contains a lot of chaff and only a little wheat. Hence, the process of finding responsive documents, but only responsive documents, is challenging. Parties often employ vendors with expertise in computer science and computer forensics, and the vendors for each party negotiate the search terms that will be used to cull the ESI for relevant material. In recent years, "predictive coding" or "technology-assisted review" (TAR) has become the norm. A lawyer or technical expert crafts an initial search, examines a sample of the documents that the search produces, and determines which documents are (and are not) responsive. The search program "learns" from that determination to refine the search. The documents produced in the new search are then examined for their responsiveness. Over several iterations of this process, a search program in the hands of sophisticated counsel and an experienced vendor can become fairly adept at producing responsive material — and only responsive material. *See* Da Silva Moore v. Publicis

Groupe, 287 F.R.D. 182, 191 (S.D.N.Y.2012) ("Computer-assisted review appears to be better than the available alternatives, and thus should be used in appropriate cases.").

TAR can be expensive, so you might think a responding party could just let the requesting party image the responder's files and then search at the requestor's expense. Responders, however, generally disfavor this course of action. When using predictive coding, the responding party also needs to set up a process (usually called a "privilege review") to ensure that the responsive material does not included any privileged or otherwise protected information — which cannot be done if the requesting party is given free rein to search the images. Sometimes a requesting party will ask to image files when there is a concern that the files may be tampered with or deleted (a particular risk with ESI). In these instances, imaging is possible, but responding parties generally resist imaging because it gives the opponent access to irrelevant information and metadata, and it becomes more difficult to control exactly what information the opponent is working with. *See generally* Javeler Marine Servs. LLC v. Cross, 175 F. Supp. 2d 756, 761-63 (S.D. Tex. 2016) (describing imaging process).

Finally, a significant issue with ESI is destruction. Let's say that you once wrote a document that becomes important in litigation years later. Every draft of that document may be relevant. Unfortunately, after you made changes to each draft, you saved the new version, thus immediately — and unthinkingly — destroying relevant evidence. Forensic computer analysis can sometimes recover this information, but at great expense. Retention of ESI generates other issues as well. For instance, many companies are moving toward cloud computing; collecting data from the cloud and preserving the data against security breaches present unique challenges. Moreover, because backing up and storing every piece of ESI is too expensive, companies typically have ESI-retention systems that routinely and automatically delete ESI after a period of time. If the deletion occurs before litigation, relevant information may be lost forever. If the litigation occurs first, the court will often enter a *litigation hold* (or *preservation order*) requiring the parties not to destroy relevant documents, including ESI. The parties must therefore suspend the operation of their automatic ESI-deletion systems — a potentially expensive process that is not always successful. Indeed, the failure to preserve relevant evidence can expose a party to a tort claim, known as "spoliation," or to sanctions. *See infra* pp. 164-65, Notes 4-5 (discussing sanctions in ESI cases).

2. Rule 26(b)(2)(B), which was promulgated in 2006, was designed to address the problem of ESI. Its innovation was to flip in part the presumption that relevant information is subject to disclosure and discovery, and to make some ESI (that which "is not reasonably accessible because of undue burden or cost") presumptively not disclosable or discoverable. That presumption can be overcome, however, by a showing of "good cause." For ESI sought from nonparties, Rule 45(e)(1)(D) adopts the same two-tier approach.

One of the concerns about the 2006 amendments was the incentive that it might give businesses to store information in hard-to-retrieve formats. Note that *Guardiola* takes a somewhat jaundiced view of such practices.

3. If ESI is "reasonably accessible," the special limits of Rule 26(b)(2)(B) do not kick in; the information is disclosable or discoverable on the same relevance-and-proportionality terms as any other information. As *Guardiola* says, many cases use a *per se* approach in deciding whether ESI is (or is not) "reasonably accessible because of undue burden or cost." On this approach information contained in certain storage formats (such as backup tapes; legacy formats; or erased, corrupted, or fragmented data) is automatically deemed inaccessible and passes straight through to the "good cause" analysis. Even ESI stored in an accessible format (for instance, on a hard drive or server) might be subject to the presumption of nondisclosure if it is difficult for some reason to cull the relevant documents. *See* W.E. Aubuchon Co. v. BeneFirst, LLC, 245 F.R.D. 38 (D. Mass. 2007).

4. Suppose that *Guardiola* had involved a $500,000 claim. If you were the judge, would you have approved a $248,000 expenditure on the gap-period emails? Should the quality of justice that parties receive depend on the amount at stake?

5. Is the structure of Rule 26(b)(2)(B) too unwieldy? As *Guardiola* says, the first issue is to engage in a cost-benefit examination in determining if inaccessible ESI is *unduly* burdensome or costly. Then, in determining "good cause," a court uses the three-factor test of Rule 26(b)(2)(C), which kicks back to the six-factor proportionality test of Rule 26(b)(1). In addition, the Advisory Committee's note to the 2006 amendment listed seven factors — which are essentially duplicative of Rule 26(b)(1)'s six factors — to aid in determining "good cause." Finally, the final sentence of Rule 26(b)(2)(B), which allows a court to "specify the conditions" for e-discovery, permits the court to order cost-shifting. As *Guardiola* states, Zubulake v. UBS Warburg LLC, 217 F.R.D. 309, 322 (S.D.N.Y. 2003), the seminal case in the field of e-discovery that shaped Rule 26(b)(2)(B) and its subsequent analysis, developed yet another seven factors to determine whether to shift costs for e-discovery. As *Guardiola* says, these factors are also for all practical purposes identical to the factors used to determine good cause and proportionality.

Do we need all these different tests? Can they be summarized by the following statement: "Permit discovery if but only if the extra cost of discovery is less than the probable incremental gain in accuracy"? This is simply the marginal-utility formula common in other areas of economic and legal analysis. Should Rule 26(b)(2) include factors that are *not* a part of a marginal-utility calculus?

6. Unwieldiness might not matter if Rule 26(b)(2)(B) is effective. Shortly after the Rule was promulgated, a survey of in-house counsel reflected disagreement about the efficacy of the 2006 amendment. *See* Fourth Annual Litigation Trends Survey Findings (2007), *available at* http://www.fulbright.com/mediaroom/files/2007/fj6438-littrends-v13.pdf (noting that more than half of counsel "detected no change in how their

companies are handling federal litigation; 18% felt the e-discovery guidelines have eased their litigation issues, while 27% said the rules have actually made their litigation lives more difficult"). *Cf.* NICHOLAS PACE & LAURA ZAKARAS, RAND CORP., WHERE THE MONEY GOES (2012) (finding, in a survey of fifty-seven large ESI productions, that document review constituted seventy-three percent of ESI expenditures, that human review of documents was highly inconsistent, and that unclear standards about preserving documents were leading to costly overpreservation of ESI).

7. Electronic discovery has shifted the nature of legal practice. Large law firms often contain an ESI group whose practice consists of parachuting in to establish effective ESI programs for its clients' lawsuits. At the same time, corporations have brought more and more e-discovery work in-house to control costs. And, as technology has become cheaper and more accurate than humans, *see* John Markoff, *Armies of Expensive Lawyers, Replaced by Cheaper Software*, N.Y. TIMES, Mar. 5, 2011, at A1, "doc review" is no longer the great engine of employment for first-year associates in large law firms.

8. The Federal Rules contain restrictions on the use of some discovery techniques. Rule 26(b)(2)(A) allows a court to limit the number of requests for admission. In addition, each side can take no more than ten depositions, which can last no more than seven hours apiece. *See* Fed. R. Civ. P. 30(a)(2)(A)(i) and –(d)(1). Finally, a party can propound no more than twenty-five interrogatories. *See* Fed. R. Civ. P. 33(a)(1). The court can change the limits on depositions and interrogatories.

2. Privilege and Work Product

Sometimes the law does not require a person to disclose relevant information to the parties or the court. In other words, the person has a "privilege" of nondisclosure. Generally, privileges arise when society values a particular relationship — and the free flow of information within that relationship — more highly than it values the marginal gains in the accuracy of judgments that forced disclosure might generate.

There are numerous privileges, including the marital privilege, the attorney-client privilege, the physician-patient privilege, the priest-penitent privilege, and the Fifth Amendment's privilege against self-incrimination. Some privileges are "absolute," which means that they cannot be overcome even if the need for the information is overwhelming. Other privileges are "qualified," which means that they can be overcome if the need for the information is great enough. *See generally* KENNETH S. BROUN ET AL., MCCORMICK ON EVIDENCE §§ 72–138 (7th ed. 2014).

In trials conducted in federal courts, Federal Rule of Evidence 501 provides the basic rule of privilege:

> The common law — as interpreted by United States courts in the light of reason and experience — governs a claim of privilege unless any of the following provides otherwise:
>
> • the United States Constitution;

- a federal statute; or
- rules prescribed by the Supreme Court.

But in a civil case, state law governs privilege regarding a claim or defense for which state law supplies the rule of decision.

A course in Evidence will teach you the content and sources of privileges. Our concern here is to see how privileges (of whatever content and derived from whatever source) and related protections intersect with the law of discovery. We focus on two doctrines that affect the work of lawyers who represent clients in litigation: attorney-client privilege and work product.

HICKMAN V. TAYLOR

329 U.S. 495 (1947)

MR. JUSTICE MURPHY delivered the opinion of the Court.

This case presents an important problem under the Federal Rules of Civil Procedure as to the extent to which a party may inquire into oral and written statements of witnesses, or other information, secured by an adverse party's counsel in the course of preparation for possible litigation after a claim has arisen. Examination into a person's files and records, including those resulting from the professional activities of an attorney, must be judged with care. It is not without reason that various safeguards have been established to preclude unwarranted excursions into the privacy of a man's work. At the same time, public policy supports reasonable and necessary inquiries. Properly to balance these competing interests is a delicate and difficult task.

On February 7, 1943, the tug "J.M. Taylor" sank while engaged in helping to tow a car float of the Baltimore & Ohio Railroad across the Delaware River at Philadelphia. The accident was apparently unusual in nature, the cause of it still being unknown. Five of the nine crew members were drowned. Three days later the tug owners and the underwriters employed a law firm, of which respondent Fortenbaugh is a member, to defend them against potential suits by representatives of the deceased crew members and to sue the railroad for damages to the tug.

A public hearing was held on March 4, 1943, before the United States Steamboat Inspectors, at which the four survivors were examined. This testimony was recorded and made available to all interested parties. Shortly thereafter, Fortenbaugh privately interviewed the survivors and took statements from them with an eye toward the anticipated litigation; the survivors signed these statements on March 29. Fortenbaugh also interviewed other persons believed to have some information relating to the accident and in some cases he made memoranda of what they told him. At the time when Fortenbaugh secured the statements of the survivors, representatives of two of the deceased crew members had been in communication with him. Ultimately claims were presented by representatives of all five of the deceased; four of the claims, however, were settled without litigation. The fifth claimant, petitioner herein, brought suit in a federal court under the Jones Act on November 26, 1943, naming as defendants the two tug owners, individually and as partners, and the railroad.

One year later, petitioner filed 39 interrogatories directed to the tug owners. The 38th interrogatory read: "State whether any statements of the members of the crews of the Tugs 'J.M. Taylor' and 'Philadelphia' or of any other vessel were taken in connection with the towing of the car float and the sinking of the Tug 'John M. Taylor.' Attach hereto exact copies of all such statements if in writing, and if oral, set forth in detail the exact provisions of any such oral statements or reports."

Supplemental interrogatories asked whether any oral or written statements, records, reports or other memoranda had been made concerning any matter relative to the towing operation, the sinking of the tug, the salvaging and repair of the tug, and the death of the deceased. If the answer was in the affirmative, the tug owners were then requested to set forth the nature of all such records, reports, statements or other memoranda.

The tug owners, through Fortenbaugh, answered all of the interrogatories except No. 38 and the supplemental ones just described. While admitting that statements of the survivors had been taken, they declined to summarize or set forth the contents. They did so on the ground that such requests called "for privileged matter obtained in preparation for litigation" and constituted "an attempt to obtain indirectly counsel's private files." It was claimed that answering these requests "would involve practically turning over not only the complete files, but also the telephone records and, almost, the thoughts of counsel."

... The District Court for the Eastern District of Pennsylvania, sitting en banc, held that the requested matters were not privileged. The court then decreed that the tug owners and Fortenbaugh, as counsel and agent for the tug owners forthwith "answer Plaintiff's 38th interrogatory and supplemental interrogatories; produce all written statements of witnesses obtained by Mr. Fortenbaugh, as counsel and agent for Defendants; state in substance any fact concerning this case which Defendants learned through oral statements made by witnesses to Mr. Fortenbaugh whether or not included in his private memoranda and produce Mr. Fortenbaugh's memoranda containing statements of fact by witnesses or to submit these memoranda to the Court for determination of those portions which should be revealed to Plaintiff." Upon their refusal, the court adjudged them in contempt and ordered them imprisoned until they complied.

The Third Circuit Court of Appeals, also sitting en banc, reversed the judgment of the District Court. It held that the information here sought was part of the "work product of the lawyer" and hence privileged from discovery under the Federal Rules of Civil Procedure. The importance of the problem, which has engendered a great divergence of views among district courts, led us to grant certiorari.

SECTION C   THE SCOPE OF AND LIMITS ON DISCOVERY

The pre-trial deposition-discovery mechanism established by Rules 26 to 37 is one of the most significant innovations of the Federal Rules of Civil Procedure. Under the prior federal practice, the pre-trial functions of notice-giving, issue-formulation, and fact-revelation were performed primarily and inadequately by the pleadings. Inquiry into the issues and the facts before trial was narrowly confined and was often cumbersome in method. The new rules, however, restrict the pleadings to the task of general notice-giving and invest the deposition-discovery process with a vital role in the preparation for trial. The various instruments of discovery now serve (1) as a device, along with the pre-trial hearing under Rule 16, to narrow and clarify the basic issues between the parties, and (2) as a device for ascertaining the facts, or information as to the existence or whereabouts of facts, relative to those issues. Thus civil trials in the federal courts no longer need be carried on in the dark. The way is now clear, consistent with recognized privileges, for the parties to obtain the fullest possible knowledge of the issues and facts before trial.

[The Court observed that the plaintiff had used the wrong method of discovery — interrogatories addressed to the tug owner — rather than a deposition of Fortenbaugh. In making this observation, the Court stated that "[a] party clearly cannot refuse to answer interrogatories on the ground that the information sought is solely within the knowledge of his attorney."]

But under the circumstances we deem it unnecessary and unwise to rest our decision upon this procedural irregularity, an irregularity which is not strongly urged upon us and which was disregarded in the two courts below. . . . The deposition-discovery rules create integrated procedural devices. And the basic question at stake is whether any of those devices may be used to inquire into materials collected by an adverse party's counsel in the course of preparation for possible litigation. . . . Having noted the proper procedure, we may accordingly turn our attention to the substance of the underlying problem.

In urging that he has a right to inquire into the materials secured and prepared by Fortenbaugh, petitioner emphasizes that the deposition-discovery portions of the Federal Rules of Civil Procedure are designed to enable the parties to discover the true facts and to compel their disclosure wherever they may be found. It is said that inquiry may be made under these rules, epitomized by Rule 26, as to any relevant matter which is not privileged; and since the discovery provisions are to be applied as broadly and liberally as possible, the privilege limitation must be restricted to its narrowest bounds. On the premise that the attorney-client privilege is the one involved in this case, petitioner argues that it must be strictly confined to confidential communications made by a client to his attorney. And since the materials here in issue were secured by Fortenbaugh from third persons rather than from his clients, the tug owners, the conclusion is reached that these materials are proper subjects for discovery under Rule 26.

As additional support for this result, petitioner claims that to prohibit discovery under these circumstances would give a corporate defendant a tremendous advantage in a suit by an individual plaintiff. Thus in a suit by an injured employee against a railroad or in a suit by an insured person against an insurance company the corporate defendant could pull a dark veil of secrecy over all the pertinent facts it can collect after the claim arises merely on the assertion that such facts were gathered by its large staff of attorneys and claim agents. At the same time, the individual plaintiff, who often has direct knowledge of the matter in issue and has no counsel until some time after his claim arises[,] could be compelled to disclose all the intimate details of his case. By endowing with immunity from disclosure all that a lawyer discovers in the course of his duties, it is said, the rights of individual litigants in such cases are drained of vitality and the lawsuit becomes more of a battle of deception than a search for truth.

But framing the problem in terms of assisting individual plaintiffs in their suits against corporate defendants is unsatisfactory. Discovery concededly may work to the disadvantage as well as to the advantage of individual plaintiffs. Discovery, in other words, is not a one-way proposition. It is available in all types of cases at the behest of any party, individual or corporate, plaintiff or defendant. The problem thus far transcends the situation confronting this petitioner. And we must view that problem in light of the limitless situations where the particular kind of discovery sought by petitioner might be used.

We agree, of course, that the deposition-discovery rules are to be accorded a broad and liberal treatment. No longer can the time-honored cry of "fishing expedition" serve to preclude a party from inquiring into the facts underlying his opponent's case. Mutual knowledge of all the relevant facts gathered by both parties is essential to proper litigation. To that end, either party may compel the other to disgorge whatever facts he has in his possession. The deposition-discovery procedure simply advances the stage at which the disclosure can be compelled from the time of trial to the period preceding it, thus reducing the possibility of surprise. But discovery, like all matters of procedure, has ultimate and necessary boundaries. . . . [L]imitations inevitably arise when it can be shown that the examination is being conducted in bad faith or in such a manner as to annoy, embarrass or oppress the person subject to the inquiry. And as Rule 26(b) provides, further limitations come into existence when the inquiry touches upon the irrelevant or encroaches upon the recognized domains of privilege.

We also agree that the memoranda, statements and mental impressions in issue in this case fall outside the scope of the attorney-client privilege and hence are not protected from discovery on that basis. It is unnecessary here to delineate the content and scope of that privilege as recognized in the federal courts. For present purposes, it suffices to note that the protective cloak of this privilege does not extend to information which an attorney secures from a witness while acting for his client in anticipation of litigation. Nor does this privilege concern the memoranda, briefs, communications and other writings prepared by counsel for his own use in prosecuting his client's case; and it is equally unrelated to writings which reflect an attorney's mental impressions, conclusions, opinions or legal theories.

But the impropriety of invoking that privilege does not provide an answer to the problem before us. Petitioner has made more than an ordinary request for relevant, non-privileged facts in the possession of his adversaries or their counsel. He has sought discovery as of right of oral and written statements of witnesses whose identity is well known and whose availability to petitioner appears unimpaired. He has sought production of these matters after making the most searching inquiries of his opponents as to the circumstances surrounding the fatal accident, which inquiries were sworn to have been answered to the best of their information and belief. Interrogatories were directed toward all the events prior to, during and subsequent to the sinking of the tug. Full and honest answers to such broad inquiries would necessarily have included all pertinent information gleaned by Fortenbaugh through his interviews with the witnesses. Petitioner makes no suggestion, and we cannot assume, that the tug owners or Fortenbaugh were incomplete or dishonest in the framing of their answers. In addition, petitioner was free to examine the public testimony of the witnesses taken before the United States Steamboat Inspectors. We are thus dealing with an attempt to secure the production of written statements and mental impressions contained in the files and the mind of the attorney Fortenbaugh without any showing of necessity or any indication or claim that denial of such production would unduly prejudice the preparation of petitioner's case or cause him any hardship or injustice. For aught that appears, the essence of what petitioner seeks either has been revealed to him already through the interrogatories or is readily available to him direct from the witnesses for the asking.

The District Court, after hearing objections to petitioner's request, commanded Fortenbaugh to produce all written statements of witnesses and to state in substance any facts learned through oral statements of witnesses to him. Fortenbaugh was to submit any memoranda he had made of the oral statements so that the court might determine what portions should be revealed to petitioner. All of this was ordered without any showing by petitioner, or any requirement that he make a proper showing, of the necessity for the production of any of this material or any demonstration that denial of production would cause hardship or injustice. The court simply ordered production on the theory that the facts sought were material and were not privileged as constituting attorney-client communications.

In our opinion, neither Rule 26 nor any other rule dealing with discovery contemplates production under such circumstances. That is not because the subject matter is privileged or irrelevant, as those concepts are used in these rules. Here is simply an attempt, without purported necessity or justification, to secure written statements, private memoranda and personal recollections prepared or formed by an adverse party's counsel in the course of his legal duties. As such, it falls outside the arena of discovery and contravenes the public policy underlying the orderly prosecution and defense of legal claims. Not even the most liberal of discovery theories can justify unwarranted inquiries into the files and the mental impressions of an attorney.

Historically, a lawyer is an officer of the court and is bound to work for the advancement of justice while faithfully protecting the rightful interests of his clients. In performing his various duties, however, it is essential that a lawyer work with a certain degree of privacy, free from unnecessary intrusion by opposing parties and their counsel. Proper preparation of a client's case demands that he assemble information, sift what he considers to be the relevant from the irrelevant facts, prepare his legal theories and plan his strategy without undue and needless interference. That is the historical and the necessary way in which lawyers act within the framework of our system of jurisprudence to promote justice and to protect their clients' interests. This work is reflected, of course, in interviews, statements, memoranda, correspondence, briefs, mental impressions, personal beliefs, and countless other tangible and intangible ways — aptly though roughly termed by the Circuit Court of Appeals in this case as the "work product of the lawyer." Were such materials open to opposing counsel on mere demand, much of what is now put down in writing would remain unwritten. An attorney's thoughts, heretofore inviolate, would not be his own. Inefficiency, unfairness and sharp practices would inevitably develop in the giving of legal advice and in the preparation of cases for trial. The effect on the legal profession would be demoralizing. And the interests of the clients and the cause of justice would be poorly served.

We do not mean to say that all written materials obtained or prepared by an adversary's counsel with an eye toward litigation are necessarily free from discovery in all cases. Where relevant and non-privileged facts remain hidden in an attorney's file and where production of those facts is essential to the preparation of one's case, discovery may properly be had. Such written statements and documents might, under certain circumstances, be admissible in evidence or give clues as to the existence or location of relevant facts. Or they might be useful for purposes of impeachment or corroboration. And production might be justified where the witnesses are no longer available or can be reached only with difficulty. Were production of written statements and documents to be precluded under such circumstances, the liberal ideals of the deposition-discovery portions of the Federal Rules of Civil Procedure would be stripped of much of their meaning. But the general policy against invading the privacy of an attorney's course of preparation is so well recognized and so essential to an orderly working of our system of legal procedure that a burden rests on the one who would invade that privacy to establish adequate reasons to justify production through a subpoena or court order. That burden, we believe, is necessarily implicit in the rules as now constituted.

Rule 30(b) [now Rule 26(c) — Ed.], as presently written, gives the trial judge the requisite discretion to make a judgment as to whether discovery should be allowed as to written statements secured from witnesses. But in the instant case there was no room for that discretion to operate in favor of the petitioner. No attempt was made to establish any reason why Fortenbaugh should be forced to produce the written statements. There was only a naked, general demand for these materials as of right and a finding by the District Court that no recognizable privilege was involved. That was insufficient to justify discovery under these circumstances and the court should have sustained the refusal of the tug owners and Fortenbaugh to produce.

But as to oral statements made by witnesses to Fortenbaugh, whether presently in the form of his mental impressions or memoranda, we do not believe that any showing of necessity can be made under the circumstances of this case so as to justify production. Under ordinary conditions, forcing an attorney to repeat or write out all that witnesses have told him and to deliver the account to his adversary gives rise to grave dangers of inaccuracy and untrustworthiness. No legitimate purpose is served by such production. The practice forces the attorney to testify as to what he remembers or what he saw fit to write down regarding witnesses' remarks. Such testimony could not qualify as evidence; and to use it for impeachment or corroborative purposes would make the attorney much less an officer of the court and much more an ordinary witness. The standards of the profession would thereby suffer.

Denial of production of this nature does not mean that any material, non-privileged facts can be hidden from the petitioner in this case. He need not be unduly hindered in the preparation of his case, in the discovery of facts or in his anticipation of his opponents' position. Searching interrogatories directed to Fortenbaugh and the tug owners, production of written documents and statements upon a proper showing and direct interviews with the witnesses themselves all serve to reveal the facts in Fortenbaugh's possession to the fullest possible extent consistent with public policy. Petitioner's counsel frankly admits that he wants the oral statements only to help prepare himself to examine witnesses and to make sure that he has overlooked nothing. That is insufficient under the circumstances to permit him an exception to the policy underlying the privacy of Fortenbaugh's professional activities. If there should be a rare situation justifying production of these matters, petitioner's case is not of that type.

We fully appreciate the wide-spread controversy among the members of the legal profession over the problem raised by this case. It is a problem that rests on what has been one of the most hazy frontiers of the discovery process. But until some rule or statute definitely prescribes otherwise, we are not justified in permitting discovery in a situation of this nature as a matter of unqualified right. When Rule 26 and the other discovery rules were adopted, this Court and the members of the bar in general certainly did not believe or contemplate that all the files and mental processes of lawyers were thereby opened to the free scrutiny of their adversaries. And we refuse to interpret the rules at this time so as to reach so harsh and unwarranted a result.

We therefore affirm the judgment of the Circuit Court of Appeals.

■ MR. JUSTICE JACKSON, concurring. . . .

The primary effect of the practice advocated here would be on the legal profession itself. But it too often is overlooked that the lawyer and the law office are indispensable parts of our administration of justice. Law-abiding people can go nowhere else to learn the ever changing and constantly multiplying rules by which they must behave and to obtain redress for their wrongs. The welfare and tone of the legal profession is therefore of prime consequence to society, which would feel the consequences of such a practice as petitioner urges secondarily but certainly. . . .

. . . [T]he statement by counsel of what a witness told him is not evidence when written. Plaintiff could not introduce it to prove his case. What, then, is the purpose sought to be served by demanding this of adverse counsel?

Counsel for the petitioner candidly said on argument that he wanted this information to help prepare himself to examine witnesses, to make sure he overlooked nothing. He bases his claim to it in his brief on the view that the Rules were to do away with the old situation where a law suit developed into "a battle of wits between counsel." But a common law trial is and always should be an adversary proceeding. Discovery was hardly intended to enable a learned profession to perform its functions either without wits or on wits borrowed from the adversary.

The real purpose and the probable effect of the practice ordered by the district court would be to put trials on a level even lower than a "battle of wits." I can conceive of no practice more demoralizing to the Bar than to require a lawyer to write out and deliver to his adversary an account of what witnesses have told him. Even if his recollection were perfect, the statement would be his language permeated with his inferences. Every one who has tried it knows that it is almost impossible so fairly to record the expressions and emphasis of a witness that when he testifies in the environment of the court and under the influence of the leading question there will not be departures in some respects. Whenever the testimony of the witness would differ from the "exact" statement the lawyer had delivered, the lawyer's statement would be whipped out to impeach the witness. Counsel producing his adversary's "inexact" statement could lose nothing by saying, "Here is a contradiction, gentlemen of the jury. I do not know whether it is my adversary or his witness who is not telling the truth, but one is not." Of course, if this practice were adopted, that scene would be repeated over and over again. The lawyer who delivers such statements often would find himself branded a deceiver afraid to take the stand to support his own version of the witness's conversation with him, or else he will have to go on the stand to defend his own credibility — perhaps against that of his chief witness, or possibly even his client.

Every lawyer dislikes to take the witness stand and will do so only for grave reasons. This is partly because it is not his role; he is almost invariably a poor witness. But he steps out of professional character to do it. He regrets it; the profession discourages it. But the practice advocated here is one which would force him to be a witness, not as to what he has seen or done but as to other witnesses' stories, and not because he wants to do so but in self-defense.

And what is the lawyer to do who has interviewed one whom he believes to be a biased, lying or hostile witness to get his unfavorable statements and know what to meet? He must record and deliver such statements even though he would not vouch for the credibility of the witness by calling him. Perhaps the other side would not want to call him either, but the attorney is open to the charge of suppressing evidence at the trial if he fails to call such a hostile witness even though he never regarded him as reliable or truthful. . . .

It is true that the literal language of the Rules would admit of an interpretation that would sustain the district court's order. . . . But all such procedural measures have a background of custom and practice which was assumed by those who wrote and should be by those who apply them. . . . Certainly nothing in the tradition or practice of discovery up to the time of these Rules would have suggested that they would authorize such a practice as here proposed.

The question remains as to signed statements or those written by witnesses. Such statements are not evidence for the defendant. Nor should I think they ordinarily could be evidence for the plaintiff. But such a statement might be useful for impeachment of the witness who signed it, if he is called and if he departs from the statement. There might be circumstances, too, where impossibility or difficulty of access to the witness or his refusal to respond to requests for information or other facts would show that the interests of justice require that such statements be made available. Production of such statements [is] governed by Rule 34 . . . .

I agree to the affirmance of the judgment of the Circuit Court of Appeals which reversed the district court.

MR. JUSTICE FRANKFURTER joins in this opinion.

Notes and Questions

1. Fortenbaugh appears to be the model of lawyerly courage, willing to risk imprisonment for the principle he wishes to vindicate on his client's behalf. There is another part to the story. Discovery rulings by a district court usually are not appealable immediately; they can be appealed only after a final judgment has been entered. But the damage would have been done had Fortenbaugh produced the requested information and appealed the decision later. One exception to the non-appealability of a discovery order is when a nonparty, such as a lawyer, disobeys the order and is found in contempt, as Fortenbaugh had been. Then the contempt order can be appealed, and the underlying reason for the contempt can be contested on appeal. So in a sense, in finding Fortenbaugh in contempt, the district court was "helping" to resolve the critical issue facing the parties and the legal system. In some cases, like Fortenbaugh's, the lawyer is exonerated. In some cases the lawyer is not exonerated, and the contempt finding stands. Would you have done what Fortenbaugh did, just to vindicate the principle at stake in *Hickman*?

2. To what extent do Rule 26(b)(2) and other recent efforts to constrain the scope of discovery suggest a retreat from *Hickman v. Taylor*'s famous assertion that "[n]o longer can the time-honored cry of 'fishing expedition' serve to preclude a party from inquiring into the facts underlying his opponent's case"?

3. Should the Federal Rules be interpreted according to their plain language? In 1947 the only express limits on discovery were relevance and privilege. In *Hickman* the Court conceded that the information sought was relevant and that it was not privileged. Under a plain reading of the Federal Rules, should that have been the end of the matter?

4. The 1970 amendments added Rule 26(b)(3), which partially codified *Hickman*'s work-product doctrine. Rule 26(b)(3) creates work-product protection for "documents and tangible things that are prepared in anticipation of litigation or for trial." It raises several important questions.

(a) When is material "prepared in anticipation of litigation or for trial"? In *Jumpsport, Inc. v. Jumpking, Inc.*, 213 F.R.D. 329, 330-31 (N.D. Cal. 2003), the court proposed a two-stage test:

> In the first stage, the court should determine whether the party trying to invoke work product protection has shown that the prospect of litigation was a substantial factor in the mix of considerations, purposes, or forces that led to the preparation of the document. . . . In [the] second stage, the court focuses on the policy objectives that the work product doctrine has been developed to promote . . . . The court would conclude that the document comes within the ambit of the Rule (was "prepared in anticipation of litigation") on a showing that a contrary conclusion would likely frustrate or interfere (more than minimally) with the promotion of the principal objectives this doctrine is designed to serve.

In answering the second-stage inquiry, the court identified two considerations: whether "a refusal to extend protection to this document [would] invade that 'zone of privacy' that courts have assumed that lawyers and clients need if they are to think reliably, critically, and creatively about their litigation" and whether "a refusal to extend protection to this document [would] damage the sets of incentives that are said to be essential to the effective functioning of the adversary system." *Id.* at 353.

(b) Is work-product material absolutely protected from discovery, or can protected documents be discovered in some situations? For *ordinary work product*, Rule 26(b)(3)(A)(ii) permits disclosure on a showing of "substantial need" and "undue hardship." Even when this showing is made, however, "the mental impressions, conclusions, opinions, or legal theories of a party's attorney or other representative" — material sometimes called *core* or *opinion work product* — receive additional protection from disclosure. Fed. R. Civ. P. 26(b)(3)(B). Is it ever possible for core work product to be disclosed? *See* Upjohn Co. v. United States, 449 U.S. 383, 399-402 (1981) (reserving question, but noting that, at a minimum, something more than "substantial need" and "undue hardship" would need to be demonstrated).

(c) When do "substantial need" and "undue hardship" exist? Suppose:

- A witness interviewed by Fortenbaugh has died.
- A witness interviewed by Fortenbaugh no longer remembers what happened by the time of her deposition.
- A witness interviewed by Fortenbaugh has related different versions of the events to different people.
- A witness interviewed by Fortenbaugh is willing to be deposed — but only in Abu Dhabi, to which he recently moved. Traveling to Abu Dhabi and back would cost $7,000 and take four days.

Can other parties get Fortenbaugh's interview notes in any of these situations? Suppose Fortenbaugh has in his possession pictures taken within an hour of the accident by the tug owner's general counsel, who was called to the scene of the accident. Protected or not?

(d) Is there any work-product protection for information not contained in "documents and tangible things"? Suppose that a party wants to take a deposition of the opposing lawyer to obtain work-product information. Rule 26(b)(3) does not preclude this form of discovery. Does *Hickman*'s common-law doctrine still apply? If so, does the "substantial need and undue hardship" exception also apply? (Note that *Hickman* never said that "substantial need" and "undue hardship" were dual necessary conditions for overcoming work-product protection.) Courts and commentators generally agree that a common-law work-product protection extends to forms of information other than "documents and tangible things." *See* United States v. Deloitte LLP, 610 F.3d 129, 136 (D.C. Cir. 2010).

5. Because it protects information other than communications, and because it can sometimes be overcome on a sufficient showing of need for the information, work product is sometimes not regarded as a true evidentiary privilege. Therefore, it is sometimes referred to as the "work-product doctrine" or "work-product protection." Little hinges on whether we regard work product as a privilege, a doctrine, or a protection.

6. *Hickman* asserts that the attorney-client privilege did not extend to the interviews that Fortenbaugh conducted. Why not? Wasn't Fortenbaugh the tug owner's lawyer? Yes, but the Court was still right. Students, and even lawyers, sometimes confuse work product with the attorney-client privilege. But it is important to distinguish them.

Though they both operate to protect information from discovery, the work-product doctrine and the attorney-client privilege serve different purposes. The purpose behind the attorney-client privilege is "to encourage clients to make full disclosure of facts to counsel so that he may properly, competently, and ethically carry out his representation. The ultimate aim is to promote the proper administration of justice." The work-product doctrine, by contrast, "promotes the adversary system directly by protecting the confidentiality of papers prepared by or on behalf of attorneys in anticipation of litigation. Protecting attorneys' work product promotes the adversary system by enabling attorneys to prepare cases without fear that their work product will be used against their clients."

In re Chevron Corp., 633 F.3d 153, 164 (3d Cir. 2011).

7. In *United States v. Mobil Corp.*, 149 F.R.D. 533, 536 (N.D. Tex. 1993), the court described the attorney-client privilege as follows:

> The attorney-client privilege protects two related, but different, communications: (1) confidential communications made by a client to his lawyer for the purpose of obtaining legal advice; and (2) any communication from an attorney to his client when made in the course of giving legal advice, whether or not that advice is based on privileged communications from the client. . . .
>
> To invoke the attorney-client privilege, the claimant must establish the following elements: (1) the asserted holder of the privilege is or sought to become a client; (2) the person to whom the communication was made is (a) a member of a bar of a court, or his subordinate, and (b) in connection with this communication is acting as a lawyer; (3) the communication relates to a fact of which the attorney was informed (a) by his client (b) without the presence of strangers (c) for the purpose of securing primarily either (i) an opinion on law or (ii) legal services (iii) or assistance in some legal proceeding, and (d) not for the purpose of committing a crime or tort; and (4) the privilege has been (a) claimed and (b) not waived by the client.

8. Although the attorney-client privilege and the work-product doctrine protect different information (attorney-client communications versus material prepared for litigation), the doctrines overlap; sometimes the same information can be protected under both doctrines. Because the attorney-client privilege is absolute unless waived, while work-product protection can sometimes be overcome on a showing of substantial need and undue hardship, parties generally prefer the protection of the attorney-client privilege. But they should assert both doctrines when appropriate.

9. One type of information brought into existence by or in anticipation of litigation is expert-witness testimony. Should experts' work receive work-product protection? Read Rules 26(a)(2) and –(b)(4) and the following case.

REPUBLIC OF ECUADOR V. HINCHEE

741 F.3d 1185 (11th Cir. 2013)

Before HULL and HILL, Circuit Judges, and PANNELL, District Judge.*

■ HULL, Circuit Judge.

Respondent-Appellant Dr. Robert Hinchee ("Dr. Hinchee"), who resides in Florida, and Intervenor-Appellant Chevron Corporation ("Chevron")

---

* Honorable Charles A. Pannell, Jr., United States District Judge for the Northern District of Georgia, sitting by designation.

appeal the district court's discovery order compelling production of Dr. Hinchee's documents to Petitioner-Appellee, the Republic of Ecuador ("the Republic"). Dr. Hinchee served as a testifying expert for Chevron in a related proceeding. Dr. Hinchee's documents at issue are (1) Dr. Hinchee's personal notes for his own use and (2) email communications between Dr. Hinchee and a group of non-attorneys consisting primarily of other Chevron experts. Dr. Hinchee and Chevron contend that these documents are shielded from discovery by the work-product doctrine, relying primarily on Rule 26(b)(3) and the 2010 Amendments to Rule 26(a)(2) of the Federal Rules of Civil Procedure.

. . . [W]e affirm the district court's order compelling the production of the documents in this case.

I. BACKGROUND

[In a case known as the "Lago Agrio litigation," a large number of indigenous persons filed suit in Ecuador claiming that oil-exploration operations by Chevron's predecessor in interest, Texaco, had caused health problems and contaminated their land. A court in Ecuador issued its judgment in 2011, awarding approximately $18.2 billion in damages against Chevron. Ecuador's highest court subsequently reduced the judgment to $9.1 billion.]

While the Lago Agrio litigation was pending in Ecuador, Chevron sought arbitration against the Republic of Ecuador ("the Republic") in front of the Permanent Court of Arbitration in The Hague, Netherlands. Chevron claimed that the Republic had violated its obligations under the Ecuador-United States Bilateral Investment Treaty ("Treaty"). Specifically, Chevron contended that the Republic breached the Treaty by: (1) failing to notify the Lago Agrio court that Chevron was fully released from any liability relating to the environmental pollution through a settlement agreement between Chevron and the Republic; (2) refusing to "indemnify, protect and defend" the rights of Chevron in connection with the Lago Agrio litigation; (3) "openly campaigning for a decision against Chevron"; and (4) engaging "in a pattern of improper and fundamentally unfair conduct."

This Treaty arbitration remains ongoing. Chevron seeks, *inter alia*, indemnification or damages from the Republic to cover the cost of the monetary award entered against Chevron in the Lago Agrio litigation. To support its position in the Treaty arbitration, Chevron has sought materials and documents in the possession of experts who testified for the plaintiffs in the Lago Agrio litigation, including experts residing in the United States. In turn, the Republic has requested discovery from Chevron's expert witnesses in the Lago Agrio litigation, including Dr. Hinchee in Florida. . . .

. . . The Republic requested this discovery to aid "in defending the validity of the Lago Agrio judgment" in the Treaty arbitration. The Republic explained that "Dr. Hinchee is an environmental engineer and an expert in the assessment and remediation of petroleum contaminated sites." Because Chevron relied on Dr. Hinchee's expert reports in both the Lago Agrio litigation and in the Treaty arbitration, the Republic contended that Dr. Hinchee and his documents were relevant to the Treaty arbitration. The Republic requested that the district court issue a subpoena to Dr. Hinchee for a deposition and production of documents pursuant to 28 U.S.C. § 1782, which allows the district court to issue orders to give "[a]ssistance to foreign and international tribunals and to litigants before such tribunals."

Chevron intervened in the district court action and opposed the subpoena. The district court granted the Republic's request for a subpoena, and Dr. Hinchee and Chevron produced approximately 94,000 pages of documents. However, Dr. Hinchee and Chevron asserted work-product protection over 1,200 documents. [The Republic moved to compel production. The district court conducted an *in camera* review (in which the court but not the opposing party views the documents) of forty of these documents. It determined that thirty-nine of them were not privileged. It then ordered Chevron to produce all remaining documents "that were not draft reports or communications between Chevron's attorneys or their staff members and Dr. Hinchee or his staff members." For documents for which Chevron and Dr. Hinchee still maintained a claim of attorney-client privilege or work-product protection, the district court ordered that the documents be submitted for *in camera* review.]

Chevron and Dr. Hinchee timely appealed the district court's order.

II. STANDARD OF REVIEW

"[D]istrict courts are entitled to broad discretion in managing pretrial discovery matters," including when ruling on the applicability of the work-product doctrine.

The issue in this appeal is whether the district court erred in its interpretation of Rule 26, including the 2010 Amendments to Rule 26. This presents a question of law subject to this Court's de novo review.

III. DISCUSSION

At issue in this appeal are (1) Dr. Hinchee's personal notes prepared for his own use and (2) email communications between Dr. Hinchee and a group of non-attorneys consisting primarily of other Chevron experts. The question is whether the Republic may discover these documents.

A. *Rule 26(b)(1) Entitles the Republic to All Relevant, Non-Privileged Information*

. . .

There is no dispute here that Dr. Hinchee's notes and email communications with non-attorneys, including other experts, are relevant within the meaning of Rule 26(b)(1). The Republic is thus entitled to discover these materials — unless Chevron and Dr. Hinchee can meet their burden of establishing that a privilege or the work-product doctrine exempts these documents from discovery.

The documents here do not involve communications between (1) Chevron's attorneys (in-house or outside counsel) or their staff members and (2) Dr. Hinchee or his staff members. Rather, Chevron and Dr. Hinchee claim that Dr. Hinchee's personal notes and email communications with non-attorneys, such as other experts, enjoy work-product protection under Rule 26(b)(3)(A). We examine this rule next.

B. *Rules 26(b)(3)(A) and (b)(4)*

First enacted in 1970, Rule 26(b)(3)(A) incorporates the attorney work-product doctrine discussed in the Supreme Court's seminal decision in *Hickman v. Taylor*, 329 U.S. 495 (1947). . . . It is undisputed that the documents at issue were prepared "in anticipation of litigation or for trial" and that Dr. Hinchee and his colleagues prepared these documents as part of their work for Chevron. It is also undisputed that Dr. Hinchee is a testifying expert for Chevron.

Chevron and Dr. Hinchee contend that Rule 26(b)(3)(A) protects the materials at issue here because Dr. Hinchee is Chevron's "representative" and, therefore, these materials were "prepared by or for a representative." Alternatively, Chevron and Dr. Hinchee argue that these materials are covered by Rule 26(b)(3)(A) because they were "prepared for a party." The threshold question is, however, whether Rule 26(b)(3)(A) even applies to a testifying expert.

The text, structure, and background of Rule 26 suggest otherwise. While Rule 26(b)(3)(A) mentions a "party or its representative," including an "attorney, consultant, surety, indemnitor, insurer, or agent," the word "expert" is noticeably absent. This silence speaks volumes, in light of the fact that right after subsection (b)(3), Rule 26 contains another provision expressly dealing with experts. Concurrent with the enactment of Rule 26(b)(3)(A) in 1970, the drafters also implemented an entirely new provision in Rule 26(b)(4)(A) to address specifically the discovery of facts known and opinions held by a testifying expert that were "acquired or developed in anticipation of litigation or for trial." . . .

The 1970 Advisory Committee noted that a "prohibition against discovery of information held by expert witnesses produces in acute form the very evils that discovery has been created to prevent." The Advisory Committee elaborated that "[e]ffective cross-examination of an expert witness requires advance preparation," and "effective rebuttal requires advance knowledge of the line of testimony of the other side." "If the latter is foreclosed by a rule against discovery, then the narrowing of issues and elimination of surprise which discovery normally produces are frustrated."

In 2010, Rule 26(b)(4) was amended again. New Rule 26(b)(4)(B) was "added to provide work-product protection under Rule 26(b)(3)(A) and (B) for drafts of expert reports or disclosures." New Rule 26(b)(4)(C) was "added to provide work-product protection for attorney-expert communications regardless of the form of the communications, whether oral, written, electronic, or otherwise." But the 2010 Advisory Committee cautioned that new Rules 26(b)(4)(B) and (C) "do not impede discovery about the opinions to be offered by the expert or the development, foundation, or basis of those opinions." . . . .

Given that the drafters explicitly and specifically address work-product claims with respect to experts in Rule 26(b)(4) and never mention experts in (b)(3), it is difficult to say, as Chevron does, that Rule 26(b)(3)(A) applies to all testifying expert materials in general and that Rule 26(b)(4) merely clarifies that general principle in a specific context. To the contrary, a reading of Rule 26(b)(3)(A) to include testifying experts would render parts of Rule 26(b)(4) superfluous, a result disfavored by our canons of statutory (or here rule) interpretation.

For example, if Rule 26(b)(3)(A) covered all trial preparation materials prepared by or for a testifying expert, there would have been little need for the rule drafters to specifically add work-product protection for draft expert reports and for attorney-expert communications in Rules 26(b)(4)(B) and (C). Draft expert reports and attorney-expert communications would already enjoy work-product protection under Rule 26(b)(3)(A).

Indeed, an overbroad reading of Rule 26(b)(3)(A) would undermine the drafters' deliberate choice in Rules 26(b)(4)(B) and (C) to extend work-product protection to only draft expert reports and attorney-expert communications. . . .

There is good reason why the general work-product doctrine of Rule 26(b)(3)(A) does not cover a testifying expert. Rule 26(b)(3)(A) traces its roots to *Hickman*'s directive that "it is essential that a *lawyer* work with a certain degree of privacy, free from unnecessary intrusion by opposing parties and their counsel." 329 U.S. at 510 (emphasis added). . . .

Unlike an "attorney, consultant, surety, indemnitor, insurer, or agent," see Fed. R. Civ. P. 26(b)(3)(A), a testifying expert's role is to provide independent, impartial, qualified opinion testimony helpful to the trier of fact. Given that testifying experts offer evidence in court, the opposing side must have the opportunity to challenge the opinions of a testifying expert, including how and why the expert formed a particular opinion. Cloaking all materials prepared by or for a testifying expert under the work-product doctrine inhibits the thorough and sharp cross examination that is vital to our adversary system. . . .

C. *Rule 26(a)(2)(B) and the 2010 Amendments*

The parties also dispute the impact of Rule 26(a)(2)(B) and the 2010 Amendment to that rule. Chevron and Dr. Hinchee argue that because the 2010 Amendments narrowed the expert disclosure requirements of Rule 26(a)(2)(B), Dr. Hinchee need not produce his notes and communications with non-attorneys that are at issue in this case. Accordingly, we discuss the history and current version of Rule 26(a)(2). . . .

[The court quoted the former version of Rule 26(a)(2)(B), which required an expert's report to include, among other things, "the data or other information considered by the witness in forming the opinions." Most cases held that this provision required a party to disclose all information provided to testifying experts, including core work product.]

To alter the outcome of these cases, the 2010 Amendments did two things. First, as outlined above, the drafters added Rules 26(b)(4)(B) and (C) to protect draft expert reports and attorney-expert communications as work product. Second, the drafters changed the language of Rule 26(a)(2)(B) from "data or other information" to "facts or data." This change rejects the outcome reached by cases that relied on the old "other information" language in Rule 26(a)(2)(B) to compel the production of draft expert reports and communications between attorneys and experts. Rule 26(a)(2)(B) was changed so that it would not conflict with new Rules 26(b)(4)(B) and (C), which now expressly exempt draft reports and attorney-expert communications from discovery. . . .

None of this suggests the drafters' intent to confer work-product status on the notes of a testifying expert or on a testifying expert's communications with other experts. Rather, the 2010 Amendment to Rule 26(a)(2)(B) was intended to protect the opinion work-product of attorneys in the context of expert discovery. As the 2010 Advisory Committee put it, "[t]he refocus of disclosure on 'facts or data' is meant to limit disclosure to material of a factual nature by excluding *theories or mental impressions of counsel*" (emphasis added). . . . In other words, the term "facts or data" includes all materials considered by a testifying expert, except the core opinion work-product of attorneys.

Notably here, Chevron and Dr. Hinchee do not argue that the discovery materials at issue in this case contain the core opinion work-product of Chevron attorneys. Instead, by withholding Dr. Hinchee's personal notes and communications with other experts, Chevron and Dr. Hinchee attempt to shield the theories and mental impressions of Dr. Hinchee and his fellow testifying experts. Rule 26 provides no basis for this, neither before nor after the 2010 Amendments.

To the extent any attorney core opinion work-product is embedded in the 1,200 documents at issue here, Chevron and Dr. Hinchee may appropriately redact such portions — subject to providing a privilege log under Rule 26(b)(5) and submitting the materials for *in camera* review if requested by the Republic and directed by the district court. Any redaction beyond attorney core opinion work-product is not allowed.

Notes and Questions

1. Parties can use expert witnesses when "scientific, technical, or other specialized knowledge will assist the trier of fact to understand the evidence or to determine a fact in issue." Fed. R. Evid. 702. Expert witnesses are not tied to their first-hand observations, and can give opinions on the ultimate

issues in a case. Fed. R. Evid. 704(a). Because expert witnesses can have a powerful influence over a trial, it is important that a person be qualified to testify as an expert; a bricklayer cannot give an expert opinion on whether a neurosurgeon performed competent brain surgery. The Supreme Court and lower federal courts have been active in policing expert qualifications and testimony. *See* Daubert v. Merrell Dow Pharm., Inc., 509 U.S. 579 (1993).

2. Expert-witness testimony is classically information prepared in anticipation of litigation or for trial. It is, in other words, work product. But trials might revert to the common-law "trial by ambush" if testifying experts' opinions received substantial protection from pretrial disclosure. Thus, Rules 26(a)(2) and –(b)(4) limit the ability of parties to throw a veil over their experts' work product. Rule 26(a)(2) requires parties both to identify expert witnesses that a party "may use at trial" and, as a general matter, to provide a report that describes these experts' opinions and the grounds for their opinions. A party who fails to comply with these disclosure-and-report obligations risks the possibility that the court will bar the expert from testifying at trial. *See* Fed. R. Civ. P. 37(c)(1).

Rule 26(b)(4) provides that the parties can obtain discovery from expert witnesses "whose opinions may be presented at trial." In *Hinchee*, Chevron argued that information not discoverable from an expert under Rule 26(b)(4) receives the work-product protection of Rule 26(b)(3). The court of appeals did not disagree with this general principle, but held that the information sought from Dr. Hinchee was discoverable under Rule 26(b)(4).

3. Sometimes parties retain or speak informally with experts but do not call them as witnesses. Rule 26(a)(2) imposes no disclosure obligations for such experts, although Rule 26(b)(4)(D) allows discovery against experts "retained or specially employed" when "exceptional circumstances" make it "impracticable . . . to obtain facts or opinions on the same subject by other means." *See In re* Zofran (Ondansetron) Prods. Liab. Litig., 392 F. Supp. 3d 179, 185-87 (D. Mass. 2019) (finding "exceptional circumstances" that required disclosure of documents between plaintiffs' attorney and an expert whose epidemiological study the attorney financed after the plaintiffs' testifying expert relied on the study). What happens if a party informally consults with, but never retains, an expert? Rule 26(b)(4) is silent, but the Advisory Committee Notes to the 1970 amendments state that Rule 26(b)(4) "precludes discovery against experts who were informally consulted in preparation for trial, but not retained or specially employed."

4. At the end of *Hinchee*, the court of appeals mentioned a *privilege log*. A privilege log is a document that Rule 26(b)(5)(A)(ii) requires a party to prepare when withholding information due to a claim of privilege or work-product protection. The log must "describe the nature of the documents, communications, or tangible things not disclosed — and do so in a manner that, without revealing information itself privileged or protected, will enable other parties to assess the claim." Rule 45(d)(2)(A) provides a comparable mechanism that nonparties must use. If a person fails to comply precisely with these requirements, is the privilege or

protection lost? *Compare* United States v. Constr. Prods. Research, Inc., 73 F.3d 464 (2d Cir. 1996) (privilege lost), *with* Mass. Sch. of Law at Andover, Inc. v. Am. Bar Ass'n, 914 F. Supp. 1172 (E.D. Pa. 1996) (failure to supply supporting documentation did not result in loss of privilege, but did limit objections that could later be made to discovery requests).

5. Another way in which privileges and other protections can be lost is waiver. Waiver can occur when a party or lawyer shares protected material with a third person, including an opponent. For privileges, disclosure to a third party not within the protected relationship is often seen as an automatic waiver. On the other hand, work-product protection is waived only by a disclosure "inconsistent with keeping [the material] from an adversary." *In re* Chevron Corp., 633 F.3d 153, 165 (3d Cir. 2011). For instance, many courts hold that parties who share a "common interest" can exchange work product, although the uncertain boundaries of this so-called *common-interest privilege* make it a minefield for litigators. *See, e.g., In re* Teleglobe Commc'ns Corp., 493 F.3d 345, 362-66 (3d Cir. 2007).

6. The traditional rule on waiver was harsh: The privilege or protection was lost — even if the disclosure was inadvertent — and the waiver encompassed not only the document disclosed but also any other document on the same subject matter. Some courts moved away from the harshness of this rule, especially when the disclosure was excusable or the consequences of waiver would be severe. In 2006, Rules 26(b)(5)(B) and 45(d)(2)(B) were added to deal with aspects of this problem. These provisions allow a person who inadvertently disclosed privileged or protected information to notify the party to whom disclosure was made of the disclosure. After receiving notice, the latter party must sequester or destroy the information and make no further use of it until the claim of privilege or protection is resolved. Neither provision, however, established a standard to resolve whether waiver occurred.

Congress stepped into the fray in 2008, enacting Federal Rule of Evidence 502 to deal with disclosures of attorney-client and work-product information. When a disclosure is "intentional," Rule 502 provides that "the waiver extends to an undisclosed communication or information in a federal or state proceeding" if "the disclosed and undisclosed communications concern the same subject matter" and "they ought in fairness to be considered together." When the disclosure is "inadvertent," Rule 502 states that disclosure "does not operate as a waiver" if the party "took reasonable steps to prevent disclosure . . . and to rectify the error, including (if applicable) following Federal Rule of Civil Procedure 26(b)(5)." Courts have identified five factors to evaluate the reasonableness of precautions: "the extent of the document production"; "[t]he number of inadvertent disclosures"; "[t]he extent of the disclosure"; "[a]ny delay and measures taken to rectify the disclosure"; and "[w]hether the overriding interests of justice would or would not be served by relieving the party of its errors." *See* Rhoads Indus., Inc. v. Bldg. Materials Corp. of Am., 254 F.R.D. 216, 219 (E.D. Pa. 2008); Absolute Activist Value Master Fund Ltd. v. Devine, 262 F. Supp. 3d 1312, 1324 (M.D. Fla. 2017).

(7) Because of the consequences of waiver, persons making disclosures or responding to discovery requests must often do a *privilege review*, in which they examine documents to determine if they contain privileged or otherwise protected information. As *Oxbow* (*supra* p. 121) and *Guardiola* (*supra* p. 130) showed, this review can be costly, especially for the production of ESI. To cut down on the expense, parties often conduct the review of ESI by using predictive coding or by searching for keywords (for instance, searching for the name of the party's attorney). In *Victor Stanley, Inc. v. Creative Pipe, Inc.*, 250 F.R.D. 251 (D. Md. 2008), the court held that defendants waived any privilege for documents that were inadvertently produced after a keyword search. The court used the five-factor test mentioned in the last Note, and concluded that the defendants had failed to take reasonable precautions to prevent inadvertent disclosure. The court relied heavily on the fact that the defendant did not sample the results of the keyword search to determine whether those results were reliable. *Id.* at 256-57. *See also The Sedona Conference Best Practices Commentary on the Use of Search & Information Retrieval Methods in E-Discovery*, 8 SEDONA CONF. J. 200 (2007).

D. HANDLING DISCLOSURE AND DISCOVERY DISPUTES: HEREIN OF SANCTIONS

In *Klipsch Group, Inc. v. ePRO E–Commerce Ltd*, 880 F.3d 620, 630-31 (2d Cir. 2018), the court observed that "compliance [with discovery obligations] is not optional or negotiable; rather, the integrity of our civil litigation process requires that the parties before us, although adversarial to one another, carry out their duties to maintain and disclose the relevant information in their possession in good faith." But the persons from whom disclosure or discovery is sought do not always comply. Sometimes the reason is the correct (or at least reasonable) belief that the requesting party is not entitled to obtain the requested information. Sometimes the reasons are less laudable: to stonewall on providing damaging information or to deplete the requesting party's resources by fighting every step of the way.

The failure to provide disclosure or discovery is usually brought to the court's attention either by means of a motion to compel filed by the party seeking the disclosure or discovery or by means of a motion for a protective order filed by the person resisting the disclosure or discovery. This section examines this process in more detail, and also explores whether sanctions should be imposed either on a party who incorrectly requests discovery or on a person who incorrectly refuses to comply. Unless sanctions exist, persons have little incentive to provide any disclosure or discovery. But what should the sanctions be? If sanctions are severe (for instance, dismissing the case or entering default judgment), we frustrate the goal of deciding cases on the merits. If sanctions are lenient, we tacitly encourage obstreperous behavior.

SECTION D HANDLING DISCLOSURE AND DISCOVERY DISPUTES

1. Motions to Compel

The basic provisions regarding sanctions are Rules 37(a)-(e), which you should read in conjunction with the following case.

NATIONAL HOCKEY LEAGUE V. METROPOLITAN HOCKEY CLUB, INC.

427 U.S. 639 (1976)

■ PER CURIAM.

This case arises out of the dismissal, under Fed. R. Civ. P. 37, of respondents' antitrust action against petitioners for failure to timely answer written interrogatories as ordered by the District Court. The Court of Appeals for the Third Circuit reversed the judgment of dismissal, finding that the District Court had abused its discretion. The question presented is whether the Court of Appeals was correct in so concluding. Rule 37 provides in pertinent part as follows:

> If a party . . . fails to obey an order to provide or permit discovery . . . the court in which the action is pending may make such orders in regard to the failure as are just, and among others the following: . . .
>
> (C) An order striking out pleadings or parts thereof, or staying further proceedings until the order is obeyed, or dismissing the action or proceeding or any part thereof, or rendering a judgment by default against the disobedient party.*

This Court held in *Societe Internationale v. Rogers*, 357 U.S. 197, 212 (1958), that Rule 37

> should not be construed to authorize dismissal of [a] complaint because of petitioner's noncompliance with a pretrial production order when it has been established that failure to comply has been due to inability, and not to willfulness, bad faith, or any fault of petitioner. . . .

The District Court, in its memorandum opinion directing that respondents' complaint be dismissed, summarized the factual history of the discovery proceeding in these words:

> After seventeen months where crucial interrogatories remained substantially unanswered despite numerous extensions granted at the eleventh hour and, in many instances, beyond the eleventh hour, and notwithstanding several admonitions by the Court and promises and commitments by the plaintiffs, the Court must and does conclude that the conduct of the plaintiffs demonstrates the callous disregard of

---

* The 2007 amendments slightly changed the quoted language, and also renumbered it. For the present text, see Fed. R. Civ. P. 37(b)(2)(A) and –(A)(iii)-(vi). In particular, Rule 37(b)(2)(A)(v) authorizes a court to issue an order "dismissing the action or proceeding in whole or in part." — ED.

responsibilities counsel owe to the Court and to their opponents. The practices of the plaintiffs exemplify flagrant bad faith when after being expressly directed to perform an act by a date certain, *viz.*, June 14, 1974, they failed to perform and compounded that noncompliance by waiting until five days afterwards before they filed any motions. Moreover, this action was taken in the face of warnings that their failure to provide certain information could result in the imposition of sanctions under Fed. R. Civ. P. 37. If the sanction of dismissal is not warranted by the circumstances of this case, then the Court can envisage no set of facts whereby that sanction should ever be applied.

The Court of Appeals, in reversing the order of the District Court by a divided vote stated:

After carefully reviewing the record, we conclude that there is insufficient evidence to support a finding that M–GB's failure to file supplemental answers by June 14, 1974 was in flagrant bad faith, willful or intentional. . . .

The Court of Appeals did not question any of the findings of historical fact which had been made by the District Court, but simply concluded that there was in the record evidence of "extenuating factors." The Court of Appeals emphasized that none of the parties had really pressed discovery until after a consent decree was entered between petitioners and all of the other original plaintiffs except the respondents approximately one year after the commencement of the litigation. It also noted that respondents' counsel took over the litigation, which previously had been managed by another attorney, after the entry of the consent decree, and that respondents' counsel encountered difficulties in obtaining some of the requested information. The Court of Appeals also referred to a colloquy during the oral argument on petitioners' motion to dismiss in which respondents' lead counsel assured the District Court that he would not knowingly and willfully disregard the final deadline.

While the Court of Appeals stated that the District Court was required to consider the full record in determining whether to dismiss for failure to comply with discovery orders, *see* Link v. Wabash R.R., 370 U.S. 626 (1962), we think that the comprehensive memorandum of the District Court supporting its order of dismissal indicates that the court did just that. That record shows that the District Court was extremely patient in its efforts to allow the respondents ample time to comply with its discovery orders. Not only did respondents fail to file their responses on time, but the responses which they ultimately did file were found by the District Court to be grossly inadequate.

The question, of course, is not whether this Court, or whether the Court of Appeals, would as an original matter have dismissed the action; it is whether the District Court abused its discretion in so doing. Certainly the findings contained in the memorandum opinion of the District Court quoted earlier in this opinion are fully supported by the record. We think that the lenity evidenced in the opinion of the Court of Appeals, while certainly a significant factor in considering the imposition of sanctions under Rule 37, cannot be allowed to wholly supplant other and equally necessary considerations embodied in that Rule.

There is a natural tendency on the part of reviewing courts, properly employing the benefit of hindsight, to be heavily influenced by the severity of outright dismissal as a sanction for failure to comply with a discovery order. It is quite reasonable to conclude that a party who has been subjected to such an order will feel duly chastened, so that even though he succeeds in having the order reversed on appeal he will nonetheless comply promptly with future discovery orders of the district court.

But here, as in other areas of the law, the most severe in the spectrum of sanctions provided by statute or rule must be available to the district court in appropriate cases, not merely to penalize those whose conduct may be deemed to warrant such a sanction, but to deter those who might be tempted to such conduct in the absence of such a deterrent. If the decision of the Court of Appeals remained undisturbed in this case, it might well be that *these* respondents would faithfully comply with all future discovery orders entered by the District Court in this case. But other parties to other lawsuits would feel freer than we think Rule 37 contemplates they should feel to flout other discovery orders of other district courts. Under the circumstances of this case, we hold that the District Judge did not abuse his discretion in finding bad faith on the part of these respondents, and concluding that the extreme sanction of dismissal was appropriate in this case by reason of respondents' "flagrant bad faith" and their counsel's "callous disregard" of their responsibilities. Therefore, the petition for a writ of certiorari is granted and the judgment of the Court of Appeals is reversed.

■ MR. JUSTICE BRENNAN and MR. JUSTICE WHITE dissent.

■ MR. JUSTICE STEVENS took no part in the consideration or decision of this case.

Notes and Questions

1. After the court determines that a person has improperly withheld information, it enters an order compelling disclosure or discovery. The real question is what additional sanction, if any, should attach to the person failing to make the disclosure or to permit discovery. Rule 37 creates two levels of sanctions: the "minor" sanctions of Rule 37(a) and the "major" sanctions of Rule 37(b). As a general matter, the "major" sanctions are not available for failure to comply with a discovery request; for these sanctions to come into play, a party must violate a court order that compels the party to produce the requested discovery. *See* Fed. R. Civ. P. 37(b)(2)(A). To get such an order, the party who fails to obtain discovery must file a motion to compel. *See* Fed. R. Civ. P. 37(a)(1), –(a)(3)(B). If the court grants the motion and orders production, it must also award, as a first level of "minor" sanctions, the reasonable expenses, including attorney's fees, that the moving party incurred in prosecuting the motion to compel — except that

expenses must not be awarded if the moving party did not attempt "in good faith" to resolve the issue before filing the motion, Fed. R. Civ. P. 37(a)(5)(A)(i); if the reason for not providing discovery is "substantially justified," Fed. R. Civ. P. 37(a)(5)(A)(ii); or if "other circumstances make an award of expenses unjust," Fed. R. Civ. P. 37(a)(5)(A)(iii). Conversely, if the motion to compel is itself not substantially justified, the court must award reasonable expenses against the moving party. Fed. R. Civ. P. 37(a)(5)(B).

2. The point of Rule 37(a) is to decide whether the information should be produced; it is not to impose sanctions on parties with a legitimate (although ultimately incorrect) basis for denying disclosure or discovery. Once the court determines that the material should be provided and issues an order accordingly, the dynamic changes. A recalcitrant party who still refuses to permit discovery is now disobeying an order of the court. Disobedience to the court kicks in the second level of "major" sanctions.

This second level of sanctions is in play in *National Hockey League*. In that case the district judge imposed the ultimate sanction — the death penalty for the plaintiffs' case. But Rule 37(b)(2)(A) provides a host of other permissible sanctions. Should judges be given a smorgasbord of sanctions, or should judicial discretion be confined by directing specific sanctions for specific types of misconduct? *National Hockey League* says that a sanction serves two purposes: punishment of recalcitrant individuals, and deterrence against similar behavior by other parties. Do these goals help you determine the appropriate sanction, either in general or in a case like *National Hockey League*?

3. Exceptional circumstances allow the imposition of the second level of sanctions without a prior order. When a party refuses to serve answers to interrogatories or to respond to requests for production, or fails to appear at a previously noticed deposition, a court can impose any of the sanctions listed in Rules 37(b)(2)(A)(i)-(vi), but not the contempt sanction of Rule 37(b)(2)(A)(vii). Fed. R. Civ. P. 37(d)(1), –(d)(3); *but see* United States v. Certain Real Prop., 126 F.3d 1314, 1317-18 (5th Cir. 1997) (suggesting that sanctions should generally be imposed only for violating a discovery order).

4. Rule 37(e) imposes a specific sanction for the destruction of ESI. Sanctions under Rule 37(e) are allowed only when two conditions pertain: first, the ESI that "should have been preserved in the anticipation or conduct of litigation is lost because a party failed to take reasonable steps to preserve it," and second, the destroyed ESI "cannot be restored or replaced through additional discovery." The level of sanction hinges on whether the ESI was unintentionally lost or the loss of ESI was intentionally designed to prevent another party from obtaining the information. If the loss is unintentional, a court must find that another party was prejudiced by the loss, and may then "order measures no greater than necessary to cure the prejudice." Fed. R. Civ. P. 37(e)(1). If the destruction is intentional, the court may presume that the destroyed information was unfavorable, may instruct the jury to presume that it was unfavorable, or may dismiss the action or enter a default judgment. Fed. R. Civ. P. 37(e)(2). Rule 37(e) does not itself impose a duty to preserve

ESI, which must derive from some other source of law. It only specifies the consequences when a party fails to meet its duty of preservation. *See* Cat3, LLC v. Black Lineage, Inc., 164 F. Supp. 3d 488 (S.D.N.Y. 2016) (holding that alteration of e-mails before their production to the other party amounted to "spoliation of evidence" that was sanctionable under Rule 37(e), even when the original e-mails were eventually restored).

5. The battle over the production of ESI has generated some of the most memorable and substantial sanctions decisions. In *United States v. Philip Morris USA, Inc.*, 327 F. Supp. 2d 21 (D.D.C. 2004), the court ordered a defendant to pay a monetary sanction of $2,750,000 for its failure to comply with a court order requiring preservation of ESI. Another court awarded $500,000 in expenses under Rule 37(c)(1) (and an additional $750,000 in expenses under Rule 11) against a party and its law firm for their failure to disclose a critical document that tended to disprove the liability of another party. The defendant had intentionally deleted the electronic version of the document, but a hard copy remained. The law firm failed to turn over the document for more than two years; in the meantime, the case settled. *See In re* Sept. 11th Liab. Ins. Coverage Cases, 243 F.R.D. 114 (S.D.N.Y. 2007).

6. In a more humorous vein, consider *Avista Management, Inc. v. Wausau Underwriters Insurance Co.*, 2006 WL 1562246 (M.D. Fla. June 6, 2006). The discovery dispute involved the location at which a deposition was to take place. The court "fashion[ed] a new form of dispute resolution":

> [A]t 4:00 P.M. on Friday, June 30, 2006, counsel shall convene at a neutral site agreeable to both parties. If counsel cannot agree on a neutral site, they shall meet on the front steps of the Sam M. Gibbons U.S. Courthouse, 801 North Florida Ave., Tampa, Florida 33602. Each lawyer shall be entitled to be accompanied by one paralegal who shall act as an attendant and witness. At that time and location, counsel shall engage in one (1) game of "rock, paper, scissors." The winner of this engagement shall be entitled to select the location for the . . . deposition . . . . [*Id.* at *1.]

7. For the most part, the sanctions of Rule 37 are geared to parties who fail to provide disclosure or discovery. Nonparties can also be required to supply deposition testimony and documents pursuant to a subpoena. Rule 37(b)(1) describes the sanction against a nonparty who fails to answer questions at a deposition. Rule 45(e) describes the sanction for failing to obey a subpoena.

8. Courts also have a statutory power under 28 U.S.C. § 1927 and an inherent power to impose sanctions for discovery abuses. *See* Chambers v. NASCO, Inc., 501 U.S. 32 (1991); Roadway Express, Inc. v. Piper, 447 U.S. 752 (1980); Link v. Wabash R.R. 370 U.S. 626 (1962). The exact scope of courts' inherent power has never been fully determined. In *Goodyear Tire & Rubber Co. v. Haeger*, 581 U.S. —, 137 S. Ct. 1178 (2017), the Supreme Court clarified some limits on courts' inherent power to award attorney's fees as a sanction for bad-faith conduct. The award of attorney's fees "must

be compensatory rather than punitive in nature," and is thus limited to "those attorney's fees incurred because of the misconduct at issue." *See Klipsch*, 880 F.3d 620 (affirming inherent-power sanctions of $2.68 million for discovery costs incurred as a result of spoliation of ESI, even though the destroyed evidence ultimately was of limited value).

9. Was the penalty in *NHL* too severe? Shouldn't cases be decided on their merits rather than on procedural prerequisites? On the other hand, would any lesser sanction have been adequate to deter violations of the discovery rules and vindicate the court's authority? Courts are generally reluctant to use the dismissal sanction of Rule 37. *Ehrenhaus v. Reynolds*, 965 F.2d 916, 920-21 (10th Cir. 1992), captured the ambivalence:

> . . . Before choosing dismissal as a just sanction, a court should ordinarily consider a number of factors, including: "(1) the degree of actual prejudice to the defendant; (2) the amount of interference with the judicial process; . . . (3) the culpability of the litigant"; (4) whether the court warned the party in advance that dismissal of the action would be a likely sanction for noncompliance; and (5) the efficacy of lesser sanctions. "Only when the aggravating factors outweigh the judicial system's strong predisposition to resolve cases on their merits is dismissal an appropriate sanction."

See also GN Network, Inc. v. Plantronics, Inc., 930 F.3d 76, 82 (3d Cir. 2019) (holding that it was not an abuse of discretion to refuse to enter a default judgment against a defendant who intentionally destroyed ESI).

2. Motions for Protective Orders

Read Rule 26(c). The Rule lists five general circumstances ("annoyance, embarrassment, oppression, or undue burden or expense") in which a party may move a court for an order protecting a party from disclosure or discovery. The Rule then amplifies those five circumstances into a list of eight specific situations in which a court may, "for good cause," issue a protective order precluding or restricting disclosure or discovery. When a party claims that disclosure or discovery should not occur at all, a motion for a protective order is essentially the mirror image of a motion to compel; rather than objecting and waiting for the motion to compel, a party preemptively moves for a protective order to block discovery.

Indeed, as evidence of the mirror-image nature of the Rule 37 motion to compel and the Rule 26 motion for a protective order, a court that denies a motion to compel in whole or part can at the same time issue a protective order. *See* Fed. R. Civ. P. 37(a)(5)(B), –(C). Furthermore, the sanctions for filing an inappropriate motion for a protective order (or, conversely, for filing an inappropriate discovery request that necessitates a motion for a protective order) are the same as the first level of minor sanctions employed with motions to compel. *See* Fed. R. Civ. P. 26(c)(3), 37(a)(5)(A).

The following case describes a different, increasingly popular function that protective orders serve in modern American litigation.

IN RE NATIONAL PRESCRIPTION OPIATE LITIGATION

927 F.3d 919 (6th Cir. 2019)

Before GUY, CLAY, and GRIFFIN, Circuit Judges.

CLAY, Circuit Judge.

Intervenors HD Media Company, LLC ("HDM") and The W.P. Company, LLC, d/b/a the Washington Post ("Washington Post") appeal the district court Opinion and Order holding that the data in the Drug Enforcement Administration's Automation of Reports and Consolidated Orders System ("ARCOS") database cannot be disclosed by Plaintiffs pursuant to state public records requests. . . .

BACKGROUND

[The plaintiffs are 1,300 public entities, including cities, counties, and Native American tribes. Defendants are manufacturers, distributors, and retailers of prescription opiate drugs. The plaintiffs sued the defendants in federal court to recover the funds expended to respond to the opioid epidemic in their communities, allegedly due to the fraudulent marketing practices of the defendants. Through a process known as multidistrict litigation ("MDL"), *see* 28 U.S.C. § 1407, the cases were consolidated before one district judge in the Northern District of Ohio.

[Using Rule 45, the plaintiffs subpoenaed the ARCOS database from the United States Drug Enforcement Administration (DEA), which was not a party. This database is a comprehensive drug reporting system that monitors the flow of controlled substances from their point of manufacture through distribution channels to point of sale or distribution at the dispensing/retail level. Following a stipulation between the plaintiffs and the DEA, the district court adopted a protective order, providing that the ARCOS data "shall remain confidential and shall be used only for litigation purposes or in connection with state and local law enforcement efforts."

[Over the DEA's objection, the district court ordered the DEA to provide ARCOS data for specific states from 2006 through 2014. The district court found that the DEA had not met its burden of showing "good cause" not to comply with the Rule 45 subpoena. Specifically, the court stated that the data were necessary to reveal the extent of the allegedly fraudulent marketing, that disclosure would not affect ongoing law-enforcement efforts, and that disclosure would not cause substantial competitive harm to the defendants. The DEA handed over the data.

[Subsequently, the intervenors filed public-records requests with some of the plaintiffs to obtain the data. The DEA and the defendants objected to disclosure of the data, and HDM and the Washington Post intervened in the case to litigate the issue.]

. . . In an Opinion and Order, the district court held that the public records requests must be denied because the requests were barred by the court's Protective Order and Defendants and the DEA had demonstrated "good cause" for the Protective Order's application to such requests, as required under Rule 26(c)(1)....

DISCUSSION

...

II. *"Good Cause" for the Protective Order*

This Court reviews the question of whether a district court's protective order was premised upon a showing of good cause for an abuse of discretion.

A protective order shall only be entered upon a showing of "good cause" by the party seeking protection. Fed. R. Civ. P. 26(c)(1).... To show good cause for a protective order, the moving party is required to make "a particular and specific demonstration of fact, as distinguished from stereotyped and conclusory statements." A district court abuses its discretion where it "ma[kes] neither factual findings nor legal arguments supporting the need for" the order. Despite these formal requirements, "it is common practice for parties to stipulate to [protective] orders." Protective orders "are often blanket in nature, and allow the parties to determine in the first instance whether particular materials fall within the order's protection."

Because parties may stipulate to a protective order, courts sometimes permit intervenors to challenge protective orders. If an intervenor challenges a protective order, "the burden of proof will remain with the party seeking protection when the protective order was a stipulated order and no party had made a 'good cause' showing."

In this case, the parties stipulated to a protective order that would prevent Plaintiffs from disclosing the ARCOS data to the media, and the district court did not make a good cause finding on this issue before entering its Protective Order....

Because the issue of public disclosure of the ARCOS data was never squarely raised before the district court, the court never had occasion to find that Defendants or the DEA had made "a particular and specific demonstration of fact" justifying the Protective Order's permanent blanket ban on such disclosure....

Despite the "substantial latitude" afforded to district courts during the discovery process, *see* Seattle Times Co. v. Rhinehart, 467 U.S. 20, 36, (1984), we hold that the district court abused its discretion in finding that good cause existed to permanently and categorically prevent the ARCOS data from being disclosed pursuant to public records requests. In considering whether good cause for protection exists, we balance the interests in favor of disclosure against the interests in favor of nondisclosure. Accordingly, we will balance Intervenors' interest in reporting on the ARCOS data and the public interest in learning what such reporting would reveal against Defendants' and the DEA's interest in keeping the ARCOS data secret....

Ironically, the best evidence that good cause did not exist for the Protective Order comes from the district court's own balancing of the interests in disclosure versus nondisclosure.

In ordering the DEA to disclose the ARCOS data to Plaintiffs, the district court specifically held that the DEA did *not* meet its burden of showing "good cause" not to comply with Plaintiffs' subpoena for the ARCOS data. The court noted that the data "provid[es] invaluable, highly-specific information regarding historic patterns of opioid sales," and emphasized that the role each Defendant played in the crisis "can be revealed *only by all of the data*." (Emphasis added.) The district court, comparing the opioid crisis to a plague, even stated that because it is possible to "discover how and where the virus grew" by studying the ARCOS data, disclosure of the ARCOS data "is a reasonable step toward defeating the disease."

In the same order concerning disclosure to Plaintiffs, the district court rejected Defendants' and the DEA's arguments that there was "good cause" for nondisclosure. The court specifically rejected the DEA's arguments that disclosing the data would interfere with law enforcement interests. . . . The court likewise rejected the argument that producing the data would cause Defendants competitive harm, explaining that "the assertion was conclusory and . . . market data over three years old carried no risk of competitive harm."

Between the time it ordered the DEA to produce the ARCOS data to Plaintiffs and the time it denied Intervenors' requests for the data, the district court seems to have done a complete about-face concerning the relevant interests at stake. It is true that this about-face might be explained in part by the different interests at stake when disclosure is made only to parties to a case pursuant to a protective order, as compared to third parties that intend to publicly report on the disclosed information. In other words, the fact that the district court ordered the DEA to disclose the ARCOS data to Plaintiffs pursuant to the Protective Order does not necessarily imply that the same considerations would require disclosing that data to Intervenors and, by extension, the public.

However, it is readily apparent from the record that the district court's analysis in its first order did take into account the public's interest in obtaining the ARCOS data and the interests of Defendants and the DEA in keeping this data from the public. . . .

. . . Our "good cause" inquiry takes into account "[t]he scope of the protective order" as it relates to the relevant interests. Because the Protective Order in this case prevented any disclosure of any ARCOS data by any Plaintiff, and because this ban on disclosure would remain in effect in perpetuity, the DEA and Defendants faced a high hurdle in demonstrating "good cause" for these extreme restrictions. . . .

For the foregoing reasons, we hold that the district court abused its discretion in finding "good cause" not to permit disclosure of the ARCOS data pursuant to state public records requests. We vacate the district court's Protective Order and remand to permit the district court to consider entering a new protective order consistent with the proper legal standards as set forth in this opinion. On remand the district court may entertain arguments by the DEA as to why particular pieces of ARCOS data that relate to specific ongoing investigations should not be disclosed; however, the district court shall not enter a blanket, wholesale ban on disclosure pursuant to state public records requests. Nor shall any modified protective order specify that the ARCOS data be destroyed or returned to the DEA at the conclusion of this litigation. . . .

■ [The opinion of GUY, Circuit Judge, concurring in part and dissenting in part, is omitted.]

Notes and Questions

1. The protective order in *Opiate Litigation* was not designed to prevent the production of information, but rather to prevent its public dissemination. The point of such protective orders is often to avoid discovery disputes. If the entity possessing discoverable information knows that its information will be made available to the public, it may fight disclosure or discovery with great vigor. As long as the material will not be disseminated widely, however, it has less reason to object. Hence, a consensual protective order reduces discovery disputes and streamlines the case. Parties also consent to protective orders in which they agree to designate documents as confidential and reserve until later any objections to their use. Under these *blanket* or *umbrella protective orders*, the parties get to see the material, much of which will probably never be used as evidence. Thus, the disputes over the discovery and admissibility of evidence are reduced from entire categories of documents to the few that really matter. These blanket protective orders also avoid the waiver problems that inadvertent disclosure can create (*see supra* pp. 159-60, Notes 5-7). Even with such an order, parties will still object to the discovery of some materials, such as those involving attorney-client privilege or work product.

2. Courts are public institutions resolving public disputes, and some have argued that the public has a right to know what is going on within those institutions and disputes. In *Seattle Times Co. v. Rhinehart*, 467 U.S. 20 (1984), a newspaper involved in litigation obtained in discovery newsworthy information that it wished to print. A state court issued a protective order preventing its publication. The newspaper protested, arguing that it enjoyed a First Amendment right to publish the information. The Supreme Court concluded that it had no such right:

> As the Rules authorizing discovery were adopted by the state legislature, the processes thereunder are a matter of legislative grace. A litigant has no First Amendment right of access to information made available only for purposes of trying his suit. Thus, continued court control over the discovered information does not raise the same specter

of government censorship that such control might suggest in other situations.

Moreover, pretrial depositions and interrogatories are not public components of a civil trial. Such proceedings were not open to the public at common law, and, in general, they are conducted in private as a matter of modern practice. . . .

There is an opportunity, therefore, for litigants to obtain — incidentally or purposefully — information that not only is irrelevant but if publicly released could be damaging to reputation and privacy. . . . The prevention of the abuse that can attend the coerced production of information under a State's discovery rule is sufficient justification for the authorization of protective orders. [*Id.* at 35-36.]

3. Protective orders have also been attacked under the common-law right of access to judicial records, which antedates the United States Constitution. "The right of access includes the right to attend court proceedings and to inspect and copy public records and documents, including judicial records and documents." *In re* Avandia Mktg., Sales Practices & Prods. Liab. Litig., 924 F.3d 662, 672 (3d Cir. 2019). Courts apply a presumption (which they sometimes characterize as "strong") of access to "pretrial motions of a nondiscovery nature"; the presumption can be overcome only by "compelling, countervailing interests." *Id.* This analysis is distinct from the "good cause" analysis of Rule 26(c), and usually comes into play when a party attaches to a motion a document that was designated as confidential under an umbrella protective order.

4. Even though doing so may disturb settled expectations, courts modify protective orders in some situations. The seminal case is *In re "Agent Orange" Product Liability Litigation*, 821 F.2d 139 (2d Cir. 1987), which permitted public disclosure even though the defendants had settled the case on the express condition that no disclosure of discovery materials would occur. The court did not allow the defendants to back out of the settlement.

5. Violations of umbrella protective orders may be sanctionable. *See Smith & Fuller P.A. v. Cooper Tire & Rubber Co.*, 685 F.3d 486 (5th Cir. 2012), (upholding a $29,668 sanction issued under Rule 37(b)(2) when attorneys who had obtained information under an umbrella protective order inadvertently disclosed it during a conference call with attorneys handling related cases). *But see* Lipscher v. LRP Publ'ns, Inc., 266 F.3d 1305, 1323 (11th Cir. 2001) ("[A] Rule 26(c) protective order is not 'an order to provide or permit discovery,' and therefore, such orders do not fall within the scope of Rule 37(b)(2)."); *see also id.* (leaving open whether violating a protective order could be sanctioned under a court's inherent power).

3. Certifications in the Discovery Process

One way to deal with discovery abuse is to sanction failures to provide appropriate discovery. Until 1983, that was the principal approach used in the Federal Rules. Another approach is to impose a specific obligation on the attorneys to engage only in responsible discovery practices, and then to call the lawyers to account when they fail to abide by this duty.

Read Rule 26(g), which was first adopted, in a slightly different form, in 1983. Rule 26(g) places affirmative obligations on lawyers and parties to eschew certain practices. The basic structure and language of Rule 26(g) should sound familiar — it is the discovery counterpart to Rule 11. (You might recall that Rule 11(d) made Rule 11 inapplicable to disclosures and to discovery requests, responses, objections, and motions.)

As with Rule 11, an attorney or unrepresented party must sign "[e]very disclosure under Rule 26(a)(1) or (a)(3) and every discovery request, response, or objection." (An opposing party has no obligation to act if the document is unsigned. *See* Fed. R. Civ. P. 26(g)(2).) As with Rule 11, the signature constitutes a certification of certain matters. For disclosures, an attorney's signature certifies that a disclosure "is complete and correct as of the time it is made." *See* Fed. R. Civ. P. 26(g)(1)(A). For discovery requests, responses, and objections, the signature certifies three things that largely overlap with each other and that echo the comparable rule 11 certifications: essentially, the party has a good legal and factual basis for its request, response, or objection. *See* Fed. R. Civ. P. 26(g)(1)(B). Note in particular Rule 26(g)(1)(B)(iii), which emphasizes yet again the proportionality requirements of Rules 26(b)(1) and –(b)(2)(C).

Sanctions for a violation of Rule 26(g) lack the specificity of Rule 37's sanctions. *See* Fed. R. Civ. P. 26(g)(3) (allowing an "appropriate sanction"). Unless the violation is "substantially justified," this sanction is mandatory, and "may include" an award of attorney's fees. Rule 26(g) contains no safe-harbor provision akin to that added to Rule 11(c)(2) in 1993. Why not? Part of the answer is that Rule 26(g) has never generated the amount of satellite litigation that the pre-1993 Rule 11 did; most discovery disputes are still handled under Rule 37. Because Rule 37 sanctions have not been abandoned, what value does Rule 26(g) add to the process of handling discovery disputes? Given the nature of the certifications, can a violation of Rule 26(g) ever be "substantially justified"? Note that Rule 11 has no similar "substantial justification" excuse for avoiding sanctions.

4. Other Sanctions

Three other sanctions merit brief mention. First, a party who fails to disclose a witness or information under Rule 26(a), or who fails to supplement a disclosure or discovery response to list a newly discovered witness or information under Rule 26(e), is subject to the sanction of Rule 37(c)(1): the party cannot use the witness or information "at a hearing, or at a trial, unless the failure was substantially justified." A failure to disclose or supplement can also lead to the award of reasonable expenses, informing "the jury of the party's failure," and the sanctions of Rules 37(b)(2)(A)(i)-(vi) (but not the contempt sanction of Rule 37(b)(2)(A)(vii)). *See* Fed. R. Civ. P. 37(c)(1). Why is there no comparable sanction for a party who fails to provide the name of a known witness in response to an interrogatory asking for such information? (Hint: recall that major discovery sanctions arise only when a party violates a court order.)

Second, Rule 37(c)(2) permits sanctions when a party fails to admit the genuineness or truth of a Rule 36 request for admission, thus forcing the other party to the time and expense of proving the proposition. The sanction is limited (paying the other party's reasonable expenses and fees for proving the point that was not admitted), and it is unavailable when the admission was "of no substantial importance," the "party failing to admit had a reasonable ground to believe that it might prevail," or "there was other good reason for the failure to admit." Isn't this sanction — especially in light of the exceptions — pretty toothless? If the Federal Rules cared about narrowing issues before trial, wouldn't the sanction be greater?

Finally, Rule 37(f) provides a sanction against a party who fails "to participate in good faith" in the framing of the Rule 26(f) discovery plan. The sanction — paying reasonable expenses, including attorney's fees, caused by the failure to participate — is not great; the real "sanction" is that the court might accept the opponent's discovery plan.

Chapter Four

Case Management, Settlement, and Alternative Dispute Resolution

This course primarily concerns judicial procedures for adjudicating civil disputes. As we have told the story so far, the point of pleading and discovery is to ready the case for adjudication, and adjudication is *the* method for resolving disputes. But that story is incomplete. Many people resolve disputes without ever entering the litigation system. Even among disputes that enter the system, the parties often settle or otherwise resolve the cases without a formal adjudication of rights and liabilities. Indeed, adjudication is the exception and not the rule — in recent years, less than one percent of civil cases filed in federal court end in a trial. Many of the remainder are dismissed on motions, dropped, or defaulted, but even more are settled.

The frequency of settlement should not be surprising. When rational parties have access to the relevant information about their dispute, they can perceive the strengths and the weaknesses of each other's cases, as well as the likely range of recovery if the plaintiff wins. With that knowledge, they will often be in a position to settle. For instance, if the plaintiff seems poised to recover $100,000 to $150,000 if he or she wins, and if the evidence developed in pretrial suggests that the plaintiff has somewhere between a 40% and a 60% chance of winning, then in a costless procedural world, rational, risk-neutral parties would probably settle the case for something between $40,000 (40% x $100,000) and $90,000 (60% x $150,000). The costs of litigation must then be factored in. If it will cost each side $10,000 to try the case, then the actual range of settlement becomes $30,000 to $100,000. There is, to be sure, no guarantee that the parties will settle the case; the plaintiff might refuse to back off from a demand for $100,000, and the defendant might dig in at $30,000. Moreover, the parties might not assess the chances of success or the likely amount of recovery the same way, or one side may be willing to take a big gamble. But in many cases, the pretrial process gives the parties something they did not have before: the information they need to resolve their dispute.

Understood from this viewpoint, the pretrial process is more about resolving the dispute than about beginning the adjudication of a claim. Adjudication is still important; it is the default dispute-resolution mechanism when others fail. The pretrial process, though, must be designed not only with adjudication in mind, but also with the goal of helping the parties come to their own resolution of the dispute. Adjudication is only one means — settlement, mediation, and arbitration are others — through which the dispute can end. Indeed, in recent decades one of the growth areas in legal practice has been the field of *alternative dispute resolution* (ADR), with some lawyers representing their clients in ADR processes and other lawyers (who sometimes describe themselves sardonically as "recovering litigators") providing ADR services as mediators or arbitrators.

As we have seen, however, the pretrial process raises two related concerns: its costliness and its relative weakness in narrowing the case down to the critical issues to be decided. The main discovery devices are not oriented toward removing the issues, claims, or defenses that turn out not to be in dispute. If anything, discovery is likely to inject new factual and legal issues into the litigation. The lawyers in an adversarial system may be good at getting facts from each other; but their duty is to represent their side with vigor, and they will not lightly concede a point to their opponents. Likewise, a lawyer representing a better-financed party has an incentive to make the litigation expensive in order to force an opponent to drop out. If costs are to be controlled and the issues narrowed, someone else must become involved.

The most logical "someone else" is the judge. This judicial function is usually called *case management*. The managerial judge assumes a very different role from that of the judge in the classic adversarial model, who stays detached from the case until the trial begins. To the contrary, the managerial judge has some similarities to the activist judge of the civil-law system.

Although they are independent ideas, both ADR and case management have a common impulse: the more efficient resolution of disputes. Unsurprisingly, both came into full flower in the 1970s and 1980s, as concerns about the costliness and breadth of modern American litigation grew more common. The two ideas can merge; one of the judge's case-management techniques is to encourage parties to use ADR methods. Both ADR and case management stretch the paradigm of an adversarial and party-controlled model of adjudication. Whether they are, independently or together, the salvation of our generally liberal pleading and discovery system, or whether they are instead ill-advised steps away from the adversarial process that is our American cultural tradition, is the ultimate question that this chapter addresses.

SECTION A: PERSPECTIVES ON CASE MANAGEMENT, SETTLEMENT, AND ALTERNATIVE DISPUTE RESOLUTION

WILLIAM W SCHWARZER, THE FEDERAL RULES, THE ADVERSARY PROCESS, AND DISCOVERY REFORM

50 U. PITT. L. REV. 703, 703-06, 713-18 (1989)

The framers of the Federal Rules of Civil Procedure had no doubts about the adversary process. Their purpose was to fashion a procedural framework in which that process could function effectively, free of surprise and technical encumbrance. In this framework, lawyers would manage their cases, would obtain all necessary information through pretrial discovery, and, if they failed to settle, would bring the case to trial promptly. As one enthusiastic commentator described it, "The 'sporting theory of justice' has been rejected. Victory is intended to go to the party entitled to it, on all the facts, rather than to the side which best uses its wits." The result would be the "just, speedy and inexpensive determination of every action."

Fifty years later, that vision has become clouded and the framers' purpose is largely unfulfilled. The staggering increase in the volume and complexity of cases has thrust case management on judges and has involved them deeply in controlling the scope and pace of litigation. Discovery, originally conceived as the servant of the litigants to assist them in reaching a just outcome, now tends to dominate the litigation and inflict disproportionate costs and burdens. Often it is conducted so aggressively and abusively that it frustrates the objectives of the Federal Rules. It has been said that now lawyers must try their cases twice, once before trial and once at trial. . . .

In the context of discovery and pretrial, adversarial techniques are generally counterproductive. They tend to interfere with disclosure — it is, after all, intuitively inconsistent with the adversarial ideal to be helpful to one's opponent. It is extraordinarily difficult for a lawyer to let her witness give damaging testimony at a deposition or for the interrogating lawyer not to try to take advantage of opportunities to trap or mislead a witness in the questioning. To have to produce a smoking gun document is a wrenching experience for a lawyer, often followed by soul searching over whether it could have been avoided. And adversarial techniques are not conducive to nonconfrontational approaches at pretrial leading to narrowing issues and expediting the litigation. It is hard for a lawyer to concede an issue that in good faith ought not to be litigated. The adversarial ideal is not to give in but to fight — fairly, to be sure, but to fight — and let the court decide. But making pretrial procedures, in particular discovery, dependent on contested proceedings culminating in court orders means that the purposes of the rules to bring about the "just, speedy and inexpensive determination of every action" will never be realized. . . .

The issue is not whether the adversary process should be abandoned.... [F]or the trial of lawsuits, the adversary process is probably superior to the alternative the continental system offers. But for the pretrial stages of litigation, the practice under the continental system bears sympathetic examination, if not emulation. That practice involves the staged development of the case under the direction of the judge, with a gradual narrowing of issues as the facts are marshalled. The process is deliberate and controlled, not competitive or confrontational.

Without acknowledging a debt to the continental system, practice under the Federal Rules has evolved in much the same direction. Under the pressure of heavier and more complex dockets, federal judges have felt compelled to modify their traditional role and take a more active part in the management of litigation. This practice has been legitimated by the amendments of Rules 16 and 26 which confirm that judges, while remaining fair and impartial, are no longer expected to be passive and ignorant.

Hand in hand has come a decline in the degree of control exercised by lawyers over their cases. Increasingly the preparation and presentation of cases is subjected to judicial supervision through the judge's control over discovery, motion practice, issue definition, scheduling, and other aspects of pretrial activity.

Judicial intervention, reinforced by the pressure of escalating litigation costs, has given powerful impetus to early disposition of cases. Trial is becoming the least favored means for resolving controversies in the opinion of probably a majority of lawyers and judges.... The system of procedural and evidentiary rules designed to ascertain the truth has therefore lost much of its significance in the disposition of civil controversies.

JUDITH RESNIK, MANAGERIAL JUDGES

96 HARV. L. REV. 374, 378, 408, 413, 417, 424-25, 427, 430 (1982)

... Judges have described their new tasks as "case management" — hence my term "managerial judges." As managers, judges learn more about cases much earlier than they did in the past. They negotiate with parties about the course, timing, and scope of both pretrial and posttrial litigation. These managerial responsibilities give judges greater power. Yet the restraints that formerly circumscribed judicial authority are conspicuously absent. Managerial judges frequently work beyond the public view, off the record, with no obligation to provide written, reasoned opinions, and out of reach of appellate review....

... Informal judge-litigant contact provides judges with information beyond that traditionally within their ken. [Pretrial conference] topics are more wide ranging and the judges' concerns are broader than either are when proceedings are conducted in court. The supposedly rigid structure of evidentiary rules, designed to insulate decision-makers from extraneous and impermissible information, is irrelevant in case management. Managerial judges are not silent auditors of retrospective events retold by first-person storytellers. Instead, judges remove their blindfolds and become part of the sagas themselves. . . .

. . . [F]ew institutional [constraints] inhibit judges during the pretrial phase. . . . During pretrial supervision, judges make many decisions informally and often meet with parties *ex parte*, and appellate review is virtually unavailable. The judge has vast influence over the course and eventual outcome of the litigation. As a result, litigants have good reason to capitulate to judicial pressure rather than risk the hostility of a judge who . . . has ongoing responsibility for the case. During pretrial management, judges are restrained only by personal beliefs about the proper role of judge-managers. . . .

Proponents of managerial judging typically assume that management enhances efficiency in three respects. They claim that case management decreases delay, produces more dispositions, and reduces litigation costs. But close examination of the currently available information reveals little support for the conclusion that management is responsible for efficiency gains (if any) at the district court level, and strong reason to suspect that many of the purported efficiency gains in the district courts are illusory. . . .

In the rush to conquer case loads, few proponents of managerial judging have examined its side effects. Judicial management has its own techniques, goals, and values, which appear to elevate speed over deliberation, impartiality, and fairness. . . .

. . . Moreover, judges are in close contact with attorneys during the course of management. Such interactions may become occasions for the development of intense feelings — admiration, friendship, or antipathy. Therefore, management becomes a fertile field for the growth of personal bias.

Further, judges with supervisory obligations may gain stakes in the cases they manage. Their prestige may ride on "efficient" management, as calculated by the speed and number of dispositions. Competition and peer pressure may tempt judges to rush litigants because of reasons unrelated to the merits of disputes. . . .

Unreviewable power, casual contact, and interest in outcome (or in aggregate outcomes) have not traditionally been associated with the "due process" decisionmaking model. These features do not evoke images of reasoned adjudication, images that form the very basis of both our faith in the judicial process and our enormous grant of power to federal judges.

Owen M. Fiss, Against Settlement

93 Yale L.J. 1073, 1073-76, 1085, 1089-90 (1984)

In a recent report . . . , Derek Bok [then the president of Harvard University — Ed.] called for a new direction in legal education. He decried "the familiar tilt in the law curriculum toward preparing students for legal combat," and asked instead that law schools train their students "for the gentler arts of reconciliation and accommodation." He sought to turn our attention from the courts to "new voluntary mechanisms" for resolving disputes. In doing so, Bok echoed themes that have long been associated with [Chief Justice Warren Burger], and that have become a rallying point for the organized bar and the source of a new movement in the law. . . . It has even received its own acronym — ADR (Alternative Dispute Resolution).

The movement . . . extends to ongoing litigation as well, and the advocates of ADR have sought new ways to facilitate and perhaps even pressure parties into settling pending cases. Just last year, Rule 16 of the Federal Rules of Civil Procedure was amended to strengthen the hand of the trial judge in brokering settlements: The "facilitation of settlement" became an explicit purpose of pre-trial conferences . . . .

The advocates of ADR are led to support such measures and to exalt the idea of settlement more generally because they view adjudication as a process to resolve disputes. They act as though courts arose to resolve quarrels between neighbors who had reached an impasse and turned to a stranger for help. . . . [Settlement] seems preferable to judgment because it rests on the consent of both parties and avoids the cost of a lengthy trial.

In my view, however, this account of adjudication and the case for settlement rest on questionable premises. I do not believe that settlement as a generic practice is preferable to judgment or should be institutionalized on a wholesale and indiscriminate basis. It should be treated instead as a highly problematic technique for streamlining dockets. Settlement is for me the civil analogue of plea bargaining: Consent is often coerced; the bargain may be struck by someone without authority; the absence of a trial and judgment renders subsequent judicial involvement troublesome; and although dockets are trimmed, justice may not be done. Like plea bargaining, settlement is a capitulation to the conditions of mass society and should be neither encouraged nor praised. . . .

The disparities in resources between the parties can influence the settlement in three ways. First, the poorer party may be less able to amass and analyze the information needed to predict the outcome of the litigation, and thus be disadvantaged in the bargaining process. Second, he may need the damages he seeks immediately and thus be induced to settle as a way of accelerating payment, even though he realizes he would get less now than he might if he awaited judgment. . . . Third, the poorer party might be forced to settle because he does not have the resources to finance the litigation, to cover either his own projected expenses, such as his lawyer's time, or the expenses his opponent can impose through the manipulation of procedural mechanisms such as discovery. It might seem that settlement benefits the plaintiff by allowing him to avoid the costs of litigation, but this is not so. The defendant can anticipate the plaintiff's costs if the case were to be tried fully and decrease his offer by that amount. The indigent plaintiff is a victim of the costs of litigation even if he settles. . . .

The dispute-resolution story makes settlement appear as a perfect substitute for judgment . . . by trivializing the remedial dimensions of a lawsuit, and also by reducing the social function of the lawsuit to one of resolving private disputes . . . .

In my view, however, the purpose of adjudication should be understood in broader terms. Adjudication uses public resources, and employs not strangers chosen by the parties but public officials chosen by a process in which the public participates. These officials, like members of the legislative and executive branches, possess a power that has been defined and conferred by public law, not by private agreement. Their job is not to maximize the ends of private parties, nor simply to secure the peace, but to explicate and give force to the values embodied in authoritative texts such as the Constitution and statutes: to interpret those values and to bring reality into accord with them. This duty is not discharged when the parties settle. . . .

To conceive of the civil lawsuit in public terms as America does might be unique. I am willing to assume that no other country . . . has a case like *Brown v. Board of Education* in which the judicial power is used to eradicate the caste structure. I am willing to assume that no other country conceives of law and uses law in quite the way we do. But this should be a source of pride rather than shame. What is unique is not the problem, that we live short of our ideals, but that we alone among the nations of the world seem willing to do something about it. Adjudication American-style is not a reflection of our combativeness but rather a tribute to our inventiveness and perhaps even more to our commitment.

Notes and Questions

1. The fulcrum for case management is Rule 16, which provides judges with substantial power to manage litigation. We will examine some of Rule 16's specific provisions shortly. As a general matter, both Judge Schwarzer (a leading proponent of case management) and Professor Resnik (a leading skeptic) agree that the point of the Rule 16 case-management process is to increase the judge's involvement during the pretrial process, with the goal of reducing or eliminating meritless factual and legal issues.

However much Rule 16 has legitimized case management, the debate over its desirability continues. Federal trial judge William Young appended this lament to a decision he had rendered:

> I conceive of trial as the primary means provided by our constitution and laws for the fair and impartial resolution of legal disputes . . . .
>
> This is, however, the minority view. Today, . . . the administrative model of the business of the district courts . . . seeks the speedy, inexpensive (to the courts), and cost-efficient resolution of every case. Trials, being costly and inefficient, are disfavored.

United States v. Massachusetts, 781 F. Supp. 2d 1, 21 (D. Mass. 2011). *See also* Stephen N. Subrin & Thomas O. Main, *The Fourth Era of American Civil Procedure*, 162 U. Pa. L. Rev. 1839, 1850 (2014) (critically appraising the post-1980 era in American civil procedure, in which "the scope of discovery was narrowed; numerical limits restricted the amount of discovery; and new discovery conferences, pre-trial conferences, mandatory disclosures, and sanction rules encouraged closer judicial supervision of discovery.").

In a sweeping historical analysis that describes the evolution from the common-law jury trial to the modern litigation system, Professor Langbein has assessed the modern approach in more favorable terms:

> The discovery regime of the Federal Rules and the associated practices of judicial case management, ostensibly directed at enabling the litigants to prepare for trial, have had the effect of displacing trial in most cases, causing ever more cases to be resolved in the pretrial process, either by settlement or by pretrial adjudication. Pretrial civil procedure has become nontrial civil procedure. . . .
>
> Settlement of a civil dispute has material advantages over adjudication. Settlement is usually cheaper and faster; the court is spared the labor of adjudication; each party is spared the risk of a less favorable outcome; and neither party is stigmatized as the loser. Thus, so long as adjudication is preserved as a viable alternative, the litigants' choice to settle a case is voluntary, and facilitating settlement is sound public policy. . . .
>
> . . . Build a better mousetrap, said Emerson, and the world will beat a path to your door. The Federal Rules built a better mousetrap: a civil procedure centered in pretrial discovery. Litigants no longer go to trial because they no longer need to. . . .
>
> Common law trial was never a particularly good way of resolving fact disputes, because the common law was never able to overcome the mistake that hobbled it from the outset in the Middle Ages, the failure to devise suitable means of investigating the facts. The discovery revolution of the Federal Rules, by overcoming that investigation deficit, set in motion changes that have made trial obsolete.

John H. Langbein, *The Disappearance of Civil Trial in the United States*, 122 YALE L.J. 522, 526, 561, 569, 572 (2012).

2. At one level, the fight over case management is a fight over values: how adversarial should our system of civil litigation be? A more activist or managerial judge does not spell the end of our adversarial system; the lawyers still maintain significant responsibilities in the pretrial process and at trial. But case management suggests possible movement toward more continental-style judge-driven civil litigation. The convergence, though, should not be overstated. American managerial judges have left fact development in parties' hands and have not gone so far as to take on some civil-law judges' inquisitorial role in that aspect of case preparation. *See* Thomas D. Rowe, Jr., *Authorized Managerialism Under the Federal Rules — and the Extent of Convergence with Civil-Law Judging*, 36 SW. U. L. REV. 191 (2007). Moreover, civil-law trial judges typically operate under the fairly tight control of their appellate courts, and do not enjoy the breadth of virtually unreviewable discretion that Professor Resnik emphasizes.

3. At a different level, the fight over case management is a fight over effectiveness: does case management deliver on its promise of more efficient and less contentious dispute resolution? Suppose that case management saved 1% of the total costs of litigation (or, conversely, added 1% to the cost of litigation). Would that affect your judgment about case management? What if the savings were 10%? Or 50%?

Some researchers have investigated whether case management results in cheaper, swifter, or more satisfactory justice. Examining the question from client, attorney, and judicial perspectives, most of the data seem inconclusive to neutral. One of the clear messages to emerge from the data is that establishing an early and firm trial date has a statistically significant effect on reducing a case's time to disposition. It also has an effect — less than statistically significant, but detectable — on the number of attorney hours spent on a case. *See* JAMES S. KAKALIK, RAND CORP., AN EVALUATION OF JUDICIAL CASE MANAGEMENT UNDER THE CIVIL JUSTICE REFORM ACT (1996). The same study found that other early case-management techniques significantly increased attorney work hours (by an average of 20 hours per case). Early case management did, however, reduce delays in litigation (by an average of 1.5 to 2 months). A subsequent study by the same researchers refined these findings: while early management significantly reduced the time to disposition, the decrease was even more dramatic when discovery and case-management planning occurred early in the litigation; and while early management increased attorney hours when it was not accompanied by discovery planning and case-management planning, attorney hours did not increase when such planning occurred. *See* James S. Kakalik et al., *Discovery Management: Further Analysis of the Civil Justice Reform Act Evaluation Data*, 39 B.C. L. REV. 613 (1998).

4. The same theoretical and empirical questions can be asked about ADR methods used in conjunction with litigation. To begin with the theoretical issue, Judge Schwarzer alludes on a couple of occasions to the benefits of ADR. Professor Fiss's article takes a critical stance toward settlement, but his comments can be generalized to other forms of ADR. Professors McThenia and Shaffer take issue with Fiss's critique:

> The "real divide" between us and Fiss may not be our differing views of the sorts of cases that now wind their way into American courts, but, more fundamentally, it may be our different views of justice. Fiss comes close to equating justice with law. He includes among the cases unsuited for settlement "those in which justice needs to be done, or to put it more modestly, where there is a genuine social need for an authoritative interpretation of the law." We do not believe that law and justice are synonymous. . . .
>
> Many advocates of ADR . . . assume not that justice is something people get from the government but that it is something people give to one another.

Andrew McThenia & Thomas Shaffer, *For Reconciliation*, 94 YALE L.J. 1660, 1664-65 (1985). For a list of other advantages of ADR, including its flexibility in meeting the parties' goals and achieving fairer, more ethical, and more democratic adjustments of competing interests than decisions made pursuant to legal rules can provide, see Carrie Menkel-Meadow, *Whose Dispute Is It Anyway? A Philosophical and Democratic Defense of Settlement (in Some Cases)*, 83 GEO. L.J. 2663, 2692 (1995).

In a quarter-century symposium on Fiss's article, *Against Settlement: Twenty-Five Years Later*, 78 FORDHAM L. REV. 1117 (2009), Professor Moffitt looks for common ground, suggesting that settlement skeptics and supporters are all concerned about power imbalances, agency costs, and barriers to court access. Proponents of settlement and of litigation "embrace the same values" of efficiency, justice, truth, and stability. "Both settlement and litigation fail on each of these measures with some reliability, and both processes continue to undergo reforms aimed at improving their performances as measured by these values. But to characterize either as unconcerned with any one of these values is . . . false." Michael Moffitt, *Three Things To Be Against ("Settlement" Not Included)*, 78 FORDHAM L. REV. 1203, 1245 (2009).

Fiss yields not an inch. "Judges are judges, not brokers of deals, and I fear that a too-ready acquiescence in the directives of those who want them to behave otherwise will — not in a day, but over time — diminish their authority in the eyes of the community. Judges must, I believe, . . . adhere to the procedures that have long allowed them to wear the mantle of the law." Owen M. Fiss, *The History of an Idea*, 78 FORDHAM L. REV. 1273, 1280 (2009).

Professor Resnik has framed the issue in terms of the centuries-old commitment to enforce private rights, modern political movements designed to assure equality, and the cost and desirability of broad access to courts:

> If persons . . . have no way to voice their claims — be they right or wrong — in court, if the ordinary civil litigant is priced out or among the millions of pro se complainants, then courts become the domain of the criminal defendant; of the well-to-do litigants who opt in rather than buying private dispute resolution services; of the few constitutional claimants able . . . to attract issue-oriented lawyers; and of the government . . . . That reduced spectrum of users becomes a problem for the democratic legitimacy of courts . . . .

Judith Resnik, *Fairness in Numbers: A Comment on* AT&T v. Concepcion, Wal-Mart v. Dukes, *and* Turner v. Rogers, 125 HARV. L. REV. 78, 170 (2011).

5. On the empirical side the data on ADR, when used in cases that have already entered the litigation system, are again inconclusive to neutral. A study of various federal district courts that employed two popular ADR methods (mediation and early neutral evaluation) found that court-required ADR did not reduce expense or delay in civil litigation; nor, on the other hand, did the use of ADR increase expense or delay. To summarize a detailed investigation briefly, the gains (in terms of reduced costs and delays) that were achieved in the cases that were disposed of through mandated ADR were evenly balanced against the additional costs and delays that ADR created in those cases that were forced to go through the ADR

process without success. Lawyer satisfaction with ADR was good; clients were somewhat less satisfied, but overall their reactions were positive. The study did not measure the cost savings from consensual ADR processes such as settlement. *See* JAMES S. KAKALIK ET AL., RAND CORP., AN EVALUATION OF MEDIATION AND EARLY NEUTRAL EVALUATION UNDER THE CIVIL JUSTICE REFORM ACT xxx-xxxv (1996). Prior work on the benefits and costs of court-run arbitration programs had similar inconclusive results. *See id.* at xxx.

SECTION B: CASE MANAGEMENT

In 1938 Rule 16 began as a modest rule that permitted, but did not require, district judges to hold pretrial conferences. Amendments to Rule 16 in 1983 and 1993 have turned it into one of the longest and most significant Federal Rules. The amendments placed great emphasis on the pretrial-conference system, and empowered judges to issue case-management orders to expedite the case.

Case management consists of a package of techniques. Some attempt to streamline discovery; others aim to make the pretrial process run smoothly; and still others seek to narrow the issues for trial. Examining all possible case-management techniques is not possible in this chapter, and is better left to an upper-level class in Complex Litigation. Instead, we choose two techniques that are applied in nearly every case — the scheduling order under Rule 16(b) and the final pretrial conference and order under Rule 16(e) — as well as a smattering of other practices grounded in Rule 16(c). The most powerful pretrial issue-narrowing device, the motion for summary judgment under Rule 56, is reserved to the following chapter.

Before you read the following materials, you should read Rule 16.

1. The Scheduling Order

One of the central features in the 1983 amendments was the requirement that, except in certain excluded cases, a judge establish a *scheduling order* for completing various pretrial tasks. Fed. R. Civ. P. 16(b). The 1993 amendments continued the strong commitment to the scheduling order. The scheduling order must issue within ninety days of service of the complaint on the defendant or sixty days after the defendant's appearance in the case (whichever is earlier). Fed. R. Civ. P. 16(b)(2).

Although a scheduling order can issue without a scheduling conference, the judge usually holds a conference with the parties' attorneys, either in person or by teleconference, before issuing the order. At least twenty-one days before the conference or order, the parties must hold a Rule 26(f) discovery-planning conference (*see supra* pp. 116-17, Note 5). Rule 26(a)(1)'s required initial disclosures (*see supra* p. 117) are then due at least seven days before the conference or order. Therefore, by the time of the conference, the judge and parties will have some sense of the litigation.

Rule 16(b)(3)(A) requires that the scheduling order contain deadlines for joining parties, for amending the pleadings, for completing discovery, and for filing motions. Rule 16(b)(3)(B) states that the scheduling order may impose other deadlines, including dates for the final pretrial conference and trial, and may also address issues relating to disclosure and discovery. Deadlines established in a scheduling order can be modified "only for good cause and with the judge's consent." Fed. R. Civ. P. 16(b)(4). Note as well the judge's power to sanction a party or attorney who "fails to obey a scheduling . . . order." Fed. R. Civ. P. 16(f)(1)(C).

McKeague v. One World Technologies, Inc.

858 F.3d 703 (1st Cir. 2017)

Before Torruella, Lynch, and Kayatta, Circuit Judges.

■ Kayatta, Circuit Judge.

This appeal arises out of a civil case in which the plaintiff's two lawyers did nothing to prosecute the plaintiff's claims within generous deadlines, received a second chance, and then failed to oppose a pending motion for summary judgment. On such a record, we find that the district court did not abuse its discretion in failing to grant yet another reprieve.

I.

Todd McKeague suffered injuries to his hand while using a table saw. In late 2014, he sued the three defendants, claiming that they were responsible for a defect in the design of the saw that proximately caused his injuries. . . . In April of 2015, the parties filed a discovery plan that the district court approved and adopted as an order under Federal Rule of Civil Procedure 16(b). [After modification, the plan required] that all discovery requests be served by December 31, 2015, with fact discovery to be completed within sixty-five days. The court also set May 31, 2016, as the deadline for filing summary judgment motions, and June 30, 2016, as the response date. Trial was scheduled for September 19, 2016. All in all, this was plenty of time within which to conduct pretrial proceedings in ordinary course.

Defendants thereupon propounded discovery, serving interrogatories and document requests and deposing plaintiff, all well within the deadlines. Inexplicably, plaintiff served no discovery before the December 31, 2015, deadline. Instead, in early February of 2016, and without leave of the court, plaintiff belatedly served written discovery requests. Plaintiff's counsel prevailed upon defendants to assent to a motion to extend the discovery deadline nunc pro tunc, but then never filed the motion.

Worse yet, apparently plaintiff's counsel did not at the outset retain an expert in this design-defect product-liability case in which plaintiff concedes an expert is required in order to get to trial. In his initial disclosures under Federal Rule of Civil Procedure 26(a)(1) filed on June 12, 2015, plaintiff identified [three experts. In answer to an interrogatory served on October 26, 2015, he identified a fourth expert.] Plaintiff's counsel, however, did not retain [any] experts at that time. The final expert disclosure deadline under the scheduling order came and went with no expert designation by plaintiff. Even when defendants subsequently and timely designated their own expert, plaintiff's lawyers were nowhere to be found, seemingly content to make no effort at a counter-designation. Nor was this merely a problem of not filing something; plaintiff's lawyers had retained no expert to designate.

Plaintiff's counsel's cumulative neglect came to a head when defendants timely and predictably filed a motion for summary judgment on May 31, 2016. . . . [D]efendants argued in their motion . . . that the absence of any expert testimony was fatal to plaintiff's case given that the table saw functioned properly and suffered from no defect obvious to any layperson.

Plaintiff's counsel thereupon threw themselves (or, rather, threw plaintiff) on the mercy of the court, asking that instead of granting the well-grounded motion for summary judgment, the court reopen discovery, set a new expert-disclosure deadline for the plaintiff, order defendants to respond to plaintiff's untimely discovery, and push back the date by which plaintiff needed to oppose the summary judgment motion. To the likely annoyance of the diligent defendants, the district court granted the delinquents all they sought. The net effect was to swap the order of production, allowing plaintiff to designate an expert after defendants had already done so, and after reviewing defendants' summary judgment motion. In other words, plaintiff received both mercy and some arguable advantage. Presumably, the district court decided that any prejudice to defendants was minimal, enough so to favor an outcome driven by the merits rather than by plaintiff's counsel's neglect. . . . The indulgence was complete, granting plaintiff all the time requested, and more, and without any sanction. Having evaded the potential consequences of their remarkable inattention to their client's case, plaintiff's lawyers unfortunately stayed their irresponsible course. The new, extended deadline for filing an opposition to the long-pending motion for summary judgment came and went without anything — even a new motion for extension — being filed on plaintiff's behalf. On August 10, 2016, two days after the new deadline passed, the district court dismissed the case for failure to prosecute and failure to comply with scheduling orders.

Twelve days after the case was dismissed — yes, twelve, not one or two — plaintiff moved for reconsideration. He argued he had timely retained an expert, but that the expert needed more time to review a large number of documents received from defendants on August 2, 2016, and that the documents should have been delivered by defendants on August 1, 2016. Unimpressed, the district court denied the motion for reconsideration. This appeal followed.

II.

Confronted with repeated failures to comply with its scheduling orders, the district court had considerable discretion in deciding what to do. Perhaps it could have granted yet another extension, although that might have caused one to wonder if the court's orders meant anything at all. The district court certainly could have imposed a monetary sanction on plaintiff or counsel. The question posed by this appeal is whether the district court also had the discretion to dismiss the case. For the following reasons, we hold that it did.

We have previously held that when a litigant fails to comply with court deadlines after having already been once granted a reprieve from such a failure, and in the absence of a good excuse, a district court's discretion in setting a sanction is broad enough to include dismissal. Tower Ventures, Inc. v. City of Westfield, 296 F.3d 43, 46 (1st Cir. 2002). *But see* García-Pérez v. Hosp. Metropolitano, 597 F.3d 6, 9 (1st Cir. 2010) (per curiam) (vacating dismissal where district court contributed to case's extremely lethargic pace and did not clearly communicate deadlines to litigants who failed to meet them). Here, plaintiff's counsel tried to excuse the ultimate failure by claiming that his expert did not have enough time to review documents and form an opinion. Plaintiff's counsel, however, provided zero support for this bald assertion. Moreover, the record shows that it took until August 2, 2016, for defendants to produce the full complement of documents only because plaintiff's counsel repeatedly neglected to send back a protective order, and that plaintiff's counsel did not even send the documents produced on August 1 and 2 to plaintiff's expert until August 13, after the court had entered its order dismissing the case. The expert, too, formed an opinion within six days and made no claim to the district court that he needed to do much other than look at information and materials that had long been available and in the hands of plaintiff's counsel.

The district court acted well within its discretion in dismissing the instant case, especially when one considers that the court's dismissal order simply ended a case that just as easily could have ended had the court chosen to rule on the unopposed, long-pending summary judgment motion.
. . .

Like the district court, we prefer that adjudications be driven by the merits of a case rather than the neglect of counsel. As the district court implicitly recognized, though, at some point this preference takes a backseat to the important goals of maintaining a fair and orderly adversarial process. Even schoolchildren know that changing the rules mid-course to benefit someone who flouted them creates subtle and even substantial risks of unfairness. Such changes increase uncertainty, introduce delay, raise costs, and invite further violations by others. . . .

The bottom line is that we grant a district court wide discretion in deciding how best to balance these considerations fairly in a particular case. The district court has a better sense of the underlying equities, the bona fides of counsel's explanations, and the likelihood that a dispensation will make a difference. Here, given the failure of plaintiff's lawyers to prosecute his claim and their repeated flouting of reasonable deadlines, the district court demonstrated a reasonable sense of nuance in doing the necessary balancing.

Notes and Questions

1. When a party misses a deadline, the court can excuse the failure by modifying the deadline retroactively or by allowing a one-time exception. In either event, the court must determine whether "good cause" exists for overlooking the deadline. *See* Fed. R. Civ. P. 16(b)(4). In a situation in which a party failed to identify a witness by the deadline established in a scheduling order, one leading case provides four factors to guide the courts' "good cause" analysis: "(1) the explanation for the failure . . . ; (2) the importance of the testimony; (3) potential prejudice in allowing the testimony; and (4) the availability of a continuance to cure such prejudice." Geiserman v. MacDonald, 893 F.2d 787, 791 (5th Cir. 1990). Unless an extension prejudices the opposing party, should our system's commitment to deciding cases on their merits lead a court to extend the deadline even for flagrant violators of deadlines? For a view opposing *McKeague*, see *Potomac Electric Power Co. v. Electric Motor Supply, Inc.*, 190 F.R.D. 372 (D. Md. 1999) (refusing to enforce deadline for disclosure of expert witness due to lack of prejudice to opposing party; $100 sanction imposed on offending counsel). *See also* Betzel v. State Farm Lloyds, 480 F.3d 704 (5th Cir. 2007) (holding that decision to exclude a late-designated expert witness was an abuse of discretion when the testimony was essential and the last three *Geiserman* factors cut against exclusion).

2. Some courts, exercising more mercy than justice, leniently allow both in-time and out-of-time extensions of the Rule 16(b) deadlines. Other courts, exercising more justice than mercy, do not. Nearly all courts agree that the decision is fact-bound, so hard-and-fast principles are difficult to find. Appellate courts are unanimous in holding that the decision on a Rule 16(b) extension lies within the district court's discretion, so variability in the treatment of similar cases can be anticipated. Is this a benefit of case management, or a drawback?

3. Rule 16(f)(1)(C) provides the authority for a court to sanction a breach of a scheduling order. The sanction of dismissal is fairly unusual. The most common sanction is to refuse to extend the deadline. That refusal may have the effect of ending the case; for instance, without an excluded expert witness, it may be impossible for the plaintiff to prevail at trial. More frequently, the offending party's case is seriously hampered, but it can still limp along. *Cf.* Rimbert v. Eli Lilly & Co., 647 F.3d 1247, 1254 (10th Cir. 2011) (noting that refusing to alter "a scheduling order can have an outcome-determinative effect on the case").

4. A frequent source of "good cause" litigation is a party's failure to amend the pleadings within the order's deadline. An out-of-time motion for leave to amend pits two rules against each other: Rule 15(a)(2), which states that the court "should freely give leave when justice so requires," and Rule 16(b)(4), which does not permit extensions of deadlines without "good cause." Courts wrestling with this tension have tended to say that the Rule 15(a) standard applies to an amendment requested within the Rule 16(b) deadline; if sought after the deadline, an amendment must satisfy both Rule 15(a) and

Rule 16(b) standards. *See* United States *ex rel* D'Agostino v. EV3, Inc., 802 F.3d 188, 194 (1st Cir. 2015).

In a similar vein, Rule 56 allows a party to file a summary-judgment motion "at any time until 30 days after the close of all discovery." Fed. R. Civ. P. 56(b). Because Rule 56(b) expressly allows courts to establish a different deadline, the district courts' power under Rule 16(b)(3)(A) to establish deadlines to "file motions" trumps Rule 56(b)'s thirty-day rule. As the 2009 Advisory Committee note for Rule 56 states, "[s]cheduling orders tailored to the needs of the specific case, perhaps adjusted as it progresses, are likely to work better than default rules."

5. Imposing deadlines seems a modest case-management tool. When the deadlines are fairly short, and they are enforced with rigor, the hoped-for effect is to focus the parties on the essential issues and prevent expensive discovery on peripheral matters. Of course, shorter deadlines might induce parties to add more lawyers, which offsets any savings from the deadline. As discussed above, the empirical data on early, firm deadlines show that deadlines reduce the time to dispose of a case, but the expense incurred is about the same. *See supra* p. 182, Note 3. If reducing expense and delay is the goal, then early, firm deadlines appear to have some positive effects and no negative ones. But this conclusion begs an important question: how important is the reduction of cost and delay in relation to other values such as party control of litigation and determining cases on their merits?

6. A common topic of discussion at scheduling and subsequent pretrial conferences is the possible use of other case-management techniques, some of which we examine in the next subsection.

2. Some Basic Case-Management Techniques

Courts often create *case-management plans* that include techniques for narrowing issues and streamlining discovery. The following materials give a sense of some devices that a case-management plan might employ.

MANUAL FOR COMPLEX LITIGATION, FOURTH

45-46 (2004)

A variety of techniques have been used to help identify, define, and resolve issues in complex litigation, including the following:

1. requiring nonbinding statements of counsel, such as those that may be required at the initial conference . . . ;

2. encouraging voluntary abandonment of tenuous claims or defenses by the parties, often after the court's probing into the likelihood of success and the potential disadvantages of pursuing them;

3. requiring counsel to list the essential elements of the cause of action — this exercise, designed to clarify the claims, may help identify

elements in dispute and result in abandonment of essentially duplicative theories of recovery; . . .

5. using the court's powers under Federal Rule of Civil Procedure 16(c)(1) [now 16(c)(2)(A) — ED.] to eliminate insubstantial claims or defenses;

6. allowing contention interrogatories . . . and requests for admission . . . , especially when served after adequate opportunity for relevant discovery;

7. ruling promptly on motions for . . . summary judgment . . . ;

8. requiring, with respect to one or more issues, that the parties present a detailed statement of their contentions, with supporting facts and evidence . . . — the statements may be exchanged, with each party marking those parts it disputes; the order directing this procedure will provide that other issues or contentions are then precluded and no additional evidence may be offered absent good cause; . . . and

9. conducting a separate trial under Federal Rule of Civil Procedure 42(b) of issues that may render unnecessary or substantially alter the scope of further discovery or trial . . . .

ACUNA V. BROWN & ROOT INC.

200 F.3d 335 (5th Cir. 2000)

Before GARWOOD, SMITH, and BENAVIDES, Circuit Judges.

■ BENAVIDES, Circuit Judge.

. . . Plaintiffs-appellants . . . appeal the imposition of certain pre-discovery orders and argue, in the alternative, that they satisfied any burdens placed upon them and that their cases should not have been dismissed. As discussed below, we find that . . . dismissal of the cases was proper.

I. *Facts and Procedural History*

Crecension Acuna and other plaintiffs, in total numbering over one thousand, brought suit . . . against defendant companies for alleged personal injuries and property damage arising from defendants' uranium mining and processing activities. Rebecca Garcia and approximately 600 other plaintiffs brought suit alleging similar claims against a partially overlapping set of defendants, most of whom were also engaged in uranium mining activities in another area of Texas.

In both cases, plaintiffs alleged that they were exposed to and injured by the defendants' mining and processing activities. Some plaintiffs worked in uranium mines or processing plants, while others alleged exposure to radiation or uranium dust or tailings through contact with family members who worked in the mines or through environmental factors such as wind and groundwater. Plaintiffs alleged a range of injuries as well as durations and intensities of exposure. . . .

First in *Acuna* and then in *Garcia*, the court issued pre-discovery scheduling orders that required plaintiffs to establish certain elements of their claims through expert affidavits. Those affidavits had to specify, for each plaintiff, the injuries or illnesses suffered by the plaintiff that were caused by the alleged uranium exposure, the materials or substances causing the injury and the facility thought to be their source, the dates or circumstances and means of exposure to the injurious materials, and the scientific and medical bases for the expert's opinions.

In response to the order issued in *Acuna*, plaintiffs submitted just over one thousand form affidavits from a single expert, Dr. Smith. Those affidavits identified a series of illnesses and effects that can occur as a result of uranium exposure and stated that the relevant plaintiff suffered from some or all of them. The affidavits stated that Dr. Smith had reviewed the plaintiff's medical data and had come to the conclusion that exposure to uranium and its byproducts had reached clinically significant doses. The affidavits went on to list all of the mining facilities covered in the lawsuit as responsible for each plaintiff's exposure and routes of exposure as including inhalation, ingestion, and direct skin contact. The affidavits also included a list of scientific studies and materials.

The magistrate judge found that the affidavits did not comply with the scheduling order, reiterated some of the requirements of the order, and gave plaintiffs an additional month to comply. Plaintiffs then submitted additional affidavits by Dr. Smith and two other experts. Some individuals were identified in these affidavits as suffering from particular diseases but the other required information was not provided regarding their claims. The supplemental affidavits did not provide any new information regarding the specific claims of the vast majority of plaintiffs. The magistrate judge found that these additional affidavits still failed to meet the specificity requirements of the order and recommended that the case be dismissed. The district court issued a memorandum and order dismissing the case.

An identical pre-discovery order was issued some months later in *Garcia*. [Plaintiffs submitted only one affidavit by Dr. Smith, designed to cover all plaintiffs' claims. The district court dismissed the case for failure to comply with the order.] Plaintiffs in both cases appeal.

II. *Analysis*

. . .

Plaintiffs contend that the pre-discovery orders requiring expert support for the details of each plaintiff's claim imposed too high a burden for that stage of litigation. In the alternative, they argue that they in fact complied with the orders and that their cases should be remanded for discovery and trial. The district court's dismissal of plaintiffs' claims in *Garcia* is reviewed for plain error, because plaintiffs did not make a timely objection to the magistrate judge's recommendation of dismissal. . . . Plaintiffs did file an objection in *Acuna*, and the district court therefore conducted a de novo review of the recommendation to dismiss. We review the district court's dismissal order under Rule 16(f) for abuse of discretion. *See* Nat'l Hockey League v. Metro. Hockey Club, Inc., 427 U.S. 639, 642 (1976) [*supra* p. 161]. . . .

The pre-discovery orders in issue are of a type known as *Lone Pine* orders, named for *Lore v. Lone Pine Corp.*, No. L-33606-85 (N.J. Super. Ct. 1986). *Lone Pine* orders are designed to handle the complex issues and potential burdens on defendants and the court in mass tort litigation. In the federal courts, such orders are issued under the wide discretion afforded district judges over the management of discovery under Rule 16.

In these two cases, treated as related in the district court, there are approximately one thousand six hundred plaintiffs suing over one hundred defendants for a range of injuries occurring over a span of up to forty years. Neither the defendants nor the court was on notice from plaintiffs' pleadings as to how many instances of which diseases were being claimed as injuries or which facilities were alleged to have caused those injuries. It was within the court's discretion to take steps to manage the complex and potentially very burdensome discovery that the cases would require.

The scheduling orders issued below essentially required that information which plaintiffs should have had before filing their claims pursuant to Rule 11(b)(3). Each plaintiff should have had at least some information regarding the nature of his injuries, the circumstances under which he could have been exposed to harmful substances, and the basis for believing that the named defendants were responsible for his injuries. . . . The affidavits supplied by plaintiffs did not provide this information. The district court did not commit clear error or an abuse of discretion in refusing to allow discovery to proceed without better definition of plaintiffs' claims.

OCEAN ATLANTIC WOODLAND CORP. v. DRH CAMBRIDGE HOMES, INC.

2004 WL 609326 (N.D. Ill. Mar. 23, 2004)

■ GUZMAN, District Judge.

Ocean Atlantic Woodland Corporation ("Ocean Atlantic") has sued DRH Cambridge Homes, Inc. ("Cambridge"), Cowhey, Gundmundson, Leder, Ltd. ("Cowhey"), and Pugsley & LaHaie, Ltd ("Pugsley") (collectively "defendants") alleging copyright infringement, unfair competition and deceptive trade practices, false designation of origin, conversion and unjust enrichment. . . .

On November 26, 2002, the defendants filed a motion pursuant to Rule 42(b) requesting the court to bifurcate liability and damages discovery. The defendants requested that the Court decline to allow the parties to enter into damages discovery until liability issues were determined. . . .

Whether to bifurcate discovery is a matter committed to the discretion of the trial court. Rule 42 specifies the factors to be weighed when considering whether or not to bifurcate: convenience, the avoidance of prejudice, expedition and economy.

The Court has the inherent power to control its docket. Separating the issues of liability and damages for the purposes of discovery will avoid unnecessary time and expense and further the interest of expedition by expediting the decision on liability. A verdict of no liability for infringement would render discovery on the damages issue unnecessary. In the instant case, this Court has already found . . . that, "[t]he record in this case . . . presents substantial issues which bear on Ocean Atlantic's likelihood of proving infringement . . . ." Thus, should plaintiff fail to establish liability in this case, the savings in time and costs with regard to discovery and discovery management would benefit both the parties and the Court.

It is clear, based on the breadth of the discovery requests, that the defendants would expend substantial amounts of time and resources responding to the discovery requests on damages. Continuation of discovery on the issue of damages would necessitate considerable operating costs in hiring accountants, researching, and calculating at a time when the [extent of damages remains uncertain]. Because, as noted above, the distinct possibility exists that the issue of damages will never be reached, bifurcating discovery as to liability from that of damages will serve the goals of convenience, expedition and economy. Moreover, evidence necessary to establish liability will nominally, if at all, overlap with evidence relating to damages and therefore the risk of duplication and delay is minimal.

Accordingly, the discovery of this case will be bifurcated into two phases. In the first, all discovery on liability will be completed. The defendants have already notified this Court that they will seek summary judgment as soon as discovery is complete. Therefore, discovery on damages is stayed pending resolution of the issue of liability.

Notes and Questions

1. The *Manual for Complex Litigation, Fourth* is a guidebook designed to give federal judges advice about how to handle complex cases. It is not binding on judges in the way that statutes or the Federal Rules of Civil Procedure are. Nonetheless, the *Manual* is influential. Although it is often said that complex cases require particularly aggressive case management, many of the *Manual*'s insights on complex litigation were imported into more routine litigation during the 1980s and 1990s.

2. Of the techniques mentioned in the *Manual*, many lack clear textual authority in the Federal Rules; a court's power to use them derives either from the penumbra of Rule 16(c) or a court's "inherent power" to control litigation. Bifurcation has clear textual authority in the Federal Rules. Fed.

R. Civ. P. 16(c)(2)(M), 42(b). But these rules talk about bifurcated *trial*, not bifurcated *pretrial* as in *Ocean Atlantic*.

3. The lack of clear authority also exists in *Acuna*. Is *Acuna* consistent with the pleading philosophy of Rule 8? With *Swierkiewicz*? With *Twombly* and *Iqbal*? With the limited initial disclosures of Rule 26(a)(1) and party-controlled interrogatories under Rule 33? Can you make an argument that the technique used in *Acuna* has textual support in Rule 11? In Rule 16? In Rule 7(a)(7)? Should judges ever employ techniques to narrow issues without clear authority in the Federal Rules? *Compare* Breslin v. Brainard, 2002 WL 31513429 (E.D. Pa. Nov. 1, 2002) (ordering use of a "RICO case statement," which requires the plaintiff to answer a detailed list of questions probing the validity of a RICO claim), *with* Wynder v. McMahon, 360 F.3d 73 (2d Cir. 2004) (holding that a court cannot dismiss a complaint complying with Rule 8 even when plaintiff fails to obey court order to provide additional factual and legal material).

4. Even if the judges in *Acuna* and *Ocean Atlantic* had the authority to use these case-management techniques, they were not required to use them; put differently, they had the discretion not to use them. In *Acuna*, the plaintiffs had actually commenced their cases in Texas state court, and the defendants had removed the cases to federal court. Had the case remained in state court, it is possible that the state judge would never have issued a *Lone Pine* order. Indeed, had a different federal district judge handled *Acuna*, he or she might not have entered a *Lone Pine* order. For instance, in *In re Digitek® Product Liability Litigation*, 264 F.R.D. 249 (S.D. W. Va. 2010), the district court denied the defendants' motion for a *Lone Pine* order. The court noted the lack of clear authority for such an order in the Federal Rules or in federal statute. The "more prudent" course was "to yield to the consistency and safeguards of the mandated rules" such as the motion to dismiss, the motion for sanctions, and the motion for summary judgment. *Id.* at 259.

Had the district court in *Acuna* similarly declined to issue a *Lone Pine* order, the outcome of the case might have been different. The same is true with respect to the decision in *Ocean Atlantic* to bifurcate discovery. A well-known effect of bifurcation is a greater likelihood of a defense verdict; one study suggested that a defendant's chance of victory rose from 43% to 76% when liability was tried before damages. *See* Hans Zeisel & Thomas Callahan, *Split Trials and Time Saving: A Statistical Analysis*, 76 HARV. L. REV. 1606, 1616-17 (1963). *See generally* Steven S. Gensler, *Bifurcation Unbound*, 75 WASH. L. REV. 705 (2000) (thorough, favorable discussion of bifurcation).

Does this type of discretionary power, in which the judge can have a significant effect on the outcome of cases, chill you? Or does the speed with which *Acuna* was resolved thrill you? In the final analysis, how much discretionary power are you willing to place in the hands of judges? *See* Nora Freeman Engstrom, *The Lessons of* Lone Pine, 129 YALE L.J. 2 (2019) (describing how *Lone Pine* orders bypass institutional constraints on judicial power).

5. Most of the questions in this section have been, by design, loaded ones. Perhaps you can now see more concretely some of the reasons why case management is controversial.

6. Rule 16(d) states that a case-management order entered at a pretrial conference "controls the course of the action unless the court modifies it." No standard for modification is stated; the Committee Note to the 1983 amendment that created what is now Rule 16(d) indicates that this omission was a conscious choice to allow the district courts maximum flexibility to manage litigation. Some courts state a standard in the pretrial order; others mistakenly apply Rule 16(e)'s "manifest injustice" standard, which applies only to modifications of final pretrial orders; and still others recite Rule 16(b)(4)'s "good cause" standard.

3. Final Disclosures and the Final Pretrial Order

According to Rule 16(e), the trial court "may" (and most often does) hold a *final pretrial conference*. This conference is usually held after the close of discovery, and focuses on the conduct of the trial. Recall Rule 16(d), which states that the court "should issue" a pretrial order after every pretrial conference. What should the *final pretrial order* include?

The answer to this last question varies from judge to judge, but most judges insist that, before the final pretrial conference, the parties submit a joint *trial plan* or *proposed final pretrial order* that includes the following elements: stipulations of law and fact on which all parties agree; a statement of the disputed issues of law and fact that will form the basis of the trial; a list of witnesses that each party may call; deposition excerpts that a party proposes to use; a list of documents that each party proposes to introduce in evidence; and any objections to opposing parties' witnesses, deposition excerpts, or documents. Some judges require additional information.

Overlapping with this requirement is Rule 26(a)(3), which requires the parties to make disclosures about the identity of witnesses and documents to be used at trial. Unless a judge alters the timing, the parties must make the disclosures at least thirty days before trial. Although many judges' final pretrial orders require these disclosures, Rule 26(a)(3) ensures disclosure of this information if a final pretrial order does not already require it. The Rule also sets a deadline for a party to object to the documentary and deposition evidence designated by other parties.

The final disclosures and/or final pretrial order usually occur after the close of discovery, and are therefore not so much about the discovery of information as about the final preparations of the parties for adjudication. They are the distillation of the lengthy process of discovery — the legal issues, the evidence, and the witnesses that emerge from the threshing floor of pretrial. They therefore close the circle on the pretrial process that has become the heart of the American civil adjudicatory system.

Final pretrial orders can be modified "only to prevent manifest injustice." Fed. R. Civ. P. 16(e). The following case explores the meaning of this phrase.

R.M.R. v. MUSCOGEE COUNTY SCHOOL DISTRICT

165 F.3d 812 (11th Cir. 1999)

Before TJOFLAT, BIRCH and MARCUS, Circuit Judges.

■ TJOFLAT, Circuit Judge.

Thirteen-year-old R.M.R. was sexually molested at school by his music teacher. R.M.R. then brought this suit against the Muscogee County School District ("Muscogee"), alleging that Muscogee was vicariously liable for this abuse under Title IX of the Education Amendments of 1972, 20 U.S.C. § 1681 ("Title IX") and under 42 U.S.C. § 1983. The jury returned a verdict in favor of Muscogee. [R.M.R.] and his mother appeal, claiming that the district court erred by . . . improperly excluding a last-minute witness who was not listed in the pretrial order. We affirm the district court's judgment for the reasons set forth below.

[In 1993 R.M.R. was a student at Richards Middle School, where he attended a boys' chorus class taught by Herman Larry Carr. Carr allegedly molested R.M.R. R.M.R. told a school counselor about the attack. The principal confronted Carr with R.M.R.'s claim, and Carr did not deny it. Later that day, Carr admitted to the Muscogee superintendent that he had molested R.M.R. Under pressure from the superintendent, Carr resigned.

[Meanwhile, the word had spread around the school that R.M.R. was responsible for Carr's suspension. Some students speculated about what had happened, and frequently told R.M.R. that they believed he was lying. The principal, Mr. Arrington, did not inform the students or their parents that Carr had confessed. Carr was arrested for child molestation on May 19, 1993. The arrest, including the fact that R.M.R. was Carr's accuser, received considerable media attention. On May 20, R.M.R. left the school, and on May 29, he and his mother moved from Georgia to Alabama.

[R.M.R.'s complaint asserted that Muscogee was liable under Title IX because it knew or should have known that Carr had molested boys in the past, and therefore constituted a danger to the children entrusted to its care. Muscogee's defense was that it did not know, and could not reasonably have known, that Carr posed a danger to children.]

In order to prove that Muscogee had prior knowledge of Carr's propensity to molest children, appellants decided to contact each of Carr's former students and ask whether Carr had molested them. To accomplish this goal, appellants served on Muscogee a set of discovery requests, including the following interrogatories:

2. Identify by title each document, including, but not limited to, class rolls, which lists the names of students who were enrolled in each class [taught by Carr]. State the location of each such document, each form in which it exists (i.e., paper record, computer file, etc.), and the name of its custodian.

3. Identify by title each document, including, but not limited to, student directories, containing "directory information" such as

name, address, and/or phone number, which lists the names of students who were enrolled in each class [taught by Carr]. State the location of each such document, each form in which it exists (i.e., paper record, computer file, etc.), and the name of its custodian.

Appellants also served on Muscogee a request to produce all documents identified in response to these two interrogatories.

Muscogee responded to Interrogatory 2 and the corresponding request for document production by identifying and producing grade books that listed the name of each student taught by Carr. In response to Interrogatory 3 and its corresponding document request, however, Muscogee objected that the discovery request was "overly broad, burdensome, and is not reasonably calculated to lead to the discovery of admissible evidence." Subject to that objection, Muscogee identified rolodex cards for each student taught by Carr between 1988 and 1993. Muscogee refused, however, to produce the rolodex cards. Appellants moved the district court to compel production of the cards but the court denied the motion, concluding that the discovery request was "overly broad."

The case went to trial before a jury on September 23, 1996. . . .

On the third day of trial, after appellants had rested their case and Muscogee had presented most of its defense — four of its six witnesses (including Arrington) — appellants moved the court for leave to reopen their case in order to call a witness whom they had not listed in the pretrial order. This witness, D.L.J., had appeared at the courthouse that morning, after hearing about the case in the media. D.L.J. had been a student in Carr's class in 1984, and, according to D.L.J., had been molested by Carr approximately fifty times. D.L.J. claimed that he repeatedly told Arrington about this sexual abuse.

Muscogee opposed appellants' motion, arguing that allowing D.L.J. to testify without first giving it an opportunity to depose him and conduct whatever investigation might be required to rebut his testimony would be highly prejudicial. The district court agreed, and therefore denied appellants' motion.

After Muscogee rested its case, appellants attempted to call D.L.J. to the stand to rebut Arrington's testimony. Arrington had testified (during Muscogee's case) that he "[a]bsolutely [did] not" have prior notice that "Carr had previously engaged in any behavior similar to what R.M.R. was saying was done. . . ." Muscogee objected, reiterating the argument it made in opposition to appellants' motion for leave to reopen their case. The court sustained their objection.

Appellants presented no rebuttal, and the evidence was closed. Following counsels' summations and the court's instructions, the jury returned a verdict for Muscogee. . . .

Appellants [contend on appeal] that the court abused its discretion when it barred D.L.J. from testifying. According to appellants, identifying other victims was crucial in order to prove that Muscogee had prior notice of Carr's propensity to molest children. . . .

A district court's decision to exclude a witness not listed on the pretrial order is reviewable only for abuse of discretion. We have previously stated that an appellate court that is reviewing the decision to exclude a witness should consider: (1) the importance of the testimony, (2) the reason for the failure to disclose the witness earlier, and (3) the prejudice to the opposing party if the witness had been allowed to testify.

Appellants assert that the court should have allowed D.L.J. to testify because his testimony was of crucial importance. If D.L.J. was allowed to testify, he would have stated that Carr molested him approximately fifty times, and that he repeatedly told Arrington about the abuse. Consequently, D.L.J.'s testimony would have refuted Muscogee's assertion that its officials did not have prior notice of Carr's propensity to molest children. Appellants argue that the importance of D.L.J.'s testimony outweighed any prejudice that would have resulted to Muscogee because D.L.J. was not listed on the pretrial order.

Furthermore, appellants contend that D.L.J. should not have been excluded because appellants had a good excuse for failing to discover his identity before he appeared on the third day of trial: at the time of trial, D.L.J. went by a different name from that which he used as a student at Richards Middle School. Although D.L.J. used his middle name while attending Richards, at the time of the trial he instead was using his first name. Consequently, appellants failed to locate D.L.J. from the grade books produced by Muscogee.

We conclude, however, that the court did not abuse its discretion in excluding D.L.J.'s testimony. It would have been extremely prejudicial to Muscogee to allow D.L.J. to testify. If Muscogee had received notice before the trial that [D.L.J.] would testify, Muscogee could have structured its defense to counter what D.L.J. had to say. By the time D.L.J. was discovered, however, Muscogee had already presented most of its defense to the jury. Had D.L.J. been allowed to testify in the middle of Muscogee's presentation of its case, it would have disrupted the flow of Muscogee's defense, and forced Muscogee to scramble at the last minute to counter his testimony.

Appellants had several options available that would have minimized the prejudice to Muscogee. First, after appellants discovered D.L.J. they could have requested that the court grant a continuance. This option would have allowed Muscogee the opportunity to depose D.L.J., investigate D.L.J.'s story, prepare cross-examination, and find witnesses to rebut his testimony. A continuance, in short, would have provided Muscogee the opportunity to counter D.L.J.'s testimony in some meaningful way. Second, appellants could have requested a mistrial. This option would have allowed both parties to investigate D.L.J.'s claims and reargue their case from the beginning, taking D.L.J.'s testimony into account.

Appellants, however, eschewed both of these less prejudicial alternatives. Instead, they presented the judge with a narrow choice: allow D.L.J. to testify immediately — and thus deny Muscogee the opportunity to depose him and prepare cross-examination — or exclude his testimony entirely. In light of the extreme prejudice to Muscogee if D.L.J. were allowed to testify, as well as appellants' failure to move for a continuance or request a mistrial in an effort to ameliorate the prejudice to Muscogee, we conclude that the district court did not abuse its discretion in barring D.L.J.'s testimony.

Notes and Questions

1. The court suggests that R.M.R.'s attorney had other alternatives to deal with the new information, and therefore blames the attorney for any miscarriage of justice. But there is no guarantee that the trial judge would have granted either a continuance or a mistrial, both of which lay within the judge's discretion. Mistrials are especially difficult to obtain. Given that the defendant had so vigorously protested the release of the information that might have led the plaintiff to a timely discovery of the damaging testimony, should the court have placed the onus on the plaintiff's attorney, in the heat of battle, to consider various alternatives to address the situation?

2. Rule 16(e) states that the standard of modification of a final pretrial order is "manifest injustice." Does this standard help to justify the result in *R.M.R.*? As *R.M.R.* says, courts of appeals review a district court's application of the "manifest injustice" standard under an abuse-of-discretion standard. Does this deferential review justify the result in *R.M.R.*?

3. Assume that the trial judge had modified the order, and then had given both sides an opportunity to conduct discovery regarding the plaintiff's new witness. If the school district had lost at trial, could it have successfully appealed from the modification of the final pretrial order? Probably not; a decision to modify (or not modify) the order likely lay within the trial judge's discretion. In a wide range of situations, therefore, the trial judge's decision on modification — as on many case-management issues — is effectively the final word. Should trial judges be able to exercise such outcome-affecting power without more specific guidance than "manifest injustice"?

4. In *Monfore v. Phillips*, 778 F.3d 849 (10th Cir. 2015) (Gorsuch, J.), a group of defendants in a medical-malpractice case jointly defended the case during pretrial on a particular legal theory. After the final pretrial order was entered, all the defendants but one settled out. The remaining doctor then wanted to modify the final pretrial order to accommodate his new theory: that the plaintiff's death resulted from the fault of his former co-defendants. The district court refused, and the jury found the doctor liable for more than $1 million. In affirming the trial judge's decision, the court of appeals noted this relationship among liberal pleading, broad discovery, and the final pretrial order: "Leaving the reins so loose at the front end of the case requires some method of gathering them up as the end approaches. . . . Final pretrial orders encourage both sides to edit their scripts, peel away any pleading and discovery bluster, and disclose something approximating their real trial intentions to opposing counsel and the court." *Id.* at 851.

The concurrence would have applied a four-factor test to determine whether a modification was appropriate: "(1) prejudice or surprise to opposing party; (2) ability of the opposing party to cure the prejudice; (3) potential disruption of trial; and (4) any bad faith of moving party." *Id.* at 854. Under this test, the concurrence argued that the trial judge could well have allowed modification of the order, but recognized that, "in light of Dr. Phillips' double burden to demonstrate manifest injustice below and an abuse of discretion on appeal, . . . Rule 16(e) did not mandate that the district court grant the motion in this case." *Id.* at 856.

5. If you believe that justice was not done in *R.M.R.*, how far have we moved from the vilified days of draconian pleading? Isn't the final pretrial order just another pleading — albeit one that closes rather than opens the pretrial process? Most final pretrial orders contain a level of detail that far exceeds the level required in either common-law or code pleading. One difference from the "bad old days" of pleading is that the final pretrial order occurs after the parties have been able to discover information relevant to the dispute. Nor is a stumble over the final pretrial order invariably fatal, as was true of stumbles in the old pleading systems. Most courts strive to do substantial justice to the parties. For a useful survey of the factors that courts use in determining whether to permit modification, see 3 JAMES WM. MOORE ET AL., MOORE'S FEDERAL PRACTICE § 16.78[4] (3d ed. 2019). Whatever the stated factors, the treatise authors note that "the intensity of judicial reluctance to modify final pretrial orders appears to vary considerably among trial judges," and that "different courts of appeal appear to send different messages about how receptive trial courts should be to motions to modify these orders." *Id.* § 16.78[4][a], at 16-213.

Do these variable outcomes suggest to you that the American experiment of notice pleading, wide-open discovery, and judicial discretion is flawed — or might it still be the least of the available evils?

SECTION C: SETTLEMENT AND ALTERNATIVE DISPUTE RESOLUTION

Parties can, and often do, settle, arbitrate, or otherwise resolve their disputes without entering the litigation system — or elect such approaches once they have already entered it. The choices, strategies, and processes involved in these decisions are best explored in upper-level electives such as Negotiation or Alternative Dispute Resolution. Here we provide a general overview of settlement and ADR, followed by an examination of the ways in which the Federal Rules, federal statutes, and case-management principles encourage, and sometimes require, parties to engage in settlement discussions or other ADR methods after a case enters the litigation system. The principal question is whether courts, which are social institutions designed to adjudicate disputes, should try to facilitate private dispute resolution when the plaintiff has opted for public adjudication.

1. An Overview

Rule 16(a)(5), the last sentence of Rule 16(c)(1), and the first clause of Rule 16(c)(2)(I) recognize that a court can discuss settlement at a pretrial conference. The second clause of Rule 16(c)(2)(I) and the catchall provisions of Rules 16(c)(2)(L) and –(P) provide a court with the authority to encourage or require the parties to engage in ADR. The following extract describes some of the methods that the parties and the court can consider.

LEONARD L. RISKIN ET AL., DISPUTE RESOLUTION AND LAWYERS

8-11, 13-14 (5th ed. 2014)

Brief descriptions of the major methods of dispute processing are set forth below. We begin with the "primary processes" — adjudicative and consensual — and then describe "mixed processes," which combine features of the primary processes. We exclude other important forms of dispute processing such as voting, fighting, and avoidance. . . .

1. ADJUDICATIVE PROCESSES

Court and Administrative Proceedings

Adjudication, the most familiar process to lawyers, features a third party with power to impose a solution upon the disputants, such as in public trials and appeals by courts and in administrative adjudication by government agencies. Adjudication usually produces a "win/lose" result. Parties have the opportunity to present evidence and arguments, and usually they do so through representatives, ordinarily lawyers.

Arbitration

In arbitration, the parties at least theoretically agree to submit their dispute to a neutral party whom they have selected to make a decision. . . . The parties can select an arbitrator with background and experience suitable for dealing with the particular issues in dispute. Because the parties can customize the proceedings to suit their needs, arbitration has the potential to be less formal, faster, and less expensive than the judicial process. The parties can agree that less importance be given to following or establishing precedent and more importance be given to other factors, such as community, industry, or workplace norms or expectations. . . .

Private Tribunals

In some jurisdictions, statutes or rules of court permit a court to refer cases to privately selected and paid third-party neutrals ("rent-a-judge"). The private judge's decision is entered as the judgment of the court. Therefore, unlike an arbitrator's award, a judgment entered by a private judge may be appealed. The parties voluntarily submit to such tribunals in order to select their own decision maker, or in the hope of eliminating delay or gaining the ability to exclude the public from the proceedings. . . .

2. CONSENSUAL PROCESSES

Negotiation

In negotiation, persons seek to resolve a disagreement or plan a transaction through discussions conducted by the parties themselves or through representatives. Much negotiation in law practice, particularly that involved in resolving disputes, is based on adversarial or value distributing assumptions — that is, that the purpose of negotiation is to divide a limited resource. Since the early 1980s, however, scholars have argued that problem-solving or value-creating approaches to negotiation, long-used in putting together business deals and other transactions, can and should be applied to dispute resolution. . . .

Mediation

Mediation is an informal process in which an impartial third party helps others resolve a dispute or plan a transaction but does not impose a solution. In other words, mediation is facilitated negotiation. The parties often enter into mediation voluntarily, but many courts have programs that require parties to mediate before proceeding to trial. The desired result is an agreement uniquely suited to the needs and interests of the parties. Normally the agreement is expressed in a contract or release and is enforceable according to the rules of contract law. Apart from negotiation, mediation has come to be the predominant alternative method of dispute resolution . . . .

Conciliation

The term "conciliation" sometimes is used interchangeably with "mediation," particularly in international settings. . . . Most broadly, conciliation generally refers to a less formal consensual process (e.g., where the neutral acts as a "go-between") or to a less active role for the neutral.

3. MIXED PROCESSES

Disputing parties frequently use so-called mixed processes, which combine elements of more than one of the primary dispute resolution processes. The following are the most common forms of mixed processes. . . .

Mediation-Arbitration

"Med-arb" begins as mediation. If the parties do not reach an agreement, they proceed to arbitration, which may be performed either by the mediator or by another neutral. . . .

Arbitration-Mediation

"Arb-med" begins as an arbitration, but converts to mediation after the presentation of evidence to the arbitrator. The arbitrator makes and records a decision, which is withheld from the parties while they attempt to mediate the dispute. If the parties reach a settlement, the arbitrator's decision is not disclosed to the parties. If the parties do not settle, then the arbitrator's award is disclosed to and binding upon the parties.

Mini-trial

"Mini-trials," or "structured settlement negotiations," refer to specially designed processes to resolve complex business disputes that would otherwise be the subject of protracted litigation. In the most common model, lawyers for both sides present their cases in abbreviated form to a panel composed of decision-making executives of the two organizations and a neutral advisor, who usually is a lawyer with expertise in relevant areas of law. Next, the executives retire to negotiate a settlement, with or without the neutral advisor. The neutral advisor may kick off these negotiations by giving her opinion about what would happen if the matter were litigated, or she may provide her opinion only if the principals fail to reach an agreement.

The mini-trial was a popular form of ADR in the early 1990s, but is costly and cumbersome, and has been less common more recently as mediation and other processes have become more popular. . . .

Early Neutral Evaluation

Early neutral evaluation (ENE) seeks to reduce pretrial costs and delay by requiring the parties to confront the strengths and weaknesses of their cases at an early stage. A neutral identifies issues on which the parties agree and disagree and provides an evaluation of each side's case. The neutral may predict the probable outcome if the case were to go to trial and estimate a range of likely damages if the plaintiff were to win. The neutral may also offer to assist the parties in settlement discussions. ENE combines elements of mediation and nonbinding court-annexed arbitration. . . .

Fact-finding

In this process, a neutral makes findings on contested issues of fact, such as the valuation of property. This can aid in negotiation, mediation, or adjudication.

Ombuds

An ombuds is an official, appointed by a public or private institution, whose job is to receive complaints and either prevent disputes or facilitate their resolution within that institution. Methods include investigating, publicizing, and recommending. Although ombuds sometimes mediate or perform other dispute resolution functions, the more classic model involves assisting complainants, directing them to other processes that might be appropriate.

Notes

1. Two major classifications of ADR types may be worth emphasizing. First, ADR — in any of several forms — may be either *extrajudicial* or *court-annexed*. With extrajudicial ADR, the parties proceed outside the regular court system, usually on their own initiative, to try to handle their dispute.

With court-annexed ADR the parties have already come to court, and the judicial system resorts to a mechanism other than traditional discovery, motion practice, and trial to seek resolution, refinement, or settlement of the litigants' dispute. Extrajudicial ADR is nearly always voluntarily chosen by the parties to a dispute, either by provision in a contract agreed to before any dispute arises or by choosing ADR (at least initially) rather than court once a dispute has arisen. Advance agreements may be less than fully "voluntary" as to one of the parties; a controversial aspect of modern ADR is widespread insistence on ADR rather than resort to court in contracts of adhesion imposed by parties who have superior bargaining power. *See infra* pp. 219-30. Court-annexed ADR is often mandatory, a required additional step for the parties — or at least one urged by the court, or from which the parties may have to move for exemption if they prefer not to go through it.

Second, ADR may be either *binding* or *nonbinding*. With binding ADR, the parties agree to accept the outcome of the ADR process and to forgo other dispute-resolution remedies (in particular, adjudication). Court-annexed ADR is virtually always nonbinding; the parties retain the right to have their dispute resolved by a judge or jury, even if the judicial system requires them to go through a nonbinding ADR stage first. Some court-annexed ADR processes, though, use incentives to induce parties to accept the result of an ADR proceeding; for instance, a party who refuses to accept an award from court-annexed arbitration may have to pay extra costs if the award at trial is not more favorable.

2. The opposing poles in dispute resolution are settlement (or negotiation) and adjudication. In settlement, the parties alone determine the outcome of the dispute, they do so by mutual agreement, and they typically "split the baby" by agreeing to a solution that lies somewhere between their ideal outcomes. (Class and other representative actions, in which settlements can bind persons not before the court, are an exception; court approval of such settlements is required. *See infra* Chapter Twelve.) Adjudication uses a government institution to resolve the dispute, the dispute is resolved under legal principles imposed by the government, and the dispute typically has a winner whose position is vindicated and a loser whose position is not. Most ADR methods have some of the features of both settlement and adjudication. Binding arbitration is the most adjudication-like ADR method; the main differences are that the arbitration results from the parties' agreement rather than government fiat, and legal principles do not necessarily form the basis for the arbitration decision. Nonbinding mediation is the most settlement-like ADR method; a third party is involved, but the dispute — if not tried — must ultimately be settled by the agreement of the parties. Other ADR methods fall in between these poles, although all of them rely to some extent on the offices of third persons.

The following three sections explore settlement (the common and long-standing alternative to adjudication) and a range of other methods conventionally grouped under the "ADR" label that parties might elect, or courts might encourage or employ, as a substitute for adjudication.

2. Settlement

Controversy exists about the desirability of settlement as opposed to adjudication, and about how far courts should go in promoting settlements. Some concerns have weight; to whatever extent a judicial officer receives information in confidence in the course of trying to facilitate a settlement, it is important to maintain confidentiality; and a judge should not promote settlement in a way that raises doubts about the judge's impartiality should the case go to trial. Be all that as it may, judges do much to try to foster settlements, and several provisions in Rule 16 make it clear that they are within their powers in trying to get parties to consider settlement.

Federal Rule of Civil Procedure 68 on offers of judgment is the rule regarded as most directly aimed at trying to promote settlements; you should read it now. In brief, Rule 68 allows defendants to make formal offers to have judgment entered against them, with the consequence that if a claimant does not accept the offer and does not do better in the end, the plaintiff is liable for the defendant's post-offer "costs" — usually not including attorney fees. (Prevailing parties are usually entitled to non-fee "costs," such as filing fees and some deposition-reporter expenses, under Federal Rule 54(d)(1) and 28 U.S.C. § 1920.) Rule 68 can function both to encourage defendants to make serious settlement offers and to give plaintiffs an incentive — the prospect of having to pay post-offer defense costs, even if they win but don't do better than the offer — to take defense offers seriously. Rule 68 has been relatively little used and consequently ineffective, in considerable part because the amounts affected by its cost-shifting rule — usually not including the big ticket, attorney fees — are often small, making it not worth using the Rule's formal-offer device.

But Rule 68 offers can sometimes have an impact on attorney-fee liability. Exploring this possibility requires a short digression into a key aspect of American civil litigation — the "American rule" on whether a losing party in a civil case should be liable in whole or in part for the winner's reasonably incurred attorney fees. Absent some statutory, decisional, or contractual exception, the default rule in all American jurisdictions (including the federal courts) save the state of Alaska is that you pay your own lawyer, win or lose. One of the most important federal fee-shifting provisions is 42 U.S.C. § 1988, which allows prevailing *plaintiffs* (but usually not defendants) to recover fees in many suits, especially for civil-rights violations, against government officials. In following the default no-fee-shifting approach America is almost unique in the world, with Japan being the only other major advanced nation that starts from the same premise. Elsewhere, including in nations such as the United Kingdom, Canada, and Australia with which the United States shares an English legal heritage, the default rule is "loser pays" — with a losing plaintiff or defendant being liable for at least some fraction of the winner's reasonable attorney fees.

Arguments over whether the United States should approach attorney-fee liability more as the rest of the world does are multifarious and recurring. They draw on themes such as not excessively inhibiting access to civil justice through the threat of fee liability, controlling the pursuit of frivolous claims and defenses, and the justice of purporting to award full compensation for substantive legal wrongs while leaving plaintiffs' lawyers to be paid out of plaintiffs' recoveries — thus compensating winning plaintiffs less than fully after they pay their lawyers.

Marek v. Chesny

473 U.S. 1 (1985)

■ Chief Justice Burger delivered the opinion of the Court.

We granted certiorari to decide whether attorney's fees incurred by a plaintiff [after] an offer of settlement under Federal Rule of Civil Procedure 68 must be paid by the defendant under 42 U.S.C. § 1988, when the plaintiff recovers a judgment less than the offer.

I

[Petitioner police officers, in answering a call on a domestic disturbance, shot and killed respondent's adult son. Respondent sued petitioners in federal court under 42 U.S.C. § 1983 and state tort law. Before trial, petitioners made a timely Rule 68 offer of judgment of $100,000, expressly including accrued costs and attorney's fees, but respondent did not accept it. The case went to trial and respondent was awarded $5,000 on the state-law claim, $52,000 on the § 1983 claim, and $3,000 in punitive damages. Respondent then filed a request for attorney's fees under 42 U.S.C. § 1988, which provides that a prevailing party in a § 1983 action may be awarded attorney's fees "as part of the costs." The claimed fees included fees for work performed after the settlement offer. The District Court declined to award these latter fees pursuant to Federal Rule of Civil Procedure 68, which provided, before stylistic changes in 2007, that if a timely pretrial offer of settlement is not accepted and "the judgment finally obtained by the offeree is not more favorable than the offer, the offeree must pay the costs incurred after the making of the offer." The Court of Appeals reversed.*]

II

. . . The plain purpose of Rule 68 is to encourage settlement and avoid litigation. The Rule prompts both parties to a suit to evaluate the risks and costs of litigation, and to balance them against the likelihood of success upon trial on the merits. This case requires us to decide whether the offer in this case was a proper one under Rule 68, and whether the term "costs" as used in Rule 68 includes attorney's fees awardable under 42 U.S.C. § 1988.

---

* This statement of facts is derived from the syllabus of the case prepared by the Reporter of Decisions. The syllabus often contains a useful summary of the opinion, but is not officially part of the opinion itself. — Ed.

A

The first question we address is whether petitioners' offer was valid under Rule 68. Respondent contends that the offer was invalid because it lumped petitioners' proposal for damages with their proposal for costs. Respondent argues that Rule 68 requires that an offer must separately recite the amount that the defendant is offering in settlement of the substantive claim and the amount he is offering to cover accrued costs. . . . We do not read Rule 68 to require that a defendant's offer itemize the respective amounts being tendered for settlement of the underlying substantive claim and for costs. . . .

B

The second question we address is whether the term "costs" in Rule 68 includes attorney's fees awardable under 42 U.S.C. § 1988. By the time the Federal Rules of Civil Procedure were adopted in 1938, federal statutes had authorized and defined awards of costs to prevailing parties for more than 85 years. . . . *[S]ee generally* Alyeska Pipeline Serv. Co. v. Wilderness Soc'y, 421 U.S. 240 (1975). Unlike in England, such "costs" generally had not included attorney's fees; under the "American Rule," each party had been required to bear its own attorney's fees. The "American Rule" as applied in federal courts, however, had become subject to certain exceptions by the late 1930's. Some of these exceptions had evolved as a product of the "inherent power in the courts to allow attorney's fees in particular situations." *Alyeska,* 421 U.S. at 259. But most of the exceptions were found in federal statutes that directed courts to award attorney's fees as part of costs in particular cases. . . .

The authors of Federal Rule of Civil Procedure 68 were fully aware of these exceptions to the American Rule. The Advisory Committee's Note to Rule 54(d) contains an extensive list of the federal statutes which allowed for costs in particular cases; of the 35 "statutes as to costs" set forth in the final paragraph of the Note, no fewer than 11 allowed for attorney's fees as part of costs. Against this background of varying definitions of "costs," the drafters of Rule 68 did not define the term; nor is there any explanation whatever as to its intended meaning in the history of the Rule.

In this setting, given the importance of "costs" to the Rule, it is very unlikely that this omission was mere oversight; on the contrary, the most reasonable inference is that the term "costs" in Rule 68 was intended to refer to all costs properly awardable under the relevant substantive statute or other authority. In other words, all costs properly awardable in an action are to be considered within the scope of Rule 68 "costs." Thus, absent congressional expressions to the contrary, where the underlying statute defines "costs" to include attorney's fees, we are satisfied such fees are to be included as costs for purposes of Rule 68.

Here, respondent sued under 42 U.S.C. § 1983. Pursuant to the Civil Rights Attorney's Fees Awards Act of 1976, as amended, 42 U.S.C. § 1988, a prevailing party in a § 1983 action may be awarded attorney's fees "as part of the costs." Since Congress expressly included attorney's fees as "costs" available to a plaintiff in a § 1983 suit, such fees are subject to the cost-shifting provision of Rule 68. This "plain meaning" interpretation of the interplay between Rule 68 and § 1988 is the only construction that gives meaning to each word in both Rule 68 and § 1988.

Unlike the Court of Appeals, we do not believe that this "plain meaning" construction of the statute and the Rule will frustrate Congress' objective in § 1988 of ensuring that civil rights plaintiffs obtain "effective access to the judicial process." Merely subjecting civil rights plaintiffs to the settlement provision of Rule 68 does not curtail their access to the courts, or significantly deter them from bringing suit. Application of Rule 68 will serve as a disincentive for the plaintiff's attorney to continue litigation after the defendant makes a settlement offer. There is no evidence, however, that Congress, in considering § 1988, had any thought that civil rights claims were to be on any different footing from other civil claims insofar as settlement is concerned. Indeed, Congress made clear its concern that civil rights plaintiffs not be penalized for "helping to lessen docket congestion" by settling their cases out of court.

Moreover, Rule 68's policy of encouraging settlements is neutral, favoring neither plaintiffs nor defendants; it expresses a clear policy of favoring settlement of all lawsuits. Civil rights plaintiffs — along with other plaintiffs — who reject an offer more favorable than what is thereafter recovered at trial will not recover attorney's fees for services performed after the offer is rejected. But, since the Rule is neutral, many civil rights plaintiffs will benefit from the offers of settlement encouraged by Rule 68. Some plaintiffs will receive compensation in settlement where, on trial, they might not have recovered, or would have recovered less than what was offered. And, even for those who would prevail at trial, settlement will provide them with compensation at an earlier date without the burdens, stress, and time of litigation. In short, settlements rather than litigation will serve the interests of plaintiffs as well as defendants.

To be sure, application of Rule 68 will require plaintiffs to "think very hard" about whether continued litigation is worthwhile; that is precisely what Rule 68 contemplates. This effect of Rule 68, however, is in no sense inconsistent with the congressional policies underlying § 1983 and § 1988. Section 1988 authorizes courts to award only "reasonable" attorney's fees to prevailing parties.... In a case where a rejected settlement offer exceeds the ultimate recovery, the plaintiff — although technically the prevailing party — has not received any monetary benefits from the postoffer services of his attorney. This case presents a good example: the $139,692 in postoffer legal services resulted in a recovery $8,000 less than petitioners' settlement offer. Given Congress' focus on the success achieved, we are not persuaded that shifting the postoffer costs to respondent in these circumstances would in any sense thwart its intent under § 1988.

Rather than "cutting against the grain" of § 1988, as the Court of Appeals held, we are convinced that applying Rule 68 in the context of a

§ 1983 action is consistent with the policies and objectives of § 1988. Section 1988 encourages plaintiffs to bring meritorious civil rights suits; Rule 68 simply encourages settlements. There is nothing incompatible in these two objectives.

III

Congress, of course, was well aware of Rule 68 when it enacted § 1988, and included attorney's fees as part of recoverable costs. The plain language of Rule 68 and § 1988 subjects such fees to the cost-shifting provision of Rule 68. Nothing revealed in our review of the policies underlying § 1988 constitutes "the necessary clear expression of congressional intent" required "to exempt . . . [the] statute from the operation of" Rule 68. We hold that petitioners are not liable for costs of $139,692 incurred by respondent after petitioners' offer of settlement.

The judgment of the Court of Appeals is reversed.

■ [The concurring opinions of JUSTICE POWELL and JUSTICE REHNQUIST, who both joined the opinion of the Court, are omitted.]

■ JUSTICE BRENNAN, with whom JUSTICE MARSHALL and JUSTICE BLACKMUN join, dissenting.

The question presented by this case is whether the term "costs" as it is used in Rule 68 of the Federal Rules of Civil Procedure and elsewhere throughout the Rules refers simply to those taxable costs defined in 28 U.S.C. § 1920 and traditionally understood as "costs" — court fees, printing expenses, and the like — or instead includes attorney's fees when an underlying fees-award statute happens to refer to fees "as part of" the awardable costs. Relying on what it recurrently emphasizes is the "plain language" of one such statute, 42 U.S.C. § 1988, the Court today holds that a prevailing civil rights litigant entitled to fees under that statute is *per se* barred by Rule 68 from recovering any fees for work performed after rejecting a settlement offer where he ultimately recovers less than the proffered amount in settlement.

I dissent. The Court's reasoning is wholly inconsistent with the history and structure of the Federal Rules, and its application to the over 100 attorney's fees statutes enacted by Congress will produce absurd variations in Rule 68's operation based on nothing more than picayune differences in statutory phraseology. Neither Congress nor the drafters of the Rules could possibly have intended such inexplicable variations in settlement incentives. Moreover, the Court's interpretation will "seriously undermine the purposes behind the attorney's fees provisions" of the civil rights laws . . . .

II

. . . Congress has instructed that attorney's fee entitlement under § 1988 be governed by a *reasonableness* standard. Until today the Court always has recognized that this standard precludes reliance on any mechanical "bright-line" rules automatically denying a portion of fees, acknowledging that such "mathematical approach[es]" provide "little aid in determining what is a reasonable fee in light of all the relevant factors." Although the starting point is always "the number of hours *reasonably* expended on the litigation," this "does not end the inquiry": a number of considerations set forth in the legislative history of § 1988 "may lead the district court to adjust the fee upward or downward." We also have emphasized that the district court "necessarily has discretion in making this equitable judgment" because of its "superior understanding of the litigation." Section 1988's reasonableness standard is, in sum, "acutely sensitive to the merits of an action and to antidiscrimination policy."

Rule 68, on the other hand, is not "sensitive" at all to the merits of an action and antidiscrimination policy. It is a mechanical *per se* provision automatically shifting "costs" incurred after an offer is rejected, and it deprives a district court of *all* discretion with respect to the matter by using "the strongest verb of its type known to the English language — 'must.' " . . .

Of course, a civil rights plaintiff who *unreasonably* fails to accept a settlement offer, and who thereafter recovers less than the proffered amount in settlement, is barred under § 1988 itself from recovering fees for unproductive work performed in the wake of the rejection. This is because "the extent of a plaintiff's success is *a* crucial factor in determining the proper amount of an award of attorney's fees"; hours that are "excessive, redundant, or otherwise unnecessary" must be excluded from that calculus. To this extent, the results might sometimes be the same under either § 1988's reasonableness inquiry or the Court's wooden application of Rule 68. . . .

But the results under § 1988 and Rule 68 will *not* always be congruent, because § 1988 mandates the careful consideration of a broad range of other factors and accords appropriate leeway to the district court's informed discretion. Contrary to the Court's protestations, it is not at all clear that "[t]his case presents a good example" of the smooth interplay of § 1988 and Rule 68, because there has never been an evidentiary consideration of the reasonableness or unreasonableness of the respondent's fee request. It *is* clear, however, that under the Court's interpretation of Rule 68 a plaintiff who ultimately recovers only slightly less than the proffered amount in settlement will *per se* be barred from recovering trial fees even if he otherwise "has obtained excellent results" in litigation that will have far-reaching benefit to the public interest. Today's decision necessarily will require the disallowance of some fees that otherwise would have passed muster under § 1988's reasonableness standard . . . .

The Court argues, however, that its interpretation of Rule 68 "is neutral, favoring neither plaintiffs nor defendants." This contention is also plainly wrong. As the Judicial Conference Advisory Committee on the Federal Rules of Civil Procedure has noted twice in recent years, Rule 68 "is a 'one-way street,' available only to those defending against claims and not to claimants." Interpreting Rule 68 in its current version to include attorney's fees will lead to a number of skewed settlement incentives that squarely conflict with Congress' intent. To discuss but one example, Rule 68 allows an offer to be made any time after the complaint is filed and gives the plaintiff only 10 [now 14 — ED.] days to accept or reject. The Court's decision inevitably will encourage defendants who know they have violated the law to make "low-ball" offers immediately after suit is filed and before plaintiffs have been able to obtain the information they are entitled to by way of discovery to assess the strength of their claims and the reasonableness of the offers. The result will put severe pressure on plaintiffs to settle on the basis of inadequate information in order to avoid the risk of bearing all of their fees even if reasonable discovery might reveal that the defendants were subject to far greater liability. Indeed, because Rule 68 offers may be made recurrently without limitation, defendants will be well advised to make ever-slightly larger offers throughout the discovery process and before plaintiffs have conducted all reasonably necessary discovery.

This sort of so-called "incentive" is fundamentally incompatible with Congress' goals. Congress intended for "private citizens . . . to be able to assert their civil rights" and for "those who violate the Nation's fundamental laws" not to be able "to proceed with impunity." Accordingly, civil rights plaintiffs "appear before the court cloaked in a mantle of public interest"; to promote the "*vigorous* enforcement of modern civil rights legislation," Congress has directed that such "private attorneys general" shall not "be deterred from bringing good faith actions to vindicate the fundamental rights here involved." Yet requiring plaintiffs to make wholly uninformed decisions on settlement offers, at the risk of *automatically* losing all of their postoffer fees no matter what the circumstances and notwithstanding the "excellent" results they might achieve after the full picture emerges, will work just such a deterrent effect.

Notes and Questions

1. The greatest controversy regarding Rule 68, to which Justice Brennan's *Marek* dissent points, is that it is one-sided: defendants, but not claimants, can use the device. Virtually all of the Federal Rules (other than some pleading rules) are facially neutral, and apply equally to plaintiffs and defendants. Why should only defendants get the benefit of Rule 68?

Before you conclude that Rule 68 is cockeyed, think about just what benefit you might give plaintiffs if they could make Rule 68 offers. If a prevailing plaintiff is already entitled to attorney fees under an exception to the American rule, should a plaintiff who makes an unaccepted, unbeaten offer get *more* than fees? If a prevailing plaintiff is entitled under the usual American rule to non-fee costs but not to attorney fees, should an unaccepted, unbeaten plaintiff's offer make the defendant liable to pay the plaintiff's post-offer attorney fees? If so, wouldn't even-handedness require that plaintiffs who don't accept and don't do better than a defense offer be generally liable for post-offer defense fees — but should plaintiffs be subject to getting hit that hard? In short, the problem of making Rule 68 something other than a one-sided rule may not be as easy as it can initially seem. Do those difficulties, and Rule 68's fairly low use and limited effectiveness, suggest that the best thing to do would be to get rid of the rule entirely? Or does it serve good enough purposes when used to warrant keeping it as is?

2. Putting aside whether the *Marek* majority or dissent had the stronger arguments as to statutory and rule interpretation, what do you think of *Marek* as a policy matter? Prevailing plaintiffs (including those who do not win more than an unaccepted Rule 68 offer) who are statutorily entitled to fees still get their pre-offer attorney fees, whether defendants make Rule 68 offers early or late. Plaintiffs who accept Rule 68 offers get what's offered — the amount of which will presumably be influenced by plaintiffs' fee entitlement. For plaintiffs who don't accept Rule 68 offers and go on to do better at trial, it is as if the offer had never been made; such plaintiffs get both pre-offer and post-offer fees. Only plaintiffs who don't accept a Rule 68 offer, and then don't do better, suffer consequences: a defense offer cuts off the defendant's fee liability as of the time of the offer (and also makes plaintiff liable for the defendant's post-offer non-fee costs). Does that setup strike you as hitting such plaintiffs too hard, or about fair as between plaintiffs and defendants?

3. The *Marek* majority states that "the plain purpose of Rule 68 is to encourage settlement and avoid litigation," and that view is widely accepted today. But Professor Bone makes a strong historical argument that the original purpose of the rule was not to encourage settlements; instead, it was to promote fairness by letting defendants escape responsibility for post-offer costs when plaintiffs kept litigating fruitlessly after the offer. *See* Robert G. Bone, *Rule 68, Offers of Judgment, and the History of the Federal Rules of Civil Procedure*, 102 Nw. U. L. Rev. 1561 (2008). Be that as it may, modern case law emphasizes the settlement-promotion purpose so heavily that it is important to keep that goal in mind when interpreting the rule.

4. A key issue that was not before the Court in *Marek* is whether a civil-rights plaintiff who did not accept a Rule 68 offer, and then went on to win some recovery but not more than the offer, should be liable for the defendant's post-offer attorney fees (such a plaintiff *is* liable for post-offer defense non-fee costs). Under many federal fee-shifting statutes including § 1988, *losing* plaintiffs are not liable for defendants' attorney fees unless the plaintiff's "claim was frivolous, unreasonable, or groundless, or . . . the plaintiff continued to litigate after it clearly became so." Christiansburg Garment Co. v. EEOC, 434 U.S. 412, 421 (1978); *see also* Fox v. Vice, 563 U.S. 826 (2011) (discussing treatment of cases involving both frivolous and nonfrivolous claims). Most lower federal courts that have considered the question have held that plaintiffs who do not accept offers but then fail to do better are not liable for post-offer defense fees. *See, e.g.,* Crossman v. Marcoccio, 806 F.2d 329, 333-34 (1st Cir. 1986). *Contra,* Smith v. Vaughn, 171 F.R.D. 323, 326-27 (M.D. Fla. 1997). *See* Megan Barbero, Note, *Interpreting Rule 68 to Conform with the Rules Enabling Act*, 57 Stan. L. Rev. 2017 (2005) (supporting majority result).

5. The Supreme Court has settled one other significant Rule 68 issue: the rule, with its consequence that a plaintiff *must* pay post-offer defense costs (usually *not* including attorney fees), has no application unless the

plaintiff wins something. If a defendant makes a Rule 68 offer, plaintiff fails to accept it, and the defendant goes on to win outright at trial, the offer has no effect; defendant is likely entitled to all its costs under Rule 54(d)(1), but the trial court has some discretion over such cost awards. *See* Delta Air Lines, Inc. v. August, 450 U.S. 346 (1981) (interpreting predecessor to Rule 68(d)'s "judgment that the offeree finally obtains" language).

6. Most recently, the Court has settled a circuit split over whether an unaccepted Rule 68 offer of judgment that would give a plaintiff all the relief (including attorneys' fees and costs) to which that plaintiff would be entitled makes the plaintiff's claim moot so that the action cannot proceed. Defendants facing possible Rule 23 class actions or "collective" actions under certain federal statutes, in which individual claims tend to be small but class or collective liability could be large, have made such offers to individual plaintiffs to stave off the threat of such larger liability. In *Campbell-Ewald Co. v. Gomez*, 577 U.S. —, 136 S. Ct. 663 (2016), the Court held that "an unaccepted settlement offer has no force. . . . With the offer off the table, and the defendant's continuing denial of liability, adversity between the parties persists." *Id.* at 666. The plaintiff can proceed with his or her individual claim, and can seek to represent the class or collective group (the court decides whether a class or collective action is procedurally appropriate).

Justice Ginsburg's opinion for five Justices relied on "basic principles of contract law" concerning unaccepted offers and language in Rule 68 (b) that "[a]n unaccepted offer is considered withdrawn" if not accepted within fourteen days of being served. *Id.* at 670-71. The majority opinion noted, but did not regard it necessary to address, the question "whether the result would be different if a defendant deposits the full amount of the plaintiff's individual claim in an account payable to the plaintiff, and the court then enters judgment for the plaintiff in that amount." *Id.* at 672. Justice Thomas concurred in the judgment. Chief Justice Roberts, joined by Justices Scalia and Alito, dissented, viewing the defendant's full-satisfaction offer as mooting the case; Justice Alito also dissented separately.

Since *Campbell-Ewald*, numerous defendants have turned to the alternative possibility mentioned — but not resolved — in the majority opinion, depositing the full amount of the plaintiff's individual claim in an account payable to the plaintiff and seeking to have the court enter judgment for the plaintiff. So far lower courts facing this situation have held, relying on language in *Campbell-Ewald*, that such plaintiffs must have a "fair opportunity to move for class certification." *See, e.g.*, Chen v. Allstate Ins. Co., 819 F.3d 1136, 1139 (9th Cir. 2016).

3. Using ADR Techniques in Litigation

Although the extent to which the courts should encourage settlement is debatable, the idea that parties should be able to resolve a dispute by their agreement is not controversial. The same cannot be said for other court-annexed ADR methods. Given that the principal charge of courts is to adjudicate, how far can a court go to steer the parties toward ADR?

UNITED STATES v. TENACIOUS HOLDINGS, INC.

6 F. Supp. 3d 1374 (Ct. Int'l Trade 2014)

■ CARMAN, Judge.

Before the Court is the Motion for Referral to Court-Annexed Mediation filed by Defendant Tenacious Holdings, Inc. ("Tenacious"). Plaintiff United States ("United States" or "Government") opposes the motion. For the reasons that follow, the Court will grant the motion....

BACKGROUND

The United States brought this penalty case against Tenacious seeking penalties for negligent misclassification of work gloves. Prior to the initiation of this action, Tenacious had already brought an action challenging the proper classification of the same work gloves at issue in this case. *See* Ergodyne Corp. v. United States, Court No. 10–00200. *Ergodyne* is also pending before the Court.

The current schedule for this case was set by a consent amended scheduling order. The current deadline for discovery is September 29, 2014, with dispositive motions to be filed on or before November 10, 2014....

Because the Court finds the potential benefits of mediation outweigh the risks, the motion will be granted.

DISCUSSION

Tenacious claims referral to mediation is appropriate here for six reasons. First, Tenacious claims that penalty actions are inherently suited to mediation because they often settle, given that the Court has wide latitude over the central issue of whether the defendant importer exercised reasonable care in classifying the goods at entry. Second, Tenacious notes that the approximately $50,000 amount sought by the government in penalties and unpaid duties could be exceeded by litigation expenses, giving the parties an incentive for early resolution. Third, Tenacious claims that the relevant provision of the tariff schedule is so ambiguous as to make it unlikely that the negligence penalty would be found appropriate. Fourth, Defendant notes that the classification provision at issue expired in 2009, so the parties have no interest in a court judgment to guide its future application. Fifth, Tenacious contends that the confidential forum of mediation may permit resolution without the waiver of attorney-client privilege that would be necessary if Tenacious were to invoke an advice-of-counsel defense to the negligent misclassification charge. While Tenacious states that it has not yet asserted an advice-of-counsel defense, it recognizes that it may eventually have to do so. Tenacious states that it "would prefer to seek a mediated resolution to this claim, if possible, so that a waiver will not become necessary," and suggests that such a waiver could impact the *Ergodyne* litigation as well. Tenacious notes that "referral to mediation may likely enhance communication between the parties because there will be no risk that evidentiary privileges will be waived in the process" given the strict confidentiality of mediation discussions. Finally, Tenacious contends that referral to mediation will promote the goal of "just, speedy, and inexpensive" resolution embodied in the Court's rules.

The United States opposes mediation. Noting that Tenacious' motion was filed the same day that Tenacious was due to produce certain discovery materials, the government claims that "Tenacious filed the present motion in hopes of avoiding its obligation to answer the Government's outstanding discovery requests." The government argues that it would be "a waste of time" to enter mediation before Tenacious produces discovery. From the government's perspective, the merits of the case cannot be properly weighed in mediation without full discovery. The government states that it is "not interested in a mediation in which Tenacious would provide a hand-picked sample of its attorney-client communications" related to a potential advice-of-counsel defense, since that would allow Tenacious to "reveal favorable advice while withholding unfavorable advice" as well as "the information that its attorneys considered before providing advice." The government also views the case "very seriously," disagreeing with Tenacious' view that the case's relatively small dollar value and lack of precedential value for future imports make it unimportant.

Court-annexed mediation in the Court of International Trade is governed by USCIT Rule 16.1 ("Rule 16.1") and the Guidelines for Court Annexed Mediation ("Guidelines") incorporated therein by reference.* Neither the consent of the parties nor a motion is required for referral to mediation; instead, CIT judges have broad authority to make a mediation referral "[a]t any time during the pendency of an action." The Guidelines provide that a CIT judge may refer a case to mediation "in response to a consent motion," "in response to a motion from one or more parties," or "sua sponte by the assigned judge." . . . At the time Tenacious filed its motion, the scheduled deadline for dispositive motions was November 10, 2014, making the present motion timely under Rule 16.1.

---

* ED. — Rule 16.1 of the Court of International Trade provides in part:

At any time during the pendency of an action before the United States Court of International Trade, any judge or three-judge panel of the court may refer the action for mediation. The matter will be referred to a judge of the court who is not assigned to the action to be mediated, who has consented to serve as a Judge Mediator in the action, and who is not otherwise disqualified to serve in accordance with Title 28 U.S.C. § 455 and the Canons of Judicial Ethics.

At any time, but not less than 30 days prior to the scheduled date for the filing of: a motion for summary judgment . . . or trial (whichever first occurs), any party may move for the referral to mediation of an action pending before the court.

The USCIT Guidelines for mediation set forth in full the procedures to be followed in actions referred to mediation. The Judge Mediator and all parties and counsel participating in a session of mediation are bound by the confidentiality provisions set forth in the Guidelines.

The parties have not provided authority regarding the manner in which the Court should decide a contested motion for referral to mediation. The basis for determining such a motion is not mentioned in [the statutes or rules that govern procedure in the Court of International Trade]. It has been held, however, that a United States district court may compel mediation pursuant to its authority under local court rule, statute, the Federal Rules of Civil Procedure, or the court's inherent powers. *In re* Atl. Pipe Corp., 304 F.3d 135, 140 (1st Cir. 2002).

1

Here, the Court's power to order mediation is grounded in Rule 16.1 and the Guidelines, which do not establish any express limitations on that authority. The matter is left to the Court's discretion, limited by the bounds of its inherent powers. In deciding how to exercise that discretion, it seems wise to accept guidance from the Court of Appeals for the First Circuit, which identified four limits to a district court's exercise of its inherent power to order mediation in *Atlantic Pipe*: (1) "inherent powers must be used in a way reasonably suited to the enhancement of the court's processes, including the orderly and expeditious disposition of pending cases"; (2) "inherent powers cannot be exercised in a manner that contradicts an applicable statute or rule"; (3) "the use of inherent powers must comport with procedural fairness"; and (4) "inherent powers must be exercised with restraint and discretion."

2

In evaluating whether mediation may assist in the orderly and expeditious disposition of this case, the Court has given careful consideration to the objections of the government. Although the government is opposed to the idea that mediation may be successful, the Court is mindful that "the results of mandatory mediation resemble those achieved in voluntary mediation in terms of settlement rates and party satisfaction." Tenacious is correct that mediation is more likely to be successful given that the amount in dispute here is relatively low and the tariff provision at issue is no longer in effect and therefore resolution of this case is unlikely to impact future cases. Noting these practical factors does not suggest that the case is unimportant, merely that it may be amenable to early resolution. Ordering mediation is consistent with Rule 16.1 and the Guidelines. Since there are no fees for court-annexed mediation in the CIT, the financial concerns that sometimes arise with mediation referrals are inapplicable. Referral to mediation will not cause any procedural unfairness, since the discovery issues at the core of the government's concerns will be fully addressable by order of the Court should mediation be unsuccessful. Although the Court acknowledges the government's concerns about mediating without the robust information that it would have after the completion of discovery, the Court does not agree that mediation is bound to fail at this stage. Many cases are resolved in mediation prior to the production of all discovery, and Rule 16.1 and the Guidelines clearly contemplate referrals to mediation prior to the completion of discovery. The government cannot accurately prejudge what information Tenacious may produce in the confidential setting of mediation; if the government approaches the process with good faith, as the Court expects it to do, it may be surprised to find that the case is more amenable to disposition than the government fears.

Notes and Questions

1. Congress created the Court of International Trade (CIT) to handle civil disputes arising out of alleged violations of customs or international-trade laws. Like the federal district courts, the CIT is established pursuant to Article III of the United States Constitution and federal statute. *See* 28 U.S.C. § 251. It operates under its own rules of procedure, which are modeled on the Federal Rules of Civil Procedure.

2. *Tenacious Holdings* notes that the court-annexed mediation program comes at no charge to the parties. Many ADR methods, however, involve third parties who expect compensation for their time and expenses. Usually one or more of the parties must come up with the necessary funds. In *In re Atlantic Pipe Corp.*, 304 F.3d 135 (1st Cir. 2002), one party balked at a district court's order to participate in mandatory mediation in part because of cost: $900 per hour and $9,000 per day for the mediator. The court of appeals rejected the argument:

> [Atlantic Pipe] also grouses that it should not be forced to share the costs of an unwanted mediation. We have held, however, that courts have the power under Rule 26(f) to issue pretrial cost-sharing orders in complex litigation. Given the difficulties facing trial courts in cases involving multiple parties and multiple claims, we are hesitant to limit that power to the traditional discovery context. This is especially true in complicated cases, where the potential value of mediation lies not only in promoting settlement but also in clarifying the issues remaining for trial.
>
> The short of the matter is that, without default cost-sharing rules, the use of valuable ADR techniques (like mediation) becomes hostage to the parties' ability to agree on the concomitant financial arrangements. . . . [T]he district court's inherent power to order private mediation in appropriate cases would be rendered nugatory absent the corollary power to order the sharing of reasonable mediation costs. To avoid this pitfall, we hold that the district court, in an appropriate case, is empowered to order the sharing of reasonable costs and expenses associated with mandatory non-binding mediation.

Id. at 146-47. Because the mediation order failed to "set reasonable limits on the duration of the mediation and on the mediator's fee," the court of appeals ultimately reversed and remanded the case for further proceedings. *Id.* at 147-48.

The time of judges and clerks in litigation is, of course, largely free (filing fees and the payment of taxes, some of which go to support the judiciary, are the exceptions to this statement). If parties were forced to internalize the costs of the judicial system, would there be more use of ADR? Would this be a good idea? If not, should courts have the power to force parties to pay for their justice in a court-annexed ADR program?

3. The parties resisting mediation in *Atlantic Pipe* also raised other objections that the court of appeals rejected:

- The chosen mediator had been nominated by one of the other parties. The court held that this fact was "insufficient to establish bias," but that "litigants are free to challenge the qualifications or neutrality of any suggested mediator (whether or not nominated by a party to the case)." *Id.* at 146.

- The mediation order failed to "contain certain procedural and substantive safeguards to ensure fairness." The court of appeals stated that, aside from imposing limits on the duration and fees of the mediator, a mediation order should make clear that "participation in mediation will not be taken as a waiver of any litigation position." *Id.* at 147.

- "[J]ustice delayed is justice denied. An unsuccessful mediation will postpone the ultimate resolution of the case — indeed, the district court has stayed all discovery pending the completion of the mediation — and, thus, prolong the litigation." True, the court of appeals acknowledged, but this concern is remediable by definite limits on the duration of the mediation. *Id.*

In *Tenacious Holdings* the government raised other objections to the process. Are you persuaded that the benefits of trying to resolve a case through mediation outweigh these concerns, as well as potential concerns for costs?

4. As we have seen, ADR in both its extrajudicial and court-annexed forms has enjoyed considerable popularity. It also has had strong theoretical defenders. *See, e.g.,* Stephen N. Subrin, *A Traditionalist Looks at Mediation: It's Here to Stay and Much Better than I Thought,* 3 Nev. L.J. 196 (2002-03); Carrie Menkel-Meadow, *Whose Dispute Is It Anyway? A Philosophical and Democratic Defense of Settlement (in Some Cases)*, 83 Geo. L.J. 2663 (1995). At the same time, ADR is often controversial not just in particular cases like *Atlantic Pipe* but on broader bases, particularly that it may raise problems of "second-class justice." This concern can take at least two forms, first that the well-off — by electing fancy, costly (and usually nonpublic) ADR for themselves — can buy their way out of the regular public system of justice with all of its down sides such as under-funding, backlogs, and perhaps uncomfortable exposure of questionable conduct to public scrutiny. (The $9,000 daily fee of the private mediator in *Atlantic Pipe* illustrates how pricey high-end ADR can be.) The rest of us could be relegated to the second-class system of regular courts — which, if the better-off can avoid them by buying their way into the litigation counterpart of a gated community, they may have less interest in improving to the benefit of all.

A somewhat converse form of second-class-justice concern with ADR starts from the premise that the public courts, for all their problems, offer protections of impartiality and regularity that private and often less formal ADR mechanisms, whether extrajudicial or court-annexed, may lack. ADR may deny these advantages to the less privileged. With respect to court-annexed ADR, then-federal Magistrate Judge Wayne Brazil — generally an ADR proponent — acknowledged one form of such concerns:

> [I]n some quarters there is suspicion of the motives of those who first supported ADR. The suspicion generally comes from the political left. It is characterized by a belief that ADR's early judicial supporters had venal motives — that they wanted to use ADR only to remove from the dockets annoying and unpopular classes of cases — so the judges would have more time to themselves and more time to spend on classes of cases with which they were more politically comfortable (e.g., big business disputes). To these critics, judges supported ADR not in order to better serve litigants' needs, but to advance the judges' selfish interests.

Wayne D. Brazil, *ADR and the Courts, Now and in the Future,* 17 ALTERNATIVES TO THE HIGH COST OF LITIGATION 85, 101 (1999).

4. Arbitration, Unconscionability, and Preemption

The second-class-justice concern about excluding the less advantaged from the protections of the regular system can also apply to extrajudicial ADR. It is one thing if parties with relatively equal bargaining power agree, before or after a dispute arises, to choose private ADR rather than public litigation. It may be quite another if parties with superior bargaining power — creditors, employers, health-care providers, your cell-phone company, etc. — include in their form contracts mandatory, binding arbitration that can keep their adversaries from seeking court redress. In general, the courts have upheld the legality of such provisions. *See, e.g.,* Rent-a-Center, West, Inc. v. Jackson, 561 U.S. 63 (2010) (upholding arbitration clause that required arbitrator, rather than a court, to determine whether the arbitration clause was enforceable); Preston v. Ferrer, 552 U.S. 346 (2008) (requiring arbitration of claims arising under a personal-services contract, even though the claims would otherwise be determined in an administrative forum); Circuit City Stores v. Adams, 532 U.S. 105 (2001) (interpreting the Federal Arbitration Act, 9 U.S.C. § 2, as not excluding most employment contracts and thus allowing employers and employees to enter into arbitration contracts; preempting state law restricting such contracts).

A particularly significant issue has been the validity of class-arbitration waiver provisions. In contracts with such clauses the potential claimant, such as a cable-TV customer, agrees to arbitrate disputes and waives the right to seek arbitration on a group basis. If valid such contracts have a double bite: no going to court (and therefore no class action before a judge), and no seeking to pool costs with many other small claimants against their provider in an arbitration proceeding. In other words, it's the solitary claimant against the company in arbitration. The pattern in lower-court decisions dealing with the validity of such contracts generally and their restrictions in particular had been mixed, with some surviving and others being struck down, somewhat qualifying the generally pro-arbitration-agreement tendency sketched in the previous paragraph. The issue came to a head in the following decision.

AT&T MOBILITY LLC v. CONCEPCION

563 U.S. 333 (2011)

■ JUSTICE SCALIA delivered the opinion of the Court.

Section 2 of the Federal Arbitration Act (FAA) makes agreements to arbitrate "valid, irrevocable, and enforceable, save upon such grounds as exist at law or in equity for the revocation of any contract." 9 U.S.C. § 2. We consider whether the FAA prohibits States from conditioning the enforceability of certain arbitration agreements on the availability of classwide arbitration procedures.

I

In February 2002, Vincent and Liza Concepcion entered into an agreement for the sale and servicing of cellular telephones with AT&T Mobility LLC (AT&T). The contract provided for arbitration of all disputes between the parties, but required that claims be brought in the parties' "individual capacity, and not as a plaintiff or class member in any purported class or representative proceeding." . . .

The . . . agreement provides that customers may initiate dispute proceedings by completing a one-page Notice of Dispute form available on AT&T's Web site. AT&T may then offer to settle the claim; if it does not, or if the dispute is not resolved within 30 days, the customer may invoke arbitration by filing a separate Demand for Arbitration, also available on AT&T's Web site. In the event the parties proceed to arbitration, the agreement specifies that AT&T must pay all costs for nonfrivolous claims; that arbitration must take place in the county in which the customer is billed; that, for claims of $10,000 or less, the customer may choose whether the arbitration proceeds in person, by telephone, or based only on submissions; that either party may bring a claim in small claims court in lieu of arbitration; and that the arbitrator may award any form of individual relief, including injunctions and presumably punitive damages. The agreement, moreover, denies AT&T any ability to seek reimbursement of its attorney's fees, and, in the event that a customer receives an arbitration award greater than AT&T's last written settlement offer, requires AT&T to pay a $7,500 minimum recovery [increased in 2009 to $10,000 — ED.] and twice the amount of the claimant's attorney's fees.

The Concepcions purchased AT&T service, which was advertised as including the provision of free phones; they were not charged for the phones, but they were charged $30.22 in sales tax based on the phones' retail value. In March 2006, the Concepcions filed a complaint against AT&T in the United States District Court for the Southern District of California. The complaint was later consolidated with a putative class action alleging, among other things, that AT&T had engaged in false advertising and fraud by charging sales tax on phones it advertised as free.

In March 2008, AT&T moved to compel arbitration under the terms of its contract with the Concepcions. The Concepcions opposed the motion, contending that the arbitration agreement was unconscionable and unlawfully exculpatory under California law because it disallowed classwide procedures. The District Court denied AT&T's motion. It described AT&T's arbitration agreement favorably, noting, for example, that the informal dispute-resolution process was "quick, easy to use" and likely to "promp[t] full or . . . even excess payment to the customer *without* the need to arbitrate or litigate"; that the $7,500 premium functioned as "a substantial inducement for the consumer to pursue the claim in arbitration" if a dispute was not resolved informally; and that consumers who were members of a class would likely be worse off. Nevertheless, relying on the California Supreme Court's decision in *Discover Bank v. Superior Court,* 113 P.3d 1100 (Cal. 2005), the court found that the arbitration provision was unconscionable because AT&T had not shown that bilateral arbitration adequately substituted for the deterrent effects of class actions.

The Ninth Circuit affirmed, also finding the provision unconscionable under California law as announced in *Discover Bank*. . . .

II

The FAA was enacted in 1925 in response to widespread judicial hostility to arbitration agreements. Section 2, the "primary substantive provision of the Act," provides, in relevant part, as follows:

> A written provision in any maritime transaction or a contract evidencing a transaction involving commerce to settle by arbitration a controversy thereafter arising out of such contract or transaction . . . shall be valid, irrevocable, and enforceable, save upon such grounds as exist at law or in equity for the revocation of any contract.

We have described this provision as reflecting both a "liberal federal policy favoring arbitration," and the "fundamental principle that arbitration is a matter of contract." In line with these principles, courts must place arbitration agreements on an equal footing with other contracts, and enforce them according to their terms.

The final phrase of § 2, however, permits arbitration agreements to be declared unenforceable "upon such grounds as exist at law or in equity for the revocation of any contract." This saving clause permits agreements to arbitrate to be invalidated by "generally applicable contract defenses, such as fraud, duress, or unconscionability," but not by defenses that apply only to arbitration or that derive their meaning from the fact that an agreement to arbitrate is at issue. The question in this case is whether § 2 preempts

California's rule classifying most collective-arbitration waivers in consumer contracts as unconscionable. We refer to this rule as the *Discover Bank* rule.

Under California law, courts may refuse to enforce any contract found "to have been unconscionable at the time it was made," or may "limit the application of any unconscionable clause." A finding of unconscionability requires "a 'procedural' and a 'substantive' element, the former focusing on 'oppression' or 'surprise' due to unequal bargaining power, the latter on 'overly harsh' or 'one-sided' results."

In *Discover Bank,* the California Supreme Court applied this framework to class-action waivers in arbitration agreements and held as follows:

> [W]hen the waiver is found in a consumer contract of adhesion in a setting in which disputes between the contracting parties predictably involve small amounts of damages, and when it is alleged that the party with the superior bargaining power has carried out a scheme to deliberately cheat large numbers of consumers out of individually small sums of money, then ... the waiver becomes in practice the exemption of the party "from responsibility for [its] own fraud, or willful injury to the person or property of another." Under these circumstances, such waivers are unconscionable under California law and should not be enforced....

III

A

The Concepcions argue that the *Discover Bank* rule, given its origins in California's unconscionability doctrine and California's policy against exculpation, is a ground that "exist[s] at law or in equity for the revocation of any contract" under FAA § 2....

When state law prohibits outright the arbitration of a particular type of claim, the analysis is straightforward: The conflicting rule is displaced by the FAA. But the inquiry becomes more complex when a doctrine normally thought to be generally applicable, such as duress or, as relevant here, unconscionability, is alleged to have been applied in a fashion that disfavors arbitration....

An obvious illustration of this point would be a case finding unconscionable or unenforceable as against public policy consumer arbitration agreements that fail to provide for judicially monitored discovery. ... A court might reason that no consumer would knowingly waive his right to full discovery, as this would enable companies to hide their wrongdoing. Or the court might simply say that such agreements are exculpatory — restricting discovery would be of greater benefit to the company than the consumer, since the former is more likely to be sued than to sue. ... In practice, of course, the rule would have a disproportionate impact on arbitration agreements; but it would presumably apply to contracts purporting to restrict discovery in litigation as well....

The Concepcions [concede] that . . . "[r]ules aimed at destroying arbitration" or "demanding procedures incompatible with arbitration" . . . "would be preempted by the FAA because they cannot sensibly be reconciled with Section 2." The "grounds" available under § 2's saving clause, they admit, "should not be construed to include a State's mere preference for procedures that are incompatible with arbitration and 'would wholly eviscerate arbitration agreements.'"

We largely agree. Although § 2's saving clause preserves generally applicable contract defenses, nothing in it suggests an intent to preserve state-law rules that stand as an obstacle to the accomplishment of the FAA's objectives. As we have said, a federal statute's saving clause "cannot in reason be construed as [allowing] a common law right, the continued existence of which would be absolutely inconsistent with the provisions of the act. In other words, the act cannot be held to destroy itself."

We differ with the Concepcions only in the application of this analysis to the matter before us. We do not agree that rules requiring judicially monitored discovery . . . are "a far cry from this case." The overarching purpose of the FAA . . . is to ensure the enforcement of arbitration agreements according to their terms so as to facilitate streamlined proceedings. Requiring the availability of classwide arbitration interferes with fundamental attributes of arbitration and thus creates a scheme inconsistent with the FAA.

B

The "principal purpose" of the FAA is to "ensur[e] that private arbitration agreements are enforced according to their terms." . . . In light of [the FAA's] provisions, we have held that parties may agree to limit the issues subject to arbitration, to arbitrate according to specific rules, and to limit *with whom* a party will arbitrate its disputes.

The point of affording parties discretion in designing arbitration processes is to allow for efficient, streamlined procedures tailored to the type of dispute. It can be specified, for example, that the decisionmaker be a specialist in the relevant field, or that proceedings be kept confidential to protect trade secrets. And the informality of arbitral proceedings is itself desirable, reducing the cost and increasing the speed of dispute resolution. . . .

California's *Discover Bank* rule . . . interferes with arbitration. Although the rule does not *require* classwide arbitration, it allows any party to a consumer contract to demand it *ex post*. The rule is limited to adhesion contracts, but the times in which consumer contracts were anything other than adhesive are long past. The rule also requires that damages be predictably small, and that the consumer allege a scheme to cheat consumers. The former requirement, however, is toothless and malleable (the Ninth Circuit has held that damages of $4,000 are sufficiently small), and the latter has no limiting effect, as all that is required is an allegation. Consumers remain free to bring and resolve their disputes on a bilateral basis under *Discover Bank,* and some may well do so; but there is little incentive for lawyers to arbitrate on behalf of individuals when they may do so for a class and reap far higher fees in the process. And faced with inevitable class arbitration, companies would have less incentive to continue resolving potentially duplicative claims on an individual basis.

. . . [T]he "changes brought about by the shift from bilateral arbitration to class-action arbitration" are "fundamental." This is obvious as a structural matter: Classwide arbitration includes absent parties, necessitating additional and different procedures and involving higher stakes. Confidentiality becomes more difficult. And while it is theoretically possible to select an arbitrator with some expertise relevant to the class-certification question, arbitrators are not generally knowledgeable in the often-dominant procedural aspects of certification, such as the protection of absent parties. The conclusion follows that class arbitration, to the extent it is manufactured by *Discover Bank* rather than consensual, is inconsistent with the FAA.

First, the switch from bilateral to class arbitration sacrifices the principal advantage of arbitration — its informality — and makes the process slower, more costly, and more likely to generate procedural morass than final judgment. . . .[7]

Second, class arbitration *requires* procedural formality. The [rules of the American Arbitration Association (AAA)] governing class arbitrations mimic the Federal Rules of Civil Procedure for class litigation. . . .

Third, class arbitration greatly increases risks to defendants. Informal procedures do of course have a cost: The absence of multilayered review makes it more likely that errors will go uncorrected. Defendants are willing to accept the costs of these errors in arbitration, since their impact is limited to the size of individual disputes, and presumably outweighed by savings from avoiding the courts. But when damages allegedly owed to tens of thousands of potential claimants are aggregated and decided at once, the risk of an error will often become unacceptable. Faced with even a small chance of a devastating loss, defendants will be pressured into settling questionable claims. . . .

The dissent claims that class proceedings are necessary to prosecute small-dollar claims that might otherwise slip through the legal system. But States cannot require a procedure that is inconsistent with the FAA, even if it is desirable for unrelated reasons. Moreover, the claim here was most unlikely to go unresolved. As noted earlier, the arbitration agreement provides that AT&T will pay claimants a minimum of $7,500 and twice their attorney's fees if they obtain an arbitration award greater than AT&T's last settlement offer. The District Court found this scheme sufficient to provide incentive for the individual prosecution of meritorious claims that are not

---

7. The dissent claims that class arbitration should be compared to class litigation, not bilateral arbitration. Whether arbitrating a class is more desirable than litigating one, however, is not relevant. A State cannot defend a rule requiring arbitration-by-jury by saying that parties will still prefer it to trial-by-jury.

immediately settled, and the Ninth Circuit admitted that aggrieved customers who filed claims would be "essentially guarantee[d]" to be made whole. Indeed, the District Court concluded that the Concepcions were *better off* under their arbitration agreement with AT&T than they would have been as participants in a class action, which "could take months, if not years, and which may merely yield an opportunity to submit a claim for recovery of a small percentage of a few dollars."

* * *

Because it "stands as an obstacle to the accomplishment and execution of the full purposes and objectives of Congress," California's *Discover Bank* rule is preempted by the FAA. The judgment of the Ninth Circuit is reversed, and the case is remanded for further proceedings consistent with this opinion.

■ JUSTICE THOMAS, concurring. . . .

. . . [W]hen possible, it is important in interpreting statutes to give lower courts guidance from a majority of the Court. Therefore, . . . I reluctantly join the Court's opinion. . . .

[The FAA requires] enforcement of an agreement to arbitrate unless a party successfully asserts a defense concerning the formation of the agreement to arbitrate, such as fraud, duress, or mutual mistake. Contract defenses unrelated to the making of the agreement — such as public policy — [can]not be the basis for declining to enforce an arbitration clause.

■ JUSTICE BREYER, with whom JUSTICE GINSBURG, JUSTICE SOTOMAYOR, and JUSTICE KAGAN join, dissenting.

The Federal Arbitration Act says that an arbitration agreement "shall be valid, irrevocable, and enforceable, *save upon such grounds as exist at law or in equity for the revocation of any contract.*" 9 U.S.C. § 2 (emphasis added). California law sets forth certain circumstances in which "class action waivers" in *any* contract are unenforceable. In my view, this rule of state law is consistent with the federal Act's language and primary objective. It does not "stan[d] as an obstacle" to the Act's "accomplishment and execution." And the Court is wrong to hold that the federal Act pre-empts the rule of state law. . . .

The *Discover Bank* rule does not create a "blanket policy in California against class action waivers in the consumer context." Instead, it represents the "application of a more general [unconscionability] principle." Courts applying California law have enforced class-action waivers where they satisfy general unconscionability standards. . . . And even when they fail, the parties remain free to devise other dispute mechanisms, including informal mechanisms, that, in context, will not prove unconscionable. . . .

The majority's . . . view (that *Discover Bank* stands as an "obstacle" to the accomplishment of the federal law's objective) rests primarily upon its claims that the *Discover Bank* rule increases the complexity of arbitration procedures, thereby discouraging parties from entering into arbitration agreements, and to that extent discriminating in practice against arbitration. These claims are not well founded.

For one thing, a state rule of law that would sometimes set aside as unconscionable a contract term that forbids class arbitration is not (as the majority claims) like a rule that would require . . . "judicially monitored discovery" . . . . Unlike the majority's example[ ], class arbitration is consistent with the use of arbitration. It is a form of arbitration that is well known in California and followed elsewhere. Indeed, the AAA has told us that it has found class arbitration to be "a fair, balanced, and efficient means of resolving class disputes." And unlike the majority's examples, the *Discover Bank* rule imposes equivalent limitations on litigation; hence it cannot fairly be characterized as a targeted attack on arbitration. . . .

For another thing, the majority's argument that the *Discover Bank* rule will discourage arbitration rests critically upon the wrong comparison. The majority compares the complexity of class arbitration with that of bilateral arbitration. And it finds the former more complex. But, if incentives are at issue, the *relevant* comparison is not "arbitration with arbitration" but a comparison between class arbitration and judicial class actions. After all, in respect to the relevant set of contracts, the *Discover Bank* rule similarly and equally sets aside clauses that forbid class procedures — whether arbitration procedures or ordinary judicial procedures are at issue.

Why would a typical defendant (say, a business) prefer a judicial class action to class arbitration? AAA statistics "suggest that class arbitration proceedings take more time than the average commercial arbitration, but may take *less time* than the average class action in court." Data from California courts confirm that class arbitrations can take considerably less time than in-court proceedings in which class certification is sought. . . . And a single class proceeding is surely more efficient than thousands of separate proceedings for identical claims. Thus, if speedy resolution of disputes were all that mattered, then the *Discover Bank* rule would reinforce, not obstruct, that objective of the Act.

The majority's related claim that the *Discover Bank* rule will discourage the use of arbitration because "[a]rbitration is poorly suited to . . . higher stakes" lacks empirical support. . . .

Further, even though contract defenses, e.g., duress and unconscionability, slow down the dispute resolution process, federal arbitration law normally leaves such matters to the States. Rent-A-Center, West, Inc. v. Jackson, 561 U.S. 63, 68 (2010) (arbitration agreements "may be invalidated by 'generally applicable contract defenses'"). . . . The *Discover Bank* rule amounts to a variation on this theme. California is free to define unconscionability as it sees fit, and its common law is of no federal concern so long as the State does not adopt a special rule that disfavors arbitration. . . .

Because California applies the same legal principles to address the unconscionability of class arbitration waivers as it does to address the unconscionability of any other contractual provision, the merits of class proceedings should not factor into our decision. If California had applied its law of duress to void an arbitration agreement, would it matter if the procedures in the coerced agreement were efficient?

Regardless, the majority highlights the disadvantages of class arbitrations, as it sees them. But class proceedings have countervailing advantages. In general agreements that forbid the consolidation of claims can lead small-dollar claimants to abandon their claims rather than to litigate. I suspect that it is true even here, for . . . AT&T can avoid the $7,500 payout (the payout that supposedly makes the Concepcions' arbitration worthwhile) simply by paying the claim's face value, such that "the maximum gain to a customer for the hassle of arbitrating a $30.22 dispute is still just $30.22."

. . . In California's perfectly rational view, nonclass arbitration over such sums will also sometimes have the effect of depriving claimants of their claims . . . . Why is this kind of decision — weighing the pros and cons of all class proceedings alike — not California's to make?

Notes and Questions

1. *Concepcion*, finding state law that held some class-arbitration waiver provisions in consumer contracts unconscionable to be preempted by the Federal Arbitration Act (FAA), was one of a trilogy of important arbitration cases that the Supreme Court decided in 2010 and 2011. In *Stolt–Nielsen S.A. v. AnimalFeeds International Corp.*, 559 U.S. 662, 684 (2010), the Court held that the FAA does not permit an arbitration panel to require a party "to submit to class arbitration unless there is a contractual basis for concluding that the party *agreed* to do so." In another case it held that a provision in an employment agreement delegating to an arbitrator exclusive authority to resolve any dispute relating to the agreement's enforceability was valid under the FAA; thus, the employee could not bring any challenge that the agreement was unconscionable before a judge. *See* Rent-A-Center, W., Inc. v. Jackson, 561 U.S. 63 (2010).

In all three cases, the division on the Court was close and consistent. The same five-Justice majority (Chief Justice Roberts and Justices Scalia, Kennedy, Thomas, and Alito) prevailed each time. When the cases pitted business against consumer or employee interests (*Concepcion*; *Rent-a-Center*), the business side won; when the decision affected the availability of class proceedings (*Concepcion*; *Stolt–Nielsen*), the ruling was negative.

The Court extended *Stolt–Nielsen* in *Lamps Plus, Inc. v. Varela*, 587 U.S. —, 139 S. Ct. 1407 (2019). In that case, the contract was ambiguous, rather than silent, on the question whether class arbitration was permitted. The Court held that "[n]either silence nor ambiguity provides a sufficient basis for concluding that parties to an arbitration agreement agreed to undermine the central benefits of arbitration itself." The Court's holding overrode the Ninth Circuit's application of a neutral California rule of contract law, that ambiguity in a contract is construed against the drafter. Relying on both

Concepcion and a subsequent case, *Epic Systems Corp. v. Lewis*, 584 U.S. —, 138 S. Ct. 1612 (2018) (*infra* Note 3), the Court held that even neutral state rules are preempted by the FAA if they interfere with "fundamental attributes of arbitration." *Id.* at 1418 (internal quotation marks omitted). Imposing classwide arbitration does so, according to the majority. As in the earlier cases, Justices Ginsburg, Breyer, Sotomayor, and Kagan dissented.

Consumers did, however, win a class-action victory outside the arbitration context in *Shady Grove Orthopedic Associates, P.A. v. Allstate Insurance Co.*, 559 U.S. 393 (2010) (*infra* p. 614). The Court allowed a class action to proceed in federal court on a state-law claim despite the fact that state law barred the particular statutory claim from proceeding as a class action in state court.

2. The Supreme Court has continued to decide significant numbers of arbitration cases. The three most important are probably *American Express Co. v. Italian Colors Restaurant*, 570 U.S. 228 (2013); *DirecTV, Inc. v. Imburgia*, 577 U.S. —, 136 S. Ct. 463 (2015); and *Epic Systems Corp. v. Lewis*, 584 U.S. —, 138 S. Ct. 1612 (2018). The issue in *Italian Colors* was whether a class-action waiver in a credit-card arbitration clause was unenforceable as a matter of *federal* (not state) law because of arguable effects on the ability of cardholders to pursue antitrust claims against issuers. The five-Justice majority held that the arbitration agreement, including the waiver of class-wide arbitration, did not preclude "effective enforcement" of the federal antitrust statute and was thus valid and enforceable. The majority drew a distinction between arbitration agreements that interfere with the ability to "pursue" statutory remedies and those that fail to alleviate the prohibitive expense to an individual litigant of hiring the economic experts required to prove an antitrust case. The dissent accused the majority of ignoring the reality of antitrust litigation, which requires expensive expert analysis. In *DirecTV*, Justice Breyer wrote for a six-Justice majority including Chief Justice Roberts and Justices Scalia, Kennedy, Alito, and Kagan. The Court reversed a California state-court decision involving a contractual arbitration clause providing that it was invalid if the "law of your state" made the clause's class-action waiver unenforceable. The state court had held that the "law of your state" included state law that was valid at the time of contracting but was later, in *Concepcion*, ruled preempted by the FAA. Justice Thomas dissented on the ground that he views the FAA as not applying to proceedings in state, as opposed to federal, courts. Justice Ginsburg's dissent, joined by Justice Sotomayor, argued that the Delphic "law of your state" term should be read "to give the customer, not the drafter, the benefit of the doubt."

3. In *Epic Systems*, the Court relied on *Concepcion* and *Italian Colors* in rejecting an argument that the National Labor Relations Act's protection of workers' rights such as to bargain collectively "and to engage in other concerted activities for the purpose of . . . other mutual aid and protection," 29 U.S.C. § 157, invalidates waivers of class or collective proceedings in employment contracts with arbitration clauses. Employees who had signed contracts with such waiver provisions sought to bring collective federal-court

actions for small individual claims of wage underpayment in violation of the federal Fair Labor Standards Act and analogous state laws. Justice Gorsuch's opinion for a five-Justice majority held that the NLRA should not be read to create an exception to the Federal Arbitration Act's general favoring of arbitration contracts' enforceability. Justice Ginsburg's dissent for herself and Justices Breyer, Sotomayor, and Kagan took a different view of the interpretation of the FAA and NLRA and cited the likely effects of the ruling, which means that employees' claims must be pursued in individual arbitrations rather than cost-effective class or collective actions, on enforcement of workers' rights. The majority replied, "The policy may be debatable but the law is clear: Congress has instructed that arbitration agreements like those before us must be enforced as written."

4. Does *Concepcion* leave any role for state unconscionability law in determining the validity of arbitration agreements? A leading case is *In re Checking Account Overdraft Litigation*, 685 F.3d 1269 (11th Cir. 2012). The court distinguished the California provision held preempted in *Concepcion* as one that the majority there viewed as being applied in such a way as to disfavor arbitration. By contrast, the South Carolina unconscionability doctrine at issue in *Overdraft Litigation* "applies to arbitration and to other agreements according to the same basic criteria, and these criteria do not disproportionately impact arbitration agreements." *Id.* at 1277. Hence it "is among the 'generally applicable contract defenses' that apply to arbitration agreements under the savings clause" of FAA § 2, and is not preempted by the FAA. *Id.* at 1279. Applying the South Carolina unconscionability doctrine, the court held a one-sided cost- and fee-shifting provision in the arbitration agreement unconscionable. The court went on, however, to hold that provision severable from the rest of the arbitration agreement and ordered arbitration, refusing to invalidate the entire agreement. *See also In re* Checking Account Overdraft Litig., 485 F. App'x 403, 406 (11th Cir. 2012) (per curiam) (similar results under North Carolina's unconscionability law). Does the court's analysis strike you as a fair reading of *Concepcion*, or fancy footwork unconvincingly trying to wriggle out from under a mandate uncongenial to a particular panel?

5. Advance agreements to arbitrate a dispute can, of course, be reached by peers (say, two businesses dealing with each other) or imposed through contracts of adhesion. Peer-to-peer arbitration agreements were probably more common than adhesive agreements in 1925, when Congress enacted the FAA to overcome then-prevalent judicial hostility even to voluntary, peer-to-peer arbitration agreements. A good deal of arbitration business continues to arise from such agreements. But a study of arbitration clauses in consumer and non-consumer contracts found that some large corporations frequently require mandatory arbitration in contracts with consumers — but rarely include such a provision in their business-to-business contracts:

> The absence of arbitration provisions in the vast majority of material contracts suggests that, *ex ante*, many firms value, even prefer, litigation over arbitration to resolve disputes with peers. Our data suggest that the frequent use of arbitration clauses in the same firms' consumer

contracts may be an effort to preclude aggregate consumer action rather than, as often claimed, an effort to promote fair and efficient dispute resolution.

Theodore Eisenberg et al., *Arbitration's Summer Soldiers: An Empirical Study of Arbitration Clauses in Consumer and Nonconsumer Contracts*, 41 U. MICH. J. L. REFORM 871, 871 (2008).

6. Even before the 2010-11 trilogy, the Supreme Court's generally pro-arbitration decision pattern had drawn sharp criticism from some academics. *See, e.g.,* Paul D. Carrington, *Self-Deregulation, the "National Policy" of the Supreme Court,* 3 NEV. L.J. 259, 264 (2002-03) (arguing that the Court's decisions allow "economic predators to contract at least partially out of the system of effective private law enforcement, thereby exposing consumers, employees, small businesses, and other persons of limited economic bargaining power to a thousand wounds"). Does this view strike you as accurate or overwrought? Even Professor Menkel-Meadow, a leading theoretical proponent of ADR, has explored such concerns. Carrie Menkel-Meadow, *Do the Haves Come Out Ahead in Alternative Judicial Systems? Repeat Players in ADR,* 15 OHIO ST. J. DISP. RESOL. 19 (1999). On the other hand, Professor Nagareda suggested that the Court's recent arbitration cases reflect an appropriate modesty about the capacity of U.S. litigation procedures "to govern the world." Richard A. Nagareda, *The Litigation-Arbitration Dichotomy Meets the Class Action,* 86 NOTRE DAME L. REV. 1069, 1076 (2011). He argued that the Court generally favors arbitration when the parties choose it as an alternative to litigation, but holds that it cannot be imposed upon parties without their consent. *See also* Suzanna Sherry, *Hogs Get Slaughtered at the Supreme Court,* 2011 SUP. CT. REV. 1 (arguing that *Concepcion* reached the right result because the waiver clause was not unconscionable, but that plaintiffs' litigating tactics and especially the positions of lower-court judges and dissenting Justices may have led to the majority's adoption of a needlessly and harmfully broad rationale).

Raising concerns about one-sidedness in ADR is not to imply that ADR does nothing but tilt the playing field in favor of the advantaged. For one thing, the "haves" often do well in adjudication too. *See* Marc Galanter, *Why the "Haves" Come Out Ahead: Speculations on the Limits of Legal Change,* 9 L. & SOC'Y REV. 95 (1974). And in many applications, ADR mechanisms do seem to produce acceptable results with reasonable cost and speed and with good satisfaction reports by those who have used them. The challenge, both for public policy and for lawyers dealing with clients' disputes, is to find ways to make good use of ADR while winnowing out its possible abuses.

CHAPTER FIVE

JUDGE AND JURY

Until now, this book has focused on the process of preparing a lawsuit for adjudication. Many lawsuits are resolved — through dismissal under Rule 12(b), dismissal for violation of court orders, voluntary dismissal, settlement, or other ADR mechanisms — during this process. But not all. In this chapter, we examine the mechanisms that our procedural system has provided to adjudicate disputes on their merits.

Adjudicating a dispute "on its merits" conjures up the image of a trial before a jury, in which the lawyers thrust and parry with blistering cross-examinations and impassioned closing arguments. If we peel back this image and ask what adjudication "on the merits" must accomplish, however, we see the matter in less theatrical terms. Someone must determine the law that governs the dispute, determine the disputed facts, apply the law to the facts to determine if liability exists, and, when appropriate, fashion a remedy. In most of the world, these functions fall solely on one person: the judge. In the United States, federal courts and most state courts divide adjudicatory responsibilities between a judge and a jury — although not in all cases. In federal court, for example, about two-thirds of civil trials are jury trials, and the remainder are *bench trials* (tried to a judge).

The standard line used to describe the division of responsibility in jury trials is that judges decide the law and juries decide the facts. That line can be difficult to draw. Consider the application of the law to the facts. Is a determination that the defendant was "negligent" a question of law for the judge or a question of fact for the jury? What if, before the trial begins, it becomes obvious that the plaintiff's evidence is so weak that no rational person would believe it? Can the judge end the case without conducting a trial? Same question, but now the weakness of the evidence emerges during trial: must the judge let the jury decide the issue (risking an irrational finding of liability), or can the judge end the trial and enter judgment for the defendant? What if the judge becomes convinced after the jury returns its verdict that the jury acted irrationally — or at least contrary to the way in which the judge would have determined the facts?

In thinking about the answers to these questions, concerns for accurate decision-making, efficient issue-narrowing, and respect for the rule of law weigh heavily. Other considerations also come into play. In the United States juries are more than factfinders — they serve as a check on the power of government, an opportunity for average citizens to express their views on the law's application, a way for parties to tell their stories to the community, and a device by which unsuccessful litigants can come to accept their fate (without the blame being thrown directly on the government itself). The jury affects the structure of the entire civil-justice system. A single, culminating trial event requires a clear division between pretrial and trial — a division whose consequences you have been studying for the past few chapters.

But the debate over the role of juries is not just a question of policy or structure. The United States Constitution also has something to say about the use of and judicial control over civil juries in federal court. The Seventh Amendment "preserve[s]" the right of jury trial in all "Suits at common law" in which the matter in controversy exceeds $20, and precludes re-examination of a jury's factual findings except "according to the rules of the common law." Most states have comparable — if not stronger — constitutional guarantees.

Increasingly the debate is also one of international practicalities. In a globalizing world, strong pressure exists for procedural systems to coordinate and harmonize. The United States remains alone in its devotion to the use of the jury in civil matters. Most of the world has no tradition of civil jury trial, and does not use the jury at all in civil matters. Even in England, the jury's birthplace, civil juries are rare. Without juries, many of these countries have organized their procedural systems in ways very different from ours. It is no exaggeration to say that America's continued adherence to civil juries is a principal factor in its procedural isolation in the world today, and it remains an open question whether the United States can afford to pay the price of that isolation in the world economy of tomorrow.

Section A: Perspectives on Jury Trial

Lawrence M. Friedman, Some Notes on the Civil Jury in Historical Perspective

48 DePaul L. Rev. 201, 202-08, 211-12, 219-20 (1998)

Alexis De Tocqueville, interestingly, thought the civil jury meant more for American democracy than the criminal jury. Juries, he thought, "communicate the spirit of the judges to the minds of all the citizens; and this spirit . . . is the soundest preparation for free institutions." The jury, in his view, was a kind of "gratuitous public school, ever open," a school that allowed jurors to become "practically acquainted with the laws." The "political good sense" of the Americans, he felt, was due to the "long use that they have made of the jury in civil cases." . . .

... [T]he right to a civil jury was never so absolute as the right to a jury in a criminal case. Historically, the jury was not available in equity or admiralty cases.... Presumably, the legislatures of the states *could* have changed these rules.... But legislatures, on the whole, did not do this....

The percentage of cases that go to the jury, in both civil and criminal cases, has probably been declining since 1800. Charles Clark and Harry Shulman found the civil jury used in less than 4% of the civil cases in New Haven and Waterbury, Connecticut in the decade of the 1920s. Notoriously, most cases never reach the jury; they get settled long in advance of trial. Nonetheless, the jury has a vast influence on the law. The whole massive law of evidence is a tribute to the jury as an institution. Without the jury, nobody would need most of these rules.... Instead, the trained judge would simply assess the evidence, and separate the wheat from the chaff. This is of course what happens in *most* legal systems....

... [A]t one point the judge could simply tell the jury to go back and try again if the verdict was not to the judge's liking. In its most exaggerated form, this power probably disappeared before the Revolution. Judges remained, of course, awesome courtroom figures — and they had, potentially at least, enormous power to influence the jury. The judge could, for example, comment freely on the evidence, but legislatures ultimately took away this power....

... [I]n the twentieth century, the judge has lost what was once an important source of power — the power to craft his or her own instructions. The judge can pick and choose among instructions that lawyers dish up. This is no small matter. The instructions, however, are pretty much confined to abstract black-letter rules. The judge cannot explain them to the jury in commonsense terms and cannot comment on the case or on the evidence. In this regard, the jury is pretty much on its own and pretty much in command....

[The jury process] is a system in which, realistically, the judges retain a quiet authority to shape the trial and its proceedings. They also have the power of the law behind them: judges can set aside bad verdicts and they can choke cases off before they ever reach that point....

Can we draw any conclusions from these two developments — curbing the judge; and curbing the jury? They seem, at first blush, to contradict each other. They might reflect nothing more than the widespread mistrust of power in the American legal system; and the taste for constant checks and balances. The jury counterbalances the judge; and the judge in turn counterbalances the jury. There may also be some kind of fundamental ambivalence toward both the judge and the jury. The jury is the people (in theory); but on the other hand, we do not really trust the people. The judge is the law, the authority, and the government. We vacillate in trusting these institutions too....

... This leads us to ask: How different are the minds and hearts of judges compared to juries? [In a 1964 article, Professor Harry Kalven reported that the] evidence suggested, pretty strongly, that judges and juries saw tort cases in almost exactly the same light. In civil cases, judge and jury agreed

79% of the time. In the other 21% of the cases, one would expect, from all the whooping and hollering, that judges would tilt more toward defendants. But in fact, disagreements were distributed equally both ways. Judges, in short, were not one whit less or more pro-plaintiff than juries. There is corroboration for this point in a study of traffic negligence cases that went to trial in the late 1920s in the Supreme Court of New York County. In this county, juries gave the nod to plaintiff in just over 70% of the cases. But plaintiffs also won 70% of the bench trials.

Nonetheless, the image of wild, runaway, populist juries shows no signs of abating. It is backed up by anecdotes and scare stories. In fact, research makes it clear that the fears are grossly exaggerated. . . .

The civil jury system unquestionably has its problems. It is an interesting — and flawed — institution. The problems may be worst in complex, technical cases — cases where the ideal decision-maker would be somebody who understood brain chemistry, computers, monopoly theory, or how to navigate through the ins and outs of some complicated financial shenanigans. The civil jury has trouble with such cases. It also has trouble grasping the *legal* complexities of cases. How could it be otherwise, when typically all the jury learns about the law comes in the form of some densely packed, technical, high-falutin' "instructions"? Presumably something could be done about *this*; the law could be changed, allowing judges to instruct juries in everyday language. There are movements in this direction — attempts to write instructions that juries can actually understand. . . .

I doubt that many people today think of the jury as a kind of school for democracy; or as necessary for a system of popular justice. Certainly, there is no such halo around the civil jury. But it is hard to separate the civil jury from the rest of the texture of the American justice system. Most cases never get to the jury; but they may be decided in the shadow of what a jury is thought likely to do.

The civil jury may also play some part in legitimating the legal system. And many of us have a certain affection for the civil jury, despite its faults. It is something we are used to. It has the comfortable and affectionate patina of history. Old cities that grow over the centuries, all higgledy-piggledy, with crooked streets and ancient, tumble-down houses, always seem more beautiful than new, planned, "rational" cities. Who knows? Some legal institutions may, in a way, be like that too.

Notes and Questions

1. Professor Friedman presents arguments on both sides of the jury-trial debate. How many of the stereotypical attitudes (whether pro- or anti-jury) that Professor Friedman identifies did you possess when you began this course?

2. Professor Friedman is correct that the last two centuries have seen increased efforts both to control the jury and to loosen those controls. However we account for this phenomenon, two points are certain. First, the

issue of judicial control over juries is hardly a new one, nor has the effort to strike the right balance yet come to a resting place. Second, judges have always had a great deal of authority in setting the balance. The question is not entirely determined by the ambiguous text of the Seventh Amendment and comparable state guarantees of jury trial.

3. Today jury trial is familiar to us. But the rise of common-law jury trial in England during the Middle Ages also displaced familiar (though hardly rational) methods of factfinding. Claims of jury tampering and jury incompetence were common. One consequence of these claims was the development of the system of equity, in which the Chancellor heard claims without a jury. Over the past 150 years, most states have abolished (or "merged") the separate systems of common law and equity. The federal courts did so with the adoption of the Federal Rules of Civil Procedure in 1938. *See* Fed. R. Civ. P. 2. But merger created its own problems, principally how to blend two procedural systems, one of which used juries and the other of which relied on the non-jury, non-trial tradition of the civil law. Professor Subrin has argued that, for the most part, the Federal Rules are closer to equity than law in spirit. Stephen N. Subrin, *How Equity Conquered Common Law: The Federal Rules of Civil Procedure in Historical Perspective*, 135 U. PA. L. REV. 909 (1987).

4. Professor Langbein has argued that this equity-inspired, discovery-based system is proving so superior to jury trial that trial is properly becoming "obsolete." John H. Langbein, *The Disappearance of Civil Trial in the United States*, 122 YALE L.J. 522, 572 (2012). From July 1, 2018, to June 30, 2019, 0.7% of federal civil cases went to trial; of that number seventy percent were jury trials. *See* ADMIN. OFFICE OF U.S. COURTS, STATISTICAL TABLES FOR THE FEDERAL JUDICIARY tbl.C–4 (2019). Whether the phenomenon of the "vanishing trial" is a good development is a matter of some debate. For an argument that the trend has gone too far, accompanied by specific proposals to make trial a more common occurrence, see Stephen B. Burbank & Stephen N. Subrin, *Litigation and Democracy: Restoring a Realistic Prospect of Trial,* 46 HARV. C.R.–C.L. L. REV. 399 (2011). *But see* Jason M. Solomon, *The Political Puzzle of the Civil Jury*, 61 EMORY L.J. 1331 (2012) (arguing that the benefits of the civil jury as a political institution are overstated and making recommendations for improvement).

5. Professor Friedman mentions some of the research that has been done regarding jury performance. The social-science research literature on juries is vast. For an excellent summary, concluding that juries perform competently, see NEIL VIDMAR & VALERIE P. HANS, AMERICAN JURIES: THE VERDICT (2007). Professors Vidmar and Hans also express concern for the decline in the number of civil jury trials.

6. According to a study of 8,038 state-court trial decisions and 549 appeals, the reversal rate is 33.7% for jury trials and 27.5% for bench trials. *See* Theodore Eisenberg & Michael Heise, *Plaintiphobia in State Courts: An Empirical Study of State Court Trials on Appeal*, 38 J. LEGAL STUD. 121, 130 tbl. 1 (2009). What do these data suggest about appellate judges' attitudes toward juries and their perceived value in the American legal system?

SECTION B: SUMMARY JUDGMENT

A good pretrial process does two things: it develops the relevant facts and issues, and then it narrows the case down to the salient points for adjudication (a task that may dispose of the entire case). As we have seen, the disclosure-and-discovery process develops the facts and issues. What narrows them? The Rule 12(b)(6) motion to dismiss and the Rule 12(c) motion for judgment on the pleadings, which require the court to accept well-pleaded, plausible factual allegations as true, cannot serve this purpose in most cases. Rule 36, which involves consensual admissions, will not eliminate truly contested factual or legal disputes. Likewise, discovery may lead a party to abandon an issue that lacks merit, but it cannot resolve legitimate disputes. Ideally, another mechanism to narrow and eliminate disputes would be useful to help judges manage and resolve cases.

But such a mechanism raises concerns. A principal concern is the effect of an issue-narrowing device on the jury's role. Relatedly, should the legal system adjudicate the merits of a case without conducting a trial — the common law's centuries-old adjudicatory method?

Into this debate steps Rule 56, which permits a party to move for *summary judgment* on some or all of the claims or defenses in a case before the trial. Unlike the Rule 12(b)(6) and Rule 12(c) motions, the motion for summary judgment is usually based on facts adduced during the pretrial process. It is a powerful device, frequently used in modern American litigation. The following cases will help you to understand the criteria under which a court may enter summary judgment — especially the critical requirement that there be "no genuine dispute as to any material fact."

CELOTEX CORP. V. CATRETT

477 U.S. 317 (1986)

■ JUSTICE REHNQUIST delivered the opinion of the Court.

The United States District Court for the District of Columbia granted the motion of petitioner Celotex Corporation for summary judgment against respondent Catrett because the latter was unable to produce evidence in support of her allegation in her wrongful-death complaint that the decedent had been exposed to petitioner's asbestos products. A divided panel of the Court of Appeals for the District of Columbia Circuit reversed, however, holding that petitioner's failure to support its motion with evidence tending to negate such exposure precluded the entry of summary judgment in its favor. This view conflicted with that of the Third Circuit.... We granted certiorari to resolve the conflict, and now reverse the decision of the District of Columbia Circuit.

[In September 1980, Catrett filed a wrongful-death action in federal court, alleging that her husband's death in 1979 resulted from his exposure to asbestos products manufactured or distributed by fifteen defendants, including Celotex. In September 1981, Celotex filed a motion for summary judgment, asserting that discovery had failed to produce any evidence to support Catrett's allegation that her husband had been exposed to Celotex's products. In particular, Celotex noted that Catrett had failed to identify, in answering interrogatories specifically requesting such information, any witnesses who could testify about her husband's exposure to Celotex's asbestos products. In response to the motion for summary judgment, Catrett produced three documents tending to show exposure in Chicago during the 1970s. Celotex argued that the documents were inadmissible hearsay and thus could not be considered in opposition to the summary-judgment motion.

[The district court granted the motion. The Court of Appeals reversed, 2-1, holding that summary judgment in Celotex's favor was precluded because Celotex failed to support its motion with evidence tending to negate exposure to *its* asbestos.] The majority therefore declined to consider petitioner's argument that none of the evidence produced by respondent in opposition to the motion for summary judgment would have been admissible at trial. The dissenting judge argued that "[t]he majority errs in supposing that a party seeking summary judgment must always make an affirmative evidentiary showing, even in cases where there is not a triable, factual dispute." According to the dissenting judge, the majority's decision "undermines the traditional authority of trial judges to grant summary judgment in meritless cases."

We think that the position taken by the majority of the Court of Appeals is inconsistent with the standard for summary judgment set forth in Rule 56(c) [now Rule 56(a) — ED.] of the Federal Rules of Civil Procedure. Under Rule 56(c), summary judgment is proper "if the pleadings, depositions, answers to interrogatories, and admissions on file, together with the affidavits, if any, show that there is no genuine issue as to any material fact and that the moving party is entitled to a judgment as a matter of law."* In our view, the plain language of Rule 56(c) mandates the entry of summary judgment, after adequate time for discovery and upon motion, against a party who fails to make a showing sufficient to establish the existence of an element essential to that party's case, and on which that party will bear the burden of proof at trial. In such a situation, there can be "no genuine issue as to any material fact," since a complete failure of proof concerning an essential element of the nonmoving party's case necessarily renders all other facts immaterial. The moving party is "entitled to a judgment as a matter of law" because the nonmoving party has failed to make a sufficient showing on an essential element of her case with respect to which she has the burden

---

* Amendments to Rule 56 in 2007 and 2010 changed this language and arranged some of it in other sections. The standard for granting a motion for summary judgment is now found in Rule 56(a), and requires that "the movant show[ ] no genuine dispute" — rather than that the pleadings, discovery, and affidavits "show no genuine issue." Rule 56(c)(1)(A) describes the types of information that a movant can use to show that "a fact cannot be or is genuinely disputed" — "depositions, documents, electronically stored information, affidavits or declarations, stipulations ..., admissions, interrogatory answers, or other materials." — ED.

of proof. "[T]h[e] standard [for granting summary judgment] mirrors the standard for a directed verdict under Federal Rule of Civil Procedure 50(a) . . . ." Anderson v. Liberty Lobby, Inc., 477 U.S. 242, 250 (1986).

Of course, a party seeking summary judgment always bears the initial responsibility of informing the district court of the basis for its motion, and identifying those portions of [the pleadings and discovery responses, as well as any affidavits,] which it believes demonstrate the absence of a genuine issue of material fact. But unlike the Court of Appeals, we find no express or implied requirement in Rule 56 that the moving party support its motion with affidavits or other similar materials negating the opponent's claim. . . . [T]he motion may, and should, be granted so long as whatever is before the district court demonstrates that the standard for the entry of summary judgment . . . is satisfied. One of the principal purposes of the summary judgment rule is to isolate and dispose of factually unsupported claims or defenses, and we think it should be interpreted in a way that allows it to accomplish this purpose. . . .

. . . [T]he nonmoving party [need not] produce evidence in a form that would be admissible at trial in order to avoid summary judgment. Obviously, Rule 56 does not require the nonmoving party to depose her own witnesses. . . .

Our conclusion is bolstered by the fact that district courts are widely acknowledged to possess the power to enter summary judgments sua sponte, so long as the losing party was on notice that she had to come forward with all of her evidence. It would surely defy common sense to hold that the District Court could have entered summary judgment sua sponte in favor of petitioner in the instant case, but that petitioner's filing of a motion requesting such a disposition precluded the District Court from ordering it.

Respondent commenced this action in September 1980, and petitioner's motion was filed in September 1981. The parties had conducted discovery, and no serious claim can be made that respondent was in any sense "railroaded" by a premature motion for summary judgment. Any potential problem with such premature motions can be adequately dealt with under Rule 56(f) [now Rule 56(d) — ED.], which allows a summary judgment motion to be denied, or the hearing on the motion to be continued, if the nonmoving party has not had an opportunity to make full discovery.

In this Court, respondent's brief and oral argument have been devoted as much to the proposition that an adequate showing of exposure to petitioner's asbestos products was made as to the proposition that no such showing should have been required. But the Court of Appeals declined to address either the adequacy of the showing made by respondent in opposition to petitioner's motion for summary judgment, or the question whether such a showing, if reduced to admissible evidence, would be sufficient to carry respondent's burden of proof at trial. We think the Court of Appeals with its superior knowledge of local law is better suited than we are to make these determinations in the first instance.

The Federal Rules of Civil Procedure have for almost 50 years authorized motions for summary judgment upon proper showings of the lack of a genuine, triable issue of material fact. Summary judgment procedure is properly regarded not as a disfavored procedural shortcut, but rather as an integral part of the Federal Rules as a whole, which are designed "to secure the just, speedy[,] and inexpensive determination of every action." Fed. R. Civ. P. 1. Before the shift to "notice pleading" accomplished by the Federal Rules, motions to dismiss a complaint or to strike a defense were the principal tools by which factually insufficient claims or defenses could be isolated and prevented from going to trial with the attendant unwarranted consumption of public and private resources. But with the advent of "notice pleading," the motion to dismiss seldom fulfills this function any more, and its place has been taken by the motion for summary judgment. Rule 56 must be construed with due regard not only for the rights of persons asserting claims and defenses that are adequately based in fact to have those claims and defenses tried to a jury, but also for the rights of persons opposing such claims and defenses to demonstrate in the manner provided by the Rule, prior to trial, that the claims and defenses have no factual basis.

The judgment of the Court of Appeals is accordingly reversed, and the case is remanded for further proceedings consistent with this opinion.

■ [The opinion of JUSTICE WHITE, concurring, is omitted.]

■ [The opinion of JUSTICE BRENNAN, with whom THE CHIEF JUSTICE and JUSTICE BLACKMUN joined, dissenting, is omitted.]

■ [The opinion of JUSTICE STEVENS, dissenting, is omitted.]

Notes and Questions

1. In responding to a prior motion for summary judgment that Celotex withdrew, the plaintiff had presented three documents from which a factfinder could arguably infer the plaintiff's decedent had been exposed to Celotex's asbestos. Because it held that Celotex needed to support its motion for summary judgment with evidence negating exposure, the court of appeals never determined whether these documents created a genuine dispute regarding the material issue of exposure. On remand, the court of appeals held that a genuine dispute of material fact existed. Catrett v. Johns–Manville Sales Corp., 826 F.2d 33 (D.C. Cir. 1987). The parties settled shortly afterwards. *See* David L. Shapiro, *The Story of Celotex: The Role of Summary Judgment in the Administration of Justice*, in CIVIL PROCEDURE STORIES 359 (Kevin M. Clermont ed., 2d ed. 2008). So what, if anything, did the Supreme Court accomplish by taking the case?

2. After reading Rule 56(c)(1)(B), you might have wondered what the fuss in *Celotex* was about. The answer is that Rule 56(c)(1)(B), which allows a party to demonstrate that a fact is not genuinely disputed by showing that "an adverse party cannot produce admissible evidence to support the fact," was not in existence when *Celotex* was decided. *Celotex* established that the party *who does not have the burden at trial* (here, Celotex) need not bring forward *positive* evidence showing its lack of liability. Although Celotex may do so, it suffices for Celotex to point, with specificity, to the *absence* of

evidence admissible at trial that would permit a rational jury to conclude that Celotex's asbestos caused the harm. The result in *Celotex* therefore fits within the somewhat broader language of present Rule 56(c)(1)(B).

3. *Celotex* was one of three summary-judgment cases — often referred to as the "trilogy" — that were decided by the Supreme Court in the same year. The other two were *Matsushita Electric Industrial Co. v. Zenith Radio Corp.*, 475 U.S. 574 (1986), and *Anderson v. Liberty Lobby, Inc.*, 477 U.S. 242 (1986). Some commentators and courts claimed that the trilogy constituted a significant shift in the Court's attitude toward summary judgment because the three cases seemed to conflict with earlier cases of the Court that evinced a stingier attitude — in particular, *Poller v. Columbia Broadcasting System, Inc.*, 368 U.S. 464 (1962), and *Adickes v. S.H. Kress & Co.*, 398 U.S. 144 (1970). To some extent, however, the trilogy was less revolutionary than evolutionary. The real upturn in summary-judgment motions may have occurred in the decade before the trilogy. In one study of six federal courts, the percentage of federal cases in which a party filed a summary-judgment motion rose from 12% in 1975 to 17% in 1986, but then rose only to 19% by 1988, fell back to 17% in 1989, and slowly rose to 21% in 2000. *See* Joe S. Cecil et al., *A Quarter Century of Summary Judgment Practice in Six Federal District Courts*, 4 J. EMPIRICAL LEGAL STUD. 861, 882 (2007).

Nonetheless, coming as it did on the heels of significant changes in the Federal Rules in 1983 — such as invigorating case-management powers under Rule 16, creating new restrictions on discovery in Rule 26, and establishing new sanctions for filing marginal claims and defenses under Rule 11 — the trilogy suggested to some observers that judges had a new role to play: gatekeepers to adjudication by trial.

4. Summary judgment has become a central feature of modern federal litigation. The percentage of cases terminated by a summary judgment rose from 3.7% in 1975 to 7.8% in 2000; over the same period, the percentage of cases in which summary judgment eliminated some of the claims or defenses rose from 2.3% to 4.2%. Motions for summary judgment are far more common in some districts and with some types of claims. *See* Cecil, *supra*, at 882-86, 896; *see also* Theodore Eisenberg & Charlotte Lanvers, *Summary Judgment Rates Over Time, Across Case Categories, and Across Districts: An Empirical Study of Three Large Federal Districts*, *in* EMPIRICAL STUDIES OF JUDICIAL SYSTEMS 2008, at 1, 23 (K.C. Huang ed. 2009) (noting that summary-judgment motions terminated between 5.0% and 10.9% of cases in three federal districts in 2001-02). If trials occur in about 0.7% of all federal civil cases, a case in federal court is at least seven times as likely to be disposed of through a summary-judgment motion than through trial.

These data do not tell the entire story. Parties often collect evidence in the pretrial process with an eye toward making, or defeating, a motion for summary judgment, whether or not one is ever filed. Moreover, many cases settle while the summary-judgment motion is pending. Using economic analysis, one article argues that summary judgment also affects the incentives of parties to litigate, largely by driving down the settlement values of all cases. *See* Samuel Issacharoff & George Loewenstein, *Second*

Thoughts About Summary Judgment, 100 YALE L.J. 73 (1990); *see also* Louis Kaplow, *Multistage Adjudication*, 126 HARV. L. REV. 1179, 1288-98 (2013) (critiquing the summary-judgment standard as "unclear, question-begging in key respects, and at bottom open-ended" in terms of how it advances the ultimate purposes of the federal civil-justice system).

5. Another way to measure the impact of the trilogy is this: in just two decades, *Anderson*, *Celotex*, and *Matsushita* — in that order — had become the most-cited Supreme Court decisions of all time in the federal courts. *See* Adam N. Steinman, *The Irrepressible Myth of* Celotex*: Reconsidering Summary Judgment Burdens Twenty Years after the Trilogy*, 63 WASH. & LEE L. REV. 81, 143-44 (2006). *Twombly* (*supra* p. 36) and *Iqbal* (*supra* p. 45) have since deposed them from the top spots. *See supra* p. 55, Note 5.

6. In *Fesler v. Whelen Engineering Co.*, 794 F. Supp. 2d 994, 1006-07 (S.D. Iowa 2011), the court nicely summarized the law and the attitude of many federal judges regarding Rule 56:

> The term "summary judgment" is something of a misnomer. It "suggests a judicial process that is simple, abbreviated, and inexpensive," while in reality, the process is complicated, time-consuming, and expensive. . . . Despite the seeming inaptness of the name, and the desire for some in the plaintiffs' bar to be rid of it, the summary judgment process is well-accepted and appears "here to stay."
>
> . . . "[S]ummary judgment is an extreme remedy, and one which is not to be granted unless the movant has established his right to a judgment with such clarity as to leave no room for controversy and that the other party is not entitled to [prevail] under any discernible circumstances." The purpose of summary judgment is not "to cut litigants off from their right of trial by jury if they really have issues to try." . . .
>
> . . . The Court does not weigh the evidence, nor does it make credibility determinations. The Court only determines whether there are any disputed issues and, if so, whether those issues are both genuine and material.
>
> . . . An issue is "genuine" if the evidence is sufficient to [permit] a reasonable jury to return a verdict for the nonmoving party. "As to materiality, the substantive law will identify which facts are material. . . . Factual disputes that are irrelevant or unnecessary will not be counted." [*Anderson*, 477 U.S. at 248.]
>
> Courts do not treat summary judgment as if it were a paper trial. . . . In a motion for summary judgment, the Court's job is only to decide, based on the evidentiary record that accompanies the moving and resistance filings of the parties, whether there really is any material dispute of fact that still requires a trial.

7. As *Fesler* notes, *Anderson* held that a "genuine" dispute under Rule 56 exists when "the evidence is such that a reasonable jury could return a verdict for the non-moving party." *Anderson*, 477 U.S. at 248. *Anderson* thus linked two procedures: the standard under which a judge can grant

summary judgment before trial under Rule 56 and the standard under which a judge can enter *judgment as a matter of law* during trial under Rule 50(a). Under the latter standard, which we study in more detail shortly (*see infra* pp. 272-81), a judge can enter judgment against a party if, based on the evidence produced at trial, "no reasonable jury" could find in favor of that party. *See* 477 U.S. at 250-51. The "no reasonable jury" standard tends to be the modern approach. In the nineteenth century, "if there was what is called a *scintilla* of evidence in support of a case the judge was bound to leave it to the jury." *See* Improvement Co. v. Munson, 81 U.S. (14 Wall.) 442, 448 (1872) (rejecting the "scintilla rule" in favor of the "no reasonable jury" approach). The scintilla rule still operates in South Carolina and Florida. *See* Ray v. City of Rock Hill, 834 S.E.2d 464 (S.C. 2019); Leybovich v. SecureAlert, Inc., 237 So. 3d 1104 (Fla. Dist. Ct. App. 2017). A few states require the nonmoving party to produce "more than a scintilla" of evidence supporting the disputed issue; in practice this standard seems akin to a "no reasonable jury" approach. Other states adopt a "no reasonable jury" or "no substantial evidence" approach.

In jury-tried cases, linking summary judgment's "no genuine dispute" standard to this "no reasonable jury" standard makes sense: if the case would be tossed out during trial, why bother to start the trial?

8. *Celotex* concerned whether a genuine dispute of material *fact* exists. When the only matter dividing the parties is a question of law for which no factual adjudication is needed, summary judgment provides an excellent vehicle for the court to resolve the case. So does a Rule 12(b)(6) motion to dismiss, but often the parties need time to conduct some discovery to frame the legal issue before they present it to the judge. Hence, they wait and file a motion for summary judgment.

Conversely, sometimes a party will file a motion to dismiss under Rule 12(b)(6) and attach evidentiary material in support. Because such a motion to dismiss is decided solely on the basis of the pleadings (*see supra* p. 69), a court cannot consider this material. Rule 12(d), however, allows the court to convert the motion to dismiss into a motion for summary judgment. When doing so, however, a court must heed *Celotex*'s admonition to allow the opposing party "adequate time for discovery" (*supra* p. 237).

9. When disputed issues of material fact exist, one concern with summary judgment is the potential intrusion of the judge into the jury's traditional (and constitutionally mandated) role as factfinder. The Supreme Court has never squarely held that summary judgment — a practice that developed in nineteenth-century England, after ratification of the Seventh Amendment — is constitutional. But the Court has held that the Seventh Amendment is no barrier to a Rule 50 entry of judgment at trial when the evidence is insufficient to maintain a verdict for the nonmoving party. *See* Galloway v. United States, 319 U.S. 372 (1943). Because, as *Celotex* and *Anderson* say, Rule 50(a)'s "reasonable jury" standard at trial equates to Rule 56(a)'s "no genuine dispute" standard before trial, it appears that no constitutional problem exists. Indeed, the Court has never expressed any constitutional concern about summary judgment. *See* Sartor v. Ark. Natural

Gas Corp., 321 U.S. 620, 627 (1944); Fid. & Deposit Co. of Md. v. United States, 187 U.S. 315, 320 (1902). *See also* Burks v. Wis. Dep't of Transp., 464 F.3d 744, 759 (7th Cir. 2006) (noting that the argument against Rule 56's constitutionality "flies in the face of firmly established law").

10. Like the "reasonable person" in Torts, the "reasonable jury" is a legal construction. In a case like *Celotex*, the answer to what a reasonable jury should do is fairly easy: if the plaintiff who bears the burden of proof on an element of a claim puts on absolutely *no* evidence at trial to support that element, a jury logically must return a verdict for the defendant. Therefore, if a plaintiff has no evidence to prove that element before the trial, "no genuine dispute" exists and summary judgment is appropriate. *Cf.* Fed. R. Civ. P. 56(e)(1)(B) (allowing a moving party to show that "an adverse party cannot produce admissible evidence to support [a] fact").

The harder question is how to handle a case in which there is some, albeit weak, evidence to support a party's claim. Does any conflict in the evidence render the dispute "genuine"? Consider the following case.

SCOTT V. HARRIS

550 U.S. 372 (2007)

■ JUSTICE SCALIA delivered the opinion of the Court.

We consider whether a law enforcement official can, consistent with the Fourth Amendment, attempt to stop a fleeing motorist from continuing his public-endangering flight by ramming the motorist's car from behind. Put another way: Can an officer take actions that place a fleeing motorist at risk of serious injury or death in order to stop the motorist's flight from endangering the lives of innocent bystanders?

I

In March 2001, a Georgia county deputy clocked respondent's vehicle traveling at 73 miles per hour on a road with a 55-mile-per-hour speed limit. The deputy activated his blue flashing lights indicating that respondent should pull over. Instead, respondent sped away, initiating a chase down what is in most portions a two-lane road, at speeds exceeding 85 miles per hour.... Petitioner, Deputy Timothy Scott, heard the radio communication and joined the pursuit along with other officers....

... Scott took over as the lead pursuit vehicle. Six minutes and nearly 10 miles after the chase had begun, Scott decided to attempt to terminate the episode by employing a "Precision Intervention Technique ('PIT') maneuver, which causes the fleeing vehicle to spin to a stop." Having radioed his supervisor for permission, Scott was told to "[g]o ahead and take him out." Instead, Scott applied his push bumper to the rear of respondent's vehicle. As a result, respondent lost control of his vehicle, which left the roadway, ran down an embankment, overturned, and crashed. Respondent was badly injured and was rendered a quadriplegic. [Scott stated that he did not employ the PIT maneuver because he was "concerned that the vehicles were moving too quickly to safely execute the maneuver."]

Respondent filed suit against Deputy Scott and others under 42 U.S.C. § 1983, alleging, *inter alia*, a violation of his federal constitutional rights, viz. use of excessive force resulting in an unreasonable seizure under the Fourth Amendment. In response, Scott filed a motion for summary judgment . . . . The District Court denied the motion . . . . On interlocutory appeal, the United States Court of Appeals for the Eleventh Circuit affirmed the District Court's decision . . . . Taking respondent's view of the facts as given, the Court of Appeals concluded that Scott's actions could constitute "deadly force" . . . , and that the use of such force in this context "would violate [respondent's] constitutional right to be free from excessive force during a seizure. Accordingly, a reasonable jury could find that Scott violated [respondent's] Fourth Amendment rights." . . . We granted certiorari, and now reverse. . . .

III

A

The first step in assessing the constitutionality of Scott's actions is to determine the relevant facts. As this case was decided on summary judgment, there have not yet been factual findings by a judge or jury, and respondent's version of events (unsurprisingly) differs substantially from Scott's version. When things are in such a posture, courts are required to view the facts and draw reasonable inferences "in the light most favorable to the party opposing the [summary judgment] motion." . . . [T]his usually means adopting (as the Court of Appeals did here) the plaintiff's version of the facts.

There is, however, an added wrinkle in this case: existence in the record of a videotape capturing the events in question. There are no allegations or indications that this videotape was doctored or altered in any way, nor any contention that what it depicts differs from what actually happened. The videotape quite clearly contradicts the version of the story told by respondent and adopted by the Court of Appeals.[5] For example, the Court of Appeals adopted respondent's assertions that, during the chase, "there was little, if any, actual threat to pedestrians or other motorists, as the roads were mostly empty and [respondent] remained in control of his vehicle." Indeed, reading the lower court's opinion, one gets the impression that respondent, rather than fleeing from police, was attempting to pass his driving test:

5. JUSTICE STEVENS suggests that our reaction to the videotape is somehow idiosyncratic, and seems to believe we are misrepresenting its contents. *See post* (dissenting opinion) ("In sum, the factual statements by the Court of Appeals quoted by the Court . . . were entirely accurate"). We are happy to allow the videotape to speak for itself. *See* Record 36, Exh. A, available at http://www.supremecourtus.gov/opinions/video/scott_v_harris.rmvb and in Clerk of Court's case file.

"[T]aking the facts from the non-movant's viewpoint, [respondent] remained in control of his vehicle, slowed for turns and intersections, and typically used his indicators for turns. He did not run any motorists off theroad. . . . Significantly, by the time . . . Scott rammed [respondent], the motorway had been cleared of motorists and pedestrians allegedly because of police blockades of the nearby intersections."

The videotape tells quite a different story. There we see respondent's vehicle racing down narrow, two-lane roads in the dead of night at speeds that are shockingly fast. We see it swerve around more than a dozen other cars, cross the double-yellow line, and force cars traveling in both directions to their respective shoulders to avoid being hit.[6] We see it run multiple red lights and travel for considerable periods of time in the occasional center left-turn-only lane, chased by numerous police cars forced to engage in the same hazardous maneuvers just to keep up. Far from being the cautious and controlled driver the lower court depicts, what we see on the video more closely resembles a Hollywood-style car chase of the most frightening sort, placing police officers and innocent bystanders alike at great risk of serious injury.[7]

At the summary judgment stage, facts must be viewed in the light most favorable to the nonmoving party only if there is a "genuine" dispute as to those facts. As we have emphasized, "[w]hen the moving party has carried its burden under Rule 56(c), its opponent must do more than simply show that there is some metaphysical doubt as to the material facts . . . . Where the record taken as a whole could not lead a rational trier of fact to find for the nonmoving party, there is no 'genuine issue for trial.'" Matsushita Elec. Indus. Co. v. Zenith Radio Corp., 475 U.S. 574, 586-87 (1986). "[T]he mere existence of some alleged factual dispute between the parties will not defeat an otherwise properly supported motion for summary judgment; the requirement is that there be no genuine issue of material fact." Anderson v. Liberty Lobby, Inc., 477 U.S. 242, 247-48 (1986). When opposing parties tell two different stories, one of which is blatantly contradicted by the record, so that no reasonable jury could believe it, a court should not adopt that version of the facts for purposes of ruling on a motion for summary judgment.

---

6. Justice Stevens hypothesizes that these cars "had already pulled to the side of the road or were driving along the shoulder because they heard the police sirens or saw the flashing lights," so that "[a] jury could certainly conclude that those motorists were exposed to no greater risk than persons who take the same action in response to a speeding ambulance." It is not our experience that ambulances and fire engines careen down two-lane roads at 85-plus miles per hour, with an unmarked scout car out in front of them. . . .

7. This is not to say that each and every factual statement made by the Court of Appeals is inaccurate. For example, the videotape validates the court's statement that when Scott rammed respondent's vehicle it was not threatening any other vehicles or pedestrians. (Undoubtedly Scott waited for the road to be clear before executing his maneuver.)

B

Judging the matter on that basis, we think it is quite clear that Deputy Scott did not violate the Fourth Amendment. . . .

The car chase that respondent initiated in this case posed a substantial and immediate risk of serious physical injury to others; no reasonable jury could conclude otherwise. Scott's attempt to terminate the chase by forcing respondent off the road was reasonable, and Scott is entitled to summary judgment. The Court of Appeals' decision to the contrary is reversed.

■ [The concurring opinion of JUSTICE GINSBURG is omitted.]

■ JUSTICE BREYER, concurring.

. . . Because watching the video footage of the car chase made a difference to my own view of the case, I suggest that the interested reader take advantage of the link in the Court's opinion, and watch it. Having done so, I do not believe a reasonable jury could, in this instance, find that Officer Timothy Scott (who joined the chase late in the day and did not know the specific reason why the respondent was being pursued) acted in violation of the Constitution. . . .

■ JUSTICE STEVENS, dissenting.

Relying on a de novo review of a videotape of a portion of a nighttime chase on a lightly traveled road in Georgia where no pedestrians or other "bystanders" were present, buttressed by uninformed speculation about the possible consequences of discontinuing the chase, eight of the jurors on this Court reach a verdict that differs from the views of the judges on both the District Court and the Court of Appeals who are surely more familiar with the hazards of driving on Georgia roads than we are. . . .

My colleagues on the jury saw respondent "swerve around more than a dozen other cars," and "force cars traveling in both directions to their respective shoulders," but they apparently discounted the possibility that those cars were already out of the pursuit's path as a result of hearing the sirens. . . . At no point during the chase did respondent pull into the opposite lane other than to pass a car in front of him; he did the latter no more than five times and, on most of those occasions, used his turn signal. On none of these occasions was there a car traveling in the opposite direction. In fact, at one point, when respondent found himself behind a car in his own lane and there were cars traveling in the other direction, he slowed and waited for the cars traveling in the other direction to pass before overtaking the car in front of him while using his turn signal to do so. This is hardly the stuff of Hollywood. To the contrary, the video does not reveal any incidents that could even be remotely characterized as "close calls." . . .

If two groups of judges can disagree so vehemently about the nature of the pursuit and the circumstances surrounding that pursuit, it seems eminently likely that a reasonable juror could disagree with this Court's characterization of events. Moreover, it is certainly possible that "a jury could conclude that Scott unreasonably used deadly force to seize Harris by ramming him off the road under the instant circumstances."

Notes and Questions

1. *Scott v. Harris* is the first opinion in which the Supreme Court created a link so that people could see the video footage on which its decision turned. You might have already looked at the footage yourself. (It is also available on YouTube. There are two videos, one shot from each of two police cars involved in the chase.) Is the Supreme Court in effect saying that "when we know exactly what happened, we don't need a jury to tell us what to decide"? If so, what is the future of the jury in a video-saturated age?

2. In thinking about these questions, consider two cases with similar facts. In *Plumhoff v. Pickard*, 572 U.S. 765 (2014), the Supreme Court held that summary judgment was warranted in favor of police officers who fired fifteen shots into a vehicle that they had been chasing at high speeds when the driver momentarily came to a stop in a parking lot but then tried again to flee. The police killed both the driver and his passenger. Although the Court's opinion does not mention it, the district court's opinion stated that the entire event had been captured on the dashboard camera of one of the police vehicles. As in *Scott*, both the district court and the court of appeals had held that the police officers were not entitled to summary judgment.

On the other hand, the Supreme Court summarily reversed a court of appeals' affirmance of a district court's grant of summary judgment in *Tolan v. Cotton*, 572 U.S. 650 (2014) (per curiam). In *Tolan*, a police officer shot an unarmed young man on his front porch. The officer claimed that the shooting did not constitute excessive force because he reasonably feared for his safety. The plaintiff and his parents described circumstances disputing this claim. There was also conflicting testimony about the plaintiff's actions, about the lighting conditions, and about plaintiff's mother's role in the incident — all of which bore on the reasonableness of the officer's actions. The Court held that, "[b]y weighing the evidence and reaching factual inferences contrary to Tolan's competent evidence, the court below neglected to adhere to the fundamental principle that at the summary judgment stage, reasonable inferences should be drawn in favor of the nonmoving party." *Id.* at 660. In *Tolan* there was no video of the altercation.

3. In a study using 1,650 randomly selected people who viewed an edited version of the videotapes in *Scott v. Harris*, a substantial majority believed that Harris's behavior posed a deadly risk to the public and that Harris was more at fault for creating the risk than the police. Nonetheless, certain groups — typically minorities, low-income people, those from the Northeast, and self-described liberals — held the opposite view. The authors of the study suggested that the Court's majority was guilty of "cognitive illiberalism," failing to respect the perceptions of — and "inevitably called into question the integrity, intelligence, and competence of" — "identifiable subcommunities whose members in fact held . . . dissenting beliefs." " Dan M. Kahan et al., *Whose Eyes Are You Going to Believe? Scott v. Harris and the Perils of Cognitive Illiberalism*, 122 HARV. L. REV. 837, 897 (2009). They contended that, "[d]ue humility obliges a judge to consider whether privileging her own view of the facts risks conveying a denigrating and exclusionary message to members of such subcommunities." *Id.* at 898-99.

4. Unlike the plaintiff in *Celotex*, who allegedly had no evidence to support an element of her case, the plaintiff in *Scott v. Harris* had some evidence to support his claim. The issue was whether the evidence was strong enough to withstand a motion for summary judgment. When conflicting evidence exists, here are a few issues that can arise:

(a) *Is the dispute material?* In *Tiso v. Blumenthal*, 371 F. Supp. 2d 135 (D. Conn. 2005), Cars A and B were stopped at a red light. Car C plowed into the back of Car B, which then hit Car A. The plaintiff, who was in Car A, sued the driver of Car B (yes, Car B!) on the theory that the driver of Car B violated a state statute requiring drivers not to follow too closely. The factual dispute concerned whether Car B was stopped "directly" behind Car A (as the police report put it) or about six feet behind Car A (the defendant's version). The court held that the statute applied only when the cars were moving in traffic. Hence, the dispute over the distance between Cars A and B was immaterial, and summary judgment in favor of the driver of Car B was proper.

Salus v. Sivan, 534 F. Supp. 2d 430 (S.D.N.Y. 2008), nicely complements *Tiso*. In *Salus*, the plaintiff stopped his car when the light turned yellow, and the defendant rear-ended him. The court granted summary judgment for the plaintiff on the issue of liability. The defendant claimed that the plaintiff had come "to a sudden stop," but the district court cited cases under New York law that found such an excuse to be unavailing. *Id.* at 431.

(b) *Can the evidence that creates the dispute be presented in an admissible form at trial?* Rule 56(c)(2) allows a party to object to "material cited to support or dispute a fact" if the fact "cannot be presented in a form that would be admissible at trial." Suppose that the dispute involved whether driver W ran a red light and hit pedestrian X. X never saw what happened, but eyewitness Y later tells X: " I saw W run a red light." Y dies before being deposed. W moves for summary judgment, using the affidavit of eyewitness Z, who says that W went through a green light and X wasn't paying attention. Under Rule 56(c)(1)(A) and –(4), W can use Z's affidavit to show that the light was green; even though W could not submit the affidavit of Z at trial, Z's evidence can be presented at trial in an admissible form (live testimony). On the other hand, X may not submit an affidavit saying "Y told me that W ran the red light" to show a factual dispute. The reason is that X could not make this statement at trial (it's hearsay), and because Y is dead, there is no way to present Y's statement in an admissible form. Unless X has other evidence, W wins the motion for summary judgment.

(c) *Does the dispute involve the inferences to be drawn from undisputed admissible evidence?* It is hornbook law that drawing inferences is the work of the jury; when conflicting inferences can reasonably be drawn from the evidence, summary judgment is inappropriate. *See, e.g.*, Hunt v. Cromartie, 526 U.S. 541, 553 (1999). Does *Scott v. Harris* revise the hornbook? For an excellent discussion of different types of inference and the policies that a court should consider in handling inferences, see Williams v. KFC Nat'l Mgmt. Co., 391 F.3d 411, 422-31 (2d Cir. 2004) (Calabresi, J., concurring).

(d) *Does biased evidence create the dispute?* An affidavit "may preclude summary judgment even if it is self-serving and uncorroborated." United States v. Stein, 881 F.3d 853, 854 (11th Cir. 2018).

5. Rule 56(a) states that, when no genuine dispute exists, and as a result the moving party is entitled to judgment, the court "shall" grant summary judgment. "Shall" is ambiguous — it could mean "must" or "may" depending on the context. That ambiguity is a studied one. In nearly all cases in which a moving party meets the standard of Rule 56(a), the district court must grant summary judgment. But in rare and perhaps close cases, a judge may see no "genuine dispute" yet prefer to see what may develop at trial. Using "shall" gives judges a modest amount of leeway to deny summary judgment even when a party was entitled to it, but less leeway than using "may" would give.

6. Rule 56(a) also requires that "the movant [be] entitled to judgment as a matter of law." Suppose that Doctor D prescribed a double dose of a medicine to Patient P. A year later, P is diagnosed with cancer. Discovery reveals that D indisputably breached her duty of care, but D has credible, admissible evidence disputing that the overdose caused P's cancer. Assuming that the relevant law requires P to prove duty, breach of duty, causation, and damages, can P move for partial summary judgment just on the issues of duty and breach? Rule 56(a) allows a party to move for summary judgment on a claim or defense "or part of [the] claim or defense." The Advisory Committee's note to a 2010 amendment to Rule 56 states suggests that P could use Rule 56 to remove the duty and breach issues from the case. Using summary judgment to narrow issues is also consistent with the case-management philosophy of the Federal Rules. *Cf.* Rule 56(g) (allowing a court to enter an order treating "any material fact . . . that is not genuinely disputed . . . as established in the case" even if "the court does not grant all the relief requested").

7. *Celotex* noted that judges can grant summary judgment sua sponte (that is, on their own initiative) rather than waiting for a motion. In a 2010 amendment, Rule 56(f) codified this long-standing practice. Court-initiated summary judgment is an inroad on the adversarial model, but it does not give judges powers to narrow issues beyond those that parties can invoke.

8. Sometimes both parties believe that no genuine disputes of material fact exist, and both move for summary judgment in their favor. With *cross motions* for summary judgment, the court is to decide each independently; denial of one doesn't require grant of the other. *See, e.g.*, Faludi v. U.S. Shale Sols., L.L.C., 936 F.3d 215, 218 (5th Cir. 2019).

SECTION C: JURY TRIAL

At last we have arrived at the moment of trial. The parties have completed discovery, and their motions for summary judgment have weeded out unsupportable claims and defenses. Let the fun and fireworks begin!

250 CHAPTER FIVE JUDGE AND JURY

Sorry, you'll have to wait. Courses like Evidence and Trial Advocacy cover the process by which evidence is admitted and good advocates use examinations, exhibits, arguments, and a dash of showmanship to build a persuasive case. This course emphasizes structural questions: allocating factfinding responsibility and ensuring the factfinder's accountability. In this section we examine when jury trial is required, how a jury is selected, and the controls that the law places on jury factfinding.

1. The Right to Trial by Jury in Federal Civil Cases

Juries have never been the only factfinders used in Anglo-American law to resolve factual disputes. In medieval England, the system of equity, which did not use juries, grew up alongside the common law, which employed juries as factfinders. For the most part, American colonists accepted the duality of equity and common law. Sometimes, however, royal governors suspended the right of jury trial — a suspension noted in the Declaration of Independence. Colonists saw civil jury trial as an important bulwark against excessive governmental power. When the United States Constitution was written in 1787, however, it did not provide expressly for jury trials in actions at common law. The Seventh Amendment, one of the Bill of Rights amendments ratified in 1791, remedied this gap. Read the Seventh Amendment, and also Rule 38. Exactly what is being "preserved"?

CHAUFFEURS, TEAMSTERS AND HELPERS, LOCAL NO. 391 V. TERRY

494 U.S. 558 (1990)

■ JUSTICE MARSHALL delivered the opinion of the Court, except as to Part III-A, in which THE CHIEF JUSTICE, JUSTICE WHITE, and JUSTICE BLACKMUN join.

This case presents the question whether an employee who seeks relief in the form of backpay for a union's alleged breach of its duty of fair representation has a right to trial by jury. We hold that the Seventh Amendment entitles such a plaintiff to a jury trial.

I

McLean Trucking Company and the Chauffeurs, Teamsters, and Helpers Local No. 391 (Union) were parties to a collective-bargaining agreement that governed the terms and conditions of employment at McLean's terminals.... In 1982 McLean [transferred the respondents, who were truck drivers and members of the Union, to a terminal in Winston-Salem. It gave the respondents special seniority rights at the terminal. When McLean began to lay off and recall drivers in a way that seemed inconsistent with these seniority rights, the respondents filed three grievances with the Union, alleging that the layoffs and recalls violated the collective-bargaining agreement. Although the Union grievance committee supported the respondents on the first occasion, it did not support them on the second occasion, and stated on the third occasion that the matter had already been determined by the second grievance proceeding.]

In July 1983, respondents filed an action in District Court, alleging that McLean had breached the collective-bargaining agreement in violation of § 301 of the Labor Management Relations Act, 1947, 29 U.S.C. § 185, and that the Union had violated its duty of fair representation. Respondents requested a permanent injunction requiring the defendants to cease their illegal acts and to reinstate them to their proper seniority status; in addition, they sought, *inter alia*, compensatory damages for lost wages and health benefits. In 1986 McLean filed for bankruptcy; subsequently, the action against it was voluntarily dismissed, along with all claims for injunctive relief.

Respondents had requested a jury trial in their pleadings. The Union moved to strike the jury demand on the ground that no right to a jury trial exists in a duty of fair representation suit. The District Court denied the motion to strike. After an interlocutory appeal, the Fourth Circuit affirmed the trial court, holding that the Seventh Amendment entitled respondents to a jury trial of their claim for monetary relief. We granted the petition for certiorari to resolve a Circuit conflict on this issue, and now affirm the judgment of the Fourth Circuit.

II

The duty of fair representation is inferred from unions' exclusive authority under the National Labor Relations Act (NLRA), 29 U.S.C. § 159(a), to represent all employees in a bargaining unit. The duty requires a union "to serve the interests of all members without hostility or discrimination toward any, to exercise its discretion with complete good faith and honesty, and to avoid arbitrary conduct." A union must discharge its duty both in bargaining with the employer and in its enforcement of the resulting collective-bargaining agreement. Thus, the Union here was required to pursue respondents' grievances in a manner consistent with the principles of fair representation.

. . . Whether the employee sues both the labor union and the employer or only one of those entities, he must prove the same two facts to recover money damages: that the employer's action violated the terms of the collective-bargaining agreement and that the union breached its duty of fair representation.

III

We turn now to the constitutional issue presented in this case — whether respondents are entitled to a jury trial. The Seventh Amendment provides that "[i]n Suits at common law, where the value in controversy shall exceed twenty dollars, the right of trial by jury shall be preserved." The right to a jury trial includes more than the common-law forms of action recognized in 1791; the phrase "Suits at common law" refers to "suits in which legal rights [are] to be ascertained and determined, in contradistinction to those where equitable rights alone [are] recognized, and equitable remedies [are] administered." Parsons v. Bedford, 28 U.S. (3 Pet.) 433, 447 (1830). The right extends to causes of action created by Congress. Since the merger of the systems of law and equity, see Fed. R. Civ. P. 2, this Court has carefully preserved the right to trial by jury where legal rights are at stake. As the Court noted in Beacon Theatres, Inc. v. Westover, 359 U.S. 500, 501 (1959), "Maintenance of the jury as a fact-finding body is of such importance and occupies so firm a place in our history and jurisprudence that any seeming curtailment of the right to a jury trial should be scrutinized with the utmost care."

To determine whether a particular action will resolve legal rights, we examine both the nature of the issues involved and the remedy sought. "First, we compare the statutory action to 18th-century actions brought in the courts of England prior to the merger of the courts of law and equity. Second, we examine the remedy sought and determine whether it is legal or equitable in nature." The second inquiry is the more important in our analysis. Granfinanciera, S.A. v. Nordberg, 492 U.S. 33, 42 (1989).[4]

A

An action for breach of a union's duty of fair representation was unknown in 18th-century England; in fact, collective bargaining was unlawful. We must therefore look for an analogous cause of action that existed in the 18th century to determine whether the nature of this duty of fair representation suit is legal or equitable.

The Union contends that this duty of fair representation action resembles a suit brought to vacate an arbitration award because respondents seek to set aside the result of the grievance process. In the 18th century, an action to set aside an arbitration award was considered equitable. . . .

The arbitration analogy is inapposite, however, to the Seventh Amendment question posed in this case. No grievance committee has considered respondents' claim that the Union violated its duty of fair representation; the grievance process was concerned only with the employer's alleged breach of the collective-bargaining agreement. . . .

---

4. JUSTICE STEVENS' analysis emphasizes a third consideration, namely whether "the issues [presented by the claim] are typical grist for the jury's judgment." This Court, however, has never relied on this consideration "as an independent basis for extending the right to a jury trial under the Seventh Amendment." We recently noted that this consideration is relevant only to the determination "whether Congress has permissibly entrusted the resolution of certain disputes to an administrative agency or specialized court of equity, and whether jury trials would impair the functioning of the legislative scheme." Granfinanciera, 492 U.S. at 42 n.4. No one disputes that an action for breach of the duty of fair representation may properly be brought in an Article III court; thus, the factor does not affect our analysis.

The Union next argues that respondents' duty of fair representation action is comparable to an action by a trust beneficiary against a trustee for breach of fiduciary duty. Such actions were within the exclusive jurisdiction of courts of equity. This analogy is far more persuasive than the arbitration analogy. Just as a trustee must act in the best interests of the beneficiaries, a union, as the exclusive representative of the workers, must exercise its power to act on behalf of the employees in good faith. Moreover, just as a beneficiary does not directly control the actions of a trustee, an individual employee lacks direct control over a union's actions taken on his behalf.

The trust analogy extends to a union's handling of grievances. In most cases, a trustee has the exclusive authority to sue third parties who injure the beneficiaries' interest in the trust, including any legal claim the trustee holds in trust for the beneficiaries. The trustee then has the sole responsibility for determining whether to settle, arbitrate, or otherwise dispose of the claim. Similarly, the union typically has broad discretion in its decision whether and how to pursue an employee's grievance against an employer. Just as a trust beneficiary can sue to enforce a contract entered into on his behalf by the trustee only if the trustee "improperly refuses or neglects to bring an action against the third person," so an employee can sue his employer for a breach of the collective-bargaining agreement only if he shows that the union breached its duty of fair representation in its handling of the grievance.

Respondents contend that their duty of fair representation suit is less like a trust action than an attorney malpractice action, which was historically an action at law....

The attorney malpractice analogy is inadequate in several respects. Although an attorney malpractice suit is in some ways similar to a suit alleging a union's breach of its fiduciary duty, the two actions are fundamentally different. The nature of an action is in large part controlled by the nature of the underlying relationship between the parties. Unlike employees represented by a union, a client controls the significant decisions concerning his representation. Moreover, a client can fire his attorney if he is dissatisfied with his attorney's performance. This option is not available to an individual employee who is unhappy with a union's representation, unless a majority of the members of the bargaining unit share his dissatisfaction. Thus, we find the malpractice analogy less convincing than the trust analogy.

Nevertheless, the trust analogy does not persuade us to characterize respondents' claim as wholly equitable. The Union's argument mischaracterizes the nature of our comparison of the action before us to 18th-century forms of action. As we observed in *Ross v. Bernhard*, 396 U.S. 531 (1970), "[t]he Seventh Amendment question depends on the nature of the *issue* to be tried rather than the character of the overall action." *Id.* at 538 (emphasis added). As discussed above, to recover from the Union here, respondents must prove both that McLean violated § 301 by breaching the collective-bargaining agreement and that the Union breached its duty of fair representation. When viewed in isolation, the duty of fair representation issue is analogous to a claim against a trustee for breach of fiduciary duty. The § 301 issue, however, is comparable to a breach of contract claim — a legal issue.

Respondents' action against the Union thus encompasses both equitable and legal issues. The first part of our Seventh Amendment inquiry, then, leaves us in equipoise as to whether respondents are entitled to a jury trial.

B

Our determination under the first part of the Seventh Amendment analysis is only preliminary. In this case, the only remedy sought is a request for compensatory damages representing backpay and benefits. Generally, an action for money damages was "the traditional form of relief offered in the courts of law." This Court has not, however, held that "any award of monetary relief must *necessarily* be 'legal' relief." Nonetheless, because we conclude that the remedy respondents seek has none of the attributes that must be present before we will find an exception to the general rule and characterize damages as equitable, we find that the remedy sought by respondents is legal.

First, we have characterized damages as equitable where they are restitutionary, such as in "action[s] for disgorgement of improper profits." Tull v. United States, 481 U.S. 412, 424 (1987). The backpay sought by respondents is not money wrongfully held by the Union, but wages and benefits they would have received from McLean had the Union processed the employees' grievances properly. Such relief is not restitutionary.

Second, a monetary award "incidental to or intertwined with injunctive relief" may be equitable. Because respondents seek only money damages, this characteristic is clearly absent from the case. . . .

We hold, then, that the remedy of backpay sought in this duty of fair representation action is legal in nature. Considering both parts of the Seventh Amendment inquiry, we find that respondents are entitled to a jury trial on all issues presented in their suit.

IV

On balance, our analysis of the nature of respondents' duty of fair representation action and the remedy they seek convinces us that this action is a legal one. Although the search for an adequate 18th-century analog revealed that the claim includes both legal and equitable issues, the money damages respondents seek are the type of relief traditionally awarded by courts of law. Thus, the Seventh Amendment entitles respondents to a jury trial, and we therefore affirm the judgment of the Court of Appeals.

■ JUSTICE BRENNAN, concurring in part and concurring in the judgment.

I agree with the Court that respondents seek a remedy that is legal in nature and that the Seventh Amendment entitles respondents to a jury trial on their duty of fair representation claims. I therefore join Parts I, II, III-B, and IV of the Court's opinion. I do not join that part of the opinion which reprises the particular historical analysis this Court has employed to determine whether a claim is a "Sui[t] at common law" under the Seventh Amendment, because I believe the historical test can and should be simplified. The current test, first expounded in *Curtis v. Loether*, 415 U.S. 189, 194 (1974), requires a court to compare the right at issue to 18th-century English forms of action to determine whether the historically analogous right was vindicated in an action at law or in equity, and to examine whether the remedy sought is legal or equitable in nature. However, this Court, in expounding the test, has repeatedly discounted the significance of the analogous form of action for deciding where the Seventh Amendment applies. I think it is time we dispense with it altogether. I would decide Seventh Amendment questions on the basis of the relief sought. If the relief is legal in nature, i.e., if it is the kind of relief that historically was available from courts of law, I would hold that the parties have a constitutional right to a trial by jury — unless Congress has permissibly delegated the particular dispute to a non-Article III decisionmaker and jury trials would frustrate Congress' purposes in enacting a particular statutory scheme. . . .

■ JUSTICE STEVENS, concurring in part and concurring in the judgment. . . .

. . . [T]he commonsense understanding of the jury, selected to represent the community, is appropriately invoked when disputes in the factory, the warehouse, and the garage must be resolved. In most duty of fair representation cases, the issues, which require an understanding of the realities of employment relationships, are typical grist for the jury's judgment. . . .

In my view, the evolution of [the duty-of-fair-representation] doctrine through suits tried to juries, the useful analogy to common-law malpractice cases, and the well-recognized duty to scrutinize any proposed curtailment of the right to a jury trial "with the utmost care" provide a plainly sufficient basis for the Court's holding today. I therefore join its judgment and all of its opinion except for Part III-A.

■ JUSTICE KENNEDY, with whom JUSTICE O'CONNOR and JUSTICE SCALIA join, dissenting.

. . . To determine whether rights and remedies in a duty of fair representation action are legal in character, we must compare the action to the 18th-century cases permitted in the law courts of England, and we must examine the nature of the relief sought. I agree also with those Members of the Court who find that the duty of fair representation action resembles an equitable trust action more than a suit for malpractice.

I disagree with the analytic innovation of the Court that identification of the trust action as a model for modern duty of fair representation actions is insufficient to decide the case. The Seventh Amendment requires us to determine whether the duty of fair representation action "is more similar to cases that were tried in courts of law than to suits tried in courts of equity." Having made this decision in favor of an equitable action, our inquiry should end. Because the Court disagrees with this proposition, I dissent.

Notes and Questions

1. Like the remainder of the Bill of Rights, the Seventh Amendment originally applied only to the national government. Since ratification of the Fourteenth Amendment in 1868, states have been required not to "deprive any person of life, liberty, or property, without due process of law." During the twentieth century, the Supreme Court made most of the Bill of Rights applicable to the states on the theory that the Fourteenth Amendment's Due Process Clause incorporated the guarantees of the Bill of Rights. Only a few guarantees have not been incorporated. One is the Seventh Amendment. *Cf.* McDonald v. City of Chi., 561 U.S. 742, 765 n.13 (2010) (noting that the decisions limiting the scope of "the Seventh Amendment's civil jury requirement long predate the era of selective incorporation").

This omission is not as shocking as it might seem. All states but three — Colorado, Louisiana and Wyoming — guarantee in their constitutions the right to a civil jury trial; and even in these three states, juries are permitted by statute or code provision. Each state has decided for itself where the line between jury-tried and judge-tried factual disputes lies. Many states have drawn the line in roughly the same place as the Seventh Amendment, but a number accord even greater protection to the right. Here we focus only on the Seventh Amendment, which applies in the federal courts.

2. As Rule 38(a) suggests, you do not come to the difficult Seventh Amendment question if Congress has enacted a statute that provides for a jury. Congress occasionally provides such a statutory right. But this is a one-way ratchet. Congress cannot take away the jury-trial right that the Seventh Amendment guarantees. *See* Granfinanciera, S.A. v. Nordberg, 492 U.S. 33 (1989).

3. A party who wishes to have a jury trial on an issue must file and serve a *jury demand* "no later than 14 days after the last pleading directed to the issue is served." Fed. R. Civ. P. 38(b)(1). (Note, for instance, the jury demand in the sample complaint, *supra* p. 27.) The consequence of failing to file and serve a jury demand is severe: jury trial is waived. Fed. R. Civ. P. 38(d); *see* Lutz v. Glendale Union High Sch., 403 F.3d 1061, 1067 (9th Cir. 2005) (a jury-trial demand first asserted in an amended complaint cannot ordinarily overcome a prior waiver).

4. One important exception to the right to jury trial involves cases seeking damages against the federal government. For many tort, contract, tax, and other claims, Congress has waived the sovereign immunity of the United States, but it conditions the waiver by requiring that the case be tried without a jury. This condition does not run afoul of the Seventh Amendment. Lehman v. Nakshian, 453 U.S. 156 (1981). In contrast, when federal and state officials are sued for damages because they have allegedly violated a plaintiff's constitutional rights, the parties may demand a jury trial. City of Monterey v. Del Monte Dunes at Monterey, Ltd., 526 U.S. 687 (1999); Carlson v. Green, 446 U.S. 14 (1980).

5. For the most part, the Seventh Amendment analysis is not that difficult. For categories of cases that correspond to the old common-law writs

— for instance, tort or contract claims seeking damages — the right to a jury is a given. Similarly, factual disputes in claims seeking an injunction (recall that the injunction was a primary remedy available in equity) are almost always going to be decided without a jury. For claims involving violations of federal or state statutes, such as in *Chauffeurs v. Terry*, injunctive relief is often the only remedy available (or at least the only remedy that the plaintiff seeks); hence, no jury. Difficult questions typically arise only when a claim for a statutory violation seeks monetary relief, Congress is silent on the jury-trial right, *and* there is no obvious analogy to a common-law form of action. *Chauffeurs v. Terry* represents the now-standard analysis.

6. The two basic prongs of the Seventh Amendment analysis — historical English practice in 1791 and the nature of the relief requested — have remained constant for many years. The weight accorded to each factor, however, has wobbled. Beginning in the 1980s, the Court made clear that the second factor carried more weight. Since the 1990s, the historical inquiry has tended to dominate the Court's analysis. *See City of Monterey*, 526 U.S. at 708; Feltner v. Columbia Pictures Television, Inc., 523 U.S. 340 (1998). Because the second factor is historically inspired (as a general rule, English common law awarded damages, while English equity awarded injunctive relief), the two factors will often point to the same answer. When the two factors point in opposite directions, how should the tie be broken? Should history win, so that the "nature of the relief requested" factor comes into play only when the historical inquiry is inconclusive? Or should the "nature of the relief requested" factor win? If the latter, isn't Justice Brennan right that the historical factor should be jettisoned?

One argument for Justice Brennan's view is that it is bad history, and a rather silly exercise, to ask what the English courts of 1791 would have done with some claim that didn't exist and was beyond the legal imagination at that time. On the other hand, does the Seventh Amendment's use of the word "preserved" demand an historical analysis? Is Justice Kennedy right — that it is the second and not the first factor that should be downplayed? For a discussion of the role that history should play — as well as the limits of historical inquiry — in Seventh Amendment analysis, see Darrell A.H. Miller, *Text, History, and Tradition: What the Seventh Amendment Can Teach Us About the Second*, 122 YALE L.J. 852, 876-86, 907-17 (2013).

7. What should eighteenth-century legal history have to do with why juries matter and what their future should be? In *Damsky v. Zavatt*, 289 F.2d 46 (2d Cir. 1961), two great judges of the last century opined that Seventh Amendment analysis "may seem to reek unduly of the study," *id.* at 48 (Friendly, J.), "if not of the museum," *id.* at 59 (Clark, J., dissenting). In editing *Chauffeurs v. Terry*, we saved you from some of the more esoteric historical analysis, and many of the recent Supreme Court opinions dwell on even more abstruse details of eighteenth-century pleading.

Is freezing the right to jury trial in its 1791 form realistic in a procedural system that has evolved considerably since then? Take two examples. At common law, no Rule 12(b)(6) motion to dismiss existed; the closest analog was a device known as the demurrer. After the Supreme Court's decisions in *Twombly* (*supra* p. 36) and *Iqbal* (*supra* p. 45), a federal court today can arguably dismiss a case that would have survived a demurrer. Likewise, there was no summary judgment until the 1800s. Are these two devices unconstitutional, on the theory that they allow a judge to decide issues that a jury would have decided in 1791? For affirmative (but controversial) answers, see Suja A. Thomas, *Why the Motion to Dismiss Is Now Unconstitutional*, 92 MINN. L. REV. 1851 (2008); Suja A. Thomas, *Why Summary Judgment Is Unconstitutional*, 93 VA. L. REV. 140 (2007). For a critique of Professor Thomas's argument about summary judgment, see Brian T. Fitzpatrick, *Originalism and Summary Judgment*, 71 OHIO ST. L.J. 919 (2010).

On the other hand, the Supreme Court has intimated that neither heightened pleading nor summary judgment infringes on the right to jury trial. *See* Tellabs, Inc. v. Makor Issues & Rights, Ltd., 551 U.S. 308, 327-28 (2007) (pleading); Sartor v. Ark. Natural Gas Corp., 321 U.S. 620, 627-28 (1944) (summary judgment). And it is worth keeping in mind Justice Brandeis's oft-quoted observation that "[n]ew devices may be used to adapt the ancient institution [of the jury] to present needs and to make of it an efficient instrument in the administration of justice." *Ex parte* Peterson, 253 U.S. 300, 309-10 (1920).

8. In *Ross v. Bernhard*, 396 U.S. 531, 538 (1970), the Court stated that "[t]he Seventh Amendment question depends on the nature of the issue to be tried rather than the character of the overall action." In a well-known footnote, it then observed that "the 'legal' nature of an issue is determined by considering, first, the pre-merger custom with reference to such questions; second, the remedy sought; and, third, the practical abilities and limitations of juries." *Id.* at 538 n.10.

This analysis presents two difficulties. First, the "nature of the issue" analysis is problematic. "Issues" are not legal or equitable in their nature. For instance, the issue whether a party breached a contract is the same regardless of whether the plaintiff requests damages (legal relief), specific performance (equitable relief), or both. Put differently, *claims* are legal or equitable, not *issues*.

Second, *Ross* cited no authority for the third factor, and did not elaborate on it. Did the Court mean that, when a case is difficult and complex, a jury can be stricken even when the first two factors favor the jury? Some courts and many commentators thought so: arguing for or against a "complexity exception" to the Seventh Amendment became a cottage industry in the 1970s and 1980s. In *Granfinanciera*, Justice Brennan tried to end the controversy by suggesting that the third factor of *Ross* had a more limited meaning, one that the majority described in footnote 4 of *Chauffeurs v. Terry* (*supra* p. 252). As Justice Stevens' concurrence in *Chauffeurs v. Terry* suggests, however, the idea that the Seventh Amendment should be interpreted functionally — by assigning to juries the type of factfinding tasks that lay people are good at — rather than historically or in terms of the relief requested is hardly illogical. Consider the following case.

MARKMAN V. WESTVIEW INSTRUMENTS, INC.

517 U.S. 370 (1996)

■ JUSTICE SOUTER delivered the opinion for a unanimous Court.

The question here is whether the interpretation of a so-called patent claim, the portion of the patent document that defines the scope of the patentee's rights, is a matter of law reserved entirely for the court, or subject to a Seventh Amendment guarantee that a jury will determine the meaning of any disputed term of art about which expert testimony is offered. We hold that the construction of a patent, including terms of art within its claim, is exclusively within the province of the court.

I

. . . It has long been understood that a patent must describe the exact scope of an invention and its manufacture to "secure to [the patentee] all to which he is entitled, [and] to apprise the public of what is still open to them." Under the modern American system, these objectives are served by two distinct elements of a patent document. First, it contains a specification describing the invention "in such full, clear, concise, and exact terms as to enable any person skilled in the art . . . to make and use the same." 35 U.S.C. § 112. Second, a patent includes one or more "claims," which "particularly poin[t] out and distinctly clai[m] the subject matter which the applicant regards as his invention." Id. § 112. "A claim covers and secures a process, a machine, a manufacture, a composition of matter, or a design, but never the function or result of either, nor the scientific explanation of their operation." The claim "define[s] the scope of a patent grant," and functions to forbid not only exact copies of an invention, but products that go to "the heart of an invention but [avoid] the literal language of the claim by making a noncritical change." In this opinion, the word "claim" is used only in this sense peculiar to patent law.

Characteristically, patent lawsuits charge what is known as infringement, and rest on allegations that the defendant "without authority ma[de], use[d] or [sold the] patented invention, within the United States during the term of the patent therefor . . . ." 35 U.S.C. § 271(a). Victory in an infringement suit requires a finding that the patent claim "covers the alleged infringer's product or process," which in turn necessitates a determination of "what the words in the claim mean."

[Markman owned the patent to a system that tracked clothing through the dry-cleaning process using a keyboard and data processor. The process generated a transaction record, including a bar code readable by optical detectors. According to the patent's "independent claim 1," Markman's product could "maintain an inventory total" and "detect and localize spurious additions to inventory." The product of Westview Instruments, Inc., also used a keyboard and processor and listed dry-cleaning charges on bar-coded tickets that could be read by optical detectors. Part of the infringement suit hinged on the meaning of the word "inventory" in independent claim 1. After hearing an expert witness testify about the meaning of the claim's language, the jury found that Westview's product had infringed Markman's patent. The district court nevertheless granted Westview's deferred motion for judgment as a matter of law, overturning the jury's verdict. It construed the word "inventory" to mean that Markman's product could track articles of clothing throughout the cleaning process and generate reports about their status and location. Because Westview's system could not do these things, no infringement occurred.]

Markman appealed, arguing it was error for the District Court to substitute its construction of the disputed claim term "inventory" for the construction the jury had presumably given it. The United States Court of Appeals for the Federal Circuit affirmed, holding the interpretation of claim terms to be the exclusive province of the court and the Seventh Amendment to be consistent with that conclusion. Markman sought our review on each point, and we granted certiorari. We now affirm.

II

. . . Since Justice Story's day, we have understood that "[t]he right of trial by jury thus preserved is the right which existed under the English common law when the Amendment was adopted." In keeping with our longstanding adherence to this "historical test," we ask, first, whether we are dealing with a cause of action that either was tried at law at the time of the founding or is at least analogous to one that was. If the action in question belongs in the law category, we then ask whether the particular trial decision must fall to the jury in order to preserve the substance of the common-law right as it existed in 1791.

A

As to the first issue, going to the character of the cause of action, "[t]he form of our analysis is familiar. 'First we compare the statutory action to 18th-century actions brought in the courts of England prior to the merger of the courts of law and equity.'" Granfinanciera, S.A. v. Nordberg, 492 U.S. 33, 42 (1989) (citation omitted). Equally familiar is the descent of today's patent infringement action from the infringement actions tried at law in the 18th century, and there is no dispute that infringement cases today must be tried to a jury, as their predecessors were more than two centuries ago.

B

This conclusion raises the second question, whether a particular issue occurring within a jury trial (here the construction of a patent claim) is itself necessarily a jury issue, the guarantee being essential to preserve the right to a jury's resolution of the ultimate dispute. In some instances the answer to this second question may be easy because of clear historical evidence that the very subsidiary question was so regarded under the English practice of leaving the issue for a jury. But when, as here, the old practice provides no clear answer, we are forced to make a judgment about the scope of the Seventh Amendment guarantee without the benefit of any foolproof test.

The Court has repeatedly said that the answer to the second question "must depend on whether the jury must shoulder this responsibility *as necessary to preserve the 'substance of the common-law right of trial by jury.'*" Tull v. United States, 481 U.S. 412, 426 (1987) (emphasis added). "Only those incidents which are regarded as fundamental, as inherent in and of the essence of the system of trial by jury, are placed beyond the reach of the legislature." *Tull*, 481 U.S. at 426 (citations [and quotation marks] omitted).

The "substance of the common-law right" is, however, a pretty blunt instrument for drawing distinctions. We have tried to sharpen it, to be sure, by reference to the distinction between substance and procedure. We have also spoken of the line as one between issues of fact and law.

But the sounder course, when available, is to classify a mongrel practice (like construing a term of art following receipt of evidence) by using the historical method, much as we do in characterizing the suits and actions within which they arise. Where there is no exact antecedent, the best hope lies in comparing the modern practice to earlier ones whose allocation to court or jury we do know, seeking the best analogy we can draw between an old and the new.

C

... Claim practice did not achieve statutory recognition until the passage of the Act of July 4, 1836, and inclusion of a claim did not become a statutory requirement until 1870 ....

The closest 18th-century analogue of modern claim construction seems, then, to have been the construction of specifications, and as to that function the mere smattering of patent cases that we have from this period shows no established jury practice sufficient to support an argument by analogy that today's construction of a claim should be a guaranteed jury issue. ...

III

Since evidence of common-law practice at the time of the framing does not entail application of the Seventh Amendment's jury guarantee to the construction of the claim document, we must look elsewhere to characterize this determination of meaning in order to allocate it as between court or jury. We accordingly consult existing precedent and consider both the relative interpretive skills of judges and juries and the statutory policies that ought to be furthered by the allocation.

A

[After reviewing relevant cases, the Court found that none] indicates that juries resolved the meaning of terms of art in construing a patent ....

B

Where history and precedent provide no clear answers, functional considerations also play their part in the choice between judge and jury to define terms of art. We said in *Miller v. Fenton*, 474 U.S. 104, 114 (1985), that when an issue "falls somewhere between a pristine legal standard and a simple historical fact, the fact/law distinction at times has turned on a determination that, as a matter of the sound administration of justice, one judicial actor is better positioned than another to decide the issue in question." So it turns out here, for judges, not juries, are the better suited to find the acquired meaning of patent terms.

The construction of written instruments is one of those things that judges often do and are likely to do better than jurors unburdened by training in exegesis. Patent construction in particular "is a special occupation, requiring, like all others, special training and practice. The judge, from his training and discipline, is more likely to give a proper interpretation to such instruments than a jury; and he is, therefore, more likely to be right, in performing such a duty, than a jury can be expected to be." Such was the understanding nearly a century and a half ago, and there is no reason to weigh the respective strengths of judge and jury differently in relation to the modern claim; quite the contrary, for "the claims of patents have become highly technical in many respects as the result of special doctrines relating to the proper form and scope of claims that have been developed by the courts and the Patent Office."

Markman would trump these considerations with his argument that a jury should decide a question of meaning peculiar to a trade or profession simply because the question is a subject of testimony requiring credibility determinations, which are the jury's forte. . . . . We . . . think there is sufficient reason to treat construction of terms of art like many other responsibilities that we cede to a judge in the normal course of trial . . . .

C

Finally, we see the importance of uniformity in the treatment of a given patent as an independent reason to allocate all issues of construction to the court. As we noted in *General Electric Co. v. Wabash Appliance Corp.*, 304 U.S. 364, 369 (1938), "[t]he limits of a patent must be known for the protection of the patentee, the encouragement of the inventive genius of others and the assurance that the subject of the patent will be dedicated ultimately to the public." Otherwise, a "zone of uncertainty which enterprise and experimentation may enter only at the risk of infringement claims would discourage invention only a little less than unequivocal foreclosure of the field," and "[t]he public [would] be deprived of rights supposed to belong to it, without being clearly told what it is that limits these rights." It was just for the sake of such desirable uniformity that Congress created the Court of Appeals for the Federal Circuit as an exclusive appellate court for patent cases, observing that increased uniformity would "strengthen the

United States patent system in such a way as to foster technological growth and industrial innovation."

Uniformity would, however, be ill served by submitting issues of document construction to juries. . . .

Accordingly, we hold that the interpretation of the word "inventory" in this case is an issue for the judge, not the jury, and affirm the decision of the Court of Appeals for the Federal Circuit.

Notes and Questions

1. Using the standard two-prong analysis described in *Chauffeurs v. Terry* (*supra* p. 252), *Markman* first held that a patent-infringement case was triable to a jury. Should that have been the end of the matter? In 1791, if a case was triable to a jury, the jury decided all of the factual issues in the case. The judge did not carve out some factual issues for his own determination. *See The Supreme Court, 1995 Term — Leading Cases*, 110 HARV. L. REV. 266, 272 (1996) (noting that *Markman* developed a "novel inquiry of its own design" and was an "extension of the historical method [that is] not quite as consistent with precedent as the Court implies"); JAMES OLDHAM, TRIAL BY JURY 14, 10-15 (2006) (stating that "[i]t was customary to send 'the whole matter' to the jury," but describing devices through which a judge could overturn the jury's finding on a particular fact after trial).

2. In deciding whether a *factual issue* is determined by a jury, *Markman* began by examining history to see whether the determination of the particular factual issue in dispute had traditionally been performed by a jury. Without a clear historical answer, it then turned to "functional considerations" to allocate responsibility for factfinding. Along the way *Markman* also acknowledged that factual determinations that are "necessary" to, "fundamental" to, "inherent in," or "of the essence" of jury trial must be decided by a jury.

First of all, how are we to know what is "of the essence" to the jury-trial right and what is not? In *Tull v. United States*, 481 U.S. 412 (1987), the question was whether a statute that allowed a judge to set the amount of a civil fine comported with the Seventh Amendment. The jury still decided the question of liability; the statute limited only its role in setting fines. The Supreme Court held that setting the amount of a civil fine was not essential to the jury's role, and upheld the statute. *See also* Hana Fin., Inc. v. Hana Bank, 574 U.S. 418, 423 (2015) ("[W]e have long recognized across a variety of doctrinal contexts that, when the relevant question is how an ordinary person or community would make an assessment, the jury is generally the decisionmaker that ought to provide the fact-intensive answer.").

Next, recall that *Granfinanciera S.A. v. Nordberg*, 492 U.S. 33 (1989), tried to confine the "practical abilities and limitations of the jury" branch of the Seventh Amendment analysis to a very small corner. *See supra* p. 258, Note 8. Doesn't *Markman* create a huge doorway in that corner, and allow the "functional" strengths and weaknesses of the jury to matter on the different, but related, question of which *factual issues* (rather than which *claims*) a jury can determine? A single lawsuit can present dozens of factual issues. Does *Markman* mean that each factual issue has to be examined to determine whether a jury or judge should decide it?

3. *Markman*'s facts suggest another jury-trial problem. Suppose that Markman wanted two remedies for patent infringement—both damages for past breaches and an injunction against future infringement. Had Markman sought only an injunction, the nature of the relief requested would point to the judge as a factfinder. Had Markman brought a case solely for damages, the nature of the relief requested would point to a jury as a factfinder for all issues other than the construction of the claim. But the Federal Rules permit Markman to bring both claims in one case. Who decides the factual questions that are relevant to deciding both the injunctive and the legal claims? The judge? The jury? Or can each decide independently?

This problem of overlapping facts is the result of the merger of law and equity into one system. *See* Fed. R. Civ. P. 2. Before 1938, when the two systems were distinct, the issue never arose; actions at law had factual issues tried by juries, and suits in equity had them tried by judges. Whichever case came to trial first determined the factfinder; and, under principles of issue preclusion that we will study in Chapter Seven, the second factfinder was usually bound to accept the facts determined in the first case. *See* Am. Life Ins. Co. v. Stewart, 300 U.S. 203 (1937). Once legal and equitable claims could be heard together, a new approach was required.

In *Beacon Theatres, Inc. v. Westover*, 359 U.S. 500 (1959), the plaintiff sought a declaratory judgment and preliminary injunction. The defendant counterclaimed for damages, demanding a jury trial. The district court decided to try the plaintiff's claim first, thus binding the jury to the judge's factual findings on overlapping issues. The Court rejected this procedure:

> [T]he use of discretion by the trial court . . . to deprive [a party asserting a legal claim] of a full jury trial . . . cannot be justified. Under the Federal Rules the same court may try both legal and equitable causes in the same action. . . . Whatever permanent injunctive relief [a party] might be entitled to on the basis of the decision in this case could, of course, be given by the court after the jury renders its verdict. In this way the issues between these parties could be settled in one suit giving [a party] a full jury trial of every . . . issue. . . .
>
> . . . This is not only in accord with the spirit of the Rules . . . but is required by the provision in the Rules that "[t]he right of trial by jury as declared by the Seventh Amendment to the Constitution or as given by a statute of the United States shall be preserved . . . inviolate." . . .
>
> [O]nly under the most imperative circumstances, circumstances which in view of the flexible procedures of the Federal Rules we cannot now anticipate, can the right to a jury trial of legal issues be lost through prior determination of equitable claims. [359 U.S. at 508-11.]

4. Later cases present variations on *Beacon Theatres*. In *Dairy Queen, Inc. v. Wood*, 369 U.S. 469 (1962), the plaintiff sought injunctive relief

against using its franchise and trademark and monetary relief for wrongful past use. It styled its monetary request as an "accounting," which was an equitable remedy to untangle complicated financial affairs. The Supreme Court rejected two alternative bases for finding the entire case equitable with no jury right: (1) that the monetary claim was equitable; and (2) that the legal relief was "incidental" to the equitable relief. On the first argument, the Court held that the claim was not too complicated for a jury to hear. On the second argument, the Court acknowledged that, before the merger of law and equity, the "clean-up" doctrine permitted a court of equity to handle a legal claim for damages if the legal claim was "incidental" to the equitable claim. Echoing *Beacon Theatres,* however, *Dairy Queen* insisted that only under the "most imperative circumstances," which it found not present, might such a justification for nonjury trial be satisfactory. This position has effectively abolished the clean-up doctrine in the federal courts, although it survives in some state systems.

The Supreme Court did find the "imperative circumstances" to which *Beacon Theatres* and *Dairy Queen* had referred in *Katchen v. Landy*, 382 U.S. 323 (1966). Bankruptcy proceedings have long been regarded as equitable and thus nonjury, and Congress had also used its constitutional power to legislate on the subject of bankruptcy to establish summary proceedings to resolve claims promptly and without juries. A bankruptcy trustee, seeking to marshal assets of the debtor for the benefit of creditors, could have brought a separate action at law to enforce a money claim that the debtor had against one of the creditors. Since the creditor was already trying to collect money from the debtor's estate in the bankruptcy proceeding, the trustee sought to pursue the claim within the nonjury bankruptcy proceeding. The Court held that the trustee could do so and found no Seventh Amendment violation. The interest in not disrupting and delaying the bankruptcy proceeding, which marshals and distributes debtors' assets among creditors as quickly as possible so that all concerned can proceed with their affairs, was great enough to excuse the trustee from bringing a separate legal action to collect on the debtor's claim.

Finally, *Ross v. Bernhard*, 396 U.S. 531 (1970), whose footnote 10 we already explored (*see supra* p. 258, Note 8), was a *shareholder's derivative action,* in which shareholders sue to try to force a corporation to pursue a claim they believe it has but is not enforcing (sometimes because it is a claim against the corporation's own officers and directors). Before the merger of law and equity, derivative actions in federal court proceeded entirely in equity — even as to damage claims that, if pursued on the corporation's own initiative, would have been legal ones with jury right. But with merger, which has the same courts handling both legal jury-trial matters and equitable nonjury ones, the Court saw insufficient reason to treat the case entirely as if it were in a court of equity. This ruling does not mean that a jury handles all issues in such a case; the judge, for example, still rules without a jury — as had equity's chancellor — on whether the case meets requirements for the use of the derivative-action device. And that decision, if it goes against the shareholders, means the case never gets on to dealing with the underlying claim. But if the judge's ruling on the appropriateness of the derivative action is favorable, then the jury right attaches to the claim for damages, being pressed on the corporation's behalf.

5. Using *Beacon Theatres* and its progeny, try your hand at figuring out whether a Seventh Amendment right exists in the following cases:

- Plaintiff seeks an injunction; defendant denies material factual allegations in the complaint.
- Plaintiff seeks an injunction; defendant counterclaims for the imposition of a trust (historically, an equitable remedy).
- Plaintiff seeks an injunction; defendant counterclaims for damages.
- Plaintiff seeks a declaratory judgment that she has not breached a contract with defendant; defendant counterclaims seeking specific performance. In answering this question, you should know that a "declaratory judgment" seeks neither money nor an injunction — just a declaration of the rights and duties of the parties. *See* 28 U.S.C. §§ 2201-2202. The declaration can then serve as the basis for additional remedies, if needed, later on. The hornbook law is that the right to jury trial in a declaratory-judgment action is determined by the type of action (legal or equitable) that would have been pursued in the absence of the declaratory-judgment device.

6. State courts are not bound to adopt the *Beacon Theatres* framework. Some states follow the federal approach, but roughly an equal number use the pre-*Beacon* practice, which allowed a court of equity to determine overlapping factual issues. *See* Eric J. Hamilton, Note, *Federalism and the State Civil Jury Trial Rights*, 65 STAN. L. REV. 851 (2013).

2. Selecting a Jury

The process of selecting a jury begins when the court sends out a notice or summons requiring that people appear for jury service. The Supreme Court has held that the United States Constitution requires that this initial group of people, often called a *venire panel*, be drawn from a fair cross section of the community whose territory the court encompasses. *See, e.g.,* Norris v. Alabama, 294 U.S. 587 (1935). Unless there is evidence that the procedures effectively discriminate against segments of the community, this obligation can be satisfied by randomly selecting names from such sources as voter-registration records, lists of licensed drivers, and the like. In the federal system, the Jury Selection and Service Act of 1968, 28 U.S.C. §§ 1861-69, controls this selection process.

According to Rule 48(a), a jury in a federal civil case must be composed of at least six members, and may consist of as many as twelve. A venire panel, however, is much larger; depending on the case, it may range from twenty to several hundred people. The venire panel is winnowed down to the six to twelve jury members through a process known as *voir dire*. The process usually begins with the court determining whether any jury members are disqualified from serving on the jury. 28 U.S.C. § 1865 states the grounds for automatic disqualification; they include illiteracy, physical or mental infirmity, and serious criminal record. Next, the prospective jurors may be asked questions (usually by the judge, but sometimes by the lawyers) to determine if they have prior knowledge or firmly formed beliefs that might make it difficult for them to deliberate dispassionately. Prospective jurors who cannot perform their factfinding tasks properly are excused *for cause*.

The final step before the court empanels the *petit jury* (the jury that hears the case) involves *peremptory challenges*. The parties are typically given the opportunity to strike, without explanation or cause, three (or sometimes more) prospective jurors. *See* Fed. R. Civ. P. 47(b); 28 U.S.C. § 1870. The use of peremptory challenges has become the subject of considerable litigation.

EDMONSON V. LEESVILLE CONCRETE CO.

500 U.S. 614 (1991)

■ JUSTICE KENNEDY delivered the opinion of the Court.

We must decide in the case before us whether a private litigant in a civil case may use peremptory challenges to exclude jurors on account of their race. Recognizing the impropriety of racial bias in the courtroom, we hold the race-based exclusion violates the equal protection rights of the challenged jurors. This civil case originated in a United States District Court, and we apply the equal protection component of the Fifth Amendment's Due Process Clause.

I

Thaddeus Donald Edmonson, a construction worker, was injured in a jobsite accident at Fort Polk, Louisiana, a federal enclave. Edmonson sued Leesville Concrete Company for negligence in the United States District Court for the Western District of Louisiana . . . . Edmonson invoked his Seventh Amendment right to a trial by jury.

During voir dire, Leesville used two of its three peremptory challenges authorized by statute to remove black persons from the prospective jury. Citing our decision in *Batson v. Kentucky*, 476 U.S. 79 (1986), Edmonson, who is himself black, requested that the District Court require Leesville to articulate a race-neutral explanation for striking the two jurors. The District Court denied the request on the ground that *Batson* does not apply in civil proceedings. As empaneled, the jury included 11 white persons and 1 black person. The jury rendered a verdict for Edmonson, assessing his total damages at $90,000. It also attributed 80% of the fault to Edmonson's contributory negligence, however, and awarded him the sum of $18,000.

Edmonson appealed . . . . [A divided Fifth Circuit panel reversed, holding that] *Batson* applies to a private attorney representing a private litigant and that peremptory challenges may not be used in a civil trial for the purpose of excluding jurors on the basis of race. [A divided en banc panel vacated this opinion and affirmed the judgment of the district court.]

. . . We granted certiorari, and now reverse the Court of Appeals.

II

A

In *Powers v. Ohio*, 499 U.S. 400 (1991), we held that a criminal defendant, regardless of his or her race, may object to a prosecutor's race-based exclusion of persons from the petit jury. Our conclusion rested on a two-part analysis. First, following our opinions in *Batson* and in *Carter v. Jury Commission of Greene County*, 396 U.S. 320 (1970), we made clear that a prosecutor's race-based peremptory challenge violates the equal protection rights of those excluded from jury service. Second, we relied on well-established rules of third-party standing to hold that a defendant may raise the excluded jurors' equal protection rights.

Powers relied upon over a century of jurisprudence dedicated to the elimination of race prejudice within the jury selection process. While these decisions were for the most part directed at discrimination by a prosecutor or other government officials in the context of criminal proceedings, we have not intimated that race discrimination is permissible in civil proceedings. See Thiel v. S. Pac. Co., 328 U.S. 217, 220-21 (1946). Indeed, discrimination on the basis of race in selecting a jury in a civil proceeding harms the excluded juror no less than discrimination in a criminal trial. In either case, race is the sole reason for denying the excluded venire-person the honor and privilege of participating in our system of justice.

That an act violates the Constitution when committed by a government official, however, does not answer the question whether the same act offends constitutional guarantees if committed by a private litigant or his attorney. The Constitution's protections of individual liberty and equal protection apply in general only to action by the government. Racial discrimination, though invidious in all contexts, violates the Constitution only when it may be attributed to state action. Thus, the legality of the exclusion at issue here turns on the extent to which a litigant in a civil case may be subject to the Constitution's restrictions.

. . . Although the conduct of private parties lies beyond the Constitution's scope in most instances, governmental authority may dominate an activity to such an extent that its participants must be deemed to act with the authority of the government and, as a result, be subject to constitutional constraints. This is the jurisprudence of state action, which explores the "essential dichotomy" between the private sphere and the public sphere, with all its attendant constitutional obligations.

We begin our discussion within the framework for state-action analysis set forth in *Lugar [v. Edmondson Oil Co.*, 457 U.S. 922, 936-37 (1982)]. We asked first whether the claimed constitutional deprivation resulted from the exercise of a right or privilege having its source in state authority; and second, whether the private party charged with the deprivation could be described in all fairness as a state actor.

There can be no question that the first part of the *Lugar* inquiry is satisfied here. By their very nature, peremptory challenges have no significance outside a court of law. Their sole purpose is to permit litigants to assist the government in the selection of an impartial trier of fact.... Peremptory challenges are permitted only when the government, by statute or decisional law, deems it appropriate to allow parties to exclude a given number of persons who otherwise would satisfy the requirements for service on the petit jury.

Legislative authorizations, as well as limitations, for the use of peremptory challenges date as far back as the founding of the Republic; and the common-law origins of peremptories predate that. Today in most jurisdictions, statutes or rules make a limited number of peremptory challenges available to parties in both civil and criminal proceedings. In the case before us, the challenges were exercised under ... 28 U.S.C. § 1870. Without this authorization, granted by an Act of Congress itself, Leesville would not have been able to engage in the alleged discriminatory acts.

Given that the statutory authorization for the challenges exercised in this case is clear, the remainder of our state-action analysis centers around the second part of the *Lugar* test, whether a private litigant in all fairness must be deemed a government actor in the use of peremptory challenges. Although we have recognized that this aspect of the analysis is often a factbound inquiry, our cases disclose certain principles of general application. Our precedents establish that, in determining whether a particular action or course of conduct is governmental in character, it is relevant to examine the following: the extent to which the actor relies on governmental assistance and benefits; whether the actor is performing a traditional governmental function; and whether the injury caused is aggravated in a unique way by the incidents of governmental authority. Based on our application of these three principles to the circumstances here, we hold that the exercise of peremptory challenges by the defendant in the District Court was pursuant to a course of state action.

Although private use of state-sanctioned private remedies or procedures does not rise, by itself, to the level of state action, our cases have found state action when private parties make extensive use of state procedures with "the overt, significant assistance of state officials." It cannot be disputed that, without the overt, significant participation of the government, the peremptory challenge system, as well as the jury trial system of which it is a part, simply could not exist. As discussed above, peremptory challenges have no utility outside the jury system, a system which the government alone administers. In the federal system, Congress has established the qualifications for jury service, see 28 U.S.C. § 1865, and has outlined the procedures by which jurors are selected. To this end, each district court in the federal system must adopt a plan for locating and summoning to the court eligible prospective jurors. *Id.* § 1863. This plan, as with all other trial court procedures, must implement statutory policies of random juror selection from a fair cross section of the community, *id.* § 1861, and non-exclusion on account of race, color, religion, sex, national origin, or economic status, 18 U.S.C. § 243; 28 U.S.C. § 1862. Statutes prescribe many of the details of the jury plan, 28 U.S.C. § 1863, defining the jury wheel, *id.* § 1863(b)(4), voter lists, *id.* §§ 1863(b)(2), 1869(c), and jury commissions, *id.* § 1863(b)(1). A statute also authorizes the establishment of procedures for assignment to grand and petit juries, *id.* § 1863(b)(8), and for lawful excuse from jury service, *id.* § 1863(b)(5), –(6).

At the outset of the selection process, prospective jurors must complete jury qualification forms as prescribed by the Administrative Office of the United States Courts. *See id.* § 1864. Failure to do so may result in fines and imprisonment, as might a willful misrepresentation of a material fact in answering a question on the form. . . . The clerk of the United States district court, a federal official, summons potential jurors from their employment or other pursuits. They are required to travel to a United States courthouse, where they must report to juror lounges, assembly rooms, and courtrooms at the direction of the court and its officers. Whether or not they are selected for a jury panel, summoned jurors receive a per diem fixed by statute for their service. *Id.* § 1871.

The trial judge exercises substantial control over voir dire in the federal system. *See* Fed. R. Civ. P. 47. The judge determines the range of information that may be discovered about a prospective juror, and so affects the exercise of both challenges for cause and peremptory challenges. In some cases, judges may even conduct the entire voir dire by themselves, a common practice in the District Court where the instant case was tried. The judge oversees the exclusion of jurors for cause, in this way determining which jurors remain eligible for the exercise of peremptory strikes. In cases involving multiple parties, the trial judge decides how peremptory challenges shall be allocated among them. 28 U.S.C. § 1870. When a lawyer exercises a peremptory challenge, the judge advises the juror he or she has been excused.

As we have outlined here, a private party could not exercise its peremptory challenges absent the overt, significant assistance of the court. . . . By enforcing a discriminatory peremptory challenge, the court "has not only made itself a party to the [biased act], but has elected to place its power, property and prestige behind the [alleged] discrimination." . . .

In determining Leesville's state-actor status, we next consider whether the action in question involves the performance of a traditional function of the government. A traditional function of government is evident here. The peremptory challenge is used in selecting an entity that is a quintessential governmental body, having no attributes of a private actor. The jury exercises the power of the court and of the government that confers the court's jurisdiction. As we noted in *Powers*, the jury system performs the critical governmental functions of guarding the rights of litigants and "ensur[ing] continued acceptance of the laws by all of the people." . . . [T]he jury becomes the principal factfinder, charged with weighing the evidence, judging the credibility of witnesses, and reaching a verdict. The jury's factual determinations as a general rule are final. . . . These are traditional functions of government, not of a select, private group beyond the reach of the Constitution. . . .

Finally, we note that the injury caused by the discrimination is made more severe because the government permits it to occur within the courthouse itself. Few places are a more real expression of the constitutional authority of the government than a courtroom, where the law itself unfolds. Within the courtroom, the government invokes its laws to determine the rights of those who stand before it. In full view of the public, litigants press their cases, witnesses give testimony, juries render verdicts, and judges act with the utmost care to ensure that justice is done.

Race discrimination within the courtroom raises serious questions as to the fairness of the proceedings conducted there. Racial bias mars the integrity of the judicial system and prevents the idea of democratic government from becoming a reality. . . . To permit racial exclusion in this official forum compounds the racial insult inherent in judging a citizen by the color of his or her skin.

B

Having held that in a civil trial exclusion on account of race violates a prospective juror's equal protection rights, we consider whether an opposing litigant may raise the excluded person's rights on his or her behalf. As we noted in *Powers*: "In the ordinary course, a litigant must assert his or her own legal rights and interests, and cannot rest a claim to relief on the legal rights or interests of third parties." We also noted, however, that this fundamental restriction on judicial authority admits of "certain, limited exceptions," and that a litigant may raise a claim on behalf of a third party if the litigant can demonstrate that he or she has suffered a concrete, redressable injury, that he or she has a close relation with the third party, and that there exists some hindrance to the third party's ability to protect his or her own interests. [The Court held that these criteria were satisfied.]

III

It remains to consider whether a prima facie case of racial discrimination has been established in the case before us, requiring Leesville to offer race-neutral explanations for its peremptory challenges. In *Batson*, we held that determining whether a prima facie case has been established requires consideration of all relevant circumstances, including whether there has been a pattern of strikes against members of a particular race. The same approach applies in the civil context, and we leave it to the trial courts in the first instance to develop evidentiary rules for implementing our decision.

The judgment is reversed, and the case is remanded for further proceedings consistent with our opinion.

- [The dissenting opinion of JUSTICE O'CONNOR, with whom THE CHIEF JUSTICE and JUSTICE SCALIA joined, is omitted.]
- [The dissenting opinion of JUSTICE SCALIA is omitted.]

Notes and Questions

1. Does the process of selecting a jury make you think more or less of jury trial?

2. In *J.E.B. v. Alabama ex rel. T.B.*, 511 U.S. 127 (1994), the Court extended *Batson* to preclude gender-based peremptory strikes in a civil case in which one party sought to strike all the men from the jury. The case arose in state court and involved application of the Fourteenth Amendment, but its rule would apply through the Fifth Amendment to federal courts.

Thus far, race and gender are the only suspect categories that the Court has recognized with regard to the exercise of peremptory challenges. How about religion? Political affiliation? Wealth? Sexual orientation? *See* SmithKline Beecham Corp. v. Abbott Labs., 740 F.3d 471, 474 (9th Cir. 2014) (holding that the Equal Protection Clause "prohibits peremptory strikes based on sexual orientation"). Is the ultimate message of *Edmonson* and *J.E.B.* that the days of peremptory challenges are numbered?

3. How serious a bar are *Batson* and *Edmonson* in the real world? In *Purkett v. Elem*, 514 U.S. 765 (1995), the prosecutor used his peremptory challenges to strike two African-Americans from the jury. The defense made a *Batson* challenge. The prosecutor justified the strikes as follows:

> I struck [juror] number twenty-two because of his long hair. He had long curly hair. He had the longest hair of anybody on the panel by far. He appeared to me to not be a good juror for that fact, the fact that he had long hair hanging down shoulder length, curly, unkempt hair. Also, he had a mustache and a goatee type beard. And juror number twenty-four also has a mustache and goatee type beard. Those are the only two people on the jury . . . with the facial hair. . . . And I don't like the way they looked, with the way the hair is cut, both of them. And the mustaches and the beards look suspicious to me. [514 U.S. at 766.]

The prosecutor also explained that he feared that one of the stricken jurors, who was once robbed at gunpoint, would believe that "to have a robbery you have to have a gun, and there is no gun in this case." *Id.*

The state trial court found these explanations to be race-neutral, and permitted the peremptories. The Supreme Court, in its limited review of state-court factfinding, did not overturn the finding.

3. Motion for Judgment as a Matter of Law

Once the jury is selected, the trial begins. What happens when, during the trial, it becomes obvious that one side has put forward no, or at least insufficient, evidence either to meet the party's burden of proof or to rebut the evidence of the opposing party who bears the burden of proof? Must the case go to the jury? Read Rule 50(a).

REEVES V. SANDERSON PLUMBING PRODUCTS, INC.

530 U.S. 133 (2000)

■ JUSTICE O'CONNOR delivered the opinion for a unanimous Court.

This case concerns the kind and amount of evidence necessary to sustain a jury's verdict that an employer unlawfully discriminated on the basis of age. Specifically, we must resolve whether a defendant is entitled to judgment as a matter of law when the plaintiff's case consists exclusively of a prima facie case of discrimination and sufficient evidence for the trier of fact to disbelieve the defendant's legitimate, nondiscriminatory explanation for its action. We must also decide whether the employer was entitled to judgment as a matter of law under the particular circumstances presented here.

I

In October 1995, petitioner Roger Reeves was 57 years old and had spent 40 years in the employ of respondent, Sanderson Plumbing Products, Inc., a manufacturer of toilet seats and covers. Petitioner worked in a department known as the "Hinge Room," where he supervised the "regular line." Joe Oswalt, in his mid-thirties, supervised the Hinge Room's "special line," and Russell Caldwell, the manager of the Hinge Room and age 45, supervised both petitioner and Oswalt. Petitioner's responsibilities included recording the attendance and hours of those under his supervision, and reviewing a weekly report that listed the hours worked by each employee.

In the summer of 1995, Caldwell informed Powe Chesnut, the director of manufacturing and the husband of company president Sandra Sanderson, that "production was down" in the Hinge Room because employees were often absent and were "coming in late and leaving early." Because the monthly attendance reports did not indicate a problem, Chesnut ordered an audit of the Hinge Room's timesheets for July, August, and September of that year. According to Chesnut's testimony, that investigation revealed "numerous timekeeping errors and misrepresentations on the part of Caldwell, Reeves, and Oswalt." Following the audit, Chesnut . . . recommended to company president Sanderson that petitioner and Caldwell be fired. In October 1995, Sanderson followed the recommendation and discharged both petitioner and Caldwell.

In June 1996, petitioner filed suit in the United States District Court for the Northern District of Mississippi, contending that he had been fired because of his age in violation of the Age Discrimination in Employment Act of 1967 (ADEA), 81 Stat. 602, as amended, 29 U.S.C. § 621 et seq. At trial, respondent contended that it had fired petitioner due to his failure to maintain accurate attendance records, while petitioner attempted to demonstrate that respondent's explanation was pretext for age discrimination. Petitioner introduced evidence that he had accurately recorded the attendance and hours of the employees under his supervision, and that Chesnut, whom Oswalt described as wielding "absolute power" within the company, had demonstrated age-based animus in his dealings with petitioner.

During the trial, the District Court twice denied oral motions by respondent for judgment as a matter of law under Rule 50 of the Federal Rules of Civil Procedure, and the case went to the jury. The court instructed the jury that "[i]f the plaintiff fails to prove age was a determinative or motivating factor in the decision to terminate him, then your verdict shall be for the defendant." So charged, the jury returned a verdict in favor of petitioner, awarding him $35,000 in compensatory damages, and found that respondent's age discrimination had been "willfu[l]." The District Court accordingly entered judgment for petitioner in the amount of $70,000, which included $35,000 in liquidated damages based on the jury's finding of willfulness. Respondent then renewed its motion for judgment as a matter of law and alternatively moved for a new trial, while petitioner moved for front pay. The District Court denied respondent's motions and granted petitioner's, awarding him $28,490.80 in front pay for two years' lost income.

The Court of Appeals for the Fifth Circuit reversed, holding that petitioner had not introduced sufficient evidence to sustain the jury's finding of unlawful discrimination. . . .

We granted certiorari to resolve a conflict among the Courts of Appeals as to whether a plaintiff's prima facie case of discrimination (as defined in *McDonnell Douglas Corp. v. Green*, 411 U.S. 792, 802 (1973)), combined with sufficient evidence for a reasonable factfinder to reject the employer's nondiscriminatory explanation for its decision, is adequate to sustain a finding of liability for intentional discrimination.

II

Under the ADEA, it is "unlawful for an employer . . . to fail or refuse to hire or to discharge any individual or otherwise discriminate against any individual with respect to his compensation, terms, conditions, or privileges of employment, because of such individual's age." 29 U.S.C. § 623(a)(1). When a plaintiff alleges disparate treatment, "liability depends on whether the protected trait (under the ADEA, age) actually motivated the employer's decision." That is, the plaintiff's age must have "actually played a role in [the employer's decisionmaking] process and had a determinative influence on the outcome." Recognizing that "the question facing triers of fact in discrimination cases is both sensitive and difficult," and that "[t]here will seldom be 'eyewitness' testimony as to the employer's mental processes," the Courts of Appeals, including the Fifth Circuit in this case, have employed some variant of the framework articulated in *McDonnell Douglas* to analyze ADEA claims that are based principally on circumstantial evidence. . . .

McDonnell Douglas and subsequent decisions have "established an allocation of the burden of production and an order for the presentation of proof in . . . discriminatory-treatment cases." St. Mary's Honor Center v. Hicks, 509 U.S. 502, 506 (1993). First, the plaintiff must establish a prima facie case of discrimination. *Id*. It is undisputed that petitioner satisfied this burden here: (i) at the time he was fired, he was a member of the class protected by the ADEA ("individuals who are at least 40 years of age," 29 U.S.C. § 631(a)), (ii) he was otherwise qualified for the position of Hinge Room supervisor, (iii) he was discharged by respondent, and (iv) respondent successively hired three persons in their thirties to fill petitioner's position. The burden therefore shifted to respondent to "produc[e] evidence that the plaintiff was rejected, or someone else was preferred, for a legitimate, nondiscriminatory reason." This burden is one of production, not persuasion; it "can involve no credibility assessment." Respondent met this burden by offering admissible evidence sufficient for the trier of fact to conclude that petitioner was fired because of his failure to maintain accurate attendance records. Accordingly, "the *McDonnell Douglas* framework — with its presumptions and burdens" — disappeared, and the sole remaining issue was "discrimination *vel non*."

Although intermediate evidentiary burdens shift back and forth under this framework, "[t]he ultimate burden of persuading the trier of fact that the defendant intentionally discriminated against the plaintiff remains at all times with the plaintiff." And in attempting to satisfy this burden, the plaintiff — once the employer produces sufficient evidence to support a nondiscriminatory explanation for its decision — must be afforded the "opportunity to prove by a preponderance of the evidence that the legitimate reasons offered by the defendant were not its true reasons, but were a pretext for discrimination." That is, the plaintiff may attempt to establish that he was the victim of intentional discrimination "by showing that the employer's proffered explanation is unworthy of credence." Moreover, although the presumption of discrimination "drops out of the picture" once the defendant meets its burden of production, the trier of fact may still consider the evidence establishing the plaintiff's prima facie case "and inferences properly drawn therefrom . . . on the issue of whether the defendant's explanation is pretextual."

In this case, the evidence supporting respondent's explanation for petitioner's discharge consisted primarily of testimony by Chesnut and Sanderson and documentation of petitioner's alleged "shoddy record keeping." Chesnut testified that a 1993 audit of Hinge Room operations revealed "a very lax assembly line" where employees were not adhering to general work rules. As a result of that audit, petitioner was placed on 90 days' probation for unsatisfactory performance. In 1995, Chesnut ordered another investigation of the Hinge Room, which, according to his testimony, revealed that petitioner was not correctly recording the absences and hours of employees. Respondent introduced summaries of that investigation documenting several attendance violations by 12 employees under petitioner's supervision, and noting that each should have been disciplined in some manner. Chesnut . . . and Sanderson also stated that petitioner's errors, by failing to adjust for hours not worked, cost the company overpaid wages. Sanderson testified that she accepted the recommendation to discharge petitioner because he had "intentionally falsif[ied] company pay records."

Petitioner, however, made a substantial showing that respondent's explanation was false. First, petitioner offered evidence that he had properly maintained the attendance records. Most of the timekeeping errors cited by respondent involved employees who were not marked late but who were recorded as having arrived at the plant at 7 a.m. for the 7 a.m. shift. Respondent contended that employees arriving at 7 a.m. could not have been at their workstations by 7 a.m., and therefore must have been late. But both petitioner and Oswalt testified that the company's automated timeclock often failed to scan employees' timecards, so that the timesheets would not record any time of arrival. On these occasions, petitioner and Oswalt would visually check the workstations and record whether the employees were present at the start of the shift. They stated that if an employee arrived promptly but the timesheet contained no time of arrival, they would reconcile the two by marking "7 a.m." as the employee's arrival time, even if the employee actually arrived at the plant earlier. On cross-examination, Chesnut acknowledged that the timeclock sometimes malfunctioned, and that if "people were there at their work station[s]" at the start of the shift, the supervisor "would write in seven o'clock." Petitioner also testified that when employees arrived before or stayed after their shifts, he would assign them additional work so they would not be overpaid.

Petitioner similarly cast doubt on whether he was responsible for any failure to discipline late and absent employees. Petitioner testified that his job only included reviewing the daily and weekly attendance reports, and that disciplinary writeups were based on the monthly reports, which were reviewed by Caldwell. Sanderson admitted that Caldwell, and not petitioner, was responsible for citing employees for violations of the company's attendance policy. Further, Chesnut conceded that there had never been a union grievance or employee complaint arising from petitioner's recordkeeping, and that the company had never calculated the amount of overpayments allegedly attributable to petitioner's errors. Petitioner also testified that, on the day he was fired, Chesnut said that his discharge was due to his failure to report as absent one employee, Gina Mae Coley, on two days in September 1995. But petitioner explained that he had spent those days in the hospital, and that Caldwell was therefore responsible for any overpayment of Coley. Finally, petitioner stated that on previous occasions that employees were paid for hours they had not worked, the company had simply adjusted those employees' next paychecks to correct the errors.

Based on this evidence, the Court of Appeals concluded that petitioner "very well may be correct" that "a reasonable jury could have found that [respondent's] explanation for its employment decision was pretextual." Nonetheless, the court held that this showing, standing alone, was insufficient to sustain the jury's finding of liability: "We must, as an essential final step, determine whether Reeves presented sufficient evidence that his age motivated [respondent's] employment decision." And in making this determination, the Court of Appeals ignored the evidence supporting petitioner's prima facie case and challenging respondent's explanation for its decision. The court confined its review of evidence favoring petitioner to that evidence showing that Chesnut had directed derogatory, age-based comments at petitioner, and that Chesnut had singled out petitioner for harsher treatment than younger employees. It is therefore apparent that the court believed that only this additional evidence of discrimination was relevant to whether the jury's verdict should stand. That is, the Court of Appeals proceeded from the assumption that a prima facie case of discrimination, combined with sufficient evidence for the trier of fact to disbelieve the defendant's legitimate, nondiscriminatory reason for its decision, is insufficient as a matter of law to sustain a jury's finding of intentional discrimination.

In so reasoning, the Court of Appeals misconceived the evidentiary burden borne by plaintiffs who attempt to prove intentional discrimination through indirect evidence. . . .

. . . [A] plaintiff's prima facie case, combined with sufficient evidence to find that the employer's asserted justification is false, may permit the trier of fact to conclude that the employer unlawfully discriminated.

This is not to say that such a showing by the plaintiff will always be adequate to sustain a jury's finding of liability. Certainly there will be instances where, although the plaintiff has established a prima facie case and set forth sufficient evidence to reject the defendant's explanation, no rational factfinder could conclude that the action was discriminatory. For instance, an employer would be entitled to judgment as a matter of law if the record conclusively revealed some other, nondiscriminatory reason for the employer's decision, or if the plaintiff created only a weak issue of fact as to whether the employer's reason was untrue and there was abundant and uncontroverted independent evidence that no discrimination had occurred. To hold otherwise would be effectively to insulate an entire category of employment discrimination cases from review under Rule 50, and we have reiterated that trial courts should not "treat discrimination differently from other ultimate questions of fact."

Whether judgment as a matter of law is appropriate in any particular case will depend on a number of factors. Those include the strength of the plaintiff's prima facie case, the probative value of the proof that the employer's explanation is false, and any other evidence that supports the employer's case and that properly may be considered on a motion for judgment as a matter of law. For purposes of this case, we need not — and could not — resolve all of the circumstances in which such factors would entitle an employer to *judgment* as a matter of law. It suffices to say that, because a prima facie case and sufficient evidence to reject the employer's explanation may permit a finding of liability, the Court of Appeals erred in proceeding from the premise that a plaintiff must always introduce additional, independent evidence of discrimination.

III

A

The remaining question is whether, despite the Court of Appeals' misconception of petitioner's evidentiary burden, respondent was nonetheless entitled to judgment as a matter of law. Under Rule 50, a court should render judgment as a matter of law when "a party has been fully heard on an issue and there is no legally sufficient evidentiary basis for a reasonable jury to find for that party on that issue."* The Courts of Appeals have articulated differing formulations as to what evidence a court is to consider in ruling on a Rule 50 motion. Some decisions have stated that review is limited to that evidence favorable to the non-moving party, while most have held that review extends to the entire record, drawing all reasonable inferences in favor of the nonmovant.

On closer examination, this conflict seems more semantic than real. Those decisions holding that review under Rule 50 should be limited to evidence favorable to the nonmovant appear to have their genesis in *Wilkerson v. McCarthy*, 336 U.S. 53 (1949). In *Wilkerson*, we stated that "in passing upon whether there is sufficient evidence to submit an issue to the jury we need look only to the evidence and reasonable inferences which tend to support the case of" the nonmoving party. But subsequent decisions have clarified that this passage was referring to the evidence to which the trial court should *give credence*, not the evidence that the court should *review*. In the analogous context of summary judgment under Rule 56, we have stated that the court must review the record "taken as a whole." Matsushita Elec. Indus. Co. v. Zenith Radio Corp., 475 U.S. 574, 587 (1986). And the standard for granting summary judgment "mirrors" the standard for judgment as a matter of law, such that "the inquiry under each is the same." Anderson v. Liberty Lobby, Inc., 477 U.S. 242, 250-51 (1986); *see also* Celotex Corp. v. Catrett, 477 U.S. 317, 323 (1986) [*supra* p. 236]. It therefore follows that, in entertaining a motion for judgment as a matter of law, the court should review all of the evidence in the record.

In doing so, however, the court must draw all reasonable inferences in favor of the nonmoving party, and it may not make credibility determinations or weigh the evidence. "Credibility determinations, the weighing of the evidence, and the drawing of legitimate inferences from the facts are jury functions, not those of a judge." *Liberty Lobby*, 477 U.S. at 255. Thus, although the court should review the record as a whole, it must disregard all evidence favorable to the moving party that the jury is not required to believe. That is, the court should give credence to the evidence favoring the nonmovant as well as that "evidence supporting the moving party that is uncontradicted and unimpeached, at least to the extent that that evidence comes from disinterested witnesses."

---

* In 2007, Rule 50(a) was amended to read: "a party has been fully heard on an issue during a jury trial and the court finds that a reasonable jury would not have a legally sufficient evidentiary basis to find for the party on that issue." — ED.

B

Applying this standard here, it is apparent that respondent was not entitled to judgment as a matter of law. In this case, in addition to establishing a prima facie case of discrimination and creating a jury issue as to the falsity of the employer's explanation, petitioner introduced additional evidence that Chesnut was motivated by age-based animus and was principally responsible for petitioner's firing. Petitioner testified that Chesnut had told him that he "was so old [he] must have come over on the Mayflower" and, on one occasion when petitioner was having difficulty starting a machine, that he "was too damn old to do [his] job." According to petitioner, Chesnut would regularly "cuss at me and shake his finger in my face." Oswalt, roughly 24 years younger than petitioner, corroborated that there was an "obvious difference" in how Chesnut treated them. He stated that, although he and Chesnut "had [their] differences," "it was nothing compared to the way [Chesnut] treated Roger." Oswalt explained that Chesnut "tolerated quite a bit" from him even though he "defied" Chesnut "quite often," but that Chesnut treated petitioner "[i]n a manner, as you would . . . treat . . . a child when . . . you're angry with [him]." Petitioner also demonstrated that, according to company records, he and Oswalt had nearly identical rates of productivity in 1993. Yet respondent conducted an efficiency study of only the regular line, supervised by petitioner, and placed only petitioner on probation. Chesnut conducted that efficiency study and, after having testified to the contrary on direct examination, acknowledged on cross-examination that he had recommended that petitioner be placed on probation following the study.

Further, petitioner introduced evidence that Chesnut was the actual decisionmaker behind his firing. Chesnut was married to Sanderson, who made the formal decision to discharge petitioner. Although Sanderson testified that she fired petitioner because he had "intentionally falsif[ied] company pay records," respondent only introduced evidence concerning the inaccuracy of the records, not their falsification. . . . Oswalt testified that all of respondent's employees feared Chesnut, and that Chesnut had exercised "absolute power" within the company for "[a]s long as [he] can remember."

In holding that the record contained insufficient evidence to sustain the jury's verdict, the Court of Appeals misapplied the standard of review dictated by Rule 50. Again, the court disregarded critical evidence favorable to petitioner — namely, the evidence supporting petitioner's prima facie case and undermining respondent's nondiscriminatory explanation. The court also failed to draw all reasonable inferences in favor of petitioner. For instance, while acknowledging "the potentially damning nature" of Chesnut's age-related comments, the court discounted them on the ground that they "were not made in the direct context of Reeves's termination." And the court discredited petitioner's evidence that Chesnut was the actual decisionmaker by giving weight to the fact that there was "no evidence to suggest that any of the other decision makers were motivated by age." Moreover, the other evidence on which the court relied — that Caldwell and Oswalt were also cited for poor recordkeeping, and that respondent employed many managers over age 50 — although relevant, is certainly not dispositive. In concluding that these circumstances so overwhelmed the evidence favoring petitioner that no rational trier of fact could have found that petitioner was fired because of his age, the Court of Appeals impermissibly substituted its judgment concerning the weight of the evidence for the jury's.

The ultimate question in every employment discrimination case involving a claim of disparate treatment is whether the plaintiff was the victim of intentional discrimination. . . . Given that petitioner established a prima facie case of discrimination, introduced enough evidence for the jury to reject respondent's explanation, and produced additional evidence of age-based animus, there was sufficient evidence for the jury to find that respondent had intentionally discriminated. The District Court was therefore correct to submit the case to the jury, and the Court of Appeals erred in overturning its verdict.

For these reasons, the judgment of the Court of Appeals is reversed.

■ [The concurring opinion of JUSTICE GINSBURG is omitted.]

Notes and Questions

1. In 1991, Rule 50 underwent a significant change in nomenclature. Before 1991, what is now called a *judgment as a matter of law* was called a *directed verdict*. Before 1991, Rule 50 also did not specify the exact standard under which a motion for a directed verdict could be granted. The standard developed through cases was for all practical purposes the same as the standard now articulated in Rule 50(a). *See supra* pp. 241-42, Note 7.

2. Unlike summary judgment, a judgment as a matter of law does not deny a jury trial *per se*, but it does deny the losing party the very point of a jury trial: jury factfinding. Take a look at the second half of the Seventh Amendment, which is often called the Re-Examination Clause. Over Justice Black's strenuous objection that a motion for directed verdict was unknown in 1791 and thus impermissibly authorized courts to re-examine the findings of a jury in a manner not in accord with the "rules of the common law," the Supreme Court held that a directed verdict (and hence, presumably, the Rule 50(a) judgment as a matter of law) did not violate the Seventh Amendment. Galloway v. United States, 319 U.S. 372 (1943).

3. As *Reeves* reminds us, the Rule 50(a) "reasonable jury" standard is intended to mirror the Rule 56(a) "no genuine dispute as to any material fact" standard. Therefore, *Reeves* provides useful principles that guide the interpretation of both Rule 50(a) and Rule 56(a); it also provides a helpful illustration of how those principles work in the context of a case involving conflicting evidence and inferences.

4. A motion for judgment as a matter of law can be made as soon as an opposing party has been "fully heard on an issue." The old rule regarding directed verdicts permitted a party to make the motion only at the end of the opponent's case. The present rule is designed to be more efficient; if the

[Margin note at top: Standard under which a judge can enter judgement as a matter of law during the trial 50(a) a judge can enter judgment against a party if, based on the evidence produced at trial, "no reasonable jury" could find in favor of that party.]

plaintiff needs to prevail on three issues, has been fully heard on the first, and needs four more weeks of trial to present the evidence on the remaining two, little is gained by delaying the decision on whether the plaintiff presented sufficient evidence on the first issue.

5. Judges will sometimes decline to rule on a Rule 50(a) motion made during the trial or at the close of the evidence. Even if the judge thinks that the motion has merit, the judge may hope that the jury will see it the same way. An appellate court is less likely to overturn a jury's verdict than to reverse a judge's decision to take a case away from the jury. Therefore, the judge declines to enter the fray until the jury has spoken.

6. Judgment as a matter of law acts as a judicial check on the work of the jury. If we don't always trust juries to get the result right, why do we use them at all? Are judges any more likely to get it right? If not, then why have any judicial control over juries at all?

Employing different methodologies, a number of studies have shown a high level of agreement between judges and juries on the outcome of cases and a high level of judicial satisfaction with juries. *See* Valerie P. Hans & Stephanie Albertson, *Empirical Research and Civil Jury Reform*, 78 NOTRE DAME L. REV. 1497, 1500-03 (2003) (analyzing studies). The most famous study, conducted in the 1950s, found that judges and juries agreed on the outcome in 78% of jury-tried civil cases, with juries very slightly favoring plaintiffs when there was disagreement. HARRY KALVEN JR. & HANS ZEISEL, THE AMERICAN JURY 63-65 (1966). In a later study of complex civil cases, judge-jury agreement dropped to 63%, with juries very slightly favoring defendants when they disagreed with judges. Larry Heuer & Steven Penrod, *Trial Complexity: A Field Investigation of Its Meaning and Its Effects*, 18 L. & HUM. BEHAV. 29, 46-48 (1994). In only a subset of the cases in which judge and jury disagree — those in which the judge finds the verdict unreasonable — will the judge grant a motion for judgment as a matter of law. Therefore, the return on the Rule 50(a) investment is a changed outcome in only a few cases on the margin. How important a procedural value is "getting it right," as opposed to "getting it acceptable," "getting it quick and cheap," and "getting it democratic"?

4. Jury Instructions, Special Verdicts, and General Verdicts with Answers to Written Questions

Jury instructions provide the jury with the legal principles that it must apply to the case. They also act as a form of jury-control device, because they limit the jury's ability to resolve a case any way it sees fit. Read Rule 51. According to this Rule, the court determines the content of the jury instructions. Typically, each party has the opportunity to draft proposed jury instructions and to object to the other side's proposed instructions. Not surprisingly, good lawyers often spend time crafting instructions that stay within the bounds of the law (an erroneous jury instruction can result in an overturned jury verdict) but still put a favorable spin on the evidence in the case. Many state courts and some federal courts now employ pattern jury instructions that a judge can read to the jury. These ready-made instructions are typically developed and approved by a state supreme court or federal appellate court.

Rule 51 addresses the timing for requesting jury instructions (when?), the manner in which an opposing party must object to an instruction (how?), the time by which the judge must inform the parties of the instructions that the jury will be read (when?), and the consequences of failing to give a correct instruction (what?). The rule does not say what the consequence is for a party who fails to make a timely objection to an instruction (or a failure to give a requested instruction), but the answer can be fairly inferred — the objection is waived. But note the exception provided in Rule 51(d)(2) for instructions involving "plain error." The committee note to the 2003 amendment suggests that four factors — the obviousness of the mistake, the importance of the error, the cost of correcting it, and the impact on nonparties — should be used to flesh out the meaning of "plain error." *See* C.B. v. City of Sonora, 769 F.3d 1005, 1016-19 (9th Cir. 2014) (discussing "plain error" factors).

One constant and consistent theme emerges in study after study of the American jury: juries do not understand more than half of the jury instructions read to them. Even when one of the jurors does correctly understand the instructions, she is as likely to be persuaded by other jurors that she is wrong as she is likely to persuade the others that they are wrong. You might think that an obvious answer to this problem would be to draft "plain English" instructions, but it is hard to convince lawyers and judges to do that. They know that, as long as the judge reads the jury the mumbo-jumbo in the approved pattern jury instruction, the case will not be reversed for instruction error on appeal and sent back for a new trial.

A court can also exercise control over a jury's factfinding function through special verdicts and general verdicts with answers to written questions. Read Rule 49. As Judge Rubin explained in *Guidry v. Kem Manufacturing Co.*, 598 F.2d 402, 405-06 (5th Cir. 1979):

> Most civil jury cases in federal courts have been, and still are, resolved by a general verdict. After receiving the court's instructions, the jury weighs the facts in light of the court's instructions and renders a verdict for the plaintiff or the defendant. Judges and lawyers and all laymen who have thought about the process know that this permits the jurors to import notions of lay justice, to temper legal rules and to render a verdict based on their consciences and their ideas of how the case ought to be decided without strict compliance with the rules laid down by the court. This flexibility is a deliberate part of the jury system, and is sanctioned so long as there is sufficient evidence to support the verdict regardless of the judge's agreement or disagreement with the outcome. . . .
>
> Rule 49 makes available alternate procedures that may be adopted by the trial judge to focus the jury's attention on the factual issues: a general verdict accompanied by answers to interrogatories [now "written questions" — ED.] about particular issues in the case (Rule 49(b)); or,

dispensing altogether with the general verdict, submission of the various fact issues to the jury in the form of questions with the answers forming a special verdict on each (Rule 49(a))....

The special verdict permitted by Rule 49(a) is a splendid device for clarification of jury verdicts and for focusing the jurors' attention on the disputed facts .... However, like all fine tools, it must be skillfully employed and its successful use requires the careful attention of counsel for all parties as well as of the court to be certain that the questions are framed to avoid the possibility of inconsistent answers.

Rule 49(b) contemplates the possibility that a jury will make findings that are inconsistent with its verdict. Does the prospect of inconsistency suggest problems with the jury system, or does the problem lie with confusing jury instructions and written questions? For a discussion of the problem of inconsistent answers in the context of special verdicts (Rule 49(a)) and general verdicts with answers to written questions (Rule 49(b)), and of important procedural differences between the two rules when the jury's answers are inconsistent, see *Whitlock v. Jackson*, 754 F. Supp. 1394 (S.D. Ind. 1991).

5. Renewed Motion for Judgment as a Matter of Law and Motion for a New Trial

After deliberating in private, the jury renders its verdict. Except for special verdicts under Rule 49(a), the verdict states the jury's view on the winner(s) and loser(s) of the case. Usually the court will then enter judgment in accordance with the verdict. *See* Fed. R. Civ. P. 58. But what if the judge does not agree with the jury's verdict? Does the judge retain some authority to review, overturn, or modify the jury's factual findings? Read Rule 50(b), on the renewed motion for judgment as a matter of law, and Rule 59(a)(1)(A), on the motion for a new trial in a jury-tried case.

a. *Renewed Motion for Judgment as a Matter of Law.* Start with Rule 50(b). Just as the 1991 amendments changed the name of the "motion for directed verdict" to "motion for judgment as a matter of law," they changed the name of the post-trial "motion for judgment notwithstanding the verdict" (or "motion j.n.o.v.") to "renewed motion for judgment as a matter of law."

(i) *Timing.* Renewed motions for judgments as a matter of law must be filed within 28 days of the entry of the judgment. The usual view is that this time limit cannot be extended by the trial court, although a party who fails to object to a late Rule 50(b) motion cannot raise untimeliness on appeal. *See* Weissman v. Dawn Joy Fashions, Inc., 214 F.3d 224 (2d Cir. 2000).

(ii) *Grounds.* The grounds for granting a renewed motion for judgment as a matter of law are identical to those for granting a motion for judgment as a matter of law: no legally sufficient evidentiary basis for a reasonable jury to find for the party opposing the motion.

(iii) *Limits on Renewed Motion.* A renewed motion for judgment as a matter of law cannot be granted unless the moving party made a motion for judgment as a matter of law during the trial itself. Moreover, a Rule 50(b) motion can assert only those grounds that were previously asserted in a Rule 50(a) motion. *See* Exxon Shipping Co. v. Baker, 554 U.S. 471, 485 (2008) ("A motion under Rule 50(b) is not allowed unless the movant sought relief on similar grounds under Rule 50(a) before the case was submitted to the jury."); *but see* SEB S.A. v. Montgomery Ward & Co., 594 F.3d 1360, 1371 (Fed. Cir. 2010) (a court may decide an issue raised for the first time in a Rule 50(b) motion "to prevent manifest injustice").

b. *New Trial.* The remedy requested by a Rule 59(a) motion is not a judgment in the verdict loser's favor, but another trial. Although a new trial seems less radical than overturning a jury's verdict, asking a court to commit its resources to try again something that was already tried once is a hard sell in a world of limited trial resources.

(i) *Timing.* Like a Rule 50(b) motion, a Rule 59(a)(1)(A) motion must be filed within 28 days of entry of the judgment. As with a Rule 50(b) motion, district courts lack the power to extend this period. *See Weissman*, 214 F.3d 224. Because both motions have the same time limit, parties typically bring both motions at the same time.

(ii) *Grounds.* Rule 59(a)(1)(A) states that new trials may be granted for "any reason for which a new trial has heretofore been granted in an action at law in federal court." At common law, new trials were ordered on numerous grounds. The classic formulation is that of *Montgomery Ward & Co. v. Duncan*, 311 U.S. 243, 251 (1940):

> The motion for a new trial may invoke the discretion of the court in so far as it is bottomed on the claim that the verdict is against the weight of the evidence, that the damages are excessive, or that, for other reasons, the trial was not fair to the party moving; and may raise questions of law arising out of alleged substantial errors in admission or rejection of evidence or instructions to the jury.

Among the reasons falling within the catchall "fairness" category are newly discovered evidence; impermissible arguments by counsel; and misbehavior by counsel, the judge, or members of the jury. *See generally* 11 CHARLES A. WRIGHT ET AL., FEDERAL PRACTICE AND PROCEDURE §§ 2805-10 (3d ed. 2012). It is often difficult to prove jury misbehavior, in part because Federal Rule of Evidence 606(b)(1) typically does not allow a court "[d]uring an inquiry into the validity of a verdict" to receive testimony or affidavits from jurors about statements made by other jurors during deliberations.

One of the most common grounds on which a new trial is granted — a ground that is essentially a specific application of the "against the weight of the evidence" standard — is an excessively large verdict. A federal judge usually cannot, consistently with the Seventh Amendment, reduce a jury's award of damages. Nevertheless, a judge who is convinced that the award is too high, and thus "shocks the conscience," can order a new trial on damages, but tell the plaintiff that the new trial will not proceed if the plaintiff accepts a stated lesser award. Thus, the plaintiff has the choice between a new trial and an immediate judgment for the lesser amount. This practice is called "remittitur," and has been employed since the early days of our republic. In addition to reducing "shock the conscience" awards (awards that exceed the highest amount that a reasonable jury could have awarded), remittitur is possible when the court can identify an error that caused the inclusion of a quantifiable amount that the jury should not have awarded. *See, e.g.*, Anderson Grp. v. City of Saratoga Springs, 805 F.3d 34, 51 (2d Cir. 2015). Because the judge cannot force the plaintiff to take the immediate payment, remittitur preserves the plaintiff's right to a jury trial, thus passing Seventh Amendment muster. 11 WRIGHT ET AL., *supra*, § 2815.

A judge can also grant a new trial when the jury's award is excessively small. Dimick v. Schiedt, 293 U.S. 474, 487 (1935); Bell v. Johnson, 404 F.3d 997, 1003 (6th Cir. 2005). In one of the odder asymmetries in procedural law, the Supreme Court has held that a judge does not have the converse power of "additur," which conditions a new-trial grant on a defendant's refusal to accept a higher judgment when the jury's award is shockingly low. *Dimick*, 293 U.S. at 485-88 (Seventh Amendment precludes additur). *Dimick* questioned the constitutionality of remittitur, but thought that the practice was of sufficiently long standing that it should not be disturbed. *Cf. In re PHC, Inc. S'holder Litig.*, 894 F.3d 419, 437 (1st Cir. 2018) (holding that additur in connection with an equitable claim is permissible).

A number of state courts, construing the jury-trial rights in their state constitutions, authorize both remittitur and additur. And the Supreme Court has hinted that it might reconsider *Dimick*'s disapproval of additur. *See* Gasperini v. Ctr. for Humanities, Inc., 518 U.S. 415, 433 n.16 (1996).

(iii) *Limits on Motion for New Trial.* Some courts hold that failing to make a Rule 50(a) motion for judgment as a matter of law precludes a party from making a Rule 59 new-trial motion premised on insufficiency of the evidence. Yohannon v. Keene Corp., 924 F.2d 1255, 1262 (3d Cir. 1991). Others do not. Oliveras v. Am. Exp. Isbrandtsen Lines, Inc., 431 F.2d 814, 817 (2d Cir. 1970).

A party's failure to move for a new trial precludes appellate review of an "against the weight of the evidence" argument, but not of an argument premised on other new-trial grounds. 11 WRIGHT ET AL., *supra*, § 2818.

c. *Constitutional Considerations.* If judgment as a matter of law runs up to the constitutional line drawn by the Seventh Amendment, how can the motion for a new trial, which grants relief even when a reasonable jury could have found as it did, be constitutional? The answer is that the motion for a new trial was well established at common law in 1791, when the Seventh Amendment was ratified. Moreover, the motion, if successful, results in a new jury trial; therefore, the right is not lost.

d. *Relationship Between Judgment as a Matter of Law and New Trial.* Rule 50(b) expressly contemplates that Rule 50(b) and 59(a)(1)(A) motions can be filed at the same time. What is the difference between a motion for a new trial because the verdict is "against the weight of the evidence" and a renewed motion for judgment as a matter of law because "no reasonable jury" could have found as the jury did? In a remedial sense, the difference is obvious: in the one case a judgment is entered for the verdict loser, while in the other the verdict loser gets a new trial. But why would anyone who could get judgment in his or her favor ask for a new trial instead? The answer lies in the standards under which the two motions are granted:

> The standards governing a district court's consideration of a Rule 59 motion for a new trial on the grounds that the verdict was against the weight of the evidence [differ] in two significant ways from the standards governing a Rule 50 motion for judgment as a matter of law. Unlike judgment as a matter of law, a new trial may be granted even if there is substantial evidence supporting the jury's verdict. Moreover, a trial judge is free to weigh the evidence himself, and need not view it in the light most favorable to the verdict winner. A court considering a Rule 59 motion for a new trial must bear in mind, however, that the court should only grant such a motion when the jury's verdict is "egregious." Accordingly, a court should rarely disturb a jury's evaluation of a witness's credibility.

DLC Mgmt. Corp. v. Town of Hyde Park, 163 F.3d 124, 133-34 (2d Cir. 1998); *accord*, Jennings v. Jones, 587 F.3d 430, 435-39 (1st Cir. 2009).

UNITHERM FOOD SYSTEMS, INC. v. SWIFT–ECKRICH, INC.

546 U.S. 394 (2006)

■ JUSTICE THOMAS delivered the opinion of the Court.

Ordinarily, a party in a civil jury trial that believes the evidence is legally insufficient to support an adverse jury verdict will seek a judgment as a matter of law by filing a motion pursuant to Federal Rule of Civil Procedure 50(a) before submission of the case to the jury, and then (if the Rule 50(a) motion is not granted and the jury subsequently decides against that party) a motion pursuant to Rule 50(b). In this case, however, the respondent filed a Rule 50(a) motion before the verdict, but did not file a Rule 50(b) motion after the verdict. Nor did respondent request a new trial under Rule 59. The Court of Appeals nevertheless proceeded to review the sufficiency of the evidence and, upon a finding that the evidence was insufficient, remanded the case for a new trial. Because our cases addressing the requirements of Rule 50 compel a contrary result, we reverse.

I

[ConAgra sent a warning to Unitherm that Unitherm was infringing one of ConAgra's patents. Unitherm filed suit, seeking a declaratory judgment that the patent was invalid and further claiming that ConAgra's accusation constituted an antitrust violation. ConAgra counterclaimed for infringement. In an earlier ruling, the district concluded that the patent was invalid, so that only Unitherm's antitrust claim remained for trial.] Prior to the court's submission of the case to the jury, ConAgra moved for a directed verdict under Rule 50(a) based on legal insufficiency of the evidence. The

District Court denied that motion. The jury returned a verdict for Unitherm, and ConAgra neither renewed its motion for judgment as a matter of law pursuant to Rule 50(b), nor moved for a new trial on antitrust liability pursuant to Rule 59.

On appeal . . . , ConAgra maintained that there was insufficient evidence to sustain the jury's [antitrust] verdict. . . . Under Tenth Circuit law, a party that has failed to file a postverdict motion challenging the sufficiency of the evidence may nonetheless raise such a claim on appeal, so long as that party filed a Rule 50(a) motion prior to submission of the case to the jury. Cummings v. Gen. Motors Corp., 365 F.3d 944, 950-51 (10th Cir. 2004). Notably, the only available relief in such a circumstance is a new trial.

Freed to examine the sufficiency of the evidence, the [court of appeals] concluded that, although Unitherm had presented sufficient evidence to support a determination that ConAgra had attempted to enforce a patent that it had obtained through fraud . . . , Unitherm had failed to present evidence sufficient to support the remaining elements of its antitrust claim. Accordingly, it vacated the jury's judgment in favor of Unitherm and remanded for a new trial. We granted certiorari, and now reverse.

II

Federal Rule of Civil Procedure 50 sets forth the procedural requirements for challenging the sufficiency of the evidence in a civil jury trial and establishes two stages for such challenges — prior to submission of the case to the jury, and after the verdict and entry of judgment. Rule 50(a) allows a party to challenge the sufficiency of the evidence prior to submission of the case to the jury, and authorizes the District Court to grant such motions at the court's discretion . . . .

Rule 50(b), by contrast, sets forth the procedural requirements for renewing a sufficiency of the evidence challenge after the jury verdict and entry of judgment. . . .

This Court has addressed the implications of a party's failure to file a postverdict motion under Rule 50(b) on several occasions and in a variety of procedural contexts. This Court has concluded that, "[i]n the absence of such a motion" an "appellate court [is] without power to direct the District Court to enter judgment contrary to the one it had permitted to stand." Cone v. W. Va. Pulp & Paper Co., 330 U.S. 212, 218 (1947). This Court has similarly concluded that a party's failure to file a Rule 50(b) motion deprives the appellate court of the power to order the entry of judgment in favor of that party where the district court directed the jury's verdict, Globe Liquor Co. v. San Roman, 332 U.S. 571 (1948), and where the district court expressly reserved a party's preverdict motion for a directed verdict and then denied that motion after the verdict was returned, Johnson v. New York, N.H. & H. R.R., 344 U.S. 48 (1952). A postverdict motion is necessary because "[d]etermination of whether a new trial should be granted or a judgment entered under Rule 50(b) calls for the judgment in the first instance of the judge who saw and heard the witnesses and has the feel of the case which no appellate printed transcript can impart." *Cone,* 330 U.S. at 216. Moreover, the "requirement of a timely application for judgment after verdict is not an idle motion" because it "is . . . an essential part of the rule, firmly grounded in principles of fairness." *Johnson,* 344 U.S. at 53.

The foregoing authorities lead us to reverse the judgment below. . . . This Court's observations about the necessity of a postverdict motion under Rule 50(b), and the benefits of the district court's input at that stage, apply with equal force whether a party is seeking judgment as a matter of law or simply a new trial. . . .

Despite the straightforward language employed in *Cone, Globe Liquors,* and *Johnson,* respondent maintains that those cases dictate affirmance here, because in each of those cases the litigants secured a new trial. But in each of those cases the appellants moved for a new trial postverdict in the District Court, and did not seek to establish their entitlement to a new trial solely on the basis of a denied Rule 50(a) motion. Accordingly, these outcomes merely underscore our holding today — a party is not entitled to pursue a new trial on appeal unless that party makes an appropriate postverdict motion in the district court.

Our determination that respondent's failure to comply with Rule 50(b) forecloses its challenge to the sufficiency of the evidence is further validated by the purported basis of respondent's appeal, namely the District Court's denial of respondent's preverdict Rule 50(a) motion. . . . But if, as in *Cone, Globe Liquors,* and *Johnson,* a litigant that has failed to file a Rule 50(b) motion is foreclosed from seeking the relief it sought in its Rule 50(a) motion — i.e., the entry of judgment — then surely respondent is foreclosed from seeking a new trial, relief it did not and could not seek in its preverdict motion. In short, respondent never sought a new trial before the District Court, and thus forfeited its right to do so on appeal.

The text of Rule 50(b) confirms that respondent's preverdict Rule 50(a) motion did not present the District Court with the option of ordering a new trial. That text provides that a district court may only order a new trial on the basis of issues raised in a preverdict Rule 50(a) motion when "ruling on a renewed motion" [now "ruling on the renewed motion" — ED.] under Rule 50(b). Accordingly, even if the District Court was inclined to grant a new trial on the basis of arguments raised in respondent's preverdict motion, it was without the power to do so under Rule 50(b) absent a postverdict motion pursuant to that Rule. Consequently, the Court of Appeals was similarly powerless.

Similarly, the text and application of Rule 50(a) support our determination . . . . The Rule provides that "the court *may* determine" that "there is no legally sufficient evidentiary basis for a reasonable jury to find for [a] party on [a given] issue," and "*may* grant a motion for judgment as a matter of law against that party . . . ."* (Emphasis added.) Thus, while a

---

* The 2007 amendments slightly reworded the quoted language, and renumbered portions of it as Rules 50(a)(1)(A) and –(B). — ED.

district court is permitted to enter judgment as a matter of law when it concludes that the evidence is legally insufficient, it is not required to do so. To the contrary, the district courts are, if anything, encouraged to submit the case to the jury, rather than granting such motions. . . . Thus, the District Court's denial of respondent's preverdict motion cannot form the basis of respondent's appeal, because the denial of that motion was not error. It was merely an exercise of the District Court's discretion, in accordance with the text of the Rule and the accepted practice of permitting the jury to make an initial judgment about the sufficiency of the evidence. The only error here was counsel's failure to file a postverdict motion pursuant to Rule 50(b).

* * *

For the foregoing reasons, we hold that since respondent failed to renew its preverdict motion as specified in Rule 50(b), there was no basis for review of respondent's sufficiency of the evidence challenge in the Court of Appeals. The judgment of the Court of Appeals is reversed.

■ JUSTICE STEVENS, with whom JUSTICE KENNEDY joins, dissenting.

Murphy's law applies to trial lawyers as well as pilots. Even an expert will occasionally blunder. . . . This is not a case, in my view, in which the authority of the appellate court is limited by an explicit statute or controlling rule. The spirit of the Federal Rules of Civil Procedure favors preservation of a court's power to avoid manifestly unjust results in exceptional cases.

Notes and Questions

1. *Unitherm* shows that a party must be careful to make the motions that preserve a party's ability to contest a jury's factual findings on appeal; ConAgra lost a case that it might have won because of the failure to preserve the issue. The need to turn square corners with these motions is a common theme in the cases. Courts want to prevent sandbagging; in requiring precision, they also afford more deference to the nonmoving party's right to have factual issues determined by a jury. On the other hand, the procedural rigor in this area grates against the modern desire to decide cases on their merits rather than on legal technicalities. Should it matter whether ConAgra's failure was the result of an honest blunder or a calculated choice?

2. When a party moves for both renewed judgment as a matter of law and a new trial, the overlapping nature of the two motions presents some difficult questions of how the district court, the appellate court, and the party who won the verdict should respond to the motions. Rules 50(c)-(e) sort out some of these issues. Their fundamental direction to the district court facing both a renewed motion for judgment as a matter of law and a motion for new trial is to decide both motions — even if a decision on one of the two disposes of the case. Of the two motions, the renewed motion must be considered first. If the district court grants the motion, then Rule 50(c)

comes into play. Although the decision to grant the renewed motion makes unnecessary any consideration of the new-trial motion, Rule 50(c) asks the district court to provide a conditional ruling on the latter motion. The reason is efficiency. If the court of appeals reverses the district court's entry of judgment as a matter of law, it can consider the new-trial question at the same time; otherwise, the court of appeals would have to remand the case to the district court to rule on a new-trial motion that may be years old. Rule 50(d) then allows the party that lost the renewed motion for judgment as a matter of law to ask for a new trial (which is something that the party had not needed to do until then, because the verdict was in the party's favor). Finally, if the district court denies the renewed motion, the court must decide the new-trial motion, and Rule 50(e) comes into play.

Rules 50(c) and –(e) do something unusual for the Federal Rules of Civil Procedure: they discuss how the court of appeals should handle the review of the district court's decisions on the two motions. A separate body of rules, the Federal Rules of Appellate Procedure, generally governs the work of the courts of appeals. Because appellate review hinges on the district court's decisions on the two motions, however, Rules 50(c) and –(e) state the responsibilities of both sets of courts. Note that Rule 50(e) also describes how the verdict-winning party can protect its interests by seeking a new trial if the court of appeals overturns the judgment in the party's favor.

3. Two reasons for the complexity of Rules 50(c) and –(e) are the varying standards of review and lurking, unanswered Seventh Amendment questions. A district court's grant or denial of a renewed motion for judgment as a matter of law is usually regarded as a question of law from which de novo review lies. Review of a trial court's decision on a motion for new trial is more complex. The district court's grant of a new trial is usually not appealable until after the second trial is held, and it is ultimately reviewed for abuse of discretion. *See* Bryant v. Egan, 890 F.3d 382, 385 (2d Cir. 2018); Manley v. AmBase Corp., 337 F.3d 237, 245 (2d Cir. 2003). When a trial court declined to order a new trial on "weight of the evidence" grounds in 1791, courts of appeals had no authority to review that decision. Therefore, the traditional view was that appellate review of the denial of a new-trial motion based on the weight of the evidence ran afoul of the Seventh Amendment's Re-examination Clause. The Second Circuit continues to adhere to this view, *see* Elyse v. Bridgeside, Inc., 367 F. App'x 266, 268 (2d Cir. 2010) (permitting review only to ensure that the district court applied the correct legal standard), but most circuits today review "weight of the evidence" denials of a new trial under an abuse-of-discretion standard. *See* 11 CHARLES A. WRIGHT ET AL., FEDERAL PRACTICE AND PROCEDURE § 2819 (3d ed. 2012) (critiquing modern view). Appellate review of the denial of a new trial on grounds other than the weight of the evidence usually occurs on an abuse-of-discretion standard.

The Supreme Court has never resolved the questions surrounding the appellate authority to review denials of new-trial motions. The language of Rules 50(c) and –(e) papers over some of the nuances and hard questions. For more guidance in sorting out these issues, see 9B CHARLES A. WRIGHT

& ARTHUR R. MILLER, FEDERAL PRACTICE AND PROCEDURE § 2540 (3d ed. 2008).

4. In *Weisgram v. Marley Co.*, 528 U.S. 440 (2000), the plaintiff's case hinged on an expert witness's testimony; without that testimony, she had no proof of an essential element of her case. The district court admitted the testimony over the defendant's objection. After the jury returned a verdict for the plaintiff, the trial court denied the defendant's Rule 50(b) and Rule 59 motions. The court of appeals held that the testimony should not have been admitted. Hence, it directed entry of judgment as a matter of law for the defendant. The Supreme Court held that the court of appeals, in the exercise of its discretion, had the power to enter judgment if, after "excision of testimony erroneously admitted, there remains insufficient evidence to support the jury's verdict." *Id.* at 457. The 2007 amendments added the final clause of Rule 50(e) to confirm this power.

5. In *Ortiz v. Jordan*, 562 U.S. 180 (2011), prison officials moved for summary judgment on the ground that they were immune from suit. The district court denied the motion. At trial, the officials failed to make a Rule 50(a) motion; and after trial, they did not make either a Rule 50(b) or a Rule 59(a) motion. On appeal, they argued that they could appeal from the denial of the motion for summary judgment. The Court held that a party may not "appeal an order denying summary judgment after a full trial on the merits." *Id.* at 184. The Court made a number of observations about Rules 50 and 59, and their relationship to Rule 56. First, citing *Unitherm*, the Court stated that, "[a]bsent [a Rule 50(b)] motion, we have repeatedly held, an appellate court is 'powerless' to review the sufficiency of the evidence after trial." *Id.* at 189. Next, the Court noted the distinction between a claim that a verdict is "against the weight of the evidence" (a Rule 59 new-trial issue) and a claim that "the evidence submitted at trial was insufficient to warrant submission of the case to the jury" (a Rule 50 judgment-as-a-matter-of-law issue), emphasizing that the two are "not equivalent." *Id.* at 189 n.6. Finally, the Court stated: "[Q]uestions going to the sufficiency of the evidence are not preserved for appellate review by a summary judgment motion alone"; rather, challenges of that order "must be renewed post-trial under Rule 50." *Id.* at 190.

6. You might have the (correct) impression that an awful lot of technical, tricky, and sometimes arcane law has sprung up around the renewed motion for judgment as a matter of law and the motion for a new trial. Some of this law reflects the traditional scope and limits of jury trial, some of it reflects our society's ambivalence about using juries at all, and some of it reflects our society's commitment to juries. With such conflicting impulses, perhaps anything other than technicality is impossible.

SECTION D: FACTFINDING IN TRIALS WITHOUT A JURY

This section examines the trial process when a judge is a factfinder. In federal courts, a judge determines the facts relevant to an equitable claim (at least if there are no overlapping facts also relevant to a legal claim), facts to which the *Markman* analysis applies (*see supra* p. 259), and facts in cases in which the parties waive their right to a jury trial. Our purpose in this section is not to analyze in exhaustive detail all aspects of a bench trial. Instead, we highlight just a few points of similarity and departure from the procedures used in jury trials. These points provide useful comparative information on the advantages and disadvantages of jury and bench trials.

1. Selecting the Factfinder: The Advisory Jury and Special Masters

The identity of the factfinder in a bench trial seems obvious: the judge. Under the Federal Rules, however, the judge can get factfinding assistance in two different ways. First, the judge can empanel an advisory jury whose function, as the name implies, is to advise the judge about how it would rule on the facts. Fed. R. Civ. P. 39(c). The ultimate factfinding responsibility still lies with the judge, who is not required to follow the jury's advice. The decision whether to use an advisory jury lies within the discretion of the trial judge, and, except in unusual cases, cannot be reviewed on appeal. 9 CHARLES A. WRIGHT & ARTHUR R. MILLER, FEDERAL PRACTICE AND PROCEDURE § 2335 (3d ed. 2008).

Advisory juries are rarely employed. A standard argument for their use is the jury's ability to provide the judge with a sense of the community's norms when they are a relevant consideration. The standard argument against their use is that advisory juries waste time and resources. If the judge agrees with the jury and finds the facts as the jury did, the device is unnecessary; and if the judge disagrees with the jury and finds the facts to be other than those found by the jury, the process is still unnecessary.

Second, a judge can refer factfinding to a person specially appointed to the task — a *special master*. The office of the special master had a long but rather checkered history in equity. Rule 53 authorizes the use of special masters to "hold trial proceedings and make or recommend findings of fact" in nonjury cases only when an "exceptional condition" or a difficult question of damages arises. Fed. R. Civ. P. 53(a)(1)(B). The master's findings of fact are usually reviewed by the trial judge de novo. Fed. R. Civ. P. 53(f)(3).

The argument for use of a special master is that someone who possesses expertise in a field can make more informed findings of fact than a judge can. The standard contrary argument is that use of a master constitutes "an abdication of the judicial function." La Buy v. Howes Leather Co., 352 U.S. 249, 256 (1957). Masters are often appointed in complex cases, but usually to perform pretrial or post-trial functions rather than factfinding at trial.

2. Findings of Fact and Conclusions of Law

In a bench trial "the court must find the facts specially and state its conclusions of law separately." Fed. R. Civ. P. 52(a)(1). Findings of fact and conclusions of law can be rendered orally in open court, but are typically written. The judge often gives the parties the opportunity to propose findings of fact and conclusions of law. Sometimes the judge adopts as the court's own the proposed findings and conclusions of the prevailing party. Courts of appeals frown on this practice, but it persists with few consequences to the judge who engages in it. *See* Anderson v. City of Bessemer City, 470 U.S. 564, 571-73 (1985).

The judge's decision may not emerge for a number of weeks or months. This hiatus gives the judge time to sift through the evidence, and to re-open the trial if the judge thinks that more information is needed to decide a particular point. Whether this approach makes the decision more accurate is a fair point for debate; it slows down the process of getting a result, but it also creates more accountability than a jury's general verdict.

3. Motions to Terminate Trial and Post-Trial Motions

A bench trial runs differently from a jury trial. For instance, rules of evidence, which were largely designed to keep prejudicial or untrustworthy information from juries, are often relaxed. Does the difference in factfinder also affect the ability of parties to bring motions akin to a motion for judgment as a matter of law, a renewed motion for judgment as a matter of law, or a motion for new trial? Read Rules 52 and 59(a)(1)(B), and compare them to Rules 50(a)-(b) and 59(a)(1)(A). Note the following differences:

1. The bench trial's equivalent to the Rule 50(a) motion for judgment as a matter of law is the Rule 52(c) motion for judgment on partial findings. Because the judge is the factfinder, Rule 52(c) does not contain a "reasonable jury" overlay. If the evidence on an issue does not persuade the judge, and the nonmoving party needs a "favorable finding" on that issue to win the case, the judge, as factfinder, can enter judgment then and there.

2. The bench trial's equivalent to the Rule 50(b) renewed motion for judgment as a matter of law is the Rule 52(b) motion to amend the judgment. Absent again is the "reasonable jury" overlay. Unlike the Rule 50(b) motion, a Rule 52(b) motion to amend need not be filed in order to preserve the right to contest the sufficiency of the evidence on appeal. *See* Fed. R. Civ. P. 52(a)(5).

3. The bench trial's equivalent for the Rule 59(a)(1)(A) motion for a new trial is Rule 59(a)(1)(B). The grounds for a new trial in equity were essentially the same as those at common law: introduction of inadmissible evidence, improper argument, incorrect statement of the law, and inaccurate factual findings. *See* 11 CHARLES A. WRIGHT ET AL., FEDERAL PRACTICE AND PROCEDURE § 2804 (3d ed. 2012). But a new bench trial is often different from a new trial in a jury-tried case. Because the judge has already heard the evidence, the new trial can often be limited to hearing new evidence on the point or points that the court believes must be amplified or corrected.

4. The standard under which the court of appeals reviews the judge's findings of fact is "clearly erroneous." Fed. R. Civ. P. 52(a)(6). In *United States v. United States Gypsum Co.*, 333 U.S. 364, 395 (1948), the Supreme Court held that "[a] finding is 'clearly erroneous' when although there is

evidence to support it, the reviewing court on the entire evidence is left with the definite and firm conviction that a mistake has been committed." In *Anderson v. City of Bessemer City*, 470 U.S. 564, 573-74 (1985), the Court expanded on this analysis:

> This standard plainly does not entitle a reviewing court to reverse the finding of the trier of fact simply because it is convinced that it would have decided the case differently. The reviewing court oversteps the bounds of its duty under Rule 52(a) if it undertakes to duplicate the role of the lower court. . . . If the district court's account of the evidence is plausible in light of the record viewed in its entirety, the court of appeals may not reverse it even though convinced that had it been sitting as the trier of fact, it would have weighed the evidence differently. Where there are two permissible views of the evidence, the factfinder's choice between them cannot be clearly erroneous.

Formally, the "clear error" standard for the review of judicial factfinding is less deferential than the "no reasonable jury" standard for the review of jury factfinding. In reality, however, some federal appellate courts draw the "clear error" and "no reasonable jury" lines in roughly the same place. *Compare* Concrete Pipe & Prods. of Cal., Inc. v. Constr. Laborers Pension Trust for S. Cal., 508 U.S. 602, 623 (1993) (stating that "review under the 'clearly erroneous' standard is significantly deferential . . . [a]nd application of a [reasonable jury] standard is even more deferential than that"), *with* Reynolds v. City of Chicago, 296 F.3d 524, 527 (7th Cir. 2002) (suggesting that the difference in the two standards of review is "a general issue of judicial epistemology" without much practical significance).

SECTION E: RELIEF FROM A JUDGMENT OR ORDER

Much energy, time, and money go into obtaining a final judgment. What happens when, after a judgment becomes final, a party believes that the judgment was entered in error? Should the district court ever be allowed to reopen and review the judgment? Suppose the judgment mistakenly adds an extra zero and provides that the plaintiff is entitled to $10,000,000 in damages, when the evidence shows that the amount was $1,000,000. Or suppose that the losing party has conclusive proof, not available at the time of trial, that the judgment was wrong. What if the conclusive proof existed at the time of trial, but the losing party neglected to uncover it? What if the losing party discovers that the winning party used fraudulent evidence or hid relevant documents?

Read Rule 60. Rule 60 seeks to strike a balance between important procedural values — in particular, ensuring finality of the judgment and obtaining accurate outcomes on the merits. Rule 60(a) provides a means to correct technical errors in the judgment, a process that seems fair enough. The harder problems are dealt with in Rule 60(b). The basic division in Rule 60(b) is between the three grounds on which a party must seek relief from the judgment within one year of the entry of the judgment and the three grounds on which a party can seek relief even beyond that year. This balance creates its own issues. Consider the following case.

ACKERMANN V. UNITED STATES

340 U.S. 193 (1950)

■ MR. JUSTICE MINTON delivered the opinion of the Court.

Petitioner Hans Ackermann filed a motion in the District Court for the Western District of Texas to set aside a judgment entered December 7, 1943, in that court cancelling his certificate of naturalization. The motion was filed March 25, 1948, pursuant to amended Rule 60(b) of the Federal Rules of Civil Procedure, which became effective March 19, 1948. The United States filed a motion to dismiss petitioner's motion. The District Court denied petitioner's motion and the Court of Appeals affirmed. We granted certiorari.

The question is whether the District Court erred in denying the motion for relief under Rule 60(b).

Petitioner and his wife Frieda were natives of Germany. They were naturalized in 1938. They resided, as now, at Taylor, Texas, where petitioner and Max Keilbar owned and operated a German language newspaper. Frieda Ackermann wrote for the paper. She was a sister of Keilbar, who was also a native of Germany and who had been naturalized in 1933.

In 1942 complaints were filed against all three to cancel their naturalization on grounds of fraud. Petitioner and Keilbar were represented by counsel and answered the complaints. After an order of consolidation, trial of the three cases began November 1, 1943, and separate judgments were entered December 7, 1943, cancelling and setting aside the orders admitting them to citizenship. Keilbar appealed to the Court of Appeals, and by stipulation with the United States Attorney his case in that court was reversed, and the complaint against him was ordered dismissed. The Ackermanns did not appeal.

Petitioner in his motion here under consideration alleges that his "failure to appeal from said judgment is excusable" for the reason that he had no money or property other than his home in Taylor, Texas, owned by him and his wife and worth $2,500, "and the costs of transcribing the evidence and printing the record and brief on appeal were estimated at not less than $5,000.00." On December 11, 1943, petitioner was detained in an Alien Detention Station at Seagoville, Texas. Before time for appeal had expired, petitioner was advised by his attorney that he and his wife could not appeal on affidavits of inability to pay costs until they had "appropriated said home to the payment of such costs to the full extent of the proceeds of a sale thereof"; that this information distressed them, and they sought advice from W. F. Kelley, "Assistant Commissioner for Alien Control,

Immigration and Naturalization Department," in whose custody petitioner and his wife were being held, "and he being a person in whom they had great confidence"; that Kelley on being informed of their financial condition and the advice of their attorney that it would be necessary for them to dispose of their home in order to appeal, advised them in substance to "hang on to their home," and told them further that they had lost their American citizenship and were stateless, and that they would be released at the end of the war; that relying upon Kelley's advice, they refrained from appealing from said judgments; that on April 29, 1944, after time for appeal had expired, they were interned, and on January 25, 1946, the Attorney General ordered them to depart within thirty days or be deported. They did not depart, and they have not been deported, although the orders of deportation are still outstanding. Petitioner further alleged that he would show that the judgment of December 7, 1943, was unlawful and erroneous by producing the record in the *Keilbar* case.

The District Court on September 28, 1948, denied petitioner's motion to vacate the judgment of denaturalization, the court stating in the order that "there is no merit to said motion."

It will be noted that petitioner alleged in his motion that his failure to appeal was *excusable*. A motion for relief because of excusable neglect as provided in Rule 60(b)(1) must, by the rule's terms, be made not more than one year after the judgment was entered. The judgment here sought to be relieved from was more than four years old. It is immediately apparent that no relief on account of "excusable neglect" was available to this petitioner on the motion under consideration.

But petitioner seeks to bring himself within Rule 60(b)(6), which applies if "any other reason justifying relief" [now "any other reason that justifies relief" — ED.] is present, as construed and applied in *Klapprott v. United States*, 335 U.S. 601 (1949). . . .

We cannot agree that petitioner has alleged circumstances showing that his failure to appeal was justifiable. It is not enough for petitioner to allege that he had confidence in Kelley. On the allegations of the motion before us, Kelley was a stranger to petitioner. In that state of the pleadings there are two reasons why petitioner cannot be heard to say his neglect to appeal brings him within the rule. First, anything said by Kelley could not be used to relieve petitioner of his duty to take legal steps to protect his interest in litigation in which the United States was a party adverse to him. Secondly, petitioner had no right to repose confidence in Kelley, a stranger. There is no allegation of any fact or circumstance which shows that Kelley had any undue influence over petitioner or practiced any fraud, deceit, misrepresentation, or duress upon him. There are no allegations of privity or any fiduciary relations existing between them. Indeed, the allegations of the motion all show the contrary. However, petitioner had a confidential adviser in his own counsel. Instead of relying upon that confidential adviser, he freely accepted the advice of a stranger, a source upon which he had no right to rely. Petitioner made a considered choice not to appeal, apparently because he did not feel that an appeal would prove to be worth what he thought was a required sacrifice of his home. His choice was a risk, but calculated and deliberate and such as follows a free choice. Petitioner cannot be relieved of such a choice because hindsight seems to indicate to him that his decision not to appeal was probably wrong, considering the outcome of the *Keilbar* case. There must be an end to litigation someday, and free, calculated, deliberate choices are not to be relieved from.

As further evidence of the inadequacy of petitioner's motion to bring himself within any division of Rule 60(b) which would excuse him from not having taken an appeal, we call attention to the fact that Keilbar got the record before the Court of Appeals, and it contained all the evidence that was introduced as to petitioner and his wife, who were tried together with Keilbar. The Ackermanns and Keilbar were related, yet no effort was made to get into the Court of Appeals and use the same record as to the evidence that Keilbar used. It certainly would not have taken five thousand dollars or one-tenth thereof for petitioner and his wife to have supplemented the *Keilbar* record with that pertaining to themselves and to prepare a brief, even if all of it were printed. We are further aware of the practice of the Courts of Appeals permitting litigants who are poor but not paupers to file typewritten records and briefs at a very small cost to them. With the same counsel representing petitioner as represented his kinsman Keilbar, and with Frieda Ackermann having funds sufficient to employ separate counsel, failure to appeal because of the fear of losing his home in defraying the expenses of the brief and record, makes it further evident that Rule 60(b) has no application to petitioner in this setting.

The *Klapprott* case was a case of extraordinary circumstances. Mr. Justice Black stated in the following words why the allegations in the *Klapprott* case, there taken as true, brought it within Rule 60(b)(6): "But petitioner's allegations set up an extraordinary situation which cannot fairly or logically be classified as mere 'neglect' on his part. The undenied facts set out in the petition reveal far more than a failure to defend the denaturalization charges due to inadvertence, indifference, or careless disregard of consequences. For before, at the time, and after the default judgment was entered, petitioner was held in jail in New York, Michigan, and the District of Columbia by the United States, his adversary in the denaturalization proceedings. Without funds to hire a lawyer, petitioner was defended by appointed counsel in the criminal cases. Thus petitioner's prayer to set aside the default judgment did not rest on mere allegations of 'excusable neglect.' The foregoing allegations and others in the petition tend to support petitioner's argument that he was deprived of any reasonable opportunity to make a defense to the criminal charges instigated by officers of the very United States agency which supplied the secondhand information upon which his citizenship was taken away from him in his absence. The basis of his petition was not that he had neglected to act in his own defense, but that in jail as he was, weakened from illness, without a lawyer in the denaturalization proceedings or funds to hire one, disturbed and fully occupied in efforts to protect himself against the gravest criminal charges, he was no more able to defend himself in the New Jersey court than he would have been had he never received notice of the charges." . . .

From a comparison of the situations shown by the allegations of Klapprott and Ackermann, it is readily apparent that the situations of the parties bore only the slightest resemblance to each other. The comparison strikingly points up the difference between no choice and choice; imprisonment and freedom of action; no trial and trial; no counsel and counsel; no chance for negligence and inexcusable negligence. Subsection 6 of Rule 60(b) has no application to the situation of petitioner. Neither the circumstances of petitioner nor his excuse for not appealing is so extraordinary as to bring him within *Klapprott* or Rule 60(b)(6).

The motion for relief was properly denied, and the judgment is affirmed.

No. 36, *Frieda Ackermann v. United States*, is a companion case to No. 35, and it was stipulated that the decision in No. 36 should be the same as in No. 35. The judgment in No. 36 therefore is also affirmed.

■ MR. JUSTICE CLARK took no part in the consideration or decision of this case.

■ MR. JUSTICE BLACK, with whom MR. JUSTICE FRANKFURTER and MR. JUSTICE DOUGLAS concur, dissenting.

The Court's interpretation of amended Rule 60(b) of the Federal Rules of Civil Procedure neutralizes the humane spirit of the Rule and thereby frustrates its purpose. The Rule empowers courts to set aside judgments under five traditional, specified types of circumstances in which it would be inequitable to permit a judgment to stand. But the draftsmen of the Rule did not intend that these specified grounds should prevent the granting of similar relief in other situations where fairness might require it. Accordingly, there was added a broad sixth ground . . . .

. . . It does no good to have liberalizing rules like 60(b) if, after they are written, their arteries are hardened by this Court's resort to ancient common-law concepts. I would reverse.

Notes and Questions

1. Isn't *Ackermann* a Rule 60(b)(1) "excusable neglect" case that is filed past the one-year limit? Is Rule 60(b)(6) a crowbar that pries open the window of Rule 60(b)(1) for longer than one year, or is it better to read Rule 60(b) literally and deny the untimely motion?

2. In answering these last questions, would you want to know the reason for the denaturalization proceedings against the Ackermanns? The Court never mentions the reason. What if the Ackermanns were members of the Communist Party? What if they were Jews who filled out false paperwork in order to escape the Nazis?

If you are interested, you can read a synopsis of the government's case against the Ackermanns in *United States v. Ackermann*, 53 F. Supp. 611 (W.D. Tex. 1943). In fact, they were outspoken supporters of Hitler and his Nazi regime. Should the Ackermanns' particular story affect the interpretation of Rule 60(b)?

3. Assuming that they had applied for relief from the judgment within a year, would Rule 60(b)(1) have given the Ackermanns the relief they sought? In interpreting the "excusable neglect" component of Rule 60(b)(1), courts consider a range of factors, including " the danger of prejudice . . . , the length of the delay and its potential impact on judicial proceedings, the reason for the delay, including whether it was within the reasonable control of the movant, and whether the movant acted in good faith." Pioneer Inv. Servs. Co. v. Brunswick Assocs. Ltd., 507 U.S. 380, 395 (1993).

4. The "newly discovered evidence" component of Rule 60(b)(2) presents a clear tension between finality and accuracy. Courts have tended to read Rule 60(b)(2) in a way that emphasizes finality. *See e.g.*, Holmes v. United States, 898 F.3d 785, 791 (8th Cir. 2018) (permitting relief when ""(1) the evidence was discovered after trial; (2) due diligence was exercised to discover the evidence; (3) the evidence is material and not merely cumulative or impeaching; and (4) the evidence is such that a new trial would probably produce a different result") (quotation marks omitted).

5. Rule 60(b)(5) is directed primarily at cases involving injunctive relief. Injunctions often enjoin the defendant in perpetuity. Sometimes, however, circumstances so change that the defendant no longer believes that it is fair for it to be subject to the injunction's restrictions. Rule 60(b)(5) provides the vehicle through which the defendant can seek relief.

In *United States v. Swift & Co.*, 286 U.S. 106, 119 (1932), the Supreme Court stated that the showing for obtaining such relief was a "clear showing of grievous wrong." In *Rufo v. Inmates of Suffolk County Jail*, 502 U.S. 367, 393 (1992), the Court relaxed the *Swift* standard for injunctions involving the reform of governmental and large private entities: "Under the flexible standard we adopt today, a party seeking modification of a consent decree must establish that a significant change in facts or law warrants revision of the decree and that the proposed modification is suitably tailored to the changed circumstance."

The Court revisited Rule 60(b)(5) in *Horne v. Flores*, 557 U.S. 433 (2009). In *Horne* governmental defendants sought relief from an order that required them to provide additional funding to comply with a federal law; they claimed relief was proper because the state was now complying with the statute. The district court denied the motion and the court of appeals affirmed. The Supreme Court reversed and remanded. The Court stressed that "Rule 60(b)(5) serves a particularly important function" in what it called "institutional reform litigation." *Id.* at 447. Injunctions that reform or restructure state and local institutions, the Court noted, often remain in force for many years, but circumstances change as new officials are elected and new laws are enacted. Moreover, "[f]ederalism concerns are heightened when, as in these cases, a federal court decree has the effect of dictating state or local budget priorities." *Id.* at 448. Finally, the Court pointed to the unusual dynamics of institutional-reform cases, in which some public officials (including some defendants) may support the federal court's intervention as a way to accomplish objectives that they are unable to accomplish through state or local legislative action.

6. Courts have not done much better than *Ackermann* in articulating the circumstances that justify Rule 60(b)(6) relief. For one effort to catalogue some of the "extraordinary circumstances" that merit relief, see *Salazar ex rel. Salazar v. District of Columbia*, 633 F.3d 1110, 1120-21 (D.C. Cir. 2011). *Salazar* emphasized that Rule 60(b)(6) "should be only sparingly used and may not be employed simply to rescue a litigant from strategic choices that later turn out to be improvident." It noted that "a more compelling showing of inequity or hardship is necessary to warrant relief under subsection (6) than under subsection (5); otherwise, the ready availability of subsection (6) would make meaningless the limitation of subsection (5)." On the other hand, *Salazar* suggested that relief might be possible if "an attorney was grossly negligent."

Would you grant Rule 60 (b)(6) relief in these situations?

- In a wrongful-death case, the plaintiffs relied on the advice of their lawyer and decided to file their case in federal court. The advice turned out to be poor, and the federal court dismissed the case for lack of jurisdiction. By the time that the case was refiled in state court, the statute of limitations had run. But the state court would have been able to extend the statute and hear the case if the federal judgment were reopened. Should Rule 60(b)(6) relief be granted? *See* McCurry *ex rel.* Turner v. Adventist Health Sys./Sunbelt, Inc., 298 F.3d 586 (6th Cir. 2002) (no).

- The defendant's lawyer essentially abandoned the defense of a case, causing the entry of a default judgment. The lawyer did not tell the defendant about the default, and even said that the litigation was proceeding smoothly. The defendant did not learn of the default until the plaintiff sought to enforce the judgment, and immediately sought relief from the judgment. Do you oblige? *See* Cmty. Dental Servs. v. Tani, 282 F.3d 1164 (9th Cir. 2002) (yes); KPS & Assocs., Inc. v. Designs by FMC, Inc., 318 F.3d 1 (1st Cir. 2003) (no).

- Plaintiffs filed a federal lawsuit claiming that, under Texas law, their home-equity lien was void. The district court dismissed the case under Rule 12(b)(6), holding that Texas's four-year statute of limitations barred the claim. After deciding that this statute of limitations applied, the court of appeals affirmed the dismissal. Three years later, the Texas Supreme Court held that the statute of limitations did not apply to claims like those that the plaintiffs asserted. More than a year later, the plaintiffs sought to vacate the federal judgment. Would you grant the plaintiffs relief under Rule 60(b)(6)? *See* Priester v. JP Morgan Chase Bank, N.A., 927 F.3d 912, 913 (5th Cir. 2019) (mem.) ("[T]he interest in getting the law 'right' must sometimes give way to an even stronger interest in finality.").

7. An appellate court reviews a district court's Rule 60(b) decision on an abuse-of-discretion standard, but questions of law are reviewed de novo. Washington v. Ryan, 833 F.3d 1087, 1091 (9th Cir. 2016). If the district court had granted the Ackermanns' request for relief from the judgment, would that order have been reversible on appeal?

CHAPTER SIX

APPEALS

SECTION A: THE STRUCTURE AND FUNCTIONS OF APPELLATE COURTS

1. Structure of Appellate-Court Systems

For present purposes, we can say that American state- and federal-court systems generally have three basic tiers — trial courts, intermediate appellate courts, and courts of last resort. Some of the less populous states have just trial courts and a state supreme court; and there can be levels within levels, such as trial courts of limited jurisdiction with no juries and "appeal" available to losers in such courts by demand for jury trial de novo in a trial court of general jurisdiction. But such variations in structure need not detain us here.

Terminology is not consistent. States need not and often do not follow the federal practice of calling trial courts *district courts*, intermediate appellate courts *courts of appeals* for the various circuits (the widely used term *circuit courts* is technically incorrect; over a century ago, Congress abolished federal courts with some trial jurisdiction that had been formally called circuit courts), and the court of last resort the Supreme Court. Some states have district courts at the trial level, while others use terms such as *circuit court* or *superior court*. In New York, the main trial court is the Supreme Court, whose judges are called justices. Intermediate appellate courts also come with different labels, often *courts of appeals* but sometimes *district courts of appeal* and, in New York, the Appellate Division of the Supreme Court. Most commonly courts of last resort are called *supreme courts*, but variations exist — Supreme Judicial Court, Court of Criminal Appeals (Oklahoma and Texas have separate final courts for criminal and civil matters), and in New York and Maryland the Court of Appeals, whose justices are called judges.

Appellate courts almost always function as multi-member bodies, whereas trial judges mostly sit solo. (Single-judge action in an appellate court is most commonly of a provisional nature on an emergency application, involving the likes of deciding whether to stay a lower court's action temporarily until the regularly composed appeals court can act.) Intermediate appellate courts often have a good many members but usually sit in panels of three or five judges, sometimes with provision for sittings *en banc* with all members or a larger panel to settle an important legal issue for that court or to review a panel decision that some members regard as especially questionable. En banc consideration — even if granted sparingly because of its heavy use of judge-power — can be important because many intermediate courts have a rule or practice, to avoid inconsistency, that law made by a single panel binds the entire court, except in cases of en banc reconsideration or change in governing law from a higher court or the legislature. *See, e.g.*, United States v. Vega-Castillo, 540 F.3d 1235, 1236 (11th Cir. 2008) (per curiam) ("Under the prior precedent rule, we are bound to follow a prior binding precedent 'unless and until it is overruled by this court en banc or by the Supreme Court.'") (citation omitted). Sometimes an intermediate appellate court has statewide jurisdiction, but in other systems the court has jurisdiction over just a geographical part of the state — with the parallel being true for the federal courts of appeals for the various circuits, most of which review judgments from federal district courts in a few or several states. Geographically based courts within a single system may disagree with each other, a situation that can call for review by the court of last resort to bring about uniformity.

Supreme courts in the United States generally have five, seven, or nine members, who usually do not sit in separate panels. Unlike the intermediate appellate courts, supreme courts' jurisdiction is often at least in considerable part discretionary, so that the justices can limit their docket to cases that particularly warrant a second appellate review. The United States Supreme Court's Rule 10, for example, identifies such considerations for granting review via the writ of "certiorari" as conflicting lower-court decisions on federal law, importance of the issue, and major departure "from the accepted and usual course of judicial proceedings." Denial of discretionary review is not regarded as endorsement of the lower court's position; its decision stands, but without the supreme court expressing any view on the merits. Even supreme courts with much discretionary jurisdiction will often have some that is mandatory; review of death-penalty cases, for example, is frequently of right and may come directly to a state supreme court from the trial court, without intermediate appellate review. And the United States Supreme Court must hear direct appeals from three-judge district courts, which usually have two district judges and one circuit judge and are used mainly for constitutional challenges to apportionment of congressional districts or state legislatures. *See* 28 U.S.C. §§ 1253 (providing for direct appeals of right from three-judge district courts), 2284(a) (requiring three-judge district courts for apportionment challenges). Some supreme courts also have power to reach down and take cases from intermediate appeals courts before judgment or even from trial courts, although such powers tend to be rarely used.

The federal and state appellate systems in the United States operate fairly independently of each other, except that the U.S. Supreme Court can review decisions on dispositive federal-law rulings from the highest state court in which a decision could be had. Also, of course, state courts (like federal ones) are bound by U.S. Supreme Court decisions on federal-law matters. Congress has not given any other federal court appellate jurisdiction over any state court,* and state courts are free to disagree with federal ones about not just state-law matters but also about federal-law issues before them until the U.S. Supreme Court speaks. But just as that court is the final word on constitutionality and interpretation of federal law, a state supreme court's decision on a state-law matter is authoritative and binds the federal courts as well as state tribunals. Nearly all states provide for some or all federal courts to certify questions of the state's law to the state supreme court; a federal court's doing so does not transfer the entire case but seeks definitive resolution of the state-law matter so that a federal court need not risk making a wrong guess on an unsettled or unclear point.

2. Correcting Error, Settling Conflicts, and Articulating the Law

Appellate courts exist to serve multiple purposes. The one that many people would probably think of first is correcting trial-court errors, and that is indeed an important function — particularly at the intermediate appellate level. But appellate courts usually have jurisdiction over several lower courts, whose judges may disagree with each other; for uniformity and clarity in the law, another important function of appellate courts is settling such conflicts. And while all courts in deciding cases say what the law is — sometimes not just applying law, but making it by choosing among different possible views on an unsettled point or by adopting a new rule to replace an old one now regarded as wrong — the function of speaking authoritatively as to the content of the law is an especially significant function of appellate courts, particularly those of last resort. This listing by no means exhausts what one might identify as functions of appellate courts, but it should suffice for what is meant as a concise survey.

To say a bit more about each of these functions: trial courts can of course make mistakes, and it is important to have means for trying to correct significant errors. At least in the federal-court system, many may be

---

* A limited but significant semi-exception is federal habeas corpus for state prisoners. After exhausting state-court remedies (and perhaps even unsuccessfully seeking U.S. Supreme Court review of the state-court judgment), a person in state custody alleging federal-law errors in conviction or sentence may bring a collateral attack on the state court's judgment in federal trial court. Such a challenge takes the form of a new civil action against the prison warden or state corrections superintendent, seeking release, retrial, or resentencing via issuance of the writ of habeas corpus. Federal-court review of state-court criminal judgments via habeas corpus is mostly quite deferential, but the state-court system's findings are not completely preclusive — as they can be on many matters not affecting freedom from confinement. *See infra* Chapter Seven.

surprised to hear, there is no constitutional right to appeal. Indeed, in early American practice there sometimes was no appeal as of right from a judgment. Now, however, with wide acceptance of the general proposition that there should usually be one appeal of right from an adverse trial-court judgment, statutes in the state and federal systems do generally provide for mandatory appellate jurisdiction at the first level above the trial court. (To keep appeals of right from being abused or overused, some systems authorize sanctions for frivolous or unsuccessful appeals.) Some exceptions exist to the principle of one review of right: Congress has, for example, disfavored what it regarded as particularly low-yield appeals in many habeas-corpus cases by requiring a certificate of appealability, based on trial or appellate judges' assessment that a rejected claim of constitutional error may nonetheless have enough possible merit to warrant allowing an appeal.

Ability to take an appeal does not mean that the appeals court will review de novo all significant aspects of the trial court's action. As discussion in the following section brings out, appellate review is often deferential, especially as to case-management orders and fact findings as opposed to rulings of law. And one does not try one's case again in the court of appeals; unlike in some civil-law systems, American appellate courts rarely allow introduction of new matter but instead consider arguments based on the record made in the trial court. The combination of (one hopes) trial-court competence, sometimes deferential appellate scrutiny, and review on the trial-court record means that much of the key action is in the trial court, and reversal rates are generally not high; in the twelve months ending June 30, 2019, for example, the federal courts of appeals reversed in 7.9% of their cases overall, with considerable rate variations between types of proceedings. *Statistical Tables for the Federal Judiciary* (June 30, 2019) tbl.B–5, https://www.uscourts.gov/statistics/table/b-5/statistical-tables-federal-judiciary/2019/06/30. Ability to appeal also does not mean that the court will hear oral argument; caseload pressures, and the weakness of many appeals, have led appellate courts to screen cases for oral argument and decide some based on just reading the briefs and reviewing the record.

As for settling conflicts, the judicial system strives for uniformity in the law's content when a single law is supposed to govern (State A may, of course, decide that its own law is different from that of State B), so that parties' rights do not turn on the court in which they litigate. Splits can arise between districts within a circuit and, more seriously, between circuits or between state and federal appellate courts about federal-law matters. The conflict-settling function is especially important at the supreme-court level and, as we have seen, is a consideration for the U.S. Supreme Court in deciding whether to grant review. For several reasons, though, conflicts may remain unresolved: conflicts are many, the Supreme Court has finite capacity to take cases, and not all conflicts may seem serious enough to need immediate settlement. If the conflict is on a point of procedure, for example, parties in different circuits may be able to play by the circuits' differing rules so that the division is less likely to change case outcomes than if the split is over substance. Further, even when a conflict is on an important substantive point, a supreme court may think that it would improve the quality of an eventual resolution to let the matter "percolate" and be considered by more lower courts before the highest court takes one of the cases to settle the conflict.

Finally, as to law-articulation: fairly often, even if reversing for error below, in deciding a case an appellate court will just be applying what appears to be settled law. But a significant portion of the time, the issue of law that the court must decide may be one about which lower courts have disagreed, or one on which the law has been somehow unclear, or a matter of first impression. In such instances the court must say what it believes the law is, and when the law is unsettled doing so can require the court to decide based on what it thinks the law should be — drawing on sources such as textual construction, relevant history, analogous precedent, and in some instances the judges' or justices' own views on what makes sound policy. This function can take place at the trial level but is more significant for appellate courts. The often discretionary jurisdiction of courts of last resort reflects this different balance in the relative importance of functions, with review of right in intermediate courts emphasizing the function of error correction (not, of course, to the exclusion of other functions). Discretionary jurisdiction in a court of last resort lets it correct individual-case errors if it has time and inclination, but allows it to concentrate on legal issues of greatest importance to the system.

SECTION B: BASIC CONCEPTS

In American practice, the building blocks of a system governing appeals are the three concepts of *appealability*, *reviewability*, and *standard of review*.

1. Appealability

The Final-Judgment Rule and Its Rationales. Appealability refers to *when* a party aggrieved by a trial-court ruling may take the matter to an appellate court. In the federal courts and in most state-court systems, the *final-judgment rule* governs, with some exceptions allowing interlocutory appeal (before final judgment in the trial court). Without a final judgment or an authorized basis for interlocutory appeal, an appellate court lacks jurisdiction and must dismiss the appeal without reaching the merits.

Finality in this context means that nothing remains to be done at the trial level except, if necessary, enforcing the judgment or — at least in federal court — ruling on a pending request for costs and attorneys' fees. When the final-judgment rule applies, then and only then may a losing party appeal. And the party *must* appeal in time, or risk having its appeal dismissed. In *Ray Haluch Gravel Co. v. Central Pension Fund of International Union of Operating Engineers & Participating Employers*, 571 U.S. 177 (2014), the Supreme Court unanimously held that an appeal filed within thirty days of a district-court ruling on an award of attorneys' fees, but more than thirty days after its order deciding the merits of the underlying claim, was untimely for the merits appeal. Section 1291 of the Judicial Code (28 U.S.C.) codifies the final-judgment rule for cases in the federal courts. Thus, a party who is dissatisfied with a pretrial or trial ruling, such as a discovery order or a ruling on the admissibility of evidence at trial, usually may not take an interlocutory appeal before final judgment, but must wait until a dipositive pretrial ruling or the end of trial and post-trial proceedings in the trial court before taking an appeal.

For the most part, United States jurisdictions regard the costs of repeated, "piecemeal" appeals in the same case as likely to exceed the value of possible correction of trial-court errors while the case is still proceeding at the trial level. Especially if trial judges are likely to be right considerably more often than they are wrong, or upheld even if arguably wrong because of a deferential standard of review, pre-finality appeals if allowed would frequently involve delay and expense but no change. Further, interlocutory appeals if readily allowed might often be about matters that ultimately made no difference and would not have been appealed had the case gone to final judgment (such as a discovery ruling against the eventual winner).

Exceptions and Qualifications. Sometimes it is particularly easy to see the importance of not allowing interlocutory appeals. For example, appeals of evidence-admissibility rulings in the middle of a jury trial would be extraordinarily disruptive. But in other situations, interlocutory review might prevent considerable harm either in the real world, for instance if a trial court has entered a quite mistaken preliminary injunction, or in the litigation, as when the judge has made a questionable ruling that could require much further wasteful proceeding if it is erroneous and not corrected before final judgment and later appeal. For such reasons, all American jurisdictions allow some degree of interlocutory review in various situations; some, such as California and New York, do so relatively liberally. California state appellate courts are somewhat, perhaps considerably, more willing than federal courts to grant "extraordinary writs" such as prohibition and mandamus ordering changes in course by trial judges as to some matters in pending cases. New York may go the farthest toward allowing interlocutory appeals, authorizing them for situations including an interlocutory trial-court ruling made after notice and motion that "involves some part of the merits" or "affects a substantial right." N.Y. C.P.L.R. 5701(a)2.(iv)-(v).

Principal explicit *exceptions* to the federal final-judgment requirement of § 1291 are:

- 28 U.S.C. § 1292(a)(1), authorizing interlocutory appeal from "orders of the district courts ... granting, continuing, modifying, refusing or dissolving injunctions."
- 28 U.S.C. § 1292(b), for when "a district judge, in making in a civil action an order not otherwise appealable under this section, shall be of opinion that such order involves a controlling question of law as to which there is substantial ground for difference of opinion and that an immediate appeal from the order may materially advance

the ultimate termination of the litigation, he shall so state in writing in such order"; the relevant Court of Appeals then *may* — not must — "in its discretion, permit an appeal to be taken from such order" upon prompt application.

- Federal Rule of Civil Procedure 23(f), authorizing courts of appeals in their discretion to "permit an appeal from an order granting or denying class-action certification" upon application within fourteen days after entry of the order (for the federal government and its agencies, officers, and employees, the period is forty-five days) — but *without* the trial-judge certification that is required for an interlocutory appeal under § 1292(b).

As may be apparent, these exceptions are framed to allow interlocutory appeals in — but also limit them to — the kinds of situations mentioned above when they may be most justifiable and necessary. Section 1292(a)(1) focuses on the possible real-world harm of erroneous grant or denial of an interlocutory injunction. Section 1292(b) creates a dual-gatekeeper situation in which the trial judge may certify that an otherwise unappealable interlocutory order meets specified conditions making it a good candidate for immediate review, but the appellate court may also decline to entertain the appeal before final judgment. Both of these exceptions, and some narrower ones, have been on the books for many decades; Rule 23(f), by contrast, took effect in 1998. It reflected a perception that a trial judge's decision to certify or not to certify a case as a class action may have make-or-break significance, either putting heavy settlement pressure on a defendant because of greatly expanded exposure or making an effort to pool many small claims uneconomical to pursue on a claim-by-claim basis.

In addition, one may speak of some *qualifications* to the federal final-judgment rule. Here, appeal is *not* explicitly interlocutory, as it is with what we above called exceptions. Rather, a perhaps somewhat borderline situation is treated as meeting the § 1291 finality requirement, even though not absolutely everything is over in the trial court. You'll no doubt see what we're calling qualifications referred to loosely as "exceptions," which is not a problem as long as you keep in mind the mostly conceptual difference between something admittedly interlocutory and something regarded as coming within a perhaps loose definition of "final." A non-exhaustive list of examples of such qualifications includes:

- Federal Rule of Civil Procedure 54(b), authorizing a federal court in a multi-claim or multi-party action to "direct entry of a final judgment as to one or more, but fewer than all, claims or parties," but "only if the court expressly determines that there is no just reason for delay." No such determination, though, is necessary when a district court dismisses one of many *separate* but related cases all pending before it. The loser need not wait to appeal until the court disposes of the related cases. Gelboim v. Bank of Am. Corp., 574 U.S. 405 (2015). The same is true with cases consolidated under Federal Rule 42(a) when one consolidated case goes to judgment while other such cases remain pending. Hall v. Hall, 584 U.S.—, 138 S. Ct. 1118 (2018).

- The decisional "collateral order" doctrine, allowing immediate appeal when a federal trial court has made a final ruling (hence the ability to regard it as "final" for § 1291 purposes, even though the whole case is not over) on an important issue involving an asserted claim of right that is separate from the merits of the case (hence the "collateral" label) and effectively unreachable on review after final judgment. For example, a trial court's denial of a government official's claim to immunity from having to stand trial when sued for actions taken within the scope of official duty — which asserts that the official is legally entitled not to be put through trial at all, not just that he or she may have to stand trial but should win on the merits — is often appealable as a collateral order. Mitchell v. Forsyth, 472 U.S. 511 (1985). Just because a ruling has important consequences, though, does not mean that it will qualify as an appealable collateral order. In *Mohawk Industries, Inc. v. Carpenter*, 558 U.S. 100 (2009), the Supreme Court held without dissent that a district court's ruling that a party had waived the attorney-client privilege — which can result in major disclosure of privileged material, toothpaste that cannot readily be put back into the tube (although it can be excluded from evidence if there is an appellate reversal after final judgment, followed by a later trial) — was not a collateral order and thus was not immediately appealable.

Finally, in federal courts the extraordinary writ of mandamus may be viewed as neither an exception allowing interlocutory appeal nor a qualification viewing an action as final, but as a *circumvention* of the finality requirement. Although a mandamus petition may obtain appellate-court review of a trial judge's action before a final decision, it does not involve formally taking an appeal — interlocutory or after final judgment — at all. Rather, a mandamus proceeding historically was in form an original action initiated in the court of appeals against the trial judge or court, alleging highly prejudicial, egregious usurpation or abuse of discretion that cannot be adequately reviewed if not handled immediately by mandamus. (In the federal courts, a 1996 amendment to Federal Rule of Appellate Procedure 21 ended the styling of a mandamus petition as one naming the trial judge. The writ if granted, though, may still be directed to the trial court.) Mandamus is fairly rarely granted and is not, the Supreme Court reiterates, to be a "substitute for appeal." An example of mandamus — under an established exception to the general rule that mandamus is for cases involving extraordinary circumstances and abuse of discretion — in these materials is *Beacon Theatres, Inc. v. Westover*, 359 U.S. 500 (1959) (*supra* p. 264, Note 3). The right to trial by jury is regarded as so important and fundamental that mandamus is available to challenge its denial at the district-court level without waiting for appeal after final judgment.

Without following all the particulars, state systems mostly have something like the federal pattern — a final-judgment requirement with some categorical exceptions allowing interlocutory appeals, often including grants and denials of preliminary injunctions because of the importance of reviewing orders dealing with claims of short-term irreparable harm. Wisconsin, with a statute based on an American Bar Association proposal, takes a less categorical, broadly discretionary approach to interlocutory appeals:

> *Appeals by permission.* A judgment or order not appealable as [from a final trial-court action] may be appealed to the court of appeals in advance of a final judgment or order upon leave granted by the court if it determines that an appeal will:
>
> (a) Materially advance the termination of the litigation or clarify further proceedings in the litigation;
>
> (b) Protect the petitioner from substantial or irreparable injury; or
>
> (c) Clarify an issue of general importance in the administration of justice.

Wis. Stat. Ann. § 808.03(2). Would such an approach be better than the present federal patchwork?

2. Reviewability

Reviewability refers to *which* trial-court rulings, once a case is before a court of appeals by interlocutory appeal or by appeal after final judgment in the trial court, the court of appeals will consider. Thus a ruling that was not itself *appealable*, such as a pretrial discovery order or the exclusion or admission of particular evidence at trial, may be *reviewable* once a later appealable order or judgment has let the case come to the court of appeals. But courts of appeals find some trial-court actions *unreviewable*: most basically, a party who suffered an adverse interlocutory ruling but then won a final trial-court judgment despite that ruling (such as a defendant who lost some evidentiary rulings at trial, but then won a verdict of no liability) may not seek review of such a ruling. Appellate courts may also decline to consider possible error that went against the appellant, if the error appears to have been harmless. *Cf.* Fed. R. Civ. P. 61 (trial courts are not to grant new trials, set aside verdicts, etc., "[u]nless justice requires otherwise"; they are to "disregard all errors and defects that do not affect any party's substantial rights").

Also, an appellate court may find even a trial-court ruling that appears to have disadvantaged the losing party to be unreviewable, for such reasons as failure to make timely objection when the trial court made its ruling. This idea is often summed up with the shorthand term that alleged error must be "properly preserved" for review. Thus under Rule 51 on jury instructions, a party's failure to make timely and specific objection to the giving of or failure to give an instruction keeps it from being considered as ground for possible reversal — except if there was "plain error . . . [that] affects substantial rights." Fed. R. Civ. P. 51(d)(2). Similarly, a party who fails to make a proper pre-verdict motion for judgment as a matter of law usually may not make such a motion after the jury returns its verdict, *see* Fed. R. Civ. P. 50(a)-(b), or urge on appeal a previously omitted ground as reason to enter judgment in its favor. Such requirements are meant to give trial courts a chance to correct possible errors in timely fashion and to keep parties from "sandbagging" — letting error go at the time to keep a possible objection as an ace in the hole for later if the case turns out badly.

3. Standard of Review

The *standard of review* determines whether a court of appeals will review a trial-court finding or ruling with or without according it some level of deference or presumption of correctness. It has been nicely described as an appellate court's "measuring stick." Steven Alan Childress, *A Primer on Standards of Review in Federal Civil Appeals*, 293 F.R.D. 156, 159 (2013). Trial-court rulings on questions of law, and sometimes on questions of mixed law and fact, are subject to de novo appellate review without deference to the trial court's view. This approach reflects the importance of attempting to assure uniformity in the definition of generally applicable legal standards.

The federal courts of appeals had been divided on the standard of review for trial courts' findings on mixed questions of law and fact. The Supreme Court stated in *U.S. Bank National Association ex rel. CWCapital Asset Management LLC v. Village at Lakeridge, LLC*, 583 U.S. —,138 S. Ct. 960 (2018), that the standard should differ depending on the type of appellate determination involved:

> Mixed questions are not all alike. . . . [S]ome require courts to expound on the law, particularly by amplifying on a broad legal standard. When that is so — when applying the law involves developing auxiliary legal principles of use in other cases — appellate courts should typically review a decision de novo. . . . But . . . other mixed questions immerse courts in case-specific factual issues — compelling them to marshal and weigh evidence, make credibility judgments, and otherwise address what we have . . . called "multifarious, fleeting, special, narrow facts that utterly resist generalization." And when that is so, appellate courts should usually review a decision with deference. . . . In short, the standard of review for a mixed question all depends — on whether answering it entails primarily legal or factual work.

Id. at 967.

By contrast to matters receiving de novo review, two important kinds of actions at the trial level are usually reviewed with deference and thus some degree of disinclination to disturb the ruling below: (1) findings of fact by a judge or especially a jury, and (2) trial judges' rulings on many matters of pretrial and trial management such as discovery. The role of the jury in American civil litigation requires limited trial- and appellate-court review of findings that are regarded as within the jury's province: if there was substantial enough evidence that a rational factfinder could have found as the jury did on a material, disputed issue of fact, or an evaluative matter such as whether certain conduct was negligent, then the trial and appellate judges may not enter a judgment contrary to the jury's finding (although the court may order a new trial if it regards the jury verdict as contrary to the weight of the evidence).

Even when factual findings are made by judges rather than juries, as may happen on pretrial motions or when a jury right does not attach or has been waived, those findings are subject to reversal only if the appellate court regards them as *clearly erroneous*, *see* Fed. R. Civ. P. 52(a)(6) — which, however it may sound, involves somewhat closer review than is given to jury findings, although the "clearly erroneous" review standard is still quite deferential. Reversal is warranted only if the reviewing court "is left with the definite and firm conviction that a mistake has been committed." United States v. U.S. Gypsum Co., 333 U.S. 364, 395 (1948). This practice reflects the idea that trial judges viewing witnesses' testimony may be in a better position to resolve such issues as credibility; a sense that appellate courts should treat trial judges with due respect; and a desire to economize by not inundating appellate courts with review of many close rulings on factual issues that will often be unique to a particular case.

Besides deferring to trial judges' and juries' fact findings, appellate courts in the United States review many actions of trial judges on the basis that they may be reversed only for *abuse of discretion*. In matters such as the sequencing or number of pretrial discovery events, or the decision whether to try together or separately claims that are joined in the parties' pleadings, American appellate courts regard it as essential for trial judges to have considerable scope for the exercise of individual judgment on how best to manage cases before them. Nor does the concept of discretion extend only to procedural and case-management issues. Trial judges must often, for example, make provisional decisions on requests for preliminary injunctions. Although these rulings are subject to interlocutory review, they are reviewed for abuse of discretion so long as the trial judge was applying the proper legal standard.

When a trial court's ruling is subject to review for abuse of discretion, an appellate court is not supposed to reverse just because its judges think that they would have made the opposite decision if they had been in the trial judge's position. To reverse, they must conclude that the ruling is outside a generally considerable range of discretion appropriately left to the trial judge. As a practical matter the degree of deference will vary depending on the type of ruling, with decisions of major impact (such as rulings on preliminary-injunction requests and entry or vacation of default judgments) getting somewhat closer scrutiny; still, abuse-of-discretion review remains deferential albeit not toothless.

If the trial judge may have applied the wrong legal standard, though, even when review of application of the *right* standard would be deferential, review of the correctness of the legal standard applied is de novo. A finding that the trial judge applied the wrong legal standard would ordinarily result in the decision's being vacated for reconsideration under the right standard, with review of that application in turn for abuse of discretion. You will encounter various articulations, with some judges thinking it makes sense to leave abuse of discretion out of the picture when a possible error of law is involved. *See, e.g.*, Plouffe v. Ligon, 606 F.3d 890, 894-95 (8th Cir. 2010) (Colloton, J., concurring) ("An error of law can always be characterized as 'an abuse of discretion,' . . . [b]ut the issue is more accurately described as a legal matter that we review de novo . . . ."). Probably more often, courts say that a trial court's making an error of law is itself an abuse of discretion. *See, e.g.*, Koon v. United States, 518 U.S. 81, 100 (1996) ("A district court by definition abuses its discretion when it makes an error of law."). Either way, the bottom line is the same: possible errors of law are reviewed de novo. As to "pure questions of law," "the Court of Appeals has no cause to defer to the District Court." United States v. Clarke, 573 U.S. 248, 257 (2014).

CHAPTER SEVEN

JUDGMENTS

Once you have litigated a civil case to a conclusion, what do you have? Have you really won (or lost) anything, or can matters that were or could have been dealt with in your case be raised or reopened later in another case? Can an adversary who claims you caused both property damage and personal injuries in the same accident sue for the property damage only, and then bring another action for the personal injuries? Or assume that one plaintiff passenger in your bus sues you for causing injuries in a collision, establishes that your negligent driving caused the crash, and wins a judgment against you. Then, when another passenger injured in the same accident sues you in a separate action for her injuries, can you contest the issue of your negligence — or may the second passenger benefit from the finding against you on that issue in the prior case?*

The area of law that deals with these types of questions is known by multiple names — *res judicata* ("a thing adjudicated"), *judgments*, *preclusion*, and *former adjudication*, to give the most prominent ones. (As we will see, the field is afflicted by multiple sets of terminologies, with some of the terms themselves at times inconsistently used. So you have to be able to translate between traditional and modern terminology, and to be alert for the sense in which a term that may have multiple meanings is being used, or even misused.) Unlike most other areas covered in Civil Procedure, the law in the former-adjudication field is largely — although not exclusively —

---

* There is also the question of how to enforce the judgment. If the loser does not pay damages awarded, perform a contractual obligation when ordered to do so, comply with an injunction, etc., the winner may have to seek judicial enforcement in the jurisdiction where the judgment was rendered or elsewhere — if, for example, the defendant's bank account, or a child subject to a custody order, is in another state or nation. Getting judgments enforced is of much practical importance and too often considerable difficulty (a problem fortunately avoided when a damage suit is settled rather than tried to a verdict — for the case to be dismissed as settled, the money must cross the table). The area involves much nitty-gritty and regulation at both state and federal levels, sometimes of general applicability and sometimes — as with support and child-custody enforcement — subject-specific. Enforcement of judgments is beyond the scope of this book.

decisional, governed by common-law principles developed by the courts without much input from constitution-makers, legislators, or rule-drafters.

The decided trend in American preclusion law over several decades, as relaxation of common-law restrictions on joinder of claims made it feasible to bring all claims arising out of a single transaction or event in one action, has been toward broader preclusive effect: generally, bring all of the related claims you have (at least against one defendant) in a single action, or lose the ones you leave out. Also, in the name of efficiency and consistency, most American jurisdictions now sometimes allow a nonparty to benefit from the results of a prior suit — as, for example, if one passenger establishes that the bus driver was negligent and a second passenger wants to take advantage of that finding in a later suit against the same defendant. Such broad preclusive effects are another respect in which American civil procedure, along with procedure in other nations of English legal heritage, is somewhat distinctive; civil-law systems tend to have considerably narrower approaches. *See, e.g.,* DAVID L. SHAPIRO, CIVIL PROCEDURE: PRECLUSION IN CIVIL ACTIONS 15-16, 154-55 n.54 (2001). (As you might expect, they nonetheless have ways of preventing inconsistency and duplicative litigation, such as judges using findings from the record of another action between the same parties as evidence. For a description of preclusion law in several systems, see Kevin M. Clermont, *Res Judicata as Requisite for Justice*, 68 RUTGERS U.L. REV. 1067 (2016).)

The following extract from the *Restatement (Second) of Judgments* gives historical and theoretical background on preclusion law and the importance of finality in matters adjudicated. The *Restatement*, although not formally binding, is widely — not, of course, universally on all points — followed, giving American preclusion law a considerable degree of consistency across jurisdictions despite its common-law nature. In this extract we encounter two generations of terminology, with the *Restatement* pressing use of the modern (and increasingly favored) terms *claim preclusion* and *issue preclusion* for the two main doctrines in the area; their traditional (and still used) counterparts are *res judicata* and *collateral estoppel* respectively. As our use of the term "res judicata" above reflected, that phrase can also — here is one example of the fractiousness of labeling in this field — be used broadly to refer to the entire body of law, as well as more narrowly to just the doctrine known as claim preclusion in the modern terminology.

SECTION A: PERSPECTIVES ON JUDGMENTS

RESTATEMENT (SECOND) OF JUDGMENTS

Ch. 1, introductory cmt., at 6-13 (AM. LAW INST. 1982)

The complementary relationship between the law of procedure and the law of res judicata is not difficult to explain. The law of res judicata expresses essentially simple principles, even though the implications of those principles are often complex. The principle underlying the rule of claim preclusion is that a party who once has had a chance to litigate a claim before an appropriate tribunal usually ought not to have another chance to do so. A related but narrower principle — that one who has actually litigated an issue should not be allowed to relitigate it — underlies the rule of issue preclusion. The legal and social purposes served by these principles will be referred to presently. The very statement of them, however, shows their dependence on presuppositions about the law of procedure. The "chance" to litigate is not simply some unspecified opportunity for disputation over legal rights; it is the opportunity to submit a dispute over legal rights to a tribunal legally empowered to decide it according to definite procedural rules. Any less formal process would be regarded as either legally inconclusive — that is, not a serious and genuine "chance" to litigate — or fundamentally unfair. Indeed, a procedure for ventilating a legal dispute that lacks certain minimal elements of form will be treated as inconclusive for the reason that it is fundamentally unfair. Putting the point differently, it may be a denial of Due Process to treat an undefined procedural mechanism as yielding a conclusive result in determination of legal rights.

The requirements of Due Process prescribe the outer constitutional limits of a procedural system that may yield a conclusive product, i.e., one entitled to res judicata effects. Within the constitutional limits, the contours of res judicata are determined by the particulars of the opportunity to litigate afforded by the system of procedure in question. The imprint of the procedural system manifests itself in the rules of both claim preclusion and issue preclusion.

Under the common law forms of action, for example, a plaintiff ordinarily was not permitted to join in one action claims formulated under different forms of action. That limitation in the original procedure properly imported a corollary in the law of res judicata that a party who had claimed through one form of action was not necessarily precluded from later claiming through another form of action, even though the same underlying grievance was involved. Also in the common law regime before the merger of law and equity, a litigant ordinarily could not assert legal and equitable claims in a single action, or assert equitable defenses in an action on the common law side. The res judicata corollary was that prosecution of an action at law did not necessarily preclude a subsequent suit in equity on the same transaction.

Under prevailing versions of the Field Code, the common law restrictions on joinder of claims were relaxed but not obliterated. For example, in most jurisdictions for many years a plaintiff could not join causes of action in contract and tort in a single suit. It followed, or should have followed, that a party who lost in an action based on a contract theory might still be able to maintain an action based on a tort theory, at least if such eventualities as the statute of limitations did not independently intervene....

Other rules of procedure influenced the definition of issue preclusion. The rule of "mutuality of estoppel" is a principal illustration. The mutuality rule was this: A party is not bound by a finding in an earlier action if the opponent in the subsequent action would not have been bound if the finding had been the other way. The mutuality rule evolved in contemplation that a lawsuit, even one arising out of a multi-party controversy, was ordinarily a two-sided affair; as a two-sided affair its effects should not go beyond the immediate parties. However, to a limited extent under the Codes, and to a very broad extent under the Federal Rules, the procedural system changed to permit a plaintiff to constitute a multi-party controversy as a multi-party lawsuit. Once the procedural system afforded a party the opportunity to bring in all adversaries, the question inevitably arose whether penalties in the form of preclusion should attach if he failed to use that opportunity. In the era of liberal joinder that question came to be answered more and more definitely in the affirmative. It has now become the rule that a party who loses the contest of an issue against one adversary is ordinarily precluded from relitigating it against any other adversary.

The proper scope of issue preclusion is also shaped by the procedural rules governing pleading and discovery. Both at common law and under the Codes the rules of pleading required a claimant to state his claim with fairly definite particulars as to time, place, cause, and consequence.... Discovery was almost non-existent at common law and very cumbersome in equity. The Codes expanded discovery only in very limited directions, at least before the adoption of 20th Century amendments. Against this backdrop, the cases applying the rule of issue preclusion — collateral estoppel as it was then called — generally applied a correspondingly narrow definition of "issue." Thus, it was often said that the issue in two actions was the same only if the evidence was the same. In effect, this gave a party a chance to relitigate if he could develop substantially different evidence even if a single underlying dispute was involved.

The provisions on pleading and discovery under the Federal Rules of Civil Procedure invite a quite different approach to the concepts of "claim" and "issue" for purposes of res judicata. So far as pleading is concerned, the premise of the Federal Rules is that a party should be able to state his claim on any and every permissible foundation available under the substantive law. Furthermore, if a pleader describes generally the transaction by which he is aggrieved, the action may not be dismissed under the Federal Rules unless it is evident that no substantive theory can support his action; he is virtually required to plead himself out of court to suffer dismissal at the pleading stage.* Similar latitude is allowed in affirmative defenses, counterclaims, and claims against third parties. "Claim" for purposes of res judicata under the Federal Rules thus ordinarily refers to the transaction involved rather than legal formulations about the transaction.

Within the spacious framework of pleading under the Federal Rules, the parties are permitted by Rule 26 to discover everything "relevant to the subject matter of the action" [now "relevant to any party's claim or defense"

---

* Subsequent developments in the federal courts and some state systems have tightened pleading requirements to some extent, *see supra* pp. 36-58, but thus far they have had no impact on preclusion law. — ED.

— ED.] through a formidable armory of devices. The concept of "issue" has been correspondingly and appropriately enlarged in the rule of issue preclusion applied under the Federal Rules. Under the Federal Rules, issue preclusion is primarily determined not by whether the evidence offered in the second action is the same as that in the first action, but by whether that evidence was fairly accessible to the party in the first action.

The law of res judicata expresses the terms for assessing whether the procedural system afforded the contending party an adequate opportunity to litigate. In the now accepted phrase, the question is whether that opportunity was "full and fair." Modern civil procedure usually does provide full and fair freedom to present substantive contentions and full and fair access to evidence. Accordingly, under that system of procedure there must be compelling reasons to sustain a plea for a second chance. Such is the general tenor of this Restatement.

The rules of res judicata in modern procedure therefore may fairly be characterized as illiberal toward the opportunity for relitigation. Their rigor contrasts sharply with the liberality of the rules governing the original event, which is the theme of the Federal Rules of Civil Procedure and similar systems. The Federal Rules direct that a party be given broad freedom in developing, and if need be in changing, position. That freedom is allowed in prosecution as well as defense, at trial as well as pretrial. The policy of the Federal Rules is epitomized in Rule 15(a), dealing with amendment of pleadings, which provides that "leave shall be freely given when justice so requires." [Rule 15(a)'s language now reads: "The court should freely give leave when justice so requires." — ED.] In contrast, the policy of the modern law of res judicata is summed up in § 26(f) of this Restatement, allowing relitigation of a claim (except on other specific grounds) only if it is "clearly and convincingly shown that the policies favoring preclusion of a second action are overcome for an extraordinary reason."

This difference does not represent a contradiction or ambivalence in procedural policy. Rather, it reflects the relationship between rules of original procedure and rules of res judicata. Inasmuch as the former are now generally permissive, the latter are correspondingly restrictive. In this connection, it is pertinent to observe that when the rules of original procedure constrain the first opportunity to litigate, the rules of res judicata are adjusted reciprocally. In some types of courts of limited jurisdiction and some types of administrative agencies, for example, the scope of substantive inquiry and the potential for development of evidence are much more restricted than the corresponding opportunity afforded in a court of general jurisdiction in a comparable case. The rules of res judicata with respect to the judgments of such tribunals are correspondingly less restrictive.

However formulated and applied, the basic principle of res judicata reflects a fundamental paradox. The law of res judicata endows judgments of courts with a peculiar finality: They are immune from examination by other authorities and may be reexamined by the courts themselves only in unusual circumstances. Yet this finality attaches not because the courts are infallible but because they are inevitably fallible. Adjudication is a procedure by which a disinterested agency — the judge or jury — is authorized to impose a binding resolution of a controversy over legal rights. Arriving at such a resolution requires either a determination of the facts or a particularization of the law as it applies to facts, or both. If there were infallible personages who could discern law and facts in a way that engendered universal assent, the process of adjudication would be socially unnecessary. Legal disputes could simply be remanded to the oracles. It is because such personages do not exist that the offices of judge and jury and a system of procedure are created by law, supplying by fiat a practical substitute for perfect intelligence. Justice Jackson's observation about the Supreme Court is true of the judicial system as a whole: "We are not final because we are infallible, but we are infallible only because we are final." Brown v. Allen, 344 U.S. 443, 540 (1953) (Jackson, J., concurring).

Finality, then, is the service rendered by the courts through operation of the law of res judicata. The finality in contemplation includes the immediate finality that is imposed on the litigation itself. It includes also imposition of finality on the dispute that gave rise to the litigation so far as it is within the means of legal process to do so. In a still broader sense, the law of res judicata cumulatively reinforces the authoritativeness of the law itself. It holds that at some point arguable questions of right and wrong for practical purposes simply cannot be argued any more. It compels repose. In substituting compulsion for persuasion, the law of res judicata trenches upon freedom to petition about grievances and autonomy of action, very serious concerns in an open society. Yet such a society requires a system of order to maintain its open structure.

Indefinite continuation of a dispute is a social burden. It consumes time and energy that may be put to other use, not only of the parties but of the community as a whole. It rewards the disputatious. It renders uncertain the working premises upon which the transactions of the day are to be conducted. The law of res judicata reduces these burdens even if it does not eliminate them, and is thus the quintessence of the law itself: A convention designed to compensate for man's incomplete knowledge and strong tendency to quarrel.

The convention concerning finality of judgments has to be accepted if the idea of law is to be accepted, certainly if there is to be practical meaning to the idea that legal disputes can be resolved by judicial process. At the same time, acceptance of the basic convention cannot conceal the fact that manifest failures of justice occur. The possibility, indeed the certainty, of such failures must be acknowledged as the price paid for the benefits of the convention. If that price is to be kept within reason, however, the convention that a judgment is justice can be accepted only with qualifications. . . . The law of res judicata therefore must provide some leeway for reexamination of judgments. Doing so is a matter not only of fairness but also of efficiency. While the rules of preclusion are supported in part by considerations of efficiency, affording the possibility of reconsideration is also a matter of efficiency, for it relaxes the requirements of procedural meticulousness in the first instance.

No perfect system of correcting a failure of justice is possible, however, any more than a perfect system of first instance justice is possible. The willingness to look through the convention of finality cannot be unconstrained. It must be tempered by recognition that beyond the appearances on which the original judgment rested lie only other appearances, perhaps substantiated by better evidence, but appearances nevertheless. It must be tempered by the further recognition that imperfections of court, counsel, and procedure may also attend a new inquiry.

The central problem in finality of judgments is how far the principle of finality is to be qualified. The law of res judicata grapples with this central problem. Its specifications endeavor to state the conditions under which the possibility of failure of civil justice is so substantial as to justify remedial action in the form of relitigation. On the one hand, judgments must in general be accorded finality despite flaws in the processes leading to decision and the unavoidable possibility that the results in some instances were wrong. On the other hand, a judgment in a particular case must be subject to reexamination in the name of substantial justice if the initial engagement of the merits was inadequate. Mediation between these opposed considerations cannot be simply ad hoc; if it were, both the finality of judgments and the opportunity for reexamination would be a function of the intuitions of judges. A measure of intuition and discretion, to be sure, is required in administering the law of res judicata, as the rules in this Restatement frankly acknowledge. However, a policy of reasonable finality requires rules that take into account the complex substantive and procedural considerations going into a civil judgment. The law of res judicata is thus a mirror of legal justice itself.

Notes

1. *Preclusion as a later-case determination.* Preclusion issues generally come up when there are two different cases. Such issues are almost entirely decided in the second case; a court rendering a judgment does not adjudicate what its preclusive effect will be in later cases. Doing so would often waste time on an abstract proposition, for a second case involving the preclusive effect of the first case may never arise. First-round courts do take steps that can influence whether a decision does or does not have preclusive effect, such as specifying that a dismissal is with or without prejudice (although a dismissal with prejudice does not invariably mean that a plaintiff cannot sue again). And when the preclusive effect of a judgment in State A is at issue in a later case in the courts of State B, the preclusion law that would apply in State A's courts is supposed to govern. But it is the job of second-round courts to figure out just what preclusive effect an initial judgment should have.

2. *Preclusion as an affirmative defense.* Federal Rule of Civil Procedure 8(c)(1) provides: "In responding to a pleading, a party must affirmatively state any avoidance or affirmative defense, including . . . estoppel [and] res

judicata...." In Chapter Two (*supra* pp. 79-80, Note 4), we saw that, if you don't raise an affirmative defense, you may lose it. "But since the rationale of preclusion doctrine draws in part on the efficiency gains to the judicial system, the matter has been held to be one that a court may recognize on its own motion if it wishes." DAVID L. SHAPIRO, CIVIL PROCEDURE: PRECLUSION IN CIVIL ACTIONS 71 (2001); *see* Arizona v. California, 530 U.S. 392, 412 (2000) (noting that the court may raise the defense "in special circumstances").

3. *Motions for relief from judgments as a sometime alternative to contesting preclusion.* This chapter focuses on preclusion issues in second-round courts. In quite limited circumstances, a party with a reason such as newly discovered evidence, or that an adverse judgment was procured by fraud, may — even after exhaustion of all appeals — seek relief from a judgment by motion in the judgment-rendering court under Federal Rule of Civil Procedure 60(b) and state counterparts. *See supra* pp. 294-300.

Some grounds for Rule 60(b) relief, such as newly discovered evidence that could not with reasonable diligence have been discovered in time to move for a new trial, would not be reason for a second-round court to make an exception to otherwise applicable preclusion. The main overlap between Rule 60(b) and grounds for resisting preclusion comes when the loser has an argument that the judgment was void, as for want of jurisdiction or notice. But if a party failed to raise an available challenge to subject-matter jurisdiction until after judgment, it is unlikely to be able to do so either by Rule 60(b) motion in the original court or to resist preclusion in another action. And if a party litigated an issue of personal or subject-matter jurisdiction and lost, that ruling is likely to have preclusive effect even if it may have been wrong. Finally, remember that the grounds for Rule 60(b) relief are indeed "quite limited"; for example, the Supreme Court's later settling a circuit split against the position that the circuit had taken in deciding a case does not suffice to get the loser relief from that judgment. *See* United States *ex rel.* Garibaldi v. Orleans Parish Sch. Bd., 397 F.3d 334 (5th Cir. 2005). *See generally, e.g.,* GEOFFREY C. HAZARD, JR. ET AL., CIVIL PROCEDURE §§ 15.14-.15, -.17 (6th ed. 2011) (discussing grounds for obtaining relief from a judgment).

SECTION B: CLAIM PRECLUSION

RESTATEMENT (SECOND) OF JUDGMENTS

(AM. LAW INST. 1982)

§ 17. Effects of Former Adjudication — General Rules

A valid and final personal judgment is conclusive between the parties, except on appeal or other direct review, to the following extent:

(1) If the judgment is in favor of the plaintiff, the claim is extinguished and merged in the judgment and a new claim may arise on the judgment . . . ;

(2) If the judgment is in favor of the defendant, the claim is extinguished and the judgment bars a subsequent action on that claim . . . ;

(3) A judgment in favor of either the plaintiff or the defendant is conclusive, in a subsequent action between them on the same or a different claim, with respect to any issue actually litigated and determined if its determination was essential to that judgment (see § 27).

§ 24. Dimensions of "Claim" for Purposes of Merger or Bar — General Rule Concerning "Splitting"

(1) When a valid and final judgment rendered in an action extinguishes the plaintiff's claim pursuant to the rules of merger or bar . . . , the claim extinguished includes all rights of the plaintiff to remedies against the defendant with respect to all or any part of the transaction, or series of connected transactions, out of which the action arose.

(2) What factual grouping constitutes a "transaction", and what groupings constitute a "series", are to be determined pragmatically, giving weight to such considerations as whether the facts are related in time, space, origin, or motivation, whether they form a convenient trial unit, and whether their treatment as a unit conforms to the parties' expectations or business understanding or usage.

Notes

1. *Terminology. Restatement (Second)* § 17 sets out the basic rules of claim preclusion (subsections (1)-(2)) and issue preclusion (subsection (3)). Claim preclusion, or res judicata in the term's narrower sense, is referred to as "merger" when the claimant won and "bar" when the claimant lost. The idea is that a winning plaintiff's claim is "merged" into the judgment, and the only claim that the plaintiff has left is to enforce the judgment if necessary. Thus a claimant who thinks it won too little in damages cannot bring another suit for more, at least against the same defendant; it no longer has the original claim and is limited by the amount awarded in the judgment. When a claimant loses, he or she does not have a judgment into which its claim is merged; instead the claim is regarded as barred by the judgment for the other side, so that the claimant cannot try again.

2. *"Claim-splitting."* The claim-preclusion rules of merger and bar thus prevent blatant second tries by claimants against the same defendant, but such efforts are few aside from instances — regrettably frequent — of harassment. As a practical matter, claim preclusion comes up much more often in connection with arguments over whether a plaintiff has acted in the

manner forbidden by *Restatement (Second)* § 24 on "claim-splitting," by bringing in two actions against the same defendant different parts of what should be regarded as a single claim that the plaintiff ought to have brought in one suit. The case after these notes illustrates the arguments over what the breadth of "claim" should be for purposes of the claim-preclusion rule against splitting, along with an unsuccessful effort to use issue preclusion that fails because claim preclusion knocks the plaintiff out of court entirely.

Declaratory judgments, in which courts adjudicate the rights and duties of the parties without ordering "coercive" relief such as damages or an injunction, are not subject to claim preclusion's rule against claim splitting. Plaintiffs can limit themselves to seeking declaratory relief and use the judgment later as a basis for coercive relief if necessary. If you think the government will obey a ruling that its policy is unlawful, you need not seek an injunction right away. If you win and the government does not obey, you can still come back and seek injunctive relief. *See, e.g.*, Harborside Refrigerated Servs., Inc. v. Vogel, 959 F.2d 368, 372-73 (2d Cir. 1992). Issues determined in a declaratory-judgment proceeding, though, can later have issue-preclusive effect in the same or a different proceeding.

3. *Finality for purposes of preclusion, and the misleading "on the merits" requisite.* A common mantra — partly but not entirely tracked in the *Restatement* — is that prerequisites for at least some kinds of preclusive effect are that a judgment be "valid, final, and on the merits." Validity, to which the *Restatement* does refer, piggybacks on basic requirements for a valid judgment such as subject-matter and personal jurisdiction, including adequate notice. Finality, also present in the *Restatement*, has a not entirely precise but somewhat specialized meaning in the preclusion context, not identical with meanings of the term in other contexts such as finality of a judgment for purposes of taking an appeal. Entry of a final judgment is obviously necessary for claim preclusion: for a claim to be merged into or barred by a judgment, there has to be a judgment in the first place. For issue preclusion, though, "'final judgment' includes any prior adjudication of an issue in another action that is determined to be sufficiently firm to be accorded conclusive effect." RESTATEMENT (SECOND) OF JUDGMENTS § 13 (AM. LAW INST. 1982). Thus a finding of liability in a bifurcated trial with proceedings on damages yet to come, even though there is no final judgment, may be conclusive enough for preclusive effect in other litigation. Other rulings, such as a finding of likelihood of success on the merits as part of a decision on a request for an interlocutory injunction, are provisional even if hotly contested and carefully considered. They would ordinarily have no preclusive effect.

The "on the merits" factor cannot be limited to a ruling on the substantive merits of a case. One may be precluded on a procedural issue, such as the existence of diversity of citizenship for purposes of federal-court jurisdiction, just as much as one may be precluded on a substantive issue such as liability. And while a decision on the merits — after trial or summary judgment, say — does qualify for claim-preclusive effect, other dispositions such as default judgments, settlements, and dismissals for discovery misconduct can also support merger or bar. The *Restatement*'s approach, rather than using "on the merits," is to specify circumstances in which a judgment does *not* have claim-preclusive effect — in the case of a judgment for defendant, for example, § 20 mentions such grounds as jurisdictional and venue dismissals, voluntary dismissals without prejudice, and dismissals for prematurity of plaintiff's action. **Read this paragraph again.** We cannot tell you how often commentators, writers of commercial outlines, and students have gotten this point wildly wrong by reading "on the merits" — which, again, the *Restatement* does *not* use — too literally.

4. *Preclusion and related claims against different parties.* Restatement *(Second)* § 24(1)'s rule against claim-splitting applies only to the claim of a plaintiff "against the defendant." However subtly stated, this limit has the important effect that **claim preclusion does not apply when P sues D1 and then sues D2 on a related claim in a separate action.** Hey! Got that? Students often miss this point. But as we shall see, D2 may be able to benefit from *issue*-preclusive effect on findings that went against P. Also, the "one-satisfaction rule" of remedial law means that P cannot collect doubly for a single loss.

RUSH V. CITY OF MAPLE HEIGHTS

147 N.E.2d 599 (Ohio 1958)

[Official syllabus by the Court*]

Where a person suffers both personal injuries and property damage as a result of the same wrongful act, only a single cause of action arises, the different injuries occasioned thereby being separate items of damage from such act. (Paragraph four of the syllabus in the case of *Vasu v. Kohlers, Inc.*, 61 N.E.2d 707 (Ohio 1945), overruled.) . . .

■ HERBERT, J.

[Plaintiff, a passenger on a motorcycle she apparently owned, was hurt in a fall allegedly resulting from the defendant city's negligent street maintenance. She sued for damages to the motorcycle; the court held that the city had been negligent in not repairing a hole, and awarded her a judgment of $100. The city appealed to the Court of Appeals and the Supreme Court of Ohio, which both affirmed. End of first litigation.

[Plaintiff then filed a second action against the city for personal injuries suffered in the accident, arguing that the issue of the city's negligence was determined by the previous litigation and seeking trial on damages alone. The city sought dismissal on the ground that by suing first for property damage alone plaintiff had split a single claim and, in the alternative if plaintiff was not out of court altogether, argued against issue-preclusive effect; but the trial judge agreed with the plaintiff and sent the case to a jury

---

* In Ohio, unlike in most jurisdictions, the syllabus of the Supreme Court constitutes an official part of the opinion. — ED.

on the issue of damages alone. The jury awarded her $12,000; the city appealed to the Court of Appeals, which affirmed.]

The eighth error assigned by the defendant is that "the trial and appellate courts committed error in permitting plaintiff to split her cause of action and to file a separate action in the Cleveland Municipal Court for her property damage and reduce same to judgment, and, thereafter, to proceed, in the Cuyahoga County Common Pleas Court, with a separate action for personal injuries, both claims arising out of a single accident." . . .

In the case of *Vasu v. Kohlers, Inc.*, 61 N.E.2d 707 (Ohio 1945), plaintiff operating an automobile came into collision with defendant's truck, in which collision he suffered personal injuries and also damage to his automobile. [Vasu's insurer paid for the property damage, and Vasu assigned his property-damage claim to the insurer. The insurer sued Kohlers and lost. Vasu separately sued Kohlers for personal injuries. Kohlers argued that the judgment against the insurer barred Vasu's claim. Kohlers lost in the trial court. The Court of Appeals upheld Kohlers' preclusion defense and reversed.]

This court reversed the judgment of the Court of Appeals, holding in the syllabus, in part, as follows:

1. If the owner of a single cause of action arising out of a single tortious act brings an action against his tort-feasor, he may have but one recovery; and, in case he fails to recover, he may not maintain a subsequent action on the same cause of action, even though he has failed to include his entire cause of action or elements of damage in his original action.

2. If an owner of a single cause of action has a recovery thereon, the cause of action is merged in the judgment; but if he fails to recover on his claimed cause of action and judgment goes against him, such judgment is *res judicata* and a bar to a second action on the same cause of action. . . .

4. Injuries to both person and property suffered by the same person as a result of the same wrongful act are infringements of different rights and give rise to distinct causes of action, with the result that the recovery or denial of recovery of compensation for damages to the property is no bar to an action subsequently prosecuted for the personal injury, unless by an adverse judgment in the first action issues are determined against the plaintiff which operate as an estoppel against him in the second action.

5. A right, question or fact in issue which was necessarily determined by a court of competent jurisdiction in a judgment which has become final, cannot be disputed or litigated in a subsequent suit between the same parties, although the subsequent suit is based upon a different cause of action.

6. Where an injury to person and to property through a single wrongful act causes a prior contract of indemnity and subrogation as to the injury to property, to come into operation for the benefit of the

person injured, the indemnitor may prosecute a separate action against the party causing such injury for reimbursement for indemnity moneys paid under such contract.

7. Parties in privy, in the sense that they are bound by a judgment, are those who acquired an interest in the subject matter after the beginning of the action or the rendition of the judgment; and if their title or interest attached before that fact, they are not bound unless made parties.

8. A grantor or assignor is not bound, as to third persons, by any judgment which such third persons may obtain against his grantee or assignee adjudicating the title to or claim for the interest transferred, unless he participated in the action in such manner as to become, in effect, a party.

. . . The first two paragraphs, although not pertinent there because of the fourth paragraph, are not only applicable but persuasive in our determination here. The sixth, seventh and eighth paragraphs deal with the factual situation which existed in the *Vasu* case, i.e., a prior contract of indemnity and subrogation. Although, as discussed *infra*, it was not actually necessary to the determination of the issue in that case, attention centers on the fourth paragraph. . . .

[Later Ohio Supreme Court cases], distinguishing and explaining the *Vasu* case, have not changed the rule established in paragraph four of the syllabus of the latter case, holding that injuries to both person and property suffered by the same person as a result of the same wrongful act are infringements of different rights and give rise to distinct causes of action.

However, it is contended here that that rule is in conflict with the great weight of authority in this country and has caused vexatious litigation. The following quotation from 1 AMERICAN JURISPRUDENCE, 494, Section 114, states this question well:

> It sometimes happens that a single wrongful or negligent act causes damage in respect of both the person and the property of the same individual, as, for instance, where the owner of a vehicle is injured in a collision which also damages the vehicle. In such a case, the question arises as to whether there are two causes of action or only one, and the authorities are in conflict concerning it. The majority rule is that only one cause of action arises, the reason of the rule being that as the defendant's wrongful act is single, the cause of action must be single, and that the different injuries occasioned by it are merely items of damage proceeding from the same wrong. . . . .
>
> In other jurisdictions, the rule is that two causes of action result from a negligent act which inflicts injury on a person and his property at the same time. This conclusion has been reached in different jurisdictions by different lines of reasoning.

Upon examination of decisions of courts of last resort, we find that the majority rule is followed in [cases from 21 states,] in each of which the action was between the person suffering injury and the person committing the tort, and where insurers were not involved, as in the case here.

The minority rule, that separate actions may be maintained to recover for personal injuries and for damages to property resulting from the same wrongful act, is set forth in [cases from five states] . . . .

The reasoning behind the majority rule seems to be well stated in the case of *Mobile & Ohio R.R. v. Matthews*, 91 S.W. 194 (Tenn. 1906), as follows:

> The negligent action of the plaintiff in error constituted but one tort. The injuries to the person and property of the defendant in error were the several results and effects of one wrongful act. A single tort can be the basis of but one action. It is not improper to declare in different counts for damages to the person and property when both result from the same tort, and it is the better practice to do so where there is any difference in the measure of damages, and all the damages sustained must be sued for in one suit. This is necessary to prevent multiplicity of suits, burdensome expense, and delays to plaintiffs, and vexatious litigation against defendants. . . .
>
> Indeed, if the plaintiff fail to sue for the entire damage done him by the tort, a second action for the damages omitted will be precluded by the judgment in the first suit brought and tried.

The minority rule would seem to stem from the English case of *Brunsden v. Humphrey* (1884), 14 Q.B. 141. The facts in that case are set forth in the opinion in the *Vasu* case, concluding with the statement:

> The Master of the Rolls, in his opinion, stated that the test is "whether the same sort of evidence would prove the plaintiff's case in the two actions," and that, in the action relating to the cab, "it would be necessary to give evidence of the damage done to the plaintiff's vehicle. In the present action it would be necessary to give evidence of the bodily injury occasioned to the plaintiff, and of the sufferings which he has undergone, and for this purpose to call medical witnesses. This one test shows that the causes of action as to the damage done to the plaintiff's cab, and as to the injury occasioned to the plaintiff's person, are distinct."

The fallacy of the reasoning in the English court is best portrayed in the dissenting opinion of Lord Coleridge, as follows:

> It appears to me that whether the negligence of the servant, or the impact of the vehicle which the servant drove, be the technical cause of action, equally the cause is one and the same: that the injury done to the plaintiff is injury done to him at one and the same moment by one and the same act in respect of different *rights*, i.e. his person and his goods, I do not in the least deny; but it seems to me a subtlety not warranted by law to hold that a man cannot bring two actions, if he is injured in his arm and in his leg, but can bring two, if besides his arm and leg being injured, his trousers which contain his leg, and his coat-sleeve which contains his arm, have been torn.

There appears to be no valid reason in these days of code pleading to adhere to the old English rule as to distinctions between injuries to the person and damages to the person's property resulting from a single tort. It would seem that the minority rule is bottomed on the proposition that the right of bodily security is fundamentally different from the right of security of property and, also, that, in actions predicated upon a negligent act, damages are a necessary element of each independent cause of action and no recovery may be had unless and until actual consequential damages are shown. . . .

The decision of the question actually in issue in the *Vasu* case is found in paragraphs six, seven and eight of the syllabus, as it is quite apparent from the facts there that the first judgment, claimed to be *res judicata* in Vasu's action against the defendant, was rendered against Vasu's insurer in an action initiated by it after having paid Vasu for the damages to his automobile. . . .

In the light of the foregoing, it is the view of this court that the so-called majority rule conforms much more properly to modern practice, and that the rule declared in the fourth paragraph of the syllabus in the *Vasu* case, on a point not actually at issue therein, should not be followed.

We, therefore, conclude and hold that, where a person suffers both personal injuries and property damage as a result of the same wrongful act, only a single cause of action arises, the different injuries occasioned thereby being separate items of damage from such act. It follows that paragraph four of the syllabus in the *Vasu case* must be overruled. . . .

Accordingly, the judgment of the Court of Appeals is reversed, and final judgment is entered for defendant. . . .

WEYGANDT, C. J., and STEWART, TAFT, MATTHIAS and BELL, JJ., concur. . . .

■ STEWART, J., concurring. . . .

. . . If it had been necessary [in *Vasu*] to decide the question whether a single tort gives rise to two causes of action as to the one injured by such tort, I would be reluctant to disturb that holding. However, neither the discussion in the *Vasu* case as to whether a single or double cause of action arises from one tort nor the language of the fourth paragraph of the syllabus was necessary to decide the issue presented in the case, and obviously both such language and such paragraph are obiter dicta and, therefore, are not as persuasive an authority as if they had been appropriate to the question presented. . . .

■ ZIMMERMAN, J., dissenting.

I am not unalterably opposed to upsetting prior decisions of this court where changing conditions and the lessons of experience clearly indicate the desirability of such course, but, where those considerations do not obtain, established law should remain undisturbed in order to insure a stability on which the lower courts and the legal profession generally may rely with some degree of confidence.

Much may be said in support of the position taken in the majority opinion herein. However, there is a sharp division in the cases.... Less than 13 years ago that question was discussed at some length in the opinion in the [*Vasu*] case, and the rule in favor of distinct causes of action was carried into the fourth paragraph of the syllabus and approved by a unanimous court....

... There is abundant and respectable authority for both ... viewpoints. Ohio has deliberately adopted one of them, and I can find no impelling reason for changing the rule at the present time....

Notes and Questions

1. Until now, this book has focused almost exclusively on federal courts implementing federal procedural rules and statutes. *Rush* is decided in state court under state law. As a general matter, federal and state courts analyze preclusion in a common-law fashion, with cases rather than rules and statutes providing the relevant principles. Hence, *Rush*'s analysis of Ohio's preclusion law can help us to understand the reasoning process and principles that federal or other state courts might adopt.

2. Why might plaintiff's counsel in *Rush* have tried the seemingly wasteful tactic of suing separately on the two claims, even if the law appeared to allow that?

3. Why did the city appeal the first judgment (in the property-damage case) to the state Supreme Court when it was for only $100?

4. In the second litigation (the personal-injury case), what is each side's position on the preclusive effect that should be given to the first case?

5. Is it fair — or, even if rough on her, in some way justifiable — to apply the new rule the court announces to Ms. Rush herself, who had not unreasonably relied on the same court's relatively recent *Vasu* opinion? Imagine yourself as her counsel, trying after everything is over to explain how the legal system can deprive her of an apparently meritorious claim for what must have been — given the effects of inflation over the past several decades — fairly serious injuries. She has a plausible complaint that she was mousetrapped: play by what we tell you are the rules, and we'll change them on you not just in the middle of the game but at the end. Is there anything that you, as a part of the system that has just seemingly pulled the rug on her, could possibly say to your client to make it seem that this is anything but an outrageous way for courts to treat a litigant? Note that this question is not about the desirability of the preclusion rule adopted by the Ohio Supreme Court in the *Rush* case; it is about whether anything justifies applying the new rule to deprive Ms. Rush of the judgment she had won in reliance on the old rule, which the same court had announced not too many years before in *Vasu*. *Cf*. Peterson v. Temple, 918 P.2d 413 (Or. 1996) (disallowing separate personal-injury and property-damage claims, but applying the decision prospectively only, because it was abandoning the old, narrower claim-preclusion rule).

Section C: Issue Preclusion

Restatement (Second) of Judgments

(Am. Law Inst. 1982)

§ 27. Issue Preclusion — General Rule

When an issue of fact or law is actually litigated and determined by a valid and final judgment, and the determination is essential to the judgment, the determination is conclusive in a subsequent action between the parties, whether on the same or a different claim.

§ 28. Exceptions to the General Rule of Issue Preclusion

Although an issue is actually litigated and determined by a valid and final judgment, and the determination is essential to the judgment, relitigation of the issue in a subsequent action between the parties is not precluded in the following circumstances:

(1) The party against whom preclusion is sought could not, as a matter of law, have obtained review of the judgment in the initial action; or

(2) The issue is one of law and (a) the two actions involve claims that are substantially unrelated, or (b) a new determination is warranted in order to take account of an intervening change in the applicable legal context or otherwise to avoid inequitable administration of the laws; or

(3) A new determination of the issue is warranted by differences in the quality or extensiveness of the procedures followed in the two courts or by factors relating to the allocation of jurisdiction between them; or

(4) The party against whom preclusion is sought had a significantly heavier burden of persuasion with respect to the issue in the initial action than in the subsequent action; the burden has shifted to his adversary; or the adversary has a significantly heavier burden than he had in the first action, or

(5) There is a clear and convincing need for a new determination of the issue (a) because of the potential adverse impact of the determination on the public interest or the interests of persons not themselves parties in the initial action, (b) because it was not sufficiently foreseeable at the time of the initial action that the issue would arise in the context of a subsequent action, or (c) because the party sought to be precluded, as a result of the conduct of his adversary or other special circumstances, did not have an adequate opportunity or incentive to obtain a full and fair adjudication in the initial action.

Notes and Questions

1. *Terminology; direct and collateral estoppel.* The basic issue-preclusion rule of *Restatement (Second)* § 27 embraces not just the collateral-estoppel doctrine referred to previously but also the little-encountered doctrine of direct estoppel. Notice the language at the end of § 27, providing for preclusion in a later action "whether on the same or a different claim." How, given claim preclusion, might there be later litigation on *the same* claim between the same parties? Easy, if not all that common: not every ground on which a claim can be dismissed precludes the plaintiff from suing on it again. A dismissal from federal court for lack of subject-matter jurisdiction, for example, based on a finding that the plaintiff was not of diverse state citizenship from the defendant, would leave the plaintiff free to bring the same claim in state court, where the same jurisdictional problem could not arise. But if the plaintiff tried (improbably) to bring it instead in another federal district court, assuming that nothing about the parties' state citizenship had changed in the meantime the plaintiff would be barred by issue preclusion from relitigating the diversity issue.

More commonly, issue preclusion comes into play when a different claim is at issue in the later litigation. "Direct estoppel," as the term was and occasionally still is used, refers to issue preclusion when the prior action was on the same claim; "collateral estoppel," still much used, refers to issue preclusion in a second action on a different claim. The *Restatement (Second)*'s articulation of the basic rule brings out the underlying similarity of direct and collateral estoppel — same idea, slightly different contexts — and, for those who choose to speak the *Restatement (Second)*'s language, makes it unnecessary to choose between the two distinct traditional terms. But others still speak traditional rather than Restatement, and pre-*Restatement (Second)* cases can remain good law whatever phrasings they used, so you may have to know both traditional terms to understand usage that you will encounter.

2. *The "actually litigated" requirement — claim vs. issue preclusion.* Why should the law require *actual* litigation and determination for *issue* preclusion, whereas it imposes *claim* preclusion for aspects of claims *not* actually litigated (as in *Rush v. City of Maple Heights*)? In other words, passing up a chance to litigate can cost you later on *claims* as it cost Ms. Rush, but passing up a chance to contest may not cost you later on *issues* — how much of a real difference is there, and does it make any sense?

3. *Determining whether an issue was actually litigated.* To illustrate some specific problems in applying *Restatement (Second)* § 27's general rule of issue preclusion in multiple-issue cases, consider the following variations on a situation involving a routine negligence case in one of the few remaining jurisdictions where plaintiff's contributory negligence is a complete defense to liability for a negligent tort. Assume — as is still the case in several states — that no compulsory-counterclaim rule exists. (If you haven't studied joinder yet, under such rules, a defendant with a claim against the plaintiff related to the plaintiff's claim against the defendant

must usually plead it in the suit brought by the plaintiff, or be precluded from bringing it in a separate action.)

- P sues and D raises the defense of contributory negligence. All issues go to the jury, which returns a general verdict (just who wins and the amount of damages, with no specific findings on issues) for P. D then sues P for damages from their accident. Can P benefit from any issue preclusion? If so, on what issues?

- Same first case, but a general verdict for D. In D's suit against P for damages, can D benefit from any issue preclusion?

- Same first case, only with a special verdict (*see* Fed. R. Civ. P. 49(a)) for D, the jury finding that D was negligent and that P was contributorily negligent. When D later sues P for damages, can P benefit from the prior finding of D's negligence?

4. *Alternative holdings.* What if any issue-preclusive effect should be given to alternative holdings each sufficient on its own to support the judgment, as if a jury made special-verdict findings that D was not negligent *and* that P was contributorily negligent? Such issues are "actually litigated and determined," but should they be regarded as "essential to the judgment"? The *Restatement (Second)* splits the baby — or tries to have it both ways — here. Comment *i* to § 27 denies preclusive effect to unreviewed alternative holdings at the trial-court level. Is it perverse to let losers relitigate when they lost on two grounds but not when they lost on just one? But then in Comment *o*, the *Restatement (Second)* favors preclusive effect for whatever an appellate court does with trial-court alternative holdings *if* an appeal is taken — for both holdings if it reaches and affirms both grounds, for just one if it reaches and affirms on one alone, etc. Is this turnaround some sort of goofy hairsplitting? Think a moment, before you go on to the next paragraph, about the possible quality of alternative holdings and the appeal incentives that losers face under different possible alternative-holding preclusion rules.

Comment *i* to § 27 gives these rationales for denying preclusive effect to trial-level alternative holdings:

> First, a determination in the alternative may not have been as carefully or rigorously considered as it would have if it had been necessary to the result, and in that sense it has some of the characteristics of dicta. Second, and of critical importance, the losing party, although entitled to appeal from both determinations, might be dissuaded from doing so because of the likelihood that at least one of them would be upheld and the other not even reached. If he were to appeal solely for the purpose of avoiding the application of the rule of issue preclusion, then the rule might be responsible for increasing the burdens of litigation on the parties and the courts rather than lightening those burdens.

But if the loser found it worthwhile to appeal for reasons other than concern about possible preclusive effect (which might happen under the contrary rule giving preclusive effect to alternative trial-level holdings), review at the appellate level reduces the problem of less careful consideration enough to support preclusion. The point, though, is a close one on which the cases and commentators are split between the *Restatement (Second)*'s approach and the position of the original *Restatement of Judgments*, which gave preclusive effect to trial-level, independently sufficient alternative holdings. The Third Circuit has come down squarely in favor of the first *Restatement*'s position. *See* Jean Alexander Cosmetics, Inc., v. L'Oreal USA, Inc., 458 F.3d 244, 250-55 (3d Cir. 2006). For a thorough discussion, see Intellectual Ventures I LLC v. Capital One Fin. Corp., 937 F.3d 1359, 1372-76 (Fed. Cir. 2019) (adopting the *Restatement (Second)*'s view but recognizing an exception when either holding is sufficient to dispose of the second case).

5. *Issue preclusion between administrative agencies and courts.* The Supreme Court has held that decisions by administrative agencies can be given preclusive effect in judicial proceedings. *See* B & B Hardware, Inc. v. Hargis Indus., Inc., 575 U.S. 138, 148 (2015) ("Both this Court's cases and the *Restatement [(Second) of Judgments]* make clear that issue preclusion is not limited to those situations in which the same issue is before two *courts*. Rather, where a single issue is before a court and an administrative agency, preclusion also often applies."). In its analysis, the Court observed that it "regularly turns to the *Restatement* . . . for a statement of the ordinary elements of issue preclusion." *Id.* On the facts, the Court concluded that preclusion was appropriate: the same legal standard applied to the agency and court proceedings; the stakes in the agency proceeding were substantial enough to expect that both sides would take the matter seriously; the agency's procedures, while somewhat different from judicial ones, did not run afoul of the relevant standard that they not be "fundamentally poor, cursory, or unfair," *id.* at 158; and the legislation under which the agency operated did not indicate that Congress wished to deny the agency's decisions preclusive effect.

6. *Exceptions to the general issue-preclusion rule. Restatement (Second)* § 28 enumerates several factors that may permit relitigation of an issue, even though it was actually litigated and determined and essential to a prior judgment. The factors seem to fall into two broad categories: indications that the proceeding in which the issue was decided before was insufficiently likely to produce a ruling worthy of preclusive effect, and public-interest considerations that support revisiting the prior determination. *See generally* DAVID L. SHAPIRO, CIVIL PROCEDURE: PRECLUSION IN CIVIL ACTIONS 56-60 (2001). Notice that the likelihood that the prior ruling itself was just plain wrong is not a factor supporting relitigation; the sheer rightness or wrongness of a determination is precisely what preclusion keeps from being reconsidered, and relitigation must be justified for some reason other than doubt about the rightness of the particular ruling.

Without going through all of § 28's exceptions, a few concrete examples may be useful. The first exception, when review is unavailable, is basic; if it was impossible for you to get an appellate court to consider possible error in a ruling against you, you should not be held to it. It can readily happen, for example, that a judge or jury finds against you on a point but you win anyway for other reasons. Someone who wins outright cannot appeal negative rulings that did not affect the ultimate result, and those rulings cannot have preclusive effect. Or a statute may make a district-court remand to state court unreviewable. *See* Kircher v. Putnam Funds Trust, 547 U.S. 633, 640-41 (2006). Classic illustrations of exceptions 2(b) for change in legal context, and 5(a) about impact on others, can involve taxpayers or importers who win once in litigation against the government as to tax liability or duty exemption, and then later decisions involving others that change or cast doubt on the legal ruling in favor of the first taxpayer or importer. Beating the government once does not immunize a taxpayer for life from taxes that others must pay, even if the issue remains the same one on which the taxpayer won; and an importer who gets a ruling that goods can come in duty-free cannot keep forever a competitive advantage if others are later held liable to pay tariffs. *See* Comm'r v. Sunnen, 333 U.S. 591 (1948) (tax liability); United States v. Stone & Downer Co., 274 U.S. 225 (1927) (import duties). Finally, the different-burden consideration in subsection 4 supports refusal to hold the government precluded if it fails to prove someone's criminal guilt beyond a reasonable doubt, but later has reason to sue the acquitted defendant for the same conduct in a civil proceeding in which it need show only a fair preponderance of the evidence.

7. *Nonmutual issue preclusion in favor of prior nonparties.* Issue preclusion often arises when the same parties litigate against each other in two successive cases, but it may also come into play when someone who was not a party to the first case seeks to take advantage of rulings against its present adversary, a party to both proceedings. The following case is a leading decision on the modern approach, followed in about two-thirds of American jurisdictions, to what is often called nonmutual issue preclusion.

PARKLANE HOSIERY CO. V. SHORE

439 U.S. 322 (1979)

■ MR. JUSTICE STEWART delivered the opinion of the Court.

[Respondent brought this stockholder's class action in the District Court for damages and other relief against petitioners, a corporation, its officers, directors, and stockholders, who allegedly had issued a materially false and misleading proxy statement in violation of the federal securities laws and Securities and Exchange Commission (SEC) regulations. Before the action came to trial the SEC sued the same defendants in the District Court alleging that the proxy statement was materially false and misleading in essentially the same respects as respondent had claimed. The District Court after a nonjury trial entered a declaratory judgment for the SEC, and the Court of Appeals affirmed. Respondent in this case then moved for partial summary judgment against petitioners, asserting that they were collaterally estopped from relitigating the issues that had been resolved against them in the SEC suit. The District Court denied the motion on the ground that such an application of collateral estoppel would deny petitioners their Seventh Amendment right to a jury trial. The Court of Appeals reversed.*]

This case presents the question whether a party who has had issues of fact adjudicated adversely to it in an equitable action may be collaterally estopped from relitigating the same issues before a jury in a subsequent legal action brought against it by a new party. . . .

I

The threshold question to be considered is whether . . . the petitioners can be precluded from relitigating facts resolved adversely to them in a prior equitable proceeding with another party under the general law of collateral estoppel. Specifically, we must determine whether a litigant who was not a party to a prior judgment may nevertheless use that judgment "offensively" to prevent a defendant from relitigating issues resolved in the earlier proceeding.[4]

A

Collateral estoppel, like the related doctrine of res judicata,[5] has the dual purpose of protecting litigants from the burden of relitigating an identical issue with the same party or his privy and of promoting judicial economy by preventing needless litigation. Until relatively recently, however, the scope of collateral estoppel was limited by the doctrine of mutuality of parties. Under this mutuality doctrine, neither party could use a prior judgment as an estoppel against the other unless both parties were bound by the judgment. Based on the premise that it is somehow unfair to allow a party to use a prior judgment when he himself would not be so bound,[7] the mutuality requirement provided a party who had litigated and lost in a previous action an opportunity to relitigate identical issues with new parties.

By failing to recognize the obvious difference in position between a party who has never litigated an issue and one who has fully litigated and lost, the

---

* This statement of facts is taken verbatim from the syllabus of the case prepared by the Reporter of Decisions. The syllabus often contains a useful summary of the opinion, but is not officially part of the opinion itself. — ED.

4. In this context, offensive use of collateral estoppel occurs when the plaintiff seeks to foreclose the defendant from litigating an issue the defendant has previously litigated unsuccessfully in an action with another party. Defensive use occurs when a defendant seeks to prevent a plaintiff from asserting a claim the plaintiff has previously litigated and lost against another defendant.

5. Under the doctrine of res judicata, a judgment on the merits in a prior suit bars a second suit involving the same parties or their privies based on the same cause of action. Under the doctrine of collateral estoppel, on the other hand, the second action is upon a different cause of action and the judgment in the prior suit precludes relitigation of issues actually litigated and necessary to the outcome of the first action.

7. It is a violation of due process for a judgment to be binding on a litigant who was not a party or a privy and therefore has never had an opportunity to be heard.

mutuality requirement was criticized almost from its inception.[8] Recognizing the validity of this criticism, the Court in *Blonder-Tongue Laboratories, Inc. v. University of Illinois Foundation*, 402 U.S. 313 (1971), abandoned the mutuality requirement, at least in cases where a patentee seeks to relitigate the validity of a patent after a federal court in a previous lawsuit has already declared it invalid. The "broader question" before the Court, however, was "whether it is any longer tenable to afford a litigant more than one full and fair opportunity for judicial resolution of the same issue." The Court strongly suggested a negative answer to that question:

> In any lawsuit where a defendant, because of the mutuality principle, is forced to present a complete defense on the merits to a claim which the plaintiff has fully litigated and lost in a prior action, there is an arguable misallocation of resources. To the extent the defendant in the second suit may not win by asserting, without contradiction, that the plaintiff had fully and fairly, but unsuccessfully, litigated the same claim in the prior suit, the defendant's time and money are diverted from alternative uses — productive or otherwise — to relitigation of a decided issue. And, still assuming that the issue was resolved correctly in the first suit, there is reason to be concerned about the plaintiff's allocation of resources. Permitting repeated litigation of the same issue as long as the supply of unrelated defendants holds out reflects either the aura of the gaming table or "a lack of discipline and of disinterestedness on the part of the lower courts, hardly a worthy or wise basis for fashioning rules of procedure." Although neither judges, the parties, nor the adversary system performs perfectly in all cases, the requirement of determining whether the party against whom an estoppel is asserted had a full and fair opportunity to litigate is a most significant safeguard.

B

The *Blonder-Tongue* case involved defensive use of collateral estoppel — a plaintiff was estopped from asserting a claim that the plaintiff had previously litigated and lost against another defendant. The present case, by contrast, involves offensive use of collateral estoppel — a plaintiff is seeking to estop a defendant from relitigating the issues which the defendant previously litigated and lost against another plaintiff. In both the offensive and defensive use situations, the party against whom estoppel is asserted has litigated and lost in an earlier action. Nevertheless, several reasons have been advanced why the two situations should be treated differently.

---

8. This criticism was summarized in the Court's opinion in *Blonder-Tongue Laboratories, Inc. v. University of Illinois Foundation*, 402 U.S. 313, 322-27 (1971). The opinion of Justice Traynor for a unanimous California Supreme Court in *Bernhard v. Bank of America National Trust & Savings Ass'n*, 122 P.2d 892, 895 (Cal. 1942), made the point succinctly:

> No satisfactory rationalization has been advanced for the requirement of mutuality. Just why a party who was not bound by a previous action should be precluded from asserting it as res judicata against a party who was bound by it is difficult to comprehend.

First, offensive use of collateral estoppel does not promote judicial economy in the same manner as defensive use does. Defensive use of collateral estoppel precludes a plaintiff from relitigating identical issues by merely "switching adversaries." Thus defensive collateral estoppel gives a plaintiff a strong incentive to join all potential defendants in the first action if possible. Offensive use of collateral estoppel, on the other hand, creates precisely the opposite incentive. Since a plaintiff will be able to rely on a previous judgment against a defendant but will not be bound by that judgment if the defendant wins, the plaintiff has every incentive to adopt a "wait and see" attitude, in the hope that the first action by another plaintiff will result in a favorable judgment. Thus offensive use of collateral estoppel will likely increase rather than decrease the total amount of litigation, since potential plaintiffs will have everything to gain and nothing to lose by not intervening in the first action.[13]

A second argument against offensive use of collateral estoppel is that it may be unfair to a defendant. If a defendant in the first action is sued for small or nominal damages, he may have little incentive to defend vigorously, particularly if future suits are not foreseeable. . . . Allowing offensive collateral estoppel may also be unfair to a defendant if the judgment relied upon as a basis for the estoppel is itself inconsistent with one or more previous judgments in favor of the defendant.[14] Still another situation where it might be unfair to apply offensive estoppel is where the second action affords the defendant procedural opportunities unavailable in the first action that could readily cause a different result.[15]

C

We have concluded that the preferable approach for dealing with these problems in the federal courts is not to preclude the use of offensive

---

13. The *Restatement (Second) of Judgments* § 88(3) (Tent. Draft No. 2, Apr. 15, 1975) [renumbered § 29(3) in final version — ED.] provides that application of collateral estoppel may be denied if the party asserting it "could have effected joinder in the first action between himself and his present adversary."

14. In Professor Currie's familiar example, a railroad collision injures 50 passengers all of whom bring separate actions against the railroad. After the railroad wins the first 25 suits, a plaintiff wins in suit 26. Professor Currie argues that offensive use of collateral estoppel should not be applied so as to allow plaintiffs 27 through 50 automatically to recover. Currie, *Mutuality of Estoppel: Limits of the* Bernhard *Doctrine,* 9 STAN. L. REV. 281, 304 (1957). *See Restatement (Second) of Judgments* § 88(4) [renumbered § 29(4) — ED.].

15. If, for example, the defendant in the first action was forced to defend in an inconvenient forum and therefore was unable to engage in full scale discovery or call witnesses, application of offensive collateral estoppel may be unwarranted. Indeed, differences in available procedures may sometimes justify not allowing a prior judgment to have estoppel effect in a subsequent action even between the same parties, or where defensive estoppel is asserted against a plaintiff who has litigated and lost. The problem of unfairness is particularly acute in cases of offensive estoppel, however, because the defendant against whom estoppel is asserted typically will not have chosen the forum in the first action. *See id.* § 88(2) [renumbered § 29(2) — ED.] and Comment *d.*

collateral estoppel, but to grant trial courts broad discretion to determine when it should be applied.[16] The general rule should be that in cases where a plaintiff could easily have joined in the earlier action or where, either for the reasons discussed above or for other reasons, the application of offensive estoppel would be unfair to a defendant, a trial judge should not allow the use of offensive collateral estoppel.

In the present case, however, none of the circumstances that might justify reluctance to allow the offensive use of collateral estoppel is present. The application of offensive collateral estoppel will not here reward a private plaintiff who could have joined in the previous action, since the respondent probably could not have joined in the injunctive action brought by the SEC even had he so desired. Similarly, there is no unfairness to the petitioners in applying offensive collateral estoppel in this case. First, in light of the serious allegations made in the SEC's complaint against the petitioners, as well as the foreseeability of subsequent private suits that typically follow a successful Government judgment, the petitioners had every incentive to litigate the SEC lawsuit fully and vigorously. Second, the judgment in the SEC action was not inconsistent with any previous decision. Finally, there will in the respondent's action be no procedural opportunities available to the petitioners that were unavailable in the first action of a kind that might be likely to cause a different result.[19]

We conclude, therefore, that none of the considerations that would justify a refusal to allow the use of offensive collateral estoppel is present in this case. Since the petitioners received a "full and fair" opportunity to litigate their claims in the SEC action, the contemporary law of collateral estoppel leads inescapably to the conclusion that the petitioners are collaterally estopped from relitigating the question of whether the proxy statement was materially false and misleading. . . .

The judgment of the Court of Appeals is affirmed.

■ MR. JUSTICE REHNQUIST, dissenting. . . .

. . . I . . . would not sanction the use of collateral estoppel in this case. . . . In my view, it is "unfair" to apply offensive collateral estoppel where the party who is sought to be estopped has not had an opportunity to have the facts of his case determined by a jury. Since in this case petitioners were not entitled to a jury trial in the Securities and Exchange Commission (SEC)

---

16. This is essentially the approach of *id.* § 88 [renumbered § 29 — ED.], which recognizes that "the distinct trend if not the clear weight of recent authority is to the effect that there is no intrinsic difference between 'offensive' as distinct from 'defensive' issue preclusion, although a stronger showing that the prior opportunity to litigate was adequate may be required in the former situation than the latter." *Id.* Reporter's Note, at 99.

19. It is true, of course, that the petitioners in the present action would be entitled to a jury trial of the issues bearing on whether the proxy statement was materially false and misleading had the SEC action never been brought . . . . But the presence or absence of a jury as factfinder is basically neutral, quite unlike, for example, the necessity of defending the first lawsuit in an inconvenient forum.

lawsuit, I would not estop them from relitigating the issues determined in the SEC suit before a jury in the private action.

Notes and Questions

1. *How essential is "essential"?* The standard articulation is that for issue-preclusive effect a finding must have been "essential to the judgment." RESTATEMENT (SECOND) OF JUDGMENTS § 27 (AM. LAW INST. 1982). Just how crucial a finding has to have been has split a Fourth Circuit panel and may divide some of the federal courts of appeals. In *In re Microsoft Corp. Antitrust Litigation,* 355 F.3d 322 (4th Cir. 2004), private plaintiffs sued Microsoft for antitrust violations and sought to take advantage of findings reached in the Government's antitrust proceeding against Microsoft, which had been affirmed in part by the District of Columbia Circuit. The district court applied a standard that gave preclusive effect to findings that were "supportive of the judgment."

All three judges on the Fourth Circuit panel agreed that standard was too lax and that findings had to be in some way "necessary" to be given preclusive effect. The majority held that the appropriate standard was "critical and necessary"; the dissenter, claiming support from two other circuits, argued for a somewhat less demanding standard of " 'distinctly put in issue and directly determined' and a material element of th[e] judgment." Judge Niemeyer's majority opinion, although recognizing the discretion afforded district judges by *Parklane Hosiery,* argued that the possible unfairness of offensive nonmutual issue preclusion required that the criteria for it be applied strictly. It also expressed concern that the "supportive of" standard would unfairly give preclusive effect to some findings that the party resisting preclusion had little or no real chance to get reviewed by an appellate court in the prior litigation. Judge Gregory's partial dissent urged that his intermediate standard would serve the purposes of preclusion to prevent burdensome relitigation and inconsistent outcomes, while adequately protecting those in Microsoft's position from unfair application of offensive preclusion.

A different possible reason for regarding a prior determination as not "essential" or "necessary" to the prior judgment, though, is generally rejected: if a court decided a case on a broad ground rather than on an available narrower ground, that is usually not regarded as sufficient cause to deny issue-preclusive effect to the ruling on the broader ground. Courts should generally "resist[ ]" the "tempt[ation] to speculate that a prior decision could have been rested on narrower grounds than those actually chosen, so that resolution of the broader issues was not necessary to the decision. . . . There is little reason to infer that broadly based decisions are reached with less care than narrow decisions . . . ." 18 CHARLES ALAN WRIGHT ET AL., FEDERAL PRACTICE AND PROCEDURE § 4421, at 594-96 (3d ed. 2016) (footnotes omitted). "We do not ask whether the resolution of the issue was necessary to reach the same outcome; rather, the inquiry is whether the issue was necessary to the decision actually rendered." Manganella v. Evanston Ins. Co., 700 F.3d 585, 594 (1st Cir. 2012).

2. *Historical exceptions to the mutuality requirement.* Just as nonmutual preclusion is subject to the many exceptions enumerated in *Restatement (Second)* §§ 28-29, the mutuality requirement even in its heyday was not absolute. Most prominently, preclusion — sometimes regarded as being of the claim rather than issue variety — applied to prevent anomaly in some indemnity situations. If P sued employee D1 and lost, then sued D1's employer, D2, on a respondeat-superior theory for the harm allegedly done by D1, letting P's second action proceed would produce a dilemma if P won. Either D2 could sue D1 for the reimbursement allowed D2 by law, which would effectively render D1's victory against P meaningless; or D2's claim against D1 could be barred, depriving D2 of its indemnity right without D2 being heard on its claim as a result of an action to which D2 was not a party. The solution while the mutuality requirement prevailed was to cut P off at the pass, treating his defeat in his first action against D1 as barring his second action against D2. *See* DAVID L. SHAPIRO, CIVIL PROCEDURE: PRECLUSION IN CIVIL ACTIONS 106-07 (2001). Under modern approaches followed in a majority of American jurisdictions, D2 could take advantage of issue preclusion as to common issues decided against P in the first action. The result could be dismissal of P's suit against D2, on grounds not of claim preclusion but of issue preclusion on an issue essential to P's case, such as negligence or causation.

3. *Exceptions to nonmutual issue preclusion.* The *Restatement (Second)*, having dealt with basic issue preclusion and its exceptions in §§ 27-28, then addresses the *Parklane* problem of nonmutual issue preclusion and exceptions thereto in § 29:

§ 29. Issue Preclusion in Subsequent Litigation with Others

A party precluded from relitigating an issue with an opposing party, in accordance with §§ 27 and 28, is also precluded from doing so with another person unless the fact that he lacked full and fair opportunity to litigate the issue in the first action or other circumstances justify affording him an opportunity to relitigate the issue. The circumstances to which consideration[ ] should be given include those enumerated in § 28 and also whether:

. . .

(2) The forum in the second action affords the party against whom preclusion is asserted procedural opportunities in the presentation and determination of the issue that were not available in the first action and could likely result in the issue being differently determined;

(3) The person seeking to invoke favorable preclusion, or to avoid unfavorable preclusion, could have effected joinder in the first action between himself and his present adversary;

(4) The determination relied on as preclusive was itself inconsistent with another determination of the same issue;

(5) The prior determination . . . apparently was based on a compromise verdict or finding; . . .

(7) The issue is one of law and treating it as conclusively determined would inappropriately foreclose opportunity for obtaining reconsideration of the legal rule upon which it was based;

(8) Other compelling circumstances make it appropriate that the party be permitted to relitigate the issue.

The *Restatement*'s laundry list in § 29 of grounds for denying nonmutual preclusion, in addition to those in § 28 that would support denying it between the same parties, is long enough that an attempt to give examples for all would be pedagogical malpractice. The *Parklane Hosiery* majority opinion gives several useful ones in its part I-B. The exception for inconsistent determinations in § 29(4) can be quite significant in practice, because a defendant anticipating multiple related suits may be able to settle stronger claims and litigate weaker ones to lay a foundation for an argument of inconsistency if it eventually loses to one or more plaintiffs on a common issue. In general, the *Restatement* avoids broad categorical approaches, as the Supreme Court reflects in its refusal to ban entirely the use of nonmutual offensive issue preclusion. The Court limited *Parklane Hosiery,* though, in a later decision holding the federal government not subject to nonmutual offensive issue preclusion, at least as to questions of law, because of the public interest in development of legal doctrine by consideration of issues in multiple courts. United States v. Mendoza, 464 U.S. 154 (1984).

4. *"Privity" and adequate representation as bases for preclusion against nonparties.* This section has dealt with situations in which prior nonparties may *benefit* from issue preclusion. *Parklane Hosiery*'s footnote 7 refers to the bedrock principle that due process forbids binding effect *against* one "who was not a party *or a privy* and therefore has never had an opportunity to be heard" (emphasis added). "Privity" refers to "a relationship between two parties that is 'sufficiently close' so as to bind them both to an initial determination, at which only one of them was present. 'Privity' is merely the term used by the courts to indicate that the relationship between the one who is a party on the record and another is close enough to include that other within the scope of claim or issue preclusion." 18 JAMES WM. MOORE ET AL., MOORE'S FEDERAL PRACTICE § 132.04[1][b][iii], at 132-147 to -148 (3d ed. 2019) (footnotes omitted). Types of relationships that can support findings of privity include successorship to a property interest and control of the original suit. The *Restatement (Second) of Judgments*, which avoids the term "privity" in favor of focusing on the "substantive legal relationships resulting in preclusion," enumerates many such relationships in its §§ 43-63.

In addition, due process can permit preclusion against one not individually named as a party whose interests were adequately represented in a prior litigation. This vital principle is the foundation of the modern class action and other forms of representative proceedings. *See* Chapter Twelve (on class actions); Chapter Nine (on personal jurisdiction, including notice and adequacy of representation in non-class representative litigation).

5. *Rejection of the doctrine of "virtual representation."* Just because due process may allow preclusion against someone not named as a party but whose interests were adequately represented in a prior case does not mean that preclusion law, which is largely decisional and nonconstitutional, will apply preclusion whenever due process might not forbid it. In *Taylor v. Sturgell*, 553 U.S. 880 (2008), for example, the Supreme Court rejected the doctrine of "virtual representation." Under this doctrine, which some lower federal courts had applied fairly expansively, a prior judgment could have claim- or issue-preclusive effect against a prior nonparty if a court concluded that there had been "virtual representation" of the nonparty's interests by a prior party. *Taylor v. Sturgell* listed six established situations — such as agreement to be bound, succession in interest (*see supra* Note 4), proper class actions (*see* Chapter Twelve), and control of the prior litigation — in which a prior judgment might preclude a nonparty. But, as a matter of the federal decisional law of preclusion, the Court unanimously rejected the idea that beyond the six exceptions a judgment can bind a nonparty.

6. *The effect of failure to intervene. Parklane Hosiery* suggests that a nonparty who fails to intervene in the first suit may not be able to benefit from nonmutual offensive preclusion. But what of a nonparty who later wants to challenge the outcome in the first suit? Must that person intervene in order to prevent the winner of the first suit from arguing that the issue should be considered settled? In *Martin v. Wilks*, 490 U.S. 755 (1989), the Supreme Court held that under existing rules intervention could not be required in the latter situation.

7. Martin v. Wilks, *the Opportunity to Intervene, and Preclusion. Martin v. Wilks* involved two consecutive suits against the city of Birmingham, Alabama. In the first suit, a group of African American firefighters alleged that the city had discriminated against them in promotions. That suit resulted in a consent decree, which is essentially a judgment negotiated by the parties and approved by the court. The decree obligated the city to promote African Americans preferentially in certain situations. A group of white firefighters then sued the city, arguing that the preferential promotion policy violated *their* rights. The city argued that because the white firefighters had notice of the original suit, and could have intervened, they should be precluded from attacking the consent decree.

The Supreme Court, 5-4, rejected the city's argument. It held that the white firefighters could not be bound by the earlier judgment:

> We begin with the words of Justice Brandeis in *Chase National Bank v. Norwalk*, 291 U.S. 431, 441 (1934):
>
>> The law does not impose upon any person absolutely entitled to a hearing the burden of voluntary intervention in a suit to which he is a stranger. . . . Unless duly summoned to appear in a legal proceeding, a person not a privy may rest assured that a judgment recovered therein will not affect his legal rights.
>
> While these words were written before the adoption of the Federal Rules of Civil Procedure, we think the Rules incorporate the same

principle; a party seeking a judgment binding on another cannot obligate that person to intervene; he must be joined.... Accordingly, Rule 19(a) provides for mandatory joinder in circumstances where a judgment rendered in the absence of a person may "leave ... persons already parties subject to a substantial risk of incurring ... inconsistent obligations...."* Rule 19(b) sets forth the factors to be considered by a court in deciding whether to allow an action to proceed in the absence of an interested party.

Joinder as a party, rather than knowledge of a lawsuit and an opportunity to intervene, is the method by which potential parties are subjected to the jurisdiction of the court and bound by a judgment or decree. The parties to a lawsuit presumably know better than anyone else the nature and scope of relief sought in the action, and at whose expense such relief might be granted. It makes sense, therefore, to place on them a burden of bringing in additional parties where such a step is indicated, rather than placing on potential additional parties a duty to intervene when they acquire knowledge of the lawsuit..... [490 U.S. at 763-65.]

Parklane Hosiery and *Restatement* § 29(3) can be read as at least usually disapproving of nonmutual offensive issue preclusion if someone who now seeks to benefit from it could easily have joined in the earlier action, as by intervening, but did not. *Martin v. Wilks,* interpreting Rule 24, refuses to require someone who could intervene to do so in order to avoid being bound by an adverse decree. Does the later case undercut the apparent rule of *Parklane Hosiery* and the *Restatement*, or are there reasons to require nonparties to take the initiative and intervene if possible in situations like *Parklane Hosiery* while not requiring that they do so in cases like *Martin v. Wilks*?

Congress partially overruled the holding of *Martin v. Wilks* in the 1991 Civil Rights Act, prohibiting subsequent challenges to employment-discrimination consent decrees and litigated judgments if the challenger had notice of the first suit and an opportunity to intervene. 42 U.S.C. § 2000e-2(n). Is that statute constitutional? Put differently, is the result in *Martin v. Wilks* constitutionally compelled?

Section D: Interjurisdictional Preclusion

The foregoing sections have treated the preclusive effects to be given judgments of one court system in later litigation within the same system. In the United States, though, the same question can arise when the later litigation takes place elsewhere — with the first judgment rendered by the courts of one state and its preclusive effects being in question in the courts

---

* The 2007 amendments slightly altered Rule 19(a), which now requires joinder, if feasible, of a party whose absence may "leave an existing party subject to a substantial risk of incurring ... inconsistent obligations." — Ed.

of another state, or in the federal courts, or with a federal court having rendered the first judgment and the preclusion issue arising in a state-court system or a different federal court. The answer to the question of how to come at determining preclusive effect in such situations turns out to be basically simple, although with some wrinkles and getting there by different routes depending on whether the court system rendering the first judgment (often referred to as F1, for the first forum) was federal or that of a particular state: the court system entertaining the second action (F2) is to give it the same preclusive effect — no more, no less — as it would have received if the second case had been filed in F1. Thus F2 is not supposed to apply its own preclusion law (although many judges and lawyers may overlook this rule), but rather to look to F1 as the *source* of applicable preclusion law. This approach when followed has the virtue of giving a judgment the same preclusive effect everywhere in the country, rather than varying depending on the preclusion law of whatever system happens to be F2. Preclusion principles across American jurisdictions tend to be fairly uniform, with the *Restatement (Second) of Judgments* quite influential; but some significant variations remain. For excellent discussion of interjurisdictional preclusion, including the finding that many state courts have seemed unaware of the very clearly established requirement to apply the preclusion law that would govern in F1, see Howard M. Erichson, *Interjurisdictional Preclusion,* 96 MICH. L. REV. 945 (1998).

When F1 is a state court, the route to applicability elsewhere of the preclusion law that would be followed in F1 starts with the Full Faith and Credit Clause of Article IV, Section 1 of the United States Constitution:

> Full Faith and Credit shall be given in each State to the . . . judicial Proceedings of every other State. And the Congress may by general Laws prescribe the Manner in which such . . . Proceedings shall be proved, and the Effect thereof.

Exercising its authority under this section, and also its powers to legislate concerning the federal courts and United States territories and possessions, Congress long ago passed a provision that in present form appears at 28 U.S.C. § 1738:

> . . . The . . . judicial proceedings of any court of any . . . State, Territory or Possession . . . shall have the same full faith and credit in every court within the United States and its Territories and Possessions as they have by law or usage in the courts of such State, Territory or Possession from which they are taken.

Two key points to note about this statute are its direction to F2s to look to the preclusion law of F1, and also its mandate to "every court within the United States" — federal, state, territorial, etc. — to look to F1 for applicable preclusion law when F1 was a court of a state, territory, or possession. Absent some specific provision to the contrary, that includes when F2 is a federal court and when F1, a state court, dealt with a federal-law matter — even if the federal court thinks the state court got the federal law wrong. The remedy of the federal-law loser is not to try getting a lower federal court to disregard the state court's federal-law ruling but to seek review of the state court's judgment in higher state courts and the Supreme Court of the United States.

That leaves what to do about judgments of federal courts, to which the Constitution's Full Faith and Credit Clause does not speak and for whose preclusive effect Congress has not legislated. The established rule is that federal common law governs the effect of federal-court judgments, in federal and state courts alike (but get ready for a significant wrinkle). An example of such federal common law is the Supreme Court's decision in *Parklane Hosiery* (*supra* p. 333) not to require mutuality of estoppel for a prior nonparty to benefit from issue-preclusive effect of a federal court's judgment. When the judgment of a federal court as F1 is on a federal-law matter, the federal preclusion law applicable in F2 is uniform federal common law of the sort articulated in *Parklane Hosiery*. But when the F1 federal court decided a state-law matter, although federal common law determines the preclusive effects to be given to its judgment (here comes the wrinkle), the *content* of that federal common law will ordinarily be borrowed from the preclusion law of the state where the F1 federal court sat. This, in brief, is the holding of *Semtek International Inc. v. Lockheed Martin Corp.*, 531 U.S. 497 (2001). *Semtek* also strongly emphasized the general principle of federal common law governing the preclusive effect of federal-court judgments:

> Since state, rather than federal, substantive law is at issue there is no need for a uniform federal rule. And indeed, nationwide uniformity in the substance of the matter is better served by having the same [preclusion] rule (the state rule) apply whether the [judgment has been rendered] by a state or a federal court. This is, it seems to us, a classic case for adopting, as the federally prescribed rule of decision, the law that would be applied by state courts in the State in which the federal diversity court sits. . . . [A]ny other rule would produce . . . "forum-shopping . . . and . . . inequitable administration of the laws" . . . since filing in, or removing to, federal court would be encouraged by the divergent effects that the litigants would anticipate [from judgments of state vs. federal courts].
>
> This federal reference to state law will not obtain, of course, in situations in which the state law is incompatible with federal interests. If, for example, state law did not accord claim-preclusive effect to dismissals for willful violation of discovery orders, federal courts' interest in the integrity of their own processes might justify a contrary federal rule. [*Id.* at 508-09.]

Applying *Semtek*, the Tennessee Supreme Court has held that state claim-preclusion law rather than Federal Rule of Civil Procedure 41(a)(1)(B) governed as to the effect of plaintiff's having taken two voluntary dismissals of state-law claims, once in California state court and once in federal district court in Tennessee, when the plaintiff filed a third time in Tennessee state court. Cooper v. Glasser, 419 S.W.3d 924 (Tenn. 2013). The Federal Rule gives a second voluntary dismissal the effect of "an adjudication on the merits"; the counterpart Tennessee rule permits plaintiffs to take two voluntary dismissals "without prejudice." With the court viewing state preclusion law as governing, plaintiff could proceed in Tennessee state court. What if the plaintiff's claims had been based on federal rather than state law?

Questions

Suppose that State A follows the *Restatement (Second)*'s approach to nonmutual issue preclusion, while State B is one of the significant minority (about a third of the states; Florida and Michigan are prominent examples) that still adhere to the old requirement of mutuality. We have also seen what the Supreme Court has had to say in *Parklane Hosiery* about allowing nonmutual issue preclusion as a matter of federal common law when it governs, and that decision remains valid precedent. In both of the following questions, assume that none of the reasons for exceptions to issue preclusion enumerated in *Restatement (Second)* § 28(1)-(5) or § 29(1)-(8) is present, and that the issues in question are identical and were actually litigated and determined and essential to the first judgment, which has become final. Also assume proper jurisdiction and venue.

- Passenger 1 sues Driver 1 on a state tort claim in state court in State A and wins a verdict that necessarily includes findings in Passenger 1's favor on negligence, causation, etc. Passenger 2, a victim of the same accident, then sues Driver 1 on a state tort claim arising out of the same accident in state court in State B. What if any issue-preclusive effect should the courts of State B give to the common issues that were litigated in the state-court proceeding in State A, and why?

- Passenger 3 sues Driver 2 on a state tort claim, arising from a completely different accident, in a diversity action in *federal* court in State B. Passenger 3 wins a verdict that necessarily involves findings in Passenger 3's favor on negligence, causation, etc. Passenger 4, a victim in the same accident as Passenger 3, then sues Driver 2 on a state tort claim in a diversity action in *federal* court in State A. What if any issue-preclusive effect should the federal court in State A give to the common issues that were litigated in the federal-court proceeding in State B, and why?

SECTION E: LAW OF THE CASE AND STARE DECISIS

1. Law of the Case

So far, what we have covered in this chapter has involved a first case litigated far enough to be regarded as "final" for purposes of preclusion, and its preclusive effects in a different case. Such preclusion, when it applies, is rock-hard — no reopening in the second litigation, period, even if the determination in question appears to have been quite wrong. Of course, many of the exceptions to preclusion try to identify types of situations in which there may be reasons to deny preclusive effect, such as informality of the prior proceeding or difference in burden; but if the situation falls into no such category, the possibility — even the overwhelming likelihood — that the determination in the prior litigation was just plain wrong is not reason to deny it preclusive effect. Message to losers: appeal, rather than expecting to attack the ruling in another litigation.

Whether to adhere to a prior determination, even if it may have been wrong, can also be an issue in successive stages of a single multi-stage litigation, as when a case goes up on interlocutory appeal, a panel decides an issue, the trial court completes its work on the case, and the case comes up on appeal after final judgment — perhaps to a different panel that might not have decided the first appeal the same way. Similar situations may arise at the trial level, as when a trial judge rules on an issue and a later judge who gets the case doubts the rightness of the ruling — or even the same judge, continuing to sit on the case, has second thoughts about the ruling. The strong, but less than rock-hard, doctrine called *law of the case* can come into play in such instances.

This doctrine "posits that when a court decides upon a rule of law, that decision should continue to govern the same issues in subsequent stages in the same case." Christianson v. Colt Indus. Operating Corp., 486 U.S. 800, 816 (1988) (internal quotation marks omitted). Unlike preclusion, though, law of the case is not always "a limit on a court's power to revisit an issue if the court feels such review is necessary"; still, a court should not "revisit its own decisions . . . absent extraordinary circumstances showing that the prior decision was clearly wrong and would work a manifest injustice." 18 JAMES WM. MOORE ET AL., MOORE'S FEDERAL PRACTICE § 134.21[1], at 134-56 (3d ed. 2019) (footnotes omitted). One such circumstance would naturally be change in applicable law, as determined in another case that the court should now follow. Other factors that could support reconsideration include the availability of new evidence and the sense that the earlier decision was not just wrong but manifestly unjust.

A few clarifications may be important to avoid confusion about law of the case. First, hierarchical relationships between courts are important: an appellate panel's interlocutory ruling binds the trial court on remand (absent, say, a supreme court decision to the contrary in a different case), even if it does not invariably bind a later appellate panel in the same case. But a trial court's ruling is not law of the case on appeal, where trial-court decisions are reviewed for error. Second, many decisions are managerial or provisional in nature, such as setting discovery deadlines or ruling on a request for a preliminary as opposed to final injunction. Such decisions are much more subject to reconsideration than firm adjudication of legal issues. Parties who have lost on fairly definitive but not yet formally final legal rulings might be all too inclined to try to reopen them before appeal if they could, and the law-of-the-case doctrine serves as both a warning to parties not to seek reconsideration all the time — and as some protection for courts against parties' inclination to pester them with requests to revisit considered rulings.

2. Stare Decisis

Beyond the doctrines of claim and issue preclusion and law of the case that are conventionally regarded as coming under the heading of former adjudication, a court's decision on an issue of law may of course have precedential effect in other litigation. The practice of not regarding already-litigated legal issues as up for grabs anew every time they come up is often referred to with the label of *stare decisis*, Latin for "to stand by things decided." Justice Zimmerman's dissenting opinion (*supra* pp. 327-28) in *Rush v. City of Maple Heights* argues that the reasons for abandoning stare decisis in that case are not persuasive enough; the majority and the concurrence by Justice Stewart (coincidentally, the father of United States Supreme Court Associate Justice Potter Stewart, author of the *Parklane Hosiery* majority opinion) find varying reasons to justify departure from precedent. Stare decisis, although not absolute, is important for several reasons including predictability, economy from not relitigating all legal issues all the time, and consistency in treating similarly situated parties alike. It can mean, though, that you are bound by a rule of law established by others in a different case without your having had anything to say about it.

Courts sometimes articulate criteria for overruling prior precedents. In *Janus v. American Federation of State, County, & Municipal Employees*, 585 U.S. —, 138 S. Ct. 2448 (2018), the Supreme Court overruled *Abood v. Detroit Board of Education*, 431 U.S. 209 (1977), which had permitted requiring non-union members to pay an "agency fee" to a union representing government workers for activities "germane" to the union's collective-bargaining activities, but not its political work. The majority listed factors relevant to whether stare decisis should be observed: the quality of the prior decision's reasoning, its workability, subsequent legal and factual developments, and real-world reliance on the precedent.

As with law of the case, hierarchical relationships between courts are important in determining the strength of a legal precedent. A lower court may not disregard (although it may distinguish) a legal holding of a court directly above it, but a court may reconsider and overrule its own precedent if it concludes that the reasons for departing from stare decisis are strong enough. And precedent from courts outside one's jurisdiction may be persuasive but is not binding; a federal court of appeals, and even a district court, may reject the position of another circuit. Also, in trial courts with multiple judges, a single trial judge's ruling on a legal issue in one case may not bind all other judges of the same court. As the Supreme Court has stated of federal district courts, "federal district judges, sitting as sole adjudicators, lack authority to render precedential decisions binding other judges, even members of the same court." Am. Elec. Power Co. v. Connecticut, 564 U.S.

410, 428 (2011). By contrast, a decision by a panel of an intermediate appellate court will often set the law for the full court, unless it is overruled by the court sitting en banc, reversed or disapproved by a court of last resort, or changed by legislation.

CHAPTER EIGHT

JOINDER OF CLAIMS AND PARTIES

Until now, this book has for the most part assumed that litigation is a simple affair, with one plaintiff pursuing one claim against one defendant. In many cases, that assumption is unrealistic. The plaintiff may have more than one claim to assert against the defendant; the defendant may have one or more claims to pursue against the plaintiff; the controversy may involve others who allegedly either harmed the plaintiff (potential additional defendants) or were harmed by the defendant (potential additional plaintiffs). Some of these parties may have still more claims to assert.

As a case gets bigger, it gets more expensive, more cumbersome, and more difficult for the decision-maker to make all of the right determinations. On the other hand, a more truncated proceeding may lead to incomplete justice and a multiplicity of lawsuits. If we expand the lawsuit beyond the one-claim, two-party model, what principle should define the scope and limits of the expansion? Should it be efficiency: permit expansion only when the benefits outweigh the costs? How about accuracy: permit expansion unless the case becomes so unwieldy that the decisionmaker cannot render a judgment based on reason and law? Some other principle?

In thinking about these questions, you must also account for a bedrock constitutional principle: persons must be afforded notice and an opportunity to be heard when a court takes action affecting their legal interests. In the American system, the usual way in which that opportunity to be heard is given effect is by means of *joining* the affected person as a party in the case. As a general rule, a person who is not a party to a case is not bound by the judgment in that case. As Justice Brandeis observed long ago, "Unless duly summoned to appear in a legal proceeding, a person not a privy may rest assured that a judgment recovered therein will not affect his legal rights." Chase Nat'l Bank v. City of Norwalk, 291 U.S. 431, 441 (1934). Chief Justice Rehnquist expressed the same principle more recently: "[T]he general rule [is] that a person cannot be deprived of his legal rights in a proceeding to which he is not a party.... Joinder as a party, rather than knowledge of a lawsuit and an opportunity to intervene, is the method by which potential parties are subjected to the jurisdiction of the court and bound by a judgment or decree." Martin v. Wilks, 490 U.S. 755, 759, 765 (1989).

SECTION A: PERSPECTIVES ON JOINDER

ABRAM CHAYES, THE ROLE OF THE JUDGE IN PUBLIC LAW LITIGATION

89 HARV. L. REV. 1281, 1282-84, 1289-90 (1976)

In our received tradition, the lawsuit is a vehicle for settling disputes between private parties about private rights. The defining features of this conception of civil adjudication are:

(1) The lawsuit is *bipolar*. Litigation is organized as a contest between two individuals or at least two unitary interests, diametrically opposed, to be decided on a winner-takes-all basis....

(3) *Right and remedy are interdependent*. The scope of the relief is derived more or less logically from the substantive violation under the general theory that the plaintiff will get compensation measured by the harm caused by the defendant's breach of duty — in contract by giving plaintiff the money he would have had absent the breach; in tort by paying the value of the damage caused.

(4) The lawsuit is a *self-contained* episode. The impact of the judgment is confined to the parties. If plaintiff prevails there is a simple compensatory transfer, usually of money, but occasionally the return of a thing or the performance of a definite act. If defendant prevails, a loss lies where it has fallen. In either case, entry of judgment ends the court's involvement.

(5) The process is *party-initiated* and *party-controlled*. The case is organized and the issues defined by exchanges between the parties. Responsibility for fact development is theirs. The trial judge is a neutral arbiter of their interactions who decides questions of law only if they are put in issue by an appropriate move of a party....

Whatever its historical validity, the traditional model is clearly invalid as a description of much current civil litigation in the federal district courts. Perhaps the dominating characteristic of modern federal litigation is that lawsuits do not arise out of disputes between private parties about private rights. Instead, the object of litigation is the vindication of constitutional or statutory policies. The shift in the legal basis of the lawsuit explains many, but not all, facets of what is going on "in fact" in federal trial courts. For this reason, although the label is not wholly satisfactory, I shall call the emerging model "public law litigation."...

Joinder of ~~parties, which~~ was strictly limited at common law, was verbally liberalized under the codes to conform with the approach of equity calling for joinder of all parties having an "interest" in the controversy. The codes, however, did not at first produce much freedom of joinder. Instead, the courts defined the concept of "interest" narrowly to exclude those without an independent legal right to the remedy to be given in the main dispute. . . . The proponents of "efficiency" argued for a more informal and flexible approach, to the end that the courts should not have to rehear the same complex of events. This argument ultimately shifted the focus of the lawsuit from legal theory to factual context — the "transaction or occurrence" from which the action arose. This in turn made it easier to view the set of events in dispute as giving rise to a range of legal consequences all of which ought to be considered together.

This more open-ended view of the subject matter of the litigation fed back upon party questions and especially intervention. Here, too, the sharp constraints dictated by the right-remedy nexus give way. And if the right to participate in litigation is no longer determined by one's claim to relief at the hands of another party or one's potential liability to satisfy the claim, it becomes hard to draw the line determining those who may participate so as to eliminate anyone who is or might be significantly (a weasel word) affected by the outcome — and the latest revision of the Federal Rules of Civil Procedure has more or less abandoned the attempt.

LON L. FULLER, THE FORMS AND LIMITS OF ADJUDICATION

92 HARV. L. REV. 353, 393-95, 397-98 (1978)

Attention is now directed to the question, What kinds of tasks are inherently unsuited to adjudication? The test here will be that used throughout. If a given task is assigned to adjudicative treatment, will it be possible to preserve the meaning of the affected party's participation through proofs and arguments? . . .

[S]uppose in a socialist regime it were decided to have all wages and prices set by courts which would proceed after the usual forms of adjudication. It is, I assume, obvious that here is a task that could not successfully be undertaken by the adjudicative method. The point that comes first to mind is that courts move too slowly to keep up with a rapidly changing economic scene. The more fundamental point is that the forms of adjudication cannot encompass and take into account the complex repercussions that may result from any change in prices or wages. . . . In such a case it is simply impossible to afford each affected party a meaningful participation through proofs and arguments. It is a matter of capital importance to note that it is not merely a question of the huge number of possibly affected parties, significant as that aspect of the thing may be. A more fundamental point is that each of the various forms that award might take (say, a three-cent increase per pound, a four-cent increase, a five-cent increase, etc.) would have a different set of repercussions and might require in each instance a redefinition of the "parties affected."

We may visualize this kind of situation by thinking of a spider web. A pull on one strand will distribute tensions after a complicated pattern throughout the web as a whole. Doubling the original pull will, in all likelihood, not simply double each of the resulting tensions but will rather create a different complicated pattern of tensions. This would certainly occur, for example, if the doubled pull caused one or more of the weaker strands to snap. This is a "polycentric" situation because it is "many centered" — each crossing of strands is a distinct center for distributing tensions. . . .

Now, if it is important to see clearly what a polycentric problem is, it is equally important to realize that the distinction involved is often a matter of degree. There are polycentric elements in almost all problems submitted to adjudication. . . . It is not, then, a question of distinguishing black from white. It is a question of knowing when the polycentric elements have become so significant and predominant that the proper limits of adjudication have been reached.

Notes and Questions

1. Professor Chayes correctly observed that a basic principle of modern joinder is "transactionalism": the ability to join in one case all of the legal theories and persons involved in a transaction or occurrence. The principle descends from equity, which prided itself on doing "complete justice" among all those interested in a dispute. In this regard, equity counterbalanced the stingy joinder rules of the common law. As long as common law and equity existed side by side, truly transactional joinder was impossible. The Federal Rules abolished the law-equity distinction in 1938, and generally permitted joinder on the equity model. A few restrictions on joinder remained, but most of those were removed in the 1966 amendments. For the most part, these joinder rules have not been substantively changed since then.

As we will see, claim joinder can extend beyond the transaction, and sometimes party joinder does not reach to the outer limits of the transaction. But the "transaction" remains the basic unit around which modern litigation is organized. This fact has a number of important consequences. The first is definitional: how closely connected must the claims or parties be to compose one "transaction or occurrence"? Next, if the transaction (however defined) is the basic unit of litigation, should joinder on a transactional scale be not merely permissible, but *required*? Put differently, in the first chapter we saw that another of the structural choices of the American procedural system is an adversarial method in which the parties, and not the court, control litigation choices. If the parties are in charge, they may choose not to include all the claims and parties that they could bring under the joinder rules. How do we reconcile the tension between the transactional and adversarial goals?

Similarly, the joinder of large numbers of transactionally related claims and parties will be more efficient in some cases, but in other cases broad joinder will be less efficient than a smaller unit of litigation. How should the tension between transactional and efficiency goals be mediated?

Allowing broad joinder also puts greater pressure on the discovery system and on juries (which, at common law, did not hear complex multi-claim, multi-party disputes). Can we simultaneously maintain an allegiance to the transaction as the unit of litigation, the open-ended spirit of our pleading and discovery rules, and the right to jury trial?

2. Professor Fuller was an ardent defender of the adversarial system. The article excerpted above had been written in the 1950s, and was posthumously published. Chayes's article, which is one of the most cited in the history of legal scholarship, was in many ways a reply to Fuller's article. Chayes and Fuller operate on different planes. Chayes describes the world as it exists; Fuller posits a theoretical model of how adjudication must function in order to be worthy of the name. Nor does Fuller critique directly the transactional orientation of the joinder rules: certain problems will be "polycentric" regardless of whether joinder rules permit multi-claim, multi-party lawsuits. But broad joinder rules make more likely the adjudication of disputes that Fuller would have regarded as polycentric.

3. To some extent, your views about joinder might be influenced by its actual consequences — the rise of "public law litigation" and the judge whose powers are broader than those of classic adversarial theory. You should remember, however, that not all joinder rules have such broad implications. Joinder devices such as counterclaims and crossclaims are largely uncontroversial and usually do not greatly expand the litigation.

SECTION B: A PRIMER ON JURISDICTION

Questions of joinder of claims and parties are invariably intertwined with issues of subject-matter jurisdiction and personal jurisdiction. This fact creates a pedagogical quandary. If jurisdiction is taught first, some basic principles of claim and party joinder must be taught at the same time in order for jurisdiction to be understood; if joinder is taught first, the converse is true. We have chosen to begin with claim and party joinder; in Chapter Nine we examine personal jurisdiction, and in Chapter Ten we examine subject-matter jurisdiction. What follows in this section, therefore, are the basic rules of federal subject-matter jurisdiction and personal jurisdiction — enough for you to understand the joinder cases in this chapter.

We begin with subject-matter jurisdiction. Federal courts, in which the Federal Rules of Civil Procedure operate, are courts of limited subject-matter jurisdiction. This means that they have the authority to decide only certain types of cases and claims; if they do not have such authority, then the cases and claims must be heard in other courts — typically the state courts. This division between federal and state courts is complicated by the fact that, in most situations, state courts can also hear cases that the federal courts have subject-matter jurisdiction to hear; when both state and federal courts have subject-matter jurisdiction, the plaintiff usually has a choice of filing the case in either state or federal court.

For a federal court to have subject-matter jurisdiction over a case, *both* the Constitution *and* a federal statute must grant jurisdiction. Because the Federal Rules of Civil Procedure are not a statute, they cannot grant jurisdiction to a federal court. *See* Fed. R. Civ. P. 82. Therefore, a federal court does not have jurisdiction just because the Federal Rules permit joinder. Joinder and jurisdiction are separate requirements, and both must be satisfied for a joined claim or party to be heard in federal court.

The most common forms of federal civil subject-matter jurisdiction are *federal-question jurisdiction*, based on 28 U.S.C. § 1331, and *diversity jurisdiction*, based on 28 U.S.C. § 1332. Federal-question jurisdiction typically exists when the plaintiff claims that the defendant has violated federal law. In contrast, diversity jurisdiction exists when the plaintiff's claim involves a violation of state law. With diversity jurisdiction, a federal court can hear a state-law claim only when (1) the plaintiff and defendant (at least one of whom must be a citizen of an American state) are citizens of different states or countries, *and* (2) the matter in controversy in the case exceeds $75,000. Therefore, if a plaintiff sues a defendant for the state-law tort of negligence, the federal court has no power to adjudicate the case if both are citizens of the same state *or* if the dispute is clearly not worth more than $75,000. You must also know another important rule of diversity jurisdiction. Under *Strawbridge v. Curtiss*, 7 U.S. (3 Cranch) 267 (1806), diversity must be *complete*: when there are multiple plaintiffs and/or multiple defendants, § 1332 requires that no plaintiff be a citizen of the same state as any defendant. Be careful: it is *not* a problem if some or all of the parties on the same side of the litigation (that is, on the same side of the "v.") are citizens of the same state.

These rules are usually not that hard to apply. Federal jurisdictional issues become trickier when it becomes possible, as our joinder rules permit in some situations, to add together multiple claims and parties in one case. Suppose that a plaintiff files a lawsuit involving multiple claims and parties in federal court. For some claims against some parties, federal subject-matter jurisdiction exists, but for other claims, no *independent* subject-matter jurisdiction would exist if the plaintiff had filed them separately. Should the court have *supplemental* jurisdiction to hear the additional claims over which no independent jurisdiction exists? In some cases, the answer is "yes," and in other cases the answer is "no." 28 U.S.C. § 1367, enacted in 1990, describes the boundaries of supplemental jurisdiction.

Personal jurisdiction is entirely distinct from subject-matter jurisdiction. While subject-matter jurisdiction concerns a court's power to adjudicate a dispute of a particular type, personal jurisdiction asks whether a court has the power to adjudicate a dispute involving particular parties. For example, if you have never been in Indiana and your dispute has nothing to do with Indiana, you might think it unfair if someone tried to sue you in a state or federal court in Indiana. As we explore in detail in Chapter Nine, your intuition has merit. A defendant must have sufficient *contacts* with a forum before a court there can adjudicate a dispute involving that party.

To illustrate the distinctness of personal jurisdiction from joinder and subject-matter jurisdiction, assume that I am a citizen of North Carolina, you and your business partner are citizens of Tennessee, and our contract dispute amounts to $500,000. You have no connections with Ohio. If I sue you and your partner in a federal court in Tennessee, the Federal Rules allow me to join you both as defendants, the federal court has jurisdiction over our dispute, and your contacts with Tennessee give the court the power over you and your partner. But if I try to sue you and your partner in federal court in Ohio, that court cannot hear your case due to a lack of personal jurisdiction — even though the Federal Rules permit the joinder and the court has diversity jurisdiction.

Therefore, joinder, subject-matter jurisdiction, and personal jurisdiction are three independent requirements that together determine the claims and parties that a federal civil case can contain. Only those claims and parties that satisfy all three criteria — that lie in the intersection of all three sets — can be properly adjudicated by the relevant court. You should train yourself to ask, for any claim or party proposed to be joined, three distinct questions: (1) Does a Federal Rule permit the joinder? (2) Does the federal court have personal jurisdiction over each defendant proposed to be joined? and (3) Does the court have either independent or supplemental subject-matter jurisdiction over each claim and party proposed to be joined? A negative answer to any of the three questions ends the inquiry; the court cannot hear the claim involving that party.

SECTION C: CLAIM JOINDER

This section examines three issues: the plaintiff's ability to join multiple claims or theories of recovery against a defendant, the defendant's ability to assert multiple defenses against the plaintiff, and the defendant's ability to assert claims against the plaintiff. As you read the following materials, keep in mind the distinction between additional claims or legal theories that arise out of the same transaction or occurrence as the first claim in the case and additional claims or theories that arise out of separate transactions or occurrences. To what extent do the rules for joinder of claims differ between these two situations — the first of which implicates the transactional principle and second of which does not?

1. Asserting Multiple Claims Against the Defendant

By this point in your legal education, you now realize that an event can implicate different legal theories, and sometimes even entirely different bodies of law. For example, when a person is injured by a product purchased from the defendant, the case sounds like a tort claim. But it also involves a contract. Both bodies of law might have something to say about how this dispute is resolved. Can the plaintiff's complaint plead both a tort and a contract theory? Or must the plaintiff file two cases? On the tort theory, suppose that the plaintiff wants to pursue both a strict-liability theory and a negligence theory. Must each theory be pursued in a separate case with a separate complaint? Now suppose that the plaintiff has an unrelated billing dispute with the defendant about another purchase. Must this claim be brought separately?

Between them, Rules 8(d)(2), 8(d)(3), and 18 permit the joinder of claims on a capacious scale: permitting joinder not only of transactionally related theories and claims, but also of claims that are not part of the same transaction. This broad scope of claim joinder was a reaction to common-law pleading, in which a plaintiff could sue on only one writ at a time. Allowing the joinder of all legal theories and claims involved in a single transaction often makes sense from the viewpoint of efficiency. The efficiency gain from joining unrelated claims may be harder to see, but the joinder of unrelated claims does not expand the party structure of the lawsuit, makes one lawsuit of two, and, if the parties choose to settle, brings together all the disputes for a single set of negotiations. It avoids costly satellite litigation about whether or not two claims are transactionally related. Moreover, in case the joinder of unrelated claims is inefficient, a judge can employ Rule 42(b), which permits aspects of the case to be tried separately.

Rules 8(d)(2), 8(d)(3), and 18 state the maximum *permissive* scope of claim joinder. These rules are not *mandatory*, in the sense of requiring joinder of all possible claims. In our adversarial system, plaintiffs are free to assert fewer than all the claims that they might assert. Often it is strategically advantageous to pursue only some claims. When claims are transactionally related, the law of preclusion, which we considered in Chapter Seven, may prevent a plaintiff from asserting additional claims in a second case after the first case goes to judgment. This fact does not compel a plaintiff to assert in the first case all the transactionally related claims against the defendant under Rules 8(d) and 18, but it imposes a consequence if the plaintiff chooses not to do so.

There is one constraint on the breadth of claim joinder. A federal court must have subject-matter jurisdiction to hear every claim asserted in the case. Even if the Federal Rules of Civil Procedure authorize multiple claims to be asserted, the requirements of subject-matter jurisdiction must also be satisfied before a court can properly entertain a claim.

Broad joinder of claims is common in modern adjudicatory systems — although some joinder rights are not as broad as those permitted under the Federal Rules. In their effort to meld the procedural approaches of various legal systems for transnational litigation, the American Law Institute and UNIDROIT proposed this principle for joining claims: "A party may assert any claim substantially connected to the subject matter of the proceeding against another party." ALI/UNIDROIT, Principles of Transnational Civil Procedure Principle 12.1 (2006).

2. Asserting Multiple Defenses Against the Plaintiff

Rules 8(d)(2) and –(d)(3) also allow the defendant to assert as many defenses as he or she has to the plaintiff's claims. This broad ability to assert defenses is the mirror image of the plaintiff's ability to join as many claims as he or she has. It is also eminently fair and reasonable in a pleading system designed to reach the merits of the controversy.

3. Asserting Claims Against the Plaintiff

Until now, we have conceived of a lawsuit as a dispute in which only the plaintiff claims an injury. Sometimes the controversy is a two-sided affair, with both the plaintiff and the defendant feeling that the other side has committed a wrong. Suppose that there is a car accident at an intersection, and both drivers are seriously injured. Both claim that they had the right of way and the other driver was negligent. If Driver A files a case for her injuries, may Driver B assert his claims for injuries in the same case? Must Driver B do so? Read Rules 13(a) and –(b).

PAINTER V. HARVEY

863 F.2d 329 (4th Cir. 1988)

Before RUSSELL, HALL, and WILKINSON, Circuit Judges.

■ WILKINSON, Circuit Judge.

In this case we must determine if the district court properly invoked its [supplemental] subject matter jurisdiction to entertain a state libel counterclaim that arose in response to a federal action under 42 U.S.C. § 1983. Plaintiff Painter alleged that defendant Harvey violated her constitutional rights while arresting her for driving under the influence in November, 1984. Defendant counterclaimed, asserting that plaintiff slandered and libeled him by filing a fabricated complaint about the circumstances of her arrest with the Town Council of Luray, Virginia, and by distributing her complaint to the local news media. Following a jury verdict in defendant's favor, plaintiff moved to dismiss defendant's counterclaim for lack of subject matter jurisdiction. The district court held defendant's counterclaim compulsory because it involved substantially the same evidence as plaintiff's claim. . . . We affirm . . . .

I.

At 12:45 a.m. on the morning of November 9, 1984, police officer Larry Harvey stopped a vehicle driven erratically by plaintiff Florhline Painter in the Town of Luray, Virginia. Both plaintiff and a companion appeared intoxicated and Harvey called for additional assistance. After the assistance arrived, Harvey placed Painter under arrest for driving while intoxicated, handcuffed her, and, with the help of another officer, placed her in the back seat of his patrol car. A plastic shield separated the front and back seats.

Harvey transported Painter at once from the scene of the arrest to a local jail. Harvey's car was preceded and followed by two other police cars and was never out of their sight. When Painter arrived at the jail, her blouse was unbuttoned, one breast was exposed, and her shoes, panty hose, and underpants were removed. She claimed Officer Harvey had raped her and initially refused to cover herself when requested to do so.

On April 9, 1985, Painter appeared before the Luray Town Council to summarize her version of the events of her arrest and to file a formal complaint against Officer Harvey. She also issued a prepared written statement to a reporter from the local newspaper, the *Page News and Courier*. The statement contained the allegation that Harvey had "jerked me out of my car, tore my blouse, put marks on my breast, and I also sustained a head and neck injury from his excessive force he used. . . ." Excerpts from the complaint were published in the *Page News and Courier* on April 12, 1985.

Painter filed suit in federal district court in February, 1985. She alleged that Harvey lacked probable cause to arrest her and had used excessive force during her arrest, all in violation of 42 U.S.C. § 1983.

Harvey counterclaimed against Painter for defamation. He alleged that Painter had falsely claimed that she was molested or raped during the November, 1984 arrest, and had submitted a false summary of the circumstances of her arrest to the Luray Town Council the following April. Harvey's version of events was starkly at variance with that of Painter. He testified that when he and Painter arrived at the jail, he noticed that Painter had opened her blouse, exposed one of her breasts, and had removed her shoes, panty hose, and underpants. Jerry Shiro, the former chief of police of the Luray Police Department, stated that the *Page News and Courier* article had created serious embarrassment for Harvey with the public, his fellow police officers, and members of the Town Council.

The case was tried before a jury. The jury found for Harvey on Painter's § 1983 claim. The jury also found in Harvey's favor on the defamation counterclaim, awarding compensatory damages of $5,000.00 and punitive damages of $15,000.00. Painter moved to set aside the verdict on the grounds that the court lacked subject matter jurisdiction over the counterclaim. . . . The district court denied [Painter's motion]. . . .

II.

The sole question on Painter's appeal is the nature of Harvey's counterclaim. If the counterclaim is compulsory, it is within the [supplemental] jurisdiction of the court to entertain and no independent basis of federal jurisdiction is required. If the counterclaim is permissive, however, it must have its own independent jurisdictional base. Since Painter and Harvey are both citizens of Virginia, and Harvey asserts no federal question, the designation of the counterclaim is critical.

. . . We hold that defendant's counterclaim is compulsory and that the district court properly exercised jurisdiction over it.

III.

In *Sue & Sam Mfg. Co. v. B-L-S Construction Co.*, 538 F.2d 1048 (4th Cir. 1976), this circuit suggested four inquiries to determine if a counterclaim is compulsory: (1) Are the issues of fact and law raised in the claim and counterclaim largely the same? (2) Would res judicata bar a subsequent suit on the party's counterclaim, absent the compulsory counterclaim rule? (3) Will substantially the same evidence support or refute the claim as well as the counterclaim? and (4) Is there any logical relationship between the claim and counterclaim? A court need not answer all these questions in the affirmative for the counterclaim to be compulsory. Rather, the tests are less a litmus, more a guideline.

Although the tests are four in number, there is an underlying thread to each of them in this case: evidentiary similarity. The claim and counterclaim both involved witness testimony directed toward the same critical event. Indeed, in applying the four *Sue & Sam* tests, the district court invariably returned to the same place. As to inquiry (1), the district court noted that: "The central issue in both the claim and counterclaim is identical: What transpired during Mrs. Painter's arrest on November 9, 1984? The jury, in essence, was faced with irreconcilably conflicting evidence and was required to choose which version to accept or reject."

As to inquiry (2), the district court stated: "Examining the facts here, one finds that the jury verdict against Mrs. Painter on her § 1983 claim necessarily determined the issue of what happened during her arrest. Thus, in subsequent state action she could well face an issue preclusion bar as to relitigating those facts."

Inquiry (3) is explicitly evidentiary in nature. Not surprisingly, the district court concluded: "All of the witnesses, except the newspaper editor and witnesses testifying to damages, limited their testimony to a single factual issue — what transpired during Mrs. Painter's arrest on November 9, 1984? It is hard to imagine a case in which the evidence bearing on the two claims is so closely identical."

With regard to inquiry (4), the district court was once again led to the differing tales of the same evening underlying both claim and counterclaim. It concluded that: "In short, the truth of Officer Harvey's version of the events of November 9, 1984, is the central issue of fact in both the claim and counterclaim. They are inextricably and logically connected."

Where, as here, the same evidence will support or refute both the claim and counterclaim, the counterclaim will almost always be compulsory. The "same evidence" test thus accomplishes the purposes of Rule 13(a), because the "very purpose of making certain types of counterclaims compulsory is to prevent the relitigation of the same set of facts." . . . Holding counterclaims compulsory avoids the burden of multiple trials with their corresponding duplication of evidence and their drain on limited judicial resources. The "same evidence" test simply makes these concerns the focal point of its determination by requiring claims and counterclaims which involve the same evidence to be heard in a single proceeding.

Although the district court appeared to apply what in essence was the "same evidence test" in this case, courts have properly cautioned that this test should not be the exclusive determinant of compulsoriness under Rule 13(a) because it is too narrow a definition of a single transaction or occurrence. Some counterclaims may thus be compulsory even though they do not involve a substantial identity of evidence with the claim. A counterclaim may still arise from the same "transaction or occurrence," as a logically related claim even though the evidence needed to prove the opposing claims may be quite different. Here, however, the claims both bear a logical relationship and an evidentiary similarity, and the problems of a divergence between the last two inquiries under *Sue & Sam* are not present.

IV.

The foregoing purposes of Rule 13(a) lead us to reject Painter's assertion that Harvey's libel counterclaim was merely permissive. We address plaintiff's arguments in turn.

Plaintiff argues that defendant's counterclaim should be found permissive because plaintiff's claim involves federal law and defendant's counterclaim state libel law. The fact that the counterclaim may be one of state law, however, says nothing about its logical relationship to the federal claim or to the evidentiary overlap between them. Where a plaintiff asserts a claim based on federal law, a counterclaim based on state law may be adjudicated as a matter of [supplemental] jurisdiction so long as the counterclaim arises from the same transaction.

Similarly, we reject plaintiff's assertion that the counterclaim is permissive because the events of November 9, 1984 became relevant to the libel counterclaim only when plaintiff responded to that counterclaim with an affirmative defense of truth. The affirmative defense, however, followed the counterclaim much as night follows day . . . .

The judgment of the district court is affirmed.

Notes and Questions

1. Typically, the party asserting a counterclaim is the defendant, and the person against whom it is asserted is the plaintiff. We will soon see that the party structure can become more complicated, and other parties can also assert counterclaims. But be clear about what a counterclaim is: Rules 13(a) and –(b) allow you to assert a claim against someone who has asserted a claim against you. A person who has not asserted a claim against you is not an "opposing party," and you cannot use Rule 13(a) or –(b) to assert a claim exclusively against that person. United States *ex rel.* Branch Consultants, L.L.C. v. Allstate Ins. Co., 265 F.R.D. 266, 269 (E.D. La. 2010).

2. Rules 8(d) and 18 allow — but do not themselves require — plaintiffs to join as many claims as they have against defendants. Other doctrines constrain the liberality of these Rules. First, although plaintiffs need not assert all their claims, claim preclusion bars the later assertion of transactionally related claims against the same defendant. *See supra* pp. 320-28. Second, a federal court cannot hear claims over which it lacks subject-matter jurisdiction. *See supra* pp. 353-54.

Rules 13(a) and –(b) reflect the same liberal attitude when defendants have claims to assert against plaintiffs: assert whatever claims you have. They also have similar side constraints in terms of preclusive effect and subject-matter jurisdiction:

(a) Preclusion: The "Compulsory-Counterclaim Rule." Rule 13(a)(1)(A) defines a compulsory counterclaim as a claim that "arises out of the transaction or occurrence that is the subject matter of the opposing party's claim." According to Rule 13(a), a party *must* assert these counterclaims (unless the claim falls within one of two exceptions listed in Rule 13(a)(2)). In contrast, Rule 13(b) states that a party *may* assert "any claim that is not compulsory." As the heading to Rule 13(b) states, these claims are usually called permissive counterclaims — claims that do not arise out of the transaction or occurrence that is the basis of the opposing party's claim.

Rule 13 never states the consequence for a party who fails to plead a compulsory counterclaim. Courts generally hold that a party who fails to plead a compulsory counterclaim is barred from asserting that claim in another case. Baker v. Gold Seal Liquors, Inc., 417 U.S. 467, 469 n.1 (1974); *see* 6 CHARLES A. WRIGHT ET AL., FEDERAL PRACTICE AND PROCEDURE § 1417 (3d ed. 2010). Barring defendants' subsequent litigation of these claims is the equivalent of the modern approach to claim preclusion, which imposes a comparable consequence on plaintiffs who fail to assert all transactionally related claims in one case. This preclusive effect is often referred to as the *compulsory-counterclaim rule*. (Here is another place where nomenclature can be tricky; "compulsory-counterclaim rule" is sometimes used to describe Rule 13(a), and sometimes to describe the preclusive consequence of failing to assert a compulsory counterclaim.) The compulsory-counterclaim rule is of more recent origin than the doctrine of claim preclusion, and is not itself a rule of claim preclusion — although, because it operates just as claim preclusion does, it is sometimes described in that way.

On the other hand, failing to plead a permissive counterclaim generally does not prevent a party from asserting the claim in later litigation. *But see* Capitol Hill Group v. Pillsbury, Winthrop, Shaw, Pittman, LLC, 569 F.3d 485, 492 (D.C. Cir. 2009) (noting that permissive counterclaims can be barred "if allowing a permissive counterclaim to go forward would nullify the earlier judgment or impair rights established in the earlier action").

(b) Subject-Matter Jurisdiction. A federal court must have subject-matter jurisdiction over each counterclaim asserted. If the court would have had jurisdiction over the counterclaim if it had been filed as its own case, the court has power to hear the counterclaim. In addition, the traditional rule, which *Painter* reflects, was that a federal court had supplemental

jurisdiction over a compulsory counterclaim even when the court would have lacked jurisdiction had the claim been filed as an independent case. That rule is still in place today. *See, e.g., Baker*, 417 U.S. at 469 n.1.

For permissive counterclaims, the traditional rule was the opposite: if a claim asserted under Rule 13(b) did not fall within a federal court's subject-matter jurisdiction, the court had no power to decide it. Some federal courts have held that they have supplemental jurisdiction over a few permissive counterclaims. Such supplemental jurisdiction is rare: the counterclaim must not be transactionally related enough to make it compulsory, but it must nevertheless be transactionally related in some way. For a recent example, see *Global Naps, Inc. v. Verizon New England, Inc.*, 603 F.3d 71, 85-89 (1st Cir. 2010) (finding supplemental jurisdiction over permissive counterclaim); for a more traditional analysis, see *Ammons v. Ally Financial, Inc.*, 305 F. Supp. 3d 818, 820-23 (M.D. Tenn. 2018) (rejecting supplemental jurisdiction over permissive counterclaim).

The reason for the traditional rules is simple. Supplemental jurisdiction exists because of the "logical relationship" among claims (some of which fall within the federal courts' original jurisdiction and some of which fall outside). Moore v. N.Y. Cotton Exch., 270 U.S. 593, 610 (1926). Compulsory counterclaims arise out of the same transaction or occurrence as the original claim; thus the claims have a logical relationship. Permissive counterclaims, which lack this transactional connection, almost always lack a logical relationship.

3. The label "compulsory" does not mean that a court will require a defendant to add a counterclaim. Rather, arguments over whether a counterclaim is compulsory or permissive tend to arise either when (1) a defendant seeks to take advantage of federal supplemental jurisdiction, and the plaintiff argues (as in *Painter*) that the court lacks such jurisdiction because the counterclaim is only permissive, or (2) when a defendant in a subsequent case (in state or federal court) asserts the compulsory-counterclaim rule to bar a claim not previously asserted.

4. Suppose that Harvey had not filed his defamation claim in Painter's case, but filed it in state court after Painter lost her § 1983 claim. Is the state court required to dismiss the claim? (You can assume that a Virginia state court must apply the same preclusion rule to Harvey's claim that a federal court would.) Perhaps the meaning of "arises out of the same transaction or occurrence" should vary depending on the context. There is little downside to interpreting it broadly in cases like *Painter*, in which it is more efficient to allow all the claims to be decided in the single federal case. But if Harvey fails to raise the counterclaim and then brings a separate suit later, concluding that his libel claim is transactionally related to Painter's § 1983 claim means that he cannot bring it at all. Doing so punishes him for what might be considered a technical mistake. For that reason, it might make sense to adopt a narrower interpretation of "arising out of the same transaction or occurrence" in the context of whether a claim is precluded than in the context of whether it is compulsory and thus within supplemental jurisdiction.

5. The four tests described in *Painter* are the ones generally used to separate the compulsory from the permissive. The "same evidence" and "logical relationship" tests are the most common, with more courts adopting the latter. In nearly all situations, however, nothing of substance hinges on the choice, because both tests usually lead to the same conclusion.

6. When a defendant asserts a claim against the plaintiff, the counterclaim is governed by Rules 13(a) and –(b). What happens when one of two or more defendants wants to assert a claim against another? These claims are not called counterclaims, but rather *crossclaims*. (Watch out for variant terminology in some state courts. What Rule 13 and many state counterparts call a counterclaim, for instance, California calls a *cross-complaint*.) Rule 13(g) addresses crossclaims. Like Rule 13(a), Rule 13(g) contains the "transaction or occurrence" limitation; it does not permit transactionally unrelated crossclaims. Unlike counterclaims under Rule 13(a), however, crossclaims are never compulsory; a defendant who fails to bring a crossclaim can later sue a co-defendant. Why should that be so?

Finally, read Rule 13(h). If a defendant believes that both the plaintiff and an as-yet-unjoined third person have caused injury, how should he or she proceed? Must the defendant join additional parties to the counterclaim? *See* Pace v. Timmermann's Ranch & Saddle Shop, Inc., 795 F.3d 748, 753-54 (7th Cir. 2015) ("Rule 13 . . . does not *require* the joinder of parties. . . . Whether a *party must* be joined in an action continues to be governed only by Rule 19.").

Although Rules 13(g) and –(h) govern the assertion of additional claims, they presuppose the presence of additional parties. Therefore, we examine Rules 13(g) and –(h) in more detail in the following section, which explores the rules governing party joinder. *See infra* pp. 375-80.

SECTION D: PARTY JOINDER

Until now, we have focused on a one-plaintiff, one-defendant lawsuit. Joining additional parties is often desirable; for instance, if the defendant's conduct injured more than one plaintiff, or if more than one defendant contributed to the plaintiff's harm, one lawsuit may be more economical than several. Of course, there are tradeoffs. This combined lawsuit will be bigger and more complicated, and will make the adversarial presentation of evidence and arguments more challenging.

In thinking through the proper scope of party joinder, we begin with one of the basic tenets of our legal system: that every party enjoys the right to a "day in court." This "day in court" ideal gives each plaintiff the autonomy to decide when, where, with whom, and against whom to bring suit, and to select the claims that he or she will pursue. In exercising this autonomy, plaintiffs may want to join together; so we must consider the circumstances in which consensual plaintiff joinder can occur. Next, we must consider if we want to place constraints on this autonomy. Required joinder of plaintiffs or defendants may be more efficient or fair than allowing each plaintiff the right to an individual day in court against each defendant. Granting complete autonomy to each plaintiff to choose her preferred party structure might also frustrate a defendant's need to add parties that the defendant believes are necessary or useful to resolve the dispute. Moreover, this autonomy can harm nonparties whose interests lead them to want to participate in the litigation.

Discerning the circumstances under which we should rely on permissive joinder of additional parties, the circumstances under which we should insist on required joinder, and the circumstances under which we should permit defendants and nonparties to alter the party structure selected by the plaintiff(s) is an important task in any set of joinder rules.

1. Permissive Party Joinder

Party joinder under the Federal Rules of Civil Procedure centers on the idea of *permissive joinder*. Permissive joinder places the decision about which parties to include in a case in the hands of each person asserting a claim. When two or more plaintiffs have claims to assert, each must consent to join; neither can be forced into the other's case. The defendant(s) are selected by the plaintiff(s). The defendant(s) do not have the same options as the plaintiff(s): a defendant, for example, cannot ordinarily "join" as additional defendants other persons that the defendant thinks the plaintiff(s) ought to have sued. But a defendant may wish to assert claims against nonparties. And each party in the case may wish to assert claims against parties that another party has joined.

What should the limits of permissive party joinder be? The following material considers this question.

a. Joining Additional Plaintiffs and Defendants

GRIGGS V. HOLT

2018 WL 5283448 (S.D. Ga. October 24, 2018)

■ J. RANDAL HALL, Chief Judge.

Before the Court are two motions to dismiss and a motion to sever. . . .

The motion to sever is filed by Defendants Jerry Beard, Trei Bluitt, Lenon Butler, Janson Creagor, Verneal Evans, Julian Greenaway, Rodgerick Nabors, Stan Shepard, and Scott Wilkes. . . . For the reasons given below, Defendants' motion to sever . . . is denied.

I. BACKGROUND

This case began with a complaint filed by Christopher Varner, Eugene Griggs, and Cameron Maddox, all inmates or former inmates at the Augusta

State Medical Prison ("ASMP"); each man alleges he was the subject of an excessive force assault by correctional officers at ASMP in violation of the Eighth and Fourteenth Amendments.

[The court here summarized the allegations of the complaint. Each plaintiff described a different incident, on a different date, involving one or more of the defendant guards.]

Plaintiffs allege the above described assaults and multiple others mentioned in the Amended Complaint represent ASMP's "longstanding pattern and practice" of correctional officers using excessive force on prisoners solely to inflict pain on inmates, many of whom suffer from debilitative physical and mental illnesses. Correctional officers use secluded areas, such as elevators, to conduct these attacks because those areas are not under video surveillance. Plaintiffs allege prison administrators, namely Defendants Stan Shepard and Scott Wilkes, have failed to correct these practices and routinely downplay or ignore credible complaints of excessive force by inmates. Finally, because Maddox and Griggs are still housed at ASMP, they face an ongoing risk of being harmed by correctional officers using excessive force.

Based on the foregoing facts, each Plaintiff brings a claim for damages against their attackers. In Count I, Varner alleges Defendants Washington, Binns, Butler, Nabors, and Greenaway violated his Eighth and Fourteenth Amendment rights during the February 13th incident. Griggs alleges Defendant Evans violated his Eighth and Fourteenth Amendment rights during the July 27th incident. Lastly, Maddox alleges Defendant Bluitt and Creagor violated his Eighth and Fourteenth Amendment rights during the September 27th incident.

In Count II, Varner brings a claim for damages against Defendants Stan Shepard and Jerry Beard, in their individual capacities, under a theory of supervisor liability for their failure to take reasonable steps to prevent the February 13th assault. Varner specifically alleges Beard "had personally ordered, authorized, or condoned the use of excessive force against prisoners" at ASMP.

Finally, in Count III, Maddox and Griggs bring a claim for declaratory and injunctive relief against Defendant Stan Shepard, Assistant Regional Director for the North Region of the [Georgia Department of Corrections ("GDC")], and Defendant Scott Wilkes, Warden of ASMP. This claim is brought against Wilkes and Shepard, in their official capacities, to prevent further violations of Griggs and Maddox's rights under the Eighth and Fourteenth Amendments. . . .

II. DISCUSSION

[The court first dismissed (without prejudice) all of Varner's claims for failure to comply with the requirements of the federal Prison Litigation Reform Act (PLRA).]

Defendants move to sever Plaintiffs' claims under Federal Rule of Civil Procedure 20. They argue that such claims do not arise out of the same transaction or occurrence because each Plaintiff's excessive force allegations involve separate incidents with different defendants. Defendants further contend that although Plaintiffs bring the same type of claims, each involves the resolution of unrelated factual disputes.

In response, Plaintiffs argue that their claims arise out of the same series of transactions or occurrences, namely that each Plaintiff was assaulted as part of a "pattern and practice" at ASMP of using excessive force solely to inflict pain on inmates.

Federal Rule of Civil Procedure 20(a)(1) governs the joinder of plaintiffs in a lawsuit and uses a flexible standard that requires the plaintiffs to "assert any right to relief . . . arising out of the same transaction, occurrence, or series of transactions or occurrences" and there be a "question of law or fact common to all plaintiffs." Fed. R. Civ. P. 20(a) (1)(A), (B). In the Eleventh Circuit, "joinder is 'strongly encouraged' and the rules are construed generously 'toward entertaining the broadest possible scope of action consistent with fairness to the parties.'" Vanover v. NCO Fin. Servs. Inc., 857 F.3d 833, 839 (11th Cir. 2017) (quoting *United Mine Workers of Am. v. Gibbs*, 383 U.S. 715, 724 (1966)). District courts are granted broad discretion when considering matters of joinder. *Id.*

Under the first part of Rule 20's test, transaction "is a word of flexible meaning. It may comprehend a series of many occurrences, depending not so much upon the immediateness of their connection as upon their logical relationship." Alexander v. Fulton Cnty., 207 F.3d 1303, 1323 (11th Cir. 2000), *overruled on other grounds by* Manders v. Lee, 338 F.3d 1304 (11th Cir. 2003). Thus, events that are "logically related" to one another are "generally regarded as comprising a transaction or occurrence." *Id.* (internal quotations omitted).

In *Alexander*, the Eleventh Circuit concluded that an allegation "of a pattern or practice of discrimination may describe such logically related events and satisfy the same transaction requirement." *Id.* Although that case concerned race discrimination by a state employer and not excessive force practices at a prison, the salient point is that an unlawful pattern or practice can satisfy the same transaction requirement. Other courts have agreed. In *Revilla v. Glanz*, 7 F. Supp. 3d 1207 (N.D. Okla. 2014), the court permitted the joinder of four prisoners who alleged Tulsa County Jail's health services had a policy or practice of providing constitutionally deficient medical care. *Id.* at 1213. Although each plaintiff's injury or death was caused by different ailments, involved different medical staff, and occurred over the span of eighteen months, the court found there was "a logical relationship between circumstances underlying the claims" that permitted joinder of the plaintiffs. *Id.*

Here, the Amended Complaint alleges a pattern or practice at ASMP of using excessive force solely to harm inmates. While each incident of excessive force occurred separately, Plaintiffs create a "logical relationship" between each event in their allegations that the use of excessive force is a routine practice at ASMP and prison administrators are aware of this practice but refuse to take reasonable steps to prevent further assaults.

Indeed, beyond the Plaintiffs' individual incidents, the complaint alleges in detail at least six other assaults by officers on non-party inmates. Many of these incidents involve the same correctional officers now joined as Defendants. Finally, while it is true each Plaintiff brings a damages claim against the officers alleged to have assaulted him, the gravamen of the complaint is to seek an end to this ongoing practice at ASMP.

The second part of Rule 20's test "does not require that all question of law and fact raised by the dispute be common, but only that *some* question of law or fact be common to all parties." *Alexander*, 207 F.3d at 1324 (emphasis in original). While Defendants correctly point out that an Eighth Amendment analysis of each of Plaintiff's individual incidents will present different facts, the determination of all other claims requires answers to overlapping questions of policies and practices at ASMP, the knowledge of prison administrators regarding the pattern of incidents, and the preventative measures those administrators did or did not take to address excessive force incidents. Thus, there are at least some shared questions of law and fact. . . . Accordingly, the Court finds that Plaintiffs satisfy Rule 20's requirements for joinder.

This holding, however, does not foreclose the possibility of severance at a later time. It may be, upon development of the evidence during discovery, Plaintiffs' claims should be severed for trial. If necessary, the Court has the ability under Federal Rule of Civil Procedure 42 to do so. Fed. R. Civ. P. 42(b). At this stage of the case, however, judicial economy is best served by joinder, rather than proceedings in duplicative suits. . . . Therefore, Defendants' motion to sever is denied without prejudice.

Notes and Questions

1. Rule 20(a) is the basic rule on the joinder of additional parties. It contains standards for both the joinder of additional plaintiffs and the joinder of additional defendants. A party who believes that a plaintiff or defendant was improperly joined may assert misjoinder under Rule 21. Because "Rule 21 does not provide any standards by which district courts can determine if parties are misjoined, courts have looked to Rule 20 for guidance." Acevedo v. Allsup's Convenience Stores, Inc., 600 F.3d 516, 521 (5th Cir. 2010).

2. The standards for joining additional plaintiffs in Rule 20(a)(1) and additional defendants in Rule 20(a)(2) appear to be essentially identical. In both cases, the two prongs are that the claims (whether asserted by the joined plaintiffs or against the joined defendants) must all arise out of "the same transaction, occurrence, or series of transactions or occurrences" and that "any" common question of law or fact exists among the joined parties.

(a) *Transaction, Occurrence, or Series of Transactions or Occurrences.* Does a "transaction or occurrence" mean the same thing here as it means in Rule 13(a)? Courts often look to Rule 13(a) in interpreting Rule 20(a). *See In re* EMC Corp., 677 F.3d 1351, 1358 (Fed. Cir. 2012) (noting that the inquiries under Rules 13(a) and 20(a) are "similar"). Recall *Painter*'s four tests to determine the meaning of "transaction or occurrence" under Rule 13(a). How many of these tests would be useful in determining the scope of Rule 20(a) joinder?

If "transaction or occurrence" means the same thing in Rule 13(a) and Rule 20(a), then what does the language "or series of transactions or occurrences" in Rule 20(a) mean? Both Rules are said to permit the maximal joinder consistent with fairness and efficiency. Perhaps the entire phrase "transaction, occurrence, or series of transactions or occurrences" in Rule 20(a) means the same thing that "transaction or occurrence" means in Rule 13(a). Should identical words used in different rules should be accorded the same meaning, or does the meaning of words shift with the context of their usage?

(b) *Any Question of Law of Fact Common to the Joined Parties*. The "common question" requirement also has interpretive challenges. Can you conceive of any circumstance in which the "transaction or occurrence" prong would be satisfied, but the "common question" prong would not? In other words, is the only limit on permissive joinder the transactional one? One way to give the commonality clause some independent meaning is to require that the common questions be "substantial" or "significant," but the text of the rule does not support that view.

3. Some courts also consider the possible unfairness to some defendants of joining a particular constellation of co-defendants in deciding whether joinder under Rule 20(a) is allowable. *See, e.g.*, Desert Empire Bank v. Ins. Co. of N. Am., 623 F.2d 1371 (9th Cir. 1980). Is there any textual support for that view in Rule 20(a), as opposed to Rule 42(b)?

4. Not all courts would have allowed the joinder in *Griggs*. In *Stojcevski v. County of Macomb*, 143 F. Supp. 3d (E.D. Mich. 2015), two brothers incarcerated in the same county jail during the same period of time were allegedly denied necessary medical care. One died and the other had to be hospitalized. The surviving brother sued various jail and county employees on his own behalf and as the administrator of his brother's estate, alleging that jail officials were "deliberately indifferent" to their medical needs (if true, that indifference would constitute a violation of their Eighth and Fourteenth Amendment rights). The court held that the claims were misjoined:

> The claims related to Vladimir and David do not "share an aggregate of operative facts." While it is true that they were incarcerated at the same jail during the same time period, they were housed in separate units, experienced different medical problems, and received different medical treatment by varying medical providers. For the most part, their claims require entirely different proof. Undoubtedly, the Amended Complaint alleges that Vladimir's and David's injuries resulted from a jail, county, and/or CCS policy and/or practice of indifference to the medical needs of inmates. Nevertheless, such similarity does not convert claims involving Vladimir and David into the same "series of transactions or occurrences" in Rule 20(a)'s terms *Id*. at 683.

Does *Griggs* or *Stojcevski* do a better job at implementing the underlying goals of Rule 20? In that regard, consider *United States v. Mississippi*, 380 U.S. 128, 143 (1965). The Supreme Court upheld the joinder of six county registrars, each of whom allegedly sought to deprive African-Americans of the right to vote, because their activities "were part of a series of transactions or occurrences the validity of which depended to a large extent upon 'question(s) of law or fact common to all of them.'"

5. Suppose that one of the plaintiffs joined under Rule 20(a) has an unrelated claim against one of the defendants joined under Rule 20(a). Can that claim also be joined? The question pits the transaction-or-less limit of Rule 20 against the transaction-and-more inclusiveness of Rule 18. Rule 18 was amended in 1966 to make clear that unrelated claims could be added to a claim against a party already properly joined under Rule 20.

6. Rule 20 is a rule of permissive (or voluntary) joinder. It stakes out the permissible scope of joinder for consenting plaintiffs; it does not compel joinder to that maximum. Potential plaintiffs who wish to bring their cases separately can refuse to join the case; nothing in Rule 20 gives any plaintiff a right to force other potential plaintiffs into the lawsuit. Nor does Rule 20 penalize potential plaintiffs who decline to join a case; because they are never made parties to the case, their claims are not precluded. Rule 20 also does not require a plaintiff to join all possible defendants — even if they are joint tortfeasors. *Compare EMC*, 677 F.3d at 1356 ("It is clear that where defendants are alleged to be jointly liable, they may be joined under Rule 20 because the transaction-or-occurrence test is always satisfied."), *with* Temple v. Synthes Corp., 498 U.S. 5 (1990) (per curiam) (recognizing that joint tortfeasors need not be joined but may be sued separately). Other doctrines, however, may provide an incentive for a plaintiff to join defendants. For instance, in circumstances that we explored in Chapter Seven, the plaintiff might be precluded from relitigating facts in cases against later defendants that were determined adversely to the plaintiff in the case against the first defendant.

In a few situations that we examine later in this chapter, the Federal Rules contemplate *required joinder*. The permissive joinder of Rule 20, however, remains the default position. The right of the individual to control the fate of his or her case, so crucial to the workings of the adversarial system, is thought to outweigh the concerns for efficiency, transactionalism, and collective fairness. Therefore, although Rule 20 makes efficient and fair joinder possible, it does not require it.

b. Impleading Third-Party Defendants

Rule 20 describes parties whom the plaintiff may permissively join. The next issue is whether the defendant may also permissively join additional parties. Read Rule 14. Like Rule 20(a), Rule 14(a)(1) speaks in terms of parties who "may" be joined, not those who must be joined. Unlike Rule 20(a), Rule 14(a)(1) significantly constricts the ability of the defendant to join additional parties. The person joined under Rule 14 is called the *third-*

party defendant; the defendant who effectuates this joinder is called the *third-party plaintiff*. Joinder of a third-party defendant under Rule 14 is often called *impleader*.

LEHMAN V. REVOLUTION PORTFOLIO LLC

166 F.3d 389 (1st Cir. 1999)

Before SELYA, Circuit Judge, CAMPBELL, Senior Circuit Judge, and LYNCH, Circuit Judge.

■ SELYA, Circuit Judge.

This appeal grows out of a triangular 1987 financial transaction that involved the Farm Street Trust (the Trust), its beneficiaries (Barry Lehman and Stuart A. Roffman), and First Mutual Bank for Savings (the Bank). In the ensuing eleven years, the transaction imploded, litigation commenced, the Bank and Lehman became insolvent, parties came and went, and the case was closed and partially reopened. In the end, only a third-party complaint proved ripe for adjudication. Even then, the district court dismissed two of its three counts, but entered summary judgment on the remaining count. The third-party defendant, Roffman, now appeals. After sorting through the muddled record and the case's serpentine procedural history, we affirm.

I. BACKGROUND

[Lehman and Roffman, joint beneficiaries of the Trust, obtained a loan from the Bank. Each personally guaranteed the loan, and Lehman put up two real estate parcels as additional collateral. The Trust defaulted on the loan, and the Bank foreclosed on Lehman's properties. Lehman sued the Bank in state court, seeking an injunction against the sale of the properties. Alternatively, he asked for rescission of the loan agreement. He alleged that Roffman had fraudulently induced the Bank to make the loan, and that the Bank violated state law in swallowing this fraud without exercising due diligence.

[Shortly afterwards the Bank failed. Acting pursuant to federal law, the Federal Deposit Insurance Corporation (FDIC) took over the Bank's responsibilities, including its role as a defendant in Lehman's case. It removed the case to federal court.... [T]he FDIC sought leave under Rule 14(a) to implead Roffman. The district judge granted the leave. The third-party complaint contained three counts. The first two sought indemnification and contribution, respectively, if the FDIC was found liable to Lehman. The third sought judgment against Roffman, as loan guarantor, for the outstanding loan balance.

[Procedural wrangling eliminated the original claim by Lehman. With this ruling, the first two counts of the FDIC's third-party complaint collapsed. But on the third count, the district court found in favor of the

II. DISCUSSION

. . .

. . . We . . . must answer the question whether the FDIC's deployment of a third-party complaint against Roffman was proper. In this regard, Roffman asserts that the district court should not have entertained the impleader, and that, therefore, the joined claim on the guaranty should fall of its own weight. We review a district court's decision to permit the filing of a third-party complaint under Rule 14(a) for abuse of discretion.

. . . [T]he FDIC impleaded Roffman as a third-party defendant on theories of indemnification and contribution (counts 1 and 2, respectively), maintaining, in essence, that if it were found to be liable to Lehman, then Roffman would in turn be liable to hold it harmless or, at least, contribute to any damages assessed against it. *See* Fed. R. Civ. P. 14(a) (contemplating the availability of third-party practice when a non-party is or may be liable "for all or part of the [ ] claim against" the defendant). In the same pleading, the FDIC asserted an independent claim for the outstanding loan balance, premised on Roffman's guaranty (count 3). RP (which now stands in the FDIC's shoes) acknowledges that the FDIC could not have brought count 3 as a stand-alone third-party claim under Rule 14(a), but asserts that count 3 was validly joined with counts 1 and 2 under Rule 18(a) (providing for permissive joinder). To parry this thrust, Roffman contends that the FDIC's claims for indemnification and contribution were not viable under state law, and thus, since the use of Rule 14(a) admittedly hinged on the propriety of those claims, the FDIC should not have been allowed to implead him at all.

We doubt that Roffman has preserved this argument inasmuch as he did not raise it below in his opposition to the FDIC's summary judgment motion. We prefer not to inquire into this apparent waiver, however, for we conclude, without serious question, that the FDIC was entitled to implead Roffman under Rule 14(a) and that it appropriately joined the guaranty claim under Rule 18(a).

A defendant, acting as a third-party plaintiff, may implead any non-party "who is or *may be* liable to the third-party plaintiff for all or part of the plaintiff's claim against the third-party plaintiff."* Fed. R. Civ. P. 14(a) (emphasis supplied). If the defendant acts within ten days of submitting his answer, he may bring a third party into the suit without leave of court.† Otherwise, the court's permission must be obtained. In that event, the determination is left to the informed discretion of the district

---

* The 2007 stylistic amendments made minor changes in the wording of this provision, and re-designated it as Rule 14(a)(2). — ED.

† A 2009 amendment to Rule 14(a)(1) changed the ten-day period (not counting weekend days) to fourteen days (inclusive of weekend days). — ED.

court, which should allow impleader on any colorable claim of derivative liability that will not unduly delay or otherwise prejudice the ongoing proceedings. Under this liberal standard, a party accused of passive negligence (here, the FDIC) assuredly is entitled to implead the party who allegedly committed the relevant active conduct (here, Roffman) on a theory of indemnification.

The FDIC's third-party claim for contribution against Roffman similarly passes muster because Roffman and the Bank (the FDIC's predecessor in interest) were putative joint tortfeasors (i.e., according to the complaint, Roffman's fraudulent acts combined with the Bank's negligent omissions to create harm). *See* Mass. Gen. Laws ch. 231B, § 1(a) (1986) (providing a right of contribution among persons who are jointly liable in tort for the same injury); *see also* Wolfe v. Ford Motor Co., 434 N.E.2d 1008 (Mass. 1982) (allowing contribution even though the two joint tortfeasors were liable under different theories of tort liability).

To be sure, Roffman argues that because Lehman's complaint sought only restraint or rescission of the property sales, and not damages, a third-party claim for contribution should not lie. But this argument gains him no ground. Even though Lehman's complaint did not explicitly seek money damages, that omission did not eliminate the possibility that damages might be awarded to him. *See* Fed. R. Civ. P. 54(c). Rule 54(c) is particularly apt in this situation, for a party may pray for rescission and be entitled to it, yet only receive damages. As long as damages may be awarded in lieu of rescission, impleader properly may be used to seek contribution toward those potential damages. It follows inexorably that the district court did not err in denying Roffman's motion to strike and allowing the FDIC's Rule 14(a) claims to stand.

Against this backdrop, the court properly assumed jurisdiction over count 3 of the third-party complaint. Rule 18(a) authorizes a third-party plaintiff to "join, . . . as independent or as alternative claims, as many claims . . . as the [third-party plaintiff] has against an opposing party." This authorization is subject only to the usual requirements of jurisdiction and venue (none of which are implicated here) and the district court's discretionary power to "direct an appropriate procedure for trying the claims." Given Rule 18(a)'s broad expanse, misjoinder of claims has become an anachronism in federal civil practice.

In this instance, Roffman signed an unconditional personal guaranty of a loan, and the borrower later defaulted. As a holder in due course of the note, the FDIC had an independent claim for the outstanding balance against Roffman. There is absolutely no reason why the FDIC could not append its independent claim on the guaranty to its other claims against Roffman.

As a fallback position, Roffman suggests that the third-party complaint against him should have been dismissed because the FDIC had a complete defense under 12 U.S.C. § 1823(e) to the claims brought by Lehman. We do not agree. Even if section 1823(e) offered the FDIC a potentially strong defense against Lehman's claims, the record fails to show that the mere existence of that statute rendered Lehman's complaint a nullity.

There is, moreover, a broader point. A district court must oversee third-party practice with the core purpose of Rule 14(a) in mind: avoiding unnecessary duplication and circuity of action. Requiring a district court to determine the merits of all defenses potentially available to the original defendant as a precondition to allowing that defendant to file a third-party complaint would frustrate this purpose and countervail the efficient allocation of judicial resources. Thus, as long as a third-party action falls within the general contours limned by Rule 14(a), does not contravene customary jurisdictional and venue requirements, and will not work unfair prejudice, a district court should not preclude its prosecution. So here.

[The court of appeals went on to hold that summary judgment had been properly entered against Roffman on the third count.]

Notes and Questions

1. A few key features of Rule 14 impleader are worth emphasizing. First, to invoke Rule 14 a party defending against a claim must have a claim for reimbursement or derivative liability (often referred to as contribution or indemnity) against the party to be joined by impleader. The defendant must be able to claim that *if* the defendant is liable to the plaintiff, *then* the third-party defendant has to pay the defendant for all or part of what the defendant owes — *not* that the third-party defendant is independently liable to the original defendant, *nor* that the third-party defendant is liable to the plaintiff *instead of or in addition to* the defendant. (Admiralty practice, mentioned in Rule 14(c), is an exception to some of these statements; it allows impleader of additional defendants who may be liable to either the original defendant or the original plaintiff.)

Second, impleader is purely procedural, itself creating no substantive obligations. It piggybacks onto the contractual or other legal relationships between the defendant and third-party defendant, such as a surety obligation or status as joint tortfeasors with right of contribution.

Third, Rules 14(a)(2) and –(3) authorize further joinder of related claims among plaintiff, defendant, and third-party defendant, such as counterclaims by the third-party defendant against the original defendant, claims by the third-party defendant against the plaintiff, and claims by the plaintiff against the third-party defendant.

Fourth, other rules dovetail with Rule 14: Rule 18(a) on permissive joinder of claims is explicit that the original defendant asserting a third-party claim may join any other claims that the defendant has against the third-party defendant. Further, Rule 13(g) makes clear that a defendant may state as a crossclaim against a co-defendant the type of derivative-liability claim that is the basis for Rule 14(a) impleader of one not a party. Finally, a third-party defendant who believes that another nonparty is or may be liable to the third-party defendant if the third-party defendant is liable to the third-party plaintiff can use Rule 14(a)(5) to implead the nonparty, who is sometimes called a *fourth-party defendant*.

2. The key to *Lehman*'s holding is Rule 18(a): once the FDIC asserted a proper third-party claim, it could join any other claims it had against Roffman. Therefore, to escape liability Roffman needed to back up a step and argue that the third-party complaint was improper. Without the third-party claims in the first two counts, the guaranty claim in the third count would have had nothing to join up with.

3. *Lehman* demonstrates the constraints on the defendant's ability to rearrange the party structure established by the plaintiff. The third count against Roffman undoubtedly arose out of the same transaction as Lehman's original claim against the bank. Lehman could have sued Roffman himself if he had chosen to do so; after all, Lehman's claim against the bank was only that it had not uncovered Roffman's wrongdoing. But Lehman sued only the bank, and the FDIC, as successor to the bank, could not join Roffman on the theory that the guaranty claim arose out of the same transaction or occurrence. If the FDIC could not have asserted a proper claim within the terms of Rule 14(a), it would have needed to pursue the guaranty claim in a separate lawsuit.

Why should there be reluctance to allow a defendant to add additional parties whose rights and liabilities arise out of the same transaction or occurrence? Presumably the answer is to respect the plaintiff's ability to structure the lawsuit as the plaintiff sees fit and to keep defendants from too readily redirecting the plaintiff's case into new channels. Rule 14 is a compromise between transactional joinder and respect for the autonomy of plaintiffs. Does *Lehman*'s holding that additional claims can be joined under Rule 18 tip the balance too far to one side? In *Lehman*, the claim joined under Rule 18 was related to the Rule 14(a) claims. But Rule 18 does not require that additional claims be transactionally related.

4. Like Rule 20 joinder by a plaintiff, Rule 14 joinder is permissive rather than mandatory. A defendant is not required to implead any third-party defendants, nor is a subsequent lawsuit against other allegedly responsible parties barred by claim preclusion. At most, issue preclusion may prevent the defendant from relitigating certain issues in the subsequent litigation.

In some cases, the risk of issue preclusion and the costs of a second case are not worth incurring; thus, the defendant will implead other responsible parties. In other cases, the calculation is different. A common strategy for defendants is to use the "empty-chair defense," in which the defendant tries to pin the entire blame for the plaintiff's injury on an absent third party. When the third party is impleaded, however, the chances of successful use of this defense plummet. The third-party defendant is unlikely to stand idly by while it is sullied; it is far more likely to throw blame back on the original defendant. This mutual finger-pointing is a dream come true for the plaintiff. Hence, when the empty-chair defense has reasonable prospects of success, the defendant may eschew resort to Rule 14.

c. Asserting Additional Claims

After the basic claim and party structure have been established, it is possible that some of the parties have claims against each other that have not been covered by any of the joinder devices we have thus far encountered. For instance, if a pedestrian sues two drivers who are allegedly responsible for her injuries, Driver A might wish to sue Driver B for the damage done to A's car. This would not be a Rule 13 counterclaim, since both drivers are defendants in the case. Nor would it be covered by Rule 14. (Quick refresher drill: why not?) Similarly, if A wished to claim that B was liable to him in the event that he was liable to the pedestrian, Rule 14 would not cover the situation. (Once again: why not?)

Rule 13(g) deals with these situations. Claims under this rule are called *crossclaims*, because they are brought against those aligned on one side of a case (as distinguished from counterclaims, which are brought against those aligned on the opposite side of the case). Although crossclaims, in conjunction with counterclaims and third-party claims, allow the assertion of many additional claims, gaps may remain.

LUYSTER V. TEXTRON, INC.

266 F.R.D. 54 (S.D.N.Y. 2010)

■ McKENNA, District Judge.

[The plaintiff was executor of the estate of two people who died in a small-airplane crash. She sued various defendants involved in the design, inspection, or maintenance of the airplane, including Superior Air Parts, Inc. ("Superior") and KS Gleitlager USA, Inc. ("KS Gleitlager"). Because federal air-traffic controllers did not give the plane's pilot directions to the closest airport when the plane developed trouble, KS Gleitlager brought a third-party complaint seeking contribution or indemnity from the United States ("the Government").]

On December 18, 2008, defendant Superior filed a cross-claim against the Government, alleging that the Government, "through its employee acting within the scope of his employment, was negligent in providing air traffic control services to [the pilot]." Superior claims that "[i]f Superior is held liable for damages to plaintiff . . . such liability will have been caused or contributed to by the negligence of Third Party Defendant the United States"; and "[t]herefore, Superior is entitled to contribution and/or indemnification from the United States for any amounts plaintiff may recover against Superior in this action." . . .

DISCUSSION

The Government seeks dismissal of Superior's purported cross-claim because, according to the Government, "it is not a cross-claim . . . ." The

Government contends that Superior's cross-claim "is more properly in the nature of a third-party complaint," and "[a] challenge to the propriety of this claim may be tested through a Motion to Dismiss under Rule 12(b)(6)." . . .

II. Rule 13(g) Cross-Claims

Rule 13(g) provides that "[a] pleading may state as a crossclaim any claim by one party against a coparty if the claim arises out of the transaction or occurrence that is the subject matter of the original action or of a counterclaim, or if the claim relates to any property that is the subject matter of the original action." Fed. R. Civ. P. 13(g). The Government has not disputed that Superior's cross-claim arises out of the same occurrence that is the subject matter of Plaintiff's original action. Rather, Superior's cross-claim is contingent upon Plaintiff obtaining a judgment against Superior. This comports with Rule 13(g), which provides that a cross-claim "may include a claim that the coparty is or may be liable to the cross-claimant for all or part of a claim asserted in the action against the cross-claimant." Fed. R. Civ. P. 13(g).

Although Rule 13(g) permits a cross-claim "by one party against a coparty," the Government asks this Court to conclude that it and Superior are not coparties. Superior and the Government were on the same side of the litigation (i.e., not opposing parties) when Superior filed its cross-claim, but they were at different levels. Superior is an original defendant to the action (i.e., a defendant sued by plaintiff), whereas the Government became a third party defendant when KS Gleitlager filed a third party complaint against it . . . . The primary issue before the Court is whether Superior and the Government are coparties for purposes of Rule 13(g); if not, then Superior's claim is not a proper cross-claim.

A. *Definition of "Coparty"*

Although Rule 13(g) allows cross-claims between coparties, the term "coparty" is not defined in the Rules. It seems clear that a coparty against whom a party can cross-claim is neither a non-party nor a party it formally opposes (i.e., a party on the opposite side of the action).

In multiparty actions, courts have disagreed regarding whether parties on the same side, but not at the same level, of an action are "coparties" that may cross-claim against each other. Faced with this question, courts generally appear to split between two constructions of the term "coparty."

Some courts have suggested that because a "coparty" must be a party of "like status," Rule 13(g) only allows cross-claims between parties both on the same side and at the same level of an action (hereinafter, the "Narrow Definition"). To illustrate, the Narrow Definition allows for a cross-claim between original defendants or between third party defendants, but does not allow a cross-claim by an original defendant against a third-party defendant or vice versa. *See, e.g.*, Int'l Paving Sys. v. Van-Tulco, Inc., 866 F. Supp. 682, 695 (E.D.N.Y. 1994) (disallowing a cross-claim by an original defendant against a fourth-party defendant); Murray v. Haverford Hosp. Corp., 278 F. Supp. 5, 6-7 (E.D. Pa. 1968) (dismissing cross-claims of defendants against a third party defendant).

Other courts have construed the term "coparty" more broadly to encompass any party that is not an opposing party (hereinafter, the "Broad Definition"). *See, e.g.*, Ga. Ports Auth. v. Construzioni Meccaniche Industriali Genovesi, S.P.A., 119 F.R.D. 693, 695 (S.D. Ga. 1988).

Under the Broad Definition, the presence of adverse interests between two parties would not, in itself, make them opposing parties rather than coparties . . . .

The Broad Definition allows for a cross-claim by an original defendant, such as Superior, against a third party defendant, such as the Government; the Narrow Definition does not. . . .

B. *The Intended Scope of Rule 13(g) Cross-Claims*

The Supreme Court has indicated that "in ascertaining [the Rules'] meaning the construction given to them by the [Advisory] Committee is of weight." Miss. Publ'g Corp. v. Murphree, 326 U.S. 438, 444 (1946). [After examining an amendment in 1946 to Rule 14 and the accompanying Advisory Committee notes, the court concluded that they appeared "to undermine the contention that the Narrow Definition was intended."] . . .

Facing the question whether third party defendants may cross-claim against an original defendant (the reverse of the case before this Court), a panel of the Fifth Circuit rejected the Narrow Definition. Thomas v. Barton Lodge II, Ltd., 174 F.3d 636, 652 (5th Cir. 1999). The *Thomas* court "agree[d] that a reading of rules 14(a) and 13(g) can lead to the conclusion that third party defendants are barred from filing cross-claims against original defendants," yet found "this reading to be a strained one and the result nonsensical." . . .

Overall, this Court is not persuaded that a plain reading of the Rules suggests that the Narrow Definition applies or that there is any compelling indication that the framers of the Rules intended such. Perhaps, as at least one court has noted, "in the formulation of the Rules, the subject of cross-claims may not have received sufficient consideration."

C. *Cross-Claims in the Framework of the Rules*

The Broad Definition appears to be the most sensible reading of the term "coparty" in the context of the Rules. As one court noted, such construction "comports with the structure of the federal rules, which envision three types of claims that may be asserted by defendants": Rule 13(a) counterclaims against opposing parties, Rule 14(a) third-party claims against non-parties, and Rule 13(g) cross-claims against coparties. *Georgia Ports Authority*, 119 F.R.D. at 695. Adopting the Broad Definition, the *Georgia Ports Authority* court stated: "Certainly, the relationship between an original defendant and a third-party defendant fits somewhere into this framework. Characterizing the relationship as that of 'co-parties' appears to be the logical choice." *Id.*

On the other hand, the Narrow Definition creates a gap in the Rules. If a defending party cannot file a cross-claim against another party on the same side, but not at the same level, of an action, then the Rules are silent regarding how such a claim might be brought. Some courts suggest that the purported cross-claimant would need to file an additional action. Other courts have recognized that this result is a strong reason not to adopt the Narrow Definition. . . . Additionally, the *Georgia Ports Authority* court found that under the Narrow Definition "[c]o-defendants are forced to race to be the first defendant to implead a particular third-party defendant" because all other defendants would then be forced to file independent actions; it rejected the idea that such a result was intended by the Rules. *Id.* at 695.

Other courts have filled the gap left by the Narrow Definition by adding procedural steps to make the parties fit the Rules. Specifically, a court can sever the claims pursuant to Rule 21 (such that the party against whom the claim is to be brought becomes a non-party to the severed claim); the claimant then impleads the non-party pursuant to Rule 14(a), and finally the two actions are reconsolidated. . . .

The Second Circuit has recognized that:

> The general purpose of [Rule 14] was to avoid two actions which should be tried together to save the time and cost of a reduplication of evidence, to obtain consistent results from identical or similar evidence, and to do away with the serious handicap to a defendant of a time difference between a judgment against him and a judgment in his favor against the third-party defendant.

Agrashell, Inc. v. Bernard Sirotta Co., 344 F.2d 583, 585 (2d Cir. 1965). Both Rules 13(g) and 14(a) avoid the delay of a subsequent judgment by allowing a defending party to bring as part of the same action a claim against one who "is or may be liable" to it for all or part of a claim asserted against it. Fed. R. Civ. P. 13(g), 14(a)(1), –(5). This allows a contingent claim for contribution or indemnity, such as Superior's claim against the Government, to be brought as part of the original action, rather than requiring that it be brought as a separate claim once mature.

Similar to the purposes underlying Rule 14 and other provisions of Rule 13, "the general policy behind allowing cross-claims is to avoid multiple suits and to encourage the determination of the entire controversy among the parties before the court with a minimum of procedural steps." 6 CHARLES ALAN WRIGHT ET AL., FEDERAL PRACTICE AND PROCEDURE § 1431, at 229 (2d ed. 1990). Accordingly, "courts generally have construed [Rule 13](g) liberally in order to settle as many related claims as possible in a single action." *Id.* at 229-30. Allowing cross-claims between coparties according to the Broad Definition furthers the purpose of Rule 13(g) by providing a mechanism for claims such as the one before the Court; the Narrow Definition does not.

Finally, and perhaps most significantly, the Rules give explicit guidance regarding how they should be interpreted. Rule 1 states that the Rules "should be construed and administered to secure the just, speedy, and inexpensive determination of every action and proceeding."* . . .

. . . It runs contrary to the purposes of Rules 13 and 14, and the mandate of Rule 1, to construe a lone reference in Rule 14(a) to limit the term "coparty" to the Narrow Definition, when doing so would require multiple actions arising from the same set of facts or add unnecessary procedural steps. Moreover, the reference merely states that "the 'third-party defendant' . . . may assert . . . any crossclaim against another third-party defendant under Rule 13(g)." Fed. R. Civ. P. 14(a). Rule 14 does not state that these are the only cross-claims that a third party defendant may bring, it does not use or define the term "coparty," and it does not state that it limits or defines the scope of Rule 13(g). . . .

CONCLUSION

For the foregoing reasons, the motion to dismiss by cross-defendant, the Government, is denied in its entirety.

Notes and Questions

1. The contribution and indemnity claims that Superior wishes to assert are the types of claims often handled through impleader. But Rule 14(a)(1), which governs impleader practice, allows a third-party claim to be asserted only against a "nonparty." Once KS Gleitlager joined the United States under Rule 14, the United States was no longer a nonparty. So Rule 14 could not be the provision on which Superior based its claim. Rule 13(g) was the obvious alternative, but the "coparty" language then became a sticking point.

2. If Superior had been unable to bring its claim against the United States, it was not the end of the world: Superior could still have asserted the claim in a subsequent case. In contrast to Rule 13(a), which contains the same "transaction or occurrence" language as Rule 13(g), joinder under Rule 13(g) is always permissive, never mandatory. In particular, the failure to file a crossclaim does not preclude a party's later assertion of the claim in separate litigation. *See* 6 CHARLES A. WRIGHT ET AL., FEDERAL PRACTICE AND PROCEDURE § 1431, at 275-76 (3d ed. 2010). Moreover, "[f]ederal courts generally do not apply collateral estoppel, or issue preclusion, between parties who were codefendants in the prior action . . . [b]ecause co-parties are usually not adversaries in fact." Alumax Mills Prods., Inc. v. Cong. Fin. Corp., 912 F.2d 996, 1012 (8th Cir. 1990).

---

* An amendment in 2015 slightly altered the scope of Rule 1, which now provides that the Federal Rules of Civil Procedure "should be construed, administered, and employed by the court and parties to secure the just, speedy, and inexpensive determination of every action and proceeding." — ED.

3. Even though Superior would have lost no legal rights by failing to assert a claim against the United States, it was arguably more efficient to resolve the disputes among all potentially responsible parties in one case. How much should efficiency matter when interpreting a term like "coparty"? How much weight should the autonomy principles that underlie the joinder rules carry? Does the term "coparty" lend itself to a "plain reading"?

4. Consider the following scenario: A sues B and C; C impleads D under Rule 14(a)(1); D impleads E under Rule 14(a)(5). Assuming that *Luyster* is correct, may D bring a claim against B? May D do so under what *Luyster* calls the "narrow definition" of Rule 13(g)? May E bring a claim against B, or B against E? At some point, isn't there a risk that the original dispute (A suing B and C) will become a sideshow?

2. Required Joinder Under Rule 19

Until now, we have focused on rules that permit the plaintiff or defendant to join additional parties. Although there might be negative consequences, such as issue preclusion, from a decision not to join certain potential parties, the Federal Rules generally have given the parties the autonomy to decide when the expected costs of a particular litigation strategy outweigh its expected benefits, and to act in their self-interest in choosing the party structure.

In some circumstances, however, the Federal Rules require the joinder of nonparties. Read Rule 19. According to Rule 19(a), certain nonparties must be "joined if feasible." Their joinder is required because their absence from the case will seriously harm someone's interest — either the plaintiff's interest in obtaining relief (Rule 19(a)(1)(A)), their own interest (Rule 19(a)(1)(B)(i)), or the defendant's interest in avoiding multiple liability for the same injury (Rule 19(a)(1)(B)(ii)). In each case, the potential for harm is thought to outweigh the plaintiff's autonomy to shape the lawsuit. In common vernacular — although not in Rule 19, whose 1966 amendment avoided the phrase in a singularly unsuccessful effort to change the legal vocabulary — these persons are called *necessary parties*. (Note that the present title of Rule 19(a)(1), added in the 2007 stylistic amendments, uses the phrase "required parties," although it remains to be seen if this phrase will displace the old "necessary parties.")

Sometimes it is not possible to join a required party. Perhaps the joinder of the party would destroy the complete diversity of citizenship needed for subject-matter jurisdiction, or perhaps the party is not subject to the personal jurisdiction of the court. *See* Fed. R. Civ. P. 19(a)(1). Perhaps the party enjoys some form of immunity from suit. In each of these situations, a hard choice confronts the judge. Should the case go forward even though a required party is not present, or should the judge dismiss the case and risk denying justice to the plaintiff? Rule 19(b) addresses this problem. Rule 19(b) balances the interests of the plaintiff, the defendant, the party that cannot be joined, and the court system. When this balance indicates that the case should not proceed, the case is to be dismissed. Until 2007, a nonparty whose absence required dismissal of the case was labeled an *indispensable party*. The 2007 amendment to Rule 19(b) eschews this phrase, although it remains to be seen whether the Rule's choice will be any more successful in changing the practicing lawyer's vocabulary than the failed effort in 1966 to halt the use of the phrase "necessary party."

The circumstances in which a nonparty's joinder is required must be limited, or else the required-joinder exception will swallow the permissive-joinder rule. An overly expansive required-joinder rule also creates the risk of dismissing more cases for reasons unrelated to their merits. Have the Federal Rules struck the right balance? Consider the following case.

MAKAH INDIAN TRIBE V. VERITY

910 F.2d 555 (9th Cir. 1990)

Before BROWNING, BEEZER, and RYMER, Circuit Judges.

■ BEEZER, Circuit Judge.

The Makah Indian Tribe brought this action to challenge federal regulations allocating the ocean harvest of migrating Columbia River salmon. The district court dismissed the action for failure to join indispensable parties. We affirm in part, reverse in part and remand.

I

The Makah Indian tribe resides at the northwest corner of the Olympic Peninsula of the State of Washington. Their historic fishing grounds extend forty miles out to sea. The Makah are guaranteed the right to fish in these grounds by treaty.

To protect such Indian treaty rights, a complex judicial and administrative scheme has evolved that regulates the harvest of salmon that pass through these waters. The State of Washington regulates the fisheries within its jurisdiction, extending three miles out to sea, under the continuing jurisdiction of the Washington district court. *See* United States v. Washington, 384 F. Supp. 312 (W.D. Wash. 1974), *aff'd*, 520 F.2d 676 (9th Cir. 1975).[2] The Columbia River harvest is allocated under a similar arrangement overseen by the Oregon district court. *See* United States v. Oregon, 699 F. Supp. 1456, 1458-60 (D. Or. 1988).[3]

Outside the three-mile limit, ocean fishing is regulated by the federal government under the Fishery Conservation and Management Act of 1976 (FCMA). The FCMA establishes the Pacific Fishery Management Council

---

2. The parties to *United States v. Washington* include the Puget Sound treaty tribes, ocean treaty tribes including the Makah, certain Columbia River tribes, and the State of Washington. The federal government is a party to the suit only in its capacity as trustee for the tribes.

3. The Makah are not a party to *United States v. Oregon* but have sought to intervene.

(PFMC), which is composed of representatives of the States of Washington, Oregon, California and Idaho, one representative of the Indian tribes, and the federal government. The PFMC develops a regional fishery management plan which must be consistent with applicable law, including Indian treaty rights, and must consider the regulations of coastal states. In 1978, the PFMC adopted a "framework plan" which calls for consideration of proposals by Indian tribes. After public meetings, the PFMC recommends yearly harvest rates to the Secretary of Commerce, who promulgates regulations detailing ocean fishing allotments. The Secretary's regulations are subject to judicial review under the standards of the Administrative Procedure Act [("APA")].

This action concerns ocean quotas that coordinate with the most recent Columbia River Fish Management Plan. The plan was negotiated by the parties to the *Oregon* suit and approved by the *Oregon* court in 1988. Although not a party to the *Oregon* suit, the federal government participated in the negotiations and signed the plan. The plan sets minimum "escapement" levels for all Columbia River runs with quotas low enough to protect the weakest runs. For 1987, it assigned most of the allowable catch of the weakest run to river fishermen, anticipating low ocean quotas.

After the plan reached final form, but before court approval, the PFMC adopted ocean harvest quotas for the 1987 season that were consistent with the plan. The Makah and three other ocean treaty tribes proposed higher ocean quotas, but their requests were rejected. The Secretary accepted the PFMC's recommendation, and corresponding regulations were published in May 1987. After a nine-day comment period, the regulations became final. Shortly thereafter, the Makah filed this suit challenging the quotas and the regulatory process. The district court dismissed the suit for failure to join the twenty-three treaty tribes of Puget Sound, the Columbia River and the ocean fishery.

. . . We review a district court's dismissal for failure to join an indispensable party for abuse of discretion.

II

The Makah make two types of claims. First, they charge that the quotas adopted violate their treaty rights and are otherwise unfair. They request declaratory relief and an injunction setting a proposed higher quota. They also request a remand to the Secretary for an equitable adjustment for their 1987 losses.

Second, they charge that the Secretary's regulations violate the FCMA. They contend that the quotas were "the product of commitments made outside the administrative process." Specifically, they allege that the Secretary adopted quotas set in secret negotiations, violated notice and comment requirements of the APA, and ignored a quota proposed by the Makah. They also argue that the regulations violate the FCMA because they are arbitrary and capricious, have no basis in the record, and fail to describe

Indian treaty rights. The Makah seek declaratory and injunctive relief requiring the Secretary to comply with the FCMA.

The district court determined that the Makah sought primarily reallocation of the harvest of Columbia River salmon. [The court accepted the government's argument that the total catch could not be increased: "Any adjustment to benefit one tribe, the Makah, must come from the remaining portion available to other treaty tribes."] The court concluded it could not grant this relief without involving the twenty-three absent tribes. Because the other tribes are immune from suit unless they explicitly waive sovereign immunity, the court found them to be indispensable parties under Rule 19(b) and dismissed the suit.

The Makah challenge the court's order. They argue that there is no negative impact on the absent parties because they seek only enforcement of their own treaty rights and an increase in the overall harvest, not a reallocation among the treaty tribes. They also argue that their challenge is to the procedures followed by the Secretary, not just the resulting quotas.

III

To determine whether a party is "indispensable" under Rule 19, a court must undertake a two-part analysis: it must first determine if an absent party is "necessary" to the suit; then if, as here, the party cannot be joined, the court must determine whether the party is "indispens[a]ble" so that in "equity and good conscience" the suit should be dismissed. The inquiry is a practical one and fact specific, *see* Provident Tradesmens Bank & Trust Co. v. Patterson, 390 U.S. 102, 118-19 (1968), and is designed to avoid the harsh results of rigid application. The moving party has the burden of persuasion in arguing for dismissal.

A. *Necessary Party*

To determine if the absent party is necessary to the suit, the court must undertake another two-part analysis.

First, the court must decide if *complete relief* is possible among those already parties to the suit. This analysis is independent of the question whether relief is available to the absent party.

Next, the court must determine whether the absent party has a *legally protected interest* in the suit. This interest must be more than a financial stake, and more than speculation about a future event. A fixed fund which a court is asked to allocate may create a protectable interest in beneficiaries of the fund. Generally, there is no legally protected interest in particular agency procedures.

If a legally protected interest exists, the court must further determine whether that interest will be *impaired or impeded* by the suit. Impairment may be minimized if the absent party is adequately represented in the suit. The United States may adequately represent an Indian tribe unless there is a conflict between the United States and the tribe.

The court must also determine whether *risk of inconsistent rulings* will affect the parties present in the suit. Allocation of a limited fund to which absent parties are entitled may create such a risk.

Applying these principles, the district court determined that the absent tribes were necessary to the suit. The court, viewing the 1987 harvest as a trust fund, held that it could not grant complete relief to the Makah because it would violate the treaty rights of other tribes. It held the absent tribes had an interest in the suit because "any share that goes to the Makah must come from [the] other tribes." It found that the federal government could not protect the interests of the absent tribes because those interests conflict among themselves. Finally, it held that the federal government could face inconsistent rulings if the Makah were awarded a quota that violated other tribes' treaty rights.

We agree that to the extent the Makah seek a reallocation of the 1987 harvest or challenge the Secretary's inter-tribal allocation decisions, the absent tribes may have an interest in the suit. The district court's conclusion that they are necessary parties to an adjudication of those claims was not an abuse of discretion.

We disagree, however, that the absent tribes are necessary to the Makah's procedural claims for which they seek prospective injunctive relief. Paragraphs 1.3.3 and 6.8.2 of the complaint go to the procedures the Secretary followed in promulgating the regulations. Procedures of the PFMC and the Secretary are subject to judicial review under the FCMA and the APA. Under the APA, any person adversely affected by agency action may seek review. Therefore, the district court has the authority to grant relief on the Makah's procedural claims without the presence of the other tribes.

To the extent that the Makah seek relief that would affect only the future conduct of the administrative process, the claims . . . are reasonably susceptible to adjudication without the presence of other tribes. The absent tribes would not be prejudiced because all of the tribes have an equal interest in an administrative process that is lawful. We conclude that the absent tribes are not necessary parties to the request for injunctive relief . . . . However, the scope of the relief available to the Makah on their procedural claims is narrow. None of the Makah's other requests for relief would be appropriately considered in the absence of the other tribes.

B. *Indispensable Party*

Only if the absent parties are "necessary" and cannot be joined must the court determine whether in "equity and good conscience" the case should be dismissed under Rule 19(b). Since we hold that the absent tribes are not necessary to the Makah's procedural challenges, we conclude that those claims should not have been dismissed and need not inquire further. With regard to the Makah's substantive claims requesting a higher quota, we must determine whether the absent tribes are indispens[a]ble under Rule 19(b), requiring another four-part analysis.

First, *prejudice* to any party resulting from a judgment militates toward dismissal of the suit. As in Rule 19(a)(2), the presence of a representative may lessen prejudice. Amicus status is not sufficient to satisfy this test, however, nor is ability to intervene if it requires waiver of immunity.

Second, *shaping of relief* to lessen prejudice may weigh against dismissal. The Supreme Court has encouraged shaping relief to avoid dismissal. *Provident*, 390 U.S. at 111-12. If there is "more than enough pie to satisfy all," then such relief may be adequate.

Third, if an *adequate remedy*, even if not complete, can be awarded without the absent party, the suit may go forward.

Finally, if no *alternative forum* is available to the plaintiff, the court should be "extra cautious" before dismissing the suit.

Applying these principles, the district court concluded that the case should be dismissed. We agree with the court's analysis of the first three factors regarding the Makah's substantive claims. The district court found that prejudice was inevitable since "any relief would be detrimental to the other tribes"; the absent tribes had no proper representative because potential intertribal conflicts meant the United States could not represent all of them. The court held that there was no way to shape relief because the 1987 harvest was a limited resource and any relief would be detrimental to either the Makah or the absent tribes. Similarly, the only "adequate" remedy would be at the cost of the absent parties because the Makah request at a minimum an equitable adjustment by the Secretary. Allowing input from all the tribes would require their participation and was therefore unacceptable.

We disagree with the district court's analysis of the fourth factor. The court suggested the Makah should have brought this action as a subproceeding in *United States v. Washington*. It is not clear, however, that a challenge to the federal regulation of ocean fishing could be brought in *Washington*. The Secretary of Commerce is not a party to that action. The suit concerns only fishing regulations promulgated by the State of Washington. The *Washington* court has not assumed jurisdiction over Columbia River runs or the ocean fishery generally.

Nevertheless, lack of an alternative forum does not automatically prevent dismissal of a suit. Sovereign immunity may leave a party with no forum for its claims. We conclude that the district court's determination that the absent tribes are indispens[a]ble to the Makah's claim for reallocation was not an abuse of discretion.

Notes and Questions

1. Rule 19 is basically a defendants' rule, even though it is in terms equally available to both sides. Plaintiffs usually do not need Rule 19; they can use Rule 20(a)(1) to join as consenting plaintiffs and Rule 20(a)(2) to join defendants. Only if a plaintiff fails to join a potential party (most commonly

a potential defendant, but possibly a party who would be aligned as a plaintiff) is a defendant likely to raise Rule 19. Defendants tend to do so for two reasons. Either they genuinely want the omitted party brought into the case; or they hope to get the case dismissed by convincing the court that the "necessary" party who cannot be joined is "indispensable." (Remember, neither of the terms in quotation marks appears in Rule 19, but courts often use them as shorthand for the Rule 19 analysis.)

2. Rule 19(c) requires a party asserting a claim to identify known necessary parties. This rule is typically honored in the breach, and it falls to the opposing parties to point out the existence of unjoined necessary parties. Failure to join a party under Rule 19 is a defense to a claim. A party that wants to assert the defense must either file a Rule 12(b)(7) motion to dismiss or plead the defense in the answer. Unlike the defenses in Rules 12(b)(2)-(5), a properly asserted Rule 12(b)(7) defense is not waived when a defendant moves to dismiss on other Rule 12(b) grounds. *See* Rule 12(h)(2).

3. *Makah* presents a classic case for the use of Rule 19(a), at least on the re-allocation claim. A pie has been cut up a certain way, with no leftovers. One recipient thinks that its slice of the pie is too small. The only way to make its slice bigger is to take some pie from the others. To do that without their participation in the process seems unfair. Joinder that brings them into the process is one solution to this problem. *Makah* therefore seems to be a straightforward application of Rule 19(a)(1)(B)(i). Can you also make an argument that it is a Rule 19(a)(1)(A) case?

4. Rule 19(a)(1) identifies three types of required parties. Which type is involved in each of these situations?

- Plaintiff Soberay contracted with IPEC to sell a machine, knowing that IPEC was going to resell the machine to MRF in a separate contract. MRF paid IPEC in full for the machine, but IPEC did not fully pay Soberay. Meanwhile, IPEC went bankrupt. Soberay sued MRF for the balance that IPEC owed. Which provision or provisions of Rule 19(a) made IPEC a required party? *See* Soberay Mach. & Equip. Co. v. MRF Ltd., 181 F.3d 759 (6th Cir. 1999).

- A baseball player who was under contract with a team in the Mexican Major Leagues (the Diablos Rojos) sued Major League Baseball and its Commissioner. Asserting interference with economic relations and related torts, the player claimed that the defendants conspired to keep him from signing with the Boston Red Sox. Which provision or provisions of Rule 19(a) made the Diablos Rojos and the Mexican Major Leagues required parties? *See* Camacho v. Major League Baseball, 297 F.R.D. 457 (S.D. Cal. 2013).

- Merrill Lynch held assets that belonged to Ferdinand Marcos, the deposed Philippine dictator. Pimentel and other victims of human-rights abuses during Marcos's regime obtained a $2 billion judgment against Marcos's estate. They sought to collect part of the judgment from the assets. Two entities associated with the Philippine government also claimed title to the assets. What provision or provisions of Rule 19(a) made these entities required parties? *See* Republic of the Philippines v. Pimentel, 553 U.S. 851 (2008).

5. Do you see a consistent thread that runs through all three types of required parties? The thread is not a transactional one; Rule 19(a) does not require the joinder of all persons involved in the transaction. Nor is it autonomy; forced joinder often violates the autonomy of the original parties who did not wish to include the required party, as well as that of the required party, who is forced to participate in the lawsuit. Nor would notions of efficiency explain the rule; Rule 19(a) is far too narrow, and dismissal under Rule 19(b) is far too draconian, to think that efficiency will regularly be advanced by Rule 19. *Cf.* Temple v. Synthes Corp., 498 U.S. 5 (1990) (per curiam) (joint tortfeasors are not required parties, even if it would be more efficient to try their cases in one suit).

6. The real bite of Rule 19 is Rule 19(b), which permits the dismissal of some lawsuits in which a party required to be joined under Rule 19(a) cannot be joined. If a court dismisses a case under the "equity and good conscience" standard of Rule 19(b), the plaintiff can sometimes refile the case in state court. In other situations, no alternate forum exists; for instance, in *Makah*, the other tribes also enjoyed an immunity from suit in state court. In the latter situations, the plaintiff is out of luck. It has lost the claim not on its merits but on a procedural deficiency.

This result does not seem consistent with the on-the-merits orientation of our procedural system. Thus, "'[f]ederal courts are extremely reluctant to grant motions to dismiss based on nonjoinder and, in general, dismissal will be ordered only when the defect cannot be cured and serious prejudice or inefficiency will result.'" Am. Trucking Ass'n v. N.Y. State Thruway Auth., 795 F.3d 351, 357 (2d Cir. 2015) (quoting 7 CHARLES ALAN WRIGHT & ARTHUR R. MILLER, FED. PRACTICE AND PROCEDURE § 1609 (3d ed. 2001)). In *Provident Tradesmens Bank & Trust Co. v. Patterson*, 390 U.S. 102, 109-11 (1968), the Supreme Court formulated the "equity and good conscience" test in this way:

> First, the plaintiff has an interest in having a forum. . . . Second, the defendant may properly wish to avoid multiple litigation, or inconsistent relief, or sole responsibility for a liability he shares with another. . . . Third, there is the interest of the outsider whom it would have been desirable to join. . . . Fourth, there remains the interest of the courts and the public in complete, consistent, and efficient settlement of controversies.

These four factors are not the four factors that Rule 19(b) lists to guide the "equity and good conscience" analysis. In *Pimentel*, the Court hewed closer to the four factors in Rule 19(b). Although the human-rights victims had been unable to collect their $2 billion judgment from any sources other than the assets in the possession of Merrill Lynch, the Court nonetheless held that the inability to join the entities associated with the Philippine government (both of which were immune from suit in American courts) required dismissal under Rule 19(b). The Court emphasized the comity interests that underlay the Philippine government's sovereign immunity, the inability to fashion relief that could avoid damaging these interests if the case proceeded, and the lawsuit's inability to end the dispute over ownership of the assets (given that the Philippine entities, as nonparties, would not be bound by any judgment entered in the case). 553 U.S. at 865-72.

3. Intervention

A different model of joinder would not require the original parties to join additional persons, but would instead give nonparties the opportunity to *intervene* in the case if they wished. Read Rule 24, which governs the ability of nonparties to intervene in other parties' lawsuits.

GRUTTER V. BOLLINGER

188 F.3d 394 (6th Cir. 1999)

Before DAUGHTREY and MOORE, Circuit Judges, and STAFFORD, District Judge.*

■ DAUGHTREY, Circuit Judge.

Before us are two cases in which proposed defendant-intervenors were denied intervention under Federal Rule of Civil Procedure 24(a) and (b), in actions brought against the University of Michigan contesting the use of an applicant's race as a factor in determining admission. The appeals come from separate district courts but present similar, and in some instances the same, issues for our consideration. We have therefore consolidated the two cases for purposes of this opinion, and we find in both instances that the district courts erred in denying intervention under Rule 24(a).

PROCEDURAL AND FACTUAL BACKGROUND

In each of the cases before the court, a group of students and one or more coalitions appeal the denial of their motion to intervene in a lawsuit brought to challenge a race-conscious admissions policy at the University of Michigan. The named plaintiffs in *Gratz v. Bollinger* are two white applicants who were denied admission to the College of Literature, Arts and Science. They allege that the College's admissions policy violates the Equal Protection Clause of the Fourteenth Amendment, 42 U.S.C. § 1981 and § 1983, and 42 U.S.C. §§ 2000d *et seq*. The plaintiffs seek compensatory and punitive damages, injunctive relief forbidding continuation of the alleged discriminatory admissions process, and admission to the College. The intervenors are 17 African-American and Latino/a individuals who have applied or intend to apply to the University, and the Citizens for Affirmative Action's Preservation (CAAP), a nonprofit organization whose stated mission

---

* The Honorable William H. Stafford, United States District Judge for the Northern District of Florida, sitting by designation.

is to preserve opportunities in higher education for African-American and Latino/a students in Michigan. The intervenors claim that the resolution of this case directly threatens the access of qualified African-American and Latino/a students to public higher education and that the University will not adequately represent their interest in educational opportunity. The district court denied their motion for intervention as of right, holding that the plaintiffs did not have a substantial interest in the litigation and that the University could adequately represent the proposed intervenors' interests. The district court also denied the proposed intervenors' alternative motion for permissive intervention.

The named plaintiff in *Grutter v. Bollinger* is a white woman challenging the admissions policy of the University of Michigan Law School [on the same grounds]. . . . The proposed intervenors are 41 students and three pro-affirmative action coalitions. As described by the district court:

> [The] individual proposed intervenors include 21 undergraduate students of various races who currently attend [various undergraduate institutions], all of whom plan to apply to the law school for admission; five black students who currently attend [local high schools] and who also plan to apply to the law school for admission; 12 students of various races who currently attend the law school; a paralegal and a Latino graduate student at the University of Texas at Austin who intend to apply to the law school for admission; and a black graduate student at the University of Michigan who is a member of the Defend Affirmative Action Party.

The plaintiff opposed the motion to intervene, but the defendants, various officials of the Law School and the University, did not oppose the motion. The district court denied the motion to intervene as of right on the basis that the intervenors failed to show that their interests would not be adequately represented by the University. The district court also denied the proposed intervenors' alternative motion for permissive intervention.

DISCUSSION

The proposed intervenors in each of these cases contend principally that the district court erred by denying their motion to intervene as of right. . . . In this circuit, proposed intervenors must establish four elements in order to be entitled to intervene as a matter of right: (1) that the motion to intervene was timely; (2) that they have a substantial legal interest in the subject matter of the case; (3) that their ability to protect that interest may be impaired in the absence of intervention; and (4) that the parties already before the court may not adequately represent their interest. *See* Jansen v. City of Cincinnati, 904 F.2d 336, 340 (6th Cir. 1990). A district court's denial of intervention as of right is reviewed de novo, except for the timeliness element, which is reviewed for an abuse of discretion. The district court held in each of these cases that the motion for intervention was timely, and the plaintiffs do not contest this finding on appeal. We will therefore consider the motions timely and need address only the three remaining elements.

Substantial Legal Interest

The proposed intervenors must show that they have a substantial interest in the subject matter of this litigation. However, in this circuit we subscribe to a "rather expansive notion of the interest sufficient to invoke intervention of right." Mich. State AFL-CIO v. Miller, 103 F.3d 1240, 1245 (6th Cir. 1997). For example, an intervenor need not have the same standing necessary to initiate a lawsuit. We have also "cited with approval decisions of other courts 'reject[ing] the notion that Rule 24(a)(2) requires a specific legal or equitable interest.'" *Miller*, 103 F.3d at 1245. "The inquiry into the substantiality of the claimed interest is necessarily fact-specific." *Id.*

The proposed intervenors argue that their interest in maintaining the use of race as a factor in the University's admissions program is a sufficient substantial legal interest to support intervention as of right. Specifically, they argue that they have a substantial legal interest in educational opportunity, which requires preserving access to the University for African-American and Latino/a students and preventing a decline in the enrollment of African-American and Latino/a students. The district court in *Grutter* "assumed without deciding" that the proposed intervenors do have a significant legal interest in this case and that their ability to protect that interest may be impaired by an adverse ruling in the underlying case. The district court in *Gratz*, however, determined that the proposed intervenors did not have a direct and substantial interest which is "legally protectable" and that they therefore failed to establish this required element. We conclude that Sixth Circuit precedent requires a finding to the contrary.

In *Jansen*, 904 F.2d at 338-39, black applicants and employees of the city's fire department sought to intervene in a reverse discrimination lawsuit challenging the department's use of a quota system. We noted that the proposed intervenors were parties to an earlier consent decree setting goals for minority hiring and found that the proposed intervenors did have a significantly protectable interest in the affirmative action challenged in the lawsuit. The district court in *Gratz* distinguished *Jansen* . . . on the basis that the proposed intervenors in . . . *Jansen* . . . had a legally protected interest only by virtue of their status as parties to a consent decree. As the proposed intervenors point out, however, [*Jansen* does not stand] for the proposition that an interest must be protected by means of a consent decree or by any other particular means in order for the proposed intervenors to be able to establish that they have a substantial legal interest.

The *Gratz* district court's opinion relies heavily on the premise that the proposed intervenors do not have a significant legal interest unless they have a "legally enforceable right to have the existing admissions policy construed." We conclude that this interpretation results from a misreading of this circuit's approach to the issue. . . . For example, in *Miller*, the Michigan Chamber of Commerce sought to intervene in a suit by labor unions challenging an amendment to Michigan's Campaign Finance Act, Mich. Comp. Laws Ann. §§ 169.201-.282 (1996), which extended the application of statutory restrictions on corporate political expenditures so that they applied to unions as well as to corporations. The majority found that the Chamber of Commerce did have a substantial legal interest by virtue of its role in the political process that resulted in the adoption of the contested amendments. The Chamber of Commerce was therefore allowed to intervene as of right, although the Chamber had no legal "right" to the enactment of the challenged legislation. We believe that the district court's attempt to distinguish *Miller* . . ., on the sole basis that [it] involved challenges to legislation, was misguided. The case law of this circuit does not limit the finding of a substantial interest to cases involving the legislative context, any more than it limits such a finding to cases involving a consent decree. . . . This case is, if anything, a significantly stronger case for intervention than *Miller* and many of the cases on which *Miller* relied.

Even if it could be said that the question raised is a close one, "close cases should be resolved in favor of recognizing an interest under Rule 24(a)." *Miller*, 103 F.3d at 1247. The proposed intervenors have enunciated a specific interest in the subject matter of this case, namely their interest in gaining admission to the University, which is considerably more direct and substantial than the interest of the Chamber of Commerce in *Miller* — a much more general interest. We therefore hold that the district court erred in *Gratz* in failing to rule that the proposed intervenors have established that they have a substantial legal interest in the subject matter of this case.

Impairment

"To satisfy this element of the intervention test, a would-be intervenor must show only that impairment of its substantial legal interest is possible if intervention is denied. This burden is minimal." *Miller*, 103 F.3d at 1247. As noted above, the district court in *Grutter* "assumed without deciding" that the proposed intervenors met this element. The district court in *Gratz*, however, determined that because "the proposed intervenors . . . failed to articulate the existence of a substantial legal interest in the subject matter of the instant litigation, it necessarily follows that the proposed intervenors cannot demonstrate an impairment of any interest." The proposed intervenors in *Gratz* continue to argue on appeal that a decision in favor of the plaintiff will adversely affect their interest in educational opportunity by diminishing their likelihood of obtaining admission to the University and by reducing the number of African-American and Latino/a students at the University.

As we have now decided, the district court erred in determining that the proposed intervenors did not have a substantial interest in the subject matter of this case. Consequently, we must likewise conclude that the district court erred in its analysis of the impairment element as well. There is little room for doubt that access to the University for African-American and Latino/a students will be impaired to some extent and that a substantial decline in the enrollment of these students may well result if the University is precluded from considering race as a factor in admissions. Recent experiences in California and Texas suggest such an outcome. The probability of similar effects in Michigan is more than sufficient to meet the minimal requirements of the impairment element.

Inadequate Representation

Finally, the prospective intervenors must show that the existing defendant, the University, may not adequately represent their interests. However, the proposed intervenors are "not required to show that the representation will in fact be inadequate." *Miller*, 103 F.3d at 1247. Indeed, "[i]t may be enough to show that the existing party who purports to seek the same outcome will not make all of the prospective intervenor's arguments." *Id.*

As a preliminary matter, there is some dispute about the relevant standard for determining whether this element has been met when the existing defendant is a governmental entity. The district court in *Gratz* mentioned that the plaintiff relied on *Hopwood v. State of Texas*, 21 F.3d 603 (5th Cir. 1994), for the proposition that a stronger showing of inadequacy is required when a governmental agency is involved as the existing defendant. On reconsideration, however, the district court made clear that it had simply noted the plaintiff's argument in regard to the higher *Hopwood* standard but had not applied this higher standard. In *Grutter*, by contrast, the district court does appear to have applied the more demanding *Hopwood* standard. However, this circuit has declined to endorse a higher standard for inadequacy when a governmental entity [is] involved. For example, in *Miller*, where the defendants included the Secretary of State and the Attorney General, this court clearly stated that the proposed intervenors were required only to show that the representation *might* be inadequate. The district court in *Grutter* therefore erred in applying the higher standard articulated by the Fifth Circuit in *Hopwood*.

The proposed intervenors insist that there is indeed a possibility that the University will inadequately represent their interests, because the University is subject to internal and external institutional pressures that may prevent it from articulating some of the defenses of affirmative action that the proposed intervenors intend to present. They also argue that the University is at less risk of harm than the applicants if it loses this case and, thus, that the University may not defend the case as vigorously as will the proposed intervenors. The district court in *Gratz*, however, found that the proposed intervenors did not identify any specific separate or additional defenses that they will present that the University will not present. The district court in *Grutter* also found that the proposed intervenors failed to show that the University would not adequately represent their interests.

We conclude that the district court erred in each of these cases. The Supreme Court has held, and we have reiterated, that the proposed intervenors' burden in showing inadequacy is "minimal." *See* Trbovich v. United Mine Workers, 404 U.S. 528, 538 n.10 (1972). The proposed intervenors need show only that there is a *potential* for inadequate representation. The proposed intervenors in these two cases have presented legitimate and reasonable concerns about whether the University will present particular defenses of the contested race-conscious admissions policies. We find persuasive their argument that the University is unlikely to present evidence of past discrimination by the University itself or of the disparate impact of some current admissions criteria, and that these may be important and relevant factors in determining the legality of a race-conscious admissions policy. We must therefore conclude that the proposed intervenors have articulated specific relevant defenses that the University may not present and, as a consequence, have established the possibility of inadequate representation.

CONCLUSION

For the reasons set out above, we find that the proposed intervenors have shown that they have a substantial legal interest in the subject matter of this matter, that this interest will be impaired by an adverse determination, and that the existing defendant, the University, may not adequately represent their interest. Hence, the proposed intervenors are entitled to intervene as of right and the district court's decision in each of these cases denying the motion for intervention as of right cannot be sustained. While this determination renders moot the question of permissive intervention under Rule 24(b), we do not believe that the denial of intervention on a permissive basis was erroneous. . . .

■ STAFFORD, District Judge, dissenting. . . .

There is nothing in the record of either case to suggest that the University of Michigan will not zealously defend its voluntarily-adopted admissions policies, will not present all relevant evidence in support of its admissions policies, will not resist unspecified pressures that could temper its ability to defend its admissions policies, or will not raise all defenses or make all arguments that the prospective intervenors may raise or make. Because I do not think that we should substitute our judgment for the informed judgment of the two respective trial judges who determined that, based on the record before them, intervention was not merited, I must respectfully dissent.

Notes and Questions

1. *Grutter* was an early procedural skirmish in the cases that ultimately went to the Supreme Court. The Supreme Court upheld affirmative action and the method of implementation used by the University of Michigan Law School; it struck down the specific method used by the University of Michigan in its undergraduate admissions program. Grutter v. Bollinger, 539 U.S. 306 (2003); Gratz v. Bollinger, 539 U.S. 244 (2003).

2. Are the putative intervenors' interests in *Grutter* sufficiently substantial or tangible to justify intervention? Different courts — and sometimes even the same court — take somewhat broader or narrower

views of Rule 24(a)(2)'s interest requirement. As one court has observed, "[r]ead literally, the 'property or transaction' reference of Rule 24(a) might appear to require a specific piece of property or contract, and the drafters may have intended a narrow reading. However, the case law has effectively rejected the narrow reading, although clear outer boundaries have yet to be developed." Daggett v. Comm'n on Governmental Ethics & Election Practices, 172 F.3d 104, 110 (1st Cir. 1999). *Grutter* claims that it is adopting a broad interpretation of the interest requirement, as do many other courts.

Whatever the exact meaning of "interest," Rule 24 does not permit intervention to the full extent of the transaction or occurrence; otherwise, Rule 24 could have been more simply drafted as "A person may intervene whenever his or her claim or defense arises out of the same transaction or occurrence as the case into which intervention is sought." What justifies our present intervention doctrine, which is consistent with neither the transactional principle nor the autonomy of the plaintiff to structure the case as he or she sees fit? *Cf.* Nuesse v. Camp, 385 F.2d 694, 700 (D.C. Cir. 1967) (noting that Rule 24(a)'s "'interest' test is primarily a practical guide to disposing of lawsuits by involving as many apparently concerned persons as is compatible with efficiency and due process").

3. Exactly what is the "impairment" of the putative intervenors' interests in *Grutter*? If they did not intervene, they would not be parties to the *Grutter* case, and thus could not be legally bound by a decision adverse to their interests. But interpreting "impairment" to mean a "legally binding determination" presents a Catch-22; the only people whose interests can be impaired are the parties, but the parties have no need to intervene. Thus, courts have argued that more practical forms of impairment satisfy the inquiry. One of the classic impairments, which is reflected to some extent in *Grutter*, is the stare-decisis effect of a judgment on the putative intervenor's interests. This form of impairment was first recognized in *Atlantis Development Corp. v. United States,* 379 F.2d 818 (5th Cir. 1967).

Reliance on stare-decisis effects to create an impairment raises some difficulties. Notice that the "impairment" language in Rule 24(a)(2) is nearly the same as (though not identical to) the "impairment" language in Rule 19(a)(1)(B)(i). If stare-decisis effects constitute a sufficient reason to permit intervention, then should these same putative intervenors be mandatorily joined under Rule 19(a)(1)(B)(i)? If they must be mandatorily joined, then what is the point of Rule 24(a)(2)? If they need not be mandatorily joined, then on what logic can you defend giving different meanings to nearly identical language in two related provisions of the Federal Rules?

4. *Grutter* mentions the concept of standing, noting that intervenors "need not have the same standing necessary to initiate a lawsuit." Standing is a constitutional doctrine, grounded in the "case or controversy" requirement of Article III of the Constitution, which requires a litigant in federal court to have a tangible interest in the outcome of the case. Technically, standing and the interest required by Rule 24 are distinct: an interest sufficient for Rule 24 may not always be sufficient under Article III.

Standing was not an issue in *Grutter* because the intervenors sought to intervene as *defendants*. At the time *Grutter* was decided, courts were divided on whether *plaintiff*-intervenors needed to satisfy the standing requirement. But in 2017, the Supreme Court stepped in and held that a plaintiff-intervenor must satisfy Article III standing requirements if he or she seeks relief beyond, or different from, the relief sought by the original plaintiff(s). Town of Chester v. Laroe Estates, Inc., 581 U.S. —, 137 S. Ct. 1645 (2017). As the Court said, "standing is not dispensed in gross," so "[f[or all relief sought, there must be a litigant with standing." *Id*. at 1650, 1651.

5. Permissive intervention remains an option for a person unable to intervene of right. "Permissive" intervention is a bit of a misnomer, at least in terms of how we have been using the phrase until now. Both intervention of right and permissive intervention are permissive in the sense that they rely on the decision of the putative intervenor to seek intervention. As used in Rule 24(b), permissive intervention has a different meaning: it is largely up to the judge's discretion to decide whether to permit the intervention. As *Grutter* reflects, it is not necessarily easier to obtain permissive intervention than intervention of right, mostly because the decision to allow or deny permissive intervention lies within the district court's discretion. The district court can, and often does, impose conditions on a permissive intervenor that limit the intervenor's rights to participate in the litigation.

6. *Grutter* states that the standard of review of a trial court's decision on intervention of right, except on the issue of timeliness, is de novo. We have seen with other joinder rules that the appellate standard is generally abuse of discretion. Is there any reason for intervention to be treated differently? Other courts of appeals state that they review all aspects of a motion to intervene under an abuse-of-discretion standard. *See, e.g.*, Ungar v. Arafat, 634 F.3d 46, 51 (1st Cir. 2011); PA Prison Soc'y v. Cortes, 622 F.3d 215, 232 (3d Cir. 2010). Would the decision not to permit intervention in *Gratz* and *Grutter* have been reversible on an abuse-of-discretion standard? For a case disagreeing with *Grutter* on nearly identical facts, see Students for Fair Admissions, Inc. v. President & Fellows of Harvard College, 807 F.3d 472 (1st Cir. 2015) (holding that the district court did not abuse its discretion in holding that Harvard College adequately represented the interests of prospective students seeking to uphold the college's affirmative-action plan).

7. A person who does not wish to intervene need not. With the narrowest of exceptions, *see* 42 U.S.C. § 2000e-2(n) (discussed *supra* pp. 341-42, Note 7), no adverse preclusion consequences attach to the decision to stay on the sidelines.

4. Other Joinder Rules

The joinder rules described above are the ones that come up most frequently in ordinary litigation. The Federal Rules of Civil Procedure contain two other joinder devices: Rule 22 (interpleader) and Rule 23 (class actions). Some statutory joinder devices and other doctrines that have the indirect effect of achieving joinder also exist. These specialized mechanisms are best studied in an advanced course in civil procedure or complex litigation. Here we briefly profile interpleader and class actions.

a. Interpleader

Modern interpleader, which is descended from the interpleader device available in equity, was designed originally to deal with this problem: Smith had possession of property, which Jones had given him for safekeeping. Johnson believed that the property actually belonged to her, as did White and, of course, Jones. If Johnson sued at common law to recover the property and won, Smith had to give the property to Johnson. But suppose that the next day White sued Smith, claiming that the property really belonged to her. At common law, if White could prove that she was the owner of the property (in other words, she had a better claim to ownership than Johnson), Smith would need to pay her the value of the property that he had given to Johnson. The entire scenario could be replayed if Jones then sued Smith.

Smith's exposure to double or even multiple liability resulted from two factors: first, the limited ability at common law to join other interested parties (no devices equivalent to Rule 19 or Rule 24 were available); and second, the principle, to which we still adhere today, that a person generally cannot be bound by a judgment to which he or she is not a party. Thus, Smith could not join White and Jones when he was first sued by Johnson, and neither White nor Jones was bound by the determination in *Johnson v. Smith* that Johnson was the owner of the property.

Persons who were in the position of Smith (called *stakeholders*) eventually prevailed on the Chancellor to create a means of avoiding the rigors and unfairness of the common law. The device, called interpleader, allowed the stakeholder to sue all of the persons claiming an interest in the property. The Chancellor decided the issue of ownership, and all the claimants, as parties to the proceeding, were bound by the determination. Although interpleader had significant limitations that we need not explore here, it worked reasonably well and was carried forward into modern times.

Two distinct forms of interpleader devices are available in federal court. The first is usually called *rule interpleader*, and is found in Rule 22. Rule interpleader is available whenever there exist "[p]ersons with claims that may expose a plaintiff to double or multiple liability." "Double or multiple liability" does not mean liability to multiple plaintiffs (like a driver who hurts two people) but *logically inconsistent* liability. The stakeholder faces conflicting claims to a single asset and forces the claimants to *interplead* (or state their claims against each other), so that the stakeholder will not have to pay twice (or more) when it should have to pay only once. The ordinary rules of subject-matter jurisdiction, personal jurisdiction, and venue apply to a rule-interpleader suit.

The second type of interpleader is called *statutory interpleader*. As the name suggests, this form of interpleader is authorized by statute rather than by the Federal Rules. The statutory provisions are found at 28 U.S.C. §§ 1335, 1397, and 2361. The remedy provided by statutory interpleader is the same as rule interpleader, but statutory interpleader contains some features that often make it a more useful device. Among the improvements are more generous provisions for subject-matter jurisdiction (instead of all defendants needing to have a different citizenship from the plaintiff, it is enough if any one of the claiming parties has a different citizenship from any other; and only $500 needs to be at stake instead of the $75,000.01 for ordinary diversity cases), for personal jurisdiction, and for venue. As a result, statutory interpleader is usually preferable to rule interpleader, but in limited situations rule interpleader can provide a remedy when statutory interpleader cannot.

Interpleader typically flips the position of the parties; the defendant in the underlying dispute becomes the plaintiff. (Note that Rule 22 provides for the possibility that the stakeholder will be the defendant, and will effect interpleader through counterclaims and crossclaims.) Joinder is permissive, in the sense that the stakeholder decides which claimants to sue.

Among interpleader's most common users are insurance companies, which invoke the device when two or more persons have a claim to a single insurance benefit. For example, both a prior and a surviving spouse might claim to be entitled to a deceased policy holder's life insurance. The insurance company pays the proceeds of the policy into court, interpleads both spouses, and lets the court settle the dispute.

b. Class Actions

Class actions likewise stretch the joinder paradigm. The theoretical and practical challenges of class actions make them the most controversial of the joinder rules, and arguably the most controversial of all the Federal Rules of Civil Procedure. As a result, we return to a fuller study of the federal class-action rule — Rule 23 — in Chapter Twelve, where we use the rule to tie together various parts of the course and to suggest an alternative model for adjudication. Here we simply mention class actions, so that you can understand where they fit into the overall structure of the Federal Rules.

The basic idea of a class action is that a large number of people — a *class* — all find themselves in a similar legal situation as a result of a transaction or series of transactions that has created possible legal liability. A case is brought by or against a representative member or members of the class on behalf of the entire class. The remainder of the class — the *class members* — is bound by the settlement or judgment that this *class representative* obtains. Thus, the class action brings together the entire class of similarly situated people in a single case, settles or adjudicates the claims or defenses of the entire class, and ends the controversy in one fell swoop, win or lose. A string of individual lawsuits is often avoided.

Rule 23 is located in the midst of the rules on party joinder. In some instances, class actions are *mandatory*, so that Rule 23 is a device akin to Rule 19 joinder. In other instances, Rule 23 allows the class members to *opt out* of the class. The right to opt out makes this form of class action somewhat like Rule 20 permissive joinder, but in Rule 20 plaintiffs must assent to joinder — in other words, opt into the case. With the opt-out class action, the presumption runs the other way; unless a class member takes affirmative steps to opt out, he or she is included in the class. Once a class member opts out, he or she is no longer a party in the case, and cannot typically be bound by or benefit from the judgment or settlement achieved in the case. This opt-out idea is a new one for us; it has no precise analogue in the other joinder rules we have studied.

We explore these concepts, as well as other doctrinal and policy features that make class actions so controversial, in Chapter Twelve.

CHAPTER NINE

PERSONAL JURISDICTION AND VENUE

In order to adjudicate a case, a court must have jurisdiction over the parties, or *personal jurisdiction*. Since plaintiffs are held to consent to jurisdiction in a particular forum when they file their case there, personal-jurisdiction questions arise primarily with regard to defendants. Under what circumstances should a defendant — especially one who is not a resident of the forum state — be required to litigate in a forum not of his or her choosing, which may be inconvenient or burdensome? Note that the question is never *whether* a defendant can be sued, but only *where*; nor, in general, have courts suggested that a particular state's exercise of jurisdiction is necessarily related to whether that state's law or another state's law should apply to the case. In the American system of justice, the question of a court's authority over a person is ultimately a constitutional question: under what circumstances does a court have authority to adjudicate the rights of a particular person?

Begin by deciding in your own mind whether the following defendants should be liable to suit in Tennessee, and what principles guide your decisions: (1) A California resident, driving through Tennessee, is involved in an accident with a Tennessee resident and is sued in Tennessee; (2) An Indiana company ships products into Tennessee, and the company is sued in Tennessee by a Tennessee resident who bought the product in Tennessee and claims that it injured her there; (3) A Tennessee resident goes to Indiana and purchases the same product, then returns to Tennessee and sues there when he is injured in Tennessee by the product (Would it matter if the Indiana company does not ship any products to Tennessee, but does ship to other states? If it ships no products out of state?); (4) A California company ships parts to a Michigan manufacturer, knowing that the manufacturer plans to ship the finished product all over the country (including Tennessee); when one of the products shipped into Tennessee injures a resident there, he sues the California company in Tennessee, alleging that the defective part caused the injury; (5) A North Carolina consumer enters into a credit-card contract with a Tennessee bank, and when she fails to pay for purchases she made in North Carolina, the bank sues her in Tennessee (Would it matter if the credit-card contract specifies that Tennessee law governs all disputes between the parties? If the contract specifies that all suits regarding the contract will be litigated in Tennessee?); (6) Can the North Carolina consumer sue the Tennessee credit-card company in North Carolina if she thinks its interest rates are illegally high? As you read through the chapter, compare your answers to those given by courts and commentators.

We begin, in Sections A through D, with an exploration of the general limits on a court's *power* to command that a party submit to its jurisdiction. Then in Section E we consider a second element of personal jurisdiction: what type of *notice* is sufficient to subject a party to the court's jurisdiction? Section F focuses on the personal jurisdiction in the federal courts in particular. Finally, Section G deals with an issue closely related to personal jurisdiction: *venue*, or the appropriate geographic choice of courts among those with both personal and subject-matter jurisdiction.

SECTION A: PERSPECTIVES ON PERSONAL JURISDICTION

In fashioning a doctrine of personal jurisdiction that limits where cases can be brought, the first thing we must decide is why there should be limits at all. In particular, we need to explain why the *Constitution* — rather than doctrines of convenience, or more easily alterable state or federal statutes — should place any limits on where suits can be brought against defendants. The following excerpt summarizes and criticizes the most common justifications for state-based geographic limits on personal jurisdiction, and provides a possible alternative. Compare these various justifications to the principles you formulated in answering the questions above.

WENDY COLLINS PERDUE, PERSONAL JURISDICTION AND THE BEETLE IN THE BOX

32 B.C. L. Rev. 529, 530-31, 533-34, 539, 541-49, 551-56, 560-64, 567-73 (1991)

[E]very few years, the Court's description of personal jurisdiction is inconsistent with its recent prior precedent. . . .

The reason for the Court's difficulty in this area appears to be that personal jurisdiction is really a solution in search of a problem. Although the Court has thought "the problem" to be sufficiently important to warrant its hearing thirteen personal jurisdiction cases in the past fourteen years, it has never explicitly defined the problem. . . .

Some commentators have attempted to describe in some detail the problem for which personal jurisdiction is the solution. They have suggested two related problems for which personal jurisdiction is supposedly the solution. The first of these perceived problems is derived from a central concern of political philosophy, that is, when may a state legitimately exercise coercive power? The second perceived problem reflects commerce clause-related concerns about burdening and discriminating against outsiders who are not represented in the state's political process. . . .

[Proponents of the "political legitimacy" approach argue] that a state can legitimately exercise authority only over those who have, through their conduct, manifested a willing affiliation with the state. "Consent" in the sense of some actual agreement is not necessary for legitimacy, but some form of voluntary affiliating conduct is required. Cases and commentators suggest different versions of this type of tacit consent. . . .

Under one version of tacit consent, obligations arise from the acceptance of benefits. . . .

. . . [But] even people who have never visited a state may benefit. . . . One need not enter a state to benefit from a state's economy or its transportation system.

In addition to these problems, a benefits analysis of state authority is incomplete. In the area of personal jurisdiction, situations can arise in which the defendant has received no benefits but jurisdiction is nonetheless appropriate. *Calder v. Jones*[, 465] U.S. 783 (1984),] is the most obvious example. In *Calder*, the Florida writer of the defamatory article about a California resident did not receive any meaningful benefits from California (at least none beyond those received by all employees of corporations doing business in California). Yet, the Supreme Court unanimously upheld personal jurisdiction. Many other tort cases may similarly prove difficult to fit into the benefits model.

The benefits approach also poses theoretical difficulties. As a theory of governmental legitimacy, it is troubling. Even if we can develop a standard for assessing whether benefits and burdens are commensurate, it is deeply disturbing to suggest that as long as government provides you with something of objective value (that you may not want), it can legitimately extract something from you (that you do not want to give up). . . .

Several commentators who have argued that personal jurisdiction should incorporate a consent theory of legitimacy have offered another variation on tacit consent. They have argued that, although consent in the form of actual agreement is not necessary to legitimacy, some form of voluntary "affiliating conduct" is required in order to protect the "right to remain unconnected to a sovereign." By requiring voluntary affiliating conduct, we limit governmental power in a way that reaffirms both the princip[le] of individual autonomy and the notion that governmental legitimacy derives from the people.

In order to use this approach to explain personal jurisdiction doctrine, rules must be developed that delineate what voluntary actions are "sufficiently affiliating" to legitimate the exercise of power. The rules for inferring consent must exist independently of the supposedly affiliating conduct and must be justified on some other basis. Thus, we need some meta theory of legitimacy, independent of consent, to justify the rules for inferring consent. . . .

Professor Brilmayer, who has argued that personal jurisdiction should be based upon a political philosophy of governmental legitimacy, has offered another approach. She has acknowledged the inadequacy of all the currently advanced theories, including those of tacit consent, observing that "theories of tacit consent assume almost exactly what they set out to prove." As an alternative to tacit consent, Professor Brilmayer has argued that we should abandon consent and apply a "fairness" inquiry that would consider "whether an individual's connections with a state are such as to make it fair to impose upon him or her the state's conception of substantive justice." A volitional act must connect a non-domiciliary with a state in order "to assure a minimal level of individual control over the legal norms to which the individual will be subjected." Although she offered this formulation of the "fairness" argument in the context of choice of law, a similar approach might be offered for personal jurisdiction.

Brilmayer's approach is a variation of the voluntary affiliation argument and shares many of the same problems. She offers little to explain what conduct should or should not be deemed an exercise of control. Consider a confused tourist visiting Washington, D.C., who gets lost and mistakenly crosses a bridge into Virginia. It is appropriate that the tourist be required to comply with Virginia traffic laws and that she be subject to suit in Virginia for any injuries that she happens to cause there. It is completely artificial, however, to suggest that by crossing the Potomac River the tourist has made a meaningful choice of legal norms.

In contrast to the confused tourist, consider a D.C. resident who regularly drives in Virginia. If the D.C. resident hits a Virginia pedestrian while driving in D.C., could she be sued in Virginia? Her regular and knowing use of Virginia roads would seem to demonstrate much more of an acceptance of the legal norms of Virginia than was demonstrated by the confused tourist. Suppose that in addition to regularly driving in Virginia, the D.C. resident participated in political campaigns and debate in Virginia. Would this be sufficient to make her subject to suit in Virginia?

In explaining why some applications should be considered sufficient and others not, Brilmayer has argued that a "state cannot justify predicating jurisdiction upon local conduct that is not legally wrongful." If the goal of jurisdiction is to assure some individual control of the applicable legal norms, however, Brilmayer has no reason to differentiate between legal and illegal conduct. In fact, engaging in illegal or wrongful conduct in a state seems on its face to demonstrate a rejection of that state's legal norms. . . .

With respect to interstate personal jurisdiction, the issue is not under what circumstances people must respect political authority or the authority of a wholly unrelated sovereign. We are already one nation of interdependent states, bound by shared values and one constitution. Inherent in our existence as a nation is that each state and its citizens necessarily accept[ ] the political legitimacy of all the other states. Concerns about political legitimacy might appropriately underlie personal jurisdiction in the international, but not in the interstate, context. The difference between Florida and California on the one hand and Florida and Iran on the other is not merely one of degree. . . .

Once one accepts that states are not wholly autonomous and separate from each other, it becomes very difficult to base personal jurisdiction doctrine on a theory of political obligation. For example, one could accept a traditional consent theory of political legitimacy yet still conclude that states have unlimited adjudicatory authority by arguing that by participating in our interdependent nation with its free interstate flow of goods and services, we have all consented to be sued in any state. The free flow of commerce among the states has many benefits, but one of its costs is that interstate commerce sometimes produces detrimental effects on places far away from one of the participants in a transaction. Having accepted the benefits of our free flowing economy, it is fair to impose the burden of possible distant litigation. . . .

[Other commentators] have suggested that a state's overly aggressive assertion of personal jurisdiction may impede interstate commerce because producers, fearful that they may have to litigate in some distant forum, may either curtail production or increase prices. Thus, proponents of this view might argue that if the car dealer in *World–Wide Volkswagen* could be sued anywhere that the car he sold blew up, then he would have to curtail his sales or raise the price of his cars in order to cover the costs of this additional risk. In effect, the risk of litigation in distant fora impedes interstate commerce. . . .

Even if a state's broad assertion of jurisdiction over out-of-state defendants did impose a burden on interstate commerce, the state's conduct would not necessarily be impermissible. Under traditional commerce clause analysis, the court would balance the state's interest in jurisdiction against the burdens imposed on the defendant. The burdens imposed by more expansive personal jurisdiction may be quite modest. The burden at issue is not the burden of litigation, because personal jurisdiction does not protect a defendant from suit, but rather the incremental additional cost that must be incurred by virtue of litigating in some forum other than one's home state. This additional cost may be quite small. On the other hand, the assertion of jurisdiction over an out-of-state defendant may serve a legitimate state interest. In the context of products liability, for example, a state might conclude that the burdens of distant litigation may be particularly onerous for plaintiffs who tend to be one-time players in the legal system, who may find it particularly difficult to find a lawyer in a different state, and who may lack the necessary resources for the upfront costs of distant litigation. . . .

. . . [I]t is not clear why states cannot be protectionist in this context. When a plaintiff and a defendant are from different states, at least one will unavoidably bear the burden of distant litigation. There are only two options — either the in-state plaintiff or the out-of-state defendant bears the burden. In this context, it seems odd to conclude that the Constitution requires states to choose to disadvantage their citizens.

It is sometimes argued that notwithstanding a state's legitimate interest in providing a forum for its local plaintiffs, a bias in favor of defendants is warranted because "society normally gives less weight to the interest of the plaintiff who disturbed the tranquility and initiated the litigation." Whatever the pedigree of the view that plaintiffs generally should be regarded as troublemakers, there are several difficulties with incorporating it into personal jurisdiction doctrine. First, as an empirical description of actual attitudes of society, it is disputable that plaintiffs are generally viewed as troublemakers. Surely most plaintiffs would describe the situation differently and argue that the defendant, not the litigation, disrupted the status quo. . . .

Second, even if an anti-plaintiff bias generally exists, the more fundamental question is whether the Constitution mandates that states adopt this anti-plaintiff view. This question reflects a classic problem of defining the appropriate constitutional baseline from which to evaluate state power. There is certainly no textual basis for concluding that states are required to treat litigation as disruptive rather than restorative of the status quo. Where states have affirmatively chosen to favor one side in litigation, there is no reason why the Constitution should displace that choice. . . .

[Thus] the traditional understanding of the problem for which personal jurisdiction is the solution is inadequate, [but nonetheless] there may be problems for which personal jurisdiction is the solution. These problems do not involve profound or abstract issues of the nature of sovereignty or the sources of governmental legitimacy. They are much more mundane and reflect the considerations that motivate actual litigants to care about personal jurisdiction.

Litigants do care about personal jurisdiction; indeed, they care enough to litigate the issue of personal jurisdiction all the way to the United States Supreme Court. They care not because of abstract philosophical reasons, but because the place where the litigation is conducted has a number of practical consequences: choice of law; convenience or inconvenience for one party; and local bias or perception that judges or juries in particular locales are more or less generous. In short, there are numerous practical reasons why choice of forum matters.

Personal jurisdiction limits the plaintiff's choice of fora. The fundamental question is whether there are reasons why the federal courts should limit the plaintiff's choice. Although my conclusions are still somewhat tentative, I believe that it is possible to justify a personal jurisdiction doctrine, the sole purpose of which is to limit plaintiff's choice of fora.

The rationale for such a doctrine would derive from three major practical reasons why litigants care about choice of forum: convenience, bias, and choice of law. All three of these considerations can be conceived of as problems for which the federal courts should supply a solution.

Notes and Questions

1. The American doctrine of state-based geographic limits on personal jurisdiction is not the only possible solution to the puzzle of jurisdiction in a federal system. Australia, for example, once allowed personal jurisdiction over a domestic defendant in any Australian court (federal, state, or territorial), but required that the case be transferred to a different court if it was "in the interests of justice." *Jurisdiction of Courts (Cross-vesting) Act 1987* (Cth) (Austl.), subsequently invalidated in *Re Wakim* [1999] 198 CLR 511 (Austl.). In the European Union — which, like our own federal system, brings together many separate sovereigns into a single union for some purposes — the focus is on the relationship between the controversy and the forum rather than that between the defendant and the forum; the purpose seems to be to limit the number of forums in which a suit can be brought rather than to protect either sovereigns or defendants. For a more detailed comparative perspective, see Linda J. Silberman, *Judicial Jurisdiction in the Conflict of Laws Course: Adding a Comparative Dimension*, 28 VAND. J. TRANSNAT'L L. 389 (1995).

2. Why should a defendant who lives in San Diego be subject to the jurisdiction of a court in San Francisco, 500 miles away, when a defendant who lives in New York City might not be subject to the jurisdiction of a court in Newark, New Jersey, just a quick trip across the Hudson River?

3. Think about how personal jurisdiction and choice of law might work, together and separately. Under current doctrine, the Supreme Court places few limits on state decisions regarding choice of law: a state is entitled to apply its own law to a dispute as long as the choice is neither arbitrary nor fundamentally unfair. Given that hands-off approach, does it make sense to impose *greater* limits on jurisdiction than on choice of law? Professor Silberman suggests that "[t]o believe that a defendant's contacts with the forum state should be stronger under the Due Process Clause for jurisdictional purposes than for choice of law is to believe that an accused is more concerned with where he will be hanged than with whether." Linda Silberman, Shaffer v. Heitner: *The End of an Era*, 53 N.Y.U. L. REV. 33, 88 (1978). Might an alternative argument be that imposing stricter limits on jurisdiction is a back-door method of preventing states from using their own substantive law in arguably inappropriate situations? If so, should courts focus more directly on choice of law?

SECTION B: FROM PRESENCE TO CONTACTS

Each American state has always had its own court system, and questions therefore arose early in our history about the extent to which a state court could exercise jurisdiction over residents of other states. (We will consider the reach of the personal jurisdiction of federal courts in Section F, but for now you can assume that a federal court is subject to the same limits that would apply to a state court in the same state.) Although it is possible to argue that every American court should have jurisdiction over every American citizen, American courts have always assumed that state territorial boundaries matter. The issue then becomes the circumstances under which a court can exercise jurisdiction over persons outside its boundaries. The cases in this section illustrate the Supreme Court's gradual evolution from a formal insistence that a state may exercise jurisdiction only over an individual "present" in the state to a more functionalist analysis of the specific connections between the defendant and the forum state. As you read these cases, consider why there should be limits on state-court power over persons, and how those limits should be structured in light of their purposes.

In order to understand the first case, *Pennoyer v. Neff,* you need to know some technical terms. *Attachment* is a formal process by which the state takes control over someone's real property. It can be initiated by individuals, as, for example, when a potential plaintiff wishes to prevent a potential defendant from selling land whose ownership is disputed. The particular formal requirements for a successful attachment are specified by state law, and usually involve law-enforcement personnel posting a notice on the property. *In rem* jurisdiction is reserved for general disputes about the property itself, such as who owns it. Attachment can also be used in narrower *quasi in rem* cases, which under *Pennoyer* could but did not have to relate to the property. Finally, if no property is attached, a suit is said to be *in personam*, that is, against the person rather than against the property. Read *Pennoyer* carefully to determine the different circumstances under which a court can exercise jurisdiction over a nonresident defendant in *in rem*, *quasi in rem*, and *in personam* suits.

PENNOYER V. NEFF

95 U.S. 714 (1878)

■ MR. JUSTICE FIELD delivered the opinion of the court. . . .

[J.H. Mitchell sued Marcus Neff in Oregon state court, on a debt owed for legal services. Mitchell claimed that he could not find Neff to serve process, and instead published notice of the suit in a newspaper. Neff, who was not an Oregon resident at the time, did not appear, and Mitchell obtained a default judgment. To satisfy the judgment, the state sold property that Neff owned in Oregon, and turned the proceeds from the sale over to Mitchell. (This is a common method of satisfying judgments if the defendant does not pay voluntarily. In this case, the property had *not* been attached before the suit.) Sylvester Pennoyer later acquired the property. When Neff returned to Oregon, he sued Pennoyer in federal court to recover his property, claiming that Mitchell's original judgment against Neff was invalid because the Oregon state court had not had jurisdiction over Neff. The federal trial court found in favor of Neff, on the ground that the defendant's proof of publication did not satisfy the requirements of Oregon law, and Pennoyer appealed to the United States Supreme Court.

[In addition to the defects in publication found by the lower court,] it was also contended in that court, and is insisted upon here, that the judgment in the State court against the plaintiff was void for want of personal service of process on him, or of his appearance in the action in which it was rendered and that the premises in controversy could not be subjected to the payment of the demand of a resident creditor except by a proceeding *in rem;* that is, by a direct proceeding against the property for that purpose. If these positions are sound, the ruling of the [trial court] as to the invalidity of that judgment must be sustained.... And that they are sound would seem to follow from two well-established principles of public law respecting the jurisdiction of an independent State over persons and property. The several States of the Union are not, it is true, in every respect independent, many of the right[s] and powers which originally belonged to them being now vested in the government created by the Constitution. But, except as restrained and limited by that instrument, they possess and exercise the authority of independent States, and the principles of public law to which we have referred are applicable to them. One of these principles is, that every State possesses exclusive jurisdiction and sovereignty over persons and property within its territory.... The other principle of public law referred to follows from the one mentioned; that is, that no State can exercise direct jurisdiction and authority over persons or property without its territory. The several States are of equal dignity and authority, and the independence of one implies the exclusion of power from all others. And so it is laid down by jurists, as an elementary principle, that the laws of one State have no operation outside of its territory, except so far as is allowed by comity; and that no tribunal established by it can extend its process beyond that territory so as to subject either persons or property to its decisions. "Any exertion of authority of this sort beyond this limit," says [Justice] Story, "is a mere nullity, and incapable of binding such persons or property in any other tribunals."

But as contracts made in one State may be enforceable only in another State, and property may be held by non-residents, the exercise of the jurisdiction which every State is admitted to possess over persons and property within its own territory will often affect persons and property without it. To any influence exerted in this way by a State affecting persons resident or property situated elsewhere, no objection can be justly taken; whilst any direct exertion of authority upon them, in an attempt to give ex-territorial operation to its laws, or to enforce an ex-territorial jurisdiction by its tribunals, would be deemed an encroachment upon the independence of the State in which the persons are domiciled or the property is situated, and be resisted as usurpation.

Thus the State, through its tribunals, may compel persons domiciled within its limits to execute, in pursuance of their contracts respecting property elsewhere situated, instruments in such form and with such solemnities as to transfer the title, so far as such formalities can be complied with; and the exercise of this jurisdiction in no manner interferes with the supreme control over the property by the State within which it is situated.

So the State, through its tribunals, may subject property situated within its limits owned by non-residents to the payment of the demand of its own citizens against them; and the exercise of this jurisdiction in no respect infringes upon the sovereignty of the State where the owners are domiciled. Every State owes protection to its own citizens; and, when non-residents deal with them, it is a legitimate and just exercise of authority to hold and appropriate any property owned by such non-residents to satisfy the claims of its citizens. It is in virtue of the State's jurisdiction over the property of the non-resident situated within its limits that its tribunals can inquire into that non-resident's obligations to its own citizens, and the inquiry can then be carried only to the extent necessary to control the disposition of the property. If the non-resident have no property in the State, there is nothing upon which the tribunals can adjudicate.

These views are not new. They have been frequently expressed, with more or less distinctness, in opinions of eminent judges, and have been carried into adjudications in numerous cases. Thus . . . Mr. Justice Story said:

> Where a party is within a territory, he may justly be subjected to its process, and bound personally by the judgment pronounced on such process against him. Where he is not within such territory, and is not personally subject to its laws, if, on account of his supposed or actual property being within the territory, process by the local laws may, by attachment, go to compel his appearance, and for his default to appear judgment may be pronounced against him, such a judgment must, upon general principles, be deemed only to bind him to the extent of such property, and cannot have the effect of a conclusive judgment *in personam* . . . .

. . . [This] is the only doctrine consistent with proper protection to citizens of other States. If, without personal service, judgments *in personam*, obtained *ex parte* [without the appearance of the other party — ED.] against non-residents and absent parties, upon mere publication of process, which, in the great majority of cases, would never be seen by the parties interested, could be upheld and enforced, they would be the constant instruments of fraud and oppression. Judgments for all sorts of claims upon contracts and for torts, real or pretended, would be thus obtained, under which property would be seized, when the evidence of the transactions upon which they were founded, if they ever had any existence, had perished.

Substituted service by publication, or in any other authorized form, may be sufficient to inform parties of the object of proceedings taken where property is once brought under the control of the court by seizure or some equivalent act. The law assumes that property is always in the possession of its owner, in person or by agent; and it proceeds upon the theory that its seizure will inform him, not only that it is taken into the custody of the court, but that he must look to any proceedings authorized by law upon such seizure for its condemnation and sale. . . . In other words, such service may answer in all actions which are substantially proceedings *in rem*. But where the entire object of the action is to determine the personal rights and obligations of the defendants, that is, where the suit is merely *in personam*, constructive service in this form upon a non-resident is ineffectual for any purpose. Process from the tribunals of one State cannot run into another State, and summon parties there domiciled to leave its territory and respond to proceedings against them. Publication of process or notice within the State where the tribunal sits cannot create any greater obligation upon the non-resident to appear. Process sent to him out of the State, and process published within it, are equally unavailing in proceedings to establish his personal liability.

The want of authority of the tribunals of a State to adjudicate upon the obligations of non-residents, where they have no property within its limits, is not denied by the court below: but the position is assumed, that, where they have property within the State, it is immaterial whether the property is in the first instance brought under the control of the court by attachment or some other equivalent act, and afterwards applied by its judgment to the satisfaction of demands against its owner; or such demands be first established in a personal action, and the property of the non-resident be afterwards seized and sold on execution. But the answer to this position has already been given in the statement, that the jurisdiction of the court to inquire into and determine his obligations at all is only incidental to its jurisdiction over the property. Its jurisdiction in that respect cannot be made to depend upon facts to be ascertained after it has tried the cause and rendered the judgment. If the judgment be previously void, it will not become valid by the subsequent discovery of property of the defendant, or by his subsequent acquisition of it. The judgment, if void when rendered, will always remain void: it cannot occupy the doubtful position of being valid if property be found, and void if there be none. . . .

Since the adoption of the Fourteenth Amendment to the Federal Constitution, the validity of such judgments [against non-residents] may be directly questioned, and their enforcement in the State resisted, on the ground that proceedings in a court of justice to determine the personal rights and obligations of parties over whom that court has no jurisdiction do not constitute due process of law. Whatever difficulty may be experienced in giving to those terms a definition which will embrace every permissible exertion of power affecting private rights, and exclude such as is forbidden, there can be no doubt of their meaning when applied to judicial proceedings. They then mean a course of legal proceedings according to those rules and principles which have been established in our systems of jurisprudence for the protection and enforcement of private rights. To give such proceedings any validity, there must be a tribunal competent by its constitution — that is, by the law of its creation — to pass upon the subject-matter of the suit; and, if that involves merely a determination of the personal liability of the defendant, he must be brought within its jurisdiction by service of process within the State, or his voluntary appearance. . . .

It follows from the views expressed that the personal judgment recovered in the State court of Oregon against the plaintiff herein, then a non-resident of the State, was without any validity, and did not authorize a sale of the property in controversy. . . .

■ [The dissenting opinion of MR. JUSTICE HUNT is omitted.]

Notes and Questions

1. Although they are not relevant to the disposition of the case, you might want to know several additional facts. Notice of the suit was published in the *Pacific Christian Advocate*, "a weekly newspaper published under the authority of the Methodist Episcopal Church and devoted primarily to religious news and inspirational articles." Wendy Collins Perdue, *Sin, Scandal, and Substantive Due Process: Personal Jurisdiction and* Pennoyer *Reconsidered*, 62 WASH. L. REV. 479, 485 (1987). After winning the default judgment, Mitchell did not immediately execute on it, but waited almost five months, until confirmation of Neff's ownership of the property had arrived from Washington, D.C. (the federal government at the time was giving away undeveloped land in Oregon to homesteaders). When the state ultimately sold Neff's property to satisfy the judgment, the buyer was Mitchell himself, who assigned it to Pennoyer three days later. Both Mitchell and Pennoyer were colorful characters. Mitchell was a seducer of teen-age girls and a bigamist who became a United States Senator, and was eventually convicted of fraud. Pennoyer became Governor of Oregon, and, in his inaugural address, decried the Supreme Court decision in *Pennoyer*, ten years after it was decided. Neff, on the other hand, "disappeared into obscurity" after the case. *Id.* at 488. Professor Perdue's wonderful article contains many other tidbits, as well as an interesting legal analysis.

2. Note that the Court finds even actual notice insufficient to confer jurisdiction over a defendant not present in the state. But in numerous cases around the same time as *Pennoyer*, the Court held that attachment of property was sufficient to confer jurisdiction by itself, without any attempt at notice. The Court's justification was that a property owner is "always in possession of his property" and thus that the attachment itself (usually by posting a notice on the property) will suffice to give him notice. Do you think that Neff, who was apparently living in California when Mitchell's suit was filed, would have been any more aware of the suit had Mitchell or the sheriff tacked a notice onto a tree on the property?

3. Imagine that the debt Neff owed Mitchell was for services relating to the property itself (it may have been; the historical record is unclear). Also assume that Mitchell had tracked Neff down in California, and had personally served him with notice of the lawsuit. Under *Pennoyer*, the Oregon court would still have lacked jurisdiction. Yet there would have been jurisdiction had Mitchell merely attached the property — even if the debt had nothing to do with the property, and even if no other notice of the suit was given. On what theory of jurisdiction can such a distinction rest? (Hint: what does the *Pennoyer* Court say about personal jurisdiction and state sovereignty?) Do you think such a distinction is fair?

4. *Pennoyer* also drew another distinction: between former residents, like Neff, who had permanently left the state, and current residents who were temporarily absent from the state. The latter could be subject to jurisdiction even though they were served with process in another state. *See* Milliken v. Meyer, 311 U.S. 457 (1940). Again, the subject of the lawsuit did not matter: even if the suit concerned a tort that the former resident had committed while still a resident, *Pennoyer* required the plaintiff to seek out the defendant in her new residence. Is *that* distinction fair?

5. The *Pennoyer* doctrine began causing serious problems around the beginning of the twentieth century, with growth in interstate commerce and the advent of the automobile. Apply *Pennoyer* to the following case. A Pennsylvania driver, driving in Massachusetts, hits a pedestrian who is a citizen of Massachusetts. After the accident, he returns home to Pennsylvania. The Massachusetts pedestrian would like to sue him in Massachusetts. Can she? In *Hess v. Pawloski*, 274 U.S. 352 (1927), the Supreme Court permitted just such a suit. A Massachusetts statute asserted jurisdiction over out-of-state drivers on the theory that they had implicitly consented to jurisdiction in Massachusetts by driving on Massachusetts public roads. The Court upheld the statute against a due-process challenge. Do you think the Pennsylvania driver thought he had consented to jurisdiction in Massachusetts? Did exercising jurisdiction over him violate the underlying theory of *Pennoyer*?

Things got even stickier with corporations that did business in multiple states. Initially, states required any corporation that wanted to do business in the state to appoint an in-state agent who could accept service of process. But as interstate business increased, such requirements became more difficult to enforce, and, inevitably, suits were brought against out-of-state corporations that had failed to appoint an agent. Despite the apparently insurmountable obstacle of *Pennoyer*, courts began upholding jurisdiction on a variety of fictions similar to the "implied consent" fiction used for out-of-state motorists. They held that doing business in the state, like driving in the state, implied consent to jurisdiction, or that doing business in the state warranted an inference that a corporation was "present" in the state. The tests for jurisdiction moved further and further from the bright line of *Pennoyer*, and led to all sorts of unjustified distinctions. For example, a corporation could avoid jurisdiction in a particular state, after causing injury there, simply by ceasing to do any business in the state.

6. Reduced to its essentials, *Pennoyer* holds that, in general, no state may exercise jurisdiction over the citizens of another state even if the out-of-stater has substantial connections to the state. (*Pennoyer* recognized two exceptions: when the in-state property was the subject of the suit, and when the defendant was served in the state.) By emphasizing territorial boundaries and each state's exclusive power over persons within its boundaries, *Pennoyer* created many problems in a society with increasing numbers of interstate corporations and increasingly mobile citizens. The Supreme Court tried to find a way out of the *Pennoyer* morass in the

following case. As you read it, think about how it treats both territorial boundaries and individual expectations.

INTERNATIONAL SHOE CO. V. WASHINGTON

326 U.S. 310 (1945)

MR. CHIEF JUSTICE STONE delivered the opinion of the Court.

The [question] for decision [is] ... whether, within the limitations of the due process clause of the Fourteenth Amendment, appellant, a Delaware corporation, has by its activities in the State of Washington rendered itself amenable to proceedings in the courts of that state to recover unpaid contributions to the state unemployment compensation fund exacted by state statutes. . . .

The statutes in question set up a comprehensive scheme of unemployment compensation, the costs of which are defrayed by contributions required to be made by employers to a state unemployment compensation fund. The contributions are a specified percentage of the wages payable annually by each employer for his employees' services in the state. . . .

In this case notice of [payments due] for the years in question was personally served upon a sales solicitor employed by appellant in the State of Washington, and a copy of the notice was mailed by registered mail to appellant at its address in St. Louis, Missouri. Appellant appeared specially* before the office of unemployment and moved to set aside the order and notice of [payments due] on the ground that ... appellant was not a corporation of the State of Washington and was not doing business within the state; [and] that it had no agent within the state upon whom service could be made . . . .

The facts as found by the appeal tribunal and accepted by the state Superior Court and Supreme Court, are not in dispute. Appellant is a Delaware corporation, having its principal place of business in St. Louis, Missouri, and is engaged in the manufacture and sale of shoes and other footwear. It maintains places of business in several states, other than Washington, at which its manufacturing is carried on and from which its merchandise is distributed interstate through several sales units or branches located outside the State of Washington.

Appellant has no office in Washington and makes no contracts either for sale or purchase of merchandise there. It maintains no stock of merchandise

---

* A "special appearance" allows a party to participate in a case solely for the purpose of contesting jurisdiction. Without a rule allowing a special appearance, a party who showed up to argue a lack of personal jurisdiction could be served with process upon entering the courtroom, thus establishing the very jurisdiction that the party was trying to contest. An equivalent to the special appearance is a motion to dismiss under Fed. R. Civ. P. 12(b)(2). For a full discussion of the issues surrounding the special appearance, see *infra* pp. 477-78, Note 4. — ED.

in that state and makes there no deliveries of goods in intrastate commerce. During the years from 1937 to 1940, now in question, appellant employed eleven to thirteen salesmen under direct supervision and control of sales managers located in St. Louis. These salesmen resided in Washington; their principal activities were confined to that state; and they were compensated by commissions based upon the amount of their sales. The commissions for each year totaled more than $31,000. Appellant supplies its salesmen with a line of samples, each consisting of one shoe of a pair, which they display to prospective purchasers. On occasion they rent permanent sample rooms, for exhibiting samples, in business buildings, or rent rooms in hotels or business buildings temporarily for that purpose. The cost of such rentals is reimbursed by appellant.

The authority of the salesmen is limited to exhibiting their samples and soliciting orders from prospective buyers, at prices and on terms fixed by appellant. The salesmen transmit the orders to appellant's office in St. Louis for acceptance or rejection, and when accepted the merchandise for filling the orders is shipped . . . from points outside Washington to the purchasers within the state. All the merchandise shipped into Washington is invoiced at the place of shipment from which collections are made. No salesman has authority to enter into contracts or to make collections.

The Supreme Court of Washington was of opinion that the regular and systematic solicitation of orders in the state by appellant's salesmen, resulting in a continuous flow of appellant's product into the state, was sufficient to constitute doing business in the state so as to make appellant amenable to suit in its courts. . . .

Appellant . . . insists that its activities within the state were not sufficient to manifest its "presence" there and that in its absence the state courts were without jurisdiction, that consequently it was a denial of due process for the state to subject appellant to suit. It refers to those cases in which it was said that the mere solicitation of orders for the purchase of goods within a state, to be accepted without the state and filled by shipment of the purchased goods interstate, does not render the corporation seller amenable to suit within the state. . . .

Historically the jurisdiction of courts to render judgment *in personam* is grounded on their de facto power over the defendant's person. Hence his presence within the territorial jurisdiction of a court was prerequisite to its rendition of a judgment personally binding him. Pennoyer v. Neff, 95 U.S. 714 (1877). But now that the *capias ad respondendum* [an old form of process involving physical detention of a defendant to secure jurisdiction — ED.] has given way to personal service of summons or other form of notice, due process requires only that in order to subject a defendant to a judgment *in personam*, if he be not present within the territory of the forum, he have certain minimum contacts with it such that the maintenance of the suit does not offend "traditional notions of fair play and substantial justice." Milliken v. Meyer, 311 U.S. 457, 463 (1940).

Since the corporate personality is a fiction, . . . it is clear that unlike an individual its "presence" without, as well as within, the state of its origin can be manifested only by activities carried on in its behalf by those who are authorized to act for it. To say that the corporation is so far "present" there as to satisfy due process requirements, for purposes of . . . the maintenance of suits against it in the courts of the state, is to beg the question to be decided. For the terms "present" or "presence" are used merely to symbolize those activities of the corporation's agent within the state which courts will deem to be sufficient to satisfy the demands of due process. . . . Those demands may be met by such contacts of the corporation with the state of the forum as make it reasonable, in the context of our federal system of government, to require the corporation to defend the particular suit which is brought there. An "estimate of the inconveniences" which would result to the corporation from a trial away from its "home" or principal place of business is relevant in this connection.

"Presence" in the state in this sense has never been doubted when the activities of the corporation there have not only been continuous and systematic, but also give rise to the liabilities sued on, even though no consent to be sued or authorization to an agent to accept service of process has been given. Conversely it has been generally recognized that the casual presence of the corporate agent or even his conduct of single or isolated items of activities in a state in the corporation's behalf are not enough to subject it to suit on causes of action unconnected with the activities there. To require the corporation in such circumstances to defend the suit away from its home or other jurisdiction where it carries on more substantial activities has been thought to lay too great and unreasonable a burden on the corporation to comport with due process.

While it has been held in cases on which appellant relies that continuous activity of some sorts within a state is not enough to support the demand that the corporation be amenable to suits unrelated to that activity, there have been instances in which the continuous corporate operations within a state were thought so substantial and of such a nature as to justify suit against it on causes of action arising from dealings entirely distinct from those activities.

Finally, although the commission of some single or occasional acts of the corporate agent in a state sufficient to impose an obligation or liability on the corporation has not been thought to confer upon the state authority to enforce it, other such acts, because of their nature and quality and the circumstances of their commission, may be deemed sufficient to render the corporation liable to suit. True, some of the decisions holding the corporation amenable to suit have been supported by resort to the legal fiction that it has given its consent to service and suit, consent being implied from its presence in the state through the acts of its authorized agents. But more realistically it may be said that those authorized acts were of such a nature as to justify the fiction.

It is evident that the criteria by which we mark the boundary line between those activities which justify the subjection of a corporation to suit, and those which do not, cannot be simply mechanical or quantitative. The test is not merely, as has sometimes been suggested, whether the activity, which the corporation has seen fit to procure through its agents in another state, is a little more or a little less. Whether due process is satisfied must depend rather upon the quality and nature of the activity in relation to the fair and orderly administration of the laws which it was the purpose of the due process clause to insure. That clause does not contemplate that a state may make binding a judgment *in personam* against an individual or corporate defendant with which the state has no contacts, ties, or relations.

But to the extent that a corporation exercises the privilege of conducting activities within a state, it enjoys the benefits and protection of the laws of that state. The exercise of that privilege may give rise to obligations; and, so far as those obligations arise out of or are connected with the activities within the state, a procedure which requires the corporation to respond to a suit brought to enforce them can, in most instances, hardly be said to be undue.

Applying these standards, the activities carried on in behalf of appellant in the State of Washington were neither irregular nor casual. They were systematic and continuous throughout the years in question. They resulted in a large volume of interstate business, in the course of which appellant received the benefits and protection of the laws of the state, including the right to resort to the courts for the enforcement of its rights. The obligation which is here sued upon arose out of those very activities. It is evident that these operations establish sufficient contacts or ties with the state of the forum to make it reasonable and just according to our traditional conception of fair play and substantial justice to permit the state to enforce the obligations which appellant has incurred there. Hence we cannot say that the maintenance of the present suit in the State of Washington involves an unreasonable or undue procedure. . . .

Appellant having rendered itself amenable to suit upon obligations arising out of the activities of its salesmen in Washington, the state may maintain the present suit *in personam* to collect the tax laid upon the exercise of the privilege of employing appellant's salesmen within the state. . . .

Affirmed.

■ MR. JUSTICE JACKSON took no part in the consideration or decision of this case.

■ [The opinion of MR. JUSTICE BLACK is omitted.]

Notes and Questions

1. Note that the Court assumes — and in later cases confirms — that the "minimum contacts" and "fair play and substantial justice" tests of *International Shoe* apply to individuals as well as corporations. Consider a situation in which a product shipped into the state by an out-of-state defendant causes harm in the state. Do you think the *International Shoe* test will produce the same results regardless of whether the defendant is a

large corporation or a Mom-and-Pop operation on a shoestring budget? Will it matter whether the *plaintiff* is another corporation or an individual consumer? If the answer to either question is affirmative, does that mean that *International Shoe* rejected state sovereignty as a basis for jurisdictional limits, in favor of notions of convenience and fairness? Should it have?

2. The Court also mentions that defendants who receive "benefits" from the "privilege" of doing business in a particular state necessarily also incur obligations, including the possibility that they might be sued in that state. Does this argument bring state sovereignty, or what Professor Perdue calls "political legitimacy" arguments, back into the jurisdiction equation? Does the reliance on *traditional* notions of justice do so, since traditionally courts have respected territorial boundaries? (Perhaps you are beginning to understand why Professor Perdue argues that the Court does not know what theory underlies its personal-jurisdiction jurisprudence.) For an argument that *Pennoyer* actually offers a better way to analyze jurisdiction than *International Shoe* does, see Stephen E. Sachs, Pennoyer *Was Right*, 95 TEX. L. REV. 1249 (2017). Sachs suggests, however, that personal jurisdiction under *Pennoyer* was a matter of common law, not constitutional law — a principle that later cases reject.

3. The Court in *International Shoe* draws a distinction between cases in which the defendant's actions in the state "give rise to the liabilities sued on," and cases in which the cause of action is "unrelated" to the defendant's activities in the state. Jurisdiction in the latter type of case, the Court suggests, requires a greater level of contacts between the defendant and the forum state. This distinction is generally referred to as the difference between *specific jurisdiction* (when the claim arises out of the contacts) and *general jurisdiction* (when the claim is unrelated to the contacts). We will return to this distinction later, in Section D-1 of this chapter. The cases in this section and Section C, however, all involve specific jurisdiction.

4. *International Shoe* extended *in personam* jurisdiction beyond the territorial boundaries established by *Pennoyer*. Recall that the *Pennoyer* regime also had a flip side: as long as the suit was *in rem* or *quasi in rem* (based on the presence in the state of the defendant's property, which the plaintiff often attached before the suit began), the court had jurisdiction over *any* defendant *anywhere*. Did that part of *Pennoyer* survive *International Shoe*?

To understand this issue, you may need some background. Most civil suits are termed *in personam*; examples are many ordinary types of claims, such as tort and contract, in which the plaintiff seeks a judgment against the defendant personally. Relief may include a money judgment against the defendant or an injunction or specific performance, again speaking to the defendant personally. *International Shoe*, departing from *Pennoyer* with that case's emphasis on the defendant's physical presence, established minimum contacts as the approach for such actions against out-of-state defendants. But some suits seek relief relating to property; examples are claims to quiet title to real estate, which can result not in a personal judgment but in a sort of "universal declaration," settling that the successful claimant owns Blackacre. Such actions are termed *in rem*. Under *Pennoyer* jurisdiction over such cases was proper based on the sheer presence of the property in the state.

There are also actions referred to as *quasi in rem*, which led to a judgment giving the successful plaintiff the interest in property that the defendant had had, rather than a judgment valid against all the world. These came in two varieties, confusingly under the same *quasi in rem* label. In one, the action is related to the property; a good example is mortgage foreclosure. A successful creditor often ends up with the property of the defaulting debtor, but not necessarily: if the creditor holds only a second mortgage, for example, then the creditor takes the place of the debtor, with the creditor's claim to the property subordinate to the interest of the holder of the first mortgage. Again, under *Pennoyer* jurisdiction was proper based on the sheer presence of the property in the state.

But there was a second variety of cases also referred to as *quasi in rem*: in these the plaintiff's claim was unrelated to the defendant's property and might be the sort of claim, such as tort or contract, that would often be brought against the defendant in an *in personam* action. Under *Pennoyer* jurisdiction was also regarded as proper based on the sheer presence of the unrelated property in the state, although relief if the plaintiff won was limited to the ownership or value of the property. So if a plaintiff had a $75,000 claim and won a *quasi in rem* judgment involving property worth only $50,000, the plaintiff was left to seek the remaining $25,000 in a separate action.

Such "unrelated" *quasi in rem* jurisdiction was extended to extreme lengths in cases involving intangible property. In one old case, *Harris v. Balk*, 198 U.S. 215 (1905), the Supreme Court upheld jurisdiction based on the presence of the defendant's property in the form of a traveling debtor: the defendant could be sued, up to the value of the debt owed to him, wherever the debtor could be found. Rest assured; that is no longer the law.

Once *International Shoe* shifted from presence to minimum contacts for *in personam* actions against out-of-state defendants, the question arose whether the presence of property in the state could still give rise to *in rem* or *quasi in rem* jurisdiction. The Supreme Court dealt with that question in *Shaffer v. Heitner*, 433 U.S. 186 (1977). Delaware law viewed stock in a corporation incorporated in Delaware as being located in Delaware, and authorized "sequestration" of such stock as a basis for requiring its owner to appear and defend in Delaware, on any claim, on pain of losing the stock. A shareholder sued Greyhound (which was incorporated in Delaware), a subsidiary, and their officers and directors in Delaware state court, basing jurisdiction over many of the officers and directors on their ownership of Greyhound stock. The claims had to do with corporate business, not the stock itself, The Delaware courts upheld jurisdiction. The Supreme Court reversed, concluding that "all assertions of state-court jurisdiction must be evaluated according to the standards set forth in *International Shoe* and its progeny." *Id.* at 212.

Thus the various forms of *in rem* and *quasi in rem* jurisdiction had to be evaluated for minimum contacts "among the defendant, the forum, and the litigation," *id.* at 204, rather than having jurisdiction rest on mere presence of the defendant's property in the forum state. What difference did that make as to the validity of jurisdiction? For pure *in rem* and "related" *quasi in rem* claims, none; a dispute about interests in a property located in the state readily satisfies the requirement of minimum contacts with the state. But an "unrelated" *quasi in rem* action lacks the required minimum contacts when a plaintiff uses the in-state property of an out-of-state defendant as the ground for jurisdiction over a claim based on out-of-state conduct.

5. Shouldn't officers and directors of a company that seeks the benefits of a state's law by incorporating there be subject to suits in the state about company business? A few weeks after *Shaffer*, the Delaware legislature adopted a law that "deemed" every nonresident director of every Delaware corporation to have consented to be sued in Delaware on matters related to corporate business. Shortly afterward, Greyhound reincorporated in Arizona, stating that it did not wish to subject its directors to suit in Delaware. The Supreme Court of Delaware later upheld the statute. Armstrong v. Pomerance, 423 A.2d 174 (Del. 1980).

6. Consider the Anticybersquatting and Consumer Protection Act (ACPA), 15 U.S.C. § 1125(d). If I register "www.nike.com" as a domain name, I can probably make a fair amount of money either by selling it to Nike or by selling pop-up or click-through ads that will confront anyone trying to find the sportswear company. The ACPA makes such practices illegal, and allows the trademark owner (in certain circumstances) to bring an *in rem* suit against the domain name itself in the jurisdiction in which the domain name was registered. Because registering the name is usually the defendant's only contact with the jurisdiction, it is important to know whether the *in rem* suit confers jurisdiction. Language in *Shaffer*, which emphasizes contacts rather than formal rules, suggests that minimum-contacts analysis applies to both *in rem* and *quasi in rem* cases. But true *in rem* suits — those that are about ownership of the property, including ownership of a trademarked domain name — are quite different from *Shaffer*: a court determining ownership of property within its jurisdiction can argue that it must have jurisdiction over anyone with claims on the property. Courts are split on this question. *Compare* FleetBoston Fin. Corp. v. fleetbostonfinancial.com, 138 F. Supp. 2d 121, 131-35 (D. Mass. 2001) (minimum contacts necessary), *with* Cable News Network L.P. v. cnnews.com, 162 F. Supp. 2d 484, 491 (E.D. Va. 2001) (minimum contacts not necessary), *aff'd in relevant part*, 56 F. App'x 599 (4th Cir. 2003). Which position do you find more sensible in light of the cases you have read, and the underlying theories of jurisdiction they embody?

7. *Shaffer* generally frowned on state assertions of jurisdiction based on the presence of property unrelated to a defendant's claim-related contacts with the forum state. At one point, however, it referred to the possibility that "a State in which property is located should have jurisdiction to attach that property, by use of proper procedures, as security for a judgment being

sought in a forum where the litigation can be maintained consistently with *International Shoe.*" *Shaffer*, 433 U.S. at 210. The constitutionality of this very limited and sensible form of "attachment jurisdiction" seems accepted. *See, e.g.*, Carolina Power & Light Co. v. Uranex, 451 F. Supp. 1044 (N.D. Cal. 1977). The procedure is available, though, only when authorized by state law, and apparently not many states provide for it. *See* 16 JAMES WM. MOORE ET AL., MOORE'S FEDERAL PRACTICE § 108.80[2][d] (3d ed. 2019).

SECTION C: APPLYING MINIMUM CONTACTS

The decision in *International Shoe* generated a great deal of litigation, some of which reached the Supreme Court, about exactly how much contact was enough to sustain jurisdiction. Each fact pattern is unique, and thus a doctrine of personal jurisdiction that depends on a test as amorphous as whether a defendant's "minimum contacts" are sufficient to withstand scrutiny under "traditional notions of fair play and substantial justice" is bound to create interpretive difficulties. This section examines the most important attempts to apply and clarify the *International Shoe* doctrine.

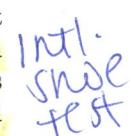

1. The First Step: Statutes or Court Rules as the Authority for Exercising Personal Jurisdiction

However much litigation *International Shoe* has spawned, the constitutional limitations of *International Shoe* and its progeny form only part of the doctrine of personal jurisdiction. Before the constitutional question even arises, a court must have a source of authority for exercising jurisdiction over a defendant. This source of jurisdictional authority comes either from a statute or from a rule of court. In federal courts, a few specialized statutes grant jurisdictional power over a defendant, but for the most part, Federal Rule of Civil Procedure 4(k) is the source of a federal court's power. Under Rule 4(k), the jurisdiction of a federal court is usually the same as that of a state court in the state in which the federal court is located. Because of that correlation, we first examine the scope and limits of a state court's power to exercise jurisdiction over a defendant, and return to consider Rule 4(k) in more depth in Section F (*infra* pp. 494-95).

State statutes and rules of court specify the precise circumstances under which a state court can exercise personal jurisdiction over defendants located either within that state or outside its borders. Provisions that permit the exercise of jurisdiction over those outside the state are usually called *long-arm provisions*: they authorize the "long arm of the law" to reach into another state so that the court can exercise jurisdiction over a nonresident. Many long-arm provisions authorize jurisdiction when the defendant has committed a tort in the state, or has committed an act outside the state that causes harm within the state. Here is a representative statute, from Massachusetts (Mass. Gen. Laws ch. 223A, §§ 2-3). Note the long-arm provision in § 3:

§ 2. A court may exercise personal jurisdiction over a person domiciled in, organized under the laws of, or maintaining his or its principal place of business in, this commonwealth as to any cause of action.

§ 3. A court may exercise jurisdiction over a person, who acts directly or by an agent, as to a cause of action in law or equity arising from the person's

(a) transacting any business in this commonwealth;

(b) contracting to supply services or things in this commonwealth;

(c) causing tortious injury by an act or omission in this commonwealth;

(d) causing tortious injury in this commonwealth by an act or omission outside this commonwealth if he regularly does or solicits business, or engages in any other persistent course of conduct, or derives substantial revenue from goods used or consumed or services rendered, in this commonwealth;

(e) having an interest in, using or possessing real property in this commonwealth; [or]

(f) contracting to insure any person, property or risk located within this commonwealth at the time of contracting . . . .

Many states have interpreted their long-arm provisions to reach to the furthest extent permitted by the Due Process Clause, but you should be careful not to overread cases using such language. Courts sometimes speak in such terms with respect to just one aspect of the state long-arm provision, leaving it explicitly or implicitly undecided whether the long arm goes to constitutional limits in all respects. Some provisions make their reach explicit: California Code of Civil Procedure § 410.10, for example, provides that "[a] court of this state may exercise jurisdiction on any basis not inconsistent with the Constitution of this state or of the United States."

Not infrequently, state courts will find that they lack power over a defendant because no statute or rule of court permits jurisdiction. In such cases, it is not necessary to consider the constitutional analysis. For this reason, lawyers almost always start the personal-jurisdiction analysis by looking to the applicable jurisdictional statute or rule. If, but only if, that authority exists must courts consider the question of their constitutional power over a defendant. Of course, if the state long-arm provision expressly or by interpretation goes to constitutional limits, the analyses under the state law and the federal Constitution become one.

2. The Second Step: Constitutional Authority and Minimum-Contacts Analysis

As we have seen, *International Shoe* keys a state court's constitutional authority to exercise jurisdiction to the contacts between the defendant and the state. One question that arises frequently is whether jurisdiction can be exercised on the basis of a defendant's single contact with the state. Recall that *International Shoe* mentioned but did not decide this question:

> Finally, although the commission of some single or occasional acts of the corporate agent in a state sufficient to impose an obligation or liability on the corporation has not been thought to confer upon the state authority to enforce it, other such acts, because of their nature and quality and the circumstances of their commission, may be deemed sufficient to render the corporation liable to suit. [326 U.S. at 318.]

In two cases decided a year apart, the Court reached opposite conclusions on the question.

In *McGee v. International Life Insurance Co.*, 355 U.S. 220 (1957), the plaintiff, a California resident, was the beneficiary of a life-insurance policy purchased by another California resident. The policyholder had purchased the policy from an Arizona company, which was later taken over by International Life, a Texas company. According to the Court:

> Respondent [International Life] then mailed a reinsurance certificate to [the policyholder] in California offering to insure him in accordance with the terms of the policy he had held with [the Arizona insurance company]. He accepted this offer and from that time until his death [two years later] paid premiums by mail from his California home to respondent's Texas office. . . . It appears that neither [the Arizona company] nor respondent has ever had any office or agent in California. And so far as the record before us shows, respondent has never solicited or done any insurance business in California apart from the policy involved here. [355 U.S. at 221-22.]

The Court held that this single insurance contract was sufficient to confer jurisdiction over International Life in California for claims arising out of the policy. Describing the history of personal jurisdiction from *Pennoyer* through *International Shoe*, the Court saw a "clearly discernible" trend "toward expanding the permissible scope of state jurisdiction over foreign corporations and other nonresidents." *Id.* at 222. It found sufficient contacts for jurisdiction in the fact that "the contract was delivered in California, the premiums were mailed from there and the insured was a resident of that State when he died." *Id.* at 223. The inconvenience to the insurer did not alter this result. The Court also noted that "California has a manifest interest in providing effective means of redress for its residents when their insurers refuse to pay claims." *Id.*

A year later, however, the Court found that a Florida court lacked jurisdiction in a similar situation. *Hanson v. Denckla*, 357 U.S. 235 (1958), involved a complicated dispute about a will and a trust fund established by Dora Donner. Donner, then a resident of Pennsylvania, established the trust in 1935 under Delaware law with a Delaware trustee. Nine years later she moved to Florida, and five years after that she changed the terms of the trust. This change provided that most of the trust — more than $1,000,000 — would pass through her will to two of her daughters. But it also allocated $200,000 each to two grandchildren by a third daughter (who was not to inherit anything herself). When Donner died (in Florida three years later), the first two sisters brought suit in Florida, where they also lived, challenging the part of the trust that gave money to their niece and nephew. They argued that the trust was invalid under Florida law, which meant that all of the estate should pass to them under the will. The Florida courts agreed. Meanwhile, Donner's two grandchildren (and their mother) brought suit in Delaware, asking the court to declare the trust valid. Although the Florida suit reached judgment first, the Delaware courts refused to give it *full faith and credit*, that is, refused to consider it a valid judgment, on the ground that the Florida court had not had personal jurisdiction over the Delaware trustee, a necessary defendant. The Delaware courts held the trust valid under Delaware law and found for the grandchildren.

Both cases landed in the Supreme Court and were decided together. The Court held that Florida did not have personal jurisdiction over the Delaware trustee. Even though the trustee had notice of the suit and an adequate opportunity to participate, the Court found insufficient contacts between the trustee and Florida. The Court distinguished *McGee*:

> The cause of action in this case is not one that arises out of an act done or transaction consummated in the forum state. In that respect, it differs from *McGee*.... In *McGee*, the nonresident defendant solicited a reinsurance agreement with a resident of California. The offer was accepted in that State, and the insurance premiums were mailed from there until the insured's death.... In contrast, this action involves the validity of an agreement that was entered into without any connection to the forum State.... The first relationship Florida had to the agreement was years later, when the settlor [Donner] became domiciled there, and the trustee remitted the trust income to her in that State. From Florida Mrs. Donner carried on several bits of trust administration that may be compared to the mailing of premiums in *McGee*. But the record discloses no instance in which the trustee performed any acts in Florida that bear the same relationship to the agreement as the solicitation in *McGee*. [357 U.S. at 251-52.]

The Court held that "it is essential" for jurisdiction "that there be some act by which the defendant purposefully avails itself of the privilege of conducting activities within the forum State, thus invoking the benefits and protections of its laws." *Id.* at 253. And the "unilateral activity" of Donner, in moving to Florida, "cannot satisfy the requirement of contact with the forum State." *Id.*

Justice Black, joined by Justices Burton and Brennan, dissented. (Justice Douglas also dissented, in a separate opinion.) Justice Black concluded — and the majority did not dispute — that Florida had sufficient connection with the lawsuit that Florida law could be applied if a court with jurisdiction chose to do so. For that reason, he thought the Florida courts ought also to have jurisdiction:

> True, the question whether the law of a State can be applied to a transaction is different from the question whether the courts of that State have jurisdiction to enter a judgment, but the two are often closely

related and to a substantial degree depend upon similar considerations. It seems to me that where a transaction has as much relationship to a State as Mrs. Donner's [change in the terms of the trust] had to Florida its courts ought to have power to adjudicate controversies arising out of that transaction, unless litigation there would impose such a heavy and disproportionate burden on a nonresident defendant that it would offend what this Court has referred to as "traditional notions of fair play and substantial justice." . . . Certainly there is nothing fundamentally unfair in subjecting the corporate trustee to the jurisdiction of the Florida courts. It chose to maintain business relations with Mrs. Donner in that State for eight years, regularly communicating with her with respect to the business of the trust including the very [change] in question. [*Id.* at 258-59.]

Justice Black also concluded that Florida had a strong interest in the validity of the trust because Florida courts administered Donner's will.

Notes and Questions

1. Are you persuaded by the Court's distinction between *McGee* and *Hanson*? Imagine that the Court had instead held the trustee subject to jurisdiction in Florida, and then think about what the trustee could have done to avoid jurisdiction in Florida after Donner moved there. Would it have been fair to subject it to jurisdiction for failure to take steps to avoid jurisdiction?

2. Several recent cases have involved variations on the "single-client" situation of *McGee* and *Hanson*: what if the only sale in the forum state is to an officer of, or investigator for, the plaintiff, who deliberately purchased the item in order to create jurisdiction? *See, e.g.,* 721 Bourbon, Inc. v. House of Auth, LLC, 140 F. Supp. 3d 586 (E.D. La. 2015) (investigator's online purchase of out-of-state vendor's allegedly infringing product insufficient to show purposeful availment); Foreign Candy Co. v. Tropical Paradise, Inc., 950 F. Supp. 2d 1017 (N.D. Iowa 2013) (plaintiff company's president's online purchase through unaffiliated third-party vendor of defendant's allegedly infringing product insufficient to support personal jurisdiction over defendant).

3. In *Hanson* the Court finds that the trustee did not "purposefully [avail] itself of the privilege of conducting activities within the forum State." If administering a trust held by a Florida resident — with correspondence back and forth, including the substantial change in the terms of the trust communicated from Florida — is not conducting business in Florida, what is? If a dispute had arisen while Donner was still alive, could *she* have sued the trustee in Florida? If so, why shouldn't her heirs be able to do so? And if not, does such a rule overly protect defendants in voluntary business relationships with those in other states?

4. Continue thinking about the theories underlying the Court's limits on personal jurisdiction. Despite the difference in result, can you see how

the Court adopts a similar theory in both cases? (Compare Justice Black's dissent in *Hanson*, which seems to focus on both the defendant's interest and the forum state's interest.)

5. Both the majority and the dissent assume that it would have been constitutional for the Delaware courts to apply Florida law to the dispute. If that is true, does it make sense to deprive Florida courts of jurisdiction? If Delaware courts applied Florida law, would they put their own spin on that law? Would a Delaware court ever have interpreted Florida law as the Florida court did, to invalidate a trust that was valid under Delaware law? Perhaps the Court got it exactly backwards: the Florida court should have had jurisdiction, but it should have applied Delaware law.

6. There is also another possible explanation for the Court's holding in *Hanson*. Had it held that the Florida court had jurisdiction, the result would have been to disinherit two grandchildren of the testator, in favor of their aunts who were already getting a million dollars. It also would have frustrated Donner's wishes.

7. The Supreme Court continued to develop its personal-jurisdiction jurisprudence in a series of cases in the 1980s. As you read these cases, think about whether they are consistent with either the results or the underlying theories of *International Shoe*, *McGee*, and *Hanson*.

WORLD–WIDE VOLKSWAGEN CORP. V. WOODSON

444 U.S. 286 (1980)

■ MR. JUSTICE WHITE delivered the opinion of the Court.

The issue before us is whether, consistently with the Due Process Clause of the Fourteenth Amendment, an Oklahoma court may exercise *in personam* jurisdiction over a nonresident automobile retailer and its wholesale distributor in a products-liability action, when the defendants' only connection with Oklahoma is the fact that an automobile sold in New York to New York residents became involved in an accident in Oklahoma.

I

Respondents Harry and Kay Robinson purchased a new Audi automobile from petitioner Seaway Volkswagen, Inc. (Seaway), in Massena, N. Y., in 1976. The following year the Robinson family, who resided in New York, left that State for a new home in Arizona. As they passed through the State of Oklahoma, another car struck their Audi in the rear, causing a fire which severely burned Kay Robinson and her two children.

The Robinsons subsequently brought a products-liability action in the District Court for Creek County, Okla., claiming that their injuries resulted from defective design and placement of the Audi's gas tank and fuel system. They joined as defendants the automobile's manufacturer, Audi NSU Auto Union Aktiengesellschaft (Audi); its importer Volkswagen of America, Inc.

(Volkswagen); its regional distributor, petitioner World–Wide Volkswagen Corp. (World–Wide); and its retail dealer, petitioner Seaway. Seaway and World–Wide entered special appearances, claiming that Oklahoma's exercise of jurisdiction over them would offend the limitations on the State's jurisdiction imposed by the Due Process Clause of the Fourteenth Amendment.

The facts presented to the District Court showed that World–Wide is incorporated and has its business office in New York. It distributes vehicles, parts, and accessories, under contract with Volkswagen, to retail dealers in New York, New Jersey, and Connecticut. Seaway, one of these retail dealers, is incorporated and has its place of business in New York. Insofar as the record reveals, Seaway and World–Wide are fully independent corporations whose relations with each other and with Volkswagen and Audi are contractual only. Respondents adduced no evidence that either World–Wide or Seaway does any business in Oklahoma, ships or sells any products to or in that State, has an agent to receive process there, or purchases advertisements in any media calculated to reach Oklahoma. In fact, as respondents' counsel conceded at oral argument, there was no showing that any automobile sold by World–Wide or Seaway has ever entered Oklahoma with the single exception of the vehicle involved in the present case.

Despite the apparent paucity of contacts between petitioners and Oklahoma, the District Court rejected their constitutional claim and reaffirmed that ruling in denying petitioners' motion for reconsideration. Petitioners then sought a writ of prohibition in the Supreme Court of Oklahoma to restrain the District Judge, respondent Charles S. Woodson, from exercising *in personam* jurisdiction over them. They renewed their contention that, because they had no "minimal contacts," with the State of Oklahoma, the actions of the District Judge were in violation of their rights under the Due Process Clause.

The Supreme Court of Oklahoma denied the writ, holding that personal jurisdiction over petitioners was authorized by Oklahoma's "long-arm" statute. Okla. Stat., Tit. 12, § 1701.03(a)(4) (1971).[7] Although the court noted that the proper approach was to test jurisdiction against both statutory and constitutional standards, its analysis did not distinguish these questions, probably because § 1701.03(a)(4) has been interpreted as conferring jurisdiction to the limits permitted by the United States Constitution. The court's rationale was contained in the following paragraph:

---

7. This subsection provides:

A court may exercise personal jurisdiction over a person, who acts directly or by an agent, as to a cause of action or claim for relief arising from the person's . . . causing tortious injury in this state by an act or omission outside this state if he regularly does or solicits business or engages in any other persistent course of conduct, or derives substantial revenue from goods used or consumed or services rendered, in this state . . . .

The State Supreme Court rejected jurisdiction based on § 1701.03(a)(3), which authorizes jurisdiction over any person "causing tortious injury in this state by an act or omission in this state." Something in addition to the infliction of tortious injury was required.

In the case before us, the product being sold and distributed by the petitioners is by its very design and purpose so mobile that petitioners can foresee its possible use in Oklahoma. This is especially true of the distributor, who has the exclusive right to distribute such automobile in New York, New Jersey and Connecticut. The evidence presented below demonstrated that goods sold and distributed by the petitioners were used in the State of Oklahoma, and under the facts we believe it reasonable to infer, given the retail value of the automobile, that the petitioners derive substantial income from automobiles which from time to time are used in the State of Oklahoma. This being the case, we hold that under the facts presented, the trial court was justified in concluding that the petitioners derive substantial revenue from goods used or consumed in this State.

We granted certiorari to consider an important constitutional question with respect to state-court jurisdiction and to resolve a conflict between the Supreme Court of Oklahoma and the highest courts of at least four other States. We reverse.

II

The Due Process Clause of the Fourteenth Amendment limits the power of a state court to render a valid personal judgment against a nonresident defendant. A judgment rendered in violation of due process is void in the rendering State and is not entitled to full faith and credit elsewhere. Due process requires that the defendant be given adequate notice of the suit, and be subject to the personal jurisdiction of the court, Int'l Shoe Co. v. Washington, 326 U.S. 310 (1945). In the present case, it is not contended that notice was inadequate; the only question is whether these particular petitioners were subject to the jurisdiction of the Oklahoma courts.

As has long been settled, and as we reaffirm today, a state court may exercise personal jurisdiction over a nonresident defendant only so long as there exist "minimum contacts" between the defendant and the forum State. The concept of minimum contacts, in turn, can be seen to perform two related, but distinguishable, functions. It protects the defendant against the burdens of litigating in a distant or inconvenient forum. And it acts to ensure that the States through their courts, do not reach out beyond the limits imposed on them by their status as coequal sovereigns in a federal system.

The protection against inconvenient litigation is typically described in terms of "reasonableness" or "fairness." We have said that the defendant's contacts with the forum State must be such that maintenance of the suit "does not offend 'traditional notions of fair play and substantial justice.'" The relationship between the defendant and the forum must be such that it is "reasonable . . . to require the corporation to defend the particular suit which is brought there." Implicit in this emphasis on reasonableness is the understanding that the burden on the defendant, while always a primary concern, will in an appropriate case be considered in light of other relevant factors, including the forum State's interest in adjudicating the dispute, *see McGee v. Int'l Life Ins. Co.*, 355 U.S. 220 (1957); the plaintiff's interest in obtaining convenient and effective relief, at least when that interest is not adequately protected by the plaintiff's power to choose the forum; the interstate judicial system's interest in obtaining the most efficient resolution of controversies; and the shared interest of the several States in furthering fundamental substantive social policies.

The limits imposed on state jurisdiction by the Due Process Clause, in its role as a guarantor against inconvenient litigation, have been substantially relaxed over the years. As we noted in *McGee*, this trend is largely attributable to a fundamental transformation in the American economy:

> Today many commercial transactions touch two or more States and may involve parties separated by the full continent. With this increasing nationalization of commerce has come a great increase in the amount of business conducted by mail across state lines. At the same time modern transportation and communication have made it much less burdensome for a party sued to defend himself in a State where he engages in economic activity.

The historical developments noted in *McGee*, of course, have only accelerated in the generation since that case was decided.

Nevertheless, we have never accepted the proposition that state lines are irrelevant for jurisdictional purposes, nor could we, and remain faithful to the principles of interstate federalism embodied in the Constitution. The economic interdependence of the States was foreseen and desired by the Framers. In the Commerce Clause, they provided that the Nation was to be a common market, a "free trade unit" in which the States are debarred from acting as separable economic entities. But the Framers also intended that the States retain many essential attributes of sovereignty, including, in particular, the sovereign power to try causes in their courts. The sovereignty of each State, in turn, implied a limitation on the sovereignty of all of its sister States — a limitation express or implicit in both the original scheme of the Constitution and the Fourteenth Amendment.

Hence, even while abandoning the shibboleth that "[t]he authority of every tribunal is necessarily restricted by the territorial limits of the State in which it is established," *Pennoyer v. Neff*, 95 U.S. 714, 720 (1877), we emphasized that the reasonableness of asserting jurisdiction over the defendant must be assessed "in the context of our federal system of government," *International Shoe*, and stressed that the Due Process Clause ensures not only fairness, but also the "orderly administration of the laws." As we noted in *Hanson v. Denckla*, 357 U.S. 235, 250-51 (1958):

> As technological progress has increased the flow of commerce between the States, the need for jurisdiction over nonresidents has undergone a similar increase. At the same time, progress in communications and transportation has made the defense of a suit in a foreign tribunal less burdensome. In response to these changes, the requirements for personal jurisdiction over nonresidents have evolved from the rigid rule

of *Pennoyer* to the flexible standard of *International Shoe*. But it is a mistake to assume that this trend heralds the eventual demise of all restrictions on the personal jurisdiction of state courts. Those restrictions are more than a guarantee of immunity from inconvenient or distant litigation. They are a consequence of territorial limitations on the power of the respective States.

Thus, the Due Process Clause "does not contemplate that a state may make binding a judgment *in personam* against an individual or corporate defendant with which the state has no contacts, ties, or relations." *International Shoe*. Even if the defendant would suffer minimal or no inconvenience from being forced to litigate before the tribunals of another State; even if the forum State has a strong interest in applying its law to the controversy; even if the forum State is the most convenient location for litigation, the Due Process Clause, acting as an instrument of interstate federalism, may sometimes act to divest the State of its power to render a valid judgment.

III

Applying these principles to the case at hand, we find in the record before us a total absence of those affiliating circumstances that are a necessary predicate to any exercise of state-court jurisdiction. Petitioners carry on no activity whatsoever in Oklahoma. They close no sales and perform no services there. They avail themselves of none of the privileges and benefits of Oklahoma law. They solicit no business there either through salespersons or through advertising reasonably calculated to reach the State. Nor does the record show that they regularly sell cars at wholesale or retail to Oklahoma customers or residents or that they indirectly, through others, serve or seek to serve the Oklahoma market. In short, respondents seek to base jurisdiction on one, isolated occurrence and whatever inferences can be drawn therefrom: the fortuitous circumstance that a single Audi automobile, sold in New York to New York residents, happened to suffer an accident while passing through Oklahoma.

It is argued, however, that because an automobile is mobile by its very design and purpose it was "foreseeable" that the Robinsons' Audi would cause injury in Oklahoma. Yet "foreseeability" alone has never been a sufficient benchmark for personal jurisdiction under the Due Process Clause. In *Hanson v. Denckla* it was no doubt foreseeable that the settlor of a Delaware trust would subsequently move to Florida and seek to exercise a power of appointment there; yet we held that Florida courts could not constitutionally exercise jurisdiction over a Delaware trustee that had no other contacts with the forum State. . . .

If foreseeability were the criterion, a local California tire retailer could be forced to defend in Pennsylvania when a blowout occurs there; a Wisconsin seller of a defective automobile jack could be haled before a distant court for damage caused in New Jersey; or a Florida soft-drink concessionaire could be summoned to Alaska to account for injuries happening there. Every seller of chattels would in effect appoint the chattel his agent for service of process. His amenability to suit would travel with the chattel....[11]

This is not to say, of course, that foreseeability is wholly irrelevant. But the foreseeability that is critical to due process analysis is not the mere likelihood that a product will find its way into the forum State. Rather, it is that the defendant's conduct and connection with the forum State are such that he should reasonably anticipate being haled into court there. The Due Process Clause, by ensuring the "orderly administration of the laws," *International Shoe*, gives a degree of predictability to the legal system that allows potential defendants to structure their primary conduct with some minimum assurance as to where that conduct will and will not render them liable to suit.

When a corporation "purposefully avails itself of the privilege of conducting activities within the forum State," *Hanson v. Denckla*, 357 U.S. at 253, it has clear notice that it is subject to suit there, and can act to alleviate the risk of burdensome litigation by procuring insurance, passing the expected costs on to customers, or, if the risks are too great, severing its connection with the State. Hence if the sale of a product of a manufacturer or distributor such as Audi or Volkswagen is not simply an isolated occurrence, but arises from the efforts of the manufacturer or distributor to serve directly or indirectly, the market for its product in other States, it is not unreasonable to subject it to suit in one of those States if its allegedly defective merchandise has there been the source of injury to its owner or to others. The forum State does not exceed its powers under the Due Process Clause if it asserts personal jurisdiction over a corporation that delivers its products into the stream of commerce with the expectation that they will be purchased by consumers in the forum State.

But there is no such or similar basis for Oklahoma jurisdiction over World–Wide or Seaway in this case. Seaway's sales are made in Massena, N.Y. World–Wide's market, although substantially larger, is limited to dealers in New York, New Jersey, and Connecticut. There is no evidence of record that any automobiles distributed by World–Wide are sold to retail customers outside this tristate area. It is foreseeable that the purchasers of automobiles sold by World–Wide and Seaway may take them to Oklahoma. But the mere "unilateral activity of those who claim some relationship with a nonresident defendant cannot satisfy the requirement of contact with the forum State." *Hanson v. Denckla*, 357 U.S. at 253.

---

11. Respondents' counsel ... sought to limit the reach of the foreseeability standard by suggesting that there is something unique about automobiles. It is true that automobiles are uniquely mobile, that they did play a crucial role in the expansion of personal jurisdiction through the fiction of implied consent, and that some of the cases have treated the automobile as a "dangerous instrumentality." But today, under the regime of *International Shoe*, we see no difference for jurisdictional purposes between an automobile and any other chattel. The "dangerous instrumentality" concept apparently was never used to support personal jurisdiction; and to the extent it has relevance today it bears not on jurisdiction but on the possible desirability of imposing substantive principles of tort law such as strict liability.

In a variant on the previous argument, it is contended that jurisdiction can be supported by the fact that petitioners earn substantial revenue from goods used in Oklahoma. The Oklahoma Supreme Court so found, drawing the inference that because one automobile sold by petitioners had been used in Oklahoma, others might have been used there also. While this inference seems less than compelling on the facts of the instant case, we need not question the court's factual findings in order to reject its reasoning.

This argument seems to make the point that the purchase of automobiles in New York, from which the petitioners earn substantial revenue, would not occur *but for* the fact that the automobiles are capable of use in distant States like Oklahoma. Respondents observe that the very purpose of an automobile is to travel, and that travel of automobiles sold by petitioners is facilitated by an extensive chain of Volkswagen service centers throughout the country, including some in Oklahoma. However, financial benefits accruing to the defendant from a collateral relation to the forum State will not support jurisdiction if they do not stem from a constitutionally cognizable contact with that State. In our view, whatever marginal revenues petitioners may receive by virtue of the fact that their products are capable of use in Oklahoma is far too attenuated a contact to justify that State's exercise of *in personam* jurisdiction over them.

Because we find that petitioners have no "contacts, ties, or relations" with the State of Oklahoma, the judgment of the Supreme Court of Oklahoma is reversed.

■ MR. JUSTICE BRENNAN, dissenting.

The Court holds that the Due Process Clause of the Fourteenth Amendment bars the States from asserting jurisdiction over the defendants in [this case].... Because I believe that the Court reads *International Shoe* and its progeny too narrowly, and because I believe that the standards enunciated by those cases may already be obsolete as constitutional boundaries, I dissent.

I

The Court's opinions focus tightly on the existence of contacts between the forum and the defendant. In so doing, they accord too little weight to the strength of the forum State's interest in the case and fail to explore whether there would be any actual inconvenience to the defendant. The essential inquiry in locating the constitutional limits on state-court jurisdiction over absent defendants is whether the particular exercise of jurisdiction offends "traditional notions of fair play and substantial justice." *International Shoe*, 326 U.S. at 316. The clear focus in *International Shoe* was on fairness and reasonableness.... The existence of contacts, so long as there were some, was merely one way of giving content to the determination of fairness and reasonableness.

Surely *International Shoe* contemplated that the significance of the contacts necessary to support jurisdiction would diminish if some other consideration helped establish that jurisdiction would be fair and reasonable. The interests of the State and other parties in proceeding with the case in a particular forum are such considerations. *McGee v. International Life Ins. Co.*, 355 U.S. 220, 223 (1957), for instance, accorded great importance to a State's "manifest interest in providing effective means of redress" for its citizens.

Another consideration is the actual burden a defendant must bear in defending the suit in the forum. Because lesser burdens reduce the unfairness to the defendant, jurisdiction may be justified despite less significant contacts. The burden, of course, must be of constitutional dimension. Due process limits on jurisdiction do not protect a defendant from all inconvenience of travel, and it would not be sensible to make the constitutional rule turn solely on the number of miles the defendant must travel to the courtroom. Instead, the constitutionally significant "burden" to be analyzed relates to the mobility of the defendant's defense. For instance, if having to travel to a foreign forum would hamper the defense because witnesses or evidence or the defendant himself were immobile, or if there were a disproportionately large number of witnesses or amount of evidence that would have to be transported at the defendant's expense, or if being away from home for the duration of the trial would work some special hardship on the defendant, then the Constitution would require special consideration for the defendant's interests.

That considerations other than contacts between the forum and the defendant are relevant necessarily means that the Constitution does not require that trial be held in the State which has the "best contacts" with the defendant. The defendant has no constitutional entitlement to the best forum or, for that matter, to any particular forum. Under even the most restrictive view of *International Shoe*, several States could have jurisdiction over a particular cause of action. We need only determine whether the forum States in these cases satisfy the constitutional minimum.

II

In [this case], I would find that the forum State has an interest in permitting the litigation to go forward, the litigation is connected to the forum, the defendant is linked to the forum, and the burden of defending is not unreasonable. Accordingly, I would hold that it is neither unfair nor unreasonable to require these defendants to defend in the forum State....

... [T]he interest of the forum State and its connection to the litigation is strong. The automobile accident underlying the litigation occurred in Oklahoma. The plaintiffs were hospitalized in Oklahoma when they brought suit. Essential witnesses and evidence were in Oklahoma. The State has a legitimate interest in enforcing its laws designed to keep its highway system safe, and the trial can proceed at least as efficiently in Oklahoma as anywhere else.

The petitioners are not unconnected with the forum. Although both sell automobiles within limited sales territories, each sold the automobile which in fact was driven to Oklahoma where it was involved in an accident....

An automobile simply is not a stationary item or one designed to be used in one place. An automobile is *intended* to be moved around. Someone in the business of selling large numbers of automobiles can hardly plead ignorance of their mobility or pretend that the automobiles stay put after they are sold. It is not merely that a dealer in automobiles foresees that they will move. The dealer actually intends that the purchasers will use the automobiles to travel to distant States where the dealer does not directly "do business." The sale of an automobile does *purposefully* inject the vehicle into the stream of interstate commerce so that it can travel to distant States. . . .

Furthermore, an automobile seller derives substantial benefits from States other than its own. A large part of the value of automobiles is the extensive, nationwide network of highways. Significant portions of that network have been constructed by and are maintained by the individual States, including Oklahoma. The States, through their highway programs, contribute in a very direct and important way to the value of petitioners' businesses. Additionally, a network of other related dealerships with their service departments operates throughout the country under the protection of the laws of the various States, including Oklahoma, and enhances the value of petitioners' businesses by facilitating their customers' traveling.

Thus, the Court errs in its conclusion that "petitioners have *no* 'contacts, ties, or relations'" with Oklahoma. There obviously are contacts, and, given Oklahoma's connection to the litigation, the contacts are sufficiently significant to make it fair and reasonable for the petitioners to submit to Oklahoma's jurisdiction. . . .

[Finally, the] Court's opinion . . . suggests that the defendant ought to be subject to a State's jurisdiction only if he has contacts with the State "such that he should reasonably anticipate being haled into court there."[18] There is nothing unreasonable or unfair, however, about recognizing commercial reality. . . . People should understand that . . . in our society most actions have consequences affecting many States. . . .

■ [The dissenting opinion of MR. JUSTICE MARSHALL, joined by MR. JUSTICE BLACKMUN, is omitted.]

■ [The dissenting opinion of MR. JUSTICE BLACKMUN is omitted.]

Notes and Questions

1. The Court describes the minimum-contacts test as serving two functions: to protect defendants and to enforce respect for the co-equal sovereignty of sister states. Is this description consistent with the underlying theories of personal jurisdiction in *McGee* and *Hanson*? In

---

18. The Court suggests that this is the critical foreseeability rather than the likelihood that the product will go to the forum State. But the reasoning begs the question. A defendant cannot know if his actions will subject him to jurisdiction in another State until we have declared what the law of jurisdiction is.

Shaffer? What interests are served by placing limits on the jurisdiction of a court in the name of "interstate federalism"?

The Court later disavowed this reliance on federalism as a basis for limits on personal jurisdiction:

> The requirement that a court have personal jurisdiction flows not from Art. III, but from the Due Process Clause. The personal jurisdiction requirement recognizes and protects an individual liberty interest. It represents a restriction on judicial power not as a matter of sovereignty, but as a matter of individual liberty.

Ins. Corp. of Ir. v. Compagnie des Bauxites de Guinee, 456 U.S. 694, 702 (1982). *Insurance Corp.* went on to hold that because personal-jurisdiction requirements rested on individual liberty, they could be — and in the particular case, had been — waived. This holding necessarily depended on the rejection of *World–Wide Volkswagen*'s reliance on state sovereignty. As you read through the rest of the cases in this section, think about whether the purported abandonment of sovereignty as one underpinning of personal-jurisdiction doctrine has endured — and whether it should. (You might focus especially on *Bristol–Myers Squibb Co. v. Superior Court* (infra p. 446).)

2. What role does foreseeability play in the majority's analysis? Think about why a defendant would (or would not) "reasonably anticipate being haled into court" in a particular state. Do you think a car dealership has any idea whether it might be subject to jurisdiction in another state? Imagine that your client asks you whether it should "reasonably anticipate being haled into court" somewhere on the basis of its actions. To answer that question, you would presumably look to the legal precedents. Doesn't the Court's definition of foreseeability translate into the proposition that if the precedents would allow jurisdiction, then there is jurisdiction because it is foreseeable that your client might be subject to jurisdiction?

3. Imagine that the suit was brought not by the Robinsons, but by a passing driver who was injured when the Robinsons' car exploded. Assume this driver was an Oklahoma citizen who had never been outside the state. Would the result have been different? Should it have been different? What theory (or theories) of jurisdiction underlies your answer?

4. Contrast the *World–Wide Volkswagen* focus on the defendant with the European focus on the harm. The European Union, like the United States, contains individual member states. Both must thus have some method of determining in which state (or country) suits may be brought. In the EU, personal jurisdiction for most civil suits is governed by Council Regulation No. 44/2001, 2001 O.J. (L 12) 1 (EC). For tort claims, Article 5(3) of the Regulation provides that jurisdiction is proper "where the harmful event occurred or may occur." How would *World–Wide Volkswagen* have come out under that standard? Which test is better?

5. Compare *World–Wide Volkswagen* with the following cases:

(a) In **Keeton v. Hustler Magazine, Inc.**, 465 U.S. 770 (1984), the plaintiff, a resident of New York, brought a libel suit in New Hampshire against Hustler, an Ohio corporation. New Hampshire, like most states, followed the "single-publication rule," which meant that if the plaintiff prevailed on the merits, she could recover damages suffered in any jurisdiction, not just in the forum state. The plaintiff's only connection with New Hampshire was that copies of a small independent magazine she helped to produce circulated there (as well as in many other states). The defendant's only connection with New Hampshire was that 10,000 to 15,000 copies of its magazine — a very small percentage of its total publication — circulated there. The plaintiff chose to sue in New Hampshire because it was the only state in which the statute of limitations on libel suits had not expired (New Hampshire had an unusually long statute of limitations).

The Court concluded that (1) the plaintiff's contacts — or lack thereof — with the forum state were irrelevant; (2) the defendant "deliberately exploited the New Hampshire market [and] must reasonably anticipate being haled into court there in a libel action based on the contents of its magazine," 465 U.S. at 781; and (3) New Hampshire had a significant interest in redressing the injury (libel) to a nonresident, because it could thereby "discourage the deception of its citizens," *id*. at 776. The Court rejected the argument that New Hampshire's long statute of limitations was unfair to the defendant, holding that the limitations period was a question of choice of law, not jurisdiction. It noted: "Petitioner's successful search for a State with a lengthy statute of limitations is no different from the litigation strategy of countless plaintiffs who seek a forum with favorable substantive or procedural rules or sympathetic local populations." *Id*. at 779.

Why should Keeton be permitted to sue Hustler in New Hampshire, when the Robinsons could not sue World-Wide and Seaway in Oklahoma, where many witnesses resided and where the plaintiffs were hospitalized?

(b) In ***Burger King Corp. v. Rudzewicz***, 471 U.S. 462 (1985), the Court found jurisdiction on the basis of a franchise contract. Burger King, a Florida corporation, entered into a franchise contract with Rudzewicz and his partner, both Michigan residents, that allowed the two partners to open a Burger King franchise in Michigan. They dealt with both the local district office and the Miami headquarters during contract negotiations. The final contract specified that Florida law would apply to all disputes, but it did not contain any reference to possible forums. When the Michigan franchise fell behind in its contractually required payments, Burger King sued the partners for breach of contract in Florida. The Court described the Due Process Clause as affording protection of "an individual's liberty interest in not being subject to the binding judgments of a forum with which he has established no meaningful 'contacts, ties, or relations.'" 471 U.S. at 471-72. It then analyzed the case under the precedents you have read so far:

> Where a forum seeks to assert specific jurisdiction over an out-of-state defendant who has not consented to suit there, [the] "fair warning" requirement is satisfied if the defendant has "purposefully directed" his activities at residents of the forum, *Keeton*, and the litigation results from alleged injuries that "arise out of or relate to" those activities. Thus, "[t]he forum State does not exceed its powers under the Due Process Clause if it asserts personal jurisdiction over a corporation that

delivers its products into the stream of commerce with the expectation that they will be purchased by consumers in the forum State" and those products subsequently injure forum consumers. *World–Wide Volkswagen.* . . . And with respect to interstate contractual obligations, we have emphasized that parties who "reach out beyond one state and create continuing relationships and obligations with citizens of another state" are subject to regulation and sanctions in the other state for the consequences of their activities. Travelers Health Ass'n v. Virginia *ex rel.* State Corp. Comm'n, 339 U.S. 643, 647 (1950). *See also McGee.* . . .

[T]he constitutional touchstone remains whether the defendant purposefully established "minimum contacts" in the forum State. *International Shoe.* . . .

Jurisdiction in these circumstances may not be avoided merely because the defendant did not *physically* enter the forum State. . . . [I]t is an inescapable fact of modern commercial life that a substantial amount of business is transacted solely by mail and wire communications across state lines, obviating the need for physical presence within a State in which business is conducted. So long as a commercial actor's efforts are "purposefully directed" toward residents of another State, we have consistently rejected the notion that an absence of physical contacts can defeat personal jurisdiction there. . . .

Applying these principles to the case at hand, we believe there is substantial record evidence supporting the District Court's conclusion that the assertion of personal jurisdiction over Rudzewicz in Florida . . . did not offend due process. . . . If the question is whether an individual's contract with an out of state party *alone* can establish sufficient minimum contacts in the other party's home forum, we believe the answer clearly is that it cannot. . . . Instead, we have emphasized the need for a "highly realistic" approach that recognizes that a "contract" is "ordinarily but an intermediate step serving to tie up prior business negotiations with future consequences which are themselves the real object of the business transaction." It is these factors — prior negotiations and contemplated future consequences, along with the terms of the contract and the parties' actual course of dealing — that must be evaluated in determining whether the defendant purposefully established minimum contacts within the forum. [*Id.* at 472-79.]

After concluding that Rudzewicz and his partner deliberately "reached out" to affiliate themselves with a Florida franchisor, and entered into a contract with "substantial connection" to the State, the Court turned to whether it was unfair for Florida to assert jurisdiction:

The Court of Appeals also concluded . . . that the parties' dealings involved "a characteristic disparity of bargaining power" and "elements of surprise," and that Rudzewicz "lacked fair notice" of the potential for litigation in Florida because the contractual provisions suggesting the contrary were merely "boilerplate declarations in a lengthy printed contract." . . . [T]he District Court found that . . . Rudzewicz and [his partner] "were and are experienced and sophisticated businessmen," and that "at no time" did they "ac[t] under economic duress or disadvantage imposed by" Burger King. . . .

Notwithstanding [the District Court's findings,] the Court of Appeals apparently believed that it was necessary to reject jurisdiction in this case as a prophylactic measure, reasoning that an affirmance of the District Court's judgment [upholding jurisdiction] would result in the exercise of jurisdiction over "out-of-state consumers to collect payments due on modest personal purchases" and would "sow the seeds of default judgments against franchisees owing smaller debts." We share the Court of Appeals' broader concerns and therefore reject any talismanic jurisdictional formulas . . . .

For the reasons set forth above, however, these dangers are not present in the instant case. [*Id.* at 484-87.]

Is this case consistent with *World–Wide Volkswagen,* in approach or in result? Does *Burger King* provide an answer to one of the questions posed at the beginning of the chapter: is a North Carolina consumer liable in Tennessee for purchases on a credit card issued by a Tennessee bank?

(c) In ***Asahi Metal Industry Co. v. Superior Court of California***, 480 U.S. 102 (1987), the Court dealt with a recurring question: what if a manufacturer in state A ships its products to state B (to a distributor or to another manufacturer to incorporate into a further product), and the state-A manufacturer knows that the final product will end up in state C, the forum state? Is there jurisdiction in state C? Note that *Burger King* repeated the statement from *World–Wide Volkswagen* that a manufacturer "that delivers its products into the stream of commerce with the expectation that they will be purchased by consumers in the forum State" is subject to jurisdiction. But in *Asahi,* the Court could not agree on whether merely placing items in the "stream of commerce," knowing that they would end up in the forum state, was enough to satisfy the minimum-contacts test. Four Justices would have held that placing an item in the stream of commerce is enough by itself; four Justices would have held that some other act directed to the forum state is required. Ultimately, however, eight Justices agreed that it would be unfair to subject the defendant to jurisdiction, regardless of whether the minimum contacts prong was satisfied.

6. After *Asahi,* lower courts divided on the appropriate standard in "stream of commerce" cases. Some concluded that because there was no majority opinion for the "minimum contacts" part of *Asahi,* the standard of *World–Wide Volkswagen* should apply, and thus that placing an item in the stream of commerce is sufficient to establish minimum contacts. *See, e.g.,* Luv n' care, Ltd. v. Insta–Mix, Inc., 438 F.3d 465 (5th Cir. 2006). Other courts adopted the reasoning of Justice O'Connor's plurality opinion, demanding some action purposefully directed toward the forum state. *See, e.g.,* Bridgeport Music, Inc. v. Still N The Water Publ'g, 327 F.3d 472 (6th Cir. 2003). The Supreme Court did not revisit the issue for more than two decades. It finally did so in the following case.

J. McIntyre Machinery, Ltd. v. Nicastro

564 U.S. 873 (2011)

■ JUSTICE KENNEDY announced the judgment of the Court and delivered an opinion, in which THE CHIEF JUSTICE, JUSTICE SCALIA, and JUSTICE THOMAS join.

Whether a person or entity is subject to the jurisdiction of a state court despite not having been present in the State either at the time of suit or at the time of the alleged injury, and despite not having consented to the exercise of jurisdiction, is a question that arises with great frequency in the routine course of litigation. The rules and standards for determining when a State does or does not have jurisdiction over an absent party have been unclear because of decades-old questions left open in *Asahi Metal Industry Co. v. Superior Court*, 480 U.S. 102 (1987).

Here, the Supreme Court of New Jersey, relying in part on *Asahi*, held that New Jersey's courts can exercise jurisdiction over a foreign manufacturer of a product so long as the manufacturer "knows or reasonably should know that its products are distributed through a nationwide distribution system that might lead to those products being sold in any of the fifty states." Applying that test, the court concluded that a British manufacturer of scrap metal machines was subject to jurisdiction in New Jersey, even though at no time had it advertised in, sent goods to, or in any relevant sense targeted the State.

That decision cannot be sustained. . . . [T]he "stream of commerce" metaphor carried the decision far afield. Due process protects the defendant's right not to be coerced except by lawful judicial power. As a general rule, the exercise of judicial power is not lawful unless the defendant "purposefully avails itself of the privilege of conducting activities within the forum State, thus invoking the benefits and protections of its laws." Hanson v. Denckla, 357 U.S. 235, 253 (1958). There may be exceptions, say, for instance, in cases involving an intentional tort. But the general rule is applicable in this products-liability case, and the so-called "stream-of-commerce" doctrine cannot displace it.

I

This case arises from a products-liability suit filed in New Jersey state court. Robert Nicastro seriously injured his hand while using a metal-shearing machine manufactured by J. McIntyre Machinery, Ltd. (J. McIntyre). The accident occurred in New Jersey, but the machine was manufactured in England, where J. McIntyre is incorporated and operates. The question here is whether the New Jersey courts have jurisdiction over J. McIntyre, notwithstanding the fact that the company at no time either marketed goods in the State or shipped them there. . . .

At oral argument . . ., Nicastro's counsel stressed three primary facts in defense of New Jersey's assertion of jurisdiction over J. McIntyre.

First, an independent company agreed to sell J. McIntyre's machines in the United States. J. McIntyre itself did not sell its machines to buyers in this country beyond the U.S. distributor, and there is no allegation that the distributor was under J. McIntyre's control.

Second, J. McIntyre officials attended annual conventions for the scrap recycling industry to advertise J. McIntyre's machines alongside the distributor. The conventions took place in various States, but never in New Jersey.

Third, no more than four machines (the record suggests only one), including the machine that caused the injuries that are the basis for this suit, ended up in New Jersey.

In addition to these facts emphasized by respondent, the New Jersey Supreme Court noted that J. McIntyre held both United States and European patents on its recycling technology. It also noted that the U.S. distributor "structured [its] advertising and sales efforts in accordance with" J. McIntyre's "direction and guidance whenever possible," and that "at least some of the machines were sold on consignment to" the distributor.

In light of these facts, the New Jersey Supreme Court concluded that New Jersey courts could exercise jurisdiction over petitioner without contravention of the Due Process Clause. Jurisdiction was proper, in that court's view, because the injury occurred in New Jersey; because petitioner knew or reasonably should have known "that its products are distributed through a nationwide distribution system that might lead to those products being sold in any of the fifty states"; and because petitioner failed to "take some reasonable step to prevent the distribution of its products in this State."

Both the New Jersey Supreme Court's holding and its account of what it called "[t]he stream-of-commerce doctrine of jurisdiction," were incorrect, however. This Court's *Asahi* decision may be responsible in part for that court's error regarding the stream of commerce, and this case presents an opportunity to provide greater clarity.

II

The Due Process Clause protects an individual's right to be deprived of life, liberty, or property only by the exercise of lawful power. . . . As a general rule, neither statute nor judicial decree may bind strangers to the State.

A court may subject a defendant to judgment only when the defendant has sufficient contacts with the sovereign "such that the maintenance of the suit does not offend traditional notions of fair play and substantial justice." Int'l Shoe Co. v. Washington, 326 U.S. 310, 316 (1945). Freeform notions of fundamental fairness divorced from traditional practice cannot transform a judgment rendered in the absence of authority into law. As a general rule, the sovereign's exercise of power requires some act by which the defendant "purposefully avails itself of the privilege of conducting activities within the forum State, thus invoking the benefits and protections of its laws," *Hanson*, 357 U.S. at 253, though in some cases, as with an intentional tort, the defendant might well fall within the State's authority by reason of his attempt to obstruct its laws. In products-liability cases like this one, it is the defendant's purposeful availment that makes jurisdiction consistent with "traditional notions of fair play and substantial justice."

A person may submit to a State's authority in a number of ways. There is, of course, explicit consent. Presence within a State at the time suit commences through service of process is another example. Citizenship or domicile — or, by analogy, incorporation or principal place of business for corporations — also indicates general submission to a State's powers. Each of these examples reveals circumstances, or a course of conduct, from which it is proper to infer an intention to benefit from and thus an intention to submit to the laws of the forum State. These examples support exercise of the general jurisdiction of the State's courts and allow the State to resolve both matters that originate within the State and those based on activities and events elsewhere. By contrast, those who live or operate primarily outside a State have a due process right not to be subjected to judgment in its courts as a general matter.

There is also a more limited form of submission to a State's authority for disputes that "arise out of or are connected with the activities within the state." *International Shoe*, 326 U.S. at 319. Where a defendant "purposefully avails itself of the privilege of conducting activities within the forum State, thus invoking the benefits and protections of its laws," *Hanson*, 357 U.S. at 253, it submits to the judicial power of an otherwise foreign sovereign to the extent that power is exercised in connection with the defendant's activities touching on the State. In other words, submission through contact with and activity directed at a sovereign may justify specific jurisdiction "in a suit arising out of or related to the defendant's contacts with the forum."

. . . This Court has stated that a defendant's placing goods into the stream of commerce "with the expectation that they will be purchased by consumers within the forum State" may indicate purposeful availment. World–Wide Volkswagen Corp. v. Woodson, 444 U.S. 286, 298 (1980) (finding that expectation lacking). But that statement does not amend the general rule of personal jurisdiction. It merely observes that a defendant may in an appropriate case be subject to jurisdiction without entering the forum — itself an unexceptional proposition — as where manufacturers or distributors "seek to serve" a given State's market. *Id.* at 295. The principal inquiry in cases of this sort is whether the defendant's activities manifest an intention to submit to the power of a sovereign. In other words, the defendant must "purposefully avai[l] itself of the privilege of conducting activities within the forum State, thus invoking the benefits and protections of its laws." *Hanson*, 357 U.S. at 253. Sometimes a defendant does so by sending its goods rather than its agents. The defendant's transmission of goods permits the exercise of jurisdiction only where the defendant can be said to have targeted the forum; as a general rule, it is not enough that the defendant might have predicted that its goods will reach the forum State.

In *Asahi*, an opinion by Justice Brennan for four Justices outlined a different approach. It discarded the central concept of sovereign authority in favor of considerations of fairness and foreseeability. . . . It was the premise of the concurring opinion that the defendant's ability to anticipate suit renders the assertion of jurisdiction fair. In this way, the opinion made foreseeability the touchstone of jurisdiction.

The standard set forth in Justice Brennan's concurrence was rejected in an opinion written by Justice O'Connor; but the relevant part of that opinion, too, commanded the assent of only four Justices, not a majority of the Court. That opinion stated: ". . . The placement of a product into the stream of commerce, without more, is not an act of the defendant purposefully directed toward the forum State."

Since *Asahi* was decided, the courts have sought to reconcile the competing opinions. But Justice Brennan's concurrence, advocating a rule based on general notions of fairness and foreseeability, is inconsistent with the premises of lawful judicial power. This Court's precedents make clear that it is the defendant's actions, not his expectations, that empower a State's courts to subject him to judgment.

. . . [J]urisdiction is in the first instance a question of authority rather than fairness . . . . [W]ere general fairness considerations the touchstone of jurisdiction, a lack of purposeful availment might be excused where carefully crafted judicial procedures could otherwise protect the defendant's interests, or where the plaintiff would suffer substantial hardship if forced to litigate in a foreign forum. That such considerations have not been deemed controlling is instructive.

Two principles are implicit in the foregoing. First, personal jurisdiction requires a forum-by-forum, or sovereign-by-sovereign, analysis. The question is whether a defendant has followed a course of conduct directed at the society or economy existing within the jurisdiction of a given sovereign, so that the sovereign has the power to subject the defendant to judgment concerning that conduct. Personal jurisdiction, of course, restricts "judicial power not as a matter of sovereignty, but as a matter of individual liberty," Ins. Corp. [of Ir. v. Compagnie des Bauxites de Guinee, 456 U.S. 694, 702 (1982)], for due process protects the individual's right to be subject only to lawful power. But whether a judicial judgment is lawful depends on whether the sovereign has authority to render it.

The second principle is a corollary of the first. Because the United States is a distinct sovereign, a defendant may in principle be subject to the jurisdiction of the courts of the United States but not of any particular State. . . .

It must be remembered . . . that although this case and *Asahi* both involve foreign manufacturers, the undesirable consequences of Justice Brennan's approach are no less significant for domestic producers. The owner of a small Florida farm might sell crops to a large nearby distributor, for example, who might then distribute them to grocers across the country. If foreseeability were the controlling criterion, the farmer could be sued in

Alaska or any number of other States' courts without ever leaving town. And the issue of foreseeability may itself be contested so that significant expenses are incurred just on the preliminary issue of jurisdiction. Jurisdictional rules should avoid these costs whenever possible. . . .

III

In this case, petitioner directed marketing and sales efforts at the United States. . . . Here the question concerns the authority of a New Jersey state court to exercise jurisdiction, so it is petitioner's purposeful contacts with New Jersey, not with the United States, that alone are relevant.

Respondent has not established that J. McIntyre engaged in conduct purposefully directed at New Jersey. . . . The British manufacturer had no office in New Jersey; it neither paid taxes nor owned property there; and it neither advertised in, nor sent any employees to, the State. Indeed, after discovery the trial court found that the "defendant does not have a single contact with New Jersey short of the machine in question ending up in this state." These facts may reveal an intent to serve the U.S. market, but they do not show that J. McIntyre purposefully availed itself of the New Jersey market. . . .

Due process protects petitioner's right to be subject only to lawful authority. At no time did petitioner engage in any activities in New Jersey that reveal an intent to invoke or benefit from the protection of its laws. New Jersey is without power to adjudge the rights and liabilities of J. McIntyre, and its exercise of jurisdiction would violate due process. The contrary judgment of the New Jersey Supreme Court is reversed.

■ JUSTICE BREYER, with whom JUSTICE ALITO joins, concurring in the judgment. . . .

None of our precedents finds that a single isolated sale, even if accompanied by the kind of sales effort indicated here, is sufficient. Rather, this Court's previous holdings suggest the contrary. The Court has held that a single sale to a customer who takes an accident-causing product to a different State (where the accident takes place) is not a sufficient basis for asserting jurisdiction. See World–Wide Volkswagen Corp. v. Woodson, 444 U.S. 286 (1980). And the Court, in separate opinions, has strongly suggested that a single sale of a product in a State does not constitute an adequate basis for asserting jurisdiction over an out-of-state defendant, even if that defendant places his goods in the stream of commerce, fully aware (and hoping) that such a sale will take place. See Asahi Metal Indus. Co. v. Superior Court, 480 U.S. 102, 111, 112 (1987) (opinion of O'Connor, J.) (requiring "something more" than simply placing "a product into the stream of commerce," even if defendant is "awar[e]" that the stream "may or will sweep the product into the forum State"); id. at 117 (Brennan, J., concurring in part and concurring in judgment) (jurisdiction should lie where a sale in a State is part of "the regular and anticipated flow" of commerce into the State, but not where that sale is only an "edd[y]," i.e., an isolated occurrence); id. at 122 (Stevens, J., concurring in part and concurring in judgment) (indicating that "the volume, the value, and the hazardous character" of a good may affect the jurisdictional inquiry and emphasizing Asahi's "regular course of dealing").

Here, the relevant facts found by the New Jersey Supreme Court show no "regular . . . flow" or "regular course" of sales in New Jersey; and there is no "something more," such as special state-related design, advertising, advice, marketing, or anything else. Mr. Nicastro . . . has not . . . shown that [J. McIntyre] "purposefully avail[ed] itself of the privilege of conducting activities" within New Jersey, or that it delivered its goods in the stream of commerce "with the expectation that they will be purchased" by New Jersey users. *World–Wide Volkswagen* 444 U.S. at 297-98. . . .

I would not go further. Because the incident at issue in this case does not implicate modern concerns, and because the factual record leaves many open questions, this is an unsuitable vehicle for making broad pronouncements that refashion basic jurisdictional rules. . . .

The plurality seems to state strict rules that limit jurisdiction where a defendant does not "inten[d] to submit to the power of a sovereign" and cannot "be said to have targeted the forum." But what do those standards mean when a company targets the world by selling products from its Web site? And does it matter if, instead of shipping the products directly, a company consigns the products through an intermediary (say, Amazon.com) who then receives and fulfills the orders? And what if the company markets its products through popup advertisements that it knows will be viewed in a forum? Those issues have serious commercial consequences but are totally absent in this case.

But though I do not agree with the plurality's seemingly strict no-jurisdiction rule, I am not persuaded by the absolute approach adopted by the New Jersey Supreme Court and urged by respondent and his *amici*. Under that view, a producer is subject to jurisdiction for a products-liability action so long as it "knows or reasonably should know that its products are distributed through a nationwide distribution system that *might* lead to those products being sold in any of the fifty states." In the context of this case, I cannot agree. . . .

. . .What might appear fair in the case of a large manufacturer which specifically seeks, or expects, an equal-sized distributor to sell its product in a distant State might seem unfair in the case of a small manufacturer (say, an Appalachian potter) who sells his product (cups and saucers) exclusively to a large distributor, who resells a single item (a coffee mug) to a buyer from a distant State (Hawaii). . . .

It may be that a larger firm can readily "alleviate the risk of burdensome litigation by procuring insurance, passing the expected costs on to customers, or, if the risks are too great, severing its connection with the State." *World–Wide Volkswagen*, 444 U.S. at 297. But manufacturers come in many shapes and sizes. It may be fundamentally unfair to require a small Egyptian shirt maker, a Brazilian manufacturing cooperative, or a Kenyan coffee farmer, selling its products through international distributors, to respond to products-liability tort suits in virtually every State in the United

States, even those in respect to which the foreign firm has no connection at all but the sale of a single (allegedly defective) good. And a rule like the New Jersey Supreme Court suggests would require every product manufacturer, large or small, selling to American distributors to understand not only the tort law of every State, but also the wide variance in the way courts within different States apply that law. . . .

■   JUSTICE GINSBURG, with whom JUSTICE SOTOMAYOR and JUSTICE KAGAN join, dissenting.

A foreign industrialist seeks to develop a market in the United States for machines it manufactures. It hopes to derive substantial revenue from sales it makes to United States purchasers. Where in the United States buyers reside does not matter to this manufacturer. Its goal is simply to sell as much as it can, wherever it can. It excludes no region or State from the market it wishes to reach. But, all things considered, it prefers to avoid products liability litigation in the United States. To that end, it engages a U.S. distributor to ship its machines stateside. Has it succeeded in escaping personal jurisdiction in a State where one of its products is sold and causes injury or even death to a local user? . . .

In a November 23, 1999 letter to [its distributor, McIntyre America, an Ohio-based company that went bankrupt in 2001], McIntyre UK's president spoke plainly about the manufacturer's objective in authorizing the exclusive distributorship: "All we wish to do is sell our products in the [United] States — and get paid!" Notably, McIntyre America was concerned about U.S. litigation involving McIntyre UK products, in which the distributor had been named as a defendant. McIntyre UK counseled McIntyre America to respond personally to the litigation, but reassured its distributor that "the product was built and designed by McIntyre Machinery in the UK and the buck stops here — if there's something wrong with the machine." . . .

. . . Nicastro's suit, I would hold, has been brought in a forum entirely appropriate for the adjudication of his claim. He alleges that McIntyre UK's shear machine was defectively designed or manufactured and, as a result, caused injury to him at his workplace. The machine arrived in Nicastro's New Jersey workplace not randomly or fortuitously, but as a result of the U.S. connections and distribution system that McIntyre UK deliberately arranged. On what sensible view of the allocation of adjudicatory authority could the place of Nicastro's injury within the United States be deemed off limits for his products liability claim against a foreign manufacturer who targeted the United States (including all the States that constitute the Nation) as the territory it sought to develop? . . . .

[T]he constitutional limits on a state court's adjudicatory authority derive from considerations of due process, not state sovereignty. As the Court clarified in *Insurance Corp. of Ireland v. Compagnie des Bauxites de Guinee*, 456 U.S. 694 (1982):

> The restriction on state sovereign power described in *World–Wide Volkswagen Corp.* . . . must be seen as ultimately a function of the individual liberty interest preserved by the Due Process Clause. That

Clause is the only source of the personal jurisdiction requirement and the Clause itself makes no mention of federalism concerns. . . . [*Id.* at 703 n.10.] . . .

The modern approach to jurisdiction over corporations and other legal entities, ushered in by *International Shoe*, gave prime place to reason and fairness. Is it not fair and reasonable, given the mode of trading of which this case is an example, to require the international seller to defend at the place its products cause injury? Do not litigational convenience and choice-of-law considerations point in that direction? On what measure of reason and fairness can it be considered undue to require McIntyre UK to defend in New Jersey as an incident of its efforts to develop a market for its industrial machines anywhere and everywhere in the United States? Is not the burden on McIntyre UK to defend in New Jersey fair, i.e., a reasonable cost of transacting business internationally, in comparison to the burden on Nicastro to go to Nottingham, England to gain recompense for an injury he sustained using McIntyre's product at his workplace in Saddle Brook, New Jersey?

McIntyre UK dealt with the United States as a single market. Like most foreign manufacturers, it was concerned not with the prospect of suit in State X as opposed to State Y, but rather with its subjection to suit anywhere in the United States. . . .

In sum, McIntyre UK, by engaging McIntyre America to promote and sell its machines in the United States, "purposefully availed itself" of the United States market nationwide, not a market in a single State or a discrete collection of States. McIntyre UK thereby availed itself of the market of all States in which its products were sold by its exclusive distributor. . . . How could McIntyre UK not have intended, by its actions targeting a national market, to sell products in the fourth largest destination for imports among all States of the United States and the largest scrap metal market? . . .

The Court's judgment also puts United States plaintiffs at a disadvantage in comparison to similarly situated complainants elsewhere in the world. . . . The European Court of Justice has [permitted] jurisdiction either where the harmful act occurred or at the place of injury.

For the reasons stated, I would hold McIntyre UK answerable in New Jersey for the harm Nicastro suffered at his workplace in that State using McIntyre UK's shearing machine. While I dissent from the Court's judgment, I take heart that the plurality opinion does not speak for the Court, for that opinion would take a giant step away from the "notions of fair play and substantial justice" underlying *International Shoe*.

Notes and Questions

1. What is the state of the law after *Nicastro*? Under what circumstances will placement of an item into the stream of commerce with knowledge that it will wind up in the forum state suffice to establish

minimum contacts? Does *Nicastro* do anything to end the confusion created by *Asahi*? Be sure to consider both Justice Kennedy's plurality opinion and Justice Breyer's opinion in answering these questions. The Supreme Court has previously held that "[w]hen a fragmented Court decides a case and no single rationale explaining the result enjoys the assent of five Justices, 'the holding of the Court may be viewed as that position taken by those Members who concurred in the judgments on the narrowest grounds . . . .'" Marks v. United States, 430 U.S. 188 (1977). Consider one lower court's analysis under *Marks*: "Because *McIntyre* did not produce a majority opinion, we must follow the narrowest holding among the plurality opinions in that case. The narrowest holding is that which can be distilled from Justice Breyer's concurrence — that the law remains the same after *McIntyre*." AFTG–TG, LLC v. Nuvoton Tech. Corp., 689 F.3d 1358, 1363 (Fed. Cir. 2012) (per curiam); *accord*, Ainsworth v. Moffett Eng'g, Ltd., 716 F.3d 174, 179 (5th Cir. 2013); Wylam v. Trader Joe's Co., 2018 WL 473022 (M.D. Pa. 2018).

2. Lower courts are divided on the effect of *Nicastro*. Compare *Ainsworth*, 716 F.3d at 178 ("We . . . find that application of the stream-of-commerce approach . . . does not run afoul of *McIntyre*'s narrow holding"), *AFTG–TG*, 689 F.3d at 1363 ("Because we must proceed on the premise that *McIntyre* did not change the Supreme Court's jurisdictional framework, we must apply our precedent that interprets the Supreme Court's existing stream-of-commerce precedents"), *and* Original Creations, Inc. v. Ready Am., Inc., 836 F. Supp. 2d 711, 717 (N.D. Ill. 2011) ("That the *Nicastro* Court does not discard the stream of commerce theory would . . . suggest that the . . . Circuit case law utilizing this approach has been left undisturbed"), *with* Keranos, LLC v. Analog Devices, Inc., 2011 WL 4027427, at *10 (E.D. Tex. Sept. 12, 2011) (*Nicastro* "announced" a "new minimum contacts analysis"), N. Ins. Co. of N.Y. v. Constr. Navale Bordeaux, 2011 WL 2682950, at *5 (S.D. Fla. July 11, 2011) (stating that "'something more' than merely placing a product into the stream of commerce is required for personal jurisdiction" (quoting *Nicastro*, 564 U.S. at 889 (Breyer, J., concurring))), *and* Oticon Inc. v. Sebotek Hearing Sys., LLC, 865 F. Supp. 2d 501, 513 (D.N.J. 2011) ("*Nicastro* stands for the proposition that targeting the national market is *not* enough to impute jurisdiction to all the forum States").

Some courts have relied on *Bristol–Myers Squibb Co. v. Superior Court of California*, 582 U.S. —, 137 S. Ct. 1773 (2017) (*infra* p. 446), to conclude that personal jurisdiction cannot be based on a stream-of-commerce theory; others disagree. *See infra* p. 452, Note 3.

3. Is *Nicastro* consistent with prior Supreme Court opinions? When you read the "stream of commerce" language in *World–Wide Volkswagen* and again in *Burger King*, did you think that anything more than placing an item in the stream of commerce (with the expectation that it would end up in the forum state) was required for minimum contacts? (Note that whatever the rule on "stream of commerce," *World–Wide* makes clear that the stream ends with the consumer.) If the franchisees in *Burger King* were "reaching out" to Florida and deriving benefits from the connection, wasn't J. McIntyre deriving benefits from the sale of its machine in New Jersey?

4. J. McIntyre Machinery eventually sold its recycling-machinery manufacturing to JMC Recycling (a company independent of, but related to, McIntyre). JMC continued to sell machines in the United States, through an independent distributor in Texas. In 2011, another worker in New Jersey was injured by a JMC machine and sued in federal court there. The court dismissed for lack of personal jurisdiction: "Following *McIntyre*, which held in the context of a practically identical defendant that merely placing goods in the stream of commerce, even with the expectation that the goods might reach consumers in the forum state, would not establish personal jurisdiction, Plaintiff's claim that the Court has personal jurisdiction over JMC is clearly unsustainable." Benitez v. JMC Recycling Sys., Ltd., 97 F. Supp. 3d 576, 584 (D.N.J. 2015).

5. The exercise of specific jurisdiction requires that the lawsuit relate to defendant's contacts with the forum. How closely connected to the lawsuit must those contacts be? The following case explores this critical issue.

BRISTOL–MYERS SQUIBB CO. v. SUPERIOR COURT OF CALIFORNIA

582 U.S. —, 137 S. Ct. 1773 (2017)

■ JUSTICE ALITO delivered the opinion of the Court.

More than 600 plaintiffs, most of whom are not California residents, filed this civil action in a California state court against Bristol-Myers Squibb Company (BMS), asserting a variety of state-law claims based on injuries allegedly caused by a BMS drug called Plavix. The California Supreme Court held that the California courts have specific jurisdiction to entertain the nonresidents' claims. We now reverse.

I

A

BMS, a large pharmaceutical company, is incorporated in Delaware and headquartered in New York, and it maintains substantial operations in both New York and New Jersey. Over 50 percent of BMS's work force in the United States is employed in those two States.

BMS also engages in business activities in other jurisdictions, including California. Five of the company's research and laboratory facilities, which employ a total of around 160 employees, are located there. BMS also employs about 250 sales representatives in California and maintains a small state-government advocacy office in Sacramento.

One of the pharmaceuticals that BMS manufactures and sells is Plavix, a prescription drug that thins the blood and inhibits blood clotting. BMS did not develop Plavix in California, did not create a marketing strategy for Plavix in California, and did not manufacture, label, package, or work on the regulatory approval of the product in California. BMS instead engaged in all of these activities in either New York or New Jersey. But BMS does sell Plavix in California. Between 2006 and 2012, it sold almost 187 million Plavix pills in the State and took in more than $900 million from those sales. This amounts to a little over one percent of the company's nationwide sales revenue.

B

A group of plaintiffs — consisting of 86 California residents and 592 residents from 33 other States — filed eight separate complaints in California Superior Court, alleging that Plavix had damaged their health. All the complaints asserted 13 claims under California law, including products liability, negligent misrepresentation, and misleading advertising claims. The nonresident plaintiffs did not allege that they obtained Plavix through California physicians or from any other California source; nor did they claim that they were injured by Plavix or were treated for their injuries in California. . . . [The California Court of Appeal found] that the California courts had specific jurisdiction over the nonresidents' claims against BMS.

The California Supreme Court affirmed. The court unanimously agreed with the Court of Appeal [that general jurisdiction was lacking], but the court was divided on the question of specific jurisdiction. The majority applied a "sliding scale approach to specific jurisdiction." Under this approach, "the more wide ranging the defendant's forum contacts, the more readily is shown a connection between the forum contacts and the claim." Applying this test, the majority concluded that "BMS's extensive contacts with California" permitted the exercise of specific jurisdiction "based on a less direct connection between BMS's forum activities and plaintiffs' claims than might otherwise be required." This attenuated requirement was met, the majority found, because the claims of the nonresidents were similar in several ways to the claims of the California residents (as to which specific jurisdiction was uncontested). The court noted that "[b]oth the resident and nonresident plaintiffs' claims are based on the same allegedly defective product and the assertedly misleading marketing and promotion of that product. And while acknowledging that "there is no claim that Plavix itself was designed and developed in [BMS's California research facilities]," the court thought it significant that other research was done in the State.

Three justices dissented. "The claims of . . . nonresidents injured by their use of Plavix they purchased and used in other states," they wrote, "in no sense arise from BMS's marketing and sales of Plavix in California," and they found that the "mere similarity" of the residents' and nonresidents' claims was not enough. . . .

We granted certiorari to decide whether the California courts' exercise of jurisdiction in this case violates the Due Process Clause of the Fourteenth Amendment.

II

A

. . .

Since our seminal decision in *International Shoe* [*v. Washington*, 326 U.S. 310 (1945)], our decisions have recognized two types of personal jurisdiction: "general" (sometimes called "all-purpose") jurisdiction and "specific" (sometimes called "case-linked") jurisdiction. Goodyear [*Dunlop Tires Operations, S.A. v. Brown*, 564 U.S. 915, 919 (2011)]. . . .

. . . In order for a state court to exercise specific jurisdiction, "the *suit*" must "aris[e] out of or relat[e] to the defendant's contacts with the *forum*." Daimler [*AG v. Bauman*, 571 U.S. 117, 127 (2014) (*infra* p. 461)] (internal quotation marks omitted; emphasis added). In other words, there must be "an affiliation between the forum and the underlying controversy, principally, [an] activity or an occurrence that takes place in the forum State and is therefore subject to the State's regulation." *Goodyear*, 564 U.S. at 919. For this reason, "specific jurisdiction is confined to adjudication of issues deriving from, or connected with, the very controversy that establishes jurisdiction." *Id.* . . .

B

In determining whether personal jurisdiction is present, a court must consider a variety of interests. These include "the interests of the forum State and of the plaintiff in proceeding with the cause in the plaintiff's forum of choice." *Kulko v. Superior Court of Calif.*, 436 U.S. 84, 92 (1978). But the "primary concern" is "the burden on the defendant." Assessing this burden obviously requires a court to consider the practical problems resulting from litigating in the forum, but it also encompasses the more abstract matter of submitting to the coercive power of a State that may have little legitimate interest in the claims in question. As we have put it, restrictions on personal jurisdiction "are more than a guarantee of immunity from inconvenient or distant litigation. They are a consequence of territorial limitations on the power of the respective States." "[T]he States retain many essential attributes of sovereignty, including, in particular, the sovereign power to try causes in their courts. The sovereignty of each State . . . implie[s] a limitation on the sovereignty of all its sister States." And at times, this federalism interest may be decisive. As we explained in *World–Wide Volkswagen* [*v. Woodson*, 444 U.S. 286, 292 (1980)], "[e]ven if the defendant would suffer minimal or no inconvenience from being forced to litigate before the tribunals of another State; even if the forum State has a strong interest in applying its law to the controversy; even if the forum State is the most convenient location for litigation, the Due Process Clause, acting as an instrument of interstate federalism, may sometimes act to divest the State of its power to render a valid judgment."

III

A

Our settled principles regarding specific jurisdiction control this case. In order for a court to exercise specific jurisdiction over a claim, there must be an "affiliation between the forum and the underlying controversy, principally, [an] activity or an occurrence that takes place in the forum State." *Goodyear*, 564 U.S. at 919. When there is no such connection, specific jurisdiction is lacking regardless of the extent of a defendant's unconnected activities in the State. *See id.* at 931 n.6 ("[E]ven regularly occurring sales of a product in a State do not justify the exercise of jurisdiction over a claim unrelated to those sales").

For this reason, the California Supreme Court's "sliding scale approach" is difficult to square with our precedents. Under the California approach, the strength of the requisite connection between the forum and the specific claims at issue is relaxed if the defendant has extensive forum contacts that are unrelated to those claims. Our cases provide no support for this approach, which resembles a loose and spurious form of general jurisdiction. For specific jurisdiction, a defendant's general connections with the forum are not enough. . . .

The present case illustrates the danger of the California approach. The State Supreme Court found that specific jurisdiction was present without identifying any adequate link between the State and the nonresidents' claims. As noted, the nonresidents were not prescribed Plavix in California, did not purchase Plavix in California, did not ingest Plavix in California, and were not injured by Plavix in California. The mere fact that *other* plaintiffs were prescribed, obtained, and ingested Plavix in California—and allegedly sustained the same injuries as did the nonresidents—does not allow the State to assert specific jurisdiction over the nonresidents' claims. As we have explained, "a defendant's relationship with a . . . third party, standing alone, is an insufficient basis for jurisdiction." Walden [v. Fiore, 571 U.S. 277, 286 (2014)]. This remains true even when third parties (here, the plaintiffs who reside in California) can bring claims similar to those brought by the nonresidents. Nor is it sufficient—or even relevant—that BMS conducted research in California on matters unrelated to Plavix. What is needed—and what is missing here—is a connection between the forum and the specific claims at issue. . . .

C

In a last ditch contention, respondents contend that BMS's "decision to contract with a California company [McKesson] to distribute [Plavix] nationally" provides a sufficient basis for personal jurisdiction. But as we have explained, "[t]he requirements of *International Shoe* . . . must be met as to each defendant over whom a state court exercises jurisdiction." In this case, it is not alleged that BMS engaged in relevant acts together with McKesson in California. Nor is it alleged that BMS is derivatively liable for

McKesson's conduct in California. And the nonresidents "have adduced no evidence to show how or by whom the Plavix they took was distributed to the pharmacies that dispensed it to them." The bare fact that BMS contracted with a California distributor is not enough to establish personal jurisdiction in the State.

IV

Our straightforward application in this case of settled principles of personal jurisdiction will not result in the parade of horribles that respondents conjure up. Our decision does not prevent the California and out-of-state plaintiffs from joining together in a consolidated action in the States that have general jurisdiction over BMS. BMS concedes that such suits could be brought in either New York or Delaware. Alternatively, the plaintiffs who are residents of a particular State — for example, the 92 plaintiffs from Texas and the 71 from Ohio — could probably sue together in their home States. In addition, since our decision concerns the due process limits on the exercise of specific jurisdiction by a State, we leave open the question whether the Fifth Amendment imposes the same restrictions on the exercise of personal jurisdiction by a federal court. See Omni Capital Int'l, Ltd. v. Rudolf Wolff & Co., 484 U. S. 97, 102 n.5 (1987).

* * *

The judgment of the California Supreme Court is reversed, and the case is remanded for further proceedings not inconsistent with this opinion.

■ JUSTICE SOTOMAYOR, dissenting.

Three years ago, the Court imposed substantial curbs on the exercise of general jurisdiction in its decision in *Daimler*. Today, the Court takes its first step toward a similar contraction of specific jurisdiction by holding that a corporation that engages in a nationwide course of conduct cannot be held accountable in a state court by a group of injured people unless all of those people were injured in the forum State.

I fear the consequences of the Court's decision today will be substantial. The majority's rule will make it difficult to aggregate the claims of plaintiffs across the country whose claims may be worth little alone. It will make it impossible to bring a nationwide mass action in state court against defendants who are "at home" in different States. And it will result in piecemeal litigation and the bifurcation of claims. None of this is necessary. A core concern in this Court's personal jurisdiction cases is fairness. And there is nothing unfair about subjecting a massive corporation to suit in a State for a nationwide course of conduct that injures both forum residents and nonresidents alike. . . .

. . . Even absent a rigid requirement that a defendant's in-state conduct must actually cause a plaintiff's claim,[3] the upshot of today's opinion is that

3. Bristol–Meyers urges such a rule upon us, but its adoption would have con- sequences far beyond those that follow from today's factbound opinion. Among

plaintiffs cannot join their claims together and sue a defendant in a State in which only some of them have been injured. That rule is likely to have consequences far beyond this case.

Notes and Questions

1. Although the Court rejects California's "sliding scale" approach, it does not specify how closely related a defendant's activities or contacts must be to the claim, and lower courts have disagreed. One court had previously summarized the state of the law:

> Three approaches predominate. The most restrictive standard is the "proximate cause" or "substantive relevance" test. Courts have articulated this test in a variety of ways. Some hold the defendant's contacts must be the "legal cause" of the plaintiff's injury "(i.e. the defendant's in-state conduct [must] g[i]ve birth to the cause of action)." Justice Brennan, dissenting in *Helicopteros*, similarly described it as a requirement that "the cause of action . . . formally 'arise out of' the [defendant's] contacts." But stated most simply, this test examines whether any of the defendant's contacts with the forum are relevant to the merits of the plaintiff's claim.
>
> A second, more relaxed test requires only "but-for" causation. As the name indicates, this standard is satisfied when the plaintiff's claim would not have arisen in the absence of the defendant's contacts. . . .
>
> A third standard looks for a "substantial connection" or "discernible relationship." Unlike the but-for test, causation is of no special importance. The critical question is whether the tie between the defendant's contacts and the plaintiff's claim is close enough to make jurisdiction fair and reasonable. . . . The degree of relatedness in a given case is inversely proportional to the overall "intensity of [the defendant's] forum contacts."

O'Connor v. Sandy Lane Hotel Co., 496 F.3d 312, 318-20 (3d Cir. 2007). The *O'Connor* court itself declined to adopt any test. It did explicitly reject the third approach, and *Bristol–Myers Squibb*'s rejection of the "sliding scale" confirms that the third approach is not viable.

2. Recall the manufacturer, Audi, in the *World–Wide Volkswagen* case. Although the Robinsons bought their car in New York, Audi sold identical cars in Oklahoma. Audi did not challenge personal jurisdiction. If it had done so, should the fortuity that the Robinsons' car came from New York deprive the Oklahoma court of jurisdiction over Audi? Think about whether *Bristol–Myers Squibb* answers the question. Justice Sotomayor's footnote 3 suggests that there would be jurisdiction over Audi. Do you agree with her reading of the majority opinion? As this edition goes to press, the Supreme

other things, it might call into question whether even a plaintiff *injured* in a State by an item identical to those sold by a defendant in that State could avail himself of that State's courts to redress his injuries — a result specifically contemplated by *World–Wide Volkswagen Corp. v. Woodson*, 444 U.S. 286, 297 (1980).

Court has granted certiorari in two consolidated cases that address that question. *See* Bandemer v. Ford Motor Co., 931 N.W.2d 744 (Minn. 2019), *cert. granted,* 2020 WL 254152 (U.S. Jan. 17, 2020) (No. 19–369); Ford Motor Co. v. Mont. Eighth Judicial Dist. Ct., 443 P.3d 407 (Mont. 2019), *cert. granted,* 2020 WL 254155 (U.S. Jan. 17, 2020) (No 19–368).

3. Does *Bristol–Myers Squibb* affect the stream-of-commerce analysis that we examined in *Nicastro*? Consider the majority's statement that "[t]he bare fact that BMS contracted with a California distributor is not enough to establish personal jurisdiction in the State." In the context of the rest of the paragraph, this seems to mean that unless the plaintiffs can show some connection between the California distributor and their own injuries in other states, this one unrelated contact is insufficient. However, some courts have focused on this statement and concluded that a majority has now definitively rejected stream-of-commerce as a method of establishing jurisdiction. *See, e.g.*, Shuker v. Smith & Nephew, 885 F.3d 760, 780 (3d Cir. 2017); A.T. *ex rel.* Travis v. Hahn, 341 F. Supp. 3d 1031, 1037 (E.D. Mo. 2018). Other courts have held that *Bristol–Myers Squibb* has no effect on stream-of-commerce jurisprudence. *See, e.g.*, Lindsley v. Am. Honda Motor Co., 2017 WL 3217140, at *2 (E.D. Pa. July 28, 2017).

4. The Court has wavered about whether personal-jurisdiction doctrine rests on individual liberty or state sovereignty (or both). *World–Wide Volkswagen* emphasized the importance of both factors, but *Insurance Corp. of Ireland* (*supra* pp. 432-33, Note 1) rejected state sovereignty, resting personal-jurisdiction limitations solely on the defendant's liberty interest. In *Nicastro*, the plurality emphasized state sovereignty but ultimately quoted and adhered to *Insurance Corp.*'s sole focus on liberty. But if state sovereignty is not important, why should the Court care about McIntyre's contacts with *New Jersey* rather than with the United States as a whole? By making territorial borders matter more than distance and convenience, the Court seems to rely on some kind of state sovereignty, under whatever label. The fact that — both before and after *Nicastro* — a defendant residing in Buffalo, New York, is automatically subject to jurisdiction in New York City 400 miles away, while a defendant residing in Newark, New Jersey (just across the Hudson River from New York City) is not subject to jurisdiction in New York City unless he or she has sufficient contacts with New York *State*, makes no sense unless state boundaries are important — which takes us back to the importance of territoriality and state sovereignty. (Recall that *Insurance Corp.* was about whether the defendant had waived its objections to personal jurisdiction, which might explain why the Court downplayed state sovereignty in that case.) In *Bristol-Myers Squibb*, the Court executed a major and unexplained conceptual about-face — whose practical impact and durability if any remain unclear — returning with extended quotation to *World–Wide Volkswagen*'s dual emphasis on both liberty interests of the defendant and state sovereignty. The majority opinion for eight Justices (including the three surviving members of the *Nicastro* plurality, which had expressly relied on *Insurance Corp.*'s treatment of the sovereignty aspect) made no mention of *Insurance Corp*. No wonder lower courts seem unsure how to apply personal-jurisdiction doctrine!

5. The Court notes that everyone agrees that the California court has personal jurisdiction over the defendant for the claims brought by California residents. If Bristol–Myers Squibb can be sued in California by *some* plaintiffs, why does it care whether it can also be sued — in the same lawsuit — by other plaintiffs? This lawsuit alleges violations of California law. It might help you understand the defendant's motive for challenging jurisdiction over the claims by non-Californians if you consider what law would likely apply if, for example, the Texas plaintiffs bring suit in Texas.

6. Having read the somewhat inconsistent precedents on personal jurisdiction in the real world, you can imagine the problems in applying them to the virtual world. Under what circumstances, for example, should a website accessible in the forum state subject its owner to suit there? In fact, courts have had less difficulty than you might think translating personal-jurisdiction doctrines to the internet. Consider the following case.

SHIPPITSA LTD. V. SLACK

2019 WL 2372687 (N.D. Tex. June 5, 2019)

■ FITZWATER, Senior [District] Judge.

[Shippitsa manufactures a dietary supplement called Phen375, which it sells through its website at the domain name phen375.com. Shippitsa contracted with MoreNiche (founded and directed by John Slack) to have MoreNiche advertise Phen375 on a MoreNiche website and provide a link to Shippitsa's own website. When the contract expired, MoreNiche instead began linking to a webpage — mixi.mn — operated by MoreNiche and Slack. The mixi.mn webpage consists only of the following lines of text: "Phen375 is no longer available via this link, we will be redirecting you to an alternative in 5 seconds. If you do not want us to do that click here."

[Shippitsa sued Slack and MoreNiche in Texas federal district court on federal and state claims including trademark infringement, unfair competition, and related claims. Slack is a citizen of the UK, and MoreNiche is incorporated under the laws of and headquartered in the UK. Both defendants moved to dismiss for lack of personal jurisdiction, and the court granted both motions. Shippitsa then moved for reconsideration.]

I

[In its first ruling,] . . . the court rejected Shippitsa's theory of personal jurisdiction: that MoreNiche and Slack have the required minimum contacts with this forum because their webpage — mixi.mn — caused visitors' web browsers — including web browsers located in this district — to connect automatically to a different website.

The court applied the test from *Zippo Manufacturing Co. v. Zippo Dot Com, Inc.*, 952 F. Supp. 1119 (W.D. Pa. 1997), as adopted by the Fifth Circuit in *Mink v. AAAA Development LLC*, 190 F.3d 333, 336 (5th Cir. 1999).

Applying this analysis, the court concluded that mixi.mn is not sufficiently commercial or interactive to support personal jurisdiction . . . .

III

In its motion for reconsideration, Shippitsa re-urges its argument that mixi.mn can support personal jurisdiction under the *Zippo* test. Shippitsa also cites, for the first time, *Wien Air Alaska, Inc. v. Brandt*, 195 F.3d 208, 213 (5th Cir. 1999), and folds the principles from that case into the present minimum-contacts analysis.

A

. . .

1

The fundamental test for whether a court has personal jurisdiction over a defendant is well-settled.

"When a nonresident defendant presents a motion to dismiss for lack of personal jurisdiction, the plaintiff bears the burden of establishing the district court's jurisdiction over the nonresident." The determination whether a federal district court has *in personam* jurisdiction over a nonresident defendant is bipartite. The court first decides whether the long-arm statute of the state in which it sits confers personal jurisdiction over the defendant. If it does, the court then resolves whether the exercise of jurisdiction is consistent with due process under the United States Constitution. Because the Texas long-arm statute extends to the limits of due process, the court need only consider whether exercising jurisdiction over the defendant would be consistent with the Due Process Clause of the Fourteenth Amendment. . . .

2

When specific jurisdiction is based on online interactions via an Internet website, the Fifth Circuit is guided by the sliding scale adopted in *Zippo*, 952 F. Supp. at 1124. *Zippo* requires the court to assess the level of interactivity of the defendant's website. It prescribes different outcomes to the personal jurisdiction question depending on which of the following three categories the website falls into: (1) where a website is nothing more than a passive advertisement, the court must decline to exercise personal jurisdiction; (2) where a website facilitates contractual relationships and the knowing and repeated transmission of computer files over the Internet, personal jurisdiction is proper; and (3) where a website falls somewhere in between, "the exercise of jurisdiction is determined by the level of interactivity and commercial nature of the exchange of information that occurs on the [w]ebsite."

As this court noted in *Shippitsa I*, "[t]he *Zippo* court did not create its sliding scale from whole cloth — the test is based on 'well developed personal jurisdiction principles.'" "Even in the strange realm of Internet-related contacts, the standard for personal jurisdiction remains that a non-resident defendant must have purposefully availed itself of the benefits and protections of the forum's laws such that it should reasonably anticipate being haled into the forum's courts." Thus while *Zippo* provides a helpful framework in which to analyze online contacts, it does not supplant the Due Process Clause or the animating principles of personal-jurisdiction jurisprudence. . . .

The *Zippo* framework nonetheless has its uses. It averts the risk that a defendant, merely by operating a globally-accessible website, might be subject to global personal jurisdiction — without any opportunity "to structure [its] primary conduct with some minimum assurance as to where that conduct will and will not render [it] liable to suit," World-Wide Volkswagen [Corp. v. Woodson, 444 U.S. 286, 297 (1980) (*supra* p. 424)]. The D.C. Circuit, in an early Internet-contacts case, explained the problem succinctly:

> When stripped to its core, [plaintiff]'s theory of jurisdiction rests on the claim that, because the defendants have acted to maximize usage of their websites in the District, mere accessibility of the defendants' websites establishes the necessary "minimum contacts" with this forum. This theory simply cannot hold water. Indeed, under this view, personal jurisdiction in Internet-related cases would almost always be found in any forum in the country. We do not believe that the advent of advanced technology, say, as with the Internet, should vitiate long-held and inviolate principles of federal court jurisdiction. The Due Process Clause exists, in part, to give "a degree of predictability to the legal system that allows potential defendants to structure their primary conduct with some minimum assurance as to where that conduct will and will not render them liable to suit." In the context of the Internet, [plaintiff]'s expansive theory of personal jurisdiction would shred these constitutional assurances out of practical existence. Our sister circuits have not accepted such an approach, and neither shall we.

GTE New Media Servs. Inc. v. BellSouth Corp., 199 F.3d 1343, 1350 (D.C. Cir. 2000) (citations omitted). The *Zippo* framework recognizes that due process cannot support this result.

Zippo instead comports with core personal-jurisdiction principles by requiring "evidence of purposeful conduct" by the defendant. It is well-established that "[a] plaintiff's or third party's unilateral activities cannot establish minimum contacts between the defendant and forum state." A user's connection to a defendant's website is initiated by the user; the process has been analogized to the defendant's receiving a phone call from a forum resident. Thus the user-driven process of connecting to a website cannot, without more, support personal jurisdiction. The lodestars of the *Zippo* analysis — the level of interactivity and the commercial nature of the exchange of information — allow courts to differentiate between defendants who merely maintain a passive Internet presence (to which users then unilaterally connect) and defendants who actively engage, and do business, with residents of the forum state via the Internet.

A corollary principle of personal jurisdiction is that a defendant should be able to structure its conduct so as to predict where it might be haled into court. *See World-Wide Volkswagen*, 444 U.S. at 297. A defendant can control the universe of those with whom it interacts and does business online; thus the *Zippo* test provides an opportunity for defendants to choose whether to subject themselves to jurisdiction in a particular forum.

Finally, where a defendant uses a website to engage in business transactions, *Zippo* reflects an extension of the principle that "when an entity intentionally reaches beyond its boundaries to conduct business with foreign residents, the exercise of specific jurisdiction is proper." *Zippo*, 952 F. Supp. at 1124 (citing Burger King [Corp. v. Rudzewicz, 471 U.S. 462, 475 (1985)]). "Different results should not be reached simply because business is conducted over the Internet." *Id.* Thus where there is "evidence that [the defendant] conducted business over the Internet by engaging in business transactions with forum residents or by entering into contracts over the Internet," personal jurisdiction is proper.

Zippo is not the only test applicable to Internet contacts. Some courts have applied the so-called "effects test" from *Calder v. Jones*, 465 U.S. 783 (1984), alongside — or in lieu of — the *Zippo* analysis. The core principle of *Calder* is that, when a defendant is "charged with intentional, tortious conduct directed toward the forum state . . . [it] must 'reasonably anticipate being haled into court there[.]'" *Wien Air*, 195 F.3d at 212 (quoting *Calder*, 465 U.S. at 789-90). Although *Calder* itself involved a defamation claim, the Fifth Circuit has extended its analysis to other intentional torts.

Like *Zippo*, *Calder* does not supersede or replace the Due Process Clause; rather, it is an application of familiar principles of personal jurisdiction in the context of intentional torts. . . .

B

In light of the above, the court remains unpersuaded that mixi.mn can support the exercise of specific personal jurisdiction under the *Zippo* test.

Shippitsa asserts that, "[t]he [c]ourt errantly considered only what could be seen by the browser's user, and ignored messages that controlled operation of the browser itself. Shippitsa's allegations against MoreNiche and Slack turn on the 'redirection' and not merely the visible content [of mixi.mn]." . . . The court's analysis focused on the visible elements of mixi.mn . . . . This was not a manifest error of law or fact.

. . . [T]he court's focus on the visible elements of mixi.mn was sensible in light of the underlying principles of personal jurisdiction embodied in the *Zippo* test. The fact that the mixi.mn page *automatically* sends redirect instructions to all visitors does not evince "purposeful conduct" on the part of MoreNiche and Slack. . . .

[If] *Zippo* were to take into account the technical instructions sent to a user's web browser, the courts would be faced with a line-drawing problem, because the number of invisible messages exchanged between users and websites is greater today than at the time when *Zippo* was decided. For example, even purely-informational websites now widely use "cookies" — "data that [are] sent from a website's host server and then stored on the user's computer" — for a variety of purposes. . . .

In any event, "doing business over the Internet," *Zippo*, 952 F. Supp. at 1124, does not include every online activity that financially benefits the defendant. Were it so, even passive online advertisements would give rise to personal jurisdiction — an outcome that is plainly foreclosed by *Mink*, 190 F.3d at 337. Rather, the second *Zippo* category is an extension of the principle that "when an entity intentionally reaches beyond its boundaries to conduct business with foreign residents, the exercise of specific jurisdiction is proper." *Zippo*, 952 F. Supp. at 1124. In support of this principle, the *Zippo* court cited *Burger King*, in which the defendant reached out to a company headquartered in the forum state and entered into a long-term contractual relationship with that company. Visitors to mixi.mn cannot contract with MoreNiche and Slack via mixi.mn. Thus here, as in *Mink*, "[t]here was no evidence that [the defendants] conducted business over the Internet by engaging in business transactions with forum residents or by entering into contracts over the Internet." Accordingly, mixi.mn falls, at best, in the middle category of *Zippo*. To support personal jurisdiction, the webpage must be sufficiently interactive in the context of the *Zippo* sliding scale. The court has already concluded that it is not.

C

The court is not persuaded by Shippitsa's references to *Wien Air* and the principles advanced therein — principles derived from *Calder*.

Shippitsa cites *Wien Air* for the proposition that "[w]hen the actual content of communications with a forum gives rise to intentional tort causes of action, this alone constitutes purposeful availment." According to Shippitsa, MoreNiche and Slack committed a number of intentional torts — including, *inter alia*, trademark infringement and false designation of origin — when they redirected Texas residents to [other] websites. These intentional torts thus arose from the digital instructions, or "communications," that mixi.mn sent to visitors' web browsers in Texas.

The instant case, however, is less like *Wien Air* than it is like *Revell* [v. *Lidov*, 317 F.3d 467 (5th Cir. 2002)]. In *Wien Air* the Fifth Circuit held that specific jurisdiction could be exercised over a defendant who directed a number of tortious and deceptive letters, faxes, and phone calls to the plaintiffs in Texas. The panel based its conclusion on the principle from *Calder* that "intentional, tortious conduct *directed toward the forum state*" can create the minimum contacts necessary to support personal jurisdiction. In *Revell* the Fifth Circuit applied the same principle to an Internet tort, and held that personal jurisdiction was lacking. The panel concluded that an allegedly-defamatory article shared via an online bulletin board did not subject the article's author and the website's owner to specific jurisdiction in Texas, the plaintiff's state of residence. The panel reasoned that "the post to the bulletin board here was presumably directed at the entire world, or perhaps just concerned U.S. citizens. But certainly it was not directed specifically at Texas[.]". . .

Finally, under Shippitsa's theory, it could have brought this lawsuit against MoreNiche and Slack in any forum in which a visitor to mixi.mn resides. This proves too much. Just as the defendants in *Revell* did not subject themselves to global personal jurisdiction by making their defamatory article available worldwide, MoreNiche and Slack did not submit themselves to personal jurisdiction everywhere by maintaining an allegedly-infringing webpage. . . .

* * *

For the foregoing reasons, the court denies Shippitsa's motion to reconsider the dismissal of defendants MoreNiche and Slack.

Notes and Questions

1. Many courts regard *Zippo* as providing the most appropriate way to apply traditional personal-jurisdiction principles to cases in which the sole or primary contact with the forum state is a website. *See, e.g.*, Best Van Lines, Inc. v. Walker, 490 F.3d 239, 252 (2d Cir. 2007) (interactivity factor, one aspect of *Zippo* sliding scale, "may be useful" "insofar as it helps to decide whether the defendant 'transacts any business' in" the forum state); Toys "R" Us, Inc. v. Step Two, S.A., 318 F.3d 446, 452 (3d Cir. 2003) ("[*Zippo*] has become a seminal authority regarding personal jurisdiction based upon the operation of an Internet web site"); ALS Scan, Inc. v. Digital Serv. Consultants, Inc., 293 F.3d 707 (4th Cir. 2002) (explicitly adopting *Zippo*).

But as *Shippitsa* indicates, *Zippo* has its limitations. As one court has noted: "Interactive websites 'where a user can exchange information with the host computer' are now extremely common." CollegeSource, Inc. v. AcademyOne, Inc., 653 F.3d 1066, 1075 (9th Cir. 2011) (quoting *Zippo*). The *Zippo* test is therefore most useful at the extremes: passive websites cannot confer jurisdiction, but companies that "do business over the Internet" should be subject to jurisdiction wherever they do business. Do we really need *Zippo* to tell us that? The Seventh Circuit has explicitly rejected it as unnecessary: "[W]e think that the traditional due process inquiry . . . is not so difficult to apply to cases involving Internet contacts that courts need some sort of easier-to-apply categorical test." Illinois v. Hemi Group LLC, 622 F.3d 754, 759 (7th Cir. 2010). Ultimately, does the *Zippo* sliding scale give the least help where help is most needed, in the middle ground?

2. Anyone who maintains a website knows that it may be accessible anywhere in the world. Business entities maintain websites for commercial

benefits: even passive websites serve as advertising and tell potential customers how to reach the company. Why shouldn't the owner of a passive website be subject to jurisdiction in any state where the site is accessible? Geolocation software can identify, with claimed accuracy between 60% and 95%, the geographical location of a user browsing the web. The software can block, or "redirect," that user away from the site. Thus, a company that does not want to be subject to jurisdiction in Ohio can prevent most Ohio residents from gaining access to its website. Should that fact influence personal-jurisdiction doctrines? What if the software's accuracy were 100%?

3. One way to look at questions arising out of internet contacts is to focus on what the Court in *World–Wide Volkswagen* labeled the "fortuitous circumstance" leading to the events in the forum state. We might argue that it is similarly "fortuitous" that a passive website is viewed in the forum state. *Shippitsa* makes that argument when it talks about companies being able to structure their conduct to avoid certain forums. But that argument can also be turned around to suggest that fortuities should not *destroy* jurisdiction any more than they should *create* it. Imagine a company that has no retail outlets but sells through a website; although it does business exclusively over the internet, and it receives and transmits information over the web, its primary business involves shipping items to customers who have ordered them. Should it be subject to jurisdiction based on its website in a state to which it had, fortuitously, shipped no products? What if it deliberately chooses not to ship products to a particular state? *See Hemi Group*, 622 F.3d at 758 ("While Hemi is correct that its contacts, or lack of contacts, with any other state has no bearing on whether it is subject to personal jurisdiction in Illinois, its election not to do business with New York demonstrates that it should have foreseen being subject to litigation in Illinois as a result of its cigarette sales to Illinois customers.").

4. The *Shippitsa* court also uses the "effects" test, which can apply to both internet and non-internet contacts. Two Supreme Court cases have delineate the boundaries of the test.

Calder v. Jones, 465 U.S. 783 (1984), was a libel suit. The plaintiff (Jones) sued the author of the article and the editor of the newspaper as well as the newspaper itself. The suit was brought in California, where the plaintiff lived; the two individual defendants lived in Florida. The editor had only two contacts with California — a pleasure trip and a trip to give testimony in an unrelated case. The author traveled to California frequently on business, but wrote this particular article in Florida, based on research that included telephone calls to California. The Court found the requisite minimum contacts for both defendants:

> The allegedly libelous story concerned the California activities of a California resident. It impugned the professionalism of an entertainer whose television career was centered in California. The article was drawn from California sources, and the brunt of the harm, in terms of both respondent's emotional distress and the injury to her professional reputation, was suffered in California. In sum, California is the focal point both of the story and of the harm suffered. Jurisdiction is therefore

proper in California based on the "effects" of their Florida conduct in California. [465 U.S. at 788-89.]

Is jurisdiction in *Calder* consistent with the lack of jurisdiction in *World–Wide Volkswagen*? Can the same "effects" argument be made in both cases? Note that the Court also pointed to the fact that the defendants' "intentional, and allegedly tortious, actions were expressly aimed at California." *Id.* at 789. Does that statement distinguish *World–Wide*?

The Court examined and distinguished *Calder* in *Walden v. Fiore*, 571 U.S. 277 (2014). In *Walden*, a federal agent in Georgia erroneously confiscated money from the plaintiffs, professional gamblers who were en route from Puerto Rico to their homes in Nevada. After the plaintiffs returned home, the agent executed a probable-cause affidavit for seizure of the money. The Assistant United States Attorney found the affidavit misleading, and the money was eventually returned to the plaintiffs, who sued the federal agent in federal court in Nevada. The Supreme Court unanimously ruled against jurisdiction, distinguishing *Calder* and elaborating on the requirements of minimum contacts:

> . . . The inquiry whether a forum State may assert specific jurisdiction over a nonresident defendant "focuses on 'the relationship among the defendant, the forum, and the litigation.'" . . . Two related aspects of this necessary relationship are relevant in this case.
>
> First, the relationship must arise out of contacts that the "defendant *himself*" creates with the forum State. . . .
>
> Second, our "minimum contacts" analysis looks to the defendant's contacts with the forum State itself, not the defendant's contacts with persons who reside there. . . .
>
> [T]he plaintiff cannot be the only link between the defendant and the forum. Rather, it is the defendant's conduct that must form the necessary connection with the forum State that is the basis for its jurisdiction over him. . . .
>
> The crux of *Calder* was that the reputation-based "effects" of the alleged libel connected the defendants to California, not just to the plaintiff. . . . [T]he reputational injury caused by the defendants' story would not have occurred but for the fact that the defendants wrote an article for publication in California that was read by a large number of California citizens. . . .
>
> . . . [In this case, the Court of Appeals erroneously found jurisdiction on the basis of] the [defendant's] knowledge of [plaintiffs'] "strong forum connections." In the court's view, that knowledge, combined with its conclusion that [plaintiffs] suffered foreseeable harm in Nevada, satisfied the "minimum contacts" inquiry.
>
> This approach to the "minimum contacts" analysis impermissibly allows a plaintiff's contacts with the defendant and forum to drive the jurisdictional analysis. Petitioner's actions in Georgia did not create sufficient contacts with Nevada simply because he alleged directed his conduct at plaintiffs whom he knew had Nevada connections. Such

reasoning improperly attributes a plaintiff's forum connections to the defendant and makes those connections "decisive in the jurisdictional" analysis. It also obscures the reality that none of petitioner's challenged conduct had anything to do with Nevada itself. [571 U.S. 283-89.]

Are *Calder* and *Walden* as distinguishable as the Court suggests, or has the Court simply cut back on its analysis in *Calder*? Most courts have concluded that, after *Walden*, mere knowledge that the brunt of the effects of an intentional tort will be felt in the forum state is not enough of a connection to satisfy minimum contacts. *See, e.g.*, Ariel Invs. v. Ariel Capital Advisors, 881 F.3d 520 (7th Cir. 2018) (knowledge that trademark holder resided in forum state insufficient in trademark-infringement suit); A Corp. v. All Am. Plumbing, Inc., 812 F.3d 54 (1st Cir. 2016) (same); Axiom Foods, Inc. v. Acerchem Int'l, Inc., 874 F.3d 1064 (9th Cir. 2017) (knowledge that copyright holder resided in forum state insufficient in copyright-infringement suit). *But see* Acorda Therapeutics Inc. v. Mylan Pharm. Inc., 817 F.3d 755 (Fed. Cir. 2016) (knowledge that patent holder resided in forum state sufficient in patent-infringement suit). For a careful parsing of *Fiore*, see Havel v. Honda Motor Eur. Ltd., 2014 WL 4967229 (S.D. Tex. Sept. 30 2014).

SECTION D: BEYOND MINIMUM CONTACTS: OTHER BASES FOR PERSONAL JURISDICTION

Satisfying the minimum-contacts test is not the only way to obtain jurisdiction over a defendant. Traditionally, three other situations gave rise to personal jurisdiction. A defendant was considered "present" by being validly served with process while in the state. A defendant could consent to jurisdiction. Or a defendant could have such significant contacts with the forum state that the plaintiff could sue a defendant even for a claim unrelated to the defendant's contacts. Citizens of a state, for example, are always subject to jurisdiction in the courts of that state. This last situation implicates the court's *general personal jurisdiction* rather than its *specific personal jurisdiction*, and requires an analysis of the level of contacts necessary to satisfy due process. This section begins with an examination of general jurisdiction, and then turns to "presence" and consent.

1. General Jurisdiction

DAIMLER AG V. BAUMAN

571 U.S. 117 (2014)

■ JUSTICE GINSBURG delivered the opinion of the Court.

This case concerns the authority of a court in the United States to entertain a claim brought by foreign plaintiffs against a foreign defendant based on events occurring entirely outside the United States. The litigation commenced in 2004, when twenty-two Argentinian residents filed a complaint in the United States District Court for the Northern District of California against DaimlerChrysler Aktiengesellschaft (Daimler), a German public stock company, headquartered in Stuttgart, that manufactures Mercedes-Benz vehicles in Germany. The complaint alleged that during Argentina's 1976-1983 "Dirty War," Daimler's Argentinian subsidiary, Mercedes-Benz Argentina (MB Argentina) collaborated with state security forces to kidnap, detain, torture, and kill certain MB Argentina workers, among them, plaintiffs or persons closely related to plaintiffs. Damages for the alleged human-rights violations were sought from Daimler under the laws of the United States, California, and Argentina. Jurisdiction over the lawsuit was predicated on the California contacts of Mercedes-Benz USA, LLC (MBUSA), a subsidiary of Daimler incorporated in Delaware with its principal place of business in New Jersey. MBUSA distributes Daimler-manufactured vehicles to independent dealerships throughout the United States, including California.

The question presented is whether the Due Process Clause of the Fourteenth Amendment precludes the District Court from exercising jurisdiction over Daimler in this case, given the absence of any California connection to the atrocities, perpetrators, or victims described in the complaint. Plaintiffs invoked the court's general or all-purpose jurisdiction. California, they urge, is a place where Daimler may be sued on any and all claims against it, wherever in the world the claims may arise. For example, as plaintiffs' counsel affirmed, under the proffered jurisdictional theory, if a Daimler-manufactured vehicle overturned in Poland, injuring a Polish driver and passenger, the injured parties could maintain a design defect suit in California. Exercises of personal jurisdiction so exorbitant, we hold, are barred by due process constraints on the assertion of adjudicatory authority.

In *Goodyear Dunlop Tires Operations, S.A. v. Brown*, 564 U.S. 915 (2011), we addressed the distinction between general or all-purpose jurisdiction, and specific or conduct-linked jurisdiction. As to the former, we held that a court may assert jurisdiction over a foreign corporation "to hear any and all claims against [it]" only when the corporation's affiliations with the State in which suit is brought are so constant and pervasive "as to render [it] essentially at home in the forum State." Instructed by *Goodyear*, we conclude Daimler is not "at home" in California, and cannot be sued there for injuries plaintiffs attribute to MB Argentina's conduct in Argentina.

I

... [P]laintiffs asserted claims under the Alien Tort Statute, 28 U.S.C. § 1350, and the Torture Victim Protection Act of 1991, 106 Stat. 73, note following 28 U.S.C. § 1350, as well as claims for wrongful death and intentional infliction of emotional distress under the laws of California and Argentina. The incidents recounted in the complaint center on MB Argentina's plant in Gonzalez Catan, Argentina; no part of MB Argentina's alleged collaboration with Argentinian authorities took place in California or anywhere else in the United States.

Plaintiffs' operative complaint names only one corporate defendant: Daimler, the petitioner here. Plaintiffs seek to hold Daimler vicariously liable for MB Argentina's alleged malfeasance. . . .

Daimler moved to dismiss the action for want of personal jurisdiction. Opposing the motion, plaintiffs submitted declarations and exhibits purporting to demonstrate the presence of Daimler itself in California. Alternatively, plaintiffs maintained that jurisdiction over Daimler could be founded on the California contacts of MBUSA, a distinct corporate entity that, according to plaintiffs, should be treated as Daimler's agent for jurisdictional purposes.

MBUSA, an indirect subsidiary of Daimler, is a Delaware limited liability corporation. MBUSA serves as Daimler's exclusive importer and distributor in the United States, purchasing Mercedes-Benz automobiles from Daimler in Germany, then importing those vehicles, and ultimately distributing them to independent dealerships located throughout the Nation. Although MBUSA's principal place of business is in New Jersey, MBUSA has multiple California-based facilities, including a regional office in Costa Mesa, a Vehicle Preparation Center in Carson, and a Classic Center in Irvine. According to the record developed below, MBUSA is the largest supplier of luxury vehicles to the California market. In particular, over 10% of all sales of new vehicles in the United States take place in California, and MBUSA's California sales account for 2.4% of Daimler's worldwide sales.

The relationship between Daimler and MBUSA is delineated in a General Distributor Agreement, which sets forth requirements for MBUSA's distribution of Mercedes-Benz vehicles in the United States. That agreement established MBUSA as an "independent contracto[r]" that "buy[s] and sell[s] [vehicles] . . . as an independent business for [its] own account." The agreement "does not make [MBUSA] . . . a general or special agent, partner, joint venturer or employee of DAIMLERCHRYSLER or any DaimlerChrysler Group Company"; MBUSA "ha[s] no authority to make binding obligations for or act on behalf of DAIMLERCHRYSLER or any DaimlerChrysler Group Company."

After allowing jurisdictional discovery on plaintiffs' agency allegations, the District Court granted Daimler's motion to dismiss. Daimler's own affiliations with California, the court first determined, were insufficient to support the exercise of all-purpose jurisdiction over the corporation. Next, the court declined to attribute MBUSA's California contacts to Daimler on an agency theory, concluding that plaintiffs failed to demonstrate that MBUSA acted as Daimler's agent.

[The Ninth Circuit ultimately reversed, adopting the theory that an agency relationship sufficient to warrant attribution of MBUSA's contacts to Daimler existed.]

We granted certiorari to decide whether, consistent with the Due Process Clause of the Fourteenth Amendment, Daimler is amenable to suit in California courts for claims involving only foreign plaintiffs and conduct occurring entirely abroad.

II

Federal courts ordinarily follow state law in determining the bounds of their jurisdiction over persons. *See* Fed. R. Civ. P. 4(k)(1)(A). Under California's long-arm statute, California state courts may exercise personal jurisdiction "on any basis not inconsistent with the Constitution of this state or of the United States." California's long-arm statute allows the exercise of personal jurisdiction to the full extent permissible under the U.S. Constitution. We therefore inquire whether the Ninth Circuit's holding comports with the limits imposed by federal due process.

III

In *Pennoyer v. Neff*, 95 U.S. 714 (1878), decided shortly after the enactment of the Fourteenth Amendment, the Court held that a tribunal's jurisdiction over persons reaches no farther than the geographic bounds of the forum. In time, however, that strict territorial approach yielded to a less rigid understanding, spurred by "changes in the technology of transportation and communication, and the tremendous growth of interstate business activity." Burnham v. Superior Court, 495 U.S. 604, 617 (1990) (opinion of SCALIA, J.).

"The canonical opinion in this area remains *International Shoe* [*Co. v. Washington*], 326 U.S. 310 (1945), in which we held that a State may authorize its courts to exercise personal jurisdiction over an out-of-state defendant if the defendant has 'certain minimum contacts with [the State] such that the maintenance of the suit does not offend traditional notions of fair play and substantial justice.'" *Goodyear*, 564 U.S. at 923 (quoting *International Shoe*, 326 U.S. at 316). Following *International Shoe*, "the relationship among the defendant, the forum, and the litigation, rather than the mutually exclusive sovereignty of the States on which the rules of *Pennoyer* rest, became the central concern of the inquiry into personal jurisdiction." Shaffer [v. Heitner], 433 U.S. [186, 204 (1977)].

International Shoe's conception of "fair play and substantial justice" presaged the development of two categories of personal jurisdiction. The first category is represented by *International Shoe* itself, a case in which the in-state activities of the corporate defendant "ha[d] not only been continuous and systematic, but also g[a]ve rise to the liabilities sued on." *International Shoe* recognized, as well, that "the commission of some single or occasional acts of the corporate agent in a state" may sometimes be enough to subject the corporation to jurisdiction in that State's tribunals with respect to suits relating to that in-state activity. Adjudicatory authority of this order, in which the suit "aris[es] out of or relate[s] to the defendant's contacts with the forum," Helicopteros Nacionales de Colombia, S.A. v. Hall, 466 U.S. 408, 414 n.8 (1984), is today called "specific jurisdiction."

International Shoe distinguished between, on the one hand, exercises of specific jurisdiction, as just described, and on the other, situations where a foreign corporation's "continuous corporate operations within a state [are] so substantial and of such a nature as to justify suit against it on causes of action arising from dealings entirely distinct from those activities." As we have since explained, "[a] court may assert general jurisdiction over foreign (sister-state or foreign-country) corporations to hear any and all claims against them when their affiliations with the State are so 'continuous and systematic' as to render them essentially at home in the forum State." *Goodyear*, 564 U.S. at 919; *Helicopteros*, 466 U.S. at 414 n.9.

Since *International Shoe*, "specific jurisdiction has become the centerpiece of modern jurisdiction theory, while general jurisdiction [has played] a reduced role." *International Shoe*'s momentous departure from *Pennoyer*'s rigidly territorial focus, we have noted, unleashed a rapid expansion of tribunals' ability to hear claims against out-of-state defendants when the episode-in-suit occurred in the forum or the defendant purposefully availed itself of the forum. Our subsequent decisions have continued to bear out the prediction that "specific jurisdiction will come into sharper relief and form a considerably more significant part of the scene."

Our post-*International Shoe* opinions on general jurisdiction, by comparison, are few. "[The Court's] 1952 decision in *Perkins v. Benguet Consol. Mining Co.* remains the textbook case of general jurisdiction appropriately exercised over a foreign corporation that has not consented to suit in the forum." *Goodyear*, 564 U.S. at 927-28 (internal quotation marks and brackets omitted). The defendant in *Perkins*, Benguet, was a company incorporated under the laws of the Philippines, where it operated gold and silver mines. Benguet ceased its mining operations during the Japanese occupation of the Philippines in World War II; its president moved to Ohio, where he kept an office, maintained the company's files, and oversaw the company's activities. Perkins v. Benguet Consol. Mining Co., 342 U.S. 437, 448 (1952). The plaintiff, an Ohio resident, sued Benguet on a claim that neither arose in Ohio nor related to the corporation's activities in that State. We held that the Ohio courts could exercise general jurisdiction over Benguet without offending due process. That was so, we later noted, because "Ohio was the corporation's principal, if temporary, place of business."

The next case on point, *Helicopteros*, arose from a helicopter crash in Peru. Four U.S. citizens perished in that accident; their survivors and representatives brought suit in Texas state court against the helicopter's owner and operator, a Colombian corporation. That company's contacts with Texas were confined to "sending its chief executive officer to Houston for a contract-negotiation session; accepting into its New York bank account checks drawn on a Houston bank; purchasing helicopters, equipment, and training services from [a Texas-based helicopter company] for substantial sums; and sending personnel to [Texas] for training." Notably, those contacts bore no apparent relationship to the accident that gave rise to the suit. We held that the company's Texas connections did not resemble the "continuous and systematic general business contacts . . . found to exist in *Perkins*." "[M]ere purchases, even if occurring at regular intervals," we clarified, "are not enough to warrant a State's assertion of in personam jurisdiction over a nonresident corporation in a cause of action not related to those purchase transactions."

Most recently, in *Goodyear*, we answered the question: "Are foreign subsidiaries of a United States parent corporation amenable to suit in state court on claims unrelated to any activity of the subsidiaries in the forum State?" That case arose from a bus accident outside Paris that killed two boys from North Carolina. The boys' parents brought a wrongful-death suit in North Carolina state court alleging that the bus's tire was defectively manufactured. The complaint named as defendants not only The Goodyear Tire and Rubber Company (Goodyear), an Ohio corporation, but also Goodyear's Turkish, French, and Luxembourgian subsidiaries. Those foreign subsidiaries, which manufactured tires for sale in Europe and Asia, lacked any affiliation with North Carolina. A small percentage of tires manufactured by the foreign subsidiaries were distributed in North Carolina, however, and on that ground, the North Carolina Court of Appeals held the subsidiaries amenable to the general jurisdiction of North Carolina courts.

We reversed, observing that the North Carolina court's analysis "elided the essential difference between case-specific and all-purpose (general) jurisdiction." Although the placement of a product into the stream of commerce "may bolster an affiliation germane to specific jurisdiction," we explained, such contacts "do not warrant a determination that, based on those ties, the forum has general jurisdiction over a defendant." As *International Shoe* itself teaches, a corporation's "continuous activity of some sorts within a state is not enough to support the demand that the corporation be amenable to suits unrelated to that activity." Because Goodyear's foreign subsidiaries were "in no sense at home in North Carolina," we held, those subsidiaries could not be required to submit to the general jurisdiction of that State's courts.

As is evident from *Perkins*, *Helicopteros*, and *Goodyear*, general and specific jurisdiction have followed markedly different trajectories post-*International Shoe*. Specific jurisdiction has been cut loose from *Pennoyer*'s sway, but we have declined to stretch general jurisdiction beyond limits traditionally recognized. As this Court has increasingly trained on the "relationship among the defendant, the forum, and the litigation," *Shaffer*, 433 U.S. at 204, i.e., specific jurisdiction, general jurisdiction has come to occupy a less dominant place in the contemporary scheme.[11]

IV

With this background, we turn directly to the question whether Daimler's affiliations with California are sufficient to subject it to the general (all-purpose) personal jurisdiction of that State's courts. In the proceedings below, the parties agreed on, or failed to contest, certain points

---

11. As the Court made plain in *Goodyear* and repeats here, general jurisdiction requires affiliations "so 'continuous and systematic' as to render [the foreign corporation] essentially at home in the forum State." 564 U.S. at 919, i.e., comparable to a domestic enterprise in that State.

we now take as given. Plaintiffs have never attempted to fit this case into the specific jurisdiction category. Nor did plaintiffs challenge on appeal the District Court's holding that Daimler's own contacts with California were, by themselves, too sporadic to justify the exercise of general jurisdiction. While plaintiffs ultimately persuaded the Ninth Circuit to impute MBUSA's California contacts to Daimler on an agency theory, at no point have they maintained that MBUSA is an alter ego of Daimler.

Daimler, on the other hand, failed to object below to plaintiffs' assertion that the California courts could exercise all-purpose jurisdiction over MBUSA.[12] We will assume then, for purposes of this decision only, that MBUSA qualifies as at home in California.

A

In sustaining the exercise of general jurisdiction over Daimler, the Ninth Circuit relied on an agency theory, determining that MBUSA acted as Daimler's agent for jurisdictional purposes and then attributing MBUSA's California contacts to Daimler. The Ninth Circuit's agency analysis derived from Circuit precedent considering principally whether the subsidiary "performs services that are sufficiently important to the foreign corporation that if it did not have a representative to perform them, the corporation's own officials would undertake to perform substantially similar services."

This Court has not yet addressed whether a foreign corporation may be subjected to a court's general jurisdiction based on the contacts of its in-state subsidiary. Daimler argues, and several Courts of Appeals have held, that a subsidiary's jurisdictional contacts can be imputed to its parent only when the former is so dominated by the latter as to be its alter ego. The Ninth Circuit adopted a less rigorous test based on what it described as an "agency" relationship. Agencies, we note, come in many sizes and shapes: "One may be an agent for some business purposes and not others so that the fact that one may be an agent for one purpose does not make him or her an agent for every purpose." A subsidiary, for example, might be its parent's agent for claims arising in the place where the subsidiary operates, yet not its agent regarding claims arising elsewhere. The Court of Appeals did not advert to that prospect. But we need not pass judgment on invocation of an agency theory in the context of general jurisdiction, for in no event can the appeals court's analysis be sustained.

The Ninth Circuit's agency finding rested primarily on its observation that MBUSA's services were "important" to Daimler, as gauged by Daimler's hypothetical readiness to perform those services itself if MBUSA did not exist. Formulated this way, the inquiry into importance stacks the deck, for it will always yield a pro-jurisdiction answer.... The Ninth Circuit's agency theory thus appears to subject foreign corporations to general jurisdiction whenever they have an in-state subsidiary or affiliate, an outcome that

---

12. MBUSA is not a defendant in this case.

would sweep beyond even the "sprawling view of general jurisdiction" we rejected in *Goodyear*.[15]

B

Even if we were to assume that MBUSA is at home in California, and further to assume MBUSA's contacts are imputable to Daimler, there would still be no basis to subject Daimler to general jurisdiction in California, for Daimler's slim contacts with the State hardly render it at home there.

Goodyear made clear that only a limited set of affiliations with a forum will render a defendant amenable to all-purpose jurisdiction there. "For an individual, the paradigm forum for the exercise of general jurisdiction is the individual's domicile; for a corporation, it is an equivalent place, one in which the corporation is fairly regarded as at home." With respect to a corporation, the place of incorporation and principal place of business are "paradig[m] . . . bases for general jurisdiction." Those affiliations have the virtue of being unique — that is, each ordinarily indicates only one place — as well as easily ascertainable. *Cf.* Hertz Corp. v. Friend, 559 U.S. 77, 94 (2010) ("Simple jurisdictional rules . . . promote greater predictability.") [*infra* p. 540]. These bases afford plaintiffs recourse to at least one clear and certain forum in which a corporate defendant may be sued on any and all claims.

Goodyear did not hold that a corporation may be subject to general jurisdiction only in a forum where it is incorporated or has its principal place of business; it simply typed those places paradigm all-purpose forums. Plaintiffs would have us look beyond the exemplar bases *Goodyear* identified, and approve the exercise of general jurisdiction in every State in which a corporation "engages in a substantial, continuous, and systematic course of business." That formulation, we hold, is unacceptably grasping.

. . . [T]he words "continuous and systematic" were used in *International Shoe* to describe instances in which the exercise of specific jurisdiction would be appropriate.[17] Turning to all-purpose jurisdiction, in contrast, *International Shoe* speaks of "instances in which the continuous corporate operations within a state [are] so substantial and of such a nature as to justify suit . . . on causes of action arising from dealings entirely distinct from those activities." Accordingly, the inquiry under *Goodyear* is not whether a foreign corporation's in-forum contacts can be said to be in some

---

15. The Ninth Circuit's agency analysis also looked to whether the parent enjoys "the right to substantially control" the subsidiary's activities. The Court of Appeals found the requisite "control" demonstrated by the General Distributor Agreement between Daimler and MBUSA, which gives Daimler the right to oversee certain of MBUSA's operations, even though that agreement expressly disavowed the creation of any agency relationship. Thus grounded, the separate inquiry into control hardly curtails the overbreadth of the Ninth Circuit's agency holding.

17. *International Shoe* also recognized . . . that "some single or occasional acts of the corporate agent in a state . . ., because of their nature and quality and the circumstances of their commission, may be deemed sufficient to render the corporation liable to suit."

sense "continuous and systematic," it is whether that corporation's "affiliations with the State are so 'continuous and systematic' as to render [it] essentially at home in the forum State."[19]

Here, neither Daimler nor MBUSA is incorporated in California, nor does either entity have its principal place of business there. If Daimler's California activities sufficed to allow adjudication of this Argentina-rooted case in California, the same global reach would presumably be available in every other State in which MBUSA's sales are sizable. Such exorbitant exercises of all-purpose jurisdiction would scarcely permit out-of-state defendants "to structure their primary conduct with some minimum assurance as to where that conduct will and will not render them liable to suit." Burger King Corp. [v. Rudzewicz], 471 U.S. [462, 472 (1985)] (internal quotation marks omitted).

It was therefore error for the Ninth Circuit to conclude that Daimler, even with MBUSA's contacts attributed to it, was at home in California, and hence subject to suit there on claims by foreign plaintiffs having nothing to do with anything that occurred or had its principal impact in California.[20]

. . .

■ JUSTICE SOTOMAYOR, concurring in the judgment.

I agree with the Court's conclusion that the Due Process Clause prohibits the exercise of personal jurisdiction over Daimler in light of the

---

19. We do not foreclose the possibility that in an exceptional case, see, e.g., Perkins, a corporation's operations in a forum other than its formal place of incorporation or principal place of business may be so substantial and of such a nature as to render the corporation at home in that State. But this case presents no occasion to explore that question, because Daimler's activities in California plainly do not approach that level. It is one thing to hold a corporation answerable for operations in the forum State, quite another to expose it to suit on claims having no connection whatever to the forum State.

20. To clarify in light of JUSTICE SOTOMAYOR's opinion concurring in the judgment, the general jurisdiction inquiry does not "focu[s] solely on the magnitude of the defendant's in-state contacts." General jurisdiction instead calls for an appraisal of a corporation's activities in their entirety, nationwide and worldwide. A corporation that operates in many places can scarcely be deemed at home in all of them. Otherwise, "at home" would be synonymous with "doing business" tests framed before specific jurisdiction evolved in the United States. Nothing in *International Shoe* and its progeny suggests that "a particular quantum of local activity" should give a State authority over a "far larger quantum of . . . activity" having no connection to any in-state activity.

JUSTICE SOTOMAYOR would reach the same result, but for a different reason. Rather than concluding that Daimler is not at home in California, JUSTICE SOTOMAYOR would hold that the exercise of general jurisdiction over Daimler would be unreasonable "in the unique circumstances of this case." In other words, she favors a resolution fit for this day and case only. True, a multipronged reasonableness check was articulated in *Asahi* [Metal Industry Co. v. Superior Court of California, 480 U.S. 102, 113-14 (1987)], but not as a free-floating test. Instead, the check was to be essayed when specific jurisdiction is at issue. First, a court is to determine whether the connection between the forum and the episode-in-suit could justify the exercise of specific jurisdiction. Then, in a second step, the court is to consider several additional factors to assess the reasonableness of entertaining the case. When a corporation is genuinely at home in the forum State, however, any second-step inquiry would be superfluous. . . .

unique circumstances of this case. I concur only in the judgment, however, because I cannot agree with the path the Court takes to arrive at that result. . . .

Our personal jurisdiction precedents call for a two-part analysis. The contacts prong asks whether the defendant has sufficient contacts with the forum State to support personal jurisdiction; the reasonableness prong asks whether the exercise of jurisdiction would be unreasonable under the circumstances. As the majority points out, all of the cases in which we have applied the reasonableness prong have involved specific as opposed to general jurisdiction. Whether the reasonableness prong should apply in the general jurisdiction context is therefore a question we have never decided,[1] and it is one on which I can appreciate the arguments on both sides. But it would be imprudent to decide that question in this case given that respondents have failed to argue against the application of the reasonableness prong during the entire 8-year history of this litigation. As a result, I would decide this case under the reasonableness prong without foreclosing future consideration of whether that prong should be limited to the specific jurisdiction context.

We identified the factors that bear on reasonableness in *Asahi Metal Industry Co. v. Superior Court*, 480 U.S. 102, 113-14 (1987): "the burden on the defendant, the interests of the forum State," "the plaintiff's interest in obtaining relief" in the forum State, and the interests of other sovereigns in resolving the dispute. We held in *Asahi* that it would be "unreasonable and unfair" for a California court to exercise jurisdiction over a claim between a Taiwanese plaintiff and a Japanese defendant that arose out of a transaction in Taiwan, particularly where the Taiwanese plaintiff had not shown that it would be more convenient to litigate in California than in Taiwan or Japan.

The same considerations resolve this case. It involves Argentine plaintiffs suing a German defendant for conduct that took place in Argentina. Like the plaintiffs in *Asahi*, respondents have failed to show that it would be more convenient to litigate in California than in Germany, a sovereign with a far greater interest in resolving the dispute. *Asahi* thus makes clear that it would be unreasonable for a court in California to subject Daimler to its jurisdiction. . . .

Because I would reverse the Ninth Circuit's decision on the narrower ground that the exercise of jurisdiction over Daimler would be unreasonable in any event, I respectfully concur in the judgment only.

Notes and Questions

1. The Court reaffirmed *Daimler*, reining in another lower court, in *BNSF Ry. Co. v. Tyrrell*, 581 U.S. —, 137 S. Ct. 1549 (2017). The Court held that a railroad incorporated elsewhere and with its principal place of

---

[1] 1. The Courts of Appeals have uniformly held that the reasonableness prong does in fact apply in the general jurisdiction context. . . .

business elsewhere had some of its track and workforce in Montana did not make it "at home" there for the purpose of general personal jurisdiction. The Court also made clear that the Due Process limit on state-court jurisdiction "does not vary with the type of claim asserted or business enterprise sued." *Id.* at 1559.

2. Note that even after *Daimler*, the core aspects of general jurisdiction remain unchanged. A court can always exercise general jurisdiction in any forum in which an individual in domiciled, or a corporation is either incorporated or has its principal place of business.

Before *Daimler* (and its predecessor *Goodyear*), however, some lower courts had held that any significant physical presence in the forum state — offices, factories, or retail outlets — constituted sufficient "continuous and systematic" contacts to reach the level of contacts required by *International Shoe*. *Daimler* and *Goodyear* make it clear that these courts were wrong. It was solely with respect to these broader assertions of general personal jurisdiction, almost entirely with respect to business entities, that there had been domestic disagreement about the proper breadth of such assertions — as well as foreign unease with expansive versions. *Goodyear* and *Daimler* sharply rein in these broad assertions. Notice the *Daimler* Court's emphasis, in part III of the opinion, on the context in which the phrase "continuous and systematic" was used in the *International Shoe* opinion — specific rather than general personal jurisdiction. The *Daimler* opinion goes on to quote what *Shoe* had to say about what is now called general jurisdiction, when it spoke of "continuous corporate operations . . . so substantial and of such a nature as to justify" suit in the state on any claim arising anywhere. Relying on *Goodyear* and *Helicopteros*, it speaks of affiliations "so 'continuous and systematic' as to render [a corporation] essentially at home in the forum State." Those formulations of the test require more than just "continuous and systematic" contacts. But the use of "continuous and systematic," without more, had become such a widely used mantra for general jurisdiction that you may have to point out to an older lawyer, or a judge for whom you are clerking or before whom you are arguing, what the Supreme Court has now said about the mantra.

3. After *Goodyear* and *Daimler*, one question is whether any general jurisdiction beyond the core of incorporation and principal place of business survives at all. The answer seems to be yes, because the Court relies on *Perkins* (its only case upholding such jurisdiction); it also speaks of "continuous and systematic general business contacts" as sufficing. Realistically, what kind of beyond-paradigm general personal jurisdiction might be upheld? Consider the case of the airplane manufacturer Boeing, a Delaware corporation with its headquarters in Illinois. Boeing used to have its headquarters in Washington state and still has nearly half its production there. Would jurisdiction over a non-Washington claim against Boeing in that state be constitutional? It might be considered "at home" in Washington based on its history and continued major presence there, or Washington might still be considered its "principal place of business" for constitutional purposes despite the headquarters move to Illinois.

4. As we discuss *infra* pp. 479-85, a court can also obtain personal jurisdiction over a party (including a defendant) who consents to the exercise of jurisdiction. All states require nonresident corporations to register with the state in order to do business in the state. After *Daimler*, the question arose whether compliance with a registration statute constitutes consent, and whether interpreting registration as consent is constitutional. Courts are divided. *See infra* pp. 484-85, Note 4.

5. *Daimler*'s restrictive view is in keeping with other countries' views. Foreign courts strongly disfavor expansive assertions of general jurisdiction, and might refuse to enforce American judgments based on such assertions.

6. The Court mentions, but does not resolve, the question whether the contacts of a subsidiary can be attributed to the parent company. (And the issue was complicated in *Daimler* by the fact that MBUSA was an "indirect" subsidiary, a fine point of corporate law that you need not worry about now.) For purposes of *specific* jurisdiction, the general rule — albeit not yet decided by the Supreme Court — is that the contacts of each defendant company must be evaluated on their own, even if the parent wholly owns the subsidiary. "The contacts of each individual entity ordinarily must be considered separately. Only when the parent corporation has sufficient control over the subsidiary, or when the appearance of separateness is actually a sham, may the contacts of one be imputed to the other." 16 JAMES WM. MOORE ET AL., MOORE'S FEDERAL PRACTICE § 108.42[3][b][iv], at 108-74.4(7) to −(8) (3d ed. 2019).

2. "Presence": Service in the Forum State

General jurisdiction is appropriate when a defendant's contacts with the state are so extensive that it is deemed to be "present" in the state. Citizens of a state are also present there, and thus are subject to general jurisdiction. But what about a defendant who has few (or no) relevant contacts with the forum state, but has the misfortune to be served with process while traveling there on an unrelated matter? Is that "presence" sufficient for the state to exercise personal jurisdiction? Consider the following case.

BURNHAM V. SUPERIOR COURT OF CALIFORNIA

495 U.S. 604 (1990)

■ JUSTICE SCALIA announced the judgment of the Court and delivered an opinion in which THE CHIEF JUSTICE and JUSTICE KENNEDY join, and in which JUSTICE WHITE joins with respect to Parts I, II-A, II-B, and II-C.

The question presented is whether the Due Process Clause of the Fourteenth Amendment denies California courts jurisdiction over a nonresident, who was personally served with process while temporarily in that State, in a suit unrelated to his activities in the State.

I

Petitioner Dennis Burnham married Francie Burnham in 1976 in West Virginia. In 1977 the couple moved to New Jersey, where their two children were born. In July 1987 the Burnhams decided to separate. They agreed that Mrs. Burnham, who intended to move to California, would take custody of the children. Shortly before Mrs. Burnham departed for California that same month, she and petitioner agreed that she would file for divorce on grounds of "irreconcilable differences."

In October 1987, petitioner filed for divorce in New Jersey state court on grounds of "desertion." Petitioner did not, however, obtain an issuance of summons against his wife and did not attempt to serve her with process. Mrs. Burnham, after unsuccessfully demanding that petitioner adhere to their prior agreement to submit to an "irreconcilable differences" divorce, brought suit for divorce in California state court in early January 1988.

In late January, petitioner visited southern California on business, after which he went north to visit his children in the San Francisco Bay area, where his wife resided. He took the older child to San Francisco for the weekend. Upon returning the child to Mrs. Burnham's home on January 24, 1988, petitioner was served with a California court summons and a copy of Mrs. Burnham's divorce petition. He then returned to New Jersey.

Later that year, petitioner made a special appearance in the California Superior Court, moving to quash the service of process on the ground that the court lacked personal jurisdiction over him because his only contacts with California were a few short visits to the State for the purposes of conducting business and visiting his children. The Superior Court denied the motion, and the California Court of Appeal denied mandamus relief, rejecting petitioner's contention that the Due Process Clause prohibited California courts from asserting jurisdiction over him because he lacked "minimum contacts" with the State. The court held it to be "a valid jurisdictional predicate for *in personam* jurisdiction" that the "defendant [was] present in the forum state and personally served with process." We granted certiorari.

II

...

B

Among the most firmly established principles of personal jurisdiction in American tradition is that the courts of a State have jurisdiction over nonresidents who are physically present in the State. The view developed early that each State had the power to hale before its courts any individual who could be found within its borders, and that once having acquired jurisdiction over such a person by properly serving him with process, the

State could retain jurisdiction to enter judgment against him, no matter how fleeting his visit....

... [That] understanding was shared by American courts at the crucial time for present purposes: 1868, when the Fourteenth Amendment was adopted....

Decisions in the courts of many States in the 19th and early 20th centuries held that personal service upon a physically present defendant sufficed to confer jurisdiction, without regard to whether the defendant was only briefly in the State or whether the cause of action was related to his activities there.... Most States, moreover, had statutes or common-law rules that exempted from service of process individuals who were brought into the forum by force or fraud, or who were there as a party or witness in unrelated judicial proceedings. These exceptions obviously rested upon the premise that service of process conferred jurisdiction. Particularly striking is the fact that, as far as we have been able to determine, *not one* American case from the period (or, for that matter, not one American case until 1978) held, or even suggested, that in-state personal service on an individual was insufficient to confer personal jurisdiction. Commentators were also seemingly unanimous on the rule.

This American jurisdictional practice is, moreover, not merely old; it is continuing. It remains the practice of, not only a substantial number of the States, but as far as we are aware *all* the States and the Federal Government — if one disregards (as one must for this purpose) the few opinions since 1978 that have erroneously said, on grounds similar to those that petitioner presses here, that this Court's due process decisions render the practice unconstitutional....

C

Despite this formidable body of precedent, petitioner contends, in reliance on our decisions applying the *International Shoe* standard, that in the absence of "continuous and systematic" contacts with the forum, a nonresident defendant can be subjected to judgment only as to matters that arise out of or relate to his contacts with the forum. This argument rests on a thorough misunderstanding of our cases....

The short of the matter is that jurisdiction based on physical presence alone constitutes due process because it is one of the continuing traditions of our legal system that define the due process standard of "traditional notions of fair play and substantial justice." That standard was developed by *analogy* to "physical presence," and it would be perverse to say it could now be turned against that touchstone of jurisdiction....

D

... For new procedures, hitherto unknown, the Due Process Clause requires analysis to determine whether "traditional notions of fair play and substantial justice" have been offended. But a doctrine of personal jurisdiction that dates back to the adoption of the Fourteenth Amendment and is still generally observed unquestionably meets that standard.

III

A few words in response to JUSTICE BRENNAN's opinion concurring in the judgment: It insists that we apply "contemporary notions of due process" to determine the constitutionality of California's assertion of jurisdiction. But our analysis today comports with that prescription, at least if we give it the only sense allowed by our precedents. The "contemporary notions of due process" applicable to personal jurisdiction are the enduring "*traditional notions of fair play and substantial justice*" established as the test by *International Shoe*. By its very language, that test is satisfied if a state court adheres to jurisdictional rules that are generally applied and have always been applied in the United States.

But the concurrence's proposed standard of "contemporary notions of due process" requires more: It measures state-court jurisdiction not only against traditional doctrines in this country, including current state-court practice, but also against each Justice's subjective assessment of what is fair and just. Authority for that seductive standard is not to be found in any of our personal jurisdiction cases. It is, indeed, an outright break with the test of "traditional notions of fair play and substantial justice," which would have to be reformulated "*our* notions of fair play and substantial justice." . . .

The difference between us and JUSTICE BRENNAN has nothing to do with whether "further progress [is] to be made" in the "evolution of our legal system." It has to do with whether changes are to be adopted as progressive by the American people or decreed as progressive by the Justices of this Court. Nothing we say today prevents individual States from limiting or entirely abandoning the in-state-service basis of jurisdiction. And nothing prevents an overwhelming majority of them from doing so, with the consequence that the "traditional notions of fairness" that this Court applies may change. But the States have overwhelmingly declined to adopt such limitation or abandonment, evidently not considering it to be progress. The question is whether, armed with no authority other than individual Justices' perceptions of fairness that conflict with both past and current practice, this Court can compel the States to make such a change on the ground that "due process" requires it. We hold that it cannot. . . .

Because the Due Process Clause does not prohibit the California courts from exercising jurisdiction over petitioner based on the fact of in-state service of process, the judgment is affirmed.

■ JUSTICE WHITE, concurring in part and concurring in the judgment.

. . . The rule allowing jurisdiction to be obtained over a nonresident by personal service in the forum State, without more, has been and is so widely accepted throughout this country that I could not possibly strike it down, either on its face or as applied in this case, on the ground that it denies due process of law guaranteed by the Fourteenth Amendment. . . .

■ JUSTICE BRENNAN, with whom JUSTICE MARSHALL, JUSTICE BLACKMUN, and JUSTICE O'CONNOR join, concurring in the judgment.

I agree with JUSTICE SCALIA that the Due Process Clause of the Fourteenth Amendment generally permits a state court to exercise jurisdiction over a defendant if he is served with process while voluntarily present in the forum State. I do not perceive the need, however, to decide that a jurisdictional rule that "has been immemorially the actual law of the land" automatically comports with due process simply by virtue of its "pedigree." Although I agree that history is an important factor in establishing whether a jurisdictional rule satisfies due process requirements, I cannot agree that it is the *only* factor such that all traditional rules of jurisdiction are, *ipso facto,* forever constitutional. Unlike JUSTICE SCALIA, I would undertake an "independent inquiry into the . . . fairness of the prevailing in-state service rule." I therefore concur only in the judgment. . . .

By visiting the forum State, a transient defendant actually "avail[s]" himself of significant benefits provided by the State. His health and safety are guaranteed by the State's police, fire, and emergency medical services; he is free to travel on the State's roads and waterways; he likely enjoys the fruits of the State's economy as well. Moreover, the Privileges and Immunities Clause of Article IV prevents a state government from discriminating against a transient defendant by denying him the protections of its law or the right of access to its courts. . . . [A]n out-of-state plaintiff may use state courts in all circumstances in which those courts would be available to state citizens. Without transient jurisdiction, an asymmetry would arise: A transient would have the full benefit of the power of the forum State's courts as a plaintiff while retaining immunity from their authority as a defendant.

The potential burdens on a transient defendant are slight. "[M]odern transportation and communications have made it much less burdensome for a party sued to defend himself" in a State outside his place of residence. That the defendant has already journeyed at least once before to the forum — as evidenced by the fact that he was served with process there — is an indication that suit in the forum likely would not be prohibitively inconvenient. Finally, any burdens that do arise can be ameliorated by a variety of procedural devices. For these reasons, as a rule the exercise of personal jurisdiction over a defendant based on his voluntary presence in the forum will satisfy the requirements of due process. . . .

■ [The opinion of JUSTICE STEVENS, concurring in the judgment, is omitted].

Notes and Questions

1. Lower courts applying *Burnham* have uniformly concluded that service in the forum state is always, without more, sufficient to confer jurisdiction over natural persons (not corporations), unless the defendant

was fraudulently lured into the state by the plaintiff or, in some cases, was in the state to participate in court proceedings. The latter exception ensures that a plaintiff cannot serve a defendant out of state, and, when the defendant comes to contest jurisdiction, re-serve her on the courthouse steps — now invoking presence as the basis for jurisdiction. In effect, the exception allows a party to contest jurisdiction in a case.

2. Although the validity of transient or "tag" jurisdiction is well established, its use is fairly rare. The availability of specific personal jurisdiction where a natural person has minimum contacts, and general jurisdiction where the person lives, usually suffices for plaintiffs' needs. And nonconstitutional doctrines such as forum non conveniens and the availability of transfer between federal courts, *see infra* pp. 498-507, can mean that even service of an out-of-stater in the state on a claim unrelated to the forum might not result in the case remaining in the original court.

3. Most courts hold that *Burnham* does not apply to corporations: one cannot obtain jurisdiction over a corporation by serving one of its officers in the forum state. *See, e.g.*, Martinez v. Aero Caribbean, 764 F.3d 1062, 1064 (9th Cir. 2014); *but see* N. Light Tech., Inc. v. N. Lights Club, 236 F.3d 57, 63 n.10 (1st Cir. 2001).

4. The idea that a defendant has a right to contest jurisdiction — without her presence in court serving as the basis for personal jurisdiction — has a long historical pedigree and remains universally accepted. Without such a right, a defendant is put on the horns of a dilemma: either appear in court and defend the case on the merits; or refuse to appear in court, suffer a default judgment, and try to attack the judgment collaterally (that is, by filing a suit attacking the judgment, as in *Pennoyer*, or by raising lack of jurisdiction when the plaintiff tries to enforce the judgment, as in *Hanson*). The former strategy, in which the defendant enters a *general appearance*, forces the defendant to sacrifice a potentially winning jurisdictional argument. The latter strategy has a different risk: if the defendant loses the jurisdictional argument in the collateral suit, the defendant cannot then defend the case on the merits, because the default in the first case precludes litigation of the merits.

To avoid this dilemma, the common law created, and virtually every state adopted, the concept of the *special appearance*. *See supra* p. 412, n.* (noting the use of the special appearance in *International Shoe*). If a court granted a defendant's request to appear specially, as it usually did, the defendant appeared in court to contest jurisdiction. (A special appearance gave only this right. If the defendant did anything to defend the case on nonjurisdictional grounds, the defendant was usually held to have appeared generally.) If the defendant won the jurisdictional issue, the case was over. If the defendant lost the jurisdictional issue, she typically could either enter a general appearance, thus contesting the case on the merits; or else stand on her jurisdictional objection and appeal the contrary ruling. The one opportunity that the special appearance sacrificed was the right of collateral attack: the court's ruling that it had jurisdiction had issue-preclusive effect in subsequent collateral proceedings.

Therefore, at common law a nonresident defendant typically had three options: enter a general appearance, enter a special appearance, or fail to appear. Over the course of the twentieth century, many states abolished the distinction between general and special appearances. In these states today, a defendant enters an appearance — and is then free to contest both the court's jurisdiction and the merits of the case. The Federal Rules adopt this modern approach. *See* Fed. R. Civ. P. 12(a)-(b) (allowing a defendant to raise both jurisdictional and merits-based defenses by answer or motion to dismiss). Under this approach, the defendant still retains the option not to appear and to challenge the court's jurisdiction collaterally. (Recall that one of the requirements for giving a judgment preclusive effect is that the judgment be valid — in other words, that the court had jurisdiction to enter the judgment. *See supra* pp. 322-23, Note 3.)

5. If a defendant is served while on board a train passing through a state, has he been served in the state? What if he is served while in an airplane flying over the state? For a classic case before *Burnham*, see Grace v. MacArthur, 170 F. Supp. 442 (E.D. Ark. 1959) (service on plane sufficient to confer jurisdiction); Peabody v. Hamilton, 106 Mass. 217 (1870) (service on board ship in harbor, not yet moored, sufficient to confer jurisdiction). Under *Burnham*, is there jurisdiction if the defendant is served at an Interstate rest stop while driving through the state? If served while visiting a dying child in the hospital in the forum state?

6. Is Justice Scalia's opinion in *Burnham* consistent with the Court's approach in *Shaffer*, decided thirteen years earlier? *Shaffer* held that mere physical presence of property within a state did not justify jurisdiction over the owner for claims unrelated to the property, despite tradition to the contrary. Should mere transient physical presence of a person within a state justify jurisdiction over that person for claims unrelated to the reasons for the person's presence or conduct within the state?

7. Notice that the *result* in *Burnham* is unanimous, but there is no majority opinion! Moreover, personal jurisdiction, however fascinating to those studying Civil Procedure, is not a topic that carries much political salience. Justice Scalia's criticism of Justice Brennan's approach seems out of proportion to the importance of the case. Why so much furor over a seemingly small issue when, after all, the Justices agree on the result? Think about Justice Scalia's argument that the issue dividing him from Justice Brennan is "whether, armed with no authority other than individual Justices' perceptions of fairness that conflict with both past and current practice, this Court can compel the States to make such a change on the ground that 'due process' requires it." Then focus on his statement that "a doctrine of personal jurisdiction that dates back to the adoption of the Fourteenth Amendment and is still generally observed" unquestionably satisfies the due process. These arguments over how judges should interpret "due process" in the personal-jurisdiction area track persisting disagreements over how judges should approach "due process" requirements in much more hot-button areas such as reproductive rights, with differences in viewpoint between the conservative "strict constructionist" Scalia and the

liberal "activist" Brennan. (The terms in quotation marks are labels often attached to the two Justices; you can consider in your Constitutional Law class whether they are fair or accurate.)

8. One major difference between Justice Scalia and Justice Brennan lies in their approach to "tradition." Justice Scalia argued that the long tradition of "tag" jurisdiction was enough to validate it. Justice Brennan, on the other hand, measured jurisdiction against contemporary standards. His argument resonates with a much earlier statement by Justice Oliver Wendell Holmes (although he did not quote it):

> It is revolting to have no better reason for a rule of law than that so it was laid down in the time of Henry IV. It is still more revolting if the grounds upon which it was laid down have vanished long since, and the rule simply persists from blind imitation of the past.

Oliver Wendell Holmes, *The Path of the Law*, 10 HARV. L. REV. 457, 469 (1897).

3. Consent and Waiver

The doctrines we have studied thus far authorize courts to exercise jurisdiction over nonconsenting defendants. A court also has jurisdiction over a party who consents to be sued in the forum. In this context, "consent" is rather broadly construed. A plaintiff, for example, by bringing suit in a forum, consents not only to the court's jurisdiction over his own claims, but also to jurisdiction over related, and perhaps unrelated, counterclaims that the defendant might bring. *See* Adam v. Saenger, 303 U.S. 59 (1938).

Related to the idea of consent is the idea of waiver. A party who fails to object to a lack of personal jurisdiction in the proper way is deemed to have waived the defense — in effect, to have consented to the court's jurisdiction over her. For instance, in the Federal Rules, personal jurisdiction is regarded as a defense. *See* Fed. R. Civ. P. 12(b)(2). That defense is waived unless it is raised either by motion or in an answer. *See* Fed. R. Civ. P. 12(h)(1)(B). The defense is also waived if a defendant makes a Rule 12 motion, but fails to include an available Rule 12(b)(2) defense. *See* Fed. R. Civ. P. 12(g), –(h)(1)(A); *supra* pp. 68-69.

Consent to suit can also be given contractually. In the following case, the Court enforced a contract's forum-selection clause so as to prohibit a suit in a *different* forum. The same rules will presumably apply to force an unwilling defendant into a forum to which she has contractually agreed.

CARNIVAL CRUISE LINES, INC. V. SHUTE

499 U.S. 585 (1991)

■ JUSTICE BLACKMUN delivered the opinion of the Court.

In this admiralty case we primarily consider whether the United States Court of Appeals for the Ninth Circuit correctly refused to enforce a forum-selection clause contained in tickets issued by petitioner Carnival Cruise Lines, Inc., to respondents Eulala and Russel Shute.

I

The Shutes, through an Arlington, Wash., travel agent, purchased passage for a 7-day cruise on petitioner's ship, the *Tropicale*.... The face of each ticket, at its left-hand lower corner, contained this admonition:

> SUBJECT TO CONDITIONS OF
> CONTRACT ON LAST PAGES
> **IMPORTANT!** PLEASE READ CONTRACT
> — ON LAST PAGES 1, 2, 3

The following appeared on "contract page 1" of each ticket:

> *TERMS AND CONDITIONS OF PASSAGE
> CONTRACT TICKET*
>
> 3. (a) The acceptance of this ticket by the person or persons named hereon as passengers shall be deemed to be an acceptance and agreement by each of them of all of the terms and conditions of this Passage Contract Ticket....
>
> 8. It is agreed by and between the passenger and the Carrier that all disputes and matters whatsoever arising under, in connection with or incident to this Contract shall be litigated, if at all, in and before a Court located in the State of Florida, U.S.A., to the exclusion of the Courts of any other state or country.

The last quoted paragraph is the forum-selection clause at issue.

II

Respondents boarded the *Tropicale* in Los Angeles, Cal. The ship sailed to Puerto Vallarta, Mexico, and then returned to Los Angeles. While the ship was in international waters off the Mexican coast, respondent Eulala Shute was injured when she slipped on a deck mat during a guided tour of the ship's galley. Respondents filed suit against petitioner in the United States District Court for the Western District of Washington, claiming that Mrs. Shute's injuries had been caused by the negligence of Carnival Cruise Lines and its employees.

Petitioner moved for summary judgment, contending that the forum clause in respondents' tickets required the Shutes to bring their suit against petitioner in a court in the State of Florida....

Turning to the forum-selection clause, the Court of Appeals acknowledged that a court concerned with the enforceability of such a clause must begin its analysis with *The Bremen v. Zapata Off-Shore Co.*, 407 U.S. 1 (1972), where this Court held that forum-selection clauses, although not "historically ... favored," are "prima facie valid." The appellate court concluded that the forum clause should not be enforced because it "was not freely bargained for." As an "independent justification" for refusing to enforce the clause, the Court of Appeals noted that there was evidence in the record to indicate that "the Shutes are physically and financially incapable of pursuing this litigation in Florida" and that the enforcement of the clause would operate to deprive them of their day in court and thereby contravene this Court's holding in *The Bremen*. . . .

Both petitioner and respondents argue vigorously that the Court's opinion in *The Bremen* governs this case, and each side purports to find ample support for its position in that opinion's broad-ranging language. This seeming paradox derives in large part from key factual differences between this case and *The Bremen,* differences that preclude an automatic and simple application of *The Bremen*'s general principles to the facts here.

In *The Bremen,* this Court addressed the enforceability of a forum-selection clause in a contract between two business corporations. An American corporation, Zapata, made a contract with Unterweser, a German corporation, for the towage of Zapata's oceangoing drilling rig from Louisiana to a point in the Adriatic Sea off the coast of Italy. The agreement provided that any dispute arising under the contract was to be resolved in the London Court of Justice. After a storm in the Gulf of Mexico seriously damaged the rig, Zapata ordered Unterweser's ship to tow the rig to Tampa, Fla., the nearest point of refuge. Thereafter, Zapata sued Unterweser in admiralty in federal court at Tampa. Citing the forum clause, Unterweser moved to dismiss. The District Court denied Unterweser's motion, and the Court of Appeals for the Fifth Circuit, sitting *en banc* on rehearing, and by a sharply divided vote, affirmed.

This Court vacated and remanded, stating that, in general, "a freely negotiated private international agreement, unaffected by fraud, undue influence, or overweening bargaining power, such as that involved here, should be given full effect." The Court further generalized that "in the light of present-day commercial realities and expanding international trade we conclude that the forum clause should control absent a strong showing that it should be set aside." The Court did not define precisely the circumstances that would make it unreasonable for a court to enforce a forum clause. Instead, the Court discussed a number of factors that made it reasonable to enforce the clause at issue in *The Bremen* and that, presumably, would be pertinent in any determination whether to enforce a similar clause.

In this respect, the Court noted that there was "strong evidence that the forum clause was a vital part of the agreement, and [that] it would be unrealistic to think that the parties did not conduct their negotiations, including fixing the monetary terms, with the consequences of the forum clause figuring prominently in their calculations." Further, the Court observed that it was not "dealing with an agreement between two Americans to resolve their essentially local disputes in a remote alien forum," and that in such a case, "the serious inconvenience of the contractual forum to one or both of the parties might carry greater weight in determining the reasonableness of the forum clause." The Court stated that even where the forum clause establishes a remote forum for resolution of conflicts, "the party claiming [unfairness] should bear a heavy burden of proof."

In applying *The Bremen,* the Court of Appeals in the present litigation took note of the foregoing "reasonableness" factors and rather automatically decided that the forum-selection clause was unenforceable because, unlike the parties in *The Bremen,* respondents are not business persons and did not negotiate the terms of the clause with petitioner. Alternatively, the Court of Appeals ruled that the clause should not be enforced because enforcement effectively would deprive respondents of an opportunity to litigate their claim against petitioner.

The Bremen concerned a "far from routine transaction between companies of two different nations contemplating the tow of an extremely costly piece of equipment from Louisiana across the Gulf of Mexico and the Atlantic Ocean, through the Mediterranean Sea to its final destination in the Adriatic Sea." These facts suggest that, even apart from the evidence of negotiation regarding the forum clause, it was entirely reasonable for the Court in *The Bremen* to have expected Unterweser and Zapata to have negotiated with care in selecting a forum for the resolution of disputes arising from their special towing contract.

In contrast, respondents' passage contract was purely routine and doubtless nearly identical to every commercial passage contract issued by petitioner and most other cruise lines. In this context, it would be entirely unreasonable for us to assume that respondents — or any other cruise passenger — would negotiate with petitioner the terms of a forum-selection clause in an ordinary commercial cruise ticket. Common sense dictates that a ticket of this kind will be a form contract the terms of which are not subject to negotiation, and that an individual purchasing the ticket will not have bargaining parity with the cruise line. But by ignoring the crucial differences in the business contexts in which the respective contracts were executed, the Court of Appeals' analysis seems to us to have distorted somewhat this Court's holding in *The Bremen.*

In evaluating the reasonableness of the forum clause at issue in this case, we must refine the analysis of *The Bremen* to account for the realities of form passage contracts. As an initial matter, we do not adopt the Court of Appeals' determination that a nonnegotiated forum-selection clause in a form ticket contract is never enforceable simply because it is not the subject of bargaining. Including a reasonable forum clause in a form contract of this kind well may be permissible for several reasons: First, a cruise line has a special interest in limiting the fora in which it potentially could be subject to suit. Because a cruise ship typically carries passengers from many locales, it is not unlikely that a mishap on a cruise could subject the cruise line to litigation in several different fora. Additionally, a clause establishing *ex ante* the forum for dispute resolution has the salutary effect of dispelling any confusion about where suits arising from the contract must be brought and defended, sparing litigants the time and expense of pretrial motions to determine the correct forum and conserving judicial resources that otherwise would be devoted to deciding those motions. Finally, it stands to reason that passengers who purchase tickets containing a forum clause like that at issue in this case benefit in the form of reduced fares reflecting the savings that the cruise line enjoys by limiting the fora in which it may be sued.

We also do not accept the Court of Appeals' "independent justification" for its conclusion that *The Bremen* dictates that the clause should not be enforced because "[t]here is evidence in the record to indicate that the Shutes are physically and financially incapable of pursuing this litigation in Florida." We do not defer to the Court of Appeals' findings of fact. In dismissing the case . . . the District Court made no finding regarding the physical and financial impediments to the Shutes' pursuing their case in Florida. The Court of Appeals' conclusory reference to the record provides no basis for this Court to validate the finding of inconvenience. Furthermore, the Court of Appeals did not place in proper context this Court's statement in *The Bremen* that "the serious inconvenience of the contractual forum to one or both of the parties might carry greater weight in determining the reasonableness of the forum clause." The Court made this statement in evaluating a hypothetical "agreement between two Americans to resolve their essentially local disputes in a remote alien forum." In the present case, Florida is not a "remote alien forum," nor — given the fact that Mrs. Shute's accident occurred off the coast of Mexico — is this dispute an essentially local one inherently more suited to resolution in the State of Washington than in Florida. In light of these distinctions, and because respondents do not claim lack of notice of the forum clause, we conclude that they have not satisfied the "heavy burden of proof," required to set aside the clause on grounds of inconvenience.

It bears emphasis that forum-selection clauses contained in form passage contracts are subject to judicial scrutiny for fundamental fairness. In this case, there is no indication that petitioner set Florida as the forum in which disputes were to be resolved as a means of discouraging cruise passengers from pursuing legitimate claims. Any suggestion of such a bad-faith motive is belied by two facts: Petitioner has its principal place of business in Florida, and many of its cruises depart from and return to Florida ports. Similarly, there is no evidence that petitioner obtained respondents' accession to the forum clause by fraud or overreaching. Finally, respondents have conceded that they were given notice of the forum provision and, therefore, presumably retained the option of rejecting the contract with impunity. In the case before us, therefore, we conclude that the Court of Appeals erred in refusing to enforce the forum-selection clause.

. . .

The judgment of the Court of Appeals is reversed.

■ JUSTICE STEVENS, with whom JUSTICE MARSHALL joins, dissenting.

The Court prefaces its legal analysis with a factual statement that implies that a purchaser of a Carnival Cruise Lines passenger ticket is fully and fairly notified about the existence of the choice of forum clause in the fine print on the back of the ticket. Even if this implication were accurate, I would disagree with the Court's analysis. But, given the Court's preface,

I begin my dissent by noting that only the most meticulous passenger is likely to become aware of the forum-selection provision [because of its type size and placement in the text of the ticket]. . . .

The Bremen, which the Court effectively treats as controlling this case, had nothing to say about stipulations printed on the back of passenger tickets. That case involved the enforceability of a forum-selection clause in a freely negotiated international agreement between two large corporations . . . .

Notes and Questions

1. The language appeared on the ticket in type approximately this size:

    It is agreed by and between the passenger and the Carrier that all disputes and matters whatsoever arising under, in connection with or incident to this Contract shall be litigated, if at all, in and before a Court located in the State of Florida, U.S.A., to the exclusion of the Courts in any other state or country.

2. Imagine a suit brought by Carnival in Florida against California passengers boarding in California who have no connection to Florida other than the ticket and who have caused damage to the ship during the voyage. Does the Florida court have jurisdiction over the defendants under *Burger King*? Under *Carnival Cruise Lines*? Should it have jurisdiction?

3. Forum-selection clauses are increasingly common, and courts are increasingly willing to enforce them. The same is true of choice-of-law clauses. Is enforcement of forum-selection clauses in situations such as *Carnival Cruise Lines* or the hypothetical reverse suit consistent with the Court's identification of the purposes of limitations on personal jurisdiction in the cases you have read? Or does the desirability of enforcing forum-selection clauses rest on a particular view of *contract* law rather than any particular view of *due process*? Can the two be so easily separated?

4. Another method of obtaining consent to jurisdiction is also used in some states, although its consistency with modern personal-jurisdiction principles is disputed. All states require nonresident corporations doing business in the state to register and appoint an agent for service of process. Some courts have construed a corporation's compliance with a state registration statute as consent to jurisdiction on any claim. *See, e.g.*, Knowlton v. Allied Van Lines, Inc., 900 F.2d 1196 (8th Cir. 1990).

After *Daimler AG v. Bauman* (*supra* p. 461), however, the question has arisen whether consent by registration is constitutionally valid. A few courts have held that it is. *See, e.g.*, AK Steel Corp. v. PAC Operating L.P., 2017 WL 3314294 (D. Kan. Aug. 3, 2017); Mitchell v. Eli Lilly & Co., 159 F. Supp. 3d 967 (E.D. Mo. 2016). Many courts have finessed the question by holding that under the state registration statute, registration does *not* constitute consent. *See, e.g.*, Waite v. All Acquisition Corp., 901 F.3d 1307 (11th Cir. 2018). The Second Circuit adopted that approach in *Brown v. Lockheed Martin Corp.*, 814 F.3d 619, 637 (2d Cir. 2016), stating that its narrow interpretation of New York's registration statute was mandated by

Daimler. See also Genuine Parts Co. v. Cepec, 137 A.3d 123 (Del. 2016) (changing its interpretation of Delaware registration statute, so that registration did not constitute consent, based on its conclusion that *Daimler* would make the statute unconstitutional otherwise). Most recently, one district court has held that Pennsylvania's registration statute, which explicitly considers registration as equivalent to consent, is unconstitutional after *Daimler*. In re Asbestos Prods. Liab. Litig., 384 F. Supp. 3d 532 (E.D. Pa. 2019). Commentators similarly disagree about the constitutionality of mandating consent by registration. *Compare* Tanya J. Monestier, *Registration Statutes, General Jurisdiction, and the Fallacy of Consent*, 36 CARDOZO L. REV. 1343 (2015) (unconstitutional), *with* Oscar G. Chase, *Consent to Judicial Jurisdiction: The Foundation of "Registration" Statutes*, 73 N.Y.U. ANN. SURV. AM. L. 159 (2018) (constitutional).

5. In light of *Daimler* and the controversy over registration statutes, consider the following. Relatives of victims of overseas terrorist attacks brought federal lawsuits, under the federal Anti-Terrorist Act of 1992, against the Palestine Liberation Organization (PLO) and the Palestine Authority (PA) for the attacks. Several courts found they lacked personal jurisdiction over the PLO and the PA. *See, e.g.*, Waldman v. Palestinian Liberation Org., 835 F.3d 317 (2d Cir. 2016). In response, Congress in late 2018 enacted 18 U.S.C. § 2334(e), which provided that any defendant who accepted certain forms of U.S. aid (which both the PLO and the PA arguably do) "shall be deemed to have consented to personal jurisdiction" in suits brought under the Anti-Terrorist Act. Is the statute constitutionally valid? In *Estate of Klieman v. Palestinian Authority*, 923 F.3d 1115 (D.C. Cir. 2019), defendant PA challenged the constitutionality of § 2334(e), but the court did not reach the question because it found that there was insufficient evidence that the PA accepted U.S. financial aid during the requisite period.

6. If you have already covered Chapter Eleven (depending on how your professor has organized the course, you might not have done so), consider the following question: if a state has a policy *against* enforcing choice-of-law clauses, should a federal court enforce such a clause in a diversity case in which that state's substantive law will apply? *See* Stewart Org., Inc. v. Ricoh Corp., 487 U.S. 22 (1988). Note that *Carnival Cruise Lines* was a case in admiralty jurisdiction, in which federal common law governs.

SECTION E: THE REQUIREMENT OF NOTICE

Just because a particular forum has the *power* to exercise jurisdiction over a person does not exhaust the inquiry under the Due Process Clause of the Constitution. Before the court can issue a judgment that affects an individual's rights or interests, it must provide appropriate notice and an opportunity to be heard. Fed. R. Civ. P. 4, which governs service of process, is designed to serve two functions: first, to provide constitutionally adequate notice to parties to a lawsuit, and, second, to act as the formal means by which a court asserts personal jurisdiction over the defendant. As we saw in Chapter Two (*see supra* pp. 58-67), Rule 4 occasionally gives rise to questions of adequate notice. But most cases raising issues regarding the constitutionality of various forms of notice arise under state statutes. The Supreme Court set the standard for evaluating such statutes in the following case.

MULLANE V. CENTRAL HANOVER BANK & TRUST CO.

339 U.S. 306 (1950)

■ MR. JUSTICE JACKSON delivered the opinion of the Court.

This controversy questions the constitutional sufficiency of notice to beneficiaries on judicial settlement of accounts by the trustee of a common trust fund established under the New York Banking Law. The New York Court of Appeals considered and overruled objections that the statutory notice contravenes requirements of the Fourteenth Amendment and that by allowance of the account beneficiaries were deprived of property without due process of law. . . .

Common trust fund legislation is addressed to a problem appropriate for state action. Mounting overheads have made administration of small trusts undesirable to corporate trustees. In order that donors and testators of moderately sized trusts may not be denied the service of corporate fiduciaries, the District of Columbia and some thirty states other than New York have permitted pooling small trust estates into one fund for investment administration. The income, capital gains, losses and expenses of the collective trust are shared by the constituent trusts in proportion to their contribution. By this plan, diversification of risk and economy of management can be extended to those whose capital standing alone would not obtain such advantage.

Statutory authorization for the establishment of such common trust funds is provided in the New York Banking Law. Under this Act a trust company may . . . establish a common fund and, within prescribed limits, invest therein the assets of an unlimited number of estates, trusts or other funds of which it is trustee. Each participating trust shares ratably in the common fund, but exclusive management and control is in the trust company as trustee, and neither a fiduciary nor any beneficiary of a participating trust is deemed to have ownership in any particular asset or investment of this common fund. The trust company must keep fund assets separate from its own, and in its fiduciary capacity may not deal with itself or any affiliate. Provisions are made for accountings twelve to fifteen months after the establishment of a fund and triennially thereafter. The decree in each such judicial settlement of accounts is made binding and conclusive as to any matter set forth in the account upon everyone having any interest in the common fund or in any participating estate, trust or fund.

In January, 1946, Central Hanover Bank and Trust Company established a common trust fund in accordance with these provisions, and in March, 1947, it petitioned the Surrogate's Court [a special New York state court with jurisdiction over trust matters – ED.] for settlement of its first account as common trustee. During the accounting period a total of 113 trusts . . . participated in the common trust fund, the gross capital of which was nearly three million dollars. The record does not show the number or residence of the beneficiaries, but they were many and it is clear that some of them were not residents of the State of New York.

The only notice given beneficiaries of this specific application was by publication in a local newspaper in strict compliance with the minimum requirements of N.Y. Banking Law § 100-c(12): "After filing such petition (for judicial settlement of its account) the petitioner shall cause to be issued by the court in which the petition is filed and shall publish not less than once in each week for four successive weeks in a newspaper to be designated by the court a notice or citation addressed generally without naming them to all parties interested in such common trust fund and in such estates, trusts or funds mentioned in the petition, all of which may be described in the notice or citation only in the manner set forth in said petition and without setting forth the residence of any such decedent or donor of any such estate, trust or fund." Thus the only notice required, and the only one given, was by newspaper publication setting forth merely the name and address of the trust company, the name and the date of establishment of the common trust fund, and a list of all participating estates, trusts or funds.

At the time the first investment in the common fund was made on behalf of each participating estate, however, the trust company, pursuant to the requirements of § 100-c(9), had notified by mail each person of full age and sound mind whose name and address was then known to it and who was "entitled to share in the income therefrom . . . (or) . . . who would be entitled to share in the principal if the event upon which such estate, trust or fund will become distributable should have occurred at the time of sending such notice." Included in the notice was a copy of those provisions of the Act relating to the sending of the notice itself and to the judicial settlement of common trust fund accounts.

Upon the filing of the petition for the settlement of accounts, appellant [Mullane] was, by order of the court pursuant to § 100-c(12), appointed special guardian and attorney for all persons known or unknown not otherwise appearing who had or might thereafter have any interest in the income of the common trust fund; and appellee Vaughan was appointed to represent those similarly interested in the principal. There were no other appearances on behalf of any one interested in either interest or principal.

Appellant appeared specially, objecting that notice and the statutory provisions for notice to beneficiaries were inadequate to afford due process under the Fourteenth Amendment, and therefore that the court was without jurisdiction to render a final and binding decree. Appellant's objections were entertained and overruled, the Surrogate holding that the notice required and given was sufficient. A final decree accepting the accounts has been entered, affirmed by the Appellate Division of the Supreme Court and by the Court of Appeals of the State of New York.

The effect of this decree, as held below, is to settle "all questions respecting the management of the common fund." We understand that every right which beneficiaries would otherwise have against the trust company, either as trustee of the common fund or as trustee of any individual trust, for improper management of the common trust fund during the period covered by the accounting is sealed and wholly terminated by the decree.

[The Court first rejected an argument that the state completely lacked power to adjudicate the interests of any nonresident beneficiaries who had not been personally served, because the proceeding should be regarded as *in personam*. It observed that the *in rem – in personam* distinction was not always clear or treated consistently in the context of trusts.] But in any event we think that the requirements of the Fourteenth Amendment to the Federal Constitution do not depend upon a classification for which the standards are so elusive and confused generally and which, being primarily for state courts to define, may and do vary from state to state. . . . [W]e do not rest the power of the State to resort to constructive service in this proceeding upon how its courts or this Court may regard this historic antithesis. It is sufficient to observe that . . . the interest of each state in providing means to close trusts that exist by the grace of its laws and are administered under the supervision of its courts is so insistent and rooted in custom as to establish beyond doubt the right of its courts to determine the interests of all claimants, resident or nonresident, provided its procedure accords full opportunity to appear and be heard.

Quite different from the question of a state's power to discharge trustees is that of the opportunity it must give beneficiaries to contest. Many controversies have raged about the cryptic and abstract words of the Due Process Clause but there can be no doubt that at a minimum they require that deprivation of life, liberty or property by adjudication be preceded by notice and opportunity for hearing appropriate to the nature of the case.

In two ways this proceeding does or may deprive beneficiaries of property. It may cut off their rights to have the trustee answer for negligent or illegal impairments of their interests. Also, their interests are presumably subject to diminution in the proceeding by allowance of fees and expenses to one who, in their names but without their knowledge, may conduct a fruitless or uncompensatory contest. Certainly the proceeding is one in which they may be deprived of property rights and hence notice and hearing must measure up to the standards of due process.

Personal service of written notice within the jurisdiction is the classic form of notice always adequate in any type of proceeding. But the vital interest of the State in bringing any issues as to its fiduciaries to a final settlement can be served only if interests or claims of individuals who are outside of the State can somehow be determined. A construction of the Due Process Clause which would place impossible or impractical obstacles in the way could not be justified.

Against this interest of the State we must balance the individual interest sought to be protected by the Fourteenth Amendment. This is defined by our holding that "The fundamental requisite of due process of law is the opportunity to be heard." This right to be heard has little reality or worth unless one is informed that the matter is pending and can choose for himself whether to appear or default, acquiesce or contest.

The Court has not committed itself to any formula achieving a balance between these interests in a particular proceeding or determining when constructive notice may be utilized or what test it must meet. Personal service has not in all circumstances been regarded as indispensable to the process due to residents, and it has more often been held unnecessary as to nonresidents. We disturb none of the established rules on these subjects. No decision constitutes a controlling or even a very illuminating precedent for the case before us. But a few general principles stand out in the books.

An elementary and fundamental requirement of due process in any proceeding which is to be accorded finality is notice reasonably calculated, under all the circumstances, to apprise interested parties of the pendency of the action and afford them an opportunity to present their objections. The notice must be of such nature as reasonably to convey the required information, and it must afford a reasonable time for those interested to make their appearance. But if with due regard for the practicalities and peculiarities of the case these conditions are reasonably met the constitutional requirements are satisfied. . . .

But when notice is a person's due, process which is a mere gesture is not due process. The means employed must be such as one desirous of actually informing the absentee might reasonably adopt to accomplish it. The reasonableness and hence the constitutional validity of any chosen method may be defended on the ground that it is in itself reasonably certain to inform those affected, or, where conditions do not reasonably permit such notice, that the form chosen is not substantially less likely to bring home notice than other of the feasible and customary substitutes.

It would be idle to pretend that publication alone as prescribed here, is a reliable means of acquainting interested parties of the fact that their rights are before the courts. It is not an accident that the greater number of cases reaching this Court on the question of adequacy of notice have been concerned with actions founded on process constructively served through local newspapers. Chance alone brings to the attention of even a local resident an advertisement in small type inserted in the back pages of a newspaper, and if he makes his home outside the area of the newspaper's normal circulation the odds that the information will never reach him are large indeed. The chance of actual notice is further reduced when as here the notice required does not even name those whose attention it is supposed to attract, and does not inform acquaintances who might call it to attention. In weighing its sufficiency on the basis of equivalence with actual notice we are unable to regard this as more than a feint.

Nor is publication here reinforced by steps likely to attract the parties' attention to the proceeding. It is true that publication traditionally has been acceptable as notification supplemental to other action which in itself may reasonably be expected to convey a warning. The ways of an owner with tangible property are such that he usually arranges means to learn of any direct attack upon his possessory or proprietary rights. Hence, . . . attachment of a chattel or entry upon real estate in the name of law may reasonably be expected to come promptly to the owner's attention. When the state within which the owner has located such property seizes it for some reason, publication or posting affords an additional measure of notification. A state may indulge the assumption that one who has left tangible property in the state either has abandoned it, in which case proceedings against it deprive him of nothing, or that he has left some caretaker under a duty to let him know that it is being jeopardized. . . .

In the case before us there is, of course, no abandonment. On the other hand these beneficiaries do have a resident fiduciary as caretaker of their interest in this property. But it is their caretaker who in the accounting becomes their adversary. Their trustee is released from giving notice of jeopardy, and no one else is expected to do so. Not even the special guardian is required or apparently expected to communicate with his ward and client . . . .

This Court has not hesitated to approve of resort to publication as a customary substitute in another class of cases where it is not reasonably possible or practicable to give more adequate warning. Thus it has been recognized that, in the case of persons missing or unknown, employment of an indirect and even a probably futile means of notification is all that the situation permits and creates no constitutional bar to a final decree foreclosing their rights.

Those beneficiaries represented by appellant whose interests or whereabouts could not with due diligence be ascertained come clearly within this category. As to them the statutory notice is sufficient. However great the odds that publication will never reach the eyes of such unknown parties, it is not in the typical case much more likely to fail than any of the choices open to legislators endeavoring to prescribe the best notice practicable.

Nor do we consider it unreasonable for the State to dispense with more certain notice to those beneficiaries whose interests are either conjectural or future or, although they could be discovered upon investigation, do not in due course of business come to knowledge of the common trustee. Whatever searches might be required in another situation under ordinary standards of diligence, in view of the character of the proceedings and the nature of the interests here involved we think them unnecessary. We recognize the practical difficulties and costs that would be attendant on frequent investigations into the status of great numbers of beneficiaries, many of whose interests in the common fund are so remote as to be ephemeral; and we have no doubt that such impracticable and extended searches are not required in the name of due process. The expense of keeping informed from day to day of substitutions among even current income beneficiaries and presumptive remaindermen, to say nothing of the far greater number of contingent beneficiaries, would impose a severe burden on the plan, and would likely dissipate its advantages. These are practical matters in which we should be reluctant to disturb the judgment of the state authorities.

Accordingly we overrule appellant's constitutional objections to published notice insofar as they are urged on behalf of any beneficiaries whose interests or addresses are unknown to the trustee.

As to known present beneficiaries of known place of residence, however, notice by publication stands on a different footing. Exceptions in the name of necessity do not sweep away the rule that within the limits of practicability notice must be such as is reasonably calculated to reach interested parties. Where the names and post office addresses of those affected by a proceeding are at hand, the reasons disappear for resort to means less likely than the mails to apprise them of its pendency.

The trustee has on its books the names and addresses of the income beneficiaries represented by appellant, and we find no tenable ground for dispensing with a serious effort to inform them personally of the accounting, at least by ordinary mail to the record addresses. Certainly sending them a copy of the statute months and perhaps years in advance does not answer this purpose. The trustee periodically remits their income to them, and we think that they might reasonably expect that with or apart from their remittances word might come to them personally that steps were being taken affecting their interests.

We need not weigh contentions that a requirement of personal service of citation on even the large number of known resident or nonresident beneficiaries would, by reasons of delay if not of expense, seriously interfere with the proper administration of the fund. Of course personal service even without the jurisdiction of the issuing authority serves the end of actual and personal notice, whatever power of compulsion it might lack. However, no such service is required under the circumstances. This type of trust presupposes a large number of small interests. The individual interest does not stand alone but is identical with that of a class. The rights of each in the integrity of the fund and the fidelity of the trustee are shared by many other beneficiaries. Therefore notice reasonably certain to reach most of those interested in objecting is likely to safeguard the interests of all, since any objections sustained would inure to the benefit of all. We think that under such circumstances reasonable risks that notice might not actually reach every beneficiary are justifiable.

The statutory notice to known beneficiaries is inadequate, not because in fact it fails to reach everyone, but because under the circumstances it is not reasonably calculated to reach those who could easily be informed by other means at hand. However it may have been in former times, the mails today are recognized as an efficient and inexpensive means of communication. Moreover, the fact that the trust company has been able to give mailed notice to known beneficiaries at the time the common trust fund was established is persuasive that postal notification at the time of accounting would not seriously burden the plan.

In some situations the law requires greater precautions in its proceedings than the business world accepts for its own purposes. In few, if any, will it be satisfied with less. Certainly it is instructive, in determining the reasonableness of the impersonal broadcast notification here used, to ask whether it would satisfy a prudent man of business, counting his pennies but finding it in his interest to convey information to many persons whose names and addresses are in his files. We are not satisfied that it would. Publication may theoretically be available for all the world to see, but it is too much in our day to suppose that each or any individual beneficiary does or could examine all that is published to see if something may be tucked away in it that affects his property interests. . . .

We hold the notice of judicial settlement of accounts required by the New York Banking Law § 100-c(12) is incompatible with the requirements of the Fourteenth Amendment as a basis for adjudication depriving known persons whose whereabouts are also known of substantial property rights. . . .

Reversed.

■ [The dissenting opinion of MR. JUSTICE BURTON is omitted.]

■ [MR. JUSTICE DOUGLAS did not participate in this case.]

Notes and Questions

1. Notice that the Court first disposes of the argument that *Pennoyer* deprives the New York court of *power* to exercise jurisdiction over the absent parties. Only five years after *International Shoe*, the Court does not rely on minimum contacts but rather on a more general recognition that states have an interest in being able to adjudicate rights held under trusts administered in the state. Would the case come out the same way under the minimum-contacts test?

2. The Court's requirement that the means of providing notice "must be reasonably calculated, under all the circumstances, to apprise interested parties" requires courts to examine the facts on a case-by-case basis. In *Greene v. Lindsey*, 456 U.S. 444 (1982), for example, the Court found that posting an eviction notice on a tenant's door was insufficient notice because such notices — in the public-housing project involved — were often removed by other tenants before they were seen by the occupant. The Court required that such notice be supplemented by notice sent through the mail. Should a plaintiff have to investigate these sorts of individual circumstances in each case? What if the plaintiff's investigation showed that mailboxes in public housing were often broken into and mail stolen?

3. In the electronic age, is notice by e-mail likely to be the most effective method in many cases? Rule 4 does not permit service of initial process by e-mail except if ordered by a court against a foreign corporation. (Recall *Rio Properties Inc. v. Rio International Interlink*, 284 F.3d 1007 (9th Cir. 2002) (*supra* p. 59).) Does that make Rule 4 unconstitutional in cases in which e-mail is the most effective form of notice? (Hint: does the Court require the *most* effective form of notice?) Service of papers other than the

summons and complaint may be made by e-mail if the person receiving it has consented in writing to that method. *See* Fed. R. Civ. P. 5(b)(2)(E).

4. *Jones v. Flowers*, 547 U.S. 220 (2006), applied *Mullane* to find notice inadequate. In *Jones*, the state had sent a notice of tax delinquency to Jones via certified mail addressed to him at the delinquent property, but the letter was returned unclaimed. Despite this knowledge that its attempt to notify Jones had failed, the state sold the property to Flowers. Although certified mail might satisfy due process in the abstract, the Court reiterated that in previous cases it had "required the government to consider unique information about an intended recipient regardless of whether a statutory scheme is reasonably calculated to provide notice in the ordinary case." *Id.* at 230. The Court analogized the situation to one in which "the Commissioner prepared a stack of letters to mail to delinquent taxpayers, handed them to the postman, and then watched as the departing postman accidentally dropped the letters down a storm drain." *Id.* at 229. It held that the state's inaction after the initial letter was returned was not "not what someone 'desirous of actually informing' Jones would do; such a person would take further reasonable steps if any were available." *Id.* at 230.

5. Although notice is a prerequisite for the exercise of personal jurisdiction, it is also an aspect of a larger constitutional requirement — contained in the Due Process Clauses of the Fifth and Fourteenth Amendments — that no one be deprived "of life, liberty, or property without due process of law." (As *World–Wide Volkswagen* makes clear, the minimum-contacts and fairness analyses are also derived from the Due Process Clause.) As *Mullane* notes, the requirements of due process include both notice and an opportunity to be heard. *Mullane* itself sets the standard for constitutionally adequate notice. A number of Supreme Court cases define the contours of the right to be heard, which varies with the context of the deprivation. Although the cases are not completely consistent with one another, two conclusions may be drawn. First, a state may not authorize pre-judgment seizure of property (real or personal) without providing either a pre-seizure opportunity for the putative property owner to be heard, or adequate safeguards against erroneous seizure and a swift post-seizure hearing. *See*, *e.g.*, Sniadach v. Family Fin. Corp. of Bay View, 395 U.S. 337 (1969); Fuentes v. Shevin, 407 U.S. 67 (1972); Mitchell v. W. T. Grant Co., 416 U.S. 600 (1974); N. Ga. Finishing, Inc. v. Di–Chem, Inc., 419 U.S. 601 (1975); Connecticut v. Doehr, 501 U.S. 1 (1991). Second, if the government itself seeks to deprive anyone of an entitlement other than real or personal property (such as welfare payments or parental rights), the Court applies a balancing test to determine how much process is due:

> [I]dentification of the specific dictates of due process generally requires consideration of three distinct factors: First, the private interest that will be affected by the official action; second, the risk of an erroneous deprivation of such interest through the procedures used, and the probable value, if any, of additional or substitute procedural safeguards; and finally, the Government's interest, including the function involved

and the fiscal and administrative burdens that the additional or substitute procedural requirement would entail.

Mathews v. Eldridge, 424 U.S. 319, 335 (1976). You may learn about some of these cases when you study Constitutional Law.

Section F: Personal Jurisdiction in Federal Court

So far, we have not distinguished between state and federal courts. As in state courts, the exercise of jurisdiction in federal court must be consistent with both statutory and constitutional doctrines. Rule 4, which deals with service of process, also governs personal jurisdiction in the federal courts. This section focuses on the meaning and interpretation of Rule 4(k), which you should read now.

Let's begin with Rule 4(k)(1)(C), which you might think is the most often used. In fact, very few federal statutes authorize nationwide service (or mention service of process at all). Among those that do so are the antitrust laws, some securities-fraud provisions, and ERISA, which governs employee pensions and other benefits. For most federal statutes, however, including such important and often-litigated statutes as federal intellectual-property laws, Title VII (prohibiting employment discrimination) and § 1983 (protecting constitutional and civil rights), Rule 4(k)(1)(C) is irrelevant. For the few cases that do rest on Rule 4(k)(1)(C), courts are split on an interesting question: what is the constitutional test for jurisdiction? Many courts allow jurisdiction if the defendant has minimum contacts with the United States as a whole, while others look to the fairness of requiring the defendant to defend in the particular federal court.

In most cases, though, personal jurisdiction in federal court will be determined under Rule 4(k)(1)(A). Read that provision carefully: now do you see why you can read personal-jurisdiction cases decided by state courts *and* federal courts and not really care about the difference? Consider again the various theories underlying limits on personal jurisdiction. Which, if any, apply to federal courts? Would it make more sense to adopt nationwide service in federal court as the default option, but provide for transfer if the forum is inconvenient? Think about how such a system would operate in both federal-question cases, and, if you have already studied Chapter Eleven, diversity cases. Might the latter explain why Rule 4(k)(1)(A) is written the way it is?

Rule 4(k)(1)(B) (the "100-mile bulge" rule) is largely self-explanatory — although it bears emphasizing that it cannot be used to start an action, only to add parties to one already properly brought. Rule 4(k)(1)(B) gives rise to the same question that arises under Rule 4(k)(1)(C): must the party joined under Rule 14 or 19 and served within the "bulge" have contacts with the "bulge" state, the forum state, either, or neither? Courts disagree. They all agree, however, that the 100-mile distance is measured as the crow flies.

Finally, consider Rule 4(k)(2). It was added to the Rules primarily in response to *Omni Capital International, Ltd. v. Rudolf Wolff & Co.*, 484 U.S. 97 (1987). In *Omni Capital*, a foreign defendant accused of violating federal securities law had significant contacts with the United States but insufficient contacts with any single state. The Court held that the defendant was not amenable to jurisdiction in federal court. Do you see how Rule 4(k)(2) solves the problem? Note that it is a fallback provision only: if there would be jurisdiction under any other provision, Rule 4(k)(2) is inapplicable. Courts applying Rule 4(k)(2) generally determine the constitutionality of the exercise of jurisdiction by looking at whether the defendant has sufficient contacts with the United States as a whole. *See*, *e.g.*, Touchcom, Inc. v. Bereskin & Parr, 574 F.3d 1403, 1416 (Fed. Cir. 2009); Mwani v. bin Laden, 417 F.3d 1, 11-12 (D.C. Cir. 2005).

SECTION G: VENUE

1. Original Venue

You already know that a court must have jurisdiction over the parties to have the authority to decide a case. The court must also be one in which venue is appropriate. Unlike personal jurisdiction, which concerns a court's power to adjudicate, venue is primarily concerned with convenience:

> Venue, though a statutory requirement, is based on [the] decision concerning where a case should be heard. It is a privilege given to the defendant primarily as a matter of convenience and is not based on an inherent power of a particular court over the parties. In general, the purpose of statutorily specified venue is to protect the defendant against the risk that a plaintiff will select an unfair or inconvenient place for trial.

Johnson Creative Arts, Inc. v. Wool Masters, Inc., 743 F.2d 947, 951 (1st Cir. 1984).

Imagine a contract between a North Carolina company and an Indiana company, to construct an office building in Tennessee. If a dispute arises, and a suit is filed for more than $75,000, *any* federal district court has subject-matter jurisdiction. There is probably personal jurisdiction over both parties in state or federal court in North Carolina, Indiana, and Tennessee, since both parties have significant contacts with each of the three states. But the federal venue statute, 28 U.S.C. § 1391, places further limits on where the suit can be brought. (States have venue provisions as well, which govern state-court suits.)

Read § 1391(a)-(d), then answer the following questions:

1. A resident of Nashville, Tennessee and a resident of Durham, North Carolina have a car accident in South Bend, Indiana. Nashville is located in the Middle District of Tennessee; Durham in the Middle District of North

Carolina; and South Bend in the Northern District of Indiana. The Tennessean files suit in federal court in the Middle District of Tennessee, alleging state-law tort claims and asking for $100,000 in damages. While the North Carolina defendant is traveling on unrelated business in Tennessee, the Tennessee plaintiff has him personally served with process.

- Does the Tennessee federal court have *subject-matter jurisdiction*? (You must have studied Chapter Ten to answer this question; if you have not done so, you should skip to the next question.)
- Does the Tennessee federal court have *personal jurisdiction* over the North Carolina defendant? (Hint: recall *Burnham v. Superior Court*, supra p. 472.)
- Is *venue* properly laid in the Tennessee federal court? (For this question, you must read § 1391(b) carefully.)

2. Imagine the same accident, but this time three cars are involved. The third driver is from South Bend, Indiana, and he wishes to sue both the Tennesseean and the North Carolinian in one action. Neither defendant has left his or her home state since the accident. Considering both personal jurisdiction and venue, and assuming that an applicable state long-arm statute exists, in what federal court(s) may the suit be brought?

3. Several persons negotiate to build a $5 million structure in Buffalo, New York, which is in the Western District of New York. The owner is a Tennessee resident who lives in Knoxville, which is located in the Eastern District of Tennessee; the builder is from Buffalo; and the architect is from Manhattan, which is located in the Southern District of New York. The negotiations are carried on by telephone, e-mail, and in person in all three locations. A contract is reached, but the deal breaks down before building begins. The Tennessee owner wants to sue the builder and the architect. New York has four federal districts (the other two are, unsurprisingly, the Northern District and the Eastern District). Again considering both personal jurisdiction and venue, in what federal court(s) may the suit be brought?

4. Imagine the same negotiations in New York and Tennessee, but this time the builder lives in Philadelphia (90 miles from Manhattan), in the Eastern District of Pennsylvania — although no negotiations were carried on in Pennsylvania. In what federal court(s) is venue proper, and why (do not consider personal jurisdiction just yet)? In how many of these courts is there a way to obtain personal jurisdiction over both defendants?

5. Finally, imagine that the builder in Philadelphia is not an individual but a corporation. Now where is venue appropriate? (Hint: read § 1391(c)(1)-(2) carefully, and figure out how it interacts with § 1391(b).)

6. If the Tennessee plaintiff, (individual) Philadelphia builder, and Buffalo architect had already entered into a contract that specified that all disputes were to be litigated in Tennessee, would venue be properly laid in federal court in Tennessee? (Hint: recall *Carnival Cruise Lines*, supra p. 479, and note that objections to venue, like objections to personal jurisdiction, may be waived.)

7. When a case is removed from state to federal court (*see infra* pp. 567-73), the venue provisions of section 1391 and other venue statutes do not apply. Removal, so to speak, makes its own venue. *See* 28 U.S.C. § 1390(c) ("This [venue] chapter shall not determine the district court to which a civil action pending in a State court may be removed . . .").

8. Section 1391(a)(2), enacted in late 2011, provides that "the proper venue for a civil action shall be determined without regard to whether the action is local or transitory in nature." What, you may wonder, is that about? The new provision finally abolishes, or attempted to abolish, for the federal courts a hoary distinction between cases tied to a locality because of the location of real property, which were triable only where the property is ("local" actions), and most civil litigation such as tort and contract claims, which were triable wherever personal jurisdiction and venue under the general provisions were proper ("transitory" actions). It generally makes sense to deal with claims affecting title to real property where that property is, and claims for damage to real property are often best tried where a jury can conveniently view the property. But the lore on just what came within the category of a "local" action was inconsistent, and at worst could deny a forum entirely if there was a problem asserting jurisdiction over a defendant where the land was located.

New § 1391(a)(2) subjects both actions formerly known as "local" and those known as "transitory" to the same federal venue rules. As to "transitory" actions, no change and no problem; the 2011 version of § 1391 is similar to its predecessor, which already governed such actions. As to actions previously known as "local," the possible problem of a hypothetical quiet-title suit in Alaska federal court against an Alaska claimant to land located in Florida would be unlikely to arise — not because venue would be improper as to the Alaska defendant, but because quiet-title actions are *in rem* and require territorial jurisdiction over the property, which would be lacking. But if applicable local-action lore had regarded a property-*damage* action as local and thus maintainable only where the allegedly damaged land was located — even if the defendant lived in a different state — the 2011 statute's abolition of the local-transitory distinction would make venue proper in the federal district where the out-of-state defendant resided (in addition, of course, to where the land was located).

Despite § 1391(a)(2)'s apparent elimination of the local-action doctrine, the Ninth Circuit reverted to it in *Eldee-K Rental Properties, LLC v. DirecTV, Inc.*, 748 F.3d 943 (9th Cir. 2014). In *Eldee-K*, the owner of an apartment building in Connecticut sued a satellite TV provider for drilling holes and making other permanent changes in the building's common areas to accommodate the necessary hardware. It brought suit in California. The defendant moved to dismiss, arguing that, under the local-action doctrine, the case could be brought only in Connecticut, where the real property at issue was located. The court of appeals, recognizing some division and uncertainty in the federal courts about whether the local-action doctrine goes just to venue or limits subject-matter jurisdiction, concluded that the doctrine is jurisdictional. As a result, § 1391(a)(2), which deals only with venue, does not overturn the doctrine. The court then held, looking to California law to determine whether the action was local or transitory, that it was a local action and affirmed dismissal of the suit.

Warning No. 1: most states retain the local-transitory distinction in their venue law (although, even in state-law cases, you may no longer have to worry about the distinction in federal court). Warning No. 2: states' definitions of the distinction vary. Actions for damage to, as opposed to title to, land, for example, are regarded as "transitory" in some states and "local" in others.

2. Change of Venue

Federal statutes also make provision for situations in which the plaintiff brings suit in the wrong venue, or in which a legally appropriate venue is nevertheless unfair or inconvenient. Read 28 U.S.C. §§ 1404(a) and 1406(a). Although the *original* venue statutes do not govern in cases removed from state to federal court, *see supra* p. 497, Note 7, the *transfer* provisions do: "This [venue] chapter ... shall govern the transfer of [a removed] action ... as between districts and divisions of the United States district courts." 28 U.S.C. § 1390(c).

Section 1404(a) permits a court in which venue is proper to transfer it to another federal district court "[f]or the convenience of parties and witnesses, in the interest of justice." The transferee court must be one in which the case might have been brought originally — unless, as a 2011 amendment to § 1404(a) now allows, all parties consent to another federal court. In determining where the suit "might have been brought," a court must find both that venue is proper there, and that the transferee court would have had personal jurisdiction over the defendant at the time the plaintiff filed suit. Under *Van Dusen v. Barrack*, 376 U.S. 612, 639 (1964) (discussed *infra* p. 504; pp. 628-29, Note 5), a "transferee court must ... apply the state law that would have been applied if there had been no change of venue."

Courts vary on exactly how to determine whether a transfer is "in the interest of justice." In *J. Lyons & Co. v. Republic of Tea, Inc.*, 892 F. Supp. 486, 492 (S.D.N.Y. 1995), the court identified nine considerations:

(1) the convenience of witnesses; (2) the location of relevant documents and the relative ease of access to sources of proof; (3) the convenience of the parties; (4) the locus of the operative facts; (5) the availability of process to compel attendance of unwilling witnesses; (6) the relative means of the parties; (7) a forum's familiarity with the governing law; (8) the weight accorded a plaintiff's choice of forum; and (9) trial efficiency and the interests of justice, based on the totality of the circumstances.

As the court explained in *Citicorp Leasing, Inc. v. United American Funding, Inc.*, 2004 WL 102761, at *3 (S.D.N.Y. Jan. 21, 2004):

"There is no rigid formula for balancing these factors and no single one of them is determinative." "In performing the analysis the Court must, however, give due deference to the plaintiff's choice of forum which should not be disturbed unless the balance of convenience and justice weigh heavily in favor of defendant's forum." Further, "[t]he balancing of these factors is an equitable task and an 'ample degree of discretion is afforded the district courts in determining a suitable forum.'" Finally, the moving parties, here the individual defendants, bear the burden of establishing by clear and convincing evidence that transfer is appropriate.

Using these guidelines, try your hand at deciding whether the following cases should be transferred under § 1404:

- An Alabama corporation sued a New York corporation and a California corporation in the Northern District of Alabama. The defendants allegedly breached an agreement to refer certain business to the plaintiff. The agreement contained a forum-selection clause requiring all claims to be brought in the Central District of California. The plaintiff contended that it could not afford to litigate the case in such a distant forum, and the docket in the Central District of California was so heavily congested that a trial might not occur there for years. Transfer? P & S Bus. Machs., Inc. v. Canon USA, Inc., 331 F.3d 804 (11th Cir. 2003) (transfer).

- The plaintiff was injured while working aboard ship on the Mississippi River, near Donaldson, Louisiana. He was a citizen of Mississippi; the defendant was a Tennessee corporation with its principal place of business in Tennessee. The plaintiff received medical treatment in Memphis, Tennessee (the Western District of Tennessee) and in a Memphis suburb in the Northern District of Mississippi. The only eyewitness is a citizen of Indiana. The plaintiff sued in the Eastern District of Louisiana; the defendant wants the case transferred to the Western District of Tennessee or the Northern District of Mississippi. What result? Williams v. S. Towing Co., 2004 WL 60314 (E.D. La. Jan. 8, 2004) (no transfer).

Section 1406(a) allows a court the option of dismissing a suit in which venue is improper, or transferring it to a district in which it could have been brought. In determining where the suit "could have been brought," a court must again find both that venue is proper there, and that the transferee court would have had personal jurisdiction over the defendant at the time the plaintiff filed suit. The Supreme Court has interpreted § 1406 to allow a court in which venue is improper *and* personal jurisdiction is lacking to transfer a case to a district where both venue and personal jurisdiction are proper. Goldlawr, Inc. v. Heiman, 369 U.S. 463 (1962). If venue, personal jurisdiction, or both were improper, *Van Dusen* does not apply and transfer*ee*-forum law governs.

The Supreme Court addressed transfers of venue in the context of contractual forum-selection clauses in *Atlantic Marine Construction Corp. v. U.S. District Court*, 571 U.S. 49 (2013). In that case, the parties had contractually agreed to litigate all disputes in state or federal court in Virginia, but when a dispute arose the plaintiff filed suit in federal court in Texas, where most of the events had occurred. The defendant moved to transfer under § 1404(a) and to dismiss under § 1406(a), and also moved to dismiss for improper venue under Rule 12(b)(3). The district court denied all the motions. It held, first, that § 1404(a) was the exclusive mechanism for enforcing the forum-selection clause because the Western District of Texas was an appropriate venue under § 1391(b)(2), thus making venue in that district neither "wrong" (hence, not implicating § 1406(a)) nor "improper" (hence, not implicating Rule 12(b)(3)). The court then concluded that the transfer was not warranted under § 1404(a), considering all the typical factors for analyzing a transfer motion. The Supreme Court ultimately reversed. It agreed that neither § 1406(a) nor Rule 12(b)(3) was an appropriate mechanism for enforcing a forum-selection clause; the determination whether venue is "wrong" or "improper" turns solely on the federal statutory venue requirements and is not influenced by the existence of a forum-selection clause. But, the Court went on to hold, "[w]hen the parties have agreed to a valid forum-selection clause, a district court should ordinarily transfer the case to the forum specified in that clause. Only under extraordinary circumstances unrelated to the convenience of the parties should a § 1404(a) motion be denied." 571 U.S. at 62. Thus, absent extraordinary circumstances, a valid forum-selection clause will be dispositive. Finally, the Court held that when a case is transferred pursuant to a forum-selection clause, *Van Dusen* does not apply; the transferee court (i.e. the one selected by the clause) should apply the law that would have been applied had the case been filed in that court originally.

Under § 1404, a federal court can transfer a case only to another federal court. What if the most convenient or just forum is a state court or a foreign court? The following case deals with exactly that situation.

PIPER AIRCRAFT CO. V. REYNO

454 U.S. 235 (1981)

■ JUSTICE MARSHALL delivered the opinion of the Court.

These cases arise out of an air crash that took place in Scotland. Respondent, acting as representative of the estates of several Scottish citizens killed in the accident, brought wrongful-death actions against petitioners that were ultimately transferred to the United States District Court for the Middle District of Pennsylvania. Petitioners moved to dismiss on the ground of *forum non conveniens*. After noting that an alternative forum existed in Scotland, the District Court granted their motions. The United States Court of Appeals for the Third Circuit reversed. The Court of Appeals based its decision, at least in part, on the ground that dismissal is automatically barred where the law of the alternative forum is less favorable to the plaintiff than the law of the forum chosen by the plaintiff. Because we conclude that the possibility of an unfavorable change in law should not, by itself, bar dismissal, and because we conclude that the District Court did not otherwise abuse its discretion, we reverse.

I

A

In July 1976, a small commercial aircraft crashed in the Scottish highlands during the course of a charter flight from Blackpool to Perth. The pilot and five passengers were killed instantly. The decedents were all Scottish subjects and residents, as are their heirs and next of kin. There were no eyewitnesses to the accident. At the time of the crash the plane was subject to Scottish air traffic control.

The aircraft, a twin-engine Piper Aztec, was manufactured in Pennsylvania by petitioner Piper Aircraft Co. (Piper). The propellers were manufactured in Ohio by petitioner Hartzell Propeller, Inc. (Hartzell). At the time of the crash the aircraft was registered in Great Britain and was owned and maintained by Air Navigation and Trading Co., Ltd. (Air Navigation). It was operated by McDonald Aviation, Ltd. (McDonald), a Scottish air taxi service. Both Air Navigation and McDonald were organized in the United Kingdom. The wreckage of the plane is now in a hangar in Farnsborough, England. . . .

In July 1977, a California probate court appointed respondent Gaynell Reyno administratrix of the estates of the five passengers. Reyno is not related to and does not know any of the decedents or their survivors; she was a legal secretary to the attorney who filed this lawsuit. Several days after her appointment, Reyno commenced separate wrongful-death actions against Piper and Hartzell in the Superior Court of California, claiming negligence and strict liability. Air Navigation, McDonald, and the estate of the pilot are not parties to this litigation. The survivors of the five passengers whose estates are represented by Reyno filed a separate action in the United Kingdom against Air Navigation, McDonald, and the pilot's estate. Reyno candidly admits that the action against Piper and Hartzell was filed in the United States because its laws regarding liability, capacity to sue, and damages are more favorable to her position than are those of Scotland. Scottish law does not recognize strict liability in tort. Moreover, it permits wrongful-death actions only when brought by a decedent's relatives. The relatives may sue only for "loss of support and society."

[Petitioners removed the suit] to the United States District Court for the Central District of California. Piper then moved for transfer to the United States District Court for the Middle District of Pennsylvania, pursuant to 28 U.S.C. § 1404(a). Hartzell moved to dismiss for lack of personal jurisdiction, or in the alternative, to transfer. In December 1977, the District Court quashed service on Hartzell and transferred the case to the Middle District of Pennsylvania. Respondent then properly served process on Hartzell.

B

In May 1978, after the suit had been transferred, both Hartzell and Piper moved to dismiss the action on the ground of *forum non conveniens*. The District Court granted these motions in October 1979. It relied on the balancing test set forth by this Court in *Gulf Oil Corp. v. Gilbert*, 330 U.S. 501 (1947), and its companion case, *Koster v. Lumbermens Mutual Casualty Co.*, 330 U.S. 518 (1947). In those decisions, the Court stated that a plaintiff's choice of forum should rarely be disturbed. However, when an alternative forum has jurisdiction to hear the case, and when trial in the chosen forum would "establish . . . oppressiveness and vexation to a defendant . . . out of all proportion to plaintiff's convenience," or when the "chosen forum [is] inappropriate because of considerations affecting the court's own administrative and legal problems," the court may, in the exercise of its sound discretion, dismiss the case. To guide trial court discretion, the Court provided a list of "private interest factors" affecting the convenience of the litigants, and a list of "public interest factors" affecting the convenience of the forum.[6] . . .

On appeal, the United States Court of Appeals for the Third Circuit reversed and remanded for trial. . . .

II

The Court of Appeals erred in holding that plaintiffs may defeat a motion to dismiss on the ground of *forum non conveniens* merely by showing that the substantive law that would be applied in the alternative forum is less favorable to the plaintiffs than that of the present forum. The possibility of a change in substantive law should ordinarily not be given conclusive or even substantial weight in the *forum non conveniens* inquiry. . . .

. . . [B]y holding that the central focus of the *forum non conveniens* inquiry is convenience, *Gilbert* implicitly recognized that dismissal may not be barred solely because of the possibility of an unfavorable change in law. Under *Gilbert*, dismissal will ordinarily be appropriate where trial in the plaintiff's chosen forum imposes a heavy burden on the defendant or the court, and where the plaintiff is unable to offer any specific reasons of convenience supporting his choice. If substantial weight were given to

---

6. The factors pertaining to the private interests of the litigants included the "relative ease of access to sources of proof; availability of compulsory process for attendance of unwilling, and the cost of obtaining attendance of willing, witnesses; possibility of view of premises, if view would be appropriate to the action; and all other practical problems that make trial of a case easy, expeditious and inexpensive." The public factors bearing on the question included the administrative difficulties flowing from court congestion; the "local interest in having localized controversies decided at home"; the interest in having the trial of a diversity case in a forum that is at home with the law that must govern the action; the avoidance of unnecessary problems in conflict of laws, or in the application of foreign law; and the unfairness of burdening citizens in an unrelated forum with jury duty.

the possibility of an unfavorable change in law, however, dismissal might be barred even where trial in the chosen forum was plainly inconvenient.

The Court of Appeals' decision is inconsistent with this Court's earlier *forum non conveniens* decisions in another respect. Those decisions have repeatedly emphasized the need to retain flexibility. In *Gilbert*, the Court refused to identify specific circumstances "which will justify or require either grant or denial of remedy." Similarly, in *Koster*, the Court rejected the contention that where a trial would involve inquiry into the internal affairs of a foreign corporation, dismissal was always appropriate. "That is one, but only one, factor which may show convenience." And in *Williams v. Green Bay & Western R.R.*, 326 U.S. 549, 557 (1946), we stated that we would not lay down a rigid rule to govern discretion, and that "[e]ach case turns on its facts." If central emphasis were placed on any one factor, the *forum non conveniens* doctrine would lose much of the very flexibility that makes it so valuable.

In fact, if conclusive or substantial weight were given to the possibility of a change in law, the *forum non conveniens* doctrine would become virtually useless. Jurisdiction and venue requirements are often easily satisfied. As a result, many plaintiffs are able to choose from among several forums. Ordinarily, these plaintiffs will select that forum whose choice-of-law rules are most advantageous. Thus, if the possibility of an unfavorable change in substantive law is given substantial weight in the *forum non conveniens* inquiry, dismissal would rarely be proper. . . .

The Court of Appeals' approach is not only inconsistent with the purpose of the *forum non conveniens* doctrine, but also poses substantial practical problems. If the possibility of a change in law were given substantial weight, deciding motions to dismiss on the ground of *forum non conveniens* would become quite difficult. Choice-of-law analysis would become extremely important, and the courts would frequently be required to interpret the law of foreign jurisdictions. First, the trial court would have to determine what law would apply if the case were tried in the chosen forum, and what law would apply if the case were tried in the alternative forum. It would then have to compare the rights, remedies, and procedures available under the law that would be applied in each forum. Dismissal would be appropriate only if the court concluded that the law applied by the alternative forum is as favorable to the plaintiff as that of the chosen forum. The doctrine of *forum non conveniens*, however, is designed in part to help courts avoid conducting complex exercises in comparative law. As we stated in *Gilbert*, the public interest factors point towards dismissal where the court would be required to "untangle problems in conflict of laws, and in law foreign to itself."

Upholding the decision of the Court of Appeals would result in other practical problems. At least where the foreign plaintiff named an American manufacturer as defendant, a court could not dismiss the case on grounds of *forum non conveniens* where dismissal might lead to an unfavorable change in law. The American courts, which are already extremely attractive to foreign plaintiffs, would become even more attractive. The flow of litigation into the United States would increase and further congest already crowded courts.¹⁹

The Court of Appeals based its decision, at least in part, on an analogy between dismissals on grounds of *forum non conveniens* and transfers between federal courts pursuant to § 1404(a). In *Van Dusen v. Barrack*, 376 U.S. 612 (1964), this Court ruled that a § 1404(a) transfer should not result in a change in the applicable law. Relying on dictum in an earlier Third Circuit opinion interpreting *Van Dusen,* the court below held that that principle is also applicable to a dismissal on *forum non conveniens* grounds. However, § 1404(a) transfers are different than dismissals on the ground of *forum non conveniens.*

Congress enacted § 1404(a) to permit change of venue between federal courts. Although the statute was drafted in accordance with the doctrine of *forum non conveniens*, it was intended to be a revision rather than a codification of the common law. District courts were given more discretion to transfer under § 1404(a) than they had to dismiss on grounds of *forum non conveniens.*

The reasoning employed in *Van Dusen v. Barrack* is simply inapplicable to dismissals on grounds of *forum non conveniens.* That case did not discuss the common-law doctrine. Rather, it focused on "the construction and application" of § 1404(a). . . . The Court feared that if a change in venue were accompanied by a change in law, forum-shopping parties would take unfair advantage of the relaxed standards for transfer. The rule was necessary to ensure the just and efficient operation of the statute.

We do not hold that the possibility of an unfavorable change in law should *never* be a relevant consideration in a *forum non conveniens* inquiry. Of course, if the remedy provided by the alternative forum is so clearly inadequate or unsatisfactory that it is no remedy at all, the unfavorable change in law may be given substantial weight; the district court may conclude that dismissal would not be in the interests of justice.²² In these

---

19. In holding that the possibility of a change in law unfavorable to the plaintiff should not be given substantial weight, we also necessarily hold that the possibility of a change in law favorable to defendant should not be considered. Respondent suggests that Piper and Hartzell filed the motion to dismiss, not simply because trial in the United States would be inconvenient, but also because they believe the laws of Scotland are more favorable. She argues that this should be taken into account in the analysis of the private interests. We recognize, of course, that Piper and Hartzell may be engaged in reverse forum-shopping. However, this possibility ordinarily should not enter into a trial court's analysis of the private interests. If the defendant is able to overcome the presumption in favor of plaintiff by showing that trial in the chosen forum would be unnecessarily burdensome, dismissal is appropriate — regardless of the fact that defendant may also be motivated by a desire to obtain a more favorable forum.

22. At the outset of any *forum non conveniens* inquiry, the court must determine whether there exists an alternative forum. Ordinarily, this requirement will be satisfied when the defendant is "amenable to process" in the other jurisdiction. In rare circumstances, however, where the remedy offered by the other forum is clearly unsatisfactory, the other forum may not be an adequate

cases, however, the remedies that would be provided by the Scottish courts do not fall within this category. Although the relatives of the decedents may not be able to rely on a strict liability theory, and although their potential damages award may be smaller, there is no danger that they will be deprived of any remedy or treated unfairly.

III

The Court of Appeals also erred in rejecting the District Court's *Gilbert* analysis. The Court of Appeals stated that more weight should have been given to the plaintiff's choice of forum, and criticized the District Court's analysis of the private and public interests. However, the District Court's decision regarding the deference due plaintiff's choice of forum was appropriate. Furthermore, we do not believe that the District Court abused its discretion in weighing the private and public interests.

A

The District Court acknowledged that there is ordinarily a strong presumption in favor of the plaintiff's choice of forum, which may be overcome only when the private and public interest factors clearly point towards trial in the alternative forum. It held, however, that the presumption applies with less force when the plaintiff or real parties in interest are foreign.

The District Court's distinction between resident or citizen plaintiffs and foreign plaintiffs is fully justified. . . . When the home forum has been chosen, it is reasonable to assume that this choice is convenient. When the plaintiff is foreign, however, this assumption is much less reasonable. Because the central purpose of any *forum non conveniens* inquiry is to ensure that the trial is convenient, a foreign plaintiff's choice deserves less deference. . . .

In analyzing the private interest factors, the District Court stated that the connections with Scotland are "overwhelming." This characterization may be somewhat exaggerated. Particularly with respect to the question of relative ease of access to sources of proof, the private interests point in both directions. As respondent emphasizes, records concerning the design, manufacture, and testing of the propeller and plane are located in the United States. She would have greater access to sources of proof relevant to her strict liability and negligence theories if trial were held here. However, the District Court did not act unreasonably in concluding that fewer evidentiary problems would be posed if the trial were held in Scotland. A large proportion of the relevant evidence is located in Great Britain. . . .

The District Court correctly concluded that the problems posed by the inability to implead potential third-party defendants clearly supported

alternative, and the initial requirement may not be satisfied. Thus, for example, dismissal would not be appropriate where the alternative forum does not permit litigation of the subject matter of the dispute.

holding the trial in Scotland. Joinder of the pilot's estate, Air Navigation, and McDonald is crucial to the presentation of petitioners' defense. If Piper and Hartzell can show that the accident was caused not by a design defect, but rather by the negligence of the pilot, the plane's owners, or the charter company, they will be relieved of all liability. It is true, of course, that if Hartzell and Piper were found liable after a trial in the United States, they could institute an action for indemnity or contribution against these parties in Scotland. It would be far more convenient, however, to resolve all claims in one trial. . . .

The District Court's review of the factors relating to the public interest was also reasonable. On the basis of its choice-of-law analysis, it concluded that if the case were tried in the Middle District of Pennsylvania, Pennsylvania law would apply to Piper and Scottish law to Hartzell. It stated that a trial involving two sets of laws would be confusing to the jury. It also noted its own lack of familiarity with Scottish law. Consideration of these problems was clearly appropriate under *Gilbert*; in that case we explicitly held that the need to apply foreign law pointed towards dismissal. . . .

Scotland has a very strong interest in this litigation. The accident occurred in its airspace. All of the decedents were Scottish. Apart from Piper and Hartzell, all potential plaintiffs and defendants are either Scottish or English. As we stated in *Gilbert*, there is "a local interest in having localized controversies decided at home." Respondent argues that American citizens have an interest in ensuring that American manufacturers are deterred from producing defective products, and that additional deterrence might be obtained if Piper and Hartzell were tried in the United States, where they could be sued on the basis of both negligence and strict liability. However, the incremental deterrence that would be gained if this trial were held in an American court is likely to be insignificant. The American interest in this accident is simply not sufficient to justify the enormous commitment of judicial time and resources that would inevitably be required if the case were to be tried here. . . .

■ JUSTICE POWELL took no part in the decision of these cases.

■ JUSTICE O'CONNOR took no part in the consideration or decision of these cases.

■ [The opinion of JUSTICE WHITE, concurring in part and dissenting in part, is omitted.]

■ [The dissenting opinion of JUSTICE STEVENS, joined by JUSTICE BRENNAN, is omitted.]

Notes and Questions

1. Note the various differences between *forum non conveniens* and transfer under § 1404(a). If transfer is meant to be easier to obtain under § 1404(a) than dismissal under traditional *forum non conveniens* doctrines,

are the other differences necessary to reduce the incentive for forum shopping in each situation? If the Scottish plaintiffs in *Piper Aircraft* had known the rules ultimately announced by the Supreme Court, do you think they would have filed suit in the United States?

2. Can you see why, after the adoption of § 1404(a), *forum non conveniens* is very rarely invoked in federal court? Some state courts still use the doctrine regularly. *See, e.g.*, Oxford Global Res., LLC v. Hernandez, 106 N.E.3d 556, 567-71 (Mass. 2018) (dismissing action by Massachusetts employer against California employee for alleged breach of employment agreement).

3. Imagine that an American passenger from New York had been aboard the plane, and that her estate (using the same California administratrix) had sued the defendants in California. How would the lawsuit have proceeded?

Chapter Ten

Subject-Matter Jurisdiction

In order to adjudicate a case before it, a court must have jurisdiction over the subject matter as well as over the parties. Jurisdiction over the parties, called *personal jurisdiction*, is covered in Chapter Nine. This chapter deals with *subject-matter jurisdiction*, and, in particular, with the subject-matter jurisdiction of the federal courts. Subject-matter jurisdiction is a *sine qua non* of adjudication. Unlike objections to personal jurisdiction, defects in subject-matter jurisdiction cannot be waived by the parties. *See* Fed. R. Civ. P. 12(h)(3). In the American system, most questions of subject-matter jurisdiction involve the allocation of jurisdiction between state courts and federal courts. That allocation is determined by a combination of federal constitutional and statutory provisions. Because most litigation about subject-matter jurisdiction concerns statutory questions, this chapter will focus primarily on federal statutory law. Interesting constitutional questions of less practical significance, mentioned in the notes, are usually covered in more detail in advanced courses such as Federal Courts.

Section A: Perspectives on Subject-Matter Jurisdiction

State-court systems have courts of *general jurisdiction*, which means that they are presumed to have jurisdiction over all subjects unless some statutory or constitutional provision deprives them of jurisdiction. Federal courts, on the other hand, are courts of *limited jurisdiction*, which means that they have only the jurisdiction affirmatively granted to them. Article III of the Constitution sets out the permissible boundaries of federal-court jurisdiction, which for our purposes includes primarily two kinds of cases: *federal-question* cases, in which the case "arises under" some federal law (including statutory law, constitutional law, and treaties), and *diversity* cases, in which the opposing parties are from different states. Pursuant to Article III, Congress has enacted statutory provisions granting jurisdiction in both types of cases. If a particular case does not meet the constitutional and statutory requirements for federal-court jurisdiction, then it must be litigated in state court — if at all. (A third important type of jurisdiction, not emphasized in first-year civil-procedure courses, is over cases involving the United States government or one of its agencies or officers as a party.)

As you read the following excerpts, think about why federal courts might be appropriate forums for these two types of cases, and where the line should be drawn between limited federal-court jurisdiction and residual state-court jurisdiction.

BURT NEUBORNE, THE MYTH OF PARITY

90 HARV. L. REV. 1105, 1120-25, 1127-28 (1977)

Concentrating . . . on an institutional comparison at the trial level, disclaiming any intent to cast aspersions on the good faith of state judges, and recognizing that both state and federal trial judges have roots in the communities they serve, three sets of reasons support a preference for a federal trial forum. First, the level of technical competence which the federal district court is likely to bring to the legal issues involved generally will be superior to that of a given state trial forum. Stated bluntly, in my experience, federal trial courts tend to be better equipped to analyze complex, often conflicting lines of authority and more likely to produce competently written, persuasive opinions than are state trial courts. Second, there are several factors, unrelated to technical competence — which, lacking a better term, I call a court's psychological set — that render it more likely that an individual with a constitutional claim will succeed in federal district court than in a state trial court. Finally, the federal judiciary's insulation from majoritarian pressures makes federal court structurally preferable to state trial court as a forum in which to challenge powerful local interests. . . .

Because it is relatively small, the federal trial bench maintains a level of competence in its pool of potential appointees which dwarfs the competence of the vastly larger pool from which state trial judges are selected. There are about twice as many trial judges in California as in the entire federal system. As in any bureaucracy, it is far easier to maintain a high level of quality when appointing a relatively small number of officials than when staffing a huge department. Additionally, there is a substantial disparity between state and federal judicial compensation which allows the federal bench to attract a higher level of legal talent than state trial courts can hope to obtain. . . .

The competence gap does not stem solely from the differences in the native ability of the judges. While it is often overlooked, the caliber of judicial clerks exerts a substantial impact on the quality of judicial output. Federal clerks at both the trial and appellate levels are chosen from among the most promising recent law school graduates for one- to two-year terms. State trial clerks, on the other hand, when available at all, tend to be either career bureaucrats or patronage employees and may lack both the ability and dedication of their federal counterparts. Moreover, while the caseload burden of the federal courts is substantial, it pales when compared to the caseload of most state trial courts of general jurisdiction. Thus, even if state and federal judges were of equal native ability, the advantages enjoyed by federal judges would probably result in a higher level of performance. When those institutional advantages are combined with the differential in native ability, the competence gap becomes pronounced. . . .

Even if state and federal forums were of equal technical competence, a series of psychological and attitudinal characteristics renders federal district judges more likely to enforce constitutional rights vigorously. First, although intangible, an elite tradition animates the federal judiciary, instilling elan and a sense of mission in federal judges and exerting, as Judge [Henry] Friendly[, an eminent twentieth-century Second Circuit judge,] has noted, a palpable influence on the quality of the judicial product. As heirs of a tradition of constitutional enforcement, federal judges feel subtle, yet nonetheless real pressures to uphold that tradition. State trial judges, on the other hand, generally seem to lack a comparable sense of tradition or institutional mission.

Second, federal judges often display an enhanced sense of bureaucratic receptivity to the pronouncements of the Supreme Court. State judges, of course, almost always recognize that they too are bound not to disregard the Supreme Court's interpretation of the Federal Constitution. Their bureaucratic relationship with the Supreme Court is, however, more attenuated than that of a district court judge. Although the effects of this difference are difficult to isolate with certainty, in my experience federal judges appear to recognize an affirmative obligation to carry out and even anticipate the direction of the Supreme Court. Many state judges, on the other hand, appear to acknowledge only an obligation not to disobey clearly established law. While this distinction is subtle, in the doubtful case it can exert a discernible impact on the trial level outcome. . . .

Constitutional adjudication inherently involves persuading a judicial forum to counter the will of the majority as expressed through its representatives. To the extent that the forum is itself subject to the political pressures which shaped the judgment it is asked to review, its capacity to provide sustained enforcement of countermajoritarian constitutional norms will be diminished. When one compares the institutional structure of the federal trial bench with state court structures, the functional superiority of federal courts as checks on majoritarian excess is pronounced.

Federal district judges, appointed for life and removable only by impeachment, are as insulated from majoritarian pressures as is functionally possible, precisely to insure their ability to enforce the Constitution without fear of reprisal. State trial judges, on the other hand, generally are elected for a fixed term, rendering them vulnerable to majoritarian pressure when deciding constitutional cases.

GIL SEINFELD, THE FEDERAL COURTS AS A FRANCHISE: RETHINKING THE JUSTIFICATIONS FOR FEDERAL QUESTION JURISDICTION

97 CAL. L. REV. 95, 97-99, 115, 124-25, 158-59 (2009)

Since 1875, the federal district courts have been vested with what is known as "general federal question jurisdiction" — original jurisdiction predicated on the presence in a suit of a [claim] of federal law. The conferral of such jurisdiction on the federal courts is typically justified on three grounds. First, state court judges are thought more likely than their federal counterparts to exhibit bias against claims sounding in federal law; second, federal courts are thought better able than state courts to supply a uniform interpretation of federal law; and third, federal judges are thought to have greater expertise than state court judges in the interpretation and application of federal law. By channeling federal question cases into the federal courts, the argument goes, we increase the likelihood of even-handed, uniform, expert adjudication of federal law. This "bias-uniformity-expertise" mantra lies at the core of judicial and scholarly discourse relating to federal question jurisdiction. It is incanted almost reflexively by courts when they craft doctrine governing the allocation of federal question cases between the state and federal judiciaries, and it is frequently the starting point for scholarly analysis of these doctrines.

Despite its prominence in judicial and academic discussions of federal jurisdiction, the bias-uniformity-expertise model has significant limitations. . . .

My critique of the bias prong of the conventional wisdom covers ground that others have been over before, so it is relatively brief. As the federal judiciary has become increasingly ideologically conservative, it has been noted that litigants pressing certain kinds of federal claims (specifically, claims of individual constitutional right) have fared increasingly poorly in federal court. It has been suggested, therefore, that it makes less sense today than it did decades ago to premise jurisdictional policy on the assumption that state courts are generally less willing than federal courts to vindicate federal claims. While it is too quick to leap from the premise that the federal judiciary has become more conservative to the conclusion that individual rights claimants will fare more poorly in the federal courts (much depends on the ideological valence of the particular claim at issue), these critiques highlight an important limit of the state bias argument for federal question jurisdiction. The argument is contingent on both historical and substantive factors, yet the conventional model makes no account of these contingencies. . . .

There are . . . myriad reasons to question the notion that the lower federal courts meaningfully advance the interest in a uniform interpretation of federal law. This notion appears to be partially premised on assumptions about the [small] overall size of the federal judiciary that are no longer valid; and it also rests on questionable assumptions about the relationship between the number of judges adjudicating a particular question and the measure of disuniformity we can expect those judges to produce. Moreover, . . . there is a growing body of evidence that when the need for a uniform interpretation of federal law is thought to be especially important, Congress and the Supreme Court are apt to channel cases away from the lower federal courts and to rely, instead, on adjudication by specialized courts and administrative agencies.

Of the conventional justifications for channeling federal question cases to the federal courts, the claim that federal judges have expertise in the interpretation of federal law is most compelling. . . . [But] federal judges are expert in the interpretation of federal law in a sense that is broad, but rather shallow, and the implications of such expertise for jurisdictional policy should be concomitantly modest. . . .

The principal challenge for the judge who would lay claim to general expertise in the interpretation of federal law is grappling with its sheer bulk. The U.S. Code currently includes some fifty Titles, while the Code of Federal Regulations has ballooned to more than 100,000 pages. Between 1974 and 1998, moreover, Congress created 474 new causes of action eligible for federal jurisdiction. . . .

Because of the explosion of federal law, it has become impossible for generalist judges sitting on federal district and circuit courts to develop specific expertise with respect to many of the subjects that come before them. . . .

[Rather,] the crucial distinctions between the state and federal courts are best captured by thinking of the federal courts as a kind of franchise — a group of local installations in a national chain, offering common rules of procedure and cultural norms, as well as a generally high measure of competence, to the litigants and lawyers who appear before them. These characteristics make the federal courts particularly attractive to lawyers and litigants who would, absent access to the federal judicial system, be forced to invest considerable time and energy getting up to speed on the distinct rules of practice and cultural norms applicable in state courtrooms across the country.

LARRY KRAMER, DIVERSITY JURISDICTION

1990 B.Y.U. L. REV. 97, 100, 102-07, 119-21

. . . Since at least the early 1970s, diversity cases have consistently accounted for 25% of the district courts' civil docket, 20% of the total district court docket, and 10 to 14% of the docket of the courts of appeals.

To gauge the full impact of diversity cases on the federal courts, we must adjust these raw caseload figures for the difficulty of diversity cases relative to other components of the courts' dockets. With respect to the district courts, two measures suggest that diversity cases are more demanding than the average case. First, diversity cases are overrepresented among trials, which place the greatest demand on the time and energy of federal district judges.... Second, diversity cases are more difficult than average according to a "time and motion" study of federal district judges conducted by the Federal Judicial Center in 1979....

A. The Case Against Diversity Jurisdiction

The numbers above suggest the most straightforward reason to eliminate diversity jurisdiction: abolishing it will significantly reduce the caseload problem in the federal courts. As Justice Frankfurter put it, "[a]n Act for the elimination of diversity jurisdiction could fairly be called an Act for the relief of the federal courts." Of course, eliminating any 25% share of the federal docket would relieve the federal caseload burden, and just as there should be no presumption in favor of retaining diversity, so there should be no presumption in favor of abolishing or curtailing it. Nonetheless, a number of additional reasons support making a cut here.

First, perhaps no other major class of cases has a weaker claim on federal judicial resources. There is no consensus on precisely how federal jurisdiction should be allocated, but there is agreement on general priorities. And one point on which there is virtual consensus is that state law cases deserve lower priority than cases based on federal law....

Second, beyond questions of federalism and the general preference for having federal courts decide federal questions and state courts decide state questions lies a simpler point about expertise and the efficient use of resources. Federal courts are capable of deciding state law questions, but they offer no special advantages in such cases; on most issues, and especially when it comes to interpreting state statutes, the state courts have greater expertise and authority. By the same token, federal jurisdiction does offer special advantages in federal question cases, where the benefits of experience and expertise undoubtedly lie in the federal courts. Thus, diversity jurisdiction forces federal courts to decide issues on which they have no special expertise at the expense of tasks they can perform significantly better than state courts.

Furthermore, federal diversity decisions are less valuable than either state court decisions or federal decisions in federal question cases. After *Erie Railroad v. Tompkins*, 304 U.S. 64 (1938) [*infra* p. 577], the opinion of a federal court sitting in diversity does not constitute precedent within the state system.... [D]iversity rulings "are in the nature of an advisory opinion whose contribution to establishing the law is at best uncertain." Diversity thus resembles arbitration because its primary value is limited to resolving the particular dispute before the court....

Third, diversity jurisdiction is frequently a source of friction between state and federal courts....

Fourth, the desire to minimize these frictions and to avoid federal interference with the development of state substantive law generates complex procedural problems that make it more expensive and time-consuming to litigate diversity cases. Some of these problems, such as the difficulties associated with administering the *Erie* doctrine, are familiar. . . .

Fifth, diversity jurisdiction reduces pressure to improve state judicial systems. Diversity provides litigants who satisfy its requirements a choice of forums, enabling them to pick the court that is "better" for them in any particular case. As such, its continued existence "diminishes the incentives for state court reform by those influential professional groups who, by virtue of diversity jurisdiction, are able to avoid litigation in the state courts."

Sixth, while it would be an overstatement to say that there are no benefits from diversity jurisdiction, most of its original justifications no longer exist. Commercial interests still appreciate the option of bringing or removing a case into federal court, but the interstate market is today sufficiently robust and established that this protection is unnecessary. . . .

One benefit of diversity jurisdiction undoubtedly remains. As the bar's overwhelming support for this jurisdiction demonstrates, diversity provides a forum that litigants (or at least their lawyers) find desirable and satisfactory. In addition to the tactical advantages a federal forum may offer, out-of-state attorneys may be more familiar with the federal rules of procedure and may desire the benefits such procedures provide. . . . [But] [f]orum shopping is regarded as an undesirable form of strategic behavior in every other context because it encourages wasteful investment of resources by both parties and courts. It is no less undesirable here. . . .

B. The Case for Diversity Jurisdiction

. . .

The "traditional, and most often cited, explanation of the purpose of diversity jurisdiction" is that it protects outsiders from state court discrimination. . . . [A]dvocates of diversity jurisdiction argue that bias is a problem and that it necessitates diversity jurisdiction, and many of their opponents regard this as the strongest argument for diversity jurisdiction.

. . . [This] bias argument is difficult to evaluate. The empirical data are sparse and inconsistent, suggesting that lawyers in some (mostly rural) areas still fear bias, while lawyers in other areas do not. Unfortunately, these studies test only lawyers' fears, not the reality of bias or even the fears of clients. . . . Advocates concede that xenophobia is less of a problem today than it was in the nineteenth century, but contend that "anyone who believes that there is no local chauvinism in the state courts is hiding his head somewhere." Opponents respond that the few cases in which bias against out-of-staters appears are the exceptions that prove the rule.

It seems clear that many other types of bias are far more prevalent today and far more likely to influence litigation than bias against citizens of other states. Judge Friendly has argued persuasively, for example, that in cases between corporations, or where the in-state party is a corporation, prejudice against the out-of-state party *qua* out-of-stater probably is non-existent. Even in personal injury cases between individuals, any prejudice against an out-of-state defendant more likely stems from the jury's suspicion that he or she is insured than from his residence.

In addition, the aid a federal court may render in the small class of cases in which bias is important is exceedingly limited. The same biased jurors serve in both state and federal courts, and the power of a federal judge to protect an out-of-stater by directing a verdict or by setting one aside is not great. . . .

Notes and Questions

1. Which is more important, federal-question jurisdiction or diversity jurisdiction? Note that Congress established diversity jurisdiction in 1789, but — except for a statute that was enacted in 1801 and repealed in 1802 — did not enact a general statute granting jurisdiction over federal-question cases until 1875. Think about how the United States has changed since 1789. Might that account for the relative importance of diversity and federal-question jurisdiction?

2. Many studies have tried to determine whether different forums produce different outcomes. They have reached conflicting results, especially on the question whether federal statutory or constitutional rights are better protected in federal court. Might it depend on the political composition of the federal courts, which depends on which party has recently been able to make appointments to the bench? Do Professor Neuborne's arguments transcend party affiliation? Professor Redish, elaborating on Professor Neuborne's thesis, has focused on cases in which plaintiffs allege that state laws (or actions by state officials) are unconstitutional. He argues that this type of case is especially inappropriate for state-court adjudication:

> Imagine, for a moment, that the Chicago Cubs announced that from this point forward, they would hire the umpires, unilaterally determine their salaries, and retain unreviewable discretion to fire them at any time. Can anyone imagine that we would trust a call at second base?

Martin H. Redish, *Judicial Parity, Litigant Choice, and Democratic Theory: A Comment on Federal Jurisdiction and Constitutional Rights*, 36 UCLA L. REV. 329, 333 (1988).

3. Are the arguments of Professors Neuborne and Seinfeld relevant to diversity jurisdiction, or only to federal-question jurisdiction? Professor Kramer suggests arguments in favor of diversity jurisdiction, and then attempts to refute them. Which side do you find more persuasive? Even if you find Professor Kramer's arguments persuasive, does it necessarily follow that we should abolish diversity jurisdiction altogether? What if lawyers — and, more important, their corporate clients — believe that local prejudice against out-of-state litigators still exists? Might abolishing diversity jurisdiction have a negative effect on interstate movement of capital? Can diversity jurisdiction be limited in ways that reduce the federal caseload but still allow the federal courts to serve a useful purpose in diversity cases?

Section B: Federal-Question Jurisdiction

Article III of the Constitution provides that "[t]he judicial power of the United States shall extend to all cases . . . arising under this Constitution, the laws of the United States, and treaties made . . . under their authority." The statutory grant of federal-question jurisdiction, 28 U.S.C. § 1331, uses almost identical language: "The district courts shall have original jurisdiction of all civil actions arising under the Constitution, laws, or treaties of the United States." What does it mean for a case to "arise under" federal law? Must the plaintiff be suing on a federal claim? What if the federal question is raised as a defense, or as part of a state-law claim? Should the "arising under" language of Article III and § 1331 be interpreted identically? Think about these questions as you read the following cases and notes.

1. The "Well-Pleaded Complaint" Rule

LOUISVILLE & NASHVILLE RAILROAD CO. V. MOTTLEY

211 U.S. 149 (1908)

Statement by MR. JUSTICE MOODY:

The appellees (husband and wife), being residents and citizens of Kentucky, brought this suit in equity in the Circuit Court of the United States for the Western District of Kentucky against the appellant, a railroad company and a citizen of the same State. The object of the suit was to compel the specific performance of [a] contract. . . .

The bill alleged that in September, 1871, plaintiffs, while passengers upon the defendant railroad, were injured by the defendant's negligence, and released their respective claims for damages in consideration of the agreement for transportation during their lives, expressed in the contract. It is alleged that the contract was performed by the defendant up to January 1, 1907, when the defendant declined to renew the passes. The bill then alleges that the refusal to comply with the contract was based solely upon that part of the act of Congress of June 29, 1906 which forbids the giving of free passes or free transportation. The bill further alleges: First, that the act of Congress referred to does not prohibit the giving of passes under the circumstances of this case; and, second, that, if the law is to be construed as prohibiting such passes, it is in conflict with the 5th Amendment of the Constitution, because it deprives the plaintiffs of their property without due process of law. . . . The judge of the Circuit Court . . . entered a decree for the relief prayed for, and the defendant appealed directly to this court.

■ MR. JUSTICE MOODY, after making the foregoing statement, delivered the opinion of the court.

Two questions of law . . . have been argued before us. They are, first, whether that part of the act of Congress of June 29, 1906 which forbids the giving of free passes or the collection of any different compensation for transportation of passengers than that specified in the tariff filed, makes it unlawful to perform a contract for transportation of persons who, in good faith, before the passage of the act, had accepted such contract in satisfaction of a valid cause of action against the railroad; and, second, whether the statute, if it should be construed to render such a contract unlawful, is in violation of the 5th Amendment of the Constitution of the United States. We do not deem it necessary, however, to consider either of these questions, because, in our opinion, the court below was without jurisdiction of the cause. Neither party has questioned that jurisdiction, but it is the duty of this court to see to it that the jurisdiction of the circuit court, which is defined and limited by statute, is not exceeded. . . .

There was no diversity of citizenship and it is not and cannot be suggested that there was any ground of jurisdiction, except that the case was a "suit . . . arising under the Constitution and laws of the United States." It is the settled interpretation of these words, as used in this statute, conferring jurisdiction, that a suit arises under the Constitution and laws of the United States only when the plaintiff's statement of his own cause of action shows that it is based upon those laws or that Constitution. It is not enough that the plaintiff alleges some anticipated defense to his cause of action and asserts that the defense is invalidated by some provision of the Constitution of the United States. Although such allegations show that very likely, in the course of the litigation, a question under the Constitution would arise, they do not show that the suit, that is, the plaintiff's original cause of action, arises under the Constitution. In *Tennessee v. Union & Planters' Bank*, 152 U. S. 454 (1894), the plaintiff, the State of Tennessee, brought suit in the circuit court of the United States to recover from the defendant certain taxes alleged to be due under the laws of the State. The plaintiff alleged that the defendant claimed an immunity from the taxation by virtue of its charter, and that therefore the tax was void, because in violation of the provision of the Constitution of the United States, which forbids any state from passing a law impairing the obligation of contracts. The cause was held to be beyond the jurisdiction of the circuit court, the court saying, by Mr. Justice Gray, "A suggestion of one party, that the other will or may set up a claim under the Constitution or laws of the United States, does not make the suit one arising under that Constitution or those laws." Again, in *Boston & Montana Consolidated Copper & Silver Mining Co. v. Montana Ore Purchasing Co.*, 188 U. S. 632 (1903), the plaintiff brought suit in the Circuit Court of the United States for the conversion of copper ore and for an injunction against its continuance. The plaintiff then alleged, for the purpose of showing jurisdiction, in substance, that the defendant would set up in defense certain laws of the United States. The cause was held to be beyond the jurisdiction of the Circuit Court, the court saying, by Mr. Justice Peckham:

> It would be wholly unnecessary and improper, in order to prove complainant's cause of action, to go into any matters of defense which the defendants might possibly set up, and then attempt to reply to such defence, and thus, if possible, to show that a Federal question might or

probably would arise in the course of the trial of the case. To allege such defence and then make an answer to it before the defendant has the opportunity to itself plead or prove its own defence is inconsistent with any known rule of pleading, so far as we are aware, and is improper.

The rule is a reasonable and just one that the complainant in the first instance shall be confined to a statement of its cause of action, leaving to the defendant to set up in his answer what his defence is, and, if anything more than a denial of complainant's cause of action, imposing upon the defendant the burden of proving such defence....

The only way in which it might be claimed that a Federal question was presented would be in the complainant's statement of what the defence of defendants would be, and complainant's answer to such defence. Under these circumstances the case is brought within the rule laid down in *Tennessee v. Union & Planters' Bank*. That case has been cited and approved many times since.

... The application of this rule to the case at bar is decisive against the jurisdiction of the Circuit Court.

It is ordered that the judgment be reversed and the case remitted to the circuit court with instructions to dismiss the suit for want of jurisdiction.

Notes and Questions

1. The rule of *Mottley* is often called the "well-pleaded complaint" rule, and is interpreted to require that the federal question be *necessary* to a well-pleaded complaint. How should we determine whether a particular federal question is necessary to a well-pleaded complaint? (Hint: what happens if you subject the Mottleys' complaint, minus the federal question, to a 12(b)(6) motion?) What should happen if there are multiple counts in a complaint, some of which rest on federal grounds and some of which do not? Think again about Rule 12(b)(6) in answering this question.

2. *Mottley* means that a case raising a federal defense (but no federal claim) cannot be brought in federal district court, even if both parties agree that the federal question is the only disputed issue in the case. Should that be the rule? If you conclude that the rule is too harsh, think about what might happen if federal defenses were held to confer federal jurisdiction, and plaintiffs could anticipate federal defenses in the complaint. Is there any middle ground between *Mottley* and a rule allowing federal jurisdiction based on the anticipation of federal defenses?

3. Does the well-pleaded complaint rule mean that litigants like the Mottleys (and the railroad) will *never* have a federal court consider their federal questions? Look at 28 U.S.C. § 1257. Is Supreme Court review of state court rulings adequate to achieve the goals noted by Professors Neuborne and Seinfeld? In fact, after the Supreme Court's decision in *Mottley*, the Mottleys sued the railroad in Kentucky state court and won. The Supreme Court ultimately reversed the Kentucky court, holding that

the federal statute precluded the issuance of passes and that the statute was constitutional. Louisville & Nashville R.R. v. Mottley, 219 U.S. 467 (1911).

4. The well-pleaded complaint rule is an interpretation of § 1331. The scope of the constitutional "arising under" language, which is nearly identical in its language to § 1331, has been interpreted more broadly. In *Osborn v. Bank of the United States*, 22 U.S. (9 Wheat.) 738 (1824), Chief Justice Marshall considered whether the Bank could sue in federal court to obtain an injunction preventing Osborn, a state official, from collecting state-imposed taxes from the Bank. The Court had already held, in *McCulloch v. Maryland*, 17 U.S. (4 Wheat.) 316 (1819), that state taxes on the national Bank were unconstitutional. The federal statute creating the Bank was first interpreted to confer federal jurisdiction on all suits brought by the Bank, and the Court in *Osborn* then had to decide whether that statutory grant of jurisdiction was constitutional.

The Bank's complaint — that Osborn would be acting in violation of the Constitution if he collected monies from the Bank — involved a federal question, and thus satisfied what would eventually become the well-pleaded complaint rule. But Marshall's opinion went further in two respects. First, he suggested that it is "a sufficient foundation for jurisdiction, that the title or right set up by the party, may be defeated by one construction of the constitution or law of the United States, and sustained by the opposite construction." Thus, Article III allows jurisdiction on the basis of federal *defenses* even in the absence of any federal *claims*. It follows that Congress could abolish the well-pleaded complaint rule by amending § 1331.

The more controversial part of Marshall's opinion addressed cases in which no federal question was actually raised by either party. He noted that whether the Bank, a federally-created entity, had a right to sue, was "an original ingredient in every [case]." 22 U.S. at 824. That question (involving federal law) served to confer federal jurisdiction on *every* case brought by the Bank, "[w]hether it be in fact relied on or not, in the defence." Justice Johnson disagreed with Marshall, saying that the "possibility" that "a constitutional question may be raised in any conceivable suit . . . would be a very insufficient ground for assuming . . . jurisdiction." *Id.* at 886-87.

Although Marshall's very broad interpretation of Article III might have been considered dictum in *Osborn*, it was relied on without discussion in a companion case, *Bank of the United States v. Planters' Bank of Georgia*, 22 U.S. (9 Wheat.) 904 (1824). In *Planters' Bank*, the national Bank brought suit in federal court to recover, under state law, on notes issued by the Planters' Bank. No federal question was raised in the case, but the Court found federal jurisdiction. Marshall disposed of the question of jurisdiction merely by noting that it was "fully considered by the Court in the case of *Osborn[ ] v. The Bank of the United States*, and it is unnecessary to repeat the reasoning used in that case." *Id.* at 905; *see also* Am. Nat'l Red Cross v. S.G., 505 U.S. 247 (1992) (holding that "sued and be sued" provision in federal statute chartering Red Cross creates federal jurisdiction in all cases involving Red Cross); Verlinden B.V. v. Cent. Bank of Nigeria, 461 U.S. 480 (1983) (implicitly reaffirming *Osborn*).

Questions have also arisen about whether Congress can constitutionally grant jurisdiction to protect federal *interests*, even when no federal question is or could be present in the case. Commentators have labeled this idea "protective jurisdiction." In *Textile Workers Union v. Lincoln Mills of Alabama*, 353 U.S. 448 (1957), two concurring Justices endorsed protective jurisdiction, but no majority opinion has either adopted or repudiated it. It seems unlikely that the Supreme Court would adopt the theory. In *Mesa v. California*, 489 U.S. 121, 136-38 (1989), a unanimous Court rejected a broad interpretation of a removal statute and expressly declined to adopt a protective-jurisdiction theory urged upon it, hinting that the idea could raise "grave constitutional questions." For further discussion of protective jurisdiction, see Paul J. Mishkin, *The Federal "Question" in the District Courts*, 53 COLUM. L. REV. 157 (1953); Herbert Wechsler, *Federal Jurisdiction and the Revision of the Judicial Code*, 13 LAW & CONTEMP. PROBS. 216 (Winter 1948).

5. Section 1331 says nothing about *concurrent state-court jurisdiction*. In fact, most cases arising under federal law can be brought in either state or federal court, at the plaintiff's option. Congress does have the power to create *exclusive federal jurisdiction*, and thereby prohibit state courts from exercising jurisdiction over particular federal questions. However, federal jurisdiction is presumed to be concurrent, rather than exclusive, unless there is evidence that Congress intended federal courts to have exclusive jurisdiction. For examples of exclusive jurisdiction, see 28 U.S.C. §§ 1333 (admiralty), 1334 (bankruptcy), and 1338 (patents and copyrights). Why might Congress have wanted federal jurisdiction to be exclusive in these sorts of cases? The Supreme Court has also confirmed that when Congress explicitly grants jurisdiction to *state* courts to adjudicate federal questions, there is a presumption of concurrent federal-court jurisdiction as well. Mims v. Arrow Fin. Servs., LLC, 565 U.S. 368 (2012).

6. Plaintiffs sometimes have related federal-law and state-law claims, which would let them bring their entire case in federal court (with the state claims coming along under the supplemental-jurisdiction statute, *see infra* pp. 556-73). If they prefer to sue in state court and not be subject to removal (*see infra* pp. 567-73) because of the federal claims, they may sue on the state claims only. If the parties are citizens of the same state, there is no basis for federal jurisdiction. But sometimes federal law does not create a claim in addition to a state claim; it takes over from or "preempts" the state claim. Many claims involving pension agreements, for example, are governed by the federal Employee Retirement Income and Security Act (ERISA), which is often interpreted to preempt what might be otherwise applicable state law in this area. So an employee with a preempted claim based on a pension contract may not stay in state court by pleading just a state-law contract claim in a suit against a nondiverse defendant. Such a claim is regarded as really an ERISA claim — preemption doesn't mean that the employee has no claim, just that it's turned into a federal claim — and the defendant may remove the case to federal court. In this situation it is said that plaintiffs cannot defeat federal jurisdiction by "artful pleading."

2. Sufficiency of the Federal Question

Under *Mottley*, a claim based on *federal* law will confer federal jurisdiction as long as the federal question is necessary to the complaint. That straightforward approach handles with little or no difficulty the jurisdictional question in the overwhelming majority of § 1331 cases. So, for example, there is always federal-question jurisdiction over an antitrust action, a Title VII suit, or a claimed violation of federal constitutional rights.

But there is a small (we do mean small, despite the amount of material that follows), vexing corner of this area that the Supreme Court has kept revisiting in a surprising number of cases for about a century now: what about a *state* claim that turns on federal law, as, for example, when a state statute incorporates a federal standard? A significant issue under § 1331 involves federal questions that are embedded in state-law claims. To the extent that such a claim turns on a question of federal law, the complaint satisfies the *Mottley* rule, but the Court has equivocated about when such a claim is sufficient to confer federal-court jurisdiction.

The line of modern cases considering embedded federal questions begins with *Smith v. Kansas City Title & Trust Co.*, 255 U.S. 180 (1921). In *Smith*, plaintiffs sued in federal court to enjoin the defendant from purchasing certain bonds. They brought suit under state-law doctrines prohibiting companies from investing in "unauthorized" bonds, and alleged that the bonds were unauthorized (under state law) because they were issued by the federal government in violation of the federal Constitution. Thus, in order to decide whether plaintiffs should prevail on their state-law claim, a court would necessarily have to decide the federal constitutional question. *Smith* held in favor of federal jurisdiction on the ground that "the right to relief depends on the construction or application of" federal law. *Id.* at 199.

Apparently contrary to *Smith* is *Moore v. Chesapeake & Ohio Railway Co.*, 291 U.S. 205 (1934). The plaintiff in that case brought suit in federal court under the state Employers' Liability Act. The state statute provided that the plaintiff-employee could not be held guilty of contributory negligence or assumption of risk — partial defenses to the defendants' liability — if the employer's actions had been in violation of "any statute, state or federal, enacted for the safety of the employee." The plaintiff claimed that the defendant had violated the Federal Safety Appliance Acts. As in *Smith*, in order to decide whether the plaintiff could recover on the particular claim at issue, a court would have to decide whether the employer had violated federal law. The Supreme Court held that the case did not "arise under" federal law for purposes of § 1331.

One way to reconcile *Smith* and *Moore* might be to apply *Mottley*: we might characterize the federal question in *Moore* as an anticipated federal defense. The Supreme Court did not take that route, however. It characterized the complaint as alleging that violation of the federal act constituted negligence *per se*, not as anticipating a defense. It also did not mention *Mottley*, but rather held that a suit that "brings within the purview of the [state] statute a breach of the duty imposed by the federal statute" does not arise under the laws of the United States. Note that the Supreme Court has never relied on *Moore*, nor is it cited at all in the most recent cases.

Merrell Dow Pharmaceuticals Inc. v. Thompson, 478 U.S. 804 (1986), is another precedent on this issue. In *Merrell Dow*, plaintiffs sued a pharmaceutical manufacturer for negligence and other state-law torts in connection with the manufacture and sale of the drug Bendectin, which they alleged caused birth defects when taken by pregnant women. In Count IV of the complaint, the plaintiffs alleged that Bendectin was "misbranded" in violation of the federal Food, Drug, and Cosmetic Act (FDCA) because it failed to provide adequate warnings. That misbranding was alleged to constitute a rebuttable presumption of negligence under state law. Recovery on this (state-law) count thus depended on the meaning of the FDCA.

The *Merrell Dow* Court nevertheless held that the case did not "arise under" federal law for purposes of § 1331. The Court first stressed that in the context of federal-law questions embedded in state causes of action, "determinations about federal jurisdiction require sensitive judgments about congressional intent, judicial power, and the federal system." *Id.* at 810. Part of that determination, the Court said (quoting Justice Cardozo in *Gully v. First National Bank*, 299 U.S. 109, 118 (1936)), involves "a selective process which picks [out] the substantial causes . . . and lays the other ones aside." 478 U.S. at 813-14. In holding that the FDCA question was not "substantial," the Court rested heavily (some might say exclusively) on the fact that Congress had not created a private cause of action under the FDCA — that is, that no individual could sue directly for a violation of the FDCA: "We conclude that a complaint alleging a violation of a federal statute as an element of a state cause of action, when Congress has determined that there should be no private, federal cause of action for the violation, does not state a claim 'arising under the Constitution, laws, or treaties of the United States.'" *Id.* at 817.

Much confusion among both scholars and lower courts followed in the wake of *Merrell Dow*. Some thought the test was a free-floating assessment of "substantiality," some thought the resolution depended entirely on whether Congress had created a private cause of action, and others tried to combine the two approaches. The Court returned to this small but difficult corner of federal-question jurisdiction in the following case.

GRABLE & SONS METAL PRODUCTS, INC. V. DARUE ENGINEERING & MANUFACTURING

545 U.S. 308 (2005)

■ JUSTICE SOUTER delivered the opinion for a unanimous Court.

The question is whether want of a federal cause of action to try claims of title to land obtained at a federal tax sale precludes removal to federal court of a state action with non-diverse parties raising a disputed issue of federal title law. We answer no, and hold that the national interest in providing a federal forum for federal tax litigation is sufficiently substantial to support the exercise of federal question jurisdiction over the disputed issue on removal, which would not distort any division of labor between the state and federal courts, provided or assumed by Congress.

I

[The Internal Revenue Service seized Grable's property because Grable owed back taxes. The IRS sold the property to Darue, after notifying Grable of the impending sale by certified mail. Grable later sued Darue in state court on a state-law claim to "quiet title" (that is, to declare Grable the owner), arguing that Darue's title was invalid because 26 U.S.C. § 6335 required the IRS to give Grable notice of the sale by personal service, not certified mail. Darue removed the case to Federal District Court because the title claim depended on an interpretation of federal tax law. The District Court and the Court of Appeals both held that there was federal jurisdiction, and both ruled for Darue on the merits.]

II

Darue was entitled to remove the quiet title action if Grable could have brought it in federal district court originally, 28 U.S.C. § 1441(a), as a civil action "arising under the Constitution, laws, or treaties of the United States," *id.* § 1331. This provision for federal-question jurisdiction is invoked by and large by plaintiffs pleading a cause of action created by federal law . . . . There is, however, another longstanding, if less frequently encountered, variety of federal "arising under" jurisdiction, this Court having recognized for nearly 100 years that in certain cases federal question jurisdiction will lie over state-law claims that implicate significant federal issues. *E.g.,* Hopkins v. Walker, 244 U.S. 486, 490-91 (1917). The doctrine captures the commonsense notion that a federal court ought to be able to hear claims recognized under state law that nonetheless turn on substantial questions of federal law, and thus justify resort to the experience, solicitude, and hope of uniformity that a federal forum offers on federal issues.

The classic example is *Smith v. Kansas City Title & Trust Co.*, 255 U.S. 180 (1921), a suit by a shareholder claiming that the defendant corporation could not lawfully buy certain bonds of the National Government because their issuance was unconstitutional. Although Missouri law provided the cause of action, the Court recognized federal-question jurisdiction because the principal issue in the case was the federal constitutionality of the bond issue. *Smith* thus held, in a somewhat generous statement of the scope of the doctrine, that a state-law claim could give rise to federal-question jurisdiction so long as it "appears from the [complaint] that the right to relief depends upon the construction or application of [federal law]."

The *Smith* statement has been subject to some trimming to fit earlier and later cases recognizing the vitality of the basic doctrine, but shying away from the expansive view that mere need to apply federal law in a state-law claim will suffice to open the "arising under" door.... It has in fact become a constant refrain in such cases that federal jurisdiction demands not only a contested federal issue, but a substantial one, indicating a serious federal interest in claiming the advantages thought to be inherent in a federal forum.

But even when the state action discloses a contested and substantial federal question, the exercise of federal jurisdiction is subject to a possible veto. For the federal issue will ultimately qualify for a federal forum only if federal jurisdiction is consistent with congressional judgment about the sound division of labor between state and federal courts governing the application of § 1331. . . . Because arising-under jurisdiction to hear a state-law claim always raises the possibility of upsetting the state-federal line drawn (or at least assumed) by Congress, the presence of a disputed federal issue and the ostensible importance of a federal forum are never necessarily dispositive; there must always be an assessment of any disruptive portent in exercising federal jurisdiction.

These considerations have kept us from stating a "single, precise, all-embracing" test for jurisdiction over federal issues embedded in state-law claims between nondiverse parties. We have not kept them out simply because they appeared in state raiment, as Justice Holmes would have done, *see Smith*, 255 U.S. at 214 (dissenting opinion), but neither have we treated "federal issue" as a password opening federal courts to any state action embracing a point of federal law. Instead, the question is, does a state-law claim necessarily raise a stated federal issue, actually disputed and substantial, which a federal forum may entertain without disturbing any congressionally approved balance of federal and state judicial responsibilities.

III

A

This case warrants federal jurisdiction. Grable's state complaint must specify "the facts establishing the superiority of [its] claim," and Grable has premised its superior title claim on a failure by the IRS to give it adequate notice, as defined by federal law. Whether Grable was given notice within the meaning of the federal statute is thus an essential element of its quiet title claim, and the meaning of the federal statute is actually in dispute; it appears to be the only legal or factual issue contested in the case. The meaning of the federal tax provision is an important issue of federal law that sensibly belongs in a federal court. The Government has a strong interest in the "prompt and certain collection of delinquent taxes," and the ability of the IRS to satisfy its claims from the property of delinquents requires clear terms of notice to allow buyers like Darue to satisfy themselves that the Service has touched the bases necessary for good title. The Government thus has a direct interest in the availability of a federal forum to vindicate its own administrative action, and buyers (as well as tax delinquents) may find it valuable to come before judges used to federal tax matters. Finally, because it will be the rare state title case that raises a contested matter of federal law, federal jurisdiction to resolve genuine disagreement over federal tax title provisions will portend only a microscopic effect on the federal-state division of labor. . . .

B

Merrell Dow Pharmaceuticals Inc. v. Thompson, 478 U.S. 804 (1986), on which Grable rests its position, is not to the contrary. *Merrell Dow* considered a state tort claim resting in part on the allegation that the defendant drug company had violated a federal misbranding prohibition, and was thus presumptively negligent under Ohio law. The Court assumed that federal law would have to be applied to resolve the claim, but after closely examining the strength of the federal interest at stake and the implications of opening the federal forum, held federal jurisdiction unavailable. Congress had not provided a private federal cause of action for violation of the federal branding requirement, and the Court found "it would . . . flout, or at least undermine, congressional intent to conclude that federal courts might nevertheless exercise federal-question jurisdiction and provide remedies for violations of that federal statute solely because the violation . . . is said to be a . . . 'proximate cause' under state law."

Because federal law provides for no quiet title action that could be brought against Darue, Grable argues that there can be no federal jurisdiction here, stressing some broad language in *Merrell Dow* (including the passage just quoted) that on its face supports Grable's position. But an opinion is to be read as a whole, and *Merrell Dow* cannot be read whole as overturning decades of precedent, as it would have done by effectively adopting the Holmes dissent in *Smith,* and converting a federal cause of action from a sufficient condition for federal-question jurisdiction into a necessary one.

. . . *Merrell Dow* disclaimed the adoption of any bright-line rule. . . . *Merrell Dow* then, did not toss out, but specifically retained the contextual enquiry that had been *Smith's* hallmark for over 60 years. . . .

Accordingly, *Merrell Dow* should be read in its entirety as treating the absence of a federal private right of action as evidence relevant to, but not dispositive of, the "sensitive judgments about congressional intent" that § 1331 requires. The absence of any federal cause of action affected *Merrell Dow's* result two ways. The Court saw the fact as worth some consideration in the assessment of substantiality. But its primary importance emerged when the Court treated the combination of no federal cause of action and no preemption of state remedies for misbranding as an important clue to Congress's conception of the scope of jurisdiction to be exercised under § 1331. The Court saw the missing cause of action not as a missing federal door key, always required, but as a missing welcome mat, required in the circumstances, when exercising federal jurisdiction over a state misbranding action would have attracted a horde of original filings and removal cases raising other state claims with embedded federal issues. For if the federal labeling standard without a federal cause of action could get a state claim into federal court, so could any other federal standard without a federal cause of action. And that would have meant a tremendous number of cases.

. . . Expressing concern over the "increased volume of federal litigation," and noting the importance of adhering to "legislative intent," *Merrell Dow* thought it improbable that the Congress, having made no provision for a federal cause of action, would have meant to welcome any state-law tort case implicating federal law "solely because the violation of the federal statute is said to [create] a rebuttable presumption [of negligence] . . . under state law." In this situation, no welcome mat meant keep out. *Merrell Dow's* analysis thus fits within the framework of examining the importance of having a federal forum for the issue, and the consistency of such a forum with Congress's intended division of labor between state and federal courts.

As already indicated, however, a comparable analysis yields a different jurisdictional conclusion in this case. Although Congress also indicated ambivalence in this case by providing no private right of action to Grable, it is the rare state quiet title action that involves contested issues of federal law. Consequently, jurisdiction over actions like Grable's would not materially affect, or threaten to affect, the normal currents of litigation. Given the absence of threatening structural consequences and the clear interest the Government, its buyers, and its delinquents have in the availability of a federal forum, there is no good reason to shirk from federal jurisdiction over the dispositive and contested federal issue at the heart of the state-law title claim.

IV

The judgment of the Court of Appeals, upholding federal jurisdiction over Grable's quiet title action, is affirmed.

■ JUSTICE THOMAS, concurring.

The Court faithfully applies our precedents interpreting 28 U.S.C. § 1331 to authorize federal-court jurisdiction over some cases in which state law creates the cause of action but requires determination of an issue of federal law. In this case, no one has asked us to overrule those precedents and adopt the rule Justice Holmes set forth in *American Well Works Co. v. Layne & Bowler Co.*, 241 U.S. 257 (1916), limiting § 1331 jurisdiction to cases in which federal law creates the cause of action pleaded on the face of the plaintiff's complaint. In an appropriate case, and perhaps with the benefit of better evidence as to the original meaning of § 1331's text, I would be willing to consider that course.

Jurisdictional rules should be clear. Whatever the virtues of the *Smith* standard, it is anything but clear. . . .

Whatever the vices of the *American Well Works* rule, it is clear. Moreover, it accounts for the "vast majority" of cases that come within § 1331 under our current case law — further indication that trying to sort out which cases fall within the smaller *Smith* category may not be worth the effort it entails.

Notes and Questions

1. The Supreme Court distinguished *Grable* in *Empire HealthChoice Assurance, Inc. v. McVeigh*, 547 U.S. 677 (2006). In *Empire HealthChoice*, an insurer contracted with the federal government to cover medical expenses for federal employees. After the insurer had paid an injured employee's medical expenses, the employee's estate settled a state-court tort suit for his injuries. The insurer then filed in federal court a subrogation claim to recover the value of the medical expenses that it had previously disbursed. While a federal statute governed the relationship between the insurer and the government, and also preempted state law on coverage and benefits, the statute said nothing about subrogation and did not expressly confer federal jurisdiction over such claims. Among other arguments, the insurer contended that the suit was within federal-question jurisdiction under *Grable* because federal law was a "necessary element" of the insurer's claim for relief. The Court rejected that argument, concluding that the case did "not fit within the special and small category" defined by *Grable*:

> This case is poles apart from *Grable*. The dispute there centered on the action of a federal agency (IRS) and its compatibility with a federal statute, the question qualified as "substantial," and its resolution was both dispositive of the case and would be controlling in numerous other cases. Here, the reimbursement claim was triggered, not by the action of any federal department, agency, or service, but by the settlement of a personal-injury action launched in state court, and the bottom-line practical issue is the share of that settlement properly payable to Empire.
>
> *Grable* presented a nearly "pure issue of law," one "that could be settled once and for all and thereafter would govern numerous tax sale cases." In contrast, Empire's reimbursement claim . . . is fact-bound and situation-specific. [*Id.* at 700-01.]

2. Lower courts had some difficulty applying the test announced in *Grable*. One recurring issue was whether state-law malpractice actions that arose from the lawyer's missteps in a federal-question case — and thus turned on an interpretation of federal law — gave rise to federal jurisdiction. The Supreme Court addressed that situation in the following case.

GUNN V. MINTON

568 U.S. 251 (2013)

■ CHIEF JUSTICE ROBERTS delivered the opinion for a unanimous Court.

Federal courts have exclusive jurisdiction over cases "arising under any Act of Congress relating to patents." 28 U.S.C. § 1338(a). The question presented is whether a state law claim alleging legal malpractice in the handling of a patent case must be brought in federal court.

I

[Minton developed a computer program and telecommunications network, and leased his inventions to a third party for more than a year before he obtained a patent. Minton later sued two defendants for patent infringement in federal court. The defendants won a summary-judgment motion because patents that have been "on sale" for more than a year are invalid. Minton's attorneys, Gunn and several others, did not raise an "experimental-use" exception to the "on sale" doctrine. When the attorneys did raise it, on a motion for reconsideration and then on appeal, the courts held that it had been waived.

[Convinced that his attorneys' failure to raise the experimental-use argument cost him the lawsuit and led to the invalidation of his patent, Minton brought a malpractice action in Texas state court. The state trial court granted summary judgment against Minton.]

On appeal, Minton raised a new argument: Because his legal malpractice claim was based on an alleged error in a patent case, it "aris[es] under" federal patent law for purposes of 28 U.S.C. § 1338(a). And because, under § 1338(a), "[n]o State court shall have jurisdiction over any claim for relief arising under any Act of Congress relating to patents," the Texas court — where Minton had originally brought his malpractice claim — lacked subject matter jurisdiction to decide the case. Accordingly, Minton argued, the trial court's order should be vacated and the case dismissed, leaving Minton free to start over in the Federal District Court.

The Supreme Court of Texas [ultimately] concluded that Minton's claim involved "a substantial federal issue" within the meaning of *Grable* [*supra* p. 522] "because the success of Minton's malpractice claim is reliant upon the viability of the experimental use exception as a defense to the on-sale bar." Adjudication of Minton's claim in federal court was consistent with the appropriate balance between federal and state judicial responsibilities, it held, because "the federal government and patent litigants have an interest in the uniform application of patent law by courts well-versed in that subject matter." . . .

II

"Federal courts are courts of limited jurisdiction," possessing "only that power authorized by Constitution and statute." There is no dispute that the Constitution permits Congress to extend federal court jurisdiction to a case such as this one, *see Osborn v. Bank of United States*, 22 U.S. (9 Wheat.) 738, 823-24 (1824); the question is whether Congress has done so.

As relevant here, Congress has authorized the federal district courts to exercise original jurisdiction in "all civil actions arising under the Constitution, laws, or treaties of the United States," 28 U.S.C. § 1331, and, more particularly, over "any civil action arising under any Act of Congress relating to patents," § 1338(a). Adhering to the demands of "[l]inguistic consistency," we have interpreted the phrase "arising under" in both sections identically, applying our § 1331 and § 1338(a) precedents interchangeably. For cases falling within the patent-specific arising under jurisdiction of § 1338(a), however, Congress has not only provided for federal jurisdiction but also eliminated state jurisdiction, decreeing that "[n]o State court shall have jurisdiction over any claim for relief arising under any Act of Congress relating to patents." § 1338(a). To determine whether jurisdiction was proper in the Texas courts, therefore, we must determine whether it would have been proper in a federal district court — whether, that is, the case "aris[es] under any Act of Congress relating to patents."

For statutory purposes, a case can "aris[e] under" federal law in two ways. Most directly, a case arises under federal law when federal law creates the cause of action asserted. *See* Am. Well Works Co. v. Layne & Bowler Co., 241 U.S. 257, 260 (1916) ("A suit arises under the law that creates the cause of action"). As a rule of inclusion, this "creation" test admits of only extremely rare exceptions, *see, e.g.*, Shoshone Mining Co. v. Rutter, 177 U.S. 505 (1900), and accounts for the vast bulk of suits that arise under federal law. . . .

But even where a claim finds its origins in state rather than federal law — as Minton's legal malpractice claim indisputably does — we have identified a "special and small category" of cases in which arising under jurisdiction still lies. In outlining the contours of this slim category, we do not paint on a blank canvas. Unfortunately, the canvas looks like one that Jackson Pollock got to first.

In an effort to bring some order to this unruly doctrine several Terms ago, we condensed our prior cases into the following inquiry: Does the "state-law claim necessarily raise a stated federal issue, actually disputed and substantial, which a federal forum may entertain without disturbing any congressionally approved balance of federal and state judicial responsibilities"? *Grable*, 545 U.S. at 314. That is, federal jurisdiction over a state law claim will lie if a federal issue is: (1) necessarily raised, (2) actually disputed, (3) substantial, and (4) capable of resolution in federal court without disrupting the federal-state balance approved by Congress. Where all four of these requirements are met, we held, jurisdiction is proper because there is a "serious federal interest in claiming the advantages thought to be inherent in a federal forum," which can be vindicated without disrupting Congress's intended division of labor between state and federal courts.

III

Applying *Grable*'s inquiry here, it is clear that Minton's legal malpractice claim does not arise under federal patent law. Indeed, for the reasons we discuss, we are comfortable concluding that state legal malpractice claims based on underlying patent matters will rarely, if ever, arise under federal patent law for purposes of § 1338(a). Although such cases may necessarily raise disputed questions of patent law, those cases are by their nature unlikely to have the sort of significance for the federal system necessary to establish jurisdiction.

A

To begin, we acknowledge that resolution of a federal patent question is "necessary" to Minton's case. Under Texas law, a plaintiff alleging legal malpractice must establish four elements: (1) that the defendant attorney owed the plaintiff a duty; (2) that the attorney breached that duty; (3) that the breach was the proximate cause of the plaintiff's injury; and (4) that damages occurred. In cases like this one, in which the attorney's alleged error came in failing to make a particular argument, the causation element requires a "case within a case" analysis of whether, had the argument been made, the outcome of the earlier litigation would have been different. To prevail on his legal malpractice claim, therefore, Minton must show that he would have prevailed in his federal patent infringement case if only petitioners had timely made an experimental-use argument on his behalf. That will necessarily require application of patent law to the facts of Minton's case.

B

The federal issue is also "actually disputed" here — indeed, on the merits, it is the central point of dispute. Minton argues that the experimental-use exception properly applied to his lease to Stark, saving his patent from the on-sale bar; petitioners argue that it did not. This is just the sort of "dispute . . . respecting the . . . effect of [federal] law" that *Grable* envisioned.

C

Minton's argument founders on *Grable*'s next requirement, however, for the federal issue in this case is not substantial in the relevant sense. In reaching the opposite conclusion, the Supreme Court of Texas focused on the importance of the issue to the plaintiff's case and to the parties before it. As our past cases show, however, it is not enough that the federal issue be significant to the particular parties in the immediate suit; that will always be true when the state claim "necessarily raise[s]" a disputed federal issue, as *Grable* separately requires. The substantiality inquiry under *Grable* looks instead to the importance of the issue to the federal system as a whole.

In *Grable* itself, for example, the Internal Revenue Service had seized property from the plaintiff and sold it to satisfy the plaintiff's federal tax delinquency. Five years later, the plaintiff filed a state law quiet title action against the third party that had purchased the property, alleging that the IRS had failed to comply with certain federally imposed notice requirements, so that the seizure and sale were invalid. In holding that the case arose under federal law, we primarily focused not on the interests of the litigants themselves, but rather on the broader significance of the notice question for the Federal Government. We emphasized the Government's "strong interest" in being able to recover delinquent taxes through seizure and sale of property, which in turn "require[d] clear terms of notice to allow buyers . . . to satisfy themselves that the Service has touched the bases necessary for good title." The Government's "direct interest in the availability of a federal forum to vindicate its own administrative action" made the question "an important issue of federal law that sensibly belong[ed] in a federal court."

A second illustration of the sort of substantiality we require comes from *Smith v. Kansas City Title & Trust Co.*, 255 U.S. 180 (1921), which *Grable* described as "[t]he classic example" of a state claim arising under federal law. In *Smith*, the plaintiff argued that the defendant bank could not purchase certain bonds issued by the Federal Government because the Government had acted unconstitutionally in issuing them. We held that the case arose under federal law, because the "decision depends upon the determination" of "the constitutional validity of an act of Congress which is directly drawn in question." Again, the relevant point was not the importance of the question to the parties alone but rather the importance more generally of a determination that the Government "securities were issued under an unconstitutional law, and hence of no validity." *See also* Merrell Dow Pharms. Inc. v. Thompson, 478 U.S. 804, 814, n.12 (1986).

Here, the federal issue carries no such significance. Because of the backward-looking nature of a legal malpractice claim, the question is posed in a merely hypothetical sense: If Minton's lawyers had raised a timely experimental-use argument, would the result in the patent infringement proceeding have been different? No matter how the state courts resolve that hypothetical "case within a case," it will not change the real-world result of the prior federal patent litigation. Minton's patent will remain invalid.

Nor will allowing state courts to resolve these cases undermine "the development of a uniform body of [patent] law." Congress ensured such uniformity by vesting exclusive jurisdiction over actual patent cases in the federal district courts and exclusive appellate jurisdiction in the Federal Circuit. In resolving the nonhypothetical patent questions those cases present, the federal courts are of course not bound by state court case-within-a-case patent rulings. In any event, the state court case-within-a-case inquiry asks what would have happened in the prior federal proceeding if a particular argument had been made. In answering that question, state courts can be expected to hew closely to the pertinent federal precedents. It is those precedents, after all, that would have applied had the argument been made.

As for more novel questions of patent law that may arise for the first time in a state court "case within a case," they will at some point be decided by a federal court in the context of an actual patent case, with review in the Federal Circuit. If the question arises frequently, it will soon be resolved within the federal system, laying to rest any contrary state court precedent; if it does not arise frequently, it is unlikely to implicate substantial federal interests. The present case is "poles apart from *Grable*," in which a state court's resolution of the federal question "would be controlling in numerous other cases." . . .

Nor can we accept the suggestion that the federal courts' greater familiarity with patent law means that legal malpractice cases like this one belong in federal court. It is true that a similar interest was among those we considered in *Grable*. But the possibility that a state court will incorrectly resolve a state claim is not, by itself, enough to trigger the federal courts' exclusive patent jurisdiction, even if the potential error finds its root in a misunderstanding of patent law.

There is no doubt that resolution of a patent issue in the context of a state legal malpractice action can be vitally important to the particular parties in that case. But something more, demonstrating that the question is significant to the federal system as a whole, is needed. That is missing here.

D

It follows from the foregoing that *Grable*'s fourth requirement is also not met. That requirement is concerned with the appropriate "balance of federal and state judicial responsibilities." We have already explained the absence of a substantial federal issue within the meaning of *Grable*. The States, on the other hand, have "a special responsibility for maintaining standards among members of the licensed professions." Their "interest . . . in regulating lawyers is especially great since lawyers are essential to the primary governmental function of administering justice, and have historically been officers of the courts." We have no reason to suppose that Congress — in establishing exclusive federal jurisdiction over patent cases — meant to bar from state courts state legal malpractice claims simply because they require resolution of a hypothetical patent issue.

* * *

As we recognized a century ago, "[t]he Federal courts have exclusive jurisdiction of all cases arising under the patent laws, but not of all questions in which a patent may be the subject-matter of the controversy." In this case, although the state courts must answer a question of patent law to resolve Minton's legal malpractice claim, their answer will have no broader effects. It will not stand as binding precedent for any future patent claim; it will not even affect the validity of Minton's patent. Accordingly, there is no "serious federal interest in claiming the advantages thought to be inherent in a federal forum," *Grable*, 545 U.S. at 313. Section 1338(a) does not deprive the state courts of subject matter jurisdiction.

The judgment of the Supreme Court of Texas is reversed, and the case is remanded for further proceedings not inconsistent with this opinion.

Notes and Questions

1. After *Gunn*, do you think that the *Grable* test will lead to a finding of jurisdiction very often? Lower courts have often but not always rejected

jurisdiction in cases with embedded federal questions. For examples of post-*Gunn* cases in which an embedded federal question gave rise to federal subject-matter jurisdiction, see Evergreen Square of Cudahy v. Wisc. Housing & Econ. Dev. Auth., 776 F.3d 463, 465-68 (7th Cir. 2015); Great Lakes Gas Transmission Ltd. P'ship v. Essar Steel Minn., LLC, 103 F. Supp. 3d 1000, 1018-25 (D. Minn. 2015).

2. Sometimes there is no federal jurisdiction even when Congress has created a cause of action. In *Shoshone Mining Co. v. Rutter*, 177 U.S. 505 (1900), Congress established a system for miners to file "patents" (in this context, a way of stating their property claims) on their land claims. The federal statute provided that adverse claimants could file challenges to the patented claims in any "court of competent jurisdiction," but that the conflicting claims were to be resolved by local law. The Court held that federal courts lacked jurisdiction because the suit would "not involve any question as to the construction or effect of the Constitution or laws of the United States."

Consider the federal September 11th Victim Compensation Fund of 2001, 49 U.S.C. § 40101 note, § 408(b):

> (1) AVAILABILITY OF ACTION. — There shall exist a Federal cause of action for damages arising out of the hijacking and subsequent crashes of American Airlines flights 11 and 77, and United Airlines flights 93 and 175, on September 11, 2001. . . . [T]his cause of action shall be the exclusive remedy for damages arising out of the hijacking and subsequent crashes of such flights.
>
> (2) SUBSTANTIVE LAW. — The substantive law for decision in any such suit shall be derived from the law, including choice of law principles, of the State in which the crash occurred unless such law is inconsistent with or preempted by Federal law.
>
> (3) JURISDICTION. — The United States District Court for the Southern District of New York shall have original and exclusive jurisdiction over all actions brought for any claim (including any claim for loss of property, personal injury, or death) resulting from or relating to the terrorist-related aircraft crashes of September 11, 2001.

Is § 408(b) consistent with *Shoshone Mining*? Does the answer depend on whether *Shoshone Mining* rests on statutory or constitutional grounds? The Second Circuit has twice questioned (without deciding) the constitutionality of § 408(b). *See* World Trade Ctr. Props., L.L.C. v. Hartford Fire Ins. Co., 345 F.3d 154, 164 (2d Cir. 2003); Canada Life Assurance Co. v. Converium Ruckversicherung (Deutschland) AG, 335 F.3d 52, 59 (2d Cir. 2003).

3. *Grable* and *Gunn* provide the test only for cases in which the federal question is embedded in a state-law claim. For cases in which the federal question stands on its own, rather than being incorporated into a state claim, the test for federal jurisdiction is more lenient: there is jurisdiction unless the federal claim "is so attenuated and unsubstantial as to be absolutely devoid of merit." Newburyport Water Co. v. City of Newburyport,

193 U.S. 561, 579 (1904); *accord* Hagans v. Lavine, 415 U.S. 528 (1974). Should the same "substantiality" test be applied in both circumstances?

Section C: Diversity Jurisdiction

Section 1331 confers federal jurisdiction based on the nature of the claim. Section 1332, by contrast, confers federal jurisdiction based on the citizenship of the parties and the apparent size of their dispute. Read § 1332(a)-(c) and –(e). Section 1332(a)(1) imposes two distinct requirements: the parties must be of *diverse citizenship* and the *amount in controversy* must exceed $75,000. (In 1996, the amount was raised from $50,000.) Think about how courts should determine whether these requirements have been met. What does it mean to be a citizen of a particular state? How should the citizenship of a corporation be determined? How should one calculate the amount in controversy if there are multiple claims or multiple parties, or if the complaint seeks injunctive relief instead of damages? These and other questions are the subject of this section.

1. Diversity of Citizenship

Both Article III of the Constitution and § 1332(a)(1) confer jurisdiction over suits between "citizens of different States." But neither Article III nor § 1332 explains what it means for a suit to be "between" citizens of different states, nor do they tell us how to determine citizenship.

a. The Complete-Diversity Rule

If a citizen of state A sues a citizen of state B, it seems obvious that the suit is "between citizens of different States." But what if a citizen of state A sues both a citizen of state A and a citizen of state B in a single lawsuit? In *Strawbridge v. Curtiss*, 7 U.S. (3 Cranch) 267 (1806), the Supreme Court held that the statutory grant of diversity jurisdiction in § 1332(a)(1) imposes a requirement of *complete diversity*: if there are multiple parties, all of the plaintiffs must be diverse from all of the defendants. Thus, a suit with a single plaintiff and two defendants, one of whom is from the same state as the plaintiff, does not fall within the § 1332(a)(1) diversity jurisdiction.

As with federal-question jurisdiction, the statutory language and the constitutional language are not identically construed. In *State Farm Fire & Casualty Co. v. Tashire*, 386 U.S. 523 (1967), the Supreme Court made clear that the *Strawbridge* requirement of complete diversity is an interpretation of § 1332 only. *Tashire* was an interpleader case, with jurisdiction determined by 28 U.S.C. § 1335 rather than § 1332 (interpleader is discussed *supra* pp. 396-97). The Court upheld the congressional use of *minimal diversity* in § 1335: Article III permits jurisdiction as long as any two opposing parties are citizens of different states. In 2002 and 2005

Congress enacted two other minimal-diversity statutes: 28 U.S.C. § 1369 (which grants jurisdiction over some cases involving a single accident causing at least 75 deaths), and 28 U.S.C. § 1332(d) (which grants jurisdiction over many large state-law class actions, and is discussed in more detail *infra* pp. 666-676). Unless Congress amends § 1332, however, *Strawbridge* remains the rule for cases brought under § 1332(a)(1). Even though the supporters of diversity jurisdiction are likely to keep it from being abolished, Congress will almost certainly not expand § 1332(a)(1) to permit minimal diversity, although it might make further targeted use of minimal diversity as it did when it enacted §§ 1369 and 1332(d).

b. Determining Citizenship

SHEEHAN V. GUSTAFSON

967 F.2d 1214 (8th Cir. 1992)

Before ARNOLD, Chief Judge, LAY, Senior Circuit Judge, and BOWMAN, Circuit Judge.

■ BOWMAN, Circuit Judge.

John D. Sheehan, Sr., appeals the order of the District Court dismissing his action for lack of subject matter jurisdiction. We affirm.

Sheehan, a Nevada citizen, commenced an action in February 1991 against Deil O. Gustafson alleging breach of an oral contract involving the proceeds of the sale of the Tropicana Hotel and Casino in Las Vegas, Nevada. Sheehan brought his action in federal court in Minnesota, asserting that diversity jurisdiction was proper under 28 U.S.C. § 1332(a), because Gustafson, according to the complaint, was a citizen of Minnesota. Gustafson moved to dismiss the complaint for lack of subject matter jurisdiction. The District Court granted that motion in July 1991, holding that Gustafson, like Sheehan, was a citizen of Nevada and thus there was no diversity of the parties. Sheehan appeals.

A district court's conclusion as to citizenship for purposes of federal diversity jurisdiction is a mixed question of law and fact (albeit primarily fact). The findings of fact upon which the legal conclusion of citizenship is based thus are subject to review by this Court under the clearly erroneous standard.

The statute conferring diversity jurisdiction in federal court requires that the parties be citizens of different states. 28 U.S.C. § 1332(a)(1). Section 1332(a) must be strictly construed, in view "of the constitutional limitations upon the judicial power of the federal courts, and of the Judiciary Acts in defining the authority of the federal courts when they sit, in effect, as state courts." Thus the burden falls upon the party seeking the federal forum, if challenged, to demonstrate by a preponderance of the evidence that the parties are citizens of different states. The District Court found facts that are not clearly erroneous and determined that Sheehan failed to carry his burden. We cannot say the court erred as a matter of law.

Courts look to the facts as of the date an action is filed to determine whether or not diversity of citizenship exists between the parties. "For purposes of diversity jurisdiction, the terms 'domicile' and 'citizenship' are synonymous." Therefore, to determine if Gustafson is a citizen of a state other than Nevada, the proper analysis is the two-part test for domicile: Gustafson's presence in the purported state of domicile and his intention to remain there indefinitely.

The facts of this case, as found by the District Court, indicate that in February 1991 Gustafson had a presence in both Nevada and Minnesota (as well as California and Florida). Gustafson was a citizen of Minnesota until 1973 when he moved to Las Vegas, Nevada, to manage the Tropicana Hotel, which he had purchased in 1972. In 1975, he sold eighty percent of his interest in the hotel. In 1983, Gustafson was convicted in federal court in Minnesota of misappropriation of bank funds and was incarcerated from 1984 to 1987.

The facts found by the District Court that are evidence of Minnesota domicile as of February 1991 include Gustafson's bank and investment accounts in the state; ownership of property in Minnesota by a corporation controlled by Gustafson, including a condominium whose address Gustafson uses as his own in his monthly reports to his probation officer; Gustafson's use of corporate vehicles when in the state; location of Gustafson's secretary and office in Minneapolis, where he regularly checks for messages and mail; location of Gustafson's physician, dentist, and attorney in the state; and his use of Minnesota addresses and bank accounts for some of his Nevada businesses.

The facts found supporting Nevada domicile include Gustafson's holding a Nevada driver's license since 1973 and the registration of his personal vehicles in the state; Gustafson's filing of Minnesota tax returns as a non-resident since 1974, with a Nevada permanent address shown; Gustafson's voter registration in Nevada since 1973; his current valid passport showing a Nevada address; Gustafson's last will (dated July 2, 1989) containing a statement that he is domiciled in Clark County, Nevada; use of his parents' home address in Boulder, Nevada, as Gustafson's permanent address since the mid-1980's; and current (as of 1991) construction of a new home on his ranch in Ely, Nevada.

The facts demonstrate Gustafson's presence and intent to remain in Nevada, that is, domicile in Nevada. Sheehan did not show by a preponderance of the evidence that Gustafson's domicile was in fact in Minnesota at the time suit was filed. Sheehan's evidence to show domicile in Minnesota primarily demonstrates Gustafson's business contacts and occasional presence in the state; the Nevada contacts are more indicative of intent to remain.

Finding no clearly erroneous findings of fact and no error of law, we affirm the decision of the District Court.

Notes and Questions

1. The story of Deil Gustafson's citizenship is both more difficult and more colorful than the court lets on. Gustafson and his partner were forced to sell the Tropicana in 1979, after FBI tapes purportedly revealed that Gustafson had allowed the hotel's entertainment director to divert hotel proceeds to the mob. The $80 million sale, and the subsequent bankruptcy of Gustafson's company, led to federal charges that Gustafson used a bankruptcy scam to hide millions of dollars in sale proceeds. He pleaded guilty to that charge in 1995, and agreed to testify against other defendants — some allegedly working for the mob — involved in the bankruptcy fraud. (They were ultimately acquitted by a jury.) The Minnesota attorney general later charged another of his companies, an electric-car dealership, with consumer fraud; the company filed for bankruptcy protection with more than $2.5 million in debts.

In 1991, Gustafson owned not only the car dealership in Minnesota, but also several Minnesota banks and miscellaneous other property including a downtown Minneapolis office building. He died in 1998 in Minnesota, and his obituary listed his residence as a suburb of Minneapolis.

2. If the district court had found Gustafson to be a citizen of Minnesota, should the court of appeals have reversed that finding as clearly erroneous? Can reasonable judges differ on questions of citizenship? Consider *Lundquist v. Precision Valley Aviation, Inc.*, 946 F.2d 8, 10 (1st Cir. 1991), in which the court had to decide whether plaintiff Lundquist was a citizen of New Hampshire or of Florida; since the defendant was a citizen of New Hampshire, federal jurisdiction turned on Lundquist's citizenship:

> Defendants' primary evidence that Lundquist was a New Hampshire citizen was as follows: (1) that Lundquist owned real property in Melvin Village, New Hampshire and paid taxes on that property; (2) that Lundquist maintained a functioning telephone in Melvin Village; (3) that Lundquist had had a New Hampshire driver's license since 1986; (4) that Lundquist was registered to vote in New Hampshire from 1976 until at least 1990, and has actually voted in New Hampshire during that time; and (5) that Lundquist or Lundquist's wife stated his address to be in Melvin Village, New Hampshire on 1986, 1987, and 1988 annual reports filed with the New Hampshire Secretary of State by Amphibair, Inc., a corporation of which Lundquist was sole director, President, and Treasurer, and Lundquist's wife was Secretary.
>
> Lundquist presented affidavits of himself and his wife setting forth primarily the following evidence that Lundquist was a citizen not of New Hampshire, but of Florida: (1) that Lundquist purchased real property in Florida and moved there in 1984, keeping his New Hampshire property as a summer home; (2) that since 1984 Lundquist has maintained several Florida bank accounts; (3) that Lundquist has a Florida driver's license; (4) that Lundquist's wife has run a horse farm continuously in Florida since 1984; (5) that Lundquist and/or his wife belong to several social organizations in Florida; (6) that Lundquist has

summered in New Hampshire, in some years spending as little as two to three weeks there; (7) that all of Lundquist's personal belongings are in Florida except for certain bank accounts and for sparse furnishings in the Melvin Village, New Hampshire residence; and (8) that Lundquist listed a Florida residence on his federal tax returns for 1987, 1988, and 1989.

How should the district court rule on this question? Should the court of appeals affirm a district-court decision *either* way?

3. Why did Sheehan want to be in federal rather than state court? Why did Gustafson prefer state court? Sheehan chose to sue in *Minnesota* federal court, so we might presume that he would prefer Minnesota state court to Nevada state court. In either case the suit would probably be in Minnesota rather than Nevada. Is Gustafson the kind of defendant who might receive more favorable treatment from a Minnesota state court? *Cf.* Rose v. Giamatti, 721 F. Supp. 906 (S.D. Ohio 1989): In 1989, Pete Rose, the manager (and former player) of the Cincinnati Reds, was accused of betting on baseball — a charge which, if proven, would likely lead to his permanent banishment from the game. Baseball Commissioner Bartlett Giamatti — formerly president of Yale University — scheduled a hearing on the charges. Rose obtained a temporary injunction against the hearing from an Ohio state-court judge in Cincinnati; the judge was up for re-election the following year. Although Giamatti was not a citizen of Ohio, Rose's state-court suit also named the Cincinnati Reds as a defendant. Giamatti removed the case to federal court on diversity grounds, arguing that the Reds were not real parties in interest and their citizenship should therefore be disregarded. (Removal jurisdiction is discussed *infra* pp. 567-73, and requires that the case could have been brought originally in federal court.) At oral argument to determine jurisdiction, Giamatti's lawyer argued:

> In the State Court in Cincinnati, I need not describe Mr. Rose's standing. He is a local hero, perhaps the first citizen of Cincinnati. And Commissioner Giamatti is viewed suspiciously as a foreigner from New York, trapped in an ivory tower, accused of bias by Mr. Rose. Your Honor, this is a textbook example of why diversity jurisdiction was created in the Federal Courts and why it exists to this very day.

How should the court rule? Note that 28 U.S.C. § 1359 prohibits "improperly or collusively" joining parties to *create* federal jurisdiction. Does anything prevent plaintiffs from joining parties deliberately in order to *avoid* federal jurisdiction? The court in *Rose* ultimately allowed jurisdiction, because "a plaintiff cannot defeat a defendant's right of removal on the basis of diversity of citizenship by the 'fraudulent joinder' of a nondiverse defendant against whom the plaintiff has no real cause of action."

4. Sometimes a party's citizenship is in flux before and during the litigation. Suppose that Smith and Jones are citizens of Michigan when Jones injures Smith, but Smith moves to Indiana shortly before filing — and because he wants to file — suit in federal court. Or suppose that A and B sue C, a citizen of Ohio. A and B allege that they are citizens of Iowa, but it later turns out that A is from Ohio. In the meantime, A has settled or been

dismissed from the case. *Sheehan* recites the classic "time-of-filing rule": diversity is determined by examining the citizenship of the parties on the date the complaint is filed. An exception exists when a nondiverse party has been dismissed and the jurisdictional issue is not raised before the jury returns its verdict. *See* Caterpillar Inc. v. Lewis, 519 U.S. 61 (1996). Be careful, however: there are exceptions to the exception, and you should do more research if you ever face a complicated "time-of-filing" question.

5. As *Sheehan* notes, domicile and citizenship are identical for purposes of diversity jurisdiction, and require both presence and an intent to remain permanently or indefinitely. Using those requirements, determine the current domicile of the following persons:

- Hannah was born in Minnesota and moved to Tennessee with her parents at the age of 10. She is now an 18-year-old freshman at Swarthmore College in Pennsylvania. She has not declared a major, and is not certain what she wants to do after college. She knows that she does not want to live in either Minnesota (too cold) or Tennessee (too hot). (Note that a minor takes on the domicile of her parents until she successfully changes her domicile by meeting the requirements for establishing a new domicile.) TN?

- Joshua, age 30, has lived in New York since graduation from college. He has a New York driver's license, pays New York taxes, and lists his residence as New York on all state and federal tax forms. He is an attorney with a New York firm and a member of the New York bar. He has recently become engaged to a woman who lives in California. He has taken the California bar exam, and has obtained a job with a California firm, which will start as soon as he is admitted to the California bar. He and his fiancée have bought a house in California, and he will be moving there in a month. NY

- Joe is a 40-year-old freelance writer. Ten years ago he moved from Huntsville, Alabama to Chicago, Illinois because, he says, he thought it might "stimulate his artistic muse." According to Joe, he never intended to stay in Illinois, and still doesn't. Once he becomes more successful, he "plans to move back to Alabama . . . or maybe to Utah." He holds driver's licenses from both Alabama and Illinois; his car is registered in Alabama. He does not file state or federal income tax forms (although the failure to file is illegal, he does not earn enough money to owe any taxes). He is not registered to vote. He has a library card from the Chicago public library. Over the past ten years, he lived in over a dozen short-term rental housing units, never for more than six months; with friends; and in his car. IL

present in the state with intention to remain indefinitely.

6. In some of these real and hypothetical cases, wouldn't it make more sense to allow a court to find that a particular person is domiciled in more than one state? For individuals the Supreme Court has definitely rejected that possibility: they can have only one domicile at a time for diversity purposes. *See* Williamson v. Osenton, 232 U.S. 619 (1914). For corporations, however, § 1332(c)(1) presumes the possibility of multiple domiciles. Determining the domicile of a corporation is more difficult than determining

the domicile of a natural person. Read § 1332(c)(1) and consider the following case.

HERTZ CORP. V. FRIEND

559 U.S. 77 (2010)

■ JUSTICE BREYER delivered the opinion for a unanimous Court.

The federal diversity jurisdiction statute provides that "a corporation shall be deemed to be a citizen of any State by which it has been incorporated *and of the State where it has its principal place of business.*" 28 U.S.C. § 1332(c)(1) (emphasis added).* We seek here to resolve different interpretations that the Circuits have given this phrase. In doing so, we place primary weight upon the need for judicial administration of a jurisdictional statute to remain as simple as possible. And we conclude that the phrase "principal place of business" refers to the place where the corporation's high level officers direct, control, and coordinate the corporation's activities. Lower federal courts have often metaphorically called that place the corporation's "nerve center." We believe that the "nerve center" will typically be found at a corporation's headquarters.

I

In September 2007, respondents Melinda Friend and John Nhieu, two California citizens, sued petitioner, the Hertz Corporation, in a California state court. They sought damages for what they claimed were violations of California's wage and hour laws. . . .

Hertz filed a notice seeking removal to a federal court. 28 U.S.C. §§ 1332(d)(2), 1441(a). Hertz claimed that the plaintiffs and the defendant were citizens of different States. *Id.* § 1332(a)(1), –(c)(1). Hence, the federal court possessed diversity-of-citizenship jurisdiction. Friend and Nhieu, however, claimed that the Hertz Corporation was a California citizen, like themselves, and that, hence, diversity jurisdiction was lacking.

To support its position, Hertz submitted a declaration by an employee relations manager that sought to show that Hertz's "principal place of business" was in New Jersey, not in California. The declaration stated, among other things, that Hertz operated facilities in 44 States; and that California — which had about 12% of the Nation's population — accounted for 273 of Hertz's 1,606 car rental locations; about 2,300 of its 11,230 full-time employees; about $811 million of its $4.371 billion in annual revenue; and about 3.8 million of its approximately 21 million annual transactions, i.e., rentals. The declaration also stated that the "leadership of Hertz and its domestic subsidiaries" is located at Hertz's "corporate

---

* In 2011 Congress amended § 1331(c)(1) by adding "and foreign state" after "citizen of any State" and "or foreign state" after "of the State." This change does not affect the reasoning or the result of *Hertz*. — ED.

headquarters" in Park Ridge, New Jersey; that its "core executive and administrative functions . . . are carried out" there and "to a lesser extent" in Oklahoma City, Oklahoma; and that its "major administrative operations . . . are found" at those two locations.

The District Court of the Northern District of California accepted Hertz's statement of the facts as undisputed. But it concluded that, given those facts, Hertz was a citizen of California. In reaching this conclusion, the court applied Ninth Circuit precedent, which instructs courts to identify a corporation's "principal place of business" by first determining the amount of a corporation's business activity State by State. If the amount of activity is "significantly larger" or "substantially predominates" in one State, then that State is the corporation's "principal place of business." If there is no such State, then the "principal place of business" is the corporation's "nerve center," i.e., the place where "the majority of its executive and administrative functions are performed."

Applying this test, the District Court found that the "plurality of each of the relevant business activities" was in California, and that "the differential between the amount of those activities" in California and the amount in "the next closest state" was "significant." Hence, Hertz's "principal place of business" was California, and diversity jurisdiction was thus lacking. The District Court consequently remanded the case to the state courts.

Hertz appealed the District Court's remand order. The Ninth Circuit affirmed in a brief memorandum opinion. Hertz filed a petition for certiorari. And, in light of differences among the Circuits in the application of the test for corporate citizenship, we granted the writ. . . .

III

We begin our "principal place of business" discussion with a brief review of relevant history. . . .

In *Louisville, Cincinnati & Charleston R.R. v. Letson*, 43 U.S. (2 How.) 497 (1844), the Court . . . held that a corporation was to be deemed an artificial person of the State by which it had been created, and its citizenship for jurisdictional purposes determined accordingly. . . . [T]he practical upshot was that, for diversity purposes, the federal courts considered a corporation to be a citizen of the State of its incorporation. . .

At the same time as federal dockets increased in size, many judges began to believe those dockets contained too many diversity cases. A committee of the Judicial Conference of the United States studied the matter. And on March 12, 1951, that committee, the Committee on Jurisdiction and Venue, issued a report.

Among its observations, the committee found a general need "to prevent frauds and abuses" with respect to jurisdiction. The committee recommended against eliminating diversity cases altogether. Instead it recommended, along with other proposals, a statutory amendment that would make a corporation a citizen both of the State of its incorporation and any State from which it received more than half of its gross income....

During the spring and summer of 1951 committee members circulated their report and attended circuit conferences at which federal judges discussed the report's recommendations. Reflecting those criticisms, the committee filed a new report in September, in which it revised its corporate citizenship recommendation. It now proposed that "a corporation shall be deemed a citizen of the state of its original creation . . . [and] shall also be deemed a citizen of a state where it has its principal place of business." ...

... Subsequently, in 1958, Congress both codified the courts' traditional place of incorporation test and also enacted into law a slightly modified version of the Conference Committee's proposed "principal place of business" language. A corporation was to "be deemed a citizen of any State by which it has been incorporated and of the State where it has its principal place of business."

IV

The phrase "principal place of business" has proved more difficult to apply than its originators likely expected....

After Congress' amendment, courts were . . . uncertain as to where to look to determine a corporation's "principal place of business" for diversity purposes. If a corporation's headquarters and executive offices were in the same State in which it did most of its business, the test seemed straightforward. The "principal place of business" was located in that State.

But suppose those corporate headquarters, including executive offices, are in one State, while the corporation's plants or other centers of business activity are located in other States? [Some courts applied a "nerve center" test, in which the principal place of corporations with "far-flung business activities" was located at the office that controlled the corporation.]

[But this "nerve center" test] did not answer what courts should do when the operations of the corporation are not "far-flung" but rather limited to only a few States. When faced with this question, various courts have focused more heavily on where a corporation's actual business activities are located.

Perhaps because corporations come in many different forms, involve many different kinds of business activities, and locate offices and plants for different reasons in different ways in different regions, a general "business activities" approach has proved unusually difficult to apply. Courts must decide which factors are more important than others: for example, plant location, sales or servicing centers; transactions, payrolls, or revenue generation.

The number of factors grew as courts explicitly combined aspects of the "nerve center" and "business activity" tests to look to a corporation's "total activities," sometimes to try to determine what treatises have described as the corporation's "center of gravity." A major treatise confirms this growing complexity, listing Circuit by Circuit, cases that highlight different factors or emphasize similar factors differently, and reporting that the "federal courts of appeals have employed various tests"—tests which "tend to overlap" and which are sometimes described in "language" that "is imprecise." 15 J. MOORE ET AL., MOORE'S FEDERAL PRACTICE § 102.54[2], at 102-112. *See also id.* §§ 102.54[2], [13], at 102-112 to 102-122 (describing, in 14 pages, major tests as looking to the "nerve center," "locus of operations," or "center of corporate activities"). Not surprisingly, different circuits (and sometimes different courts within a single circuit) have applied these highly general multifactor tests in different ways.

This complexity may reflect an unmediated judicial effort to apply the statutory phrase "principal place of business" in light of the general purpose of diversity jurisdiction, i.e., an effort to find the State where a corporation is least likely to suffer out-of-state prejudice when it is sued in a local court. But, if so, that task seems doomed to failure. After all, the relevant purposive concern — prejudice against an out-of-state party — will often depend upon factors that courts cannot easily measure, for example, a corporation's image, its history, and its advertising, while the factors that courts can more easily measure, for example, its office or plant location, its sales, its employment, or the nature of the goods or services it supplies, will sometimes bear no more than a distant relation to the likelihood of prejudice. At the same time, this approach is at war with administrative simplicity. And it has failed to achieve a nationally uniform interpretation of federal law, an unfortunate consequence in a federal legal system.

V

A

. . . We conclude that "principal place of business" is best read as referring to the place where a corporation's officers direct, control, and coordinate the corporation's activities. It is the place that Courts of Appeals have called the corporation's "nerve center." And in practice it should normally be the place where the corporation maintains its headquarters — provided that the headquarters is the actual center of direction, control, and coordination, i.e., the "nerve center," and not simply an office where the corporation holds its board meetings (for example, attended by directors and officers who have traveled there for the occasion).

Three sets of considerations, taken together, convince us that this approach, while imperfect, is superior to other possibilities. First, the statute's language supports the approach. The statute's text deems a corporation a citizen of the "State where it has its principal place of business." 28 U.S.C. § 1332(c)(1). The word "place" is in the singular, not the plural. The word "principal" requires us to pick out the "main, prominent" or "leading" place. 12 OXFORD ENGLISH DICTIONARY 495 (2d ed. 1989) (def.(A)(I)(2)). And the fact that the word "place" follows the words "State where' means that the "place" is a place *within* a State. It is not the State itself.

A corporation's "nerve center," usually its main headquarters, is a single place. The public often (though not always) considers it the corporation's main place of business. And it is a place within a State. By contrast, the application of a more general business activities test has led some courts, as in the present case, to look, not at a particular place within a State, but incorrectly at the State itself, measuring the total amount of business activities that the corporation conducts there and determining whether they are "significantly larger" than in the next-ranking State.

This approach invites greater litigation and can lead to strange results, as the Ninth Circuit has since recognized. Namely, if a "corporation may be deemed a citizen of California on th[e] basis" of "activities [that] roughly reflect California's larger population . . . nearly every national retailer — no matter how far flung its operations — will be deemed a citizen of California for diversity purposes." But why award or decline diversity jurisdiction on the basis of a State's population, whether measured directly, indirectly (say proportionately), or with modifications?

Second, administrative simplicity is a major virtue in a jurisdictional statute. Complex jurisdictional tests complicate a case, eating up time and money as the parties litigate, not the merits of their claims, but which court is the right court to decide those claims. Complex tests produce appeals and reversals, encourage gamesmanship, and, again, diminish the likelihood that results and settlements will reflect a claim's legal and factual merits. Judicial resources too are at stake. Courts have an independent obligation to determine whether subject-matter jurisdiction exists, even when no party challenges it. So courts benefit from straightforward rules under which they can readily assure themselves of their power to hear a case.

Simple jurisdictional rules also promote greater predictability. Predictability is valuable to corporations making business and investment decisions. Predictability also benefits plaintiffs deciding whether to file suit in a state or federal court.

A "nerve center" approach, which ordinarily equates that "center" with a corporation's headquarters, is simple to apply *comparatively speaking*. The metaphor of a corporate "brain," while not precise, suggests a single location. By contrast, a corporation's general business activities more often lack a single principal place where they take place. That is to say, the corporation may have several plants, many sales locations, and employees located in many different places. If so, it will not be as easy to determine which of these different business locales is the "principal" or most important "place."

Third, the statute's legislative history, for those who accept it, offers a simplicity-related interpretive benchmark. The Judicial Conference provided an initial version of its proposal that suggested a numerical test. A corporation would be deemed a citizen of the State that accounted for more than half of its gross income. The Conference changed its mind in light of criticism that such a test would prove too complex and impractical to apply. That history suggests that the words "principal place of business" should be interpreted to be no more complex than the initial "half of gross income" test. A "nerve center" test offers such a possibility. A general business activities test does not.

B

We recognize that there may be no perfect test that satisfies all administrative and purposive criteria. We recognize as well that, under the "nerve center" test we adopt today, there will be hard cases. For example, in this era of telecommuting, some corporations may divide their command and coordinating functions among officers who work at several different locations, perhaps communicating over the Internet. That said, our test nonetheless points courts in a single direction, towards the center of overall direction, control, and coordination. Courts do not have to try to weigh corporate functions, assets, or revenues different in kind, one from the other. Our approach provides a sensible test that is relatively easier to apply, not a test that will, in all instances, automatically generate a result.

We also recognize that the use of a "nerve center" test may in some cases produce results that seem to cut against the basic rationale for 28 U.S.C. § 1332. For example, if the bulk of a company's business activities visible to the public take place in New Jersey, while its top officers direct those activities just across the river in New York, the "principal place of business" is New York. One could argue that members of the public in New Jersey would be *less* likely to be prejudiced against the corporation than persons in New York — yet the corporation will still be entitled to remove a New Jersey state case to federal court. And note too that the same corporation would be unable to remove a New York state case to federal court, despite the New York public's presumed prejudice against the corporation.

We understand that such seeming anomalies will arise. However, in view of the necessity of having a clearer rule, we must accept them. Accepting occasionally counterintuitive results is the price the legal system must pay to avoid overly complex jurisdictional administration while producing the benefits that accompany a more uniform legal system.

The burden of persuasion for establishing diversity jurisdiction, of course, remains on the party asserting it. When challenged on allegations of jurisdictional facts, the parties must support their allegations by competent proof. And when faced with such a challenge, we reject suggestions such as, for example, the one made by petitioner that the mere filing of a form like the Securities and Exchange Commission's Form 10-K listing a corporation's "principal executive offices" would, without more, be sufficient proof to establish a corporation's "nerve center." Such possibilities would readily permit jurisdictional manipulation, thereby subverting a major reason for the insertion of the "principal place of business" language in the diversity statute. Indeed, if the record reveals attempts at manipulation — for example, that the alleged "nerve center" is nothing more than a mail drop box, a bare office with a computer, or the location of an annual executive retreat — the courts should instead take as the "nerve center" the place of actual direction, control, and coordination, in the absence of such manipulation.

VI

Petitioner's unchallenged declaration suggests that Hertz's center of direction, control, and coordination, its "nerve center," and its corporate headquarters are one and the same, and they are located in New Jersey, not in California. Because respondents should have a fair opportunity to litigate their case in light of our holding, however, we vacate the Ninth Circuit's judgment and remand the case for further proceedings consistent with this opinion.

Notes and Questions

1. *Hertz* relied in part on administrative convenience in adopting the "nerve center" approach. Will the "nerve center" test always be easier to apply than the "total activities" test? Can you make an argument that what matters most is that *Hertz* chose *one* test — settling a circuit split — and thus that the particular test is of secondary importance? For an example of a difficult application of *Hertz*, see Johnson v. SmithKline Beecham Corp., 724 F.3d 337, 349-57 (3d Cir. 2013) (determining that principal place of business of incorporated holding company, which conducts no business except occasional board meetings, is the place of those meetings).

2. The Court also relied on one of the rationales for diversity jurisdiction: the possibility that an out-of-state party might suffer prejudice in the courts of the state. But under § 1332, the only thing that matters is whether the plaintiff and defendant are citizens of different states; it does not matter whether the suit is brought in the home state of one of the parties. Why, then, should we care *which* state counts as the corporation's principal place of business? Either the parties are diverse, in which case the suit can be brought in any federal court including the corporation's home state or the other party's home state; or the parties are not diverse, in which case the suit will be brought in a state court somewhere. Isn't one test as good as any other as long as it is clear? The answer might be different in cases like *Hertz*, in which the suit is brought in state court and the defendant wishes to remove it to federal court. Under § 1441(b), a defendant may not remove a case that is filed in state court in the defendant's home state. Given the Court's rationale of avoiding prejudice to the corporation, was the Court correct to hold that a corporation's principal place of business is always its "nerve center," even when the case is filed in federal court originally? Should § 1332 be amended to prohibit a party from bringing a diversity suit in its own state's federal court?

3. A corporation can have only one principal place of business, but it is considered a citizen of every state in which it is incorporated. In practice, however, multiple incorporations are now very rare.

4. Unincorporated associations — including partnerships, labor unions, trade associations, charitable organizations, and the like — are treated differently for diversity purposes. No statute directly addresses the

citizenship of such organizations, but under decisional law their citizenship is determined by the citizenship of *all* their members. Thus, if any member of the association is a citizen of the same state as one of the adverse parties, there will be no diversity jurisdiction. *See, e.g.*, Americold Realty Trust v. ConAgra Foods, Inc., 577 U.S. —, 136 S. Ct. 1012 (2016) (citizenship of trust is determined by looking at citizenship of all its members or shareholders); Carden v. Arkoma Assocs., 494 U.S. 185 (1990) (for limited partnership, citizenship of limited partners — in addition to that of general partner or partners — counts for diversity determination). Every court of appeals that has considered the issue has treated American limited liability companies (LLCs) as unincorporated associations. *See, e.g.*, Harvey v. Grey Wolf Drilling Co., 542 F.3d 1077, 1080 (5th Cir. 2008) (listing cases). Foreign LLCs, however, are sometimes treated as corporations. *See, e.g.*, Lear Corp. v. Johnson Elec. Holdings Ltd., 353 F.3d 580 (7th Cir. 2003) (Bermuda "limited" entity had legal attributes similar to corporation and was therefore treated as corporation).

5. Note that § 1332 provides for jurisdiction not only when the parties are citizens of different states, but also in some cases when foreign citizens or foreign states are involved. Those provisions raise important questions that are beyond the scope of an introductory course. "Stateless" persons who are not citizens of any nation, and American-citizen expatriates domiciled abroad, are not citizens of any state or foreign nation and cannot be original parties to a suit that requires complete diversity. *See* Newman–Green, Inc. v. Alfonzo-Larrain, 490 U.S. 826 (1989). What result when a citizen of a state sues a number of defendants, including a law firm with one American partner domiciled in the United Kingdom? *See* Swiger v. Allegheny Energy, Inc., 540 F.3d 179 (3d Cir. 2008) (no diversity).

2. Amount in Controversy

JTH TAX, INC. V. FRASHIER

624 F.3d 635 (4th Cir. 2010)

Before MOTZ, KING, and DAVIS, Circuit Judges.

MOTZ, Circuit Judge.

JTH Tax, Inc. ("Liberty") appeals from an order dismissing its complaint for lack of subject matter jurisdiction. Liberty contends that the district court erred in holding that its complaint failed to meet the $75,000 amount in controversy requirement for diversity jurisdiction under 28 U.S.C. § 1332(a). We agree and so reverse.

I.

Liberty franchises thousands of tax preparation offices nationwide. The dispute before us arises from its relationship with Harry Frashier, one of its franchisees. In 2006, Frashier signed a franchise agreement with Liberty granting him the right to operate Liberty Tax Service franchises in a designated area of West Virginia. In return, Frashier agreed to several post-termination provisions, including a covenant not to compete and a requirement that he return all customer lists and equipment to Liberty.

Frashier operated a Liberty franchise tax office without incident until 2008. On August 26 of that year . . . Frashier offered to sell Liberty a right of first refusal for the purchase of Frashier's franchise territory for $80,000. When the parties failed to agree on the terms of a sale, Frashier closed his franchise, which prompted Liberty to terminate its agreement with Frashier.

This dispute centers on what happened next. On January 28, 2009, Liberty filed a complaint in the Eastern District of Virginia, seeking $80,000 in damages and a permanent injunction compelling Frashier's compliance with the post-termination provisions of the franchise agreement. Specifically, Liberty claimed that Frashier breached his post-termination duties by using his former office to support a competing tax enterprise and by failing to return the requisite materials to Liberty. . . .

Liberty never amended its complaint, but in its subsequent motion for summary judgment, Liberty refined its damages calculation, seeking $60,456.25 in money damages and injunctive relief. The district court *sua sponte* dismissed Liberty's complaint for failure to meet the $75,000 amount in controversy requirement for diversity jurisdiction. . . .

Liberty then noted this appeal. We review de novo the judgment of the district court dismissing the complaint for lack of subject matter jurisdiction.

II.

In most cases, the "sum claimed by the plaintiff controls" the amount in controversy determination. St. Paul Mercury Indem. Co. v. Red Cab Co., 303 U.S. 283, 288 (1938). If the plaintiff claims a sum sufficient to satisfy the statutory requirement, a federal court may dismiss only if "it is apparent, *to a legal certainty,* that the plaintiff cannot recover the amount claimed." *Id.* at 289 (emphasis added).

Defendants, seeking dismissal of diversity actions for lack of a sufficient amount in controversy, must therefore shoulder a heavy burden. They must show "the legal impossibility of recovery" to be "so certain as virtually to negative the plaintiff's good faith in asserting the claim." Wiggins v. N. Am. Equitable Life Assurance Co., 644 F.2d 1014, 1017 (4th Cir. 1981). A mere dispute over the mathematical accuracy of a plaintiff's damages calculation does not constitute such a showing. *See* McDonald v. Patton, 240 F.2d 424, 425 (4th Cir. 1957) (noting that plaintiffs may secure federal jurisdiction even when "it is apparent on the face of the claim" that the claim to the requisite amount is subject to a "valid defense").

With these controlling principles in mind, we turn to the case at hand.

III.

Courts generally determine the amount in controversy by reference to the plaintiff's complaint. *See Wiggins,* 644 F.2d at 1016 ("Ordinarily the jurisdictional amount is determined by the amount of the plaintiff's original claim, provided that the claim is made in good faith."). If the complaint in good faith alleges a sufficient amount in controversy, "[e]vents occurring subsequent" to the filing of the complaint "which reduce the amount recoverable below the statutory limit do not oust jurisdiction." *St. Paul Mercury,* 303 U.S. at 289-90.

Here, Liberty's complaint — which it has not amended — alleges $80,000 in damages, a sum sufficient to exceed the $75,000 amount necessary for diversity jurisdiction. Liberty's later downward adjustment made in its motion for summary judgment (but not in any amended complaint) does not constitute a "subsequent reduction of the amount claimed" sufficient to "oust the district court's jurisdiction." *Id.* at 295.

In other words, jurisdiction turns not on the sum contained in Liberty's summary judgment motion, but on the good faith of the allegation in its complaint of an adequate jurisdictional amount. The district court did not find, nor has Frashier even argued, that Liberty made a bad faith claim of $80,000 in its complaint. Accordingly, the complaint appears sufficient to allege an adequate jurisdictional amount.

IV.

To be sure, even a plaintiff whose complaint alleges a sufficient amount in controversy cannot secure jurisdiction "if, from the proofs, the court is satisfied to a [legal] certainty that the plaintiff never was entitled to recover that amount." *Id.* at 289. But even if Liberty's reassessment of its damages demonstrated to a legal certainty that it could recover only the $60,456.25 requested in its summary judgment motion, dismissal for lack of jurisdiction would still constitute error here.

This is so because, like requests for money damages, requests for injunctive relief must be valued in determining whether the plaintiff has alleged a sufficient amount in controversy. Moreover, plaintiffs may aggregate smaller claims in order to reach the jurisdictional threshold. Therefore, the district court should have considered not only the amount of money damages Liberty requested but also the injunctive relief it sought when determining jurisdiction.

Consideration of the requested injunctive relief compels the conclusion that Liberty's claim alleges a sufficient amount in controversy. Even if the $60,456.25 alleged in its summary judgment motion constitutes the sole money damages sought by Liberty, its requested injunctive relief need only have a good faith worth of $14,543.76, i.e. the amount necessary to yield a combined value in excess of $75,000.

We ascertain the value of an injunction for amount in controversy purposes by reference to the larger of two figures: the injunction's worth to the plaintiff or its cost to the defendant. In this case, Liberty has demonstrated that the injunction, whether valued for the benefit it confers on Liberty or the detriment it imposes on Frashier, arguably yields a figure that exceeds the necessary jurisdictional amount. . . .

We pass no judgment on the merits of any of [Liberty's suggested calculations of the worth of the injunction]. For our purposes, all that matters is that we cannot say *with legal certainty* that Liberty's injunction is worth less than the requisite amount. Indeed, all of Liberty's calculations employ reasoning that is at least facially plausible, and Frashier proposes no methodology of his own suggesting that the injunction lacks the requisite value.

V.

For the foregoing reasons, the judgment of the district court is reversed.

Notes and Questions

1. As *JTH* notes, allegations that more than $75,000 is in controversy will suffice to confer jurisdiction unless it appears "to a legal certainty" that plaintiff cannot recover more than the jurisdictional amount. In *Freeland v. Liberty Mutual Fire Insurance Co.*, 632 F.3d 250 (6th Cir. 2011), the court held that it had no jurisdiction when the amount in controversy was *exactly* $75,000.

2. Claims for punitive damages, if there is a basis in law and fact for their availability, do count toward satisfying the amount-in-controversy requirement and can be added to compensatory-damage claims that by themselves do not exceed $75,000. But courts are likely to subject them to closer scrutiny than claims for actual damages — especially if they may be necessary to, or appear to have been asserted for the purpose of securing, federal jurisdiction. *See generally*, *e.g.*, Missouri *ex rel.* Pemiscot Cty. v. W. Sur. Co., 51 F.3d 170, 173 (8th Cir. 1995) ("When determining the amount in controversy, we scrutinize a claim for punitive damages more closely than a claim for actual damages to ensure that Congress's limits on diversity jurisdiction are properly observed.") Should punitive damages be counted toward the jurisdictional amount at all?

3. The Fourth Circuit follows the "either viewpoint" rule for valuing injunctive relief: if either the benefit to the plaintiff or the cost to the defendant meets the jurisdictional minimum, then the court has jurisdiction. The circuits are split on this issue. Some agree with the Fourth Circuit, but others determine the value of an injunction by looking solely at the benefit to the plaintiff and still others by looking solely at the cost to the defendant. *Compare* Cleveland Hous. Renewal Project v. Deutsche Bank Trust Co., 621 F.3d 554 (6th Cir. 2010) (defendant's cost can establish amount in controversy), *with* Correspondent Servs. Corp. v. First Equities Corp. of Fla., 442 F.3d 767 (2d Cir. 2006) (only plaintiff's benefit can establish amount in controversy).

4. The *JTH* case involved a single plaintiff suing a single defendant. A single plaintiff may combine as many claims as she has against a single defendant, and jurisdiction is determined by the total amount sought in the complaint, even if the claims are entirely unrelated. What about multiple plaintiffs or defendants? The basic rule is that multiple plaintiffs cannot aggregate their individual claims to reach the jurisdictional amount, unless there is one *res*, or, as some other courts describe it, the plaintiffs have suffered a "single indivisible harm" or claim a "common undivided interest." (as is the case, for instance, with joint tenants claiming damage to property they own together). Similarly, claims against multiple defendants cannot be aggregated unless the defendants are jointly liable. Do these rules make any sense? Courts have had some difficulty in determining when multiple plaintiffs can aggregate. Should punitive damages count as a common undivided interest? Should damages to a partnership count when, if recovered, they will be divided among the partners? Should claims by a union? By minority shareholders in a corporation? By time-share owners? Courts are divided on some of these questions. *See* 14AA CHARLES ALAN WRIGHT ET AL., FEDERAL PRACTICE AND PROCEDURE § 3704 (4th ed. 2011).

5. Imagine that a complaint seeks $50,000 and the defendant files a counterclaim that would be considered compulsory under Rule 13(a) (discussed *supra* pp. 357-63) for either $50,000 or $100,000. Can either case be brought in, or removed to, federal court? (Remember, whether a case can be removed to federal court under § 1441 generally depends on whether it satisfies the requirements for original federal jurisdiction.) The answer should be clear from *Mottley* (quick, what does that case suggest?), and indeed most courts do not consider the value of counterclaims in calculating the amount in controversy. The problem arises infrequently in cases originally filed in federal court because the plaintiff's own claim usually satisfies the amount-in-controversy requirement. In cases removed from state court, a minority of courts has considered the value of a defendant's compulsory counterclaim, especially when the counterclaim satisfies the requirement on its own. *See* 14AA WRIGHT ET AL., *supra*, § 3706.

SECTION D: SUPPLEMENTAL JURISDICTION

Many lawsuits involve more than one claim, and there may be federal jurisdiction over one of the claims but not others. Doctrines of *supplemental jurisdiction*, once called *ancillary* or *pendent* jurisdiction, determine whether the federal courts may (or must) decide these add-on or tag-along claims. The doctrines began as judicial interpretations of the term "case or controversy." In 1990, Congress codified supplemental jurisdiction in a new provision, 28 U.S.C. § 1367. As you read the cases and notes in this section, think about why federal courts should have jurisdiction over otherwise nonfederal (and nondiverse) claims and parties, and what limits should be placed on that jurisdiction.

United Mine Workers of America v. Gibbs

383 U.S. 715 (1966)

■ Mr. Justice Brennan delivered the opinion of the Court.

Respondent Paul Gibbs was awarded compensatory and punitive damages in this action against petitioner United Mine Workers of America (UMW) for alleged violations of § 303 of the [Federal] Labor Management Relations Act, and of the common law of Tennessee. The case grew out of the rivalry between the United Mine Workers and the Southern Labor Union over representation of workers in the southern Appalachian coal fields.... [In 1960,] Grundy Company ... hired respondent as mine superintendent to attempt to open a new mine.... As part of the arrangement, Grundy also gave respondent a contract to haul the mine's coal to the nearest railroad loading point.

On August 15 and 16, 1960, armed members of Local 5881 [of the United Mine Workers] forcibly prevented the opening of the mine, threatening respondent and beating an organizer for the rival union. The members of the local believed [that Grundy's parent corporation] had promised them the jobs at the new mine; they insisted that if anyone would do the work, they would. At this time, no representative of the UMW, their international union, was present.... There was no further violence at the mine site; a picket line was maintained there for nine months; and no further attempts were made to open the mine during that period.

Respondent lost his job as superintendent, and never entered into performance of his haulage contract. He testified that he soon began to lose other trucking contracts and mine leases he held in nearby areas. Claiming these effects to be the result of a concerted union plan against him, he sought recovery not against Local 5881 or its members, but only against petitioner, the international union. The suit was brought in the United States District Court for the Eastern District of Tennessee, and jurisdiction was premised on allegations of secondary boycotts under § 303. The state law claim, for which jurisdiction was based upon the doctrine of pendent jurisdiction, asserted "an unlawful conspiracy and an unlawful boycott aimed at him and [Grundy] to maliciously, wantonly and willfully interfere with his contract of employment and with his contract of haulage." ...

I.

A threshold question is whether the District Court properly entertained jurisdiction of the claim based on Tennessee law....

... Under the [Federal Rules of Civil Procedure], the impulse is toward entertaining the broadest possible scope of action consistent with fairness to the parties; joinder of claims, parties and remedies is strongly encouraged. Yet ... there has been some tendency to limit its application to cases in which the state and federal claims are ... "little more than the equivalent of different epithets to characterize the same group of circumstances."

This limited approach is unnecessarily grudging. Pendent jurisdiction, in the sense of judicial *power*, exists whenever there is a claim "arising under [the] Constitution, the Laws of the United States, and Treaties made, or which shall be made, under their Authority . . . ," U.S. CONST. art. III, § 2, and the relationship between that claim and the state claim permits the conclusion that the entire action before the court comprises but one constitutional "case." The federal claim must have substance sufficient to confer subject matter jurisdiction on the court. The state and federal claims must derive from a common nucleus of operative fact. But if, considered without regard to their federal or state character, a plaintiff's claims are such that he would ordinarily be expected to try them all in one judicial proceeding, then, assuming substantiality of the federal issues, there is power in federal courts to hear the whole.

That power need not be exercised in every case in which it is found to exist. It has consistently been recognized that pendent jurisdiction is a doctrine of discretion, not of plaintiff's right. Its justification lies in considerations of judicial economy, convenience and fairness to litigants; if these are not present a federal court should hesitate to exercise jurisdiction over state claims . . . . Needless decisions of state law should be avoided both as a matter of comity and to promote justice between the parties, by procuring for them a surer-footed reading of applicable law. Certainly, if the federal claims are dismissed before trial, even though not insubstantial in a jurisdictional sense, the state claims should be dismissed as well. Similarly, if it appears that the state issues substantially predominate, whether in terms of proof, of the scope of the issues raised, or of the comprehensiveness of the remedy sought, the state claims may be dismissed without prejudice and left for resolution to state tribunals. There may, on the other hand, be situations in which the state claim is so closely tied to questions of federal policy that the argument for exercise of pendent jurisdiction is particularly strong. . . . Finally, there may be reasons independent of jurisdictional considerations, such as the likelihood of jury confusion in treating divergent legal theories of relief, that would justify separating state and federal claims for trial. If so, jurisdiction should ordinarily be refused.

We are not prepared to say that in the present case the District Court exceeded its discretion in proceeding to judgment on the state claim. . . . [T]he state and federal claims arose from the same nucleus of operative fact and reflected alternative remedies. Indeed, the verdict sheet sent in to the jury authorized only one award of damages, so that recovery could not be given separately on the federal and state claims. . . .

- THE CHIEF JUSTICE took no part in the decision of this case.
- [The concurring opinion of MR. JUSTICE HARLAN, with whom MR. JUSTICE CLARK joined, is omitted.]

Notes and Questions

1. *Gibbs* represents a shift from the narrow pre-Rules view of when it is appropriate to join state and federal claims together. As the opinion notes, the federal courts have power over any claim that is so related to a federal claim that it forms a part of the same case or controversy, and the Court defines case or controversy very broadly to include any claims that arise from a "common nucleus of operative fact."

2. Recall Rule 18(a), which allows a party to join "as many claims" as the party has against an opposing party, regardless of whether those claims are related to one another. How is the test adopted in *Gibbs* different? Why is it different? (Hint: think about the underlying limits on federal-court jurisdiction derived from Article III.)

3. As we have learned in this chapter, federal jurisdiction requires two things: constitutional authority *and* congressional authorization to use that authority. *Gibbs* addresses the question of the breadth of constitutional authority. But no statute authorized federal courts to accept jurisdiction. Was the ultimate result in *Gibbs* therefore wrong, or do federal courts possess some inherent authority to exercise their constitutional jurisdiction in the interests of "judicial economy, convenience and fairness to litigants"?

4. There are three somewhat different situations in which a court must decide whether it can exercise jurisdiction over a claim if that claim provides no independent basis for jurisdiction. *Gibbs* addressed jurisdiction over additional claims asserted by the plaintiff against the defendant (sometimes called *pendent* (or *pendent-claim*) *jurisdiction*). Questions also arose about subject-matter jurisdiction over other claims that could be asserted under the rules of claim and party joinder. One subset of these claims involved *ancillary jurisdiction*. The idea of ancillary jurisdiction was that, once a federal court had jurisdiction over the main controversy, it also had jurisdiction to resolve closely connected claims that defendants and third parties needed to assert in order to protect their interests. Compulsory counterclaims, crossclaims, and third-party claims by defendants, as well as claims by intervenors of right, were the classic ancillary claims. (These claims are described in more detail in Chapter Eight.) The most commonly cited test for ancillary jurisdiction derived from *Moore v. New York Cotton Exchange*, 270 U.S. 593 (1926), which authorized ancillary jurisdiction over a compulsory counterclaim. *Moore* spoke of a "logical relationship" and a "close . . . connection" between the main and ancillary claim. *Id.* at 610.

Pendent and ancillary jurisdiction were traditionally distinguished from a third form of jurisdiction, often called *pendent-party jurisdiction*. Pendent-party claims were claims asserted by additional plaintiffs or against additional defendants. (Remember, the court must have jurisdiction over a claim of at least one plaintiff against one defendant, and the question is whether it may also exercise jurisdiction over other claims, which, on their own, would not be within federal jurisdiction.) On the one hand, pendent-party claims lack the quality that defines most ancillary claims — the need of defendants or third parties to assert additional claims to protect their interests. On the other hand, they often possess the quality that defines pendent jurisdiction — the efficiency and convenience of trying related claims in one proceeding. So which approach, if either, should apply?

5. The Court vacillated about the rules governing pendent-party jurisdiction. In *Aldinger v. Howard*, 427 U.S. 1 (1976), it seemed that the Court might be leaving open the possibility that such jurisdiction existed unless Congress explicitly or implicitly negated it. The most important "implicit negation" case is *Owen Equipment & Erection Co. v. Kroger*, 437 U.S. 365 (1978). In *Kroger*, plaintiff, a citizen of Iowa, sued a Nebraska corporation for the wrongful death of her husband. The Nebraska defendant in turn used Rule 14(a) to implead an Iowa corporation. Plaintiff sought to amend her complaint to state a wrongful-death claim against the impleaded party. Rule 14 permits the plaintiff to raise (related) claims against a third-party defendant. Is there pendent-party jurisdiction over the plaintiff's claim against the third-party defendant? *Kroger* ruled against jurisdiction in exactly this situation:

> ... [I]n determining whether jurisdiction over a nonfederal claim exists, the context in which the nonfederal claim is asserted is crucial. And the claim here arises in a setting quite different from the kinds of nonfederal claims that have been viewed in other cases as falling within the ancillary jurisdiction of the federal courts.
>
> First, the nonfederal claim in this case was simply not ancillary to the federal one in the same sense that, for example, the impleader by a defendant of a third-party defendant always is. A third-party complaint depends at least in part upon the resolution of the primary lawsuit. Its relation to the original complaint is thus not mere factual similarity but logical dependence. The respondent's claim against the petitioner, however, was entirely separate from her original claim against [the Nebraska defendant], since the petitioner's liability to her depended not at all upon whether or not [the Nebraska defendant] was also liable. Far from being an ancillary and dependent claim, it was a new and independent one.
>
> Second, the nonfederal claim here was asserted by the plaintiff, who voluntarily chose to bring suit upon a state-law claim in a federal court. By contrast, ancillary jurisdiction typically involves claims by a defending party haled into court against his will, or by another person whose rights might be irretrievably lost unless he could assert them in an ongoing action in a federal court. A plaintiff cannot complain if ancillary jurisdiction does not encompass all of his possible claims in a case such as this one, since it is he who has chosen the federal rather than the state forum and must thus accept its limitations. "[T]he efficiency plaintiff seeks so avidly is available without question in the state courts."
>
> It is not unreasonable to assume that, in generally requiring complete diversity, Congress did not intend to confine the jurisdiction of the federal courts so inflexibly that they are unable to protect legal rights or effectively to resolve an entire, logically intertwined lawsuit.

Those practical needs are the basis of the doctrine of ancillary jurisdiction. But neither the convenience of litigants nor considerations of judicial economy can suffice to justify extension of the doctrine of ancillary jurisdiction to a plaintiff's cause of action against a citizen of the same State in a diversity case. Congress has established the basic rule that diversity jurisdiction exists under 28 U.S.C. § 1332 only when there is complete diversity of citizenship. "The policy of the statute calls for its strict construction." To allow the requirement of complete diversity to be circumvented as it was in this case would simply flout the congressional command. [437 U.S. at 375-77.]

If *Kroger* had held the opposite, what could plaintiffs who desired a federal forum do when seeking to sue multiple but incompletely diverse defendants?

6. In 1989, the Court revisited the issue of pendent-party jurisdiction in *Finley v. United States*, 490 U.S. 545 (1989). *Finley* involved a plaintiff whose husband and two of her children died when their small airplane struck electric transmission lines on approaching a landing. She sued the Federal Aviation Administration under the Federal Tort Claims Act (FTCA), alleging that it was responsible for both runway lights and air-traffic control functions that contributed to the crash. She also sought to include state-law claims against the city (San Diego) and the utility company for their role in maintaining the transmission lines. The district court concluded that all the claims arose from a common nucleus of operative fact and asserted pendent jurisdiction over the state-law claims. The Supreme Court ultimately disagreed, finding no jurisdiction.

The Court distinguished the pendent-*claim* jurisdiction permitted in *Gibbs*: "with respect to the addition of parties, as opposed to the addition of only claims, we will not assume that the full constitutional power has been congressionally authorized, and will not read jurisdictional statutes broadly." *Id.* at 549. It concluded that *Gibbs* had not been (and should not be) extended to pendent-*party* jurisdiction:

> The *Gibbs* line of cases was a departure from prior practice, and a departure that we have no intent to limit or impair. But *Aldinger* indicated that the *Gibbs* approach would not be extended to the pendent-party field, and we decide today to retain that line. Whatever we say regarding the scope of jurisdiction conferred by a particular statute can of course be changed by Congress. What is of paramount importance is that Congress be able to legislate against a background of clear interpretive rules, so that it may know the effect of the language it adopts. . . . [A] grant of jurisdiction over claims involving particular parties does not itself confer jurisdiction over additional claims by or against different parties. [490 U.S. at 556.]

Since the FTCA did not explicitly create pendent-party jurisdiction, the Court found that the federal courts had no jurisdiction over the state-law claims against additional parties.

7. In response to *Finley*, Congress enacted the supplemental jurisdiction statute, 28 U.S.C. § 1367. The legislative history strongly suggests that § 1367 was meant to overrule *Finley* but to codify the results

in most cases decided before *Finley*. Read § 1367. How does it confer pendent-party jurisdiction in cases that resemble *Finley*? How does it avoid creating pendent-party jurisdiction in cases that resemble *Kroger*?

8. Before the enactment of § 1367, each plaintiff in a diversity case had to individually satisfy the minimum amount in controversy. That rule was first applied to plaintiffs who join together under Rule 20 in *Clark v. Paul Gray, Inc.*, 306 U.S. 583 (1939). It was extended to class actions in *Zahn v. International Paper Co.*, 414 U.S. 291 (1973), so that each member of the class must individually satisfy the minimum amount in controversy. Does § 1367(b) change the *Clark/Zahn* rule in cases in which one plaintiff meets the jurisdictional minimum but others do not? We consider the question of *Zahn* and class actions *infra* pp. 665-66. With regard to *Clark* and Rule 20, consider the following case.

EXXON MOBIL CORP. V. ALLAPATTAH SERVICES, INC.

545 U.S. 546 (2005)

■ JUSTICE KENNEDY delivered the opinion of the Court.

[This case] present[s] the question whether a federal court in a diversity action may exercise supplemental jurisdiction over additional plaintiffs whose claims do not satisfy the minimum amount-in-controversy requirement, provided the claims are part of the same case or controversy as the claims of plaintiffs who do allege a sufficient amount in controversy. Our decision turns on the correct interpretation of 28 U.S.C. § 1367. The question has divided the Courts of Appeals, and we granted certiorari to resolve the conflict.

We hold that, where the other elements of jurisdiction are present and at least one named plaintiff in the action satisfies the amount-in-controversy requirement, § 1367 does authorize supplemental jurisdiction over the claims of other plaintiffs in the same Article III case or controversy, even if those claims are for less than the jurisdictional amount specified in the statute setting forth the requirements for diversity jurisdiction. . . .

I

[The Court decided two consolidated cases. The *Allapattah* case — from which the case derives its name — involved a class action. The other case, *Rosario Ortega v. Star-Kist Foods*, involved joinder under Rule 20. In *Rosario Ortega*, a 9-year-old girl sued Star-Kist in a diversity action in district court, seeking damages for unusually severe injuries she received when she sliced her finger on a tuna can. Her parents and sister joined in the suit, seeking damages for emotional distress and medical expenses. The District Court granted summary judgment to Star-Kist, finding that none of the plaintiffs met the minimum amount-in-controversy requirement. The Court of Appeals for the First Circuit ruled that the injured girl, but not her family members, met the jurisdictional minimum. It then held that supplemental jurisdiction over the family's claims was improper.]

II

A

The district courts of the United States, as we have said many times, are "courts of limited jurisdiction. They possess only that power authorized by Constitution and statute." In order to provide a federal forum for plaintiffs who seek to vindicate federal rights, Congress has conferred on the district courts original jurisdiction in federal-question cases — civil actions that arise under the Constitution, laws, or treaties of the United States. 28 U.S.C. § 1331. In order to provide a neutral forum for what have come to be known as diversity cases, Congress also has granted district courts original jurisdiction in civil actions between citizens of different States, between U.S. citizens and foreign citizens, or by foreign states against U.S. citizens. § 1332. To ensure that diversity jurisdiction does not flood the federal courts with minor disputes, § 1332(a) requires that the matter in controversy in a diversity case exceed a specified amount, currently $75,000.

Although the district courts may not exercise jurisdiction absent a statutory basis, it is well established — in certain classes of cases — that, once a court has original jurisdiction over some claims in the action, it may exercise supplemental jurisdiction over additional claims that are part of the same case or controversy. The leading modern case for this principle is *Mine Workers v. Gibbs*, 383 U.S. 715 (1966). In *Gibbs*, the plaintiff alleged the defendant's conduct violated both federal and state law. The District Court, *Gibbs* held, had original jurisdiction over the action based on the federal claims. *Gibbs* confirmed that the District Court had the additional power (though not the obligation) to exercise supplemental jurisdiction over related state claims that arose from the same Article III case or controversy.

As we later noted, the decision allowing jurisdiction over pendent state claims in *Gibbs* did not mention, let alone come to grips with, the text of the jurisdictional statutes and the bedrock principle that federal courts have no jurisdiction without statutory authorization. Finley v. United States, 490 U.S. 545, 548 (1989). In *Finley*, we nonetheless reaffirmed and rationalized *Gibbs* and its progeny by inferring from it the interpretive principle that, in cases involving supplemental jurisdiction over additional claims between parties properly in federal court, the jurisdictional statutes should be read broadly, on the assumption that in this context Congress intended to authorize courts to exercise their full Article III power to dispose of an "entire action before the court [which] comprises but one constitutional 'case.'"

We have not, however, applied *Gibbs*' expansive interpretive approach to other aspects of the jurisdictional statutes. For instance, we have consistently interpreted § 1332 as requiring complete diversity: In a case with multiple plaintiffs and multiple defendants, the presence in the action of a single plaintiff from the same State as a single defendant deprives the district court of original diversity jurisdiction over the entire action. Strawbridge v. Curtiss, 7 U.S. (3 Cranch) 267 (1806); Owen Equip. & Erection Co. v. Kroger, 437 U.S. 365, 375 (1978).... The Court... has adhered to the complete diversity rule in light of the purpose of the diversity requirement, which is to provide a federal forum for important disputes where state courts might favor, or be perceived as favoring, home-state litigants. The presence of parties from the same State on both sides of a case dispels this concern, eliminating a principal reason for conferring § 1332 jurisdiction over any of the claims in the action. The specific purpose of the complete diversity rule explains both why we have not adopted *Gibbs*' expansive interpretive approach to this aspect of the jurisdictional statute and why *Gibbs* does not undermine the complete diversity rule. In order for a federal court to invoke supplemental jurisdiction under *Gibbs*, it must first have original jurisdiction over at least one claim in the action. Incomplete diversity destroys original jurisdiction with respect to all claims, so there is nothing to which supplemental jurisdiction can adhere.

In contrast to the diversity requirement, most of the other statutory prerequisites for federal jurisdiction, including the federal-question and amount-in-controversy requirements, can be analyzed claim by claim. True, it does not follow by necessity from this that a district court has authority to exercise supplemental jurisdiction over all claims provided there is original jurisdiction over just one. Before the enactment of § 1367, the Court declined in contexts other than the pendent-claim instance to follow *Gibbs*' expansive approach to interpretation of the jurisdictional statutes. The Court took a more restrictive view of the proper interpretation of these statutes in so-called pendent-party cases involving supplemental jurisdiction over claims involving additional parties — plaintiffs or defendants — where the district courts would lack original jurisdiction over claims by each of the parties standing alone.

Thus, with respect to plaintiff-specific jurisdictional requirements, the Court held in *Clark v. Paul Gray, Inc.*, 306 U.S. 583 (1939), that every plaintiff must separately satisfy the amount-in-controversy requirement. Though *Clark* was a federal-question case, at that time federal-question jurisdiction had an amount-in-controversy requirement analogous to the amount-in-controversy requirement for diversity cases. "Proper practice," *Clark* held, "requires that where each of several plaintiffs is bound to establish the jurisdictional amount with respect to his own claim, the suit should be dismissed as to those who fail to show that the requisite amount is involved." The Court reaffirmed this rule ... in *Zahn v. International Paper Co.*, 414 U.S. 291 (1973). It follows "inescapably" from *Clark* ... that "any plaintiff without the jurisdictional amount must be dismissed from the case, even though others allege jurisdictionally sufficient claims." 414 U.S. at 300.

The Court took a similar approach with respect to supplemental jurisdiction over claims against additional defendants that fall outside the district courts' original jurisdiction. [The Court then discussed *Finley v. United States* (*supra* p. 556, Note 6).]

As the jurisdictional statutes existed in 1989, then, here is how matters stood: First, the diversity requirement in § 1332(a) required complete diversity; absent complete diversity, the district court lacked original jurisdiction over all of the claims in the action. *Strawbridge*; *Kroger*. Second, if the district court had original jurisdiction over at least one claim, the jurisdictional statutes implicitly authorized supplemental jurisdiction over all other claims between the same parties arising out of the same Article III case or controversy. *Gibbs*. Third, even when the district court had original jurisdiction over one or more claims between particular parties, the jurisdictional statutes did not authorize supplemental jurisdiction over additional claims involving other parties. *Clark*; *Finley*.

B

In *Finley* we emphasized that "[w]hatever we say regarding the scope of jurisdiction conferred by a particular statute can of course be changed by Congress." In 1990, Congress accepted the invitation. It passed the Judicial Improvements Act, which enacted § 1367, the provision which controls these cases. . . .

All parties to this litigation and all courts to consider the question agree that § 1367 overturned the result in *Finley*. There is no warrant, however, for assuming that § 1367 did no more than to overrule *Finley* and otherwise to codify the existing state of the law of supplemental jurisdiction. We must not give jurisdictional statutes a more expansive interpretation than their text warrants; but it is just as important not to adopt an artificial construction that is narrower than what the text provides. No sound canon of interpretation requires Congress to speak with extraordinary clarity in order to modify the rules of federal jurisdiction within appropriate constitutional bounds. Ordinary principles of statutory construction apply. In order to determine the scope of supplemental jurisdiction authorized by § 1367, then, we must examine the statute's text in light of context, structure, and related statutory provisions.

Section 1367(a) is a broad grant of supplemental jurisdiction over other claims within the same case or controversy, as long as the action is one in which the district courts would have original jurisdiction. The last sentence of § 1367(a) makes it clear that the grant of supplemental jurisdiction extends to claims involving joinder or intervention of additional parties. The single question before us, therefore, is whether a diversity case in which the claims of some plaintiffs satisfy the amount-in-controversy requirement, but the claims of other plaintiffs do not, presents a "civil action of which the district courts have original jurisdiction." If the answer is yes, § 1367(a) confers supplemental jurisdiction over all claims, including those that do not independently satisfy the amount-in-controversy requirement, if the claims are part of the same Article III case or controversy. If the answer is no, § 1367(a) is inapplicable and, in light of our holdings in *Clark* and *Zahn*, the district court has no statutory basis for exercising supplemental jurisdiction over the additional claims.

We now conclude the answer must be yes. When the well-pleaded complaint contains at least one claim that satisfies the amount-in-controversy requirement, and there are no other relevant jurisdictional defects, the district court, beyond all question, has original jurisdiction over that claim. The presence of other claims in the complaint, over which the district court may lack original jurisdiction, is of no moment. If the court has original jurisdiction over a single claim in the complaint, it has original jurisdiction over a "civil action" within the meaning of § 1367(a), even if the civil action over which it has jurisdiction comprises fewer claims than were included in the complaint. Once the court determines it has original jurisdiction over the civil action, it can turn to the question whether it has a constitutional and statutory basis for exercising supplemental jurisdiction over the other claims in the action.

Section 1367(a) commences with the direction that § 1367(b) and –(c), or other relevant statutes, may provide specific exceptions, but otherwise § 1367(a) is a broad jurisdictional grant, with no distinction drawn between pendent-claim and pendent-party cases. In fact, the last sentence of § 1367(a) makes clear that the provision grants supplemental jurisdiction over claims involving joinder or intervention of additional parties. The terms of § 1367 do not acknowledge any distinction between pendent jurisdiction and the doctrine of so-called ancillary jurisdiction. Though the doctrines of pendent and ancillary jurisdiction developed separately as a historical matter, the Court has recognized that the doctrines are "two species of the same generic problem." *Kroger*. Nothing in § 1367 indicates a congressional intent to recognize, preserve, or create some meaningful, substantive distinction between the jurisdictional categories we have historically labeled pendent and ancillary.

If § 1367(a) were the sum total of the relevant statutory language, our holding would rest on that language alone. The statute, of course, instructs us to examine § 1367(b) to determine if any of its exceptions apply, so we proceed to that section. While § 1367(b) qualifies the broad rule of § 1367(a), it does not withdraw supplemental jurisdiction over the claims of the additional parties at issue here. The specific exceptions to § 1367(a) contained in § 1367(b), moreover, provide additional support for our conclusion that § 1367(a) confers supplemental jurisdiction over these claims. Section 1367(b), which applies only to diversity cases, withholds supplemental jurisdiction over the claims of plaintiffs proposed to be joined as indispensable parties under Federal Rule of Civil Procedure 19, or who seek to intervene pursuant to Rule 24. Nothing in the text of § 1367(b), however, withholds supplemental jurisdiction over the claims of plaintiffs permissively joined under Rule 20 . . . . The natural, indeed the necessary, inference is that § 1367 confers supplemental jurisdiction over claims by Rule 20 . . . plaintiffs. This inference . . . is strengthened by the fact that § 1367(b) explicitly excludes supplemental jurisdiction over claims against defendants joined under Rule 20.

We cannot accept the view, urged by some of the parties, commentators, and Courts of Appeals, that a district court lacks original jurisdiction over a civil action unless the court has original jurisdiction over every claim in the complaint. As we understand this position, it requires assuming either that all claims in the complaint must stand or fall as a single, indivisible "civil action" as a matter of definitional necessity — what we will refer to as the "indivisibility theory" — or else that the inclusion of a claim or party falling outside the district court's original jurisdiction somehow contaminates every other claim in the complaint, depriving the court of original jurisdiction over any of these claims — what we will refer to as the "contamination theory."

The indivisibility theory is easily dismissed, as it is inconsistent with the whole notion of supplemental jurisdiction. If a district court must have original jurisdiction over every claim in the complaint in order to have "original jurisdiction" over a "civil action," then in *Gibbs* there was no civil action of which the district court could assume original jurisdiction under § 1331, and so no basis for exercising supplemental jurisdiction over any of the claims. The indivisibility theory is further belied by our practice — in both federal-question and diversity cases — of allowing federal courts to cure jurisdictional defects by dismissing the offending parties rather than dismissing the entire action. *Clark*, for example, makes clear that claims that are jurisdictionally defective as to amount in controversy do not destroy original jurisdiction over other claims. 306 U.S. at 590 (dismissing parties who failed to meet the amount-in-controversy requirement but retaining jurisdiction over the remaining party). If the presence of jurisdictionally problematic claims in the complaint meant the district court was without original jurisdiction over the single, indivisible civil action before it, then the district court would have to dismiss the whole action rather than particular parties....

The contamination theory, as we have noted, can make some sense in the special context of the complete diversity requirement because the presence of nondiverse parties on both sides of a lawsuit eliminates the justification for providing a federal forum. The theory, however, makes little sense with respect to the amount-in-controversy requirement, which is meant to ensure that a dispute is sufficiently important to warrant federal-court attention. The presence of a single nondiverse party may eliminate the fear of bias with respect to all claims, but the presence of a claim that falls short of the minimum amount in controversy does nothing to reduce the importance of the claims that do meet this requirement....

Finally, it is suggested that our interpretation of § 1367(a) creates an anomaly regarding the exceptions listed in § 1367(b): It is not immediately obvious why Congress would withhold supplemental jurisdiction over plaintiffs joined as parties "needed for just adjudication" under Rule 19 but would allow supplemental jurisdiction over plaintiffs permissively joined under Rule 20. The omission of Rule 20 plaintiffs from the list of exceptions in § 1367(b) may have been an "unintentional drafting gap." If that is the case, it is up to Congress rather than the courts to fix it. The omission may seem odd, but it is not absurd....

And so we circle back to the original question. When the well-pleaded complaint in district court includes multiple claims, all part of the same case or controversy, and some, but not all, of the claims are within the court's original jurisdiction, does the court have before it "any civil action of which the district courts have original jurisdiction"? It does. Under § 1367, the court has original jurisdiction over the civil action comprising the claims for which there is no jurisdictional defect. No other reading of § 1367 is plausible in light of the text and structure of the jurisdictional statute. Though the special nature and purpose of the diversity requirement mean that a single nondiverse party can contaminate every other claim in the lawsuit, the contamination does not occur with respect to jurisdictional defects that go only to the substantive importance of individual claims.

It follows from this conclusion that the threshold requirement of § 1367(a) is satisfied in cases, like those now before us, where some, but not all, of the plaintiffs in a diversity action allege a sufficient amount in controversy. We hold that § 1367 by its plain text overruled *Clark* . . . and authorized supplemental jurisdiction over all claims by diverse parties arising out of the same Article III case or controversy, subject only to enumerated exceptions not applicable in the cases now before us.

C

The proponents of the alternative view of § 1367 insist that the statute is at least ambiguous and that we should look to other interpretive tools, including the legislative history of § 1367, which supposedly demonstrate Congress did not intend § 1367 to overrule [*Clark*]. We can reject this argument at the very outset simply because § 1367 is not ambiguous. . . . For the reasons elaborated above, interpreting § 1367 to foreclose supplemental jurisdiction over plaintiffs in diversity cases who do not meet the minimum amount in controversy is inconsistent with the text, read in light of other statutory provisions and our established jurisprudence. . . .

The judgment . . . of the Court of Appeals for the First Circuit is reversed, and the case is remanded for proceedings consistent with this opinion.

■ [The dissenting opinion of JUSTICE STEVENS, joined by JUSTICE BREYER, is omitted.]

■ JUSTICE GINSBURG, with whom JUSTICE STEVENS, JUSTICE O'CONNOR, and JUSTICE BREYER join, dissenting . . .

Section 1367, by its terms, operates only in civil actions "of which the district courts have original jurisdiction." The "original jurisdiction" relevant here is diversity-of-citizenship jurisdiction, conferred by § 1332. . . .

[Section] 1332, like all its predecessors, incorporates both a diverse-citizenship requirement and an amount-in-controversy specification.[5] . . .

---

5. Endeavoring to preserve the "complete diversity" rule first stated in *Strawbridge v. Curtiss*, 7 U.S. (3 Cranch) 267 (1806), the Court's opinion drives a wedge between the two components of 28 U.S.C. § 1332, treating the diversity-of-

These cases present the question whether Congress abrogated the nonaggregation rule long tied to § 1332 when it enacted § 1367. In answering that question, "context [should provide] a crucial guide." The Court should assume, as it ordinarily does, that Congress legislated against a background of law already in place and the historical development of that law. Here, that background is the statutory grant of diversity jurisdiction, the amount-in-controversy condition that Congress, from the start, has tied to the grant, and the nonaggregation rule this Court has long applied to the determination of the "matter in controversy." . . .

The Court is unanimous in reading § 1367(a) to permit pendent-party jurisdiction in federal-question cases, and thus, to overrule *Finley*. . . .

The Court divides, however, on the impact of § 1367(a) on diversity cases controlled by § 1332. Under the majority's reading, § 1367(a) permits the joinder of related claims cut loose from the nonaggregation rule that has long attended actions under § 1332. Only the claims specified in § 1367(b) would be excluded from § 1367(a)'s expansion of § 1332's grant of diversity jurisdiction. And because § 1367(b) contains no exception for joinder of plaintiffs under Rule 20 . . . , the Court concludes, *Clark* [has] been overruled.

The Court's reading is surely plausible, especially if one detaches § 1367(a) from its context and attempts no reconciliation with prior interpretations of § 1332's amount-in-controversy requirement. But § 1367(a)'s text, as the First Circuit held, can be read another way, one that would involve no rejection of *Clark* . . . .

As explained by the First Circuit . . . § 1367(a) addresses "civil action[s] of which the district courts have original jurisdiction," a formulation that, in diversity cases, is sensibly read to incorporate the rules on joinder and aggregation tightly tied to § 1332 at the time of § 1367's enactment. On this reading, a complaint must first meet that "original jurisdiction" measurement. If it does not, no supplemental jurisdiction is authorized. If it does, § 1367(a) authorizes "supplemental jurisdiction" over related claims. In other words, § 1367(a) would preserve undiminished, as part and parcel of § 1332 "original jurisdiction" determinations, both the "complete diversity" rule and the decisions restricting aggregation to arrive at the amount in controversy. . . . In contrast to the Court's construction of § 1367, which draws a sharp line between the diversity and amount-in-controversy components of § 1332, the interpretation presented here does not sever the two jurisdictional requirements. . . .

citizenship requirement as essential, the amount-in-controversy requirement as more readily disposable. Section 1332 itself, however, does not rank order the two requirements. What "[o]rdinary principl[e] of statutory construction" or "sound canon of interpretation," allows the Court to slice up § 1332 this way? In partial explanation, the Court asserts that amount in controversy can be analyzed claim-by-claim, but the diversity requirement cannot. It is not altogether clear why that should be so. The cure for improper joinder of a nondiverse party is the same as the cure for improper joinder of a plaintiff who does not satisfy the jurisdictional amount. In both cases, original jurisdiction can be preserved by dismissing the nonqualifying party. *See* Caterpillar Inc. v. Lewis, 519 U.S. 61, 64 (1996).

While § 1367's enigmatic text defies flawless interpretation, the precedent-preservative reading . . . does not attribute to Congress a jurisdictional enlargement broader than the one to which the legislators adverted, and it follows the sound counsel that "close questions of [statutory] construction should be resolved in favor of continuity and against change." Shapiro, *Continuity and Change in Statutory Interpretation*, 67 N.Y.U. L. REV. 921, 925 (1992).

For the reasons stated, I would hold that § 1367 does not overrule *Clark*. . . . I would therefore affirm the judgment of the Court of Appeals for the First Circuit . . . .

Notes and Questions

1. Note that all the Justices agree on two points about § 1367: it was meant to overrule *Finley* by providing a statutory basis for pendent-party jurisdiction, and it piggybacks on the "common nucleus of operative fact" test from *Gibbs*, despite the somewhat different language. They disagree on the limits that § 1367 imposes on the scope of pendent-party jurisdiction.

2. According to the majority, is there jurisdiction under § 1367 if two plaintiffs bring suit together for the same occurrence, each seeking $80,000 in damages, but one plaintiff is diverse from the defendant and one is not? How, if at all, is that different from *Allapattah* itself? Reread footnote 5 of the dissent. In *Newman-Green, Inc. v. Alfonzo-Larrain*, 490 U.S. 826, 832 (1989), the Court held — over a dissent by Justices Kennedy and Scalia — that Rule 21 "invests district courts with authority to allow a dispensable nondiverse party to be dropped at any time." Is that still good law after *Allapattah*'s holdings that "the presence in the action of a single plaintiff from the same State as a single defendant deprives the district court of original jurisdiction over the entire action," and that "[i]ncomplete diversity jurisdiction destroys original jurisdiction with respect to all claims"?

3. Recall that Rule 20 allows the inclusion of multiple defendants as well as multiple plaintiffs. Reread § 1367(b) carefully, looking for all mentions of Rule 20. Under *Allapattah*, there is jurisdiction over all claims arising out of the same occurrence if two plaintiffs sue a diverse defendant, one asking for $100,000 and the other asking for $50,000. Is there jurisdiction if a single plaintiff sues two diverse defendants on claims arising out of the same occurrence, one for $100,000 and one for $50,000? What if two plaintiffs sue two defendants (again on claims arising out of the same occurrence, and with complete diversity): one plaintiff asks for $100,000 from each defendant, and the other asks for $50,000 from each defendant? Do your answers make sense? In the multiple-plaintiff, multiple-defendant situation, are there *any* sensible answers that are consistent with *Allapattah*'s approach to § 1367?

4. Does *Allapattah* allow supplemental jurisdiction if two plaintiffs bring suit against a single defendant of diverse citizenship from the plaintiffs for the same occurrence, each seeking $50,000 in damages?

5. Assume that Congress intended *not* to overrule *Clark*, or any case except *Finley*. Rewrite § 1367 — especially § 1367(b) — to achieve that end.

6. *Allapattah* raises a particularly difficult problem under § 1367. You should be able to determine more easily whether there is supplemental jurisdiction in the following situations, just by reading the statute:

- Plaintiff sues (diverse) defendant on a state-law claim for more than $75,000, and defendant impleads under Rule 14 a third party who is from the same state as the defendant. Is there supplemental jurisdiction over the defendant's state-law claim against the third party for contribution or indemnification?
- Plaintiff sues a (diverse) defendant on a state-law claim for more than $75,000, and defendant impleads under Rule 14 a third party who is from the same state as the *plaintiff*. May the original plaintiff bring a state-law claim against the impleaded party?
- Plaintiff sues a (diverse) defendant on a state-law claim for more than $75,000, and defendant impleads under Rule 14 a third party who is from the same state as the plaintiff. Can the third party bring a state-law claim against the original plaintiff if it arises out of the same transaction or occurrence as the plaintiff's claim against the defendant?
- Same situation, but plaintiff now wants to bring a compulsory state-law counterclaim against the third-party defendant. May she?
- Plaintiff sues a (diverse) defendant on a state-law claim for more than $75,000, and a third party from defendant's state wishes to *intervene* as a plaintiff under Rule 24. May she? (You need not know anything about Rule 24 intervention to answer this question.)

7. Recall that traditionally permissive counterclaims did not fall within supplemental (or ancillary) jurisdiction. (*See supra* pp. 361-62, Note 2(b).) A few courts, however, have interpreted the "same case or controversy" language of § 1367 more broadly than the "transaction or occurrence" language of Rule 13. They have thus held a permissive counterclaim with an attenuated relationship to the original claim to be within supplemental jurisdiction. *See, e.g.*, Global Naps, Inc. v. Verizon New Eng., Inc., 603 F.3d 71 (1st Cir. 2010); Jones v. Ford Motor Credit, 358 F.3d 205 (2d Cir 2004); Channell v. Citicorp Nat'l Servs., Inc., 89 F.3d 379 (7th Cir. 1996). *But see* Ammons v. Ally Fin., Inc., 305 F. Supp. 3d 818, 820-23 (M.D. Tenn. 2018) (rejecting supplemental jurisdiction over permissive counterclaim).

8. Section 1367(c) gives courts discretion to decline supplemental jurisdiction in some situations. Is that discretion consistent with *Gibbs*? The Supreme Court has confirmed that § 1367(c) is discretionary; a decision to decline jurisdiction does not remove the underlying subject-matter jurisdiction. "[W]hether a court has subject-matter jurisdiction over a claim is distinct from whether a court chooses to exercise [its] discretion." Carlsbad Tech., Inc., v. HIF Bio, Inc., 556 U.S. 635 (2009). If the court does dismiss a state-law claim, the statute of limitations for that claim is tolled during the entire period that the federal court is considering it, plus thirty

days after dismissal. Thus, if there is one year left on the statute of limitations at the time the case is filed, the plaintiff has a year and thirty days to refile in state court after the federal dismissal. Artis v. Dist. of Columbia, 583 U.S. —, 138 S. Ct. 594 (2018).

SECTION E: REMOVAL JURISDICTION AND PROCEDURE

Just because a claim can be brought in federal court does not mean it must be. Federal-court jurisdiction is *presumptively concurrent*: absent evidence of congressional intent to give federal courts *exclusive jurisdiction* over a particular type of case, plaintiffs may choose to bring a claim over which there is federal jurisdiction in either federal court or state court. If a plaintiff brings such a case in state court, however, the defendant is sometimes given the option to *remove* it to federal court. Notice that removal is a one-way ratchet: if a plaintiff chooses to file in federal court (and there is federal jurisdiction), the defendant usually has no choice but to remain there. As you read through this section, think about why each party should be given an option to choose federal court, and what limits on removal jurisdiction follow from your explanation.

Begin by reading § 1441(a)-(c) and –(f). (Those provisions were revised in late 2011, but not in ways that would affect the reasoning or result in the *Spencer* case, below.) Then consider the following case.

SPENCER V. U.S. DISTRICT COURT FOR THE NORTHERN DISTRICT OF CALIFORNIA

393 F.3d 867 (9th Cir. 2004)

Before REINHARDT, THOMPSON, and BERZON, Circuit Judges.

THOMPSON, Senior Circuit Judge.

Petitioners seek a writ of mandamus ordering the district court to remand this action to state court. Petitioners . . . contend that the joinder of a local, albeit diverse, defendant following removal from state to federal court destroyed subject-matter jurisdiction, requiring remand. *See* 28 U.S.C. §§ 1441(b), 1447(c). Because . . . we find no error in the district court's determination that federal diversity jurisdiction is not destroyed by the joinder of a local, diverse defendant subsequent to removal, we deny the petition for a writ of mandamus.

I.

Lindsay C. Spencer, an electrical lineman, died as a result of injuries he sustained while working in an aerial lift bucket to repair and upgrade a Pacific Gas & Electric Company ("PG & E") utility pole. According to the petitioners, the operating controls of the lift bucket were unintentionally activated, causing the lift mechanism and the bucket to move suddenly and forcefully into the adjacent utility pole, injuring Mr. Spencer. The aerial lift truck then catapulted Mr. Spencer into the air, throwing him against a high voltage wire, causing his death by electrocution.

Mr. Spencer's son and estate brought the present wrongful death action in the superior court in California, alleging state law product liability claims against the manufacturer of the lift bucket, Altec Industries . . . .

Altec timely removed the case to the United States District Court for the Northern District of California on the basis of federal diversity jurisdiction. The plaintiffs are resident citizens of Alaska, and Altec asserts it is a citizen of Alabama. There is no dispute that the parties are diverse and that the required statutory amount in controversy is satisfied.

During discovery in the district court, the Spencers learned that possible negligence by PG & E may have caused or contributed to activating the lift bucket controls. They then moved to amend their complaint to name PG & E as a defendant . . . . The Spencers concurrently moved to remand the action to state court, arguing that remand would be required due to the joinder of PG & E. Specifically, the Spencers contended that because PG & E is a citizen of California for purposes of diversity jurisdiction, and because 28 U.S.C. § 1441(b) prohibits removal from state to federal court when at least one defendant is a citizen of the state in which the action is filed, the joinder of PG & E would destroy federal removal jurisdiction and require remand under 28 U.S.C. § 1447(c). . . .

The district court granted the Spencers' motion to join PG & E as a defendant, but denied their motion to remand the action to state court. . . . The district court declined to certify its order for interlocutory appeal, and the petitioners then filed this petition for a writ of mandamus.

II.

[The Court first held that the district court did not commit clear error by failing to abstain from the exercise of jurisdiction.]

We next consider the petitioners' contention that the district court should have remanded the case to state court because, once PG & E was added as a defendant, the district court lost subject-matter jurisdiction.

A civil action brought in a state court over which federal courts have original jurisdiction may be removed by the defendant to the appropriate district court. 28 U.S.C. § 1441(a). However, § 1441(b) imposes a limitation on actions removed pursuant to diversity jurisdiction: "such action[s] shall be removable only if none of the parties in interest properly joined and served as defendants is a citizen of the State in which such action is brought." 28 U.S.C. § 1441(b).* This "forum defendant" rule "reflects the belief that [federal] diversity jurisdiction is unnecessary because there is

---

* In 2011 Congress amended § 1441. This limitation, slightly revised in wording but unchanged in effect, now appears in § 1441(b)(2). — Ed.

less reason to fear state court prejudice against the defendants if one or more of them is from the forum state." ERWIN CHEMERINSKY, FEDERAL JURISDICTION § 5.5, at 345 (4th ed. 2003).

It is thus clear that the presence of a local defendant at the time removal is sought bars removal. 28 U.S.C. § 1441(b).

What is less clear is whether the joinder of a local, but completely diverse defendant, after an action has been removed to federal court, requires remand. This is the question we confront in this case. The district court concluded it was not required to remand the case to state court, and we agree.

Challenges to removal jurisdiction require an inquiry into the circumstances at the time the notice of removal is filed. When removal is proper at that time, subsequent events, at least those that do not destroy original subject-matter jurisdiction, do not require remand. *See, e.g.*, Van Meter v. State Farm Fire & Cas. Co., 1 F.3d 445, 450 (6th Cir. 1993) (characterizing removal jurisdiction as "necessarily tied to a temporal reference point, namely the time of removal"); *In re* Shell Oil, 966 F.2d 1130, 1133 (7th Cir. 1992) (stating that nothing in the text or legislative history of § 1447(c) alters the "traditional view" that "jurisdiction present at the time a suit is filed or removed is unaffected by subsequent acts").

Because the joinder of PG & E did not affect the propriety of the district court's original subject-matter jurisdiction, we need not decide whether an event occurring subsequent to removal which would defeat original subject-matter jurisdiction divests a district court of jurisdiction and requires remand. *Compare Van Meter*, 1 F.3d at 450, *Shell Oil*, 966 F.3d at 1133, *and* Poore v. Am.-Amicable Life Ins. Co. of Tex., 218 F.3d 1287 (11th Cir. 2000) (events subsequent to removal do not divest a district court of subject-matter jurisdiction), *with* Mayes v. Rapoport, 198 F.3d 457, 461-63 (4th Cir. 1999), Cobb v. Delta Exps., Inc., 186 F.3d 675, 677 (5th Cir. 1999), *and* Casas Office Mach., Inc. v. Mita Copystar Am., Inc., 42 F.3d 668, 673-75 (1st Cir. 1995) (events subsequent to removal which destroy federal subject-matter jurisdiction require remand).

We conclude that the post-removal joinder of PG & E, a "forum defendant," did not oust the district court of subject-matter jurisdiction. The forum defendant rule of 28 U.S.C. § 1441(b) is only applicable at the time a notice of removal is filed. Because no local defendant was a party to the action at that time, and given the preservation of complete diversity of the parties thereafter, the district court did not err in denying the Spencers' motion to remand. As stated above, we do not decide what the result would be if PG & E were a non-diverse defendant.

Petition for mandamus denied.

Notes and Questions

1. In addition to the late-joinder issue raised in *Spencer*, the language of § 1441(b) has given rise to another question. If the bar on removal applies

only to parties "properly joined and served as defendants," may a putative defendant remove *before* being served? Sometimes called "snap removal," this tactic is increasingly available as defendants can electronically monitor dockets and catch lawsuits as they are filed, before actual service. District courts are split on whether such removals are valid. The two courts of appeals to rule on the question have held that an in-state defendant *may* remove if it does so before being served. Gibbons v. Bristol–Myers Squibb Co., 919 F.3d 699 (2d Cir. 2019); Encompass Ins. Co. v. Stone Mansion Rest. Inc., 902 F.3d 147 (3d Cir. 2018). Both courts relied on the text of 1441(a).

2. A refusal to remand is not ordinarily appealable, because it is not a final order (recall the discussion of appealability in Chapter Six). The defendants in *Spencer* moved in the district court to certify the issue for interlocutory appeal under 28 U.S.C. § 1292(b), but the district court denied the motion. They therefore sought a writ of mandamus from the Court of Appeals, which would have ordered the district court to remand the case. This is why the defendant in the Court of Appeals was the district court.

On the other hand, if a district court orders the remand of a case to state court, the order is ordinarily neither appealable nor otherwise reviewable on appeal. 28 U.S.C. § 1447(d); *see* Powerex Corp. v. Reliant Energy Servs., Inc., 551 U.S. 224 (2007). There are a few exceptions to or routes around this limitation. *See, e.g.,* 28 U.S.C. § 1447(d) (allowing appeal of an order remanding a case removed under § 1443); *id.* § 1453(c) (allowing appeal of a remand order in certain class actions); Thermtron Prods., Inc. v. Hermansdorfer, 423 U.S. 336 (1976) (permitting use of mandamus when a judge orders remand for a reason unrelated to a lack of subject-matter jurisdiction; Osborn v. Haley, 549 U.S. 225 (2007) (permitting appeal of an order remanding a case against a federal official). A decision to decline the exercise of jurisdiction under § 1367(c), and to remand the state-law claims to state court, is not a remand for lack of jurisdiction and thus is reviewable on appeal. Carlsbad Tech., Inc. v. HIF Bio, Inc., 556 U.S. 635 (2009).

3. Section 1441(a) allows a defendant to remove a case only when it might have been filed in federal court in the first place. Therefore, all of the doctrines governing §§ 1331 and 1332, discussed in earlier sections of this chapter, govern removal cases. For example, a case cannot be successfully removed on the ground that a counterclaim or defense raises a federal question (due to the well-pleaded complaint rule of *Mottley*). Nor can a case raising state-law claims be successfully removed when the claims of multiple plaintiffs satisfy the amount-in-controversy rule in the aggregate, but no plaintiff's claim meets the jurisdictional amount of § 1332(a) (due to the rule of *Clark v. Paul Gray*, which survives § 1367).

4. Although the existence of original federal jurisdiction over the case is a necessary prerequisite for removal, it is not sufficient. Sections 1441, 1446, and 1447 limit the right of removal in various ways. First, some parties have no right of removal. Plaintiffs are not permitted to remove under any circumstances—even if the defendant brings a counterclaim that lies within federal jurisdiction. Shamrock Oil & Gas Corp. v. Sheets, 313 U.S. 100 (1941).

Second, courts are split on whether third-party defendants are permitted to remove, although the majority holds that they may not do so. *Compare* First Nat'l Bank of Pulaski v. Curry, 301 F.3d 456 (6th Cir. 2002) (removal not permitted), Lewis v. Windsor Door Co., 926 F.2d 729 (8th Cir. 1991) (same), *and* Thomas v. Shelton, 740 F.2d 478 (7th Cir. 1984) (same), *with* Texas *ex rel.* Bd. of Regents v. Walker, 142 F.3d 813 (5th Cir. 1998) (removal permitted). In *Home Depot U.S.A., Inc. v. Jackson*, 587 U.S. —, 139 S. Ct. 1743 (2019), the Court held that a party brought into a lawsuit through a counterclaim filed by the original defendant (using the state equivalent of Fed. R. Civ. P. 13(h)) may not remove. Citibank had sued Jackson in state court to collect a credit-card debt; Jackson responded by counterclaiming against Citibank and joining both Home Depot and another party to the counterclaim. After Citibank settled, Home Depot removed the case to federal court. The district court, court of appeals, and Supreme Court all held that § 1441(a) did not authorize the removal. The majority's language and reasoning suggest strongly that third-party (impleaded) defendants are similarly prohibited from removing cases from state to federal court: "in the context of [the] removal provisions the term 'defendant' refers only to the party sued by the original plaintiff." 139 S. Ct. at 1746.

Third, in most cases, "all defendants who have been properly joined and served must join in or consent to the removal of the action." 28 U.S.C. § 1446(b)(2)(A). If even one defendant refuses to do so, the case cannot properly be removed.

Fourth, § 1446(b) contains two timing limitations. A notice of removal must be filed within 30 days of the defendant's receipt (or, in a multi-defendant case, the last-served defendant's receipt) of a pleading that contains removable claims; and, in diversity cases only, no case may be removed more than one year after its commencement in state court, "unless the district court finds that the plaintiff has acted in bad faith in order to prevent a defendant from removing the action." 28 U.S.C. § 1446(c)(1).

5. Determining whether the amount-in-controversy requirement for diversity jurisdiction is satisfied in cases removed from state court has sometimes been a vexing problem. To discourage headline-grabbing, some states forbid stating large alleged damage amounts, at least in some kinds of cases; state-court plaintiffs may be able to recover more than the amount claimed in the complaint; some claims are for injunctive or declaratory relief and may be hard to value in monetary terms; and sometimes plaintiffs have tried to make removal impossible by claiming a sum that does not satisfy the federal amount-in-controversy requirement — but then, after a removal deadline has passed, claiming more. Jurisdictional incentives have resulted in contorted positions, with defendants seeking removal, for instance, arguing that they face large damage exposure (but, of course, are not ultimately liable for such sums).

Congress addressed these problems in the Jurisdiction and Venue Clarification Act of 2011. To summarize briefly many lines of statutory text in 28 U.S.C. § 1446(c)(2)-(3): the basic rule remains the same as for diversity cases originally filed in federal court, with "the sum demanded in good faith in the initial pleading" controlling—but with exceptions allowing the notice of removal to state an amount in cases for nonmonetary relief or when state law forbids demands for a specific sum or allows recovery above the amount claimed; or when state-court proceedings including discovery support a larger amount than originally claimed; or when the federal court finds "that the plaintiff deliberately failed to disclose the actual amount in controversy to prevent removal" until after the one-year period for removals based on diversity.

6. *Spencer* does not fully explain why the "forum defendant" rule prevents removal to federal court in a diversity case that the out-of-state plaintiff could have filed in federal court. (Hint: which party, home-stater or out-of-stater, is choosing the federal forum in the cases of original filing in federal court and removal from state court?) Why does § 1441(b)(2) draw a distinction between federal-question and diversity cases? Is that distinction consistent with allowing a *plaintiff* to file a diversity action in federal court in his own state?

7. What should happen if plaintiff files in state court a claim over which federal courts have exclusive jurisdiction? Can the case be removed? (Hint: re-read § 1441(f).)

8. Section 1441 provides the usual basis for removal, but other sections of the United States Code also govern removal jurisdiction. For instance, §§ 1442 and 1443 concern removal in specialized circumstances. Congress has passed a number of other context-specific removal provisions, including some that do not require all defendants to consent to removal. Conversely, Congress has also made certain types of cases nonremovable even though they come within federal-question jurisdiction, thus creating exceptions to § 1441(a). Most of these exceptions are contained in § 1445.

9. The basic procedures for removal and remand are specified in §§ 1446 and 1447. In addition, the Supreme Court has placed a judicial gloss on many removal issues. The most important cases include: *Dart Cherokee Basin Operating Co. v. Owens*, 574 U.S. 81 (2014) (notice of removal "need include only a plausible allegation that the amount in controversy exceeds the jurisdictional threshold"); *Beneficial National Bank v. Anderson*, 539 U.S. 1 (2003) (removal permitted if purported state-law claim is actually a federal claim "artfully pleaded" to look as if it raises only state-law questions); *Syngenta Crop Protection, Inc. v. Henson*, 537 U.S. 28 (2002) (removal permitted only under removal statutes, not under All Writs Act, 28 U.S.C. § 1651); *Murphy Bros. v. Michetti Pipe Stringing, Inc.*, 526 U.S. 344 (1999) (30-day clock in § 1446(b) begins at service of summons and complaint); and *Rivet v. Regions Bank of Louisiana*, 522 U.S. 470 (1998) (claim preclusion from a prior federal judgment is a defensive plea, not a basis for removal).

10. If you have studied claim joinder by this point in your course, you know that Federal Rule of Civil Procedure 18(a) permits a plaintiff to join both related and unrelated claims against a defendant. State claim-joinder rules are similar. What happens when a state-court plaintiff brings an action against a citizen of the same state and includes both a federal-law

claim and a state-law claim that is *not* related to the federal-law claim, and the defendant wants to remove? That doesn't happen all that frequently, but it occurs often enough that Congress has made repeated efforts to deal with the situation. (Trust us: you really, *really* don't want to know the history.) Look again at 28 U.S.C. § 1441(c), the current version of which got onto the books in a revision of jurisdiction and venue statutes in late 2011. Note that removal under § 1441(c) is of "the entire action" — including the unrelated state-law claim that is not within statutory original or supplemental jurisdiction (and is presumably outside federal Article III judicial power as well). Should that create any problems with the constitutionality of the statute?

11. Assuming that the statute is constitutional, consider a case in which a state-court plaintiff sues a co-citizen on a federal-law claim, a *related* state-law claim, and an *unrelated* state-law claim. The defendant removes the case to federal court. What are the federal court's options with respect to each of the three claims? (Hint: if you have not yet studied supplemental jurisdiction, read 28 U.S.C. § 1367(c).)

Chapter Eleven

State Law in Federal Courts (The *Erie* Doctrine)

In any system with multiple sources of law, courts will face questions of *choice of law*. State courts must decide, for example, whether to apply their law or another state's law to cases involving out-of-state parties or events. International disputes raise the same problem: if a French corporation and an American corporation enter into a contract, what law governs if the parties disagree? Most questions of this sort — often labeled *horizontal* choice-of-law questions — are addressed in courses on Conflict of Laws.

In the American federal system, a more specialized choice-of-law problem — often called a *vertical* choice-of-law question — also arises. When parties are suing in federal-question jurisdiction, a federal statutory or constitutional provision usually governs, and courts can apply that federal law. But what if parties are suing in diversity jurisdiction, for example for breach of contract? No federal statute governs most private contracts; should there be a federal common law of contracts, or should federal courts apply state law? If the federal courts apply state substantive law, where does that leave the Federal Rules of Civil Procedure? Are they applicable only in federal-question cases? These and related questions are the subject of this chapter.

Section A: Perspectives on *Erie*

Congress enacted the Rules of Decision Act, dealing with some aspects of choice of law, in 1789, and the statute has changed little since then. Nevertheless, the Supreme Court has, over the years, adopted two quite different interpretations of the law. As you read the Act, the Supreme Court cases staking out opposite positions, and commentary on the two cases, consider the underlying question of why we might want state law to apply in diversity cases (and why we might not).

RULES OF DECISION ACT

28 U.S.C. § 1652

The laws of the several states, except where the Constitution or treaties of the United States or Acts of Congress otherwise require or provide, shall be regarded as rules of decision in civil actions in the courts of the United States, in cases where they apply.

SWIFT V. TYSON

41 U.S. (16 Pet.) 1 (1842)

[Defendant Tyson gave a bill of exchange (a negotiable instrument, like a check) to a third party in payment for land that the third party in fact did not own and thus could not sell. The third party endorsed the bill over to plaintiff Swift in payment of a pre-existing debt. When Swift tried to collect from Tyson, Tyson claimed that the third party's fraud effectively nullified the bill of exchange. New York courts had uniformly held that fraud in the transaction provided a defense against payment if the bill was offered in payment for a pre-existing debt. Other courts had begun to extend the holder-in-due-course doctrine (that one who accepts a note without knowledge of its fraudulent origins can still recover) to cases of pre-existing debt. Because the case was in federal court in New York on diversity grounds, the question was which doctrine applied: the New York doctrine, favoring Tyson, or the holder-in-due-course doctrine, favoring Swift.]

■ MR. JUSTICE STORY delivered the opinion of the Court. . . .

There is no doubt, that a *bona fide* holder of a negotiable instrument, for a valuable consideration, without any notice of facts which impeach its validity as between the antecedent parties, if he takes it under an endorsement made before the same becomes due, holds the title unaffected by these facts, and may recover thereon, although as between the antecedent parties the transaction may be without any legal validity. This is a doctrine so long and so well established, and so essential to the security of negotiable paper, that it is laid up among the fundamentals of the law, and requires no authority or reasoning to be now brought in its support. . . .

In the present case, the plaintiff is a *bona fide* holder without notice for what the law deems a good and valid consideration, that is, for a preexisting debt; and the only real question in the cause is, whether, under the circumstances of the present case, such a pre-existing debt constitutes a valuable consideration, in the sense of the general rule applicable to negotiable instruments. . . . [T]he acceptance having been made in New York, the argument on behalf of the defendant is, that the contract is to be treated as a New York contract, and therefore to be governed by the laws of New York, as expounded by its Courts. . . . And then it is further contended, that by the law of New York, as thus expounded by its Courts, a pre-existing debt does not constitute, in the sense of the general rule, a valuable consideration applicable to negotiable instruments. . . .

But, admitting the doctrine to be fully settled in New York, it remains to be considered, whether it is obligatory upon this Court, if it differs from the principles established in the general commercial law. It is observable, that the Courts of New York do not found their decisions upon this point, upon any local statute, or positive, fixed or ancient local usage: but they deduce the doctrine from the general principles of commercial law. It is, however, contended, that [the Rules of Decision Act] furnishes a rule obligatory upon this court to follow the decisions of the state tribunals in all cases to which they apply. That section provides "that the laws of the several states . . . shall be regarded as rules of decision . . . ." In order to maintain the argument, it is essential, therefore, to hold, that the word "laws," in this section, includes within the scope of its meaning, the decisions of the local tribunals. In the ordinary use of language, it will hardly be contended, that the decisions of courts constitute laws. They are, at most, only evidence of what the laws are; and are not of themselves laws. They are often re-examined, reversed and qualified by the Courts themselves, whenever they are found to be either defective, or ill-founded, or otherwise incorrect. The laws of a state are more usually understood to mean the rules and enactments promulgated by the legislative authority thereof, or long-established local customs having the force of laws. In all the various cases which have hitherto come before us for decision, this Court have uniformly supposed, that the true interpretation of the [Act] limited its application to state laws strictly local, that is to say, to the positive statutes of the state, and the construction thereof adopted by the local tribunals, and to rights and titles to things having a permanent locality, such as the rights and titles to real estate, and other matters immovable and intraterritorial in their nature and character. It never has been supposed by us, that the section did apply, or was designed to apply, to questions of a more general nature, not at all dependent upon local statutes or local usages of a fixed and permanent operation, as, for example, to the construction of ordinary contracts or other written instruments, and especially to questions of general commercial law, where the state tribunals are called upon to perform the like functions as ourselves, that is, to ascertain, upon general reasoning and legal analogies, what is the true exposition of the contract or instrument, or what is the just rule furnished by the principles of commercial law to govern the case. And we have not now the slightest difficulty in holding, that this section, upon its true intendment and construction, is strictly limited to local statutes and local usages of the character before stated, and does not extend to contracts and other instruments of a commercial nature, the true interpretation and effect whereof are to be sought, not in the decisions of the local tribunals, but in the general principles and doctrines of commercial jurisprudence. Undoubtedly, the decisions of the local tribunals upon such subjects are entitled to, and will receive, the most deliberate attention and respect of this Court; but they cannot furnish positive rules, or conclusive authority, by which our own judgments are to be bound up and governed. The law respecting negotiable instruments may be truly declared . . . to be in a great measure, not the law of a single country only, but of the commercial world....

It becomes necessary for us, therefore, upon the present occasion, to express our own opinion of the true result of the commercial law upon the question now before us. And we have no hesitation in saying, that a pre-existing debt does constitute a valuable consideration in the sense of the general rule already stated, as applicable to negotiable instruments.... It is for the benefit and convenience of the commercial world to give as wide an extent as practicable to the credit and circulation of negotiable paper.... But establish the opposite conclusion, that negotiable paper cannot be applied in payment of or as security for pre-existing debts, without letting in all the equities between the original and antecedent parties, and the value and circulation of such securities must be essentially diminished, and the debtor driven to the embarrassment of making a sale thereof, often at a ruinous discount, to some third person, and then by circuity to apply the proceeds to the payment of his debts. What, indeed, upon such a doctrine, would become of that large class of cases, where new notes are given by the same or by other parties, by way of renewal or security to banks, in lieu of old securities discounted by them, which have arrived at maturity? Probably more than one-half of all bank transactions in our country, as well as those of other countries, are of this nature. The doctrine would strike a fatal blow at all discounts of negotiable securities for pre-existing debts....

■ [The concurring opinion of MR. JUSTICE CATRON is omitted.]

ERIE RAILROAD CO. V. TOMPKINS

304 U.S. 64 (1938)

■ MR. JUSTICE BRANDEIS delivered the opinion of the Court.

The question for decision is whether the oft-challenged doctrine of *Swift v. Tyson*, 41 U.S. (16 Pet.) 1 (1842), shall now be disapproved.

Tompkins, a citizen of Pennsylvania, was injured on a dark night by a passing freight train of the Erie Railroad Company while walking along its right of way at Hughestown in that state. He claimed that the accident occurred through negligence in the operation, or maintenance, of the train; that he was rightfully on the premises as licensee because on a commonly used beaten footpath which ran for a short distance alongside the tracks; and that he was struck by something which looked like a door projecting from one of the moving cars. To enforce that claim he brought an action in the federal court for Southern New York, which had jurisdiction because the company is a corporation of that state. It denied liability; and the case was tried by a jury.

The Erie insisted that its duty to Tompkins was no greater than that owed to a trespasser. It contended, among other things, that its duty to Tompkins, and hence its liability, should be determined in accordance with the Pennsylvania law; that under the law of Pennsylvania, as declared by its highest court, persons who use pathways along the railroad right of way — that is, a longitudinal pathway as distinguished from a crossing — are to be deemed trespassers; and that the railroad is not liable for injuries to undiscovered trespassers resulting from its negligence, unless it be wanton or willful. Tompkins denied that any such rule had been established by the decisions of the Pennsylvania courts; and contended that, since there was no statute of the state on the subject, the railroad's duty and liability is to be determined in federal courts as a matter of general law.

The trial judge refused to rule that the applicable law precluded recovery. The jury brought in a verdict of $30,000; and the judgment entered thereon was affirmed by the Circuit Court of Appeals, which held that it was unnecessary to consider whether the law of Pennsylvania was as contended, because the question was one not of local, but of general, law, and that "upon questions of general law the federal courts are free, in absence of a local statute, to exercise their independent judgment as to what the law is; and it is well settled that the question of the responsibility of a railroad for injuries caused by its servants is one of general law." . . .

The Erie had contended that application of the Pennsylvania rule was required, among other things, by [the Rules of Decision Act]. . . .

Because of the importance of the question whether the federal court was free to disregard the alleged rule of the Pennsylvania common law, we granted certiorari.

First. Swift v. Tyson held that federal courts exercising jurisdiction on the ground of diversity of citizenship need not, in matters of general jurisprudence, apply the unwritten law of the state as declared by its highest court; that they are free to exercise an independent judgment as to what the common law of the state is — or should be . . . .

Doubt was repeatedly expressed as to the correctness of the construction [in *Swift*], and as to the soundness of the rule which it introduced. But it was the more recent research of a competent scholar, who examined the original document, which established that the construction given to [the statute] by the Court was erroneous; and that the purpose of the section was merely to make certain that, in all matters except those in which some federal law is controlling, the federal courts exercising jurisdiction in diversity of citizenship cases would apply as their rules of decision the law of the state, unwritten as well as written.[5]

Criticism of the doctrine became widespread after the decision of *Black & White Taxicab Co. v. Brown & Yellow Taxicab Co.*, 276 U.S. 518 (1928). There, Brown and Yellow, a Kentucky corporation owned by Kentuckians, and the Louisville & Nashville Railroad, also a Kentucky corporation, wished that the former should have the exclusive privilege of soliciting passenger and baggage transportation at the Bowling Green, Kentucky, railroad station; and that the Black and White, a competing Kentucky corporation, should be prevented from interfering with that privilege.

5. Charles Warren, *New Light on the History of the Federal Judiciary Act of 1789*, 37 HARV. L. REV. 49, 51-52, 81-88, 108 (1923).

Knowing that such a contract would be void under the common law of Kentucky, it was arranged that the Brown and Yellow reincorporate under the law of Tennessee, and that the contract with the railroad should be executed there. The suit was then brought by the Tennessee corporation in the federal court for western Kentucky to enjoin competition by the Black and White; an injunction issued by the District Court was sustained by the Court of Appeals; and this Court, citing many decisions in which the doctrine of *Swift v. Tyson* had been applied, affirmed the decree.

Second. Experience in applying the doctrine of *Swift v. Tyson*, had revealed its defects, political and social; and the benefits expected to flow from the rule did not accrue. Persistence of state courts in their own opinions on questions of common law prevented uniformity; and the impossibility of discovering a satisfactory line of demarcation between the province of general law and that of local law developed a new well of uncertainties.

On the other hand, the mischievous results of the doctrine had become apparent. Diversity of citizenship jurisdiction was conferred in order to prevent apprehended discrimination in state courts against those not citizens of the state. *Swift v. Tyson* introduced grave discrimination by noncitizens against citizens. It made rights enjoyed under the unwritten "general law" vary according to whether enforcement was sought in the state or in the federal court; and the privilege of selecting the court in which the right should be determined was conferred upon the noncitizen. Thus, the doctrine rendered impossible equal protection of the law. In attempting to promote uniformity of law throughout the United States, the doctrine had prevented uniformity in the administration of the law of the state.

The discrimination resulting became in practice far-reaching. This resulted in part from the broad province accorded to the so-called "general law" as to which federal courts exercised an independent judgment. In addition to questions of purely commercial law, "general law" was held to include the obligations under contracts entered into and to be performed within the state, the extent to which a carrier operating within a state may stipulate for exemption from liability for his own negligence or that of his employee; the liability for torts committed within the state upon persons resident or property located there, even where the question of liability depended upon the scope of a property right conferred by the state; and the right to exemplary or punitive damages. Furthermore, state decisions construing local deeds, mineral conveyances, and even devises of real estate, were disregarded.

In part the discrimination resulted from the wide range of persons held entitled to avail themselves of the federal rule by resort to the diversity of citizenship jurisdiction. Through this jurisdiction individual citizens willing to remove from their own state and become citizens of another might avail themselves of the federal rule. And, without even change of residence, a corporate citizen of the state could avail itself of the federal rule by reincorporating under the laws of another state, as was done in the *Taxicab* case.

The injustice and confusion incident to the doctrine of *Swift v. Tyson* have been repeatedly urged as reasons for abolishing or limiting diversity of citizenship jurisdiction. Other legislative relief has been proposed. If only a question of statutory construction were involved, we should not be prepared to abandon a doctrine so widely applied throughout nearly a century. But the unconstitutionality of the course pursued has now been made clear, and compels us to do so.

Third. Except in matters governed by the Federal Constitution or by acts of Congress, the law to be applied in any case is the law of the state. And whether the law of the state shall be declared by its Legislature in a statute or by its highest court in a decision is not a matter of federal concern. There is no federal general common law. Congress has no power to declare substantive rules of common law applicable in a state whether they be local in their nature or "general," be they commercial law or a part of the law of torts. And no clause in the Constitution purports to confer such a power upon the federal courts. As stated by Mr. Justice Field when protesting in *Baltimore & Ohio R.R. v. Baugh*, 149 U.S. 368, 401 (1893), against ignoring the Ohio common law of fellow servant liability:

> I am aware that what has been termed the general law of the country — which is often little less than what the judge advancing the doctrine thinks at the time should be the general law on a particular subject — has been often advanced in judicial opinions of this court to control a conflicting law of a state. I admit that learned judges have fallen into the habit of repeating this doctrine as a convenient mode of brushing aside the law of a state in conflict with their views. And I confess that, moved and governed by the authority of the great names of those judges, I have, myself, in many instances, unhesitatingly and confidently, but I think now erroneously, repeated the same doctrine. But . . . there stands, as a perpetual protest against its repetition, the Constitution of the United States, which recognizes and preserves the autonomy and independence of the States — independence in their legislative and independence in their judicial departments. Supervision over either the legislative or the judicial action of the states is in no case permissible except as to matters by the Constitution specifically authorized or delegated to the United States. Any interference with either, except as thus permitted, is an invasion of the authority of the state, and, to that extent, a denial of its independence.

The fallacy underlying the rule declared in *Swift v. Tyson* is made clear by Mr. Justice Holmes. The doctrine rests upon the assumption that there is "a transcendental body of law outside of any particular State but obligatory within it unless and until changed by statute," that federal courts have the power to use their judgment as to what the rules of common law are; and that in the federal courts "the parties are entitled to an independent judgment on matters of general law":

> But law in the sense in which courts speak of it today does not exist without some definite authority behind it. The common law so far as it is enforced in a State, whether called common law or not, is not the

common law generally but the law of that State existing by the authority of that State without regard to what it may have been in England or anywhere else. . . .

The authority and only authority is the State, and if that be so, the voice adopted by the State as its own [whether it be of its Legislature or of its Supreme Court] should utter the last word.

Thus the doctrine of *Swift v. Tyson* is, as Mr. Justice Holmes said, "an unconstitutional assumption of powers by the Courts of the United States which no lapse of time or respectable array of opinion should make us hesitate to correct." In disapproving that doctrine we do not hold unconstitutional [the Rules of Decision Act] or any other Act of Congress. We merely declare that in applying the doctrine this Court and the lower courts have invaded rights which in our opinion are reserved by the Constitution to the several States.

Fourth. The defendant contended that by the common law of Pennsylvania as declared by its highest court . . . , the only duty owed to the plaintiff was to refrain from willful or wanton injury. The plaintiff denied that such is the Pennsylvania law. In support of their respective contentions the parties discussed and cited many decisions of the Supreme Court of the State. The Circuit Court of Appeals ruled that the question of liability is one of general law; and on that ground declined to decide the issue of state law. As we hold this was error, the judgment is reversed and the case remanded to it for further proceedings in conformity with our opinion.

Reversed.

■ MR. JUSTICE CARDOZO took no part in the consideration or decision of this case.

■ [The dissenting opinion of MR. JUSTICE BUTLER, joined by MR. JUSTICE MCREYNOLDS, is omitted.]

■ MR. JUSTICE REED.

I concur in the conclusion reached in this case, in the disapproval of the doctrine of *Swift v. Tyson*, 41 U.S. (16 Pet.) 1 (1842), and in the reasoning of the majority opinion, except in so far as it relies upon the unconstitutionality of the "course pursued" by the federal courts.

The "doctrine of *Swift v. Tyson*," as I understand it, is that the words "the laws," as used in [the Rules of Decision Act], do not include in their meaning "the decisions of the local tribunals." . . .

To decide the case now before us and to "disapprove" the doctrine of *Swift v. Tyson* requires only that we say that the words "the laws" include in their meaning the decisions of the local tribunals. As the majority opinion shows, by . . . the first quotation from Mr. Justice Holmes, that this Court is now of the view that "laws" includes "decisions," it is unnecessary to go further and declare that the "course pursued" was "unconstitutional," instead of merely erroneous.

The "unconstitutional" course referred to in the majority opinion is apparently the ruling in *Swift v. Tyson* that the supposed omission of

Congress to legislate as to the effect of decisions leaves federal courts free to interpret general law for themselves. I am not at all sure whether, in the absence of federal statutory direction, federal courts would be compelled to follow state decisions. There was sufficient doubt about the matter in 1789 to induce the first Congress to legislate. No former opinions of this Court have passed upon it. Mr. Justice Holmes evidently saw nothing "unconstitutional" which required the overruling of *Swift v. Tyson*, for he said in the very opinion quoted by the majority, "I should leave *Swift v. Tyson* undisturbed, . . . but I would not allow it to spread the assumed dominion into new fields." If the opinion commits this Court to the position that the Congress is without power to declare what rules of substantive law shall govern the federal courts, that conclusion also seems questionable. The line between procedural and substantive law is hazy, but no one doubts federal power over procedure.

EDWARD A. PURCELL, JR., BRANDEIS AND THE PROGRESSIVE CONSTITUTION

201-03, 215-16, 229, 246-48 (2000)

The new [post-1937] Court's primary goals were to reorient the Constitution, validate the New Deal, and constrain the power of the federal courts. The Court buried the doctrine of liberty of contract, interpreted federal law more favorably toward organized labor, and expanded the reach of federal legislative power while allowing wide latitude for state economic regulation. . . .

The Roosevelt justices rejected what they regarded as the "activism" of the old Court and proclaimed the constitutional theory of Progressivism, the wisdom and necessity of "judicial restraint." The courts, they maintained, should defer broadly to legislative efforts and construe statutes sympathetically to achieve their underlying purposes. Similarly, the justices developed doctrines designed to restrict the opportunities of the lower courts to "intrude" into areas of state and congressional authority. . . .

Similarly, the Roosevelt Court readily effectuated what its members considered *Erie*'s social goal. They sought to prevent parties from using diversity jurisdiction to avoid state laws and policies, and they were sensitive to the need to control corporate litigation tactics. Consequently, the justices implemented *Erie* vigorously to minimize incentives for forum shopping between federal and state courts.

Although they readily adopted a policy against forum shopping, the Roosevelt justices shared a common concern about the opinion's constitutional language. They feared that it might lead to substantive limitations on the power of Congress. . . . *Erie*, [Chief Justice Stone] explained . . . in 1941, had not settled the issue of whether Congress could enact substantive rules of law for the federal courts in diversity suits "notwithstanding some unfortunate dicta in the opinion." Unsure of the nature of Brandeis's constitutional theory, but anxious about its implications, the Roosevelt Court vigorously enforced its anti-forum-shopping interpretation of *Erie* while ignoring Brandeis's constitutional language. . . .

In turning the Court away from *Erie*'s constitutional foundation, Frankfurter's role was pivotal. . . .

By substituting a monolithic "anti-forum-shopping" policy for the broader social concerns that had animated Brandeis, Frankfurter identified *Erie* with a practical purpose that was not only narrow but rigid and ultimately formalistic. [Frankfurter] focused the "*Erie* doctrine" on one type of forum shopping and on one particular goal. It thereby ignored the broader concerns with unfair and abusive litigation tactics that had engaged Brandeis and helped inform his thinking about *Swift* and diversity jurisdiction. . . .

[In the 1950s Professor Henry Hart] produced a powerful vision of the national judiciary and a compelling new image of *Erie* that elided its Progressive political and social values and transformed it into an abstract symbol of federalism and the rule of law. . . .

[Diversity] jurisdiction was rooted in the specific language of the Constitution, [Hart] argued, and it was a crucial symbol and instrument of national unity. More practically, it was the method by which the federal courts could, even though they applied state substantive law, provide a "juster justice than state courts." . . . Hart defended diversity, the jurisdiction that Brandeis and Frankfurter had attacked as disruptive and unnecessary, precisely because it offered an expanded arena for the federal courts to demonstrate their superiority and to develop more fully the basic principles of a sound national jurisprudence.

From such a perspective, *Erie* emerged reborn and luminous. [Hart had originally been ambivalent about *Erie*.] . . .

By the early 1950s Hart saw a dramatically different *Erie*. . . . Gone . . . were the Progressive concerns over the ability of foreign corporations to exploit jurisdictional rules and the danger that the decision might impose limitations on congressional power. Gone, finally, were doubts about the opinion's constitutional rationale. *Erie*, in fact, embodied fundamental constitutional principles. It was, Hart proclaimed grandly, "superbly right." . . .

In the context of Hart's powerful and compelling image of the federal system, *Erie* indeed seemed seminal. . . . To those who reflected on history or the opinion's author, it seemed fitting that Brandeis had produced a monument to the "principle of federalism."

Federalism was an important element of *Erie*, as were both the axiom of coextensive powers and a powerful concern for practical justice. But Hart's *Erie* was not Brandeis's *Erie*. Hart's version denied both the social and political purposes that had animated Brandeis's efforts. It was even more abstract than Brandeis's version. . . . For Hart, *Erie* represented a neutral allocation principle unrelated to either social issues or problems of economic inequality. Absent were both Brandeis's profound commitment to legislative primacy and his concern with the practical advantages that wealth and power bestowed on private litigants. Hart elevated *Erie* to the rank of first principles by stripping it of political and social content and by denying the Progressive values that had inspired it.

Notes and Questions

1. Congress did not amend the Rules of Decision Act between *Swift* and *Erie* (although it did make some stylistic changes after *Erie*). If the statute remained unaltered, what changes might explain *Erie*'s reversal of a nearly century-old precedent? What did Justice Holmes (quoted by Brandeis) mean when he criticized *Swift* as resting on an assumption of "a transcendental body of law"? As Holmes put it in one dissent: "The common law is not a brooding omnipresence in the sky, but the articulate voice of some sovereign or quasi sovereign that can be identified." S. Pac. Co. v. Jensen, 244 U.S. 205, 222 (1917). Do you think that by 1938, most American judges would have regarded the common law as being "discovered" — or made by judges?

2. Justice Brandeis cites Charles Warren's historical work to support the claim that *Swift* misinterpreted the Rules of Decision Act. Warren discovered an early draft of the Rules of Decision Act directing federal courts to follow both state "statute law" and state "unwritten or common law." The final statute reduced this language to the simple "laws." There is some controversy about who made the change and why, but does the change to "laws" necessarily mean that "laws" was intended to cover both types of law, or might it instead mean that the drafter thought better of including common law in the Rules of Decision Act? Should it matter, since Congress had acquiesced in the *Swift* interpretation for almost a century?

More recent historical scholarship has suggested that Warren was completely wrong: the original Rules of Decision Act was meant as a directive to apply *American* rather than *English* law, and was not concerned with whether diversity courts would apply state common law. *See* WILFRED J. RITZ, REWRITING THE HISTORY OF THE JUDICIARY ACT OF 1789: EXPOSING MYTHS, CHALLENGING PREMISES, AND USING NEW EVIDENCE 126-48 (1990); Suzanna Sherry, *Wrong, Out of Step, and Pernicious:* Erie *as the Worst Decision of All Time*, 39 PEPP. L. REV. 129 (2011); Patrick J. Borchers, *The Origins of Diversity Jurisdiction, The Rise of Legal Positivism, and a Brave New World for* Erie *and* Klaxon, 72 TEX. L. REV. 79 (1993). Indeed, this research suggests that even *Swift* was incorrect insofar as it applied to state *statutory* law in diversity cases. As Ritz puts it: "American law is to be found in the 'laws of the several states' viewed as a group of eleven states in 1789, and not viewed separately and individually. It is not a direction to apply the law of a particular state, for if it had been so intended, the section would have referred to the 'laws of the respective states.'" RITZ, *supra*, at 148.

3. Consider also the social context of *Swift* and *Erie*. What results might have followed if, in 1842 (and for the remainder of the nineteenth

century), federal courts were required to apply state common law in commercial cases brought under diversity jurisdiction? Story alludes to the problem in his last paragraph; does his rationale sufficiently justify *Swift*'s holding? Brandeis's opinion in *Erie* is less explicitly attentive to social context, but Professor Purcell makes clear that one of Brandeis's primary concerns was abusive and manipulative litigation strategies by large corporations. Note that counsel for the railroad carefully avoided arguing that *Swift* be overruled: although Pennsylvania law was more favorable to the railroad in the *Erie* case itself, railroads and other large corporations were still generally better off under federal common law than under state common law; that advantage did not diminish much between 1842 and 1938. Can *Erie* be justified by changes in other social or economic conditions?

4. While Purcell emphasizes the Progressive elements of *Erie*, he describes Hart's alternative view of the case as primarily about federalism. Might it also be about separation of powers? Craft an argument that when neither the Constitution nor Congress gives specific content to federal law, federal courts ought not either — especially in light of the Rules of Decision Act. (You might get help from Stephen B. Burbank, *Of Rules and Discretion: The Supreme Court, Federal Rules and The Common Law*, 63 NOTRE DAME L. REV. 693 (1988).) If you have had Constitutional Law, think also about what you know of the post-1937 New Deal Court from that course: was that Court (the same one that decided *Erie* in 1938) interested in federalism, that is, transferring power from the federal government to the states?

5. *Erie* applies to all state claims in federal court, whether brought there under diversity jurisdiction or under supplemental jurisdiction.

6. Despite *Erie*'s statement that "[t]here is no federal general common law," in a few situations federal common law applies. In admiralty cases or cases touching on foreign relations, for example, there is often no federal statute, but courts develop and apply federal common law. *See* Kossick v. United Fruit Co., 365 U.S. 731 (1961); Banco Nacional de Cuba v. Sabbatino, 376 U.S. 398 (1964). *See also* Boyle v. United Techs. Corp., 487 U.S. 500 (1988) (tort defense for military contractors); Clearfield Trust Co. v. United States, 318 U.S. 363 (1943) (liability of United States).

7. State courts also face choice-of-law issues when considering whether to apply their own law or the law of another state (for example, if the events giving rise to the lawsuit occurred in another state). There is a whole course, Conflict of Laws, devoted to such horizontal choice-of-law questions. But you might be interested to learn that one state (that we know of) still follows *Swift*: while Georgia courts sometimes apply the statutory law of sister states, they will not apply another state's common-law doctrines. *See, e.g.*, Coon v. The Medical Ctr., Inc., 797 S.E.2d 828 (Ga. 2017).

8. For a deep dive into the facts of *Erie*, concluding that Harry Tompkins lied about how he was injured, see Brian L. Frye, *The Ballad of Harry James Tompkins*, 52 AKRON L. REV. 531 (2019).

9. *Erie* remains a bedrock of the American judicial system. In most instances, *Erie* is applied without controversy or difficulty. It is universally

accepted that, in the absence of controlling federal law, a federal court will apply the relevant state's *substantive* law. And federal *procedural* law almost always governs in federal court. But *Erie* has generated serious difficulties in the borderland between substance and procedure, the focus of the next section. As you study these hard questions, however, do not forget that the core of *Erie* — the use of state *substantive* law — remains intact.

SECTION B: DEVELOPING AND APPLYING *ERIE* IN THE PROCEDURAL CONTEXT

1938 was a banner year for civil procedure. Not only was *Erie* decided, but the Federal Rules of Civil Procedure took effect. These two events turned federal diversity litigation on its head. Before *Erie*, federal courts applied federal substantive common law under *Swift*; before the Federal Rules of Civil Procedure, federal courts applied state procedural rules under the federal Conformity Act in common-law matters. A key question after *Erie* was thus the extent to which the decision might jeopardize the newly-enacted Federal Rules. That fear was heightened by several cases in the 1940s in which the Supreme Court appeared to extend *Erie* to matters that appeared more procedural than substantive. In reading the following cases, think about the ways one might characterize the relationship between *Erie* and the Federal Rules. As you read, you will notice that the Supreme Court takes different or partial approaches at different times, and seems not to reach a fully elaborated view until at least 1965, and perhaps not until 1980.

GUARANTY TRUST CO. OF NEW YORK v. YORK

326 U.S. 99 (1945)

■ MR. JUSTICE FRANKFURTER delivered the opinion of the Court.

[Plaintiff York sued Guaranty Trust in federal court in diversity jurisdiction, alleging state-law breach of trust, an equitable claim. The suit was filed after the state statute of limitations expired. After holding that the *Erie* doctrine applied to cases in equity as well as law, the Court had to decide whether the action, barred in state court by the state statute of limitations, was nevertheless maintainable in federal court. It might have been if the federal version of the equitable doctrine of "laches" (which imposes no hard cutoff but considers whether a plaintiff's delay in bringing suit was justifiable and not prejudicial to the defendant) governed instead of the state statute of limitations.]

And so this case reduces itself to the narrow question whether, when no recovery could be had in a State court because the action is barred by the statute of limitations, a federal court in equity can take cognizance of the suit because there is diversity of citizenship between the parties. Is the outlawry, according to State law, of a claim created by the States a matter of "substantive rights" to be respected by a federal court of equity when that court's jurisdiction is dependent on the fact that there is a State-created right, or is such statute of "a mere remedial character," which a federal court may disregard?

Matters of "substance" and matters of "procedure" are much talked about in the books as though they defined a great divide cutting across the whole domain of law. But, of course, "substance" and "procedure" are the same key-words to very different problems. Neither "substance" nor "procedure" represents the same invariants. Each implies different variables depending upon the particular problem for which it is used. And the different problems are only distantly related at best, for the terms are in common use in connection with situations turning on such different considerations as those that are relevant to questions pertaining to *ex post facto* legislation, the impairment of the obligations of contract, the enforcement of federal rights in the State courts and the multitudinous phases of the conflict of laws.

Here we are dealing with a right to recover derived not from the United States but from one of the States. When, because the plaintiff happens to be a nonresident, such a right is enforceable in a federal as well as in a State court, the forms and mode of enforcing the right may at times, naturally enough, vary because the two judicial systems are not identic[al]. But since a federal court adjudicating a state-created right solely because of the diversity of citizenship of the parties is for that purpose, in effect, only another court of the State, it cannot afford recovery if the right to recover is made unavailable by the State nor can it substantially affect the enforcement of the right as given by the State.

And so the question is not whether a statute of limitations is deemed a matter of "procedure" in some sense. The question is whether such a statute concerns merely the manner and the means by which a right to recover, as recognized by the State, is enforced, or whether such statutory limitation is a matter of substance in the aspect that alone is relevant to our problem, namely, does it significantly affect the result of a litigation for a federal court to disregard a law of a State that would be controlling in an action upon the same claim by the same parties in a State court?

It is therefore immaterial whether statutes of limitation are characterized either as "substantive" or "procedural" in State court opinions in any use of those terms unrelated to the specific issue before us. *Erie Railroad Co. v. Tompkins*, 304 U.S. 64 (1938), was not an endeavor to formulate scientific legal terminology. It expressed a policy that touches vitally the proper distribution of judicial power between State and federal courts. In essence, the intent of that decision was to insure that, in all cases where a federal court is exercising jurisdiction solely because of the diversity of citizenship of the parties, the outcome of the litigation in the federal court should be substantially the same, so far as legal rules determine the outcome of a litigation, as it would be if tried in a State court. The nub of the policy that underlies *Erie* is that for the same transaction the accident of a suit by a non-resident litigant in a federal court instead of in a State court a block away, should not lead to a substantially different result. And so, putting to one side abstractions regarding "substance" and "procedure," we have held that in diversity cases the federal courts must follow the law of the State as to burden of proof, as to conflict of laws, [and] as to contributory negligence. *Erie* has been applied with an eye alert to essentials in avoiding disregard of State law in diversity cases in the federal courts. A policy so important to our federalism must be kept free from entanglements with analytical or terminological niceties.

Plainly enough, a statute that would completely bar recovery in a suit if brought in a State court bears on a State-created right vitally and not merely formally or negligibly. As to consequences that so intimately affect recovery or non-recovery a federal court in a diversity case should follow State law. . . .

Diversity jurisdiction is founded on assurance to non-resident litigants of courts free from susceptibility to potential local bias. . . . And so Congress afforded out-of-State litigants another tribunal, not another body of law. The operation of a double system of conflicting laws in the same State is plainly hostile to the reign of law. Certainly, the fortuitous circumstance of residence out of a State of one of the parties to a litigation ought not to give rise to a discrimination against others equally concerned but locally resident. The source of substantive rights enforced by a federal court under diversity jurisdiction, it cannot be said too often, is the law of the States. Whenever that law is authoritatively declared by a State, whether its voice be the legislature or its highest court, such law ought to govern in litigation founded on that law, whether the forum of application is a State or a federal court and whether the remedies be sought at law or may be had in equity. . . .

■ MR. JUSTICE ROBERTS and MR. JUSTICE DOUGLAS took no part in the consideration or decision of this case.

■ [The dissenting opinion of MR. JUSTICE RUTLEDGE, joined by MR. JUSTICE MURPHY, is omitted.]

RAGAN V. MERCHANTS TRANSFER & WAREHOUSE CO.

337 U.S. 530 (1949)

■ MR. JUSTICE DOUGLAS delivered the opinion of the Court.

This case, involving a highway accident which occurred on October 1, 1943, came to the District Court for Kansas by reason of diversity of citizenship. Petitioner instituted it there on September 4, 1945, by filing the complaint with the court — the procedure specified by the Federal Rules of Civil Procedure.[1] As prescribed by those Rules, a summons was issued.

1. Rule 3 provides, "A civil action is commenced by filing a complaint with the court."

Service was had on December 28, 1945. Kansas has a two-year statute of limitations applicable to such tort claims. Respondent pleaded it and moved for summary judgment. Petitioner claimed that the filing of the complaint tolled the statute. Respondent argued that by reason of a Kansas statute the statute of limitations was not tolled until service of the summons.

The District Court struck the defense and denied respondent's motion. A trial was had and a verdict rendered for petitioner. The Court of Appeals reversed. It ruled, after a review of Kansas authorities, that the requirement of service of summons within the statutory period was an integral part of that state's statute of limitations. It accordingly held that *Guaranty Trust Co. v. York*, 326 U.S. 99 (1945), governed and that respondent's motion for summary judgment should have been sustained. The case is here on a petition for certiorari which we granted because of the importance of the question presented.

Erie Railroad Co. v. Tompkins, 304 U.S. 64 (1938), was premised on the theory that in diversity cases the rights enjoyed under local law should not vary because enforcement of those rights was sought in the federal court rather than in the state court. If recovery could not be had in the state court, it should be denied in the federal court. Otherwise, those authorized to invoke the diversity jurisdiction would gain advantages over those confined to state courts. *Guaranty Trust* applied that principle to statutes of limitations on the theory that, where one is barred from recovery in the state court, he should likewise be barred in the federal court.

It is conceded that if the present case were in a Kansas court it would be barred. The theory of *Guaranty Trust* would therefore seem to bar it in the federal court, as the Court of Appeals held. The force of that reasoning is sought to be avoided by the argument that the Federal Rules of Civil Procedure determine the manner in which an action is commenced in the federal courts — a matter of procedure which the principle of *Erie* does not control. It is accordingly argued that since the suit was properly commenced in the federal court before the Kansas statute of limitations ran, it tolled the statute.

That was the reasoning and result in *Bomar v. Keyes*, 162 F.2d 136, 141 (2d Cir. 1947). But that case was a suit to enforce rights under a federal statute. Here, as in that case, there can be no doubt that the suit was properly commenced in the federal court. But in the present case we look to local law to find the cause of action on which suit is brought. Since that cause of action is created by local law, the measure of it is to be found only in local law. It carries the same burden and is subject to the same defenses in the federal court as in the state court. It accrues and comes to an end when local law so declares. Where local law qualifies or abridges it, the federal court must follow suit. Otherwise there is a different measure of the cause of action in one court than in the other, and the principle of *Erie* is transgressed....

Affirmed.

■ MR. JUSTICE RUTLEDGE dissents. See his dissenting opinion in *Cohen v. Beneficial Industrial Loan Corp.*, 337 U.S. 541 (1949).

[Following are some excerpts from Justice Rutledge's dissent in *Cohen*, which was intended to apply to *Cohen*, *Ragan*, and a third case decided on the same day, *Woods v. Interstate Realty Co.*, 337 U.S. 535 (1949).]

... Without undertaking to discuss each case in detail, I think the three decisions taken together demonstrate the extreme extent to which the Court is going in submitting the control of diversity litigation in the federal courts to the states rather than to Congress, where it properly belongs. This is done in the guise of applying the rule of *Erie Railroad Co. v. Tompkins*, 304 U.S. 64 (1938). But in my opinion it was never the purpose of that decision to put such matters as those involved here outside the power of Congress to regulate and to confer that authority exclusively upon the states....

The accepted dichotomy is the familiar "procedural-substantive" one. This of course is a subject of endless discussion, which hardly needs to be repeated here. Suffice it to say that actually in many situations procedure and substance are so interwoven that rational separation becomes well-nigh impossible. But, even so, this fact cannot dispense with the necessity of making a distinction. For, as the matter stands, it is Congress which has the power to govern the procedure of the federal courts in diversity cases, and the states which have that power over matters clearly substantive in nature. Judges therefore cannot escape making the division. And they must make it where the two constituent elements are Siamese twins as well as where they are not twins or even blood brothers. The real question is not whether the separation shall be made, but how it shall be made: whether mechanically by reference to whether the state courts' doors are open or closed, or by a consideration of the policies which close them and their relation to accommodating the policy of the *Erie* rule with Congress' power to govern the incidents of litigation in diversity suits....

Notes and Questions

1. Notice how Justice Reed's concurring opinion in *Erie* itself — which disagrees with Brandeis' notion that *Erie* rests on a constitutional foundation — is echoed in Justice Rutledge's dissent. Are *York* and *Ragan* examples of the Court fixating on the "trivial" problem of forum-shopping, or might they stem also from an overly formalistic focus on whether the outcome would be different in state court?

2. Both *York* and *Ragan* suggest that the test under *Erie* should be whether the rule in question affects the outcome of the case. If it does, then state law applies. But don't all rules affect the outcome, at least at the point at which they become an issue? Imagine that a state rule allows less time to file a motion to dismiss than does the relevant federal rule. If the movant fails to comply with the shorter deadline, doesn't the decision whether to apply the state or federal deadline affect the outcome? *York* focuses on the need to avoid forum-shopping by litigants: does that help solve this puzzle? (Hint: at what point in the litigation should we ask whether the particular rule is likely to affect the outcome of the case?)

3. As Justice Rutledge's dissent indicates, *Ragan* is one of several cases decided in the late 1940s that seemed to stretch the idea of "substance" and create a fear that neither congressional power nor the Federal Rules of Civil Procedure would survive the *Erie* doctrine.

But in a single case in 1958, the Court appeared to swing in a rather different direction without attempting to reconcile the earlier cases. In *Byrd v. Blue Ridge Rural Electric Cooperative, Inc.*, 356 U.S. 525 (1958), the plaintiff brought a diversity suit in federal court, alleging that he was injured because of negligence on the part of the defendant electric company, with which plaintiff's employer had contracted. Defendant argued that the suit was precluded by South Carolina's Workmen's Compensation Act, because plaintiff, as a "statutory employee" of defendant, was limited to the relief afforded by the Act and could not bring a negligence action. The Supreme Court remanded for further evidence on whether plaintiff was a "statutory employee," but also had to confront an additional issue. Under previous decisions by the South Carolina Supreme Court, the judge, not the jury, decided whether plaintiff was a "statutory employee," although the plaintiff was entitled to have a jury decide other questions. Defendant argued that this South Carolina procedure should prevail, and that, on remand, the judge should rule on the "statutory employee" defense rather than submitting it to a jury. A divided Supreme Court rejected the argument, apparently recasting *Erie* as a test that balances state and federal interests:

> *First*. It was decided in *Erie Railroad Co. v. Tompkins*, 304 U.S. 64 (1938), that the federal courts in diversity cases must respect the definition of state-created rights and obligations by the state courts. We must, therefore, first examine the [South Carolina] rule to determine whether it is bound up with these rights and obligations in such a way that its application in the federal court is required.
>
> . . . A State may, of course, distribute the functions of its judicial machinery as it sees fit. The decisions relied upon, however, furnish no reason for selecting the judge rather than the jury to decide this single affirmative defense in the negligence action. They simply reflect a policy that administrative determination of "jurisdictional facts" should not be final but subject to judicial review. The conclusion is inescapable that the [South Carolina Supreme Court precedent] is grounded in the practical consideration that the question had theretofore come before the South Carolina courts from the Industrial Commission and the courts had become accustomed to deciding the factual issue of immunity without the aid of juries. We find nothing to suggest that this rule was announced as an integral part of the special relationship created by the statute. Thus the requirement appears to be merely a form and mode of enforcing the immunity, Guaranty Trust Co. v. York, 326 U.S. 99 (1945), and not a rule intended to be bound up with the definition of the rights and obligations of the parties. . . .
>
> *Second*. But cases following *Erie* have evinced a broader policy to the effect that the federal courts should conform as near as may be — in the

absence of other considerations — to state rules even of form and mode where the state rules may bear substantially on the question whether the litigation would come out one way in the federal court and another way in the state court if the federal court failed to apply a particular local rule. *E.g., Guaranty Trust, supra*. . . . It may well be that in the instant personal-injury case the outcome would be substantially affected by whether the issue of immunity is decided by a judge or a jury. Therefore, were "outcome" the only consideration, a strong case might appear for saying that the federal court should follow the state practice.

But there are affirmative countervailing considerations at work here. The federal system is an independent system for administering justice to litigants who properly invoke its jurisdiction. An essential characteristic of that system is the manner in which, in civil common-law actions, it distributes trial functions between judge and jury and, under the influence — if not the command — of the Seventh Amendment, assigns the decisions of disputed questions of fact to the jury. The policy of uniform enforcement of state-created rights and obligations cannot in every case exact compliance with a state rule — not bound up with rights and obligations — which disrupts the federal system of allocating functions between judge and jury. Thus the inquiry here is whether the federal policy favoring jury decisions of disputed fact questions should yield to the state rule in the interest of furthering the objective that the litigation should not come out one way in the federal court and another way in the state court.

We think that in the circumstances of this case the federal court should not follow the state rule. It cannot be gainsaid that there is a strong federal policy against allowing state rules to disrupt the judge-jury relationship in the federal courts. . . .

Third. We have discussed the problem upon the assumption that the outcome of the litigation may be substantially affected by whether the issue of immunity is decided by a judge or a jury. But clearly there is not present here the certainty that a different result would follow, *cf. Guaranty Trust, supra*, or even the strong possibility that this would be the case. . . . We do not think the likelihood of a different result is so strong as to require the federal practice of jury determination of disputed factual issues to yield to the state rule in the interest of uniformity of outcome. [356 U.S. at 535-40.]

The Court has rarely cited *Byrd* since it was decided, and never unequivocally for the proposition that a countervailing federal interest overcomes the *Erie-York* determination that use of a federal rule would result in an impermissibly different outcome in federal court. *Byrd* might rest instead on the implication of the Court's "*Third*" point: that in order for *York* to apply, there must be a high likelihood of differential outcomes. Nevertheless, some lower courts have concluded that in some situations a federal countervailing interest might outweigh the *Erie* command that state law apply. *See, e.g.*, Esfeld v. Costa Crociere, S.P.A., 289 F.3d 1300 (11th Cir. 2002) (federal interests in providing U.S. forum for U.S. citizens, in foreign relations, and in uniform venue rules within federal judicial system require application of federal *forum non conveniens* law in diversity case even though not following different state law would be outcome-determinative).

4. In addition to the confusion generated by *Byrd*, the relationship between *Erie* and the Federal Rules of Civil Procedure was complicated by the fact that the Court in 1941 upheld the validity of a challenged Federal Rule of Civil Procedure without mentioning *Erie* at all. Sibbach v. Wilson & Co., 312 U.S. 1 (1941). Recall that the Federal Rules were adopted pursuant to the Rules Enabling Act, 28 U.S.C. § 2072, which provides:

> (a) The Supreme Court shall have the power to prescribe general rules of practice and procedure and rules of evidence for cases in the United States district courts . . . and courts of appeals.
>
> (b) Such rules shall not abridge, enlarge or modify any substantive right. All laws which conflict with such rules shall be of no further force or effect after such rules have taken effect.

If Congress does not veto or amend Rules adopted by the Supreme Court within a certain time period, they automatically take effect.

In *Sibbach*, a diversity case, the plaintiff argued that she need not submit to a physical examination, ordered by the federal district court pursuant to Fed. R. Civ. P. 35, because Rule 35 was beyond the authority of the Rules Enabling Act. Noting that "the courts of Indiana, the state where the cause of action arose, hold such an order proper, whereas the courts of Illinois, the state in which the trial court sat, hold that such an order cannot be made,"* the Supreme Court upheld the validity of Rule 35 by a 5-4 vote:

> Congress has undoubted power to regulate the practice and procedure of federal courts, and may exercise that power by delegating to this or other federal courts authority to make rules not inconsistent with the statutes or constitution of the United States; but it has never essayed to declare the substantive state law, or to abolish or nullify a right recognized by the substantive law of the state where the cause of action arose, save where a right or duty is imposed in a field committed to Congress by the Constitution. On the contrary it has enacted that the state law shall be the rule of decision in the federal courts.
>
> Hence we conclude that the [Rules Enabling Act] was purposely restricted in its operation to matters of pleading and court practice and procedure. Its two provisos or caveats emphasize this restriction. The first is that the court shall not "abridge, enlarge, nor modify the substantive rights", in the guise of regulating procedure. . . .
>
> [P]etitioner admits, and, we think, correctly, that [Rule 35 is a rule] of procedure. She insists, nevertheless, that by the prohibition against challenged. In order to reach this result she translates "substantive"

---

* The Illinois decisions did not positively ban such court-ordered examinations, but rested instead on the absence of any grant of authority to Illinois courts to order them. Although the Court did not discuss this point, it seems to support the Court's apparent view that the "substantive right" limitation of the Rules Enabling Act was not implicated. — ED.

into "important" or "substantial" rights. And she urges that if a rule affects such a right, albeit the rule is one of procedure merely, its prescription is not within the statutory grant of power embodied in the Act....

... The test must be whether a rule really regulates procedure, — the judicial process for enforcing rights and duties recognized by substantive law and for justly administering remedy and redress for disregard or infraction of them. That the rules in question are such is admitted....

We conclude that the rules under attack are within the authority granted. [312 U.S. at 9-11, 14, 16.]

How could Rule 35, providing for court-ordered physical examinations, be "procedural," when the Court found the statute of limitations "substantive" in *York* and refused to allow Rule 3 — which provides only that an action commences upon filing — to govern in a diversity case in *Ragan*? Are *York* and *Ragan* consistent with *Sibbach*? (Hint: think about whether the real issue here, notwithstanding the Court's language, is a question of "substance" versus "procedure" or a question whether the federal rule was enacted pursuant to congressional authority or merely by the ordinary judicial process of common-law development. Going back to the underlying purposes of *Erie* might help.)

5. The Supreme Court finally resolved much of the confusion spawned by earlier cases, including questions about the power of Congress and the relationship between the *Erie* doctrine and the Federal Rules of Civil Procedure, in the following case.

HANNA V. PLUMER

380 U.S. 460 (1965)

■ MR. CHIEF JUSTICE WARREN delivered the opinion of the Court.

The question to be decided is whether, in a civil action where the jurisdiction of the United States district court is based upon diversity of citizenship between the parties, service of process shall be made in the manner prescribed by state law or that set forth in Rule 4(d)(1) [now Rule 4(e)(2)(B) — ED.] of the Federal Rules of Civil Procedure.

On February 6, 1963, petitioner, a citizen of Ohio, filed her complaint in the District Court for the District of Massachusetts, claiming damages in excess of $10,000 for personal injuries resulting from an automobile accident in South Carolina, allegedly caused by the negligence of one Louise Plumer Osgood, a Massachusetts citizen deceased at the time of the filing of the complaint. Respondent, Mrs. Osgood's executor and also a Massachusetts citizen, was named as defendant. On February 8, service was made by leaving copies of the summons and the complaint with respondent's wife at his residence, concededly in compliance with Rule 4(d)(1), which provides [that service may be effected on an individual by leaving a copy of the summons and complaint at his "dwelling" or "usual place of abode" with someone "of suitable age and discretion."]

Respondent filed his answer on February 26, alleging, *inter alia*, that the action could not be maintained because it had been brought "contrary to and in violation of the provisions of Massachusetts General Laws (Ter. Ed.) Chapter 197, Section 9." That section provides:

> Except as provided in this chapter, an executor or administrator shall not be held to answer to an action by a creditor of the deceased . . . unless . . . the writ in such action has been served by delivery in hand upon such executor or administrator or service thereof accepted by him . . . .

On October 17, 1963, the District Court granted respondent's motion for summary judgment, citing *Ragan v. Merchants Transfer & Warehouse Co.*, 337 U.S. 530 (1949), and *Guaranty Trust Co. v. York*, 326 U.S. 99 (1945), in support of its conclusion that the adequacy of the service was to be measured by § 9, with which, the court held, petitioner had not complied. On appeal, petitioner admitted noncompliance with § 9, but argued that Rule 4(d)(1) defines the method by which service of process is to be effected in diversity actions. The Court of Appeals for the First Circuit, finding that "[r]elatively recent amendments [to § 9] evince a clear legislative purpose to require personal notification . . . ," concluded that the conflict of state and federal rules was over "a substantive rather than a procedural matter," and unanimously affirmed. Because of the threat to the goal of uniformity of federal procedure posed by the decision below, we granted certiorari.

We conclude that the adoption of Rule 4(d)(1), designed to control service of process in diversity actions, neither exceeded the congressional mandate embodied in the Rules Enabling Act nor transgressed constitutional bounds, and that the Rule is therefore the standard against which the District Court should have measured the adequacy of the service. Accordingly, we reverse the decision of the Court of Appeals. . . .

[The Court concluded, based on *Sibbach v. Wilson & Co.*, 312 U.S. 1 (1941), and other cases, that Rule 4(d)(1) is valid under the Rules Enabling Act because it "really regulates procedure." It stated that "[p]rescribing the manner in which a defendant is to be notified that a suit has been instituted against him . . . relates to the 'practice and procedure of the district courts.'" It also noted, quoting another case, that merely "incidental" effects on parties' rights might not run afoul of the Enabling Act:]

> . . . Undoubtedly most alterations of the rules of practice and procedure may and often do affect the rights of litigants. Congress' prohibition of any alteration of substantive rights of litigants was obviously not addressed to such incidental effects as necessarily attend the adoption of the prescribed new rules of procedure upon the rights of litigants who, agreeably to rules of practice and procedure, have been brought before a court authorized to determine their rights. . . .

Thus were there no conflicting state procedure, Rule 4(d)(1) would clearly control. However, respondent, focusing on the contrary Massachusetts rule, calls to the Court's attention another line of cases, a line which — like the Federal Rules — had its birth in 1938. *Erie Railroad Co. v. Tompkins,* 304 U.S. 64 (1938), overruling *Swift v. Tyson,* 41 U.S. (16 Pet.) 1 (1842), held that federal courts sitting in diversity cases, when deciding questions of "substantive" law, are bound by state court decisions as well as state statutes. The broad command of *Erie* was therefore identical to that of the Enabling Act: federal courts are to apply state substantive law and federal procedural law. However, as subsequent cases sharpened the distinction between substance and procedure, the line of cases following *Erie* diverged markedly from the line construing the Enabling Act....

Respondent, by placing primary reliance on *York* and *Ragan,* suggests that the *Erie* doctrine acts as a check on the Federal Rules of Civil Procedure, that despite the clear command of Rule 4(d)(1), *Erie* and its progeny demand the application of the Massachusetts rule. Reduced to essentials, the argument is: (1) *Erie,* as refined in *York,* demands that federal courts apply state law whenever application of federal law in its stead will alter the outcome of the case. (2) In this case, a determination that the Massachusetts service requirements obtain will result in immediate victory for respondent. If, on the other hand, it should be held that Rule 4(d)(1) is applicable, the litigation will continue, with possible victory for petitioner. (3) Therefore, *Erie* demands application of the Massachusetts rule. The syllogism possesses an appealing simplicity, but is for several reasons invalid.

In the first place, it is doubtful that, even if there were no Federal Rule making it clear that in-hand service is not required in diversity actions, the *Erie* rule would have obligated the District Court to follow the Massachusetts procedure. "Outcome-determination" analysis was never intended to serve as a talisman. Byrd v. Blue Ridge Rural Elec. Coop., Inc., 356 U.S. 525, 537 (1958). Indeed, the message of *York* itself is that choices between state and federal law are to be made not by application of any automatic, "litmus paper" criterion, but rather by reference to the policies underlying the *Erie* rule.

The *Erie* rule is rooted in part in a realization that it would be unfair for the character or result of a litigation materially to differ because the suit had been brought in a federal court.... The decision was also in part a reaction to the practice of "forum-shopping" which had grown up in response to the rule of *Swift v. Tyson.* That the *York* test was an attempt to effectuate these policies is demonstrated by the fact that the opinion framed the inquiry in terms of "substantial" variations between state and federal litigation. Not only are nonsubstantial, or trivial, variations not likely to raise the sort of equal protection problems which troubled the Court in *Erie;* they are also unlikely to influence the choice of a forum. The "outcome-determination" test therefore cannot be read without reference to the twin aims of the *Erie* rule: discouragement of forum-shopping and avoidance of inequitable administration of the laws.[9]

---

9. The Court of Appeals seemed to frame the inquiry in terms of how "important" § 9 is to the State.... [I]t is not clear to what sort of question the

The difference between the conclusion that the Massachusetts rule is applicable, and the conclusion that it is not, is of course at this point "outcome-determinative" in the sense that if we hold the state rule to apply, respondent prevails, whereas if we hold that Rule 4(d)(1) governs, the litigation will continue. But in this sense *every* procedural variation is "outcome-determinative." For example, having brought suit in a federal court, a plaintiff cannot then insist on the right to file subsequent pleadings in accord with the time limits applicable in state courts, even though enforcement of the federal timetable will, if he continues to insist that he must meet only the state time limit, result in determination of the controversy against him. So it is here. Though choice of the federal or state rule will at this point have a marked effect upon the outcome of the litigation, the difference between the two rules would be of scant, if any, relevance to the choice of a forum. Petitioner, in choosing her forum, was not presented with a situation where application of the state rule would wholly bar recovery; rather, adherence to the state rule would have resulted only in altering the way in which process was served. Moreover, it is difficult to argue that permitting service of defendant's wife to take the place of in-hand service of defendant himself alters the mode of enforcement of state-created rights in a fashion sufficiently "substantial" to raise the sort of equal protection problems to which the *Erie* opinion alluded.

There is, however, a more fundamental flaw in respondent's syllogism: the incorrect assumption that the rule of *Erie* constitutes the appropriate test of the validity and therefore the applicability of a Federal Rule of Civil Procedure. The *Erie* rule has never been invoked to void a Federal Rule. It is true that there have been cases where this Court has held applicable a state rule in the face of an argument that the situation was governed by one of the Federal Rules. But the holding of each such case was not that *Erie* commanded displacement of a Federal Rule by an inconsistent state rule, but rather that the scope of the Federal Rule was not as broad as the losing party urged, and therefore, there being no Federal Rule which covered the point in dispute, *Erie* commanded the enforcement of state law.... (Here, of course, the clash is unavoidable; Rule 4(d)(1) says — implicitly, but with unmistakable clarity — that in-hand service is not required in federal courts.) At the same time, in cases adjudicating the validity of Federal Rules, we have not applied the *York* rule or other refinements of *Erie*, but have to this day continued to decide questions concerning the scope of the Enabling Act and the constitutionality of specific Federal Rules in light of the distinction set forth in *Sibbach*.

Court of Appeals was addressing itself. One cannot meaningfully ask how important something is without first asking "important for what purpose?" *Erie* and its progeny make clear that when a federal court sitting in a diversity case is faced with a question of whether or not to apply state law, the importance of a state rule is indeed relevant, but only in the context of asking whether application of the rule would make so important a difference to the character or result of the litigation that failure to enforce it would unfairly discriminate against citizens of the forum State, or whether application of the rule would have so important an effect upon the fortunes of one or both of the litigants that failure to enforce it would be likely to cause a plaintiff to choose the federal court.

Nor has the development of two separate lines of cases been inadvertent. The line between "substance" and "procedure" shifts as the legal context changes. . . . It is true that both the Enabling Act and the *Erie* rule say, roughly, that federal courts are to apply state "substantive" law and federal "procedural" law, but from that it need not follow that the tests are identical. For they were designed to control very different sorts of decisions. When a situation is covered by one of the Federal Rules, the question facing the court is a far cry from the typical, relatively unguided *Erie* choice: the court has been instructed to apply the Federal Rule, and can refuse to do so only if the Advisory Committee, this Court, and Congress erred in their prima facie judgment that the Rule in question transgresses neither the terms of the Enabling Act nor constitutional restrictions.

We are reminded by the *Erie* opinion that neither Congress nor the federal courts can, under the guise of formulating rules of decision for federal courts, fashion rules which are not supported by a grant of federal authority contained in Article I or some other section of the Constitution; in such areas state law must govern because there can be no other law. But the opinion in *Erie*, which involved no Federal Rule and dealt with a question which was "substantive" in every traditional sense (whether the railroad owed a duty of care to Tompkins as a trespasser or a licensee), surely neither said nor implied that measures like Rule 4(d)(1) are unconstitutional. For the constitutional provision for a federal court system (augmented by the Necessary and Proper Clause) carries with it congressional power to make rules governing the practice and pleading in those courts, which in turn includes a power to regulate matters which, though falling within the uncertain area between substance and procedure, are rationally capable of classification as either. Neither *York* nor the cases following it ever suggested that the rule there laid down for coping with situations where no Federal Rule applies is coextensive with the limitation on Congress to which *Erie* had adverted. . . .

Erie and its offspring cast no doubt on the long-recognized power of Congress to prescribe housekeeping rules for federal courts even though some of those rules will inevitably differ from comparable state rules. . . . Thus, though a court, in measuring a Federal Rule against the standards contained in the Enabling Act and the Constitution, need not wholly blind itself to the degree to which the Rule makes the character and result of the federal litigation stray from the course it would follow in state courts, it cannot be forgotten that the *Erie* rule, and the guidelines suggested in *York*, were created to serve another purpose altogether. To hold that a Federal Rule of Civil Procedure must cease to function whenever it alters the mode of enforcing state-created rights would be to disembowel either the Constitution's grant of power over federal procedure or Congress' attempt to exercise that power in the Enabling Act. Rule 4(d)(1) is valid and controls the instant case.

Reversed.

- MR. JUSTICE BLACK concurs in the result.
- MR. JUSTICE HARLAN, concurring.

It is unquestionably true that up to now *Erie* and the cases following it have not succeeded in articulating a workable doctrine governing choice of law in diversity actions. I respect the Court's effort to clarify the situation in today's opinion. However, in doing so I think it has misconceived the constitutional premises of *Erie Railroad Co. v. Tompkins*, 304 U.S. 64 (1938), and has failed to deal adequately with those past decisions upon which the courts below relied.

Erie was something more than an opinion which worried about "forum-shopping and avoidance of inequitable administration of the laws," although to be sure these were important elements of the decision. I have always regarded that decision as one of the modern cornerstones of our federalism, expressing policies that profoundly touch the allocation of judicial power between the state and federal systems. *Erie* recognized that there should not be two conflicting systems of law controlling the primary activity of citizens, for such alternative governing authority must necessarily give rise to a debilitating uncertainty in the planning of everyday affairs. And it recognized that the scheme of our Constitution envisions an allocation of law-making functions between state and federal legislative processes which is undercut if the federal judiciary can make substantive law affecting state affairs beyond the bounds of congressional legislative powers in this regard. Thus, in diversity cases *Erie* commands that it be the state law governing primary private activity which prevails.

The shorthand formulations which have appeared in some past decisions are prone to carry untoward results that frequently arise from oversimplification. The Court is quite right in stating that the "outcome-determinative" test of *Guaranty Trust Co. v. York*, 326 U.S. 99 (1945), if taken literally, proves too much, for any rule, no matter how clearly "procedural," can affect the outcome of litigation if it is not obeyed. In turning from the "outcome" test of *York* back to the unadorned forum-shopping rationale of *Erie*, however, the Court falls prey to like oversimplification, for a simple forum-shopping rule also proves too much; litigants often choose a federal forum merely to obtain what they consider the advantages of the Federal Rules of Civil Procedure or to try their cases before a supposedly more favorable judge. To my mind the proper line of approach in determining whether to apply a state or a federal rule, whether "substantive" or "procedural," is to stay close to basic principles by inquiring if the choice of rule would substantially affect those primary decisions respecting human conduct which our constitutional system leaves to state regulation.[2] If so, *Erie* and the Constitution require that the state rule prevail, even in the face of a conflicting federal rule.

The Court weakens, if indeed it does not submerge, this basic principle by finding, in effect, a grant of substantive legislative power in the constitutional provision for a federal court system and through it, setting up the Federal Rules as a body of law inviolate. So long as a reasonable man

---

2. *See* HART AND WECHSLER, THE FEDERAL COURT[S] AND THE FEDERAL SYSTEM 678 [1953]. [Note: The "Hart" of "Hart and Wechsler" is Henry Hart, whose federalism theories of *Erie* were discussed in the first section of this chapter. — ED.]

could characterize any duly adopted federal rule as "procedural," the Court, unless I misapprehend what is said, would have it apply no matter how seriously it frustrated a State's substantive regulation of the primary conduct and affairs of its citizens. Since the members of the Advisory Committee, the Judicial Conference, and this Court who formulated the Federal Rules are presumably reasonable men, it follows that the integrity of the Federal Rules is absolute. Whereas the unadulterated outcome and forum-shopping tests may err too far toward honoring state rules, I submit that the Court's "arguably procedural, ergo constitutional" test moves too fast and far in the other direction. . . .

It remains to apply what has been said to the present case. . . . If the Federal District Court in Massachusetts applies Rule 4(d)(1) of the Federal Rules of Civil Procedure instead of the Massachusetts service rule, what effect would that have on the speed and assurance with which estates are distributed? As I see it, the effect would not be substantial. . . . As [the federal rule] does not seem enough to give rise to any real impingement on the vitality of the state policy which the Massachusetts rule is intended to serve, I concur in the judgment of the Court.

Notes and Questions

1. *Hanna* ties up many of the loose ends left by earlier cases. How does it resolve the troubling implication of *York* that *every* dispute over whether the federal or state rule governs will be outcome-determinative? How does it integrate *York*'s "outcome-determinative" test with the purposes of *Erie*? Would Professor Hart or Professor Purcell agree with Chief Justice Warren's description of the purposes of *Erie*? Would Justice Harlan?

2. The most important part of *Hanna* is the distinction it draws between cases such as *York*, in which no Federal Rule of Civil Procedure is on point, and *Sibbach* and *Hanna*, in which there are such Rules. In the former circumstance, state law applies if the application of federal law would be outcome-determinative in the way that *Hanna*, building on but modifying *York*, indicates with its twin-aims formulation — likely to cause forum shopping or inequitable administration of the laws. In the latter circumstance, the Federal Rule applies as long as it "really regulates procedure," or, in other words, is "arguably procedural" and does not impermissibly affect substantive rights. And *Sibbach* makes clear that *all* of the Federal Rules should be considered arguably procedural: Rule 35, which authorizes involuntary physical and mental examinations, was upheld in *Sibbach*, and is among the least "procedural" of all the Rules.

Why should the existence of a Federal Rule (as opposed to a judicially developed federal doctrine or practice) make such a difference? Think again about the constitutional structure underlying *Erie*: what is wrong with federal courts applying federal common law? Does the same problem arise when federal courts apply a Federal Rule of Civil Procedure? Justice Frankfurter dissented in *Sibbach* on the ground that the Federal Rules should not be treated with the same deference as a federal statute, because Congress did not actually enact the Rules but simply failed to veto them. (By the time *Hanna* was decided, Justice Frankfurter had retired from the Court.) Should the test for whether a Federal Rule applies be less deferential than whether it is "arguably procedural"? Professor John Hart Ely, in a classic article, sorted out these issues:

> My suggestion in this Article will be that the indiscriminate admixture of all questions respecting choices between federal and state law in diversity cases, under the single rubric of "the *Erie* doctrine" or "the *Erie* problem," has served to make a major mystery out of what are really three distinct and rather ordinary problems of statutory and constitutional interpretation.... The United States Constitution, I shall argue, constitutes the relevant text only where Congress has passed a statute creating law for diversity actions, and it is in this situation alone that *Hanna*'s "arguably procedural" test controls. Where a nonstatutory rule is involved, the Constitution remains in the background.... Thus, where there is no relevant Federal Rule of Civil Procedure or other Rule promulgated pursuant to the Enabling Act and the federal rule in issue is therefore wholly judge-made, whether state or federal law should be applied is controlled by the Rules of Decision Act, the statute construed in *Erie* and *York*. Where the matter in issue is covered by a Federal Rule, however, the Enabling Act — and not the Rules of Decision Act itself or the line of cases construing it — constitutes the relevant standard. To say that, however, . . . is by no means to concede the validity of all Federal Rules, for the Enabling Act contains significant limiting language of its own....
>
> [The Rules Enabling Act] begins with a checklist approach — anything that relates to process, writs, pleadings, motions, or to practice and procedure generally, is authorized; anything else is not.... The second sentence, however, provides that "Such rules shall not abridge, enlarge or modify any substantive right . . . ." . . . Not only must a Rule be procedural; it must in addition abridge, enlarge or modify no substantive right.
>
> You would never know it from the case law, though. In the landmark Enabling Act case, *Sibbach v. Wilson & Co.*, the Court construed the Act as a checklist only . . . . [T]he possibility that a Rule could fairly be labeled procedural and at the same time abridge or modify substantive rights was one the Court was unwilling to accept; by its lights, either a Rule was procedural or it affected substantive rights. Thus, the Act's two questions were collapsed into one . . . .
>
> Nor was the *Hanna* opinion much help in this regard. . . .
>
> The most helpful way, it seems to me, of defining a substantive rule — or more particularly a substantive right, which is what the Act refers to — is as a right granted for one or more nonprocedural reasons, for some purpose or purposes not having to do with the fairness or efficiency of the litigation process.

John Hart Ely, *The Irrepressible Myth of Erie*, 87 HARV. L. REV. 693, 697-98, 718-20, 724 (1974). Ely's trisection of "*Erie* questions" is exemplary, but his interpretation of the Rules Enabling Act is controversial. Do you agree that *Sibbach* and *Hanna* improperly eviscerated the limits of the Enabling Act? The Court's neglect of the second sentence of the Rules Enabling Act has continued, at least for a plurality of Justices. *See* Shady Grove Orthopedic Assocs. v. Allstate Ins. Co., 559 U.S. 393 (2010) (*infra* p. 614).

3. As for what constitutes a substantive right, see Thomas D. Rowe, Jr., *Not Bad For Government Work: Does Anyone Else Think the Supreme Court is Doing a Halfway Decent Job in its* Erie-Hanna *Jurisprudence?*, 73 NOTRE DAME L. REV. 963, 978 n.64 (1998):

> Professor Ely's concise and useful if somewhat circular definition is "a right granted for one or more nonprocedural reasons, for some purpose or purposes not having to do with the fairness or efficiency of the litigation process." He goes on to note "the possibility that a rule can be both procedural and substantive, when it is informed by both procedural and nonprocedural purposes." Professor Ides uses terms that also refer to the aims underlying a rule of law, in a definition that seems as if it would work in much the same way as Ely's: "Substantive law refers to that body of principles designed to regulate primary human activity; procedural law refers to that body of principles designed to provide a means for adjudicating controversies over rights derived from the substantive law."

An alternative formulation of the line between substance and procedure, in the context of both the "unguided" *Erie* choice and the limits of the Rules Enabling Act, is suggested in Jay Tidmarsh, *Procedure, Substance, and* Erie, 64 VAND. L. REV. 877, 880-81 (2011):

> [I]f we assume a world in which processing a state-law claim from filing through settlement or judgment is costless and outcome-neutral, the claim has an expected value at the time of its hypothetical filing in a state court. This value is a product of the probability of recovery and the amount of the remedy if liability is found. What a federal court cannot do — whether its choice involves a Federal Rule or a common-law procedural rule — is to choose a rule that affects this expected value. What a federal court can do is to choose its own rules to transmute the claim from this expected value to its actual value — even when those rules differ from the rules that a state court would use to process the claim, and even when those rules result in a recovery different from the recovery that the plaintiff(s) would have enjoyed in state court.

4. Recall *Ragan v. Merchants Transfer & Warehouse Co.*, 337 U.S. 530 (1940) (*supra* p. 588), which involved an apparent clash between Federal Rule 3 and Kansas law. Rule 3 states: "A civil action is commenced by filing a complaint with the court" — which could mean that in federal court, you've done what it takes to beat any statute of limitations if you just *file* before the statute runs. But Kansas required that to beat the statute on state-law claims in its courts, you had to *serve the defendant* before the statute ran. In *Ragan*, a diversity plaintiff in Kansas federal court had filed

in time but not served the defendant until after the statute ran. The Court — with little attention to the potential conflict — held that the state's service requirement governed in federal court. Does *Hanna* overrule *Ragan*? Consider the following case.

WALKER V. ARMCO STEEL CORP.

446 U.S. 740 (1980)

■ MR. JUSTICE MARSHALL delivered the opinion for a unanimous Court.

This case presents the issue whether in a diversity action the federal court should follow state law or, alternatively, Rule 3 of the Federal Rules of Civil Procedure in determining when an action is commenced for the purpose of tolling the state statute of limitations.

I

According to the allegations of the complaint, petitioner, a carpenter, was injured on August 22, 1975, in Oklahoma City, Okla., while pounding a Sheffield nail into a cement wall. Respondent was the manufacturer of the nail. Petitioner claimed that the nail contained a defect which caused its head to shatter and strike him in the right eye, resulting in permanent injuries. The defect was allegedly caused by respondent's negligence in manufacture and design.

Petitioner is a resident of Oklahoma, and respondent is a foreign corporation having its principal place of business in a State other than Oklahoma. Since there was diversity of citizenship, petitioner brought suit in the United States District Court for the Western District of Oklahoma. The complaint was filed on August 19, 1977. Although summons was issued that same day, service of process was not made on respondent's authorized service agent until December 1, 1977. . . . [R]espondent filed a motion to dismiss the complaint on the ground that the action was barred by the applicable Oklahoma statute of limitations. Although the complaint had been filed within the 2-year statute of limitations, state law does not deem the action "commenced" for purposes of the statute of limitations until service of the summons on the defendant. . . . Petitioner in his reply brief to the motion to dismiss admitted that his case would be foreclosed in state court, but he argued that Rule 3 of the Federal Rules of Civil Procedure governs the manner in which an action is commenced in federal court for all purposes, including the tolling of the state statute of limitations.

The District Court dismissed the complaint as barred by the Oklahoma statute of limitations. . . . The court rejected the argument that *Ragan v. Merchants Transfer & Warehouse Co.*, 337 U.S. 530 (1949), had been implicitly overruled in *Hanna v. Plumer*, 380 U.S. 460 (1965).

The United States Court of Appeals for the Tenth Circuit affirmed. That court concluded that [the state law] was in "direct conflict" with Rule 3.

However, the Oklahoma statute was "indistinguishable" from the statute involved in *Ragan*, and the court felt itself "constrained" to follow *Ragan*.

We granted certiorari because of a conflict among the Courts of Appeals. We now affirm.

II

The question whether state or federal law should apply on various issues arising in an action based on state law which has been brought in federal court under diversity of citizenship jurisdiction has troubled this Court for many years. . . .

In *Guaranty Trust Co. v. York*, 326 U.S. 99 (1945), we addressed ourselves to "the narrow question whether, when no recovery could be had in a State court because the action is barred by the statute of limitations, a federal court in equity can take cognizance of the suit because there is diversity of citizenship between the parties." The Court held that the *Erie* doctrine applied to suits in equity as well as to actions at law. In construing *Erie* we noted that "[i]n essence, the intent of that decision was to insure that, in all cases where a federal court is exercising jurisdiction solely because of the diversity of citizenship of the parties, the outcome of the litigation in the federal court should be substantially the same, so far as legal rules determine the outcome of a litigation, as it would be if tried in a State court." We concluded that the state statute of limitations should be applied. . . .

The decision in *York* led logically to our holding in *Ragan*. . . . It was conceded that had the case been brought in Kansas state court it would have been barred. Nonetheless, the District Court held that the statute had been tolled by the filing of the complaint. The Court of Appeals reversed because "the requirement of service of summons within the statutory period was an integral part of that state's statute of limitations."

We affirmed, relying on *Erie* and *York*. . . . We rejected the argument that Rule 3 of the Federal Rules of Civil Procedure governed the manner in which an action was commenced in federal court for purposes of tolling the state statute of limitations. Instead, we held that the service of summons statute controlled because it was an integral part of the state statute of limitations, and under *York* that statute of limitations was part of the state-law cause of action.

Ragan was not our last pronouncement in this difficult area, however. In 1965 we decided *Hanna*, holding that in a civil action where federal jurisdiction was based upon diversity of citizenship, Rule 4(d)(1) of the Federal Rules of Civil Procedure, rather than state law, governed the manner in which process was served. . . .

The Court in *Hanna* . . . pointed out "a more fundamental flaw" in the defendant's argument in that case. The Court concluded that the *Erie* doctrine was simply not the appropriate test of the validity and applicability of one of the Federal Rules of Civil Procedure . . . . The Court explained that where the Federal Rule was clearly applicable, as in *Hanna*, the test was whether the Rule was within the scope of the Rules Enabling Act . . . .

III

The present case is indistinguishable from *Ragan*. The statutes in both cases require service of process to toll the statute of limitations, and in fact the predecessor to the Oklahoma statute in this case was derived from the predecessor to the Kansas statute in *Ragan*. . . . Accordingly, as the Court of Appeals held below, the instant action is barred by the statute of limitations unless *Ragan* is no longer good law.

Petitioner argues that the analysis and holding of *Ragan* did not survive our decision in *Hanna*. Petitioner's position is that [the Oklahoma tolling statute] is in direct conflict with the Federal Rule. Under *Hanna*, petitioner contends, the appropriate question is whether Rule 3 is within the scope of the Rules Enabling Act and, if so, within the constitutional power of Congress. In petitioner's view, the Federal Rule is to be applied unless it violates one of those two restrictions. This argument ignores both the force of stare decisis and the specific limitations that we carefully placed on the *Hanna* analysis.

We note at the outset that the doctrine of stare decisis weighs heavily against petitioner in this case. Petitioner seeks to have us overrule our decision in *Ragan*. Stare decisis does not mandate that earlier decisions be enshrined forever, of course, but it does counsel that we use caution in rejecting established law. In this case, the reasons petitioner asserts for overruling *Ragan* are the same factors which we concluded in *Hanna* did not undermine the validity of *Ragan*. A litigant who in effect asks us to reconsider not one but two prior decisions bears a heavy burden of supporting such a change in our jurisprudence. Petitioner here has not met that burden.

This Court in *Hanna* distinguished *Ragan* rather than overruled it, and for good reason. Application of the *Hanna* analysis is premised on a "direct collision" between the Federal Rule and the state law. In *Hanna* itself the "clash" between Rule 4(d)(1) and the state in-hand service requirement was "unavoidable." The first question must therefore be whether the scope of the Federal Rule in fact is sufficiently broad to control the issue before the Court. It is only if that question is answered affirmatively that the *Hanna* analysis applies.[9]

As has already been noted, we recognized in *Hanna* that the present case is an instance where "the scope of the Federal Rule [is] not as broad as the losing party urge[s], and therefore, there being no Federal Rule which cover[s] the point in dispute, *Erie* command[s] the enforcement of state law." Rule 3 simply states that "[a] civil action is commenced by filing a complaint

---

9. This is not to suggest that the Federal Rules of Civil Procedure are to be narrowly construed in order to avoid a "direct collision" with state law. The Federal Rules should be given their plain meaning. If a direct collision with state law arises from that plain meaning, then the analysis developed in *Hanna* applies.

with the court." There is no indication that the Rule was intended to toll a state statute of limitations,[10] much less that it purported to displace state tolling rules for purposes of state statutes of limitations. In our view, in diversity actions[11] Rule 3 governs the date from which various timing requirements of the Federal Rules begin to run, but does not affect state statutes of limitations.

In contrast to Rule 3, the Oklahoma statute is a statement of a substantive decision by that State that actual service on, and accordingly actual notice by, the defendant is an integral part of the several policies served by the statute of limitations. The statute of limitations establishes a deadline after which the defendant may legitimately have peace of mind; it also recognizes that after a certain period of time it is unfair to require the defendant to attempt to piece together his defense to an old claim. A requirement of actual service promotes both of those functions of the statute. It is these policy aspects which make the service requirement an "integral" part of the statute of limitations both in this case and in *Ragan*. As such, the service rule must be considered part and parcel of the statute of limitations. Rule 3 does not replace such policy determinations found in state law. Rule 3 and [the Oklahoma tolling statute] can exist side by side, therefore, each controlling its own intended sphere of coverage without conflict.

Since there is no direct conflict between the Federal Rule and the state law, the *Hanna* analysis does not apply. Instead, the policies behind *Erie* and *Ragan* control the issue whether, in the absence of a federal rule directly on point, state service requirements which are an integral part of the state statute of limitations should control in an action based on state law which is filed in federal court under diversity jurisdiction. The reasons for the application of such a state service requirement in a diversity action in

---

10. . . . The Note of the Advisory Committee on the Rules states:

> When a Federal or State statute of limitations is pleaded as a defense, a question may arise under this rule whether the mere filing of the complaint stops the running of the statute, or whether any further step is required, such as, service of the summons and complaint or their delivery to the marshal for service. The answer to this question may depend on whether it is competent for the Supreme Court, exercising the power to make rules of procedure without affecting substantive rights, to vary the operation of statutes of limitations. The requirement of Rule 4(a) that the clerk shall forthwith issue the summons and deliver it to the marshal for service will reduce the chances of such a question arising.

This Note establishes that the Advisory Committee predicted the problem which arose in *Ragan* and arises again in the instant case. It does not indicate, however, that Rule 3 was *intended* to serve as a tolling provision for statute of limitations purposes; it only suggests that the Advisory Committee thought the Rule *might* have that effect.

11. The Court suggested in *Ragan* that in suits to enforce rights under a federal statute Rule 3 means that filing of the complaint tolls the applicable statute of limitations. [It] distinguish[ed] *Bomar v. Keyes,* 162 F.2d 136, 140-141 (2d Cir. 1947). We do not here address the role of Rule 3 as a tolling provision for a statute of limitations, whether set by federal law or borrowed from state law, if the cause of action is based on federal law.

the absence of a conflicting federal rule are well explained in *Erie* and *Ragan*, and need not be repeated here. It is sufficient to note that although in this case failure to apply the state service law might not create any problem of forum shopping, the result would be an "inequitable administration" of the law. There is simply no reason why, in the absence of a controlling federal rule, an action based on state law which concededly would be barred in the state courts by the state statute of limitations should proceed through litigation to judgment in federal court solely because of the fortuity that there is diversity of citizenship between the litigants. The policies underlying diversity jurisdiction do not support such a distinction between state and federal plaintiffs, and *Erie* and its progeny do not permit it.

The judgment of the Court of Appeals is affirmed.

Notes and Questions

1. The Court notes that Federal Rules of Civil Procedure should be read according to their "plain meaning," and not "narrowly construed in order to 'avoid a direct collision'" with a state law. Do you think the Court read Rule 3 according to its "plain meaning"? (Note especially the discussion in footnotes 10 and 11 of the Court's opinion. You might also want to know that the Court later interpreted Rule 3 in a federal-question case, holding that filing the complaint tolled the statute of limitations. West v. Conrail, 481 U.S. 35 (1987).) Why might the Court have been particularly inclined to construe Rule 3 narrowly in *Walker*?

2. Think about the cases in this chapter. Try to construct a flow chart that identifies each question that must be asked in a choice-of-law situation, with arrows that point to the consequences of each answer. For example, *Walker* tells us that we must ask whether there is a "direct collision" between a Federal Rule of Civil Procedure and a state rule (or, in other words, whether the Federal Rule is "sufficiently broad to control" the issue). If the answer is "yes," then the *Hanna* analysis applies and we ask whether the Rule "really regulates procedure." (This question is often phrased as whether the Rule is "arguably procedural.") If the answer to the "direct collision" question is no, what does *Walker* instruct? If you get stuck assembling a flow chart that accounts for all the cases, there is a handy chart in Thomas D. Rowe, Jr., *Not Bad For Government Work: Does Anyone Else Think the Supreme Court is Doing a Halfway Decent Job in its* Erie-Hanna *Jurisprudence?*, 73 NOTRE DAME L. REV. 963, 990 (1998).

3. While *Walker* seems to put the last piece of the puzzle in place, application of the fully developed *Erie* doctrine is still not easy. How should the following cases come out?

- Alabama state law embodies a policy against enforcement of contractual forum-selection clauses. The federal statute governing transfers of venue, 28 U.S.C. § 1404, provides that "[f]or the convenience of parties and witnesses, in the interest of justice, a district court may transfer any civil action to any other district or division where it might have been brought." Section 1404 has been interpreted to direct federal courts to conduct an "individualized, case-by-case consideration of convenience and fairness." May an Alabama federal court in a diversity case transfer the case to the district specified in the contract, if it is otherwise one where the case might have been brought? (Hint: knowing how the Court treats Federal Rules of Civil Procedure that are in conflict with state law, can you figure out what to do with a federal *statute*?) *See* Stewart Org., Inc. v. Ricoh Corp., 487 U.S. 22 (1988).

- An Alabama statute imposes a 10% penalty on any appellant who posts a bond to stay the trial-court damages judgment pending appeal and then loses that appeal. Fed. R. App. P. 38, on the other hand, provides that "[i]f the court of appeals shall determine that an appeal is frivolous, it may award just damages and single or double costs to the appellee." Must a federal court in a diversity case in which Alabama substantive law applies impose the penalty? *See* Burlington N.R.R. v. Woods, 480 U.S. 1 (1987).

- A Florida statute requires a plaintiff to obtain leave of the court before including a request for punitive damages in her complaint. Fed. R. Civ. P. 8(a)(3) provides that a complaint "must contain . . . a demand for the relief sought." Must a plaintiff in a diversity action in Florida federal court obtain leave of the court in order to ask for punitive damages? *Compare* Cohen v. Office Depot, Inc., 184 F.3d 1292 (11th Cir. 1999) (direct conflict and federal law applies), *vacated in part on reh'g on other grounds*, 204 F.3d 1069 (11th Cir. 2000), *with* Jones v. Krautheim, 208 F. Supp. 2d 1173 (D. Colo. 2002) (no direct conflict and state law applies).

- A state rule of procedure requires a plaintiff to submit a "certificate of merit" in medical and legal malpractice cases. The certificate attests that a licensed professional verifies the claim's merit. Rule 8(a)(2) requires "a short and plain statement of the claim showing the pleader is entitled to relief," and Rule 11 provides that an attorney's signature on a complaint attests that the factual and legal contentions in the complaint are warranted. Must a federal court in a diversity case dismiss a malpractice filing that does not include a certificate of merit? *Compare* Liggon-Redding v. Estate of Sugarman, 659 F.3d 258 (3d Cir. 2011) (no direct conflict), *with* Braddock v. Orlando Reg'l Health Care Sys., Inc., 881 F. Supp. 580 (M.D. Fla. 1995) (direct conflict). (Most courts find no direct conflict.)

- Some states have enacted anti-SLAPP statutes. SLAPP ("Strategic Lawsuits Against Public Participation") suits are baseless suits brought to deter or punish private citizens for exercising their political or legal rights, such as a newspaper's criticism of a particular corporation or a consumer complaint about a business practice; the plaintiff's purpose is not to win but to make the litigation so expensive that the defendant will cease his or her perfectly legal activity. Anti-SLAPP laws make such suits easier to dismiss. Do such provisions conflict with Fed. R. Civ. P. 12 or 56, which govern dismissals? Federal courts are divided on whether state anti-SLAPP laws should apply in federal court. *Compare e.g.* Klocke v. Watson, 936 F.3d 240 (5th Cir. 2019) (Texas anti-SLAPP laws do not apply), Carbone v. Cable News Network, Inc., 910 F.3d 1345 (11th Cir. 2018) (Georgia anti-SLAPP laws do not apply), *and* Abbas v. Foreign Policy Grp., LLC, 783 F.3d 1328 (2015) (D.C. anti-SLAPP laws do not apply), *with* United States *ex rel.* Newsham v. Lockheed Missiles & Space Co., 190 F.3d 963 (9th Cir. 1999) (California anti-SLAPP laws apply), *reconsideration en banc denied in* Makaeff v. Trump Univ. LLC, 736 F.3d 1180 (9th Cir. 2013).

4. If you are somewhat confused about how to draw the line between substance and procedure in this context, you're not alone. Even the Supreme Court struggles with applying the doctrine developed in *Hanna* and its progeny. Consider the following cases.

GASPERINI V. CENTER FOR HUMANITIES, INC.

518 U.S. 415 (1996)

■ JUSTICE GINSBURG delivered the opinion of the Court.

[William Gasperini, a photojournalist, lent 300 color transparencies to the Center for Humanities for use in an educational videotape. The Center lost the transparencies, and Gasperini sued in federal court in the Southern District of New York for state-law claims of negligence, breach of contract, and conversion. Jurisdiction was based on diversity, and New York provided the substantive law. Gasperini's expert testified that the "industry standard" for each lost transparency was $1,500. Gasperini testified that between 1984 and 1993 he had earned a total of approximately $10,000 from his photography work. A jury awarded Gasperini $450,000 in compensatory damages (or $1,500 for each of the 300 lost slides). The Center moved for a new trial on several grounds, including that the verdict was excessive. The district court denied the motion. The Second Circuit reversed, relying on a New York statute that required an appellate court to find an award excessive if it "materially deviates from what is reasonable compensation." It ordered a new trial unless Gasperini agreed to an award of $100,000.]

II

Before 1986, state and federal courts in New York generally invoked the same judge-made formulation in responding to excessiveness attacks on jury verdicts: courts would not disturb an award unless the amount was so exorbitant that it "shocked the conscience of the court." . . .

In both state and federal courts, trial judges made the excessiveness assessment in the first instance, and appellate judges ordinarily deferred to the trial court's judgment.

In 1986, as part of a series of tort reform measures, New York codified a standard for judicial review of the size of jury awards. Placed in CPLR § 5501(c), the prescription reads:

> In reviewing a money judgment . . . in which it is contended that the award is excessive or inadequate and that a new trial should have been granted unless a stipulation is entered to a different award, the appellate division shall determine that an award is excessive or inadequate if it deviates materially from what would be reasonable compensation.

As stated in Legislative Findings and Declarations accompanying New York's adoption of the "deviates materially" formulation, the lawmakers found the "shock the conscience" test an insufficient check on damage awards; the legislature therefore installed a standard "invit[ing] more careful appellate scrutiny." . . .

New York state-court opinions confirm that § 5501(c)'s "deviates materially" standard calls for closer surveillance than "shock the conscience" oversight.

Although phrased as a direction to New York's intermediate appellate courts, § 5501(c)'s "deviates materially" standard, as construed by New York's courts, instructs state trial judges as well. Application of § 5501(c) at the trial level is key to this case.

. . . The "deviates materially" standard . . . in design and operation, influences outcomes by tightening the range of tolerable awards.

III

In cases like Gasperini's, in which New York law governs the claims for relief, does New York law also supply the test for federal-court review of the size of the verdict? The Center [argues that the] "deviates materially" standard . . . is a substantive standard that must be applied by federal appellate courts in diversity cases. The Second Circuit agreed. Gasperini, emphasizing that § 5501(c) trains on the New York Appellate Division, characterizes the provision as procedural, an allocation of decisionmaking authority regarding damages, not a hard cap on the amount recoverable. . . .

As the parties' arguments suggest, CPLR § 5501(c), appraised under *Erie Railroad Co. v. Tompkins*, 304 U.S. 64 (1938), and decisions in *Erie*'s path, is both "substantive" and "procedural": "substantive" in that § 5501(c)'s "deviates materially" standard controls how much a plaintiff can be awarded; "procedural" in that § 5501(c) assigns decisionmaking authority to New York's Appellate Division. Parallel application of § 5501(c) at the federal appellate level would be out of sync with the federal system's division of trial and appellate court functions, an allocation weighted by the Seventh Amendment. The dispositive question, therefore, is whether federal courts can give effect to the substantive thrust of § 5501(c) without untoward alteration of the federal scheme for the trial and decision of civil cases.

A

. . .

Classification of a law as "substantive" or "procedural" for *Erie* purposes is sometimes a challenging endeavor.

Informed by [precedent], we address the question whether New York's "deviates materially" standard, codified in CPLR § 5501(c), is outcome affective in this sense: Would "application of the [standard] . . . have so important an effect upon the fortunes of one or both of the litigants that failure to [apply] it would [unfairly discriminate against citizens of the forum State, or] be likely to cause a plaintiff to choose the federal court"? Hanna v. Plumer, 380 U.S. 460, 468 n.9 (1965).

We start from a point the parties do not debate. Gasperini acknowledges that a statutory cap on damages would supply substantive law for *Erie* purposes. Although CPLR § 5501(c) is less readily classified, it was designed to provide an analogous control.

New York's Legislature codified in § 5501(c) a new standard, one that requires closer court review than the common-law "shock the conscience" test. More rigorous comparative evaluations attend application of § 5501(c)'s "deviates materially" standard. To foster predictability, the legislature required the reviewing court, when overturning a verdict under § 5501(c), to state its reasons, including the factors it considered relevant. We think it a fair conclusion that CPLR § 5501(c) differs from a statutory cap principally "in that the maximum amount recoverable is not set forth by statute, but rather is determined by case law." In sum, § 5501(c) contains a procedural instruction, but the State's objective is manifestly substantive.

It thus appears that if federal courts ignore the change in the New York standard and persist in applying the "shock the conscience" test to damage awards on claims governed by New York law, "'substantial' variations between state and federal [money judgments]" may be expected. We therefore agree with the Second Circuit that New York's check on excessive damages implicates what we have called *Erie*'s "twin aims." Just as the *Erie* principle precludes a federal court from giving a state-created claim "longer life . . . than [the claim] would have had in the state court," so *Erie* precludes a recovery in federal court significantly larger than the recovery that would have been tolerated in state court. . . .

C

In *Byrd v. Blue Ridge Rural Electric Cooperative, Inc.*, 356 U.S. 525 (1958), the Court faced a one-or-the-other choice: trial by judge as in state court, or trial by jury according to the federal practice. In the case before us, a choice of that order is not required, for the principal state and federal interests can be accommodated. The Second Circuit correctly recognized that when New York substantive law governs a claim for relief, New York law and decisions guide the allowable damages. But that court did not take into account the characteristic of the federal court system that caused us to reaffirm: "The proper role of the trial and appellate courts in the federal system in reviewing the size of jury verdicts is . . . a matter of federal law."

New York's dominant interest can be respected, without disrupting the federal system, once it is recognized that the federal district court is capable of performing the checking function, i.e., that court can apply the State's "deviates materially" standard in line with New York case law evolving under CPLR § 5501(c). We recall, in this regard, that the "deviates materially" standard serves as the guide to be applied in trial as well as appellate courts in New York.

Within the federal system, practical reasons combine with Seventh Amendment constraints to lodge in the district court, not the court of appeals, primary responsibility for application of § 5501(c)'s "deviates materially" check. Trial judges have the "unique opportunity to consider the evidence in the living courtroom context," while appellate judges see only the "cold paper record."

District court applications of the "deviates materially" standard would be subject to appellate review under the standard the Circuits now employ when inadequacy or excessiveness is asserted on appeal: abuse of discretion. In light of *Erie*'s doctrine, the federal appeals court must be guided by the damage-control standard state law supplies, but as the Second Circuit itself has said [in a different case]: "If we reverse, it must be because of an abuse of discretion. . . . The very nature of the problem counsels restraint . . . . We must give the benefit of every doubt to the judgment of the trial judge."

IV

It does not appear that the District Court checked the jury's verdict against the relevant New York decisions demanding more than "industry standard" testimony to support an award of the size the jury returned in this case. As the Court of Appeals recognized, the uniqueness of the photographs and the plaintiff's earnings as photographer — past and reasonably projected — are factors relevant to appraisal of the award. Accordingly, we vacate the judgment of the Court of Appeals and instruct that court to remand the case to the District Court so that the trial judge, revisiting his ruling on the new trial motion, may test the jury's verdict against CPLR § 5501(c)'s "deviates materially" standard.

■ [The dissenting opinion of JUSTICE STEVENS is omitted.]

■ [The dissenting opinion of JUSTICE SCALIA, with whom THE CHIEF JUSTICE and JUSTICE THOMAS joined, is omitted.]

Notes and Questions

1. Justice Scalia's dissent in *Gasperini* made two main arguments. First, the Seventh Amendment's re-examination clause ("no fact tried by a jury, shall be otherwise re-examined in any Court of the United States, than

according to the rules of the common law") barred federal courts of appeals from reviewing verdicts for alleged excessiveness. Second, Federal Rule of Civil Procedure 59, which authorizes grants of new trials in jury cases "for any reason for which a new trial has heretofore been granted in an action at law in federal court" had to be interpreted as mandating deferential federal-court review of jury verdicts for excessiveness or inadequacy. So interpreted, Rule 59 provided a standard different from New York's rule calling for more intensive scrutiny, and under the Supreme Court's *Erie-Hanna* jurisprudence the Federal Rule had to prevail.

The *Gasperini* majority responded that although the *ground* of excessiveness was encompassed by Rule 59, the *standard* for excessiveness came from the law — New York's — that gave rise to the underlying claim for relief. Justice Scalia argued that the majority's "accommodation" of federal and state approaches disrupted the judge-jury relation in federal court, and disagreed about regarding New York's review standard as "substantive" for *Erie* purposes.

2. The *Erie* question does not arise in *Gasperini* if Rule 59 is read as dictating a federal standard for grants of new trials. *Hanna* interpreted Rule 4 relatively broadly, and *Walker* (despite its ultimate holding) instructed that the "Federal Rules should be given their plain meaning" and not "narrowly construed in order to avoid a 'direct collision' with state law." Does Justice Ginsburg's opinion deviate from those instructions?

3. Did the Court's citation to *Byrd* — after years of neglect — surprise you? Consider Thomas D. Rowe, Jr., *Not Bad For Government Work: Does Anyone Else Think the Supreme Court is Doing a Halfway Decent Job in its Erie-Hanna Jurisprudence?*, 73 NOTRE DAME L. REV. 963, 998-99 (1998):

> [E]ven though the Court goes on to make some use of *Byrd* for the first time in almost two decades, it is significant that the discussion in part III.A on the choice of review standard relies entirely on the *Hanna* "twin aims" rendition of *Erie* and *York* and — like every other Supreme Court invocation of the "twin aims" test — conspicuously omits *Byrd*. . . .
>
> . . . [T]he majority's exclusive reliance on the *Hanna* rendition . . . shows that despite its later invocation of *Byrd*, use of that case's multi-factor balancing approach is to be confined to some subset of this one category of the *Erie-Hanna* area. . . . This seeming limit on the scope of *Byrd*'s applicability is all the more apparent because *Byrd* balancing would have been easy enough to apply in *Gasperini* and would have pointed toward the majority's result . . . .

4. The result in *Gasperini* is to apply the New York state standard for appellate review of jury verdicts at the trial-court level in diversity cases in federal court. We might read the dispute between the majority and dissent in *Gasperini* as an argument about the breadth of the *Erie* doctrine and the extent to which *Hanna* limited it: the majority wants to read *Erie* broadly, accommodating state policy judgments as much as possible; the dissent would prefer to rely on what it perceives as *Hanna*'s strong preference for Federal Rules. That disagreement continues in the following case.

SHADY GROVE ORTHOPEDIC ASSOCIATES, P.A. v. ALLSTATE INSURANCE CO.

559 U.S. 393 (2010)

■ JUSTICE SCALIA announced the judgment of the Court and delivered the opinion of the Court with respect to Parts I and II-A, an opinion with respect to Parts II-B and II-D, in which the CHIEF JUSTICE, JUSTICE THOMAS, and JUSTICE SOTOMAYOR join, and an opinion with respect to Part II-C, in which the CHIEF JUSTICE and JUSTICE THOMAS join.

New York law prohibits class actions in suits seeking penalties or statutory minimum damages. We consider whether this precludes a federal district court sitting in diversity from entertaining a class action under Federal Rule of Civil Procedure 23.

I

[Shady Grove tendered a claim to Allstate for the medical care it had provided to one of Allstate's insureds. Under New York law, Allstate had 30 days to pay the claim or deny it. Allstate paid, but not on time, and it refused to pay the interest that the statute required for late payments. Shady Grove filed a class action lawsuit (authorized by Fed. R. Civ. P. 23) in federal court on the basis of diversity, on behalf of itself and others to whom Allstate owed interest. The district court dismissed the lawsuit on the ground that New York law (N.Y. C.P.L.R. 901(b)) provides that "an action to recover a penalty, or minimum measure of recovery created or imposed by statute may not by maintained as a class action." In the absence of a class action, Shady Grove's claim did not reach the minimum jurisdictional amount. The Second Circuit affirmed, holding that Rule 23 did not conflict with § 901(b) and that § 901(b) was "substantive," and therefore that New York law precluded the class action.]

II

The framework for our decision is familiar. We must first determine whether Rule 23 answers the question in dispute. Burlington N. R.R. v. Woods, 480 U.S. 1, 4-5 (1987). If it does, it governs — New York's law notwithstanding — unless it exceeds statutory authorization or Congress's rulemaking power. *Id.* at 5; *see* Hanna v. Plumer, 380 U.S. 460 (1965). We do not wade into *Erie*'s murky waters unless the federal rule is inapplicable or invalid. *See* 380 U.S. at 469-71.

A

The question in dispute is whether Shady Grove's suit may proceed as a class action. Rule 23 provides an answer. It states that "[a] class action may be maintained" if two conditions are met: The suit must satisfy the criteria set forth in subdivision (a) (i.e., numerosity, commonality, typicality, and adequacy of representation), and it also must fit into one of the three categories described in subdivision (b). By its terms this creates a categorical rule entitling a plaintiff whose suit meets the specified criteria to pursue his claim as a class action. (The Federal Rules regularly use "may" to confer categorical permission, *see, e.g.,* Fed. R. Civ. P. 8(d)(2)-(3), 14(a)(1), 18(a)-(b), 20(a)(1)-(2), as do federal statutes that establish procedural entitlements.) Thus, Rule 23 provides a one-size-fits-all formula for deciding the class-action question. Because § 901(b) attempts to answer the same question — i.e., it states that Shady Grove's suit "may *not* be maintained as a class action" (emphasis added) because of the relief it seeks — it cannot apply in diversity suits unless Rule 23 is ultra vires.

The Second Circuit believed that § 901(b) and Rule 23 do not conflict because they address different issues. Rule 23, it said, concerns only the criteria for determining whether a given class can and should be certified; section 901(b), on the other hand, addresses an antecedent question: whether the particular type of claim is eligible for class treatment in the first place — a question on which Rule 23 is silent. . . .

We disagree. To begin with, the line between eligibility and certifiability is entirely artificial. . . .

There is no reason, in any event, to read Rule 23 as addressing only whether claims made eligible for class treatment by some *other* law should be certified as class actions. Allstate asserts that Rule 23 neither explicitly nor implicitly empowers a federal court "to certify a class in each and every case" where the Rule's criteria are met. But that is *exactly* what Rule 23 does: It says that if the prescribed preconditions are satisfied "[a] class action *may be maintained*" (emphasis added) — not "a class action may be permitted." Courts do not maintain actions; litigants do. The discretion suggested by Rule 23's "may" is discretion residing in the plaintiff: He may bring his claim in a class action if he wishes. And like the rest of the Federal Rules of Civil Procedure, Rule 23 *automatically* applies "in all civil actions and proceedings in the United States district courts," Fed. R. Civ. P. 1. . . .

The dissent argues that § 901(b) has nothing to do with whether Shady Grove may maintain its suit as a class action, but affects only the *remedy* it may obtain if it wins. . . . Accordingly, the dissent says, Rule 23 and New York's law may coexist in peace.

We need not decide whether a state law that limits the remedies available in an existing class action would conflict with Rule 23; that is not what § 901(b) does. By its terms, the provision precludes a plaintiff from "maintain[ing]" a class action seeking statutory penalties. Unlike a law that sets a ceiling on damages (or puts other remedies out of reach) in properly filed class actions, § 901(b) says nothing about what remedies a court may award; it prevents the class actions it covers from coming into existence at all. . . .

The dissent all but admits that the literal terms of § 901(b) address the same subject as Rule 23 — i.e., whether a class action may be maintained — but insists the provision's *purpose* is to restrict only remedies. . . .

. . . [The] evidence of the New York Legislature's purpose is pretty sparse. But even accepting the dissent's account of the Legislature's objective at face value, it cannot override the statute's clear text. Even if its aim is to restrict the remedy a plaintiff can obtain, § 901(b) achieves that end by limiting a plaintiff's power to maintain a class action. The manner in which the law "could have been written," has no bearing; what matters is the law the Legislature *did* enact. We cannot rewrite that to reflect our perception of legislative purpose. The dissent's concern for state prerogatives is frustrated rather than furthered by revising state laws when a potential conflict with a Federal Rule arises; the state-friendly approach would be to accept the law as written and test the validity of the Federal Rule. . . .

But while the dissent does indeed artificially narrow the scope of § 901(b) by finding that it pursues only substantive policies, that is not the central difficulty of the dissent's position. The central difficulty is that even artificial narrowing cannot render § 901(b) compatible with Rule 23. *Whatever* the policies they pursue, they flatly contradict each other. Allstate asserts (and the dissent implies) that we can (and must) *interpret* Rule 23 in a manner that avoids overstepping its authorizing statute. If the Rule were susceptible of two meanings — one that would violate § 2072(b) and another that would not — we would agree. But it is not. Rule 23 unambiguously authorizes *any* plaintiff, in *any* federal civil proceeding, to maintain a class action if the Rule's prerequisites are met. We cannot contort its text, even to avert a collision with state law that might render it invalid. *See* Walker v. Armco Steel Corp., 446 U.S. 740, 750 n.9 (1980).[8] What the dissent's approach achieves is not the avoiding of a "conflict between Rule 23 and § 901(b)," but rather the invalidation of Rule 23 (pursuant to § 2072(b) of the Rules Enabling Act) to the extent that it conflicts with the substantive policies of § 901. There is no other way to reach the dissent's destination. We must therefore confront head-on whether Rule 23 falls within the statutory authorization.

B

. . . In the Rules Enabling Act, Congress authorized this Court to promulgate rules of procedure subject to its review, 28 U.S.C. § 2072(a), but with the limitation that those rules "shall not abridge, enlarge or modify any substantive right," § 2072(b).

We have long held that this limitation means that the Rule must "really regulat[e] procedure, — the judicial process for enforcing rights and duties recognized by substantive law and for justly administering remedy and redress for disregard or infraction of them," *Sibbach*, 312 U.S. at 14; *see*

---

8. The cases chronicled by the dissent each involved a Federal Rule that we concluded could fairly be read not to "control the issue" addressed by the pertinent state law, thus avoiding a "direct collision" between federal and state law, *Walker*, 446 U.S. at 749. But here, as in *Hanna*, 380 U.S. at 470, a collision is "unavoidable."

Hanna, 380 U.S. at 464; *Burlington*, 480 U.S. at 8. The test is not whether the rule affects a litigant's substantive rights; most procedural rules do. What matters is what the rule itself regulates: If it governs only "the manner and the means" by which the litigants' rights are "enforced," it is valid; if it alters "the rules of decision by which [the] court will adjudicate [those] rights," it is not.

Applying that test, we have rejected every statutory challenge to a Federal Rule that has come before us. . . . Each of these rules had some practical effect on the parties' rights, but each undeniably regulated only the process for enforcing those rights; none altered the rights themselves, the available remedies, or the rules of decision by which the court adjudicated either.

Applying that criterion, we think it obvious that [joinder] rules . . . are also valid. Such rules neither change plaintiffs' separate entitlements to relief nor abridge defendants' rights; they alter only how the claims are processed. For the same reason, Rule 23 — at least insofar as it allows willing plaintiffs to join their separate claims against the same defendants in a class action — falls within § 2072(b)'s authorization. A class action, no less than traditional joinder . . . leaves the parties' legal rights and duties intact and the rules of decision unchanged. . . .

. . . [T]he substantive nature of New York's law, or its substantive purpose, *makes no difference*. A Federal Rule of Procedure is not valid in some jurisdictions and invalid in others — or valid in some cases and invalid in others — depending upon whether its effect is to frustrate a state substantive law (or a state procedural law enacted for substantive purposes). . . . If [a Federal Rule regulates procedure], it is authorized by § 2072 and is valid in all jurisdictions, with respect to all claims, regardless of its incidental effect upon state-created rights.

C

A few words in response to the concurrence. We understand it to accept the framework we apply — which requires first, determining whether the federal and state rules can be reconciled (because they answer different questions), and second, if they cannot, determining whether the Federal Rule runs afoul of § 2072(b). The concurrence agrees with us that Rule 23 and § 901(b) conflict, and departs from us only with respect to the second part of the test, i.e., whether application of the Federal Rule violates § 2072(b). Like us, it answers no, but for a reason different from ours.

The concurrence would decide this case on the basis, not that Rule 23 is procedural, but that the state law it displaces is procedural, in the sense that it does not "function as a part of the State's definition of substantive rights and remedies." A state procedural rule is not preempted, according to the concurrence, so long as it is "so bound up with," or "sufficiently intertwined with," a substantive state-law right or remedy "that it defines the scope of that substantive right or remedy."

This analysis squarely conflicts with *Sibbach,* which established the rule we apply. . . .

In reality, the concurrence seeks not to apply *Sibbach,* but to overrule it (or, what is the same, to rewrite it). Its approach, the concurrence insists, gives short shrift to the statutory text forbidding the Federal Rules from "abridg[ing], enlarg[ing], or modify[ing] any substantive right," § 2072(b). There is something to that. It is possible to understand how it can be determined whether a Federal Rule "enlarges" substantive rights without consulting State law: If the Rule creates a substantive right, even one that duplicates some state-created rights, it establishes a new *federal* right. But it is hard to understand how it can be determined whether a Federal Rule "abridges" or "modifies" substantive rights without knowing what state-created rights would obtain if the Federal Rule did not exist. *Sibbach*'s exclusive focus on the challenged Federal Rule — driven by the very real concern that Federal Rules which vary from State to State would be chaos — is hard to square with § 2072(b)'s terms.

Sibbach has been settled law, however, for nearly seven decades. Setting aside any precedent requires a "special justification" beyond a bare belief that it was wrong. And a party seeking to overturn a *statutory* precedent bears an even greater burden, since Congress remains free to correct us, and adhering to our precedent enables it do so. . . . In all events, Allstate has not even asked us to overrule *Sibbach*, let alone carried its burden of persuading us to do so. . . .

D

We must acknowledge the reality that keeping the federal-court door open to class actions that cannot proceed in state court will produce forum shopping. That is unacceptable when it comes as the consequence of judge-made rules created to fill supposed "gaps" in positive federal law. . . . But divergence from state law, with the attendant consequence of forum shopping, is the inevitable (indeed, one might say the intended) result of a uniform system of federal procedure. Congress itself has created the possibility that the same case may follow a different course if filed in federal instead of state court. *Cf. Hanna,* 380 U.S. at 472-73. The short of the matter is that a Federal Rule governing procedure is valid whether or not it alters the outcome of the case in a way that induces forum shopping. . . .

* * *

The judgment of the Court of Appeals is reversed, and the case is remanded for further proceedings.

■ JUSTICE STEVENS, concurring in part and concurring in the judgment.

The New York law at issue . . . is a procedural rule that is not part of New York's substantive law. Accordingly, I agree with JUSTICE SCALIA that Federal Rule of Civil Procedure 23 must apply in this case and join Parts I and II-A of the Court's opinion. But I also agree with JUSTICE GINSBURG that there are some state procedural rules that federal courts must apply in diversity cases because they function as a part of the State's definition of substantive rights and remedies.

I

. . .

[*Hanna v. Plumer*'s approach to the Rules Enabling Act] does not mean . . . that the federal rule always governs. . . . [W]hile Congress may have the constitutional power to prescribe procedural rules that interfere with state substantive law in any number of respects, that is not what Congress has done. Instead, it has provided in the Enabling Act that although "[t]he Supreme Court" may "prescribe general rules of practice and procedure," § 2072(a), those rules "shall not abridge, enlarge or modify any substantive right," § 2072(b). . . .

. . . The Enabling Act's limitation does not mean that federal rules cannot displace state policy judgments; it means only that federal rules cannot displace a State's definition of its own rights or remedies. . . .

It is important to observe that the balance Congress has struck turns, in part, on the nature of the state law that is being displaced by a federal rule. And in my view, the application of that balance does not necessarily turn on whether the state law at issue takes the *form* of what is traditionally described as substantive or procedural. Rather, it turns on whether the state law actually is part of a State's framework of substantive rights or remedies. *See* § 2072(b); *cf. Hanna,* 380 U.S. at 471 ("The line between 'substance' and 'procedure' shifts as the legal context changes"); Guaranty Trust Co. v. York, 326 U.S. 99, 108 (1945) (noting that the words "substance" and "procedure" "[e]ach impl[y] different variables depending upon the particular problem for which [they] are used"). . . .

II

. . .

If . . . the federal rule is "sufficiently broad to control the issue before the Court," such that there is a "direct collision," *Walker,* 446 U.S. at 749-50, the court must decide whether application of the federal rule "represents a valid exercise" of the "rulemaking authority . . . bestowed on this Court by the Rules Enabling Act." *Burlington N.R.R.,* 480 U.S. at 5. That Act requires, *inter alia,* that federal rules "not abridge, enlarge or modify *any* substantive right." 28 U.S.C. § 2072(b) (emphasis added). Unlike JUSTICE SCALIA, I believe that an application of a federal rule that effectively abridges, enlarges, or modifies a state-created right or remedy violates this command. . . .

Thus, the second step of the inquiry may well bleed back into the first. When a federal rule appears to abridge, enlarge, or modify a substantive right, federal courts must consider whether the rule can reasonably be interpreted to avoid that impermissible result. . . . And when such a "saving" construction is not possible and the rule would violate the Enabling Act, federal courts cannot apply the rule. A federal rule, therefore, cannot govern a particular case in which the rule would displace a state law that is procedural in the ordinary use of the term but is so intertwined with a state right or remedy that it functions to define the scope of the state-created right. . . .

JUSTICE SCALIA believes that the sole Enabling Act question is whether the federal rule "really regulates procedure," which means, apparently, whether it regulates "the manner and the means by which the litigants' rights are enforced." I respectfully disagree.[7] This interpretation of the Enabling Act is consonant with the Act's first limitation to "general rules of practice and procedure," § 2072(a). But it ignores the second limitation that such rules also "not abridge, enlarge or modify *any* substantive right," § 2072(b) (emphasis added), and in so doing ignores the balance that Congress struck between uniform rules of federal procedure and respect for a State's construction of its own rights and remedies. . . .

Although the plurality appears to agree with much of my interpretation of § 2072, it nonetheless rejects that approach for two reasons, both of which are mistaken. First, JUSTICE SCALIA worries that if federal courts inquire into the effect of federal rules on state law, it will enmesh federal courts in difficult determinations about whether application of a given rule would displace a state determination about substantive rights. I do not see why an Enabling Act inquiry that looks to state law necessarily is more taxing than JUSTICE SCALIA's. But in any event, that inquiry is what the Enabling Act requires. . . . The question, therefore, is not what rule *we* think would be easiest on federal courts. The question is what rule Congress established. Although JUSTICE SCALIA may generally prefer easily administrable, bright-line rules, his preference does not give us license to adopt a second-best interpretation of the Rules Enabling Act. Courts cannot ignore text and context in the service of simplicity.

Second, the plurality argues that its interpretation of the Enabling Act is dictated by this Court's decision in *Sibbach,* which applied a Federal Rule about when parties must submit to medical examinations. But the plurality misreads that opinion. . . . To understand *Sibbach,* it is first necessary to understand the issue that was before the Court. The petitioner [in *Sibbach*] raised only the facial question whether "Rules 35 and 37 [of the Federal Rules of Civil Procedure] are . . . within the mandate of Congress to this court" and not the specific question of "the obligation of federal courts to apply the substantive law of a state." The Court, therefore, had no occasion to consider whether the particular application of the Federal Rules in question would offend the Enabling Act.

---

7. This understanding of the Enabling Act has been the subject of substantial academic criticism, and rightfully so. *See, e.g.,* Ely, *The Irrepressible Myth of* Erie, 87 HARV. L. REV. 693, 719 (1974).

Nor, in *Sibbach,* was any further analysis necessary to the resolution of the case because the matter at issue, requiring medical exams for litigants, did not pertain to "substantive rights" under the Enabling Act. . . . If the Federal Rule had in fact displaced a state rule that was sufficiently intertwined with a state right or remedy, then perhaps the Enabling Act analysis would have been different.[13] Our subsequent cases are not to the contrary. . . .

[Justice Stevens concurred in the judgment because he found that § 901(b) did *not* "serve[ ] the function of defining . . . rights or remedies."]

■ JUSTICE GINSBURG, with whom JUSTICE KENNEDY, JUSTICE BREYER, and JUSTICE ALITO join, dissenting. . . .

In our prior decisions in point, many of them not mentioned in the Court's opinion, we have avoided immoderate interpretations of the Federal Rules that would trench on state prerogatives without serving any countervailing federal interest. "Application of the *Hanna* analysis," we have said, "is premised on a 'direct collision' between the Federal Rule and the state law." Walker v. Armco Steel Corp., 446 U.S. 740, 749-50 (1980) (quoting *Hanna,* 380 U.S. at 472). To displace state law, a Federal Rule, "when fairly construed," must be "sufficiently broad" so as "to 'control the issue' before the court, thereby leaving *no room* for the operation of that law." Burlington N.R.R. v. Woods, 480 U.S. 1, 4-5 (1987) (quoting *Walker,* 446 U.S. at 749-50 & n.9; emphasis added); *cf.* Stewart Org., Inc. v. Ricoh Corp., 487 U.S. 22, 37-38 (1988) (SCALIA, J., dissenting) ("[I]n deciding whether a federal . . . Rule of Procedure encompasses a particular issue, a broad reading that would create significant disuniformity between state and federal courts should be avoided if the text permits.").

In pre-*Hanna* decisions, the Court vigilantly read the Federal Rules to avoid conflict with state laws. . . .

. . . In *Hanna* itself, the Court found the clash "unavoidable," *ibid.* . . . Even as it rejected the Massachusetts prescription in favor of the federal procedure, however, "[t]he majority in *Hanna* recognized . . . that federal rules . . . must be interpreted by the courts applying them, and that the process of interpretation can and should reflect an awareness of legitimate state interests." RICHARD H. FALLON, JR. ET AL., HART AND WECHSLER'S THE FEDERAL COURTS AND THE FEDERAL SYSTEM 593 (6th ed. 2009). . . .

In sum, both before and after *Hanna,* the above-described decisions show, federal courts have been cautioned by this Court to "interpre[t] the Federal Rules . . . with sensitivity to important state interests," *Gasperini,* 518 U.S. at 427 n.7, and a will "to avoid conflict with important state regulatory policies," *id.* at 438 n.22. The Court veers away from that approach . . . in favor of a mechanical reading of Federal Rules, insensitive to state interests and productive of discord. . . .

---

13. Put another way, even if a federal rule in most cases "really regulates procedure," *Sibbach,* 312 U.S. at 14, it does not "really regulat[e] procedure" when it displaces those rare state rules that, although "procedural" in the ordinary sense of the term, operate to define the rights and remedies available in a case. . . .

I would continue to approach *Erie* questions in a manner mindful of the purposes underlying the Rules of Decision Act and the Rules Enabling Act, faithful to precedent, and respectful of important state interests. I would therefore hold that the New York Legislature's limitation on the recovery of statutory damages applies in this case, and would affirm the Second Circuit's judgment.

Notes and Questions

1. Trace the views of Justices Ginsburg (who wrote the majority opinion in *Gasperini* and the dissenting opinion in *Shady Grove*) and Scalia (who wrote the dissenting opinion in *Gasperini* and the plurality opinion in *Shady Grove*). Can you see a consistent pattern in how each judge approaches *Erie* questions?

2. Consider the alignment of Justices in both this case and *Gasperini*. In many other contexts, Justice Ginsburg favors national power and Justice Scalia favored states' rights. Note also that Justice Ginsburg often sides with — and Justice Scalia sided against — plaintiffs, especially in class actions. Do their votes in these cases reflect their usual positions? Finally, note that in *Shady Grove*, Justice Sotomayor (who usually votes with the more liberal Justices) joined most of Justice Scalia's opinion, and Justices Kennedy and Alito (who usually voted with the more conservative Justices) joined Justice Ginsburg's dissent. It seems that *Erie* questions create strange bedfellows indeed.

3. Justice Stevens relies on both the "bound up with rights and obligations" language of *Byrd* and Professor Ely's argument that a mechanical approach to *Hanna* neglects the limitation contained in § 2072(b). He seems to be attempting to bring back together the "unguided" *Erie* analysis and the Rules Enabling Act analysis that were separated in *Hanna*. Does it work? For an example of a case applying Justice Stevens' approach, see *Garman v. Campbell County School District No. 1*, 630 F.3d 977 (10th Cir. 2010) (concluding that a Wyoming pleading requirement was part of the state's "framework of substantive rights or remedies" and thus was applicable despite the conflict with Fed. R. Civ. P. 8(a)(1)).

4. How should lower courts apply *Shady Grove*, given that there was no majority opinion? Recall that under *Marks v. United States*, 430 U.S. 188 (1977), the controlling opinion is whichever one rests on the narrowest grounds. See *supra* pp. 444-45, Note 1. Several courts have treated Justice Stevens' as the controlling opinion. *See, e.g.*, Vang v. PNC Mortg., Inc., 517 F. App'x 523, 527 (8th Cir. 2013) (per curiam); James River Ins. Co. v. Rapid Funding, LLC, 658 F.3d 1207, 1217 (10th Cir. 2011). Others apply the plurality opinion without analyzing the question under *Marks*. *See, e.g.*, Fed. Treasury Enter. Sojuzplodoimport v. SPI Spirits Ltd., 726 F.3d 62, 83 (2d Cir. 2013); Yates-Williams v. El Nihum, 268 F.R.D. 566, 568 (S.D. Tex. 2010). One court has concluded that *none* of the opinions is controlling. Abbas v. Foreign Policy Group, LLC, 783 F.3d 1328, 1336-37 (D.C. Cir. 2015).

5. The *Shady Grove* problem — what to do about a Federal Rule of Civil Procedure (or Appellate Procedure) that clashes with state substantive policies

— turns up in many Supreme Court cases in the *Erie* line, including *Walker* and *Burlington Northern*, although the Court has not answered the question consistently. For a discussion of how this problem undermines the whole *Erie* doctrine, see Suzanna Sherry, *A Pox on Both Your Houses: Why the Court Can't Fix the* Erie *Doctrine*, 10 J. L. ECON & POL'Y 173 (2013). For a wide-ranging defense of *Erie*, see Ernest A. Young, *A General Defense of* Erie Railroad Co. v. Tompkins, 10 J.L. ECON. & POL'Y 17 (2013).

6. Recall that federal jurisdiction is presumptively concurrent: most cases over which there is federal jurisdiction can also be brought in state court instead. If a plaintiff brings a *federal* claim in *state* court (and the defendant does not remove to federal court), what law should apply? *See* Dice v. Akron, Canton & Youngstown R.R., 342 U.S. 359 (1952). State courts usually follow their own procedural rules in federal-law cases, but in *Dice* the Supreme Court interpreted the Federal Employers' Liability Act to require jury trials and to govern in state court on some aspects of cases as to which state law would have left decisions to the judge. To put the point more broadly if not with high precision, state procedure can govern so long as it does not unduly burden the federal right — but if it does, state courts hearing federal-law claims must follow federal procedure.

SECTION C: ASCERTAINING THE CONTENT OF STATE LAW

Once a court has determined that state law rather than federal law applies, the court must still determine the content of state law. That question involves not only a further choice-of-law issue — *which* state's law? — but also the problem of identifying the substantive content of the chosen state's law. This section addresses those questions.

WEBBER V. SOBBA

322 F.3d 1032 (8th Cir. 2003)

Before BOWMAN, RICHARD S. ARNOLD, and BYE, Circuit Judges.

■ BOWMAN, Circuit Judge.

David Webber sued Brandy Sobba for negligence and damages arising out of injuries he sustained in a single-car accident on a rural road in Fulton County, Arkansas, on August 22, 1997. Webber was a passenger in a vehicle driven by Sobba and owned by Holly Bray, another passenger in the car....

I.

During the late afternoon of August 22, 1997, Webber, age 23, met his friend Bray, age 20, in a parking lot in Salem, Arkansas, and the two drove in Webber's pickup truck to a liquor store in Lanton, Missouri, where Webber purchased several cases of beer and wine coolers. Webber put the alcohol in a cooler in his truck, and the two drank during their drive back to Salem. Upon their return, Webber parked his pickup truck, transferred the cooler to Bray's car, and the two then proceeded to drive Bray's car around town. Approximately an hour later, Webber and Bray stopped at a convenience store in Salem and encountered Sobba, age 18, whom Webber had previously dated. Sobba joined them, and the three continued to drink and drive around Salem. Later that evening, they drove to neighboring Viola, Arkansas, so Webber could visit his sister. Sobba and Bray sat in the car while Webber talked to his sister. Thirty minutes later, Webber returned and told Sobba, who was now the driver, to take the back road to Salem so as to avoid the police. Webber gave Sobba driving directions because she was unfamiliar with the route. Webber sat in the front seat (half on the console and half on the passenger-side bucket seat) between Sobba and Bray, who had passed out by this time. At trial, Sobba testified that while she was driving Webber began trying to kiss and touch her. Sobba's last recollection before the car left the road and hit a bridge abutment was trying to push Webber off of her. In his testimony, Webber denied making any physical advances toward Sobba while she was driving. Although all three survived, each suffered serious injuries from the accident.

Webber initially filed his negligence and damages suit against Sobba in Arkansas state court. Sobba pleaded comparative fault and joint enterprise as defenses.* In response, Webber moved for partial summary judgment on Sobba's joint-enterprise defense. The state court denied Webber's motion and the case proceeded to trial. After the court empaneled the jury, Webber nonsuited and his case was dismissed without prejudice. Subsequently, Webber refiled the instant action in the United States District Court for the Eastern District of Arkansas [under diversity jurisdiction] and again sought summary judgment on Sobba's joint-enterprise defense, arguing that, under Arkansas law, negligence is not imputed to the passenger in an action between a passenger and a negligent driver. The District Court denied the motion, holding that, based on a review of applicable Arkansas precedent, the Arkansas Supreme Court would allow Sobba to raise this defense. . . . The District Court also overruled Webber's objection to the jury instruction on the defense, which stated that the jury should return a verdict in favor of Sobba if they found that Webber and Sobba were engaged in a joint enterprise. The District Court also gave a comparative fault instruction, stating that if Webber's negligence was equal or greater in degree than Sobba's negligence, then the jury verdict should be for Sobba. The jury returned a general verdict in favor of Sobba, but it is not clear on which ground it based its verdict. This appeal followed.

II.

In a diversity case, we review a district court's interpretation of state law de novo, giving no deference to that interpretation. When state law is unsettled

---

* A "joint enterprise" defense exists when a member of a joint enterprise sues a third party (not a member of the enterprise). The third party is permitted to attribute the negligence of another member of the enterprise to the plaintiff. — ED.

or unclear on a particular question, it is our duty to apply the rule we believe the state supreme court would follow.

Here, we are not aware of, nor did the parties direct us to, any Arkansas Supreme Court decision that squarely addresses the narrow question now before us: whether the joint-enterprise defense can be asserted against another member of the enterprise. Consequently, we look to resources that the Arkansas Supreme Court has relied on in the past to determine whether the defense is permissible: related Arkansas case law, the Restatement of Torts, and authority from other states. *See* Reliance Nat. Indem. Co. v. Jennings, 189 F.3d 689, 694 (8th Cir. 1999) ("When the highest court in a state has not declared its law on an issue, we are 'to ascertain from all the available data what the state law is and apply it.'"). We also examine what policy justifications exist for Arkansas to depart from the majority rule on the joint-enterprise defense, as embodied in the Restatement. Based on our consideration of the foregoing, we conclude that the Arkansas Supreme Court would reject the application of the joint-enterprise defense in these circumstances.

Although there is no Arkansas case directly on point, Sobba urges us to read three other Arkansas appellate decisions as recognizing the joint-enterprise defense in an action brought by a passenger against a driver. We find those cases distinguishable. There is nothing in the Arkansas Supreme Court's decision in *Rone v. Miller*, 520 S.W.2d 268, 272 (Ark. 1975), that suggests either party challenged the applicability of the joint-enterprise defense in an action between members of a joint enterprise, and thus we cannot draw any conclusion from the court's silence on the question.[2] Similarly, the decisions of the Arkansas Supreme Court in *RLI Insurance Co. v. Coe,* 813 S.W.2d 783 (Ark. 1991), and the Arkansas Court of Appeals in *Southern Farm Bureau Casualty Insurance Co. v. Pettie*, 924 S.W.2d 828 (Ark. Ct. App. 1996), fail to support Sobba's position on the applicability of the defense because in both cases the courts found that no joint enterprise existed between members of the enterprise. Neither case reached the question before us.

In light of the dearth of Arkansas authority on this issue, we think it helpful to examine what other state supreme courts have decided when they have squarely addressed this question. The overwhelming majority rule rejects

---

2. At first blush, *Rone* appears to support Sobba's contention regarding the applicability of the joint-enterprise defense in these circumstances. In that case, Edward Floyd, Ricky Rone and another passenger were killed in a single-car accident. Floyd's estate sued Rone's estate, alleging Rone was driving when the accident happened. In response, the defendant raised the affirmative defenses of joint venture, assumption of risk, and contributory negligence and offered evidence as to who drove the car. The trial court excluded that evidence and the jury returned a verdict for the plaintiff. On appeal, the Arkansas Supreme Court found that "the rejected proffer of evidence was relevant to the affirmative defenses of joint venture, assumption of risk and the degree of contributory negligence by [plaintiff]" and that the defendant "would be entitled to appropriate instructions upon these affirmative defenses whenever evidence is adduced to justify them." We do not believe *Rone* supports the applicability of the joint-enterprise defense here. Unlike the plaintiff in the instant case, the plaintiff in *Rone* never questioned the applicability of the defense. Thus, the Arkansas Supreme Court was not confronted with the issue now before us. As discussed *infra*, we do not think the Arkansas Supreme Court would adopt such a rule.

the joint-enterprise defense as applied to members of joint enterprises who assert negligence claims against one another.

. . . The Arkansas Supreme Court frequently looks to the *Restatement* to answer unsettled questions of tort law. Given its practice of looking to the *Restatement* and the wide acceptance by other courts of the *Restatement*'s rule, we think it likely that the Arkansas Supreme Court would follow the overwhelming majority rule on this issue and not allow Sobba to raise the joint-enterprise defense. *See* Sproles v. Associated Brigham Contractors, Inc., 889 S.W.2d 740, 742 (Ark. 1994) (describing the *Restatement of Torts* and the law of other jurisdictions as "forceful authority").

While Arkansas law occasionally diverges from the majority rule on tort liability questions, our examination of the trend in Arkansas in expanding tort liability and the policy undergirding the application of the joint-enterprise defense convince us that the Arkansas Supreme Court would not find a justification for departing from the majority rule in this case.

Generally speaking, the zone of tort liability in Arkansas has been expanding. We believe that this trend would continue absent some principled policy reason to the contrary.

We can find no policy reason to protect one member of a joint enterprise from suit by a fellow member. Imputation of negligence in these circumstances would allow a negligent party to use his or her own culpability as a shield from any liability. Whatever we might think of Webber's conduct, if Sobba was negligent and if that negligence was the primary cause of Webber's injuries, then Sobba should be held responsible for her actions. We do not believe the law permits Sobba to escape liability solely on the ground that if the jury finds she and Webber were engaged in a joint enterprise, her negligence should be imputed to Webber.

Moreover, we think the joint-enterprise defense is unnecessary in these circumstances because the doctrine of comparative fault allows the jury to weigh the relative negligence of the two parties and determine whether the injured party should be held culpable for his own contribution to his injury. Given the evidence in this case, it is easy to imagine a jury holding Webber accountable for his own injuries given that he supplied alcohol to Sobba, a minor, got her to take unfamiliar roads at night, and allegedly groped her while she was driving.

In summary, we find no clear answer in Arkansas's case law to the question of whether the joint-enterprise defense applies to suits between members of the joint enterprise. We believe the Arkansas Supreme Court would adopt the *Restatement* position, which is accepted in virtually every jurisdiction that has addressed this question, absent some justifiable reason not to. Upon examination, we think there is no principled justification for applying the joint-enterprise defense to suits among members of the enterprise. The concerns that the joint-enterprise defense attempts to satisfy are already addressed in Arkansas's comparative-fault scheme, thus making the rule an unnecessary anachronism. We find it very likely that the Arkansas Supreme Court would decline to extend the rule's application to suits between joint-enterprise members. For this reason, we conclude the District Court was in error when it instructed the jury on the joint-enterprise defense. This instruction should not have been given. . . .

For the reasons stated, the judgment is reversed, and the case is remanded for a new trial.

Notes and Questions

1. The court distinguishes Arkansas precedent and then goes on to describe (and adopt) the majority rule and the policy reasons for adopting it. How different is that from what courts did under *Swift v. Tyson*? Were you persuaded by the court's distinguishing of Arkansas precedent (look especially at footnote 2)? Notice that the plaintiff dropped his suit in state court after the state trial court rejected his argument against the joint-enterprise defense; does the Eighth Circuit's ruling encourage that sort of forum shopping?

2. *Webber* is one example of how federal courts predict state law in the absence of definitive guidance from state courts. *Nationwide Mutual Insurance Co. v. Buffetta*, 230 F.3d 634, 637 (3d Cir. 2000), provides more general guidance:

> . . . In [predicting how the state supreme court would rule,] a federal court can . . . give due regard, but not conclusive effect, to the decisional law of lower state courts. The opinions of intermediate appellate state courts are "not to be disregarded by the federal court unless it is convinced by other persuasive data that the highest court of the state would decide otherwise."
>
> . . . In predicting how the highest court of the state would resolve the issue, we must consider "relevant state precedents, analogous decisions, considered dicta, scholarly works, and any other reliable data tending convincingly to show how the highest court in the state would decide the issue at hand."

Can a federal court ever disregard precedent from the state's highest court, if it believes that the state court would no longer adhere to that precedent? *Compare* Microvote Corp. v. Montgomery Cty., 942 F. Supp. 1046, 1049 (E.D. Pa. 1996) ("We must follow the ruling of the highest court of Pennsylvania even if the precedent is old [and] even if we think that the state Supreme Court would change its mind were it ever to revisit the subject."), *with* Mason v. Am. Emery Wheel Works, 241 F.2d 906, 909 (1st Cir. 1957) ("[I]t is not necessary that the decisions of a state court be explicitly overruled in order to lose their persuasive force as indications of what the law is."), *and* N.A. Burkitt, Inc. v. J.I. Case Co., 597 F. Supp. 1086, 1089 (D. Me. 1984) (stating that a federal court need not follow existing state precedent "if there are strongly persuasive reasons for the federal court's belief that the state's highest court would no longer adhere to its own decision"). Might one characterize the *Webber* court as paying lip service to the former principle but practicing the latter?

3. *Webber* gave no deference to the ruling of the district court. Until 1991, courts of appeals deferred to district court interpretations of state law. In *Salve*

Regina College v. Russell, 499 U.S. 225 (1991), however, the Supreme Court held that federal appellate courts (including both the Supreme Court and courts of appeals) should review determinations of local law de novo, without giving any deference to the trial court's ruling. Who is likely to be more familiar with Arkansas law, a district-court judge sitting in Arkansas or a panel of the Eighth Circuit, which includes six other states besides Arkansas? The panel in *Webber* included one judge from Missouri, one from North Dakota, and one (Judge Arnold) who was a judge in the Western District of Arkansas before he was elevated to the Court of Appeals. Should the composition of the panel matter?

4. An Indiana plaintiff sues a Tennessee defendant, in Tennessee federal court, for an accident that happened in North Carolina. Assuming that state law should apply, how should the federal court determine *which* state's law should apply? In *Klaxon Co. v. Stentor Electric Manufacturing Co.*, 313 U.S. 487 (1941), the Supreme Court held that *Erie* applied to choice-of-law questions: a federal court must apply whatever law would be applied by a court of the state in which the federal court is located. In our example, then, the Tennessee federal court would look to Tennessee choice-of-law doctrines to determine which state's law to apply. This can result in rather circuitous analysis. As one judge noted in a case in which the New York federal court determined that New York state courts would apply California law, "[o]ur principal task . . . is to determine what the New York courts would think the California courts would think on an issue about which neither has thought." Nolan v. Transocean Air Lines, 276 F.2d 280, 281 (2d Cir. 1960) (Friendly, J.), *set aside and remanded on other grounds*, 365 U.S. 293 (1961).

5. The *Erie* doctrine is designed, in part, to prevent forum shopping between state and federal courts. Does it instead encourage forum shopping *among* federal courts, with each party seeking to litigate in a federal court located in the state with the most favorable laws? Consider 28 U.S.C. § 1404, which allows a district court to transfer a case to another federal district, "for the convenience of parties and witnesses." If the suit in the previous note is brought in Tennessee and transferred to North Carolina under § 1404, which state's choice-of-law doctrines should govern? In *Van Dusen v. Barrack,* 376 U.S. 612, 639 (1964), the Supreme Court held: "[T]he transferee district court must be obligated to apply the state law that would have been applied if there had been no change of venue. A change of venue under § 1404(a) generally should be, with respect to state law, but a change of courtrooms." Does this ruling encourage a diversity plaintiff to file in federal court in the state with the most favorable laws, knowing that the court might well transfer the case to a more convenient, but less favorable, forum? (*Van Dusen* involved a transfer at the request of the defendant, but § 1404 allows transfers on motion of either party or on the court's own initiative. *See* Ferens v. John Deere Co., 494 U.S. 516 (1990) (applying *Van Dusen* rule to § 1404 transfer request by a plaintiff).)

In *Atlantic Marine Construction Corp. v. U.S. District Court*, 571 U.S. 49 (2013), the Supreme Court created an exception to the *Van Dusen* doctrine. *Atlantic Marine* held, first, that if a plaintiff files suit in a forum other than one specified in a contractual forum-selection clause, the court should grant the defendant's § 1404 motion to transfer to the selected forum (absent exceptional circumstances). Second, the Court held that when the case is transferred pursuant to a forum-selection clause, the transferee court should apply the choice-of-law doctrines of the state in which *it* sits, not those of the state in which the transferor court sits. Such an exception to *Van Dusen* is necessary, according to the Court, because "[n]ot only would it be inequitable to allow the plaintiff to fasten its choice of substantive law to the venue transfer, but it would also encourage gamesmanship." *Id.* at 583.

6. A federal court unsure of state law has another choice besides making what many courts refer to as an "*Erie* guess." Forty-eight states have enacted valid *certification* statutes, which permit the state's highest court to answer questions certified to it by other courts. (Only Missouri and North Carolina lack such statutes.) Minnesota, for example, has a typical certification statute:

> The Supreme Court of this state may answer a question of law certified to it by a court of the United States or by an appellate court of another state, of a tribe, of Canada or a Canadian province or territory, or of Mexico or a Mexican state, if the answer may be determinative of an issue in pending litigation in the certifying court and there is no controlling appellate decision, constitutional provision, or statute of this state. [Minn. Stat. § 480.065 (2002).]

Should federal courts always use certification if it is available? Consider *Goodlett v. Kalishek*, 223 F.3d 32 (2d Cir. 2000). Plaintiff's husband, a participant in an airplane race, was killed in a crash with defendant's plane fourteen seconds after the end of the race, when both planes were preparing to land. New York law, which applied, provided for "primary assumption of the risk" for those who participate in sports or recreational activities with known risks, thus immunizing other participants from liability for any conduct short of recklessness. Everyone agreed that, had the crash occurred during the race itself, this New York doctrine would have provided a complete defense to the suit. The majority concluded that the doctrine applied even though the crash did not occur during the race, a question the New York courts had never confronted. One judge dissented, arguing that the issue should have been certified to New York's highest court (the Court of Appeals):

> If we do not certify the issue now, the New York Court of Appeals can at any time in the future reject the majority's interpretation of New York law, as it has occasionally done in the past. If it does so, the decedent's estate will have been denied the benefit of the state's highest court on a controlling issue of state law.
>
> One of the basic reasons for a certification statute is to avoid the possibility of our misinterpreting state law. [223 F.3d at 40.]

The majority responded:

> The dissent's concern that the New York Court of Appeals could reject our interpretation of New York law, thereby denying plaintiff "the benefit of the ruling of the state's highest court on a controlling issue of state law" is misplaced. By filing her state law claim in a federal court, plaintiff "knew that any open question of state law would be decided by a federal as opposed to a New York state court." Thus, even assuming *both* that the New York

Court of Appeals is someday confronted with the question presented by this case *and* decides the question differently — possibilities we consider extremely remote — the state court's decision would "not impugn the integrity of [our] decision or the fairness of the process that was accorded [the plaintiff]." . . . "[P]laintiffs elected to proceed in the federal forum, thereby voluntarily depriving themselves of the opportunity to attempt to persuade the [state court]." [*Id.* at 37 n.4.]

Would the majority's argument work if the federal court had concluded that New York law did *not* immunize the defendant? Once the plaintiff chose federal court — and the court had jurisdiction — the defendant could never get the benefit of a state-court ruling. Does this suggest that *Erie* did not eliminate forum shopping? Would using certification more frequently help?

7. Note that a federal court's determination of state law in a diversity case is not binding on state courts. Indeed, if a federal district court decides a state question, and, while the case is on appeal, the state supreme court reaches an opposite conclusion in another case, the federal Court of Appeals is bound to follow the state court and reverse the district court even if the district court's "*Erie* guess" was perfectly reasonable at the time. *See, e.g.,* McMahan v. Toto, 311 F.3d 1077 (11th Cir. 2002).

8. Do all the complications of *Erie* — from determining whether state law applies to ascertaining the content of state law — persuade you that diversity jurisdiction is more trouble than it's worth?

CHAPTER татTWELVE

CLASS ACTIONS

We bring this initial study of civil procedure to a close with a look at class actions. In a class action, one person or group of people — called the *class representative(s)* — represents other people — called the *class members* — who have claims or defenses similar to those of the class representatives. The lawyers who represent the class are called *class counsel*. The judgment or settlement that is obtained — whether favorable or unfavorable — binds both the class representatives *and* the class members.

The class action possesses a collective power and a potential for efficient adjudication unrivaled in other forms of litigation. If a million victims have allegedly been defrauded of $100 apiece, few, if any, of the victims will sue individually. The class action creates the lawsuit — a $100 million lawsuit at that. If the plaintiffs' claims are strong, the class action provides a useful deterrent to misbehavior — although some might argue that the law should not deal in, much less encourage, lawsuits over trifling harms.

On the other hand, if the plaintiffs' claims are weak, the Damoclean sword of a $100 million judgment might induce the defendant to settle the case for a substantial amount — perhaps $10 million — even if it did nothing wrong. Moreover, class actions can involve massive discovery, case-management headaches, and intractable problems at trial. Finally, the idea that your legal rights can be determined in a lawsuit in which you did not personally participate seems antithetical to the autonomy on which the procedural system that we have studied is premised.

The ethical and practical challenges that class counsel face are enormous. Class counsel, who often front the litigation expenses and stand to receive a portion of any judgment or settlement, usually have a greater financial stake in the case than the class representatives or class members. Nor can counsel possibly represent with the adversarial vigor we expect of individual litigation the possibly varying interests of each class member.

A creature of Anglo-American law, the class action was unknown to civil-law systems. Numerous innovations made class actions much more common in the United States than in other common-law countries. That reality is changing, as more than three dozen nations have created some form of class action in the past thirty years. But foreign class actions often contain significant limits. American-style class actions remain another instance of "American exceptionalism" in civil procedure.

Federal Rule of Civil Procedure 23, the class-action rule, is probably the most contentious — and arguably least procedural — of all the federal procedural rules. Upper-level courses such as Complex Civil Litigation may treat the many interpretive issues of Rule 23 in greater depth. This chapter hopes to accomplish three simpler objectives. The first is to provide you with a foundation in the basic doctrinal and policy dimensions of class actions. The second is to use the class action as a capstone that reviews — even as it challenges — procedural and jurisdictional doctrines that this course has examined. The third is to leave you with a sense of an alternative to the one-on-one adversarial model that dominates modern American litigation.

Section A: Perspectives on Class Actions

David L. Shapiro, Class Actions: The Class as Party and Client

73 Notre Dame L. Rev. 913, 913-14, 918-19, 923-24, 926-34 (1998)

Perhaps the most dramatic development in civil procedure in recent decades has been the growth of interest in the class action as an actual and potential means of resolving a wide range of disputes. This interest, of course, extends far beyond the bounds of civil procedure itself into the domains of substantive tort and contract law, federalism, and the proper interpretation of the constitutional guarantee of due process. Indeed, it is partly through the class action device that we may be witnessing, and taking part in, a sea change in our understanding of both substantive and procedural law....

In the interest of oversimplification, take two models of "group litigation." The first — what might be called the aggregation model — sees the various joinder devices, including the class action, as essentially techniques for allowing individuals to achieve the benefits of pooling resources against a common adversary. Under this view, the individual who is part of the aggregate surrenders as little autonomy as possible (although some sacrifices are undoubtedly inevitable if the group effort is to have any utility and to afford any economies of scale). Thus the individual retains his own counsel, retains the right to leave the group before, during, and after the litigation, and can insist on playing a significant role in the operations of the group so long as he chooses to remain a part of that group.

The second . . . I call the "entity" model. In this view, . . . the entity is the litigant and the client. Moreover, in the situations in which class action treatment is warranted, the individual who is a member of the class, for whatever purpose, is and must remain a member of that class, and as a result must tie his fortunes to those of the group with respect to the litigation, its progress, and its outcome. Of course, even this entity model does not deny the class member the opportunity to seek private advice, or to contribute in some way to the progress of the litigation, but it severely limits such aspects of individual autonomy as the range of choice to move in or out of the class or to be represented before the court by counsel entirely of one's own selection. . . .

The conclusion that the entity model is preferable is not an easy one for a person like me, who believes in the virtues of autonomy and individual choice. If, as has been forcefully argued, those virtues include the value to the individual of a personal "day in court" — of the ability to participate in the fullest sense in the adjudication of a claim of right — the conclusion becomes an especially difficult one. . . .

. . . The most helpful starting point may reside in the "small claim" class action — an action defined here to embrace those cases in which the claim of any individual class member for harm done is too small to provide any rational justification to the individual for incurring the costs of litigation. As an example of such a case, take a claim on behalf of many purchasers that defendants have engaged in a price-fixing conspiracy to violate the federal antitrust laws. The . . . amount due any single purchaser would not exceed, say, $100.

In such cases, I submit . . . the soundest approach is to view the cause of action as essentially a group claim fitting the characteristics of the second model, with all the consequences that entails. . . . [T]he small claim class action strikes me as one that serves the purpose not of compensating those harmed in any significant sense, or of providing them a sense of personal vindication, but rather, and perhaps entirely, the purpose of allowing a private attorney general to contribute to social welfare by bringing an action whose effect is to internalize to the wrongdoer the cost of the wrong. The purpose of the action, in other words, is solely to deter the kind of wrong that causes a small injury to a large number . . . .

That it makes eminent sense to view the class as the aggrieved claimant in such instances . . . strikes me as more than a trivial conclusion. It suggests that notions of individual choice, autonomy, and participation — and their resonance in the constitutional guarantee of due process — are not so rigid that they cannot yield to practical arguments . . . .

. . . Remaining for consideration are the cases that, in the view of most, are the hardest to bring within the second model . . . . Perhaps the most challenging of these cases is one involving a mass tort in which there are a large number of victims, all of whom have suffered, or are threatened with, substantial injury as a result of the defendant's conduct and who would be likely (if the class action format did not exist) to bring individual actions seeking redress. . . .

. . . [In these cases] the argument for the first model — treating the class action as essentially an aggregation of individual actions for purposes of convenience — is strong. After all, if each individual claim is substantial, each potential claimant probably has both the motive and the wherewithal (given the blessings of the contingent fee) to bring a separate action, an action in which he chooses his own counsel, develops his own strategy, decides when and whether to settle, and does all the other things that constitute the core of litigation as we know it. Why should that claimant be deprived of an interest that many view as rooted in due process and some view as firmly entrenched in natural law? . . .

There are responses on several levels that, for me at least, are ultimately convincing despite my own reluctance to be convinced. . . . [I]t is important to stress the considerations of efficiency that serve in the aggregate to offer a substantial promise of a better substantive outcome for a class member — and certainly for the average class member — than as a litigant in a series of individual actions. . . . If we attribute rationality to victims (and put to one side the possibly separate interests of their lawyers), many if not most class members would doubtless see these efficiencies and distributional equities as critical to their choice of models, especially if the choice has to be made "behind a veil" of a substantial degree of ignorance about the outcome of their own individual action.

But the argument for efficiency may justify aggregation without mandating or even warranting adoption of the entity model. And the efficiency arguments may be balanced by the hazards in any process of group litigation in which individuals and their own lawyers play little or no role: that the attorneys for the group and their adversaries (the defendants) will manage to pick up most of the goodies at the settlement table, leaving only the scraps for the almost anonymous and faceless members of the injured class. Although I believe these hazards tend to be overstated by some critics of class action settlements, it remains important to make a substantive case for different treatment of a mass tort. . . .

First, while there is seldom any question whose car hit whom in the auto accident case, there may often be a total lack of proof as to whose product affected which class member in the toxic tort case, and thus the most meaningful way of addressing the issue of exposure is with respect to the class as a whole. If defendant A had a one-third market share of a fungible product that was evenly distributed throughout the affected area by all manufacturers, we can say with considerable confidence that defendant A was responsible for one-third of the class's exposure to the product, even though we can only say with respect to any individual class member that (absent other information) there is one chance in three that he was exposed to the product of defendant A.

Second, . . . we may not have sufficient data to say with any reasonable degree of assurance (and certainly not by a preponderance of the evidence) that an individual's exposure to the defendant's product was in fact the cause of his disease. Yet with the same data, we may be able to say with considerable confidence that a specified increase in the rate of the disease with respect to the class as a whole was caused by exposure to the product in question — that X members of the class would not have contracted the disease in the absence of exposure.

Thus far, the problem has been primarily addressed from the standpoint of the members of the class, whose interests in autonomy and in individual choice have been the major factors weighed against the gains to class members from entity treatment. But the broader social interests at stake need to be recognized too, since the measure of efficiency and due process does require a balancing of the interest of the individual against the other social concerns that are affected. In this case, the second model seems preferable both for the administration of the civil justice system and for the interests of litigants other than the plaintiff class.... The gain is that the overall outcome will either exonerate the defendant in a single, fully, and thoroughly litigated proceeding or, if fault is found and if adequate safeguards are observed, will end in an award more likely to approximate the actual measure of harm caused by the wrongful conduct than could the sum total awarded in a relatively arbitrary group of individual actions that are filed and pursued to judgment....

... Thus the choice is not so much between two workable models as between a model that offers some hope of a reasonably prompt and fair disposition and one that does not.

Notes and Questions

1. Professor Shapiro goes on to discuss other difficult problems that class actions create, among them ethical challenges for counsel representing a class whose members' individual interests may diverge; the necessarily expanded (and less neutral) role that the judge must play; potential harm to principles of federalism if federal courts entertain nationwide class actions; and potential harm to the legislative prerogative and separation-of-powers principles if class actions effectively create a substantive law unto themselves. He discusses the ways in which his entity model better negotiates some of these concerns than an aggregation model, but he does not suggest that the entity model makes these issues disappear.

2. We could add to the list of concerns the potential distortion of litigation incentives and dynamics that we discussed at the outset of the chapter. Although class actions aid deterrence by forcing a defendant to internalize a far greater share of the cost of its wrongful behavior, they also make it risky for a defendant to litigate even when the claims are weak. Indeed, an early critique called class actions "a form of legalized blackmail." Milton Handler, *The Shift from Substantive to Procedural Innovations in Antitrust Suits — The Twenty-Third Annual Antitrust Review*, 71 COLUM. L. REV. 1, 9 (1971). Judge Posner summed up the problem this way: "[There] is a concern with forcing these defendants to stake their companies on the outcome of a single jury trial, or be forced by fear of the risk of bankruptcy to settle even if they have no legal liability...." *In re* Rhone–Poulenc Rorer, Inc., 51 F.3d 1293, 1299 (7th Cir. 1995) (*infra* p. 683). The blackmail argument is hotly disputed. *See* Charles Silver, *We're Scared to Death: Class Certification and Blackmail,* 78 N.Y.U. L. REV. 1357 (2003).

3. Yet another problem is "agency cost": that the agents (here, class representatives and class counsel) will pursue their own interests at the expense of the interests of the principal (the class itself). *See* Jonathan R. Macey & Geoffrey P. Miller, *The Plaintiffs' Attorney's Role in Class Action and Derivative Litigation: Economic Analysis and Recommendations for Reform*, 58 U. CHI. L. REV. 1, 12-27 (1991) (discussing agency-cost theory and its application to class actions). One aspect of the agency-cost concern is the urban legend, to which Professor Shapiro alludes, that class actions enrich class counsel and rarely yield more than token relief for class members. Anecdotes involving unconscionable class settlements keep the legend alive. Except for a few outlier cases, however, one study found no support for this claim; the median fees in class actions ranged from 27% to 30% of the class's recovery — less than the 33-40% contingency fee standard in many civil cases. THOMAS E. WILLGING ET AL., EMPIRICAL STUDY OF CLASS ACTIONS IN FOUR FEDERAL DISTRICT COURTS 68-69 (1996). Another study showed that the median recovery in class settlements in state court was $850,000 and the median recovery in federal-court settlements was $300,000. Those numbers worked out to a median recovery of $350 per class member in state court and $517 per class member in federal court. *See* Thomas E. Willging & Shannon R Wheatman, *Attorney Choice of Forum in Class Action Litigation: What Difference Does It Make?*, 81 NOTRE DAME L. REV. 591, 639-40 & tbl. 15 (2006); *id.* at 640 (finding that the typical state court awarded 30% of the value of the settlement as attorneys' fees, while the typical federal-court award was 25%).

4. For trenchant criticism of class actions, see MARTIN H. REDISH, WHOLESALE JUSTICE (2009). For other appraisals, see PRINCIPLES OF THE LAW OF AGGREGATE LITIGATION (AM. LAW INST. 2010); JOHN C. COFFEE, JR., ENTREPRENEURIAL LITIGATION (2015); BRIAN T. FITZPATRICK, THE CONSERVATIVE CASE FOR CLASS ACTIONS (2020).

B. CLASS ACTIONS: THE BASICS

Rule 23 is one of the longest Federal Rules. For now, read Rules 23(a), –(b), and –(g), which are the parts of the Rule that describe when a case can be *certified* as a class action. To obtain class certification, a class representative must demonstrate that all of the requirements of Rules 23(a) and –(g) are met, plus one (or more) of the requirements of Rule 23(b).

1. Rule 23(a)

Rule 23(a) lists a set of prerequisites that every class action must meet. One advantage of class actions is their ability to resolve large numbers of related claims efficiently; one criticism of class actions is the loss of class members' autonomy to control their own lawsuits. Taken together, the elements of Rule 23(a) seek to maximize efficiency while minimizing the effects of class members' loss of individual control.

To compensate for the loss of individual control, Rule 23(a) requires class representatives to *adequately represent* the interests of class members. Grounded in the Due Process Clause, the adequacy-of-representation requirement has its origin in *Hansberry v. Lee*, 311 U.S. 32 (1940). In *Hansberry*, white residents of a Chicago neighborhood signed a racially restrictive covenant to prevent property owners from selling or renting their properties to African-Americans. The covenant was to become effective after the owners of 95% of the frontage in the neighborhood had signed and purportedly took effect in 1928. In 1932, an owner of a property subject to the covenant rented an apartment to an African-American doctor. Neighbors brought a class action in state court to enforce the covenant. Following a stipulation that the lawyers signed, the court found that the requisite percentage had signed the covenant, thus making it enforceable.

In 1937, the Hansberrys, a prominent African-American family, bought a home in the same neighborhood.* Neighbors again brought a class action to enforce the covenant. The Hansberrys contested the factual validity of the covenant, as well as its legal validity (raising constitutional and other grounds not raised in the prior class action). Although the trial judge did not believe that the covenant was effective (even stating that only 54% of the covenanted frontage had signed), the Illinois courts held that the owner of the property the Hansberrys later bought was a member of the prior class action. As successors to the prior owners, the Hansberrys were precluded from contesting the stipulation or challenging the covenant on grounds that could have been raised, but were not, in the prior class action.

Because the case involved a state-court judgment, the United States Supreme Court could overturn the Illinois judgment only if the Illinois courts had violated a federally protected right. The Supreme Court found such a right in the Due Process Clause:

> It is familiar doctrine of the federal courts that members of a class not present as parties to the litigation may be bound by the judgment where they are in fact adequately represented by parties who are present, or where they actually participate in the conduct of the litigation in which members of the class are present as parties, or where the interest of the members of the class, some of whom are present as parties, is joint, or where for any other reason the relationship between the parties present and those who are absent is such as legally to entitle the former to stand in judgment for the latter. [311 U.S. at 42-43.]

Applying this principle to the case, the Court held that class members in the prior class action had divergent interests; some wanted the covenant enforced, and others did not. The class representatives were therefore representing "dual and potentially conflicting interests." *Id.* at 44. "Such a selection of representatives for purposes of litigation, whose substantial interests are not necessarily or even probably the same as those whom they

---

* The plans of an African-American family to move into a hostile white neighborhood served as a backdrop for the award-winning 1959 play, *A Raisin in the Sun*. The author of the play, Lorraine Hansberry, was the daughter of the home owners. She was seven years old when the litigation began.

are deemed to represent, does not afford that protection to absent parties which due process requires." *Id.* at 45. The Hansberrys were therefore free to contest the validity of the covenant despite the earlier class judgment.

Hansberry stated a constitutional rule of claim preclusion: a judgment cannot bind class members whose interests a class representative has inadequately represented. The converse proposition — when the class representation is adequate, a judgment precludes further litigation of the class members' claims — became the principle on which Rule 23(a) was built. Together Rule 23(a)'s requirements interlock to meet *Hansberry*'s constitutional demand, while also ensuring that a class action will be an efficient vehicle for resolving the dispute.

Analytically, Rule 23(a) contains six elements. The first two, teased out of Rule 23(a)'s introductory text, are unnumbered:

- a definable class must exist; and
- the class representative must usually be a member of that class.

Cf. Carrera v. Bayer Corp., 727 F.3d 300 (3d Cir. 2013) (vacating class certification when class members could not be readily ascertained); *but see* Mullins v. Direct Digital, LLC, 795 F.3d 654 (7th Cir. 2015) (refusing to impose a separate ascertainability requirement). The class definition cannot be "fail-safe," in which only class members with valid claims belong to the class; otherwise, defendants could never enjoy the preclusive effect of a class judgment in their favor. *See, e.g.*, MSC Recovery Claims v. Plymouth Rock Assurance Corp., 404 F. Supp. 3d 470, 485 (D. Mass. 2019).

The next four elements are numbered:

- the class must be so numerous that individual joinder is impracticable (the *numerosity* requirement of (a)(1));
- questions of law or fact common to the class must exist (the *commonality* requirement of (a)(2));
- the claims or defenses of the representative parties must be typical of those of the class (the *typicality* requirement of (a)(3)); and
- the representative parties must fairly and adequately protect the interests of the class (the *adequacy* requirement of (a)(4)).

A large body of case law has sprung up around each of these elements. Each element serves a distinct purpose, but at the same time each reinforces the other elements. The Supreme Court has noted this interrelationship on several occasions. For instance, in *General Telephone Co. of the Southwest v. Falcon*, 457 U.S. 147 (1982), the Court held that a Mexican-American with a failure-to-promote discrimination claim could not represent Mexican-Americans with failure-to-hire discrimination claims. It is hard to tell from the Court's analysis whether the specific problem was an (a)(2) or (a)(3) deficiency. The Court refused to be pinned down:

> The commonality and typicality requirements of Rule 23(a) tend to merge. Both serve as guideposts for determining whether . . . maintenance of a class action is economical and whether the named plaintiff's claim and the class claims are so interrelated that the

interests of the class members will be fairly and adequately protected in their absence. Those requirements therefore also tend to merge with the adequacy-of-representation requirement, although the latter requirement also raises concerns about the competency of class counsel and conflicts of interest. [*Id.* at 157 n.13.]

Rule 23(a) thus provides guideposts, each of which must be independently satisfied — but efficient adjudication and adequacy in a constitutional sense remain the bottom line.

Nearly every state has a class-action rule or statute, and most track the requirements of Federal Rule 23(a). A few omit the typicality element. Be careful, though: state courts may interpret their class-action rules, even those with language similar or identical to Rule 23, in a manner different from federal courts' interpretations of Rule 23.

2. Rule 23(g)

Ordinarily, the court appoints counsel to represent the class. As *Falcon*'s footnote 13 shows, courts used to imply an adequacy-of-counsel requirement into the text of Rule 23(a)(4). A 2003 amendment added subsection (g) to Rule 23. Rule 23(g) now makes the adequacy-of-counsel requirement explicit. Rule 23(g)(1)(A) specifies the factors that a court must examine when appointing class counsel; Rule 23(g)(1)(B) permits the court to consider other matters as well.

3. Rule 23(b)

Once a class action meets each element of subdivisions (a) and –(g), it must then meet one final requirement: it must fall within one of the four categories of Rule 23(b). If a class action fits within more than one category, the court may certify the class under each applicable standard.

An important distinction exists between the first three categories (the (b)(1)(A), (b)(1)(B), and (b)(2) classes) and the fourth (the (b)(3) class). The first three class actions are *mandatory*; class members usually cannot exit the case even if they want to. The (b)(3) class action, on the other hand, is an *opt-out* class action; class members must be given notice of the case and afforded the opportunity to remove themselves. *Compare* Fed. R. Civ. P. 23(c)(2)(B) (requiring that class members in a (b)(3) class action receive notice the case and of their opt-out right), *with* Fed. R. Civ. P. 23(c)(2)(A) (making notice optional and providing no opt-out right in (b)(1)(A), (b)(1)(B), and (b)(2) class actions). The first three class actions involve circumstances in which individual litigation would create unfairness or hardship for the class representative, the class's adversary, or absent class members. In contrast, the (b)(3) class action, which permits class treatment when other forms of dispute resolution are less efficient, allows class members who just want to get out, or to sue on their own, to do so.

Like the requirements of Rule 23(a), a large body of law surrounds each of these four types of class action. The least common forms are the (b)(1)(A) and (b)(1)(B) class actions, which descend from English equity practice. Because the common law had no mechanism for joining related cases, a party sometimes faced the prospect of repetitive actions at law. Eventually equity developed a device — the bill of peace — to prevent harmful or needless relitigation. Although Rules 23(b)(1)(A) and 23(b)(1)(B) have expanded beyond these historical antecedents, Rule 23(b)(1) restates, more or less, two traditional uses of bills of peace. The (b)(1)(A) class action protects a defendant from "incompatible standards of conduct" that separate lawsuits by class members might create. The (b)(1)(B) class action has as its principal concern the negative effects that individual lawsuits might have on the rights of others in the class. A paradigm situation for the (b)(1)(B) action is the presence of multiple claims against a limited fund: early-filing individual claimants might deplete the fund, leaving later-filing claimants with little or nothing. With both (b)(1)(A) and (b)(1)(B), gathering all those who might assert claims into a single class action avoids the negative effects of individual litigation on others.

The last two class actions — the (b)(2) and (b)(3) class actions — are products of the 1966 amendments that expanded Rule 23 to its present form. They are also the most common forms of class action. Rule 23(b)(2), which permits class actions when injunctive or declaratory relief "is appropriate respecting the class as a whole," was added to make clear that class actions were available in the nascent field of civil-rights litigation. *See* David Marcus, *Flawed but Noble: Desegregation Litigation and Its Implications for the Modern Class Action*, 63 FLA. L. REV. 657 (2011). But this form of class action has applications beyond civil-rights litigation.

In contrast, Rule 23(b)(3) class actions, which allow an opt-out right, exist to achieve greater economy and efficiency. Class actions under Rule 23(b)(3) must meet two requirements: (1) the questions of law or fact common to the class (which were identified in the (a)(2) commonality analysis) must "predominate over any questions affecting only individual members"; and (2) a class action must be "superior to other available methods for fairly and efficiently adjudicating the controversy." These criteria are called *predominance* and *superiority*. Rule 23(b)(3) also lists four factors to guide the predominance and superiority analysis. The four factors test the strength of class members' autonomy interests in pursuing their own litigation, the extent of other litigation, the desirability of concentrating the case in one forum, and the court's ability to manage litigation that will likely have some issues that vary from class member to class member.

This last factor, sometimes called *manageability*, is often the critical question in (b)(3) cases. A court will not certify a class action that presents insuperable management problems; after all, an unmanageable class action is not superior to other methods for handling the dispute. But be careful: "manageability" and "superiority" are terms of art. For instance, a case is not unmanageable simply because it is easier to manage a single plaintiff's case than a class action; the court needs to consider whether the totality of individual cases will consume more judicial resources than the class action. Moreover, in some (b)(3) class actions that involve small claims — say, a million people have allegedly been cheated out of $10 each — it is highly unlikely that any will sue in the absence of a class action. You might think that, in such a case, doing nothing is superior to certifying a class action; the court will have management headaches if the class action is certified but no headaches if the class action is not. But that reasoning doesn't work: giving plaintiffs access to a cost-effective way to press meritorious claims also factors into the superiority-manageability analysis.

The superiority analysis requires a court to compare the class action to a range of alternatives for resolving a mass dispute. In this course we have examined some of these alternatives — such as voluntary joinder under Rule 20 or allowing intervention under Rule 24 — but a full examination of the various methods to achieve aggregation and of their comparative advantages and disadvantages to class actions lies beyond this course.

Before Rule 23(b)(3), monetary claims had not generally been amenable to class-action treatment. With the advent of Rule 23(b)(3), the collectivization of the monetary claims of large numbers of people became possible. The drafters of the 1966 amendment urged some caution in using Rule 23 too expansively, especially in the area of mass torts. Much of the debate over Rule 23 since 1966 has been about the wisdom of Rule 23(b)(3) — about whether aggregating monetary claims is a good idea. Supporters of Rule 23(b) argued that, for the first time in history, procedural rules fully and effectively delivered the enforcement of the substantive law, especially in small-stakes cases for which individual adjudication was not worthwhile. Others expressed concerns about the collective power of the class action, which could be harnessed to browbeat innocent defendants unwilling to risk a massive verdict into unreasonably large settlements. From a different perspective, still others worried that rapacious class counsel would collude with defendants to bilk class members out of their valid claims.

One way in which Rule 23(b)(3) balanced these concerns was to permit class members to opt out. To ensure the effective exercise of this right, the court, on certification of a (b)(3) class, must provide notice to class members of their right to exclude themselves within the time period that the court specifies. This notice must be "the best notice that is practicable under the circumstances, including individual notice to all members who can be identified through reasonable effort." Fed. R. Civ. P. 23(c)(2)(B). "Individual notice" typically means notice by first-class mail or another method of equal reliability. *See generally* Eisen v. Carlisle & Jacquelin, 417 U.S. 156 (1974) (imposing a requirement of individual notice to reasonably identifiable class members). You may also have seen class-action notices in newspapers, on television, or (increasingly) on social media like YouTube, Facebook, or Twitter to reach those who are not readily identifiable.

Class members may be bound by the outcome of a case in which they did not participate and may not have known about. In some (b)(3) class actions, notice fails to reach some class members. In (b)(1) and (b)(2) class actions, class members may never receive a notice about the case at all: other than notice of a settlement, *see* Fed. R. Civ. P. 23(e)(1), a court need not (although it may) provide any notice about the case. See Fed. R. Civ. P. 23(c)(2)(A).

4. Applying Rule 23

No case captures more than a sliver of the issues that Rule 23 presents, but the following two cases illustrate major themes.

HALEY V. MEDTRONIC, INC.

169 F.R.D. 643 (C.D. Cal. 1996)

■ REA, District Judge.

[Plaintiff received a pacemaker manufactured by the defendant. One part of the pacemaker — the "lead" — was allegedly defective. The plaintiff's pacemaker had not yet failed, but she alleged that she suffered emotional distress and other injuries because of her fear of a failure and the future possibility of needing to undergo surgery to remove the pacemaker.

[Nationwide, more than 66,000 people had received the defendant's pacemakers. The plaintiff moved for certification of a class action on behalf of all the recipients. She alleged various theories of liability, including negligence, products liability, breach of warranty, and fraud. She sought both damages and an order that would require the defendant to establish a program to monitor the health of the class members. For her damages claim, she moved to certify a class under Rule 23(b)(3); for her medical-monitoring claim, she sought certification under Rule 23(b)(2).]

A. *Class Actions in General*

Class actions have two primary purposes: (1) to accomplish judicial economy by avoiding multiple suits; and (2) to protect the rights of persons who might not be able to present claims on an individual basis.

As the party seeking class certification, the burden is on plaintiff to establish a prima facie showing of each of the prerequisites of Rule 23(a) of the Federal Rules of Civil Procedure and to establish an appropriate ground for class action under Rule 23(b). . . .

B. *Rule 23(a)'s Requirements*

. . .

1. *Numerosity*

. . . The courts have made clear that plaintiff does not need to show that it would be impossible to join every class member, as "impracticability" does not mean "impossibility." Because no exact numerical cut-off exists, the specific facts of each case must be examined to determine if impracticability exists.

In assessing whether the numerosity standard is met, the Court will consider the following factors: "the geographical diversity of class members, the ability of individual claimants to institute separate suits, and whether injunctive or declaratory relief is sought." ...

Applying this standard to the facts of the present case, it seems clear that the numerosity requirement is satisfied. Approximately 66,166 of the defective leads have been implanted and over 43,000 of these leads are still active. Moreover, these leads have been implanted across the United States such that potential plaintiffs are spread out and are not in one confined geographical area. . . .

2. *Commonality*

... [C]lass certification is proper only where the common issues of fact or law are of sufficient importance to the case that the Court is convinced that the most efficient method of determining the rights of the parties is through a class action.

In the instant case, where the underlying defect in the leads is all related to the same defective material in the leads — regardless of the particular individual in whom the lead is implanted — it appears that commonality is present. . . .

In addition, in mass tort cases like the present where a single product is involved, the requirement of commonality is satisfied by a showing of a common question of defendant's conduct with regard to liability. In the instant case, where defendant's representations and misrepresentations to the FDA and to the public are all the same, there clearly appears to be an issue of commonality. . . .

Although commonality may be found lacking where a common fact issue would be resolved differently under different state laws applicable to the facts of the case, a sufficient number of common issues are present in the instant case to satisfy the commonality requirement.

It should also be noted that in suits seeking joint relief — e.g., injunctions — commonality usually exists by its very nature, unless the injunction sought turns on individual circumstances. In the instant case, the medical treatment program would seem to fall in the former situation, as the medical monitoring program would not be based on individual circumstances.

3. *Typicality*

... To see if typicality exists, the Court does not need to find that the claims of the purported class representative are identical to the claims of the other class members. Instead, the test is that the class representative "must be part of the class and possess the same interest and suffer the same injury as the class members." In other words, a claim is typical if it: (1) arises from the same event or practice or course of conduct that gives rise to the claims of other class members; and (2) is based on the same legal theory as their claims.

In the instant case, defendant's "course of conduct" with respect to the various plaintiffs — i.e., its design, manufacture and sale of the leads — was exactly the same. In addition, plaintiff's claim is also based on the same basic legal theory as the other class members — defendant's design, manufacture and testing of the leads was improper, negligent and resulted in harm to the recipients. Thus, it would seem that plaintiff's claim is "typical" of those of the rest of the class.

In addition, it is clear that — notwithstanding defendant's arguments — it is not necessary that all class members suffer the same exact injury as the class representative. Indeed, the named plaintiff's claim may be "typical" even if other members of the class suffered lesser injuries. Even more importantly, plaintiff's claim can still be typical even if the class members' injuries were suffered at different times. On the other hand, class action is not appropriate where a different "type" of injury was suffered.

. . . [T]he different damages based on the individual characteristics of the recipients does not render plaintiff's claim atypical. . . .

4. *Adequacy of Representation*

. . . [R]epresentation is "adequate" if: (1) the attorney representing the class is qualified and competent; and (2) the class representatives do not have interests antagonistic to the remainder of the class.

To see if the attorney representing the class is qualified, the Court will look to the professional qualifications, skills, experience and resources of the lawyers. As the extensive firm resumes of plaintiff's lawyers make clear, plaintiff's lawyers clearly seem to meet this standard. In addition, plaintiff's lawyers do not possess any conflicts of interest that might hamper their ability to adequately represent the class.

To see if the named plaintiff will adequately represent the class, the Court focuses on whether the representative's individual interests are the same or similar to those of the other class members — i.e., much like was done with respect to typicality. . . .

In the instant case, plaintiff's adequate representation of the class is also guaranteed by the fact that plaintiff's interest is clearly large enough — i.e., she has enough at stake — to ensure a vigorous prosecution of the action. Furthermore, as far as can be seen, the named plaintiff here is not subject to any unique defenses not assertable against the other class members. Finally, there do not appear to be any conflicts between the class members that are either serious or irreconcil[a]ble enough to defeat the adequacy of representation.

C. *Rule 23(b)(3)*

. . .

Although the question of whether common issues predominate over individual issues and the question of whether a class action would be superior are interconnected inquiries, the Court will follow the traditional approach of addressing each of these issues independently.

1. *Predominates*

Although the Court has already found that common questions of law and fact exist in the instant action, the Court must now go one step further and find that such common questions "predominate" the action, or else class certification is inappropriate. . . . [I]n order to determine if common issues of fact and law "predominate," the Court will have to decide whether there are so many questions common to all of the plaintiffs that having class action treatment would be far more efficient than having a number of separate trials.

In arguing that common issues do not predominate in this matter, defendant focused on the fact that with implantable medical devices, individual questions for each plaintiff will be critical since each plaintiff's body will respond differently to the implanted leads. Defendant's argument, while critical to the Court's later analysis of whether class action treatment is "superior," is not as essential for assessing whether common questions predominate. This is because defendant's argument ignores the fact that plaintiffs' claims actually focus on defendant's liability and defendant's conduct with regard to the leads — not on their effect on the plaintiffs. . . .

Defendant also emphasized that because plaintiffs' claims revolve around defendant's alleged fraudulent misrepresentations, plaintiffs will have to prove individual reliance on these misrepresentations, making such individual questions more important than the common questions. Defendant is correct that individual issues will need to be considered by the Court in determining whether plaintiffs have a valid claim for fraudulent misrepresentation. As will shortly be made clear, however, this situation is more important to the Court's "superiority" analysis . . . .

As for the issue of damages, it seems clear that the fact that plaintiffs will be entitled to different damages does not mean that common questions do not predominate. . . .

2. *Superiority of Class Action Treatment*

. . .

Traditionally, courts have been reluctant to certify class actions in mass tort, product liability litigation. . . .

In determining whether a class action is superior, courts will consider four factors under Rule 23(b)(3).

A. *Rule 23(b)(3)(A)*

. . . [Individual control of litigation] is most relevant where each class member has suffered sizeable damages or has an emotional stake in the litigation. In the instant case, where the damages each plaintiff suffered are not that great, this factor weighs in favor of certifying a class action. While the damages present here are clearly of emotional import, because the amount sought — or so plaintiff claims — is so small in many of the cases, there appears to be no special desire to maintain individual actions.

B. *Rule 23(b)(3)(B)*

[There were twenty-five other pending lawsuits with the same basic theories of liability. The court found that] this factor also slightly weighs in favor of granting class certification.

C. *Rule 23(b)(3)(C)*

. . . In this case, where the potential plaintiffs are located across the country and where the witnesses and the particular evidence will also be found across the country, plaintiffs have failed to establish any particular reason why it would be especially efficient for this Court to hear such a massive class action lawsuit. Indeed, plaintiffs have not even established that the vast majority of the individual lawsuits that have been filed — or that will be filed — should be brought in the Central District of California. Absent such evidence, it seems clear that this factor indicates that class action treatment is inappropriate in the instant circumstances.

D. *Rule 23(b)(3)(D)*

. . . The Supreme Court has described the manageability issue as "encompass[ing] the whole range of practical problems that may render the class format inappropriate for a particular suit." It is because of this factor in particular that the Court feels class certification is inappropriate. First, the larger the class, the more costly and difficult it will be to provide adequate notice, to determine individual damage claims, and to distribute any recovery.

In addition, because plaintiffs' claims are all state law claims, class action treatment would present the Court with the particularly "unmanageable" task of having to apply so many different state laws. Although plaintiff contends that this hurdle is not a major problem in the instant case since state laws on negligence and fraud are likely to be quite similar, the problems and complexities raised by having to consider so many different state laws — even if they are relatively the same — convince the Court that class certification would be inappropriate in the instant litigation. . . . As a result, the Court would be forced to go through — and to have the jury go through — an individual analysis of each state's negligence law in order to determine defendant's liability for negligence with regard to each individual defendant. . . . In other words, the complexities that class action treatment would create would more than outweigh any benefits from considering the common issues in one trial, making class action treatment less efficient and definitely not "superior."

Furthermore, with this nationwide class, any measurements of compensatory and punitive damages would need to be measured individually, based on the individual circumstances and individual state laws. . . .

. . . Here, the allegedly negligent pacemaker leads were implanted in different individuals in different states by different doctors. . . . Given the fact that approximately 66,000 individuals had these leads implanted, there are potentially 66,000 different instances that the Court would have to examine to determine if defendant's conduct was the real cause of injury for each potential plaintiff. Under these circumstances, there are just too many individual issues for the Court to manage for class adjudication to be deemed superior, even though there is a common nucleus of facts concerning defendant's conduct. . . .

As a final note, it seems particularly unwise for the Court to certify a class action where fraud is one of the principal claims set forth by plaintiffs. Because proving fraud requires plaintiffs to show that the misrepresentations to each class member were the same or substantially similar, this impliedly would require the Court to hear from every single plaintiff and physician as to the representations they individually relied upon. . . .

D. *The Medical Monitoring Program*

. . .

It is clear that [the language of Rule 23(b)(2)] does not mean that every single class member must have been injured or aggrieved in the same way by defendant's conduct. Instead, it is sufficient if the defendant has adopted a pattern of activity that is likely to be the same as to all members of the class. In the instant situation, such class treatment seems appropriate since the plaintiffs have all been dealt with in identical manners by defendant. However, because class certification is inappropriate for plaintiffs' principal claims, class treatment here would be misplaced and unmanageable.

In addition, and more importantly, Rule 23(b)(2) treatment is clearly unavailable where the principal relief sought is money damages. Although plaintiffs claim that this request for a medical monitoring program is not merely incidental to their action for monetary damages, it seems clear that the primary goal of plaintiffs is in fact monetary damages. . . .

As a result, certifying a class under Rule 23(b)(2) where the declaratory relief sought is secondary to larger claims for monetary damages would be contrary to the purposes of Rule 23(b)(2). Thus, at this time, it seems wise for the Court to deny class certification here also.

Notes and Questions

1. Note how concerns for manageability sneak into the court's analysis on the (b)(2) issue. A number of courts have indicated that Rule 23(b)(2)

contains an implicit "cohesiveness" element that operates something like the (b)(3) predominance-and-superiority requirements. *See In re* St. Jude Med., Inc., Silzone Heart Valve Prods. Liab. Litig., 425 F.3d 1116, 1121-22 (8th Cir. 2005) ("Although Rule 23(b)(2) contains no predominance or superiority requirements, class claims thereunder still must be cohesive.")

2. Suppose that the class representative in *Haley* had forsworn any intention to bring damage claims, and sought only a medical-monitoring program. Would Rule 23(b)(1)(A) or –(b)(2) treatment then be appropriate? For a time during the 1990s, medical-monitoring claims were the darling of plaintiffs' class-action lawyers who were seeking a way to certify tort claims on a mandatory basis. Despite some early successes, plaintiffs saw courts swing decisively against the theory.

3. *Haley*'s (b)(3) analysis is fairly representative of the reasons why (b)(3) certification is so difficult in mass-tort cases. The only anomaly is the court's decision to analyze the problem of variant state law as a superiority rather than a predominance question. Most courts treat the problem as one of predominance. *See, e.g.*, Castano v. Am. Tobacco Co., 84 F.3d 734 (5th Cir. 1996); *In re* Am. Med. Sys., Inc., 75 F.3d 1069 (6th Cir. 1996). But the result is usually the same as in *Haley*: no class action. We return to the problems of certifying mass-tort class actions *infra* pp. 689-96.

4. Outside the mass-tort area, Rule 23(b)(3) is sometimes used with better effect. In many securities, antitrust, and consumer class actions, (b)(3) certification, while hardly automatic, is common. Tort claims are often large-stakes cases that are viable on an individual basis, while many securities, antitrust, and consumer cases are small-stakes cases in which it is, quite literally, class treatment or nothing. The present consensus is that Rule 23(b)(3) is designed principally for small-stakes cases. *See In re* Rhone–Poulenc Rorer, Inc., 51 F.3d 1293 (7th Cir. 1995) (*infra* p. 683); *Castano*, 84 F.3d 734. *Haley* was a middle-range case; it was a mass tort, but the emotional injuries did not have great value.

WAL–MART STORES, INC. V. DUKES

564 U.S. 338 (2011)

■ JUSTICE SCALIA delivered the opinion of the Court, in which CHIEF JUSTICE ROBERTS and JUSTICE KENNEDY, JUSTICE THOMAS, and JUSTICE ALITO joined, and in which JUSTICE GINSBURG, JUSTICE BREYER, JUSTICE SOTOMAYOR, and JUSTICE KAGAN joined as to Parts I and III.

We are presented with one of the most expansive class actions ever. The District Court and the Court of Appeals approved the certification of a class comprising about one and a half million plaintiffs, current and former female employees of petitioner Wal–Mart who allege that the discretion exercised by their local supervisors over pay and promotion matters violates Title VII by discriminating against women. In addition to injunctive and declaratory relief, the plaintiffs seek an award of backpay. We consider whether the certification of the plaintiff class was consistent with Federal Rules of Civil Procedure 23(a) and (b)(2).

I

A

Petitioner Wal–Mart is the Nation's largest private employer. It operates four types of retail stores throughout the country: Discount Stores, Supercenters, Neighborhood Markets, and Sam's Clubs. Those stores are divided into seven nationwide divisions, which in turn comprise 41 regions of 80 to 85 stores apiece. Each store has between 40 and 53 separate departments and 80 to 500 staff positions. In all, Wal–Mart operates approximately 3,400 stores and employs more than one million people.

Pay and promotion decisions at Wal–Mart are generally committed to local managers' broad discretion, which is exercised "in a largely subjective manner." Local store managers may increase the wages of hourly employees (within limits) with only limited corporate oversight. As for salaried employees, such as store managers and their deputies, higher corporate authorities have discretion to set their pay within preestablished ranges.

Promotions work in a similar fashion. . . .

B

The named plaintiffs in this lawsuit, representing the 1.5 million members of the certified class, are three current or former Wal–Mart employees who allege that the company discriminated against them on the basis of their sex by denying them equal pay or promotions, in violation of Title VII of the Civil Rights Act of 1964. . . .

These plaintiffs, respondents here, do not allege that Wal–Mart has any express corporate policy against the advancement of women. Rather, they claim that their local managers' discretion over pay and promotions is exercised disproportionately in favor of men, leading to an unlawful disparate impact on female employees. And, respondents say, because Wal–Mart is aware of this effect, its refusal to cabin its managers' authority amounts to disparate treatment. Their complaint seeks injunctive and declaratory relief, punitive damages, and backpay. It does not ask for compensatory damages.

Importantly for our purposes, respondents claim that the discrimination to which they have been subjected is common to *all* Wal–Mart's female employees. The basic theory of their case is that a strong and uniform "corporate culture" permits bias against women to infect, perhaps subconsciously, the discretionary decisionmaking of each one of Wal–Mart's thousands of managers — thereby making every woman at the company the victim of one common discriminatory practice. Respondents therefore wish to litigate the Title VII claims of all female employees at Wal–Mart's stores in a nationwide class action. . . .

II. Finding the commonality

The class action is "an exception to the usual rule that litigation is conducted by and on behalf of the individual named parties only." In order to justify a departure from that rule, "a class representative must be part of the class and 'possess the same interest and suffer the same injury' as the class members." Rule 23(a) ensures that the named plaintiffs are appropriate representatives of the class whose claims they wish to litigate. The Rule's four requirements — numerosity, commonality, typicality, and adequate representation — "effectively limit the class claims to those fairly encompassed by the named plaintiff's claims."

A

The crux of this case is commonality — the rule requiring a plaintiff to show that "there are questions of law or fact common to the class." Rule 23(a)(2). That language is easy to misread, since "[a]ny competently crafted class complaint literally raises common 'questions.'" Nagareda, *Class Certification in the Age of Aggregate Proof*, 84 N.Y.U. L. REV. 97, 131-32 (2009). For example: Do all of us plaintiffs indeed work for Wal–Mart? Do our managers have discretion over pay? Is that an unlawful employment practice? What remedies should we get? Reciting these questions is not sufficient to obtain class certification. Commonality requires the plaintiff to demonstrate that the class members "have suffered the same injury." This does not mean merely that they have all suffered a violation of the same provision of law. . . . Their claims must depend upon a common contention — for example, the assertion of discriminatory bias on the part of the same supervisor. That common contention, moreover, must be of such a nature that it is capable of classwide resolution — which means that determination of its truth or falsity will resolve an issue that is central to the validity of each one of the claims in one stroke.

"What matters to class certification . . . is not the raising of common 'questions' — even in droves — but, rather the capacity of a classwide proceeding to generate common answers apt to drive the resolution of the litigation. Dissimilarities within the proposed class are what have the potential to impede the generation of common answers." Nagareda, *supra*, at 132.

Rule 23 does not set forth a mere pleading standard. A party seeking class certification must affirmatively demonstrate his compliance with the Rule — that is, he must be prepared to prove that there are *in fact* sufficiently numerous parties, common questions of law or fact, etc. . . . . "[S]ometimes it may be necessary for the court to probe behind the pleadings before coming to rest on the certification question," and that certification is proper only if "the trial court is satisfied, after a rigorous analysis, that the prerequisites of Rule 23(a) have been satisfied." Frequently that "rigorous analysis" will entail some overlap with the merits of the plaintiff's underlying claim. That cannot be helped. . . .

In this case, proof of commonality necessarily overlaps with respondents' merits contention that Wal–Mart engages in a *pattern or practice* of discrimination. That is so because, in resolving an individual's Title VII claim, the crux of the inquiry is "the reason for a particular employment decision." Here respondents wish to sue about literally millions of employment decisions at once. Without some glue holding the alleged *reasons* for all those decisions together, it will be impossible to say that examination of all the class members' claims for relief will produce a common answer to the crucial question *why was I disfavored*.

B

. . .

. . . Wal–Mart's announced policy forbids sex discrimination, and as the District Court recognized the company imposes penalties for denials of equal employment opportunity. The only evidence of a "general policy of discrimination" respondents produced was the testimony of Dr. William Bielby, their sociological expert. Relying on "social framework" analysis, Bielby testified that Wal–Mart has a "strong corporate culture," that makes it "vulnerable" to "gender bias." He could not, however, "determine with any specificity how regularly stereotypes play a meaningful role in employment decisions at Wal–Mart. At his deposition . . . Dr. Bielby conceded that he could not calculate whether 0.5 percent or 95 percent of the employment decisions at Wal–Mart might be determined by stereotyped thinking." . . . Bielby's testimony does nothing to advance respondents' case. "[W]hether 0.5 percent or 95 percent of the employment decisions at Wal–Mart might be determined by stereotyped thinking" is the essential question on which respondents' theory of commonality depends. If Bielby admittedly has no answer to that question, we can safely disregard what he has to say. It is worlds away from "significant proof" that Wal–Mart "operated under a general policy of discrimination."

C

The only corporate policy that the plaintiffs' evidence convincingly establishes is Wal–Mart's "policy" of allowing discretion by local supervisors over employment matters. On its face, of course, that is just the opposite of a uniform employment practice that would provide the commonality needed for a class action; it is a policy against having uniform employment practices. It is also a very common and presumptively reasonable way of doing business — one that we have said "should itself raise no inference of discriminatory conduct."

To be sure, we have recognized that, "in appropriate cases," giving discretion to lower-level supervisors can be the basis of Title VII liability under a disparate-impact theory — since "an employer's undisciplined system of subjective decisionmaking [can have] precisely the same effects as a system pervaded by impermissible intentional discrimination." But the recognition that this type of Title VII claim "can" exist does not lead to the conclusion that every employee in a company using a system of discretion has such a claim in common. To the contrary, left to their own devices most managers in any corporation — and surely most managers in a corporation that forbids sex discrimination — would select sex-neutral, performance-based criteria for hiring and promotion that produce no actionable disparity at all. Others may choose to reward various attributes that produce disparate impact — such as scores on general aptitude tests or educational achievements. And still other managers may be guilty of intentional discrimination that produces a sex-based disparity. In such a company, demonstrating the invalidity of one manager's use of discretion will do nothing to demonstrate the invalidity of another's. A party seeking to certify a nationwide class will be unable to show that all the employees' Title VII claims will in fact depend on the answers to common questions.

Respondents have not identified a common mode of exercising discretion that pervades the entire company — aside from their reliance on Dr. Bielby's social framework analysis that we have rejected. In a company of Wal–Mart's size and geographical scope, it is quite unbelievable that all managers would exercise their discretion in a common way without some common direction. Respondents attempt to make that showing by means of statistical and anecdotal evidence, but their evidence falls well short. . . .

[With respect to the statistical evidence of pay disparity, the Court noted that the disparity "may be attributable to only a small set of Wal–Mart stores, and cannot by itself establish the uniform, store-by-store disparity upon which the plaintiffs' theory of commonality depends." Responding to the anecdotal evidence of discrimination, the Court observed that "[e]ven if every single one of these accounts is true, that would not demonstrate that the entire company 'operate[s] under a general policy of discrimination,' which is what respondents must show to certify a companywide class."]

. . . We quite agree that for purposes of Rule 23(a)(2) "[e]ven a single [common] question" will do. We consider dissimilarities not in order to determine (as Rule 23(b)(3) requires) whether common questions predominate, but in order to determine (as Rule 23(a)(2) requires) whether there *is* "[e]ven a single [common] question." And there is not here. Because respondents provide no convincing proof of a companywide discriminatory pay and promotion policy, we have concluded that they have not established the existence of any common question. . . .

III

We also conclude that respondents' claims for backpay were improperly certified under Federal Rule of Civil Procedure 23(b)(2). . . .

A

Rule 23(b)(2) allows class treatment when "the party opposing the class has acted or refused to act on grounds that apply generally to the class, so that final injunctive relief or corresponding declaratory relief is appropriate respecting the class as a whole." . . . [C]laims for *individualized* relief (like the backpay at issue here) do not satisfy the Rule. The key to the (b)(2) class is "the indivisible nature of the injunctive or declaratory remedy warranted — the notion that the conduct is such that it can be enjoined or declared unlawful only as to all of the class members or as to none of them." Nagareda, *supra*, at 132. In other words, Rule 23(b)(2) applies only when a single injunction or declaratory judgment would provide relief to each member of the class. It does not authorize class certification when each individual class member would be entitled to a *different* injunction or declaratory judgment against the defendant. Similarly, it does not authorize class certification when each class member would be entitled to an individualized award of monetary damages.

That interpretation accords with the history of the Rule. . . . [T]he Rule reflects a series of decisions involving challenges to racial segregation — conduct that was remedied by a single classwide order. In none of the cases cited by the Advisory Committee as examples of (b)(2)'s antecedents did the plaintiffs combine any claim for individualized relief with their classwide injunction.

Permitting the combination of individualized and classwide relief in a (b)(2) class is also inconsistent with the structure of Rule 23(b). Classes certified under (b)(1) and (b)(2) share the most traditional justifications for class treatment — that individual adjudications would be impossible or unworkable, as in a (b)(1) class, or that the relief sought must perforce affect the entire class at once, as in a (b)(2) class. For that reason these are also mandatory classes: The Rule provides no opportunity for (b)(1) or (b)(2) class members to opt out, and does not even oblige the District Court to afford them notice of the action. Rule 23(b)(3), by contrast, is an "adventuresome innovation" of the 1966 amendments, framed for situations "in which class-action treatment is not as clearly called for." It allows class certification in a much wider set of circumstances but with greater procedural protections. . . . And unlike (b)(1) and (b)(2) classes, the (b)(3) class is not mandatory; class members are entitled to receive "the best notice that is practicable under the circumstances" and to withdraw from the class at their option. *See* Rule 23(c)(2)(B).

Given that structure, we think it clear that individualized monetary claims belong in Rule 23(b)(3). The procedural protections attending the (b)(3) class — predominance, superiority, mandatory notice, and the right to opt out — are missing from (b)(2) not because the Rule considers them unnecessary, but because it considers them unnecessary *to a (b)(2) class*. When a class seeks an indivisible injunction benefiting all its members at once, there is no reason to undertake a case-specific inquiry into whether class issues predominate or whether class action is a superior method of adjudicating the dispute. Predominance and superiority are self-evident. But with respect to each class member's individualized claim for money, that is not so — which is precisely why (b)(3) requires the judge to make findings about predominance and superiority before allowing the class. Similarly, (b)(2) does not require that class members be given notice and opt-out rights, presumably because it is thought (rightly or wrongly) that notice has no purpose when the class is mandatory, and that depriving people of their right to sue in this manner complies with the Due Process Clause. In the context of a class action predominantly for money damages we have held that absence of notice and opt-out violates due process. *See* Phillips Petroleum Co. v. Shutts, 472 U. S. 797, 812 (1985) [*infra* p. 658]. While we have never held that to be so where the monetary claims do not predominate, the serious possibility that it may be so provides an additional reason not to read Rule 23(b)(2) to include the monetary claims here.

B

Against that conclusion, respondents argue that their claims for backpay were appropriately certified as part of a class under Rule 23(b)(2) because those claims do not "predominate" over their requests for injunctive and declaratory relief. They rely upon the Advisory Committee's statement that Rule 23(b)(2) "does not extend to cases in which the appropriate final relief relates *exclusively or predominantly* to money damages." 39 F.R.D. at 102 (emphasis added). The negative implication, they argue, is that it does extend to cases in which the appropriate final relief relates only partially and nonpredominantly to money damages. Of course it is the Rule itself, not the Advisory Committee's description of it, that governs. And a mere negative inference does not in our view suffice to establish a disposition that has no basis in the Rule's text, and that does obvious violence to the Rule's structural features. . . .

Respondents' predominance test, moreover, creates perverse incentives for class representatives to place at risk potentially valid claims for monetary relief. In this case, for example, the named plaintiffs declined to include employees' claims for compensatory damages in their complaint. That strategy of including only backpay claims made it more likely that monetary relief would not "predominate." But it also created the possibility (if the predominance test were correct) that individual class members' compensatory-damages claims would be *precluded* by litigation they had no power to hold themselves apart from. . . . That possibility underscores the need for plaintiffs with individual monetary claims to decide *for themselves* whether to tie their fates to the class representatives' or go it alone — a choice Rule 23(b)(2) does not ensure that they have. . . .

C

. . .

We have established a procedure for trying pattern-or-practice cases that gives effect to [Title VII's] statutory requirements. When the plaintiff seeks individual relief such as reinstatement or backpay after establishing a pattern or practice of discrimination, "a district court must usually conduct additional proceedings . . . to determine the scope of individual relief." At this phase, the burden of proof will shift to the company, but it will have the right to raise any individual affirmative defenses it may have, and to "demonstrate that the individual applicant was denied an employment opportunity for lawful reasons."

The Court of Appeals believed that it was possible to replace such proceedings with Trial by Formula. A sample set of the class members would be selected, as to whom liability for sex discrimination and the backpay owing as a result would be determined in depositions supervised by a master. The percentage of claims determined to be valid would then be applied to the entire remaining class, and the number of (presumptively) valid claims thus derived would be multiplied by the average backpay award in the sample set to arrive at the entire class recovery — without further individualized proceedings. We disapprove that novel project. Because the Rules Enabling Act forbids interpreting Rule 23 to "abridge, enlarge or modify any substantive right," 28 U.S.C. § 2072(b), a class cannot be certified on the premise that Wal–Mart will not be entitled to litigate its statutory defenses to individual claims. And because the necessity of that litigation will prevent backpay from being "incidental" to the classwide injunction, respondents' class could not be certified even assuming, arguendo, that "incidental" monetary relief can be awarded to a 23(b)(2) class.

* * *

The judgment of the Court of Appeals is reversed.

■ JUSTICE GINSBURG, with whom JUSTICE BREYER, JUSTICE SOTOMAYOR, and JUSTICE KAGAN join, concurring in part and dissenting in part.

The class in this case, I agree with the Court, should not have been certified under Federal Rule of Civil Procedure 23(b)(2). . . . A putative class of this type may be certifiable under Rule 23(b)(3), if the plaintiffs show that common class questions "predominate" over issues affecting individuals — e.g., qualification for, and the amount of, backpay or compensatory damages — and that a class action is "superior" to other modes of adjudication.

Whether the class the plaintiffs describe meets the specific requirements of Rule 23(b)(3) is not before the Court, and I would reserve that matter for consideration and decision on remand. The Court, however, disqualifies the class at the starting gate, holding that the plaintiffs cannot cross the "commonality" line set by Rule 23(a)(2). In so ruling, the Court imports into the Rule 23(a) determination concerns properly addressed in a Rule 23(b)(3) assessment. . . .

. . . [B]y asking whether the individual differences "impede" common adjudication, the Court duplicates 23(b)(3)'s question whether "a class action is superior" to other modes of adjudication. . . . If courts must conduct a "dissimilarities" analysis at the Rule 23(a)(2) stage, no mission remains for Rule 23(b)(3). . . .

. . . I therefore cannot join Part II of the Court's opinion.

Notes

1. Over the past ten years, the Supreme Court has been exceptionally active in rendering decisions that have shaped the boundaries of Rule 23. In addition to *Wal–Mart*, see, *e.g.*, Tyson Foods, Inc. v. Bouaphakeo, 577 U.S. —, 136 S. Ct. 1036 (2016) (holding that, because plaintiffs could have used statistical evidence derived from a representative sample to prove liability in individual unpaid-overtime suits, the same statistical evidence could be used to meet the "predominance" element in Rule 23(b)(3)); Campbell–Ewald Co. v. Gomez, 577 U.S. —, 136 S. Ct. 663 (2016) (holding that an unaccepted Rule 68 offer of judgment that fully satisfied the class representative's individual claim did not moot a Rule 23(b)(3) class action); Amgen Inc. v. Conn. Ret. Plans & Trust Funds, 568 U.S. 455 (2013) (holding that proof of "materiality" is not needed to ensure that questions of law predominate in a Rule 23(b)(3) securities-fraud class action); Comcast Corp. v. Behrend, 569 U.S. 27 (2013) (holding that an antitrust class action was improperly certified under Rule 23(b)(3) when the plaintiffs' expert failed to establish that damages could be measured on a classwide basis); Erica P. John Fund, Inc. v. Halliburton Co., 563 U.S. 804 (2011) (holding that individual class members in a Rule 23(b)(3) securities-fraud class action did not need to prove loss causation obtain certification). A number of cases have also considered the circumstances under which pre-dispute consumer-arbitration clauses may ban consumers' use of class actions in litigation or arbitration, nearly all of which have been favorable to these bans. *See supra* pp. 219-30. As this list of cases shows, the issues are often intricate and complex.

2. Many, although by no means all, of the Supreme Court's cases have limited the use of class actions. For an argument that these restrictions have undermined the compensation, deterrence, and efficiency functions of class actions, see Robert H. Klonoff, *The Decline of Class Actions*, 90 WASH. U. L. REV. 729 (2013).

3. *Wal–Mart* was arguably the most significant of the recent Supreme Court decisions. One reason was the sheer size of the case: if successful as a class action, the case might have changed the employment practices of, and visited enormous liability on, the largest private employer in America. *Wal–Mart* was also significant for its resolution or discussion of a number of important class-action issues that had been percolating in the lower federal courts. The Court seemed to tighten the Rule 23(a)(2) commonality element, which many courts had not treated as stringently as *Wal–Mart* did. Second, *Wal–Mart* squelched efforts in some lower courts — ongoing since the 1970s — to allow plaintiffs to seek "incidental" monetary damages in (b)(2) class actions. (In a part of the opinion that we edited out because it required familiarity with lower-court decisions, the Court left the door open to very limited monetary relief.) Third, the Court cleared up a debate among the lower courts, holding that courts should rigorously analyze class-certification issues that overlap with the merits of the case. Fourth, at the end of Part III-A, the Court intimated how it would resolve a due-process argument that has loomed over mandatory class actions seeking monetary relief for thirty years (and that we examine *infra* pp. 658-65). Finally, the

Court spoke unfavorably about "trial by formula," a method that had gained acceptance in some lower courts to address the manageability problems of proving causation or calculating damages for individual class members. We examine this issue in more depth *infra* pp. 687-88.

In short, across a range of issues affecting Rule 23, *Wal–Mart* appeared to take the less class-action-friendly position. For an argument that *Wal–Mart*'s legal analysis did not contract the availability of class actions, but that some of the Court's language might be read to do so, see Suzanna Sherry, *Hogs Get Slaughtered at the Supreme Court*, 2011 SUP. CT. REV. 1.

4. After the Court's decision the *Wal–Mart* plaintiffs sought to certify a smaller class action alleging discrimination in Wal–Mart's California region, but the district court ultimately denied certification because the smaller class suffered from the same problems as the larger one. *See* Dukes v. Wal–Mart Stores, Inc., 964 F. Supp. 2d 1115 (N.D. Cal. 2013).

5. The court's decision on class certification is often the single most significant event in the case. A ruling for the plaintiff often means that the defendant will start considering a large-figure settlement; a loss means that it may not be economically viable for the plaintiffs to continue the case.

Because the court's decision on class certification is not a final judgment, however, the losing party cannot file an immediate appeal under 28 U.S.C. § 1291. Nor is an appeal years down the line a realistic option; the case might settle (if the class is certified) or be dropped (if it is not). To address this difficulty, Rule 23(f) was added in 1998. It provides a discretionary appeal from a certification decision. *See* Blair v. Equifax Check Service, Inc., 181 F.3d 832, 834-35 (7th Cir. 1999) (permitting appeal when denial of class certification sounds the death knell of the case, when certification puts untoward pressure on a defendant to settle a case of little merit, or when an appeal will facilitate development of the law). *Cf.* Microsoft Corp. v. Baker, 582 U.S. —, 137 S. Ct. 1702 (2017) (holding that plaintiffs who were denied Rule 23(f) permission to appeal the denial of class certification could not create an appealable "final decision" by voluntarily dismissing their case).

6. On appeal, the district court's class-certification decision is reviewed for abuse of discretion. Factual findings are reviewed for clear error, and conclusions of law are reviewed de novo. *See* Martin v. Behr Dayton Thermal Prods. LLC, 896 F.3d 405, 411 (6th Cir. 2018). One court holds that review is more deferential when a class is certified than when it is not. *See* Torres v. Mercer Canyons, Inc., 835 F.3d 1125, 1132 (9th Cir. 2016).

C. PROCEDURAL DOCTRINES RECONSIDERED

Class actions place pressure on established procedural doctrines. In this section, we return to a few of the procedural doctrines we have already examined — personal jurisdiction, subject-matter jurisdiction, preclusion, *Erie*, and trial — and view them through the prism of class actions. In some cases, we can see class actions transforming traditional doctrine, in others traditional doctrine transforming class actions. In each of these areas, the final word on the transformation process has yet to be written.

1. Personal Jurisdiction

Our study of personal jurisdiction in Chapter Nine focused exclusively on the *defendant's* contacts with the forum state. The plaintiff's contacts were irrelevant; because the plaintiff chose to bring a case in that forum, the plaintiff is viewed as consenting to that state's authority to enter a binding judgment. With class actions, plaintiffs are swept into cases without their consent. Consent can arguably be implied in (b)(3) class actions; the failure to opt out can be so construed, although that consent is fictional in many cases. In (b)(1) and (b)(2) mandatory class actions, even this fictional consent does not exist. Must a class member have minimum contacts with the forum state before he or she can be bound by the class action's outcome?

PHILLIPS PETROLEUM CO. V. SHUTTS

472 U.S. 797 (1985)

■ JUSTICE REHNQUIST delivered the opinion of the Court.*

Petitioner is a Delaware corporation which has its principal place of business in Oklahoma. During the 1970s it produced or purchased natural gas from leased land located in 11 different States, and sold most of the gas in interstate commerce. . . .

Respondents Irl Shutts, Robert Anderson, and Betty Anderson filed suit against petitioner in Kansas state court, seeking interest payments on their suspended royalties . . . . Shutts is a resident of Kansas, and the Andersons live in Oklahoma. Shutts and the Andersons own gas leases in Oklahoma and Texas. Over petitioner's objection the Kansas trial court granted respondents' motion to certify the suit as a class action under Kansas law. The class as certified [consisted] of 33,000 royalty owners who had royalties suspended by petitioner. The average claim of each royalty owner for interest on the suspended royalties was $100.

After the class was certified respondents provided each class member with notice through first-class mail. The notice described the action and informed each class member that he could appear in person or by counsel; otherwise each member would be represented by Shutts and the Andersons, the named plaintiffs. The notices also stated that class members would be included in the class and bound by the judgment unless they "opted out" of the lawsuit by executing and returning a "request for exclusion" that was included with the notice. The final class as certified contained 28,100

---

* For the portions excerpted here, all eight Justices who participated in the decision joined the opinion of the Court. — ED.

members; 3,400 had "opted out" of the class by returning the request for exclusion, and notice could not be delivered to another 1,500 members, who were also excluded. Less than 1,000 of the class members resided in Kansas. Only a minuscule amount, approximately one quarter of one percent, of the gas leases involved in the lawsuit were on Kansas land.

. . . [T]he case was tried to the court. The court found petitioner liable under Kansas law for interest on the suspended royalties to all class members. . . .

Petitioner . . . in its appeal to the Supreme Court of Kansas . . . asserted that the Kansas trial court did not possess personal jurisdiction over absent plaintiff class members as required by *International Shoe Co. v. Washington*, 326 U.S. 310 (1945) [*supra* p. 412], and similar cases. Related to this . . . claim was petitioner's contention that the "opt-out" notice to absent class members, which forced them to return the request for exclusion in order to avoid the suit, was insufficient to bind class members who were not residents of Kansas or who did not possess "minimum contacts" with Kansas. . . .

II

Reduced to its essentials, petitioner's argument is that unless out-of-state plaintiffs affirmatively consent, the Kansas courts may not exert jurisdiction over their claims. Petitioner claims that failure to execute and return the "request for exclusion" provided with the class notice cannot constitute consent of the out-of-state plaintiffs; thus Kansas courts may exercise jurisdiction over these plaintiffs only if the plaintiffs possess the sufficient "minimum contacts" with Kansas as that term is used in cases involving personal jurisdiction over out-of-state defendants. *E.g., International Shoe*, 326 U.S. 310; Shaffer v. Heitner, 433 U.S. 186 (1977); World-Wide Volkswagen Corp. v. Woodson, 444 U.S. 286 (1980) [*supra* p. 424]. Since Kansas had no prelitigation contact with many of the plaintiffs and leases involved, petitioner claims that Kansas has exceeded its jurisdictional reach and thereby violated the due process rights of the absent plaintiffs.

In *International Shoe* we . . . held that the extent of the defendant's due process protection would depend "upon the quality and nature of the activity in relation to the fair and orderly administration of the laws . . . ." We noted that the Due Process Clause did not permit a State to make a binding judgment against a person with whom the State had no contacts, ties, or relations. If the defendant possessed certain minimum contacts with the State, so that it was "reasonable and just, according to our traditional conception of fair play and substantial justice" for a State to exercise personal jurisdiction, the State could force the defendant to defend himself in the forum, upon pain of default, and could bind him to a judgment.

The purpose of this test, of course, is to protect a defendant from the travail of defending in a distant forum, unless the defendant's contacts with the forum make it just to force him to defend there. As we explained in

Woodson, 444 U.S. at 297, the defendant's contacts should be such that "he should reasonably anticipate being haled" into the forum. . . .

Although the cases like *Shaffer* and *Woodson* which petitioner relies on for a minimum contacts requirement all dealt with out-of-state defendants or parties in the procedural posture of a defendant, petitioner claims that the same analysis must apply to absent class-action plaintiffs. In this regard petitioner correctly points out that a chose in action is a constitutionally recognized property interest possessed by each of the plaintiffs. Mullane v. Cent. Hanover Bank & Trust Co., 339 U.S. 306 (1950) [*supra* p. 486]. An adverse judgment by Kansas courts in this case may extinguish the chose in action forever through res judicata. Such an adverse judgment, petitioner claims, would be every bit as onerous to an absent plaintiff as an adverse judgment on the merits would be to a defendant. Thus, the same due process protections should apply to absent plaintiffs: Kansas should not be able to exert jurisdiction over the plaintiffs' claims unless the plaintiffs have sufficient minimum contacts with Kansas.

We think petitioner's premise is in error. The burdens placed by a State upon an absent class-action plaintiff are not of the same order or magnitude as those it places upon an absent defendant. An out-of-state defendant summoned by a plaintiff is faced with the full powers of the forum State to render judgment *against* it. The defendant must generally hire counsel and travel to the forum to defend itself from the plaintiff's claim, or suffer a default judgment. The defendant may be forced to participate in extended and often costly discovery, and will be forced to respond in damages or to comply with some other form of remedy imposed by the court should it lose the suit. The defendant may also face liability for court costs and attorney's fees. These burdens are substantial, and the minimum contacts requirement of the Due Process Clause prevents the forum State from unfairly imposing them upon the defendant. . . .

In sharp contrast to the predicament of a defendant haled into an out-of-state forum, the plaintiffs in this suit were not haled anywhere to defend themselves upon pain of a default judgment. . . .

A plaintiff class in Kansas and numerous other jurisdictions cannot first be certified unless the judge, with the aid of the named plaintiffs and defendant, conducts an inquiry into the common nature of the named plaintiffs' and the absent plaintiffs' claims, the adequacy of representation, the jurisdiction possessed over the class, and any other matters that will bear upon proper representation of the absent plaintiffs' interest. Unlike a defendant in a civil suit, a class-action plaintiff is not required to fend for himself. The court and named plaintiffs protect his interests. . . .

The concern of the typical class-action rules for the absent plaintiffs is manifested in other ways. Most jurisdictions, including Kansas, require that a class action, once certified, may not be dismissed or compromised without the approval of the court. In many jurisdictions such as Kansas the court may amend the pleadings to ensure that all sections of the class are represented adequately.

Besides this continuing solicitude for their rights, absent plaintiff class members are not subject to other burdens imposed upon defendants. They need not hire counsel or appear. They are almost never subject to counterclaims or cross-claims, or liability for fees or costs. Absent plaintiff class members are not subject to coercive or punitive remedies. Nor will an adverse judgment typically bind an absent plaintiff for any damages, although a valid adverse judgment may extinguish any of the plaintiff's claims which were litigated.

Unlike a defendant in a normal civil suit, an absent class-action plaintiff is not required to do anything. He may sit back and allow the litigation to run its course, content in knowing that there are safeguards provided for his protection. In most class actions an absent plaintiff is provided at least with an opportunity to "opt out" of the class, and if he takes advantage of that opportunity he is removed from the litigation entirely. This was true of the Kansas proceedings in this case. . . .

Petitioner contends, however, that the "opt out" procedure provided by Kansas is not good enough, and that an "opt in" procedure is required to satisfy the Due Process Clause of the Fourteenth Amendment. Insofar as plaintiffs who have no minimum contacts with the forum State are concerned, an "opt in" provision would require that each class member affirmatively consent to his inclusion within the class.

Because States place fewer burdens upon absent class plaintiffs than they do upon absent defendants in nonclass suits, the Due Process Clause need not and does not afford the former as much protection from state-court jurisdiction as it does the latter. The Fourteenth Amendment does protect "persons," not "defendants," however, so absent plaintiffs as well as absent defendants are entitled to some protection from the jurisdiction of a forum State which seeks to adjudicate their claims. In this case we hold that a forum State may exercise jurisdiction over the claim of an absent class-action plaintiff, even though that plaintiff may not possess the minimum contacts with the forum which would support personal jurisdiction over a defendant. If the forum State wishes to bind an absent plaintiff concerning a claim for money damages or similar relief at law,[3] it must provide minimal procedural due process protection. The plaintiff must receive notice plus an opportunity to be heard and participate in the litigation, whether in person or through counsel. The notice must be the best practicable, "reasonably calculated, under all the circumstances, to apprise interested parties of the pendency of the action and afford them an opportunity to present their objections." *Mullane*, 339 U.S. at 314-15. The notice should describe the action and the plaintiffs' rights in it. Additionally, we hold that due process requires at a minimum that an absent plaintiff be provided with an opportunity to remove himself from the class by executing and returning an

---

3. Our holding today is limited to those class actions which seek to bind known plaintiffs concerning claims wholly or predominately for money judgments. We intimate no view concerning other types of class actions, such as those seeking equitable relief. Nor, of course, does our discussion of personal jurisdiction address class actions where the jurisdiction is asserted against a *defendant* class.

"opt out" or "request for exclusion" form to the court. Finally, the Due Process Clause of course requires that the named plaintiff at all times adequately represent the interests of the absent class members.

We reject petitioner's contention that the Due Process Clause of the Fourteenth Amendment requires that absent plaintiffs affirmatively "opt in" to the class, rather than be deemed members of the class if they do not "opt out." We think that such a contention is supported by little, if any precedent, and that it ignores the differences between class-action plaintiffs, on the one hand, and defendants in nonclass civil suits on the other. Any plaintiff may consent to jurisdiction. The essential question, then, is how stringent the requirement for a showing of consent will be.

We think that the procedure followed by Kansas, where a fully descriptive notice is sent first-class mail to each class member, with an explanation of the right to "opt out," satisfies due process. Requiring a plaintiff to affirmatively request inclusion would probably impede the prosecution of those class actions involving an aggregation of small individual claims, where a large number of claims are required to make it economical to bring suit. . . . If, on the other hand, the plaintiff's claim is sufficiently large or important that he wishes to litigate it on his own, he will likely have retained an attorney or have thought about filing suit, and should be fully capable of exercising his right to "opt out."

In this case over 3,400 members of the potential class did "opt out," which belies the contention that "opt out" procedures result in guaranteed jurisdiction by inertia. Another 1,500 were excluded because the notice and "opt out" form was undeliverable. We think that such results show that the "opt out" procedure provided by Kansas is by no means *pro forma*, and that the Constitution does not require more to protect what must be the somewhat rare species of class member who is unwilling to execute an "opt out" form, but whose claim is nonetheless so important that he cannot be presumed to consent to being a member of the class by his failure to do so. Petitioner's "opt in" requirement would require the invalidation of scores of state statutes and of the class-action provision of the Federal Rules of Civil Procedure, and for the reasons stated we do not think that the Constitution requires the State to sacrifice the obvious advantages in judicial efficiency resulting from the "opt out" approach for the protection of the *rara avis* portrayed by petitioner.

We therefore hold that the protection afforded the plaintiff class members by the Kansas statute satisfies the Due Process Clause. The interests of the absent plaintiffs are sufficiently protected by the forum State when those plaintiffs are provided with a request for exclusion that can be returned within a reasonable time to the court. Both the Kansas trial court and the Supreme Court of Kansas held that the class received adequate representation, and no party disputes that conclusion here. . . .

We therefore affirm the judgment of the Supreme Court of Kansas insofar as it upheld the jurisdiction of the Kansas courts over the plaintiff class members in this case . . . .

■ JUSTICE POWELL took no part in the decision of this case.

■ [The opinion of JUSTICE STEVENS, concurring in part and dissenting in part, is omitted.]

Notes and Questions

1. *Shutts* describes the due-process concern about personal jurisdiction as a question of the imposition of an undue burden on a party, not as a question of a court's power to issue a binding judgment. If this is so, then why is the minimum-contacts test still appropriate for *defendants*? In other words, why not permit a court to assert jurisdiction over defendants as long as their participation in the case is not unduly burdensome or inconvenient? (Recall Justice Brennan's arguments along these lines.) For all its citation and discussion of *International Shoe* and its progeny, is *Shutts* inconsistent with the personal-jurisdiction cases that you read in Chapter Nine?

2. The $64,000 question after *Shutts* is whether the Due Process Clause forbids *mandatory*, multistate, state-law class actions in which some class members lack contact with the state in which the action is being litigated. If so, then plaintiffs who wished to bring such class actions would have to proceed state by state, or class members with insufficient contacts would need to be given notice of their right to opt out. In neither case might the action run as efficiently as one mandatory, multistate class action.

Shutts never decides the effect of its holding on mandatory class actions, because the case involved a Kansas opt-out class action. Indeed, footnote 3 refuses to answer whether the Due Process Clause forbids mandatory class actions in cases seeking injunctive or monetary relief. Since *Shutts*, courts and commentators have disagreed about its exact scope. Because most mandatory (b)(1) and (b)(2) classes seek injunctive relief, some have argued that *Shutts* has little effect on mandatory class actions. Other have argued that the Due Process Clause should be understood in historical terms; a class action that would have been acceptable in equity practice (including an action that sought monetary relief by divvying up a "limited fund," in which a pool of assets is insufficient to satisfy all of the claims of class members against those assets) should not invoke *Shutts*'s opt-out right. Still others have suggested that *Shutts* is a limitation only on state-court class actions; for a class action filed in federal court, the relevant issue is whether class members have contact with the United States as a whole. A few regard mandatory, multistate state-law class actions as unconstitutional.

Courts tend to read *Shutts* as a limitation only on damages class actions, and not even then in the case of a limited fund. *See* Robert H. Klonoff, *Class Actions for Monetary Relief Under Rule 23(b)(1)(A) and (b)(1)(B): Does Due Process Require Notice and Opt-Out Rights?*, 82 GEO. WASH. L. REV. 798 (2014) (answering yes for notice but no for an opt-out right).

3. The Supreme Court has twice granted certiorari in cases to decide the question of *Shutts*'s application to mandatory class actions, but it dismissed the cases without reaching the issue. Adams v. Robertson, 520

U.S. 83 (1997); Ticor Title Ins. Co. v. Brown, 511 U.S. 117 (1994). The question was squarely presented again in *Ortiz v. Fibreboard Corp.*, 527 U.S. 815 (1999), but the Court decided the case on grounds that mooted consideration of the *Shutts* issue. In dicta, however, the Court observed:

> The inherent tension between representative suits and the day-in-court ideal is only magnified if applied to damage claims gathered in a mandatory class. Unlike Rule 23(b)(3) class members, objectors to the collectivism of a mandatory subdivision (b)(1)(B) action have no inherent right to abstain. The legal rights of absent class members . . . are resolved regardless either of their consent, or, in a class with objectors, their express wish to the contrary. . . . [527 U.S. at 846-47.]

In a footnote, the Court added: "In *Shutts*, as an important caveat to our holding, we made clear that we were only examining the procedural protections attendant on binding out-of-state class members whose claims were 'wholly or predominately for money damages.'" *Id.* at 848 n.24.

The Court again ducked the *Shutts* issue in *Smith v. Bayer Corp.*, 564 U.S. 299, 308 n.7 (2011). But a week later, in *Wal–Mart Stores, Inc. v. Dukes*, 564 U.S. 338 (2011) (*supra* pp. 653-54), the Court addressed the scope of *Shutts* directly. *Wal–Mart* held that the plaintiffs could not use a mandatory (b)(2) class action to obtain monetary relief. *Wal–Mart* reiterated *Shutts*'s holding that mandatory class actions "predominantly for money damages" ran afoul of the Due Process Clause. It implied — albeit in language that left the issue open — that mandatory class actions seeking injunctive relief did not violate the Due Process Clause. For class actions seeking both injunctive and nonpredominant monetary relief, it held that plaintiffs could not use Rule 23(b)(2) to assert their monetary claims — in part because such a use raised serious constitutional questions.

4. Assuming that an opt-out right must in some circumstances be afforded to some absent members in mandatory class actions, exactly which class members get the right? All class members? Or just those who lack sufficient contacts with the forum state? If the latter (which seems likely), what test do we use to sort those with sufficient contacts from those without? Do we use a simple presence test — domicile or property within the state that is related to the dispute? Or do we develop a minimum-contacts approach? Applying an individualized minimum-contacts test to determine who gets *Shutts*'s opt-out right could be very time-consuming and expensive.

5. In unique circumstances, some courts permit class members to opt out in mandatory class actions. *Compare* County of Suffolk v. Long Island Lighting Co., 907 F.2d 1295 (2d Cir. 1990) (permitting plaintiff to opt out of limited-fund class action), *with* Thomas v. Albright, 139 F.3d 227 (D.C. Cir. 1998) (district court abused its discretion in permitting plaintiffs to opt out).

6. As we saw in Chapter Nine, the Due Process Clause requires not only minimum contacts but also adequate notice. Mullane v. Cent. Hanover Bank & Trust Co., 339 U.S. 306 (1950) (*supra* p. 486). Rule 23(c)(2)(B) requires notice to class members of their right to opt out of a (b)(3) class

action. The cost of preparing and sending notice is often substantial. Avoidance of this cost, which is borne by the class (and as a practical matter by class counsel), had been one reason underlying efforts to expand the scope of mandatory class actions.

7. The Eleventh Circuit held that *Shutts* does not require a court to provide an opt-out right in a Rule 23(b)(1)(B) limited-fund class action, even when class members receive monetary distributions. *See* Juris v. Inamed Corp., 685 F.3d 1294, 1329-33 (11th Cir. 2012). *Juris* arose when a class member was trying to bring suit in California state court to recover for her injuries, even though those injuries had been previously settled in the (b)(1)(B) class action. The court of appeals held that she was bound by the settlement, despite her lack of an opt-out right, and that the federal court in which the class settlement had occurred had the power to enjoin her from proceeding with her state-court lawsuit.

2. Subject-Matter Jurisdiction

The jurisdictional rules that we studied in Chapter Ten ("well-pleaded complaint" and "arising under" for federal questions, and "complete diversity" and "amount in controversy" for diversity) are clear in the main. Supplemental jurisdiction complicates matters a bit, especially because of the textual ambiguities in 28 U.S.C. § 1367(b). How do these rules apply to class actions?

For cases arising under federal-question jurisdiction, the rules are the same regardless of whether the case involves a single plaintiff or a class. A claim arising under federal law must appear on the face of the well-pleaded class complaint.

For diversity cases, however, the situation is different. In a class action, must each member of the class be of different citizenship from the opposing parties? Must each member of the class have more than $75,000 at stake? The answers to these questions have varied over the years.

To begin, in *Supreme Tribe of Ben–Hur v. Cauble*, 255 U.S. 356 (1921), the Supreme Court held that diversity of citizenship was determined by comparing the citizenship of the class representatives to the citizenship of the parties opposing the class. The citizenship of the absent class members was ignored; even if some class members had the same citizenship as some of the opposing parties, jurisdiction under § 1332 existed. This holding constituted a modest breach of the usual rule of complete diversity.

In *Snyder v. Harris*, 394 U.S. 332 (1969), the Court addressed 1332(a)'s amount-in-controversy requirement. In *Snyder*, none of the 4,000 class members could individually claim the requisite amount in controversy, but added together their claims exceeded $1.2 million. Following the usual rule that plaintiffs could not aggregate jurisdictionally insufficient individual claims, *Snyder* held that subject-matter jurisdiction was lacking. Four years later, in *Zahn v. International Paper Co.*, 414 U.S. 291 (1973), the Court addressed the situation in which *some*, but not all, class members had claims that met the amount-in-controversy requirement. *Zahn* held that the individual claim of *each* class member needed to be jurisdictionally sufficient; the claims of class members with insufficient claims could not be tacked onto the claims of class members with sufficient claims.

The upshot of *Ben–Hur* and *Zahn* was that incomplete diversity of class members was ignored for diversity jurisdiction, but the inadequacy of the amount of a class member's claims was not. These rules might not have been entirely consistent, but there they were.

The passage of § 1367 in 1990 unsettled these rules. In Chapter Ten we examined an important ambiguity in § 1367(b): whether failing to mention *plaintiffs* joined under Rule 20(a) grants supplemental jurisdiction over the state-law claims of Rule 20 plaintiffs who destroy complete diversity or have jurisdictionally insufficient claims. As we saw, in *Exxon Mobil Corp. v. Allapattah Services, Inc.*, 545 U.S. 546 (2005) (*supra* p. 557), the Supreme Court held that § 1367(b)'s failure to mention Rule 20 plaintiffs did not override § 1332(a)'s requirement that each plaintiff joined under Rule 20 have a citizenship diverse from that of the defendant(s), but did override the rule that a plaintiff with a monetarily insufficient claim could not join with a plaintiff who had a sufficient claim.

Just as it was silent about Rule 20 plaintiffs, § 1367(b) failed to mention Rule 23. Did this omission mean that federal jurisdiction over diversity class actions exists as long as any class representative (*or* even a single class member) is diverse from any party opposing the class? Did the omission also mean that Congress had overruled *Zahn*, allowing jurisdiction over diversity-based class actions when one diverse class member has more than $75,000 at stake, and the claims of other members form part of the same case or controversy under § 1367(a)? (Note that § 1367 does not affect the rule in *Snyder*. Section 1367(a) permits supplemental jurisdiction only when at least one claim lies within original federal jurisdiction.)

Allapattah, which involved a Rule 23 class action as well as Rule 20 joinder, held that federal courts had jurisdiction over the claims of class members who failed to meet the amount-in-controversy requirement. As the Court said, "We hold that § 1367 by its plain text overruled . . . *Zahn* and authorized supplemental jurisdiction over all claims by diverse parties arising out of the same Article III case or controversy." 545 U.S. at 566.

For most practical purposes, *Allapattah* was already a dead letter when it was decided. Earlier in 2005, responding to the perception that state-court class actions were leading to unfairly generous awards injuring American business interests, Congress gave federal courts considerably more original and removal jurisdiction over class actions. *See* Class Action Fairness Act of 2005, Pub. L. No. 109-2, 119 Stat. 4 (2005) ("CAFA"). CAFA created a new § 1332(d), which is one of the most complex jurisdictional grants ever enacted. CAFA also created a new § 1453, which relaxed some limitations on the removal of class actions filed in state court. Read §§ 1332(d) and 1453. CAFA is based on the idea of minimal, rather than complete, diversity. If *any* class member has different citizenship from *any* defendant, the diversity requirement is met. 28 U.S.C. § 1332(d)(2)(A)-(C). Likewise, CAFA altered the amount-in-controversy requirement from a per-plaintiff amount to an aggregate class amount of more than $5 million. *Id.* § 1332(d)(2).

The following cases illustrate some of CAFA's jurisdictional nuances.

STANDARD FIRE INSURANCE CO. V. KNOWLES

568 U.S. 588 (2013)

■ JUSTICE BREYER delivered the opinion for a unanimous Court.

The Class Action Fairness Act of 2005 (CAFA) provides that the federal "district courts shall have original jurisdiction" over a civil "class action" if, among other things, the "matter in controversy exceeds the sum or value of $5,000,000." 28 U.S.C. §§ 1332(d)(2), (5). The statute adds that "to determine whether the matter in controversy exceeds the sum or value of $5,000,000," the "claims of the individual class members shall be aggregated." *Id.* § 1332(d)(6).

The question presented concerns a class-action plaintiff who stipulates, prior to certification of the class, that he, and the class he seeks to represent, will not seek damages that exceed $5 million in total. Does that stipulation remove the case from CAFA's scope? In our view, it does not.

I

In April 2011 respondent, Greg Knowles, filed this proposed class action in an Arkansas state court against petitioner, the Standard Fire Insurance Company. Knowles claimed that, when the company had made certain homeowner's insurance loss payments, it had unlawfully failed to include a general contractor fee. And Knowles sought to certify a class of "hundreds, and possibly thousands" of similarly harmed Arkansas policyholders. In describing the relief sought, the complaint says that the "Plaintiff and Class stipulate they will seek to recover total aggregate damages of less than five million dollars." An attached affidavit stipulates that Knowles "will not at any time during this case . . . seek damages for the class . . . in excess of $5,000,000 in the aggregate."

On May 18, 2011, the company, pointing to CAFA's jurisdictional provision, removed the case to Federal District Court. See 28 U.S.C. § 1332(d); *id.* § 1453. Knowles argued for remand on the ground that the District Court lacked jurisdiction. . . . On the basis of evidence presented by the company, the District Court found that the "sum or value" of the "amount in controversy" would, in the absence of the stipulation, have fallen just above the $5 million threshold. Nonetheless, in light of Knowles' stipulation, the court concluded that the amount fell beneath the threshold. The court consequently ordered the case remanded to the state court.

The company appealed from the remand order, but the Eighth Circuit declined to hear the appeal. *See* 28 U.S.C. § 1453(c)(1) (providing discretion to hear an appeal from a remand order). . . .

II

CAFA provides the federal district courts with "original jurisdiction" to hear a "class action" if the class has more than 100 members, the parties are minimally diverse, and the "matter in controversy exceeds the sum or value of $5,000,000." 28 U.S.C. §§ 1332(d)(2), (5)(B). To "determine whether the matter in controversy" exceeds that sum, "the claims of the individual class members shall be aggregated." *Id.* § 1332(d)(6). And those "class members" include "persons (named or unnamed) who fall within the definition of the *proposed* or certified class." *Id.* § 1332(d) (1)(D) (emphasis added).

As applied here, the statute tells the District Court to determine whether it has jurisdiction by adding up the value of the claim of each person who falls within the definition of Knowles' proposed class and determine whether the resulting sum exceeds $5 million. If so, there is jurisdiction and the court may proceed with the case. The District Court in this case found that resulting sum would have exceeded $5 million but for the stipulation. And we must decide whether the stipulation makes a critical difference.

In our view, it does not. Our reason is a simple one: Stipulations must be binding. The stipulation Knowles proffered to the District Court, however, does not speak for those he purports to represent.

That is because a plaintiff who files a proposed class action cannot legally bind members of the proposed class before the class is certified. Because his precertification stipulation does not bind anyone but himself, Knowles has not reduced the value of the putative class members' claims. For jurisdictional purposes, our inquiry is limited to examining the case "as of the time it was filed in state court." At that point, Knowles lacked the authority to concede the amount-in-controversy issue for the absent class members. . . .

If . . . "hundreds, and possibly thousands" of persons in Arkansas have similar claims, and if each of those claims places a significant sum in controversy, the state court might certify the class and permit the case to proceed, but only on the condition that the stipulation be excised. Or a court might find that Knowles is an inadequate representative due to the artificial cap he purports to impose on the class' recovery. Similarly, another class member could intervene with an amended complaint (without a stipulation), and the District Court might permit the action to proceed with a new representative. Even were these possibilities remote in Knowles' own case, there is no reason to think them farfetched in other cases where similar stipulations could have more dramatic amount-lowering effects. . . .

. . . CAFA [permits] the federal court to consider, for purposes of determining the amount in controversy, the very real possibility that a nonbinding, amount-limiting, stipulation may not survive the class certification process. This potential outcome does not result in the creation of a new case not now before the federal court. To hold otherwise would, for CAFA jurisdictional purposes, treat a nonbinding stipulation as if it were binding, exalt form over substance, and run directly counter to CAFA's primary objective: ensuring "Federal court consideration of interstate cases of national importance." § 2(b)(2), 119 Stat. 5. . . .

We agree with Knowles that a federal district court might find it simpler to value the amount in controversy on the basis of a stipulation than to aggregate the value of the individual claims of all who meet the class description. We also agree that, when judges must decide jurisdictional matters, simplicity is a virtue. *See* Hertz Corp. v. Friend, 559 U. S. 77, 94 (2010) [*supra* p. 540]. But to ignore a nonbinding stipulation does no more than require the federal judge to do what she must do in cases without a stipulation and what the statute requires, namely "aggregat[e]" the "claims of the individual class members." 28 U. S. C. § 1332(d)(6).

Knowles also points out that federal courts permit individual plaintiffs, who are the masters of their complaints, to avoid removal to federal court, and to obtain a remand to state court, by stipulating to amounts at issue that fall below the federal jurisdictional requirement. That is so. *See* St. Paul Mercury Indem. Co. v. Red Cab Co., 303 U. S. 283, 294 (1938). But the key characteristic about those stipulations is that they are legally binding on all plaintiffs. That essential feature is missing here, as Knowles cannot yet bind the absent class. . . .

. . . [W]e vacate the judgment below and remand the case for further proceedings consistent with this opinion.

PRESTON V. TENET HEALTHSYSTEM MEMORIAL MEDICAL CENTER, INC.

485 F.3d 804 (5th Cir. 2007)

Before DEMOSS, STEWART, and PRADO, Circuit Judges.

■ STEWART, Circuit Judge.

. . .

I. FACTUAL AND PROCEDURAL BACKGROUND

Preston represents a putative class of patients and the relatives of deceased and allegedly injured patients hospitalized at [Tenet Health Systems Memorial Medical Center ("Memorial")] when Hurricane Katrina made landfall in New Orleans, Louisiana. Memorial owned and operated the hospital, and [LifeCare Hospitals of New Orleans, L.L.C. (collectively "LifeCare")] leased the seventh floor of the facility for an acute care center. On October 6, 2005, Preston brought suit against Memorial in the Civil District Court for the Parish of Orleans. Preston asserted claims for negligence and intentional misconduct . . . and involuntary euthanization. Preston alleged that Memorial failed to design and maintain the premises in a manner that avoided loss of power in the building. Preston further alleged that Memorial and LifeCare failed to develop and implement an evacuation plan for the patients. According to the petition, Memorial's and LifeCare's failure to maintain the premises and timely evacuate the facility resulted in the deaths and injuries of hospitalized patients. . . .

. . . LifeCare filed a timely notice of removal. Memorial never consented to removal from the state court. . . . Preston filed a motion to remand under the local controversy exception of CAFA. [Memorial later renewed this motion.] On November 21, 2006, the district court remanded the lawsuit to state court under the local controversy exception [of 28 U.S.C. § 1332(d)(4)(A)], home state exception [of § 1332(d)(4)(B)], and the discretionary jurisdiction provision [of § 1332(d)(3)]. . . . LifeCare filed a timely petition for appeal pursuant to 28 U.S.C. § 1453. On February 5, 2007, this court granted permission to appeal. LifeCare only contests the district court's citizenship findings under CAFA's exceptions to federal jurisdiction.

II. STANDARD OF REVIEW

We review the district court's factual findings as to the citizenship of the parties for clear error. . . .

The standard of review for a district court's remand under the discretionary provision constitutes an issue of first impression. We review the district court's remand order for abuse of discretion. . . .

. . . [T]he local controversy and home state exceptions read that the "district courts shall decline to exercise jurisdiction," while the discretionary provision provides that the district court " may in the interests of justice and looking at the totality of the circumstances" decline to exercise jurisdiction. *Compare id.* § 1332[(d)](2) & –(4) *with* § 1332[(d)](3). LifeCare cogently argues that the local controversy and home state exceptions should be construed narrowly and resolved in favor of federal jurisdiction based on the "shall decline to exercise jurisdiction" language . . . , which represents the classic formulation for abstention. Under the discretionary jurisdiction provision, however, Congress permitted the district court greater latitude to remand class actions to state court. . . . [T]he district court does not wield unfettered discretion over whether to remand a case; instead Congress provided a list of factors to guide the district court's consideration.

III. DISCUSSION

A. *Statutory Background*

. . . CAFA contains a basic jurisdictional test for removal, which requires the removing defendant to prove minimal diversity and an aggregated amount in controversy of $5,000,000 or more. *Id.* § 1332(d). CAFA eliminates the standard requirements of unanimous consent among the defendants and the one-year removal deadline. *Id.* § 1453(b). The district court can decline jurisdiction under three provisions: (1) the home state exception, *id.* § 1332(d)(4)(B); (2) the local controversy exception, *id.* § 1332(d)(4)(A); and (3) discretionary jurisdiction, *id.* § 1332(d)(3).

Pursuant to the local controversy exception, the district court "shall decline to exercise jurisdiction" when the class action meets the following criteria.... [Here the court quoted the language of § 1332(d)(4)(A). One of the criteria is that "greater than two-thirds of the members of all proposed plaintiff classes in the aggregate are citizens of the State in which the action was originally filed."] The home state exception provides that the district court "shall decline to exercise jurisdiction" when "two-thirds or more of the members of all proposed plaintiff classes in the aggregate, and the primary defendants, are citizens of the State in which the action was originally filed." *Id.* § 1332(4)(B).

Under the discretionary jurisdiction provision [of § 1332(d)(3)], a "district court may, in the interests of justice and looking at the totality of the circumstances, decline to exercise jurisdiction ... over a class action in which greater than one-third but less than two-thirds of the members of all proposed plaintiff classes in the aggregate and the primary defendants are citizens of the State in which the action was originally filed ...." The district court must consider [six factors, which the Court quoted in full.]

B. *Discretionary Jurisdiction Provision*

The district court remanded this class action lawsuit to state court under all three carve-outs to federal jurisdiction: the local controversy exception, the home state exception, and the discretionary jurisdiction provision. Each CAFA exception requires the court to make an objective factual finding regarding the percentage of class members that were citizens of Louisiana at the time of filing the class petition. The local controversy and home state exceptions to federal jurisdiction are separate and distinct statutory provisions [that require, respectively, "greater than two-thirds" or "two-thirds or more" of class members to be citizens of the state in which the case was filed]." LifeCare concedes that this class action lawsuit satisfies the distinguishable remaining elements of the two exceptions.

Under CAFA's discretionary jurisdiction provision, the citizenship requirement lowers to require that "greater than one-third but less than two-thirds of the members of all proposed plaintiff classes in the aggregate ... are citizens of the State in which the action was originally filed...." *Id.* § 1332(d)(3). The movants must satisfy the citizenship requirement as a prerequisite to the district court weighing the additional statutory factors enumerated to guide the court's remand determination. The same legal principles apply to the discretionary jurisdiction provision as apply to the local controversy and home state exceptions. Despite the burden to prove a lesser percentage of class members were citizens of Louisiana, which party bears the burden of proof and the sufficiency of evidence necessary to satisfy the citizenship requirements remains consistent throughout either analysis.

Congress crafted CAFA to exclude only a narrow category of truly localized controversies, and § 1332(d)(3) provides a discretionary vehicle for district courts to ferret out the "controversy that uniquely affects a particular locality to the exclusion of all others." After careful review of the record, the discretionary jurisdiction provision proves to be a particularly well-suited framework for considering the interconnections between the underlying facts giving rise to the alleged legal claims and the extenuating circumstances affecting this preliminary jurisdictional determination. The district court determined that a distinct nexus exists between the forum of Louisiana, the Defendants, and the proposed class. We observe, more specifically, that Preston alleges that LifeCare and Memorial, citizens of Louisiana, committed acts in Louisiana causing injuries and deaths to patients hospitalized in New Orleans, Louisiana, when Hurricane Katrina made landfall. The claims asserted in the petition involve issues of negligence governed by state law. Memorial does not contest that the instant lawsuit fulfills the threshold requirements for removal under CAFA, i.e. the requisite number of proposed class members, minimal diversity, and the necessary aggregate amount in controversy. *See id.* § 1332(d)(2). Accordingly, we limit our review to whether Memorial presented sufficient evidence to show that at least one-third of the putative class members were citizens of Louisiana at the time that the suit was filed.

1. *Burden of Proof*

. . . Under CAFA, the moving party on the remand motion, not the defendant seeking federal jurisdiction, bears the burden to establish the domicile of at least one-third of the class members at the time of filing the lawsuit. . . .

2. *Evidentiary Standard for Proving Citizenship*

Memorial must prove that greater than one-third of the putative class members were citizens of Louisiana at the time of filing the class action petition. 28 U.S.C. § 1332(d)(7) . . . . Preston filed this class action lawsuit on October 6, 2005; therefore, Memorial must prove citizenship as of this date. The parties contest the quantum of proof necessary to sustain the moving party's burden. Pursuant to well-settled principles of law, we hold that the party moving for remand under the CAFA exceptions to federal jurisdiction must prove the citizenship requirement by a preponderance of the evidence. This holding means that Memorial, as the movant, must demonstrate by a preponderance of the evidence that at least one-third of the putative class members were citizens of Louisiana. . . .

[The court then analyzed the evidence submitted by the parties, including an investigation into some of the individual class members that revealed that 49 of 146 identified class members resided outside Louisiana at the time of the investigation; affidavits submitted by six named plaintiffs and two members of the class, each of which indicated the affiant's intent to return to Louisiana; and the addresses listed on the medical records for 256 class members, all but seven of whom gave a Louisiana address.]

. . . Therefore, based on the record as a whole, the district court made a reasonable assumption that at least one-third of the class were Louisiana citizens at the time of filing the lawsuit on October 6, 2005, less than two months after the storm hit New Orleans. We do not find the district court's findings of fact clearly erroneous. . . .

4. *Determination of Class Size*

LifeCare argues that Memorial fails to establish the number of people composing the proposed class. Arguably, without knowing the number of persons in the class, the court cannot determine whether one-third of the class members are citizens of Louisiana. . . .

Here, we conclude that the submitted evidence provides an adequate basis for the district court to make a credible estimate of the class members domiciled in Louisiana. CAFA requires the district court to make a threshold jurisdictional determination. Thus, the district court must balance the need for discovery while not unduly delaying the resolution of this preliminary question. . . .

. . . The record reflects that the plaintiffs defined a reasonably confined class and the district court, based on a preponderance of the evidence, made a credible estimate that at least one-third of the class were citizens of Louisiana at the time of filing suit.

5. *Statutory Factors for Determining the Interest of Justice*

[The court then examined the six factors in 28 U.S.C. § 1332(d)(3). Although it acknowledged that "the nation takes [an] interest in Hurricane Katrina," it found that the dispute involved Louisiana defendants being sued, in the main, by Louisiana residents for breaches of Louisiana law. There had also been no other similar class action filed in the prior three years on the same subject. Thus, the six factors did not favor retention of federal jurisdiction.]

IV. CONCLUSION

. . . This particular Hurricane Katrina case symbolizes a quintessential example of Congress' intent to carve out exceptions to CAFA's expansive grant of federal jurisdiction when our courts confront a truly localized controversy. Based on the medical records, affidavits, and attending factual circumstances, we determine that the district court did not clearly err in finding that one-third of the class members were citizens of Louisiana at the time of filing suit. Accordingly, we affirm the district court's judgment.

Notes

1. CAFA does not affect jurisdiction over class actions that plead a federal question. With respect to diversity cases, *Standard Fire* and *Preston* show ways in which CAFA affirms some of the standard rules of diversity jurisdiction even as it departs from others. In common with other diversity cases, jurisdiction (including citizenship and amount in controversy) is

determined as of the time that the case is filed, and citizenship in a diversity case is based on the test of presence plus intent to remain. Likewise, a notice of removal must be filed within thirty days of the date on which the case first becomes removable. In other ways, however, the departures from traditional jurisdictional principles are substantial:

- Minimal diversity replaces complete diversity. The diversity of a single class member creates federal jurisdiction, even if all other plaintiffs and all defendants are citizens of one state. 28 U.S.C. § 1332(d).

- A more-than-$5,000,000 threshold, measured from the viewpoint of the defendant, replaces a more-than-$75,000 amount in controversy, measured from the amount in controversy as to each plaintiff. *Id.*

- A class plaintiff cannot avoid federal court by seeking less than the amount in controversy, unlike an ordinary plaintiff, who can.

- Meeting citizenship and amount-in-controversy requirements does not automatically create jurisdiction. Federal courts must decline jurisdiction in two instances (the local-controversy and home-state exceptions of 28 U.S.C. § 1332(d)(4)) and may decline jurisdiction under the discretionary exception outlined in § 1332(d)(3).

- A class action can be removed from a court in one of the defendants' home states; there is no "forum defendant" rule. *Id.* § 1453(b).

- Removal is effective when any defendant, rather than all served defendants, files a notice of removal; indeed, removal is effective even "without the consent of all defendants." *Id.*

- The usual presumptive rule that a diversity case cannot be removed more than one year after it is filed in state court is abolished. *Id.*

- The decision of a federal court to remand a removed class action is immediately appealable, provided that the court of appeals accepts the appeal. *Id.* § 1453(c)(1). In ordinary litigation, a remand on jurisdictional grounds is never appealable, and denial of remand is appealable only at the end of the case.

    2. One other way in which CAFA does not change the traditional rules of jurisdiction concerns removal by parties other than original defendants. As a rule, counterclaim defendants, third-party defendants, and the like are not regarded as "defendants" under 28 U.S.C. § 1441(a); thus, they may not file a notice of removal. *See supra* pp. 570-71, Note 4. In *Home Depot U.S.A., Inc. v. Jackson*, 587 U.S. —, 139 S. Ct. 1743 (2019), a consumer who was sued in state court on a credit-card debt filed a counterclaim class action on behalf of all similar consumers, alleging deceptive trade practices in violation of state law. The counterclaim joined an additional defendant. The Supreme Court held that the added defendant could not remove the case under either § 1441(a) or § 1453(b).

    3. CAFA imposes limits on its expansion of diversity jurisdiction:

- CAFA does not apply to class actions with fewer than 100 members. *Id.* § 1332(d)(5)(B).

- It does not apply to class actions in which the court could probably not grant relief against government officials or entities in any event. *Id.* § 1332(d)(5)(A).

- It does not apply to class actions involving shareholder claims against a corporation's management or certain state-law claims alleging securities fraud. *Id.* § 1332(d)(9). Federal jurisdiction over state-law securities-fraud class actions is already covered in other provisions of the United States Code.

For the second and third exclusions, as well as for shareholder claims, federal jurisdiction presumably could be obtained under the traditional jurisdictional rules, as modified by § 1367.

4. Note the importance of the burden of proof. It may be impossible or cost-prohibitive to make individualized determinations of the exact size of the class and each class member's citizenship. The party bearing the burden of proof on these issues is at a disadvantage. To some extent the burden depends on whether the case was originally filed in, or removed to, federal court, and to some extent on whether the party is contesting jurisdiction under the minimal-diversity and amount-in-controversy requirements of § 1332(d)(2) or under the discretionary or mandatory declination-of-jurisdiction provisions of § 1332(d)(3) and –(4). *See* Bartels *ex rel.* Bartels v. Saber Healthcare Grp., LLC, 880 F.3d 668, 681 (4th Cir. 2018); Life of the S. Ins. Co. v. Carzell, 851 F.3d 1341, 1343-44 (11th Cir. 2017).

5. As *Preston* shows, CAFA also contains complex provisions, driven by concerns for federalism, that carve certain state-law class actions that are truly local in nature out of federal jurisdiction. The first exception, in § 1332(d)(3), is discretionary. We previously encountered the idea of a discretionary refusal to exercise jurisdiction in *United Mine Workers of America v. Gibbs,* 383 U.S. 715 (1966) (*supra* p. 552), and in 28 U.S.C. § 1367(c) (*supra* pp. 566-67, Note 8). Although the idea of § 1332(d)(3) is similar, be careful: the six factors listed in § 1332(d)(3) bear only a modest resemblance to the four factors listed in § 1367(c).

The latter two exceptions — the local-controversy exception of § 1332(d)(4)(A) and the home-state exception of § 1332(d)(4)(B) — are mandatory; if the terms of either are met, a court must decline jurisdiction. We have not previously encountered this idea of mandatory declination of jurisdiction; Congress employs it only rarely for unique statutory schemes. For cases analyzing these exceptions in depth, see Kaufman v. Allstate N.J. Ins. Co., 561 F.3d 144 (3d Cir. 2009) (vacating an order remanding a case to state court under the local-controversy exception); *In re* Hannaford Bros. Co. Customer Data Sec. Breach Litig., 564 F.3d 75 (1st Cir. 2009) (ordering remand based on the home-state exception).

6. In *Dart Cherokee Basin Operating Co. v. Owens*, 574 U.S. 81 (2014), the defendant's notice of removal asserted that the case met the federal amount-in-controversy requirement, but failed to support that allegation with evidence. The district court therefore remanded the case. The court of appeals declined to accept the defendant's appeal, presumably because

circuit law required evidence to support an amount-in-controversy allegation in ordinary cases. The Supreme Court held that a defendant's notice of removal need not include such extrinsic evidence but needs to "include only a plausible allegation that the amount in controversy exceeds the jurisdictional threshold." *Id.* at 89. The Court also noted that, whether or not a presumption [against broad removal rights] is proper in mine-run diversity cases[,] . . . no antiremoval presumption attends cases invoking CAFA, which Congress enacted to facilitate adjudication of certain class actions in federal court." *Id.*

7. Even if a federal district court decides not to certify a class action, it retains jurisdiction over a case removed under CAFA. *See* Cunningham Charter Corp. v. Learjet, Inc., 592 F.3d 805, 806-07 (7th Cir.2010); Vega v. T–Mobile USA, Inc., 564 F.3d 1256, 1269 (11th Cir. 2009).

8. In *Exxon Mobil Corp. v. Allapattah Services, Inc.*, 545 U.S. 546, 571-72 (2005) (*supra* p. 557), the Court noted that the passage of CAFA did not affect its interpretation of § 1367. Nonetheless, the generous jurisdictional and removal provisions of §§ 1332(d) and 1453 effectively moot the traditional jurisdictional rules, as modified by § 1367, in all but a small set of class actions. Principally, this set includes class actions with fewer than 100 class members or less than $5 million in aggregate claim value; the traditional rules might also be relevant when either § 1332(d)(3) permits or § 1332(d)(4) requires a federal court to decline jurisdiction.

3. Preclusion

As we learned in Chapter Seven, a party is generally precluded from bringing a second suit involving the same claim after the first suit is concluded; conversely, nonparties are not precluded. Class members are "parties" only in a fictional sense; they trade their right to pursue their claims for a guarantee of adequate representation. When can a class member escape the preclusive effect of a class judgment?

STEPHENSON V. DOW CHEMICAL CO.

273 F.3d 249 (2d Cir. 2001), *aff'd in part by an equally divided Court and vacated in part*, 539 U.S. 111 (2003)

Before CARDAMONE and F.I. PARKER, Circuit Judges, and SPATT, District Judge.*

■ PARKER, Circuit Judge.

. . . Daniel Stephenson and Joe Isaacson are two Vietnam War veterans who allege that they were injured by exposure to Agent Orange while serving in the military in Vietnam. In the late 1990s, Stephenson and

---

* The Honorable Arthur D. Spatt, of the United States District Court for the Eastern District of New York, sitting by designation.

Isaacson (along with their families) filed separate lawsuits against manufacturers of Agent Orange. . . .

In 1984, however, some twelve years before these suits, virtually identical claims against these defendants, brought by a class of military personnel who were exposed to Agent Orange while in Vietnam between 1961 and 1972, were globally settled. . . . Judge Weinstein, who presided over the 1984 settlement, dismissed the claims of Stephenson and Isaacson, concluding that the prior settlement barred their suits. On appeal, plaintiffs chiefly contend . . . that they were inadequately represented and, therefore, due process considerations prevent the earlier class action settlement from precluding their claims. . . . [W]e vacate the district court's dismissal and remand for further proceedings.

I. BACKGROUND

. . .

In 1983, the district court certified the following class under Federal Rule of Civil Procedure 23(b)(3):

> those persons who were in the United States, New Zealand or Australian Armed Forces at any time from 1961 to 1972 who were injured while in or near Vietnam by exposure to Agent Orange or other phenoxy herbicides . . . . The class also includes spouses, parents, and children of the veterans born before January 1, 1984, directly or derivatively injured as a result of the exposure.

The court also ordered notice by mail, print media, radio and television to be provided to class members, providing in part that persons who wished to opt out must do so by May 1, 1984.

[On the eve of trial, the parties reached a settlement for $180 million. The settlement agreement provided: "The Class specifically includes persons who have not yet manifested injury."]

The district court held fairness hearings throughout the country, and approved the settlement as fair, reasonable and adequate. . . .

Seventy-five percent of the $180 million was to be distributed directly "to exposed veterans who suffer from long-term total disabilities and to the surviving spouses or children of exposed veterans who have died." . . . Payments were to be made for ten years, beginning January 1, 1985 and ending December 31, 1994:

> No payment will be made for death or disability occurring after December 31, 1994. . . . Payments will be made for compensable disability to the extent that the period of disability falls within the ten years of the program's operation. . . .

[On appeal, this court] affirmed class certification, settlement approval and much of the distribution plan. . . . We specifically rejected an attack based on adequacy of representation . . . . We additionally concluded that the notice scheme devised by Judge Weinstein was the "best notice practicable" under Federal Rule of Civil Procedure 23(c)(2). Finally, we affirmed the settlement as fair, reasonable and adequate, given the serious weaknesses of the plaintiffs' claims.

[In 1989 and 1990, two class actions, known as the *Ivy/Hartman* litigation, were filed on behalf of Vietnam veterans exposed to Agent Orange. The plaintiffs alleged that their injuries and the injuries of fellow class members manifested themselves only after the May 7, 1984 settlement. The district court held that the veterans were bound by the settlement, and dismissed the cases. The court of appeals affirmed the dismissals. Ivy v. Diamond Shamrock Chems. Co., 996 F.2d 1425, 1429-30 (2d Cir. 1993).]

II. DISCUSSION

. . .

B. *Collateral Attack*

. . . Plaintiffs assert that, since the Supreme Court's decision in *Hansberry v. Lee*, 311 U.S. 32 (1940), courts have allowed collateral attacks on class action judgments based upon due process concerns. Defendants strenuously disagree and contend that to allow plaintiffs' suit to go forward, in the face of the 1984 global settlement, would "violate defendants' right to due process of law." . . .

. . . . According to defendants, because the "due process rights of absent class members have been extensively litigated in the *Agent Orange* litigation," these plaintiffs cannot now attack those prior determinations. We reject defendants' arguments and conclude that plaintiffs' collateral attack, which seeks only to prevent the prior settlement from operating as res judicata to their claims, is permissible.

First, even if, as defendants contend, collateral attack is only permitted where there has been no prior determination of the absent class members' rights, plaintiffs' collateral attack is allowed. It is true that, on direct appeal and in the *Ivy/Hartman* litigation, we previously concluded that there was adequate representation of all class members in the original *Agent Orange* settlement. However, neither this Court nor the district court has addressed specifically the adequacy of representation for those members of the class whose injuries manifested after depletion of the settlement[ ] funds. . . .

Second, the propriety of a collateral attack such as this is amply supported by precedent. In *Hansberry*, the Supreme Court entertained a collateral attack on an Illinois state court class action judgment that purported to bind the plaintiffs. The Court held that class action judgments can only bind absent class members where "the interests of those not joined are of the same class as the interests of those who are, and where it is considered that the latter fairly represent the former in the prosecution of the litigation." Additionally, we have previously stated that a "[j]udgment in a class action is not secure from collateral attack unless the absentees were adequately and vigorously represented." . . .

... Plaintiffs do not attack the merits or finality of the settlement itself, but instead argue that they were not proper parties to that judgment. If plaintiffs were not proper parties to that judgment, as we conclude below, res judicata cannot defeat their claims. Further, such collateral review would not, as defendants maintain, violate defendants' due process rights by exposing them to double liability. Exposure to liability here is not duplicative if plaintiffs were never proper parties to the prior judgment in the first place.

We therefore hold that a collateral attack to contest the application of res judicata is available. We turn next to the merits of this attack.

C. *Due Process Considerations and Res Judicata*

The doctrine of res judicata dictates that "a final judgment on the merits of an action precludes the parties or their privies from relitigating issues that were or could have been raised in that action." Res judicata ordinarily applies "if the earlier decision was (1) a final judgment on the merits, (2) by a court of competent jurisdiction, (3) in a case involving the same parties or their privies, and (4) involving the same cause of action." ....

Plaintiffs' argument focuses on element number three in the res judicata analysis: whether they are parties bound by the settlement. Plaintiffs rely primarily on the United States Supreme Court's decisions in *Amchem Products, Inc. v. Windsor*, 521 U.S. 591 (1997) [*infra* p. 689], and *Ortiz v. Fibreboard Corp.*, 527 U.S. 815 (1999).

In *Amchem*, the Supreme Court confronted, on direct appeal, a challenge to class certification for settlement purposes in an asbestos litigation. The class defined in the complaint included both individuals who were presently injured as well as individuals who had only been exposed to asbestos. The Supreme Court held that this "sprawling" class was improperly certified under Federal Rules of Civil Procedure 23(a) and (b). Specifically, the Court held that Rule 23(a)(4)'s requirement that the named parties "will fairly and adequately protect the interests of the class" had not been satisfied. The Court reasoned that

> named parties with diverse medical conditions sought to act on behalf of a single giant class rather than on behalf of discrete subclasses. In significant respects, the interests of those within the single class are not aligned. Most saliently, for the currently injured, the critical goal is generous immediate payments. That goal tugs against the interest of exposure-only plaintiffs in ensuring an ample, inflation-protected fund for the future. . . .

In *Ortiz*, the Supreme Court again addressed a settlement only class action in the asbestos litigation context. *Ortiz*, however, involved a settlement-only limited fund class under Rule 23(b)(1)(B). The Supreme Court ultimately held that the class could not be maintained under Rule 23(b)(1)(B), because "the limit of the fund was determined by treating the settlement agreement as dispositive, an error magnified" by conflicted counsel. In so holding, *Ortiz* noted that "it is obvious after *Amchem* that a class divided between holders of present and future claims (some of the latter involving no physical injury and attributable to claimants not yet born) requires division into homogeneous subclasses under Rule 23(c)(4)(B), with separate representation to eliminate conflicting interests of counsel."

Res judicata generally applies to bind absent class members except where to do so would violate due process. Due process requires adequate representation "at all times" throughout the litigation, notice "reasonably calculated . . . to apprise interested parties of the pendency of the action," and an opportunity to opt out. Phillips Petroleum Co. v. Shutts, 472 U.S. 797, 811-12 (1985) [*supra* p. 658].

Both Stephenson and Isaacson fall within the class definition of the prior litigation: they served in the United States military, stationed in Vietnam, between 1961 and 1972, and were allegedly injured by exposure to Agent Orange. However, they both learned of their allegedly Agent Orange-related injuries only after the 1984 settlement fund had expired in 1994. Because the prior litigation purported to settle all future claims, but only provided for recovery for those whose death or disability was discovered prior to 1994, the conflict between Stephenson and Isaacson and the class representatives becomes apparent. No provision was made for post-1994 claimants, and the settlement fund was permitted to terminate in 1994. *Amchem* and *Ortiz* suggest that Stephenson and Isaacson were not adequately represented in the prior *Agent Orange* litigation.[8] Those cases indicate that a class which purports to represent both present and future claimants may encounter internal conflicts.

Defendants contend that there was, in fact, no conflict because all class members' claims were equally meritless . . . . This argument misses the mark. At this stage, we are only addressing whether plaintiffs' claims should be barred by res judicata. We are therefore concerned only with whether they were afforded due process in the earlier litigation. Part of the due process inquiry (and part of the Rule 23(a) class certification requirements) involves assessing adequacy of representation and intra-class conflicts. The ultimate merits of the claims have no bearing on whether the class previously certified adequately represented these plaintiffs.

Because these plaintiffs were inadequately represented in the prior litigation, they were not proper parties and cannot be bound by the settlement. We therefore must vacate the district court's dismissal and remand for further proceedings. We, of course, express no opinion as to the ultimate merits of plaintiffs' claims.

Notes and Questions

1. Although distinctions between the cases can be made, *Stephenson* conflicted with another appellate decision, *Epstein v. MCA, Inc.*, 179 F.3d

---

8. We also note that plaintiffs likely received inadequate notice. *Shutts* provides that adequate notice is necessary to bind absent class members. . . .

641 (9th Cir. 1999). The Supreme Court granted certiorari in *Stephenson* to resolve the conflict. The Court was stalemated on the preclusion issue, 4-4, with Justice Stevens not participating. The tie affirmed the collateral-attack ruling in *Stephenson*, but created no precedent. The Court then vacated a portion of the judgment on an unrelated issue regarding removal.

2. The term of art for a class member's attempt to contest the adequacy of representation in a separate lawsuit is *collateral attack*. By contrast, *direct review* is an appeal from a lower-court judgment as opposed to an attempt to attack the judgment in a later, separate proceeding.

3. *Stephenson*'s collateral attack involves an issue-preclusion question wrapped up within a claim-preclusion question. The claim-preclusion question is obvious: if the *Stephenson* plaintiffs are proper members of the prior class action, its settlement and judgment bind them. As *Hansberry* holds, however, claim preclusion applies only if they are adequately represented in the first class action. The district court in the first action found that the class members, including the *Stephenson* plaintiffs, had been adequately represented. Hence, the question is whether, in their new cases, the *Stephenson* plaintiffs are precluded from contesting the finding of adequate representation made in the first litigation — a classic question of issue preclusion. If they are precluded, then *Hansberry* avails them not, and claim preclusion ends their cases. If issue preclusion does not bind them to the adequacy finding, then they can contest adequacy; and if they are successful in proving inadequacy (as the court of appeals held they were), then *Hansberry* destroys the claim-preclusive effect of the first litigation.

Although *Hansberry* is the starting point for thinking about collateral attacks, the case itself provides little direct guidance. In the prior class action that was under attack in *Hansberry*, the trial court had never made any findings about adequacy of representation.

4. Strong arguments can be made on both sides of the collateral-attack question. At stake, from one perspective, is the finality of judgments, and of class judgments in particular; having expended resources to litigate a case to conclusion, and having spent perhaps an enormous sum to settle the case, the defendant does not want the case reopened fifteen or twenty years down the line. If the class action cannot promise perpetual peace from litigation, then its utility as a device to decide all related claims has been curtailed. From the opposite perspective, however, if class members are unable to disavow a deal that turns out to be collusive or otherwise disastrous to their interests because of the inadequacy of their representatives or counsel, then the loss of their autonomy in class proceedings is dear indeed. Adequate representation is the constitutional foundation on which modern class actions have been built, and its absence should never be countenanced.

Both sides in this debate have valid points, don't they? The issue cuts to the very heart of what class actions are and should be. Perhaps you can see why the Supreme Court was as closely divided as it was, and why the issue creates strong feelings among those who work with class actions. Can you think of any reasonable middle ground between the poles of "no collateral attacks" and "always collateral attacks"?

5. The *Epstein-Stephenson* question has generated significant judicial and academic debate. It is fair to say that the cases are strongly trending toward the *Epstein* approach, and away from *Stephenson*. Indeed, even the Second Circuit has limited *Stephenson* to its facts:

> *Stephenson* is not directly on point, however, because that case involved future claimants, whereas this case does not. Here, injured parties may obtain remuneration from the settlement fund . . . . [T]he essential question in determining whether the Settlement complies with the adequate representation doctrine is whether the interests that were served by the Settlement were compatible with those of [the class members] when plaintiffs negotiated a release of the . . . claims [that the class members were pursuing in separate litigation].

Wal–Mart Stores, Inc. v. Visa U.S.A., Inc., 396 F.3d 96, 110 (2d Cir. 2005). Other courts have rejected *Stephenson*. See In re Diet Drugs (Phentermine/Fenfluramine/Dexfenfluramine) Prods. Liab. Litig., 431 F.3d 141 (3d Cir. 2005); Gough v. Transamerica Life Ins. Co., 781 F. Supp. 2d 498 (W.D. Ky. 2011); Lamarque v. Fairbanks Capital Corp., 927 A.2d 753 (R.I. 2007); Hospitality Mgmt. Assocs., Inc. v. Shell Oil Co., 591 S.E.2d 611 (S.C. 2004). *But see In re* Payment Card Interchange Fee & Merch. Discount Antitrust Litig., 827 F.3d 223, 239 (2d Cir. 2016) (reversing a class settlement and reaffirming *Stephenson* when the class members challenging the settlement were "future claimants who had their claims settled for nothing").

The American Law Institute has sided with the courts that would give broad preclusive effect to a class judgment or settlement. PRINCIPLES OF THE LAW OF AGGREGATE LITIGATION § 2.07 (AM. LAW INST. 2010).

6. Class actions bend the usual rules of preclusion in another way. Suppose that a class member has both a claim in common with other class members and a related claim that is unique to him or her. Under the preclusion rules applicable in most jurisdictions, a plaintiff's failure to bring a transactionally related claim in a case bars any future cases asserting that claim. Nonetheless, in *Cooper v. Federal Reserve Bank of Richmond*, 467 U.S. 867 (1984), the Supreme Court held that class members did not lose their individual claims when the claims were not asserted in the class action. *Cooper* involved employment discrimination; the class action alleged a policy of discrimination against an entire racial group. The district court did not find class-wide discrimination. Several class members then brought claims that the defendant had discriminated against them personally. The Court said that the efficiency of class actions would be lost if every class member had to intervene to assert individual claims. The Court noted that some of the findings from the prior class action might nonetheless have issue-preclusive effect in the individual cases.

4. *Erie*

In Chapter Eleven, we explored the *Erie* doctrine, which requires federal courts to apply state substantive law and, in some instances, state procedural law as well. Class actions based on state law raise challenging

IN RE RHONE–POULENC RORER, INC.

51 F.3d 1293 (7th Cir. 1995)

Before POSNER, Chief Judge, and BAUER and ROVNER, Circuit Judges.

■ POSNER, Chief Judge.

[Manufacturers of blood products that were widely used by persons with hemophilia allegedly failed to take adequate precautions in screening blood donors. The result was that thousands of persons with hemophilia, their spouses and lovers, and their children were infected with the human immunodeficiency virus (HIV). The district court certified a Rule 23(b)(3) class action. The manufacturers sought a writ of mandamus to undo the certification. (Recall that interlocutory appeal under Rule 23(f) was not available until 1998.) The Seventh Circuit granted the writ for several reasons. One reason was the district judge's proposal to try the case by using a jury instruction on the issue of negligence that was, in the words of Chief Judge Posner, "a kind of Esperanto instruction, merging the negligence standards of the 50 states and the District of Columbia."]

[The district court] proposes to have a jury determine the negligence of the defendants under a legal standard that does not actually exist anywhere in the world. One is put in mind of the concept of "general" common law that prevailed in the era of *Swift v. Tyson*, 41 U.S. (16 Pet.) 1 (1842). The assumption is that the common law of the 50 states and the District of Columbia, at least so far as bears on a claim of negligence against drug companies, is basically uniform and can be abstracted in a single instruction. It is no doubt true that at some level of generality the law of negligence is one, not only nationwide but worldwide. Negligence is a failure to take due care, and due care a function of the probability and magnitude of an accident and the costs of avoiding it. A jury can be asked whether the defendants took due care. And in many cases such differences as there are among the tort rules of the different states would not affect the outcome....

[One of the plaintiffs' theories of negligence, however, was novel, and no state courts had yet considered it.] ... If one instruction on negligence will serve to instruct the jury on the legal standard of every state of the United States applicable to a novel claim, implying that the claim despite its controversiality would be decided identically in all 50 states and the District of Columbia, one wonders what the Supreme Court thought it was doing in the *Erie* case when it held that it was *unconstitutional* for federal courts in diversity cases to apply general common law rather than the common law of the state whose law would apply if the case were being tried in state rather than federal court.... The law of negligence, including subsidiary concepts such as duty of care, foreseeability, and proximate cause, may as the plaintiffs have argued forcefully to us differ among the states only in nuance, though we think not . . . But nuance can be important, and its significance is suggested by a comparison of differing state pattern instructions on negligence and differing judicial formulations of the meaning of negligence and the subordinate concepts. . . . The voices of the quasi-sovereigns that are the states of the United States sing negligence with a different pitch. . . .

The diversity jurisdiction of the federal courts is, after *Erie*, designed merely to provide an alternative forum for the litigation of state-law claims, not an alternative system of substantive law for diversity cases. But under the district judge's plan the thousands of members of the plaintiff class will have their rights determined, and the four defendant manufacturers will have their duties determined, under a law that is merely an amalgam, an averaging, of the nonidentical negligence laws of 51 jurisdictions. No one doubts that Congress could constitutionally prescribe a uniform standard of liability for manufacturers of blood solids. It might we suppose promulgate pertinent provisions of the *Restatement (Second) of Torts*. The point of *Erie* is that Article III of the Constitution does not empower the federal courts to create such a regime for diversity cases. . . .

■ [The dissenting opinion of JUDGE ROVNER is omitted.]

SHADY GROVE ORTHOPEDIC ASSOCIATES, P.A. v. ALLSTATE INSURANCE CO.

559 U.S. 393 (2010)

[An edited version of the opinion appears *supra* p. 614.]

Notes and Questions

1. *Rhone–Poulenc* refuses to bend *Erie*'s requirement that a federal court apply state substantive law to each class member. Its approach reflects the prevailing attitude of the federal bench today. Having to apply multiple states' substantive law may doom class treatment in many cases; the requirements of commonality and typicality — in addition to those of predominance and superiority in (b)(3) class actions — are very difficult to meet when state-law variations exist. A leading case on the issue is *Castano v. American Tobacco Co.*, 84 F.3d 734 (5th Cir. 1996), in which the court of appeals reversed certification of a nationwide class of smokers suing the tobacco companies in part because of the wide variations in state law.

Academic commentary has sometimes chafed against this reality. For instance, Professor Shapiro believed that "the very concept of a tort committed against the entire class, with the incidents I have suggested, militates strongly against the idea of having the laws of different jurisdictions apply to different members of the class. A single applicable law is almost a sine qua non." David L. Shapiro, *Class Actions: The Class as*

Party and Client, 78 NOTRE DAME L. REV. 913, 942 (1998). More recently, Professor Rosenberg and one of his students have proposed a novel way to "average" the laws of the various states in a class action. Luke McCloud & David Rosenberg, *A Solution to the Choice of Law Problem of Differing State Laws in Class Actions: Average Law*, 79 GEO. WASH. L. REV. 374 (2011). The American Law Institute has called for congressional adoption of a uniform set of choice-of-law principles in complex cases; these principles would often lead to the selection of a single substantive law. COMPLEX LITIGATION ch. 6 (AM. LAW INST. 1994). One commentator has made the radical suggestion that CAFA, by placing most multistate class actions in federal court, should be read to overrule *Erie* for covered class actions. Suzanna Sherry, *Overruling* Erie: *Nationwide Class Actions and National Common Law*, 156 U. PA. L. REV. 2135 (2008).

Courts have also developed creative (and controversial) responses to the problem of variations in state law, sometimes finding ways to use one state's (or a few states') law. *See* JAY TIDMARSH & ROGER H. TRANGSRUD, MODERN COMPLEX LITIGATION 668-706 (2d ed. 2010). Class actions are grating against the *Erie* doctrine and may slowly change its contours.

2. *Rhone–Poulenc* deals with state *substantive* law in federal class actions. What about state *procedural* law, when the federal class action is decided under state substantive law? In particular, what if the state whose substantive law applies has a more generous, or less generous, class-action rule than Rule 23? Must Rule 23 be followed in federal court?

Shady Grove answered this question in the affirmative, holding that Rule 23 governs in federal court even when a state court would apply a different class-action rule. This result stands on somewhat shaky ground, because there was no majority opinion on the reason *why* Rule 23 applied (as opposed to *whether* Rule 23 applied). Justice Scalia's four-member plurality opinion stated broadly that Rule 23, which it found to be in direct conflict with New York's law, did not violate the terms of the Rules Enabling Act, 28 U.S.C. § 2072. Justice Stevens agreed that Rule 23 did not violate the Act in the context presented in *Shady Grove*, but he left open the possibility that Rule 23 could violate the Enabling Act if the state rule is "so intertwined with a state right or remedy that it functions to define the scope of the state-created right." 559 U.S. at 423. The four-member dissent did not address whether Rule 23 violated the Enabling Act, because it believed that Rule 23 was not in direct conflict with New York law and thus did not apply. *Cf.* Garman v. Campbell Cty. Sch. Dist. No. 1, 630 F.3d 977, 983 n.6 (10th Cir. 2010) (noting that, because it was the narrowest ground for the *Shady Grove* result, Justice Stevens' concurrence controlled).

3. Even if Rule 23 passes muster under the Enabling Act, the Act still exercises an important influence over the shape of Rule 23. On three occasions the Court has cautioned against broad readings of Rule 23 to avoid potential conflict with § 2072. Wal–Mart Stores, Inc. v. Dukes, 564 U.S. 338, 367 (2011) (*supra* p. 655); Ortiz v. Fibreboard Corp., 527 U.S. 815, 845 (1999); Amchem Prods., Inc. v. Windsor, 521 U.S. 591, 613, 629 (1997) (*infra* p. 693). *Cf.* Sullivan v. DB Invs., Inc., 667 F.3d 273, 352-54 (3d Cir. 2011) (en

banc) (Jordan, J., dissenting) (arguing that certifying the class action at issue enlarged the plaintiffs' substantive rights in violation of the Enabling Act).

4. One of the ironies of *Shady Grove*'s result, noted by Justice Ginsburg in her dissent, is that the case could not have made its way to federal court but for CAFA (the plaintiff's individual claim was worth only $500, but the claims of the class exceeded $5 million). Even though CAFA's purpose was to restrict the scope of class-action practice in state court, the result in *Shady Grove* allowed a class action to be maintained in federal court when no comparable class action could have been maintained in a New York state court. *See* 559 U.S. at 436 (Ginsburg, J., dissenting) (noting that the use of Rule 23 "transform[s] a $500 case into a $5,000,000 award"); *id.* at 445 n.3 ("A court's decision to certify a class accordingly places pressure on the defendant to settle even unmeritorious claims.").

In the main, however, *Shady Grove*, when combined with CAFA, puts federal courts more clearly in charge of large-scale state-law class actions than ever before. CAFA sweeps more class actions into federal court. *Shady Grove* means that federal, not state, standards will dictate whether these class actions will be certified. Does this combination of developments offend the proper distribution of power between the state and federal courts?

5. Trial

A large class action makes the traditional trial — in which individual evidence is presented for and against the claims or defenses of each class member — almost unimaginable. Of course, trial is not a likely outcome for a class action; like other lawsuits, many class actions settle or are otherwise resolved short of trial. Except for settlement class actions (*see infra* pp. 688-99), however, trial is the default method for resolving the dispute. A court is unlikely to certify a class if it believes that the case cannot be tried. This problem is especially acute in Rule 23(b)(3) cases seeking damages; in Rule 23(b)(2) class actions, the common injunctive or declaratory relief often makes a single trial manageable. But if the class seeks damages, and if the amount of damage varies for each plaintiff, the prospect of individualizing the relief for each class member presents an obstacle to satisfying the predominance and superiority requirements of Rule 23(b)(3).

This course is not the place to consider all the options that a court has to try a class action. We will, however, mention four. The first is to separate common issues (often, whether the defendant's conduct violated the law or was even capable of causing the type of harm from which the class members suffer) from individual issues (often, questions of individual causation, individual defenses such as comparative negligence, and damages). The first trial then focuses only on the common issues. This process is usually called *bifurcation*, and is provided for in Rules 16(c)(2)(M) and 42(b). Bifurcation works well when the relevant decision-maker (judge or jury) determines that the defendant is not liable; the case ends before the intractable individual issues become relevant. But it works less well if the defendant's liability is proven; in this situation, bifurcation delays the day of reckoning rather than avoids it.

Bifurcation is controversial, for reasons ranging from the constitutional to the practical. For a discussion, see JAY TIDMARSH & ROGER H. TRANGSRUD, MODERN COMPLEX LITIGATION 1033-48 (2d ed. 2010).

A second option is to use statistical sampling. A random, sufficiently large sample of the class has its cases tried to conclusion. The results are then averaged out, and the average award given to each remaining class member. Both liability and damages factor into the award; if some of the sample lose their cases, the awards are assigned a zero value in calculating the average. Thus, the risk of loss is built into the average award. This "trial by statistics" method avoids the need to try the liability and damage cases for most class members. On the other hand, some class members (those who would have lost and those whose damages are low) will receive too much, while others (those whose damages are high) may well receive too little.

The most noteworthy example of a case employing trial by statistics is *Hilao v. Estate of Marcos,* 103 F.3d 767 (9th Cir. 1996), which upheld this method over the defendant's objection that it violated the Due Process Clause of the Fifth Amendment. Other courts have rejected this approach. *See, e.g.*, Cimino v. Raymark Indus., Inc., 151 F.3d 297 (5th Cir. 1998) (holding that trial by statistics violated due process, the defendants' right to jury trial under the Seventh Amendment, and the Rules Enabling Act). The final nail in the coffin for the *Hilao* approach was *Wal–Mart Stores, Inc. v. Dukes,* 564 U.S. 338, 367 (2011) (*supra* pp. 654-55), in which the Court spoke dubiously about the "Trial by Formula" method for determining class members' damages. While not necessary to the holding, the unanimous view of the Court to "disapprove that novel project" because it would risk violating the Rules Enabling Act makes the statistical approach untenable if it is used to determine both liability and damages issues.

More recently, however, the Court has recognized that statistical proof may be used in conjunction with other evidence when the only issue is the amount of damages. *See* Tyson Foods, Inc. v. Bouaphakeo, 577 U.S. —, 136 S. Ct. 1036 (2016). For a short, accessible argument in favor of sampling — arguing that sampling can be justified not only because it is less costly but also because it leads to more accurate results than individual trials — see Edward K. Cheng, *When 10 Trials Are Better Than 10,000: An Evidentiary Perspective on Trial Sampling*, 160 U. PA. L. REV. 955 (2012).

Related to trial by formula are methods — useful in a narrow range of cases — by which each class member's damages can be calculated by computer program or can be calculated in the aggregate, even if each member's share of damages is uncertain. In *Smilow v. Southwestern Bell Mobile Systems, Inc.*, 323 F.3d 32 (1st Cir. 2003), the defendant allegedly overcharged class members for incoming cell-phone calls. In responding to the defendant's argument that individual variation in damages made the (b)(3) class unmanageable, the plaintiff claimed that its computer experts could design a program that would determine the number of minutes that each class member had been overcharged and thus each class member's damage. The court certified the class. In *In re Pharmaceutical Industry Average Wholesale Price Litigation*, 582 F.3d 156 (1st Cir. 2009), the defendant allegedly overcharged for its prescription drugs. The total amount of the overcharge was ascertainable by examining the defendant's sales records, but the exact amount owed to each victim was more difficult to determine. The court of appeals rejected the argument that the plaintiffs needed to prove the damages of each class member, holding that the method of working backwards from the defendant's sales to establish aggregate damages was proper. *Average Wholesale Price Litigation* did not discuss how the district court was to allocate the aggregate award among class members.

A final method for trying a class action is to use *bellwether trials*. A bellwether trial picks the cases of a few class members and tries them. The idea behind the bellwether trial is to provide the parties with information about the likelihood that individual claims will succeed and with the value of those claims. Armed with this information, the parties may then be able to settle remaining claims. For discussion of the device, see *In re Chevron U.S.A., Inc.*, 109 F.3d 1016 (5th Cir. 1997); Alexandra D. Lahav, *Bellwether Trials*, 76 GEO. WASH. L. REV. 576 (2008).

The future of the (b)(3) class action may depend on courts' ability to find ways to try damages class actions. At the same time, techniques to do so grate against the individualized common-law trial ingrained in the American psyche. Must each plaintiff and defendant have a meaningful day in court? Or must we adjust our notions of trial to the modern reality of mass injuries? Reconsider your answer after reading the following section.

D. SETTLEMENT CLASS ACTIONS: RESOLVING WIDESPREAD DISPUTES WITHOUT ADVERSARY LITIGATION

Until now, we have examined class actions in which the party seeking certification intends to try the case and obtain a judgment (although many such cases, of course, settle). We call these cases *litigation class actions*.

In the 1970s a new type of class action arose: the *settlement class action*. In a settlement class action, the parties never intend to litigate the case. Before it is filed, the defendants strike a deal with a lawyer who negotiates on behalf of a putative class. The lawyer then files a class action, and the parties ask the court to approve the settlement. Thus, defendants use the class device to resolve the claims of all or most actual or potential plaintiffs. This strategy manages the defendants' litigation risks, but puts the parties and the court in an odd position. The class representatives and the defendant do not stand in an adversarial posture to each other. Both sides want the same outcome — the district court's approval of the settlement as "fair, reasonable, and adequate." *See* Fed. R. Civ. P. 23(e)(2). Collusive behavior is therefore a concern. Because the court too is often interested in a mechanism that will resolve many claims without litigation, the fear is that no one is watching out for the class's interests. Sometimes a degree of adversariness is introduced by class-member *objectors* to the settlement, who can under some circumstances appear and be heard.

The settlement terms often establish quasi-administrative structures, operating under the court's aegis, that dispense compensation. Is the court in these cases any longer engaging in traditional adjudicatory behavior? What alternative vision of the court's dispute-resolution function and its role in civil society does the settlement class action suggest?

AMCHEM PRODUCTS, INC. V. WINDSOR

521 U.S. 591 (1997)

■ JUSTICE GINSBURG delivered the opinion of the Court.

This case concerns the legitimacy under Rule 23 of the Federal Rules of Civil Procedure of a class-action certification sought to achieve global settlement of current and future asbestos-related claims. The class proposed for certification potentially encompasses hundreds of thousands, perhaps millions, of individuals tied together by this commonality: each was, or some day may be, adversely affected by past exposure to asbestos products manufactured by one or more of 20 companies [collectively known as the CCR defendants]. Those companies, defendants in the lower courts, are petitioners here.

The United States District Court for the Eastern District of Pennsylvania certified the class for settlement only, finding that the proposed settlement was fair and that representation and notice had been adequate. . . . The Court of Appeals for the Third Circuit vacated the District Court's orders, holding that the class certification failed to satisfy Rule 23's requirements in several critical respects. We affirm the Court of Appeals' judgment.

I

A

The settlement-class certification we confront evolved in response to an asbestos-litigation crisis. . . . A United States Judicial Conference Ad Hoc Committee on Asbestos Litigation, appointed by the Chief Justice in September 1990, described facets of the problem in a 1991 report:

> The most objectionable aspects of asbestos litigation can be briefly summarized: dockets in both federal and state courts continue to grow; long delays are routine; trials are too long; the same issues are litigated over and over; transaction costs exceed the victims' recovery by nearly two to one; exhaustion of assets threatens and distorts the process; and future claimants may lose altogether. . . .

In the face of legislative inaction, the federal courts — lacking authority to replace state tort systems with a national toxic tort compensation regime

— endeavored to work with the procedural tools available to improve management of federal asbestos litigation. . . .

B

. . . [A]ttorneys for plaintiffs and defendants formed separate steering committees and began settlement negotiations. . . .

Settlement talks . . . concentrated on devising an administrative scheme for disposition of asbestos claims not yet in litigation. In these negotiations, counsel for [plaintiffs with already-filed claims] endeavored to represent the interests of the anticipated future claimants, although those lawyers then had no attorney-client relationship with such claimants.

Once negotiations seemed likely to produce an agreement purporting to bind potential plaintiffs, [the defendants] agreed to settle, through separate agreements, the claims of plaintiffs who had already filed asbestos-related lawsuits. In one such agreement, . . . defendants promised to pay more than $200 million to gain release of the claims of [these] plaintiffs. . . .

C

The class action thus instituted was not intended to be litigated. Rather, within the space of a single day, January 15, 1993, the settling parties — CCR defendants and the representatives of the plaintiff class described below — presented to the District Court a complaint, an answer, a proposed settlement agreement, and a joint motion for conditional class certification.

The complaint identified nine lead plaintiffs, designating them and members of their families as representatives of a class comprising all persons who had not filed an asbestos-related lawsuit against a CCR defendant as of the date the class action commenced, but who (1) had been exposed — occupationally or through the occupational exposure of a spouse or household member — to asbestos or products containing asbestos attributable to a CCR defendant, or (2) whose spouse or family member had been so exposed. Untold numbers of individuals may fall within this description. . . . More than half of the named plaintiffs alleged that they or their family members had already suffered various physical injuries as a result of the exposure. The others alleged that they had not yet manifested any asbestos-related condition. The complaint delineated no subclasses; all named plaintiffs were designated as representatives of the class as a whole. . . .

A stipulation of settlement accompanied the pleadings . . . An exhaustive document exceeding 100 pages, the stipulation presents in detail an administrative mechanism and a schedule of payments to compensate class members who meet defined asbestos-exposure and medical requirements. The stipulation describes four categories of compensable disease: mesothelioma; lung cancer; certain "other cancers" (colon-rectal, laryngeal, esophageal, and stomach cancer); and "non-malignant conditions" (asbestosis and bilateral pleural thickening). Persons with "exceptional" medical claims — claims that do not fall within the four described diagnostic categories — may in some instances qualify for compensation, but the settlement caps the number of "exceptional" claims CCR must cover.

For each qualifying disease category, the stipulation specifies the range of damages CCR will pay to qualifying claimants. Payments under the settlement are not adjustable for inflation. Mesothelioma claimants — the most highly compensated category — are scheduled to receive between $20,000 and $200,000. . . .

Compensation above the fixed ranges may be obtained for "extraordinary" claims. But the settlement places both numerical caps and dollar limits on such claims. The settlement also imposes "case flow maximums," which cap the number of claims payable for each disease in a given year.

Class members are to receive no compensation for certain kinds of claims, even if otherwise applicable state law recognizes such claims. Claims that garner no compensation under the settlement include claims by family members of asbestos-exposed individuals for loss of consortium, and claims by so-called "exposure-only" plaintiffs for increased risk of cancer, fear of future asbestos-related injury, and medical monitoring. "Pleural" claims, which might be asserted by persons with asbestos-related plaques on their lungs but no accompanying physical impairment, are also excluded. Although not entitled to present compensation, exposure-only claimants and pleural claimants may qualify for benefits when and if they develop a compensable disease and meet the relevant exposure and medical criteria. Defendants forgo defenses to liability, including statute of limitations pleas.

Class members, in the main, are bound by the settlement in perpetuity, while CCR defendants may choose to withdraw from the settlement after ten years. A small number of class members — only a few per year — may reject the settlement and pursue their claims in court. . . .

III

. . .

In the 1966 class-action amendments, Rule 23(b)(3), the category at issue here, was "the most adventuresome" innovation. Rule 23(b)(3) added to the complex-litigation arsenal class actions for damages designed to secure judgments binding all class members save those who affirmatively elected to be excluded. . . .

Framed for situations in which "class-action treatment is not as clearly called for" as it is in Rule 23(b)(1) and (b)(2) situations, Rule 23(b)(3) permits certification where class suit "may nevertheless be convenient and desirable." . . . [T]he Advisory Committee sought to cover cases "in which a class action would achieve economies of time, effort, and expense, and promote . . . uniformity of decision as to persons similarly situated, without sacrificing procedural fairness or bringing about other undesirable results." Sensitive to the competing tugs of individual autonomy for those who might prefer to go it alone or in a smaller unit, on the one hand, and systemic efficiency on the other, the Reporter for the 1966 amendments cautioned: "The new provision invites a close look at the case before it is accepted as a class action...." ...

While the text of Rule 23(b)(3) does not exclude from certification cases in which individual damages run high, the Advisory Committee had dominantly in mind vindication of "the rights of groups of people who individually would be without effective strength to bring their opponents into court at all." As concisely recalled in a recent Seventh Circuit opinion:

> The policy at the very core of the class action mechanism is to overcome the problem that small recoveries do not provide the incentive for any individual to bring a solo action prosecuting his or her rights. A class action solves this problem by aggregating the relatively paltry potential recoveries into something worth someone's (usually an attorney's) labor. [Mace v. Van Ru Credit Corp., 109 F.3d 338, 344 (1997).] ...

In the decades since the 1966 revision of Rule 23, class action practice has become ever more "adventuresome" as a means of coping with claims too numerous to secure their "just, speedy, and inexpensive determination" one by one. *See* Fed. R. Civ. P. 1. The development reflects concerns about the efficient use of court resources and the conservation of funds to compensate claimants who do not line up early in a litigation queue. . . .

Among current applications of Rule 23(b)(3), the "settlement only" class has become a stock device. . . .

IV

We granted review to decide the role settlement may play, under existing Rule 23, in determining the propriety of class certification. The Third Circuit's opinion stated that each of the requirements of Rule 23(a) and (b)(3) "must be satisfied without taking into account the settlement." That statement, petitioners urge, is incorrect.

We agree with petitioners to this limited extent: Settlement is relevant to a class certification. The Third Circuit's opinion bears modification in that respect. But, as we earlier observed, the Court of Appeals in fact did not ignore the settlement; instead, that court homed in on settlement terms in explaining why it found the absentees' interests inadequately represented. The Third Circuit's close inspection of the settlement in that regard was altogether proper.

Confronted with a request for settlement-only class certification, a district court need not inquire whether the case, if tried, would present intractable management problems, *see* Fed. R. Civ. P. 23(b)(3)(D), for the proposal is that there be no trial. But other specifications of the rule — those designed to protect absentees by blocking unwarranted or overbroad class definitions — demand undiluted, even heightened, attention in the settlement context. Such attention is of vital importance, for a court asked to certify a settlement class will lack the opportunity, present when a case is litigated, to adjust the class, informed by the proceedings as they unfold.

And, of overriding importance, courts must be mindful that the rule as now composed sets the requirements they are bound to enforce. Federal Rules take effect after an extensive deliberative process involving many reviewers: a Rules Advisory Committee, public commenters, the Judicial Conference, this Court, the Congress. *See* 28 U.S.C. §§ 2073, 2074. The text of a rule thus proposed and reviewed limits judicial inventiveness. Courts are not free to amend a rule outside the process Congress ordered, a process properly tuned to the instruction that rules of procedure "shall not abridge . . . any substantive right." *Id.* § 2072(b). . . .

The safeguards provided by the Rule 23(a) and (b) class-qualifying criteria, we emphasize, are not impractical impediments — checks shorn of utility — in the settlement class context. First, the standards set for the protection of absent class members serve to inhibit appraisals of the chancellor's foot kind — class certifications dependent upon the court's gestalt judgment or overarching impression of the settlement's fairness.

Second, if a fairness inquiry under Rule 23(e) controlled certification, eclipsing Rule 23(a) and (b), and permitting class designation despite the impossibility of litigation, both class counsel and court would be disarmed. Class counsel confined to settlement negotiations could not use the threat of litigation to press for a better offer, . . . and the court would face a bargain proffered for its approval without benefit of adversarial investigation . . . .

Federal courts, in any case, lack authority to substitute for Rule 23's certification criteria a standard never adopted — that if a settlement is "fair," then certification is proper. . . . The Court of Appeals' opinion amply demonstrates why — with or without a settlement on the table — the sprawling class the District Court certified does not satisfy Rule 23's requirements.

A

We address first the requirement of Rule 23(b)(3) that "[common] questions of law or fact . . . predominate over any questions affecting only individual members." The District Court concluded that predominance was satisfied based on two factors: class members' shared experience of asbestos exposure and their common "interest in receiving prompt and fair compensation for their claims, while minimizing the risks and transaction costs inherent in the asbestos litigation process as it occurs presently in the tort system." The settling parties also contend that the settlement's fairness is a common question, predominating over disparate legal issues that might be pivotal in litigation but become irrelevant under the settlement.

The predominance requirement stated in Rule 23(b)(3), we hold, is not met by the factors on which the District Court relied. The benefits asbestos-exposed persons might gain from the establishment of a grand-scale compensation scheme is a matter fit for legislative consideration, but it is not pertinent to the predominance inquiry. That inquiry trains on the legal or factual questions that qualify each class member's case as a genuine controversy, questions that preexist any settlement.

The Rule 23(b)(3) predominance inquiry tests whether proposed classes are sufficiently cohesive to warrant adjudication by representation. . . . If a common interest in a fair compromise could satisfy the predominance requirement of Rule 23(b)(3), that vital prescription would be stripped of any meaning in the settlement context.

The District Court also relied upon this commonality: "The members of the class have all been exposed to asbestos products supplied by the defendants. . . ." Even if Rule 23(a)'s commonality requirement may be satisfied by that shared experience, the predominance criterion is far more demanding. Given the greater number of questions peculiar to the several categories of class members, and to individuals within each category, and the significance of those uncommon questions, any overarching dispute about the health consequences of asbestos exposure cannot satisfy the Rule 23(b)(3) predominance standard.

The Third Circuit highlighted the disparate questions undermining class cohesion in this case:

> Class members were exposed to different asbestos-containing products, for different amounts of time, in different ways, and over different periods. Some class members suffer no physical injury or have only asymptomatic pleural changes, while others suffer from lung cancer, disabling asbestosis, or from mesothelioma. . . . Each has a different history of cigarette smoking, a factor that complicates the causation inquiry.
>
> The [exposure-only] plaintiffs especially share little in common, either with each other or with the presently injured class members. It is unclear whether they will contract asbestos-related disease and, if so, what disease each will suffer. They will also incur different medical expenses because their monitoring and treatment will depend on singular circumstances and individual medical histories.

Differences in state law, the Court of Appeals observed, compound these disparities.

No settlement class called to our attention is as sprawling as this one. Predominance is a test readily met in certain cases alleging consumer or securities fraud or violations of the antitrust laws. Even mass tort cases arising from a common cause or disaster may, depending upon the circumstances, satisfy the predominance requirement. The Advisory Committee for the 1966 revision of Rule 23, it is true, noted that "mass accident" cases are likely to present "significant questions, not only of damages but of liability and defenses of liability, . . . affecting the individuals in different ways." And the Committee advised that such cases are "ordinarily not appropriate" for class treatment. But the text of the rule does not categorically exclude mass tort cases from class certification, and district courts, since the late 1970s, have been certifying such cases in increasing number. . . . The Committee's warning, however, continues to call for caution when individual stakes are high and disparities among class members great. As the Third Circuit's opinion makes plain, the certification in this case does not follow the counsel of caution. That certification cannot be upheld, for it rests on a conception of Rule 23(b)(3)'s predominance requirement irreconcilable with the rule's design.

B

Nor can the class approved by the District Court satisfy Rule 23(a)(4)'s requirement that the named parties "will fairly and adequately protect the interests of the class." The adequacy inquiry under Rule 23(a)(4) serves to uncover conflicts of interest between named parties and the class they seek to represent. "[A] class representative must be part of the class and 'possess the same interest and suffer the same injury' as the class members." . . .[20]

As the Third Circuit pointed out, named parties with diverse medical conditions sought to act on behalf of a single giant class rather than on behalf of discrete subclasses. In significant respects, the interests of those within the single class are not aligned. Most saliently, for the currently injured, the critical goal is generous immediate payments. That goal tugs against the interest of exposure-only plaintiffs in ensuring an ample, inflation-protected fund for the future. . . .

The disparity between the currently injured and [exposure]-only categories of plaintiffs, and the diversity within each category are not made insignificant by the District Court's finding that petitioners' assets suffice to pay claims under the settlement. Although this is not a "limited fund" case certified under Rule 23(b)(1)(B), the terms of the settlement reflect essential allocation decisions designed to confine compensation and to limit defendants' liability. For example, as earlier described, the settlement includes no adjustment for inflation; only a few claimants per year can opt out at the back end; and loss-of-consortium claims are extinguished with no compensation.

The settling parties, in sum, achieved a global compromise with no structural assurance of fair and adequate representation for the diverse groups and individuals affected. Although the named parties alleged a range of complaints, each served generally as representative for the whole, not for a separate constituency. In another asbestos class action, the Second Circuit spoke precisely to this point:

> [W]here differences among members of a class are such that subclasses must be established, we know of no authority that permits a court to approve a settlement without creating subclasses on the basis of consents by members of a unitary class, some of whom happen to be members of the distinct subgroups. The class representatives may well

---

20. The adequacy-of-representation requirement "tend[s] to merge" with the commonality and typicality criteria of Rule 23(a) . . . . Gen. Tel Co. of Sw. v. Falcon, 457 U.S. 147, 157, n.13 (1982). The adequacy heading also factors in competency and conflicts of class counsel. Like the Third Circuit, we decline to address adequacy-of-counsel issues discretely in light of our conclusions that common questions of law or fact do not predominate and that the named plaintiffs cannot adequately represent the interests of this enormous class. . . .

have thought that the Settlement serves the aggregate interests of the entire class. But the adversity among subgroups requires that the members of each subgroup cannot be bound to a settlement except by consents given by those who understand that their role is to represent solely the members of their respective subgroups.

The Third Circuit found no assurance here — either in the terms of the settlement or in the structure of the negotiations — that the named plaintiffs operated under a proper understanding of their representational responsibilities. That assessment, we conclude, is on the mark.

C

Because we have concluded that the class in this case cannot satisfy the requirements of common issue predominance and adequacy of representation, we need not rule, definitively, on the notice given here. In accord with the Third Circuit, however, we recognize the gravity of the question whether class action notice sufficient under the Constitution and Rule 23 could ever be given to legions so unselfconscious and amorphous.

V

The argument is sensibly made that a nationwide administrative claims processing regime would provide the most secure, fair, and efficient means of compensating victims of asbestos exposure. Congress, however, has not adopted such a solution. And Rule 23, which must be interpreted with fidelity to the Rules Enabling Act and applied with the interests of absent class members in close view, cannot carry the large load CCR, class counsel, and the District Court heaped upon it. As this case exemplifies, the rulemakers' prescriptions for class actions may be endangered by "those who embrace [Rule 23] too enthusiastically just as [they are by] those who approach [the rule] with distaste." . . .

For the reasons stated, the judgment of the Court of Appeals for the Third Circuit is affirmed.

■ JUSTICE O'CONNOR took no part in the consideration or decision of this case.

■ [The opinion of JUSTICE BREYER, with whom JUSTICE STEVENS joined, concurring in part and dissenting in part, is omitted.]

Notes and Questions

1. *Amchem* is careful to keep the possibility of settlement class actions open, even as it makes the settlement of many mass claims more difficult. Under what circumstances could you imagine a settlement class action being approved? Put differently, what were the fatal defects in *Amchem*? Was it the attempt to settle the claims of present victims and future victims on different terms? Was it trying to settle the claims of differently situated

future victims? Was it the overwhelming size of the class and the differences among the claims?

In *Ortiz v. Fibreboard Corp.*, 527 U.S. 815 (1999), the Supreme Court reviewed another asbestos settlement class action. Unlike *Amchem*, the class was certified under Rule 23(b)(1)(B), on the theory that the settlement proceeds constituted a "limited fund" that required equitable apportionment among future plaintiffs whose potential claims far exceeded the settlement fund. The *Ortiz* settlement was patterned on the *Amchem* settlement but with various changes that avoided some of the problems in *Amchem* (among them, a right to opt out of the settlement in favor of a trial at the time that the asbestos-related disease manifested itself and an award scale that was pegged to historical averages and could rise with time). But the settlement also suffered from some of *Amchem*'s defects (including a separate favorable settlement with class counsel's present clients) and some new problems (including equal treatment of claimants whose individual recoveries would have varied a great deal because of Fibreboard's complicated insurance-coverage issues). The Supreme Court overturned class certification, holding that the settlement did not meet the requirements of a classic "limited fund" under Rule 23(b)(1)(B). Although its holding was limited to Rule 23(b)(1)(B), the Court acknowledged that some of its concerns — such as the equal treatment of people whose claims varied — could have resulted in Rule 23(a)(4) adequacy problems as well.

2. Settlement class actions first developed in securities, antitrust, and consumer cases, which typically involve only presently injured claimants. What effect should *Amchem* and *Ortiz* have on the use of settlement class actions in these areas? Although approvals of settlement class actions are sparser, such class actions have not ceased. *See* Hanlon v. Chrysler Corp., 150 F.3d 1011 (9th Cir. 1998) (settlement class action certified in defective minivan litigation); *In re* Volkswagen "Clean Diesel" Mktg., Sales Practices & Prods. Liab. Litig., 229 F. Supp. 3d 1052 (N.D. Cal. 2017) (approving settlement class action in actions for breach of contract and fraud).

3. In *In re National Football League Players Concussion Injury Litigation*, 821 F.3d 410 (3d Cir. 2016), more than 5,000 individual lawsuits brought by former National Football League players against the NFL alleged that the League failed to protect them against traumatic brain injuries. The parties eventually agreed to settle the case on a class-action basis. Of the 5,000 cases, 3,900 involved players who had yet to develop symptoms of brain injury. In affirming the approval of a roughly $1 billion settlement, the court of appeals noted that the district court had created separate subclasses for present and future victims and had also appointed separate counsel to negotiate on behalf of each subclass (although the counsel for the future-victim class also represented some presently injured clients). "Simply put," the court said, "this case is not *Amchem*":

> The most important distinction is that class counsel here took *Amchem* into account by using the subclass structure to protect the sometimes divergent interests of the retired players. The subclasses were represented in the negotiations by separate class representatives with

separate counsel, and . . . each was an adequate representative. This alone is a significant structural protection for the class that weighs in favor of finding adequacy.

Moreover, the . . . [Monetary Award] Fund is uncapped and inflation-adjusted, protecting the interests of those who worry about developing injuries in the future. The NFL and class counsel must meet every ten years and confer in good faith about "prospective modifications to the definitions of Qualifying Diagnoses and/or the protocols for making Qualifying Diagnoses, in light of generally accepted advances in medical science. This allows the settlement to keep pace with changing science regarding the existing Qualifying Diagnoses. . . .

Finally, one of the principal concerns driving *Amchem*'s strict analysis of adequacy of representation was the worry that persons with a nebulous risk of developing injuries would have little or no reason to protect their rights and interests in the settlement. We have evidence that in this case the concern is misplaced because many retired players with no currently compensable injuries have already taken significant steps to protect their rights and interests. [*Id.* at 432-33.]

Do you agree that *Amchem* is so readily distinguished?

4. Another adventuresome step is the "negotiation class action," in which plaintiffs' counsel and defendants negotiate a settlement structure in advance of negotiating the settlement itself. The parties then seek class certification: without yet knowing whether the defendants will settle or for how much, class members in effect agree how to distribute the proceeds of a possible settlement among themselves. Class members have a right to opt out at this point; thus, the defendant knows before undertaking settlement negotiations how broad the binding effect of the settlement will be. Should a settlement be achieved, class members then vote to approve or reject the settlement, with approval requiring the favorable vote of a supermajority. Class members also retain rights to object to the settlement before the judge decides whether to approve it. The first case to adopt this controversial approach is *In re* Nat'l Prescription Opiate Litig., 332 F.R.D. 532 (N.D. Ohio 2019), *appeal docketed*, No. 19–306 (6th Cir. Sept. 26, 2019).

5. In 2018, amendments to Rule 23(e)(2) established clear standards for a court to evaluate whether a class settlement is "fair, reasonable, and adequate." The amendments were not radical; they conformed Rule 23 to the best practices that courts had already developed.

6. The Class Action Fairness Act of 2005 (CAFA) also affects the settlement of federal class actions in several ways. First, 28 U.S.C. § 1712 limits the fees awardable to class counsel in "coupon settlements" in order to discourage their use. Coupon settlements provide class members with discounts on future purchases of a defendant's product or service. Although rare and not necessarily without value, coupon settlements obtained the status of urban legend, with detractors claiming that they enriched plaintiffs' lawyers, let defendants off the hook for next to nothing, and left class members holding the bag.

Second, responding to an infamous (although apparently *sui generis*) settlement in which some class members ended up worse off after the settlement because of small recoveries and large attorneys' fees, CAFA establishes a "net benefit" rule: class members cannot be required to pay fees to class counsel unless the settlement's combination of monetary and injunctive relief is a net benefit to the class members. *Id.* § 1713. Third, under a curious provision that does not appear to relate to any known instance or pattern of abuse, some class members cannot receive greater benefits than others just because they are geographically closer to the courthouse. *Id.* § 1714.

Finally, CAFA requires the parties to notify the "appropriate" federal or state official within ten days of reaching a settlement. *Id.* § 1715(b). The court must wait at least ninety days after notification to approve the settlement. *Id.* § 1715(d). Although the official need not do anything after receiving notice of the settlement, the purposes of the requirement are to ensure that the settlement does not frustrate the government's enforcement objectives and to give the official an opportunity to protect the interests of class members when the settlement appears inadequate. The "appropriate" official varies with the nature of the case; as a default, the official is the relevant state or federal Attorney General, but in some cases another official is appropriate. *See id.* § 1715(a), –(c).

7. Professor Lon Fuller was a great believer in the adversarial system. In a famous paper, Fuller argued that the adversarial system was an optimal, and arguably a necessary, feature of adjudication. Lon L. Fuller, *The Forms and Limits of Adjudication*, 92 HARV. L. REV. 353 (1978). For Fuller, the touchstone of adjudication was the right to participate in the decision by means of proofs and reasoned arguments. When a dispute became too large or many-sided — Fuller coined the word "polycentric" to describe such disputes — he thought that all affected parties could no longer meaningfully participate in the decision, and the case could not be adjudicated. The only means for resolving such disputes are the political process or negotiation.

Asbestos litigation seems to fit Fuller's description of polycentrism. Before *Amchem,* all individual-litigation solutions to resolve the asbestos crisis had failed. Since legislation (one of Fuller's means for resolving polycentric matters) was not forthcoming, the parties attempted to effect a settlement (Fuller's other means for handling polycentric disputes). Should the Court have recognized the situation's polycentrism, and lent its judicial imprimatur to a negotiated solution? (For an argument somewhat along these lines, you might want to look at Justice Breyer's dissent in *Ortiz*, 527 U.S. at 865-68.) Or is it the business of courts only to adjudicate disputes? Does the answer depend on our view of how central the adversarial ideal of litigation is in modern American courts?

We opened this book by examining the justifications for the adversarial system. And so we end.

INDEX

ABUSE OF DISCRETION (See **APPEAL** — Standard of review)

ACCURACY, 3, 4-5, 10-11

ADDITUR (See **TRIAL** — Post-trial motions)

ADJUDICATION
Goals of, 2-11, 231
Preliminary tasks in, 24-25, 107-08

ADMISSIONS
In answer (See **PLEADINGS** — Answer)
In discovery (See **DISCLOSURE AND DISCOVERY** — Discovery)

ADVERSARIAL SYSTEM
  Generally, 5-11, 350-53, 631, 699
Advantages and disadvantages of, 5-11
Alternative dispute resolution and, 175
Case management and, 176-78, 181
Class actions and, 631, 688-99
Comparison to inquisitorial system, 5-6, 7-9, 22, 108-10
Disclosure and, 117
Discovery and, 108-09, 115-16
Ethics and, 9-10, 106
Joinder and, 350-53, 363-64, 369, 631-32, 688-89, 699
Rule 11 and, 94-95, 106

ADVISORY JURY (See **TRIAL** — Bench trial)

AFFIRMATIVE DEFENSES (See **PLEADING** — Defenses)

ALTERNATIVE DISPUTE RESOLUTION
  Generally, 20, 174-75, 178-84, 200-30
Authority to order in litigation, 213-19
Binding vs. nonbinding, 204
Class actions and, 688-99
Comparison to adjudication, 201-03

ALTERNATIVE DISPUTE RESOLUTION — Cont'd
Court-annexed vs. extrajudicial, 203-04
Efficiency and, 175
Perspectives on, 178-84
Techniques
  Arbitration, 201, 202-03, 219-30
  Early neutral evaluation, 183-84, 203
  Mediation, 183-84, 202-03, 214-19
  Mini-trial, 203
  Private tribunals, 201-02
  Settlement, 174-75, 178-80, 202, 205-13

AMENDMENTS (See **PLEADINGS** — Amendments)

AMOUNT IN CONTROVERSY (See **SUBJECT-MATTER JURISDICTION** — Diversity jurisdiction)

ANCILLARY JURISDICTION (See **SUBJECT-MATTER JURISDICTION** — Supplemental jurisdiction)

ANSWER (See **PLEADING** — Answer)

APPEAL
  Generally, 16-17, 20, 301-12
Appealability
  Generally, 305-09
  Exceptions to final-judgment rule
    Class certification, 307, 657
    Injunctions, 306
    Interlocutory appeal, 306-07
  Final-judgment rule, 305-06
  Of remand order after removal, 570, 674
  Qualifications to final-judgment rule
    Collateral-order doctrine, 308
    Partial judgment, 307-08
Certiorari review, 17, 302, 304-05
En banc review, 302
Functions of, 303-05
Mandamus (See **MANDAMUS**)

APPEAL — Cont'd
Reviewability
    Generally, 309-10
    Harmless error, 309
    Preservation of objection, 309-10
Standard of review
    Generally, 310-12
    Discretionary rulings (abuse of discretion standard), 311-12
    Factual findings in bench trials (clear-error standard), 294, 311
    Factual findings in jury trials (reasonable-jury standard), 248-49, 280-89, 291, 311-12, 318
    Legal questions (de novo standard), 310
Structure of appellate system, 16-17, 301-03
Supreme courts, 16-17, 301-03
United States Supreme Court (See **UNITED STATES SUPREME COURT**)

APPEARANCES (See **PERSONAL JURISDICTION** — Appearances)

ARBITRATION (See **ALTERNATIVE DISPUTE RESOLUTION** — Techniques)

ATTORNEY-CLIENT PRIVILEGE (See **DISCLOSURE AND DISCOVERY** — Scope of)

ATTORNEYS' FEES
"American Rule," 22, 205-06
Class actions and, 636, 688-89
Rule 68 and, 206-13

BIFURCATION (See **CASE MANAGEMENT** — Techniques)

BURDENS
Burden of proof
    Burden of persuasion, 35-36
    Burden of production, 35
Pleading burden, 35

CASE MANAGEMENT
    Generally, 20, 26, 85-86, 117, 175-78, 180-82, 184-200
Adversarial system and, 175, 176-77, 181
Case-management order, 195
Case-management plan, 182, 189
Deadlines in, 85-86, 182, 184-89
Discovery-planning conference, 116-17, 173, 182, 184

CASE MANAGEMENT — Cont'd
Discretion and, 188, 194, 200
Efficiency and, 175, 182, 189
Final pretrial order, 195-200
Issue narrowing and, 184, 189-95
Perspectives on, 176-78, 180-82
Scheduling conference, 116-17, 184
Scheduling order, 85-86, 116-17, 184-89
Techniques
    Generally, 184-200
    Bifurcation, 192-94, 686-87
    Lone Pine order, 190-92, 194
    Summary judgment (See **SUMMARY JUDGMENT**)

CERTIFICATION TO STATE SUPREME COURT, 303, 629-30

CERTIORARI (See **APPEAL** — Certiorari review)

CHANCELLOR (See **EQUITY**)

CHANCERY (See **EQUITY**)

CITIZENSHIP
For personal jurisdiction (See **PERSONAL JURISDICTION** — Citizenship)
For subject-matter jurisdiction (See **SUBJECT-MATTER JURISDICTION** — Diversity jurisdiction)

CIVIL-LAW SYSTEM (See **INQUISITORIAL SYSTEM**)

CLAIM JOINDER (See **JOINDER** — Claims)

CLAIM PRECLUSION (See **PRECLUSION** — Claim preclusion)

CLASS ACTIONS
    Generally, 20, 397-98, 631-99
Appeal of certification decision, 307, 657
Appeal of remand order, 570, 674
Class Action Fairness Act of 2005, 666-76, 698-99
Due process considerations, 637-38, 658-65, 676-82, 687
Employment discrimination and, 648-57
Erie considerations, 614-23, 682-86
Litigation class actions, 688
Mass torts and, 641-48, 683-84, 693-96
Notice to class members, 639, 641, 653-54, 661-62, 664-65, 680, 696

CLASS ACTIONS — Cont'd
Personal jurisdiction over class members, 658-65
Perspectives on, 632-36
Preclusive effect of judgment, 631, 676-82
Requirements of
    All class actions
        Adequacy of class counsel, 639, 644
        Adequacy of class representative, 637-39, 644, 660, 678-80, 695-96
        Ascertainability of class members, 638
        Commonality, 638-39, 643, 650-52, 655, 656
        Existence of definable class, 638
        Fail-safe class, 638
        Membership of representative in class, 638
        Numerosity, 638, 642-43
        Typicality, 638-39, 643-44
    Mandatory class actions
        (b)(1)(A) and (b)(1)(B) classes, 639-40, 641, 647-48, 658, 663-65
        (b)(2) classes, 639-40, 641, 647-48, 652-55, 658, 663-64, 686
    Negotiation class actions, 698
    Opt-out (or (b)(3)) class actions
        Generally, 639-41, 644-47, 648, 653-54, 658, 693-95
        Manageability, 640-41, 646-47, 692
        Predominance, 640, 645, 693-95
        Superiority, 640-41, 645-47
Settlement class actions, 688-99
Settlement of class actions, 641, 688-89, 696-99
Subject-matter jurisdiction (See **SUBJECT-MATTER JURISDICTION** — Class actions)
Trial, 656-57, 686-88

CLEAR ERROR (See **APPEAL** — Standard of review)

COLLATERAL ESTOPPEL (See **PRECLUSION** — Issue preclusion)

COLLATERAL-ORDER DOCTRINE — (See **APPEAL** — Appealability)

COMMON LAW
Definitions of, 5
Federal, 344, 574, 585, 600

COMMON LAW — Cont'd
History of, 11-14
Jury trials and, 12, 13-14, 20, 232-35, 249-65
Pleading (See **PLEADING** — Common-law pleading)
Preclusion and, 313-14, 315, 344

COMPARATIVE PERSPECTIVES
    Generally, 7-9, 21-22
Class actions, 631-32
Discovery, 21, 108-11
Joinder, 356
Jury trial, 21, 232
Personal jurisdiction, 405, 433, 444
Preclusion, 314

COMPLAINT (See **PLEADING** — Complaint)

COUNTERCLAIMS (See **JOINDER** — Claims)

CROSSCLAIMS (See **JOINDER** — Claims)

DAMAGES (See **REMEDIES** — Damages)

DEFAULT JUDGMENT (See **JUDGMENT** — Default judgment)

DEFENSES (See **PLEADING** — Defenses)

DEFENSIVE COLLATERAL ESTOPPEL (See **PRECLUSION** — Issue preclusion)

DENIALS
In answers (See **PLEADING** — Answer)
In requests for admission (See **DISCLOSURE AND DISCOVERY**— Discovery; **DISCLOSURE AND DISCOVERY** — Sanctions)

DE NOVO REVIEW (See **APPEAL** — Standard of review)

DEPOSITIONS (See **DISCLOSURE AND DISCOVERY** — Discovery)

DISCLOSURE AND DISCOVERY
    Generally, 19, 107-73
Certifications in discovery, 171-72

DISCLOSURE AND DISCOVERY —
    Cont'd
Disclosure
    Adversarial system and, 176-77
    Case management and, 176-77
    Forms of disclosure
        Expert witness, 152-58
        Final pretrial, 195, 199-200
        Required initial, 117
Discovery
    Abuse of, 110, 115, 165-66, 172-73
    Adversarial system and, 108-09, 115-16, 147-49
    Case management and, 117, 182
    Comparative perspective (See **COMPARATIVE PERSPECTIVES** — Discovery)
    Cutoff of, 184-88
    Expense of, 111-13, 116, 121-40
    Expert witness, 152-58
    History of, 12-13, 14-15, 110-11
    Limits on, 114, 118-20, 140
    Methods of discovery
        Depositions, 114, 116
        Document production, 114
        Interrogatories, 114-15
        Physical or mental examinations
            Generally, 114
            Erie considerations, 593-94, 600, 620-21
        Requests for admission, 114, 115
    Discovery-planning conference, 116-17, 173, 182, 184
    Electronically stored information
        Generally, 130-40
        Cost shifting, 136, 139
        "Good cause" requirement for inaccessible information, 134-36, 139
        "Reasonably accessible" requirement, 132-34, 139
        Sanctions for destruction of (See **DISCLOSURE AND DISCOVERY** — Sanctions)
    Motion for a protective order, 120, 160, 166-71
    Motion to compel, 120, 161-66
    Objections
        Limits on, 116
        Grounds for, 116, 121
        Privilege log, 157, 158-59
        Waiver of, 159-60
    Perspectives on, 108-13
    Sanctions
        Generally, 160-66, 171-73
        For destruction of electronically stored information, 138, 164-65

DISCLOSURE AND DISCOVERY —
    Cont'd
    For failure to admit genuineness of request for admission, 173
    For failure to disclose a witness, 172, 196-200
    For failure to participate in discovery planning, 173
    For failure to respond to subpoena, 165
    For failure to supplement, 172
    For improper certification, 172
Scope of and limits on
    Generally, 118-19
    Privilege
        Generally, 119, 140-41
        Attorney-client privilege, 144, 151-52
    Proportionality, 119-40
    Relevance, 119-40
    Work-product doctrine
        Generally, 119, 141-52
        Expert witnesses and, 152-58
        Extent of protection, 149-51
Signature as certification, 172
Subpoena, 114, 165
Supplementation of, 118, 172

DISCOVERY (See **DISCLOSURE AND DISCOVERY** — Discovery)

DISCRETION
Abuse-of-discretion standard of review (See **APPEAL** — Standard of review)
Case management and (See **CASE MANAGEMENT** — Discretion)
Federal Rules of Civil Procedure and, 15

DISMISSAL OF CLAIMS (See **MOTIONS** — Motions to dismiss; **SUMMARY JUDGMENT**)

DOCUMENT PRODUCTION (See **DISCLOSURE AND DISCOVERY** — Discovery)

DUE PROCESS
Choice of law and, 405
Notice and (See **NOTICE** — Due process considerations of)
Opportunity to be heard and (See **OPPORTUNITY TO BE HEARD** — Due process considerations of)
Personal jurisdiction and (See **PERSONAL JURISDICTION** — Due process)

DUE PROCESS — Cont'd
Preclusion (See **PRECLUSION** — Due process considerations of)

EFFICIENCY
As influence on alternative dispute resolution, 175, 183-84
As influence on appellate system, 306
As influence on case management, 117, 175, 182, 189
As influence on scope of joinder, 349, 351, 353, 356, 362, 368, 369, 373, 380, 387, 394
As influence on preclusion, 314, 318
As influence on pretrial process, 107, 117, 232
As influence on subject-matter jurisdiction, 553
As influence on venue transfer, 498-500
Importance as a procedural principle, 2-3, 4-5

ELECTRONIC DISCOVERY (See **DISCLOSURE AND DISCOVERY** — Electronically stored information)

ELECTRONICALLY STORED INFORMATION (See **DISCLOSURE AND DISCOVERY** — Electronically stored information)

EQUITY
History of (See **HISTORY** — English civil procedure; **HISTORY** — American civil procedure)
Jury trial and, 13, 19, 233, 250

ERIE **DOCTRINE**
Generally, 18-19, 574-630
Ascertaining content of state law, 623-30
Class actions and, 614-22, 682-86
Federal common law and, 585
Perspectives on, 574-86
Procedural law and, 586-623
Rules of Decision Act and, 574-75, 576, 578, 581, 584-85, 601, 622
Rules Enabling Act and, 593-602, 605, 616, 619-22
Statute of limitations and, 586-90, 603-07
Substantive law and, 575-82, 585-86

EXPERT WITNESSES (See **DISCLOSURE AND DISCOVERY** — Disclosure; **DISCLOSURE AND DISCOVERY** — Discovery)

FEDERAL RULES OF CIVIL PROCEDURE
Effect of *Erie* doctrine on, 586-623
History of, 15
Principles for interpretation of, 34-35
Promulgation of, 15
Rules Enabling Act and, 15

FEDERAL-QUESTION JURISDICTION (See **SUBJECT-MATTER JURISDICTION**—Federal-question jurisdiction)

FEDERALISM
Generally, 16-18
Personal jurisdiction and, 18, 427-28, 432-33, 440-41, 443-44, 448, 452
Preclusion and, 342-45
Subject-matter jurisdiction and, 17-18, 513, 522, 532

FIELD CODE, 14, 315

FINAL-JUDGMENT RULE (See **APPEAL** — Appealability)

FINAL PRETRIAL ORDER (See **CASE MANAGEMENT** — Techniques)

FORMER ADJUDICATION (See **PRECLUSION**)

FORUM NON CONVENIENS (See **VENUE** — *Forum non conveniens*)

GENERAL VERDICT (See **TRIAL** — Verdicts)

HISTORY
American civil procedure, 14-15
English civil procedure
    Common law, 11-12, 13-14
    Equity, 12-14
Merger of law and equity, 14, 15, 19, 235, 252, 264

IMPLEADER (See **JOINDER**— Parties)

INJUNCTIONS (See **REMEDIES** — Injunctions)

INQUISITORIAL SYSTEM
Comparison to adversarial system, 5-9
Equity and, 12-13
Features of, 5, 7-9

INSTRUCTIONS (See **JURY TRIAL** — Jury instructions)

INTERLOCUTORY APPEAL (See **APPEAL** — Interlocutory appeal)

INTERPLEADER (See **JOINDER** — Parties)

INTERROGATORIES
As discovery device (See **DISCLOSURE AND DISCOVERY** — Discovery)
With general verdicts (See **TRIAL** — Verdicts)

INTERVENTION (See **JOINDER** — Parties)

ISSUE NARROWING
Generally, 19, 24-26, 107-08, 143, 175, 176, 184, 189, 194, 231, 236, 249
Techniques
Answer (See **PLEADINGS** — Answer)
Motion to dismiss (See **MOTIONS** — Motion to dismiss)
Requests for admission (See **DISCLOSURE AND DISCOVERY** — Discovery)
Summary judgment (See **SUMMARY JUDGMENT** — As issue-narrowing device)

ISSUE PRECLUSION (See **PRECLUSION** — Issue preclusion)

JOINDER
Adversarial system and (See **ADVERSARIAL SYSTEM** — Joinder)
Claims
Additional claims
Generally, 355-63
Subject-matter jurisdiction, 353-54, 551-55
Counterclaims
Compulsory, 353, 357-63
Permissive, 357-63
Subject-matter jurisdiction over, 358, 361-62, 551, 554, 566, 570-71
Crossclaims
Generally, 353, 363, 373, 375-80
Subject-matter jurisdiction over, 554
Deadlines for, 185
Defenses, 357

JOINDER — Cont'd
Parties
Generally, 363-98
Class actions (See **CLASS ACTIONS**)
Impleader under Rule 14
Generally, 369-74
Subject-matter jurisdiction over, 554
Interpleader
Generally, 396-97
Distinction between statutory and rule, 396-97
Subject-matter jurisdiction over, 397
Intervention under Rule 24
Of right
Generally, 388-95
Comparison to joinder under Rule 19, 394
Preclusion and, 395
Permissive, 395
Permissive joinder under Rule 20
Generally, 364-69
Subject-matter jurisdiction over, 534-35, 555-57
Personal jurisdiction and, 354-55
Required joinder under Rule 19
Generally, 380-88, 394
Subject-matter jurisdiction and, 380, 562
Third-party claims (See *supra* Impleader under Rule 14)
Perspectives on, 350-53

JUDGE
As factfinder at trial, 292-93
Role of judge in case management (See **CASE MANAGEMENT**)

JUDGMENT
Default judgment, 27, 58, 408, 477
Effect of prior judgment (See **PRECLUSION**)
Enforcement of judgment, 313
Entry of judgment, 283
Judgment as a matter of law (See **TRIAL** — Motions during trial; **TRIAL** — Post-trial motions)
Relief from judgment (See **TRIAL** – Post-trial motions)
Summary judgment (See **SUMMARY JUDGMENT**)

JUDGMENT AS A MATTER OF LAW (See **TRIAL** — Motions during trial; **TRIAL** — Post-trial motions)

JURISDICTION (See **PERSONAL JURISDICTION; SUBJECT-MATTER JURISDICTION**)

JURY INSTRUCTIONS (See **JURY TRIAL** — Jury instructions)

JURY TRIAL (See also **TRIAL**)
    Generally, 11-12, 13-14, 16, 20, 21, 232-35, 249-91
    Advisory jury (See **TRIAL** — Bench trial)
    As influence on procedural system, 232, 224-35
    Demand for jury trial, 27, 251, 256
    History of, 11-12, 232-35
    Jury-control devices
        General verdict with answers to written questions (See **TRIAL** — Verdicts)
        Judgment as a matter of law (See **TRIAL** — Motions during trial)
        Jury instructions (See **JURY TRIAL** — Jury instructions)
        New trial (See **TRIAL** — Post-trial motions)
        Renewal of motion for judgment as a matter of law (See **TRIAL** — Post-trial motions)
        Special verdict (See **TRIAL** — Verdicts)
        Summary judgment (See **SUMMARY JUDGMENT**)
    Jury instructions, 233-34, 281-82
    Perspectives on, 232-35
    Right to jury trial (See **JURY TRIAL** — Seventh Amendment)
    Selection of the jury
        Generally, 266-72
        Peremptory challenges, 267-72
        Voir dire, 266-67, 270
    Seventh Amendment
        Re-examination Clause, 232, 280, 290, 612-13
        Right to jury trial, 250-66
    Summary jury trial (See **ALTERNATIVE DISPUTE RESOLUTION** — Techniques)
    Verdicts (See **TRIAL** — Verdicts)
    Waiver of, 256

LAW OF THE CASE, 345-47

MAGISTRATE JUDGES, 72, 128

MANAGEMENT OF LITIGATION (See **CASE MANAGEMENT**)

MANDAMUS, 128, 306, 308, 570

MEDIATION (See **ALTERNATIVE DISPUTE RESOLUTION** — Techniques)

MERGER AND BAR (See **PRECLUSION** — Claim preclusion)

MERGER OF LAW AND EQUITY — (See **HISTORY** — Merger of law and equity)

MOTIONS
    Generally, 26, 67-70
    Motion for judgment as a matter of law (See **TRIAL** — Motions during trial)
    Motion for judgment on partial findings (See **TRIAL** — Motions during trial)
    Motion for judgment on the pleadings, 69-70
    Motion for more definite statement, 33, 67-68
    Motion for new trial (See **TRIAL** — Post-trial motions)
    Motion for a protective order (See **DISCLOSURE AND DISCOVERY** — Motion for a protective order)
    Motion for relief from judgment (See **TRIAL** — Post-trial motions)
    Motion for summary judgment (See **SUMMARY JUDGMENT**)
    Motion to compel (See **DISCLOSURE AND DISCOVERY** — Motion to compel)
    Motion to dismiss under Rule 12(b)
        Effect of granting motion, 68
        For failure to join a required party, 68, 386
        For failure to state a claim, 28-58, 68
        For improper venue, 68, 500
        For insufficiency of process, 68
        For insufficiency of service of process, 58-67, 68
        For lack of personal jurisdiction, 68, 478
        For lack of subject-matter jurisdiction, 68
        Waiver of right to assert, 68-69, 479
    Motion to strike under Rule 12(f), 67-68
    Renewal of motion for judgment as a matter of law (See **TRIAL** — Post-trial motions)
    Sanctions (See **RULE 11**)

MOTIONS TO DISMISS (See **MOTIONS** — Motion to dismiss)

NOTICE
Adversarial system and, 58
Class actions (See **CLASS ACTIONS** — Notice to class members)
Due process considerations of, 58-59, 485-94
Joinder and, 349
Notice pleading (See **PLEADING** — Notice pleading)
Requirements of, 61-67, 485-94
Service of process (See **PROCESS** — Service of process)
Summons (See **PROCESS** — Summons)

OFFENSIVE COLLATERAL ESTOPPEL (See **PRECLUSION** — Issue preclusion)

OPPORTUNITY TO BE HEARD
Adversarial system and, 58
Due process considerations of, 485, 488, 493-94
Joinder and, 349

PARTY JOINDER (See **JOINDER** — Parties)

PENDENT JURISDICTION (See **SUBJECT MATTER JURISDICTION** — Supplemental jurisdiction)

PENDENT-PARTY JURISDICTION (See **SUBJECT-MATTER JURISDICTION** — Supplemental jurisdiction)

PEREMPTORY CHALLENGES (See **JURY TRIAL** — Selection of the jury)

PERSONAL JURISDICTION
Generally, 18, 354-55, 399-485, 494-95
Appearance
    General appearance, 477-78
    Rule 12(b)(2) and, 478
    Special appearance, 412, 477-78
Citizenship and, 439, 461, 468
Class actions, 658-65
Consent as basis for, 411, 439, 479-85
Due process, 400-19, 420-85
"Effects" test, 456, 459-61
Federal courts and, 419, 494-95
General jurisdiction as basis for, 416, 461-72
Internet and, 442, 453-59
Long-arm statutes, 419-20

PERSONAL JURISDICTION — Cont'd
Minimum contacts (See **PERSONAL JURISDICTION**—Specific jurisdiction as basis for)
Notice (See **NOTICE**)
Over plaintiffs, 479, 658-65
Perspectives on, 400-05
Presence as basis for, 405-12, 472-79
Property as basis for
    In rem, 406, 416-18
    Quasi in rem, 406, 416-18
Specific jurisdiction as basis for
    Constitutional requirement of minimum contacts, 412-19, 420-61
    Statutory or rule requirement, 419-20, 494-95
State sovereignty and, 401-04, 405, 407-08, 410, 416, 426-27, 432-33, 438-40, 442, 443, 448, 452, 464, 470
Stream-of-commerce theory, 428-32, 436-46, 451-52, 466
Waiver of, 68-69, 479

PHYSICAL OR MENTAL EXAMINATION (See **DISCLOSURE AND DISCOVERY** — Discovery)

PLEADING
Generally, 19, 24-58, 70-90
Amendments
    Generally, 80-90
    Answer, 74
    Deadline for, 85-86, 185
    Relation back, 86-90
Answer
    Generally, 70-80
    Admissions in, 73-74
    Affirmative defenses, 74-80
    Denials in, 72-73
    Effect of failure to deny, 70-73
Code pleading, 14, 25, 26, 48, 200
Common-law pleading, 12, 25, 26, 257, 315, 356
Complaint
    Generally, 26-67
    Service of (See **PROCESS** — Service of process)
    Sufficiency of (See **MOTIONS** — Motions to dismiss under Rule 12(b))
Defenses
    Affirmative defenses (See **PLEADING** — Answer)
    Forfeiture of, 68-69, 79-80
    Rule 12(b) defenses (See **MOTIONS** — Motions to dismiss under Rule 12(b))

PLEADING — Cont'd
Fact pleading (See **PLEADING** — Code pleading)
Issue pleading (See **PLEADING** — Common-law pleading)
Notice pleading
    Generally, 15, 25-26, 28-36, 38-39, 40, 45, 53, 58, 72, 74, 78, 80, 105, 200
    Heightened-pleading exceptions, 33, 34-35, 41-42, 51
Perspectives on, 24-26
Reply, 26, 80
Sanctions in pleading (See **RULE 11**)
Types of pleadings, 26

PRECLUSION
    Generally, 20, 313-48
As affirmative defense, 319-20
Claim preclusion
    Claim-splitting, 321-22, 323, 324
    Compulsory-counterclaim rule and, 361
    Counterclaims and
        Compulsory, 361, 362
        Permissive, 361-62
    Crossclaims and, 363
    Elements of
        Finality of the judgment, 322-23
        On the merits, 322-23
        Same "transaction or occurrence," 314, 316, 321
        Validity of the judgment, 322, 477-78
    Impleader and, 374
    Merger and bar, 320-21
Class actions and, 631, 676-82
Due process considerations of, 315, 334, 340, 341, 349-50
Federalism and, 342-45
Issue preclusion
    Elements of
        Actually litigated, 315, 321, 329, 330-32, 334
        Alternate holdings, 331-32
        Essential to the judgment, 321, 329, 331, 338-39
        Finality of the judgment, 320, 322, 329
        Validity of the judgment, 320, 322, 329
    Exceptions to, 329, 332-33
    Parties precluded
        Defensive collateral estoppel, 334, 335-36, 337
        Mutuality rule, 315-16, 333, 334-35, 339, 344, 345

PRECLUSION — Cont'd
        Offensive collateral estoppel
            Generally, 333-42
            Exceptions to, 336, 339-40
    Types of
        Collateral estoppel, 330
        Direct estoppel, 330
Nonparties
    Claim preclusion of, 323, 349-50
    Issue preclusion of, 340-42
    Virtual representation of, 341
Perspectives on, 314-20
Relationship to law of the case, 345-46
Relationship to stare decisis, 347
Res judicata, 313, 314, 319-20

PRETRIAL PROCEEDINGS (See **CASE MANAGEMENT; DISCLOSURE AND DISCOVERY; DISCRETION, ISSUE NARROWING; SUMMARY JUDGMENT**)

PRIVILEGES (See **DISCLOSURE AND DISCOVERY** — Scope of)

PROCEDURAL THEORY, 2-11

PROCESS
Service of, 58-67
Summons, 58
Waiver of service, 59, 65

PROPORTIONALITY (See **DISCLOSURE AND DISCOVERY** — Scope of)

RELEVANCE (See **DISCLOSURE AND DISCOVERY** — Scope of)

RELIEF FROM JUDGMENT (See **TRIAL** – Post-trial motions)

REMEDIES
Attachment, 406, 408, 409, 410, 416-19, 490
Damages, 2, 14, 254, 256, 263-64
Declaratory judgment
    Generally, 322
    Jury trial and, 264, 266
    Preclusive effect of, 322
Injunctions
    Generally, 2, 14, 254, 257, 264-66
    Valuation for amount-in-controversy purposes, 534, 549-50, 570
Punitive damages and the amount-in-controversy requirement, 550

REMEDIES — Cont'd
Sequestration, 417

REMITTITUR (See **TRIAL** — Post-trial motions)

REMOVAL JURISDICTION AND PROCEDURE (See **SUBJECT-MATTER JURISDICTION** — Removal jurisdiction)

RENEWED MOTION FOR JUDGMENT AS A MATTER OF LAW (See **TRIAL** — Post-trial motions)

REQUESTS FOR ADMISSION (See **DISCLOSURE AND DISCOVERY** — Discovery)

RES JUDICATA (See also **PRECLUSION**)
Meanings of, 313, 314

RULE 11
Generally, 90-106
Attorney good faith and, 90-98
Certifications
    Factual assertions, 90-102
    Legal assertions, 102-06
History of, 98-99
Safe harbor, 95-99, 102
Sanctions, 100-01, 105-06

RULES ENABLING ACT
Generally, 15
Class actions and, 655, 685-86, 687, 696
Effect on pleading rules, 43
Erie doctrine and, 593-94, 595, 597-98, 601-02, 605, 618-21, 622
Rule 11 and, 102

RULES OF DECISION ACT, 574-75, 576, 578, 581, 584-85, 601, 622

SANCTIONS (See **DISCLOSURE AND DISCOVERY** — Sanctions; **RULE 11** — Sanctions)

SCHEDULING ORDER (See **CASE MANAGEMENT** — Techniques)

SERVICE OF LITIGATION DOCUMENTS, 67

SERVICE OF PROCESS (See **PROCESS** — Service of process)

SETTLEMENT (See **ALTERNATIVE DISPUTE RESOLUTION** — Techniques)

SEVENTH AMENDMENT (See **JURY TRIAL** — Seventh Amendment)

SPECIAL MASTERS, 292

SPECIAL VERDICTS (See **TRIAL** — Verdicts)

STANDING, 390, 394-95

STARE DECISIS
Generally, 347-48
As impairment of intervenor's interest, 394

SUBJECT-MATTER JURISDICTION
Generally, 17-18, 353-54, 508-73
Class actions
    Amount in controversy in diversity-based class actions, 535, 557, 665-69, 673-74, 675-76
    Appeal of remand order, 570, 667, 674
    Class Action Fairness Act and, 666-67
    Removal jurisdiction for, 666, 674
    Supplemental jurisdiction over class members' claims, 557, 666, 676
    Traditional jurisdiction, 557, 665-66
Concurrent jurisdiction, 18, 520, 567
Diversity jurisdiction
    Generally, 17, 354, 508-09, 512-15, 533-51
    Citizenship
        Of corporation, 540-46
        Of individual, 535-40
        Of partnership, 546-47
        Of unincorporated entity, 546-47
    Constitutional requirement, 534
    Statutory requirements of § 1332(a)
        Amount in controversy, 547-51
        Complete diversity, 534, 555-56
Exclusive federal jurisdiction, 18, 520, 527, 531-32, 533, 567, 572
Federal-question jurisdiction
    Generally, 17, 354, 508-12, 516-34
    Constitutional requirement, 516, 519-20
    Statutory requirements
        "Arising under"
            Generally, 516, 521-22
            Embedded federal questions, 521-34

SUBJECT-MATTER JURISDICTION
— Cont'd
    Well-pleaded complaint rule, 516-20
General-jurisdiction court, 18, 508, 510
Inability to waive, 68-69
Joinder and, 353-54, 358-59, 361-62, 380, 551-67, 572-73
Limited-jurisdiction court, 18, 508-09, 528, 558
Motion to dismiss for lack of, 68
Perspectives on, 508-15
Removal jurisdiction
    By counterclaim defendant or party joined by counterclaim, 570, 674
    By plaintiff, 570
    By third-party defendant, 571
    Class actions, 666, 674
    Diversity cases, 567-71
    Exclusive jurisdiction and, 572
    Federal-question cases, 570-73
    Limits on removal, 570-71
    Procedure for removal, 572
    Remand, 567-68, 570, 572, 667, 674
    Supplemental jurisdiction and, 572-73
State-court jurisdiction, 18, 508
Supplemental jurisdiction
    Generally, 354, 551-67, 666, 676
    Amount-in-controversy rule for, 557-66
    Class actions and, 557, 666, 676
    Counterclaims under Rule 13, 358, 361-62, 551, 554
    Crossclaims under Rule 13, 554
    Declining jurisdiction, 553, 566-67
    Former rules
        Ancillary jurisdiction, 551, 554, 555-56, 561, 566
        Pendent jurisdiction, 551, 552-53, 554-55, 556, 558, 559, 561
        Pendent-party jurisdiction, 554-67
    Joinder of additional claims under Rule 18, 552-53
    Joinder of additional plaintiffs under Rule 20 in diversity cases, 554-67, 666
    Removal and, 572-73
    Third-party claims under Rule 14, 554

SUBPOENA (See **DISCLOSURE AND DISCOVERY** — Subpoena)

SUMMARY JUDGMENT
    Generally, 19, 236-49
As issue-narrowing device, 19, 26, 33, 40, 42, 184, 190, 236, 249
Case management and, 184, 190
Constitutionality of, 242-43, 258
Cross-motions, 249
Frequency of, 240-41
History of, 242-43, 258
Jury trial and, 236, 239, 242-43, 258, 280
Relationship to judgment as a matter of law, 237-38, 241-42, 280
Relationship to motion to dismiss, 69, 242
Standard for granting motion, 236, 237, 241-42, 244-45, 248-49
Sua sponte grant, 238, 249
Time to file, 69, 189, 237, 242

SUMMONS (See **PROCESS** — Summons)

SUPPLEMENTAL JURISDICTION (See **SUBJECT-MATTER JURISDICTION** — Supplemental jurisdiction)

SUPREME COURT (See **APPEAL** — Supreme courts; **UNITED STATES SUPREME COURT**)

THIRD-PARTY CLAIMS (See **JOINDER** — Parties)

TRANSACTIONALISM
Amendment and, 86-89
Joinder and, 351, 352-53, 355-56, 357-63, 364-69, 374, 376, 379, 387, 394
Preclusion and, 314, 316, 324, 321
Supplemental jurisdiction and, 551-67

TRANSFERS (See **VENUE** — Transfer)

TRANS-SUBSTANTIVITY, 4

TRIAL (See also **JURY TRIAL**)
    Generally, 249-94
Bench trial
    Advisory jury, 292
    Conclusions of law, 292-93
    Findings of fact, 292-93
    Special masters, 292
Class actions, 686-88
Jury instructions (See **JURY TRIAL** — Jury instructions)
Jury trial (See **JURY TRIAL**)

TRIAL — Cont'd
Motions during trial
    Motion for judgment as a matter of law
        Generally, 272-81
        Constitutionality of, 242-43, 280
        Relationship to juries, 280
        Relationship to motion for new trial, 285-91
        Relationship to motion for summary judgment, 237-38, 241-42, 280
        Standard for granting motion, 278, 280
        Timing of, 280-81
    Motion for judgment on partial findings, 293
Post-trial motions
    Motion for new trial
        In bench trial, 293
        In jury trial
            Generally, 283-91
            Additur, 285
            Constitutionality of, 285, 290-91
            Relationship to motion for judgment as a matter of law, 285-91
            Remittitur
                Definition of, 284-85
                Seventh Amendment and, 285
            Standard for granting motion, 284-85
            Timing of, 294
    Motion for relief from judgment, 294-300, 320
    Motion to amend the judgment, 293
    Renewal of motion for judgment as a matter of law
        Generally, 283-84
        Standard for granting motion, 283

TRIAL — Cont'd
    Timing, 283
Right to jury trial (See **JURY TRIAL** — Seventh Amendment)
Seventh Amendment (See **JURY TRIAL** — Seventh Amendment)
Trial by statistics, 655, 656-57, 687-88
Verdicts
    General verdict, 282
    General verdict with answers to written questions, 282-83
    Special verdict, 282-83

TRIAL BY STATISTICS (See **TRIAL** — Trial by statistics)

UNITED STATES SUPREME COURT
Appeal to, 16-17
Certiorari to, 17, 302
Role in promulgation of Federal Rules of Civil Procedure, 15

VENUE
    Generally, 19, 495-507
Forum non conveniens, 500-07
Motion to dismiss for lack of, 68
Original venue, 495-98
Relationship to personal jurisdiction, 495
Transfer, 498-500

VERDICTS (See **TRIAL** — Verdicts)

VOIR DIRE (See **JURY TRIAL** — Selection of jury)

WORK-PRODUCT DOCTRINE (See **DISCLOSURE AND DISCOVERY** — Scope of)

WRIT SYSTEM (See **PLEADING** — Common-Law Pleading)